CASES AND MATERIALS ON ADMINISTRATIVE LAW

By

S. H. BAILEY, M.A., LL.B. (Cantab)
Professor of Public Law
University of Nottingham

B. L. JONES, M.A., LL.B. (Cantab)
Lecturer in Law, and Director
Centre for Environmental Law
University of Nottingham

A. R. MOWBRAY, LL.B. (Warw), Ph.D. (Edin)
Lecturer in Law
University of Nottingham

SECOND EDITION

LONDON
SWEET & MAXWELL LTD
1992

First Edition 1977
Second Edition 1992

Published in 1992 by
Sweet & Maxwell Ltd.; South Quay Plaza,
183 Marsh Wall, London E14 9FT
Computerset by
MFK Typesetting Ltd., Hitchin
Printed in England by
Clays Ltd., St Ives plc

A CIP catalogue record
for this book is available
from The British Library

ISBN 0 421 31290 4

The front cover photograph shows the arrest of Councillor Albert Baker, one of thirty Poplar councillors arrested in 1921 for disobeying an order of mandamus. Poplar Borough Council had been ordered to levy a rate to pay precepts issued by London County Council and some other bodies for 1921-22, but Poplar Council had refused, as part of its campaign for equalisation of the rates for the benefit of the poor London Boroughs. As Noreen Branson wrote in her book, *Poplarism, 1919-1925: George Lansbury and the Councillors' Revolt* (1979), the arrests were

> "conducted with courtesy in order to avoid disturbances and accusations of ill-treatment . . . The result was a long drawn-out and somewhat ceremonious affair which lasted for many days . . . On September 3, George Lansbury telephoned the Sheriff for an appointment. Having fixed 11.30 he got in touch with his son, Edgar, with David Adams and Albert Baker. The three met Lansbury at his home in Bow Road and after making speeches and being photographed, they were driven away . . ." (pp. 63, 65).

The councillors were released after six weeks.

For further references on Poplarism see below, pp. 370 and 778. A subsequent confrontation between the Poplar councillors and the district auditor culminated in the well-known case of *Roberts* v. *Hopwood*, below, p. 363.

PREFACE

This is the second edition of a book first published in 1977 under the authorship of S. H. Bailey, C. A. Cross and J. F. Garner. Since then, Charles Cross and Jack Garner have retired (although both are continuing their contributions to legal scholarship) and the first-named author has been joined by two colleagues from the Department of Law, University of Nottingham. The elapse of time since the first edition has necessitated more rewriting than is normally the case with a second edition, and this is reflected in the reference to the three current authors in the title to the present edition. Any errors and omissions are entirely our responsibility. The last fifteen years has seen many significant changes in the structure and processes of government, and a substantial increase in the jurisprudence of judicial review. Particularly significant has been the introduction of the application for judicial review procedure in 1977. These developments have made the task of selection even more difficult than it was for the first edition.

We would like to express our thanks to the publishers for their support in the preparation of this edition.

We have endeavoured to deal with the law as at the end of April 1992, but we have been able to take account of some later developments, such as the consolidation of the Tribunals and Inquiries Act, which completed its stages in July 1992.

S.H.B.
B.L.J.
A.R.M.
14.7.92

ACKNOWLEDGEMENTS

Grateful acknowledgement is made to the following authors and publishers for permission to quote from their works:

ACAS: Extracts from Annual Report 1989 Chapter Two: Collective Conciliation; Chapter Four: Individual Conciliation

BUTTERWORTH LAW PUBLISHERS LTD.: Extracts from the All England Law Reports

CAMBRIDGE UNIVERSITY PRESS: Extract from A. Bradley: The Role of the Ombudsman in Relation to the Protection of Citizen Rights 1980 C.L.J. 304

CHARLES KNIGHT AND CO. LTD.: Extract from the judgment in *Re Hurle-Hobbs, ex p. Riley* taken from The Law Relating to District Audit (Second Ed., 1955)

COMMISSION FOR LOCAL ADMINISTRATION IN ENGLAND: Extracts from annual reports of The Local Ombudsmen

DAINTITH T.: Extract from Regulation by Contract: The New Prerogative (1979) C.L.P. 41 Oxford University Press

DIGNAN J.: Extract from Policy-Making, Local Authorities and Courts: The GLC Fare's Case (1983) 99 LQR 605

GANZ G.: Extract from Allocation of Decision-Making Functions 1972 Public Law

HMSO: Controller of HMSO for extracts from Cabinet Office Efficiency Unit: Improving Management in Government: The Next Steps; extracts from Department of Environment Review of the Development Control System. Extracts from various Acts © Crown copyright. Extracts from Parliamentary papers © Parliamentary copyright

THE INCORPORATED COUNCIL OF LAW REPORTING FOR ENGLAND AND WALES: Extracts from the Law Reports

JACKSON P.: Extract from Fairness and Natural Justice (1980) 96 LQR 497

MCAUSLAN P.: Extract from Administrative Law—Collective Consumption and Judicial Policy (1983) 46 M.L.R. 1

WALSH B.: Extract from Judicial Review of Dismissal from Employment: Conference or Confusion? 1989 Public Law

CONTENTS

TABLE OF CASES

TABLE OF STATUTES

TABLE OF STATUTORY INSTRUMENTS

TABLE OF REPORTS

ABBREVIATIONS

Allen: Sir Carleton Kemp Allen, *Law and Orders* (3rd ed., 1965, Stevens)

Cane: P. Cane, *An Introduction to Administrative Law* (1986, Clarendon Press, Oxford)

Craig: P. P. Craig, *Administrative Law* (2nd ed., 1989, Sweet & Maxwell)

Cross: S. H. Bailey, *Cross on Local Government Law* (8th ed., 1991, Sweet & Maxwell)

de Smith: J. M. Evans, *de Smith's Judicial Review of Administrative Action* (4th ed., 1980, Stevens)

de Smith CA: S. A. de Smith and R. Brazier, *Constitutional and Administrative Law* (6th ed., 1989, Penguin)

Emery and Smythe: C. T. Emery and B. Smythe, *Judicial Review: Legal Limits of Official Power* (1986, Sweet & Maxwell)

Garner: B. L. Jones, *Garner's Administrative Law* (7th ed., 1989, Butterworths)

Harlow and Rawlings: C. Harlow and R. Rawlings, *Law and Administration* (1984, Weidenfeld & Nicholson)

Lewis: C. Lewis, *Judicial Remedies in Public Law* (1992, Sweet & Maxwell)

Wade: Sir William Wade, *Administrative Law* (6th ed., 1988, Clarendon Press, Oxford)

Part I

ADMINISTRATIVE AUTHORITIES AND PROCEDURES

CHAPTER 1

THE ALLOCATION OF FUNCTIONS

ADMINISTRATIVE lawyers need to be aware of the processes by which governmental functions are allocated. Such knowledge is crucial if we are effectively to understand the operation of the current administrative system and the legal controls regulating that system's actions. Without this insight we cannot comprehend why particular activities are performed by specific bodies, nor can we seek to exert an influence on the future evolution of the administrative system.

See *Craig*, Ch. 3; *Garner*, pp. 26–27; *Wade*, pp. 156–164.

(A) THE CONCEPTUAL APPROACH

REPORT OF THE COMMITTEE ON MINISTERS' POWERS

(H.M.S.O., Cmd. 4060, April 1932)

Chairman: Lord Donoughmore (succeeded by Lord Justice Scott)

Section III: Judicial or Quasi-Judicial Decision

2. *The difference between judicial and quasi-judicial decisions*

Meaning of "quasi"

The word "quasi," when prefixed to a legal term, generally means that the thing which is described by the word has some of the legal attributes denoted and connoted by the legal term, but that it has not all of them. For instance, if a transaction is described as a quasi-contract it means that the transaction has some of the attributes of a contract but not all. Perhaps the best translation of the word "quasi," as thus used by lawyers, is "not exactly." A "quasi-judicial" decision is thus one which has some of the attributes of a judicial decision, but not all. In order, therefore, to define the term "quasi-judicial decision," as it is used in our terms of reference, we must discover which of the attributes of a true judicial decision are included and which are excluded.

Nature of true judicial decisions

A true judicial decision presupposes an existing dispute between two or more parties, and then involves four requisites:

(1) the presentation (not necessarily orally) of their case by the parties to the dispute; (2) if the dispute between them is a question of fact, the

ascertainment of the fact by means of evidence adduced by the parties to the dispute and often with the assistance of argument by or on behalf of the parties on the evidence; (3) if the dispute between them is a question of law, the submission of legal argument by the parties; and (4) a decision which disposes of the whole matter by a finding upon the facts in dispute and an application of the law of the land to the facts so found, including where required a ruling upon any disputed question of law.

Nature of quasi-judicial decisions

A quasi-judicial decision equally presupposes an existing dispute between two or more parties and involves (1) and (2), but does not necessarily involve (3), and never involves (4). The place of (4) is in fact taken by administrative action, the character of which is determined by the Minister's free choice.

For example, suppose a statute empowers a Minister to take action if certain facts are proved, and in that event gives him an absolute discretion whether or not he will take action.[1] In such a case he must consider the representations of the parties and ascertain the facts—to that extent the decision contains a judicial element. But, the facts once ascertained, his decision does not depend on any legal or statutory direction, for *ex hypothesi* he is left free within his statutory powers to take such administrative action as he may think fit: that is to say the matter is not finally disposed of by the process of (4). Whereas it is of the essence of a judicial decision that the matter is finally disposed of by that process and nothing remains to be done except the execution of the judgment, a step which the law of the land compels automatically, in the case of the quasi-judicial decision the finality of (4) is absent; another and a different kind of step has to be taken; the Minister—who for this purpose personifies the whole administrative department of state—has to make up his mind whether he will or will not take administrative action and if so what action. His ultimate decision is "quasi-judicial," and not judicial, because it is governed, not by a statutory direction to him to apply the law of the land to the facts and act accordingly, but by a statutory permission to use his discretion after he has ascertained the facts and to be guided by considerations of public policy. This option would not be open to him if he were exercising a purely judicial function.

Decisions may be truly judicial though not given by a court of law

It is obvious that if all four of the above-named requisites to a decision are present, if, for instance, a Minister, having ascertained the facts, is

[1] *e.g.* s.91 of the Road Traffic Act 1930, under which the Minister of Transport is directed to consider the report of the person appointed by him to hold a public inquiry, the responsibility for deciding the question of fact and considering the arguments of the parties being left by the section upon the Minister's own shoulders. See *R.* v. *The Minister of Transport, ex p. Southend Carriers Ltd.*, *The Times*, December 18, 1931.

obliged by the statute to decide solely in accordance with the law, the decision is judicial. The fact that it is not reached by a court so-called, but by a Minister acting under statutory powers and under specialised procedure, will not make the decision any the less judicial.

[The committee gave as an example the question whether a person was an "employed person" under the Unemployment Insurance Acts 1920 to 1930, which was decided by the Minister of Labour unless he elected to refer it for decision to the High Court. The same question is now decided by the Secretary of State under section 17(1)(*d*) of the Social Security Administration Act 1992.] . . .

4. *Administrative decisions to be distinguished*

Distinction between administrative and judicial decisions

Decisions which are purely administrative stand on a wholly different footing from quasi-judicial as well as from judicial decisions and must be distinguished accordingly. Indeed the very word "decision" has a different meaning in the one sphere of activity and the other. When a person resolves to act in a particular way, the mental step may be described as a "decision." Again, when a judge determines an issue of fact upon conflicting evidence, or a question of law upon forensic argument, he gives a "decision." But the two mental acts differ. In the case of the administrative decision, there is no legal obligation upon the person charged with the duty of reaching the decision to consider and weigh submissions and arguments, or to collate any evidence, or to solve any issue. The grounds upon which he acts, and the means which he takes to inform himself before acting, are left entirely to his discretion. We may illustrate our meaning by two examples of such a "decision": (1) the decision of the Admiralty to place a departmental contract for stores—an act of a purely "business" character; (2) the decision of the Home Secretary to grant naturalization to a particular alien, a matter upon which Parliament has given him an absolute discretion.

Judicial elements in administrative decisions

But even a large number of administrative decisions may and do involve, in greater or less degree, at some stage in the procedure which eventuates in executive action, certain of the attributes of a judicial decision. Indeed generally speaking a quasi-judicial decision is only an administrative decision, some stage or some element of which possesses judicial characteristics. And it is doubtless because so many administrative acts have this character that our terms of reference have specially included quasi-judicial decisions.

The intermingling of the two elements in one composite "decision" is well illustrated by the type of case where the judicial element looms large in proportion to the administrative, although the final act is administrative. Instances we have in mind are the decisions of licensing authorities constituted under an Act of Parliament with an obligation to grant licences to fit and proper persons in accordance with the intentions and under the conditions of the Acts; as for example the Licensing Justices in their annual meeting under the Licensing Acts, 1910 [s.10] and 1921 [s.12]; the Traffic Commissioners under Part IV of the Road Traffic Act 1930; or the Minister of Transport himself on appeal from the Commissioners under section 81 of that Act. The ultimate decision is administrative and not judicial in each case—whether given by a justice, a commissioner, or the Minister. But evidence has to be considered and weighed; arguments on fact and possibly law have to be heard, and conclusions reached; irrelevant and improper considerations have to be excluded; and the body hearing the application must be disinterested and free from bias. And it is only after they have taken all the above preliminary steps judicially that they pass into pure administration and in the exercise of administrative discretion on grounds of public policy choose to grant or withhold a licence.[2] . . .

Some principles

9. It is obvious that the separation of powers is prima facie the guiding principle by which Parliament when legislating should allocate the executive and judicial tasks involved in its legislative plan. If the statute is in general concerned with administration, an executive department should be entrusted with its execution; but if the measure is one in which justiciable issues will be raised in the course of carrying the Act into effect, and truly judicial determination will be needed in order to reach decisions, then prima facie that part of the task should be separated from the rest, and reserved for decision by a court of law—whether ordinary or specialised, as in the circumstances Parliament may think right.

It is only on special grounds that judicial functions should be assigned by Parliament to Ministers or ministerial tribunals. That there may be occasions where Parliament may rightly think the public interest best served by such assignment, we readily recognise; but Parliament when so deciding should still remember that such a legislative provision is exceptional in character—however numerous the individual cases may seem likely to be under the particular legislative scheme which gives rise to them. And this observation remains none the less true although in modern social legislation it may often be wise for Parliament to take the exceptional course; . . .

But quasi-judicial decisions stand on a different footing. The presumption as to the correct legislative course is the other way; for a decision

[2] Lord Halsbury's exposition of the duty of justices to exercise their discretion to grant or not to grant a licence judicially in *Sharp* v. *Wakefield* [1891] A.C. 173 at pp. 178–182, may be consulted by those who wish to pursue the analysis further.

which ultimately turns on administrative policy should normally be taken by the executive Minister. . . .

Just as some elements of the judicial function may thus enter into activities which are mainly administrative, so where the problem is in essence or predominatingly judicial—*i.e.* not merely quasi-judicial—there may be executive or legislative elements involved in the performance of the particular judicial task, or so inseparably connected with it that Parliament in working out its statutory plan will have to choose between (1) splitting the problem into two so as to leave the judicial side to a court, whilst entrusting the non-judicial side to the Minister whose department is concerned, and (2) assigning certain limited functions of an executive or legislative order to the court charged with the judicial decision.

That such things should be done by Parliament need not shock the most rigid constitutional purist. The doctrine of the separation of powers is not sacrosanct. We have seen that the separation of powers is not and never was complete in England; and as the writers of the *Federalist*[3] truly said, "No skill in the science of government has yet been able to discriminate and define with sufficient certainty its three great provinces, the legislative, executive and judiciary." The separation of powers is merely a rule of political wisdom, and must give way where sound reasons of public policy so require. Where a problem has a strongly marked judicial side, but it is difficult to detach the non-judicial side—be it administrative or be it legislative—Parliament may in some cases be well advised to entrust the whole to a court of law. If the particular task is not suited to the ordinary courts of law, it may properly be assigned to some special tribunal already existing, or to be newly-created for the purpose, which is better adapted in personnel or procedure. . . .

We recognise that such ministerial tribunals have much to recommend them. In cases where justice can only be done if it is done at a minimum cost, such tribunals, which are likely to be cheaper to the parties, may on this ground be preferred to the ordinary courts of law. In addition they may be more readily accessible, freer from technicality, and—where relief must be given quickly—more expeditious. They possess the requisite expert knowledge of their subject—a specialised court may often be better for the exercise of a special jurisdiction. Such tribunals may also be better able at least than the inferior courts of law to establish uniformity of practice.

But while we recognise these advantages we repeat that such tribunals should be set up only in those cases in which the conditions beyond all question demand it. It is in the ordinary courts, higher or inferior, that justiciable issues, whether between subject and subject or between Crown and subject, ought as a rule to be determined. . . .

Our conclusion on the whole matter is that there is nothing radically wrong about the existing practice of Parliament in permitting the exercise

[3] No. XXXVI.

of judicial and quasi-judicial powers by Ministers and of judicial power by ministerial tribunals, but that the practice is capable of abuse, that dangers are incidental to it if not guarded against, and that certain safeguards are essential if the rule of law and the liberty of the subject are to be maintained.

Notes

1. Professor W. A Robson regarded the classification adopted as "almost naïve" (*Justice and Administrative Law* (3rd ed., (1951)), p. 446). "The truth of the matter appears to be that the committee lacked the frankness or the insight to admit that the exercise of true judicial powers frequently permits a substantial degree of discretion, in which considerations of policy often enter. For them any admixture of "policy" in the virgin purity of a judicial determination immediately reduces it to the ranks of a quasi-judicial decision" (*ibid.* pp. 448–449). He asked whether the committee had taken into account the view of the judicial process put forward by Mr. Justice Cardozo in *The Nature of the Judicial Process*. The result of the committee's recommendations, which meant in effect "that decisions which require consideration of social policy in the field of public administration shall, as hitherto, remain within the sphere of ministerial action" was "not altogether unsatisfactory as a guide to action. But one can only deplore the fallacious reasoning by which this incidental benefit was attained."

2. For other discussion of the definitions propounded by the Donoughmore Committee, see C. K. Allen, *Law and Orders* (1st ed.), pp. 68–73, *cf.* 3rd ed., pp. 349–360; W. I. Jennings, "Report on Ministers' Powers," 10 *Public Administration* 333–351 (and note the bibliography at p. 333).

3. The Franks Committee on Administrative Tribunals and Enquiries did not find the distinction between "administrative" and "judicial" useful as a guide in the allocation of functions (below, p. 70). They also possessed a different perception of the nature of tribunals from that held by the Committee on Ministers' Powers (below, p. 72).

4. Professor de Smith observed that the courts have been inconsistent in their elaboration of the meaning of the terms "judicial," "quasi-judicial" and "administrative," when classifying functions for the purposes of judicial review: see *de Smith*, p. 69.

(B) The Historical Approach

ALLOCATION OF DECISION-MAKING FUNCTIONS

G. Ganz [1972] P.L. 215–231 and 299–308*

Before one can discuss the desirability of allocating power to make particular decisions to a certain body the nature of decision-making in the field of administration must be analysed briefly.

Every decision in this area has two elements—the establishment of the facts and their evaluation. It is the various methods of evaluation which will be investigated here. These range from the decision according to fixed rules at one end of the spectrum to a purely discretionary act at the

* Some footnotes have been omitted.

other. No clear lines can be drawn where the one activity stops and the other begins as they shade off into one another imperceptibly. . . .

Therefore, when the problem arises of who should make decisions in a particular field the controversy should centre not on whether these involve the application of rules or discretion but on who should make the necessary value judgments. Looking at this from the point of view of the legislature there is a wide area of choice. . . .

Courts

. . . The debate about whether a Minister or a court should have jurisdiction has raged in a rather different context over investment grants under the Industrial Development Act 1966.[1] The Opposition strenuously attacked the substitution of discretionary grants for investment allowances which could be set off against tax as of right. The Government made it clear that one of the reasons for this change of policy was to keep the courts out of this area because of the wide interpretation they had given to the Finance Act 1954 in *Hinton* v. *Maden*.[2] Though the grants were discretionary under the provisions of the Act it was made clear during the debates on the Bill that the discretion would be limited to interpreting the terms of the Act. It was because the Government felt that a court or a tribunal could only be entrusted with the Act's interpretation if very narrow definitions were laid down that it reserved this power to the Minister. This example shows that even a fairly detailed provision may not be entrusted to the courts for interpretation.

Tribunals

. . . On the other hand when the Immigration Appeals Act 1969 was going through Parliament the Government rejected the Opposition's amendment to give jurisdiction in appeals from immigration officers to county courts instead of adjudicators with a further appeal to the Immigration Appeal Tribunal. The main reason given was the need for speed. It was also thought best by the Government that adjudicators should be appointed by the Home Secretary from outside the public service. The county courts were also rejected as an appeal body from the adjudicators. One Appeal Tribunal, it was said, would give more consistency to decisions and the members are appointed by the Lord Chancellor. . . .

Having looked at tribunals *vis-à-vis* the courts we must now investigate their relationship with the Minister. The Franks Committee came out firmly in favour of treating tribunals as part of machinery for adjudication rather than administration. It wanted chairman and members to be made independent of Ministers both in respect of appointment and dismissal. The Tribunals and Inquiries Act 1958 only partially achieved these aims.[3]

[1] These have now been abolished by the Investment and Building Grants Act 1971.
[2] [1959] 1 W.L.R. 875.
[3] See now Tribunals and Inquiries Act 1971 [now the 1992 Act], ss.5, 7 and 8.

It is the shortness of tenure of most tribunal members rather than a power of dismissal which is a threat to their independence. . . .

Public Corporations

Another method of taking decisions out of the political arena without giving them to the courts is to give jurisdiction to a public corporation created ad hoc for this purpose. Most of the public corporations created after 1945 were set up to run the nationalised industries or non-commercial public services. . . .

The object of creating independent corporations is to take the individual decisions out of politics. This is reflected in the provisions relating to members of the boards. Most of the Acts contain provisions which add membership of the board to the list of disqualifying offices in the House of Commons Disqualification Act 1957. Members of boards are also sent a letter by the Treasury setting out the rules about political activities from which they are expected to abstain. However, members are in every case appointed and removable by the Minister on stated grounds. In practice, as has been shown by the example of the nationalised industries, a member will resign rather than be removed by the Minister and as in the case of administrative tribunals it is the shortness of tenure and therefore the ability not to reappoint which in practice gives the Minister power over the boards.

Ministers

. . . [I]t should be mentioned that some decisions are vested in Ministers as a matter of history and convenience rather than on principle. The Minister has to decide under the National Insurance Act whether contribution conditions are satisfied, the class of insured person in which a claimant is to be placed and the priority of rival claimants to an increase of benefit.[4] These provisions were an inheritance from previous Acts but they were also defended before the Franks Committee on their merits, particularly the question whether contribution conditions have been satisfied which is a matter of fact that can be determined only from the departmental records.

An example of giving decisions to a Minister on grounds of convenience is the distribution of the fund provided under the Anglo-German Agreement of 1964 for victims of Nazi persecution. This was distributed by the Foreign Office rather than the Foreign Compensation Commission to avoid delay but with dire consequences for the Foreign Office.[5]

[4] National Insurance Act 1965, s.64 (see now the Social Security Administration Act 1992, s.17).

[5] See Report of Parliamentary Commissioner for Administration, H.C. 54 (1967–68).

Conclusion

The greatest challenge which has been presented to administrative law in recent times is the development towards selectivity and discrimination. This is nothing but the old problem of discretionary power in a new guise and it, therefore, raises the fundamental distinction between discretion and arbitrariness. The difference lies in the criteria according to which the decision is made. There can be no absolute rules as to which criteria are relevant or irrelevant as we are here in the realm of values and not facts. To whom these value judgments are entrusted is, therefore, of vital importance. This is the problem which has been investigated in the preceding pages and we must now see whether any pattern emerges from them.

One of the criteria put forward for allocating decisions to a Minister is that "the decision is largely determined by policy based on a consideration of what is desirable in the future in the public interest rather than on a finding as to past fact or an interpretation of a statute or accepted principle of common law or equity.[6] But this is by no means a decisive factor in practice. Decisions of this nature have been conferred on independent bodies such as the Traffic Commissioners, the Independent Broadcasting Authority and the Civil Aviation Authority even if one excludes the Restrictive Practices Court which gave rise to considerable controversy on this point. On the other hand the interpretation of the Housing Act 1957, s.4 (unfitness for human habitation) and the Industrial Development Act 1966 (investment grants) was entrusted to a Minister rather than a court or tribunal.

Similarly the lack of "fixed or measurable criteria" has not been the determining factor in allocating decisions to Ministers. It has been the justification for ministerial decisions in the case of office and industrial development certificates and appeals against refusal of planning permission but there were no fixed criteria for the allocation of television contracts or for licensing private airlines or for some of the decisions which the immigration tribunals will have to take.

The scale of a decision is also not decisive. In the case of schemes under the Highlands and Islands Development Act 1965 and to some extent in the case of slum clearance this has been the justification for reserving decisions to Ministers but the Minister also retained control over investment grants.

Questions of national security are always reserved for the Government but in other areas it is impossible to generalise. The decisions which are regarded as non-delegable will vary with the Government in power. Whether an area should be taken out of politics and given to an independent body may be a matter of acute political controversy as in the case of the Restrictive Practices Court and immigration appeals. On the other

[6] Thesiger Committee, *Report on Licensing of Road Passenger Services* 1953, para. 196.

hand there may be all-party agreement as in the case of the allocation of television contracts. In this area as in others such as licensing of private airlines, governments both Labour and Conservative have felt that political considerations should be eliminated. This does, however, raise the question of what should be put in their place because decisions cannot be made without evaluating criteria. If political criteria are taboo then more undesirable criteria may take their place. Expertise does not provide criteria for judging between competing interests. It is of great help in assessing the facts from a technical point of view but not in making value judgments about those facts. As we have seen, there is in England a great deal of political control over independent bodies other than the courts either by way of appeal or by the power to give general directions as well as by informal contacts and sometimes more specific controls. This still leaves considerable discretionary powers in such bodies and the quality of their decisions will depend on the calibre of their members. Taking decisions out of politics is not a panacea, it may be merely passing the buck. . . .

Note

P. P. Craig believes that the United Kingdom has always had "a rather messy set of administrative institutions." (*Administrative Law*, 1st ed., p. 3.) Does Professor Ganz's analysis provide an explanation for this state of affairs?

(C) The Contemporary Approach

THE FUTURE OF TELECOMMUNICATIONS IN BRITAIN

Cmnd. 8610 (1982)

[The following extracts are from a statement made in the House of Commons by the Secretary of State for Industry (Patrick Jenkins)].

It is the Government's aim to promote consumer choice. Wherever possible, we want industrial and commercial decisions to be determined by the market and not by the state. We believe that consumer choice and the disciplines of the market lead to more stable prices, improved efficiency and a higher quality of service.

Since the British Telecommunications Act 1981 received Royal Assent less than a year ago, some progress has been made in breaking the state monopoly in telecommunications. I have licensed the Mercury Consortium to provide a new telecommunications network in competition with BT. I intend shortly to issue a general licence permitting all bona fide value-added network service operators to use the BT and Mercury networks. The way is now opening for the private sector to sell telephone apparatus direct to the public. Liberalisation of telecommunications has started and we intend to see it through. For BT, the prospect of competition and the advent of new technology are now stimulating them to provide a wider range of competitive services. I pay tribute to the way Sir George Jefferson and his Board are transforming what was not so long ago a government department into a commercially orientated business. Mr. Speaker, we now want to take the next step.

As a nationalised industry BT does not have direct access to financial markets. Its borrowing is controlled by Government and counts against the PSBR.[1] To bring inflation under control these borrowings have inevitably to be subject to strict limits. But external finance is only part of the picture. In the past monopoly power has allowed BT to raise prices to finance investment without doing all that could be done to increase efficiency. Around 90 per cent. of BT's investment programme, about £2,200 million this year, has been self-financed. By "self-financed," I mean of course "customer financed"; BT's charges to customers not only cover current running costs, but are also paying for 90 per cent of new investment. As a result, charges have risen steeply while investment is still not enough. Unless something is done radically to change the capital structure and ownership of BT and to provide a direct spur to efficiency, higher investment would mean still higher charges for the customer. The Government, BT and the general public would find that unacceptable. We need to free BT from traditional forms of government control.

We will therefore take the earliest opportunity to introduce legislation which, while keeping BT as a single enterprise, will enable it to be converted into a Companies Act company, "British Telecommunications plc." The legislation will allow the sale of shares in that company to the public. It is our intention, after the next election, to offer up to 51 per cent. of the shares on the market in one or more tranches.

Once half of the shares have been sold, the Government will give up control over the commercial decisions of BT plc. BT plc will be outside the public sector; its borrowing will cease to be subject to Exchequer control, and it will look to its shareholders and the markets for its external financing. . . .

BT plc will nevertheless dominate the British market for telecommunications for some years yet. The Government considers therefore that there will be a need for regulatory arrangements for the industry to balance the interests of those supplying telecommunications services, their customers, their competitors, their employees, their investors and their suppliers. The legislation will reform the arrangements for licensing telecommunications so as to end BT's exclusive privilege and its role in licensing. Instead, there will be a new Office of Telecommunications, modelled on the Office of Fair Trading, under a Director General appointed by me. He will have powers similar to those of the Director General of Fair Trading. He will operate with the same degree of independence from Government. It will be his job to ensure fair competition and fair prices.

[1] Public Sector Borrowing Requirement—a measure of public sector debt.

Notes

1. The Telecommunications Act 1984 provided the legal basis for the privatisation of BT. Subsequently, all of the shares in British Telecommunications plc were sold to individual and institutional shareholders.

2. Many other public utilities and publicly owned bodies (such as the former British National Oil Corporation) have been, or are in the process of being, privatised; *e.g.* British Gas plc by the Gas Act 1986, the public water authorities by the Water Act 1989, and the electricity generation/supply organisations by the Electricity Act 1989. Consequently the practice of privatisation represents a major feature of the allocation of functions during the last decade.

3. T. Prosser and C. Graham consider that the privatisation programme can be divided into three eras. First, between 1979–1983, when the main objective was to dispose of publicly owned assets in order to reduce the Public Sector Borrowing Requirement (basically the deficit between government income and expenditure). Secondly, between 1984–1986, when the target annual income from the sale of public utilities was raised to nearly £5 billion by the 1984 Public Expenditure White Paper (Cmnd. 9143). Thirdly, since 1986, when there has been political confusion over the disposal of some assets, (*e.g.* the abortive discussions on the sale of British Leyland to the Ford Motor Company; eventually the car division of British Leyland was sold to the already privatised British Aerospace conglomerate). See "Privatising Nationalised Industries: Constitutional Issues and New Legal Techniques" (1987) 50 M.L.R. 16.

These writers have also noted that the Thatcher government's justification of privatisation varied during this period, from the need to expose state enterprises to competitive forces, through to the objective of reducing the size of the state. However, they observe that the Government retains many sources of power and influence over the newly privatised companies, including the machinery of competition control (notably the Monopolies and Mergers Commission) and the influence of the Government as a major purchaser of the goods and services offered by these companies (see below, p. 113). Therefore:

> ". . . to see privatisation as a straightforward example of the rolling back of the state would be misleading; although it limits the ownership of industry by the state, it is compatible with an extensive governmental role in the economy."

Graham and Prosser, "Rolling Back the Frontiers?" p. 88 in *Waiving the Rules: The Constitution Under Thatcherism*, ed. Graham and Prosser (1988): on a related topic see also their "Golden Shares: Industrial Policy by Stealth?" [1988] P.L. 413.

For other views on the privatisation programme see: D. Thompson, J. A. Kay and C. Mayer (eds.), *Privatisation and Regulation: The U.K. Experience* (1986); D. Steel and D. Heald (eds.), *Privatising Public Enterprises* (1984) and N. Lewis and I. Harden, "Privatisation, De-Regulation and Constitutionality: Some Anglo-American Comparisons" (1983) 34 N.I.L.Q. 207; D. Marsh, "Privatization under Mrs. Thatcher: a review of the literature" (1991) 61 *Public Administration* 459.

CHAPTER 2

ADMINISTRATIVE INSTITUTIONS

(A) CENTRAL GOVERNMENT

THE central government exercises its many functions nominally by way of advice to the Crown, although statute in some instances confers powers on ministers personally.[1] These functions so exercised by Ministers of the Crown may take the form of initiating delegated legislation (by Orders in Council or by Regulations, orders, directions, etc., made by ministers), of exercising discretionary powers,[1a] of determining appeals from the decisions of other government agencies, such as local authorities, and by carrying on the every day activities of administration. These and other administrative procedures are exercised over a wide field of activity, especially in the fields of social security, town and country planning and the environment generally, immigration and foreign and commonwealth affairs, the regulation of the economy and industrial relations, etc.

In the exercise of their functions, the decisions of ministers are as subject to judicial review as are the decisions of other agencies, subject always of course to the terms of any relevant enabling statutes.

For further reading see *Garner*, Ch. 2; *Wade*, Ch. 3; *Craig*, Ch. 3.

(i) Departments

Until recently almost all of the administrative tasks allocated to ministers have been performed by government departments. These are "branches of the central administration which are staffed by civil servants, paid for out of Exchequer funds and headed by a minister responsible to Parliament."[1b] In 1988 the following report to the Prime Minister, from a group in the Cabinet Office concerned with efficiency inside the government machine, was published. The report derived from interviews with 150 ministers and officials, together with the evidence collected by earlier investigations into the civil service.

EFFICIENCY UNIT; IMPROVING MANAGEMENT IN GOVERNMENT: THE NEXT STEPS

(H.M.S.O.) 1988

10. **Seventh, the Civil Service is too big and too diverse to manage as a single entity. With 600,000 employees it is an enormous organisation compared with any private sector company and most public sector**

[1] In such instances the minister may be sued in the courts: see, *e.g. Padfield* v. *Minister of Agriculture, Fisheries and Food* below, p. 343. A decision by a subordinate in the name of the minister will normally be accepted by the courts without proof of express delegation: *Carltona Ltd* v. *Commissioners of Works* below, p. 277.

[1a] *e.g.* as in *British Oxygen Co. Ltd.* v. *Minister of Technology* below, p. 292.

[1b] Wade and Bradley, *Constitutional and Administrative Law* (10th ed., 1985), p. 270.

organisations. A single organisation of this size which attempts to provide a detailed structure within which to carry out functions as diverse as driver licensing, fisheries protection, the catching of drug smugglers and the processing of Parliamentary Questions is bound to develop in a way which fits no single operation effectively.

11. At present the freedom of an individual manager to manage effectively and responsibly in the Civil Service is severely circumscribed. There are controls not only on resources and objectives, as there should be in any effective system, but also on the way in which resources can be managed. Recruitment, dismissal, choice of staff, promotion, pay, hours of work, accommodation, grading, organisation of work, the use of IT equipment, are all outside the control of most Civil Service managers at any level. . . .

12. In our discussions it was clear that the advantages which a unified Civil Service are intended to bring are seen as outweighed by the practical disadvantages, particularly beyond Whitehall itself. We were told that the advantages of an all-embracing pay structure are breaking down, that the uniformity of grading frequently inhibits effective management and that the concept of a career in a unified Civil Service has little relevance for most civil servants, whose horizons are bounded by their local office or, at most, by their department.

19. **We recommend that "agencies" should be established to carry out the executive functions of government within a policy and resources framework set by a department.** An "agency" of this kind may be part of government and the public service, or it may be more effective outside government. We use the term "agency" not in its technical sense but to describe any executive unit that delivers a service for government. The choice and definition of suitable agencies is primarily for Ministers and senior management in departments to decide. In some instances very large blocks of work comprising virtually a whole department will be suitable to be managed in this way. In other instances, where the scale of activity is too small for an entirely separate organisation, it may be better to have one or even several smaller agencies within departments.

20. These units, large or small, need to be given a well defined framework in which to operate, which sets out the policy, the budget, specific targets and the results to be achieved. It must also specify how politically sensitive issues are to be dealt with and the extent of the delegated authority of management. The management of the agency must be held rigorously to account by their department for the results they achieve.

21. The framework will need to be set and updated as part of a formal annual review with the responsible Minister, based on a long-term plan and an annual report. The main strategic control must lie with the Minister and Permanent Secretary. But once the policy objectives and budgets within the framework are set, the management of the agency should then have as much independence as possible in deciding how those objectives are met. . . .

To strengthen operational effectiveness, there must be freedom to recruit, pay, grade and structure in the most effective way as the framework becomes sufficiently robust and there is confidence in the capacity of management to handle the task.

23. Placing responsibility for performance squarely on the shoulders of the manager of an agency also has implications for the way in which Ministers answer to Parliament on operational issues. Clearly Ministers have to be wholly responsible for policy, but it is unrealistic to suppose that they can actually have knowledge in depth about every operational question. The convention that they do is in part the cause of the overload we observed. We believe it is possible for Parliament, through Ministers, to regard managers as directly responsible for operational matters and that there are precedents for this and precisely defined ways in which it can be handled.

24. The detailed nature of the relationship between a department and an agency will vary with the job to be done or the service to be delivered. The agency structure could be used to cover a substantial proportion of the activities of the Civil Service. It is clear from our discussions with Permanent Secretaries that some departments are already moving towards this concept. What is needed is a substantial acceleration and broadening of this trend through a major initiative. Ultimately some agencies could be in a position where they are no longer inside the Civil Service in the sense they are today. Any decision of this kind should be taken pragmatically—the test must always be adopting the structure which best fits the job to be done.

44. The aim should be to establish a quite different way of conducting the business of government. The central Civil Service should consist of a relatively small core engaged in the function of servicing Ministers and managing departments, who will be the "sponsors" of particular government policies and services. Responding to these departments will be a range of agencies employing their own staff, who may or may not have the status of Crown servants, and concentrating on the delivery of their particular service, with clearly defined responsibilities between the Secretary of State and the Permanent Secretary on the one hand and the Chairmen or Chief Executives of the agencies on the other. Both departments and their agencies should have a more open and simplified structure.

Notes

1. In February 1988, Mrs. Thatcher gave her general endorsement to the report. She expressed the view that the new agencies would "generally be within the Civil Service, and their staff will continue to be civil servants."[2]

2. By July 1988, the Minister for the Civil Service stated that 29 activities, involving 170,000 persons in central government, had been identified as potential agency functions. These included Her Majesty's Stationery Office, the Meteorological Office and the Companies Registration Office.[3]

[2] H.C.Deb., Vol. 127, cols. 1149–56.

[3] Annexe, *Treasury & Civil Service Select Committee 8th Report 1987–88*, H.C. 494 (1987–88).

3. The House of Commons Select Committee on the Treasury has expressed concern about the vagueness of the Report, particularly in relation to the accountability of the new agencies to Parliament, and noted that 20 years earlier the Fulton Committee on the Civil Service had recommended the "hiving off" of discrete responsibilities to autonomous agencies (Cmnd. 3638).[4]

4. An expert in public administration has summed up these plans in the following way;

> "we are in any case probably talking about a reform that falls a long way short of a constitutional revolution. It may help to consolidate and develop the changes in Whitehall culture—towards a more businesslike way of conducting the affairs of government. . . . It may also help to weaken the concept of a unitary civil service, that has in many respects been an obstacle to improving efficiency. But the agencies are to be staffed by civil servants, by definition answerable in that capacity to ministers, and the traditional ground-rule of accountability to Parliament via ministers will remain intact."[5]

However, more recently, a well known commentator has observed:

> "if the cross-party consensus holds (and the signs are that it will), three quarters of the Civil Service, in terms of numbers, will be agencies of various kinds by the turn of the century, the most significant reform of Whitehall this century by far."[6]

5. At the end of 1991, approximately 200,000 officials were working in agencies (the largest group of them, 65,600 staffed the Social Security Benefits Agency, which administers the payment of benefits. The Inland Revenue plans to transfer 85 per cent. of its 60,000 staff to 34 "executive offices" by 1992 and 30 Executive Units have been established by the Customs and Excise Commissioners.[7] The government intends that all its executive activities will, as far as practicable, be operating on "Next Steps" lines by the end of 1993.[8]

(ii) Non-Departmental Public Bodies

During the eighteenth and nineteenth centuries, the Board system was a commonly used form of administrative organisation. The key feature of these organisations (ranging from the Poor Law Commission to the General Board of Health) was that they were not directly accountable to Parliament. However, they were gradually replaced by departments as the dominant form of central government administration. Nevertheless, there remain a number of bodies which perform public functions at the national government level that are not part of the ordinary departmental structure. Indeed, the implementation of the "Next Steps" programme (above) may contribute significantly to the growth of these bodies. Administrative lawyers are particularly interested in the legal personality of such Non-Departmental Public Bodies (hereafter N.D.P.B.s) and the judicial remedies available to control them. But, first it is necessary to consider the general issues of the modern functions performed by N.D.P.B.s, together with their accountability to Parliament, Ministers and the public generally.

[4] *Ibid.*
[5] G. Drewry, "Forward from F.M.I.: The Next Steps" [1988] P.L. 505 at p. 515.
[6] P. Hennessy, "The Last Retreat of Fame: Mrs Thatcher as History" (1991) 54 M.L.R. 492 at p. 496.
[7] *The Next Steps Agencies: Review 1991* (Cm. 1760) and *The Independent*, February 11, 1991.
[8] *The Citizen's Charter* (Cm. 1599, 1991), p. 36.

For further reading see *Craig*, pp. 71–92. I. Harden, N. Lewis and P. Birkinshaw, *Government by Moonlight* (1989). N. Lewis, "Regulating Non-Government Bodies," in J. Jowell & D. Oliver (eds.), *The Changing Constitution* (2nd ed. 1989).

REPORT ON NON-DEPARTMENTAL PUBLIC BODIES (PLIATZKY REPORT)

Cmnd. 7797 (1979)

[Soon after the election of the Conservative government in 1979, this report was prepared with the objectives of, *inter alia*, surveying the existing N.D.P.B.s and commenting upon the arrangements for their control and accountability. This report divided N.D.P.B.s into three categories, "executive bodies" that carried out a wide range of operational or regulatory functions, various scientific and cultural activities, and some commercial work; "advisory bodies" which provided external advice to ministers; and "tribunals." In this section we shall concentrate upon the first two categories and tribunals will be examined in the next chapter.]

3. Organisations in the executive etc. group generally employ staff and spend money, in some cases large amounts, on their own account. Advisory bodies and tribunals are not normally employers of staff or spenders of money themselves, but their expenses and the cost of staff working on their behalf are met by their sponsor Departments, that is, the Government Departments concerned with their affairs. In addition, Departments incur staff costs, in some cases substantial, through their own Departmental functions arising from their sponsorship role in relation to all three types of body.

4. Some non-Departmental organisations cover the whole of Great Britain, and a few cover the whole of the United Kingdom, *i.e.* including Northern Ireland. But in many cases Scotland, Wales and Northern Ireland have separate institutions.

5. At the start of this review there were 489 bodies in the executive group. Between them last year they were the channel for expenditure on capital and current account approaching £5,800 million and had around 217,000 staff. In addition Departments spent about £24 million in their sponsoring capacity for these bodies.

7. At the same date there were 1,561 advisory bodies, involving expenditure of about £13 million by their sponsor Departments. Two-thirds of this total is accounted for by as few as 22 networks of advisory bodies, each of which includes eight or more separate bodies, in some cases as many as 100 or 200, so as to cover all areas.

11. Executive-type bodies are mostly set up under a specific Act of Parliament, though some are set up by administrative action—in some cases by forming a company under the Companies Acts; a Department does not need specific legislation in order to form a company, though it needs Parliamentary approval for any money provided to the company. With advisory bodies the reverse is the case; that is to say, most of them

are set up by purely administrative action, but some of them have a statutory basis. Tribunals and other judicial bodies are set up to meet a specific statutory requirement. The feature common to all these cases is that they are in some sense part of the apparatus of government, without being Government Departments or divisions or branches or directorates of Departments, so that they do not come under the day to day direction of Ministers and Permanent Secretaries in charge of Departments; nor are they part of a local authority Department.

12. The case in principle for having an advisory committee with representation from outside the Department (as distinct from the justification in detail for all the committees which exist) is that the Department's own staff cannot provide the necessary advice by themselves, or that it may be desirable to enlist the participation of outside interests in order to formulate publicly acceptable proposals.

14. The case for having bodies of the executive type is more complex. It is that Parliament, or the Government with Parliamentary approval for the money involved, have decided that a certain function should be carried out for reasons of public policy, but that it is best carried out at arm's length from central government. There can be a number of reasons for this—because the work is of an executive character which does not require Ministers to take responsibility for its day to day management; because the work is more effectively carried out by a single-purpose organisation rather than by a Government Department with a wide range of functions; in order to involve people from outside government in the direction of the organisation; or, as a self-denying ordinance on the part of Government and Parliament, in order to place the performance of particular functions outside the party political arena.

15. Some fringe bodies go back a long way. The Development Commission, for instance, was set up in 1909, and the Horserace Totalisator Board—the Tote—goes back in one form or another to 1928. Organisations handling large sums of money, such as the New Town Development Corporations, have been set up by successive Governments since the second world war. A further fillip was given to this trend by the Fulton Committee's Report on the Civil Service in 1968 (Cmnd 3638) which recommended the creation of accountable units of management within Departments and examination of the possibility of a considerable extension of "hiving off" of autonomous bodies from Departments. Subsequent developments included the hiving off of a large part of the functions of the Department of Employment to the Manpower Services Commission, the Health and Safety Commission and the Advisory, Conciliation and Arbitration Service.

34. What is involved in being on a non-Departmental body differs a great deal from one kind of body to another. Generally speaking it is in the executive group that salaried posts are to be found, and even there a typical board will consist of a full-time or less than full-time chairman with a number of part-time members, though there are full-time members in

some cases; a board of this kind tends to have a full-time chief executive or equivalent officer whom it appoints.

35. The arrangements for advisory committees vary a great deal from case to case, as does the amount of work involved. Any remuneration paid usually takes the form of an honorarium or daily fee, but a high proportion of these appointments are unpaid.

38. The feature common to non-Departmental bodies generally is that Ministers appoint the chairman and members (though not the staff of bodies which have their own employees) and are accountable to Parliament for these appointments. In the case of some public appointments, not confined to those covered by this report, the relevant legislation provides for certain bodies, such as local authorities or representative organisations of employers or employees, to be consulted about appointments or to make nominations, or requires that the people appointed must have certain qualifications or experience. Otherwise, and subject to the special arrangements for tribunals, Ministers are free to seek the names of possible candidates from any source.

39. There is a Public Appointments Unit in the Civil Service Department which keeps a central list of potential members of public bodies, and some Departments keep a list of people with special qualifications for appointment to the bodies with which they are concerned. Departmental Ministers can obtain names from these sources but are free to seek suggestions from other sources within and outside government circles.

41. . . On various major appointments, such as the chairmanship of an executive board, Departmental Ministers naturally seek the Prime Minister's concurrence.

74. Legislation under which fringe bodies are set up, whether they are financed by grants or by other methods, generally gives the Minister concerned powers to give directions of at least a general character. Suitable powers of direction are an appropriate safeguard, though they are no substitute for an effective financial regime and a sensible working relationship.

75. Annual reports and accounts of fringe bodies, whether financed by grant in aid or from other sources, should be as informative as possible, not simply in giving news about their activities but also, in all cases where the nature of the operation lends itself to this approach, in providing material designed to help in forming a judgment on the cost-effectiveness of the organisation's activities or on the costs and benefits involved, where this is a more relevant concept.

76. Reports and accounts should include enough information about the remuneration and expenses of the chairman and members of the governing body and its employees to obviate any reasonable grounds for concern on this score. The material published about remuneration should go at least as far as that required of companies by the Companies Act. . . .

77. When a new fringe body is set up with a fairly finite mission, the legislation should contain provisions for its winding up when the mission

is complete. But in general it would not make for good management and morale and successful recruitment to go beyond this and give it only a short initial lease of life, subject to periodical renewal. On the other hand, fringe bodies should not be allowed to continue indefinitely in set ways without a fresh look being taken from time to time both at the need for their continued existence and at the success or otherwise of their form of organisation and method of operations.

79. As a general rule advisory committees should be set up either with a finite remit, which will automatically lead to the dissolution of the committee when the remit is discharged, or with a finite lease of life, after which the Committee would be disbanded unless a positive decision is taken to give it a new lease of life.

81. Between them these suggestions contain most of the ingredients indicated by experience for making up an alternative to a competitive market régime for those public bodies to which in their nature such a régime cannot apply. Within a framework of this kind the function of securing efficiency and economy must rest with the organisation's own management, while the main responsibility for oversight of its performance lies with its sponsoring Minister and Department.

82. There remains one further important ingredient in a régime of this kind, that is, monitoring by an external body. An important part of this function is discharged by the audit-based scrutinies carried out by the Public Accounts Committee of those bodies whose accounts are audited by the Comptroller and Auditor General, or his audits of Departmental expenditure involving non-Departmental bodies to whose books he has access. For the future, a further important contribution will be made by the 14 new Select Committees of the House of Commons set up in response to recommendations from the Select Committee on Procedure to examine the expenditure, administration and policy of the principal Government Departments and associated public bodies, and similar matters within the responsibilities of the Secretary of State for Northern Ireland.

Notes

1. Following the publication of the Pliatzky Report (above), the Civil Service Department issued a document in 1981 entitled *Non-Departmental Public Bodies: A Guide for Departments* and a second edition of this guide was promulgated during 1985. The Guide has been described as the informal constitution for N.D.P.B.s because, whilst primarily addressed to officials, it details both current government policy towards these bodies and the basic legal/administrative processes for their creation and dissolution. The Guide begins by stating that, "new N.D.P.B.s should be set up only if the functions they are to carry out are essential and need to be in the public sector, and it is clear that an N.D.P.B. is the most suitable and cost-effective machinery."[9] Subsequent chapters identify the legal means by which N.D.P.B.s may be created, (*e.g.* through being granted a Royal Charter or incorporation under the Companies Act); advice on the appointment and condi-

[9] p. 4.

tions of service of members; the forms of public disclosure of information relating to N.D.P.B.s, (*e.g.* through annual reports and accounts); and the procedures for dissolving such bodies, (*e.g.* how to wind-up a Royal Commission).

Harden has made a number of criticisms of the Guide. He believes that it fails to provide an accurate demarcation between government and non-government bodies, and is opaque about the appointments process. Furthermore:

> "the constitutional danger is that the publicly visible 'N.D.P.B. regime' embodied in the guide, and the limited form of public accountability through Parliament which it endorses, will be outflanked in a number of ways. First, 'ministerial responsibility' may become almost as much of a shield for the real activities of quasi-government as it is for those of government itself. Whilst, secondly, bargaining over public policy with powerful interest groups will be structured through quasi-non-government processes and institutions which remain unacknowledged even as 'public.' "

I. Harden, "A Constitution for Quangos?" [1987] P.L. 27 at p. 35.

2. For examples of judicial scrutiny of N.D.P.B.s see *R.* v. *Criminal Injuries Compensation Board, ex p. Lain* (below, p. 693); *Laker Airways Ltd.* v. *Department of Trade* (below, p. 433); *R.* v. *Monopolies and Mergers Commission, ex p. Argyll Group plc.* (below, p. 774).

Questions

1. In what ways does the legal form of a N.D.P.B. affect its accountability to Parliament, Ministers and the Courts?

2. Are there similarities between N.D.P.B.s and voluntary self-regulatory agencies (such as the Take-Over Panel or the Jockey Club) and, if so, should they be subject to a common administrative law framework?

(iii) Public Corporations

Public Corporations are a particular sub-species of N.D.P.B.s with the distinguishing feature that they always have a separate corporate personality. Very largely a creation of the twentieth century, they give rise to few technical legal problems, as in practice such sweeping powers are given to them by their constituent statutes, that the courts are virtually powerless to exercise any substantial supervision. In practice the problem that has most frequently come before the courts is the extent to which a particular corporation may be entitled to Crown immunity from suit or from the application of particular statutes.

For general reading see *Garner*, Ch. 12; *Wade*, Ch. 6. T. Prosser, *Nationalised Industries and Public Control* (1988).

NOTTINGHAM NO. 1 AREA HOSPITAL MANAGEMENT COMMITTEE v. OWEN

[1958] 1 Q.B. 50; [1957] 3 W.L.R. 707; 122 J.P. 5; 100 S.J. 852; [1957] 3 All E.R. 358, D.C. (Queen's Bench Division)

The Town Clerk of Nottingham took criminal proceedings under section 103 of the Public Health Act 1936 for a smoke nuisance caused, it was alleged, by smoke emitted from a chimney of a local hospital belonging to the Management Committee, a public corporation constituted under the National Health Service Act 1946.

The committee were required by statute to carry out their duties on behalf of the Minister of Health, and he was required to hold all the national health hospitals on trust for the Crown. In these circumstances, the court found that this was Crown property, and was therefore exempt from the penal provisions of section 103, especially in view of the alternative procedure provided under section 106 of the 1936 Act.

LORD GODDARD C.J.: . . . It is submitted that the hospital, being a hospital which is vested in the Minister, constitutes premises occupied for the public service of the Crown, and we have to see whether that is a well-founded submission. Before considering the provisions of the National Health Service Act 1946, it is necessary to glance at the provisions of the Public Health Act 1936. Under certain sections in that Act there are set out matters which are known as statutory nuisances. A bench of justices sitting as a court of summary jurisdiction do not have authority to make abatement orders in respect of every nuisance, but there are certain nuisances which are prescribed by statute as being fit matters for this summary jurisdiction. Among them is smoke nuisance; that is to say, the emission of large quantities of black smoke so as to be a nuisance and deleterious to the health of the neighbourhood. Sections 101 to 106 of the Public Health Act 1936, contain provisions with regard to smoke nuisances, and by section 103 if, in the opinion of the proper authority, a smoke nuisance exists by the emission of black smoke from chimneys which are not chimneys of private houses, proceedings can be taken before the justices and an application made for an order compelling the owner of the chimney to abate the nuisance. But, for some reason upon which we need not speculate, section 106 of the Act contains a provision—which does not appear in the statute book for the first time but was in the previous Public Health Acts, in substantially though not quite the same terms—that: "If it appears to a local authority that a smoke nuisance within, or affecting any part of, their district exists on any premises occupied for the public service of the Crown, they shall report the circumstances to the appropriate Government department, and, if the Minister responsible for that department is satisfied that after due inquiry that such a nuisance exists, he shall cause such steps to be taken as may be necessary to abate the nuisance and to prevent a recurrence thereof." Therefore, it seems clear under that section that the simple and speedy procedure which may be taken against private persons in respect of a smoke nuisance cannot be taken in respect of the emission of smoke from premises which are occupied for the public service of the Crown, but that in such a case the duty is on the local authority to report the matter to the Minister, who may, if he is satisfied that a nuisance exists, take such steps as may be necessary to abate the nuisance. It does seem, although it is not necessary to decide the point, that this provision only applies to summary proceedings taken under the Act and does not prevent the local authority from bringing an action for an injunction or the abatement of a nuisance as the case may be, but the question which we have to decide is whether this hospital comes within the expression "premises occupied for the public service of the Crown."

Section 1 of the National Health Service Act 1946, provides that: "It shall be the duty of the Minister of Health (hereafter in this Act referred to as 'the Minister') to promote the establishment in England and Wales of a comprehensive health service designed to secure improvement in the physical and mental health of the people of England and Wales and the prevention, diagnosis and treatment of illness, and for that purpose to provide or secure the effective provision of services in accordance with the following provisions of this Act," and one of the services that has to be provided is hospital accommodation and hospital treatment.

Section 3(1) provides: "As from the appointed day, it shall be the duty of the Minister to provide throughout England and Wales, to such extent as he considers necessary to meet all reasonable requirements, accommodation and services of the following descriptions, that is to say: (*a*) hospital accommodation." Then section 6 makes provision for the transfer of hospitals to the Minister. The hospitals are transferred to the Minister, who becomes the owner of them, and by section 7(3) of the Ministry of Health Act 1919: "For the purpose of acquiring and holding land, the Minister for the time being shall be a corporation sole by the name of the Minister of Health, and all land vested in the Minister shall be held in trust for His Majesty for the purposes of the Ministry of Health." So that once this hospital is transferred to the Minister under the National Health Service Act 1946, it seems to be clear that he holds it in trust for the Crown.

The Act of 1946 then goes on to provide how the Minister is to carry out his duties. Different provisions apply to teaching hospitals from those applying to general hospitals but, generally speaking, without going into it in too great detail, by section 11(1) "The Minister shall by order constitute, in accordance with Part I of the Third Schedule to this Act, boards, to be called regional hospital boards," and they have functions with respect to hospitals and specialist services. Then by subsection (3): "Every regional hospital board shall, within such period as the Minister may by direction specify, submit to the Minister a scheme for the appointment by them of committees, to be called hospital management committees, for the purpose of exercising functions with respect to the management and control of individual hospitals or groups of hospitals, other than teaching hospitals, providing hospital and specialist services in the area of the board."

It is not disputed that the Nottingham Area No. 1 Hospital Management Committee administers this hospital. By the Third Schedule, Part 4, both the regional board and the hospital management committee are made corporations, so they are corporate bodies and, as such corporate bodies, carry out the administration of this hospital, subject, of course, to the control of the Minister, and they are to carry it out on behalf of the Minister, whose duty it is to provide hospital accommodation.

The first thing to be noted in section 106 of the Public Health Act 1936, is that the section applies to premises "occupied for the public service of the Crown" and not to the occupiers: that is to say, it does not matter who occupies the premises; if they are occupied for the public service of the Crown the section applies, and there is no doubt that the occupiers of these premises are the hospital management committee. As the hospital management committee they are carrying on the duties which are imposed on the Minister, and I should find it very difficult to say that considering that this service, the hospital service, is a service which is provided by the Minister in pursuance of his duty to carry out the provisions of the Act of Parliament, that this is not a public service of the Crown.

At a late stage in this case Mr. Rodger Winn called our attention to an authority which seems to be of assistance. It is a quotation from the speech of Lord Westbury L.C. in *Mersey Docks and Harbour Board Trustees* v. *Cameron* (1864) 11 H.L.C. 443, 504, 505, where he said: "At last, in the case of the *Tyne Improvement Commissioners* v. *Chirton* (1859) 1 El. & El. 516, the Court of Queen's Bench recurred to that, which is in my opinion the true principle, namely, that the only ground of exemption from the statute of Elizabeth is that which is furnished by the rule, that the Sovereign is not bound by that statute, and that consequently when valuable property (that is, property capable of yielding a net rent above what is required for its maintenance), is sought to be exempted on the ground that it is occupied by bare trustees for public purposes, the public purposes must be such as are required and created by the government of the country, and are therefore to be deemed part of the use and service of the Crown." These purposes are such as are required and created by the statute for the Government of the country and are deemed to be part of the use and service of the Crown. In my opinion, it would be impossible to say that the provision of hospitals for the purposes of the National Health Service Act 1946, and the carrying on of a hospital is not for the public service of the Crown, and therefore I think that these premises are occupied for the public service of the Crown. As I say, I have some regret in this matter. This nuisance has been going on for a very long time. If the hospital had remained as it was before the Act, the justices would unquestionably have had jurisdiction to act in the way they did, and I can well understand their believing that the hospital management committee were amenable to their jurisdiction. However, for the reasons which I have endeavoured to state briefly I am of opinion that they were not, and that, therefore, this appeal must be allowed.

DONOVAN J. I agree. I think that the provisions of section 106 of the Public Health Act 1936 apply, and that they are too strong in their terms for the respondent local authority.

HAVERS J. I agree.

Appeal allowed.

Notes

1. In a Scottish case the House of Lords has held that an area health board is not immune from interdict proceedings by virtue of the Crown Proceedings Act 1947, s.21: *British Medical Association* v. *Greater Glasgow Health Board* [1989] A.C. 1211. See J. Wolffe, [1990] P.L. 14; and see generally P. Jackson, "The Crown and Statutes" [1990] Denning L.J. 45.

2. As we have already seen (above, Chapter 1) a major element in the post-1979 Conservative government's strategy towards public corporations owning and operating public utilities or other commercial undertakings, has been to subject them to various forms of privatisation. This development has resulted in relatively little direct litigation. One exception concerned the floatation of the trustee savings banks on the stock market in 1986. Under the Trustee Savings Banks Act 1985, the existing statutory trustee savings banks were abolished and replaced by successor limited liability companies. Depositors in the statutory banks brought actions in which they claimed that they were entitled to the surplus assets of the statutory banks when they were abolished. The House of Lords determined that the depositors' rights were limited to receiving their principal sums invested together with the interest due on those investments. Consequently, the surplus assets of the banks would pass to the successor companies and their new private shareholders: *Ross* v. *Lord Advocate* [1986] 1 W.L.R. 1078.

Later, several local authorities had their claim that the privatisation of public water authorities, by the Water Act 1989, infringed valuable property rights possessed by the councils struckout. Sir Nicolas Browne-Wilkinson V.C. concluded that the councils had no legal or equitable interests in the assets of the water authorities which were privatised. See *Sheffield City Council* v. *Yorkshire Water Services Ltd. and related actions* [1991] 2 All E.R. 280.

Question

Should the activities of public corporations be subject to greater judicial scrutiny?

(B) Local Government

In this section we will deal with the special position of local authorities, the relationship between members and officers *inter se* and in relation to other persons. Many of the problems that arise in connection with local authorities, in particular in relation to judicial control over their discretionary powers, are similar to those that arise in connection with agencies of central government and public corporations, and are considered elsewhere in this book. For general reading see *Garner*, Chs. 13–18; *Wade*, Ch. 4; *Craig*, Ch. 3; M. Loughlin, *Local Government in the Modern State* (1987). Detailed consideration of the law relating to local government can be found in the C. A. Cross (ed.) *Encyclopedia of Local Government Law*, and *Cross*.

Particular aspects of local government, law illustrated elsewhere in this book include: the application of the *ultra vires* principle to local authorities (below pp. 200 *et seq.*); delegation (pp. 282 *et seq.*); assurances given by officers to members of the public (pp. 336 *et seq.*), the fiduciary duty owed by local authorities to their rate/charge-payers (pp. 363 *et seq.*); appeals against local authority decisions (pp. 609 *et seq.*); and the liability of local authorities in tort and contract (Ch. 13).

(i) The Characteristics and Value of Local Government

THE CONDUCT OF LOCAL AUTHORITY BUSINESS

Cmnd. 9797 (1986)

Committee of Inquiry chaired by D. Widdicombe Q.C.

The constitutional position of local government

3.3 In Great Britain Parliament is sovereign. Although local government has origins pre-dating the sovereignty of Parliament, all current local authorities are the statutory creations of Parliament and have no independent status or right to exist. The whole system of local government could lawfully be abolished by Act of Parliament. Central government is not itself sovereign, and indeed its powers are—or may be—circumscribed by Parliament just as much as those of local government. In practice however central government is drawn from the political party with a majority in Parliament and its de facto political strength is accordingly much greater than that of local government.

The legislative form of local government

3.7 The principal characteristics of modern local authorities in Great Britain can be traced to the origins of elected local government in the 19th century. There have however been important changes, particularly in the functions they undertake and in their size. The system has never been a static one. Major re-organisations took place in 1974 and, in Scotland 1975, following the reports of the Redcliffe-Maud[1] and Wheatley[2] Commissions. Although a further re-organisation took place in London and the metropolitan counties on April 1, 1986 the characteristics of the great majority of local authorities were determined by those re-organisations, and can be summarised as follows:

(a) they are directly elected by popular franchise;

(b) they are multi-purpose: in most areas responsibilities are divided between two tiers of multi-purpose authorities;

(c) they cover large areas as measured in population (about 120,000 people on average for lower tier authorities);

(d) they have substantial responsibilities for the delivery of services. Indeed this is one of the reasons why it has been felt necessary to create such large authorities. The extent of autonomy from central government in the delivery of services varies between services;

[1] Report of the Royal Commission on Local Government in England, 1969. Cmnd. 4040.
[2] Report of the Royal Commission on Local Government in Scotland, 1969. Cmnd. 4150.

(e) they may only act within the specific powers set by Parliament. It would be possible for Parliament to grant local government a "general competence" to act for the good of its area. Instead they rely primarily on specific powers granted service by service;

(f) they may raise their own revenue. About 60 per cent. of national local government expenditure is currently financed from locally determined and collected rates* and rents, from other charges for services and from borrowing. The balance is financed from central government grant;

(g) they are corporate bodies. The powers of local authorities are vested corporately in their councillors as a whole. They are not vested in the majority party, nor in individual councillors, nor in officers. They rely on full-time professional officers, however, for the day-to-day discharge of their functions.

THE VALUE OF LOCAL GOVERNMENT

3.11 The value of local government stems from its three attributes of:

(a) pluralism, through which it contributes to the national political system;

(b) participation, through which it contributes to local democracy;

(c) responsiveness, through which it contributes to the provision of local needs through the delivery of services.

Pluralism

3.13 The case for pluralism is that power should not be concentrated in one organ of state but should be dispersed, thereby providing political checks and balances, and a restraint on arbitrary government and absolutism. This is not an argument for fragmentation of the state, nor for divided sovereignty, but rather for increasing the cohesiveness and stability of the state by making it less brittle and allowing within it some safety valve for the expression of contrary views.

Participation

3.18 Arguments about participation are less concerned with local government's position in the wider political system and more concerned with the quality of democracy within local government. As such they are relatively modern arguments, originating with the introduction of a popular franchise and remain in a continuing state of development as the nature of democracy itself continues to develop.

3.20 Local government offers two kinds of participation; participation in the expression of community views and participation in the actual

* Subsequently replaced by the Community Charge (Poll Tax) in relation to domestic dwellings in England and Wales (Local Government Finance Act 1988) and now by the Council Tax (Local Government Finance Act 1992) (Ed.).

delivery of services. It does so both through the process of electing representatives as councillors and through the opportunity to influence local government more directly through consultation, co-option, and local lobbying. These factors have led to much recent debate as to the quality of local democracy and how it might best be promoted.

Responsiveness

3.26 Proponents of local government argue that it is an **effective** means of delivering services because it has the ability, unlike a non-elected system of local administration, to be responsive to local needs. There is an important distinction between efficiency and effectiveness. Efficiency is concerned solely with output, effectiveness is concerned also with the meeting of needs. It is a distinction which applies in industry as much as it does in government. Efficiency in the production of manufactured goods is of little value if there is no market for those goods. A successful private industry needs to be responsive to its customers. Similarly those delivering local services need to be responsive to the local community, and it is argued that local government alone possesses that ability.

Notes

1. For an analysis of this report in its political context see P. McAuslan, "The Widdicombe Report: Local Government Business or Politics?" [1987] P.L. 154. Professor McAuslan describes recent central-local government relations thus, "the government's overriding aim which it has pursued with a fair degree of consistency since 1979 is to reduce the role, status, powers, financial independence, functions and, in some cases, the very existence of local government" (p. 162).

2. The views of councillors and other academics on the Widdicombe report can be found in a special edition of the journal *Local Government Studies*, Vol. 12, No. 6 (1986).

3. Part II of the Local Government Act 1992 establishes a Local Government Commission for England (replacing the Local Government Boundary Commission for England), whose remit includes the task of examining the structure of local government in England outside London with a view to moving where appropriate to single-tier authorities.

(ii) The Control by District Audit

PICKWELL v. CAMDEN LONDON BOROUGH COUNCIL

[1983] 1 Q.B. 962; [1983] 1 All E.R. 602; 80 L.G.R. 798, D.C. (Q.B.D.)

In February 1979 members of the National Union of Public Employees (N.U.P.E.) began indefinite strike action in the London Borough of Camden with a serious effect upon council services. The controlling group of Labour councillors agreed to negotiate with the local branch of N.U.P.E., despite the existence of contemporaneous national negotiations over local authority wage rates. A local settlement between N.U.P.E. and Camden resulted in an agreement that the relevant employees would receive at least £60 for a 35 hour week, which was approved by the Council on March 7, 1979. The next day the national negotiations resulted in a nationwide settlement which was less favourable to employees. However, the Camden employees continued to receive their extra pay. The District Auditor considered that the Camden pay settlement resulted in a £950,000 excess payment by the Council between 1978–81. He accordingly applied to the High Court for a declaration under s.161(1) of the Local Government Act 1972, that these items of account were contrary to law. In addition he sought an order under s.161(2) of the Act, in terms the court thought fit to make. The respondents were the Council and the 31 Labour councillors who had voted for the local settlement.

FORBES J. . . . I should now look at the provisions of the Local Government Act 1972 which govern these proceedings before this court, but before doing so I propose to glance briefly at the statutory provisions which preceded them. In doing this I am not seeking to derive assistance in the interpretation of the Act of 1972 but to contrast the past and present position of the court and the district auditor and to indicate the statutory background against which some of the authorities were decided.

The first situation to look at is that obtaining before 1933 under the Public Health Act 1875 (38 & 39 Vict. c. 55). I do not propose to read the statute in extenso. It is sufficient to say that it provided for the annual audit of local accounts by district auditors and contained these provisions:

> "247 . . . (6) Any ratepayer or owner of property in the district may be present at the audit, and may make any objection to such accounts before the auditor; and such ratepayers and owners shall have the same right of appeal against allowances by an auditor as they have by law against disallowances: (7) Any auditor acting in pursuance of this section shall disallow every item of account contrary to law, and surcharge the same on the person making or authorising the making of the illegal payment, and shall charge against any person accounting the amount of any deficiency or loss incurred by the negligence or misconduct of that person, or of any sum which ought to have been but is not brought into account by that person, and shall in every such case certify the amount due from such person, and on application by any party aggrieved shall state in writing the reasons for his decision . . ."

The section also provides so far as is relevant that any person so surcharged, or any ratepayer or owner aggrieved by a refusal to disallow, may apply to the Divisional Court for certiorari or alternatively appeal to the Local Government Board. The duties of that board were subsequently taken over by the Minister of Health.

The features of this procedure were thus that the district auditor himself made the surcharge, and he was under a mandatory duty to do so, wherever the item of account was contrary to law. The challenge to that decision before the courts was by certiorari. This inevitably meant that the court was exercising a supervisory and not an appellate jurisdiction. It also meant that the onus was on the applicant to show that the district auditor was wrong. Where the court is exercising a supervisory jurisdiction its approach to the matter in hand is necessarily different from its approach when acting as a Court of Appeal. The approach is often referred to as the *Wednesbury* doctrine because the elements are conveniently summarised in the judgment of Lord Greene M.R. in *Associated Provincial Picture Houses Ltd.* v. *Wednesbury Corporation* [1948] 1 K.B. 223. . . .

The principles of *Wednesbury* can therefore be seen as the corollary of the assertion of a supervisory rather than an appellate jurisdiction and involve, so far as is material here, the three brief propositions: (1) an authority must not be affected by immaterial nor ignore material considerations: (2) an authority must not act in such a way that it can be said of it that no reasonable authority, properly directing itself to what was material, could have concluded that it was entitled so to act: and (3) in reviewing the acts of an authority the court will not substitute its own view of how a discretion should be exercised for that of the authority entrusted by Parliament with the discretion. . . .

The Local Government Act 1933 repealed the provisions of the Public Health Act 1875. The provisions relating to district auditors are to be found in Part X. There is again a provision for a right of objection to the accounts which the district auditor is engaged in auditing. The right was given, not to a ratepayer or property owner, as in the Act of 1875, but, curiously, to any local government elector for the local authority area. The duties of the district auditor, however, remained the same, and in the same mandatory form. The arrangements for challenging the district auditor's decisions were markedly different. Any person aggrieved by any decision of the district auditor, whether to disallow or to refuse to do so, could appeal either to the High Court or Minister. The powers of the court or Minister are given in section 229(2) which, so far as is relevant, is in these terms:

> "The court or Minister on such an appeal shall have power to confirm, vary or quash the decision of the auditor, and to remit the case to the auditor with such directions as the court or Minister thinks fit for giving effect to the decision on appeal . . ."

I think that it has never been doubted that these words effectively mean that the court's jurisdiction was still intended to be a supervisory one and that therefore the principles which, merely as a convenient shorthand, one refers to as the *Wednesbury* principles apply. Subject to that explanation the position remained precisely as it was under the Act of 1875: the mandatory duty lay on the district auditor, the onus lay on the party aggrieved to show that he had been wrong, and the question still remained: Was the item of account contrary to law?

The modern position is to be found in section 161 of the Local Government Act 1972. I need not look at the provisions governing the audit itself. A local government elector for the area still has his right of objection to the accounts. I should read section 161(1) to (3):

"(1) Where the audit of any accounts under this Part of this Act is carried out by a district auditor and it appears to him that any item of account is contrary to law he may apply to the court for a declaration that the item is contrary to law except where it is sanctioned by the Secretary of State. (2) On an application under subsection (1) above the court may make or refuse to make the declaration asked for, and where the court makes that declaration then, subject to subsection (3) below, it may also—(*a*) order that any person responsible for incurring or authorising any expenditure declared unlawful shall repay it in whole or in part to the body in question and, where two or more persons are found to be responsible, that they shall be jointly and severally liable to repay it as aforesaid; and (*b*) if any such expenditure exceeds £2,000 and the person responsible for incurring or authorising it is a member of a local authority, order him to be disqualified from being a member of a local authority for a specified period; and (*c*) order rectification of the accounts. (3) The court shall not make an order under subsection (2)(*a*) or (*b*) above if the court is satisfied that the person responsible for incurring or authorising any such expenditure acted reasonably or in the belief that the expenditure was authorised by law, and in any other case shall have regard to all the circumstances, including that person's means and ability to repay that expenditure or any part of it."

It is clear that there has been a fundamental change in the position of the district auditor in relation to items in the account which may be contrary to law. The district auditor is no longer under a duty to disallow such items nor to surcharge the amounts on the persons responsible. He has a discretionary power to make an application to the court for a declaration. The court, too, is in a fundamentally different situation. It is not to embark on the process of seeing whether the district auditor was right. It must itself decide all questions which arise, both of fact and law. The onus is also altered: the onus of satisfying the court that the item of account is contrary to law is now on the district auditor. . . .

[After citing *Roberts* v. *Hopwood* [1925] A.C. 578: see below, p. 363]

The case seems to me to decide no more than this, that where the inevitable inference which must be drawn is that an obviously excessive wage payment was agreed to be paid without any regard to any commercial consideration and solely on some extraneous principle, as, for instance, philanthropy, such a payment can only be regarded as a gift and is not covered by a statutory power to pay reasonable wages. Looking back, as we do, over 60 years of progress in the field of social reform and industrial relations some of their Lordships' observations may, with the benefit of this hindsight, appear unsympathetic. But what has changed over those years is our attitudes to what should be regarded as pure philanthropy; the basic legal principle, that a payment is illegal which cannot be justified by reference to the objects for which a statutory power is granted, still remains. . . .

Of course it is plain that a local authority owes a fiduciary duty to its ratepayers: it also owes a duty, laid on it specifically by Parliament, to provide a wide range of services for its inhabitants, be they ratepayers, electors or neither. It is entitled as an employer to have regard to the interests and welfare of its workforce, as any good employer should. It must therefore often be involved in balancing fairly these interests which may frequently conflict. . . .

But I think despite this the district auditor in considering the accounts, and certainly the court in considering any application for a declaration under section 161, must have due regard to the other duties which the local authority has to discharge. If it can be shown, and the onus is now on the district auditor to show it, that a local authority has deliberately topped the balance in favour of one interest over others then, whether this be put as taking into account irrelevant material or as the brand of unreasonableness to which *Wednesbury* refers, it is plainly something beyond the power which was entrusted to it. . . .

The position is thus that on February 13, 1979, the Labour group's decision to agree to a £60 minimum earnings level and a 35-hour week was not taken freely and voluntarily and without pressure. The council was faced with a position where vital services had been so disrupted that real hardship was being caused, not only to the elderly and handicapped, but to the commercial concerns who pay rates but have no elective voice, and where the whole administrative machine of the borough was in imminent danger of having to close down. To this should be added a belief, not unreasonable in the circumstances, that negotiations at national level were not being pursued as effectively or speedily as was required. It seems to me that in this climate we are worlds away from Poplar in the 1920s where a calm and deliberate decision to indulge in what then passed for philanthropy was being taken. Nor do I regard it as the inevitable inference to be drawn from the payment in those circumstances of what might in others be regarded as excessive wages that the group ignored the interests of the ratepayers or any other relevant consideration or in any way can be regarded as unreasonable as that term is understood in *Associated Provincial Picture Houses Ltd.* v. *Wednesbury Corporation* [1948] 1 K.B. 223. I remain wholly unsatisfied that the district auditor has made out a case for declaring the decision to concede the £60 minimum and the 35-hour week unlawful. . . .

The district auditor was of course right to make this application. The power to do so falls just as much within his discretion as did the power to pay the wages he seeks to challenge, and, although different factors affect the two discretions. I do not wish to give any impression that the district auditor exercised his discretion wrongly in this matter. Much publicity, and much of it hostile, was attracted to the Camden decision. It is clear that the district auditor thought that Camden had given in too easily, and without a fight, to the strikers' demands. But there is nothing here to suggest that there was any collusion or collaboration between councillors and the strikers. If there had been this would of course have been wholly improper and would have struck directly at the good faith of the council's decision to pay these wages. But as it is I can reiterate that in my view it is not possible in the circumstances of this case to draw the inference that the council here ignored relevant material, were guided by improper motives, or acted in such a way as no reasonable council could properly act. I would refuse the declaration asked.

ORMROD L.J., gave a separate judgment in which he upheld the lawfulness of the expenditure.

Notes

1. Crawford believed that the case clarified the role of the auditor and the courts in relation to the burden of proof under s.161 of the 1972 Act; he also reported that some local authorities had greeted the decision with euphoria as an important defence against the value-judgments of the auditor: C. Crawford, "Auditors, Local Government and the Fiduciary Duty" [1983] P.L. 248.

2. The system of local government audit was subject to further reforms by the Local Government Finance Act 1982. The Act, *inter alia*, created a new body called the Audit Commission appointed by the Secretary of State. It has three main functions: (a) to appoint auditors for local authorities in England and Wales; (b) to prepare a code of audit practice to govern local authority audits; and (c) to undertake studies to promote economy, efficiency and effectiveness in the provision of local government services. Currently 70 per cent. of local authority audits are conducted by members of the District Audit Service, who are part of the Audit Commission. During the late 1980s the Commission expressed its concern about "creative accounting" devices used by some councils to enable the latter to balance their budgets. In the words of the Commission, "the general picture, however, is of loopholes being identified and exploited until blocked by fresh controls: after which the emphasis moves on to identify fresh loopholes."[10] A revised version of the original code of practice was approved by Parliament in 1988. The Commission have stated that their value for money studies, on topics such as highways maintenance, have resulted in savings of £219m since 1983.[11] For a brief account of the background to the creation of the Audit Commission see, R. Shaw, "The Audit Commission and its Role," Vol. 9 *Local Government Studies*, p. 19 (1983).

3. The House of Lords has held that in the performance of certain district functions (notably the issuing of a certificate under the Local Government Finance Act 1982, s.20(1), that a member of a local authority has been guilty of wilful misconduct which has caused the authority to incur a financial loss) the District Auditor is required to act fairly: see *Lloyd* v. *McMahon* [1987] A.C. 625, below p. 541.

4. On local government expenditure, see also *Roberts* v. *Hopwood* (below, p. 363) and the *Bromley* case (below, p. 372).

[10] *Audit Commission Annual Report 1988* (H.M.S.O.).
[11] *Ibid.*

(iii) Disclosure of Interest by Members

RANDS v. OLDROYD

[1959] 1 Q.B. 204; [1958] 3 W.L.R. 583; 128 J.P. 1; 102 S.J. 811; [1958] 3 All E.R. 344; 56 L.G.R. 429, D.C. (Q.B.D.)

The defendant was managing director of and held a controlling interest in a building company and was also a member of the local council. The company had taken part in various building contracts for the council, but had not tendered for any such contracts since 1954. In 1956, in view of his position on the council, the defendant decided that the company would not tender in future for any building contracts for the council. In 1957, at a meeting of the council, a motion was proposed that, where it was required that tenders should be obtained, the borough engineer should submit a tender on behalf of his department, and where necessary, the direct labour force should be increased to implement that policy. The motion was subsequently amended by deleting that part referring to the increase of the direct labour force, and the defendant voted in favour of the motion as amended. An information was preferred against the defendant under section 76 of the Local Government Act 1933 (now section 94 of the Local Government Act 1972, below, p. 587).

LORD PARKER C.J. . . . It is clear that the member of the council concerned, namely, the defendant, can only have an indirect pecuniary interest in this case if the company itself has a direct pecuniary interest. Therefore one can limit the matter to simply this: Did Henry Rands & Son Ltd. in the circumstances of this case have a direct pecuniary interest in any contract or proposed contract or other matter which was the subject of discussion at the meeting? There is no question here of any contract or proposed contract. If the company had a direct pecuniary interest it was because they had a direct pecuniary interest in an "other matter," and what is said quite shortly is this, that the matter under discussion was a matter which, to put it generally, seriously affected the company in a pecuniary way in that, if the original motion was carried, the company of the borough engineer might well be such as to prevent the company, if they tendered, from ever getting a contract. It is said that, accordingly, they had a financial interest and a direct financial interest in the matter to be discussed, and which was discussed at that meeting.

The all-important matter is to consider the mischief aimed at by section 76. One can say it is obvious, and indeed it is. It was put by Lord Esher M.R. in *Nutton* v. *Wilson* (1889) 22 Q.B.D. 744 at p. 747) a case considering a rather similar provision in the Public Health Act, 1875 in these words: "I adhere to what I have before said with regard to provisions of this kind. They are intended to prevent the members of local boards, which may have occasion to enter into contracts, from being exposed to temptation, or even to the semblance of temptation." Lindley L.J. in the same case said (at p. 748): "To interpret words of this kind, which have no very definite meaning, and which perhaps were purposely employed for that very reason, we must look at the object to be attained. The object obviously was to prevent the conflict between interest and duty that might otherwise inevitably arise."

That is clearly the object of section 76 of the Local Government Act, 1933, and whereas, of course, a consideration of the mischief aimed at does not enable the court to construe the words in a wider sense than they appear, it at least means that the court would not be acute to cut down words otherwise wide merely because this was a penal statute. Mr. Wilson in his very able argument has contended that, nevertheless, the words "having a direct pecuniary interest in any contract or proposed contract or other matter," are not as wide, properly construed, as one would otherwise think. He relies in particular on the words "or other matter," and he says that whether one looks at the matter as a case of *ejusdem generis* or of *noscitur a sociis*, at any rate "other matter" must be something confined to what he would say was a specific transaction, and not a matter of what might be said to be general policy. Apart from relying on that principle he also points out that in the Municipal Corporations Act, 1882, which was repealed by the Local Government Act, 1933, the corresponding section, section 22(3), was in these terms: "A member of the council shall not vote or take part in the discussion of any matter before the council, or a committee, in which he has, directly or indirectly, by himself or by his partner, any pecuniary interest." He points out that that is quite general; there is no reference there to a specific contract or proposed contract, and he invites the court to say that section 76 was intended to be a limitation on what heretofore had been a very general provision. I find it impossible to give any satisfactory narrower meaning, even if I were so minded, to those words "any contract or proposed contract or other matter." I do not propose to go through the number of illustrations which have been canvassed in this court, but the more one does consider the matter the more difficult and impossible it is to cut down those words "or other matter" to something which was definable and which was a limitation on what appear to be general words. Bearing in mind the mischief aimed at by this Act, I do not think those words are to be read in other than a very general way, and I see no ground for introducing a limitation which, as I said, is one which cannot satisfactorily be defined.

Mr. Wilson pointed out that if you construe section 76 in a very wide way you may make business at council meetings impossible, it may stultify the whole proceedings, and that he invokes as another ground for cutting down the general meaning of those words. I quite appreciate the force of that argument, but I think the limitation to be found in section 76 is not in regard to the words "in any contract or proposed contract or other matter," but in the consideration of whether the person under consideration—the company here—had a direct pecuniary interest. I think the limitation is to be found in that word "direct" as opposed to a pecuniary interest which is too remote. In the present case I am satisfied that the company did have a direct pecuniary interest, and that that interest was not too remote to bring them within the words of the section. All these cases, of course, must be determined ultimately on their particular facts, but I think that some help is to be gained by a consideration of one of the only two cases which have come before this court on this question, namely, *Brown* v. *Director of Public Prosecutions* ([1956] 2 Q.B. 369; [1956] 2 W.L.R. 1087; [1956] 2 All E.R. 189). The question there to be debated was as to lodgers' allowances to be paid by tenants of council houses, and three of the councillors who were on the council considering this matter were in fact tenants of council houses, albeit they had not any lodgers. The court were clearly of opinion that those councillors who were already tenants, albeit they did not have lodgers as yet and might never have lodgers, did have a pecuniary interest in the contract or proposed contract of tenancy. The court went on to contrast the position of those councillors who might become tenants of a council house in the future but who as yet had not become tenants. It is enough, I think, to refer to two passages, first, in the judgment of Lord Goddard C.J., where he said ([1956] 2 Q.B. 369 at p. 376): "I think that Parliament has laid down that on any matter in which a member of a local authority has a pecuniary interest—and he undoubtedly has a pecuniary interest if he is paying rent for a house owned by the council—he should not vote at all. . . ." A little further on he refers to what might be thought to be anomalies; he said (at p. 377): "It is true that anomalies may occur—if they are really anomalies, though I do not think they are—for instance, councillors might vote on those matters knowing, perhaps, that in a few months' time they might themselves be the occupiers of council houses and pay rent to the council. One cannot deal with every point which arises, but if a person occupies a council house, I think that he is debarred by the terms of section 76 from voting. Again, Donovan J. in his judgment ([1956] 2 Q.B. 369 at p. 378) after stating: "The object of section 76(1) is clearly to prevent councillors from voting on a matter which may affect their own pockets and which may therefore affect their judgment," goes on to say: "I am referring to the three who had not taken any lodgers or sublet at the time, but who each had a council house which was a potential income-producing asset. Their case is different from a councillor who merely had a hope of obtaining such a house in the future." The facts there were quite different. What was being considered was a contract of tenancy, but I think the relevance of it is that in laying down the limitation in the case of councillors who had not yet got tenancies, the court were making the very point I am trying to make, namely, that one has to consider whether the pecuniary interest was direct or remote, and they were really saying that the interest of councillors who had not a council house was too remote, whereas those that did have a council house came within the words of the section. In the present case the company clearly had a direct pecuniary interest in the matter under discussion.

Finally, I should say this: The justices found that not only since 1954 had the company not tendered, but that the defendant himself had decided that in view of his position as vice-chairman of the housing and town planning committee of the council, his company would not tender in the future for any building contracts of the council. Further, the justices say: "We were of opinion that the [defendant] was sincere in his statement to us that his company did not intend to tender for any further council work." I cannot think that that can affect the question whether there has been an offence committed or not. It goes very clearly to mitigation but not, I think, to defence because at any time the defendant and the company could have changed their minds and could have tendered. It is a matter which the justices very properly took into consideration in mitigation and they gave what I think is a very appropriate sentence namely an absolute discharge. In my view, the justices, who dealt very ably with a difficult case, came to a correct decision, and I would dismiss this appeal.

CASSELS and STREATFEILD JJ. delivered concurring judgments.

Appeal dismissed.

Notes

1. In 1975 the Government and local authorities agreed a voluntary National Code of Local Government Conduct. Paragraph 3 of the Code required councillors to withdraw from meetings where they had relevant non-pecuniary interests, (*e.g.* friendship with a person affected by the local authority's decision). The Widdicombe Report disclosed that the Code had been formally adopted by 82 per cent. of local authorities,[12] while the Local Government Ombudsmen normally regarded breaches of the Code as maladministration in so far as the Code related to matters within their jurisdiction.

2. Now, the Local Government and Housing Act 1989, s.31, empowers the Secretary of State, after consultation with local authorities, to issue a statutory code, which must be approved by both Houses of Parliament. Where the Local Ombudsmen find a councillor has acted in breach of the statutory code they must generally name the councillor in their report (s.32). See DoE Circular No. 8/90.

3. The Widdicombe Report also noted that 50 per cent. of local authorities had introduced non-statutory registers of members' interests.[13] They favoured this development and recommended that all councils should be obliged to produce a public register of their members' pecuniary and non-pecuniary interests. Section 19 of the Local Government and Housing Act 1989 enables the Secretary of State to promulgate regulations obliging councillors to notify their authority of the councillors' prescribed direct and indirect pecuniary interests. Failure to supply the prescribed information or supplying false/misleading information is made a criminal offence. The regulations may require the registers to be kept open for public inspection. See the Local Authorities (Members' Interests) Regulations 1992 (S.I. 1992 No. 618). See *Garner*, pp. 401–404.

Questions

1. The defendant in *Rands* v. *Oldroyd* contended that the *ejusdem generis* rule or the *noscitur a sociis* rule should be applied to the words "other matter" in the

[12] Report, para. 6:17.
[13] Report, para. 6:44.

phrase "having a direct pecuniary interest in any contract or proposed contract or other matter." What, in your view, would have been the consequence in practical terms if the court had accepted this contention?

2. If a member having an interest votes on a matter in contravention of these provisions, is the decision of the authority (or committee) void in law?

3. Compare the cases on the rules against interest and bias (the *nemo judex* rule of natural justice) below pp. 565 *et seq.*

(iv) Rights of the Public to Attend Meetings

R. v. LIVERPOOL CITY COUNCIL, ex p. LIVERPOOL TAXI FLEET OPERATORS' ASSOCIATION

[1975] 1 All E.R. 379; [1975] 1 W.L.R. 701; 119 S.J. 166; (1974) 73 L.G.R. 143, D.C. (Q.B.D.)

[The relevant facts appear in the judgment.]

LORD WIDGERY C.J.: In these proceedings counsel moves on behalf of the Liverpool Taxi Fleet Operators' Association for a variety of forms of relief under the prerogative orders. More especially, and in my judgment central to his motion, is an application for an order of certiorari to remove into this court with a view to its being quashed a resolution of the Liverpool City Council ("the corporation") dated October 9, 1974, the effect of which was to authorise the grant of an increased number of hackney carriage licences to operate within the city boundaries.

The substantial ground for the relief sought is that the committee meeting leading up to the decision of the corporation on October 9, 1974 was itself held in breach of the provisions of the Public Bodies (Admission to Meetings) Act 1960 in that it is alleged the public were not admitted to the relevant committee meeting as required by that Act.

There is a certain history to this application. I mention it very briefly because it seems to me to have no real bearing on the issue which is before the court. A very similar matter was before this court, and subsequently the Court of Appeal, in *Re Liverpool Taxi Owners' Association* ([1972] 2 All E.R. 589; [1972] 2 Q.B. 299, below, p. 502). That was a case which again had raised the vexed issue of whether there should be additional hackney carriage licences in Liverpool, this being a matter of very considerable interest to those whose livelihood depends on obtaining and retaining licences to operate such cabs, and indeed to those who already operate such cabs and who wish to be protected against unfair competition by an undue increase in the number. In the matter which was before the court in 1972 it was laid down that the corporation in exercising their undoubted jurisdiction to grant or withhold the grant of licences were required to act fairly, and in particular were required to give interested parties an opportunity of making representations before any decision in regard to the grant of new licences was taken.

Further intervention by this court occurred as recently as July 1974 because the corporation, being minded to alter the number of hackney carriage licences, and mindful of the directions of this court and the Court of Appeal in 1972, had invited representations before embarking on their decision but unhappily had not made that invitation sufficiently all embracing to bring in all those who were interested, and accordingly an application for prohibition in this court on 19th July to prohibit the corporation from acting on the then current resolution was successful because the corporation conceded that it was in the wrong and the resolution then made by the corporation was duly set aside.

It is in the autumn of 1974 that the corporation make their third attempt to deal with this problem and they began by publishing a public notice dealing with their plans. The notice went out on or about 14th August and it says in the plainest terms, it being a notice in the public press, that the corporation are proposing to review the present issue of licences for taxi cabs. It recognises in terms that the corporation are under a duty to hear representations before reaching a conclusion and invites all those who wish to make representations to attend at a meeting of the Highways and Environment Committee to be held on September 18, 1974.

If I may pause there, so far so good. The corporation appear to be following to the letter the lessons which they have learnt, if I may say so without giving offence, in the two previous proceedings before us here. The notice of course came to the attention of the applicants, who are a representation of a very large number of taxi drivers in Liverpool. In the first instance the applicants seem to have been minded to appear at the committee meeting fixed for 18th September and to make representations. But in the end they decided that they would not make representations, but they informed the corporation that they wished to attend the meeting in order to listen to the representations which were made by other people.

So one comes to the meeting of 18th September. It is at this meeting that the resolution was passed, which on adoption by the corporation on 9th October becomes the resolution under attack in the present case. On 18th September the room set aside for the meeting of the committee had 55 seats. When those concerned began to assemble it became apparent that there were 22 members of the corporation who wished to sit on the committee on that day, or at least to be present on that day. That in itself was some indication of how keen is the interest in this matter in Liverpool. In addition to the 22 members of the corporation who wanted seats there were 17 officials. One feels bound to say that seems rather a large number of officials, but it is not for us in this court to decide what was or was not necessary in that respect. There were also two police officers. So of the original 55 seats, 41 were absorbed in that way, leaving only 14 vacant. Those 14 had to serve for the claims of the press, the public and those individuals who were making representations to the committee.

It is not difficult to understand that the number of seats was clearly inadequate for that purpose: all the more so, because when the meeting was about to start there were something like 40 people outside waiting to come in being either members of the public or interested persons minded to make representations or otherwise concerned to be present. There were 40 of them there, coming to deal with a subject on which, as I have said, feelings ran high.

The decision as to what to do in that event fell on Mrs. Jones, who was the chairman of the committee, and she tells us in her affidavit what the position was. She said that having regard to the numbers to which I have already referred it was clear that it was not possible to throw the meeting open to members of the public in the ordinary sense of the word. There just was not room for that purpose. Again there was no very obvious way in which individual members of the public could be selected to occupy such seats as there were. This was not a case where there was a public gallery set aside and marked out for use as such, and it was not a case where there was an orderly queue of people from whom the first six or eight, or whatever number it was, could be taken. If there had been an indication to the assembled 40 outside that there were 14 seats, the possibility of an ugly rush was clear enough.

But not only that, in Mrs. Jones's mind there were strong reasons for saying in this case that each person coming forward to make his representations about the issue should be entitled to make those representations to the committee not in the presence of others making conflicting representations. Whether that was a sensible point of view or not is not for us to comment on, but I am bound to say that I see no reason at all why that should be regarded as other than a tenable conclusion in the rather unusual facts and circumstances of this case.

Having regard to all those matters, Mrs. Jones put it to the committee and the committee agreed that the public should be excluded from the meeting but the press should be allowed to attend. No doubt Mrs. Jones thought there would probably be room for the press, and this on the face of it, it may be, was a perfectly sensible compromise. But be that as it may, the committee adopted Mrs. Jones's suggestion on those lines and the resolution makes reference to that fact. It is resolution 101 of the relevant committee on the 18th September, and it says:

> "Exclusion of Public. Resolved that members of the public, with the exception of the Press, be excluded from the meeting during consideration of the following item in view of the limitations of available space and in order that the business of the Committee may be carried out satisfactorily."

That is the reason recorded in the minutes for the exclusion of the public. The contention that these proceedings were irregular, and irregular to the point that the resolution should be set aside, is entirely based on the provisions of the 1960 Act to which I have already referred. Section 1(1) provides:

> "Subject to subsection (2) below, any licence of a local authority or other body exercising public functions, being an authority or other body to which this Act applies, shall be open to the public."

The expression "body" there does include, as counsel have been kind enough to agree, this committee by virtue of the extension of the 1960 Act produced by s.100 of the Local Government Act 1972. So the committee was a body within the meaning of that subsection and thus required to open its proceedings to the public subject to s.1(2) of the 1960 Act, which s.1(2) says:

> "A body may, by resolution, exclude the public from a meeting (whether during the whole or part of the proceedings) whenever publicity would be prejudicial to the public interest by reason of the confidential nature of the business to be transacted or for other special reasons stated in the resolution and arising from the nature of that business or of the proceedings; and where such a resolution is passed, this Act shall not require the meeting to be open to the public during proceedings to which the resolution applies."

So under s.1(2) it is permissible for the committee to resolve to exclude the public for special reasons stated in the resolution and arising from the nature of that business, that is to say the business of the body or of the proceedings.

The first question I think we have to decide here is whether the public really were excluded or not in this particular case. It is, I think, important to stress that authorities arranging committee meetings and other meetings to which the 1960 Act applies must have regard to their duty to the public. That means they must have regard when making the arrangements for the committee meeting to the provision of reasonable accommodation for the public. If a committee was minded to choose to meet in a very small room and turned round and said "We cannot have the public in because there is no room," it would be acting in bad faith and it would not be beyond the long arm of this court. The committee must in the first instance so organise its affairs as to recognise its obligation to the public. But of course if the interest in the matter is unexpectedly great, if the estimates of persons attending are proved to be too low, and if the accommodation reasonably allotted to the public is filled up, then other members of the public will be excluded but not excluded by order of the committee; they will be excluded for the simple reason that no more can get in the space provided.

If that situation is reached, it is wrong to speak of the exclusion of the public at all in the context in which we use the phrase in this case, but in my judgment that was not this case, and I am moved to that conclusion most by the fact that the committee themselves did not regard this as a case in which the public were only turned back because the last seat had gone. The last seat indeed had not gone. The committee quite deliberately decided to exclude the public, and their conduct must be justified, if at all, under the terms of s.1(2) of the 1960 Act.

Next I turn to consider what was the reason which prompted the exclusion order and we cannot do better than take the account given by Mrs. Jones. Indeed I think that is the only source to which one can go. As I read her affidavit, extracts from which I have already given, there were really two reasons in her mind somewhat overlapping and perhaps slightly confusing each other because they do overlap.

I think she was mindful of the fact that with only a minimum number of seats available there was no practical way in which the public could be selected to come and occupy those seats. In so far as that was her reason, and later the reason of the committee which adopted her suggestion, I would have thought that was a perfectly good reason under s.1(2). It would not be a case of a body declining to face up to its responsibility and provide accommodation for the public. It would be a case of a body which found that its arrangements, apparently sensibly made, had been swamped by the number of people who sought to attend. If in those circumstances the committee said "The only way out of this is to keep all the members of the public out," and if they took that view fairly and honestly, then I think that that would be a reason arising from the nature of the business or the proceedings within the meaning of s.1(2).

But, equally, as it seems to me, the second reason which Mrs. Jones put forward is a valid one as well. The second reason, it will be remembered, was that it was desirable that individual applicants should be heard in the absence of competing applicants. That seems to me to be a conclusion which could properly be reached by this committee if so minded, and indeed there is a hint of something rather like that in s.1(3), a subsection to which I need not refer in detail.

Accordingly, if the committee had said either separately or in addition to their first reason that they wanted to exclude the public in order that individual applicants could be individually heard, I would have thought that could be regarded as a special reason arising from the nature of the business or the proceedings within the terms of s. 1(2).

So it seems to me that the acceptable reasons were there and that they were the reasons which caused Mrs. Jones to give the committee the advice she did and caused the committee to adopt the resolution which it adopted.

The only remaining stumbling block is whether those reasons have been correctly stated in the minute as required by the section. I have read the minute and in so far as the reason was based on lack of available space that reason is mentioned in the minute. But in so far as the refusal of admission to the public was based on the desire to hear applicants individually, then in my judgment that reason cannot be discovered from the terms of the minute itself. It seems to me that the expression "that the business of the committee may be carried out satisfactorily," is too vague to meet the requirement of the statute where it insists that reasons for this kind of decision be given. Therefore I would be bound to say that looked at by themselves those words did not adequately show as a reason why the committee thought that individual applicants should be individually heard.

Accordingly, the final question which has to be decided is whether, given adequate reasons, the decision of the committee becomes irregular, whether as a nullity or otherwise by reason of the failure properly to state the reasons in the resolution.

At this point I think that one must distinguish between statutory provisions which are clearly imperative or mandatory and those which are merely directory. In my opinion the requirement that the reasons shall be stated in the resolution is a purely directory requirement. The effect of that is that the resolution does not automatically become a nullity by reason of the failure to state the reasons within its terms. It stands unless and until set aside by this court, and it would not be set aside by this court unless there were good reasons for setting it aside on the footing that someone had suffered a significant injury as a consequence of the irregularity. No such injury is suggested in this case, and it seems to me therefore that the corporation has perhaps at long last produced a resolution on this subject which is not subject to attack in this court. For the reasons I have given I would refuse the application.

MELFORD STEVENSON and WATKINS JJ. agreed.

Application refused.

Notes

1. In *R.* v. *Brent Health Authority, ex p. Francis* [1985] 1 Q.B. 869, the district health authority had convened three meetings to approve reductions in expenditure and each session had been disrupted by members of the public present at the meetings. Therefore, the chairman resolved to hold a fourth meeting with the press in attendance, but other members of the public being excluded. That meeting was held and approved the chairman's decision to exclude the public. On an application for certiorari to quash the chairman's decision brought by a member of the public, the High Court held that section 1(8) of the 1960 Act preserved the common law power of exclusion from meetings of disorderly citizens. Furthermore, the court interpreted the power of exclusion to include the prevention of persons coming to a meeting and the expulsion of those already present at a meeting. In the context of the previous disruptions to their meetings the health authority's resolution to exclude the public was, therefore, lawful.

2. Whilst the 1960 Act continues to apply to meetings of certain public bodies, (*e.g.* parish councils and district health authorities) it has been supplemented by the Local Government (Access to Information) Act 1985, inserting a new Part VA in the Local Government Act 1972, which governs the major local authorities (*i.e.* county and district councils). The latter Act extends the public's right of access to the meetings of committees and sub-committees of these authorities. However, the public must be excluded when confidential information is discussed and they may be excluded in a range of designated circumstances, (*e.g.* when personal information about council employees is being considered). There are also rights of

access to agenda and connected reports, minutes and other documents after meetings and background papers. See further, *Garner*, pp. 417–420.

Questions

1. Towards the end of his judgment Lord Widgery C.J. said "I think one must distinguish between statutory provisions which are clearly imperative or mandatory and those which are merely directory. In my opinion the requirement that the reasons shall be stated in the resolution is a purely directory requirement." On what grounds did the Lord Chief Justice come to this conclusion? What was the effect of his reaching this conclusion?

2. From the principles emerging in this case can you visualise a circumstance where a person who considered himself improperly excluded from a local authority committee meeting could apply for an order of certiorari to remove a resolution of the committee into the court with a view to its being quashed?

(v) The Duties of Officers

Re HURLE-HOBBS, ex p. RILEY AND ANOTHER

(Unreported) Divisional Court (Q.B.D.)

[This case is not reported, but a full note of the judgment appears in the appendix to C. R. H. Hurle-Hobbs, *The Law Relating to District Audit* (2nd ed., 1955, Charles Knight & Co. Ltd.).]

At the beginning of 1939 the Council of the Borough of Finsbury were greatly concerned about the provision of shelters for the people of Finsbury. The second appellant, the Town Clerk of Finsbury, was closely associated with the first appellant Alderman Riley in this project. The respondent in the case was the District Auditor. He had caused a surcharge to be made against each of the appellants in respect of certain expenditure incurred in an abortive deep shelter project. He had taken the view after a long inquiry, that a contract in respect of this shelter, and which was the cause of the surcharge, was one which was open to grave criticism, that it called for the exercise by the council, as trustees of public funds, of the highest degree of care in their examination of it and of the scheme for which it provided; that the council entirely failed to exercise that care, and that such failure was due to the fact that they were kept by the appellants in complete ignorance of almost everything material to be considered. The District Auditor was satisfied that in order to get the agreements sealed, the council were deliberately kept in the dark by the appellants as to the material parts of the agreement, as to the adverse criticism of the London County Council and as to the condemnation of the scheme by an independent consulting engineer, whose opinion had been sought on the advice of Counsel, and that the appellants so acted in flagrant disregard of the liabilities and risks involved. In the District Auditor's view the council might well have rejected the scheme if they had known the truth, and it was for that reason that the appellants hid the truth from them.

The Town Clerk's answer to the Auditor's criticism was that while he knew that there ought to have been a fuller and better disclosure of information, especially the consultant's report, to the council, he was under the domination of Alderman Riley, who threatened him at least once with dismissal from his post, and that if he had taken steps to let the council have all the proper information, he would have lost his position.

LORD CALDECOTE C.J.: . . . I can deal more shortly with the case as it concerns the Town Clerk. Mr. Turner did not dispute that the Town Clerk had a duty to disclose information which was in fact kept back, but he submitted that being subordinate to Alderman Riley, he was not guilty of misconduct. Imprudence there may have been, but imprudence is not misconduct. Notwithstanding the strenuous contention of Counsel on his behalf, the Town Clerk seems to me wholly to misconceive his duty when he says that although he thought that the matters I have discussed ought to have been disclosed to the Council, he was entitled to stand by without taking such steps as were open to him merely because he would otherwise have been liable to dismissal from his office without notice. It was a little surprising to me that such an argument should be advanced on his behalf. It seems to me to be tantamount to an admission of misconduct. It suggests that the Town Clerk put his private interests above his duty in his office. The office of Town Clerk is an important part of the machinery of local government. He may be said to stand between the Borough Council and the ratepayers. He is there to assist by his advice and action the conduct of public affairs in the Borough, and if there is a disposition on the part of the Council, still more on the part of any member of the Council, to ride roughshod over his opinions, the question must at once arise as to whether it is not his duty forthwith to resign his office or, at any rate, to do what he thinks right and await the consequences. This is not so dangerous or heroic a course as it may seem. The integrity of the administration of public affairs is such that publicity may be safely relied upon to secure protection for anyone in the position in which the Town Clerk was said to have been placed.

I think the Respondent was right in holding that the Town Clerk was a party to Alderman Riley's scheme and that without the Town Clerk's assistance Alderman Riley could not have carried it through the Council.

On the whole case, therefore, I am of opinion that the Respondent rightly found that the sums which he has surcharged on these two Appellants represent losses incurred by their negligence and misconduct.

Appeal dismissed.

THE BOGNOR REGIS INQUIRY

[The Report of the Bognor Regis Inquiry presented by the Minister of Housing and Local Government and the Chairman and Members of the Bognor Regis Urban District Council by Mr. J. Ramsay Willis Q.C. (H.M.S.O., 1965) contains, at p. 64, the following comments on the observations of the Lord Chief Justice quoted above. The Inquiry was appointed to examine the circumstances leading to the dismissal of Mr. Paul Smith as Clerk of the Council.]

231. Mr. Smith considers that the Clerk of a Council, if he is a lawyer, should act as the Council's legal adviser; in so doing he is advising the Council in his speciality just as the Engineer advises on engineering matters, and all other Chief Officers provide the Council with the benefit

of their professional and technical knowledge. But the Clerk is also the Chief Administrative Officer of the Council, unless it is specifically stated to the contrary, and as such the Clerk is "first among equals" in his relationship with the Council's other Chief Officers.

232. With this view of the office of Clerk, the Bognor Regis Council, the Society of Clerks of Urban District Councils and nearly everyone in the world of local government would, I think, agree with Mr. Smith.

233. Mr. Smith, however, goes further, and believes that the Clerk of a Council bears a unique responsibility among Chief Officers in that he enjoys a very special relationship with the ratepayers. He finds support for this view, as he has said on a number of occasions, in the judgment given by Lord Chief Justice Caldecote in the case of Hurle-Hobbs ex. p. Riley, 1944, known as the "Finsbury Case," which is concerned with district audit. The section of the judgment which Mr. Smith considers to be relevant appears in his letter of 25th May to all Councillors (see Chapter 28(b)) and is as follows. [Mr. Ramsay Willis then quoted the passage printed above beginning with the words "The office of Town Clerk is an important part of the machinery of local government."]

234. The observations of the Lord Chief Justice were made in the context of the facts of the Finsbury Case and seem to me not to have been necessary to his decision on that case. Whether I am right or not, I think it is clear that Lord Caldecote was not intending to lay down a principle of local government practice of universal application and irrespective of the circumstances.

235. The acceptance of the passage quoted above as definitive of the Clerk's duties in all circumstances and at all times would place him in a unique position indeed. It would seem to follow from the acceptance of that view that in any situation in which a Clerk found himself in conflict with his Council over an important issue of policy, he would have a duty, if it was his opinion that the wishes of the Council were opposed to the best interests of the ratepayers, "to do what he thinks right"; indeed, the Clerk might conceive it to be his duty to make every effort to frustrate the will of his Council and to appeal, over their heads, for the support of the ratepayers. If a Clerk were to interpret the words of Lord Caldecote in the way suggested above, it is clear that he would consider that his first duty was to the ratepayers and that he was virtually independent of his council.

236. But if a Clerk is not answerable to his Council he is answerable to no one. In my view he is the employee of his Council and it is to them that his primary loyalty and duty lie and it is to them that he is answerable for his actions. In the course of advising his Council there is clearly no objection to a Clerk telling them that he considers their proposals to be wrong and, if he thinks fit, submitting his views to them in writing. I consider, however, that he should express his opinion in a manner that will not embarrass his Council and that once his view is known to them he should leave them to come to their own decision. It is the duty of

Councillors to formulate the policy for the local authority and they are directly answerable for their actions to the ratepayers at the polls. This was the view of their own and their Clerk's function that was held by the Bognor Regis Council, as I think, correctly.

237. In exceptional circumstances, such as those in the Finsbury Case, there could well be a justification for a Clerk departing from what I have suggested should be his normal behaviour *vis-à-vis* Councillors. If he believes that a member of the Council has either consciously or unconsciously committed, or is putting himself in a position in which he might commit, an offence then I think he should first broach the matter with the Councillor himself; if that fails he should inform the Chairman of the Council of his concern and, perhaps, consult the Leader on the Council of the Party to which the Councillor in question belongs. If after all these efforts the Clerk finds that no notice has been taken of his warning, naturally, he finds himself in a difficult situation. If he is satisfied that there is a prima facie case of, for example, an offence under section 76 of the Local Government Act, 1933 [now section 94 of the Local Government Act 1972], after making efforts to alert the Chairman and Councillor concerned, I think he would be justified in confiding his suspicions to the Director of Public Prosecutions.

238. However, it seems to me that it would be quite improper if the Clerk were to do anything which might create the impression in the minds of the public or the Press that he was suspicious of his Council or any member of it. It is perhaps otiose to add that a man is innocent until the Courts have found him guilty, but the public seems all too ready to believe that the mere suggestion of impropriety is sufficient proof of guilt.

239. I have heard evidence from the Society of Clerks of Urban District Councils and from people who have served for many years in local government either as Councillors or Officers. I am satisfied that none of them share the view—quoted by Mr. Smith on several occasions—that the Clerk "may be said to stand between the Borough Council and the ratepayers."

Note

The Widdicombe report considered that "the chief executive should be head of the authority's paid staff with clear authority over other officers, and should have ultimate managerial responsibility for the way in which officers discharge the functions of the council."[14] In addition the Committee of Inquiry recommended that all councils should be statutorily required to appoint a chief executive. By section 4 of the Local Government and Housing Act 1989, local authorities (primarily county councils, district councils and London borough councils) must designate one of their officers as "head of paid service." This officer must be provided with sufficient staff and other resources to perform his duties laid down under the section. The major obligations of such an officer are to report to the authority on the way in which the discharge of its functions are co-ordinated, and the organisation of its staff. Section 5 of the 1989 Act requires these authorities to

[14] Report, para. 6:151.

appoint a "monitoring officer," who must report to the authority if it appears that any proposal, decision or omission by the authority (or one of its committee or officers) may be contrary to law or a statutory code of practice, or maladministration. The report must be considered within 21 days and implementation is postponed until then. The report is not binding on the authority, but members who decline to follow its recommendations may open themselves to action by the auditor. The authority's chief financial officer has similar responsibilities in respect of unlawful expenditure (Local Government Finance Act 1988, s.114). The monitoring officer may be the head of paid service but may not be the chief finance officer.

Questions

Until the coming into force of the Local Government Act 1972 certain officers of local authorities (including the clerk of a county council) could not be dismissed except with the consent of a minister. This change in the law was in line with government policy to reduce the degree of central control over the exercise of local authority discretion. Is there, in your view, a case for the re-introduction of ministerial control over the dismissal of officers? If you see a case for such control to which officer or officers should it be extended? If you see no case for ministerial control what safeguards, if any, already exist for the protection of officers who may be placed in the situation of the town clerk in the *Finsbury* case? If there are such safeguards, are they, in your view, adequate? Could and should they be strengthened, and in what way?

(vi) The Powers of Members

R v. BIRMINGHAM CITY DISTRICT COUNCIL, ex p. O

[1983] A.C. 578; [1983] 1 All E.R. 497; 81 L.G.R. 259 (House of Lords)

The council acted as an adoption agency (under the Adoption Act 1958 and the Local Authority Social Services Act 1970) and had delegated its powers and duties under those Acts to a social services committee. During 1976 the social services department of the council "fostered out" a child with the applicants (a married couple with four children). Later, the applicants fell into arrears with their council tenancy and appeared before the council's housing committee. A member of that committee, Mrs. Willetts, became alarmed at the suitability of the applicants to foster or adopt the child. After communication with the social services department and the chairperson of the social services committee, Councillor Willetts sought access to the social services' files concerning the applicants. The council's solicitor advised that it was reasonably necessary for Councillor Willetts to see the files in order to properly carry out her duties as a councillor. However, before Councillor Willetts was given access to the files, the applicants sought an order of prohibition to prevent the council disclosing the files to her on the grounds that she was not a member of the social services committee and, therefore, had no duties which required her to be acquainted with social services' files. The Divisional Court refused the application. On appeal by the applicants, the Court of Appeal (by a majority) allowed the appeal. The council appealed to the House of Lords.

LORD BRIGHTMAN [with whom all the other Law Lords agreed]:

My Lords, I entertain no doubt as to the correctness of the decision of the Divisional Court and of Donaldson L.J. The general principle must be, that a councillor is entitled by virtue of his office to have access to all written material in the possession of the local authority of which he is a member, provided that he has good reason for such access. I apprehend that there can be no challenge to that general principle, which was undisputed half a century ago: see *R.* v. *Barnes Borough Council, ex p. Conlan* [1938] 3 All E.R. 226. At the risk of being repetitive, I would like to read an extract from the judgment of the Divisional Court in that case, at p. 230, which was quoted by Donaldson L.J. in his written judgment:

> "As to the right of a councillor to inspect all documents in possession of the council, there was no dispute at the bar that such a right exists, so far as his access to the documents is reasonably necessary to enable the councillor properly to perform his duties as a member of the council. The common law right of a councillor to inspect documents in the possession of the council arises from his common law duty to keep himself informed of all matters necessary to enable him properly to discharge his duty as a councillor. There must be some limit to this duty. To hold that each councillor of such a body as, for instance, the London County Council, is charged with the duty of making himself familiar with every document in the possession of that body would be to impose an impossible burden upon individual councillors. The duties are therefore divided amongst various committees and sub-committees. In our judgment, it is plain that, as was decided in *R.* v. *Southwold Corporation, Ex parte Wrightson* (1908) 97 L.T. 431: 'a councillor has no right to a roving commission to go and examine books or documents of a corporation because he is a councillor. Mere curiosity or desire to see and inspect documents is not sufficient.' "

In the case of a committee of which he is a member, a councillor as a general rule will ex hypothesi have good reason for access to all written material of such committee. So I do not doubt that each member of the social services committee is entitled by virtue of his office to see all the papers which have come into the possession of a social worker in the course of his duties as an employee of the council. There is no room for any secrecy as between a social worker and a member of the social services committee.

In the case of a committee of which the councillor is not a member, different considerations must apply. The outside councillor, as I will call him, has no automatic right of access to documentary material. Of him, it cannot be said that he necessarily has good reason, and is necessarily entitled, to inspect all written material in the possession of the council and every committee and the officers thereof. What Donaldson L.J. described as a "need to know" must be demonstrated. As he put it, [1982] 1 W.L.R. 690:

> "No official has any right to acquire any part of the authority's stock of

information, whether or not confidential, save in so far as it is needed by him in order that he should be able to do his job. In a word, he has to have a 'need to know.' "

The "need to know" test involves the application of a screening process, and this in turn raises the question of the nature of the screen and who is to apply it. To my mind, in the case of an area as delicate and confidential as that of child care and adoption, the screening process should be administered with great strictness. The utmost care must be taken to prevent the unnecessary dissemination within the council of details relating to the child, to its natural parents, to any foster or adoptive parents, and of sources of information. More than that need not be said, because the subject matter sufficiently speaks for itself.

The decision whether the outside councillor has a good reason for access to the information is ultimately one to be taken by the councillors themselves sitting in council. But the council may expressly, or by implication, delegate to others the right to decide whether an application for access to material is to be acceded to, subject to resort to a meeting of the council if the decision of the delegate is challenged. . . .

The decision of the council is the final word, subject only to an application for judical review under section 31 of the Supreme Court Act 1981 on *Wednesbury* principles: see *Associated Provincial Picture Houses Ltd.* v. *Wednesbury Corporation* [1948] 1 K.B. 223. . . .

This leads to the final question arising on this appeal, namely, whether the decision to permit access to relevant files was one which could have been taken by a reasonable local authority. Unless this question is decided in the negative, this appeal must inevitably succeed. . . .

I would urge your Lordships to hesitate before deciding that access to information is being unreasonably allowed, particularly when such access is approved by the immediate possessor of the information, namely, the social services committee, as well as by the council's solicitor, the council's general purposes committee, and the council itself. Viewing the matter broadly, I do not think that there is anything unreasonable in the council's forming the view that the interests of Emma and the legitimate interests of the applicants will in no way be prejudiced by the fact that Mrs. Willetts is permitted to have access in confidence to files about her and about those who desire to adopt her.

Appeal allowed.

Notes

1. One commentator fears that this decision may encourage a more cautious attitude to note-making by social workers, a less candid flow of information from clients and external bodies, together with the increased danger of politically motivated intervention in social work decision-making. See H. Carty, (1983) *Journal of Social Welfare Law* 179.

2. The principle endorsed in the *Birmingham* case has now been extended to

encompass a councillor's right to attend appropriate committee and sub-committee meetings. In *R.* v. *Hackney London Borough Council, ex p. Gamper* [1985] 1 W.L.R. 1229, the applicant councillor was a member of the authority's Public Services Committee, but he had been prevented from attending the meetings of the Direct Labour Organisation sub-committee. After citing the *Birmingham* decision, Lloyd L.J. stated (at p. 1240):

> "there is no logical distinction between access to documents and attendance at meetings. As in the case of access to documents, the answer must depend on whether the councillor needs to attend the meeting in order to perform his duties properly as a member of the council."

The court declared that the council had acted unlawfully in denying councillor Gamper access to the sub-committee meetings.

3. Parliament has supplemented the above common law powers of councillors by enacting the Local Government (Access to Information) Act 1985, which amended the Local Government Act 1972. Section 100F of the 1972 Act provides councillors with a general right of access to documents in the possession of their council, but this right is subject to the numerous exempted categories of information listed in Schedule 12A, (*e.g.* action taken in connection with the prevention of crime).

Question

What remedy is available to a member who believes that he is improperly prevented from seeing a document held by the authority? Against whom will the remedy lie?

CHAPTER 3

ADMINISTRATIVE PROCEDURES

DECISION-MAKING in government may take many forms and different processes are used to arrive at various decisions. In the course of these processes the law has a variety of roles to play.

A full study of decision-making is not here possible;[1] suffice it for us to examine a few of the materials dealing with the following important administrative procedures.

(A) PUBLIC PARTICIPATION

During the last three decades, there has been much debate as to the proper role of the general or interested public in decision-making. It is accepted by many (although not all: note in the planning context the views of Sir Desmond Heap, *The Land and the Development* (1976), pp. 34–41) that the public should be involved directly, and not merely through their elected representatives on local councils and in Parliament. Key issues include the general openness of government (a certain basis of information must be available to the public just for them to be able to exert democratic pressure intelligently);[2] the kinds of general information collected by government, and the methods of collection; the publicity given to specific issues on which a decision is to be taken, where the initiative in participation lies with the public; the processes of consultation whereby the views of specific individuals or interest groups are actively sought. For a useful examination of the legal provisions regulating governmental secrecy, see P. Birkinshaw, *Government and Information—The Law Relating to Access, Disclosure and Regulation* (1990).

Much of the debate concerning public participation has related to town and country planning. The question of public involvement in planning was discussed by George Dobry Q.C. in his Report (below).

The consultation of individuals and interest groups is a well-established feature of the process of making subordinate legislation (see *Garner*, pp. 68–70).[3] The meaning of "consultation" was discussed in *Rollo* v. *Minister of Town and Country Planning* [1948] 1 All E.R. 13 and *Agriculture, etc. Training Board* v. *Aylesbury Mushrooms Ltd.* [1972] 1 All E.R. 280 (below, p. 454). The legal limits to consultation between government departments are discussed in *Lavender* v. *Minister of Housing and Local Government* [1970] 1 W.L.R. 1231 (below, p. 287).

[1] For a valuable snapshot of organisation theory see *Craig*, pp. 304–305.

[2] See the Local Government (Access to Information) Act 1985, discussed in the previous chapter.

[3] And also J. F. Garner, [1964] P.L. 105.

REVIEW OF THE DEVELOPMENT CONTROL SYSTEM

Final Report by George Dobry Q.C. (H.M.S.O., February 1975)

Chapter 10

PUBLIC INVOLVEMENT

Section I: General

10.1 Role of public involvement. Other chapters of this report give substantial coverage to many aspects of public involvement. Nonetheless, it is a topic of universal interest. At virtually every meeting arranged in connection with this review, public involvement in some form or other was one of the first and most frequent topics raised. I therefore devote a separate chapter to it, which provides the background for more specific conclusions and recommendations elsewhere in this report.

10.2 Definitions. In this chapter it will be convenient to use the following expressions:

(*a*) **Public involvement**, which covers both public participation and public consultation.

(*b*) **Public participation**, which means taking an active part—from the outset—in the formulation of development plans and the making of major planning decisions of strategic importance.

(*c*) **Public consultation**, which means giving the public an opportunity to express views on planning applications.

(*d*) **Interested parties.** The public are often described as "third parties" (the owners or the tenants of land in respect of which an application has been made being known as "section 29 parties" or, alternatively, as "interested parties"). I use the expression "interested parties" in relation to all the participants, other than the applicant and district and county councils.

(*e*) **Individual rights.** . . . [T]he text of Circular 77/73 merits quotation. It says: "Planning is concerned to ensure that in the development of land the public interest is taken fully into account. Its objective is not the safeguarding of private property rights as such; nor in particular, to protect the value of individual properties or the views to be had from them. There are, however, occasions when the public interest may require that the interests of those immediately affected by even a comparatively minor proposal should be taken into account as a planning consideration."

10.3 Arguments for public involvement. The practical help the public can give in planning control has lately assumed a new and very considerable importance.

(1) **Changes in local government.** The elected member now generally represents many more constituents spread over a far wider area. He cannot now be expected to know in detail all relevant circumstances in every locality. The public has more detailed, first-hand knowledge and can be of vital importance in reaching sound decisions.
(2) **"Community land."** The proposed legislation on community land will involve local planning authorities very much more in acquisition and development of land. The reactions of interested parties will assume a new importance. There may often be no one else ready to draw attention strongly enough to the possible damaging effects of a proposal to which the local authority is a party.
(3) **Amenity societies.** Local and central government can profit from the special expertise of amenity societies and from the voluntary efforts of the public.
(4) **Public confidence in planning.** In many ways, therefore, the public can now offer information and points of view *not otherwise available.* Confidence in planning will be strengthened if the public feel they have the opportunity to make their contribution at an early stage.

10.4 Arguments against public involvement. The main difficulties in this area arise from a real or apparent conflict of interest between on the one hand the proposed developer and the planning authorities (even though these two may have opposing objectives); and on the other hand ordinary people who would be affected by the development (and who again may have opposing views about it). Because planning is a complex technical process, conflicts may arise through lack of understanding on either side: ordinary people may not appreciate the complexities, but the "professionals" (developers or planning authorities) may not be sufficiently in sympathy with the justifiable fears of the public. Those against public involvement argue:

(1) that some members of the public, perhaps inevitably, lack sufficient understanding of how planning control works;
(2) that in particular they may fail to understand which are valid or relevant grounds on which to base objections to a development proposal;
(3) that they often find it difficult to understand what plans and applications are really saying;
(4) that they add to the work of planning officers, of elected members and central government;
(5) that people do not understand the limits set by statute and national policy to a local planning authority's freedom to decide applications or impose conditions as it wishes. They are, however, not alone in finding such matters troublesome.

10.5 Complaints from the public. These are often overlooked. The faults are not necessarily all on one side, however. The more frequently-voiced complaints by members of the public about shortcomings in public involvement include:

(1) Too little notice is given of development proposals. By the time the public are aware of a proposal, either no time or too little remains for them to make effective comments or objections.
(2) Information is difficult to get at, whether contained in public registers or elsewhere. Plans cannot be produced when asked for.
(3) No one explains to them what effect, if any, their representations have had.
(4) Elected members do not always sufficiently understand the function of public involvement in planning, or in some cases, of the planning system itself.

10.6 Proper function of public involvement. It is, therefore, important that the proper function of public involvement should be clearly understood and not exceeded. It should assist elected members and central government by giving them information and other help they may need, but should not impinge on their prerogative of decision-making.

10.7 In order that it may continue and become increasingly useful, public involvement must be:

(1) relevant: *i.e.* limited to planning considerations affecting the matters for decision;
(2) more efficient: this will be achieved gradually as the public learns more about planning, and planners learn how to involve the public more effectively;
(3) constructive and selective: whilst anybody likely to be adversely affected by a proposed development should have an opportunity to make a representation, those who object to all development all the time, everywhere, can do great harm by discrediting public involvement.

Section II: Public Consultation

10.8 Early consultation is best. All forms of public involvement including consultation about planning applications should take place at the earliest possible opportunity.

10.9 Statutory publicity. Section 26 of the [Town and Country Planning Act 1971] requires the publication of notices of applications in a wide range of "bad neighbour" cases, such as those where it is proposed to build public conveniences, scrap yards, high buildings or motor-racing tracks (see article 8(1) of the General Development Order). The General Development Order prescribes a form of notice which must be advertised by the applicant in a local newspaper of his choice. Paragraph 20 of Schedule 16 of the Local Government Act 1972 deals with notification of parish and community councils. The 1971 Act and the Town and Country Amenities Act 1974 cover publicity in conservation areas. Statute now recognises public involvement: it has become an integral part of the planning process.

10.10 Further publicity for applications and decisions. I have already indicated in paragraphs 7.29, 7.30 and 7.48 the need for *site notices* or neighbour notification for all applications, and for the giving of publicity to decisions.

10.11 Neighbour notification. This method of notifying the public is strongly supported: more than four-fifths of all councils say they use it, and many consider it more effective than site notices in highlighting controversial proposals. However, it is regarded by some as an incitement to neighbours to complain about each other and some people who make representations are upset when the local planning authority approves an application despite their objections.

10.12 Who is a "neighbour"? One or two of the comments queried the definition of "immediate" neighbours, as complaints may arise when some, but not all, nearby owners are notified. This point was conveniently answered by "the Procedure for Notification of Surrounding Residents," issued by one district . . .

10.13 The role of the parish council. Parish councils (community councils in Wales) are entitled to be consulted on planning applications. . . . It is unfortunate that many large urban areas have no such bodies to represent them. It is beyond the scope of my review to recommend how this omission should be remedied, but the creation of neighbourhood councils may well fill the gap.

10.14 Public access to registers. If public consultation is to be effective, and the public is to accept a speeding up of the planning decision process, they must have very much better access to registers of planning applications.

(1) **Duplicate registers.** I understand that there is no insuperable reason why the new and larger district councils should not display details of applications in several duplicate registers at convenient places in their areas. Anyway, Article 17(8) of the General Development (Amendment) Order 1974 enables that to be done.

(2) **Hot lines to local authority offices.** District councils should provide at least lists of applications in convenient local places with direct telephone links to the register.

(3) **Open at lunchtime and evenings.** Registers should be accessible during weekday lunch-hours and on at least one evening each week.

(4) **Explanations to hand.** If possible, a member of the planning office staff should be available to explain entries in a helpful and sympathetic way. Many authorities already see that this is done.
(5) **Help with staffing.** Where a local planning authority has staffing difficulties, but is on good terms with a local amenity society, volunteer help in manning the register might be the answer.
(6) **Application plans.** The legislative changes suggested in paragraphs 11.30–11.40 will, if adopted, establish beyond doubt the right to copy plans.

Major Applications

10.15 Major applications. In Chapter 7 I suggested that, in addition to consultation procedures on these lines, there was also scope for special publicity arrangements in the case of major Class B applications (7.66 and 7.67). The applications I have in mind are those concerning areas of national or regional importance, and I suggest that exhibitions or meetings should be held before the application is made (except where they are initiated by an interested party when the meeting will come later).

10.16 Meetings. Several kinds of meetings are possible:

(1) Called at the initiative of an applicant,
(2) Organised by the council or its officers,
(3) Initiated by those affected by the application, by the parish council or an amenity society.

10.17 Exhibitions. Exhibitions could be linked to public meetings and should, if possible, take place on neutral ground (see paragraph 10.49 dealing with urban study centres).

DIRECT PARTICIPATION OF LOCAL SOCIETIES IN THE WORK OF LOCAL AUTHORITIES

10.18 Co-option to committees. I have dealt in Chapter 7 and in 10.3(3), with the need to consult amenity societies on planning applications in some cases. Local authorities should also consider arrangements for enabling members of such bodies to contribute directly to the consideration of planning issues by co-opting them to serve on committees. I know this would not always be acceptable but precedents for making such arrangements already exist (for instance the London Borough of Lewisham's planning committee) and co-option of interested outsiders is, of course, the invariable rule with education committees.

10.19 Terms of co-option. It may be argued against this suggestion that such bodies are often partisan in their point of view, and that the duty of actually deciding issues should rest with elected councillors responsible to the community as a whole. However, where co-option takes place, elected representatives are in a majority, and co-option of members of such bodies seems to me a valuable way of enabling them to contribute directly to the work of the local authority, provided that the record of those bodies does not indicate a general bias in approach and that co-option is understood to be conditional on the co-opted member taking a broad view and not simply acting as a delegate to a sponsoring body. This practice might also help the applicant as he would seek to satisfy a single co-ordinated body . . .

Section III: Public Participation

10.38 Publicity for plan making and B applications. The 1971 Act makes various statutory provisions for publicity. Section 8 deals with publicity in the preparation of structure and local plans. These procedures are outside my terms of reference. Nonetheless, I refer to them, as public participation in local plan making and public consultation on Class B applications tend to give rise to the same kind of problems.

10.39 Choosing the right methods. At present funds are limited; if money is to be spent on public involvement the right method must be carefully chosen. Local planning authorities' attempts at public involvement have often failed because they chose the wrong approach for the particular circumstances or a particular "public." The appropriate methods must depend partly on the degree of active interest found in those the planners seek to involve.

10.40 Need to reach the "non-joiners." Planners should beware of ignoring, or making assumptions about, the attitudes of neighbourhoods which ordinarily display little interest in civic affairs. They must not write off the "non-joiners": people who belong to no societies, shun public meetings, never reply to questionnaires and do not take local papers. These people have a right to be consulted. Moreover, they may react sharply if development takes them by surprise.

10.41 Every household. In some cases where a particularly significant B proposal affects a public which clearly includes this "non-responding" element, the only effective way to reach them is by distributing to all households a single, small information sheet giving details of what is proposed. . . . Door-to-door or sample surveys of public opinion are suggested as an alternative.

10.42 Early involvement vital. I have stressed elsewhere that public involvement must take place early to be effective. For most planning applications, this means the public participation process should begin just as soon as the local planning authority receives them. But for some major or particularly significant Class B proposals, it should begin earlier. The process needs to be in effect "participation" rather than "consultation." The public needs to feel it can make its views felt before either developers or the local planning authority is fully committed to particular proposals. Here the involvement process—publicity, exhibitions, meetings and, sometimes, door-to-door leaflets and surveys (if there is money for them) need to start at the pre-application stage. . . .

Notes

1. The conclusions of the Secretary of State on Mr. Dobry's recommendations were contained in Department of the Environment Circular 113/75. While accepting that there was a clear distinction between "minor" and "major" planning applications, albeit with difficult borderline cases, it was not considered possible to enforce classification by statute with the suggested fixed timetables. The Secretary of State generally agreed with Mr. Dobry's views on public involvement, emphasising again "that public involvement needs to be planned and subject to appropriate time disciplines." However, he did not propose to introduce any new publicity requirements, with one exception, to provide that local authorities' own proposals for development should be given the same publicity as equivalent applications by the general public. He pointed out that most authorities already carry out publicity beyond that required under statute (see Circular 71/73). See also [1976] J.P.L. 4. On the Report in general see J. Jowell, (1975) 38 M.L.R. 543 and (1975) 46 *Political Quarterly* 340.

2. The 1980s witnessed a changing official attitude towards public participation in the planning sphere. As one professional body observed:

> "of most importance has been the decline of the loose political consensus of the early 1970s, committed to increased public participation. A divergence between the desire of the public for more participation and that of the Government for less is becoming ever more apparent; too often public participation is being equated in local and central government circles with delay, excessive cost and inefficiency"

(*The Public and Planning: Means to Better Participation*, Royal Town Planning Institute (1982)).

Indeed, a later management report exhorted local planning authorities to adopt a more rigorous approach to the regulation and monitoring of public consultations regarding individual planning applications: see *Local Planning: The Development Control Function*, Dept. of the Environment Audit Inspectorate (1983).

3. The major statutory requirements for publicity concerning individual planning applications were consolidated in the Town and Country Planning Act 1990, ss.65–69; all but s.69 were then replaced by a new s.65, substituted by the Planning and Compensation Act 1991, s.16, with effect from May 4, 1992. In future, the detailed requirements as to publicity will be found in delegated rather than primary legislation. Section 65 enables the arrangements to be included in the General Development Order. A Consultation Paper, *Planning Applications: Publicity and Notification* was issued by the DoE in August 1991. The government's position was set out in a written answer, H.C. Deb., Vol. 203, cols. 166–167:

> "**Mr Yeo:** I am pleased to announce today arrangements for compulsory publicity for all planning applications. The new procedures will ensure that interested parties have the opportunity to comment on all planning applications affecting them.
>
> The new arrangement will allow local planning authorities the maximum possible discretion to continue using the procedures which many of them have had in place for a long time. They are as follows:
>
> (*a*) local planning authorities will be responsible for publicising planning applications;

(*b*) the list of so-called "bad neighbour" developments in Article 11 of the General Development Order 1988 will be abolished, and the link with environmental statements, required under Regulation 12 of the Environmental Assessment Regulations, will be severed;
(*c*) developments requiring environmental statements, departures from the development plan, and those affecting rights of way will be subject to compulsory site notices and newspaper advertising;
(*d*) for other major development, site notices or neighbour notification (as appropriate) and newspaper advertising will be required;
(*e*) for minor development, site notices or neighbour notification (as appropriate) will be required;
(*f*) publicity for reserved matters and amendments to planning applications will be at the discretion of local planning authorities;
(*g*) the same procedures will apply to development by the Crown, and to local authorities' own development;
(*h*) my Department will issue a circular in advance of the new legislation. It will give advice on best practice, including what constitutes 'major' and 'minor' development, and on notification of decisions to those who have commented on planning applications."

The minister noted that the extension of publicity requirements to all applications should not lead to a significant increase in cost overall. As Crawford noted (*Current Law Statutes Annotated 1991*) in commenting on the new section 65,

> "most local planning authorities have engaged in wider consultation and notification than demanded by law, through a variety of devices. Public expectation is higher than the statutory minimum, and many adverse reports of the Local Ombudsman have been concerned with such procedures."

4. On participation through public inquiries, see below, pp. 86–102.

(B) Conciliation

Conciliation is a well-developed process which is, for example, used for the resolving of industrial disputes (see the Conciliation Act 1896, s.2 and the Industrial Courts Act 1919, s.2(1)). Since 1974 such conciliation has been one major function of a public body, the Advisory, Conciliation and Arbitration Service (commonly called ACAS).[4] ACAS seeks to achieve agreed solutions to both collective disputes (those between a union and an employer) and individual disputes (those involving a specific worker and an employer).

ACAS ANNUAL REPORT 1989

CHAPTER 2: COLLECTIVE CONCILIATION

Section 2 of the Employment Protection Act 1975 empowers ACAS to offer conciliation as a means of settling industrial disputes either at the request of one or more parties to the dispute or on its own initiative. Use of conciliation is voluntary and, in view of its duty to promote good industrial relations practice, the Service does not normally intervene

[4] See the Employment Protection Act 1975, s.1(2) and Sched. 1.

unless and until any agreed procedures for direct negotiations or for the resolution of difficulties by internal appeals machinery have been exhausted.

The acceptability of ACAS conciliation to all parties in a dispute grew steadily throughout the 1980s, during which conciliation was completed in over 14,000 disputes. Increasingly, ACAS is written into agreed procedures as the final stage for the settlement of disputes. In 1980 a little under one-third of requests for collective conciliation were made jointly by managements and trade unions. In 1989 conciliation was jointly sought in 54 per cent. of all completed cases.

During 1989 ACAS received 1,164 requests for collective conciliation, and completed action in 1,070 cases, a slight increase on the previous year. Additionally, ACAS maintained private and informal contact in another 423 disputes in which it was ready to offer assistance if necessary without becoming actually involved in conciliation. Even when not formally involved, conciliation staff often served as a confidential channel of communication or sounding board for the parties.

ACAS endeavours to prevent industrial action by bringing the parties to a dispute together in conciliation before a strike or lockout occurs or before attitudes become entrenched. No industrial action took place in over four-fifths of the cases we completed in 1989. Settlement or progress towards a settlement was achieved in 85 per cent. of all cases. Even when settlements were not reached directly under ACAS auspices, conciliation often helped to clarify the issues and contributed to a better understanding between the parties which helped them subsequently to resolve their differences. . . .

. . . As in previous years most of the disputes we dealt with in 1989 were handled at local level by staff in our seven regional offices and our offices in Scotland and Wales. Our Head Office, which generally conciliates in industry-wide disputes or those involving issues of national significance and public concern, dealt with 100 cases.

Conciliation was provided in most sectors of the economy, notably the food and drink industry, which accounted for 18 per cent. of completed cases; the finance sector (8 per cent.); engineering and transport (both 7 per cent.); and newspapers and publishing (6 per cent.). By contrast, the main industries in which ACAS conciliated at the beginning of the decade were engineering, with 14 per cent. of our completed caseload; food and drink (12 per cent.); distributive trades (7 per cent.); and transport (6 per cent.).

COMPLEXITY AND CHANGE

The 1980s have witnessed a sea-change in collective bargaining. The environment within which ACAS collective conciliation now operates has seen significant changes in bargaining arrangements, organisational structures and employment law. Many disputes have taken on a complexity that has challenged ACAS resourcefulness and flexibility.

The increasing complexity of collective bargaining issues was amply demonstrated in the case of Pura (MFP) Ltd., a food manufacturing company, and the Union of Shop Distributive and Allied Workers (USDAW). Pura operated from two sites, one in Liverpool and one in London. Prior to 1989, the Liverpool workforce had received payments under the company's profit-share scheme but Pura's parent company announced that its 1988 financial results did not warrant a payment under the scheme in 1989. USDAW maintained that organisational changes had resulted in profitable manufacturing capacity being transferred from Liverpool to establish the London site and that there had been no diminution of effort by the workforce. At a series of conciliation meetings, the talks were moved away from the question of whether profit-sharing was a discretionary or a negotiable matter towards a practical solution to the issue. Following the fourth meeting, a settlement was eventually reached which satisfied both sides and ended the dispute. . . .

CHAPTER 4: INDIVIDUAL CONCILIATION

By the beginning of the 1980s a range of individual employment rights applying to relationships between employees and employers had existed for some years and the Service's statutory role in conciliating between the parties in cases brought under them had become well established. As the decade progressed a number of important changes affected the Service's work in this area. On the one hand, the qualifying periods of service necessary before individuals could benefit under the unfair dismissal jurisdiction were extended, reducing the number of cases which went to industrial tribunals. On the other, the range of statutory rights available to workers was enlarged to cover new areas, with employees being given rights, for example, to equal pay for work of equal value, to certain protections where their employer's undertaking was transferred to another employer, and to protections against unlawful deductions from their pay. Individual workers were also given the right not to be unreasonably excluded or expelled from a trade union in cases where closed shops operated, or to be unjustifiably disciplined by their union. The effect of all these changes is that ACAS handled more cases in 1989 than it did at the beginning of the decade. . . .

CASELOADS IN 1989

ACAS received 48,817 cases for individual conciliation in 1989. These represented a 10 per cent. increase over the number of cases received in 1988. . . .

As in 1988, a large rise in complaints under the Wages Act 1986 made the most significant contribution to this overall increase, but claims of unfair dismissal, sex discrimination and race discrimination, and equal pay cases (including equal value) were also higher than in 1988. . . .

UNFAIR DISMISSAL

The total of 37,324 unfair dismissal complaints we received in 1989 represented an increase of 3 per cent. over 1988. These cases continued to form the largest part (76 per cent.) of the total caseload in 1989, though their proportion was lower than in 1988 due to increases in other jurisdictions. . . .

EQUAL PAY FOR WORK OF EQUAL VALUE

ACAS received 733 equal value cases in 1989. This figure is considerably higher than the previous year's total of 120. However, 88 per cent. of the cases consisted of two large multiple cases and if these are considered separately the number of cases remained low. . . .

People in a variety of occupations lodged equal value claims in 1989 including, among others, secretaries, packers, nurses, word processing operators, typists, teachers, clerks, process workers, speech therapists, technicians and weavers. . . .

SEX DISCRIMINATION

One feature of the individual conciliation scene over the 1980s was the steady increase in the number of cases we received under the Sex Discrimination Act 1975. 1,249 cases were received in 1989, the highest total yet presented in one year and an increase of 23 per cent. over 1988. The caseload has more than doubled since 1985. The proportion of cases settled in conciliation increased to 40 per cent., the highest ever so concluded. . . . The rise in caseload may be attributed to various factors. In 1987 it became unlawful for an employer to differentiate between men and women in comparable positions as to the date at which they must retire. Claimants affected by discrimination can complain irrespective of their length of service with employers, whereas with unfair dismissal a two-year period is necessary. There have also been developments in tribunal decisions, notably in the field of dismissal for pregnancy, which have been widely publicised and which may significantly affect practice among employers. . . .

RACE DISCRIMINATION

Applications under race discrimination legislation have also increased significantly in recent years. In 1989 we received 1,008 cases, the highest annual figure so far and more than double the 1980 total of 463 cases. Part of the reason is again, no doubt, the increasing publicity being given in the media to the circumstances in which cases arise, together with growing awards of compensation at tribunal for successful applicants.

The Service continues to ensure that specially trained conciliation officers are available to undertake individual conciliation in discrimination and equal pay cases, which are often complex with sensitive and emotive issues.

Notes

1. ACAS has proposed that where a legal action is begun in relation to an industrial dispute, the judge should have the power to stay the proceedings whilst ACAS seek to obtain a conciliated settlement of the dispute. This change in the law could enable reductions in the costs and acrimony of resolving industrial disputes. However, the Government has not acted upon this suggestion: see ACAS Annual Report 1983, para. 1:16, and more generally I. T. Smith and J. C. Wood, *Industrial law* (4th ed., 1989), pp. 31–34.

2. Conciliation is also used by other public agencies, including the Equal Opportunities Commission in the field of gender discrimination and rent officers in disagreements between landlords and tenants (see the Report of the Francis Committee on the Rent Acts (Cmnd. 4609 (1971)) and *R.* v. *Brighton Rent Officers, ex p. Elliott* (1975) 29 P. & C.R. 456.

(C) ADJUDICATION

A proportion of the disputes generated in the field of administrative law can be resolved by the application of pre-existing rules. These rules vary in precision and in origin (see Administrative Rule-making, below). The application of reasonably precise rules of law in the resolution of a dispute is a function typically performed by a court of law, although there are many examples of such processes being entrusted to other institutions, and courts of law do fulfil other kinds of function. The task of adjudication in a particular area may be divided among several persons or bodies. For example, Part II of the Social Security Administration Act 1992, "Adjudication," includes examples of adjudication (1) by the Secretary of State, on such matters as whether a person is an earner (s.17(1)(*a*)); (2) by an Adjudication Officer, on "any claim for benefit" (s.20(1)(*a*)); (3) by a local Social Security Appeal Tribunal, on an appeal from the decision of an Adjudication Officer (s.22); and (4) by a Social Security Commissioner, on appeal on a point of law from any decision of a local tribunal (s.23).

Adjudication by tribunals was considered over three decades ago by the Franks Committee (below). Part II of their Report concerned "Tribunals in General" (below). Many, although not all, of its recommendations were accepted, the main ones being included in the Tribunals and Inquiries Act 1958 (consolidated in the Act of 1992, below), and see Chapter 4 regarding the Council on Tribunals.

There have been a number of research studies on tribunals in general and on particular tribunals. Official and semi-official studies include the Francis Committee on the Rent Acts (Cmnd. 4609 (1971)) and the work of Professor Kathleen Bell, "National Insurance Local Tribunals: A Research Study," 3 *Journal of Social Policy* 289; and "Research Study on Supplementary Benefit Appeal Tribunals" (H.M.S.O. 1975). For other references see the annual reports of the Council on Tribunals. More recent research on social security adjudication is contained in J. Baldwin, N. Wikeley and R. Young, *Judging Social Security* (1992).

Generally see *Garner*, Ch. 10; *Wade*, Ch. 23; *Craig*, Ch. 4; P. Birkinshaw, *Grievances, Remedies and the State* (1985); H. W. R. Wade, "Administrative Tribunals and Administrative Justice" 55 *Australian Law Journal* 374 (1981); N. V. Lowe &

H. F. Rawlings, "Tribunals and the Laws Protecting the Administration of Justice" [1982] P.L. 418; A. R. Mowbray, "Customs and Excise Public Notices: The Tribunal Response" 11 *British Tax Review* 381 (1987). R. Sainsbury, "Social Security Appeals: in Need of Review?" in W. Finnie *et al.*, *Edinburgh Essays in Public Law* (1991), N. Wikeley and R. Young," The Administration of Benefits in Britain" [1992] P.L. 238.

REPORT OF THE COMMITTEE ON ADMINISTRATIVE TRIBUNALS AND ENQUIRIES

(H.M.S.O., Cmnd. 218, July 1957)

CHAIRMAN: Sir Oliver Franks.

[The Committee's terms of reference were:

"To consider and make recommendations on:

(*a*) The constitution and working of tribunals other than the ordinary courts of law, constituted under any Act of Parliament by a Minister of the Crown or for the purposes of a Minister's functions.

(*b*) The working of such administrative procedures as include the holding of an enquiry or hearing by or on behalf of a Minister on an appeal or as the result of objections or representations, and in particular the procedure for the compulsory purchase of land."]

PART I: *INTRODUCTION*

CHAPTER 2: THE SCOPE AND NATURE OF OUR ENQUIRY

5. Our terms of reference involve the consideration of an important part of the relationship between the individual and authority. At different times in the history of this country it has been necessary to adjust this relationship and to seek a new balance between private right and public advantage, between fair play for the individual and efficiency of administration. The balance found has varied with different governmental systems and different social patterns. Since the war the British electorate has chosen governments which accepted general responsibilities for the provision of extended social services and for the broad management of the economy. It has consequently become desirable to consider afresh the procedures by which the rights of individual citizens can be harmonised with wider public interests.

6. The problem is not confined to this country. In recent years most other Western governments have been called upon to govern more extensively and more intensively, and finding a right relationship between authority and the individual has consequently become a matter of concern on both sides of the Atlantic.

Disputes between the individual and authority

7. How do disputes between the individual and authority arise in this country at the present time? In general the starting point is the enactment of legislation by Parliament. Many statutes apply detailed schemes to the whole or to large classes of the community (for example national insurance) or lay on a Minister and other authorities a general duty to provide a service (for example education or health). Such legislation is rarely sufficient in itself to achieve all its objects, and a series of decisions by administrative bodies, such as government departments and local authorities is often required. For example, in a national insurance scheme decisions have to be given on claims to benefit, and in providing an educational service decisions have to be taken on the siting of new schools. Many of these decisions affect the rights of individual citizens, who may then object.

8. Once objection has been raised, a further decision becomes inevitable. This further decision is of a different kind: whether to confirm, cancel or vary the original decision. In reaching it account must be taken not only of the original decision but also of the objection.

The resolution of these disputes

9. These further decisions are made in various ways. Some are made in courts of law and therefore by the procedure of a court of law. For example, an order made by a local authority for the demolition of an insanitary house may be appealed against to the county court. Frequently the statutes lay down that these further decisions are to be made by a special tribunal or a Minister. For example, a contested claim to national insurance benefit has to be determined by a special tribunal, and the decision whether or not to confirm an opposed scheme for the compulsory acquisition of land by a local authority must be made by the Minister concerned. In these cases the procedure to be followed in dealing with objections to the first decision and in arriving at the further decision is laid down in the statute or in regulations made thereunder.

10. But over most of the field of public administration no formal procedure is provided for objecting or deciding on objections. For example, when foreign currency or a scarce commodity such as petrol or coal is rationed or allocated, there is no other body to which an individual applicant can appeal if the responsible administrative authority decides to allow him less than he has requested. Of course the aggrieved individual can always complain to the appropriate administrative authority, to his Member of Parliament, to a representative organisation or to the Press. But there is no formal procedure on which he can insist.

11. There are therefore two broad distinctions to be made among these further decisions which we have been discussing. The first is between those decisions which follow a statutory procedure and those which do not. The second distinction is within the group of decisions subject to a

statutory procedure. Some of these decisions are taken in the ordinary courts and some are taken by tribunals or by Ministers after a special procedure.

12. These two distinctions are essential for understanding our terms of reference. We are not instructed to consider those many cases in which no formal procedure has been prescribed. Nor are we instructed to consider decisions made in the ordinary courts. What we are instructed to consider are the cases in which the decision on objections, the further decision as we have called it, is taken by a tribunal or by a Minister after a special procedure has been followed.

13. At this stage two comments may be added. First, although the foregoing broad analysis holds good over nearly all the field covered by our terms of reference, there are a few tribunals (for example Rent Tribunals) which determine disputes not between the individual and authority but between citizen and citizen. Secondly, we have said that we are not required to consider decisions made in the ordinary courts. This is adequate as a general statement, but it should be qualified by adding that our terms of reference clearly permit us to consider appeals to the courts from decisions of tribunals or of Ministers after a special procedure.

14. We have already said that our terms of reference do not instruct us to consider the vast majority of what we have termed further decisions—because they do not result from a formal procedure involving a tribunal or inquiry. It may be thought that in these cases the individual is less protected against unfair or wrong decision. But we are not asked to go into questions of maladministration which may arise in such cases.

15. It follows therefore that the celebrated case of Crichel Down, which is widely regarded as a principal reason for our appointment, itself in fact falls outside the subjects with which we have been asked to deal. It is true that an inquiry was held in this case, but it was an ad hoc inquiry for which there was no statutory requirement. It resulted from the exercise of those informal methods of raising objection to which we have referred in paragraph 10, and was therefore unlike the inquiries with which we are concerned.

Developments since the Donoughmore Report

16. Our subject corresponds broadly to that defined by the second part of the terms of reference of the Committee on Ministers' Powers, which reported in 1932 (Cmd. 4060). The first part of its terms of reference related to delegated legislation, which we were not asked to consider. That Committee is generally referred to as the Donoughmore Committee, and for convenience we use this short title in the rest of this Report.

17. At the time when the Donoughmore Committee was appointed there already existed a number of tribunals, almost entirely in the field of unemployment insurance and contributory and war pensions; and local authorities already possessed considerable powers to acquire or restrict

the use of private land. Since then the expansion of governmental activities and responsibilities has led to corresponding developments and innovations in our field on a large scale. Old tribunals have been adapted to wider purposes, and new tribunals have been established. More extensive powers exist, and more extensive use is made of powers, to acquire land and control its use.

18. The general impact of decisions by tribunals and Ministers on the public today is illustrated by the fact that Rent Tribunals have in some recent years dealt with as many as 15,000 cases and that the annual number of planning appeals is about 6,000. Although the number of cases heard by National Insurance and Industrial Injuries Local Tribunals (50,000 to 60,000 annually) is smaller than the number of unemployment insurance cases heard in the years just before the war, the scheme is now on a wider basis and potentially affects nearly everyone.

19. The subject of our inquiry, though only part of the relationship between authority and the individual, is thus large and important. The sketch which we have given of its increasingly widespread impact upon the individual illustrates the living background to the abstract formulations of our terms of reference.

CHAPTER 3: THE TWO PARTS OF THE TERMS OF REFERENCE

20. It is noteworthy that Parliament, having decided that the decisions with which we are concerned should not be remitted to the ordinary courts, should also have decided that they should not be left to be reached in the normal course of administration. Parliament has considered it essential to lay down special procedures for them.

Good administration

21. This must have been to promote good administration. Administration must not only be efficient in the sense that the objectives of policy are securely attained without delay. It must also satisfy the general body of citizens that it is proceeding with reasonable regard to the balance between the public interest which it promotes and the private interest which it disturbs. Parliament has, we infer, intended in relation to the subject-matter of our terms of reference that the further decisions or, as they may rightly be termed in this context, adjudications must be acceptable as having been properly made.

22. It is natural that Parliament should have taken this view of what constitutes good administration. In this country government rests fundamentally upon the consent of the governed. The general acceptability of these adjudications is one of the vital elements in sustaining that consent.

Openness, fairness and impartiality

23. When we regard our subject in this light, it is clear that there are certain general and closely linked characteristics which should mark these special procedures. We call these characteristics openness, fairness and impartiality.

24. Here we need only give brief examples of their application. Take openness. If these procedures were wholly secret, the basis of confidence and acceptability would be lacking. Next take fairness. If the objector were not allowed to state his case, there would be nothing to stop oppression. Thirdly, there is impartiality. How can the citizen be satisfied unless he feels that those who decide his case come to their decision with open minds?

25. To assert that openness, fairness and impartiality are essential characteristics of our subject-matter is not to say that they must be present in the same way and to the same extent in all its parts. Difference in the nature of the issue for adjudication may give good reason for difference in the degree to which the three general characteristics should be developed and applied. Again, the method by which a Minister arrives at a decision after a hearing or inquiry cannot be the same as that by which a tribunal arrives at a decision. This difference is brought out later in the Report. For the moment it is sufficient to point out that when Parliament sets up a tribunal to decide cases, the adjudication is placed outside the department concerned. The members of the tribunal are neutral and impartial in relation to the policy of the Minister, except in so far as that policy is contained in the rules which the tribunal has been set up to apply. But the Minister, deciding in the cases under the second part of our terms of reference, is committed to a policy which he has been charged by Parliament to carry out. In this sense he is not, and cannot be, impartial.

The allocation of decisions to tribunals and Ministers

26. At this stage another question naturally arises. On what principle has it been decided that some adjudications should be made by tribunals and some by Ministers? If from a study of the history of the subject we could discover such a principle, we should have a criterion which would be a guide for any future allocation of these decisions between tribunals and Ministers.

27. The search for this principle has usually involved the application of one or both of two notions, each with its antithesis. Both notions are famous and have long histories. They are the notion of what is judicial, its antithesis being what is administrative, and the notion of what is according to the rule of law, its antithesis being what is arbitrary.

28. What is judicial has been worked out and given expression by generations of judges. Its distinction from what is administrative recalls great constitutional victories and marks the essential difference in the nature of the decisions of the judiciary and of the executive.

29. The rule of law stands for the view that decisions should be made by the application of known principles or laws. In general such decisions will be predictable, and the citizen will know where he is. On the other hand there is what is arbitrary. A decision may be made without principle, without any rules. It is therefore unpredictable, the antithesis of a decision taken in accordance with the rule of law.

30. Nothing that we say diminishes the importance of these pairs of antitheses. But it must be confessed that neither pair yields a valid principle on which one can decide whether the duty of making a certain decision should be laid upon a tribunal or upon a Minister or whether the existing allocation of decisions between tribunals and Ministers is appropriate. But even if there is no such principle and we cannot explain the facts, we can at least start with them. An empirical approach may be the most useful.

31. Starting with the facts, we observe that the methods of adjudication by tribunals are in general not the same as those of adjudication by Ministers. All or nearly all tribunals apply rules. No ministerial decisions of the kind denoted by the second part of our terms of reference is reached in this way. Many matters remitted to tribunals and Ministers appear to have, as it were, a natural affinity with one or other method of adjudication. Sometimes the policy of the legislation can be embodied in a system of detailed regulations. Particular decisions cannot, single case by single case, alter the Minister's policy. Where this is so, it is natural to entrust the decisions to a tribunal, if not to the courts. On the other hand it is sometimes desirable to preserve flexibility of decision in the pursuance of public policy. Then a wise expediency is the proper basis of right adjudication, and the decision must be left with a Minister.

32. But in other instances there seems to be no such natural affinity. For example, there seems to be no natural affinity which makes it clearly appropriate for appeals in goods vehicle licence cases to be decided by the Transport Tribunal when appeals in a number of road passenger cases are decided by the Minister.

33. We shall therefore respect this factual difference between tribunals and Ministers and deal separately with the two parts of the subject. When considering tribunals we shall see how far the three characteristics of openness, fairness and impartiality can be developed and applied in general and how far their development and application must be adapted to the circumstances of particular tribunals. We shall then proceed to the decisions of Ministers after a hearing or inquiry and consider how far the difference in method of adjudication requires a different development and application of the three characteristics.

Policy is not our concern

34. Before concluding this Introduction we wish to emphasise that our terms of reference relate to the "constitution and working" of tribunals and to the "working" of certain administrative procedures. We have no concern with the policies which have given rise to the various tribunals or administrative procedures, and are not to be understood as approving or disapproving of these policies.

PART II: *TRIBUNALS IN GENERAL*

CHAPTER 4: INTRODUCTORY

The choice between tribunals and courts of law

38. We agree with the Donoughmore Committee that tribunals have certain characteristics which often give them advantages over the courts. These are cheapness, accessibility, freedom from technicality, expedition and expert knowledge of their particular subject. It is no doubt because of these advantages that Parliament, once it has decided that certain decisions ought not to be made by normal executive or departmental processes, often entrusts them to tribunals rather than to the ordinary courts. But as a matter of general principle we are firmly of the opinion that a decision should be entrusted to a court rather than to a tribunal in the absence of special considerations which make a tribunal more suitable.

39. Moreover, if all decisions arising from new legislation were automatically vested in the ordinary courts the judiciary would by now have been grossly overburdened. The Permanent Secretary to the Lord Chancellor said in his written evidence (Days 6–7, pp. 191–192):—"It is plain, I think, that if all the disputes now determined by administrative tribunals had to be transferred to the ordinary courts, such a transfer would necessarily involve the creation of a large number of additional judges, particularly in the county court. . . . many of the disputes in question do not warrant, at least in my judgment, the services of a highly remunerated judge. . . . I believe that it is essential for the administration of justice as a whole that, because the Bench should be of the highest possible quality, any proposals for dilution should be jealously regarded. . . . These are some of the reasons why I believe, with others, that the system of administrative tribunals as it has grown up in this country has positively contributed to the preservation of our ordinary judicial system." We agree with the Permanent Secretary to the Lord Chancellor that any wholesale transfer to the courts of the work of tribunals would be undesirable. We have not excluded from consideration whether the jurisdiction of any existing tribunal should be transferred to the ordinary courts, though we make no such recommendation. We therefore proceed to consider what improvements and safeguards, including appeals to the courts, should be introduced into the present structure.

Tribunals as machinery for adjudication

40. Tribunals are not ordinary courts, but neither are they appendages of government departments. Much of the official evidence, including that of the Joint Permanent Secretary to the Treasury, appeared to reflect the view that tribunals should properly be regarded as part of the machinery of administration, for which the Government must retain a close and continuing responsibility. Thus, for example, tribunals in the social service field would be regarded as adjuncts to the administration of the services themselves. We do not accept this view. We consider that tribunals should properly be regarded as machinery provided by Parliament for adjudication rather than as part of the machinery of administration. The essential point is that in all these cases Parliament has deliberately provided for a decision outside and independent of the department concerned, either at first instance (for example in the case of Rent Tribunals and the Licensing Authorities for Public Service and Goods Vehicles) or on appeal from a decision of a Minister or of an official in a special statutory position (for example a valuation officer or an insurance officer). Although the relevant statutes do not in all cases expressly enact that tribunals are to consist entirely of persons outside the government service, the use of the term "tribunal" in legislation undoubtedly bears this connotation, and the intention of Parliament to provide for the independence of tribunals is clear and unmistakable.

The application of the principles of openness, fairness and impartiality

41. We have already expressed our belief, in Part I, that Parliament in deciding that certain decisions should be reached only after a special procedure must have intended that they should manifest three basic characteristics: openness, fairness and impartiality. The choice of a tribunal rather than a Minister as the deciding authority is itself a considerable step towards the realisation of these objectives, particularly the third. But in some cases the statutory provisions and the regulations thereunder fall short of what is required to secure these objectives. Our main task in this Part and in Part III will be to assess the extent to which the three objectives are capable of attainment in the field of tribunals and to suggest appropriate measures.

42. In the field of tribunals openness appears to us to require the publicity of proceedings and knowledge of the essential reasoning underlying the decisions; fairness to require the adoption of a clear procedure which enables parties to know their rights, to present their case fully and to know the case which they have to meet; and impartiality to require the freedom of tribunals from the influence, real or apparent, of departments concerned with the subject-matter of their decisions.

Notes

1. J. A. Farmer, *Tribunals and Government* should be read as a corrective to the assumption that tribunals can and do operate solely as part of the judicial system. He points out that "some tribunals really constitute alternatives to departmental or ministerial decision-making rather than court substitutes" (*ibid.* p. 3), that "the judicial system itself cannot necessarily be regarded as falling outside the business of the State" (*ibid.* p. 4), and that the allocation of new jurisdiction to courts or tribunals has not always been done "as a rational exercise in decision-making" (*ibid.* p. 4). In his concluding chapter on "The role of administrative tribunals," Farmer shows that there is a fundamental distinction between "policy-oriented tribunals" (such as the Transport Tribunal, the transport licensing authorities, and the Civil Aviation Authority) and courts and "court-substitute tribunals" (such as the majority of those subject to the supervision of the Council on Tribunals), in that the former remain subject to ministerial control over important matters of policy. He suggests that there is "enormous potential . . . for the growth and greater use of policy-oriented tribunals" (*ibid.* p. 191) in the administration and application of general policies laid down by Ministers. Another important point made is that the differences between courts and court-substitute tribunals have been greatly exaggerated (*ibid.* p. 192) in that various tribunals have established informal systems of precedents while denying that precedents are formally binding (*ibid.* Chap. 7).

2. It must not be thought that the quality of decision-making by tribunals is always ideal. Farmer (*op. cit.* pp. 167–169) lists 10 illustrations of "the fragile nature of the procedures by which tribunals obtain the material upon which their decisions as to the facts of cases must be based," and which might be said to constitute procedural unfairness. The former Supplementary Benefit Appeal Tribunals (now superseded by Social Security Appeal Tribunals) were subject to particular criticism. H. Hodge considered that they could not distinguish policy from law, they allowed presenting officers (from the D.H.S.S.) to introduce entirely irrelevant prejudicial matter, and they had little concept of how to weigh up evidence (*L.A.G. Bulletin*, February 1973). Furthermore, N. Lewis believed that the decision-making of these tribunals did not fulfil the basic standards required by law, for example the rules against fettering or abuse of discretion ([1973] P.L. 257).

3. The Franks Report is discussed in the following articles apart from the textbooks already cited: J. A. G. Griffith, (1956) III J.S.P.T.L.(N.S.) 207–219; G. W. Keeton, (1958) 11 C.L.P. 88–103; W. A. Robson, [1958] P.L. 12–31; E. C. S. Wade, (1957) 73 L.Q.R. 470–491.

TRIBUNALS AND INQUIRIES ACT 1992

(An Act to consolidate the Tribunals and Inquiries Act 1971 and certain other enactments relating to tribunals and inquiries.)

[Sections 1 to 4 prescribe the constitution and functions of the Council on Tribunals established by the 1958 Act. These provisions are summarised in the Council's Annual Report for 1990–91, Appendix D (below, Chap. 4 pp. 126–128.]

Composition and procedure of tribunals and inquiries

Recommendations of Council as to appointment of members of tribunals

5.—(1) Subject to section 6 but without prejudice to the generality of section 1(1)(*a*), the Council may make to the appropriate Minister general recommendations as to the making of appointments to membership of any tribunals mentioned in Schedule 1 or of panels constituted for the purposes of any such tribunals; and (without prejudice to any statutory provisions having effect with respect to such appointments) the appropriate Minister shall have regard to recommendations under this section.

(2) In this section "the appropriate Minister", in relation to appointments of any description, means the Minister making the appointments or, if they are not made by a Minister, the Minister in charge of the government department concerned with the tribunals in question. . . .

Appointment of chairmen of certain tribunals

6.—(1) The chairman, or any person appointed to act as chairman, of any of the tribunals to which this subsection applies shall (without prejudice to any statutory provisions as to qualifications) be selected by the appropriate authority from a panel of persons appointed by the Lord Chancellor.

(2) Members of panels constituted under this section shall hold and vacate office under the terms of the instruments under which they are appointed, but may resign office by notice in writing to the Lord Chancellor; and any such member who ceases to hold office shall be eligible for re-appointment.

(3) Subsection (1) applies to any tribunal specified in paragraph 7, 38(*a*), 41(*a*), (*b*), (*c*) or (*e*) or 43 of Schedule 1.

(4) In relation to the tribunals specified in paragraph 41(*a*), (*b*) and (*c*) of Schedule 1, this section has effect subject to sections 41 (social security appeal tribunals), 43 (disability appeal tribunals) and 50 (medical appeal tribunals) of the Social Security Administration Act 1992.

(5) The person or persons constituting any tribunal specified in paragraph 31 of Schedule 1 shall be appointed by the Lord Chancellor, and where such a tribunal consists of more than one person the Lord Chancellor shall designate which of them is to be the chairman.

(6) In this section, "the appropriate authority" means the Minister who apart from this Act would be empowered to appoint or select the chairman, person to act as chairman, members or member of the tribunal in question.

(7) A panel may be constituted under this section for the purposes either of a single tribunal or of two or more tribunals, whether or not of the same description. . . .

Concurrence required for removal of members of certain tribunals

7.—(1) Subject to subsection (2), the power of a Minister, other than the Lord Chancellor, to terminate a person's membership of any tribunal specified in Schedule 1, or of a panel constituted for the purposes of any such tribunal, shall be exercisable only with the consent of—

(*a*) the Lord Chancellor, the Lord President of the Court of Session and the Lord Chief Justice of Northern Ireland, if the tribunal sits in all parts of the United Kingdom;
(*b*) the Lord Chancellor and the Lord President of the Court of Session, if the tribunal sits in all parts of the Great Britain;
(*c*) the Lord Chancellor and the Lord Chief Justice of Northern Ireland, if the tribunal sits both in England and Wales and in Northern Ireland;
(*d*) the Lord Chancellor, if the tribunal does not sit outside England and Wales;
(*e*) the Lord President of the Court of Session, if the tribunal sits only in Scotland;
(*f*) the Lord Chief Justice of Northern Ireland, if the tribunal sits only in Northern Ireland.

(2) This section does not apply to any tribunal specified in paragraph 3, 4, 12, 14, 17, 18, 26, 33(*a*), 34, 35(*d*) or (*e*), 36(*a*), 39(*b*), 40, 43, 48 or 56(*a*) of Schedule 1.

(3) For the purposes of this section in its application to any tribunal specified in paragraph 22(*a*) of Schedule 1, an adjudicator who has sat only in England and Wales, who has sat only in Scotland or who has sat only in Northern Ireland shall be deemed to constitute a tribunal which does not sit outside England and Wales, which sits only in Scotland or which sits only in Northern Ireland, as the case may be.

Procedural rules for tribunals

8.—(1) The power of a Minister, the Lord President of the Court of Session, the Commissioners of Inland Revenue or the Foreign Compensation Commission to make, approve, confirm or concur in procedural rules for any tribunal specified in Schedule 1 shall be exercisable only after consultation with the Council.

(2) The power of the Treasury to make—

(*a*) regulations under section 48(3) of the Building Societies Act 1986 (regulations with respect to appeals to the tribunal established under section 47 of that Act), or
(*b*) regulations under section 30 of the Banking Act 1987 (regulations with respect to appeals under Part I of that Act),

shall be exercisable only after consultation with the Council. . . .

(4) In this section "procedural rules" includes any statutory provision relating to the procedure of the tribunal in question.

Procedure in connection with statutory inquiries

9.—(1) Subject to section 14, the Lord Chancellor, after consultation with the Council, may make rules regulating the procedure to be followed in connection with statutory inquiries held by or on behalf of Ministers; and different provision may be made by any such rules in relation to different classes of such inquiries.

(2) Any rules made by the Lord Chancellor under this section shall have effect, in relation to any statutory inquiry, subject to the provisions of the enactment under which the inquiry is held, and of any rules or regulations made under that enactment.

(3) Subject to subsection (2), rules made under this section may regulate procedure in connection with matters preparatory to such statutory inquiries as are mentioned in subsection (1), and in connection with matters subsequent to such inquiries, as well as in connection with the conduct of proceedings at such inquiries. . . .

Judicial control of tribunals etc.

Reasons to be given for decisions of tribunals and Ministers

10.—(1) Subject to the provisions of this section and of section 14, where—

(*a*) any tribunal specified in Schedule 1 gives any decision, or
(*b*) any Minister notifies any decision taken by him—
 (i) after a statutory inquiry has been held by him or on his behalf, or
 (ii) in a case in which a person concerned could (whether by objecting or otherwise) have required a statutory inquiry to be so held,

it shall be the duty of the tribunal or Minister to furnish a statement, either written or oral, of the reasons for the decision if requested, on or before the giving or notification of the decision, to state the reasons.

(2) The statement referred to in subsection (1) may be refused, or the specification of the reasons restricted, on grounds of national security.

(3) A tribunal or Minister may refuse to furnish a statement under subsection (1) to a person not primarily concerned with the decision if of the opinion that to furnish it would be contrary to the interests of any person primarily concerned.

(4) Subsection (1) does not apply to any decision taken by a Minister after the holding by him or on his behalf of an inquiry or hearing which is a statutory inquiry by virtue only of an order made under section 16(2) unless the order contains a direction that this section is to apply in relation to any inquiry or hearing to which the order applies.

(5) Subsection (1) does not apply—

(*a*) to decisions in respect of which any statutory provision has effect, apart from this section, as to the giving of reasons,
(*b*) to decisions of a Minister in connection with the preparation, making, approval, confirmation, or concurrence in regulations, rules or byelaws, or orders or schemes of a legislative and not executive character, or
(*c*) to decisions of the Occupational Pensions Board referred to in paragraph 35(*d*) of Schedule 1.

(6) Any statement of the reasons for a decision referred to in paragraph (*a*) or (*b*) of subsection (1), whether given in pursuance of that subsection or of any other statutory provision, shall be taken to form part of the decision and accordingly to be incorporated in the record.

(7) If, after consultation with the Council, it appears to the Lord Chancellor and the Lord Advocate that it is expedient that—

(*a*) decisions of any particular tribunal or any description of such decisions, or
(*b*) any description of decisions of a Minister,

should be excluded from the operation of subsection (1) on the ground that the subject-matter of such decisions, or the circumstances in which they are made, make the giving of reasons unnecessary or impracticable, the Lord Chancellor and the Lord Advocate may by order direct that subsection (1) shall not apply to such decisions.

(8) Where an order relating to any decisions has been made under subsection (7), the Lord Chancellor and the Lord Advocate may, by a subsequent order made after consultation with the Council, revoke or vary the earlier order so that subsection (1) applies to any of those decisions.

Appeals from certain tribunals

11.—(1) Subject to subsection (2), if any party to proceedings before any tribunal specified in paragraph 8, 15(*a*), 16, 18, 24, 26, 31, 33(*b*), 37, 44 or 45 of Schedule 1 is dissatisfied in point of law with a decision of the tribunal he may, according as rules of court may provide, either appeal from the tribunal to the High Court or require the tribunal to state and sign a case for the opinion of the High Court.

(2) Subsection (1) shall not apply in relation to proceedings before industrial tribunals which arise under or by virtue of any of the enactments mentioned in section 136(1) of the Employment Protection (Consolidation) Act 1978.

(3) Rules of court made with respect to all or any of the tribunals

referred to in subsection (1) may provide for authorising or requiring a tribunal, in the course of proceedings before it, to state, in the form of a special case for the decision of the High Court, any question of law arising in the proceedings; and a decision of the High Court on a case stated by virtue of this subsection shall be deemed to be a judgment of the Court within the meaning of section 16 of the Supreme Court Act 1981 (jurisdiction of Court of Appeal to hear and determine appeals from judgments of the High Court).

(4) In relation to proceedings in the High Court or the Court of Appeal brought by virtue of this section, the power to make rules of court shall include power to make rules prescribing the powers of the High Court or the Court of Appeal with respect to—

(*a*) the giving of any decision which might have been given by the tribunal;
(*b*) the remitting of the matter with the opinion or direction of the court for re-hearing and determination by the tribunal;
(*c*) the giving of directions to the tribunal;

and different provisions may be made for different tribunals.

(5) An appeal to the Court of Appeal shall not be brought by virtue of this section except with the leave of the High Court or the Court of Appeal.

(6) Subsection (1) shall apply to a decision of the Secretary of State on an appeal under section 41 of the Consumer Credit Act 1974 from a determination of the Director General of Fair Trading as it applies to a decision of any of the tribunals mentioned in that subsection, but with the substitution for the reference to a party to proceedings of a reference to any person who had a right to appeal to the Secretary of State (whether or not he has exercised that right); and accordingly references in subsections (1) and (4) to a tribunal shall be construed, in relation to such an appeal, as references to the Secretary of State. . . .

(10) In this section "decision" includes any direction or order, and references to the giving of a decision shall be construed accordingly.

Supervisory functions of superior courts not excluded by Acts passed before August 1, 1958

12.—(1) As respects England and Wales—

(*a*) any provision in an Act passed before August 1, 1958 that any order or determination shall not be called into question in any court, or
(*b*) any provision in such an Act which by similar words excludes any of the powers of the High Court.

shall not have effect so as to prevent the removal of the proceedings into the High Court by order of certiorari or to prejudice the powers of the High Court to make orders of mandamus. . . .

(3) Nothing in this section shall apply—

(*a*) to any order or determination of a court of law, or

(*b*) where an Act makes special provision for application to the High Court or the Court of Session within a time limited by the Act.

Power to apply Act to additional tribunals and to repeal or amend certain provisions

13.—(1) The Lord Chancellor and the Lord Advocate may by order amend Part I or Part II of Schedule 1 by adding to that Part any such tribunals, other than any of the ordinary courts of law, as may be provided by the order.

(2) The Lord Chancellor and the Lord Advocate may by order make provision, as respects any tribunal for the time being specified in Schedule 1, not being a tribunal mentioned in section 6, for amending that section so as to apply any of the provisions of that section to the tribunal or for providing for the appointment by the Lord Chancellor, the Lord President of the Court of Session or the Lord Chief Justice of Northern Ireland of the chairman of the tribunal and of any person to be appointed to act as chairman.

(3) The Lord Chancellor and the Lord Advocate may by order amend section 11 so as to apply that section to any tribunal for the time being specified in Schedule 1.

(4) Any order under subsection (1), (2) or (3) may make any such adaptations of the provisions of this Act as may be necessary or expedient in consequence of the order.

(5) The Lord Chancellor and the Lord Advocate may by order—

(*a*) repeal or amend section 7(3) of this Act or any of paragraphs 5, 6, 9, 13, 16, 20, 22, 23, 24, 29, 30, 32, 35(*a*) and (*d*), 37, 39(*c*), 43, 44, 47, 49, 51, 54, 55, 56(*d*), 57(*a*), 58, 59 and 63 of Schedule 1;

(*b*) repeal the reference in section 6 to paragraph 43 of Schedule 1;

(*c*) repeal the reference in section 8(1) to the Foreign Compensation Commission and the reference in section 14(1) to paragraph 20 of Schedule 1;

(*d*) repeal the references in section 11 to any of paragraphs 16, 24, 37, 44, 51, 59 and 63 of Schedule 1; and

(*e*) repeal the references in paragraphs 21 and 53 of Schedule 1 to sections 16, 17B and 25 of the Forestry Act 1967. . . .

Restricted application of Act in relation to certain tribunals

14.—(1) References in this Act to the working or a decision of, or procedural rules, for,—

(*a*) any tribunals specified in paragraph 14(a), 20, 33, 34, 39(*a*) or (*b*), 40, 48, 56 or 60 of Schedule 1,
(*b*) the Director General of Fair Trading referred to in paragraph 17 of Schedule 1, or
(*c*) the Controller of Plant Variety Rights referred to in paragraph 36(*a*) of Schedule 1,

do not include references to their working, decisions or procedure in the exercise of executive functions.

(2) In this Act, references to the working of the Occupational Pensions Board referred to in paragraph 35(*d*) of Schedule 1 are references to their working so far as relating to matters dealt with by the Board by means of a formal hearing or on review; and references to procedural rules for the Board are references to regulations under section 66(7) of the Social Security Act 1973 so far as relating to procedure on any formal hearing by the Board.

(3) For the purposes of this Act, the functions of the Civil Aviation Authority referred to in paragraph 3 of Schedule 1 are to be taken to be confined to those prescribed for the purposes of section 7(2) of the Civil Aviation Act 1982.

Rules and orders

15. Any power of the Lord Chancellor and the Lord Advocate or either of them to make rules or orders under this Act shall be exercisable by statutory instrument subject to annulment in pursuance of a resolution of either House of Parliament.

Interpretation

16.—(1) In this Act, except where the context otherwise requires—

"decision," "procedural rules" and "working," in relation to a tribunal, shall be construed subject to section 14,

"Council" means the Council on Tribunals,

"Minister" includes any Board presided over by a Minister,

"Scottish Committee" means the Scottish Committee of the Council on Tribunals,

"statutory inquiry" means—

(*a*) an inquiry or hearing held or to be held in pursuance of a duty imposed by any statutory provision, or

(*b*) an inquiry or hearing, or an inquiry or hearing of a class, designated for the purposes of this section by an order under subsection (2), and

"statutory provision" means a provision contained in, or having effect under, any enactment.

(2) The Lord Chancellor and the Lord Advocate may by order designate

for the purposes of this section any inquiry or hearing held or to be held in pursuance of a power conferred by any statutory provision specified or described in the order, or any class of such inquiries or hearings.

(3) References in this Act to members of tribunals include references to the person constituting a tribunal consisting of one person. . . .

SCHEDULE 1

TRIBUNALS UNDER GENERAL SUPERVISION OF COUNCIL

PART I

TRIBUNALS UNDER DIRECT SUPERVISION OF COUNCIL

Matters with which tribunal concerned	*Tribunal and statutory authority*
Agriculture	1.(*a*) the Agricultural Land Tribunals established under section 73 of the Agriculture Act 1947; (*b*) arbitrators appointed (otherwise than by agreement) under Schedule 11 to the Agricultural Holdings Act 1986.
Aircraft and shipbuilding industries	2. The Aircraft and Shipbuilding Industries Arbitration Tribunal established under section 42 of the Aircraft and Shipbuilding Industries Act 1977.
Aviation	3. The Civil Aviation Authority established under section 2 of the Civil Aviation Act 1982.
Banking	4. An appeal tribunal constituted under section 28 of the Banking Act 1987.
Betting levy	5. An appeal tribunal for England and Wales established under section 29 of the Betting, Gaming and Lotteries Act 1963.
Building societies	6. The tribunal constituted in accordance with section 47 of the Building Societies Act 1986.
Child support maintenance	7. (*a*) The child support appeal tribunals established under section 19 of the Child Support Act 1991; (*b*) a Child Support Commissioner appointed under section 20 of that Act and any tribunal presided over by such a Commissioner.

Matters with which tribunal concerned	*Tribunal and statutory authority*
Children's homes, voluntary homes, nursing homes, mental nursing homes and residential care homes.	8. Registered Homes Tribunals constituted under Part III of the Registered Homes Act 1984.
Commons	9. The Commons Commissioners and assessors appointed under section 17(2) and (3) of the Commons Registration Act 1965.
Conveyancing	10. A Conveyancing Appeals Tribunal constitued under section 39 of the Courts and Legal Services Act 1990.
Copyright	11. The Copyright Tribunal constituted under section 145 of the Copyright, Designs and Patents Act 1988.
Criminal injuries compensation	12. The Criminal Injuries Compensation Board constituted under Part VII of the Criminal Justice Act 1988.
Dairy produce quotas	13. The Dairy Produce Quota Tribunal for England and Wales constituted under regulation 35(1) of the Dairy Produce Quotas Regulations 1991 (S.I. 1991/2232).
Data protection	14. (*a*) The Data Protection Registrar appointed under section 3 of the Data Protection Act 1984; (*b*) the Data Protection Tribunal constituted under that section.
Education	15. (*a*) Independent Schools Tribunals constituted under section 72 of, and Schedule 6 to, the Education Act 1944; (*b*) appeal committees constituted in accordance with Part I of Schedule 2 to the Education Act 1980; (*c*) appeal committees constituted for the purposes of section 58(5)(*d*) of the Education Reform Act 1988; (*d*) a tribunal constituted in accordance with Schedule 3 to the Education (Schools) Act 1992.
Employment	16. The industrial tribunals for England and Wales established under section 128 of the Employment Protection (Consolidation) Act 1978.

Matters with which tribunal concerned	*Tribunal and statutory authority*
Fair trading	17. The Director General of Fair Trading in respect of his functions under the Consumer Credit Act 1974 and the Estate Agents Act 1979, and any member of the Director's staff authorised to exercise those functions under paragraph 7 of Schedule 1 to the Fair Trading Act 1973.
Financial services	18. The Financial Services Tribunal established by section 96 of the Financial Services Act 1986.
Food	19. Tribunals constituted in accordance with regulations under Part II of the Food Safety Act 1990.
Foreign compensation	20. The Foreign Compensation Commission constituted under section 1 of the Foreign Compensation Act 1950.
Forestry	21. Committees appointed for the purposes of section 16, 17B, 20, 21 or 25 of the Forestry Act 1967, being committees the members of which are appointed by the Minister having functions under those sections as respects England or Wales.
Immigration appeals	22. (*a*) The adjudicators established under section 12 of the Immigration Act 1971; (*b*) the Immigration Appeal Tribunal establishesd under that section.
Indemnification of justices and clerks	23. Any person appointed under section 53(3) of the Justices of the Peace Act 1979.
Industrial training levy exemption	24. Referees established by the Industrial Training (Levy Exemption References) Regulations 1974 (S.I. 1974/1335).
Industry	25. An arbitration tribunal established under Schedule 3 to the Industry Act 1975.
Insolvency practitioners	26. The Insolvency Practitioners Tribunal referred to in section 396 of the Insolvency Act 1986.
Land	27. The Lands Tribunal constituted under section 1(1)(*b*) of the Lands Tribunal Act 1949.

Matters with which tribunal concerned	*Tribunal and statutory authority*
Local taxation	28. Valuation tribunals established by regulations under Schedule 11 to the Local Government Finance Act 1988.
London Building Acts	29. The tribunals of appeal constituted in accordance with section 109 of the London Building Acts (Amendment) Act 1939.
Mental health	30. The Mental Health Review Tribunals constituted or having effect as if constituted under section 65 of the Mental Health Act 1983.
Mines and quarries	31. Tribunals for the purposes of section 150 of the Mines and Quarries Act 1954.
Misuse of drugs	32. The Misuse of Drugs Tribunal in England and Wales constituted under Part I of Schedule 3 to the Misuse of Drugs Act 1971.
National Health Service	33. (*a*) Family Health Services Authorities established in pursuance of section 10 of the National Health Service Act 1977; (*b*) the tribunal constituted under section 46 of that Act; (*c*) service committees of Family Health Services Authorities, being committees constituted in accordance with regulations made under that Act.
Patents, designs, trade marks and service marks	34. The comptroller-general of patents, designs, and trade marks, and any officer authorised to exercise the functions of the comptroller under section 62(3) of the Patents and Designs Act 1907.
Pensions	35. (*a*) Pensions Appeal Tribunals for England and Wales established under section 8 of the War Pensions (Administrative Provisions) Act 1919; (*b*) Pensions Appeal Tribunals constituted under the Pensions Appeal Tribunals Act 1943, being tribunals appointed for England and Wales; (*c*) appeal tribunals constituted in accordance with a scheme in force under section 26 of the Fire Services Act 1947;

Matters with which tribunal concerned	*Tribunal and statutory authority*
	(*d*) the Occupational Pensions Board established by section 66 of the Social Security Act 1973; (*e*) the Pensions Ombudsman established under Part IVA of the Social Security Pensions Act 1975 in respect of his functions under or by virtue of section 59C(2) of that Act; (*f*) tribunals appointed under regulations under section 1 of the Police Pensions Act 1976 to hear such appeals as by virtue of the regulations lie to tribunals so appointed.
Plant varieties	36. (*a*) The Controller of Plant Variety Rights and any officer authorised to exercise the functions of the Controller under section 11(5) of the Plant Varieties and Seeds Act 1964; (*b*) the Plant Varieties and Seeds Tribunal established by section 10 of that Act.
Rents	37. Rent assessment committees constituted in accordance with Schedule 10 to the Rent Act 1977.
Reserve forces	38. (*a*) The Reinstatement Committees appointed under paragraph 1 of Schedule 2 to the Reserve Forces (Safeguard of Employment) Act 1985; (*b*) the umpire and any deputy umpire appointed under paragraph 5 of Schedule 2 to that Act.
Revenue	39. (*a*) The Commissioners for the general purposes of the income tax acting under section 2 of the Taxes Management Act 1970 for any division in England and Wales; (*b*) the Commissioners for the special purposes of the Income Tax Acts appointed under section 4 of that Act; (*c*) the tribunal constituted for the purposes of Chapter I of Part XVII of the Income and Corporation Taxes Act 1988.
Road traffic	40. (*a*) The traffic commissioner for any area constituted for the purposes of the Public Passenger Vehicles Act 1981; (*b*) a parking adjudicator appointed under section 73(3)(a) of the Road Traffic Act 1991.

Matters with which tribunal concerned	*Tribunal and statutory authority*
Social security	41. (*a*) Social security appeal tribunals constituted under section 41 of the Social Security Administration Act 1992; (*b*) disability appeal tribunals constituted under section 43 of that Act; (*c*) medical appeal tribunals constituted under section 50 of that Act; (*d*) a Commissioner appointed under section 52 of that Act and any tribunal presided over by a Commissioner so appointed; (*e*) a tribunal constituted under regulations made under section 58 of that Act.
Transport	42. The Transport Tribunal constituted as provided in Schedule 4 to the Transport Act 1985.
Vaccine damage	43. The tribunals constituted under section 4 of the Vaccine Damage Payments Act 1979.
Value added tax	44. Value added tax tribunals for England and Wales and for Northern Ireland, constituted under section 40 of, and Schedule 8 to, the Value Added Tax Act 1983.
Wireless telegraphy	45. The tribunal established under section 9 of the Wireless Telegraphy Act 1949.

PART II

TRIBUNALS UNDER SUPERVISION OF SCOTTISH COMMITTEE. . . .

Note

For a criticism of the Tribunals and Inquiries Act 1958, see J. A. G. Griffith, (1959) 22 M.L.R. 145.

(D) INQUIRIES

Public inquiries are held for many different purposes. The most formal ones are those constituted under the Tribunals of Inquiry (Evidence) Act 1921, to inquire into matters of "urgent public importance." However, only 19 such bodies have been created (*e.g.* to examine the Aberfan landslide disaster: H.C. 33 (1967–68)), with the result that one commentator has criticised successive governments for their reluctance to invoke this power of investigation (see Z. Segal, "Tribunals of Inquiry: A British Invention Ignored in Britain" [1984] P.L. 207). According to R. E. Wraith and G. B. Lamb, *Public Inquiries as an Instrument of Government* (1971), other functions performed by inquiries include (1) "post-mortems" into public scandals or major disasters (*e.g.* the inquiry chaired by Desmond Fennell Q.C. into the King's Cross Underground Fire: H.C. 499 (1987–88)); (2) considering objections to administrative decisions (*e.g.* the public local inquiry held to investigate objections to the draft M40 motorway extension which featured in *Bushell* v. *Secretary of State for the Environment* [1981] A.C. 75, below, p. 550); and (3), most frequently, hearing appeals against administrative decisions (particularly in the field of town and country planning applications).

For further reading see *Garner*, Ch. 11; *Wade*, Ch. 24; *Craig*, Ch. 4; JUSTICE—All Souls Review of Administrative Law, *Administrative Justice: Some Necessary Reforms*, Ch. 11; D. G. T. Williams, "Public Local Inquiries—Formal Administrative Adjudication" (1980) 29 I.C.L.Q. 701; W. Le-Las, *Playing the Public Inquiry Game* (1987).

For a detailed study of the longest public inquiry held in the United Kingdom (the Sizewell B pressurised water nuclear power station inquiry chaired by Sir Frank Layfield Q.C., which opened in January 1983, closed in March 1985, with the report being presented to the Secretary of State for Energy in December 1986) see T. O'Riordan, R. Kemp and M. Purdue, *Sizewell B: An Anatomy of the Inquiry* (1988).

THE TOWN AND COUNTRY PLANNING (INQUIRIES PROCEDURE) RULES 1988

(S.I. 1988 No. 944)

The Lord Chancellor, in exercise of the powers conferred on him by section 11 of the Tribunals and Inquiries Act 1971, and after consultation with the Council on Tribunals, hereby makes the following Rules:

Citation and Commencement

1. These Rules may be cited as the Town and Country Planning (Inquiries Procedure) Rules 1988 and shall come into force on July 7, 1988.

Interpretation

2. In these Rules, unless the context otherwise requires, references to sections and Schedules are references to sections of, and Schedules to, the Town and Country Planning Act 1971[4a] and—

"applicant," in the case of an appeal, means the appellant;
"assessor" means a person appointed by the Secretary of State to sit with an inspector at an inquiry or re-opened inquiry to advise the inspector on such matters arising as the Secretary of State may specify;
"the Commission" means the Historic Buildings and Monuments Commission for England;

[4a] [Ed. note this Act has been consolidated in the "planning Acts" of 1990 *i.e.* the Town and Country Planning Act 1990, Planning (Listed Buildings and Conservation Areas) Act 1990, Planning (Hazardous Substances) Act 1990, Planning (Consequential Provisions) Act 1990, and amended by the Planning and Compensation Act 1991.]

"conservation area consent" means consent required by section 277A(2);
"development order" has the meaning assigned to it by section 24;
"document" includes a photograph, map or plan;
"inquiry" means a local inquiry in relation to which these Rules apply;
"inspector" means a person appointed by the Secretary of State to hold an inquiry or a re-opened inquiry;
"land" means the land, tree or building to which an inquiry relates;
"listed building consent" has the meaning assigned to it by section 55(3A);
"local authority" has the meaning assigned to it by section 290(1);
"local planning authority" means—

(i) in relation to a referred application, the body who would otherwise have dealt with the application;
(ii) in relation to an appeal, the body who were responsible for dealing with the application occasioning the appeal;

"outline statement" means a written statement of the principal submissions which a person proposes to put forward at an inquiry;
"pre-inquiry meeting" means a meeting held before an inquiry to consider what may be done with a view to securing that the inquiry is conducted efficiently and expeditiously, and where two or more such meetings are held references to the conclusion of a pre-inquiry meeting are references to the conclusion of the final meeting;
"referred application" means an application of any description mentioned in rule 3(1) which is referred to the Secretary of State for determination;
"relevant date" means the date of the Secretary of State's written notice to the applicant and the local planning authority of his intention to cause an inquiry to be held, and "relevant notice" means that notice;
"the 1974 Rules" means the Town and Country Planning (Inquiries Procedure) Rules 1974;
"section 29(3) party" means—

(*a*) a person whose representations the Secretary of State is required by the application of section 29(3) or by regulations under Part I of Schedule 11 to take into account in determining the referred application or appeal to which an inquiry relates; and
(*b*) in the case of an appeal, a person whose representations the local planning authority were required by section 29(3) or those regulations to take into account in determining the application occasioning the appeal;

"statement of case" means a written statement which contains full particulars of the case which a person proposes to put forward at an

inquiry and a list of any documents which that person intends to refer to or put in evidence;
"tree preservation order" means an order under section 60.

Application of Rules

3.—(1) These Rules apply in relation to any local inquiry caused by the Secretary of State to be held in England or Wales before he determines—

(*a*) an application in relation to planning permission referred to him under section 35 or an appeal to him under section 36, or under section 36 as applied by section 37;
(*b*) an application for consent referred to him under a tree preservation order or an appeal to him under such an order, with the exceptions that rule 4(1) shall not apply and the references to a section 29(3) party shall be omitted;
(*c*) an application in relation to listed building consent referred to him under paragraph 4 of Schedule 11 or an appeal to him under paragraph 8 of Schedule 11, or under paragraph 8 as applied by paragraph 9 of that Schedule, including an application or appeal referred or made under any of those paragraphs as applied by section 56B(2);
(*d*) an application in relation to conservation area consent referred to him under paragraph 4 of Schedule 11 or an appeal to him under paragraph 8 of Schedule 11, or under paragraph 8 as applied by paragraph 9 of that Schedule, as those paragraphs are applied in the case of such an application or appeal by virtue of section 277A, including an application or appeal to which section 56B(2) is applied by section 277A,

but do not apply in relation to any local inquiry by reason of the application of any provision mentioned in this paragraph by any other enactment.

(2) Where these Rules apply in relation to an appeal which at some time fell to be disposed of in accordance with the Town and Country Planning Appeals (Determination by Inspectors) (Inquiries Procedure) Rules 1988 or Rules superseded by those Rules, any step taken or thing done under those Rules which could have been done under any corresponding provision of these Rules shall have effect as if it had been taken or done under that corresponding provision.

Preliminary information to be supplied by local planning authority

4.—(1) The local planning authority shall, on receipt of a notice from the Secretary of State of his intention to cause an inquiry to be held ("the relevant notice"), forthwith inform him and the applicant in writing of the name and address of any section 29(3) party who has made representations to them; and the Secretary of State shall as soon as practicable thereafter inform the applicant and the local planning authority in writing of the name and address of any section 29(3) party who has made representations to him.

(2) This paragraph applies where—

(*a*) the Secretary of State or any local authority has given to the local planning authority a direction restricting the grant of planning permission for which application was made; or

(*b*) in a case relating to listed building consent, the Commission has given a direction to the local planning authority pursuant to paragraph 6(2)(*b*) of Schedule 11 as to how the application is to be determined; or

(*c*) the Secretary of State or any other Minister of the Crown or any government department or local authority has expressed in writing to the local planning authority the view that the application should not be granted either wholly or in part, or should be granted only subject to conditions, or, in the case of an application for consent under a tree preservation order, should be granted together with a direction requiring replanting; or

(*d*) any authority or person consulted in pursuance of a development order has made representations to the local planning authority about the application.

(3) Where paragraph (2) applies, the local planning authority shall forthwith after the date of the relevant notice ("the relevant date") inform the person or body concerned of the inquiry and, unless they have already done so, that person or body shall thereupon give the local planning authority a written statement of the reasons for making the direction, expressing the view or making the representations, as the case may be.

Procedure where Secretary of State causes pre-inquiry meeting to be held

5.—(1) The Secretary of State may cause a pre-inquiry meeting to be held if it appears to him desirable and where he does so the following paragraphs apply.

(2) The Secretary of State shall serve with the relevant notice a notification of his intention to cause a meeting to be held and a statement of the matters which appear to him to be likely to be relevant to his consideration of the application or appeal in question; and where another Minister of the Crown or a government department has expressed in writing to the Secretary of State a view which is mentioned in rule 4(2)(*c*), the Secretary

of State shall set this out in his statement and shall supply a copy of the statement to the Minister or government department concerned.

(3) The local planning authority shall cause to be published in a newspaper circulating in the locality in which the land is situated a notice of the Secretary of State's intention to cause a meeting to be held and of the statement served in accordance with paragraph (2) in such form as the Secretary of State may specify.

(4) The local planning authority and the applicant shall, not later than 8 weeks after the relevant date, each serve an outline statement on the other and on the Secretary of State.

(5) Where rule 4(2) applies, the local planning authority shall—

(*a*) include in their outline statement the terms of—
   (i) any direction given together with a statement of the reasons therefor; and;
   (ii) any view expressed or representation made on which they intend to rely in their submissions at the inquiry; and

(*b*) within the period mentioned in paragraph (4), supply a copy of their statement to the person or body concerned.

(6) The Secretary of State may in writing require any other person who has notified him of an intention or a wish to appear at the inquiry to serve, within 4 weeks of being so required, an outline statement on him, the applicant and the local planning authority.

(7) The meeting (or, where there is more than one, the first meeting) shall be held not later than 16 weeks after the relevant date.

(8) The Secretary of State shall give not less than 21 days written notice of the meeting to the local planning authority, the applicant, any person known at the date of the notice to be entitled to appear at the inquiry and any other person whose presence at the meeting seems to him to be desirable; and he may require the local planning authority to take, in relation to notification of the meeting, one or more of the steps which he may under rule 10(6) require them to take in relation to notification of the inquiry.

(9) The inspector shall preside at the meeting and shall determine the matters to be discussed and the procedure to be followed, and he may require any person present at the meeting who, in his opinion, is behaving in a disruptive manner to leave and may refuse to permit that person to return or to attend any further meeting, or may permit him to return or attend only on such conditions as he may specify.

(10) Where a pre-inquiry meeting has been held pursuant to paragraph (1), the inspector may hold a further meeting. He shall arrange for such notice to be given of a further meeting as appears to him necessary; and paragraph (9) shall apply to such a meeting.

Service of statements of case etc.

6.—(1) The local planning authority shall, not later than—

(*a*) 6 weeks after the relevant date, or
(*b*) where a pre-inquiry meeting is held pursuant to rule 5, 4 weeks after the conclusion of that meeting,

serve a statement of case on the Secretary of State, the applicant and any section 29(3) party.

(2) Where rule 4(2) applies, the local planning authority shall, unless they have already done so in an outline statement, include in their statement of case the matters mentioned in rule 5(5)(a) and shall supply a copy of the statement to the person or body concerned.

(3) The applicant shall, not later than—

(*a*) in the case of a referred application where no pre-inquiry meeting is held pursuant to rule 5, 6 weeks after the relevant date, or
(*b*) in the case of an appeal where no such meeting is held, 9 weeks after the relevant date, or
(*c*) in any case where a pre-inquiry meeting is held pursuant to rule 5, 4 weeks after the conclusion of that meeting,

serve a statement of case on the Secretary of State, the local planning authority and any section 29(3) party.

(4) The Secretary of State may in writing require any other person who has notified him of an intention or a wish to appear at an inquiry to serve a statement of case, within 4 weeks of being so required, on the applicant, the local planning authority, the Secretary of State and any (or any other) section 29(3) party.

(5) The Secretary of State shall supply any person from whom he requires a statement of case in accordance with paragraph (4) with a copy of the local planning authority's and the applicant's statement of case and shall inform that person of the name and address of every person on whom his statement of case is required to be served.

(6) The Secretary of State or an inspector may require any person who has served a statement of case in accordance with this rule to provide such further information about the matters contained in the statement as he may specify.

(7) Any person serving a statement of case on the local planning authority shall serve with it a copy of any document, or of the relevant part of any document, referred to in it.

(8) Unless he has already done so, the Secretary of State, in the case of a referred application, shall, and, in the case of an appeal, may, not later than 12 weeks from the relevant date, serve a written statement of the matters referred to in that paragraph on the applicant, the local planning authority, any section 29(3) party and any person from whom he has required a statement of case.

(9) The local planning authority shall afford to any person who so requests a reasonable opportunity to inspect and, where practicable, take copies of any statement or document which, or a copy of which, has been served on them in accordance with any of the preceding paragraphs of this rule, and of any statement so served by them together with a copy of any document, or of the relevant part of any document, referred to in it; and shall specify in the statement served in accordance with paragraph (1) the time and place at which the opportunity will be afforded.

Further power of inspector to hold pre-inquiry meetings

7.—(1) Where no pre-inquiry meeting is held pursuant to rule 5, an inspector may hold one if he thinks it desirable.

(2) An inspector shall arrange for not less than 14 days written notice of a meeting he proposes to hold under paragraph (1) to be given to the applicant, the local planning authority, any person known at the date of the notice to be entitled to appear at the inquiry and any other person whose presence at the meeting appears to him to be desirable.

(3) Rule 5(9) shall apply to a meeting held under this rule.

Inquiry time-table

8. Where a pre-inquiry meeting is held pursuant to rule 5 an inspector shall, and in any other case may, arrange a time-table for the proceedings at, or at part of, an inquiry and may at any time vary the time-table.

Notification of appointment of assessor

9. Where the Secretary of State appoints an assessor, he shall notify every person entitled to appear at the inquiry of the name of the assessor and of the matters on which he is to advise the inspector.

Date and notification of inquiry

10.—(1) The date fixed by the Secretary of State for the holding of an inquiry shall be, unless he considers such a date impracticable, not later than—

(*a*) 22 weeks after the relevant date; or
(*b*) in a case where a pre-inquiry meeting is held pursuant to rule 5, 8 weeks after the conclusion of that meeting.

(2) Where the Secretary of State considers it impracticable to fix a date in accordance with paragraph (1), the date fixed shall be the earliest date after the end of the relevant period mentioned in that paragraph which he considers to be practicable.

(3) Unless the Secretary of State agrees a lesser period of notice with the applicant and the local planning authority, he shall give not less than 28

days written notice of the date, time and place fixed by him for the holding of an inquiry to every person entitled to appear at the inquiry.

(4) The Secretary of State may vary the date fixed for the holding of an inquiry, whether or not the date as varied is within the relevant period mentioned in paragraph (1); and paragraph (3) shall apply to a variation of a date as it applied to the date originally fixed.

(5) The Secretary of State may also vary the time or place for the holding of an inquiry and shall give such notice of any such variation as appears to him to be reasonable.

(6) The Secretary of State may require the local planning authority to take one or more of the following steps—

(*a*) to publish not less than 14 days before the date fixed for the holding of an inquiry in one or more newspapers circulating in the locality in which the land is situated such notice of the inquiry as he may direct;

(*b*) to serve within such period as he may specify notice of an inquiry in such form and on such persons or classes of persons as he may specify;

(*c*) to post within such period as he may specify such notice of an inquiry as he may direct in a conspicuous place near to the land.

(7) Where the land is under the control of the applicant he shall, if so required by the Secretary of State, affix firmly to the land or to some object on or near the land, in such manner as to be readily visible to and legible by members of the public, such notice of the inquiry as the Secretary of State may specify; and he shall not remove the notice, or cause or permit it to be removed, for such period before the inquiry as the Secretary of State may specify.

Appearances at inquiry

11.—(1) The persons entitled to appear at an inquiry are—

(*a*) the applicant;

(*b*) the local planning authority;

(*c*) any of the following bodies if the land is situated in their area and they are not the local planning authority—

(i) a county or district council;

(ii) a National Park Committee within the meaning of paragraph 5 of Schedule 17 to the Local Government Act 1972;

(iii) a joint planning board constituted under section 1(2) or a joint planning board or special planning board reconstituted under Part I of Schedule 17 to the Local Government Act 1972;

(iv) an urban development corporation established under section 135 of the Local Government, Planning and Land Act 1980;

(*d*) where the land is in an area designated as a new town, the development corporation for the new town or the Commission for the New Towns as its successor;

(*e*) a section 29(3) party;

(*f*) the council of the parish or community in which the land is situated, if that council made representations to the local planning authority in respect of the application in pursuance of a provision of a development order;

(*g*) where the application was required to be notified to the Commission under paragraph 6 of Schedule 11 (listed building consent in Greater London), the Commission;

(*h*) any other person who has served a statement of case in accordance with rule 6(4) or who has served an outline statement in accordance with rule 5(6).

(2) Any other person may appear at an inquiry at the discretion of the inspector.

(3) Any person entitled or permitted to appear may do so on his own behalf or be represented by counsel, solicitor or any other person.

(4) An inspector may allow one or more persons to appear for the benefit of some or all of any persons having a similar interest in the matter under inquiry.

Representatives of government departments and other authorities at inquiry

12.—(1) Where—

(*a*) the Secretary of State, any local authority or the Commission have given a direction such as is described in rule 4(2)(*a*) or (*b*); or

(*b*) the Secretary of State or any other Minister of the Crown or any government department or local authority has expressed a view such as is described in rule 4(2)(*c*) and the local planning authority have included the terms of the expression of view in a statement served in accordance with rule 5(4) or 6(1); or

(*c*) another Minister of the Crown or any government department has expressed a view such as is mentioned in rule 4(2)(*c*) and the Secretary of State has included its terms in a statement served in accordance with rule 5(2) or rule 6(8),

the applicant may, not later than 14 days before the date of an inquiry, apply in writing to the Secretary of State for a representative of the Secretary of State or of the other Minister, department or body concerned to be made available at the inquiry.

(2) Where an application is made in accordance with paragraph (1), the Secretary of State shall make a representative available to attend the inquiry or, as the case may be, transmit the application to the other Minister, department or body concerned, who shall make a representative available to attend the inquiry.

(3) A person attending an inquiry as a representative in pursuance of this rule shall state the reasons for the direction or expression of view in question and shall give evidence and be subject to cross-examination to the same extent as any other witness.

(4) Nothing in paragraph (3) shall require a representative of a Minister or a government department to answer any question which in the opinion of the inspector is directed to the merits of government policy.

Statements of evidence

13.—(1) A person entitled to appear at an inquiry who proposes to give, or to call another person to give, evidence at the inquiry by reading a written statement shall send a copy of the statement to the inspector and shall, if so required by the inspector, supply a written summary of that evidence.

(2) The statement shall be sent to the inspector not later than 3 weeks before the date on which the person is due to give evidence in accordance with the time-table arranged pursuant to rule 8 or, if there is no such time-table, 3 weeks before the date fixed for the inquiry, and the summary shall be sent within such period as may be specified by the inspector.

(3) Where the applicant or the local planning authority send a copy of a statement of evidence or a summary to an inspector in accordance with paragraph (1) they shall at the same time send a copy to the other party; and where any other party so sends such a copy statement or summary he shall at the same time send a copy to the applicant and the local planning authority.

(4) Where the inspector has required a written summary of evidence in accordance with paragraph (1), the person giving that evidence at the inquiry shall do so only by reading the written summary, unless permitted by the inspector to do otherwise.

(5) Any person required by this rule to send a copy of a statement of evidence to any other person shall send with it a copy of the whole, or the relevant part, of any documents referred to in it, unless copies of the documents or parts of documents in question have already been made available by the local planning authority pursuant to rule 6(9).

Procedure at inquiry

14.—(1) Except as otherwise provided in these Rules, the inspector shall determine the procedure at an inquiry.

(2) Unless in any particular case the inspector with the consent of the

applicant otherwise determines, the applicant shall begin and shall have the right of final reply; and the other persons entitled or permitted to appear shall be heard in such order as the inspector may determine.

(3) A person entitled to appear at an inquiry shall be entitled to call evidence and the applicant, the local planning authority and a section 29(3) party shall be entitled to cross-examine persons giving evidence, but, subject to the foregoing and paragraphs (4) and (5), the calling of evidence and the cross-examination of persons giving evidence shall otherwise be at the inspector's discretion.

(4) The inspector may refuse to permit—

(*a*) the giving or production of evidence,
(*b*) the cross-examination of persons giving evidence, or
(*c*) the presentation of any other matter,

which he considers to be irrelevant or repetitious; but where he refuses to permit the giving of oral evidence, the person wishing to give the evidence may submit to him any evidence or other matter in writing before the close of the inquiry.

(5) Where a person gives evidence at an inquiry by reading a summary of his evidence in accordance with rule 13(4), the statement of evidence referred to in rule 13(1) may be tendered in evidence, and the person whose evidence the statement contains shall then be subject to cross-examination on it to the same extent as if it were evidence he had given orally.

(6) The inspector may direct that facilities shall be afforded to any person appearing at an inquiry to take or obtain copies of documentary evidence open to public inspection.

(7) The inspector may require any person appearing or present at an inquiry who, in his opinion, is behaving in a disruptive manner to leave and may refuse to permit that person to return, or may permit him to return only on such conditions as he may specify; but any such person may submit to him any evidence or other matter in writing before the close of the inquiry.

(8) The inspector may allow any person to alter or add to a statement of case served under rule 6 so far as may be necessary for the purposes of the inquiry; but he shall (if necessary by adjourning the inquiry) give every other person entitled to appear who is appearing at the inquiry an adequate opportunity of considering any fresh matter or document.

(9) The inspector may proceed with an inquiry in the absence of any person entitled to appear at it.

(10) The inspector may take into account any written representation or evidence or any other document received by him from any person before an inquiry opens or during the inquiry provided that he discloses it at the inquiry.

(11) The inspector may from time to time adjourn an inquiry and, if the

date, time and place of the adjourned inquiry are announced at the inquiry before the adjournment, no further notice shall be required.

Site inspections

15.—(1) The inspector may make an unaccompanied inspection of the land before or during an inquiry without giving notice of his intention to the persons entitled to appear at the inquiry.

(2) The inspector may, during an inquiry or after its close, inspect the land in the company of the applicant, the local planning authority and any section 29(3) party; and he shall make such an inspection if so requested by the applicant or the local planning authority before or during an inquiry.

(3) In all cases where the inspector intends to make an inspection of the kind referred to in paragraph (2) he shall announce during the inquiry the date and time at which he proposes to make it.

(4) The inspector shall not be bound to defer an inspection of the kind referred to in paragraph (2) where any person mentioned in that paragraph is not present at the time appointed.

Procedure after inquiry

16.—(1) After the close of an inquiry, the inspector shall make a report in writing to the Secretary of State which shall include his conclusions and his recommendations or his reasons for not making any recommendations.

(2) Where an assessor has been appointed, he may, after the close of the inquiry, make a report in writing to the inspector in respect of the matters on which he was appointed to advise.

(3) Where an assessor makes a report in accordance with paragraph (2), the inspector shall append it to his own report and shall state in his own report how far he agrees or disagrees with the assessor's report and, where he disagrees with the assessor, his reasons for that disagreement.

(4) If, after the close of an inquiry, the Secretary of State—

(*a*) differs from the inspector on any matter of fact mentioned in, or appearing to him to be material to, a conclusion reached by the inspector, or

(*b*) takes into consideration any new evidence or new matter of fact (not being a matter of government policy),

and is for that reason disposed to disagree with a recommendation made by the inspector, he shall not come to a decision which is at variance with that recommendation without first notifying the persons entitled to appear at the inquiry who appeared at it of his disagreement and the reasons for it; and affording to them an opportunity of making written representations to him within 21 days of the date of the notification, or (if the Secretary of State has taken into consideration any new evidence or new matter of fact, not being a matter of government policy) of asking within that period for the re-opening of the inquiry.

(5) The Secretary of State may, as he thinks fit, cause an inquiry to be re-opened to afford an opportunity for persons to be heard on such matters relating to an application or appeal as he may specify, and he shall do so if asked by the applicant or the local planning authority in the circumstances and within the period mentioned in paragraph (4); and where an inquiry is re-opened (whether by the same or a different inspector)—

(*a*) the Secretary of State shall send to the persons entitled to appear at the inquiry who appeared at it a written statement of the specified matters; and
(*b*) paragraphs (3) to (7) of rule 10 shall apply as if the references to an inquiry were references to a re-opened inquiry.

Notification of decision

17.—(1) The Secretary of State shall notify his decision on an application or appeal, and his reasons for it, in writing to all persons entitled to appear at the inquiry who did appear, and to any other person who, having appeared at the inquiry, has asked to be notified of the decision.

(2) Where a copy of the inspector's report is not sent with the notification of the decision, the notification shall be accompanied by a statement of his conclusions and of any recommendations made by him; and if a person entitled to be notified of the decision has not received a copy of that report, he shall be supplied with a copy of it on written application made to the Secretary of State within 4 weeks of the date of the decision.

(3) In this rule "report" includes any assessor's report appended to the inspector's report but does not include any other documents so appended; but any person who has received a copy of the report may apply to the Secretary of State in writing, within 6 weeks of the date of the Secretary of State's decision, for an opportunity of inspecting any such documents and the Secretary of State shall afford him that opportunity.

Procedure following quashing of decision

18. Where a decision of the Secretary of State on an application or appeal in respect of which an inquiry has been held is quashed in proceedings before any court, the Secretary of State—

(*a*) shall send to the persons entitled to appear at the inquiry who appeared at it a written statement of the matters with respect to which further representations are invited for the purposes of his further consideration of the application or appeal; and (*b*) shall afford to those persons the opportunity of making, within 21 days of the date of the written statement, written representations to him in respect of those matters or of asking for the re-opening of the inquiry; and

(*c*) may, as he thinks fit, cause the inquiry to be reopened (whether by the same or a different inspector) and if he does so paragraphs (3) to (7) of rule 10 shall apply as if the references to an inquiry were references to a re-opened inquiry.

Allowing further time

19. The Secretary of State may at any time in any particular case allow further time for the taking of any step which is required or enabled to be taken by virtue of these Rules, and references in these Rules to a day by which, or a period within which, any step is required or enabled to be taken shall be construed accordingly. . . .

Notes

1. The Government explained, "the main objective of the new Rules is to make the inquiry process at all stages as efficient and effective as possible, whilst impairing neither the fairness and impartiality of the proceedings, nor the ability of participants to make representations which are relevant to the decision." (Joint Dept. of the Environment/Welsh Office Circular 10/88 (DoE), 15/88/WO, para. 6.) The major changes, introduced since the previous Rules were promulgated in 1974, include (1) the enhancement of information exchanges between the parties prior to the commencement of the inquiry; (2) the specific power of the Secretary of State to appoint assessors to advise inspectors; and (3) the explicit power of inspectors to regulate conduct at inquiries. See generally, R. Carnwath, *et al.*, *Blundell and Dobry's Planning Appeals and Inquiries* (4th ed., 1990).

2. The role of the Council on Tribunals in the evolution of these Rules is considered in Chapter 4 at p. 138.

3. It has been noted that apart from condemnation in costs the Rules contain no effective sanction to secure compliance with their requirements. And, it appears that few Inspectors have utilised that sanction. See V. Moore, [1988] J.P.L. 596 and [1989] J.P.L. 398.

4. The Secretary of State's obligation to give reasons for his decision under rule 17(1) has been considered by the House of Lords in *Save Britain's Heritage* v. *No. 1 Poultry Ltd.* [1991] 1 W.L.R. 153. The case concerned extremely valuable land in the City of London (the Mappin & Webb site). The property developers who owned the land sought permission from the local authority to demolish the existing listed buildings on the site and replace them with a prestigious new development. Permission was refused and the developers appealed to the Secretary of State who appointed an inspector to hold an inquiry into the matter. The Inspector recommended allowing the development to take place, and the Secretary of State accepted that advice by incorporating the Inspector's major reasoning in his formal decision letter. A preservation group, which had objected to the development, applied to the court challenging the Secretary's decision on the ground that he had failed to give adequate reasons for the decision as required by rule 17(1). Lord Bridge held that: "Whatever may be the position in any other legislative context, under the planning legislation, when it comes to deciding in any particular case whether the reasons given are deficient, the question is not to be answered *in vacuo*. The alleged deficiency will only afford a ground for quash-

ing the decision if the court is satisfied that the interests of the applicant have been substantially prejudiced by it." (pp. 166–167). In this case his Lordship concluded that the Secretary's reasons were adequate and that the granting of planning permission was therefore lawful. See further, below, p. 660.

5. Other important sets of inquiry rules include the Town and Country Planning Appeals (Determination by Inspectors) (Inquiry Procedure) Rules 1988, S.I. 1988 No. 945 and the Highways (Inquiry Procedure) Rules 1976, S.I. 1976 No. 721. Highways inquiries were particularly controversial in the 1970s, when a number were disrupted by objectors (see J. Tyme, *Motorways versus Democracy* (1978): Mr. Tyme was one of the best-known objectors; F. Sharman, [1977] J.P.L. 293; D. G. T. Williams, (1980) 29 I.C.L.Q. 701, 708–709). Steps were taken to improve the amount of information made available to objectors (see the *Report on the Review of Highway Inquiry Procedures* (Cmnd. 7133, 1978). Note, however, P. McAuslan's view that notwithstanding these developments, and, more generally, the changes brought about by the Franks Report, "the overriding purpose of the public local inquiry . . . was and is to advance the administration's version of the public interest" (*The Ideologies of Planning Law* (1980), p. 73; road inquiries are considered at pp. 55–73). For a recent general survey, see S. Tromans, "Roads to Prosperity or Roads to Ruin? Transport and the Environment in England and Wales" (1991) 3 J.E.L. 1.

6. Where an application for development under the Planning Acts in England and Wales is of major public interest because of its national or regional implications, or the extent or complexity of the environmental, safety, technical or scientific issues involved, the relevant department may decide to apply a non-statutory Code of Practice to the procedures leading up to the public inquiry into the application. The Code is contained in Annex 1 to the above Joint Circular 10/88. Its purpose is "to enable the Inspector to structure the inquiry in such a way as to ensure that the proceedings run smoothly, speedily and efficiently, and to help participants to concentrate on the real issues that have to be resolved" (para. 1). This is achieved by, *inter alia*, the establishment of an inquiry secretariat which will register interested participants and the holding of a pre-inquiry "programme meeting" at which the administrative arrangements for the inquiry will be determined.

7. A significant development in recent years has been the desire of certain pressure groups (particularly environmental groups) to question matters of national government policy before specific inquiries. The judiciary have sought to limit the legal obligations on inspectors to hear such challenges (*Bushell* v. *Secretary of State for the Environment*, below, p. 550) and reach conclusions on them (*R.* v. *Secretary of State for Transport, ex p. Gwent County Council* [1988] Q.B. 429 and see A. R. Mowbray, "Public Inquiries and Government Policy" (1987) 137 N.L.J. 418). Furthermore, studies have demonstrated the weaknesses in this use of inquiries. "Where Government policy is fundamental to the issues which are the subject-matter of an inquiry, a Government witness provides a useful function in explaining and elaborating this policy. . . . However, if Government policies are unclear or in a state of flux, the witness will be put in a difficult position. In the case of the Sizewell B Inquiry this tendency has been increased by the length of the inquiry. As a result, we would argue that it would be unwise to look to public inquiries as a formal mechanism for any definitive assessment of Government policy, especially in those areas which are either unclear or prone to substantial policy flux" M. Purdue *et al.*, "The Government at the Sizewell B Inquiry" [1985] P.L. 475 at pp. 488–489.

8. The procedure for the making, alteration and replacement of development plans, including the arrangements for public participation at public local inquiries and examinations in public have recently been revised: see the White Paper on *The Future of Development Plans* (Cm. 569, 1989); the Planning and Compensation Act 1991, Sched. 4 (amending the Town and Country Planning Act 1990); the Town

and Country Planning (Development Plan) Regulations 1991 (S.I. 1991 No. 2794); DoE Circular 18/91; Planning Policy Guidance Note 12, *Development Plans and Regional Planning Guidance*. It will be left to the discretion of local authorities what degree of publicity and consultation is appropriate, apart from requirements to consult such bodies as English Heritage and the Countryside Commission. The Secretary of State has reserve powers to direct an authority to carry out further public participation. For a case study of the effectiveness of the previous arrangements, see B. Webster and A. Laver, [1991] J.P.L. 803.

(E) Inspection[5]

Inspection involves the direct examination of an activity or object by an official. "Inspectors" may be employed by central or local government and in turn the subject of their inspections may be private citizens or their property (*e.g.* M.O.T. tests on motor cars), an institution (*e.g.* factory inspections), or a public authority (*e.g.* inspection of schools or police). Some inspectors in central government are dignified by a Crown appointment (*e.g.* "Her Majesty's Chief Inspector of Prisons"). Some so-called "inspectors" do not in fact inspect anything, except incidentally in the performance of their main functions. The main examples of these are housing and planning inspectors of the Department of the Environment who conduct inquiries on behalf of the Secretary of State (see *Wade*, pp. 992–994). The purposes of inspection include the enforcement of law, the enforcement of standards of efficiency, the giving of advice, and the obtaining of information. Emphasis today is often placed on giving advice.

REPORT OF HER MAJESTY'S CHIEF INSPECTOR OF PRISONS 1989

(1989–90) H.C. 598

Preface

. . . Inspection remains our primary function and here, as in our reviews, we aim to achieve practical results which will be of assistance to Ministers and promote the efficiency of the Prison Service . . .

Chapter I—The Inspectorate's Year

1.01 1989 was a year of solid achievement for the Inspectorate. The number of full and short inspections was increased and we adhered fully to our remit to examine and report on the treatment of prisoners and conditions in prisons. Having completed a thematic review on integral sanitation we began work on a wide-ranging review of regimes. We continued to take part in the wider debate on penal affairs and to develop contacts with outside bodies which were of direct benefit to the Inspec-

[5] See: *Garner*, pp. 28–29; Owen A. Hartley, "Inspectorates in British Central Government" [1972] *Public Administration* 447; K. Hawkins, *Environment and Enforcement* (1984); B. Hutter, "An Inspector Calls: The Importance of Proactive Enforcement in the Regulatory Context" (1986) 26 *British Journal of Criminology* 114.

torate and to the Prison Service. The end of the year saw the completion of a full and demanding programme and the Inspectorate in good heart to move into the nineties.

1.02. . . It might be helpful to set out in broad terms how the Inspectorate carries out its inspectorial function under section 5A of the Prison Act 1952, as amended:

> (2) It shall be the duty of the Chief Inspector to inspect or arrange for the inspection of prisons in England and Wales and to report to the Secretary of State on them.
> (3) The Chief Inspector shall in particular report to the Secretary of State on the treatment of prisoners and conditions in prisons.
> (4) The Secretary of State may refer specific matters connected with prisons in England and Wales and prisoners in them to the Chief Inspector and direct him to report on them.

1.03 The main thrust of the inspection programme is the full inspection. There are two core inspection teams. Each comprises a Governor 1 team leader, a Home Office Grade 7 (Principal) and a Governor 4. Each team undertakes about 10 full inspections a year. Full inspections usually last from Monday to Thursday and sometimes Fridays. They will include late night and early morning visits and, in addition, weekend visits can be made. The programme for full inspections is announced at the beginning of each year. Before any inspection a considerable amount of briefing is obtained from headquarters, the regional office and the establishment concerned.

1.04 For full inspections the core teams are accompanied by our Buildings Consultant and Medical Inspector. The Chief Inspector normally opens the inspection and during the course of his visit has discussions with the Governor, Chairman of the Board of Visitors and groups of inmates. The inspection team is usually augmented by the Chief Inspector's Staff Officer and by the Deputy Chief Inspector. In the case of large establishments the team membership is widened to include members of the other team and office based staff with inspectorial experience.

1.05 It is inevitable that with so many people examining aspects of life at an establishment there will be a large number of recommendations. These are addressed variously to the Director General, Regional Director and Governor, depending on who has the major responsibility. The most serious matters are addressed to the Home Secretary. Recommendations which require action by headquarters, or are of a national concern, are directed to the Director General. Those which require regional oversight are addressed to the Regional Director. Local issues are referred to the Governor. Many recommendations to the Governor are of a minor or housekeeping nature. These are referred direct to him when the report is submitted to the Home Secretary but are not necessarily included in the published report.

1.06 Short inspections are usually led by a Governor 1 who is normally supported by two inspectors, not necessarily from his team. Some have been undertaken by the Deputy Chief Inspector and some by the Office Grade 7 (Principal). The services of the Buildings Consultant and Medical Inspector can be called on if necessary. The inspections normally last between two and three days and while they aim to cover aspects of life in an establishment directly related to the treatment of inmates and include late night and early morning visits, the resulting recommendations tend to concentrate on local issues. The reports are submitted to the Home Secretary.

1.07 Short notice visits are normally undertaken by the Chief Inspector. There is no formal programme and they provide an opportunity for him to visit establishments and to meet Governors in a less formal atmosphere than would be the case with an inspection. The Inspectorate is also able to undertake unannounced visits.

1.08 Clearly our main concern must be to inspect establishments and report to the Home Secretary. Our annual programme for full and short inspections should enable us to cover between 40–50 establishments a year. Add to this a number of unannounced and short notice visits, and we should hope to visit each establishment in some way once every two years.

1.10 During 1989 we carried out a programme of 21 full inspections of establishments in England and Wales. This compares favourably with the 16 in 1988. In addition 17 short inspections were completed. We hope to increase the number of short inspections in 1990 to between 20–30. We also made a small number of unannounced visits. In total 43 different establishments in England and Wales were visited by the Inspectorate with inspections at 38.

1.11 Three formal recommendations arising from full inspections were made to the Secretary of State. Over 311 recommendations were addressed to the Director General, 194 to Regional Directors and an average of 104 recommendations to the Governor of each establishment inspected. Short inspections resulted in 44 recommendations to the Director General, 24 to Regional Directors and an average of 20 to Governors.

1.12 We have striven to produce reports of full inspections within a reasonable time, taking into account the complexity and, in some cases, the need to check recommendations of reports. We have set ourselves a target of submitting a report to the Home Secretary within some eight weeks of an inspection. We have been able sometimes to meet this target but the average time taken is 13 weeks. This is, of course, a vast improvement on previous years, but we feel we can still do better. Whatever our efforts the impact and the currency of recommendations can be undermined if the department is unable to consider reports and agree publication in at most the same length of time it takes us to prepare them. During the year some reports were with the department for as long as seven months before publication. We recognise that the Prison Department comprises a number of headquarters divisions which have to be consulted about each report as well as Regional Offices and the establishment itself. It is not an easy process and in 1988 we tried to help by splitting recommendations to the Governor into those which were important and required comment and those which were of a minor housekeeping nature. The Prison Department is due to embark on a fundamental reorganisation in 1990 and it remains to be seen how the procedures for processing of our reports will fit into the new system. But we would want to see a system which would allow for the speedy publication of reports. We have no executive authority to follow up our reports and recommendations. Our job is to advise Ministers: after our advice is submitted it is for the Prison Department to take matters forward.

1.15 We are often asked what happens to our reports and recommendations. As we have said above, we have no remit to follow up our inspections. It would be inappropriate for us, as advisers, to do so, save in very exceptional cases, and we do not, in any event, have the necessary staff. At present follow-up action is overseen by the Deputy Director General's Office and we receive reports on the implementation of our recommendations or the reasons why they are not accepted. We would wish to see a similar arrangement established in the forthcoming reorganisation and relocation of the Prison Department headquarters.

1.16 Some recommendations are very serious and in our view deserve to be implemented speedily. In our report on Parkhurst (published in November 1988) we drew attention to a wing of over 300 cells which at that time had been empty for nine years and which had fallen into a state of disrepair. The then Home Secretary's response to our report was that work to refurbish the wing would commence in July 1989. As we prepare this report in February 1990 the work has not yet started and is not scheduled to do so until the summer of this year—12 months late.

CHAPTER II—CONDITIONS

2.01 Conditions can often set the tone for inmate and staff relations. Spending long periods behind doors can be made more tolerable if there is little or no overcrowding, if the cell and furniture are properly maintained and if there is integral sanitation. An inmate is unlikely to have any respect for a cell decorated with other inmates' graffiti, with damaged windows and furniture and a smell of urine. The crude process of slopping out is made worse by the close proximity of the sluice sinks to hand basins and the generally poor state of recesses. It is equally degrading for staff to have to supervise such procedures, and very difficult indeed to elicit any form of positive response from inmates who all too easily come to accept their situation as the norm. At Wandsworth we found that spartan and basic conditions were accepted by both inmates and the staff as standard. Inmates saw them as part of the package for being in a "hard" prison. Many staff took the view that such conditions kept inmates in their place. The inmates knew what was expected of them and saw no way of rising above such a low level of expectation. It was a deadening experience for both groups.

2.02 Throughout the year we found a surprisingly high number of buildings which had leaking roofs. Although some were minor leaks many were not and all caused deterioration. On the older structures defective roof coverings or flashings were the usual source of water penetration, while in the newer buildings the common reasons were poorly designed and constructed flat roofs. The older prisons, usually but not always dating back to the nineteenth century, were found to have extensive areas of brickwork in need of repointing and, to a lesser extent, replacement due to serious spalling. It was clear that there was a large and serious backlog of building work which should be carried out to preserve the fabric and prevent further deterioration. The Planned Inspection of Buildings System which is being introduced should help identify this type of defect and should be introduced more rapidly.

2.07 In those prisons where inmates spend a reasonable amount of time out of their cells, their accommodation is important mainly as a place where they can have some privacy and keep belongings and mementoes and where they sleep. For inmates who may be expected to spend upwards of 20 hours a day in their cell it is their home and its importance becomes even more significant. During 1989 we were confronted by the good, the bad and the ugly.

2.08 By and large the standard of accommodation in female establishments was good and respected by inmates. . . .

2.09 Provision for male inmates varied far more. At Manchester 67 inmates were held in single cells, 296 holding two to a cell and 82 three to a cell. Most cells had recently been redecorated but had quickly developed a tatty and seedy appearance. There was a general absence of picture boards. At Wandsworth most inmates were held one or two to a cell with a relatively low level of overcrowding. Many of the cells were without picture boards and, like Manchester, had a seedy appearance. Portacabin accommodation was being used for 40 inmates at Ranby. . . .

2.10 Each inmate should have his own cell with a bed, table, locker and chair. However, without the benefits of a positive and full regime this could be counter-productive; it would be considered inhuman to hold someone on their own for some 20 hours a day even if he were in a fully furnished cell. And there is no doubt that for many, sharing a cell with another is a welcome relief from the sheer boredom of imprisonment. But this can cause problems in cells which were originally designed for one. . . .

. . . In Birmingham almost 600 inmates, both convicted and unconvicted, were held three to a cell. There was insufficient space for each inmate to have a chair, locker and table. Meals were taken sitting on beds. While in certain circumstances two inmates to a cell can be acceptable triple occupation is intolerable and should be phased out as a matter of urgency.

2.11 During the year we visited a number of establishments which had dormitory accommodation either in whole or in part. Our view has been that dormitories provide no privacy or peace and quiet and that they can bring out the worst in inmates—bullying, theft and physical abuse. Many resembled transit camps and showed signs of continual occupation. On the plus side they were usually, but not always, fitted with toilets and sinks to which there was 24-hour access.

2.15 Television would be a welcome diversion for those locked up for long periods each day but it should not be seen as an easy alternative to the development of meaningful regimes. Out-of-cell activities must remain paramount. We believe that the benefits of in-cell television far outweigh the disadvantages. Such a system would encourage and reward hard work, replace the current use of videos, many of which show scenes of violence and are inappropriate; be susceptible to censorship by staff where desirable; bring about in time the replacement of electric batteries by the use of cheaper electric socket outlets; and be seen as a valuable adjunct to education (*e.g.* the Open University) and as a preparation for release.

2.17 The quality of facilities available to inmates varied as much as that of accommodation. We comment on the installation of integral sanitation in Chapter 6. Its value cannot be overstated and apart from ending slopping out its installation should enable recesses (toilets) to be converted to shower areas. Toilet and bathing facilities in women's prisons tended to be better and appreciated by inmates but slopping out remained in a number of establishments. . . . In Birmingham the bath-house used by convicted inmates was seriously damaged and infested by cockroaches and rats.

2.18 Inmates who are lucky enough to be involved in active regimes should be able to shower daily. Those who are forced to spend long periods each day cooped up with one or two other inmates equally need to have daily access to showers. The present provision in many establishments discourages personal hygiene. Standards of cleanliness and personal hygiene must be accorded a high priority in every establishment and be rigorously enforced by staff. Management should be encouraged and supported by headquarters.

. . .

Notes

1. Regular summaries of the Prison Inspectorate's work can be found in the "Penal Policies File" section of the *Howard Journal of Criminal Justice*.

2. For the role of the judiciary in reviewing the actions of the prison authorities see *R.* v. *Hull Prison Board of Visitors, ex p. St. Germain* [1979] 1 All E.R. 701; *Leech* v. *Parkhurst Prison Deputy Governor* [1988] 1 All E.R. 485; *R.* v. *Deputy Governor of Parkhurst Prison, ex p. Hague* [1992] 1 A.C. 58 and note the commentary by A. R.

Mowbray [1991] 2 *Journal of Forensic Psychiatry* 90 (on the Court of Appeal's decision). More generally on prisoners' rights see G. D. Treverton-Jones, *Imprisonment: The Legal Status and Rights of Prisoners* (1989) and S. H. Bailey, D. J. Harris & B. L. Jones, *Civil Liberties: Cases and Materials*, 3rd ed., (1991) Ch. 12.

Question
Will the implementation of inspectors' reports be dependent upon the legal sanctions available to them?

(F) LICENSING[6]

This is an extremely common administrative device. Street[7] gives over 60 examples. The typical purpose of licensing is to ensure governmental control of some or all aspects of an activity. The best-known example is the sale by retail of intoxicating liquor, which is regulated by a large and complex body of law. This was considered at length in the *Report of the Departmental Committee on Liquor Licensing*.[8] The control of development under the Town and Country Planning Acts can also be regarded as a licensing process.

Other examples, illustrated by cases cited elsewhere in this book, are trading licences (*Nakkuda Ali* v. *Jayaratne*, p. 404); hackney carriage licences (*R.* v. *Liverpool Corporation*, p. 502) and gaming licences (*R.* v. *Gaming Board*, p. 525).

One point of particular difficulty has been whether an authority in deciding to grant, renew or revoke a licence is required to observe any form of natural justice. See the latter two cases mentioned above and *McInnes* v. *Onslow-Fane* [1978] 1 W.L.R. 1520 (below, p. 507).

Throughout the 1980s a major element in the Government's economic policy was to promote enterprise by reducing the burdens imposed via administrative and legislative regulation. In a White Paper entitled "Lifting the Burden"[9] the view was expressed that "too many people in central and local government spend too much of their time regulating the activities of others."[10] Subsequently a central body, the Enterprise and Deregulation Unit, was established to promote deregulation throughout Whitehall.[11] The life of this Unit was extended in 1988 and all departments were obliged to develop a "rolling annual programme" of reviewing existing regulations.[12]

More generally see G. Baldwin and C. McCrudden (eds.), *Regulation and Public Law* (1987).

(G) PROSECUTION[13]

Under this heading may be included offences such as the following:

(1) failure to obtain a licence before commencing or continuing an activity, or acting in breach of licence conditions (*e.g.* breaches of planning control: Planning and Compensation Act 1991);

[6] See *Garner*, pp. 29–31.
[7] H. Street, *Justice in the Welfare State* (2nd ed., 1975), pp. 70–95.
[8] Cmnd. 5154.
[9] Cmnd. 9571 (1985).
[10] *Ibid.* para. 1:7.
[11] See *Building Businesses . . . Not Barriers* (Cmnd. 9794 (1986)), Ch. 3.
[12] *Releasing Enterprise* (Cm. 512 (1988)).
[13] See *Garner*, pp. 34–35.

(2) failing to observe prescribed standards (*e.g.* in relation to clean food, weights and measures or factories legislation);

(3) false claims for rights and privileges, such as social security benefits (see the Report of the Fisher Committee, *Abuse of Social Security Benefits*);[14]

(4) obstruction of public officials when exercising statutory functions (*e.g.* *Stroud* v. *Bradbury* (below, p. 789).

Notes

1. A major official study concluded that prosecutions by central and local government bodies, excluding the police (and now, of course, the Crown Prosecution Service), amounted to almost one-fifth of non-traffic criminal cases. These agencies included the following in descending order of their use of the courts: the Post Office (television licence prosecutions), the British Transport Police (rail fare "dodgers"), the Department of the Environment (vehicle excise tax cases), local authorities (numerous types of criminal behaviour), and the revenue departments (tax fraud, etc.). See K. W. Lidstone *et al.*, *Royal Commission on Criminal Procedure: Prosecutions by Private Individuals and Non-Police Agencies*, Research Study No. 10, (H.M.S.O.) (1980).

2. Against the background of an expanding "black economy" (see the *National Federation* case below, p. 744) and growing sophistication in tax avoidance schemes, the prosecution practices of the Inland Revenue, together with the Customs and Excise, were subject to detailed scrutiny by the Committee on Enforcement Powers of the Revenue Departments (chaired by Lord Keith), Cmnd. 8822 and see the commentary by D. W. Williams, [1984] P.L. 28.

3. Research indicates that administrative bodies may for a variety of reasons prefer to use other enforcement strategies, rather than prosecution. For example, the Commissioners of Customs and Excise use their statutory power to compound proceedings (*i.e.* refrain from prosecuting an alleged offender in return for a monetary penalty being paid) in thousands of petty smuggling cases per year. Such alternatives to prosecution raise important legal questions concerning the basic rights of individuals, including the procedure by which such offers are made, the legal status of these agreements and the forms of redress available to aggrieved individuals. For a detailed study see A. R. Mowbray, "The Compounding of Proceedings by the Customs and Excise: Calculating the Legal Implications" (1988) *British Tax Review* 290.

Question

Should all agencies bringing prosecutions on behalf of the public observe the same evidential and public interest criteria in deciding whether to prosecute in particular cases? Note the Director of Public Prosecutions' Code of Practice to Crown Prosecutors, which governs their discretion to prosecute: see J. R. Spencer, *Jackson's Machinery of Justice* (1989), pp. 237–240 and S. H. Bailey and M. J. Gunn, *Smith and Bailey on the Modern English Legal System* (2nd ed., 1991), pp. 630–637.

(H) Default Powers

A number of statutes give powers to Ministers to act in default of proper action taken by local authorities (*e.g.* the Public Health Act 1936 and the Education Act 1944 as amended by the Education Reform Act 1988). See, for example, *Wade*,

[14] Cmnd. 5228 (1973).

pp. 747–750 and *Craig*, pp. 409–410. Whilst these powers are not formally invoked frequently, their use may be threatened against recalcitrant authorities and Ministers have had resort to them in periods of intense central-local government conflict (see, *e.g. Asher (and Others)* v. *Secretary of State for the Environment* [1974] 1 Ch. 208). Local authorities also have default powers to take action where individuals fail to comply with statutory notices (*e.g.* to repair unfit houses under the Housing Act 1985); see *Garner*, pp. 33–34. Another respect in which the existence of a default power may be significant is where a person aggrieved by administrative action is refused a remedy in the courts as a result. A request to the authority with power to act in default, or to give instructions to the recalcitrant authority is regarded as the proper course of action; see *Watt* v. *Kesteven County Council* [1955] 1 Q.B. 408.

R. v. SECRETARY OF STATE FOR THE ENVIRONMENT, ex p. NORWICH CITY COUNCIL

[1982] 1 Q.B. 808; [1982] 1 All E.R. 737; 80 L.G.R. 498 (Court of Appeal)

The Housing Act 1980 provided local authority tenants with the right to buy their homes. Under section 10(1) the landlord council had "as soon as practicable" to serve on a tenant, with an established right to buy, a notice stating what, in the council's opinion, was to be the price for the conveyance and what provisions should be contained therein. Section 11 enabled the tenant to have the value determined by the district valuer. By section 23(1),

> "where it appears to the Secretary of State that tenants of a particular landlord . . . have or may have difficulty in exercising the right to buy effectively and expeditiously, he may, after giving the landlord . . . notice in writing of his intention to do so . . . use his powers under the . . . section."

Subsection (3) empowers the Secretary of State to "do all such things as appear to him necessary or expedient" to enable the tenant to exercise the right to buy.

Within the first month Norwich Council had received 452 applications to buy, but after seven months no sales had been completed. Tenants began to complain about the time taken by the council to complete sales and meetings were held between officials of both the department and the council. These were followed by meetings between Ministers and councillors.

In December 1981, the Secretary of State made an order under section 23 of the Act and wrote to the leader of Norwich Council in the following terms:

> "in my view the conduct of your council with respect to the notices required to be served on your council's secure tenants under section 10 of the Housing Act 1980 could well amount to non-compliance with the statutory requirements of Chapter 1 of Part 1 of that Act. But whether or not this is the case I would still conclude that secure tenants of your council have or may have difficulty in exercising the right to buy effectively and expeditiously . . . I cannot however ignore the further delays and difficulties referred to above."

On the same day the council applied to the High Court for an order of certiorari to quash the decision of the Secretary of State. The Divisional Court dismissed the application and the council appealed to the Court of Appeal.

LORD DENNING M.R. . . .

"Default power"

. . . Our present statute, the Housing Act 1980, in section 23 goes as far as anything that I have seen hitherto. It enables the Minister to take over the function himself—to do it all himself by his own civil servants—and to charge the cost to the local authority. . . .

This "default power" enables the central government to interfere with a high hand over local authorities. Local self-government is such an important part of our constitution that, to my mind, the courts should be vigilant to see that this power of the central government is not exceeded or misused. Wherever the wording of the statute permits, the courts should read into it a provision that the "default power" should not be exercised except in accordance with the rules of natural justice. That follows from such cases as *Board of Education* v. *Rice* [1911] A.C. 179 and *Ridge* v. *Baldwin* [1964] A.C. 40. After all, the Minister is dismissing the local authority for default in carrying out their duty. He is replacing them by his own civil servants. He is making them pay all the costs and depriving them of the interest they would have received. Simple fairness requires that this should not be done unless they are told what is alleged against them and they have had an opportunity of answering it.

Apart from this, the very decision of the Minister himself is open to judicial review. If the Minister does not act in good faith, or if he acts on extraneous considerations which ought not to influence him, or if he misdirects himself in fact or in law, the court will in a proper case intervene and set his order aside. That follows from such cases as *Padfield* v. *Minister of Agriculture, Fisheries and Food* [1968] A.C. 997 and *Secretary of State for Employment* v. *ASLEF (No. 2)* [1972] 2 Q.B. 455, 493, approved by Lord Wilberforce in *Secretary of State for Education and Science* v. *Tameside Metropolitan Borough Council* [1977] A.C. 1014, 1047. Also if the Minister assumes to interfere with a decision of the local authority to which they came quite reasonably and sensibly, the court may intervene to stop the Minister. . . .

The district valuer

It is quite clear that many local councils, in order to state the price under section 10(1) at which they were ready to sell, consulted the district valuer at the outset. He made the initial valuation on which that price was fixed. That saved the council time and money. Instead of their own staff making the initial valuation in the council's time—and instead of putting out the work to private valuers—the council got the district valuer to do it at no expense to the council at all. This speeded up valuations greatly in many of the other councils. . . .

Pointing to section 11, the Norwich City Council said that the district valuer was like an appeal body. He should not be employed to make the initial valuation where he would sit on appeal from it to make the final valuation. That point impressed me much for some time. It seemed contrary to the accepted principle that "justice should not only be done, but should manifestly and undoubtedly be seen to be done": see *per* Lord Hewart C.J. in *R.* v. *Sussex Justices, ex p. McCarthy* [1924] 1 K.B. 256, 259 and *F.G.C. Metropolitan Properties Co. Ltd.* v. *Lannon* [1969] 1 Q.B. 577, 599. But this principle—like that of natural justice—must not be carried too far. It is flexible and must be adapted as the case may require.

[After detailing the method of calculation of rateable values.] A similar system is applied in these valuations under the Housing Act 1980. The initial valuation under section 10(1) (on which the local council fixes the price) is made by one of the clerks in the office. If the tenant takes objection and refers the matter to the district valuer under section 11, then the decision is made by the valuation officer himself or his deputy. This system works perfectly well. That is shown by the fact that in 50 per cent. of the cases the valuation is reduced: and also by the even more striking fact that no tenant has ever taken any objection to the system. The only person to take objection has been the Norwich City Council.

So justice is *in fact* done by reason of the final valuation being done by a senior officer quite distinct from the one who made the initial valuation. It is *seen* to be done by reason of the fact that no tenant has ever complained of it.

Application to this case

. . . the concern of this court, as always, is to protect the individual from the misuse or abuse of power by those in authority. The individual here is the tenant. He has been given by Parliament the right to buy the house in which he lives. Yet in the exercise of that right he has met with intolerable delay. The responsibility for that delay is, beyond doubt, the responsibility of the Norwich City Council. They acted—or failed to act—in complete good faith. But they were misguided. And they must answer for it. They were badly advised on many matters; such as to insist on scale 1:500 when scale 1:1250 would do. They were badly advised to refuse to employ the district valuer, when it would have speeded things up greatly. No one can excuse himself for his own mistakes by saying that he did it on bad advice: see *Federal Commerce & Navigation Co. Ltd.* v. *Molena Alpha Inc.* [1978] Q.B. 927, 979. The council here showed too little concern for the rights of the tenants. They should have given them higher priority. They were unreasonable not to do so.

What is the remedy? What recourse have the tenants for redress? None by coming to the courts. Nothing could be done effectively by mandamus. The statute has provided a remedy. It has enabled the Secretary of State to make a "default order." It is a very great power to be used only after careful consideration. The Secretary of State here did give it careful consideration. He gave the council every opportunity to mend their ways. He gave them ample notice of what was alleged against them. He heard all that they had to say before he made his order. He gave them clear warning of the consequences. His order, strong as it was, was within his statutory powers. It cannot be upset in this court.

We were told that, pending these proceedings, the Secretary of State had allowed the Norwich City Council to carry on with the selling of the houses, and had not taken them out of their hands. This holds out hope for a solution. Surely the City Council will agree now to use the district valuer to make the initial valuations. Surely they will speed up the procedure so as to avoid any further complaints. If they do this, there may be no need for the Secretary of State to act upon his order. But that his order was good, I have no doubt. I would dismiss this appeal.

KERR and MAY LJJ. gave separate judgments dismissing the appeal.

Note

Following the Court of Appeal's decision, Norwich Council co-operated with the Secretary of State by providing an office for his representatives, taking on more staff to process tenants' applications and using the district valuer for first valuations of properties. The Secretary of State withdrew his section 23 notice after three-and-a-half years in May 1985. Two academic commentators assessed the outcome of the Environment Secretary's actions in the following terms:

> "in the aftermath of the service of notice of intervention Norwich had held on to administration and co-operated in the best interests of tenants and ratepayers. Although defeat in the courts was unfortunate and the notice had remained in operation longer than had been hoped Norwich can reasonably be regarded to have coped satisfactorily with the circumstances. For central government the outcome was more favourable. Success in the courts had strengthened their hand in relations with other authorities, closeness to detailed day-to-day administration had informed them of problems and issues and again strengthened their position through increasing knowledge."

R. Forrest and A. Murie, *An Unreasonable Act? Central-Local Government Conflict and the Housing Act 1980*, pp. 129–130 (1985). See also the case commentary by S. H. Bailey, [1983] P.L. 8.

Question

Is Parliament too willing to grant coercive default powers to Ministers?

(I) CONTRACTING

This section will examine the use of contractual powers by central and local government for the purpose of securing policy goals. The liability of such bodies is considered later at p. 791.

For general reading see *Garner*, pp. 243–244 and 263–265; *Craig*, pp. 499–502; *Wade*, pp. 788–790; S. Arrowsmith, *Government Procurement and Judicial Review* (1988) [for a Commonwealth perspective]; C. Turpin, *Government Procurement and Contracts* (1989).

REGULATION BY CONTRACT: THE NEW PREROGATIVE*

Terence Daintith, (1979) Current Legal Problems 41

The anti-inflation policy pursued by the last Labour Government from 1975 to 1979[1] had many striking features, but for lawyers, that which surely still demands discussion and analysis is the reinforcement of this "voluntary" policy, until December 1978, by a programme of sanctions upon employers operated almost entirely without statutory support. During this period, an undertaking to comply with the policy was a prerequisite for the award of almost all government contracts and of some government industrial assistance; a known breach of the policy disqualified from consideration for such contracts and assistance; compliance with the policy was secured for the future as a legally enforceable term thereof.[2] The purpose of this paper is not to discuss the details of the incomes policy, but to attempt to place the tools for its enforcement in an appropriate legal context, as an example—the most egregious to date—of the use by the Government of its contractual forms and procedures as an instrument of regulation of the behaviour of the subject.[3]

Obviously, any government contract constrains, by law, the behaviour of both contracting parties, for the purpose of achieving their joint objective—the erection of an office building, say, or the provision of 10,000 pairs of wellington boots. In the traditional conception of contract, the legal obligations imposed are individualised by reference to this particular objective. With the widespread adoption, in ordinary commerce, of the standard form contract, the distinction between the consensual, individualised contract and the imposed, general regulation is already blurred. Government contracting shares fully in this movement but also, in the examples I wish to discuss, goes far beyond it; for it incorporates, into standard terms and allocation procedures, clauses and requirements

* Note: some footnotes have been omitted.

[1] See references in the White Papers: *The Attack on Inflation*, Cmnd. 6151 (1975), paras. 22–23; *The Attack on Inflation, the Second Year*, Cmnd. 6507 (1976), para. 21; *The Attack on Inflation after July 31, 1977*, Cmnd. 6882 (1977), para. 16; *Winning the Battle against Inflation*, Cmnd. 7293 (1978), para. 25. Sanctions were withdrawn by the Government following an adverse vote in the House of Commons in December 1978: see 960 H.C. Deb., col. 920 (December 14, 1978).

[2] See, *e.g.* Department of Environment, PSA General Conditions GC/Works/1, Supplementary Condition No. 186 (Counter-Inflation—Incomes Policy) (February 1978), and for an earlier, less draconian example, Supplementary Condition No. 163, Disallowance in Prices of Increases in Remuneration (November 1975).

[3] A comprehensive and perceptive discussion of the legality of sanctions is provided by Ferguson and Page, "Pay Restraint: the Legal Constraints" (1978) 128 N.L.J. 515. See also, on this topic, Harden and Scott, "Sound administration must rest on a sound legal basis" (1978) 128 N.L.J. 4; M. Elliott, "Government Contracts and Counter-Inflation Policy," (1978) 7 Ind.L.J. 120. There is little writing on the general issue of the regulatory use of government contracts in the U.K. See in general Turpin, *Government Contracts* (1972), Ch. 9, and on the Fair Wages clause Kahn-Freund, "Legislation through Adjudication: the Legal Aspect of Fair Wages Clauses and Recognised Conditions" (1948) 11 M.L.R. 269, 429; B. Bercusson, *Fair Wages Resolutions* (1978).

reflecting public interests which by their breadth and importance pass far beyond the mutual objectives of the contracting parties and which, therefore, might normally be promoted by statutory regulation. This is why the paper's title refers to prerogative: government has discovered means of using its increasing economic strength *vis-à-vis* private industry so as to promote certain policies in a style, and with results, which for a long time we have assumed must be the hallmark of parliamentary legislation: that is to say, officially promulgated rules backed by effective general compulsion. This means the power to rule without parliamentary consent, which is the hallmark of prerogative. . . .

Such an inquiry falls naturally into two parts, corresponding to the two types of power related to government contracts: first, the power of Government to decide who will be its contractors, and on what terms; secondly, its power to control contractors' (and indeed subcontractors') behaviour in terms of the contract itself. These powers will be referred to respectively as *Precontractual* and *Contractual*.

Precontractual Powers

In discussing the precontractual phase, it is necessary to distinguish the position of the Crown—that is to say, the legal personification of central government—from that of most other public authorities. The reason is that the Crown enjoys a common law capacity to make contracts, while most other public authorities, being created by statute, only enjoy such contractual capacity as their constitutive statute allots them. . . .

To sum up, therefore, on the precontractual phase, in which the public authority is taking its unilateral decision as to who shall be its contractor and on what terms, the situation of the public authority, reflecting the common law respect for freedom of contract in general, is in domestic law one of almost complete discretion. This is so whether the power to contract is based in common law or in statute. The discretion is large enough to permit the pursuit of a wide range of regulatory policies through the contractual process—a very convenient discovery in a period of minority government. Such real legal constraints as exist are external, the product of the system of EEC law, operating on some central and local government contracts through the medium of co-ordination of contractual procedures, and on some of the contractual activity of public enterprises through the rules of competition policy.

Contractual Powers

. . .

Let us, then, look back over the different phases of the exercise of contractual powers by Government, to see what is the effect, in law, of using these powers, rather than statutory powers, as an instrument of public regulation. We have just noted that, with minor exceptions, the courts have applied, to the exercise of purely contractual powers, techniques of review of a type and intensity broadly similar to those which fill the pages of de Smith's *Judicial Review of Administrative Action*. At this stage, therefore, there is little to be gained, in terms of administrative freedom of manoeuvre, from the use of contractual techniques. But in the precontractual phase, in selecting contractual partners and deciding the terms it will offer them, the Government enjoys almost unfettered freedom and total immunity from judicial review by reason of the absence of general rules of domestic law to control this process. There are important constraints on this process stemming from the activity of the European Community in the fields of public procurement and of competition law, but their full potential, and the possibility of their operation in the domestic legal arena have not yet been adequately appreciated. In consequence Government enjoys far greater freedom and discretion in the elaboration of contractual schemes of regulation than it could reasonably hope to possess as the operator of a statutory scheme under powers conferred by Parliament. Moreover, even if Parliament might itself on occasion be prepared to grant Government such wide and ill-defined powers by statute, the availability to Government of the contractual option denies to Parliament the very possibility of discussing and deciding the issue. In a recent report, the parliamentary select committee on the ombudsman showed its sensitivity to the problem of contractual regulation in recommending that the ombudsman's powers be extended to enable him to look at the process of awarding government contracts.[4] Consideration of this sensible proposal must not distract Parliament from the far more fundamental question of whether it is prepared to see a reduction of its formal supremacy by allowing Government to develop and ramify a technique of regulation in which legislative authorisation plays no effective part. It would be sad, but not surprising, if Parliament, at the time of its greatest real authority over Government in recent years, were to sit quietly by while Government fashioned for itself a new prerogative.

Note

Subsequently, Professor Daintith has classified the power of government contracting as an element of "dominium" (*i.e.* the ability of Government to secure its policy objectives through the use of public wealth). He argued:

> "a case might also be made for subjecting the use by central government of a dominant economic position to the same kinds of constraints as are imposed on private firms and some public-sector bodies by competition legislation, in particular the Fair Trading Act 1973. Useful as such improvements might be, we should not expect them to hold government back on the occasions when it feels

[4] Fourth Report from the Select Committee on the Parliamentary Commissioner for Administration (1977–78) H.C. 444. [(ed.) See further Ch. 5 below, p. 158]

that major political or economic gains can result from sweeping or unorthodox use of its dominium powers."

"The Executive Power Today: Bargaining and Economic Control," in J. Jowell & D. Oliver, *The Changing Constitution* (2nd ed., 1989), Ch. 8 at p. 217.

LOCAL GOVERNMENT ACT 1988

Local and other public authority contracts: exclusion of non-commercial considerations

17.—(1) It is the duty of every public authority to which this section applies, in exercising, in relation to its public supply or works contracts, any proposed or any subsisting such contract, as the case may be, any function regulated by this section to exercise that function without reference to matters which are non-commercial matters for the purposes of this section.

(2) The public authorities to which this section applies are those specified in Schedule 2 to this Act.

(3) The contracts which are public supply or works contracts for the purposes of this section are contracts for the supply of goods or materials, for the supply of services or for the execution of works; but this section does not apply in relation to contracts entered into before the commencement of this section.

(4) The functions regulated by this section are—

(*a*) the inclusion of persons in or the exclusion of persons from—
 (i) any list of persons approved for the purposes of public supply or works contracts with the authority, or
 (ii) any list of persons from whom tenders for such contracts may be invited;

(*b*) in relation to a proposed public supply or works contract with the authority—
 (i) the inclusion of persons in or the exclusion of persons from the group of persons from whom tenders are invited,
 (ii) the accepting or not accepting the submission of tenders for the contract,
 (iii) the selecting the person with whom to enter into the contract, or
 (iv) the giving or withholding approval for, or the selecting or nominating, persons to be sub-contractors for the purposes of the contract; and

(*c*) in relation to a subsisting public supply or works contract with the authority—
 (i) the giving or withholding approval for, or the selecting or nominating, persons to be sub-contractors for the purposes of the contract, or
 (ii) the termination of the contract.

(5) The following matters are non-commercial matters as regards the public supply or works contracts of a public authority, any proposed or any subsisting such contract, as the case may be, that is to say—

(*a*) the terms and conditions of employment by contractors of their workers or the composition of, the arrangements for the promotion, transfer or training of or the other opportunities afforded to, their workforces;
(*b*) whether the terms on which contractors contract with their sub-contractors constitute, in the case of contracts with individuals, contracts for the provision by them as self-employed persons of their services only;
(*c*) any involvement of the business activities or interests of contractors with irrelevant fields of Government policy;
(*d*) the conduct of contractors or workers in industrial disputes between them or any involvement of the business activities of contractors in industrial disputes between other persons;
(*e*) the country or territory of origin of supplies to, or the location in any country or territory of the business activities or interests of, contractors;
(*f*) any political, industrial or sectarian affiliations or interests of contractors or their directors, partners or employees;
(*g*) financial support or lack of financial support by contractors for any institution to or from which the authority gives or withholds support;
(*h*) use or non-use by contractors of technical or professional services provided by the authority under the Building Act 1984 or the Building (Scotland) Act 1959.

(6) The matters specified in subsection (5) above include matters which have occurred in the past as well as matters which subsist when the function in question falls to be exercised.

(7) Where any matter referable to a contractor would, as a matter specified in subsection (5) above, be a non-commercial matter in relation to him, the corresponding matter referable to—

(*a*) a supplier or customer of the contractor;
(*b*) a sub-contractor of the contractor or his supplier or customer;
(*c*) an associated body of the contractor or his supplier or customer; or
(*d*) a sub-contractor of an associated body of the contractor or his supplier or customer;

is also, in relation to the contractor, a non-commercial matter for the purposes of this section.

(8) In this section—

"approved list" means such a list as is mentioned in subsection (4)(a) above;

"associated body," in relation to a contractor, means any company which (within the meaning of the Companies Act 1985) is the contractor's holding company or subsidiary or is a subsidiary of the contractor's holding company;

"business" includes any trade or profession;

"business activities" and "business interests," in relation to a contractor or other person, mean respectively any activities comprised in, or any investments employed in or attributable to, the carrying on of his business and "activity" includes receiving the benefit of the performance of any contract;

"contractor," except in relation to a subsisting contract, means a "potential contractor," that is to say—

(*a*) in relation to functions as respects an approved list, any person who is or seeks to be included in the list; and

(*b*) in relation to functions as respects a proposed public supply or works contract, any person who is or seeks to be included in the group of persons from whom tenders are invited or who seeks to submit a tender for or enter into the proposed contract, as the case may be;

"exclusion" includes removal;

"Government policy" falls within "irrelevant fields" for the purposes of this section if it concerns matters of defence or foreign or Commonwealth policy and "involve," as regards business activities and any such field or policy, includes the supply of goods or materials or services to, or the execution of works for, any authority or person having functions or carrying on business in that field and, as regards business interests and any such field of policy, includes investments in any authority or person whose business activities are so involved;

"industrial dispute" has, as regards a dispute in Great Britain, the same meaning as trade dispute in the Trade Union and Labour Relations Act 1974 and "involve," as regards business activities and an industrial dispute, includes the supply of goods, materials or services to or by, or the execution of works for or by, any party to the dispute, any other person affected by the dispute, or any authority concerned with the enforcement of law and order in relation to the dispute;

"political, industrial or sectarian affiliations or interests" means actual or potential membership of, or actual or potential support for, respectively, any political party, any employers' association or trade union or any society, fraternity or other association;

"suppliers or customers" and "sub-contractors" includes prospective suppliers or customers and sub-contractors; and "supplier," in relation to a contractor, includes any person who, in the course of business, supplies him with services or facilities of any description for purposes of his business.

and "employers' association" and "trade union" have, as regards bodies constituted under the law of England and Wales or Scotland, the same meaning as in the Trade Union and Labour Relations Act 1974.

(9) This section is subject to section 18 below.

Notes

1. Schedule 2 to the Act subjects many public bodies to the above restrictions, including local authorities, police authorities and national parks planning boards.

2. Breach of section 17 does not amount to a criminal offence, but is actionable by any person who in consequence suffers loss or damage. Furthermore, potential or former potential contractors are given *locus standi* for the purposes of bringing judicial review proceedings (s.19(7)).

3. As to the scope of section 17, a departmental circular has expressed the view that the section prohibits relevant local authorities from banning contracts with contractors who have worked on nuclear missile sites, but enables authorities to make reasonable inquiries about contractors' health and safety records: Department of the Environment Circular 8/88.

4. Section 18 of the 1988 Act entitles local authorities to ask questions about contractors'/potential contractors' behaviour under race relations legislation, provided that the Secretary of State has approved the questions asked. The Environment Secretary has, after consultation with the Commission for Racial Equality, approved six questions under section 18; *e.g.* "in the last three years has any finding of unlawful racial discrimination been made against your organisation by any court or industrial tribunal?" All the authorised questions are listed in Annex B to Circular 8/88.

Question

Should the same legal principles apply to the processes of government contracting at the central and local authority levels?

(J) Administrative Rule-Making

Following the pioneering writings of the American commentator Professor K. C. Davis (particularly in his book *Discretionary Justice: A Preliminary Inquiry* (1969)), recent years have witnessed a growing interest by British academics in the important process of administrative rule-making. Despite the lack of publicity surrounding many of these provisions it is now generally recognised that the creation of non-statutory rules by central government departments, together with other public bodies, has significant influence on the actual operation of numerous administrative programmes and, consequently, raises many fundamental legal questions about the creation, status and enforcement of such norms. Craig suggests that there are at least four explanations for the creation of administrative rules:

(1) the organisational needs of bureaucratic agencies when faced with the obligation to exercise discretionary powers;
(2) the ability to use non-technical language in such provisions (*e.g.* in the Highway Code);
(3) the flexibility of these provisions compared with formal delegated legislation;
(4) the assertion that such provisions are not legally binding (but see below).

General readings:
Craig, pp. 188–195 and 310–319; *Wade*, pp. 858–860; *Harlow and Rawlings*, Ch. 5; G. Ganz, *Quasi-Legislation: Recent Developments in Secondary Legislation* (1987).

THE PARLIAMENTARY COMMISSIONER AND ADMINISTRATIVE GUIDANCE

Alastair R. Mowbray, [1987] P.L. 570*

Study of the P.C.A.'s reports soon discloses that there is a myriad of individual pieces of administrative guidance being used by departments, not necessarily under this name.[1] Consequently it is necessary to devise a method of classifying these provisions which allows the aggregation of similar forms of guidance into distinct classes. For the purpose of the present study, a threefold functional classification, which in part was derived from United States law,[2] has been adopted. This classification distinguishes between forms of administrative guidance which relate to (a) policy, (b) procedure and (c) interpretation. The first class, *policy* guidance, specifies the formal objectives of a departmental programme, such as the designation of approved company auditors, and provides the detailed criteria by which officials are to determine the cases of individuals affected by the programme. The source of this guidance is to be found in the political value judgments espoused by Ministers.[3] Secondly, *procedural* guidance informs subordinate officials and/or persons outside the department of the form to be followed in the relevant decision-making process.[4] This guidance is derived from the organisational expertise possessed by departments, supplemented occasionally by legal norms. Finally, *interpretative* guidance seeks to explain the departmental view of

* Note: some footnotes have been omitted.

[1] Thus the Scottish Office terms these provisions "guidelines" C126/77 H.C. 126 (1977–78) p. 268; the Inland Revenue calls them "departmental instructions" C87/82 H.C. 8 (1982–83) p. 92; and the Home Office refers to them as "standing orders" C264/G H.C. 290 (1972–73) p. 119.

[2] See Administrative Procedure Act, s.553 and more generally the discussion of American rulemaking in K. C. Davis, *Discretionary Justice: A Preliminary Inquiry*; R. Baldwin and K. Hawkins, "Discretionary Justice: Davis Reconsidered" [1984] P.L. 570; M. Asimow, "Delegated Legislation: U.S. and U.K." (1983) 3 O.J.L.S. 253.

[3] See the P.C.A.'s explanation of why the rules governing the sale of surplus government land were changed in 1980, C384/81 H.C. 132 (1981–82) p. 8.

[4] *e.g.* the procedure to be observed by war pension medical boards, C260/77 H.C. 126 (1977–78) p. 108. Also see A. D. Jergesen, "The Enforcement of Administrative Procedures in G.B. and the U.S." (1982) 30 Am.J.Comp.L. 267 and P. Birkinshaw, "Departments of State, Citizens and the Internal Resolution of Grievances" (1985) C.J.Q. 15.

what Parliament or any other legislator (in the case of delegated legislation) meant by enacting a particular provision.[5] Inevitably this class of guidance relies upon legal knowledge derived from lawyers. . . .

(a) Policy guidance

Provisions falling within this class of guidance are utilised by virtually all the departments subject to the scrutiny of the P.C.A. Examples extend from the Ministry of Overseas Development's rules stating eligibility for foreign income supplements to the D.H.S.S.'s criteria entitling disabled persons to financial help towards the costs of running a private car. The bulk of policy guidance encountered was concerned with the departments' aims towards the public at large who came within their responsibilities. These aims encompassed all the major functions of the modern state, including regulating conduct, providing benefits (in kind or in cash), and taxing. Such guidance regulated all types of discretionary powers, with 21 instances governing statutory and prerogative powers, 10 applying to extra-statutory discretions (mainly in the field of taxation), and the remaining two sets of provisions having no direct link with any statutory scheme. . . .

(b) Procedural guidance

The overwhelming majority of pieces of procedural guidance discovered by the P.C.A. regulated civil servants' conduct towards members of the public, with the remainder governing the form of relations between departments and other public authorities. The largest number of cases dealing with procedural guidance affecting the public elaborated the practices to be followed for the allocation of public largesse (such as the process of determining eligibility for war pensions), although a significant minority of cases concerned procedural guidance controlling the actions of officials in the revenue departments.

(c) Interpretative guidance

Unsurprisingly, six of the eight cases revealing interpretative guidance contained interpretations of primary legislation, which ranged in subject-matter from the Purchase Tax Act 1963 to the Countryside Act 1968. However, this category of guidance differed from the two previous categories in that almost all the individual pieces of interpretative guidance had been published. One explanation for this distinction may have been the departments' desire to persuade affected citizens of the accuracy and legitimacy of their interpretations, which could be achieved only via a public promulgation of the interpretations. . . .

[5] *e.g.* the Public Notices issued by the Customs and Excise on the scope of the legislation administered by their department, C316/68 H.C. 129 (1968–69) p. 20.

CONCLUSIONS

From the reports of the P.C.A. that were surveyed for the purposes of the present article, valuable insight may be gained into the significant role played by administrative guidance in decision-making across the whole spectrum of central government departments. The reports have disclosed, *inter alia*, policy guidance detailing when the former Ministry of Transport would refuse to appoint garages as approved vehicle testing stations; procedural guidance specifying the method by which capital grants for farmers could be obtained from the Ministry of Agriculture, Fisheries and Food; and interpretative guidance issued by the Department of the Environment elaborating the duties of councils as highway authorities. Hence there is a pressing need for a deeper consideration of the status of such provisions in contemporary public law. Definitive answers have yet to be established regarding the circumstances in which departments should be able to create and use these provisions, the situations in which departments ought to be bound by the terms of their guidance, and the grounds upon which affected individuals can challenge the content and application of guidance. The broader constitutional issues include the extent to which departments should be under a legal duty to consult the public about the creation of individual pieces of administrative guidance (particularly policy guidance), and to publish (or at least make available to the public) the final version of their internally promulgated guidance.[6]

From the perspective of the P.C.A., the adaptable concept of maladministration has been used to examine the departmental application of all three classes of guidance. Successive Commissioners have scrutinised officials' decision-making to ensure that relevant guidance has been applied with regard to all the material facts of the case. Furthermore, the P.C.A. now demands that officials should not deviate from the requirements of their procedural guidance without good reason. Departments have also had the substance of their procedural, and in exceptional circumstances their interpretative, guidance subjected to critical evaluation by the P.C.A. In developing these responses towards administrative guidance, the P.C.A. has demonstrated a marked tendency towards consistency in assessing whether departmental utilisation of guidance violates the concept of maladministration. Yet this consistency has been obtained without the explicit reference to previous cases that one expects in a formal system of precedential decision-making.

By undertaking the above investigations, the P.C.A. has helped to protect the vital rights, interests and duties of citizens[7] from some of the adverse effects of the creation and application of administrative guidance

6 On the issue of publication see Donald C. Rowat (ed.), *Administrative Society in Developed Countries* (1979).

7 Including, their right to legal advice in quasi-criminal proceedings (C486/81 n. 66 *supra*); their interest in securing lawful consideration of their parole applications (C264/G n. 20 *supra*); their duty to pay the correct amount of tax (C316/68 n. 46 *supra*).

by departments. His role has been particularly valuable in cases where the relevant guidance had not been published and consequently it would have been virtually impossible for the citizen to seek a judicial remedy. Furthermore, the P.C.A.'s responses towards administrative guidance are in many ways more advanced than the newly emerging judicial cognisance of these provisions. For example, since the earliest post-Sachsenhausen days, the P.C.A. has operated on the basis of the presumption that departments should apply their policy guidance to determine all individual cases coming within its scope, unless there are exceptional circumstances; whereas the courts have only recognised a similar legal presumption since 1984. Nevertheless, there is a great potential for the cross-fertilisation of ideas between the P.C.A. and the courts, in their respective assessments of the limits placed upon the departmental creation and utilisation of guidance by the standards of maladministration and illegality (*e.g.* the acceptability of particular pieces of procedural guidance when assessed against the criteria of "good administrative practice" and procedural fairness/impropriety). It may be concluded that the Parliamentary Commissioner deserves a central place in lawyers' understanding of the mechanisms that currently provide a check on the administration's use of administrative guidance in its decision-making.

Notes

1. A landmark decision in the judicial scrutiny of the way in which public authorities utilise administrative rules was delivered by the House of Lords in *British Oxygen Co. Ltd.* v. *Minister of Technology* [1971] A.C. 610 (see below, p. 292). In *R.* v. *Secretary of State for the Home Department, ex p. Khan* [1984] 1 W.L.R. 1337, the Court of Appeal reached an equally significant decision by upholding a claim that the Home Secretary was legally obliged to observe the requirements of his own administrative rules which he had published. Hence, English law was beginning to accord legal weight to the contents of such provisions (see A. R. Mowbray, "Administrative Guidance and Judicial Review" [1985] P.L. 558). After a wide-ranging study of the use and legal characteristics of administrative rules R. Baldwin and J. Houghton concluded:

> "the seeds of a more rational approach do exist, but a disinclination to deal with the effects of informal rules has rendered rule-makers unaccountable and exposed a useful device to exploitation. Questionable decisions have been taken to use informal rules in areas where fundamental liberties and issues of central political contention have been involved (*e.g.* picketing, policing, immigration, prisons). More than anything, such executive activity should prompt the courts to take action."

"Circular Arguments: The Status and Legitimacy of Administrative Rules" [1986] P.L. 239.

2. Professor Ganz has produced an alternative agenda to regulate the creation and use of administrative rules. She proposes the development of a Code of Practice to control the procedures followed by administrative bodies when making such rules (and see below, note 4). In addition she advocates the establishment of a permanent agency:

"to advise on the creation of quasi-legal or voluntary rules instead of legal rules and evolve criteria for their use. At present they seem to come into existence largely on an ad hoc basis, often as an afterthought, in response to conflicting pressures to do nothing or to legislate. If the rules are to be observed, rather than be political window dressing, they must be adopted for better reasons than political expediency"

(*Quasi-Legislation: Recent Developments in Secondary Legislation*, p. 108)

3. Administrative rules may also come within the purview of particular administrative tribunals. In a study of Value Added Tax Tribunals, it was discovered that the tribunals' response to such rules depended on (a) the breadth of the jurisdiction granted to the tribunals by Parliament and (b) the legal form of the specific administrative rule at issue. Generally, V.A.T. tribunals asserted their independence from the executive by proclaiming their unwillingness to be bound by the Customs and Excise's interpretations of legislative provisions contained in administrative rules. See A. R. Mowbray, "Customs and Excise Public Notices: The Tribunal Response" (1987) *British Tax Review* 381.

4. There are also many hybrid forms of guidance created by public authorities which have a statutory basis, but are not subordinate legislation.[15] One particular form of such guidance is the statutory code of practice. There are now over 40 different statutory provisions relating to codes of practice, most of which have been enacted since 1974. Because of the increasing practical importance of these codes, Parliament expressed its concern that not all the codes were subject to parliamentary proceedings.[16] The Government responded by producing a document entitled "Guidance on Codes of Practice and Legislation,"[17] directed at officials and parliamentary draftsmen contemplating the proposing of new statutory provisions empowering the issuing of codes of practice. The document states that "a code of practice is an authoritative statement of practice to be followed in some field." (para. 2:1) Codes differ from legislation because, (1) they offer guidance rather than imposing obligations; (2) their provisions are not directly enforceable in legal proceedings and (3) they often contain explanatory materials and argument. The document asserts that codes should not be used to impose specific legal obligations (para. 4:1); their contents should clearly distinguish between prescriptive and explanatory text (para. 9:3); and where their contents have indirect legal effects (either civil or criminal) they ought to be subject to parliamentary proceedings (*e.g.* affirmative or negative resolutions) (para. 10:1).

See further: Lord Campbell, "Codes of Practice as an Alternative to Legislation" [1985] Stat.L.R. 127; A. Samuels, "Codes of Practice and Legislation" [1986] Stat.L.R. 29; C. McCrudden, "Codes in a Cold Climate: Administrative Rule-Making by the Commission for Racial Equality" (1988) 51 M.L.R. 409.

[15] See S. H. Bailey and M. J. Gunn, *Smith and Bailey on The Modern English Legal System* (2nd ed., 1991) p. 278.

[16] Debate in the House of Lords, January 15, 1986: Hansard Vol. 469, cols. 1075–1104.

[17] Produced in December 1987 by H.M. Government: the full text of the document is reproduced in 10 Stat.L.R. 214 (1989).

CHAPTER 4

THE COUNCIL ON TRIBUNALS

THE Franks Committee[1] recommended the creation of two standing councils, one for England/Wales and one for Scotland, to keep the constitution and working of tribunals under constant review. Although the Committee perceived the councils as primarily having an advisory role it also recommended the allocation of certain executive functions to the councils, (*e.g.* the power to appoint members of tribunals).[2] Parliament, however, created a single council with limited advisory powers by the Tribunals and Inquiries Act 1958. This Act was broadened by the Tribunals and Inquiries Act 1966, and by numerous statutory instruments and was continued in existence by the (consolidating) Tribunals and Inquiries Acts 1971 and 1992.

In an early assessment of the Council's work, Professor Garner concluded that its scrutiny of draft rules governing the procedure of individual tribunals was "extremely valuable" and that the Council acted as a useful interface between senior civil servants and informed outsiders.[3] But, the Council was generally unable to provide redress for specific complainants and the Council needed a clear mandate for departments to consult it about primary legislation involving tribunals. More recently Professor Sir David Williams, a former member of the Council, has noted that despite its restricted formal powers the Council has built up a strong relationship with departments. Consequently, they regularly consult the Council about new legislation affecting tribunals and allow members of the Council to participate in departmental working parties considering such matters.[4]

Further discussion of the Council's activities can be found in *Garner*, Ch. 10; *Wade*, Ch. 23; *Harlow and Rawlings*, Ch. 6; *Craig*, Ch. 4; H. W. R. Wade, "Administrative Tribunals and Administrative Justice" 55 *Australian Law Journal* 374 (1981).

(A) CONSTITUTION AND POWERS

A NOTE ON THE CONSTITUTION AND FUNCTIONS OF THE COUNCIL

Annual Report of the Council on Tribunals 1990–91: Appendix D

H.C. 97 (1991–92)

1. The Council were set up by the Tribunals and Inquiries Act 1958 and now operate under the Tribunals and Inquiries Act 1971, as read with the Transfer of Functions (Secretary of State and Lord Advocate) Order 1972 (S.I. 1972 No. 2002).

[1] *Report of the Committee on Administrative Tribunals and Enquiries* (Cmnd. 218) (1957).
[2] *Ibid.* Chap. 11.
[3] J. F. Garner, "The Council on Tribunals" [1965] P.L. 321.
[4] D. G. T. Williams, "The Council on Tribunals: The First 25 Years" [1984] P.L. 73.

2. The Council are to consist of not more than 15 nor less than 10 members appointed by the Lord Chancellor and the Lord Advocate. In addition, the Parliamentary Commissioner for Administration (the Parliamentary Ombudsman) is a member by virtue of his office. In appointing members, regard is to be had to the need for representation of the interests of persons in Wales.

3. The Scottish Committee of the Council is to consist of two or three members of the Council designated by the Lord Advocate, and three or four non-members of the Council appointed by him. The Parliamentary Ombudsman is also an *ex officio* member of the Committee.

4. The Council at present have 15 members, of whom one has been appointed primarily to represent the interests of persons in Wales. The Scottish Committee has seven members, of whom three are members of the Council.

5. The principal functions of the Council as laid down in the Tribunals and Inquiries Act 1971 are—

(a) to keep under review the constitution and working of the tribunals specified in Schedule 1 to the Act, and, from time to time, to report on their constitution and working;

(b) to consider and report on matters referred to the Council under the Act with respect to tribunals other than the ordinary courts of law, whether or not specified in Schedule 1 to the Act; and

(c) to consider and report on these matters, or matters the Council may consider to be of special importance, with respect to administrative procedures which involve or may involve the holding of a statutory inquiry by or on behalf of a Minister.

6. The Lord Chancellor and the Lord Advocate have made orders which have the effect of adding tribunals to Schedule 1 to the Act, as is provided for in the Act.

7. The term "statutory inquiry" means (i) an inquiry or hearing held in pursuance of a statutory duty, or (ii) a discretionary inquiry or hearing designated by an order under section 19(2) of the Act. The relevant order now in force is the Tribunals and Inquiries (Discretionary Inquiries) Order 1975 (S.I. 1975 No. 1379) as amended (S.I. 1976 No. 293 and S.I. 1983 No. 1287).

8. The Council must be consulted before procedural rules are made for any tribunal specified in Schedule 1 to the 1971 Act, and on procedural rules made by the Lord Chancellor or the Lord Advocate in connection with statutory inquiries. They must also be consulted before any exemption is granted from the requirement in section 12 of the Act to give reasons for decisions. They may make general recommendations to Ministers about appointments to membership of the scheduled tribunals.

9. The jurisdiction of the Council extends over the whole of Great

Britain but they have no authority to deal with any matter in respect of which the Parliament of Northern Ireland would have power to make laws if the Northern Ireland Constitution Act 1973 had not been passed.

10. The Council are required to make an annual report which must be laid before Parliament and may, at any time, make a special report on their own initiative under (a) or (c) of paragraph 5 above.

11. Reference to the Council or reports by them are normally made by or to the Lord Chancellor and the Lord Advocate, either both or one or other of them according as the matter in question relates to Great Britain as a whole, to England and Wales or to Scotland.

12. Certain tribunals operating in Scotland, which are specified in Part II of Schedule 1 to the Act of 1971, came under the particular supervision of the Scottish Committee. Before making any reports in regard to these, or on any matter referred by the Lord Advocate, the Council must consult the Scottish Committee. In addition, the Scottish Committee have the right in certain circumstances to report directly to the Lord Advocate.

The Council's Committees

Appendix E. (Supra)

1. There are at present six Committees of the Council, apart from the Scottish Committee.

2. Much Committee business is transacted by correspondence, but meetings are held as and when required, generally on the day of the monthly Council meeting. In practice, Committees (or, in cases of great urgency, their chairmen) deal with straightforward business within their sphere of interest, reporting to the Council as necessary.

3. The Committees, with an indication of their respective areas of activity, are (in alphabetical order):—

Education Tribunals Committee	The procedures of Education Appeal Committees (both local authority and grant-maintained).
Health and Social Security Committee	Most matters concerning social security, health and related subjects, including tribunals and inquiries dealing with social security or medical issues.
Legal Committee	Matters having a strong legal content, including the drafting of primary and subordinate legislation.

Planning Procedures Committee	Town and country planning, highway and other related subjects which may involve public inquiries or related procedures, including the drafting of primary and subordinate legislation.
Representation and Assistance Committee	Matters concerning the provision of professional or other representation or assistance in tribunal and inquiry proceedings.
Visits Committee	The planning and organisation of visits by members of the Council to tribunals and inquiries.

THE FUNCTIONS OF THE COUNCIL ON TRIBUNALS: SPECIAL REPORT

(Cmnd. 7805 (1980))

5.1 The Functions of the Council Committee examined a number of weaknesses in our statutory powers and material resources.

5.2 These weaknesses are particularly striking when the scope of our statutory task is taken into account. The number of different types of tribunal within our jurisdiction has greatly increased since the Tribunals and Inquiries Act 1958 was passed, and now exceeds 50. Tribunals placed under our supervision since that time include the Local Valuation Courts, Immigration Adjudicators and the Immigration Appeal Tribunal, the Director General of Fair Trading (in respect of certain of his functions), Mental Health Review Tribunals, Rent Assessment Committees, Value Added Tax Tribunals, Children's Hearings (in Scotland) and Industrial Tribunals.

5.4 Under the heading of matters requiring statutory attention, our committee considered the lack of clarity as to the extent of our general jurisdiction in relation to tribunals; our lack of a specific power to investigate complaints; and the absence of any requirement that we be consulted on proposed primary legislation affecting tribunals or inquiries, and of any power to require our views (expressed in response to statutorily prescribed consultation) to be made public.

5.6 Other matters governed by statute are the difference between the statutory expression of our powers in relation to inquiries and that in relation to tribunals; the absence of any obligation on the part of Ministers (other than the Lord Chancellor) to consult us on draft rules in connection with statutory inquiries; and the need to clarify the right of our members to attend private hearings and to remain at the deliberation stage of tribunals' proceedings . . . we consider that all of them require suitable attention from Parliament, so that we can act with greater confidence and authority under a clear, logical and somewhat broadened remit.

5.7 Under the heading of resources, we refer to our constitution. . . . We believe that the Council should not be larger than now, and should continue to rely on the standing and the distinctive contribution of each member; but there is an obvious connection between our resources and the strength of our secretariat. A part-time body requires a great deal of professional and technical support if it is to do its job effectively. A staff as small as ours must be occupied almost exclusively by day-to-day business, and find hardly any opportunity for undertaking the wider studies and preparation of background material which are so important in our specialist field of work. We therefore recommend a modest increase in our staff.

8.6 Lord Franks made it clear, in discussion with our Functions of the Council Committee, that after a period of more than 20 years he still attached significance to the phrase "supervision of tribunals" which appears in his report as the heading to the chapter dealing with the creation of the Council of Tribunals. He felt that we should not lose sight of this rôle, because for him it still embodied the Council's essential function. Other witnesses, with practical experience as tribunal chairmen, voiced their concern about the lack of supervision of the kind envisaged by the Franks Committee—notably the absence of detailed knowledge about how tribunals are actually working, the appropriateness of their jurisdictions, the quality of decision-making in different classes of tribunals and, in general, what in fact happens at ground level. Sporadic visiting, although valuable in other respects, cannot provide this kind of systematic knowledge. It can come only from studies in depth.

8.10 We envisage that some of the research to which we have just referred would be carried out directly by our own staff. Particularly sensitive subjects would certainly have to be dealt with in this way. On other matters we would commission studies from outside researchers, or advise on research mounted on their own initiative by academic investigators. We see particular scope for directly commissioning research by academic consultants. The Administrative Conference of the United States succeeds in engaging consultants at a very modest cost to prepare reports on specific subjects in collaboration with committees of the Conference.

9.9 Looking ahead, therefore, we see an increasingly important constitutional rôle for the Council on Tribunals. In the changing constitutional climate our organisation has potentialities as yet unrealised—a point of view we share with all those with whom we had discussions. At present, movement generally is towards greater openness in public administration; there is growing demand for opening up procedures which have hitherto been closed, for explanations of how official decisions have been reached and for adjudication external to the agency in cases of unresolved disputes. Emphasis is on the legal aspects of citizens' rights and on effective procedures for their protection. In fact, the reconciliation of the requirements of efficient government with the rule of law has assumed greater significance within recent years. Indeed, some authorities are thinking in terms of a new constitutional settlement starting from a reaffirmation of the fundamental importance of the rule of law.

SPECIFIC RECOMMENDATIONS

10.1 We divide our proposals into those which would require legislation and those which could be given effect by administrative action, either with or without accompanying legislation.

Proposals requiring legislation

(i) The Council should be given a clear general power (in addition to the supervision of the tribunals named in Schedule 1 to the Act of 1971) to act as an advisory body over the whole area of administrative adjudication and the general pattern and organisation of tribunal structure.

(ii) The Council should be given a clear right to be consulted, and empowered to offer views, in relation to matters arising on draft primary legislation affecting our area of jurisdiction.

(iii) The entitlement of the Council to be consulted about procedural rules should be restated in clearer and more general terms.

(iv) When primary or secondary legislation on which the Council have been consulted is brought before Parliament, the Minister concerned should be obliged to disclose the substance of the Council's final advice.

(v) The differences between the wording of the Council's jurisdiction in connection with tribunals and that in connection with inquiries should be removed. In relation to both tribunals and inquiries, the Council should have a wide power to offer advice on general or particular matters, whether or not on request and without a matter having to be regarded as one of "special importance".

(vi) The Council should have a statutory power to investigate and issue findings upon certain complaints raising matters of principle in relation to the proceedings of tribunals and inquiries. In this connection the Council should be empowered to call for relevant papers from tribunals and government departments.

(vii) Members of the Council should be specifically empowered to visit private hearings of tribunals under the Council's supervision and to attend the deliberation stage of the proceedings of those tribunals.

(viii) At an appropriate time, further consideration should be given to the supervision of administrative tribunals and public inquiries in Northern Ireland.

Proposals not requiring legislation

(ix) A code for consultation with the Council should be agreed by the Lord Chancellor and government departments.
(x) The financial and staff resources of the Council should be strengthened.

10.2 We appreciate that the developments advocated in this report will need to be spread over a period of time. We are also mindful of economic restraints. The intention, therefore, is to indicate the way forward by setting out a programme which can be initiated in the near future and thereafter progressively implemented.

. . .

Notes

1. Lord Tweedsmuir delivered the Government's formal response to the Special Report on April 27, 1981. The Government considered that the case for substantially widening the Council's powers had not been made out. It was also concerned about the public expenditure implications of the Council's recommendations. However, the Government accepted that it would be desirable for the Council's right to be consulted about procedural rules to be restated in clearer terms. Furthermore, it was often appropriate for departments to consult the Council about draft primary legislation affecting matters within the latter's jurisdiction. In reply the Council regretted that its major recommendations had not been accepted (Annual Report [hereafter A.R.] 1980–81, H.C. 89 (1981–82) p. 7).

2. The above extracts demonstrate that the procedure of departments consulting the Council is central to the latter's working. Therefore in 1981 the Council formulated a Code of Practice on Consultation with the Council, which was accepted by the Lord Chancellor (and the Lord Advocate for Scotland). It then sent it to Ministers in relevant departments asking them to bring it to the attention of their officials working on appropriate draft legislation. The Code states that departments should always allow the Council as much time as possible to prepare and submit their comments on proposed legislation. The minimum periods for consideration by the Council should be four weeks for routine proposals which do not raise major questions of principle, and six weeks where major issues of principle are involved. The Code also emphasises that where the Council has expressed views on an important question of principle and a Minister intends to make public the fact of consultation he ought to state the general tenor of the Council's advice. In 1983 the Government refused to provide a statutory endorsement of the latter requirement. (A.R. 1983–84), H.C. 42 (1984–85) para. 2.6.) Next year the Council reported that there had been a general improvement in the way in which departments consulted the Council. However, it was still not always given adequate time for consultation (*e.g.* by the D.H.S.S. (as it was then called) who sent them draft Regulations on July 26 and then laid them before Parliament on August 2—A.R. 1984–85, H.C. 54 (1985–86) para. 2.3). In an attempt to encourage wider adherence to the code, the Council re-issued it to departments during 1986. But, some departments are still failing to observe its terms (for further examples see A.R. 1986–87, H.C. 234 (1987–88)). The full text of the Code can be found in Appendix C to the 1986–87 Annual Report.

3. In order to promote academic research into tribunals the Council appointed a part-time research co-ordinator in 1987. His work resulted in the publication of the Council's first Research Bulletin in 1989. The bulletin contained a 24-page compi-

lation of current and proposed research into tribunals by academics, and indicated areas of study which the Council believed worthy of investigation. A second bulletin was published in 1990, and a third in 1991, and annual updates are expected in the future.

4. Professor Sir David Williams has predicted that the Council will continue in its present form for some time to come ([1984] P.L. 87). The *JUSTICE/All Souls Review* (1988) recommended that the Council should continue in existence with a widened jurisdiction covering all tribunals and with greater financial resources (Ch. 9). Furthermore, the Review proposed the creation of a permanent and independent Administrative Review Commission to exercise general oversight across the whole administrative system. Close collaboration, possibly including overlapping membership, between the Council and the Commission was advocated (Ch. 4). Whilst welcoming the creation of such a new institution Professor Williams believes that it is unlikely to command governmental support for some years and, therefore, the Council will remain the dominant standing body in administrative law ("The Tribunal System—Its Future Control and Supervision," (1990) 9 C.J.Q. 27).

5. Recently the Council has renewed the plea for new legislation to enable its functions to be clarified and widened. The Council believes that reference to the 1980 Special Report "as a touchstone of our aims is subject inevitably to the law of diminishing returns." Nevertheless, legislation ought to empower the Council to advise departments on proposals to establish new tribunals, and those affecting the constitution and working of scheduled tribunals. Secondly, the Council wishes to be entitled to advise on proposals which would affect the administrative procedures involving a statutory inquiry. Thirdly, the Council wants the removal of inconsistencies in its current powers (*e.g.* its differential powers of scrutiny over tribunals and inquiries contained in Tribunals and Inquiries Act 1992, s.1). The Council has discussed these changes with the Lord Chancellor and his officials, but Government approval and the finding of legislative time is still awaited. (A.R. 1988–89, H.C. 114 (1989–90) pp. 14–18.) Subsequently, the Council has had further discussions with the Lord Chancellor's department and there is "general agreement in principle that there is considerable merit in our proposals"; but no legislative measures have yet been laid before Parliament (A.R. 1989–90, H.C. 64 (1990–91) p. 30; A.R. 1990–91, H.C. 97 (1991–92), pp. 37–38.) These questions are not addressed by the consolidation of the Tribunals and Inquiries Act in 1992.

(B) The Work of the Council on Tribunals

(i) The Scrutiny of Tribunal Procedures

ANNUAL REPORT OF THE COUNCIL ON TRIBUNALS 1985–86

H.C. 42 (1986–87)

2.5. In all our work we have been persistent in pursuing certain basic aims, as illustrated below. A good general guide to the Council's approach is embodied in the phrase "openness, fairness and impartiality". This was a constant theme of the Franks Report. However, over the years other standards have been significant. For example, efficiency, expedition and economy have also been prominent. Openness has to be expressed in practical steps to ensure accountability, so that it is clear where the responsibilities for different tribunals lie. The needs of users of the system have, rightly, received more emphasis.

2.6. We recommend that tribunals be clearly independent of the bodies over whose decisions they adjudicate: this has recently been implemented in connection with Social Security Appeal Tribunals: their members are no longer appointed by the Secretary of State in the department which was seen to be a party to appeals; they are now appointed and administered by the President of S.S.A.T.s. It has been implemented in other ways in connection with Social Security Commissioners and specialist tax appeals (VAT Tribunals and Special Commissioners of Income Tax): the administrative responsibility for these tribunals has been transferred to the Lord Chancellor's Department.

2.8. We have been vigilant in seeking to ensure that people are granted a hearing in connection with proposals which affect their interests; that rights of appeal against administrative decisions are given wherever appropriate and are not eroded where they already exist, *e.g.* concerning the Social Fund, immigration appeals, expulsion and suspension from school, the Social Security Commissioners, the Transport Tribunal, and patents; that parties to tribunal proceedings are treated equitably and neither side is given an unfair advantage; that clerks to tribunals play a defined and appropriate part in the proceedings; that reasons are normally given in writing for all decisions and that they are adequate and comprehensible; that proceedings should be simple and clear, and should normally be in public: the proceedings must be "not done in a corner"; and that resources should not be wasted— for example in Local Valuation Panels where many appeals are lodged but few are heard.

2.9. In short the procedure should make the tribunal easily accessible to the public; it should be cheap, swift and free from technicality. The whole proceedings should be, and be seen to be, independent and impartial, and fair to the powerful and the professional, but also to the vulnerable.

2.11. We have long stood out for the right of representation for parties before tribunals and inquiries. We believe that non-legal aid would sometimes be more suitable for parties before tribunals than professional assistance from a lawyer. We also believe that legal aid or assistance by way of representation should be extended to virtually all kinds of tribunal but subject to a "sieve" to ensure that it would not be granted in cases which did not really merit it. At present legal aid is only available in the Lands Tribunals and the Commons Commissioners, and free legal representation before Mental Health Review Tribunals.

Notes

1. This is the most important function performed by the Council. A very dramatic example of this process in operation occurred in relation to appeals under the Social Fund. During 1985 the Government announced that it intended to replace single payments under the supplementary benefits system (for items such as replacement furniture) with loans and grants payable out of a new Social

Fund.[5] Under these proposals claimants would lose their right of appeal to a Social Security Appeal Tribunal against an adjudication officer's decision regarding their claim for a single payment. The Council felt so strongly about this alteration in appellate rights that it issued a special report.[6] The report stated that annually around 36,000 appeals regarding single payments were heard by S.S.A.T.s and that 25 per cent. of them were successful. The Council concluded:

> "the people most affected by this proposal are amongst the most vulnerable in our society. Very good reasons are needed before the abolition of the right to an independent appeal in such circumstances, an appeal which has existed for over 50 years. It would probably be the most substantial abolition of a right of appeal to an independent tribunal since the Council on Tribunals were set up by Parliament in 1958, following the Franks Report. It is for these reasons that we are so critical of the proposal."[7]

Despite the Council's offer to advise the Government on a modified right of appeal for Social Fund disputes, the Government made no formal response to the Council until after the enactment of the Social Security Act 1986, which created the Fund.[8] However, during the report stage of the Bill the Government responded to parliamentary pressure and introduced a scheme for reviewing most challenged Social Fund decisions by a new group of Social Fund Inspectors appointed by a Social Fund Commissioner. Drabble and Lynes found that the Social Fund Inspectors were "approaching their task with a commendable degree of objectivity."[9] But, "it is too early to say how well a cadre of some 40 legally unqualified inspectors under the part-time supervision of a solicitor will perform the essentially legal task that has been assigned to them."[10] The Council has maintained its view that Social Fund appeals should be determined by an independent tribunal.[11] For a detailed account of the Social Fund see A. I. Ogus & E. M. Barendt, *The Law of Social Security*, 3rd ed. (1988), Chap. 14; also D. Feldman, "The Constitution and the Social Fund: A Novel Form of Legislation" (1991) 41 L.Q.R. 39.

2. In its Annual Report for 1989–90[12] the Council expresses the fear that financial considerations may be establishing a trend of compromising the standards expected of adjudicative bodies under their supervision. Apart from the failure to provide appeals to an independent tribunal for Social Fund disputes, the Council notes that the Government have encouraged local authorities to create internal review procedures for homeless persons seeking assistance from authorities. The Council objects to this proposal because:

> "we have consistently taken the view that the important influence of the subject-matter here on the lives of those affected demands a decision from an independent adjudicative body, and we regard some kind of internal administrative review to be adopted by local authorities at their discretion, which is apparently contemplated by the Government, as highly unsatisfactory."[13]

[5] *Reform of Social Security*, Vol. 1, Cmnd. 9517 (1985).
[6] *Social Security—Abolition of Independent Appeals Under the Proposed Social Fund*, Cmnd. 9722 (1986).
[7] *Supra*, pp. 6–7.
[8] *Annual Report 1985–86*, H.C. 42 (1986–87) para. 3.85.
[9] R. Drabble and T. Lynes, "The Social Fund—Discretion or Control?" [1989] P.L. 297 at p. 315.
[10] *Ibid.* p. 318.
[11] A.R. 1987–88, H.C. 102 (1988–89) para. 3.36.
[12] H.C. 64 (1990–91).
[13] *Ibid.* para. 1.8.

Also the Council is critical of the Government for creating one-person tribunals, an example being the Pensions Ombudsman established by the Social Security Act 1990.

> "The more usual tripartite constitution of the majority of tribunals possesses distinct advantages where the jurisdiction of the tribunal comprehends subject-matters of substantial complexity affecting the status, livelihood or financial well-being of individual appellants, permitting as it does the combination of an independent, adjudicative approach with the availability of expertise in, or experience of the subject-matter in question."[14]

Generally, the Council concluded,

> "we believe that where a decision affects a citizen's liberty, livelihood, status or other basic rights, particularly where a grievance concerns a decision of a public authority, nothing less is apt for the purpose than a properly equipped independent body able to bring an adjudicative approach to bear on the matter at issue. . . . we shall be vigilant in assessing appeals procedures on the general criteria indicated and in warning the Government and the public in cases where new appeal or review procedures are in our view inadequate for the purposes for which they are proposed."[15]

The following year, the Council voiced its "strong concern" at the state of affairs revealed by a report on housing benefit review boards (R. Sainsbury and T. Eardley, *Housing Benefit Reviews* (D.S.S. Research Report Series No. 3, H.M.S.O., 1991), which found that the system was failing to serve the interests of the majority of claimants. (See the Annual Report for 1990–91.[15a]) The report noted, *inter alia*, that there was no right of appeal from review board decisions and inconsistency in decision-making; that claimants were vulnerable to housing benefit department practices which might deter or prevent them from pursuing their right of appeal effectively; and that boards were not truly independent of the local authorities whose decisions were under review.

(ii) Visits to Tribunals and Inquiries

ANNUAL REPORT OF THE COUNCIL ON TRIBUNALS 1985–86

H.C. 42 (1986–87)

The Council's policy on visiting

6.17. Our object in visiting tribunals and inquiries is to obtain practical experience of their working, so that we can be better informed in exercising our functions. It enables us not only to obtain a useful general picture of how different tribunal systems and procedures work in practice but also to observe in operation the procedures on which we have advised. This visiting of tribunals and inquiries is not referred to in the Tribunals and Inquiries Act 1971, but is carried out as a necessary means of fulfilling our statutory duty to "keep under review the constitution and working"

[14] *Ibid.* para. 1.11.
[15] *Ibid.* para. 1.14.
[15a] H.C. 97 (1991–92), paras. 3.20–3.24.

of the tribunals under our jurisdiction, and our similar function in relation to public inquiries.

6.18. In arranging visits, care is taken to avoid giving the impression of an "inspection" of the tribunal personnel. Visits are always made by appointment, and not anonymously. Ever since the Council were established we have always thought it right to give advance notice to the tribunal. Our visits include an inspectorial element but that is related to the working and procedures of the various types of tribunals and inquiries rather than to the performance of any particular chairman, member, inspector or clerk; however, if there was an instance of that performance clearly being substantially below what is acceptable, we would take steps to prevent a recurrence. Our letters to tribunals in advance of visits refer specifically to our independence, to the fact that we take no part in the proceedings of the tribunal but observe the procedures as a whole, and to the desire of our visiting member to have discussions with the tribunal members before or after a sitting and to hear the tribunal's own views about any procedural problems. We request information on certain statistics concerning caseload and representation of parties.

6.19. There would be considerable problems in our having a role as inspectors of tribunal personnel in the course of our visits. First, because of the very small proportion of tribunal personnel whom we see in action, it would be a very hit-and-miss affair. There is also a real danger that, if we saw an individual performing unsatisfactorily, it might be isolated or untypical behaviour. It is also important that we are not equipped to carry out this kind of investigation or to see that any resulting recommendations are implemented. There would also be practical problems, because it would be difficult to keep visits unannounced as we would have to obtain details of the date, time and place of a hearing—so revealing the likelihood of a visit. In addition, because of our constitutional position and our position under the Tribunals and Inquiries Act 1971, we would not seek unnecessarily to spoil relations with tribunals and departments. We generally find that co-operation works better than confrontation, wherever possible. We also have to bear in mind the fact that the vast and changing number of tribunal personnel find it difficult to be familiar with the role and functions of the Council.

6.20. Each visit is the subject of a confidential report by the Council member to the Council as a whole. It may be the subject of discussion particularly where a visiting member draws attention to a problem. If matters of concern do arise, for example, where a possible defect has been found in procedure, we take them up with those involved. Clearly much of the knowledge of the problems and performance of the tribunals under our supervision is obtained from such visits as our individual members are able to make and from the co-operation of the tribunal secretariat.

6.21. In selecting tribunals and inquiries to be visited we aim to secure not only a planned allocation of visits between the different types of tribunals but also an equitable geographical coverage. We concentrate some of our visiting on those kinds of tribunals where there is reason to think that there may be difficulties or on tribunals which are new, are undergoing some important changes, or are the subject of a review. We also take a particular interest in attending conferences or training seminars for the chairmen, members or clerks of tribunals, because they often involve an emphasis on procedural matters, on training, and on sharing experience.

Notes

1. The late Professor Street expressed the view, in his Hamlyn lectures, that the underfunding of the Council meant "... that its supervision of tribunals is so slight as to be ineffective. It is unlikely to discover the existence of incompetent tribunal members."[16]

2. During the year 1990–91, members of the Council and its Scottish Committee visited individual tribunals on 141 occasions and made 11 visits to inquiries.[17] In the same period Social Security Appeal Tribunals, alone, decided 67,369 cases.[18]

Question

Who should have the primary responsibility for monitoring the administrative performance of tribunals—Presidents of Tribunals, the Parliamentary Commissioner for Administration, the courts or some other institution?

(iii) The Scrutiny of Inquiry Procedures

ANNUAL REPORT OF THE COUNCIL ON TRIBUNALS 1987–88

H.C. 102 (1988–89)

Review of the Planning Inquiries Procedure Rules

2.76 The publication and coming into force of new statutory Rules for the holding of Planning Appeal Inquiries is a major step forward. We survey the improvements in procedure which we have advocated in our representations and consultations over the last 10 years.

2.77 The publication of the new Planning Inquiry Procedure Rules, comprising the Secretary of State Rules[1] and the Inspectors' Rules[2], at the end of May 1988 was the culmination of much effort over the years, first on our part and latterly by the Department of the Environment. Both sets of rules came into force on July 7, 1988. No less important was the publication of the Code of Practice for Major Inquiries which has been adjusted many times since it first emerged in 1981. The Rules and the Code will operate in conjunction with each other; we have long campaigned for some of the changes in procedure they introduce. They should speed up inquiries without detracting from the rights of objectors

[16] H. Street, *Justice in the Welfare State* (2nd ed., 1975), p. 63.
[17] A.R. 1990–91, H.C. 97 (1991–92), Appendix A.
[18] *Ibid.* Appendix C.
[1] The Town and Country Planning (Inquiries Procedure) Rules 1988, S.I. 1988 No. 944.
[2] The Town and Country Planning Appeals (Determination by Inspectors) (Inquiries Procedure) Rules 1988, S.I. 1988 No. 945.

to participate fully in them. At the final stages of negotiations on the Rules we were consulted on a comprehensive draft circular, incorporating the Code of Practice, and now published as a joint circular[3] the purpose of which is to explain the Rules and their background.

2.78 One of the most important changes to these Rules stemmed from a recommendation of a government scrutiny of the arrangements for planning appeal inquiries. While it was evident that the provisions of the previous Rules were based on the right principles, the fact that time limits operated backward from the date of an inquiry rather than forward from notification to the parties that an inquiry would be held (as in the present Rules) was seen as a recipe for unnecessary delays.

2.79 It has long been our aim that there should be more equal treatment of statutory objectors having direct interests in the land involved and other parties whose interest may be less capable of definition. The Code admirably effects this by allowing the registration at an early stage of all those interested in participating in an inquiry. According to their degree of interest they may or may not be categorised as major participants, but in any event the Code ensures that everyone is given equal opportunity to put their case to the inspector.

2.80 Since 1975, pre-inquiry meetings have contributed greatly to the efficiency of inquiries. However, it became evident that, because these meetings were not subject to the rules, inspectors had no explicit powers to support the decisions taken at them. Consequently, disruptive elements whose sole desire was to obstruct the proceedings and, by this means, the development, exploited this to the full. The common enemy of disruption was thus instrumental in forging a greater co-operation between government departments involved in inquiries. They determined to amend their Inquiry Rules to avoid such abuse. We greatly welcomed this opportunity to effect amendments such as making pre-inquiry meetings subject to the Rules (Rules 5 and 7 (Secretary of State Rules) and Rule 7 (Inspectors' Rules)), and taking evidence as read (Rule 13(4) (Secretary of State Rules) and Rule 14(4) (Inspectors' Rules)), which we had earlier pressed during negotiations with the Departments of Environment and Transport for improving the Highway Inquiry Procedure Rules. At the time those negotiations had foundered because the two departments took the view that one set of rules could not be amended without involving others which were interdependent. Now that the Planning Inquiry Rules have been amended, we hope that the Department of Transport will soon produce amended Highway Inquiries Rules. Until they do, those rules which give the inspector explicit powers to deal with disruptive elements at an inquiry will not be adequately tested. The events at the most recent North Circular Road Inquiry into the Department of Transport's proposals for the junction with the A1 Falloden Way

[3] Circulars 10/88 (Department of the Environment) and 15/88 (Welsh Office) dated June 16, 1988.

and Great North Way, which commenced on February 4, 1988, were sufficient proof that such controls are still necessary.

2.81 Other improvements allow for an inquiry timetable (Rule 8 in both sets of Rules). This has already proved successful in practice by curtailing unnecessary repetition designed to prolong an earlier North Circular Road Inquiry (which took place in 1983). The power to require advance statements of case from those participating in an inquiry should prove an important means in controlling the length of inquiries. Another improvement, which we have advocated ever since the Windscale Inquiry in 1977, is that the inspector should have a power to require that a proof of evidence should not be read out in full but that a summary should replace it. This enables the time taken for reception of such evidence to be reduced, especially at inquiries where much technical evidence has to be given.

2.82 It is clear from the department's internal practice that the Secretary of State, on receipt of new evidence after an inquiry, either reopens the inquiry or refers the new evidence to those appearing at the inquiry, even though he is disposed to agree with the inspector's recommendation. During consultations this year we were unable to persuade the department to amend the rule which deals with procedure after the inquiry so as to reflect this practice. As worded, the rule only bites if the Secretary of State is disposed to disagree with the inspector's recommendations. We were unable to persuade the department to incorporate in the rule their view, as expressed in paragraph 53 of the joint circular, that there may be circumstances other than those indicated in the rule where a reference back should take place in the interests of natural justice. They considered it inappropriate for statutory rules to contain an expression of intent; they were an indication of procedural requirements for the generality of cases and identifiable specific circumstances. We accepted this but felt bound to point out the vulnerability of the Secretary of State to judicial review from parties having an interest who are opposed to an inspector's recommendation and who believe that their case is prejudiced by their having no specific right to challenge the new information.

2.83 The Planning Rules were intended to be the precedent on which the other departments would model their own rules. However, because of delay in the final publication of the Planning Rules, the Department of Energy, who were arranging a major public inquiry into a proposal for a new nuclear power station, published new rules for such inquiries in advance, after consulting us during 1987. We had already agreed the amendments of substance referred to above through the Department of the Environment but we were also able to suggest other improvements which were accepted. The Department of Energy, like the Department of the Environment, also issued a Code of Practice. There was little material difference between the two sets of Rules and their Codes. Such difference as there was reflected the difference in the technical background and the roles of the local authority.

2.85 We very much hope that the effect of this new series of Rules will be greatly to reduce the time spent on inquiries by encouraging co-operation amongst those participating in them with a view to assisting the inspector to come to a fair conclusion. **We emphasise the value of the new provisions for which we in particular pressed—**

- **specific provisions to clamp down on disruptive elements at inquiries;**
- **recognition in the Rules of the value of pre-inquiry meetings; and**
- **eliminating the need to take up valuable inquiry time by reading out lengthy technical evidence.**

Note

These provisions are set out in greater detail above at p. 87.

(iv) Examining Complaints from Individuals

ANNUAL REPORT OF THE COUNCIL ON TRIBUNALS 1985–86

H.C. 42 (1986–87)

2.15. The Council also received a small number of complaints. We have no statutory authority to deal with complaints, and have no investigatory powers of the kind enjoyed by the Ombudsmen, but we make inquiries in a case where a complainant has no reasonable access to any other remedy and it appears that the proper procedures may not have been followed or that the procedures may be unfair in themselves. However, we have no power to redress any wrong suffered by a complainant, and any action taken to correct procedural deficiencies is likely to be of general benefit rather than of direct benefit to the person who has complained. Indeed, we do not normally investigate a complaint until the decision has been given following the tribunal hearing or inquiry, to avoid any suspicion that we might influence a decision in a particular case.

Notes

During 1987–88, the Council dealt with four complaints involving tribunals and its Scottish Committee handled eight tribunal complaints.[19] The Annual Report does not indicate the outcome of these complaints for the complainant personally or the relevant tribunals. In 1990–91, the Council received a total of 10 complaints from members of the public.[20]

[19] A.R. 1987–88, H.C. 102 (1988–89), para. 3.6.
[20] A.R. 1990–91, H.C. 97 (1991–92), para. 3.15.

CHAPTER 5

THE OMBUDSMAN PRINCIPLE

(A) INTRODUCTION

THE idea of an "Ombudsman," or inquirer into the complaints of grievances suffered by citizens at the hands of some organ of the administration, is of Scandinavian origin, where it was conceived as a check on abuses of Royal power. Imported from Sweden into Denmark in 1954 where he is almost an inspector of the administration, the Ombudsman acts on his own motion, and relies on publicity and public opinion to achieve the redress of grievances. The idea was familiarised in this country chiefly by the activities of JUSTICE. A Parliamentary Commissioner was established by the Act of 1967, and he was followed by the Health Service Commissioners for Scotland (National Health Service Reorganisation Act 1972), and for England and Wales (National Health Service Reorganisation Act 1973), and by the Commissions for Local Administration (Local Government Act 1974). Meanwhile, the Parliamentary Commissioner (Northern Ireland) Act was passed in 1969, and also that jurisdiction established a separate local government commissioner, by the Commissioner for Complaints (Northern Ireland) Act 1969.

In the United Kingdom, the Parliamentary Commissioner for Administration (hereafter the P.C.A.) was initially limited to investigating complaints (referred by Members of Parliament) of "maladministration" causing injustice created by central government departments. However, in 1987 his jurisdiction was extended to encompass over 50 Non-Departmental Public Bodies, (*e.g.* the Sports Council).

During the 1960s and the 1970s the Ombudsman idea spread across many legal systems, (*e.g.* the New Zealand Ombudsman was created in 1962 and the French Mediateur in 1973). Whilst the 1980s witnessed the emergence of private sector Ombudsmen in the United Kingdom (notably to deal with consumer complaints in the financial services industries—see below p. 188). And, the current decade opened with Parliament establishing the Legal Services Ombudsman under the Courts and Legal Services Act 1990. The creation of these various Ombudsmen has enabled many grievances to be resolved by the distinct techniques adopted by such officers.

Selected general readings include *Garner*, pp. 90–106. *Craig*, pp. 102–113. *Wade*, pp. 79–101. *Harlow and Rawlings*, Ch. 7. JUSTICE, *Our Fettered Ombudsman* (1977). F. Stacey, *Ombudsmen Compared* (1978). JUSTICE—All Souls Report, Ch. 5; P. Birkinshaw, *Grievances, Remedies and the State* (1985), Ch. 5.

(B) THE PARLIAMENTARY COMMISSIONER FOR ADMINISTRATION

(i) Constitutional and Jurisdictional Matters

PARLIAMENTARY COMMISSIONER ACT 1967

Appointment and tenure of office

1.—(1) For the purpose of conducting investigations in accordance with the following provisions of this Act there shall be appointed a Commissioner, to be known as the Parliamentary Commissioner for Administration.

(2) Her Majesty may by Letters Patent from time to time appoint a person to be the Commissioner, and any person so appointed shall (subject to [subsections (3) and (3A)] of this section) hold office during good behaviour.

(3) A person appointed to be the Commissioner may be relieved of office by Her Majesty at his own request, or may be removed from office by Her Majesty in consequence of Addresses from both Houses of Parliament, and shall in any case vacate office on completing the year of service in which he attains the age of sixty-five years.

[(3A) Her Majesty may declare the office of Commissioner to have been vacated if satisfied that the person appointed to be the Commissioner is incapable for medical reasons—

(*a*) of performing duties of his office; and
(*b*) of requesting to be relieved of it.] . . .[1]

Salary and pension

2.—(1) There shall be paid to the holder of the office of Commissioner a salary at the rate (subject to subsection (2) of this section) of £8,600 a year.

(2) The House of Commons may from time to time by resolution increase the rate of the salary payable under this section, and any such resolution may take effect from the date on which it is passed or such other date as may be specified therein. . . .

(5) Any salary, pension or other benefit payable by virtue of this section shall be charged on and issued out of the Consolidated Fund.

Administrative provisions

3.—(1) The Commissioner may appoint such officers as he may determine with the approval of the Treasury as to numbers and conditions of service.

(2) Any function of the Commissioner under this Act may be performed by any officer of the Commissioner authorised for that purpose by the Commissioner [or may be performed by any officer so authorised—

(*a*) of the Health Service Commissioner for England;
(*b*) of the Health Service Commissioner for Scotland; or
(*c*) of the Health Service Commissioner for Wales].[2]

[1] Subsection (3A) added by the Parliamentary and Health Service Commissioners Act 1987, s.2(1).
[2] Amended by the Parliamentary and Health Service Commissioners Act 1987, s.3.

(3) The expenses of the Commissioner under this Act, to such amount as may be sanctioned by the Treasury, shall be defrayed out of moneys provided by Parliament.

Appointment of acting Commissioners

[**3A.**—(1) Where the Officer of Commissioner becomes vacant, Her Majesty may, pending the appointment of a new Commissioner, appoint a person under this section to act as the Commissioner at any time during the period of twelve months beginning with the date on which the vacancy arose.

(2) A person appointed under this section shall hold office during Her Majesty's pleasure and, subject to that, shall hold office—

(*a*) until the appointment of a new Commissioner or the expiry of the period of twelve months beginning with the date on which the vacancy arose, whichever occurs first; and

(*b*) in other respects, in accordance with the terms and conditions of his appointment which shall be such as the Treasury may determine.

(3) A person appointed under this section shall, while he holds office, be treated for all purposes, except those of section 2 of this Act, as the Commissioner.

(4) Any salary, pension or other benefit payable by virtue of this section shall be charged on and issued out of the Consolidated Fund.][3]

Departments, etc., subject to investigation

[**4.**—(1) Subject to the provisions of this section and to the notes contained in Schedule 2 to this Act, this Act applies to the government departments, corporations and unincorporated bodies listed in that Schedule; and references in this Act to an authority to which this Act applies are references to any such corporation or body.

(2) Her Majesty may by Order in Council amend Schedule 2 to this Act by the alteration of any entry or note, the removal of any entry or note or the insertion of any additional entry or note.

(3) An Order in Council may only insert an entry if—

(*a*) it relates—

(i) to a government department; or

(ii) to a corporation or body whose functions are exercised on behalf of the Crown; or

(*b*) it relates to a corporation or body—

(i) which is established by virtue of Her Majesty's prerogative

[3] Added by the Parliamentary and Health Service Commissioners Act 1987, s.6(1).

or by an Act of Parliament or on Order in Council or order made under an Act of Parliament or which is established in any other way by a Minister of the Crown in his capacity as a Minister or by a government department;

(ii) at least half of whose revenues derive directly from money provided by Parliament, a levy authorised by an enactment, a fee or charge of any other description so authorised or more than one of those sources; and

(iii) which is wholly or partly constituted by appointment made by Her Majesty or a Minister of the Crown or government department.

(4) No entry shall be made in respect of a corporation or body whose sole activity is, or whose main activities are, included among the activities specified in subsection (5) below.

(5) The activities mentioned in subsection (4) above are—

(*a*) the provision of education, or the provision of training otherwise than under the Industrial Training Act 1982;

(*b*) the development of curricula, the conduct of examinations or the validation of educational courses;

(*c*) the control of entry to any profession or the regulation of the conduct of members of any profession;

(*d*) the investigation of complaints by members of the public regarding the actions of any person or body, or the supervision or review of such investigations or of steps taken following them.

(6) No entry shall be made in respect of a corporation or body operating in an exclusively or predominantly commercial manner or a corporation carrying on under national ownership an industry or undertaking or part of an industry or undertaking.

(7) Any statutory instrument made by virtue of this section shall be subject to annulment in pursuance of a resolution of either House of Parliament.

(8) In this Act—

(*a*) any reference to a government department to which this Act applies includes a reference to any of the Ministers or officers of such a department; and

(*b*) any reference to an authority to which this Act applies includes a reference to any members or officers of such an authority.][4]

Matters subject to investigation

5.—(1) Subject to the provisions of this section, the Commissioner may investigate an action taken by or on behalf of a government department or

[4] Substituted by the Parliamentary and Health Services Commissioners Act 1987, s.1(1).

other authority to which this Act applies, being action taken in the exercise of administrative functions of that department or authority, in any case where—

(*a*) a written complaint is duly made to a member of the House of Commons by a member of the public who claims to have sustained injustice in consequence of maladministration in connection with the action so taken; and

(*b*) the complaint is referred to the Commissioner, with the consent of the person who made it, by a member of that House with a request to conduct an investigation thereon.

(2) Except as hereinafter provided, the Commissioner shall not conduct an investigation under this Act in respect of any of the following matters, that is to say—

(*a*) any action in respect of which the person aggrieved has or had a right of appeal, reference or review to or before a tribunal constituted by or under any enactment or by virtue of Her Majesty's prerogative;

(*b*) any action in respect of which the person aggrieved has or had a remedy by way of proceedings in any court of law;

Provided that the Commissioner may conduct an investigation notwithstanding that the person aggrieved has or had such a right or remedy if satisfied that in the particular circumstances it is not reasonable to expect him to resort or have resorted to it.

(3) Without prejudice to subsection (2) of this section, the Commissioner shall not conduct an investigation under this Act in respect of any such action or matter as is described in Schedule 3 to this Act.

(4) Her Majesty may by Order in Council amend the said Schedule 3 so as to exclude from the provisions of that Schedule such actions or matters as may be described in the Order; and any statutory instrument made by virtue of this subsection shall be subject to annulment in pursuance of a resolution of either House of Parliament.

(5) In determining whether to initiate, continue or discontinue an investigation under this Act, the Commissioner shall, subject to the foregoing provisions of this section, act in accordance with his own discretion; and any question whether a complaint is duly made under this Act shall be determined by the Commissioner.

[(6) For the purposes of this section, administrative functions exercisable by any person appointed by the Lord Chancellor as a member of the administrative staff of any court or tribunal shall be taken to be administrative functions of the Lord Chancellor's Department or, in Northern Ireland, of the Northern Ireland Court Service.][5];

[5] Added by the Courts and Legal Services Act 1990, s.110(1).

Provisions relating to complaints

6.—(1) A complaint under this Act may be made by any individual, or by any body of persons whether incorporated or not, not being—

(*a*) a local authority or other authority or body constituted for purposes of the public service or of local government or for the purposes of carrying on under national ownership any industry or undertaking or part of an industry or undertaking;

(*b*) any other authority or body whose members are appointed by Her Majesty or any Minister of the Crown or government department, or whose revenues consist wholly or mainly of moneys provided by Parliament.

(2) Where the person by whom a complaint might have been made under the foregoing provisions of this Act has died or is for any reason unable to act for himself, the complaint may be made by his personal representative or by a member of his family or other individual suitable to represent him; but except as aforesaid a complaint shall not be entertained under this Act unless made by the person aggrieved himself.

(3) A complaint shall not be entertained under this Act unless it is made to a member of the House of Commons not later than twelve months from the day on which the person aggrieved first had notice of the matters alleged in the complaint; but the Commissioner may conduct an investigation pursuant to a complaint not made within that period if he considers that there are special circumstances which make it proper to do so.

(4) [Except as provided in subsection (5) below] a complaint shall not be entertained under this Act unless the person aggrieved is resident in the United Kingdom (or, if he is dead, was so resident at the time of his death) or the complaint relates to action taken in relation to him while he was present in the United Kingdom or on an installation in a designated area within the meaning of the Continental Shelf Act 1964 or on a ship registered in the United Kingdom or an aircraft so registered, or in relation to rights or obligations which accrued or arose in the United Kingdom or on such an installation, a ship or aircraft.

[(5) A complaint may be entertained under this Act in circumstances not falling within subsection (4) above where—

(*a*) the complaint relates to action taken in any country or territory outside the United Kingdom by an officer (not being an honorary consular officer) in the exercise of a consular function on behalf of the Government of the United Kingdom; and

(*b*) the person aggrieved is a citizen of the United Kingdom and Colonies who, under section 2 of the Immigration Act 1971, has the right of abode in the United Kingdom.][6]

[6] Added by the Parliamentary Commissioner (Consular Complaints) Act 1981, s.1.

Procedures in respect of investigations

7.—(1) Where the Commissioner proposes to conduct an investigation pursuant to a complaint under this Act, he shall afford to the principal officer of the department of authority concerned, and to any person who is alleged in the complaint to have taken or authorised the action complained of, an opportunity to comment on any allegations contained in the complaint.

(2) Every such investigation shall be conducted in private, but except as aforesaid the procedure for conducting an investigation shall be such as the Commissioner considers appropriate in the circumstances of the case; and without prejudice to the generality of the foregoing provision the Commissioner may obtain information from such persons and in such manner, and make such inquiries, as he thinks fit, and may determine whether any person may be represented, by counsel or solicitor or otherwise, in the investigation.

(3) The Commissioner may, if he thinks fit, pay to the person by whom the complaint was made and to any other person who attends or furnishes information for the purposes of an investigation under this Act—

(*a*) sums in respect of expenses properly incurred by them;
(*b*) allowances by way of compensation for the loss of their time,

in accordance with such scales and subject to such conditions as may be determined by the Treasury.

(4) The conduct of an investigation under this Act shall not affect any action taken by the department or authority concerned, or any power or duty of that department or authority to take further action with respect to any matters subject to the investigation; but where the person aggrieved has been removed from the United Kingdom under any Order in force under the Aliens Restriction Acts 1914 and 1919 or under the Commonwealth Immigrants Act 1962, he shall, if the Commissioner so directs, be permitted to re-enter and remain in the United Kingdom, subject to such conditions as the Secretary of State may direct, for the purposes of the investigation.

Evidence

8.—(1) For the purposes of an investigation under this Act the Commissioner may require any Minister, officer or member of the department or authority concerned or any other person who in his opinion is able to furnish information or produce documents relevant to the investigation to furnish any such information or produce any such document.

(2) For the purposes of any such investigation the Commissioner shall have the same powers as the Court in respect of the attendance and examination of witnesses (including the administration of oaths or affir-

mations and the examination of witnesses abroad) and in respect of the production of documents.

(3) No obligation to maintain secrecy or other restriction upon the disclosure of information obtained by or furnished to persons in Her Majesty's service, whether imposed by any enactment or by any rule of law, shall apply to the disclosure of information for the purposes of an investigation under this Act; and the Crown shall not be entitled in relation to any such investigation to any such privilege in respect of the production of documents or the giving of evidence as is allowed by law in legal proceedings.

(4) No person shall be required or authorised by virtue of this Act to furnish any information or answer any question relating to proceedings of the Cabinet or of any committee of the Cabinet or to produce so much of any document as relates to such proceedings; and for the purposes of this subsection a certificate issued by the Secretary of the Cabinet with the approval of the Prime Minister and certifying that any information, question, document or part of a document so relates shall be conclusive.

(5) Subject to subsection (3) of this section, no person shall be compelled for the purposes of an investigation under this Act to give any evidence or produce any document which he could not be compelled to give or produce in [civil][7] proceedings before the Court.

Obstruction and contempt

9.—(1) If any person without lawful excuse obstructs the Commissioner or any officer of the Commissioner in the performance of his functions under this Act, or is guilty of any act or omission in relation to any investigation under this Act which, if that investigation were a proceeding in the Court, would constitute contempt of court, the Commissioner may certify the offence to the Court.

(2) Where an offence is certified under this section, the Court may inquire into the matter and, after hearing any witnesses who may be produced against or on behalf of the person charged with the offence, and after hearing any statement that may be offered in defence, deal with him in any manner in which the Court could deal with him if he had committed the like offence in relation to the Court.

(3) Nothing in this section shall be construed as applying to the taking of any such action as is mentioned in subsection (4) of section 7 of this Act.

Reports by Commissioner

10.—(1) In any case where the Commissioner conducts an investigation under this Act or decides not to conduct such an investigation, he shall

[7] Added by the Civil Evidence Act 1968, s.17(1)(*b*).

send to the member of the House of Commons by whom the request for investigation was made (or if he is no longer a member of that House, to such member of that House as the Commissioner thinks appropriate) a report of the results of the investigation or, as the case may be, a statement of his reasons for not conducting an investigation.

(2) In any case where the Commissioner conducts an investigation under this Act, he shall also send a report of the results of the investigation to the principal officer of the department or authority concerned and to any other person who is alleged in the relevant complaint to have taken or authorised the action complained of.

(3) If, after conducting an investigation under this Act, it appears to the Commissioner that injustice has been caused to the person aggrieved in consequence of maladministration and that the injustice has not been, or will not be, remedied, he may, if he thinks fit, lay before each House of Parliament a special report upon the case.

(4) The Commissioner shall annually lay before each House of Parliament a general report on the performance of his functions under this Act and may from time to time lay before each House of Parliament such other reports with respect to those functions as he thinks fit.

(5) For the purposes of the law of defamation, any such publication as is hereinafter mentioned shall be absolutely privileged, that is to say—

(*a*) the publication of any matter by the Commissioner in making a report to either House of Parliament for the purposes of this Act;

(*b*) the publication of any matter by a member of the House of Commons in communicating with the Commissioner or his officers for those purposes or by the Commissioner or his officers in communicating with such a member for those purposes;

(*c*) the publication by such a member to the person by whom a complaint was made under this Act of a report or statement sent to the member in respect of the complaint in pursuance of section (1) of this section;

(*d*) the publication by the Commissioner to such a person as is mentioned in subsection (2) of this section of a report to that person in pursuance of that subsection.

Provision for secrecy of information

11.—(1) . . .[8]

(2) Information obtained by the Commissioner or his officers in the course of or for the purposes of an investigation under this Act shall not be disclosed except—

[8] Repealed by the Official Secrets Act 1989, s.16(4), Sched. 2.

(*a*) for the purposes of the investigation and of any report to be made thereon under this Act;

(*b*) for the purposes of any proceedings for an offence under [the Official Secrets Act 1911 to 1989][9] alleged to have been committed in respect of information obtained by the Commissioner or any of his officers by virtue of this Act or for an offence of perjury alleged to have been committed in the course of an investigation under this Act or for the purposes of an inquiry with a view to the taking of such proceedings; or

(*c*) for the purposes of any proceedings under section 9 of this Act;

and the Commissioner and his officers shall not be called upon to give evidence in any proceedings (other than such proceedings as aforesaid) of matters coming to his or their knowledge in the course of an investigation under this Act.

[(2A) Where the Commissioner also holds office as a Health Service Commissioner and a person initiates a complaint to him in his capacity as such a Commissioner which relates partly to a matter with respect to which that person has previously initiated a complaint under this Act, or subsequently initiates such a complaint, information obtained by the Commissioner or his officers in the course of or for the purposes of investigating the complaint under this Act may be disclosed for the purposes of his carrying out his functions in relation to the other complaint.][10]

(3) A Minister of the Crown may give notice in writing to the Commissioner, with respect to any document or information specified in the notice, or any class of documents or information so specified, that in the opinion of the Minister the disclosure of that document or information, or of documents or information of that class, would be prejudicial to the safety of the State or otherwise contrary to the public interest; and where such a notice is given nothing in this Act shall be construed as authorising or requiring the Commissioner or any officer of the Commissioner to communicate to any person or for any purpose any document or information specified in the notice, or any document or information of a class so specified.

(4) The references in this section to a Minister of the Crown include references to the Commissioners of Customs and Excise and the Commissioners of Inland Revenue.

Consultations between Parliamentary Commissioner and Health Service Commissioners

[**11.A.**—(1) Where, at any stage in the course of conducting an investigation under this Act, the Commissioner forms the opinions that the

[9] Substituted by the Official Secrets Act 1989, s.16(3), Sched. 1, para. 1.
[10] Added by the Parliamentary and Health Service Commissioners Act 1987, s.4(1).

complaint relates partly to a matter within the jurisdiction of the Health Service Commissioner for England, Wales or Scotland, he shall—

(*a*) unless he also holds office as that Commissioner, consult about the complaint with him; and

(*b*) if he considers it necessary, inform the person initiating the complaint under this Act of the steps necessary to initiate a complaint under Part V of the National Health Service Act 1977 (Health Service Commissioner for England and for Wales) or, as the case may be, Part VI of the National Health Service (Scotland) Act 1978 (Health Service Commissioner for Scotland).

(2) Where by virtue of subsection (1) above the Commissioner consults with the Health Service Commissioner in relation to a complaint under this Act, he may consult him about any matter relating to the complaint, including—

(*a*) the conduct of any investigation into the complaint; and

(*b*) the form, content and publication of any report of the results of such an investigation.

(3) Nothing in section 11(2) of this Act shall apply in relation to the disclosure of information by the Commissioner or any of his officers in the course of consultations held in accordance with this section.][11]

Interpretation

12.—(1) In this Act the following expressions have the meanings hereby respectively assigned to them, that is to say—

"action" includes failure to act, and other expressions connoting action shall be construed accordingly;

"the Commissioner" means the Parliamentary Commissioner for Administration;

"the Court" means, in relation to England and Wales the High Court, in relation to Scotland the Court of Session, and in relation to Northern Ireland the High Court of Northern Ireland;

"enactment" includes an enactment of the Parliament of Northern Ireland and any instrument made by virtue of an enactment;

"officer" includes employee;

"person aggrieved" means the person who claims or is alleged to have sustained such injustice as is mentioned in section 5(1)(a) of this Act;

"tribunal" includes the person constituting a tribunal consisting of one person.

(2) References to this Act to any enactment are references to that enactment as amended or extended by or under any other enactment.

(3) It is hereby declared that nothing in this Act authorises or requires

[11] Added by the Parliamentary and Health Service Commissioners Act 1987, s.4(2).

the Commissioner to question the merits of a decision taken without maladministration by a government department or other authority in the exercise of a discretion vested in that department or authority. . . .

SCHEDULE 2

DEPARTMENTS, ETC., SUBJECT TO INVESTIGATION

Advisory, Conciliation and Arbitration Service.
Agricultural wages committees.
Ministry of Agriculture, Fisheries and Food.
Arts Council of Great Britain.
British Council.
British Library Board.
Building Societies Commission.
The Central Statistical Office of the Chancellor of the Exchequer.
Certification Officer.
Charity Commission.
Civil Service Commission.
Office of the Minister for the Civil Service.
Office of the Commissioner for the Rights of Trade Union Members.
Co-operative Development Agency.
Countryside Commission.
Countryside Commission for Scotland.
Countryside Council for Wales.
Crafts Council.
Crofters Commission.
Crown Estate Office.
Customs and Excise.
Data Protection Registrar.
Ministry of Defence.
Development Commission.
Department of Education and Science.
Central Bureau for Educational Visits and Exchanges.
Education Assets Board.
Office of the Director General of Electricity Supply.
Department of Employment.
Department of Energy.
Department of the Environment.
Equal Opportunities Commission.
Export Credits Guarantee Department.
Office of the Director General of Fair Trading.
British Film Institute.
Foreign and Commonwealth Office.
Forestry Commission.
Registry of Friendly Societies.
Office of the Director General of Gas Supply.
Health and Safety Commission.
Health and Safety Executive.
Department of Health.
Highlands and Islands Development Board.
Historic Buildings and Monuments Commission for England.
Home Office.
Horserace Betting Levy Board.

Housing Corporation.
Housing for Wales.
Human Fertilisation and Embryology Authority.
Central Office of Information.
Inland Revenue.
Intervention Board for Agricultural Produce.
Land Registry.
Legal Aid Board.
The following general lighthouse authorities—
(*a*) the Corporation of the Trinity House of Deptford Strond;
(*b*) the Commissioners of Northern Lighthouses.
The Lord Chancellor's Department.
Lord President of the Council's Office.
Medical Practices Committee.
Scottish Medical Practices Committee.
Museums and Galleries Commission.
National Debt Office.
Trustees of the National Heritage Memorial Fund.
National Rivers Authority.
Department for National Savings.
Nature Conservancy Council for England.
Nature Conservancy Council for Scotland.
Commission for the New Towns.
Development corporations for new towns.
Northern Ireland Court Service.
Northern Ireland Office.
Ordnance Survey.
Office of Population Censuses and Surveys.
Registrar of Public Lending Right.
Public Record Office.
Scottish Record Office.
Commission for Racial Equality.
Red Deer Commission.
Department of the Registers of Scotland.
General Register Office, Scotland.
Agricultural and Food Research Council.
Economic and Social Research Council.
Medical Research Council.
Natural Environment Research Council.
Science and Engineering Research Council.
Residuary Bodies.
Royal Mint.
Scottish Courts Administration.
Scottish Homes.
Scottish Legal Aid Board.
Scottish Office.
Council for Small Industries in Rural Areas.
Central Council for Education and Training in Social Work.
Department of Social Security.
Sports Council.
Scottish Sports Council.
Sports Council for Wales.
Stationery Office.
Office of the Director General of Telecommunication.
English Tourist Board.
Scottish Tourist Board.

Wales Tourist Board.
Board of Trade.
Department of Trade and Industry.
Agricultural Training Board.
Clothing and Allied Products Industry Training Board.
Construction Industry Training Board.
Engineering Industry Training Board.
Hotel and Catering Industry Training Board.
Plastics Processing Industry Training Board.
Road Transport Industry Training Board.
Department of Transport.
Treasury.
Treasury Solicitor.
Urban development corporations.
Development Board for Rural Wales.
Office of the Director General of Water Services.
Welsh Office.[12]

SCHEDULE 3

MATTERS NOT SUBJECT TO INVESTIGATION

1. Action taken in matters certified by a Secretary of State or other Minister of the Crown to affect relations or dealings between the Government of the United Kingdom and any other Government or any international organisation of States or Governments.

2. Action taken, in any country or territory outside the United Kingdom, by or on behalf of any officer representing or acting under the authority of Her Majesty in respect of the United Kingdom, or any other officer of the Government of the United Kingdom other than action which is taken by an officer (not being an honorary consular officer) in the exercise of a consular function on behalf of the Government of the United Kingdom. . . .

3. Action taken in connection with the administration of the government of any country or territory outside the United Kingdom which forms part of Her Majesty's dominions or in which Her Majesty has jurisdiction.

4. Action taken by the Secretary of State under the Extradition Act 1870 or the Fugitive Offenders Act 1881, the Fugitive Offenders Act 1967 or the Extradition Act 1989.

5. Action taken by or with the authority of the Secretary of State for the purposes of investigating crime or of protecting the security of the State, including action so taken with respect to passports.

6. The commencement or conduct of civil or criminal proceedings

[12] For reasons of space it is not possible to include the Notes which detailed the specific functions of the above bodies that may be investigated by the Parliamentary Commissioner. Nor is it possible to specify the precise legislative basis for the many additions and deletions to the above Schedule.

before any court of law in the United Kingdom, of proceedings at any place under the Naval Discipline Act 1957, the Army Act 1955 or the Air Force Act 1955, or of proceedings before any international court or tribunal.

6A. Action taken by any person appointed by the Lord Chancellor as a member of the administrative staff of any court or tribunal, so far as that action is taken at the direction, or on the authority (whether express or implied), of any person acting in a judicial capacity or in his capacity as a member of the tribunal.

7. Any exercise of the prerogative of mercy or of the power of a Secretary of State to make a reference in respect of any person to the Court of Appeal, the High Court of Justiciary or the Courts-Martial Appeal Court.

8. Action taken on behalf of the Minister of Health or the Secretary of State by a Regional Health Authority, an Area Health Authority, a District Health Authority, a special health authority, except the Rampton Hospital Review Board . . . the Rampton Hospital Board, the Broadmoor Hospital Board or the Moss Side and Park Lane Hospitals Board, a Family Practitioner Committee, a Health Board or the Common Services Agency for the Scottish Health Service, or by the Public Health Laboratory Service Board.

9. Action taken in matters relating to contractual or other commercial transactions, whether within the United Kingdom or elsewhere, being transactions of a government department or authority to which this Act applies or of any such authority or body as is mentioned in paragraph (a) or (b) of subsection (1) of section 6 of this Act and not being transactions for or relating to—

(a) the acquisition of land compulsorily or in circumstances in which it could be acquired compulsorily;

(b) the disposal as surplus of land acquired compulsorily or in such circumstances as aforesaid.

10.—(1) Action taken in respect of appointments or removals, pay, discipline, superannuation or other personnel matters, in relation to—

(a) service in any of the armed forces of the Crown, including reserve and auxiliary and cadet forces;

(b) service in any office or employment under the Crown or under any authority to which this Act applies; or

(c) service in any office or employment, or under any contract for services, in respect of which power to take action, or to determine or approve the action to be taken, in such matters is vested in Her Majesty, any Minister of the Crown or any such authority as aforesaid.

(2) Sub-paragraph (1)(c) above shall not apply to any action (not otherwise excluded from investigation by this Schedule) which is taken by the Secretary of State in connection with:

(*a*) the provision of information relating to the terms and conditions of any employment covered by an agreement entered into by him under section 12(1) of the Overseas Development and Cooperation Act 1980 or

(*b*) the provision of any allowance, grant or supplement or any benefit (other than those relating to superannuation) arising from the designation of any person in accordance with such an agreement.

11. The grant of honours, awards or privileges within the gift of the Crown, including the grant of Royal Charters.[13]

Notes

1. The key concept in delimiting the jurisdictional powers of the P.C.A. is that of "maladministration." This concept had its origins in the JUSTICE report of 1961,[1] as they believed that this norm of administrative behaviour would prevent the Parliamentary Commissioner from unduly encroaching upon the exercise of discretionary powers by examining if the particular decisions reached were "wrong or unwelcome." During the enactment of the 1967 Act, the Leader of the House of Commons (Richard Crossman) acknowledged that the government had not been able to define comprehensively the concept of maladministration. Instead, he proposed a non-statutory list containing some of the characteristics of this concept including, "bias, neglect, inattention, delay, incompetence, ineptitude, perversity, turpitude, arbitrariness and so on."[2] Subsequently, this description of maladministration has become known as the "Crossman catalogue."

After several years the P.C.A.'s use of maladministration was analysed by Dr. G. Marshall. He concluded, "the view (that certainly follows from the Crossman catalogue approach) that maladministration may be inferred from, and can consist in, a complete lack of merits implies that the distinction between merits and maladministration drawn in the 1967 Act is incoherent. . . ."[3] Consequently, he favoured the abandonment of the concept of maladministration with all its ambiguities as the foundation of the P.C.A.'s jurisdiction.

In 1977 another report from JUSTICE[4] suggested the replacement of "maladministration," with the P.C.A. being empowered to investigate "unreasonable, unjust, or oppressive action" by government departments. However, this idea was rejected by the Select Committee on the P.C.A. as they did not believe that the new jurisdiction would enable the Parliamentary Commissioner to investigate or criticise anything that did not already come within his authority.[5]

The JUSTICE-All Souls report accepted the view of Sir Cecil Clothier (who was P.C.A. during the early 1980s) that "maladministration" was "a wholly adequate basis for his investigations." Therefore, they did not propose any alterations to this concept.[6]

A practical appreciation of the way in which the concept of maladministration

[13] The legislative origins of the amendments to this Schedule are not included for reasons of space.

[1] *The Citizen and the Administration* (1961).

[2] H.C.Deb. Vol. 754, col. 51 (1966).

[3] G. Marshall, "Maladministration" [1973] P.L. 32.

[4] *Our Fettered Ombudsman*.

[5] *Review of Access and Jurisdiction* (1977–78) H.C. 615.

[6] Report Ch. 5.

has been invoked by various Parliamentary Commissioners can be ascertained from the extracts below at p. 165 examining the casework of the Ombudsman.

2. Another issue of contention involving the scope of the P.C.A.'s powers concerns the exclusion of complaints regarding contractual/commercial matters and public service personnel disputes from his remit. On several occasions the Select Committee on the P.C.A. has advocated the extension of the P.C.A.'s jurisdiction to cover these topics. The Committee has stated that, "the Government has a duty to administer its purchasing policies fairly and equitably, and if those policies are the subject of complaint then the complaints should be investigated; this is particularly important if any future Government were again to use the award of contracts as a political weapon."[7] (*cf.* the earlier section of this book on Government Contracting). Furthermore, the Committee has reported that there is evidence of a demand for P.C.A. investigations into the administrative decisions of departments in the field of employment matters.[8] However, the government has consistently refused to accept the need for such expansions in the jurisdiction of the P.C.A.[9] Nevertheless, individual Commissioners have continued to press for such an extension of their powers. Sir Cecil Clothier has argued:

> "it is because of the size, power and relative unaccountability of administrative machinery that democratic governments have increasingly come to adopt the ombudsman system. And if it is necessary to provide for review of the administrative process on behalf of citizens, then civil servants are individually citizens obliged to deal with a most powerful employer and the need for accountability is no less. I would not of course suggest that pay and conditions of service were administrative matters suitable for review by Ombudsmen.... As to commercial matters, there are of course many hundreds of contractors providing goods and services to government departments.... If they are suddenly removed from a tendering list, or without explanation omitted from an invitation to tender, they may suffer considerable hardship.... For these and other commercial activities where the law offers no or no practicable remedy for apparent maladministration, the inquisitorial process of the ombudsman is well suited."[10]

So far both the Government and Parliament had remained immune to these arguments. The exact scope of the current exclusion of commercial matters is causing uncertainty to the P.C.A. and he has had to seek advice from Speaker's Counsel on this question.[11]

3. Recently other jurisdictional problems have revolved around the susceptibility of court staff and social fund officers to investigation by the P.C.A. In his Annual Report for 1988,[12] the Commissioner noted that the Lord Chancellor's Department had obtained advice, from Treasury Counsel, that the P.C.A. did not have jurisdiction over the administrative work of court staff. Subsequently, the Lord Chancellor had raised the issue with the Council of Judges and they had supported the view of Treasury Counsel. The P.C.A. continued to disagree with his interpretation of the 1967 Act. Little progress was made for over a year.[13] However, the Government has now sought to clarify this aspect of the P.C.A.'s

[7] *The Jurisdiction of the P.C.A.* (1979–80) H.C. 593, para. 8.
[8] *Supra*, para. 15.
[9] *e.g. Fourth Report from The Select Committee on the P.C.A., Session 1979/80. Observations by the Government*, Cmnd. 8274 (1981).
[10] "The Value of an Ombudsman" [1986] P.L. 204 at pp. 210–211.
[11] *Annual Report 1989*, (1989–90) H.C. 353, para. 5.
[12] (1988–89) H.C. 301.
[13] *Annual Report 1989*, (1989–90) H.C. 353, para. 4.

jurisdiction by amendments to the 1967 legislation introduced by the Courts and Legal Services Act 1990. Section 110 of the 1990 Act, provides that administrative functions undertaken by any person appointed by the Lord Chancellor as a member of the staff of courts or tribunals shall be treated as administrative action of the Lord Chancellor's Department. Such action will, therefore, be within the jurisdiction of the P.C.A., unless the specific action complained of had been taken at the direction or authority of a person acting in a judicial capacity.

Unfortunately, there has not as yet been any similar resolution of the jurisdictional dispute involving social fund officers and inspectors (for the background and role of these officials see Ch. 4 at p. 134). The Department of Social Security has continued to assert that these two groups of officials do not act as agents of the Secretary of State and are not, therefore, within the scrutiny of the P.C.A. Despite the limited external review of social fund decisions, the P.C.A. has not received any viable complaints concerning this system of social assistance, consequently at present no practical difficulties have arisen from this jurisdictional disagreement.[14]

(ii) The Work of the Parliamentary Commissioner

(a) Workload

P.C.A. ANNUAL REPORT FOR 1991

H.C. 347 (1991–92)

III Statistics

Complaints received

110. I received a total of 801 complaints during 1991—97 more than in 1990. The complaints were referred to me by 432 Members of Parliament, 278 cases had been carried forward from 1990 and, of the combined total of 1079 complaints, 769 were disposed of during the year. 580 of these were rejected, 183 full investigations were completed and the results reported to Members, and 6 investigations were discontinued (either for jurisdictional reasons or in exercise of my statutory discretion). There was a surge of referrals in November and December and 310 cases were carried forward into 1992, of which 187 were under investigation as the year began (26 more than last year). Of these, 3 of the investigations were, for various reasons, temporarily suspended. The remaining cases carried forward were still at a preliminary stage of consideration. A summary of the main statistics is given in paragraph 115 below.... Appendix C provides a more detailed analysis.

Rejections

111. As in previous years, most of the cases considered by me for investigation (including those carried forward from 1990) were rejected.

[14] *Annual Report 1989*, (1989–90) H.C. 353, para. 29.

The proportion of cases accepted for investigation was 25 per cent. (23 per cent. in 1990). The reasons why complaints were not accepted, or were not investigated to a conclusion, are set out in the table at Appendix C. The following summary shows (by reference to the relevant provisions of the Parliamentary Commissioner Act 1967) the main reasons for rejection or discontinuation and the percentage of cases in each category.

Section 5(1)	Complaint did not concern administrative actions	56 57
Section 4(1)	Authorities outside scope	13 10
Section 5(2)(a)	Right to appeal to tribunals	12 13
Schedule 3(10)	Public service personnel matters	6 7
Section 5(5)	Parliamentary Commissioner's discretion	5 8

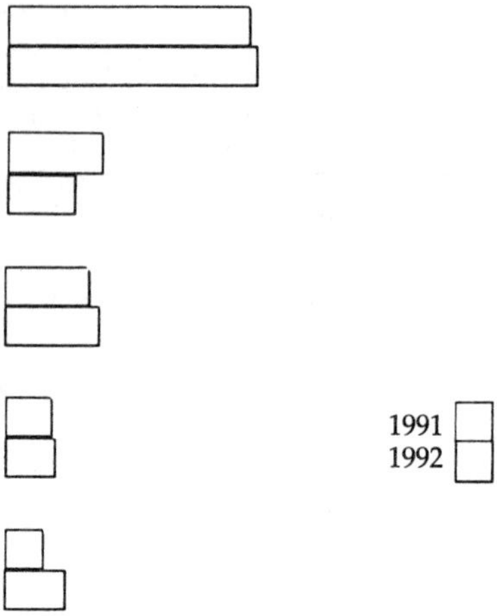

Complaints partly or wholly justified

112. The table at Appendix C shows how many complaints involved each department or authority within my jurisdiction and to what extent I upheld the complaints in the investigations which were completed during the year. In 87 of the completed cases (47 per cent.), I found the complaint against the body principally concerned wholly justified; in 78 cases (43 per cent.) I found it necessary (while not upholding the main complaint) to criticise at least some aspects of the body's handling of

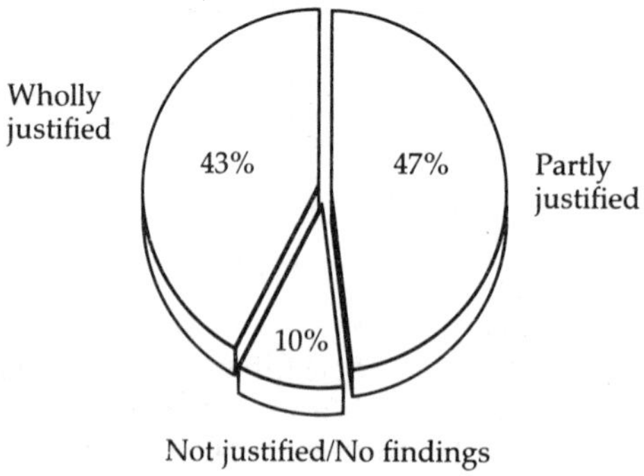

matters; and of the remaining 18 cases (10 per cent.) I found no justification for the complaint in 17 cases, and made no findings in 1 case.

83. The Departments which had 20 or more complaints directed against them (as the principal department concerned) during 1990 were as follows:

	Percentage of total referrals	Complaints and investigations
Department of Social Security	28	221 77
Inland Revenue	16	131 37
Department of the Environment	7	53 9
Home Office	5	40 10
Department of Transport	5	38 12
Department of Employment	4	30 10
Customs and Excise	3	26 7

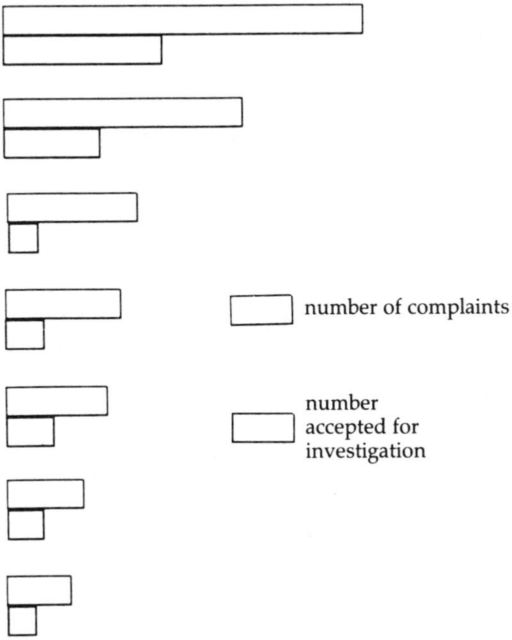

The Department of Social Security and the Inland Revenue again attracted most complaints, their combined share having fallen (from 42 per cent. in 1990) to 40 per cent.—which is around the average percentage they have accounted for over the past ten years or so. Against the general trend the Department of the Environment and Customs and Excise were the targets of fewer complaints.

Enquiries

114. The enquiries section of my Office received 1,344 telephone enquiries during the year and dealt with 1,116 letters (1,045 relating to particular complaints and 71 to more general matters). They also saw 25

Appendix C

Analysis of complaints

Workload			Cases rejected and investigations discontinued under Section/Schedule of the Act								Cases investigated to conclusion and results reported				Cases in action at 31.12.91	
Brought forward from 1990	Received in 1991	**Total**	Authorities outside scope S.4(1)	Not properly referred, not about administrative actions, S.5(1)	Right of appeal to tribunal S.5(2)a	Parliamentary Commissioner's discretion S.5(5)	Contractual and other commercial transactions Sch. 3, Para. 9	Public Service personnel matters Sch. 3, Para. 10	Miscellaneous	**Total**	Complaints upheld	Complaints not upheld, but departmental actions criticised	Complaints not upheld	**Total** showing balancing factor[a]		
10	12	22	–	9	–	–	–	–	–	9	–	4	2	6	7	Ministry of Agriculture, Fisheries and Food
–	1	1	–	1	–	–	–	–	–	1	–	–	–	–	–	Arts Council of Great Britain
2	4	6	–	2	–	–	–	–	–	2	1	–	–	1	3	Charity Commission
–	1	1	–	–	–	–	–	1	–	1	–	–	–	–	–	Office of the Minister for the Civil Service
1	3	4	–	–	–	–	–	4	–	4	–	–	–	–	–	Civil Service Commission
1	1	2	–	–	–	–	2	–	–	2	–	–	–	–	–	Crown Estate Office
9	26	35	–	10	7	–	–	–	1	18	3	2	–	5	12	Customs and Excise
4	15	19	–	1	–	–	1	11	2	15	–	–	–	–	4	Ministry of Defence
5	15	20	–	8	–	1	–	3	–	12	1	1	–	2	6	Department of Education and Science
13	30	43	–	12	5	3	–	–	–	20	3	4	1	6(+2)	17	Department of Employment
1	6	7	–	3	–	–	4	–	–	7	–	–	–	–	–	Department of Energy
8	53	61	–	40	–	1	–	3	1	45	2	1	1	3(+1)	13	Department of the Environment

[a] A balancing factor is necessary because cases involving more than one department are shown against each of those departments in the preceding three columns, but elsewhere in this table against only one of them.

–	1	1	–	1	–	–	–	–	–	1	–	–	–	–	–	Office of Fair Trading
4	5	9	–	3	1	–	–	3	–	7	2	–	–	1(+1)	1	Foreign and Commonwealth Office
–	1	1	–	–	–	–	1	–	–	1	–	–	–	–	–	Forestry Commission
–	2	2	–	2	–	–	–	–	–	2	–	–	–	–	–	Registry of Friendly Societies
1	2	3	–	1	–	–	–	–	–	1	1	–	–	1	1	Health and Safety Executive
9	14	23	–	10	–	1	1	1	7	20	–	–	–	–	3	Department of Health
–	1	1	–	–	–	–	–	–	–	–	–	–	–	–	1	Historic Building and Monuments Commission
12	40	52	–	22	1	3	1	2	2	31	4	8	–	11(+1)	10	Home Office
–	5	5	–	3	–	–	–	–	–	3	–	–	–	–	2	Housing Corporation
48	131	179	–	50	20	6	1	–	3	80	17	11	8	30(+6)	69	Inland Revenue
1	12	13	–	5	–	1	–	–	2	8	–	–	–	–	5	Land Registry
6	6	12	–	6	–	–	–	–	1	7	1	3	–	3(+1)	2	Legal Aid Board
4	16	20	–	6	–	–	–	–	2	8	2	2	1	5	7	Lord Chancellor's Department
1	2	3	–	2	–	–	–	–	–	2	–	–	–	–	1	National Rivers Authority
–	4	4	–	2	1	–	1	–	–	4	–	–	–	–	–	Department for National Savings
–	1	1	–	1	–	–	–	–	–	1	–	–	–	–	–	Northern Ireland Court Service
1	1	2	–	1	–	–	–	–	1	2	–	–	–	–	–	Northern Ireland Office
–	2	2	–	–	–	–	–	–	1	1	–	–	–	–	1	Commission for Racial Equality
–	1	1	–	–	–	–	–	1	–	1	–	–	–	–	–	Science and Engineering Research Council
–	1	1	–	–	–	–	1	–	–	1	–	–	–	–	–	Residuary Bodies
1	–	1	–	–	–	–	–	–	–	–	1	–	–	1	–	Rural Development Commission
1	2	3	–	3	–	–	–	–	–	3	–	–	–	–	–	Scottish Legal Aid Board
6	15	21	–	9	–	–	–	2	1	12	–	3	1	3(+1)	6	Scottish Office
101	221	322	–	83	36	10	–	2	3	134	48	32	9	85(+4)	103	Department of Social Security
–	2	2	–	2	–	–	–	–	–	2	–	–	–	–	–	Wales Tourist Board
6	13	19	–	5	–	1	–	–	–	6	1	5	1	6(+1)	7	Department of Trade and Industry
13	38	51	–	16	–	3	2	–	–	21	5	7	–	11(+1)	19	Department of Transport
1	5	6	–	2	1	–	–	1	1	5	–	–	–	–	1	Treasury
1	1	2	–	1	–	–	–	–	–	1	1	1	–	1(+1)	–	Treasury Solicitor
–	1	1	–	–	–	–	–	–	–	–	–	–	–	–	1	Development Board for Rural Wales
4	9	13	–	4	–	1	–	–	1	6	2	–	–	2	5	Welsh Office
1	22	23	21	–	–	–	–	–	–	21	–	–	–	–	2	Legal Bodies
–	17	17	17	–	–	–	–	–	–	17	–	–	–	–	–	Local Authorities
–	1	1	1	–	–	–	–	–	–	1	–	–	–	–	–	Nationalised Industries

Appendic C: Analysis of complaints—*cont.*

	Workload			Cases rejected and investigations discontinued under Section/Schedule of the Act								Cases investigated to conclusion and results reported				Cases in action at 31.12.91
	Brought forward from 1990	Received in 1991	**Total**	Authorities outside scope S.4(1)	Not properly referred, not about administrative actions, S.5(1)	Right of appeal to tribunal S.5(2)a	Parliamentary Commissioner's discretion S.5(5)	Contractual and other commercial transactions Sch. 3, Para. 9	Public Service personnel matters Sch. 3, Para. 10	Miscellaneous	**Total**	Complaints upheld	Complaints not upheld, but departmental actions criticised	Complaints not upheld	**Total** showing balancing factor[a]	
Police	1	1	2	2	–	–	–	–	–	–	2	–	–	–	–	–
Post Office	–	3	3	3	–	–	–	–	–	–	3	–	–	–	–	–
Tribunals	–	5	5	5	–	–	–	–	–	–	5	–	–	–	–	–
Other Public Bodies	–	4	4	4	–	–	–	–	–	–	4	–	–	–	–	–
Miscellaneous	1	26	27	26	–	–	–	–	–	–	26	–	–	–	–	1
Totals	278	801	1079	79	326	72	31	15	34	29[b]	586	95	84	24[c]	183(+20)	310
Totals for 1990	298	704	1002	53	312	72	45	2	37	26	547	79	90	22	177(+14)	278

[b]Breakdown: S.5(2)b: remedy available through legal proceedings 23
S.6(1)a: complaint by local authority 2
S.6(3): out of time 1
Sch.3(2): action outside UK 1
Sch.3(6): conduct of court proceedings 2

[c]of which 1 report was issued without findings.

individuals who called at the office to make their enquiries in person. As in previous years, my Office received and re-directed a number of complaints which were found to be proper to the Commissioners for Local Administration (Local Government Ombudsman) and they took similar action in relation to complaints meant for me but misdirected to them.

Note

In recent times it has on average taken the P.C.A. 15 months and four days to complete an investigation, (*i.e.* the time taken from receipt of the complaint to the issuing of the Commissioner's report).[15] The P.C.A. has articulated the goal of reducing this to nine months, but does not conceive of this as an "immediately achievable" target.

(b) Casework

THE BARLOW CLOWES AFFAIR

P.C.A. Annual Report for 1989: H.C. 353 (1989–90)

64. [This investigation report] was by far the longest and most detailed produced by the Office. It also resulted in the provision of the most substantial financial remedy ever to result from an investigation. I refer to my investigation into the Barlow Clowes affair—which I had decided to conduct following the publication, in October 1988, of the report[1] on the fact-finding investigation carried out by Sir Godfray Le Quesne QC at the request of the then Secretary of State for Trade and Industry. My own investigation was the subject of a special report[2] which I made to Parliament (under the provisions of section 10(4) of the Parliamentary Commissioner Act) on December 19, 1989. The investigation involved my enquiring into the exercise of licensing duties under the Prevention of Fraud (Investments) Act 1958 by the Department of Trade and Industry over a period of some 14 years. I found that there had been significant maladministration by the Department, in their dealings with Barlow Clowes' partnerships and their successor companies, in five main areas. The businesses concerned had been engaged in the management of client monies running into millions of pounds. They had led the investors to believe that their monies were being put into British Government stocks. Much of the marketing of the businesses' services had been directed to those in retirement and others seeking a risk-free but tax-efficient form of investment, and a substantial part of the attraction to investors had been the use—until it was severely curtailed in 1985—of the tax-avoidance device known as "bond-washing." The volume of the business thus transacted had already grown considerably when, in 1984, the Department sought to bring the operation within the licensing framework

[15] *Annual Report 1989*, para. 10.

[1] Barlow Clowes Report of Sir Godfray Le Quesne Q.C. to the Secretary of State for Trade and Industry H.C. 671.

[2] First Report—Session 1989–90 H.C. 76.

having, in 1976 and in the intervening years, allowed it—as described in my report—to continue unlicensed. Partnerships, with identical names but with differing members, had been operating in both the United Kingdom and in Jersey, but the Department had failed to realise that a separate Jersey partnership existed, or to appreciate the need to extend to the Jersey partnership the enquiries they proposed to make into the suitability of the United Kingdom partnership for a licence. I concluded that an examination of the Jersey partnership's affairs would have disclosed that its role was more than that of an investment vehicle for expatriates (as had been represented to DTI), that there had been intermingling between the funds it managed and those of the mainland partnership, and that—at the audit date selected for the examination of the mainland partnership's funds—securities held by the Jersey partnership on behalf of clients fell short of the amount needed to discharge obligations to investors by at least £3.65m. Had these facts been discovered, the firm's operations would in my view almost certainly have been brought to an end early in 1985. As it was, licences were issued to the United Kingdom business in 1985, 1986 and 1987 (that in 1987 being closely followed by the appointment of Inspectors by the Secretary of State to investigate the company's affairs in the light of serious concerns about its viability and integrity); and, in 1988, the United Kingdom and offshore branches of the business were put into liquidation owing investors many millions of pounds. The final total of the losses had not emerged when my report was issued, but seemed likely to exceed £100m. Apart from the centrally important errors in relation to the Jersey partnership, I also found that the viability of the schemes offered by Barlow Clowes had not been adequately considered, and that the decision to renew the licence for a third time, in 1987, had involved both excessive delay in responding to worrying information about the company and errors in correctly identifying the options available to the Department.

65. When I put my findings to the Department they told me, to my disappointment, that the Government disagreed with them and proposed to set out its own views in a separate document to be published at the same time as my report. The Department also said that my report raised a number of important issues about the responsibilities of regulators (on which the document to be published by the Government would also set out the Government's views). They went on to say, however, that the Government recognised that the case had created very great hardship and involved a unique combination of unusual features. In the light of that the Government was, in the exceptional circumstances and without admission of fault or liability, prepared to make a substantial payment to investors who had suffered loss. This payment (the proposed detailed calculation of which the Department explained to me) would be made to investors in both Barlow Clowes Gilt Managers Limited and Barlow Clowes International Limited in return for their assigning to the Secretary of State their rights in the liquidation and against third parties,

and giving an undertaking to provide reasonable assistance in the pursuit of those rights. The payments would not distinguish between early and late investors.

66. I concluded that this outcome of the investigation—providing as it would for more than 99 per cent. of the investors to receive at least 85 per cent. of their capital (and 90 per cent. in the case of those with investments of £50,000 or less) and, in addition, payments in lieu of interest lost on that amount since the collapse—was not unsatisfactory. The Government published its observations[3] on my Findings on December 19. However, I saw ground for satisfaction in that the Government—with whatever reservations—was prepared to act as it proposed in providing a fair remedy for what, as I had seen things, had been an injustice suffered by investors as a result of maladministration.

Note

For an analysis of this major investigation, see R. Gregory and G. Drewry, "Barlow Clowes and the Ombudsman" [1991] P.L. 192 and 408.

Right to Advice: A Case Study

A RIGHT TO OFFICIAL ADVICE: THE PARLIAMENTARY COMMISSIONER'S PERSPECTIVE*

Alastair R. Mowbray, [1990] P.L. 68

In the context of our contemporary society, it is inevitable that a great deal of sought after information is located within government departments, particularly where they are responsible for generating the detailed provisions that govern today's numerous administrative programmes. Therefore, a vital element in the relationship between citizens and the state concerns the nature of the obligation on the latter to provide advice to citizens regarding matters falling within the competence and expertise of those departments.

Of all the administrative grievance-handling agencies, it is the Parliamentary Commissioner for Administration (hereafter the P.C.A. or the Commissioner) who has contributed the most towards the development of a citizen's right to advice from the government in our modern public law. . . .

Today, the importance of the right to advice is reflected in the fact that during recent years advice cases have represented approximately 20 per cent. of all the investigations published by the P.C.A. in his selected case reports (see table below).

[3] Observations by the Government on the Report of the Parliamentary Commissioner for Administration on Barlow Clowes H.C. 99.

* *Note—not all the footnotes have been reproduced.*

Year	Number of Reported Cases	Number of Advice Cases
1985	59	12
1986	63	13
1987	51	9
Totals	173	34

THE SCOPE OF THE RIGHT TO ADVICE

A study of the Commissioner's published cases during 1985–87 enables us to delimit the boundaries of the right as currently enforced by the P.C.A. A clear example of the principle that individuals have a right to advice is given by a complaint against the D.H.S.S.[1] The complainant asked an officer at the local office whether he would be entitled to an increase in his supplementary benefit payments if he was to take out a mortgage on a new house. Because of a confusion over case papers the office failed to provide the complainant with a reply to his request and subsequently the building society refused to grant the complainant a mortgage. The P.C.A. concluded that the department's failure to provide the requested information meant that the complainant's criticisms were fully justified. Moreover, the P.C.A. has adopted a wide usage of the concept of "advice." He treats both the provision of essentially factual information to individuals (*e.g.* the extent of a complainant's pension contributions[2]) and the expression of officers' opinions as amounting to statements of advice. Officers' opinions can be about matters of current departmental policy (*e.g.* whether a company's short-time working schedule complied with existing departmental rules governing the payment of unemployment benefit[3]) or future situations involving the department (*e.g.* the level of benefits an individual would receive if she began reclaiming social security allowances in several months' time[4]).

(a) *The subject-matter of official advice*

Of the 34 advice cases published during 1985–87, the overwhelming majority concerned what may be termed personal queries, where individuals sought advice from departments about their eligibility for public benefit (21 cases) or liability to make a payment to the state (four cases). . . .

(b) *The form of official advice*

. . . In half the cases studied (17), the relevant advice took the form of a personal letter sent to the complainant. A typical example of advice being presented in such a form arose in a case involving the overseas branch of

[1] C573/84 (1984–85) H.C. 150.
[2] C223/85 (1984–85) H.C. 590.
[3] C466/84 (1984–85) H.C. 324.
[4] C665/84 (1984–85) H.C. 590.

the D.H.S.S.[5] The complainant was a United Kingdom citizen who had taken up employment in France and he sought advice from the department about his future entitlement to retirement pensions in Britain and France. The department wrote expressing their views on the levels of pensions he could expect from both countries under European Community regulations. Later the complainant received a much lower French pension than the D.H.S.S. had predicted and he complained to the P.C.A. The Commissioner found that the department had inadvertently misinterpreted the E.C. regulations.

The second most common form of advice was that of oral statements (14 cases). This type of advice was normally given in two distinct circumstances. First, in response to a personal visit by a citizen to departmental premises. An example occurred where a managing director went to his local VAT office to discover if a proposed purchase of manufacturing assets would be liable to tax.[6] He was informed by the officer at the counter that VAT would be payable; but the District Surveyor later determined that tax was not due. The other context in which oral advice was obviously present was where an individual telephoned the department for advice. For example, a complainant telephoned his local D.H.S.S. office to seek advice on social security benefits he could claim whilst undergoing a M.S.C. training course.[7] In reply the officer expressed a view as to what types of benefits would be payable. When it subsequently transpired that not all these benefits were available the P.C.A. was asked to investigate.

Lastly, in three of the cases studied, advice took the form of leaflets and booklets published by the department. In a case against the Department of Employment,[8] a woman complained that she satisfied the conditions required for employment under the Job Release Scheme, administered by the department, as explained in an official leaflet. But the department refused to allow her to take up such a post, because they asserted that she did not meet all the requirements laid down for the scheme. The P.C.A. upheld her complaint, noting that,

> "there was nothing in the leaflet then current to suggest that eligibility was also governed by other rules . . . the leaflet was clearly misleading in this respect and the Principal Officer of D.E. has acknowledged that it should have provided a clearer definition of the term 'unemployed.' "

In such a case the offending advice was directed towards sections of the community at large. . . .

[5] C494/83 (1984–85) H.C. 150.
[6] C567/84 (1984–85) H.C. 590.
[7] C712/86 (1987–88) H.C. 103.
[8] C313/84 (1984–85) H.C. 150.

THE QUALITY OF OFFICIAL ADVICE

As members of the public have a prima facie right to advice concerning their personal queries about programmes being administered by departments, what is the quality of the advice they can expect from officials? The P.C.A. has invoked the adaptable concept of maladministration to condemn advice which he considers to be defective. Incorrect and misleading statements were the most common forms of defects found in the cases studied, 10 cases involving incorrect advice and eight misleading advice. Although the Commissioner has not provided specific definitions of these terms, we can gain an understanding of his usage by examining the substance of his criticisms in individual cases.

The P.C.A. equates the notion of "wholy wrong" with the term "incorrect" as a characteristic of defective advice. For example, after a complainant received a reduction in his social security benefits he queried the level of his new payments with the department. The local office replied that the change was caused by the fact that the department would now be paying his rent and rates directly to the local authority. Subsequently, it emerged that this was not the true position and his benefits had been reduced because his wife had become entitled to a pension in her own right. The P.C.A. noted, "it is clear from my investigation that . . . the local office did inform the complainant quite specifically and *quite wrongly*, that from November 22 he would no longer have to pay rent and rates."[9]

In contrast, the Commissioner uses the term "misleading" advice in relation to statements which are partially wrong, with the consequence that the citizen is unable to comprehend his true position. An example involved a case where a woman was receiving benefits from the D.H.S.S. including a higher long-term scale rate of supplementary benefit. The claimant asked the local office what her entitlements would be if she were to register for a training course and then later reclaim social security benefits. The office replied that her attendance on the course would have no effect on her future eligibility for supplementary benefit. Some months later, after completing the course, the woman re-applied for supplementary benefit, but was awarded only a lower rate payment, because the rules provided that where a person receiving a higher rate benefit stopped claiming the benefit for more than eight weeks they were subsequently entitled only to the lower rate. The P.C.A. considered that the office had given the complainant misleading advice and criticised them "for their failure to provide the complainant with a *full and correct* explanation of the consequences of her planned attendance on the T.O.P.S. course."[10]

"Inadequate" advice also results in citizens being incompletely informed of their true position. The P.C.A. found that the D.H.S.S. had

[9] C701/84 (1985–86) H.C. 536.
[10] C665/84 (1984–85) H.C. 590.

provided a widow with inadequate advice about her eligibility for invalidity benefit by failing to warn her of the need to submit medical evidence regularly to the local office.[11] The difference between misleading and inadequate advice, therefore, appears to be that the former category contains statements which are partially erroneous whereas in the latter case the advice is correct but incomplete. . . .

THE INJUSTICE SUFFERED THROUGH RELIANCE ON DEFECTIVE OFFICIAL ADVICE

According to section 5(1)(*a*) of the Parliamentary Commissioner Act 1967, the P.C.A. can investigate complaints only where, *inter alia*, the complainant claims to have "sustained injustice in consequence of maladministration." So if the P.C.A. is to uphold a citizen's complaint in regard to defective advice he must also find that he or she has sustained an injustice through relying or acting upon the advice. In contrast to the Local Ombudsman, the P.C.A. tends not to make an express finding of both maladministration and injustice, but instead concludes that he upholds the citizen's complaint. However, according to the substance of his reports in this context, the P.C.A. has generally equated injustice with a tangible and direct financial disadvantage experienced by the citizen relying upon the defective advice.

The most common form of financial disadvantage experienced by complainants was a loss of state benefits, which occurred in eight of the 34 cases. One example involved a woman who suffered from agoraphobia with the result that she could not use public transport.[12] The complainant asked the D.H.S.S. mobility allowance unit if she was entitled to any form of benefit to help pay the cost of taxi fares to work. The unit informed her that she was not entitled to mobility allowance and failed to provide her with a leaflet listing other available benefits as their internal procedures required. Eight months later the complainant was awarded one of these other benefits, the existence of which she had discovered from a magazine. The P.C.A. criticised the unit's failure and approved the payment of an *ex gratia* sum equivalent to the lost eight months' benefit. . . .

CONCLUSIONS

What then are the contours of the right to advice from departments of state as currently enforced by the P.C.A.? Provided citizens have complied with a series of preliminary obligations, including the full disclosure of relevant information and the seeking of advice at the earliest opportunity, they can legitimately expect answers to the overwhelming majority of queries concerning the application of departmental programmes to their personal circumstances. If the answers are incorrect, misleading or

[11] C277/86 (1986–87) H.C. 312.
[12] C141/86 (1987–88) H.C. 41.

inadequate, the P.C.A. will characterise the department's conduct as amounting to maladministration. He will then determine whether the citizen has suffered a direct financial loss through acting or relying upon the defective advice. Where such a loss is established the P.C.A. will then treat the citizen as having sustained an injustice in consequence of maladministration. A suitable remedy will then be recommended by the P.C.A., in most cases involving the department in making a quantified *ex gratia* payment to the citizen to compensate for his or her loss.

The only significant weakness discovered in the P.C.A.'s response to advice complaints was the lack of clarity in his reports regarding the calculation of the level of financial loss suffered by citizens and the corresponding compensation required to alleviate the injustice. The inclusion of a more precise assessment of the extent of the pecuniary loss flowing from the defective advice would end any lingering suspicion that the P.C.A.'s calculations are based more on subjective inclination than objective evaluation. . . .

Despite persistent criticisms of the notion of "maladministration," the reports disclose that the indefinite nature of the concept has enabled the P.C.A. to develop and refine its application to cover virtually all forms of departmental advice concerning personal queries about collective consumption programmes. Furthermore, the success of the P.C.A. in securing redress for justified complaints (financial compensation was paid in 20 cases), means that despite his lack of formal coercive powers the P.C.A.'s findings in advice cases satisfy the minimum jurisprudential requirements of a right. As Stoljar explains, "you cannot have a right unless it can be claimed or demanded or insisted upon, indeed claimed effectively or enforceably."[13] The achievements of the Commissioner in relation to advice complaints certainly enable individuals effectively to insist upon the provision of accurate advice within the limits elucidated in this article.

Finally, we can assess the value of this right in the context of the continuing debate over freedom of information in the United Kingdom. Marsh observes that one justification put forward by proponents of a statutory right of access to government information is that the current position reflects:

> "disequilibrium between the state with its command over a wide field of information and the private organisation or individual, from whom information of all kinds is demanded by the state, from which, however, information can only be obtained with difficulty, or not at all."[14]

Against this backdrop, the right to official advice has the potential to help redress that imbalance on the level of dealings between individuals and

[13] S. Stoljar, *An Analysis of Rights* (1984) pp. 3–4.
[14] N.S. Marsh (ed.), *Public Access to Government Held Information* (1987) p. 4.

departments, because it can assist a citizen in discovering his or her position in relation to the administrative norms governing specific programmes. However, the right only extends to those activities which fall within the P.C.A.'s jurisdiction and it fails to provide a general right of access to governmental information for interested citizens (qua campaigners, journalists or academics) where they are not directly affected by a particular administrative scheme. Therefore, whilst the right is clearly not a substitute for a balanced Freedom of Information Act, it offers a modest ray of sunshine in an otherwise gloomy landscape of increasing official secrecy.

Notes

1. The right to advice is merely one of many administrative norms developed by the P.C.A. in his casework (*cf.* his principles governing the use of administrative guidance noted previously in Ch. 3 at p. 121). Professor Bradley has analysed this aspect of the P.C.A.'s work in the following terms:

> "it was to be expected that 'arbitrary discretion' of the kind which the 1967 Act vested in the British Ombudsman should evolve into a more or less settled body of ascertainable principles which might even harden into rules. . . . Thus, inevitably, the British Ombudsman has developed principles, standards and rules of what he believes to constitute good administration, since otherwise no notion of maladministration could have emerged. As the process of investigation and report continues in every fresh case, so the individual complainant receives the benefit of the Ombudsman's enforcement of the rules and principles which have emerged from the previous case-work. And it may not be pressing this analysis too far to conclude that the individual citizen thus acquires what may properly be called new rights to the maintenance of a certain quality of administration."

"The Role of the Ombudsman in Relation to the Protection of Citizens' Rights" [1980] C.L.J. 304 at pp. 310–311.

2. Because of the need for an M.P. to refer a complaint to the P.C.A. the relationship between Members of the House of Commons and the Parliamentary Commissioner is crucial to the effective operation of the ombudsman scheme. A contemporary study based on the responses of 235 M.P.s reveals a worrying lack of enthusiasm for the P.C.A.'s activities by a number of M.P.s. Professors Drewry and Harlow found that 67 per cent. of their respondents considered the P.C.A. to be only slightly useful to them and 11 per cent. felt he was of no use at all. These commentators placed part of the problem on the method of operation ("House-style") of the P.C.A. They believe that ". . . the P.C.A. and his staff seem unaware of the way in which M.P.s work and even perhaps of the pressures on them. They function more as, and relate more closely to, the civil servants whose work they are called upon to investigate than to the M.P.s whose servants they are supposed to be" ("A 'Cutting Edge?' The Parliamentary Commissioner and M.P.s" (1990) 53 M.L.R. 745 at p. 767). To deal with these perceived difficulties the authors recommend a series of radical alterations to the procedures and organisational structure of the Parliamentary Commissioner's office. "A parliamentary office plus a determined publicity campaign aimed at M.P.s and—far more important—their staff, are both essential. The introduction of new and less formal investigatory procedures is another essential. This would entail some more imaginative recruitment policies; lawyers and civil servants are of course necessary, but new blood—investigative journalists, academics, people seconded from foreign ombudsmen's

offices or industry—would also bring a welcome dilution of the prevalent civil service genes" (pp. 768–769).

3. Another, more positive, aspect of the P.C.A.'s relationship with the House of Commons has been the support given to him by the Select Committee on the P.C.A., created in 1967 to monitor his work. Professor Gregory found that the Select Committee concentrated upon three tasks. First, seeking to ensure that remedies were provided for complainants where the P.C.A. upheld their claims against departments. If a department was unwilling to provide the redress suggested by the P.C.A., then the Select Committee would call the Permanent Secretary of the department before them to explain the department's conduct. Secondly, to examine defects in administrative procedures discovered by the P.C.A. in the course of his investigations. And, thirdly, to keep under review the adequacy of the P.C.A.'s powers. Gregory concluded that the Select Committee, despite the absence of "political heavyweights" amongst its' members, had been successful in performing the first two functions, but had not been able to achieve any significant expansion of the P.C.A.'s formal powers. These successes were, according to Gregory, due to the parliamentary significance of reports concerned with persons rather than abstract jurisdictional proposals:

> "explaining and defending in Parliament a decision to reject not only the findings of the Commissioner but also the considered recommendations of a select committee of the House, on a matter of personal injustice, is not a prospect that greatly appeals to Ministers, the more so as cases of this kind often have about them just that element of 'human interest' which naturally attracts the attention of the media and general public"

("The Select Committee on the P.C.A., 1967–80" [1982] P.L. 49 at pp. 86–87.)

(C) The Local Government Ombudsmen

(i) Constitutional and Jurisdictional Matters

Once again it was a report by JUSTICE[16] that advocated the creation of ombudsmen for local government. Because of the large number of local authorities and their responsibility for the provision of many direct services to the public, thereby increasing the likelihood of consumer complaints, it was not considered possible to appoint a single local ombudsman. Instead, the idea of several local commissioners was proposed. When local authorities in England and Wales were restructured during 1974, Parliament took the opportunity to create separate local ombudsman systems for these two parts of the United Kingdom. Northern Ireland's Parliament had already established a local ombudsman (the Commissioner for Complaints) and separate legislation[17] has instituted a Local Commissioner for Scotland.

Part III of the Local Government Act 1974 creates the Commission for Local Administration in England which currently has three full time Commissioners (commonly called the Local Government Ombudsmen). The Commissioners are appointed by the Queen on the advice of the Environment Secretary. Each Commissioner deals with complaints originating from different regions of England. Originally there was a "councillor filter" requirement for complainants, but since 1988[18] the Local Government Ombudsmen can receive complaints

[16] *The Citizen and his Council* (1969).
[17] Local Government (Scotland) Act 1975.
[18] Local Government Act 1988.

directly from members of the public. They may investigate complaints against a number of specified local bodies including, county councils, district councils and urban development corporations.[19] Much of their jurisdiction is modelled on the language of the Parliamentary Commissioner Act 1967. Hence, the Local Government Ombudsmen can investigate complaints that members of the public have "sustained injustice in consequence of maladministration" in connection with the performance of administrative functions by local authorities.[20] However, certain functions are excluded from the Local Government Ombudsmen's remit, *e.g.* contractual/commercial transactions and personnel matters.[21] Their investigations are to be conducted in private and have the backing of the High Court's powers of contempt.[22] When a Local Government Ombudsman has conducted an investigation he or she must send copies of his or her report to, *inter alios*, the complainant and the local authority. As with the Parliamentary Commissioner, the Local Government Ombudsmen have no power to compel the provision of redress by local authorities where they uphold a complaint.

Note

On several occasions, notably in 1978, 1980 and 1984, the English Local Government Ombudsmen formally reviewed their existing jurisdiction. After each review they sought to have their remit extended, but with little support from local authorities or the Environment Secretary. Before the Widdicombe Committee examining "The Conduct of Local Government Business," the Local Government Ombudsmen renewed their jurisdictional pleas—in particular for:

(1) direct access by complainants;
(2) contractual/commercial transactions and personnel matters to be open to investigation;
(3) the Local Ombudsmen to be given the power to investigate on their own motion without receiving a specific complaint from a member of the public.

The Committee favoured direct access to the Local Government Ombudsmen because:

> ". . . we believe it is wrong in principle that complainants should be expected to direct their complaints against a council through a member of the executive decision making body for that council."[23]

The Local Government Ombudsmen's desire to investigate commercial transactions was also endorsed:

> "we have not been convinced that cases involving commercial and contractual transactions with members of the public are different in kind from cases involving other local authority dealings with the public and that they should therefore as a matter of general principle be excluded from the ombudsman's remit."[24]

But, the Committee was only willing to recommend that complaints about appointment procedures used by councils should be within the Ombudsmen's

[19] 1974 Act, s.25.
[20] *Ibid.* s.26(1).
[21] *Ibid.* Sched. 5.
[22] *Ibid.* ss.28–29.
[23] *The Conduct of Local Government Business* (Cmnd. 9797, 1986) para. 9.64.
[24] *Ibid.* para. 9.73.

jurisdiction, not general personnel matters. This was due to the Committee's belief that "... the primary function of the ombudsmen is in our view to provide support for the consumers of local government services rather than for those who are employed to provide them."[25] The Committee approved a modified power for the Local Government Ombudsmen to initiate investigations, provided they were based upon "good grounds for concern" and directed towards individual injustice.[26]

As indicated above, the Government accepted the desirability of direct public access to the Local Government Ombudsmen and this was enacted in 1988. However, the other proposed changes to the Ombudsmen's jurisdiction were not so well received. Regarding commercial transactions the Government felt:

> "Ombudsmen—central and local—are concerned with the inter-action between the executive arm of government and the general public. Actions taken by public bodies in buying and selling goods and services are fundamentally different. The law already provides various safeguards and remedies for the parties involved in such commercial transactions, and there is no case for providing further protection through the local Ombudsman. . . ."[27]

For the same underlying reason the Government did not accept that personnel complaints were appropriate for Local Government Ombudsmen. The idea of self-initiated action by the Ombudsmen was rejected, because the Government felt that it could result in the Ombudsmen losing goodwill if they were perceived as general purpose watchdogs. Instead the Government proposed that the Ombudsmen be given a new power to publish general guidance to local authorities on good administrative practice. This has now been enacted in section 23 of the Local Government and Housing Act 1989.

(ii) The Courts and the Local Government Ombudsmen

R v. LOCAL COMMISSIONER FOR ADMINISTRATION FOR THE SOUTH, ex p. EASTLEIGH B.C.

[1988] 1 Q.B. 855; [1988] 3 All E.R. 151 (Court of Appeal)

A householder complained to the Local Government Ombudsman, for his area of England, that Eastleigh B.C. had failed properly to inspect the construction of a defective sewer connected to his house as required by the Building Regulations 1976. The Local Ombudsman produced a report (extracts of which appear in the judgment below) in which he stated that the Council had not inspected the sewer at all the relevant stages of its construction and consequently the sewer had not been thoroughly inspected. He went on to find that the householder had sustained injustice as a consequence of the Council's maladministration, but that even if the final inspection of the sewer had been carried out properly he could not be certain that the defect would have been discovered. Therefore, the Ombudsman recommended that Eastleigh B.C. pay only a part of the costs of remedial work.

The Council sought judicial review of the Local Ombudsman's report on the

[25] *Ibid.* para. 9.72.
[26] *Ibid.* para. 9.76.
[27] *The Government's Response to the Report of the Widdicombe Committee of Inquiry* (Cm. 433, 1988), para. 6.27.

grounds that (1) it was contrary to section 34(3) of the Local Government Act 1974, in that the Ombudsman had questioned a discretionary decision taken without maladministration by the council and (2) it was also contrary to section 26(1) of the 1974 Act, in that the Ombudsman had made a report when it was not certain that the householder had suffered injustice in consequence of an act of maladministration by Eastleigh B.C. In the High Court Nolan J. upheld the Council's submissions, but refused to grant them a declaration. The Council appealed against the refusal of a remedy and the Local Government Ombudsman cross-appealed against the findings of *ultra vires*.

LORD DONALDSON OF LYMINGTON M.R.: . . . The ombudsman's conclusions are stated in paragraphs 30 and 31 of his report:

> "30. In my view good administration dictates that the council should carry out an inspection under the Building Regulations in respect of all stage inspections for which they have received notice from the owner or builder as the case may be. Where inspections have not been made at a particular stage I consider that special attention should be given on the final inspection to remedy the omission. In the case of drains it is a relatively easy matter to carry out a full test, such as a ball test or its equivalent, at the final inspection stage and I consider that a council have a duty to ensure that this is done because a final inspection should mean that, so far as the council are concerned, they have with reasonable diligence and expenditure of officer time found no defect under the Building Regulations. I am satisfied that in this case the private foul sewer in question was not fully or thoroughly inspected. The defects in piping discovered as a result of the soil and vent pipe test should have alerted officers to the possibility of other defects in the pipe work.
>
> "31. I find, therefore, that the complainant has sustained injustice as a result of the council's maladministration. However, I cannot say, categorically, whether had the council carried out the final inspection in accordance with the dictates of good administration, the trouble at the centre of this complaint would not have arisen. Equally, I have taken account of the argument that with synthetic piping of the sort employed in this case soil compaction can cause undulation at a later date. I have also considered the fact that the original fault was the builder's and that that (and the council's fault) occurred some years ago. On the other hand the final inspection was, in my view, incomplete and the council could have become aware of the problem at an early stage because of the difficulties experienced by the owner of house 3. Having considered these factors I feel on balance it would be inequitable to ask the council to defray the whole cost of the necessary remedial work. Accordingly, upon the residents' agreement to pay a proportion of the reasonable cost, I consider that the council themselves should take the action which the Assistant Director of Technical Services commended to the residents (see paragraph 29, above)."

The action referred to in paragraph 29 consisted of exposing that part of the sewer which lay between two manholes and adjusting the pipe work to eliminate the undulation.

The ombudsman's cross-appeal

Section 34(3)

This subsection is in the following terms:

> "It is hereby declared that nothing in this Part of this Act authorises or requires a Local Commissioner to question the merits of a decision taken without maladministration by an authority in the exercise of a discretion vested in that authority."

"Maladministration" is not defined in the Act, but its meaning was considered in *R.* v. *Local Commissioner for Administration for the North and East Area of England, ex p. Bradford Metropolitan City Council* [1979] Q.B. 287. All three judges (Lord Denning M.R., at p. 311, Eveleigh L.J., at p. 314, and Sir David Cairns, at p. 319) expressed themselves differently, but in substance each was saying the same thing, namely, that administration and maladministration in the context of the work of a local authority is concerned with the *manner* in which decisions by the authority are reached and the *manner* in which they are or are not implemented. Administration and maladministration have nothing to do with the nature, quality or reasonableness of the decision itself.

The key to this part of the cross-appeal lies in identifying the policy decision of the council in relation to the inspection of drains. This was, as I have stated, to inspect at four of the more important of nine stages in construction. It did not condescend to the nature of the inspections. . . .

Nolan J. read paragraph 30 of the ombudsman's report, which I have set out in full, as questioning the merits of that policy. I do not so read it. I can best illustrate my understanding of that paragraph by adding words which render explicit what, in my judgment, is implicit:

> "In my view good administration dictates that the council should carry out an inspection under the Building Regulations in respect of all stage inspections for which they have received notice from the owner or builder as the case may be. [However I recognise that, on the authority of *Anns'* case [1978] A.C. 728 to which I have referred at length earlier in this report, it was open to the council in the exercise of their discretion and taking account of the competing claims of efficiency and thrift to decide to inspect on fewer occasions. This the council has done and I accept its decisions. That said] Where inspections have not been made at a particular stage I consider that special attention should be given on the final inspection to remedying the omission. [In saying this I am not calling for an expenditure of time and effort which would nullify the council's discretionary decision on the resources to be devoted to

building regulation inspections.] In the case of drains it is a relatively easy matter to carry out a full test, such as a ball test or its equivalent, at the final inspection stage. . . . [The choice of test must be a matter for the council's officers and I would not criticise them for not using the ball test, if they had used some equivalent test. However an air pressure test, such as the council's officers used, is not such an equivalent, because it only reveals whether or not the sewer is watertight. It tells the inspector nothing about its gradient or its ability to self-clear and efficiently carry away matter discharged into it as required by regulation N10.] I consider that [this is of considerable importance and that] a council have a duty to ensure that this is done because a final inspection [if the council decide to make one, as this council did] should mean that, so far as the council are concerned, they have with reasonable diligence and expenditure of officer time found no defect under the Building Regulations. I am satisfied that in this case the private foul sewer in question was not fully or thoroughly inspected [in terms of the council's own 1977 policy. Even if in other circumstances a lesser inspection might have been justified in terms of that policy] the defects in piping discovered as a result of the soil and vent pipe tests should have alerted officers to the possibility of other defects in the pipe work."

So read, and I do so read it, paragraph 30 loyally accepts the council's discretionary decision on the inspection of drains. It simply criticises the way in which that decision was implemented. I do not, therefore, think that this complaint by the council is made out.

Section 26(1)

This subsection is in the following terms:

"Subject to the provisions of this Part of this Act where a written complaint is made by or on behalf of a member of the public who claims to have sustained injustice in consequence of maladministration in connection with action taken by or on behalf of an authority to which this Part of this Act applies, being action taken in the exercise of administrative functions of that authority, a Local Commissioner may investigate that complaint."

. . . [I]t does mean that he cannot report adversely upon an authority unless his investigation reveals not only maladministration, but injustice to the complainant sustained as a consequence of that maladministration.

The mischief at which this subsection is directed is not difficult to detect. Every local authority has living within its boundaries a small cadre of citizens who would like nothing better than to spend their spare time complaining of maladministration. The subsection limits the extent to which they can involve the ombudsman by requiring, as a condition precedent to his involvement, that the complainant shall personally have been adversely affected by the alleged maladministration. If he was not so affected, he did not himself suffer injustice. If he was, he did. . . .

Like Nolan J., I am loath to criticise a busy Local Commissioner on merely semantic grounds, but I think that he laid himself open to criticism by finding maladministration in paragraph 30 and then proceeding, without any explanation, to his conclusion of consequential injustice. . . .

. . . [I]n the end I have come to the conclusion that the ombudsman was intending to say that, whilst there could be no absolute certainty that a proper inspection would have revealed the defects and it was a possibility that the undulation occurred after the date of the inspection, on the balance of probabilities he was satisfied that the defects were present at the time of the inspection, that a proper inspection would have revealed them and that he was therefore satisfied that the complainant had suffered injustice in consequence of the maladministration.

An ombudsman's report is neither a statute nor a judgment. It is a report to the council and to the ratepayers of the area. It has to be written in everyday language and convey a message. This report has been subjected to a microscopic and somewhat legalistic analysis which it was not intended to undergo. Valid criticisms have been made, particularly of paragraph 31, but in my judgment they go to form rather than substance and, notwithstanding occasional dicta to the contrary, judicial review is concerned with substance. I would therefore allow the ombudsman's cross-appeal.

The council's appeal

As Parker and Taylor L.JJ. are minded to dismiss the ombudsman's appeal, it is necessary to consider the council's appeal. I would allow it.

Nolan J. considered that there was no need for any declaration that the ombudsman had exceeded his remit by contravening the limits upon his jurisdiction set by section 34(3). He said that this was a free country and that there was nothing to prevent the council responding to the report with equal publicity. He concluded by saying that, since Parliament had not thought it necessary to create a right of appeal against the findings in the Local Commissioner's report, and in the absence of impropriety, it seemed to him that the courts ought not to provide the equivalent of such a right by judicial review.

I have to say that I profoundly disagree with this approach. Let me start with the fact that Parliament has not created a right of appeal against the findings in a Local Commissioner's report. It is this very fact, coupled with the public law character of the ombudsman's office and powers, which is the foundation of the right to relief by way of judicial review.

Next there is the suggestion that the council should issue a statement disputing the right of the ombudsman to make his findings and that this would provide the council with an adequate remedy. Such an action would wholly undermine the system of ombudsman's reports and would, in effect, provide for an appeal to the media against his findings. The Parliamentary intention was that reports by ombudsmen should be loyally accepted by the local authorities concerned. This is clear from section 30(4) and (5), which require the local authority to make the report available for inspection by the public and to advertise this fact, from section 31(1), which requires the local authority to notify the ombudsman of the action which it has taken and proposes to take in the light of his report and from section 31(2), which entitles the ombudsman to make a further report if the local authority's response is not satisfactory.

Whilst I am very far from encouraging councils to seek judicial review of an ombudsman's report, which, bearing in mind the nature of his office and duties and the qualifications of those who hold that office, is inherently unlikely to succeed, in the absence of a successful application for judicial review and the giving of relief by the court, local authorities should not dispute an ombudsman's report and should carry out their statutory duties in relation to it.

If Nolan J. thought that the publication of his judgment in favour of the council was itself an adequate remedy, he did not say so, and, in any event, I think that he would have been mistaken, because this by itself does not relieve the council of its obligations to respond to the report in accordance with section 31(1) and, assuming that the report should never had been made, it is wrong that the council should be expected to respond.

I would grant a declaration in terms which reflect the decision of this court on the ombudsman's appeal against the decision of Nolan J.

PARKER L.J.: . . . On a fair reading of the whole of paragraph 30 it appears to me that the ombudsman is not concluding that there was maladministration because there was no inspection at all nine stages, but merely that the inspections of the sewer which were called for by the policy of inspecting at the four most important stages were not fully or thoroughly carried out. This conclusion was not dependent upon the view expressed in the opening sentence and indeed it could not have been because the policy did call for drain inspections, indeed two drain inspections. . . .

I conclude therefore that the ombudsman's conclusion in paragraph 30 was valid, but if the council felt it necessary to seek some declaratory relief with regard to the opening words of the paragraph I would be prepared to consider granting it.

I turn to the second question raised on the cross-appeal, namely, whether the conclusion that the complainant had suffered injustice as a result of the maladministration can be sustained. This depends upon paragraph 31 of the report. Had the ombudsman stopped at the first sentence, I should have had no doubt that the decision was sustainable. It seems to me abundantly clear that the complainant had suffered injustice if the failure to inspect properly led to the subsequent expenditure and the ombudsman could in my view easily have determined that it had. It is submitted however that, having stated his conclusion in the opening sentence, he proceeds to negate it and that the paragraph read as a whole really amounts to this: "I cannot say whether the failure to inspect led to the expenditure, but as the council were at fault it would be fair that they should contribute to the cost of remedial measures." For the ombudsman it is submitted that this is not so and that on a fair reading the paragraph says no more than: "I cannot be absolutely sure, but on the balance of probabilities I conclude. . . ."

I regret to say that, unlike Lord Donaldson M.R. I cannot accept this construction. It appears to me that to do so involves applying legal concepts of differing standards of proof in order to uphold a paragraph which, like its predecessor, must be broadly considered. I have, despite its opening words, been able, by a broad reading and the correctness of the ombudsman's directions to himself on the law, to uphold the conclusion in paragraph 30. In the case of paragraph 31 I am unable to do so.

I would therefore dismiss the cross-appeal and allow the appeal.

TAYLOR L.J.: . . . The crucial issue therefore is whether the ombudsman's findings in both paragraphs 30 and 31 of his report can be upheld and his cross-appeal thus allowed. I agree with Nolan J. that both paragraphs contain findings which cannot be justified.

[Regarding paragraph 30.] In my judgment its tenor shows the ombudsman to be trespassing into the field of discretion by laying down what policy as to inspections the dictates of good administration require, and what tests the council ought to ensure are carried out. That is quite different from finding that a test specifically required by the council's policy has not been carried out or has been carried out inefficiently. I therefore agree with Nolan J. that the ombudsman was in breach of section 34(3) of the Local Government Act 1974 in his conclusion that maladministration was established.

As to paragraph 31, I agree with Parker L.J. Only by straining the language used by the ombudsman and attributing to him speculatively considerations as to the burden of proof, could one render his finding on causation sound. I do not think such straining and speculation is justified.

Accordingly I conclude that in respect of both paragraphs 30 and 31 of the report, Nolan J. reached the correct conclusions. I would therefore dismiss the cross-appeal and allow the council's appeal.

Notes

1. M. Jones comments: "in *Eastleigh*, the court's interpretation of s.34(3) affirms the orthodox view, and the legislature's intent, that the Commissioners ought not to usurp the policy-making discretions of democratically elected local authorities; . . . [nevertheless] the local ombudsmen may continue to find maladministration in the processes by which discretionary decisions are made upon grounds which closely resemble the *Wednesbury* principles of review employed by the courts—

relevancy, proper purposes and so on. And there may still be room for a finding of maladministration where a Commissioner considers that the terms of an authority's policy transcend to the bounds of reasonableness, and step into perversity, capriciousness, or what the courts now term 'irrationality' " ("The Local Ombudsman and Judicial Review" [1988] P.L. 608 at pp. 615–616.)

Whilst, on the issue of whether the Local Government Ombudsman had found that the complainant's injustice was caused by the Council's maladministration, Mowbray observed:

> "the division of opinion on this question by the Court of Appeal again clearly reflected the differing judicial attitudes towards the margin of appreciation to be accorded to the Local Ombudsman in performing his functions. Lord Donaldson was willing to allow the Ombudsman a wide latitude of freedom because, in his opinion, the Ombudsman was not required to produce the kind of reasoned decision expected of a superior court of law. But the majority were unwilling to make similar allowances when scrutinising the Ombudsman's logic. Therefore, if the Local Ombudsman is to avoid such criticisms in the future his reports will have to adopt a more precise and definitive form of reasoning."

("Maladministration and the Local Ombudsmen" (1988) S.J. 1442 at p. 1444.)

2. Despite the above opinion of Lord Donaldson that an action for judicial review of a Local Government Ombudsman's report "is inherently unlikely to succeed," the High Court found that a report made in 1986 by the Chairman of the English Commission for Local Administration was *ultra vires*. In *R.* v. *Commissioner for Local Administration, ex p. Croydon L.B.C.* [1989] 1 All E.R. 1033, the Local Government Ombudsman had investigated a complaint by parents about the way in which an education appeal committee, established by the council, had rejected their appeal regarding which school their daughter should attend. The Ombudsman concluded that the committee had been guilty of maladministration by giving undue weight to council policy concerning school admissions. In response, the council sought judicial review of the report arguing, *inter alia*, that the Ombudsman should not have investigated this complaint as the parents had a remedy before a court of law (section 26(6) of the Local Government Act 1974 provides: "A Local Commissioner shall not conduct an investigation . . . in respect of the following matters, . . . (*c*) any action in respect of which the person aggrieved has or had a remedy by way of proceedings in any court of law: Provided that a Local Commissioner may conduct an investigation notwithstanding the existence of such a right or remedy if satisfied that in the particular circumstances it is not reasonable to expect the person aggrieved to resort or have resorted to it. . . .").

In the judgment of Woolf L.J., the Ombudsman must consider whether the complainant comes within section 26(6) both before and during the course of an investigation. Furthermore, the High Court stressed its predominant role in the scrutiny of tribunals:

> "the Commissioner should also have well in mind, even when the holder of the office is a distinguished lawyer as in the case here, that his expertise is not the same as that of a court of law. Issues whether an administrative tribunal has properly understood the relevant law and the legal obligations which it is under when conducting an inquiry are more appropriate for resolution by the High Court than by a Commissioner, however eminent." (p. 1045)

The Court went on to conclude that there was no foundation for the Ombudsman's finding of maladministration.

Writing extra-judicially, Sir Harry Woolf has suggested that the Ombudsman (whether central or local) should have an express power to refer an issue to the court, whether before, during or after an investigation, "either because there is a point of law of significance involved or because the courts are in a better situation to provide a remedy than he is" (*Protection of the Public—A New Challenge* (1990), pp. 90–91). This would "make the best of both systems available to the public" (*ibid.*).

3. The willingness of some local authorities to seek judicial review of the Local Commissioners' reports (which can be contrasted with the absence of such litigation by central government bodies against the Parliamentary Commissioner) indicates that the relationship between councils and Local Government Ombudsmen is not always harmonious. A continuing example of this discord is the fact that in about 5 per cent. of cases where the Ombudsmen find a local authority guilty of maladministration causing injustice the authority fails to provide a remedy that is acceptable to the Ombudsmen. Consequently, the Local Government Ombudsmen argued before the Widdicombe Committee that, as in Northern Ireland, where a local authority failed to provide a suitable remedy the complainant should have the right to go to the County/Sheriff Court for a binding judicial order of compensation or remedial action. The Committee endorsed this method of strengthening the remedial powers of the Local Government Ombudsmen (Report para. 9.69).

At about the same time, the Select Committee on the P.C.A. proposed an alternative system for dealing with recalcitrant local authorities, that involved the Select Committee extending its remit to encompass such bodies. The Select Committee suggested that where a council failed to provide a suitable remedy then the leaders of the council could be called to give evidence before the Committee which, as we have already noted, is how reluctant Departments are dealt with. (*Local Government Cases: Enforcement of Remedies* H.C. 448 (1985–86)).

The Government accepted that non-compliance was a problem, "although a rate of compliance of 95 per cent. might in other circumstances be considered good for a voluntary system, it is the other 5 per cent. of "failures" which not unnaturally attract attention. There is no doubt that these cases serve to produce a particularly marked sense of grievance on the part of the complainants, as well as undermining the creditibility of the Local Ombudsman system as a whole."[28] However, the Government rejected the solution of judicial enforcement because, ". . . local authorities might be less willing to co-operate, and investigations would become increasingly formalised, lengthy, legalistic and costly. Complainants might find the process more intimidating and flexibility would be lost."[29] Moreover, the Select Committee's idea was also dismissed:

> "although this has its attractions in that it builds on the existing voluntary principle, it is unlikely to be readily acceptable to local government who do not see themselves as accountable to Parliament—though recognising that they operate within a statutory framework laid down by Parliament."[30]

Instead it was decided to increase the local pressure on councils to comply with Ombudsmen's reports. This approach has now been enacted in Part II of the Local Government and Housing Act 1989. Where a report finding injustice in consequence of maladministration has been made the relevant local authority must

[28] *The Government's Response to the Report of the Widdicombe Committee of Inquiry*, para. 6.21.
[29] *Ibid.* para. 6.22.
[30] *Ibid.* para. 6.23.

consider the report and notify the Local Government Ombudsman of the action they have taken within three months. If the authority does not notify the Ombudsman, or he is not satisfied with the action taken, he may issue a second report. Again, the authority must consider and notify the Ombudsman of its action regarding the second report. If the Ombudsman is still not satisfied with the authority's conduct he may publish an account of his recommendations in two editions of a local newspaper. This lengthy process is clearly less forceful than the Local Government Ombudsmen's desire for judicial enforcement of their reports. But, one commentator believes that the Local Government Ombudsmen should not seek outside help in strengthening their position *vis-à-vis* councils:

> "Ombudsmen may have to accept that their influence will depend upon the prestige generated by their own offices in their own political systems. To look for external buttresses from ministers, courts or select committees may do more to undermine than to support their authority"

(C. M. G. Himsworth, "Parliamentary Teeth for Local Ombudsmen?" [1986] P.L. 546 at p. 550).

(iii) The Work of the Local Ombudsmen

THE LOCAL OMBUDSMEN: ANNUAL REPORT 1990–91

Appendix 3(b) and para. 412, Appendix 3(d)

4.12
The 9,033 complaints on which decisions were made during the year were composed of:

8,551 (95%) in which investigation was not pursued beyond the stage of considering the authority's detailed comments on them. In 1,462 cases the complaints were settled locally. The average time taken to consider complaints to this stage was 18 weeks—the same as in the previous year.

163 (2%) in which investigation was discontinued at a later stage because it became clear that there had been no maladministration (90 cases) or the complaint was settled locally (73 cases). The average time taken for these investigations was 53½ weeks compared with 47½ weeks in the previous year.

319 (4%) in which investigation was continued to the issue of a formal report. In such cases everyone involved in the complaint would have been interviewed and all the relevant council files and documents examined. The average time for these investigations was 69½ weeks compared with 58 weeks in the previous year.

Appendix 3(b)

ANALYSIS OF TREATMENT OF COMPLAINTS 1990/91

Local Government Ombudsman	Total Complaints Considered	Concluded after initial enquiries	Formal investigation discontinued	Formal investigation reports issued			Complaints settled locally	Further reports issued
				MI	M	NM		
Dr Yardley	3,415	3,285	34	70	12	14	726	2
Mr Laws	2,515	2,387	50	58	6	14	292	11
Mrs Thomas	3,103	2,879	79	88	20	37	517	22
Totals	9,033	8,551	163	216	38	65	1,535	35

Note
The complaints 'concluded after initial enquiries' are those which were examined but investigation was not pursued beyond the stage of considering the authorities' detailed comments on them. For example, the council settled the complaint satisfactorily; or there was no evidence of maladministration by the council; or the matter was not one which the law allows the Local Government Ombudsman to investigate.

The abbreviations for the findings in formal reports mean:

MI —maladministration causing injustice
M —maladministration, no injustice
NM—no maladministration

Appendix 3(d)

SUBJECTS OF INVESTIGATION REPORTS 1990/91

	Dr Yardley		Mr Laws		Mrs Thomas		Totals	
Housing:								
Council Housing Management	18		7		15		40	
Council Housing Repairs	14		–		14		28	
Right to Buy Mortgages	7		3		12		22	
Housing Benefit	–		1		4		5	
Housing Grants	–		3		9		12	
Homelessness	–		4		1		5	
Private Housing Notices	5		–		–		5	
Harassment Eviction	4		–		–		4	
Other	1		–		1		2	
Housing Total		49		18		56		123
Planning:								
Neighbour Notification/ Consultation	6		9		19		34	
Enforcement	4		2		10		16	
Other	15		27		22		64	
Planning Total		25		38		51		114
Education		3		4		13		20
Social Services		5		4		8		17
Highways		4		1		4		9
Land		3		2		3		8
Environmental Health		5		3		4		12
Commercial		–		–		2		2
Leisure & Recreation		–		1		1		2
Rating/Community Charge		–		1		–		1
Drainage		–		4		–		4
Water		–		–		1		1
Consumer Protection		1		1		2		4
Miscellaneous		1		1		–		2
Totals		96		78		145		319

Notes

1. After a major empirical study, Professor N. Lewis and his colleagues reported that, "the impact of the Local Ombudsman upon local government has been impressive, both in relation to securing redress for complainants and in improving procedures" (Report p. 59) They were impressed with the general quality of the investigations conducted by the Ombudsmen. However, despite the efforts of the Ombudsmen, public awareness about the Local Commissioners was low (a survey indicated that only 38 per cent. of the electorate were aware of the Ombudsmen's existence). The researchers were critical of the concept of "maladministration"; "the interpretation afforded to maladministration has been inconsistent and unpredictable" (Report p. 228) They, consequently, suggested empowering the Local Ombudsmen to investigate "a matter relating to administration" with the objective of discovering if it complied with statutory codes of good administrative practice. Also these commentators recommended the abolition of the Representative Body (comprised wholly of local authority nominees) to whom the Local Ombudsmen historically reported. They felt that it was too executive minded. Instead, the Report proposed a new body with a wider membership, including consumer interests (N. Lewis, M. Seneviratne, S. Cracknell, *Complaints Procedures in Local Government*, (University of Sheffield) (1987)).

2. In another study, C. Crawford and B. Thompson concluded that it was difficult to determine the specific reasoning and principles behind many reports of the Local Ombudsmen. *Decisions of Local Ombudsmen* (Dept. of the Environment/Scottish and Welsh Offices) (1987, unpublished). Does this finding support the stance taken by the local authority in the *Eastleigh* case above?

3. Crawford has advocated the creation of a new institution ("the Commission for Local Administration") to whom the Local Ombudsmen would be responsible. The Commission would have a broad composition, including local authorities' representatives (but not a dominant number), private sector groups, legal and other professional associations, and lay bodies. Amongst the proposed functions of the Commission would be:

(1) enforcement of the Ombudsmen's reports by means of second opinions;
(2) administrative audit through the issuing of codes of guidance on administrative behaviour;
(3) keeping under review the jurisdiction and casework of the Local Ombudsmen.

He believes that the creation of such an institution would help to secure the provision of an integrated complaints system for local government (C. Crawford, "Complaints, Codes, and Ombudsmen in Local Government" [1988] P.L. 246).

4. Parliament has now abolished the Representative Bodies for England and Wales (Local Government and Housing Act 1989, s.25). From 1989 onwards the English and Welsh Local Government Ombudsmen must submit their annual reports to persons who represent local authorities (*e.g.* organisations like the Association of District Councils). The funding of the Local Government Ombudsmen has been transferred to central government (1989 Act, s.24). Also they may have advisers appointed as fellow members of their respective Commissions (1989 Act, s.22).

(D) Private Sector Ombudsmen

The financial services industry has taken the lead in the creation of ombudsmen to resolve disputes between consumers and commercial organisations. In 1980 three insurance companies agreed to create a voluntary ombudsman scheme for this industry and their innovative arrangements were later developed by the banking and building society industries. The insurance scheme has no statutory basis and, therefore, utilises the legal concept of a private unlimited company. A Board of Directors (dominated by representatives of the insurance industry) is responsible for the financing of the scheme. Whilst a lay dominated Council appoints the Insurance Ombudsman and receives his annual report. The Insurance Ombudsman is an independent person who can investigate specified consumer complaints against member companies. Where he upholds the complaint he can make a binding award of up to £100,000 against the member company. Five years later the major high street banks decided to follow the example of the insurance industry. The Banking Ombudsman scheme is broadly similar, though banks can remove individual complaints from the Ombudsman's remit where novel points of law are involved. Subsequently, Parliament passed the Building Societies Act 1986, which provided the impetus for the establishment of a Building Societies Ombudsman whose jurisdiction is based upon the requirements laid down in this Act.

The above ombudsmen have maintained close links and adopted a common conception of their role as impartial decision-makers. They tend to use similar techniques of investigation (notably the reliance on documentary evidence and the utilisation of experts to resolve questions of fact). Complainants were successful in 20–30 per cent. of the cases which were subject to formal reports by the various ombudsmen. Although these figures may appear low when compared with the public sector ombudsmen, they can be explained by the need for complainants to have exhausted internal redress before raising the matter with the private sector ombudsmen and the latter's attempts to achieve conciliated settlements.

Criticisms of the banking scheme have been made by the Jack Committee on Banking Services.[31] The Committee were particularly concerned about the apparent influence of the Board of Directors over the terms of reference of the Banking Ombudsman and the failure of some smaller banks to join the scheme. One structural reform might be the integration of the Banking and Building Societies Ombudsmen into one combined Commission (analogous to the Commission for Local Administration in England) dealing with complaints against both of these industries now that many of their services are similar.

Overall, the financial services ombudsmen have evolved without many express references to the heritage of the public sector ombudsmen. But, their original methods of investigation may be of relevance to the public sector ombudsmen (especially the P.C.A.) in developing a range of efficient techniques adapted to different types of complaints. See further, A. R. Mowbray, "Ombudsmen: The Private Sector Dimension" Finnie, Himsworth & Walker (eds.) *Edinburgh Essays in Public Law* (1991); R. James, "The Building Societies Ombudsman Scheme" (1992) 11 C.J.Q. 157; R. W. Hodges, "Ombudsman and other Complaints Procedures in the Financial Services Sector in the U.K." (1992) 21 Anglo-Am. L.R. 1. A. R. Mowbray, "Newspaper Ombudsmen: the British Experience" (1991) 12 *Journal of Media Law* 91.

(E) Other Complaints Mechanisms

The various Ombudsmen's offices discussed in this Chapter must be seen in the wider context of the formal and informal complaint mechanisms that exist in respect of the multifarious activities of the state, and which have come under increasing scrutiny in recent years. On the role of M.P.s in handling complaints,

[31] *Banking Services: Law and Practice* (Cm. 622, 1989).

see R. Rawlings, "Parliamentary Redress of Grievance" in C. Harlow (ed.), Public Law and Politics (1986) and "The MP's Complaints Service" (1990) 53 M.L.R. 22 and 149. On the handling of complaints in local government, see N. Lewis and P. Birkinshaw, "Taking Complaints Seriously: A Study in Local Government Practice" in M. Partington and J. Jowell, *Welfare Law and Social Policy* (1979); N. Lewis, M. Seneviratne and S. Cracknell, *Complaints Procedures in Local Government* (1987), summarised by the latter two authors at (1988) 66 *Public Administration* 181; P. McCarthy, *et al., Grievances, Complaints and Local Government* (1992). In 1978, the Local Authorities Association published a Code of Practice, *Complaints Procedures. A Code of Practice for Local Government and Waters Authorities for dealing with queries and complaints.* More generally, see P. Burkinshaw, *Grievances, Remedies and the State* (1985), Ch. 2.

Birkinshaw (*op. cit.*) has noted the "pervasive" practice among government departments of adopting informal or formal but unpublished mechanisms for dealing with complaints, as an aid to discretion or as a means of avoiding "a more rigorous and formal statutory process of hearing grievances or complaints" (Birkinshaw, in P. McAuslan and John F. McEldowney (eds.), *Law, Legitimacy and the Constitution* (1985), pp. 164–165). These processes are generally relatively obscure. ". . . [T]here is little to believe other than that the standard of decision is high;" on the other hand, "[p]owerful institutions can use the informality of relationship, especially if it is a continuing one with a department, to negotiate a favourable position against other competitors or interests" (Birkinshaw, *op. cit.*, p. 165). The Council on Tribunals has protested against the introduction of internal review procedures as a substitute for a right of appeal to an independent body: see Annual Reports for 1989–90 (1990–91 H.C. 64), paras. 1.6–1.10, and 1990–91 (1991–92 H.C. 97), paras. 3.25–3.28, and see above, p. 135.

The importance of complaints procedures has received a new emphasis in the government's *Citizen's Charter* (Cm. 1599, 1991). The Charter applies to all public services, including government departments and agencies, nationalised industries, local authorities, the NHS, the courts, police and emergency services, and to the key utilities in the private sector. The following extract sets out what the citizen is entitled to expect.

THE CITIZEN'S CHARTER: RAISING THE STANDARD

Cm. 1599, 1991

The Principles of Public Service

Every citizen is entitled to expect:

• Standards
Explicit standards, published and prominently displayed at the point of delivery. These standards should invariably include courtesy and helpfulness from staff, accuracy in accordance with statutory entitlements, and a commitment to prompt action, which might be expressed in terms of a target response or waiting time. If targets are to be stretched, it may not be possible to guarantee them in every case; minimum, as well as average, standards may be necessary. There should be a clear presumption that standards will be progressively improved as services become more efficient.

• Openness
There should be no secrecy about how public services are run, how much

they cost, who is in charge, and whether or not they are meeting their standards. Public servants should not be anonymous. Save only where there is a real threat to their safety, all those who deal directly with the public should wear name badges and give their name on the telephone and in letters.

- **Information**

Full, accurate information should be readily available, in plain language, about what services are being provided. Targets should be published, together with full and audited information about the results achieved. Wherever possible, information should be in comparable form, so that there is a pressure to emulate the best.

- **Choice**

The public sector should provide choice wherever practicable. The people affected by services should be consulted. Their views about the services they use should be sought regularly and systematically to inform decisions about what services should be provided.

- **Non-discrimination**

Services should be available regardless of race or sex. Leaflets are being printed in minority languages where there is a need. In Wales public bodies are aware of the needs of Welsh speakers.

- **Accessibility**

Services should be run to suit the convenience of customers, not staff. This means flexible opening hours, and telephone inquiry points that direct callers quickly to someone who can help them.

- **And if things go wrong?**

At the very least, the citizen is entitled to a good explanation, or an apology. He or she should be told **why** the train is late, or **why** the doctor could not keep the appointment. There should be a well-publicised and readily available complaints procedure. If there is a serious problem, it should be put right. And lessons must be learnt so that mistakes are not repeated. Nobody wants to see money diverted from service improvement into large-scale compensation for indifferent services. But the Government intends to introduce new forms of redress where these can be made to stimulate rather than distract from efficiency.

Note

The Select Committee on the Parliamentary Commissioner has noted:

> "In several ways the charter programme provides an opportunity to raise standards in public services, and thus hopefully reduce the number of grievances which might come to the Commissioner. The standards set out in individual charters should also provide the Commissioner with benchmarks (albeit not the only benchmarks) against which he can determine whether there has been maladministration. Time and the Commissioner's reports will tell how effective the charter programme has been in those areas subject to his jurisdiction" ((1991–92) H.C. 158 at p. ix).

Part II

JUDICIAL REVIEW

INTRODUCTORY NOTE TO PART II

The remainder of this book is concerned with the role of the courts in relation to the administration of government. A person affected by an act or omission of a public authority may be able to bring the matter before a court in any of the following circumstances:

(i) where the act is *ultra vires* (*i.e.* beyond the powers of the authority); or where the authority has omitted to perform a legal duty of a public nature;

(ii) where an error of law appears "on the face of the record" of a decision taken,

In each of these situations the normal, if not only procedure, will be to seek an *application for judicial review* in the High Court under Ord. 53 R.S.C. The various *grounds of challenge* for judicial review will be considered in detail in Ch. 6–10: matters of *procedure and remedy* in applications for judicial review will be dealt with in Ch. 12.

In addition to proceedings for judicial review a matter may be taken to a court:

(iii) where statute provides for a right of *appeal* to a court against a decision taken or a proposed course of action. Such appeal will be to the kind of court specified in the statutory provision, and the grounds of appeal will be as wide or as narrow as there defined. In this context we shall have occasion to note in certain contexts—"statutory applications to quash"—in which although in form the procedure resembles an appeal, in terms of the grounds of challenge the *substance* is more akin to judicial review. These various matters will form the subject-matter of Ch. 11.

(iv) where the act or omission constitutes the commission of a tort or a breach of contract in respect of which redress may be obtained through the courts. The liability of public authorities in contract and tort is considered in Ch. 13. Such claims may either be brought by the ordinary procedures of civil litigation, or may form a part of the remedies sought in an application for judicial review.

Although, understandably, of particular concern to lawyers, it will be apparent from the materials in Part I of this book that recourse to the courts is but one way of seeking redress of a grievance. We have already considered, and stressed the importance of, other non-judicial procedures—appeals to specially created tribunals, opportunities to raise objections at public inquiries, complaints to and investigations by Ombudsmen, intervention of M.P.s or local councillors to seek to secure resolution of the matter.

Appreciation that judicial review is one of a number of means of seeking redress should not, however, lead to its significance being underestimated. The last three decades have witnessed notable developments in the substance, and the improvement and simplification of the procedures, of judicial review. A period of "judicial activism" dating from the early 1960s has developed and refined the various grounds of challenge; and the "new" R.S.C. Ord. 53 introduced in 1977 rationalised procedures for judicial review challenge. At the same time there has been a very considerable increase in the number of judicial review applications being brought before the courts, a specialist Bar has emerged, and the procedural reforms have led to these cases (the Crown Office List) being handled by a nucleus of designated judges with expertise in this area.

Moreover, the significance of judicial review should not be measured by the quantity of case-law generated. At its heart is the notion of the "rule of law"—that government has only those powers which have been bestowed upon it, and must exercise those powers in accordance with certain principles of presumed Parliamentary intention. The substance of judicial review is an examination of how the judges have operated this "police" jurisdiction over the administration. The principles of judicial review should, in outline at least, be known to administrators and influence the exercise of their functions. Concern that this was not sufficiently the case led the Treasury to issue to administrators, in 1987, a brief guide to the grounds of judicial review (*The Judge Over Your Shoulder*—Treasury Solicitor's Department). The purpose of the guide was stated to be to give administrators some basic grounding in the principles of review so that they would be less likely to act in ways which would give rise to a successful challenge. It is significant that on the first page of the document it is stated that "scarcely a day passes without the *Times Law Report* containing one or more cases where someone is challenging the decisions, or actions, of central or local government or a public body."

The next five chapters will comprise a detailed examination of the various grounds of challenge by way of judicial review. Most of the various grounds of challenge are, at root, aspects of the notion of *ultra vires*, and it may be helpful if this notion and the essence of each of the grounds of challenge is explained before they are tackled in detail.

The Ultra Vires Principle—Grounds of Challenge by way of Judicial Review

The essence of the supervisory, judicial review, jurisdiction inherent in the High Court is to ensure that persons or bodies exercising functions under statute or, exceptionally, the royal prerogative, do not exceed or abuse their powers; and also to ensure that such persons or bodies perform such duties as have been imposed upon them. An act or decision which is beyond the powers of the actor/decision-maker is *ultra vires*, and, subject to the matters to be discussed below in Chapters 14 and 15, may be regarded as having no legal validity.

There are a variety of ways in which a body may act in excess of its powers or may abuse its powers. This is reflected in the emergence of judicial opinions and in the writings of commentators of a "catalogue" of grounds of challenge.

Each of these grounds is no more than a sub-species of the broader governing notion of *ultra vires*. Some of the grounds "overlap," so that it may sometimes be successfully argued that a decision is tainted on more than one ground—and some decisions of courts expressly taken on the basis of one ground of challenge might equally well have been based on one of the other grounds. Moreover, the various grounds may not, as we shall see, cover the entire field of *ultra vires*—the door remains open for further grounds of challenge to develop. Nevertheless, the various grounds of challenge are of considerable value as a check-list by which to assess the *vires* of an act or decision. The "catalogue" is also of importance for its explanatory power—helping in the demonstration of, and providing constant reminder of, the subtlety and sophistication of the judicial elaboration of the *ultra vires* doctrine. For these reasons we have in this book preferred the traditional categorisation of the grounds of review to that suggested by Lord Diplock in the *CCSU* case (see below). His Lordship's simple division of challenges into those alleging "illegality," those alleging "irrationality," and those alleging "procedural impropriety" is valuable in drawing important distinctions between the bases of the various traditional grounds of review. We do not, however, consider that this trilogy of labels should become a substitute for the traditional "catalogue."

The traditional catalogue—in outline

i. "Simple" *ultra vires* and "jurisdictional control"

By "simple" *ultra vires* we mean the situation where a body which has power to do X and Y, in fact does Z. The purported act or decision Z will be *ultra vires*. See below, pp. 200–210.

By "jurisdictional control" we mean the situation where a body's power to do X is not conferred "at large," but has been conferred to be exercisable only in certain circumstances defined in the legislation: *i.e.* power to do X where conditions A and B prevail. In this situation if the body purports to do X in circumstances where A and B do not prevail its act or decision will be *ultra vires*. See below, pp. 210–262.

In each of these situations the task for the reviewing court is to determine the meaning in law of the jurisdictional parameters to the conferment of power, and then to determine whether on the facts the body challenged has acted within or beyond its powers. A body which has exceeded its powers may have done so because of its erroneous view as to the scope of its powers (errors of jurisdictional law) or because of an erroneous understanding of prevailing fact (error of jurisdictional fact).

ii. Failure to retain discretion as to exercise of power

Here the challenger does not dispute that a particular power is possessed in the circumstances by the body challenged. The challenge is based on failure to comply with an obligation, which the courts imply from the legislative grant of power, to retain and to exercise a free and unfettered discretion as to the exercise or non-exercise of that power. Such fettering of discretion may occur in various ways, and gives rise to sub-divisions of this ground of challenge. See below pp. 263–267 (acting under dictation), pp. 284–295 (over-rigid adherence to self-created policy), pp. 295–319 (fettering discretion by contractual or other undertakings affecting exercise of power), pp. 338–339 (fettering discretion by unduly narrow construction of scope of discretionary power).

In this section it will be appropriate also to consider the "rule against delegation" of powers (this can be regarded as a want of power in the delegate, or a failure personally to exercise the power by the delegator), see below pp. 267–284; and also the issue of estoppel in public law—to what extent may a body's past assertion/assurance as to the scope of its powers, or as to how it will exercise its powers, prevent it from subsequently denying such power or prevent it from exercising powers so as to defeat expectations which its assurances may have engendered—see below pp. 319–338 and 419–437.

iii. Challenge for "abuse of discretion"

Such challenges are based on argument that a power has been exercised by the body in question for a purpose other than one for which the power was conferred—below pp. 340–362; or that in determining how to exercise the power the body took into account considerations which were irrelevant to the proper exercise of the power; or that there was a failure to have taken into account all the considerations which were relevant—below, pp. 362–394; or on the ground that the manner of exercise of the power was patently unreasonable—not such as any reasonable body could have determined—below, pp. 394–418.

iv. Challenge on grounds of procedural irregularity

This covers:

(a) failure to have complied with a procedural requirement expressly provided in the legislative grant of power. The task for the reviewing court is to determine whether or not in all the circumstances the failure to comply makes the decision or act invalid. See below pp. 448–468.

(b) failure to comply with natural justice requirements which are implied by the judges, in some contexts, into statutory conferments of power. The rules of natural justice are two:
- that a decision-maker should not decide a matter in respect of which he has a financial interest or in respect of which there may be reason to suspect he may be biased—see below pp. 565–592;
- that no person should be seriously affected by the exercise of power without having first been informed of the intention to exercise the power and been given an appropriate opportunity to make representations before a final decision is taken—see below pp. 469–565.

v. Challenge for error of law on the face of the record

This ground of challenge differs from those outlined above in that it is not based on the notion of *ultra vires*. The ground of challenge has a long history—the court of King's Bench seeking to impose its view as to the law on courts of inferior jurisdiction. It is not any matter of surprise that where a reviewing court can see from the "record" of a decision of a body subject to judicial review that that body has adopted an erroneous interpretation of law in coming to a conclusion the reviewing court will want to intervene. It will, understandably, be of significance to examine the notion of the "record." See below pp. 593–604. Errors of law not apparent from the "record" will only ground a successful judicial review challenge where the matter can be brought within one of the grounds of review outlined earlier.

Notes

1. Judicial decision-making in any branch of law is not simply a mechanical process of logical reasoning, with the judges finding the facts and applying precisely formulated legal rules to those facts. This is perhaps particularly true of decision-making in public law, where many of the "rules" (especially the grounds for judicial review) are in fact broadly drawn principles, and where the trend is, if anything, for the grounds of review to become less rather than more specific (see for example, the case law on procedural *ultra vires*, on the duty to act fairly and on standing (below, pp. 448–468, 494–502). Moreover, remedies in administrative law are almost invariably discretionary (pp. 764–774). Thus, in practice, the judges possess considerable leeways of choice, and it becomes particularly important to attempt to discern the values that may influence their decision-making. One difficulty here is that it is unusual for these values to be expressly articulated.

Commentators have identified a variety of themes. J.A.G. Griffith (*The Politics of the Judiciary* (4th ed., 1991)) notes the homogeneity of the background of the judiciary (almost all male, predominantly public school and Oxbridge) and argues that:

> "These judges have by their education and training and the pursuit of their profession as barristers, acquired a strikingly homogenous collection of atti-

tudes, beliefs and principles, which to them represent the public interest. . . . The judicial conception of the public interest, seen in the cases discussed in this book, is threefold. It concerns, first, the interest of the state (including its moral welfare); secondly, the preservation of law and order, broadly interpreted; and, thirdly, the promotion of certain political views normally associated with the Conservative Party" (pp. 275, 278).

One of his chapters (Ch. 4) deals with cases on the control of discretionary powers. For criticism, see Lord Devlin, (1978) 41 M.L.R. 501; S. Lee, *Judging Judges* (1988), Ch. 4. Lee comments (p. 35):

> "Yet Griffith is merely saying that he disagrees with the decisions. One would get the impression that he would almost always decide the opposite way against property, stability, the Conservative Party, etc. But would this be preferable? Would it be more democratic? . . . Does the evidence really show that judges act in this way? Is law really explicable in terms of class interests?"

P. McAuslan ("Administrative Law, Collective Consumption and Judicial Policy" (1983) 46 M.L.R. 1) detected from case-law in the 1970s and early 1980s (such as the *Bromley* case (below, pp. 372–384)) the "only coherent jurisprudence of administrative law" that had emerged was "basically antipathetic" to the processes of "collective consumption." This term refers to the services (such as education, health care, social welfare, environmental and cultural facilities, highways, public transport, public housing, land use regulation and urban planning) that are organised, planned and managed on a collective public basis by central or local government or quangos, and are consumed collectively ((1983) 46 M.L.R. at p. 2). McAuslan also detected a "most significant division of judicial opinions":

> "This is between the Divisional Court, staffed for the most part by judges whose whole working life and success has coincided with, and indeed has been in large part formed by, the growth of the processes of collective consumption and the judges in the Court of Appeal and House of Lords, who for the most part either passed their formative and working years in different political milieu, or are generally not over-sympathetic to or understanding of the processes of collective consumption. The former judges with their greater understanding of modern administration and politics, and their more recent involvement as lawyers in those processes, are clearly much more reluctant to get drawn into the maelstrom of political and ideological conflicts which masquerade as legal issues justiciable in courts. They appear to be more sensibly aware of the long-term dangers of judges appearing to adopt a partisan political role through their judgments in the courts. In the higher reaches of the judiciary, it seems to be believed that if your judgment is long and full of extracts of statutes and previous decisions, no one will notice that it is a political statement and if anybody does and says so, they can be dismissed as "prejudiced" and in some obscure way "failing to uphold the rule of law."[11] (footnotes omitted; *ibid.*, p. 19).

D. Feldman ("Public Law Values in the House of Lords" (1990) 106 L.Q.R. 246) suggests that the dominant political theory among law lords since 1981 has been "democratic elitism," which:

> "restricts public participation to a periodic take-it-or-leave-it choice between competing political élites, freeing the elected group to do much as it will between elections."

(*ibid.*, at p. 247). Feldman notes the restrictions on judicial review inherent in cases on the limited applicability of review for irrationality where action has been approved by Parliament (below, pp. 400–403) on where the decision-maker is responsible to Parliament, (*e.g. R.* v. *Secretary of State for Trade and Industry, ex p. Lonrho plc.*, below, pp. 351–358; the marked deference to the political judgment of ministers where national security is in issue; and a lack of enthusiasm for a more participatory model of democracy (*cf.* the *Bushell* case, below, p. 550). Other values identified include deference to the professional expertise of administrators (*cf.* the *Puhlhofer* case, below pp. 226–231) and the limited recognition of individual rights.

> "Where rights are recognised they are important: schemes which interfere with rights will be zealously scrutinised; but those dependent on public benefits are not generally seen as having rights, so administrators of schemes conferring benefits are given a freer rein"

(*ibid.* at p. 259). Moreover, the European Convention on Human Rights has not been seen as conferring on individuals rights to be protected by English law, (*cf.* the *Brind* case, decided more recently than Feldman's article). Finally, Feldman notes that "principled consistency" has tended to give way to pragmatism, usually in the interests of government, (*e.g.* the comparison between *Manchester City Council* v. *Greater Manchester County Council* (below, p. 202) and *Re Westminster City Council* (below, p. 202)). In developing this analysis Feldman points out that the general picture does conceal heterogeneous approaches, with certain judges giving greater weight (usually in dissent) to rights or to principled consistency.

It may be helpful to keep these perspectives in mind when considering cases set out in this book. For example, how far do the cases bear out Feldman's argument that the judges in the House of Lords are tending, following the era of development in the 1960s and 1970s, towards a more restrictive approach to the availability of judicial review?

One factor that should not simply be assumed to be constant is the extent to which public authorities have been willing to take action known or suspected to be unlawful. There are well-known cases where Labour local councils have taken steps fairly clearly in defiance of the law, (*e.g.* some aspects of "Poplarism" in the 1920s: see below, p. 363; the Clay Cross affair: below, p. 110; the proceedings arising out of the wilful misconduct of Liverpool City councillors in delaying making a rate: below, pp. 541–545). On the other hand, it has been said that the (Conservative):

> "governments since 1979 have become increasingly careless of their obligations to comply with the law in the implementation of their policies. Indeed so general has become this abuse and excess of power, and the taking of actions of doubtful legality that observers would be forgiven for thinking that there was a studied practice of such behaviour."

(P. McAuslan and J.F. McEldowney, "Legitimacy and the Constitution: the Dissonance between Theory and Practice" in McAuslan and McEldowney (eds.), *Law, Legitimacy and the Constitution* (1985), Ch. 1, p. 28, giving (at pp. 28–31) 12 of the "more noteworthy examples of this casual approach to the use of governmental power" between 1979 and 1985).

2. Research on the statistics of judicial review has been conducted by Maurice Sunkin (see "What has been happening to applications for judicial review" (1987) 50 M.L.R. 432 (covering 1981–86) and "The Judicial Review Case-Load 1987–1989" [1991] P.L. 490). This shows that while the overall figures show a substantial growth in applications for judicial review in civil matters (356 applications for

leave in 1981; 938 in 1986; over 1350 in 1989), the figures are dominated by applications in particular subject areas, especially immigration and housing. However, the immigration cases peaked in 1985 (particularly with "genuine visitor" cases) and 1987 (with asylum cases), and there is in fact an increasing range of central government departments appearing as respondents in judicial review cases, with the commonest respondent, the Home Office, counting for a reducing proportion of the cases.

It is wrong to judge the efficacy of judicial review solely by reference to the case load. Harlow and Rawlings (*Law and Administration* (1984), p. 258) note not only that "the number of cases is infinitesimal compared with the millions of decisions taken daily by public authorities" but also that one court decision may affect "perhaps thousands of similar cases" and that "the mere existence of judicial review and the creation of precedent may influence administrative behaviour" (*ibid.* p. 261).

M. Sunkin and A. P. Le Sueur ("Can Government Control Judicial Review?" (1991) C.L.P. 161) record the establishment of an official group of high level civil servants to examine the perceived growth in the number of successful applications against government departments, and the consequent steps taken within the civil service. Civil servants were encouraged to reduce the risks of legal challenge by anticipating and planning for challenge throughout their decision-making, rather than simply reacting after the event. Legislation should be expressed in the clearest possible terms; steps should be taken to improve and broaden the quality of legal awareness, with the circulation of the pamphlet *The Judge Over Your Shoulder* and improved training, and the development of closer relationships between policy-makers and departmental lawyers. Moreover, the aim seems not to be entirely negative and defensive. Interviewees told the researchers that, for example, legal awareness training was "aimed at inculcating habits of good administrative conduct" (p. 172). The overall impression was:

> "that if the new ethos is having an effect it is to encourage officials to become more cautious in their work and more aware of the need to explain and justify action"

(p. 175). Judicial review was, moreover, only one of many external constraints, which included the P.C.A., M.P.s, Select Committees, the media, pressure and interest groups and, increasingly, the EC and the ECHR; these had to be set alongside the "internal organisational, policy, financial and other constraints which encroach upon operational practice" (*ibid.*).

> "When decision-makers are constantly forced to balance competing and possibly conflicting constraints, risks of challenge are incurred as an inevitable part of administrative life. The new ethos can do little to change this, save that by obliging decision-takers consciously to address the legal implications of their action, risk-taking may become a more informed, deliberate and explicit process"

(*ibid.*).

The point is also made that:

> "despite the perceptions of the senior officials that we interviewed, ignorance of the most elementary legal principles (let alone understanding of how they will be applied by the courts) is still likely to be endemic particularly amongst those charged with routine decision-making."

(*ibid.*). Examples are provided by the administration of the Social Fund (see R. Drabble and T. Lynes, [1989] P.L. 297 and the Annual Reports of the Social Fund Commissioner, noting recurring weaknesses in the decision-making of Social Fund Officers) and housing benefits (see I. Loveland, "Housing benefit: Administrative Law and Administrative Practice" (1988) 66 *Public Administration* 57.

On the involvement of lawyers in local government decision-making, see Lee Bridges, *et al.*, *Legality and Local Politics* (1987). For comments on *The Judge Over Your Shoulder*, see A.W. Bradley, [1987] P.L. 485 and [1988] P.L. 1.

3. The vast majority of the cases on judicial review concern powers based on statute. However, exercises of power by reference to the royal prerogative are also subject to judicial review. The courts have for centuries asserted the power to ensure that a prerogative power which is relied upon does in truth exist (*Case of Proclamations* (1611) 12 Co.Rep. 74; *Burmah Oil Co.* v. *Lord Advocate* [1965] A.C. 75) and has not been superseded by statute (*Att.-Gen.* v. *De Keyser's Royal Hotel Ltd.* [1920] A.C. 508; *R.* v. *Secretary of State for the Home Department, ex p. Northumbria Police Authority* [1989] Q.B. 26).

The House of Lords in *Council of Civil Service Unions* v. *Minister for the Civil Service* [1985] A.C. 374 held that at least delegated powers referable to the prerogative were in principle subject to judicial review for abuse of discretion or procedural impropriety. However, not all the prerogative powers were justiciable; *per* Lord Roskill at p. 418:

> "Prerogative powers such as those relating to the making of treaties, the defence of the realm, the prerogative of mercy, the grant of honours, the dissolution of Parliament and the appointment of ministers as well as others are not, I think, susceptible to judicial review because their nature and subject matter is such as not to be amenable to the judicial process."

Powers that have been held to be justiciable include the administration of the civil service, other than where action was necessitated by the requirements of national security (the *C.C.S.U.* case); the issue or denial of passports (*R.* v. *Secretary of State for Foreign and Commonwealth Affairs, ex p. Everett, The Independent*, December 4, 1987); the case of a warrant authorising telephone tapping (*R.* v. *Secretary of State for the Home Department, ex p. Ruddock* [1987] 1 W.L.R. 1482, below, p. 434 see now the Interception of Communications Act 1985).

The exercise of contractual powers by public authorities has also been held to be subject to judicial review in some contexts. See below, pp. 714–715.

On the *C.C.S.U.* case, see H.W.R. Wade, (1985) 101 L.Q.R. 153; G.S. Morris, [1985] P.L. 177; S. Lee, [1985] P.L. 186; K. Ewing, [1985] C.L.J. 1; C.F. Forsyth, (1985) 36 N.I.L.Q. 25; I.S. Dickinson, (1985) 30 J.L.S. 112.

On judicial review and the prerogative, see C. Walker, "Review of the Prerogative: The Remaining Issues" [1987] P.L. 62; B. Hough, "Judicial review where the Attorney-General refuses to act: time for a change" (1988) 8 L.S. 189; B.V. Harris, "Judicial review of the prerogative of mercy?" [1991] P.L. 386.

For a general survey of the modern scope of judicial review, see D. Oliver, "Is the *ultra vires* rule the Basis of Judicial Review?" [1987] P.L. 543.

CHAPTER 6

JURISDICTIONAL CONTROL

(A) "SIMPLE" ULTRA VIRES—THE BASIC PRINCIPLES

ATTORNEY-GENERAL v. FULHAM CORPORATION

[1921] 1 Ch. 440; 90 L.J. Ch. 281; 125 L.T. 14; 85 J.P. 213; 37 T.L.R. 156
(Chancery Division, Sargant J.)

THE defendant, a statutory authority, had power under the Baths and Wash-houses Acts 1846 to 1878 to establish baths, wash-houses and open bathing places. In the exercise of these powers it had for many years operated a wash-house at which persons coming to the wash-house had an opportunity of washing their clothes. The only assistance given, beyond the provision of the facilities, was that an attendant operated the "hydro-extractor" (wringer), and another attendant controlled the "box mangle." In due course, the corporation resolved to "confer a lasting benefit on all classes of the community" by "establishing a system of mechanical washing" in the borough. A public notice was issued, headed—"Household problem solved! A boon to housewives!!!." The notice continued: "the Council has established a department at the baths and wash-house, for the purpose of relieving Housewives to a great extent of this most laborious work." The new scheme involved the purchase of a bag. This the customer would fill with washing and leave at the wash-house. The laundered washing would later be delivered to the customer, or the customer could collect.

SARGANT J. This is an action by the Attorney-General, at the relation of the ratepayers of Fulham, against the municipal borough of Fulham, to restrain it, to use a short phrase, from carrying on a laundry, or something in the nature of a laundry.

In considering what the corporation may do, and what it may not do, I have to take as my guiding authority the words of Lord Selborne L.C. in *Attorney-General* v. *Great Eastern Ry. Co.* (1880) 5 App.Cas. 473, 478. He says: "I assume that your Lordships will not now recede from anything that was determined in *Ashbury Ry. Co.* v. *Riche* (1875) L.R. 7 H.L. 653. It appears to me to be important that the doctrine of *ultra vires*, as it was explained in that case, should be maintained. But I agree with James L.J. that this doctrine ought to be reasonably, and not unreasonably, understood and applied, and that whatever may fairly be regarded as incidental to, or consequential upon, those things which the Legislature has authorized, ought not (unless expressly prohibited) to be held, by judicial construction, to be *ultra vires*." That recognizes that in every case it is for a corporation of this kind to show that it has affirmatively an authority to do particular acts; but that in applying that principle, the rule is not to be applied too narrowly, and the corporation is entitled to do not only that which is expressly authorized but that which is reasonably incidental to or consequential upon that which is in terms authorized. And it is, of course, for the defendant corporation to point out the authority under which it has acted in what it has done. [His Lordship stated the facts, as set out above, including the new laundry scheme, and continued:] Now that is the new scheme and the method of carrying it out, and the question I have to consider is this, whether that scheme is authorized by the Baths and Wash-houses Act 1846, and the Baths and Wash-houses Act, 1847.

It is quite clear that the new scheme of the corporation is not directly authorized by those Acts, but I have also to see, whether, although it is not authorized in terms by the Acts, it is something which in the language I have cited, "may fairly be regarded as incidental to or consequent upon those things which the Legislature has authorized." For that purpose I have to look at the two Acts. [His Lordship summarised the principal provisions of the Acts, and continued:]

Now what is the effect of that legislation? It appears to me to be quite clear that the whole scheme is to afford facilities for persons who have not such facilities themselves and cannot pay for them, so that they may, so far as the wash-houses are concerned, do their own washing. Throughout there is no sort of suggestion, as far as I can see, that anything is to be provided for those persons except facilities for their doing the work themselves. . . .

Under the new system which has been inaugurated what has been provided for the persons who become customers is, in my judgment, not facilities for doing their own washing, but the washing itself. It seems to me that, in view of the fact that the control of the articles in question is entirely parted with, that the articles are washed up to a certain point absolutely and entirely irrespective of the labours or attention or care of the customers, and that the articles when that process has been gone through are redelivered in their semi-finished state to the customers, it is impossible to say that the council have been doing anything else except the washing of the clothes down to a certain point for the particular customers. Now is that something which may fairly be regarded as incidental to or consequential upon the provision of facilities for washing? In my judgment, it is not. . . .

There will therefore be a declaration that the defendant corporation is not entitled to carry on any enterprise which involves the total or partial washing of clothes for others by the defendant corporation, as distinguished from facilities for enabling others to come to the wash-house to wash their clothes; and there will be an injunction to restrain the defendant corporation, its officers, servants and agents, acting in contravention of this declaration. . . .

Notes

1. A feature of the case which seems to have weighed with Sargant J. in reaching his decision that the municipal enterprise of operating the laundry was *ultra vires*

was that, notwithstanding the opinion of the council sub-committee which had recommended the scheme, it appeared that the laundry was to be a substantial loss-making activity. Sargant J. discussed, in this connection, the economics of an aspect of this scheme that involved the establishment of a horse and van delivery service, and concluded:

> "the service is being performed at about half . . . of the cost to the Council. That is an instance I think . . . of the light way in which operations are conducted by persons who have not their own pockets to consider, but who have behind them what they regard as the unlimited or nearly unlimited purse of the ratepayers."

2. The notion of implied incidental/consequential powers was first worked out in the nineteenth century in relation to the powers of statutory undertakers such as the railway companies. Hence the cases referred to in *Fulham*. Note also, *Baroness Wenlock* v. *River Dee Company* (1884–85) 10 App.Cas. 354. The respondent company was empowered by an Act of 1851 to borrow up to £25,000 on mortgage. The company subsequently borrowed on mortgage over £150,000. The House of Lords held that the lender's executors could only recover £25,000. In the course of his speech Lord Watson said (at p. 362): "I am of opinion not only that the objects which the corporation may legitimately pursue must be ascertained from the Act itself, but that the powers which the corporation may lawfully use in furtherance of those objects must be expressly conferred or derived by reasonable implication from its provisions. That appears to me to be the principle recognised by this House in *Ashbury Company* v. *Riche* . . ., and in *Attorney-General* v. *Great Eastern Railway Company*. . . ."

3. This is an example of a relator action: see further below, p. 781.

4. Other recent examples of successful challenges of this sort include the following. In *R.* v. *Manchester City Council, ex p. Fulford* (1982) 81 L.G.R. 292, the schools sub-committee of the education committee resolved that corporal punishment should be abolished in all the city's schools. This resolution was confirmed by the education committee and the council, but was quashed by certiorari on the ground that it concerned the general direction of the conduct of the school rather than its general educational character and was thus for the school governors to determine and not the council, in accordance with the Articles of Government for County Secondary Schools.

In *Re Westminster City Council* [1986] A.C. 668, the House of Lords held that a proposed grant of £40m to the Inner London Education Authority by the Greater London Council, approved shortly before the latter's abolition under the Local Government Act 1985, was *ultra vires*. The 1985 Act made complete and comprehensive provision for the financing of the new ILEA, and only a clear express provision in the Act enabling the GLC to make such a grant could have given it power to do so. Moreover, grants to certain "umbrella bodies" for distribution to named voluntary associations after abolition should they not otherwise be funded, and to the revenue reserve for the funding of an arts centre, were also *ultra vires*. These grants offended the principle that local government finance is conducted on an annual basis. (*Cf. R.* v. *Greater London Council, ex p. London Residuary Body* (1986) 19 H.L.R. 175.)

Most spectacularly, the House of Lords held in *Hazell* v. *Hammersmith and Fulham London Borough Council* [1991] 2 W.L.R. 372 that interest rate swap transactions entered into on behalf of the council (and many other local authorities) were *ultra vires*. These were speculative transactions on the money markets, entered into in order to make a profit; profits were dependent on interest rates falling, but in fact they increased. The council's auditor obtained a declaration under section 19 of the Local Government Finance Act 1982 that these transactions were contrary to law; otherwise, the council stood to lose in excess of £100m. The transactions were not authorised by Schedule 13 to the Local Government Act 1972, which covered borrowing by local authorities, or by section 111 of that Act (see below, p. 207). (Litigation is proceeding on the question whether these sums are nevertheless recoverable by the banks as a matter of private law, with some cases having been settled). See generally, M. Loughlin, "Innovative Financing in Local Government Law: The Limits of Legal Instrumentalism" [1990] P.L. 372 and [1991] P.L. 568.

ATTORNEY-GENERAL v. CRAYFORD URBAN DISTRICT COUNCIL

[1962] 1 Ch. 575; [1962] 2 W.L.R. 998; 126 J.P. 308; 106 S.J. 175; [1962] 2 All E.R. 147; 60 L.G.R. 261; (Court of Appeal)

The defendant council as housing authority entered into an arrangement with the Municipal Mutual Insurance Ltd. whereby they agreed to recommend to their tenants that they should insure their household furniture and effects with that insurance company. The council acted as agents for the company, the insurance premiums (5d. per week) being collected by council rent-collectors with the rent and rates. The council retained 15 per cent. of the premiums as commission, and made a profit out of the transaction; 893 out of 3,100 tenants took advantage of the scheme.

The Attorney-General, at and by the relation of the Prudential Staff Union, a trade union established with the object, *inter alia*, of maintaining, protecting and advancing the interests of its members, sought a declaration that the council was not empowered to effect the insurance of the personal and household goods belonging to persons occupying housing accommodation provided by it or to collect premiums in respect of such insurance and that the effecting of the insurance and the collection of the premiums were *ultra vires* the council, and an injunction to restrain the council by itself, its servants or agents or otherwise from so acting.

It was established in evidence that since 1945 similar collective insurances had been made by the company with 53 local authorities. The scheme was started as it was felt that the tenants were as a rule weekly wage earners or elderly people, who, when faced with the financial strain of burglary, fire or other disaster, would either be unable to pay their rent or would have to be supported by the council. There had been flooding in the area in 1958. The council relied on their powers of "general management" under the Housing Act 1957. No evidence was tendered on behalf of the plaintiffs.

Pennycuick J. held, dismissing the action, that the power of a local authority under section 111 (1) of the Housing Act 1957 to manage its houses was limited to such acts as might fairly be regarded as acts of general management by a prudent landlord of property in the ordinary sense of that term, and that the facilitation of insurance of household goods and personal effects by way of a collective policy in the particular circumstances was such an act of management notwithstanding that it was incidentally concerned with the private possessions of the tenants.

The Attorney-General appealed.

LORD EVERSHED M.R.: . . . The real complaint . . . is that the council is acting as agent for a particular insurance company in effecting insurances of the private effects of the tenants. The interest of the relators is because they represent, as their name implies, persons interested in a rival insurance business. The union as such is not a ratepayer, and, in any event, it is clear that the effect of what the council is doing does not impose any burden on the ratepayers. It is perhaps to be noted that the challenge was first contained in a letter in which the protest, vigorously made, was stated to be on the grounds: "(a) The district council are restricting insurance to one specific office. (b) They are instructing rent collectors to become part-time insurance men in the ratepayers' time. (c) They are depriving full-time agents, who are ratepayers, of remuneration. (d) The insurance office concerned has a very bad record regarding recognition of a bona fide trade union."

When the case was opened, we expressed some curiosity in regard to the action, brought as it is by the Attorney-General at the relation of the union. It seems, however, quite clear that once the Attorney-General has initiated such proceedings, no question can be raised in regard to the nature of the action by reason of the interest or the lack of interest of the relator as a ratepayer or otherwise. . . .

[His Lordship stated further facts and continued:] Section 111 (1) of the Housing Act 1957 reads as follows: "The general management, regulation and control of houses provided by a local authority under this Part of this Act shall be vested in and exercised by the authority, and the authority may make such reasonable charges for the tenancy or occupation of the houses as they may determine." The question involved may, then, be simply stated thus: Are the activities, above described and challenged by the plaintiff, acts of "general management," within the terms of the subsection? . . .

The principle of law to be applied I take from the speech of Lord Selborne L.C. in *Attorney-General* v. *Great Eastern Railway Co.* The noble Lord there states (1880) 5 App.Cas. 473, 478 H.L., after reference to *Ashbury Railway Carriage and Iron Co.* v. *Riche* (1875) L.R. 7 H.L. 653: "I agree with James L.J. that this doctrine ought to be reasonably and not unreasonably, understood and applied, and that whatever may fairly be regarded as incidental to, or consequential upon, those things which the legislature has authorised, ought not (unless expressly prohibited) to be held, by judicial construction, to be *ultra vires*." . . . The evidence also showed quite clearly . . . that the class comprehended in the term "Council house tenants" consists generally of persons of small means who are, in the ordinary course, unable to find substantial sums, whether for the purpose of replacing losses or damage through such calamities as fire, flood, burglary and the like, and equally unable to find substantial sums at intervals in the way of insurance premiums, payment of electricity and other like charges. It was also proved that in the event of losses of their effects through calamities of the kind mentioned, the tenants were frequently inclined to default in their rent payments and, indeed, to come to the council for assistance in replacing their lost effects. In the light of these circumstances, the evidence also showed that it was the fairly general practice of councils, and had been for some time, to make arrangements for insuring the tenants, as well as themselves, against liabilities arising from that common phenomenon of the day and age, namely, the erection of television aerials, and also for the payment of electricity charges by way in each case of collecting small sums weekly from the tenants with the rent, the councils themselves paying the premiums or charges on their respective due dates. In my view it is legitimate, in considering the question before us, to take these facts into account, to have regard to the well-known and established facts as to the resources of council house tenants and also to the consequences as regards rent payment of such losses as these policies covered. In other words, we are, as it seems to me, concerned with the standard of management appropriate not to a private land owner concerned to turn to account to his best advantage his own estate but with the standard of management appropriate to a local authority providing dwellings for a particular class of the community under a statutory duty so to do, such class of the community having the limitations to which I have referred.

It must be the concern, if not the duty, of a local authority to maintain the general quality and standard of its housing estate which it is its duty to provide and to take such steps as may fairly be regarded as prudent to that end, and also so as to ensure, so far as may be, that the rents due to it will be paid and that the council will not be unduly involved in the consequences that would follow from a tenant's failure to pay his rent and observe the ordinary obligations of his tenancy. [Counsel for the Att.Gen.] said that these objectives could be achieved if the council were to enter itself into a policy covering failure to recover rent from its tenants. But apart from the fact that such a course would be much more expensive to the council than the present activities, the objectives would not be achieved of maintaining the standards of the dwellings in the way I have indicated or the avoidance of the consequences of defaults by the tenants.

I refer to certain other sections of the Part of the Act, Part V, in which section 111 occurs. The Part begins at section 91 and is headed in the statute: "Provision of housing accommodation. General powers and duties of local authorities." The first example I take is from section 93, the first subsection of which states: "The powers of a local authority under this Part of this Act to provide housing accommodation shall include a power (either by themselves or jointly with any other person) to provide and maintain with the consent of the Minister in connection with any such housing accommodation any building adapted for use as a shop, any recreation grounds, or other buildings or land which in the opinion of the Minister will serve a beneficial purpose in connection with the requirements of the persons for whom the housing accommodation is provided." Section 94 contains a power to ". . . fit out, furnish and supply any house erected, converted or acquired by them under section 92 of this Act with all requisite furniture, fittings and conveniences," and goes on to provide that they may let and sell furniture under hire-purchase contracts. Section 95 contains a power to provide, among other things, laundry facilities for the council house tenants. I pass over a number of sections and will content myself finally with a reference to section 113 which, in the statement of the arrangement of sections at the beginning of the Act, is described as "Conditions to be observed in management of local authority's houses." Subsection (2) states: "The local authority shall secure that in the selection of their tenants a reasonable preference is given to persons who are occupying insanitary or overcrowded houses, have large families or are living under unsatisfactory housing conditions." It is true, as [Counsel for the Att.-Gen.] observed, that certain things are specifically mentioned and specific power in regard to them is given to local authorities, and so, as he submitted, according to ordinary principles, these express references should be taken to exclude other activities of a comparable nature not expressly mentioned. I see the force of the argument, but I still think that it is shown by the references I have made that a council housing estate is, from the point of view of management, *sui generis*. If the plaintiffs are right, it would appear inevitably to follow that the arrangements such as those relating to insurance of television aerials and arrangements in regard to Electricity Board charges and the like would be equally open to challenge—a challenge that has never hitherto been suggested.

[Counsel for the council] went further and said that the true inference from the circumstances and from Part V of the Act was that the management of council housing estates comprehended what could be fairly described as welfare considerations of all kinds and he referred to a statement of Romer J. in *Belcher* v. *Reading Corporation* [1950] Ch. 380, 391. Pennycuick J. rejected this broad argument and in the circumstances it is unnecessary for me to express a view upon it, though I am for my part disposed to think that the obligations of the council do, as Romer J. thought, at least comprehend a welfare element. At least, such considerations would justify the view taken by my predecessor, Lord Greene M.R., in *Shelley* v. *London County Council* [1948] 1 K.B. 274, 286 affd. [1949] A.C. 56 that the widest significance should be given to the word "management" in this connection . . . I think this appeal fails and should be dismissed.

HARMAN and DONOVAN L.JJ. delivered concurring judgments.

Notes

1. The notion of implied or incidental powers gives some flexibility to the courts in their operation of the doctrine of *ultra vires*. See also, *Att.-Gen.* v. *Manchester Corpn.* [1906] 1 Ch. 643—extent to which a parcels service could be regarded as ancillary to express powers to operate a tramway service; and *Att.-Gen.* v. *Smethwick Corpn.* [1932] 1 Ch. 562—establishment of printing, bookbinding and stationery works *intra vires* as being incidental to performance by local authority of its express functions.

This beneficial principle must not, however, be pressed too far. In *London County Council* v. *Attorney-General* [1902] A.C. 165, the House of Lords held *ultra vires* the operation of an unauthorised omnibus service by a local authority authorised to operate tramways. In the words of Lord Macnaghten: "It is quite true that the two businesses can be worked conveniently together; but the one is not incidental to the other. The business of an omnibus proprietor is no more incidental to the business of a tramway company than the business of steamship owners is incidental to the undertaking of a railway company which has its terminus at a seaport." Likewise in a decision denying that legislation of 1871 conferred on trade unions power to collect and administer funds for political purposes, Lord Macnaghten insisted that the incidental powers idea should not be used to *enlarge* upon the powers conferred by Parliament, as distinct from simply sanctioning matters which by reasonable implication Parliament must have intended to authorise: see *Amalgamated Society of Railway Servants* v. *Osborne* [1910] A.C. 87.

2. Note the terms of section 111 of the Local Government Act 1972:

> "**Subsidiary powers of local authorities**
>
> **111.**—(1) Without prejudice to any powers exercisable apart from this section but subject to the provisions of this Act and any other enactment passed before or after this Act, a local authority shall have power to do any thing (whether or not involving the expenditure, borrowing or lending of money or the acquisition or disposal of any property or rights) which is calculated to facilitate, or is conducive or incidental to, the discharge of any of their functions. . . .
>
> (3) A local authority shall not by virtue of this section raise money, whether by means of rates, precepts or borrowing, or lend money except in accordance with the enactments relating to those matters respectively. . . ."

This gives statutory force in the context of local government to the common law doctrine of incidental powers.

Section 111 has been held to authorise the release of a member of staff to a joint committee of trade unions in the interests of good industrial relations (but not the release of staff in support of a campaign against government policy) (*R.* v. *Greater London Council and Another, ex p. Westminster City Council, The Times*, December 27, 1984); and the establishment of a council working party comprising staff and officers to consider ways of improving the council's structure and efficiency (*R.* v. *Eden District Council, ex p. Moffatt, The Times*, November 24, 1988).

The courts have recently adopted an apparently more restrictive attitude. In *Hazell* v. *Hammersmith and Fulham London Borough Council* [1990] 2 Q.B. 722–723, Woolf L.J. said:

> "What is a function for the purposes of the subsection is not expressly defined but in our view there can be little doubt that in this context 'functions' refers to the multiplicity of specific statutory activities the council is expressly or impliedly under a duty to perform or has power to perform under the other provisions of the Act of 1972 or other relevant legislation. The subsection does not of itself, independently of any other provision, authorise the performance of any activity. It only confers, as the sidenote to the section indicates, a subsidiary power. A subsidiary power which authorises an activity where some other statutory provision has vested a specific function or functions in the council and the performance of the activity will assist in some way in the discharge of that function or those functions."

This was approved by the Court of Appeal, [1990] 2 Q.B. 697, 785, and the House of Lords, [1991] 2 W.L.R. 372, 383. In the House of Lords, Lord Templeman accepted that "borrowing" was a "function" for these purposes, but that interest rate swap transactions neither "facilitated" nor were "conducive" or "incidental to" borrowing. A power was not incidental merely because it was convenient or desirable or profitable. *Cf. R.* v. *Wirral Metropolitan Borough Council, ex p. Milstead* (1989) 87 L.G.R. 611, where the Divisional Court held that a "factoring" agreement to sell, for a current payment, the right to receive the proceeds of future sales of land was not lawful under section 111. Entering the agreement was not incidental to the sale of the land, but was concerned with the sale of sums of money cleaved from the proceeds of sale of the land.

Then, in *R.* v. *Richmond upon Thames London Borough Council, ex p. McCarthy & Stone (Developments) Ltd.* [1991] 3 W.L.R. 941, the House of Lords, reversing the Court of Appeal, held that section 111 did not authorise the levy of a charge on developers in respect of pre-planning application meetings and discussions. The consideration and determining of planning applications *was* a function of the council; the giving of pre-application advice facilitated and was conducive and incidental to that function, but was not *itself* a "function." Charging was thus "incidental to the incidental," which was too remote a relationship (*cf.* Farwell J. in *Att.-Gen.* v. *Manchester Corporation* [1906] 1 Ch. 643, 656). Lord Lowry rejected the Court of Appeal's argument that while no charge could be made without express authority in respect of the performance of a *duty*, a charge could be made in respect of a function which it had *power* to provide.

Finally, in *R.* v. *North Tyneside Metropolitan Borough Council, ex p. Allsop, The Times*, March 12, 1992, the Court of Appeal held that section 111 did not authorise payments under a voluntary redundancy scheme in excess of the limits permitted under statutory regulations authorising redundancy payments. These regulations took effect by virtue of the Superannuation Act 1972, which was an "other enactment" for the purposes of section 111.

3. A further general power is conferred by the following section (set out as amended).

"Power of local authorities to incur expenditure for certain purposes not otherwise authorised

137.—(1) A local authority may, subject to the provisions of this section, incur expenditure which in their opinion is in the interests of [, and will bring direct benefit to,] their area or any part of it or all or some of its inhabitants, but a local authority shall not, by virtue of this subsection, incur any expenditure—

[(*a*)] for a purpose for which they are, either unconditionally or subject to any limitation or to the satisfaction of any condition, authorised or required to make any payment by or by virtue of any other enactment [; nor

(*b*) unless the direct benefit accruing to their area or any part of it or to all or some of the inhabitants of their area will be commensurate with the expenditure to be incurred].

[(1A) In any case where—

(*a*) by virtue of paragraph (*a*) of subsection (1) above, a local authority are prohibited from incurring expenditure for a particular purpose, and

(*b*) the power or duty of the authority to incur expenditure for that purpose is in any respect limited or conditional (whether by being restricted to a particular group of persons or in any other way),

the prohibition in that paragraph shall extend to all expenditure to which that power or duty would apply if it were not subject to any limitation or condition.]

(2) It is hereby declared that the power of a local authority to incur expenditure under subsection (1) above includes power to do so by contributing

towards the defraying of expenditure by another local authority in or in connection with the exercise of that other authority's functions. . . .

[(2C) A local authority may incur expenditure under subsection (1) above on publicity only—

(*a*) [. . .]

(*b*) by way of assistance to a public body or voluntary organisation where the publicity is incidental to the main purpose for which the assistance is given;

but the following provisions of this section apply to expenditure incurred by the local authority under section 142 below on information as to the services provided by them under this section, or otherwise relating to their functions under this section, as they apply to expenditure incurred under this section.

(2D) In subsection (2C) above—

"publicity" means any communication, in whatever form, addressed to the public at large or to a section of the public; and

"voluntary organisation" means a body which is not a public body but whose activities are carried on otherwise than for profit.]

(3) A local authority may, subject [to the following provisions of this section], incur expenditure on contributions to any of the following funds, that is to say—

(*a*) the funds of any charitable body in furtherance of its work in the United Kingdom; or

(*b*) the funds of any body which provides any public service [(whether to the public at large or to any section of it)] in the United Kingdom otherwise than for the purposes of gain; or

(*c*) any fund which is raised in connection with a particular event directly affecting persons resident in the United Kingdom on behalf of whom a public appeal for contributions has been made by the Lord Mayor of London or the chairman of a principal council or by a committee of which the Lord Mayor of London or the chairman of a principal council is a member. . . ."

The amount that can be spent was formerly the product of a 2p rate. Following the abolition of domestic rating, it is now calculated by multiplying the local authority's "relevant population" by £2.50 (county and non-metropolitan district councils); £5.00 (metropolitan district and London borough councils and the Common Council of the City of London); or £3.50 (parish and community councils). A separate account must be kept of expenditure under s.137.

Section 137 was substantially amended by the Local Government and Housing Act 1989. Part III of this Act now makes express provision in respect of the promotion of economic development by local authorities, which now falls outside section 137.

The use of section 137 in practice was considered by C. Crawford and V. Moore, *The Free Two Pence* (CIPFA, 1983). In *Manchester City Council* v. *Greater Manchester Metropolitan County Council* (1980) 78 L.G.R. 560, the House of Lords upheld the validity of payments under section 137 by the county council to a trust established by that council for the provision of free or assisted places at independent schools for children of parents in the area. (Education was not one of the county council's functions.) The payment was held not to infringe the principle that local government expenditure be conducted on an annual basis; although most of the money would be held by the trustees for expenditure in future years, the expenditure was properly incurred within the county council's budget in one year. (*Cf. Re Westminster City Council* [1986] A.C. 668 above, p. 202.)

4. From time to time concern has been expressed that the *ultra vires* doctrine

may unduly cramp municipal enterprise and initiative. The Committee on the-Management of Local Government (Chairman: Sir John Maud (later Lord Redcliffe-Maud)) (HMSO, 1967) considered that the *ultra vires* doctrine had "a deleterious effect on local government because of the narrowness of the legislation governing local authorities' activities. The specific nature of legislation discourages enterprise, handicaps development, robs the community of services which the local authority might render, and encourages too rigorous oversight by the central government. It contributes to the excessive concern over legalities and fosters the idea that the clerk should be a lawyer" (para. 283). They recommended the enactment of a "general competence" clause, of the kind now incorporated in section 137 of the Local Government Act 1972 (above) although they did *not* recommend financial limits.

Similarly, the Royal Commission on Local Government in England 1966–69 (Chairman: Lord Redcliffe-Maud, Cmnd. 4040) suggested that the only limit on a "general power to spend money for the benefit of their areas or inhabitants" should be "the wishes of the electors and such restrictions as have to be placed on local government expenditure in the interests of national economic and financial policy" (para. 323). This suggestion was not accepted.

(B) Jurisdictional Review

In the cases considered so far the principal question for the courts has been whether the actions of a public body were, or were not, actions which were authorised by the legislation. We now turn to cases which also raise this same essential question, but in a rather different way. In these cases there may be no dispute that in certain circumstances the body in question may act in the way that it has. The challenge, however, is founded on the contention that the power to do those things has not been granted by the legislation to be exercised "at large," whenever the body in question so pleases—but has, instead, been conferred subject to limitations as to the circumstances which must prevail for the power to be operable. It is the difference between grants of power which simply authorise a body to do "X," and grants of power which authorise the body to do "X" in (and, implicitly, only in) defined circumstances. In cases where the legislation is of the latter kind there is much scope for dispute to centre on what circumstances the legislation requires to exist before the body has power to behave as it has (a matter of interpreting the legislation), or to centre on whether those required circumstances did in fact exist. It will also be critical to determine whose decision on these questions should in the last resort be decisive.

Re RIPON (HIGHFIELD) CONFIRMATION ORDER 1938, WHITE & COLLINS v. MINISTER OF HEALTH

[1939] 2 K.B. 838; 180 L.J.K.B. 768; 161 L.T. 109; 55 T.L.R. 956; 83 S.J. 622; [1939] 3 All E.R. 548; 103 J.P. 331 (Court of Appeal)

Under Part V of the Housing Act 1936, a local authority had power to acquire land compulsorily for the provision of houses for the working classes. By section 75 nothing in the Act was to authorise the compulsory acquisition of land "which at the date of the compulsory purchase forms part of any park, garden or pleasure ground or is otherwise required for the amenity or convenience of any house." Ripon Borough Council made an order for the compulsory purchase of about 23 acres of land, forming part of the grounds of a house at Ripon called "Highfield," which comprised in all about 35 acres. The 23 acres were at the time let for grazing purposes. The owners (the present appellants) objected that the land was part of a park and required for the amenity or convenience of the house, and that the order was therefore contrary to section 75. The Minister, after causing a public inquiry to be held, confirmed the order. The owners applied to the High Court for the order to be quashed. Further evidence was given by affidavit. Charles J. dismissed the motion on the ground that the question was one of fact, and that it was not open to the court to interfere by rehearing the case and evidence. The owners appealed to the Court of Appeal.

MacKinnon L.J.: . . . The only evidence filed on this motion was three affidavits by Mr. Rennoldson, and Mr. Denman, for the applicants, and by Mr. Wrigley for the respondents. The only material evidence on the question whether this land is part of a park is that of Mr. Denman, who says: [*inter alia*] . . . "The house itself is an imposing stone-built residence. It is a house of the type and size to which it is invariably expected to find paddock and park land attached. Without them the house and grounds are not such as to attract a purchaser or tenant. To the west and north-west of the dwelling house and gardens lies an expanse of open grass land studded with trees of an approximate acreage of 23·46. This land is undoubtedly the park land attaching to the house of "Highfield." It is obvious on inspection of the site that the architect in designing "Highfield" so placed the house as to benefit by the amenity of the open stretch of land on its west side. . . . Often the land can be utilized for running horses, etc., but usually it is let off to neighbouring farmers or owners for grazing purposes, and the fact that this land is so let does not render it the less properly described in the market as park land. . . ."

. . . Upon the evidence before us I am satisfied that this land was part of a park within the meaning of section 75 of the Act of 1936, that its compulsory purchase was therefore not within the powers of the Act, and that therefore the order of the Minister ought to be quashed. I say "upon the evidence before us." I have said that we do not know what materials were before the Minister, though para. 3 of Mr. Wrigley's affidavit refers to but does not specify those materials. But I would add that, if Mr. Hall [the inspector] and the Minister in his turn accepted the contention of Mr. Peaker at the inquiry—that this land had ceased to be a park when, and because, it was let for grazing—that was manifestly an erroneous view. It is notorious that hundreds of undoubted "parks" throughout the country are so let for grazing. I should not be surprised to hear that this obtains at Chatsworth or Badminton, or even in Windsor Great Park. . . .

Mr. Valentine Holmes impressed upon us the importance of the duties of local authorities as to rehousing under this Act, and deprecated interference with them. I appreciate that importance, but it must be subject to observance of the clear words of section 75 of the Act, and I might point out that that section only refers to land "which forms *part* of any park," etc. There would be nothing to prevent the Ripon Council acquiring compulsorily the whole of the Highfield property, including the house, or the whole of the Holmfield property, as to part of which they made a previous unsuccessful attempt. The owners would have no power to interfere with them. Perhaps they would have the consolation that, however much they suffered sentimentally, they did not suffer financially.

In the result, I think Charles J. was wrong in dismissing this application, that the appeal should be allowed, and the Minister's order be quashed.

LUXMOORE L.J.: . . . The evidence before the inspector was not given on oath, and the proceedings were necessarily far less formal than in a court of law. I have carefully considered the transcript and can find but little evidence directed to prove that the land in question is part of the park of Highfield and none to justify a finding that it is not part thereof: but there is some evidence to support the view that the land is not required for the amenities or convenience of the house. The evidence in the affidavits in support of the application is uncontradicted, and leads only to the conclusion that the land is part of the park. This evidence was not before the Minister, and, although it was before Charles J. when he heard the motion, he does not appear to have considered it, for, in refusing to quash the order of the borough council and its confirmation by the Minister, he based that refusal on the ground that the Minister had decided that the land in question was not part of the park or required for the amenity or convenience of the house, and that, as these were questions of fact, he would not interfere with the findings, as he had no power to retry or to rehear the case.

In my judgment Charles J. was in error in deciding as he did. As I have already pointed out, the proceeding before Charles J. was not by way of appeal from any order made by the borough council or its confirmation by the Minister of Health, but was a new and independent proceeding and not a rehearing or a retrial.

The first and most important matter to bear in mind is that the jurisdiction to make the order is dependent on a finding of fact; for, unless the land can be held not to be part of a park or not to be required for amenity or convenience, there is no jurisdiction in the borough council to make, or in the Minister to confirm, the order. In such a case it seems almost self-evident that the court which has to consider whether there is jurisdiction to make or confirm the order must be entitled to review the vital finding on which the existence of the jurisdiction relied upon depends. If this were not so, the right to apply to the court would be illusory.

There is however ample authority that the court is entitled so to act, for the point has been considered in a number of cases. It is sufficient to refer to the case of *Bunbury* v. *Fuller* (9 Ex. 111, 140). In that case Coleridge J. delivering the judgment of the Court of Exchequer Chamber said: "it is a general rule, that no court of limited jurisdiction can give itself jurisdiction by a wrong decision on a point collateral to the merits of the case upon which the limit to its jurisdiction depends; and however its decision may be final on all particulars, making up together that subject-matter which, if true, is within its jurisdiction, and however necessary in many cases it may be for it to make a preliminary inquiry, whether some collateral matter be or be not within the limits, yet, upon this preliminary question, its decision must always be open to inquiry in the superior court. Then to take the simplest case—suppose a judge with jurisdiction limited to a particular hundred, and a matter is brought before him as having arisen within it, but the party charged contends that it arose in another hundred, this is clearly a collateral matter independent of the merits; on its being presented, the judge must not immediately forbear to proceed, but must inquire into its truth or falsehood and for the time decide it, and either proceed or not with the principal subject-matter according as he finds on that point; but this decision must be open to question, and if he has improperly either forborne or proceeded on the main matter in consequence of an error, on this the Court of Queen's Bench will issue its mandamus or prohibition to correct his mistake."

As in *Bunbury* v. *Fuller* and also in *R.* v. *Bradford* [1908] 1 K.B. 365, so also in the present case, the decision on the question whether the particular land is part of a park or not is preliminary to the exercise of the jurisdiction to make and confirm the order conferred by the Housing Act 1936, s.75, and is therefore open to review in this court. Charles J. in arriving at his decision stated that he agreed with the decision of du Parcq J. in *Re Newhill Compulsory Purchase Order*, 1937, *Payne's Application* [1938] 2 All E.R. 163, and of Swift J. in *Bowman's* case [1932] 2 K.B. 621, 627, 634 in support of the view that he had no power to review the decision of the Minister of Health, because the question to be determined was one of fact. [His Lordship summarised *Re Bowman*, see below, pp. 625–627.]

. . . Reliance in this Court was placed on the statement of Swift J. that an aggrieved person "is not entitled to come here and complain that the local authority have made a mistake of fact in making the order. He is not entitled to say that his house is not insanitary or unfit for human habitation and therefore the order should not have been made." If this statement was intended by the learned judge to be of universal application to all cases under section 11(3) of the 1930 Act, and therefore also to all cases under the second clause of the Second Schedule to the 1936 Act, I should have no hesitation in saying that it went too far, for it ignores the rule laid down in *Bunbury* v. *Fuller* to which reference has already been made: a decision which Swift J. had no power to overrule; indeed no reference appears to have been made to it during the argument of *Bowman's* case. I think the remarks of Swift J. must be read in the light of the facts of the case before him, and especially with regard to the provisions of the Act of 1930, s.1, which appear in express terms to make the local authority the judge whether the houses in question are fit for habitation or not; for the material words of that section are: "Where a local authority upon consideration of an official representation or other information in their possession are satisfied" that the houses in the area are unfit, then an order may be made.

This provision differs materially from the present case; section 75 of the Act of 1936 does not refer in terms to the local authority being satisfied that the land is not part of a park. The making of the order for compulsory purchase is prohibited if the land is part of a park, a matter which can only be proved or disproved by evidence. . . .

The true position with regard to applications under cl. 2 of the Second Schedule to the 1936 Act appears to me to be that the judge to whom the application is made is bound to consider the available evidence, whether given at the local inquiry or by the affidavits in support of or in opposition to the motion, and, if there is a conflict with regard to the facts raised, or if the evidence is insufficient to enable him to come to a conclusion, he is free to direct that oral evidence be given, whether by way of cross-examination or of additional evidence. . . .

In the present case, as I have already stated, I am satisfied that there was no evidence before the inspector sufficient to entitle the local authority or the Minister to come to a conclusion that the land in question was not part of the park of Highfield; I am further satisfied that on the affidavit evidence . . . the only conclusion open to the court is that the land was part of the park of Highfield. . . . In my judgment the appeal must be allowed.

HUMPHREYS J. agreed.

Order quashed.

Notes

1. These proceedings were in the form of a "statutory application to quash"—proceedings which are something of a hybrid between appeal and review. See further on this procedure below, p. 622. The statements in the case about the basis and scope of review for error of jurisdictional fact remain authoritative as to the substance of this ground of judicial review, although in the particular context of statutory applications to quash the modern approach may now be as stated by Lord Denning M.R. in *Ashbridge Investments Ltd.* v. *Minister of Housing and Local Government*—see further below, p. 627.

2. The reasons given in the case for distinguishing *Re Bowman* may not reflect the more recent approach of the courts to powers conferred in "subjective" form—*i.e.* power to do "X" where *in the opinion* of the body in question "Y" exists. See further, below p. 408.

R. v. SECRETARY OF STATE FOR THE HOME DEPARTMENT, ex p. KHAWAJA

[1984] A.C. 74; [1983] 1 All E.R. 765; [1983] 2 W.L.R. 32
(House of Lords)

In this case two separate appeals to the House of Lords raising the same legal issues were heard together. The appellants, Khera and Khawaja, were both persons who, having been admitted to the United Kingdom as immigrants, had later been detained and ordered for removal as "illegal entrants" under the Immigration Act 1971. Argument centred on two questions—(i) the meaning of the term "illegal entrant" and (ii) the scope of review of the exercise of power to remove such persons from the United Kingdom.

These two questions had earlier been considered by the House of Lords in *Zamir v. Secretary of State for the Home Department* [1980] A.C. 930. In that case it had been held that the term "illegal entrant" included one who had obtained permission to enter having failed positively to disclose some matter which would have led to the refusal of permission to enter had that information been known at the time. This was so even though no request for such information may have been made by any official—in other words, *Zamir* imposed a positive duty to disclose relevant information to immigration officers, even beyond answering truthfully the various questions which might specifically have been asked by the officers. In *Khawaja* the House of Lords overruled *Zamir* on this point, holding that a person who had been admitted entry was only an "illegal entrant" where some positive deception had been practised.

Our concern, however, is with the second of the two questions: in proceedings for judicial review is it sufficient for the Secretary of State to satisfy the court that when he exercised his power to order removal he had reasonable grounds to believe the appellant to be an illegal entrant? Or is not the critical issue whether the appellant does, or does not, in fact fall within that statutory category? *Zamir* had decided that the scope of review was of the former extent. The appellants called upon the House of Lords to reconsider the matter.

LORD FRASER: . . . The second general issue relates to the function of the courts and of this House in its judicial capacity when dealing with applications for judicial review in cases of this sort: is their function limited to deciding whether there was evidence on which the immigration officer or other appropriate official in the Home Office could reasonably come to his decision (provided he acted fairly and not in breach of the rules of natural justice), or does it extend to deciding whether the decision was justified and in accordance with the evidence? On this question I agree with my noble and learned friends Lord Scarman and Lord Bridge that an immigration officer is only entitled to order the detention and removal of a person who has entered the country by virtue of an *ex facie* valid permission if the person *is* an illegal entrant. That is a "precedent fact" which has to be established. It is not enough that the immigration officer reasonably believes him to be an illegal entrant if the evidence does not justify his belief. Accordingly, the duty of the court must be beyond inquiring only whether he had reasonable grounds for his belief. In both the present cases the immigration officers stated, in what appears to be a standard formula, that there were "reasonable grounds to conclude, etc." That formula indicates, in my opinion, that they applied the wrong test. . . .

LORD SCARMAN: . . . [In *Zamir*] . . . [t]he House approved a line of authority (beginning with *R.* v. *Secretary of State for the Home Department, ex p. Hussain* [1978] 1 W.L.R. 700) which put a gloss on the words of the critical provision in the 1971 Act, *i.e.* Sched. 2, para. 9 to the Act. The paragraph declares an illegal entrant to be liable to removal. It provides that where an illegal entrant is not given leave to enter or remain in the United Kingdom an immigration officer may give directions for his removal. Unless he (or the Secretary of State, para. 10) gives such directions, no power to detain him arises; for para. 16(2) provides a power to detain only in respect of a person who may be so removed. . . .

The gloss which the House in *Zamir's* case put on the words of para. 9 was to read them as meaning not "where a person *is* an illegal entrant" but "where the immigration officer *has reasonable grounds for believing a person to be* an illegal entrant" he may be removed if not given leave to enter. If it be sought to justify the gloss as a proper construction of the statutory language, there is a difficulty. The gloss requires the introduction into the paragraph of words that are not there. Must they, then, be implied? This question lies at the heart of the problem.

In *Zamir's* case the House was impressed with the difficulties arising if the implication were not to be made. The House attached importance to three considerations: (1) the line of cases beginning with *Hussain*, in which the Court of Appeal had held it necessary to make the implication; (2) the scheme of the Immigration Act; and, especially, (3) the nature and process of the power of decision conferred by the Act on immigration officers.

These considerations, in the view of the House, made it necessary to reject the appellant's argument based on the well-established principle that, where the exercise of an executive power depends on the precedent establishment of an objective fact, it is for the court, if there be a challenge by way of judicial review, to decide whether the precedent requirement has been satisfied. In *R.* v. *Governor of Pentonville Prison, ex p. Azam* [1974] A.C. 18, 34 Lord Denning M.R. (in the Court of Appeal) considered the principle applicable in the case of removal of an illegal entrant. The House recognised the existence of the principle, but, following and approving *Hussain's* case, opted for a construction of the legislation which would oust it.

In rejecting the appellant's argument based on the "precedent fact" principle of review Lord Wilberforce said [in *Zamir*] [1980] A.C. 930, 948:

> "My Lords, for the reasons I have given I am of opinion that the whole scheme of the Act is against this argument. It is true that it does not, in relation to the decisions in question, use such words as 'in the opinion of the Secretary of State' or 'the Secretary of State must be satisfied,' but it is not necessary for such a formula to be used in order to take the case out of the 'precedent fact' category. The nature and process of decision conferred on immigration officers by existing legislation is incompatible with any requirement for the establishment of precedent objective facts whose existence the court may verify."

He therefore implied into para. 9 the words needed to bring it outside the "precedent fact" category of provision. My Lords, in most cases I would defer to a recent decision of your Lordships' House on a question of construction, even if I thought it wrong. I do not do so in this context because for reasons which I shall develop I am convinced that the *Zamir* reasoning gave insufficient weight to the important (I would say fundamental) consideration that we are here concerned with, the scope of judicial review of a power which inevitably infringes the liberty of those subjected to it. This consideration, if it be good, outweighs, in my judgment, any difficulties in the administration of immigration control to which the application of the principle might give rise. The *Zamir* construction of para. 9 deprives those subjected to the power of that degree of judicial protection which I think can be shown to have been the policy of our law to afford to persons with whose liberty the executive is seeking to interfere. It does therefore, in my view, tend to obstruct the proper development and application of the safeguards our law provides for the liberty of those within its jurisdiction. . . .

Accordingly, faced with the jealous care our law traditionally devotes to the protection of the liberty of those who are subject to its jurisdiction, I find it impossible to imply into the statute words the effect of which would be to take the provision, para. 9 of Sched. 2 to the 1971 Act, "out of the 'precedent fact' category" (see *Zamir* [1980] A.C. 930 at 948, *per* Lord Wilberforce). If Parliament intends to exclude effective judicial review of the exercise of a power in restraint of liberty, it must make its meaning crystal clear.

LORD BRIDGE: . . . [T]he authorities from *R.* v. *Secretary of State for the Home Department, ex p. Hussain* to *Zamir* have consistently affirmed the principle that the decision of an immigration officer to detain and remove a person as an illegal entrant under these provisions can only be attacked successfully on the ground that there was no evidence on which the immigration officer could reasonably conclude that he was an illegal entrant.

It will be seen at once that this principle gives to an executive officer, subject, no doubt, in reaching his conclusions of fact to a duty to act fairly, a draconian power of arrest and expulsion based on his own decision of fact. . . . It will be further observed that to justify the principle important words have to be read into para. 9 of Sched. 2 by implication. That paragraph, on the face of the language used, authorises the removal of a person who is an illegal entrant. The courts have applied it as if it authorised the removal of a person whom an immigration officer on reasonable grounds believes to be an illegal entrant. The all-important question is whether such an implication can be justified.

The presently prevailing doctrine was first enunciated in *R.* v. *Secretary of State for the Home Department, ex p. Hussain* by Geoffrey Lane L.J. He explained the suggested basis of the doctrine rather more fully in *R.* v. *Secretary of State for the Home Department, ex p. Choudhary* [1978] 1 W.L.R. 1177, 1183, where he said:

"The whole object of this part of the Immigration Act 1971, read as a whole, is to ensure that there is a procedure, and a readily available and easy procedure, whereby the Secretary of State can detain pending removal any person such as the appellant in this case. The Secretary of State obviously, from the nature of things, has no desire to detain a man longer than is necessary to get him out of this country and back to Pakistan, or wherever it was he came from. It is conceded by [counsel for Mr. Choudhary], and, if I may say so, rightly conceded, that a reasonable belief held by the Secretary of State is sufficient to justify the initial detention of the man; but it is said that, once the Secretary of State's inquiries are at an end, then one has to examine the basis of fact and, if that shows that the Secretary of State had got the factual basis wrong, then the whole of the detention from the moment the inquiries have come to an end and onwards is unlawful. With that submission I cannot agree. It seems to me that the detention in circumstances such as these is throughout a matter for the discretion of the Secretary of State; and, if he was acting on reasonable grounds and acting *bona fide* on those reasonable grounds, then he is protected."

In *Zamir* [1980] A.C. 930, 948–949 Lord Wilberforce said:

"The nature and process of decision conferred on immigration officers by existing legislation is incompatible with any requirement for the establishment of precedent objective facts whose existence the court may verify.

The immigration officer, whether at the stage of entry or at that of removal, has to consider a complex of statutory rules and non-statutory guidelines. He has to act on documentary evidence and such other evidence as inquiries may provide. Often there will be documents whose genuineness is doubtful, statements which cannot be verified, misunderstandings as to what was said, practices and attitudes in a foreign state which have to be estimated. There is room for appreciation, even for discretion."

He proceeds to contrast the disadvantageous position of the Divisional Court as a fact-finding tribunal in the relevant field. . . .

My Lords, we should, I submit, regard with extreme jealousy any claim by the executive to imprison a citizen without trial and allow it only if it is clearly justified by the statutory language relied on. The fact that, in the case we are considering, detention is preliminary and incidental to expulsion from the country in my view strengthens rather than weakens the case for a robust exercise of the judicial function in safeguarding the citizen's rights.

So far as I know, no case before the decisions under the Act which we are presently considering has held imprisonment without trial by executive order to be justified by anything less than the plainest statutory language, with the sole exception of the majority decision of your Lordships' House in *Liversidge* v. *Anderson* [1942] A.C. 206. No one needs to be reminded of the now celebrated dissenting speech of Lord Atkin in that case, or of his withering condemnation of the process of writing into the statutory language there under consideration the words which were necessary to sustain the decision of the majority. Lord Atkin's dissent now has the approval of your Lordships' House in *R.* v. *Inland Revenue Commissioners, ex p. Rossminster Ltd.* [1980] A.C. 952.

A person who has entered the United Kingdom with leave and who is detained under Sched. 2, para. 16(2) pending removal as an illegal entrant on the ground that he obtained leave to enter by fraud is entitled to challenge the action taken and proposed to be taken against him both by application for habeas corpus and by application for judicial review. On the view I take, para. 9 of Sched. 2 must be construed as meaning no more and no less than it says. There is no room for any implication qualifying the words "illegal entrant." From this it would follow that, while, prima facie, the order for detention under para. 16(2) would be a sufficient return to the writ of habeas corpus, proof by the applicant that he had been granted leave to enter would shift the onus back to the immigration officer to prove that the leave had been obtained in contravention of s.26(1)(*c*) of the Act, in other words by fraud. . . .

LORDS WILBERFORCE and TEMPLEMAN delivered concurring speeches.

Note

See N. P. Gravells, (1983) 99 L.Q.R. 363; I. A. Macdonald, and N. J. Blake, *Macdonald's Immigration Law and Practice* (3rd ed., 1991), Chs. 16, 18; G. L. Peiris, "Judicial review and immigration policy: emerging trends" (1988) 8 L.S. 201.

We have assumed, so far, that a body which has powers stated in the legislation to be exercisable only in certain defined circumstances cannot by its *own* decision determine *conclusively* that those circumstances exist. It may make a preliminary determination of this matter, and proceed accordingly—but if its decision on this question is challenged, the reviewing court will itself determine whether the body has come to a correct decision in law and on the facts as to the scope of its powers. Has it correctly understood *what* precedent facts must exist? *Do* those necessary precedent facts exist?

These questions may arise not only in respect of the exercise of administrative powers (as in *White* and in *Khawaja*); they may arise equally in relation to the jurisdiction of an adjudicatory body—a tribunal. Such a body may have to consider whether a particular claim falls, in law and in fact, within the category of cases it has power to hear. A purported decision on a matter not within its jurisdiction will be *ultra vires*. A classic statement of jurisdictional review as applied to tribunals is to be found in *R.* v. *Shoreditch Assessment Committee, ex p. Morgan* (below).

R. v. SHOREDITCH ASSESSMENT COMMITTEE, ex p. MORGAN

[1910] 2 K.B. 859; 80 L.J.K.B. 185; 103 L.T. 262; 74 J.P. 361; 26 T.L.R. 663; 8 L.G.R. 744 (Court of Appeal)

The Court of Appeal upheld the decision of the Divisional Court to issue mandamus to compel the assessment committee to initiate the procedure whereby the rateable value of premises would be reduced to take account of a fall in the value of the premises. The first step was to order a valuer to make out a provisional valuation list. The committee refused to give that order, but the courts held that they were under a duty to do so. Farwell L.J. summarised the principles of jurisdictional control as follows (at pp. 879–880).

FARWELL L.J.: . . . The existence of the provisional list is a condition precedent to their jurisdiction to hear and determine, and as the claimant is entitled to require them to hear and determine, they cannot refuse to take the steps necessary to give rise to such jurisdiction; if they do, their refusal may be called in question in the High Court. No tribunal of inferior jurisdiction can by its own decision finally decide on the question of the existence or extent of such jurisdiction: such question is always subject to review by the High Court, which does not permit the inferior tribunal either to usurp a jurisdiction which it does not possess, whether at all or to the extent claimed, or to refuse to exercise a jurisdiction which it has and ought to exercise. Subjection in this respect to the High Court is a necessary and inseparable incident to all tribunals of limited jurisdiction; for the existence of the limit necessitates an authority to determine and enforce it: it is a contradiction in terms to create a tribunal with limited jurisdiction and unlimited power to determine such limits at its own will and pleasure—such a tribunal would be autocratic, not limited—and it is immaterial whether the decision of the inferior tribunal on the question of the existence or non-existence of its own jurisdiction is founded on law or fact; a court with jurisdiction confined to the City of London cannot extend such jurisdiction by finding as a fact that Piccadilly Circus is in the ward of Chepe.

These words, although expressing the normal approach of the courts, overstate the matter in so far as they assert that it is a "necessary and inseparable incident" of limited jurisdiction that such a wide power of judicial review shall exist. As Parliament is sovereign it is possible for a legislative grant of power to state that the power is exercisable only in certain defined circumstances and then make the donee of the power the conclusive judge of the existence of those circumstances. This possibility was clearly stated in the much-quoted words of Lord Esher M.R. in *R.* v. *Income Tax Special Commissioners* (below).

R. v. INCOME TAX SPECIAL COMMISSIONERS

(1888) 21 Q.B.D. 313 (Court of Appeal)

A tax statute (5 & 6 Vict. c. 35, s.133) provided that "if within or at the end of the year" of assessment a Schedule D taxpayer could prove to the satisfaction of the Income Tax Commissioners for General Purposes that they had made an overpayment of tax, the Commissioners could certify the sum overpaid to the Commissioners for Special Purposes, in which case "the last-mentioned Commissioners shall issue an order for the repayment of such sum. . . ." The Cape Copper Mining Co. Ltd. applied in March 1887 for certificates in respect of the tax years 1883–84, 1884–85 and 1885–86. The certificates were granted but the Special Commissioners refused to pay in respect of the first two of these years, arguing that the General Commissioners had no jurisdiction to grant certificates for those years, the necessary proof not having been supplied "within or at the end of the [tax] year." The Court of Appeal granted mandamus, holding that this expression could not mean "immediately on the year's ending" and did not mean "at any time after the end of the year" or "within a reasonable time." Instead, the proper construction was that the overpayment had to be proved "in as short a time after the end of the year as is possible in the particular case with exertion on the part of the person claiming repayment." (*per* Lord Esher M.R. at p. 318). The question arose, who was to decide this issue?

LORD ESHER M.R.: . . . This view of the section involves the result that the question, whether the party claiming has so satisfied the terms of the section, must be the subject of inquiry with reference to the particular circumstances in each case. I have been laying down what in my opinion is the general rule of conduct for those charged with that inquiry, but the question arises who are to make that inquiry. In the first instance obviously the Commissioners for General Purposes. They have to determine that question, and they must determine it, as it seems to me, according to the rule I have laid down. But when they have determined it, can their decision be questioned afterwards? It will be said on the one side that their jurisdiction depends on the decision of that question and, applying a well-known formula, that they cannot give themselves jurisdiction by a wrong decision on the facts. I have considered that formula with great care and, though it is correct enough for certain purposes, I think its application is often misleading. When an inferior court or tribunal or body, which has to exercise the power of deciding facts, is first established by Act of Parliament, the legislature has to consider what powers it will give that tribunal or body. It may in effect say that, if a certain state of facts exists and is shewn to such tribunal or body before it proceeds to do certain things, it shall have jurisdiction to do such things, but not otherwise. There it is not for them conclusively to decide whether that state of facts exists, and, if they exercise the jurisdiction without its existence, what they do may be questioned, and it will be held that they have acted without jurisdiction. But there is another state of things which may exist. The legislature may intrust the tribunal or body with a jurisdiction, which includes the jurisdiction to determine whether the preliminary state of facts exists as well as the jurisdiction, on finding that it does exist, to proceed further or do something more. When the legislature are establishing such a tribunal or body with limited jurisdiction, they also have to consider, whatever jurisdiction they give them, whether there shall be any appeal from their decision, for otherwise there will be none. In the second of the two cases I have mentioned it is an erroneous application of the formula to say that the tribunal cannot give themselves jurisdiction by wrongly deciding certain facts to exist, because the legislature gave them jurisdiction to determine all the facts, including the existence of the preliminary facts on which the further exercise of their jurisdiction depends; and if they were given jurisdiction so to decide, without any appeal being given, there is no appeal from such exercise of their jurisdiction. In this case I think the Act gave the Commissioners for General Purposes jurisdiction to inquire into and finally determine the question whether the applicant has brought his case within the terms "at the end of the year" interpreted in the sense I have mentioned. . . . It may be perhaps more satisfactory that I should state that, if I thought that we had to determine that question, I should be of opinion that the Crown had not brought forward any facts which shewed that the Commissioners for General Purposes had decided wrongly on this question. . . .

Notes

1. The problem for the courts is, therefore, to determine in any particular case whether the grant of power should be construed as falling within the former or the latter of Lord Esher's two categories. Most commonly, the courts opt for the former, witness the cases considered so far in this section—but the following two cases show that in certain circumstances a court may think that its powers of review should be of a more limited scope, and interpret the legislation as providing a grant of power falling within the latter of the categories.

2. Lord Esher's judgment can be analysed in two ways. First, it can be argued that the question whether the proof had been supplied "within or at the end of the year" was properly analysed as a collateral or jurisdictional question, but one which, exceptionally, it was for the tribunal to decide (see *de Smith*, p. 119). Alternatively, it can be argued that the question was *not* collateral, but "within the central area of [the Commissioners'] jurisdiction" (see *Wade*, pp. 286–287). These approaches produce the same result, but are analytically distinct (*de Smith* (3rd ed.), p. 104). Does it matter which is to be adopted? Consider *R.* v. *Ludlow, ex p. Barnsley Corporation* [1947] 1 K.B. 634.

DOWTY BOULTON PAUL LTD. v. WOLVERHAMPTON CORPORATION (No. 2)

[1976] Ch. 13 [1973] 2 W.L.R. 618; [1973] 2 All E.R. 491; 71 L.G.R. 323; 25 P. & C.R. 282 (Court of Appeal)

On August 27, 1935, the plaintiffs entered into an agreement with the defendants. The agreement stated that the Corporation would apply to the Air Council, under the Air Navigation Act 1920, for permission to establish and maintain an aerodrome on land to be acquired by them; that they would lease a site on the western side of the aerodrome to the plaintiffs for the purpose of a factory and that they would allow the plaintiffs to use the aerodrome in connection with their business of manufacturing aircraft.

In 1936 the Corporation conveyed the fee simple of the factory site to the plaintiffs instead of leasing it. By clause 2 of the conveyance, the plaintiffs covenanted to erect a factory and use it for the purpose of manufacturing, etc., aircraft and aeronautical equipment or parts thereof and for the purpose of carrying on a school for the training and teaching of flying. By clause 3 the Corporation covenanted to allow the plaintiffs to use the airport for the purpose of test, delivery and other flights in connection with their business, and for the purpose of flying in connection with the flying school, for 99 years from December 1, 1935, or as long as the corporation maintained the airport as a municipal aerodrome whichever was longer. The conveyance further provided that, without prejudice to the Corporation's powers to deal with the aerodrome, they should not, in exercise of their powers, unreasonably affect the plaintiff's rights. At the time the Corporation welcomed the establishment of a factory which would be a substantial employer of labour in the area.

By 1957, the plaintiffs were no longer manufacturing aircraft, and thereafter used the factory for making airframes and equipment. They no longer used the aerodrome for test flying, but only for executive flights. They had never operated a flying school. There were only 26 flights by the plaintiffs to or from the aerodrome in 1967, 56 in 1968, 16 in 1969 and none in 1970. The need in the area for land for housing purposes had substantially increased, and in 1971 the Corporation resolved to re-appropriate the land forming the aerodrome for planning purposes, namely a comprehensive development for housing, shops and schools, acting under section 163 (1) of the Local Government Act 1933. This provided that: "Any land belonging to a local authority and not required for the purposes for which it was acquired or has since been appropriated may be appropriated for any other purpose approved by the Minister for which the local authority are authorised to acquire land. . . ."

Once planning permission for the redevelopment was granted, the Corporation would have power under section 127 of the Town and Country Planning Act 1971 (formerly s.81 of the 1962 Act and now s.237 of the 1990 Act) to carry out works which in effect would destroy the plaintiffs' airfield rights, on payment of compensation. By writ dated September 22, 1970, the plaintiffs sought, *inter alia*, declarations that, so long as the plaintiffs used the land in accordance with the conveyance and required the aerodrome for their purposes, the Corporation were under an obligation to maintain it; the plaintiffs were entitled to use it; and, in the event of the Corporation, in breach of contract, failing to maintain it, the plaintiffs were entitled to maintain it. By originating summons taken out in 1971, the plaintiffs sought declarations that on the true construction of (1) sections 81 and 87 of the Town and Country Planning Act 1962 and section 163 of the Local Government Act 1933, (2) the conveyance and (3) the agreement, the Corporation were not entitled to vary the appropriation of the land in breach of convenant so that the aerodrome could be used for a purpose other than that of an aerodrome.

The case came before Pennycuick V.-C. in November, 1970 on a motion for interlocutory relief, in anticipation of the Corporation's resolution, which was refused: see [1971] 1 W.L.R. 204, below, p. 305. Plowman J. heard the action and summons together, and dismissed them both ([1973] Ch. 94). The plaintiffs appealed. They contended that there had not been a valid appropriation for planning purposes on the ground that it could not be said that the airfield site was not required for use as an airfield, having regard to the existence of the rights of the plaintiffs under the 1936 conveyance. They contended that it was for the court to decide whether the factual precondition of a non-requirement existed; that it was not necessary to show that the Corporation had acted mala fide, nor that no local authority on the facts could reasonably form the view that land was not required for airfield purposes; that the airfield purpose of the original appropriation or acquisition included flight use by the plaintiffs who still required so to use it, and accordingly the airfield purpose was not spent; that on the evidence the land was required for use as such by the plaintiffs both now and potentially to a greater extent in the future should they revert to manufacture of aircraft requiring flight testing.

The Corporation relied on the decision of Maugham J. in *Att.-Gen* v. *Manchester*

Corp. [1931] 1 Ch. 254 that the question whether the land was not relevantly required was for the decision of the local authority acting bona fide and not for the court.

RUSSELL L.J.: . . . The question whether land is not required for the purpose for which it was acquired has long been posed in statutory enactments relating to corporations and authorities with the ability compulsorily to acquire land. In general the situation was that land not so required had to be disposed of: it was regarded as basically wrong that it should be retained for some other purpose when the authority no longer needed it for the purpose for which is was compulsorily acquired. Subsequently, the statutory system has been to allow a local authority in such a case to appropriate the land to some other purpose for which it has powers of compulsory acquisition, I suppose to avoid the double step of (a) sale and (b) further compulsory acquisition. Section 163 of the Local Government Act 1933 is one example: as originally enacted, the exercise of the power of appropriation required the approval of the Minister, but that requirement was later dropped by amendment. It is a curious fact that no decision directly on this point is to be found, save in that of Maugham J. in *Attorney-General* v. *Manchester Corporation* [1931] 1 Ch. 254: the question there arose under section 175 of the Public Health Act 1875, as amended by section 95 of the Public Health Acts (Amendment) Act 1907: thereunder land not required for the purpose for which it had been acquired might be appropriated for any other purpose, etc. The terms of the statutory provision were not relevantly different from that now under consideration. The land in question had been acquired for street improvements, and the corporation purported to appropriate it for the purpose of a tuberculosis dispensary with the approval (then required) of the Minister of Health. One argument was whether inconsistent public rights had been acquired over the site; but the question was also raised whether the site could be said to be not required for the purpose for which it had been acquired. Maugham J. said, at p. 269:

"I have already said that in my view prima facie the defendant corporation, having acquired lands for a particular purpose, and having applied the lands with an intention that that application should be permanent, are not entitled to alter the purpose in question and to apply the land for a different one except under proper statutory authority or except under, it may be, the provisions of a general Act enabling them to do so. This leads me to what I consider to be the real point of this case—namely, the true construction of section 95 of the Public Health Acts (Amendment) Act 1907, which I have already mentioned. That section was no doubt passed, or partly passed, to prevent the evil which it was thought arose from the decision of the Court of Appeal in the case of *Attorney-General* v. *Hanwell Urban District Council* [1900] 2 Ch. 377. The headnote says (inter alia): 'A local authority have no power to apply permanently land which they have acquired for one purpose to another purpose inconsistent with the original purpose, even though the land cannot possibly be required for that original purpose, and they will be restrained from so doing at the suit of the Attorney-General.' Section 95 provides that [His Lordship read the section, and continued:] Two questions arise under that section which are, I think, of considerable importance and of some difficulty. In the first place the question arises, What is the meaning of the phrase 'not required for the purposes for which those lands have been acquired'? Who is to be the judge of that? Is it a question of fact on which the court may express an opinion, or is it a question on which the determination of the local authority is to prevail? In answering that question, I think that I have to compare section 175 of the Public Health Act 1875. That section, after providing power to purchase, goes on to say: [His Lordship read the section, and continued:] I think that in such a case, either under section 175 of the earlier Act or under section 95 of the amending Act, the local authority, acting in good faith, must be the sole judges of whether the land is no longer required, or is not required for the purpose for which the land was acquired. Of course they must act honestly. I need hardly say that the contrary is not suggested here. But I do not see any ground for thinking that the court can substitute its judgment upon such a question for the local authority who are given by these Acts wide powers of local government. Accordingly, I must take it that, in the circumstances of this case, it has been determined in good faith by the corporation that the land in question is not required for the purpose for which it was acquired in 1875. . . ."

Now that decision, on an indistinguishable section, has we are told been ever since noticed in relevant textbooks without adverse comment. Counsel were unable to find any criticism in any learned articles, over a period in which there has been intensive study and analysis of the powers of the court to disagree with and substitute its own view of the validity of administrative acts for that of, for example, a local authority. Moreover, it is by no means without significance, and is indeed persuasive—though not, of course, conclusive—that the legislature has enacted the same formula in statutes subsequent to that clear decision. Further, for my part, I consider the decision to be correct. It is a function of a local authority to study and keep under review the needs of the inhabitants of the locality and to exercise to the best of its ability its powers with those needs in mind. This must involve the authority in consideration of the relative importance of different needs, not least in connection with the use to which lands of the authority are to be put for the public benefit. I would construe "not required" in the section as meaning "not needed in the public interest of the locality" for the original purpose: and it appears that Maugham J. so construed them. Now that question, it is plain to me, involves matters both of degree and of comparative needs, as to which there can be no question but that the local authority is better qualified than the court to judge, assuming it to be acting bona fide and not upon a view that no reasonable local authority could possibly take. In the present case lack of bona fides is no longer pursued, the abandonment of the site as a municipal airport is in no way criticised, and I can see no ground for holding that the decision of Maugham J., with which I agree, is not directly applicable. Moreover, in so far as the degree of *private* need for use of the airfield as such is said to be relevant, the evidence of likely need to use it for purposes of the plaintiffs' business (other than flight testing of aircraft manufactured at the plaintiffs' factory) is extremely small in extent, and related to convenience rather than need: and the evidence directed to the possibility of future manufacture of aircraft, for which it might fairly be said that there would be a need for the airfield, is purely speculative and on balance of probability unlikely. . . . It was argued for the plaintiffs that authority showed that the court will always inquire into and decide upon the existence of a factual pre-condition of an administrative step; that non-requirement here was such; and that the views of Maugham J. were erroneous. It seems to me that this depends on what is meant by a factual pre-condition, or rather what sort of factual pre-condition is in question. We were referred to *Eleko* v. *Officer Administering the Government of Nigeria* [1931] A.C. 662, where the administrative or executive step that was challenged could only be taken if the appellant was a native chief in the particular area. That, of course, was a simple factual pre-condition which the court was as competent to decide as anyone else. In *In re Ripon (Highfield) Housing Confirmation Order 1938; White and Collins* v. *Minister of Health* [1939] 2 K.B. 838 a compulsory order was quashed on the ground that the land formed part of a park, and such land was excluded from the power of compulsory purchase: a similar type of case. . . .

Accordingly, in my judgment, the contention that the appropriate resolution was invalid on the ground that the land was still required for the purpose for which it was originally acquired or appropriated is unsound and the appeal should be dismissed.

BUCKLEY L.J. (*dubitante*) and LAWTON L.J. delivered concurring judgments.

Appeal dismissed.

Note

Section 163 was re-enacted, with modifications, as section 122 of the Local Government Act 1972.

R. v. HILLINGDON LONDON BOROUGH COUNCIL, ex p. PUHLHOFER

[1986] 1 A.C. 484; [1986] 2 W.L.R. 259; [1986] 1 All E.R. 467
(House of Lords)

LORD BRIGHTMAN. My Lords, the Housing (Homeless Persons) Act 1977 [see now the Housing Act 1985 Part III] has generated a mass of litigation, at the receiving end of which are local authorities endeavouring to cope with intractable housing problems and to balance competing claims to limited housing resources. The present appeal is the first case to reach your Lordships' House, or indeed the Court of Appeal, that is directly concerned with the meaning to be given in the Act to the word "accommodation," a word which is central to the operation of the Act and has a place in almost every section.

The statutory scheme is well known, and needs only a brief introduction. . . . [T]he Homeless Persons Act (as I will call it) imposed for the first time on a local housing authority a positive duty to accommodate homeless persons, as distinct from assisting them through welfare departments. Section 1 of the Act is a definition section. It defines when a person is "homeless" within the meaning of the Act. The key words are: "A person is homeless for the purposes of this Act if he has no accommodation. . . ." The section then sets out circumstances in which a person is to be treated as having no accommodation. These circumstances bring the homeless person's family within the shelter of the Act; a person is to be treated as having no accommodation if there is no accommodation which he, together with any other person who normally resides with him as a member of his family, is entitled to occupy. The second part of the section specifies when a person is to be treated as homeless although he has accommodation, *e.g.* if he cannot secure entry to it. There is also a definition of a person threatened with homelessness. This category of homeless person need not be distinguished for the purposes of the present appeal.

Section 2 in effect divides homeless persons into those who have and those who have not a priority need. The "priority need" class includes, for example, a person who has dependent children residing with him. Section 4 defines the principal duties of the local authority towards the homeless. There are three categories of homeless persons. The highest category, towards whom the local authority has the highest statutory duty, is the homeless person who has a priority need and who is not intentionally homeless. The duty of the local authority is "to secure that accommodation becomes available for his occupation." The next category is the homeless person who has a priority need but became homeless intentionally (as defined in section 17). In this case the duty of the local authority is twofold, to furnish him with advice and appropriate assistance, and to "secure that accommodation is made available for his occupation [including his family, *per* section 16] for such period as they consider will give him a reasonable opportunity of himself securing accommodation for his occupation." The third category is the homeless person with no priority need, whether homeless intentionally or unintentionally. In this case the duty of the local authority is confined to furnishing advice and appropriate assistance. The duty of the local authority to secure that accommodation is made available to the homeless person is accordingly confined to the homeless person with a priority need: indefinite accommodation if not intentionally homeless, temporary accommodation if intentionally homeless.

It will be seen from a reading of the Act that it contains a statutory definition of "homeless" (section 1), "threatened with homelessness" (section 1), "priority need" (section 2), "accommodation . . . available for a person's occupation" (section 16), and "homeless intentionally" (section 17). There is no statutory definition of the word "accommodation" although it is a component of the meaning of each of these expressions. Nor is there any definition in the rest of the housing legislation; the different expression "housing accommodation" is used and defined, in different terms, in the Housing Acts of 1957 and 1974.

I turn to a brief narrative of the facts. The applicants are Mr. and Mrs. Puhlhofer, to whom I will refer as the husband and the wife. The wife, then unmarried, applied to the London Borough of Hillingdon for assistance under the Act of 1977 in June 1983. She had a son born in April 1982 and was treated therefore as having a priority need. . . . The local authority placed her in the Rosslyn Guest House, Harrow, used by the borough for homeless persons within their area. In July 1983 the husband, who was also homeless, applied to the borough for assistance. They introduced him, by way of advice and appropriate assistance, to the same guest house. In September 1983 the husband and the wife married. In April 1984 a child was born of the marriage. In May 1984 the husband and the wife applied jointly to the borough for assistance under the Act. At that time they and the two children were in occupation of one room at the guest house, on a bed-and-breakfast basis. The applicants claimed that this room was not accommodation which answered the statutory duty of the borough under the Homeless Persons Act. The housing officer disagreed. He formally notified the husband and the wife by letter dated May 11, 1984 that they were not homeless or threatened with homelessness "because you have accommodation available for your occupation" at the guest house. The applicants were not satisfied with this answer and obtained leave to apply for judicial review of the local authority's decision. The relief sought by the applicants was an order of certiorari to quash the decision that they were neither homeless nor threatened with homelessness, and a declaration (so far as material) that "the accommodation available to the applicants is such that they are homeless" within the meaning of the Homeless Persons Act.

The applicants were at the date of the application in occupation of one room at the guest house containing a double and a single bed, a baby's cradle, dressing table, pram and steriliser unit. There were no cooking or washing facilities in the room. There were three bathrooms in the guest house, the total capacity of the guest house being 36 people or thereabouts. The applicants were in consequence compelled to eat out and to use a launderette for washing their own and the children's clothing. This expense absorbed most of their state benefit of £78 a week.

It is the submission of the applicants that a person does not have "accommodation" within the meaning of the Act and is therefore "homeless" if he occupies premises which either are not large enough to accommodate the family unit or lack the basic amenities of family life; such basic amenities should include not only sleeping facilities, but also cooking, washing and eating facilities. If the premises are deficient in any of these respects, they are not accommodation. The local authority have to take into account the size of the family, and whether the premises occupied are capable of being regarded as a "home" for that family. Put shortly, "accommodation" must provide the ordinary facilities of a residence. Therefore no local authority properly directing themselves could have formed the view that the room allotted to the applicants at the Rosslyn Guest House was "accommodation" within the meaning of section 1, at least after the child of the marriage was born in April 1984, because it was then overcrowded in the statutory sense, and lacked both exclusive and communal facilities for cooking and clothes washing. So ran the argument for the applicants.

[Lord Brightman noted that Hodgson J., at first instance, had held that the expression "accommodation" meant accommodation appropriate to the needs of the family, and had held that no reasonable housing authority could have come to the conclusion that the accommodation in question was appropriate. On appeal, the Court of Appeal had allowed the housing authority's appeal, Ackner, Slade and Glidewell L.JJ. each rejecting the view that the term "accommodation" meant "appropriate" accommodation. Each considered that, adopting a broader view of "accommodation," there was evidence on which a housing authority could have come to the conclusion that the applicants were not homeless. Lord Brightman continued:]

There are several features of the Act which in my respectful opinion have to be borne in mind. First, although the Act bears the word "Housing" in its short title, it is not an Act which imposes any duty upon a local authority to house the homeless. As the long title indicates, its object is to make "further provision as to the functions of local authorities with respect to persons who are homeless or threatened with homelessness; . . ." It is an Act to assist persons who are homeless, not an Act to provide them with homes. It is an Act which came into operation in England and Wales only four months, and in Scotland only seven months, after it was passed (section 21); not sufficient time to enable a local authority to achieve any dramatic increase in their available housing stock. It is intended to provide for the homeless a lifeline of last resort; not to enable them to make inroads into the local authority's waiting list of applicants for housing. Some inroads there probably are bound to be, but in the end the local authority will have to balance the priority needs of the homeless on the one hand, and the legitimate aspirations of those on their housing waiting list on the other hand.

In this situation, Parliament plainly, and wisely, placed no qualifying adjective before the word "accommodation" in section 1 or section 4 of the

Act, and none is to be implied. The word "appropriate" or "reasonable" is not to be imported. Nor is accommodation not accommodation because it might in certain circumstances be unfit for habitation for the purposes of Part II of the Housing Act 1957 or might involve overcrowding within the meaning of Part IV. [See now Parts IX and X of the 1985 Act]. Those particular statutory criteria are not to be imported into the Homeless Persons Act for any purpose. What is properly to be regarded as accommodation is a question of fact to be decided by the local authority. There are no rules. Clearly some places in which a person might choose or be constrained to live could not properly be regarded as accommodation at all; it would be a misuse of language to describe Diogenes as having occupied accommodation within the meaning of the Act. What the local authority have to consider, in reaching a decision whether a person is homeless for the purposes of the Act, is whether he has what can properly be described as accommodation within the ordinary meaning of that word in the English language.

I do not, however, accept that overcrowding is a factor to be disregarded, as Glidewell L.J. apparently thought. I agree that the statutory definition of overcrowding has no relevance. But accommodation must, by definition, be capable of accommodating. If, therefore, a place is properly capable of being regarded as accommodation from an objective standpoint, but is so small a space that it is incapable of accommodating the applicant together with other persons who normally reside with him as members of his family, then on the facts of such a case the applicant would be homeless because he would have no accommodation in any relevant sense.

In the instant case the bona fides of the borough is not in dispute. On the facts in evidence, it is in my opinion plain that the council were entitled to find that the applicants were not homeless for the purposes of the Homeless Persons Act because they had accommodation within the ordinary meaning of that expression.

My Lords, I am troubled at the prolific use of judicial review for the purpose of challenging the performance by local authorities of their functions under the Act of 1977. Parliament intended the local authority to be the judge of fact. The Act abounds with the formula when, or if, the housing authority are satisfied as to this, or that, or have reason to believe this, or that. Although the action or inaction of a local authority is clearly susceptible to judicial review where they have misconstrued the Act, or abused their powers or otherwise acted perversely, I think that great restraint should be exercised in giving leave to proceed by judicial review. The plight of the homeless is a desperate one, and the plight of the applicants in the present case commands the deepest sympathy. But it is not, in my opinion, appropriate that the remedy of judicial review, which is a discretionary remedy, should be made use of to monitor the actions of local authorities under the Act save in the exceptional case. The ground upon which the courts will review the exercise of an administrative discretion is abuse of power—*e.g.* bad faith, a mistake in construing the limits of the power, a procedural irregularity, or unreasonableness in the *Wednesbury* sense—unreasonableness verging on an absurdity: see the speech of Lord Scarman in *R.* v. *Secretary of State for the Environment, ex p. Nottinghamshire County Council* [1986] A.C. 240, 247–248. Where the existence or non-existence of a fact is left to the judgment and discretion of a public body and that fact involves a broad spectrum ranging from the obvious to the debatable to the just conceivable, it is the duty of the court to leave the decision of that fact to the public body to whom Parliament has entrusted the decision-making power save in a case where it is obvious that the public body, consciously or unconsciously, are acting perversely.

My Lords, I would dismiss this appeal. And I express the hope that there will be a lessening in the number of challenges which are mounted against local authorities who are endeavouring, in extremely difficult circumstances, to perform their duties under the Homeless Persons Act with due regard for all their other housing problems.

LORDS KEITH, ROSKILL, BRANDON and MACKAY agreed.

Appeal dismissed.

Note

The effect of this decision was reversed by the Housing and Planning Act 1986, s.14, which amended sections 58 and 69 of the Housing Act 1985. Section 58(2A) now provides that:

> "A person shall not be treated as having accommodation unless it is accommodation which it would be reasonable for him to continue to occupy."

The authority's duties under sections 65 to 68 of the 1985 Act now involve the securing of "suitable accommodation." In the materials presented so far we have concentrated on the concept of jurisdictional control as it has been applied to the actions of administrative bodies.

We now need to consider certain refinements, and sad to say, further complexities, which are introduced when these principles are applied to the decisions of adjudicatory bodies such as statutory tribunals.

The law which is relevant to an adjudicatory body in the exercise of its functions will cover a variety of matters. In respect of each matter it will be necessary for the body to come to determinations—the issue for us to consider is: in relation to what kinds of such questions will a wrong decision by the adjudicatory body result in its proceedings or decision being *ultra vires* and void?

We need first to consider the kinds of legal questions such a body may have to decide. These may relate to any, or all, of the following matters:

—the proper composition of the tribunal
—the kinds of case which the tribunal has power to hear
—the procedural rules to be followed in hearing and determining such cases
—the substantive rules to be applied to the facts found in order to come to a decision
—the order to be made consequent upon the decision reached.

It will be noted from this list that bodies which adjudicate in accordance with prescribed substantive rules have a potential for making a wider range of kinds of errors than the administrative authorities whose actions we have considered up to now. By analogy with the scope of supervisory control in relation to administrative bodies one would expect that tribunal decisions should be reviewable on the following grounds:

—that the body was not properly constituted when it heard the case
—that the body has heard a type of case which it has no power to hear; or, that it has refused to hear a case which it was under a duty to hear
—that in the course of its hearing the body failed to comply with obligations as to fair procedure
—that the body has made an order, or imposed some penalty, which it has no power to impose.

It is not difficult to see that a statutory tribunal's actions and decisions may be reviewed on these various grounds. What has given rise to more difficulty is the question whether judicial review, as distinct from any right of appeal (which may or may not exist), lies in circumstances where the allegation of the applicant is that the tribunal has come to a "wrong" decision, on the facts or as to the law, on the "merits" of the case. In other words can a tribunal which is properly constituted, which hears a case of a kind in respect of which it has jurisdiction, which conducts itself impeccably in terms of procedure, and which imposes an order which is within its powers, find its decision successfully challenged because of an error made in its decision on the substance of the claim. As we shall see in the cases which follow the courts have been willing to extend review into this area, as part of the High Court's remit in controlling the activities of inferior, limited jurisdiction, bodies. The difficulty has been in drawing a reasonably clear and appropriate line between errors which "go to jurisdiction" and errors which merely "go to the merits," whilst maintaining some distinction of substance between the notions of "appeal" and "review." As the cases which follow demonstrate, this is a matter on which the judges have not all spoken with one voice; nor has the law remained constant through time.

R. v. CITY OF LONDON, ETC., RENT TRIBUNAL, ex p. HONIG

[1951] 1 K.B. 641; [1951] 1 T.L.R. 41; [1951] 1 All E.R. 195; 115 J.P. 42; 49 L.G.R. 252, D.C. (King's Bench Division)

In 1949, the applicant, Emanuel Honig, let two furnished rooms in a house to one Albert Shomade, on a weekly tenancy. In 1950, S. was given a week's notice to quit, to expire on a Monday. A month later, having remained in possession, he referred his contract of tenancy to the rent tribunal under the Furnished Houses (Rent Control) Act 1946, in order to secure a reduction of rent. At the rent tribunal hearing, H. argued that the notice to quit was valid and that therefore there was no "contract of tenancy" subsisting which could be referred to the tribunal. The tribunal held, however, that as the notice to quit was invalid, the tenancy being from Saturday to Saturday, they had jurisdiction to reduce the rent. H. applied for certiorari to quash this reduction, on the ground that the tribunal had no jurisdiction to inquire whether the notice to quit was good or bad.

LORD GODDARD C.J.: The question in the present case is whether the tribunal can, first of all, decide the question of the existence of a tenancy.

Unless they can do so, they can only proceed in a case in which both parties agree that a contract is in existence. If they did not so agree, it would, of course, always be open to a landlord to dispute the existence of the tenancy, in which case the parties would first of all be relegated to the county court to have that preliminary matter determined. . . . I cannot think that it was intended that anything of that kind should take place in connection with proceedings under this Act.

It is not necessary, however, to embark upon any inquiry of that kind because the principles upon which these tribunals can act appear to me to be well established by decided cases. The first thing to consider is whether the tribunal, in order to obtain jurisdiction, must find that a certain state of affairs exists which is collateral to the main question. The question whether there is a contract or not seems to me to be collateral, and clearly collateral, to the main question which the tribunal have jurisdiction to decide, namely, what is the fair rent under a contract of tenancy. If there is no contract, they cannot, of course, determine that question. If there is a contract, they can determine it, and therefore they must decide for themselves in the first instance whether or not the contract exists. . . .

[His Lordship cited *R.* v. *Commissioners for Special Purposes of the Income Tax*, 21 Q.B.D. 313, 319, *per* Lord Esher M.R. (see above, p. 220) and *R.* v. *Lincolnshire JJ., ex p. Brett* [1926] 2 K.B. 192, 201.]

I am of opinion that the tribunal in the present case had power to inquire into the collateral fact, namely, whether there was a contract, because it was only if there was a contract that they could exercise the jurisdiction which the Act of Parliament has given them. When they have decided that, it is open to the person who complains of that decision to ask this court to inquire into it by means of certiorari. In many cases—at any rate in some cases—this court has been able to inquire into the matter by means of documents and other information put before it and has come to the conclusion in some cases that the tribunal decided erroneously, and in others that it acted rightly.

In a case like the present, depending as it did on oral statement against oral statement, although it is not impossible for this court to inquire into the matter it appears to me to be quite impossible for us to hold that the tribunal below were wrong. At any rate, the onus of showing that they were wrong is upon the person who applies for certiorari. The matter here depended entirely on oral statements, and the tribunal saw the witnesses and heard them. It is true that they were not cross-examined on oath, because the proceedings before the tribunals are not conducted on oath. That, again, is a matter for the legislature and not for the courts. These tribunals act on all kinds of evidence which no court of law would look at for a minute. That is one of the difficulties which frequently arise in these cases, and very often arguments are addressed to the court on that ground. But this court has nothing to do with that. If Parliament chooses to set up a tribunal to decide disputed questions of fact not on oath, that is a matter for Parliament and not for this court. Where, as in the present instance, the matter depends on oral statements with flat contradictions on one side or the other, the only people who can come to a decision are those who see and hear the witnesses—I use that word in the colloquial sense of people called before a tribunal to depose to certain facts. The tribunal here heard both parties and came to a decision on the question of fact, and there is nothing before us which can satisfy us that they came to a wrong conclusion. Therefore, certiorari cannot issue and the application must be refused.

HILBERY J. and PARKER J. concurred.

Application refused.

Notes

1. In *R.* v. *Blackpool Rent Tribunal, ex p. Ashton* [1948] 2 K.B. 277, the Divisional Court granted certiorari to quash a determination of a tribunal with jurisdiction over furnished premises. The tribunal had assumed jurisdiction on the ground that the landlord had left in the flat an electric clock, curtains in two rooms, a gas cooker and a water heater. The court held that the first two items could be ignored on the *de minimis* principle, and the second two were not "furniture" at all. Lord Goddard C.J. stated at p. 283:

> "We desire to emphasize that it is no part of a tribunal's duty to endeavour to obtain, by giving a strained construction to ordinary language, a means of exercising their control over unfurnished lettings."

2. In *R.* v. *Fulham, Hammersmith and Kensington Rent Tribunal, ex p. Zerek* [1951] 2 K.B. 1, the tribunal had jurisdiction over unfurnished lettings. The tenant of two rooms let by Z. referred the letting to the tribunal. At the hearing, Z. produced a document signed by the tenant, in which the tenant had agreed to take two furnished rooms. Z. argued that this showed conclusively that the tribunal had no jurisdiction. The tenant's story was that it was originally an unfurnished letting, but when he arrived with his furniture, the landlord refused to let him in unless he agreed first to hire to the landlord his (the tenant's) furniture for a year and then to take the rooms "furnished." The tribunal held they had jurisdiction and reduced the rent. The Divisional Court refused Z.'s application for certiorari to quash the reduction. Counsel for Z. argued that there was a boundary beyond which an administrative tribunal should not be allowed to pursue issues collateral to their jurisdiction. In particular it was unreasonable to permit collateral issues of fraud, forgery or duress to be decided by a tribunal who might make their own rules of evidence and before whom there was no right of cross-examination and no power to subpoena witnesses.

Devlin J. said at pp. 10–11:

> "In my opinion the argument on behalf of the applicant is based on a misconception of what it is that a tribunal in cases such as this is doing. When, at the inception of an inquiry by a tribunal of limited jurisdiction, a challenge is made to their jurisdiction, the tribunal have to make up their minds whether they will act or not, and for that purpose to arrive at some decision on whether they have jurisdiction or not. If their jurisdiction depends upon the existence of

a state of facts, they must inform themselves about them, and if the facts are in dispute reach some conclusion on the merits of the dispute. If they reach a wrong conclusion, the rights of the parties against each other are not affected. For, if the tribunal wrongly assume jurisdiction, the party who apparently obtains an order from it in reality takes nothing. The whole proceeding is, in the phrase used in the old reports, *coram non judice*. If, for example, the applicant in this case wishes, he can sue for his 35s. rent. He will be met with the defence that by the order of the tribunal it has been reduced to 15s. He can reply that that order is bad for want of jurisdiction, and the defendant will have to justify the order on which he relies and so prove the facts which give the tribunal jurisdiction. . . . In such an action, I apprehend, the findings of the tribunal would be irrelevant and inadmissible. They are findings in a preliminary inquiry whose only object is to enable the tribunal to decide for themselves how to act. They are findings, therefore, that cannot ultimately prejudice either party. In these circumstances, I am unable to see why the tribunal should, in making their preliminary inquiry, be restricted to any particular class of case, or how they can be restrained from investigating for their own purposes any point which they think it necessary to determine so that they can decide upon their course of action. . . .

Orders of certiorari and prohibition are concerned principally with public order, it being part of the duty of the High Court to see that inferior courts confine themselves to their own limited sphere. They also afford speedy and effective remedy to a person aggrieved by a clear excess of jurisdiction by an inferior tribunal. But they are not designed to raise issues of fact for the High Court to determine de novo. Accordingly, it has never been the practice to put the party who asserts that the inferior court has jurisdiction to proof of the facts upon which he relies. It is recognized that the inferior court will have made a preliminary inquiry itself and the superior court is generally content to act upon the materials disclosed at that inquiry and to review in the light of them the decision to assume jurisdiction. This is possible only because the court is not, as I conceive it, finally determining the validity of the tribunal's order as between the parties themselves (except, perhaps, in a case such as *Symons* v. *Rees* (1876) 1 Ex.D. 416, where the court investigated for itself the facts and pronounced upon them), but is merely deciding whether there has been a plain excess of jurisdiction or not. Where the question of jurisdiction turns solely on a disputed point of law, it is obviously convenient that the court should determine it then and there. But where the dispute turns on a question of fact, about which there is a conflict of evidence, the court will generally decline to interfere."

The court held that the evidence showed overwhelmingly that the document produced by Z. was a sham.

3. For other examples of cases from this era see *R.* v. *Hampstead and St. Pancras Furnished Houses Rent Tribunal, ex p. Ascot Lodge Ltd.* [1947] K.B. 973; *R.* v. *Fulham, Hammersmith and Kensington Rent Tribunal, ex p. Philippe* [1950] 2 All E.R. 211. The Divisional Court seemed anxious to ensure that tribunals kept within their jurisdiction. There were also doubts over aspects of their procedures: see for example Lord Goddard C.J.'s remarks at the end of the extract from *ex p. Honig*. Might these two concerns be connected?

The jurisdiction of rent tribunals and rent assessment committees has been substantially altered over the years with changes in the substantive law in the area of rent control.

4. The proper composition of a tribunal is usually a jurisdictional matter. For example, in *Howard* v. *Borneman (No. 2)* [1976] A.C. 301, the House of Lords had to decide whether a provision (the Finance Act 1960, s.28(7)) that a tribunal shall consist of a chairman "and two or more persons appointed by the Lord Chancellor

as having special knowledge of and experience in financial or commercial matters" meant that the tribunal was only validly constituted for a particular case if all the appointed members took part. The House decided that the tribunal was validly constituted provided that the chairman and not less than two of the appointed members took part.

5. It is quite common for Parliament to provide that the acts of a tribunal or other body shall be valid notwithstanding a defect in the appointment of a person purporting to be a member. An example is paragraph 20(2) of Schedule IX to the Agriculture Act 1947, which was held by the Court of Appeal to cure the defective appointments of two members of an agricultural land tribunal in *Woollett* v. *Minister of Agriculture* [1955] 1 Q.B. 103. (The defects were that they were appointed neither by the Minister as specified by para. 15 of Sched. IX, nor by a properly authorised civil servant.) Denning L.J. said at page 121:

> "I cannot help remarking that it would be most unfortunate if we came to any other conclusion. The members of the land tribunals in the eastern province have been appointed in this way for several years. They have made decisions in a great many disputes and people have acted on the faith of their decisions. Indeed, we have had cases in this court where these tribunals have given consent to notices to quit by landlords to tenants; and many landlords have recovered their lands on the basis that the decisions are valid: see *Martin-Smith* v. *Smale* [1954] 1 W.L.R. 247. If all the decisions were now invalidated by a technical defect, it would produce great confusion and injustice. It is just the thing which paragraph 20(2) was made to avoid."

Other similar statutory provisions include section 82 of the Local Government Act 1972 (members of local authorities), section 193 of the Licensing Act 1964 (licensing justices (see *Paterson's Licensing Acts* (1991 ed.), pp. 510 *et seq.*)).

The question of the proper composition of a tribunal may be described as a preliminary jurisdictional requirement, or equally properly as a question of procedural *ultra vires*. Questions of composition are also raised by allegations of bias against a tribunal member, on which see pp. 565–592 below, and by the general rule that no person ought to participate in the deliberations of a judicial or quasi-judicial body unless he is a member of it (see *Ward* v. *Bradford Corporation* (1971) 70 L.G.R. 27). See further: P. Jackson, (1974) 90 L.Q.R. 158 and (1975) 91 L.Q.R. 469.

6. The geographical competence of a tribunal is usually regarded as a jurisdictional question. For example, each panel of General Commissioners for Income Tax exercises jurisdiction in respect of a particular geographical area or "division." The allocation of the various kinds of proceedings which may come before the General Commissioners, to the appropriate panel, is governed by section 44 and Schedule 3 to the Taxes Management Act 1970. These rules may include the determination of such questions as where trade is "carried on," or where the appellant "ordinarily resides." See *Lack* v. *Doggett* (1970) 46 T.C. 497, C.A. and *R.* v. *Inland Revenue Commissioners, ex p. Knight* [1973] 3 All E.R. 721, C.A.

7. A tribunal may lack jurisdiction where proceedings before it are not properly instituted. *Cf. Campbell* v. *Wallsend Slipway & Engineering Co. Ltd.* [1978] I.C.R. 1015 where the Divisional Court held that justices did have jurisdiction to proceed with certain informations laid by an inspector of the Health and Safety Executive. The justices had dismissed the informations on the ground that the inspector was not competent to prosecute. The court held (1) that the presumption *omnia praesumuntur rite esse acta* applied in favour of the validity of the appointment of the Executive, and of the inspector, which presumption could only be rebutted by evidence; and (2) that provisions of the Health and Safety at Work Act etc. 1974, requiring certain formalities on the appointment of the Executive, were directory only.

ANISMINIC LTD. v. THE FOREIGN COMPENSATION COMMISSION AND ANOTHER

[1969] 2 A.C. 147; [1969] 2 W.L.R. 163; 113 S.J. 55; [1969] 1 All E.R. 208 (House of Lords)

Anisminic Ltd. was a British company which in 1956 owned a mining property in Egypt, which they claimed was worth over £4 million. On the outbreak of hostilities between Israel and Egypt the property was occupied by Israeli forces and damaged to the extent of some £500,000. On November 1, 1956, property in Egypt belonging to British subjects had been sequestrated by the Egyptian Government. On April 29, 1957, after the Israeli forces had withdrawn, the Egyptian Government authorised a sale of the appellants' property, and it was sold to an Egyptian organisation, T.E.D.O. The appellants' property had included a large quantity of manganese ore, and they took steps to dissuade their customers from buying ore from T.E.D.O. This apparently embarrassed the Egyptian authorities, and on November 23, 1957, an agreement was made between the appellants, T.E.D.O. and the Sequestrator General whereby the appellants purported to sell to T.E.D.O., for £500,000, their whole business in Egypt. This was not, however, to include any claim which the appellants might "be entitled to assert against any governmental authority other than the Egyptian Government, as a result of loss suffered by, or of damage to or reduction in the value of" their business or assets during the events of October and November 1956.

In 1959 a treaty was concluded between the British and Egyptian Governments under which compensation was paid to the British Government in respect of certain properties, including the appellants', listed in Annex E to the treaty. It was accepted that at that stage the disposal of the sum was in the discretion of the British Government. The distribution of the compensation was entrusted to the Foreign Compensation Commission by the Foreign Compensation (Egypt) (Determination and Registration of Claims) Order 1959 (subsequently amended), made under the Foreign Compensation Act 1950. Article 4 of the 1962 Order provided that:

> "(1) The Commission shall treat a claim under this Part of the Order as established if the applicant satisfies them of the following matters:—(*a*) that his application relates to property in Egypt which is referred to in Annex E; (*b*) if the property is referred to in paragraph (1)(*a*) or paragraph (2) of Annex E—(i) that the applicant is the person referred to in paragraph (1)(*a*) or in paragraph (2), as the case may be, as the owner of the property or is the successor in title of such person; and (ii) that the person referred to as aforesaid and any person who became successor in title of such person on or before February 28, 1959, were British nationals on October 31, 1956, and February 28, 1959; . . .
>
> (2) . . .
>
> (3) For the purposes of sub-paragraphs (*b*)(ii) and (*c*)(ii) of paragraph (1) of this article, a British national who died, or in the case of a corporation or association ceased to exist, between October 31, 1956, and February 28, 1959, shall be deemed to have been a British national on the latter date and a person who had not been born, or in the case of a corporation or association had not been constituted, on October 31, 1956, shall be deemed to have been a British national on that date if such person became a British national at birth or when constituted, as the case may be; provided that a converted company shall for the

> purposes of sub-paragraphs (*b*)(ii) and (*c*)(ii) of paragraph (1) of this article be deemed not to have been a British national. . . .

The appellants submitted a claim for compensation to the Commission. After various proceedings, the Commission made a provisional determination to the effect that Anisminic Ltd. had failed to establish entitlement to a claim under the Order, in respect of the sequestrated property, on the ground that T.E.D.O., which had become the successor in title to the appellants, was not at any time a British national. Section 4(4) of the 1950 Act provided that "The determination by the Commission of any application made to them under this Act shall not be called in question in any court of law." Browne J. ([1969] 2 A.C. 223; [1969] C.L.J. 230) made a declaration that the Commission's provisional determination was a nullity, and that the Commission were under a statutory duty to treat the appellants' claim as established. The Court of Appeal ([1968] 2 Q.B. 852) set aside his judgment. Anisminic Ltd. appealed to the House of Lords.

The main questions were as follows:

(1) Was the nationality of a "successor-in-title" relevant where the claimant was the original owner of property mentioned in Annex E of the Treaty? Lords Reid, Pearce and Wilberforce held that it was not. In their view, Article 4(1) was defectively drafted. It was meant to convey (1) that if a person claimed as the original owner, he had to show he was a British national on the dates specified, and (2) that if he claimed as the universal successor, for example after the death of an original owner or the liquidation of an original owning company, he had to show that both he and the original owner were British nationals. (See Lord Reid [1969] 2 A.C. 173–175; Lord Pearce, pp. 201–205; Lord Wilberforce, pp. 212–214.) Lord Morris of Borth-y-Gest did not express a final opinion on this point. Lord Pearson (pp. 219–223) thought the Commission correct in holding that "successor-in-title" meant "successor-in-title" to the claim of the owners against the Egyptian Government, and that this claim had been sold to T.E.D.O. as part of the business assets in Egypt.

(2) Did the error cause the Commission to exceed their jurisdiction, or was it an error within jurisdiction? Lords Reid, Pearce and Wilberforce held that there was an excess of jurisdiction. Lord Pearson (p. 215) accepted that had they made such an error it would have taken them outside their jurisdiction. Lord Morris was of the opinion that it was a matter within their jurisdiction.

(3) If the determination was made in excess of jurisdiction, was it nevertheless protected by section 4(4)? All five members of the House of Lords were agreed that it was not. (Exclusion of judicial review is considered further in Ch. 15.)

[The extracts given here are mainly concerned with the second and third questions.]

LORD REID: . . . The next argument was that, by reason of the provisions of section 4(4) of the 1950 Act, the courts are precluded from considering whether the respondent's determination was a nullity, and therefore it must be treated as valid whether or not inquiry would disclose that it was a nullity. Section 4(4) is in these terms:

> "The determination by the commission of any application made to them under this Act shall not be called in question in any court of law."

The respondent maintains that these are plain words only capable of having one meaning. Here is a determination which is apparently valid: there is nothing on the face of the document to cast any doubt on its validity. If it is a nullity, that could only be established by raising some kind of proceedings in court. But that would be calling the determination in question, and that is expressly prohibited by the statute. The appellants maintain that that is not the meaning of the words of this provision. They say that "determination" means a real determination and does not include an apparent or purported determination which in the eyes of the law has no existence because it is a nullity. Or, putting it in another way, if you seek to show that a determination is a nullity you are not questioning the purported determination—you are maintaining that it does not exist as a determination. It is one thing to question a determination which does exist: it is quite another thing to say that there is nothing to be questioned.

Let me illustrate the matter by supposing a simple case. A statute provides that a certain order may be made by a person who holds a specified qualification or appointment, and it contains a provision, similar to section 4(4), that such an order made by such a person shall not be called in question in any court of law. A person aggrieved by an order alleges that it is a forgery or that the person who made the order did not hold that qualification or appointment. Does such a provision require the court to treat that order as a valid order? It is a well established principle that a provision ousting the ordinary jurisdiction of the court must be construed strictly—meaning, I think, that, if such a provision is reasonably capable of having two meanings, that meaning shall be taken which preserves the ordinary jurisdiction of the court.

Statutory provisions which seek to limit the ordinary jurisdiction of the court have a long history. No case has been cited in which any other form of words limiting the jurisdiction of the court has been held to protect a nullity. If the draftsman or Parliament had intended to introduce a new kind of ouster clause so as to prevent any inquiry even as to whether the document relied on was a forgery, I would have expected to find something much more specific than the bald statement that a determination shall not be called in question in any court of law. Undoubtedly such a provision protects every determination which is not a nullity. But I do not think that it is necessary or even reasonable to construe the word "determination" as including everything which purports to be a determination but which is in fact no determination at all. And there are no degrees of nullity. There are a number of reasons why the law will hold a purported decision to be a nullity. I do not see how it could be said that such a provision protects some kinds of nullity but not others: if that were intended it would be easy to say so.

The case which gives most difficulty is *Smith* v. *East Elloe Rural District Council* [1956] A.C. 736 where the form of ouster clause was similar to that in the present case. But I cannot regard it as a very satisfactory case. The plaintiff was aggrieved by a compulsory purchase order. After two unsuccessful actions she tried again after six years. As this case never reached the stage of a statement of claim we do not know whether her case was that the clerk of the council had fraudulently misled the council and the

Ministry, or whether it was that the council and the Ministry were parties to the fraud. The result would be quite different, in my view, for it is only if the authority which made the order had itself acted in mala fide that the order would be a nullity. I think that the case which it was intended to present must have been that the fraud was only the fraud of the clerk because almost the whole of the argument was on the question whether a time limit in the Act applied where fraud was alleged; there was no citation of the authorities on the question whether a clause ousting the jurisdiction of the court applied when nullity was in question, and there was little about this matter in the speeches. I do not therefore regard this case as a binding authority on this question. The other authorities are dealt with in the speeches of my noble and learned friends, and it is unnecessary for me to deal with them in detail. I have come without hesitation to the conclusion that in this case we are not prevented from inquiring whether the order of the commission was a nullity.

It has sometimes been said that it is only where a tribunal acts without jurisdiction that its decision is a nullity. But in such cases the word "jurisdiction" has been used in a very wide sense, and I have come to the conclusion that it is better not to use the term except in the narrow and original sense of the tribunal being entitled to enter on the inquiry in question. But there are many cases where, although the tribunal had jurisdiction to enter on the inquiry, it has done or failed to do something in the course of the inquiry which is of such a nature that its decision is a nullity. It may have given its decision in bad faith. It may have made a decision which it had no power to make. It may have failed in the course of the inquiry to comply with the requirements of natural justice. It may in perfect good faith have misconstrued the provisions giving it power to act so that it failed to deal with the question remitted to it and decided some question which was not remitted to it. It may have refused to take into account something which it was required to take into account. Or it may have based its decision on some matter which, under the provisions setting it up, it had no right to take into account. I do not intend this list to be exhaustive. But if it decides a question remitted to it for decision without committing any of these errors it is as much entitled to decide that question wrongly as it is to decide it rightly. I understand that some confusion has been caused by my having said in *Reg.* v. *Governor of Brixton Prison, ex p. Armah* [1968] A.C. 192, 234 that if a tribunal has jurisdiction to go right it has jurisdiction to go wrong. So it has, if one uses "jurisdiction" in the narrow original sense. If it is entitled to enter on the inquiry and does not do any of those things which I have mentioned in the course of the proceedings, then its decision is equally valid whether it is right or wrong subject only to the power of the court in certain circumstances to correct an error of law. I think that, if these views are correct, the only case cited which was plainly wrongly decided is *Davies* v. *Price* [1958] 1 W.L.R. 434. But in a number of other cases some of the grounds of judgment are questionable.

I can now turn to the provisions of the Order under which the commission acted, and to the way in which the commission reached their decision. It was said in the Court of Appeal that publication of their reasons was unnecessary and perhaps undesirable. Whether or not they could have been required to publish their reasons, I dissent emphatically from the view that publication may have been undesirable. In my view, the commission acted with complete propriety, as one would expect looking to its membership.

The meaning of the important parts of this Order is extremely difficult to discover, and, in my view, a main cause of this is the deplorable modern drafting practice of compressing to the point of obscurity provisions which would not be difficult to understand if written out at rather greater length.

The effect of the Order was to confer legal rights on persons who might previously have hoped or expected that in allocating any sums available discretion would be exercised in their favour. We are concerned in this case with article 4 of the Order and more particularly with para. (1)(*b*)(ii) of the article. Article 4 is as follows:

[His Lordship read Article 4.]

The task of the commission was to receive claims and to determine the rights of each applicant. It is enacted that they shall treat a claim as established if the applicant satisfies them of certain matters. . . .

The main difficulty in this case springs from the fact that the draftsman did not state separately what conditions have to be satisfied (1) where the applicant is the original owner and (2) where the applicant claims as the successor in title of the original owner. It is clear that where the applicant is the original owner he must prove that he was a British national on the dates stated. And it is equally clear that where the applicant claims as being the original owner's successor in title he must prove that both he and the original owner were British nationals on those dates, subject to later provisions in the article about persons who had died or had been born within the relevant period. What is left in obscurity is whether the provisions with regard to successors in title have any application at all in cases where the applicant is himself the original owner. If this provision had been split up as it should have been, and the conditions, to be satisfied where the original owner is the applicant had been set out, there could have been no such obscurity.

This is the crucial question in this case. It appears from the commission's reasons that they construed this provision as requiring them to inquire, when the applicant is himself the original owner, whether he had a successor in title. So they made that inquiry in this case and held that T.E.D.O. was the applicant's successor in title. As T.E.D.O. was not a British national they rejected the appellants' claim. But if, on a true construction of the Order, a claimant who is an original owner does not have to prove anything about successors in title, then the commission made an inquiry which the Order did not empower them to make, and they based their decision on a matter which they had no right to take into account. If one uses the word "jurisdiction" in its wider sense, they went beyond their jurisdiction in considering this matter. It was argued that the whole matter of construing the Order was something remitted to the commission for their decision. I cannot accept that argument. I find nothing in the Order to support it. The Order requires the commission to consider whether they are satisfied with regard to the prescribed matters. That is all they have to do. It cannot be for the commission to determine the limits of its powers. Of course if one party submits to a tribunal that its powers are wider than in fact they are, then the tribunal must deal with that submission. But if they reach a wrong conclusion as to the width of their powers, the court must be able to correct that—not because the tribunal has made an error of law, but because as a result of making an error of law they have dealt with and based their decision on a matter with which, on a true construction of their powers, they had no right to deal. If they base their decision on some matter which is not prescribed for their adjudication, they are doing something which they have no right to do and, if the view which I expressed earlier is right, their decision is a nullity. So the question is whether on a true construction of the Order the applicants did or did not have to prove anything with regard to successors in title. If the commission were entitled to enter on the inquiry whether the applicants had a successor in title, then their decision as to whether T.E.D.O. was their successor in title would I think be unassailable whether it was right or wrong: it would be a decision on a matter remitted to them for their decision. The question I have to consider is not whether they made a wrong decision but whether they inquired into and decided a matter which they had no right to consider.

. . . In themselves the words "successor in title" are, in my opinion, inappropriate in the circumstances of this Order to denote any person while the original owner is still in existence, and I think it most improbable that they were ever intended to denote any such person. There is no necessity to stretch them to cover any such person. I would therefore hold that the words "and any person who became successor in title to such person" in Article 4(1)(*b*)(ii) have no application to a case where the applicant is the original owner. It follows that the commission rejected the appellants' claim on a ground which they had no right to take into account and that their decision was a nullity. I would allow this appeal.

LORD MORRIS OF BORTH-Y-GEST: [dissenting: stated the facts and continued:] This is not a case in which there has been any sort of suggestion of irregularity either of conduct or procedure on the part of the commission. It has not been said that anything took place which disqualified the commission from making a determination. No occasion arises, therefore, to refer to decisions which have pointed to the consequences of failing to obey or of defying the rules of natural justice: nor to decisions relating to bias in a tribunal: nor to decisions in cases where bad faith has been alleged: nor to decisions in cases where a tribunal has not been properly constituted. If a case arose where bad faith was alleged the difficult case of *Smith* v. *East Elloe Rural District Council* [1956] A.C. 736 would need consideration: but the present case can, in my view, be approached without any examination of or reliance upon that case.

The provisions of section 4(4) of the Act do not, in my view, operate to debar any inquiry that may be necessary to decide whether the commission has acted within its authority or jurisdiction. The provisions do operate to debar contentions that the commission while acting within its jurisdiction has come to wrong or erroneous conclusions. There would be no difficulty in pursuing, and in adducing evidence in support of, an allegation such as an allegation that those who heard a claim had never been appointed or that those who had been appointed had by some irregular conduct disqualified themselves from adjudicating or continuing to adjudicate. There would be no difficulty in raising any matter that goes to the right or power of the commission to adjudicate (see *R.* v. *Bolton* (1841) 1 Q.B. 66). What is forbidden is to question the correctness of a decision or determination which it was within the area of their jurisdiction to make.

It is, of course, clear that no appeal is given from a determination of the commission. When Parliament sets up a tribunal and refers matters to it, it becomes a question of policy as to whether to provide for an appeal. Sometimes that is thought to be appropriate. Thus, where (by the Indemnity Act, 1920), provision was made for the assessment by the War Compensation Court of certain claims for compensation for acts done in pursuance of prerogative powers it was enacted that though the decision of the tribunal (presided over by a judge) was to be final there could be an appeal by a party aggrieved by a direction or determination of the tribunal on any point of law. Sometimes, on the other hand, it is not thought appropriate to provide for an appeal. In reference to the Foreign Compensation Tribunal it was presumably thought that the advantages of securing finality of decision outweighed any disadvantages that might possibly result from having no appeal procedure. It was presumably thought that there was every prospect that right determinations would be reached if those appointed to reach them were persons in whom there could be every confidence.

I return, then, to the question as to how the appellants can justify the calling in question by them of the determination of the commission. The answer is that they boldly say that what looks like a determination was in fact no determination but was a mere nullity. That which, they say, should be disregarded as being null and void, is a determination explained in a carefully reasoned document nearly 10 pages in length which is signed by the chairman of the commission. There is no question here of a sham or spurious or merely purported determination. Why, then, is it said to be null and void? The answer given is that it contains errors in law which have caused the commission to exceed their jurisdiction. When analysed this really means that it is contended that when the commission considered the meaning of certain words in Article 4 of the Order in Council they gave them a wrong construction with the consequence that they had no jurisdiction to disallow the claim of the applicants.

It is not suggested that the commission were not acting within their jurisdiction when they entertained the application of the appellants and gave it their consideration nor when they heard argument and submissions for four days in regard to it. The moment when it is said that they strayed outside their allotted jurisdiction must, therefore, have been at the moment when they gave their "determination."

The control which is exercised by the High Court over inferior tribunals (a categorising but not a derogatory description) is of a supervisory but not of an appellate nature. It enables the High Court to correct errors of law if they are revealed on the face of the record. The control cannot, however, be exercised if there is some provision (such as a "no certiorari" clause) which prohibits removal to the High Court. But it is well settled that even such a clause is of no avail if the inferior tribunal acts without jurisdiction or exceeds the limit of its jurisdiction.

In all cases similar to the present one it becomes necessary, therefore, to ascertain what was the question submitted for the determination of a tribunal. What were its terms of reference? What was its remit? What were the questions left to it or sent to it for its decision? What were the limits of its duties and powers? Were there any conditions precedent which had to be satisfied before its functions began? If there were, was it or was it not left to the tribunal itself to decide whether or not the conditions precedent were satisfied? If Parliament has enacted that provided a certain situation exists then a tribunal may have certain powers, it is clear that the tribunal will not have those powers unless the situation exists. The decided cases illustrate the infinite variety of the situations which may exist and the variations of statutory wording which have called for consideration. Most of the cases depend, therefore, upon an examination of their own particular facts and of particular sets of words. It is, however, abundantly clear that questions of law as well as of fact can be remitted for the determination of a tribunal.

If a tribunal while acting within its jurisdiction makes an error of law which it reveals on the face of its recorded determination, then the court, in the exercise of its supervisory function, may correct the error unless there is some provision preventing a review by a court of law. If a particular issue is left to a tribunal to decide, then even where it is shown (in cases where it is possible to show) that in deciding the issue left to it the tribunal has come to a wrong conclusion, that does not involve that the tribunal has gone outside its jurisdiction. It follows that if any errors of law are made in deciding matters which are left to a tribunal for its decision such errors will be errors within jurisdiction. If issues of law as well as of fact are referred to a tribunal for its determination, then its determination cannot be asserted to be wrong if Parliament has enacted that the determination is not to be called in question in any court of law.

[His Lordship cited passages from the judgments in *R.* v. *Governor of Brixton Prison, ex p. Armah* [1968] A.C. 192, 234 (Lord Reid); *R.* v. *Northumberland C.A.T., ex p. Shaw* [1952] 1 K.B. 338, 346 (Denning L.J.); *R.* v. *Nat Bell Liquors Ltd.* [1922] 2 A.C. 128, 156 (Lord Sumner).]

If, therefore, a tribunal while within the area of its jurisdiction committed some error of law and if such error was made apparent in the determination itself (or, as it is often expressed, on the face of the record) then the superior court could correct that error unless it was forbidden to do so. It would be so forbidden if the determination was "not to be called in question in any court of law." If so forbidden it could not then even hear argument which suggested that error of law had been made. It could, however, still consider whether the determination was within "the area of the inferior jurisdiction."

So the question is raised whether in the present case the commission went out of bounds. Did it wander outside its designated area? Did it outstep the confines of the territory of its inquiry? Did it digress away from its allotted task? Was there some preliminary inquiry upon the correct determination of which its later jurisdiction was dependent?

For the reasons which I will endeavour to explain it seems to me that at no time did the commission stray from the direct path which it was required to tread. Under Article 4 of the Order in Council the commission was under a positive duty to treat a claim under Part III as established if the applicant satisfied them of certain matters. If they had stated that they were satisfied of those matters but had then declined to treat a claim as established, there would have been a situation very different from that now under consideration and one in which the court could clearly act. So also if they had stated that they were not satisfied of the matters but had nevertheless treated the claim as established. They would have had no right to treat the claim as established unless they were satisfied of the matters. The present is a case in which, faithfully following the wording of Article 4, they stated that they were not satisfied of the matters and, therefore, did not treat the claim as established. In stating why they were not satisfied of the matters they have set out the processes of their reasoning. The more that reasoning is examined the more apparent does it, in my view, become that the members of the commission applied their minds very carefully to a consideration of the matters about which the applicant had to satisfy "them." To no one else were the matters remitted but to "them." It was for them to be satisfied and not for anyone else. The words of Article 4 state their terms of reference. In those terms were certain words and certain phrases. The commission could not possibly discharge their duty without considering those words and phrases and without reaching a decision as to their meaning. The commission could not burke that task. It seems to me that the words which stated that it was for the commission to be satisfied of certain matters, and defined those matters, inevitably involved that any necessary interpretation of words within the compass of those matters was for the commission. They could not come to a conclusion as to whether they were satisfied as to the specified matters unless and until they gave meaning to the words which they had to follow. Unless such a phrase as "successor in title" was defined in the Order—and it was not—it was an inescapable duty of the commission to consider and to decide what the phrase signified. Doubtless they heard ample argument before forming a view. The same applies in regard to many other words and sequences of words in Article 4. But the forming of views as to these matters lay in the direct path of the commission's duties. They were duties that could not be shirked. They were central to the exercise of their jurisdiction. When their fully reasoned statement of their conclusions (which in this case can be regarded as a part of their "determination") is studied it becomes possible for someone to contend that an alternative construction of Article 4 should be preferred to that which was thought correct by the commission. But this calling in question cannot, in my view, take place in any court of law. Parliament has forbidden it. . . .

In this case there has been much concentration on the question whether the commission correctly decided that the phrase "successor in title" included an assignee. But this was but one of very many matters which might receive determination by the commission. A perusal of the Orders in Council shows that they bristle with words and phrases needing construction. For my part I cannot accept that if, in regard to any one of the many points in respect of which interpretation and construction became necessary a view can be formed that the commission made an error, the consequence follows that their determination became a nullity as being made in excess of jurisdiction. . . .

The claim of the applicants had to be determined by the commission and the applicants were under the obligation of satisfying the commission as to certain stated matters. They could not decide whether or not they were satisfied until they had construed the relevant parts of the Order in Council. When they were hearing argument as to the meaning of those relevant parts they were not acting without jurisdiction. They were at the very heart of their duty, their task and their jurisdiction. It cannot be that their necessary duty of deciding as to the meaning would be or could be followed by the result that if they took one view they would be within jurisdiction and if they took another view that they would be without. If at the moment of decision they were inevitably within their jurisdiction because they were doing what they had to do, I cannot think that a later view of someone else, if it differed from theirs, could involve that they trespassed from within their jurisdiction at the moment of decision.

It is sometimes the case that the jurisdiction of a tribunal is made dependent upon or subject to some condition. Parliament may enact that if a certain state of affairs exists then there will be jurisdiction. If in such case it appears that the state of affairs did not exist, then it follows that there would be no jurisdiction. Sometimes, however, a tribunal might undertake the task of considering whether the state of affairs existed. If it made error in that task such error would be in regard to a matter preliminary to the existence of jurisdiction. It would not be an error within the limited jurisdiction intended to be conferred. An illustration of this appeared in 1853 in *Bunbury* v. *Fuller* (1853) 9 Ex. 111. . . . [T]here is here no room for any suggestion that the commission failed to satisfy any condition precedent or failed to state the existence of any matter essential to their jurisdiction. . . .

In the submissions on behalf of the appellants a phrase much used was that the commission had asked themselves wrong questions. The phrase can be employed when consideration is being given to a question whether a tribunal has correctly decided some point of construction. If, however, the point of construction is fairly and squarely within the jurisdiction of the tribunal for them to decide, then a suggestion that a wrong question has been posed is no more than a means of deploying an argument: and if construction has been left to the tribunal the argument is unavailing. The phrase is, however, valuable and relevent in cases where it can be suggested that some condition precedent has not been satisfied or where jurisdiction is related to the existence of some state of affairs. . . . So in some cases a tribunal may reveal that by asking some wrong question it fails to bring itself within the area of the demarcation of its jurisdiction. In *Maradana Mosque Trustees* v. *Mahmud* [1967] 1 A.C. 13, P.C., one part of the decision was that the rules of natural justice had been violated. The other part of the decision, relevant for present purposes, was that where statutory authority was given to a Minister to act if he was satisfied that a school *is* being administered in a certain way he was not given authority to act because he was satisfied that the school *had been* administered in that way. It could be said that the Minister had asked himself the wrong question: so he had, but the relevant result was that he never brought himself within the area of his jurisdiction. . . .

I would dismiss the appeal.

LORD PEARCE. My Lords, the courts have a general jurisdiction over the administration of justice in this country. From time to time Parliament sets up special tribunals to deal with special matters and gives them jurisdiction to decide these matters without any appeal to the courts. When this happens the courts cannot hear appeals from such a tribunal or substitute their own views on any matters which have been specifically committed by Parliament to the tribunal.

Such tribunals must, however, confine themselves within the powers specially committed to them on a true construction of the relevant Acts of Parliament. It would lead to an absurd situation if a tribunal, having been given a circumscribed area of inquiry, carved out from the general jurisdiction of the courts, were entitled of its own motion to extend that area by misconstruing the limits of its mandate to inquire and decide as set out in the Act of Parliament.

If, for instance, Parliament were to carve out an area of inquiry within which an inferior domestic tribunal could give certain relief to wives against their husbands, it would not lie within the power of that tribunal to extend the area of inquiry and decision, that is, jurisdiction, thus committed to it by construing "wives" as including all women who have, without marriage, cohabitated with a man for a substantial period, or by misconstruing the limits of that into which they were to inquire. It would equally not be within the power of that tribunal to reduce the area committed to it by construing "wives" as excluding all those who, though married, have not been recently co-habiting with their husbands. Again, if it is instructed to give relief wherever on inquiry it finds that two stated conditions are satisfied, it cannot alter or restrict its jurisdiction by adding a third condition which has to be satisfied before it will give relief. It is, therefore, for the courts to decide the true construction of the statute which defines the area of a tribunal's jurisdiction. This is the only logical way of dealing with the situation and it is the way in which the courts have acted in a supervisory capacity.

Lack of jurisdiction may arise in various ways. There may be an absence of those formalities or things which are conditions precedent to the tribunal having any jurisdiction to embark on an inquiry. Or the tribunal may at the end make an order that it has no jurisdiction to make. Or in the intervening stage, while engaged on a proper inquiry, the tribunal may depart from the rules of natural justice; or it may ask itself the wrong questions; or it may take into account matters which it was not directed to take into account. Thereby it would step outside its jurisdiction. It would turn its inquiry into something not directed by Parliament and fail to make the inquiry which Parliament did direct. Any of these things would cause its purported decision to be a nullity.

Further, it is assumed, unless special provisions provide otherwise, that the tribunal will make its inquiry and decision according to the law of the land. For that reason the courts will intervene when it is manifest from the record that the tribunal, though keeping within its mandated area of jurisdiction, comes to an erroneous decision through an error of law. In such a case the courts have intervened to correct the error.

The courts have, however, always been careful to distinguish their intervention whether on excess of jurisdiction or error of law from an appellate function. Their jurisdiction over inferior tribunals is supervision, not review:

> "That supervision goes to two points: one is the area of the inferior jurisdiction and the qualifications and conditions of its exercise; the other is the observance of the law in the course of its exercise" (*R.* v. *Nat Bell Liquors Ltd.* [1922] 2 A.C. 128, 156).

It is simply an enforcement of Parliament's mandate to the tribunal. If the tribunal is intended on a true construction of the Act to inquire into and finally decide questions within a certain area, the courts' supervisory duty is to see that it makes the authorised inquiry according to natural justice and arrives at a decision whether right or wrong. They will intervene if the tribunal asks itself the wrong questions (that is, questions other than those which Parliament directed it to ask itself). But if it directs itself to the right inquiry, asking the right questions, they will not intervene merely because it has or may have come to the wrong answer, provided that this is an answer that lies within its jurisdiction.

It is convenient to set out the matter in broad outline because there has been evolution over the centuries and there have been many technicalities. There have also been many border-line cases. And the courts have at times taken a more robust line to see that the law is carried out and justice administered by inferior tribunals, and at times taken a more cautious and reluctant line in their anxiety not to seem to encroach or to assume an appellate function which they have not got. . . .

[His Lordship held that section 4(4) did not protect a purported determination made without jurisdiction.]

In my opinion, the subsequent case of *Smith* v. *East Elloe Rural District Council* [1956] A.C. 736 does not compel your Lordships to decide otherwise. If it seemed to do so, I would think it necessary to reconsider the case in the light of the powerful dissenting opinions of my noble and learned friends, Lord Reid and Lord Somervell. It might possibly be said that it related to an administrative or executive decision, not a judicial decision, and somewhat different considerations might have applied; certainly none of the authorities relating to absence or excess of jurisdiction were cited to the House. I agree with Browne J. that it is not a compelling authority in the present case. Again, the fact that this commission was expressly exempted from the provisions of section 11 of the Tribunals and Inquiries Act passed in 1958, though no doubt a tribute to the high standard of the commission and the fact that its chairman was a lawyer of distinction, cannot have any bearing on the construction of the Foreign Compensation Act, 1950.

If, therefore, the commission by misconstruing the Order in Council which gave them their jurisdiction and laid down the precise limit of their duty to inquire and determine, exceeded or departed from their mandate, their determination was without jurisdiction and Brown J. was right in making the order appealed from.

Pursuant to the Foreign Compensation Act 1950 the Order in Council which deals with the present claim gave a wide power to determine the amount of compensation. But with regard to the establishment of the claims under Article 4 it gave narrow powers. It gave no general discretion at all. If the applicant satisfies them of certain listed matters, the commission shall treat the claim as established. The only listed matters so far as relevant to the present claim were, the appellants argue, (1) the fact that the property referred to in Annex E was in Egypt; (2) the identity of the claimant as referred to in Annex E; and (3) the nationality of the claimant on certain dates. There is no dispute that on these matters they satisfied the commission. Therefore, on the appellants' argument, the commission had a mandatory duty to treat their claim as established. If their construction of Article 4 is correct, the appellants are right in this contention. There was no discretion in the commission, no jurisdiction to put further hurdles, other than those listed, in the path of the appellants' claim or to embark on inquiries other than those which the Order in Council directed. The commission, on the other hand, construed the Order as giving them jurisdiction to inquire and be satisfied on two further points; since they were not satisfied on these they rejected the claim. If *their* construction is correct, they were entitled to do so and have not exceeded their jurisdiction.

[His Lordship held that the commission's construction was erroneous.]

LORD WILBERFORCE: . . . In every case, whatever the character of a tribunal, however wide the range of questions remitted to it, however great the permissible margin of mistake, the essential point remains that the tribunal has a derived authority, derived, that is, from statute: at some point, and to be found from a consideration of the legislation, the field within which it operates is marked out and limited. There is always an area, narrow or wide, which is the tribunal's area; a residual area, wide or narrow, in which the legislature has previously expressed its will and into which the tribunal may not enter. Equally, though this is not something that arises in the present case, there are certain fundamental assumptions, which without explicit restatement in every case, necessarily underlie the remission of power to decide such as (I do not attempt more than a general reference, since the strength and shade of these matters will depend upon the nature of the tribunal and the kind of question it has to decide) the requirement that a decision must be made in accordance with principles of natural justice and good faith. The principle that failure to fulfil these assumptions may be equivalent to a departure from the remitted area must be taken to follow from the decision of this House in *Ridge* v. *Baldwin* [1964] A.C. 40. Although, in theory perhaps, it may be possible for Parliament to set up a tribunal which has full and autonomous powers to fix its own area of operation, that has, so far, not been done in this country. The question, what is the tribunal's proper area, is one which it has always been permissible to ask and to answer, and it must follow that examination of its extent is not precluded by a clause conferring conclusiveness, finality, or unquestionability upon its decisions. These clauses in their nature can only relate to decisions given within the field of operation entrusted to the tribunal. They may, according to the width and emphasis of their formulation, help to ascertain the extent of that field, to narrow it or to enlarge it, but unless one is to deny the statutory origin of the tribunal and of its powers, they cannot preclude examination of that extent. . . .

The courts, when they decide that a "decision" is a "nullity," are not disregarding the preclusive clause. For, just as it is their duty to attribute autonomy of decision of action to the tribunal within the designated area, so, as the counterpart of this autonomy, they must ensure that the limits of that area which have been laid down are observed (see the formulation of Lord Sumner in *Rex* v. *Nat Bell Liquors Ltd.* [1922] 2 A.C. 128, 156). In each task they are carrying out the intention of the legislature, and it would be misdescription to state it in terms of a struggle between the courts and the executive. What would be the purpose of defining by statute the limit of a tribunal's powers if, by means of a clause inserted in the instrument of definition, those limits could safely be passed? . . .

[His Lordship cited *R.* v. *Commissioners for Special Purposes of the Income Tax* (1888) 21 Q.B.D. 313, 319 (Lord Esher M.R.); *R.* v. *Shoreditch Assessment Committee, ex p. Morgan* [1910] 2 K.B. 859, 880 (Farwell L.J.); and *R.* v. *Northumberland C.A.T., ex p. Shaw* [1952] 1 K.B. 338, 346 (Denning L.J.).]

These passages at least answer one of the respondents' main arguments, to some extent accepted by the members of the Court of Appeal, which is that *because* the commission has (admittedly) been given power, indeed required, to decide some questions of law, arising out of the construction of the relevant Order in Council, it must necessarily have power to decide those questions which relate to the delimitation of its powers; or conversely that if the court has power to review the latter, it must also have power to review the former. But the one does not follow from the other: there is no reason why the Order in Council should not (as a matter of construction to be decided by the court) limit the tribunal's powers and at the same time (by the same process of construction) confer upon the tribunal power, in the exercise of its permitted task, to decide other questions of law, including questions of construction of the Order. I shall endeavour to show that this is what the Order has done.

The extent of the interpretatory power conferred upon the tribunal may sometimes be difficult to ascertain and argument may be possible whether this or that question of construction has been left to the tribunal, that is, is within the tribunal's field, or whether, because it pertains to the delimitation of the tribunal's area by the legislature, it is reserved for decision by the courts. Sometimes it will be possible to form a conclusion from the form and subject-matter of the legislation. In one case it may be seen that the legislature, while stating general objectives, is prepared to concede a wide area to the authority it establishes: this will often be the case where the decision involves a degree of policy-making rather than fact-finding, especially if the authority is a department of government or the Minister at its head. I think that we have reached a stage in our administrative law when we can view this question quite objectively, without any necessary predisposition towards one that questions of law, or questions of construction, are necessarily for the courts. In the kind of case I have mentioned there is no need to make this assumption. In another type of case it may be apparent that Parliament is itself directly and closely concerned with the definition and delimitation of certain matters of comparative detail and has marked by its language the intention that these shall accurately be observed. If *R.* v. *Minister of Health* [1939] 1 K.B. 232 was rightly decided, it must be because it was a case of the former type. The dispute related to a superannuation allowance and the statute provided that "any dispute" should be determined by the Minister. The basis of the decision is not very clearly expressed but can, I think, be taken to be that, as the context and subject-matter showed, the Minister had a field of decision extending to the construction of the superannuation provisions of the Act. The present case, by contrast, as examination of the relevant Order in Council will show, is clearly of the latter category.

I do not think it desirable to discuss further in detail the many decisions in the reports in this field. But two points may perhaps be made. First, the cases in which a tribunal has been held to have passed outside its proper limits are not limited to those in which it had no power to enter upon its inquiry or its jurisdiction, or has not satisfied a condition precedent. Certainly such cases exist (for example *ex p. Bradlaugh* (1878) 3 Q.B.D. 509) but they do not exhaust the principle. A tribunal may quite properly validly enter upon its task and in the course of carrying it out may make a decision which is invalid—not merely erroneous. This may be described as "asking the wrong question" or "applying the wrong test"—expressions not wholly satisfactory since they do not, in themselves, distinguish between doing something which is not in the tribunal's area and doing something wrong within that area—a crucial distinction which the court has to make. Cases held to be of the former kind (whether, on their facts, correctly or not does not affect the principle) are *Estate and Trust Agencies (1927) Ltd.* v. *Singapore Improvement Trust* [1937] A.C. 898, 915–917; *Seereelall Jhuggroo* v. *Central Arbitration and Control Board* [1953] A.C. 151, 161

> ("whether [the board] took into consideration matters outside the ambit of its jurisdiction and beyond the matters which it was entitled to consider");

R. v. *Fulham, Hammersmith and Kensington Rent Tribunal, ex p. Hierowski* [1953] 2 Q.B. 147. The present case, in my opinion, and it is at this point that I respectfully differ from the Court of Appeal, is of this kind. Secondly, I find myself obliged to state that I cannot regard *Smith* v. *East Elloe Rural District Council* [1956] A.C. 736 as a reliable solvent of this appeal, or of any case where similar questions arise. The preclusive clause was indeed very similar to the present but, however inevitable the particular decision may have been, it was given on too narrow a basis to assist us here. I agree with my noble and learned friends, Lord Reid and Lord Pearce, on this matter.

LORD PEARSON dissented.

Appeal allowed.

Notes

1. This is the most significant modern case on jurisdictional control, and it generated a series of important articles; see H. W. R. Wade, (1969) 85 L.Q.R. 198; S. A. de Smith, [1969] C.L.J. 161; B. C. Gould, [1970] P.L. 358; J. A. Smillie, (1969) 47 Can.Bar Rev. 623; D. Gordon, (1971) 34 M.L.R. 1. See also D. G. T. Williams, [1969] A.S.C.L. 125–126, 129–130; Cooke J. [1975] N.Z.L.J. 529; Sykes and Maher, (1970) 7 Melbourne U.L.R. 385; J. K. Bentil, (1976) U. of W.A.L.R. 543.

2. The judgments of Browne J. and of Diplock L.J. are valuable analyses of the issues and of the case law.

3. The Court of Appeal in *R.* v. *Secretary of State for the Environment, ex p. Ostler* (below, pp. 880–886) has held that despite *Anisminic, Smith* v. *East Elloe R.D.C.* (below, pp. 871–880) is still good law on the effect of clauses excluding judicial review beyond a time limitation.

4. In *R.* v. *Southampton JJ., ex p. Green* [1975] 2 All E.R. 1073 the Court of Appeal granted certiorari to quash a decision by the justices to order forfeiture of the whole of a recognisance entered by Mrs. Green as surety for her husband when he was granted bail. They held that the justices had failed to have regard to a relevant consideration: *i.e.* Mrs. Green's culpability for her husband's disappearance; and had taken into account irrelevant considerations: *i.e.* means which were not, or were not solely Mrs. Green's means (Green's boat, and the matrimonial home which was owned jointly). Lord Denning M.R. held this resulted in "want of jurisdiction" (applying Lord Pearce in *Anisminic*). Browne L.J. felt "very doubtful whether the exercise of a discretion on wrong principles can really be said to be a case of lack or excess of jurisdiction" (p. 1080). Instead his Lordship held that the error was shown by affidavits which were "material which we are entitled to treat as being part of the record" on the principles stated by Lord Denning in *ex p. Shaw* (below, p. 593). Brightman J. agreed with both Lord Denning M.R., and Browne L.J., and Lord Denning M.R. added that he agreed "with the alternative way in which Browne L.J. puts it."

5. The sequel to *Anisminic* was summarised by S. A. de Smith, [1969] C.L.J. at pp. 164–166. See the Foreign Compensation Act 1969, s.3. Points of interest in section 3 include the express power of the Commission "to determine any question as to the construction or interpretation of any provision of an Order in Council under section 3 of the 1950 Act with respect to claims failing to be determined by them" (1969 Act, s.3(1)); the provision of an appeal by way of case stated on a point of law to the Court of Appeal (s.3(4)–(7)); and the provision that a "determination" (which includes a "provisional determination" and "anything which purports to be a determination" (s.3(3)) is not to be called in question in any court of law (s.3(9)) except on the ground of breach of natural justice (s.3(10)).

6. The question whether all errors of *law* are to be regarded as going to jurisdiction has been considered in subsequent cases: see *Re Racal Communications Ltd.*, below, p. 254. A possible corollary might have been that the courts would no longer redetermine for themselves jurisdictional *facts*. This development has not taken place: see, *e.g. Khawaja* v. *Secretary of State for the Home Department*, above, p. 214. A recent illustration is *R.* v. *Secretary of State for the Environment, ex p. Davies* (1990) 61 P. & C.R. 487, where the Court of Appeal held that the question whether a person had an "interest in land" to which an enforcement notice related, and so was entitled to appeal to the Secretary of State under the Town and Country Planning Act 1971, s.88 (now the 1990 Act, s.174), was a matter that went to the jurisdiction of the Secretary of State. Neill L.J. said (at p. 492) that

> "it is now clear that it is common ground that where the decision-maker had to determine a preliminary question as to his own jurisdiction and this determination involved the inferences to be drawn from correspondence and other documents, the test to be applied by the court on judicial review is not that of

perversity or unreasonableness. It is accepted that the court is entitled to look at the matter afresh and make up its own mind.

The only remaining question between the parties on this first issue is as to the weight, if any, to be attached to the decision of the Secretary of State. . . .

As will become clear, we are concerned in this case with a claim by the appellant that at the material time she was in adverse possession of land and thus, it is said, had an interest in the land for the purposes of section 88(1) of the 1971 Act. It is necessary for her to establish an interest in land in order that she can appeal to the Secretary of State. It seems to me that in such circumstances, where the decision impugned involves a question as to the jurisdiction of the decision-maker and where the primary facts are contained in documents and do not involve any questions of credibility or policy, the court should look at the matter afresh and make up its own mind. That means, however, that the court must look at the matter on the basis of the evidence which was before the Secretary of State at the time when he reached his decision, because it is his decision against which judicial review is sought."

(The court concluded on the facts, in agreement with the Secretary of State, that the applicant did not have an interest in the land).

Questions

1. Is anything more than lip-service paid to the freedom of an inferior tribunal to make errors of law within jurisdiction? What errors might the commission have made without exceeding their jurisdiction? Can *Anisminic* be reconciled with *R.* v. *Northumberland C.A.T., ex p. Shaw* (below, p. 593) where the error in question was regarded as non-jurisdictional?

2. Can it be said that the conditions which had to be established as to the status of a claimant were collateral to the main question as to the amount of compensation which should be paid? Did their Lordships adopt that approach?

IN RE RACAL COMMUNICATIONS LTD.

[1981] A.C. 374; [1980] 3 W.L.R. 181 (*sub nom. Re A Company*); [1980] 2 All E.R. 634 (House of Lords)

Racal were suspected by the police of having inflated cost items in estimates submitted to the Ministry of Defence, thereby obtaining profit percentages substantially above those to which they were contractually entitled. It was suspected that this dishonest practice emanated from instructions given to employees by the head of Racal's quotations department. The D.P.P., prior to the institution of any criminal proceedings, sought sight of the company's records under the *ex parte* procedure provided for in section 441(1), Companies Act 1948. Vinelott J. refused the application, holding that the expression in section 441(1)—"an offence in connection with the management of the company's affairs"—was confined to offences committed in the course of the internal management of the company, and did not cover the offences of which Racal was suspected.

By virtue of section 441(3)—"the decision of a judge of the High Court . . . on an application under this section shall not be appealable." Notwithstanding this provision, the Court of Appeal heard an appeal against Vinelott J.'s decision, and reversing that decision, made an order in favour of the D.P.P. ([1980] Ch. 138). Racal appealed to the House of Lords.

LORD DIPLOCK: . . . The first reason that Racal rely upon is that the Court of Appeal had no jurisdiction to entertain an appeal from a decision of a

High Court judge made in the exercise of the statutory jurisdiction conferred on him by section 441(1) of the Companies Act 1948. Their argument is simplicity itself and can be stated in a single sentence. Subsection (3) provides that his decision shall *not* be appealable. One asks oneself rhetorically: "What could be plainer than that?" What principle of statutory interpretation can lead one to suppose that Parliament when it said "not appealable" really meant "appealable on some grounds but not on others?" To give to the phrase "shall not be appealable" its ordinary and, linguistically, its only possible meaning, does not lead to results so manifestly absurd or unjust as to drive one to the conclusion that Parliament must have intended that, despite the unqualified language used, the judge's decision should be unappealable on some grounds only but appealable to the Court of Appeal on others. . . .

My Lords, I can see no ground for saying that the consequences of denying all appeals from the decision of a High Court judge granting or refusing an order for production and inspection of a company's documents under section 441 are so absurd or unjust that Parliament cannot have meant what it so plainly said but must have intended the unappealability to be subject to implied exceptions. On the contrary, there seem to me to be cogent reasons for denying any right of appeal. So on the sole and simple ground that the statute says the judge's decision shall not be appealable I would hold the Court of Appeal had no jurisdiction to entertain an appeal from Vinelott J.'s decision to refuse the order applied for by the Director of Public Prosecutions and that the order that they purported to make ordering production and inspection of Racal's papers is a nullity and must be set aside.

It follows that your Lordships, in your turn, have no jurisdiction to enter on a consideration of whether or not the judge's decision was right or wrong. Nevertheless, to understand the reasoning by which the Court of Appeal reached the conclusion that it was entitled to exercise appellate jurisdiction in the instant case it is necessary to refer briefly to the judge's reasons for refusing to make the order that was applied for. He gave to the expression "an offence in connection with the management of the company's affairs" in section 441(1) a construction which the Court of Appeal regarded as too narrow. In the context of the Act he regarded it as confined to offences committed in the course of the internal management of the company and held that the particular offences of which an employee of Racal was suspected did not fall within the section. He also doubted whether the employee fell within the class of "officer of a company" within the meaning of the Companies Act 1948. The ground on which he dismissed the application was therefore one of law. The Court of Appeal were of opinion, rightly or wrongly, that the learned judge had misconstrued the statute and held further that section 441(3) did not render his decision unappealable if it were based on a mistake of law.

The question of jurisdiction was disposed of somewhat summarily in the judgments of the Court of Appeal. . . .

Lord Denning M.R., in a passage that is set out in full in the speech of Lord Scarman, referred to two authorities: *Anisminic Ltd.* v. *Foreign Compensation Commission* [1969] 2 A.C. 147 and a passage from his own judgment in *Pearlman* v. *Keepers and Governors of Harrow School* [1979] Q.B. 56, 70: "... no court or tribunal has any jurisdiction to make an error of law on which the decision of the case depends." He described the decision of the learned judge to dismiss the application in the instant case as refusing a jurisdiction which he ought to have entertained. Shaw L.J. [1980] Ch. 138, 144 referred to him as having "renounced jurisdiction." Templeman L.J. added nothing on the jurisdiction point. He agreed with the two previous judgments.

My Lords, this summary way of disposing of the question of jurisdiction appears to me to overlook (1) the distinction between the appellate jurisdiction of the Court of Appeal and the original jurisdiction exercisable only by the High Court (as successor to the old Court of King's Bench) to review decisions of inferior tribunals for error of law, by use of the prerogative writs of certiorari, prohibition and mandamus which have now been replaced by orders obtainable on application for judicial review, (2) the distinction between courts of law and tribunals or courts exercising administrative functions ..., and (3) the distinction between the High Court and an inferior court of law.

The jurisdiction of the Court of Appeal is wholly statutory; it is appellate only. The court has no original jurisdiction. It has no jurisdiction itself to entertain any original application for judicial review; it has appellate jurisdiction over judgments and orders of the High Court made by that court on applications for judicial review. Both the cases referred to in the Court of Appeal's judgment in the instant case were cases of judicial review which started in the High Court and came up on appeal in the ordinary way, to this House in *Anisminic* [1969] 2 A.C. 147 and to the Court of Appeal in *Pearlman* [1979] Q.B. 56. The judgment in the instant case, however, does not differentiate between appeal and judicial review. On the face of it, it appears to treat the jurisdiction in both kinds of procedure as identical. This, it may be, reflects a view expressed obiter by Lord Denning M.R. in *Pearlman* at p. 71. That was a case in which an order of certiorari was sought in respect of a determination of a county court judge made in the exercise of his statutory jurisdiction under Sched. 8 to the Housing Act 1974, which provided that this determination should be "final and conclusive." The Master of the Rolls overruling the Divisional Court, held that certiorari would lie but added that if he had come to the contrary conclusion he would have held that "final and conclusive" excluded appeal from the county court to the Court of Appeal on questions of fact only but not on questions of law.

My Lords, with great respect, I think that this dictum, on which counsel for the respondent strongly relied, is wrong; but in any event it has no application to the instant case. The expression with which your Lordships are concerned instead of being "final and conclusive" is "not appealable," which perhaps makes the point even clearer, but I agree with counsel for the respondent that there is no relevant distinction between the two. The general jurisdiction of the Court of Appeal to hear and determine appeals from any order of the High Court is conferred by section 27(1) of the Supreme Court of Judicature (Consolidation) Act 1925, but this is subject to the restrictions specified in section 31(1), of which the relevant provision is:

> "No appeal shall lie . . . (*d*) from the decision of the High Court or of any judge thereof where it is provided by any Act that the decision of any court or judge, the jurisdiction of which or of whom is now vested in the High Court, is to be final."

There is no room here for distinguishing between appeals on matters of fact and appeals on matters of law. I would, therefore, conclude that even if Vinelott J.'s decision were open to attack on judicial review the Court of Appeal would have had no original jurisdiction to entertain it.

I turn next to the question of the availability of judicial review instead of appeal as a means of correcting mistakes of law made by a court of law as distinct from an administrative tribunal or other administrative authority, however described when it is exercising quasi-judicial functions. In *Anisminic* [1969] 2 A.C. 147 this House was concerned only with decisions of administrative tribunals. Nothing I say is intended to detract from the breadth of the scope of application to administrative tribunals of the principles laid down in that case. It is a legal landmark; it has made possible the rapid development in England of a rational and comprehensive system of administrative law on the foundation of the concept of *ultra vires*. It proceeds on the presumption that where Parliament confers on an administrative tribunal or authority, as distinct from a court of law, power to decide particular questions defined by the Act conferring the power, Parliament intends to confine that power to answering the question as it has been so defined, and if there has been any doubt as to what that question is this is a matter for courts of law to resolve in fulfilment of their constitutional role as interpreters of the written law and expounders of the common law and rules of equity. So, if the administrative tribunal or authority have asked themselves the wrong question and answered that, they have done something that the Act does not empower them to do and their decision is a nullity. Parliament can, of course, if it so desires, confer on administrative tribunals or authorities power to decide questions of law as well as questions of fact or of administrative policy; but this requires clear words, for the presumption is that where a decision-making power is conferred on a tribunal or authority that is not a court of law, Parliament did not intend to do so. The breakthrough made by *Anisminic* [1969] 2 A.C. 147 was that, as respects administrative tribunals and authorities, the old distinction between errors of law that went to jurisdiction and errors of law that did not was for practical purposes abolished. Any error of law that could be shown to have been made by them in the course of reaching their decision on matters of fact or of administrative policy would result in their having asked themselves the wrong question with the result that the decision they reached would be a nullity. . . .

But there is no similar presumption that where a decision-making power is conferred by statute on a court of law, Parliament did not intend to confer on it power to decide questions of law as well as questions of fact. Whether it did or not and, in the case of inferior courts, what limits are imposed on the kinds of questions of law they are empowered to decide, depends on the construction of the statute unencumbered by any such presumption. In the case of inferior courts where the decision of the court is made final and conclusive by the statute, this may involve the survival of those subtle distinctions formerly drawn between errors of law which go to jurisdiction and errors of law which do not that did so much to confuse English administrative law before *Anisminic* [1969] 2 A.C. 147; but upon any application for judicial review of a decision of an inferior court in a matter which involves, as so many do, interrelated questions of law, fact and degree the superior court conducting the review should not be astute to hold that Parliament did not intend the inferior court to have jurisdiction to decide for itself the meaning of ordinary words used in the statute to define the question which it has to decide. This, in my view, is the error into which the majority of the Court of Appeal fell in *Pearlman* [1979] Q.B. 56. The question for decision by the county court judge under para. 1(2) of Sched. 8 to the Housing Act 1974 was whether the installation of central heating in a particular dwelling house amounted to "structural alteration, extension or addition." If the meaning of ordinary words when used in a statute becomes a question of law, here was a typical question of mixed law, fact and degree which only a scholiast would think it appropriate to dissect into two separate questions, one, for decision by the superior court, *viz.* the meaning of those words—a question which must entail considerations of degree; and the other for decision by the county court, *viz.* the application of the words to the particular installation—a question which also entails considerations of degree. The county court judge had not ventured on any definition of the words "structural alteration, extension or addition." So there was really no material on which to hold that he had got the meaning wrong rather than its application to the facts. Nevertheless the majority of the Court of Appeal in *Pearlman* [1979] Q.B. 56 held that Parliament had indeed intended that such a dissection should be made and since they would not have come to the same conclusion themselves on the facts of the case they inferred that the judge's error was one of interpretation of the words "structural alteration, extension or addition." This was in the face of a powerful dissent by Geoffrey Lane L.J. Notwithstanding that on the facts of the case he too would have reached a different conclusion from that of the county court judge, he was of opinion that the statute conferred on the judge jurisdiction to decide finally and conclusively a question which did involve interrelated questions of law, fact and degree, and that the Supreme Court had no jurisdiction to interfere with his decision by way of judicial review. For my part, I find the reasoning in his minority judgment conclusive.

There is in my view, however, also an obvious distinction between jurisdiction conferred by a statute on a court of law of limited jurisdiction to decide a defined question finally and conclusively or unappealably, and a similar jurisdiction conferred on the High Court or a judge of the High Court acting in his judicial capacity. The High Court is not a court of limited jurisdiction and its constitutional role includes the interpretation of written laws. There is thus no room for the inference that Parliament did not intend the High Court or the judge of the High Court acting in his judicial capacity to be entitled and, indeed, required to construe the words of the statute by which the question submitted to his decision was defined. There is simply no room for error going to his jurisdiction, nor, as is conceded by counsel for the respondent, is there any room for judicial review. Judicial review is available as a remedy for mistakes of law made by inferior courts and tribunals only. Mistakes of law made by judges of the High Court acting in their judicial capacity as such can be corrected only by means of appeal to an appellate court; and if, as in the instant case, the statute provides that the judge's decision shall not be appealable, they cannot be corrected at all. . . .

For all these reasons, I do not think that any sufficient grounds have been shown why this appeal ought not to be allowed for the very simple reason with which I started: that the words of the statute "shall not be appealable" mean what they say.

LORD SALMON: . . . The Court of Appeal . . . relied strongly on the decision of your Lordship's House in *Anisminic Ltd.* v. *Foreign Compensation Commission* [1969] 2 A.C. 147. That decision, however, was not, in my respectful view, in any way relevant to the present appeal. It has no application to any decision or order made at first instance in the High Court of Justice. It is confined to decisions made by commissioners, tribunals or inferior courts which can now be reviewed by the High Court of Justice—just as the decision of inferior courts used to be reviewed by the old Court of King's Bench under the prerogative writs. If and when any such review is made by the High Court, it can be appealed to the Court of Appeal and thence, by leave, to your Lordships' House. . . .

LORD EDMUND-DAVIES: . . . [In *Pearlman*] . . . Lord Denning M.R. said [1979] Q.B. 56 at pp. 69–70):

> ". . . the distinction between an error which entails *absence* of jurisdiction—and an error made *within* the jurisdiction—is very fine. So fine indeed that it is rapidly being eroded. Take this very case . . . [The judge's] error can be described on the one hand as an error which went

to his jurisdiction . . . By holding that it was not a 'structural alteration . . . or addition' he deprived himself of jurisdiction to determine those matters. On the other hand . . . it can plausibly be said that he had jurisdiction to enquire into the meaning of the words . . . and that his wrong interpretation of them was only an error within his jurisdiction, and not an error taking him outside it. . . . I would suggest that this distinction should now be discarded. The High Court has, and should have, jurisdiction to control the proceedings of inferior courts and tribunals by way of judicial review. When they go wrong in law, the High Court should have power to put them right . . . The way to get things right is to hold thus: no court or tribunal has any jurisdiction to make an error of law on which the decision of the case depends. If it makes such an error, it goes outside its jurisdiction and certiorari will lie to correct it. . . ."

In his dissenting judgment, Geoffrey Lane L.J. . . . quoted from the county court judge's judgment, and commented, [1979] Q.B. 56 at p. 76):

"The judge is considering the words . . . which he ought to consider. He is not embarking on some unauthorised or extraneous or irrelevant exercise. All he has done is to come to what appears to this court to be a wrong conclusion on a difficult question. It seems to me that, if this judge is acting outside his jurisdiction, so then is every judge who comes to a wrong decision on a point of law. Accordingly, I take the view that no form of certiorari is available to the tenant."

My Lords, like the Judicial Committee of the Privy Council in a recent decision to which I was a party (*South East Asia Fire Bricks Sdn. Bhd.* v. *Non-Metallic Mineral Products Manufacturing Employees Union* [1981] A.C. 363), I have to say respectfully that the existing law is, in my judgment, to be found in the dissenting judgment of Geoffrey Lane L.J. in *Pearlman* and that the majority view was erroneous.

Turning to the present case, I hold that the effect of section 441(3) could not be clearer in depriving the Court of Appeal of jurisdiction. . . .

LORD KEITH of KINKEL agreed with the speech of LORD DIPLOCK. LORD SCARMAN delivered a concurring speech.

Notes

1. In *South East Asia Fire Bricks Sdn. Bhd.* v. *Non-Metallic Mineral Products Manufacturing Employees Union* [1981] A.C. 363, Lord Fraser, giving the opinion of the Judicial Committee a matter of days before the House of Lords decision in *Racal*, said (at p. 370):

". . . In *Pearlman* . . . Lord Denning M.R. suggested that the distinction between an error of law which affected jurisdiction and one which did not should now be 'discarded.' Their Lordships do not accept that suggestion. They consider that the law was correctly applied to the circumstances of that case in the dissenting opinion of Geoffrey Lane L.J. . . ."

Lord Diplock was not a member of the Judicial Committee hearing the *SE Asia* case.

2. Note the extra-judicial words of Lord Diplock in 1972: "If the material before the reviewing court discloses that the decision under review is one which the court would have reversed if it had come up on an appeal from a lower court of law, legal reasoning is never at a loss to find a way of reversing it. . . . Current trends may soon enable us to say . . . 'There is no question that cannot be turned into a jurisdictional question.' " Foreword to B. Schwartz and H. W. R. Wade, *Legal Control of Government* (1972), p. xiii. Note also his views expressed at [1974] C.L.J. 233.

3. In *R.* v. *Chief Immigration Officer, Gatwick Airport, ex p. Kharrazi* [1980] 1 W.L.R. 1396, Lord Denning M.R. referred to:

> "the important observations of Lord Diplock in *Re Racal*. . . . These do away with long-standing distinctions between errors within the jurisdiction and errors without it, by the simple device which was adumbrated in *Pearlman*. . . . No administrative tribunal or administrative authority has jurisdiction to make an error of law on which the decision in the case depends. The House said in *Re Racal* that we were wrong to apply that concept to the High Court; but it left it intact with regard to administrative tribunals and other administrative bodies. Meaning thereby, as I understand it, all statutory tribunals and authorities other than regular courts of law. . . . Incidentally I would make this comment: although we were wrong, according to the House of Lords, in *Pearlman* . . . and [*Racal*] . . . we did clear up the legal position. We did give guidance to the judges below as to the way in which the statute in question should be interpreted. Whereas the House of Lords gave no guidance. They left every judge to do as he liked. Each one could interpret the statute as he wished, according to the length of his foot, and no one could correct him. . . . What a state of affairs."

4. In *O'Reilly* v. *Mackman* [1983] 2 A.C. 237, H.L., Lord Diplock had occasion, *obiter*, to reformulate his statements in *Re Racal* as to the bodies in respect of which "error of law within jurisdiction" remained a significant concept, and those bodies in respect of which that concept should no longer, in his view, apply. He said:

> "*Anisminic* . . . liberated English public law from the fetters that the courts had theretofore imposed on themselves so far as determinations of inferior courts and statutory tribunals were concerned, by drawing esoteric distinctions between errors of law committed by such tribunals that went to their jurisdiction, and errors of law committed by them within their jurisdiction. The breakthrough that *Anisminic* made was the recognition by the majority of this House that if a tribunal whose jurisdiction was limited by statute or subordinate legislation mistook the law applicable to the facts as it had found them, it must have asked itself the wrong question, *i.e.* one into which it was not empowered to inquire and so had no jurisdiction to determine. Its purported 'determination,' not being a 'determination' within the meaning of the empowering legislation, was accordingly a nullity."

Following this statement in *O'Reilly*, the Divisional Court, in *R.* v. *Greater Manchester Coroner, ex p. Tal* [1985] Q.B. 67, declined to follow its earlier decision in *R.* v. *Surrey Coroner, ex p. Campbell* [1982] Q.B. 661. In the *Campbell* case the Divisional Court had categorised a coroner's inquest as a body *not* subject to review for error of law regardless of the question of jurisdiction—*i.e.* review in the full Anisminic sense. In *ex p. Tal*, the Divisional Court noted that "inferior courts" were, according to Lord Diplock in *O'Reilly*, to be set alongside administrative/statutory tribunals and administrative authorities as being subject to this intensive scope of review—leaving only courts of law of limited jurisdiction (like in *Pearlman*) subject to the traditional concept of error within jurisdiction.

Is a distinction between "courts" and "tribunals" for the purpose of the scope of jurisdictional control (or indeed for any other purpose) workable? Note that only Lord Diplock in *Re Racal* (with whose speech Lord Keith agreed) considered the scope of *Anisminic* in respect of *inferior* courts and tribunals. Is it likely that Lord Diplock intended by his brief remarks in *O'Reilly* v. *Mackman* to discard the court/tribunal distinction?

5. It now seems customary to refer to the notion that all errors of law should found judicial review as the "*Anisminic* principle." This terminology is likely only to confuse. The speeches in *Anisminic*, as we have seen, sought explicitly to preserve the notion of "error of law within jurisdiction." Subsequently, commentators and judges noted that, given the statements in *Anisminic* about the ways in which a decision-maker may in the course of coming to his decision make an error which goes to jurisdiction, the substance of the preserved concept had, in reality, been much reduced. In practical terms, it was said, we may consider all errors of law go to jurisdiction—though the dangers of such a bold approach were subsequently demonstrated in the House of Lord's approach to *Pearlman*. In due course this rationalisation of the practical effect of *Anisminic* has itself become labelled "the *Anisminic* doctrine"!

6. If all errors of law *do* go to jurisdiction, the precise scope of the concept "error of law" becomes crucial. See below, pp. 639–663.

7. The modern case-law on jurisdictional control is considered by J. Beatson, "The Scope of Judicial Review for Error of Law" (1984) 4 O.J.L.S. 22; G. L. Peiris, "Patent error of law and the borders of jurisdiction: the Commonwealth experience" (1984) 4 L.S. 271, and "Jurisdictional Review and Judicial Policy: the Evolving Mosaic" (1987) 103 L.Q.R. 66.

On *Pearlman*, see J. F. Garner, (1979) 42 M.L.R. 578; J. Griffiths, [1979] C.L.J. 11; H. F. Rawlings, [1979] P. L. 404; H. W. R. W[ade], (1979) 95 L.Q.R. 163. On *Racal*, see H. W. R. W[ade], (1980) 96 L.Q.R. 492.

8. Note that there is no need to distinguish between jurisdictional and non-jurisdictional errors of law where statute provides an *appeal* on a point of law (see below, pp. 639–651). Moreover, a broad view has been taken of the scope of statutory applications to quash to include the correction of any error of law (see below, pp. 622–639). In practice, it is normally only where a statutory clause purports to exclude judicial review that the question becomes crucial. *Anisminic* (above pp. 237–252) involved a "shall not be questioned" clause and *Pearlman* a "no certiorari" clause. These clauses take away the court's power to quash for error of law on the face of the record, but not to quash for lack of jurisdiction (see below, pp. 866–886).

CHAPTER 7

REVIEW OF THE EXERCISE OF DISCRETION—RETENTION OF DISCRETION

IN this and the following chapter we shall be considering judicial review in relation to the exercise of discretionary powers. By "discretionary power" we mean the situation where a body has a power of choice, in the circumstances, to do "X" or not to do "X"; or to do "X" and/or "Y" or do neither. We shall be concerned to see what principles of review are applied by the courts in supervising such discretionary powers. We are not here concerned with the situation where a body has had a "duty" imposed upon it to act in a designated way in defined circumstances, involving no exercise of discretion on the part of that body.

In the cases which follow there is usually no argument as to whether the body challenged has, in the circumstances, the discretionary power in question. In this way the cases differ from those which have formed the subject-matter of Chapter 6. In the cases which follow the challenge is made on the ground that a body on which the statutory power in question has been conferred *either*:

(i) **has failed properly to retain that degree of free and unfettered power of judgment** as to whether, and, if so how, it should exercise its discretionary powers, which Parliament is assumed by the courts to have intended that donees of such powers should have retained. Such failure may arise in a number of ways, and we shall look at the decisions under the following sub-headings—"acting under dictation," "failure to retain discretion by unauthorised delegation of power," "over-rigid adherence to self-created rules of policy," "fettering discretion by contractual or similar undertakings," and "fettering discretion by estoppel." These matters are considered in this chapter.

or,

(ii) **has exercised its powers in a way which the reviewing court may categorise as an "abuse of power."** The courts have consistently stated that powers must be exercised for "proper purposes," must be exercised on the basis of consideration of "relevant" matters and the exclusion from consideration of "irrelevant" matters, and the manner of the exercise of power must not in substance be "unreasonable"—must not be a manner of exercising the power which no reasonable person/body could have chosen. These various grounds of challenge for "abuse of power" form the principal subject-matter of Chapter 8.

(A) ACTING UNDER DICTATION

R. v. THE MAYOR, ALDERMEN AND COUNCILLORS OF STEPNEY

[1902] 1 K.B. 317; 71 L.J.K.B. 238; 86 L.T. 21; 18 T.L.R. 98; 66 J.P. 183; 46 S.J. 106; 50 W.R. 412, D.C. (King's Bench Division)

Mr. Jutsum was clerk to the vestry of Mile End Old Town from 1872 to 1901. In 1901 this parish was included in the new metropolitan borough of Stepney. The existing parish officers were transferred to the borough council. Under the London Government Act 1899, s.30(1), the council had power to abolish the office of any officer transferred to them, whose office they deemed unnecessary. They accordingly abolished J.'s office. He was now entitled to compensation calculated in accordance with the Local Government Act 1888, s.120. This stated that regard should be had, *inter alia*, to the conditions on which his appointment was made, to the nature of his office or employment, to the duration of his service . . . " and to all the other circumstances of the case, and the compensation shall not exceed the amount which, under the Acts and Rules relating to Her Majesty's Civil Service, is paid to a person on abolition of office."

J. held his post on a part-time basis, as he was also a solicitor in private practice. The town clerk of Stepney wrote to the Treasury asking what their rule was as to the amount of compensation paid to a person in the Civil Service on abolition of an office, held part time. The reply was that the Treasury's practice was to calculate the compensation allowance as if the office was full time, but to deduct a quarter of the amount so arrived at. The council acted on this letter and assessed the compensation accordingly.

J. applied for mandamus to compel the council to deal with his claim properly. He could have appealed to the Treasury under section 120(4), who had power to determine what sum "ought to be granted."

CHANNELL J. . . . I think that the mandamus ought to go because the local authority have not in fact exercised their discretion upon this matter. They have, by a mistake, thought that they were bound by a practice of the Treasury as though it were a rule, and consequently they exercised no discretion in the matter. In my opinion, if they had said "We quite know that we are not bound by this absolutely, but we think it right to follow the Treasury practice," and had so followed it, they would have exercised their discretion and would have been right; but they thought that they were bound when they were not bound, and consequently it is a case for a mandamus calling upon them to exercise their discretion in the matter. . . . It is clearly settled that the Court does not grant a prerogative writ of mandamus when there is another remedy, if that other remedy is equally convenient and adequate. . . . I think he has another remedy; but I do not think on the whole, after some consideration, that it is equally convenient, because I think that the local tribunal is the one that is best to investigate in the first instance the particular facts about this gentleman's employment. They will know much more about it than the Treasury can know, and it is much better that they should investigate the facts in the first instance. I think, therefore, that although the applicant here could, in the present state of things, go to the Treasury and get them to decide finally the amount of the allowance which he ought to have—and very likely he will have to go there in the end, and the Treasury will ultimately have to decide the matter—yet I do not think that that is an equally convenient remedy where the local authority have not exercised their discretion, because if he goes to the Treasury now he will have to go without the preliminary investigation, which might or might not be useful to him in going there. . . .

LORD ALVERSTONE C.J. and DARLING J. delivered concurring judgments.

Notes

1. In *Roncarelli* v. *Duplessis* (1959) 16 D.L.R. (2d) 689, it was found that D., the Prime Minister and Attorney-General of Quebec, ordered the Quebec Licensing Commission to revoke R.'s liquor permit, in response to R.'s activities in acting in over 380 cases as surety for Jehovah's Witnesses charged with distributing literature (some of which was thought to be seditious) without a licence. The discretion to revoke was legally the Commission's, but there was "ample evidence to sustain the finding of the trial judge that the cancellation . . . was the result of instructions given by the respondent to the Managers of the Commission" (Martland J. at p. 737). D stated in a press interview: "It was I, as Attorney-General of the Province charged with the protection of good order, who gave the order to annul [R.'s] permit. By so doing not only have we exercised a right but we have fulfilled an imperious duty. The permit was cancelled not temporarily but definitely and for always." This was held to be unlawful on the ground that the Commission acted under dictation, and also because "it was a gross abuse of legal power expressly intended to punish [R.] for an act wholly irrelevant to the statute. . . ." (Rand J. at p. 706).

2. In Part I (above p. 52) we drew attention to the common practice of Parliament, in conferring grants of power, of imposing an obligation to consult with specified or unspecified persons or bodies prior to exercising the power. As will be seen when we consider review for failure to comply with procedural requirements, this obligation to consult is one which the courts have regarded as of being of a "mandatory" nature. See below, p. 451. Even beyond instances where an express statutory obligation to consult may exist, the process of consultation prior to coming to a decision may be regarded as part of the required process by which, as we shall see (below, p. 362), a decision-maker must seek to inform himself of *all relevant circumstances* in relation to the decision he is to take. More generally still, the process of consultation has been regarded as part and parcel of the process of "good administration"—as providing a mechanism, by which decision-makers may take account of, and benefit from, a broad range of expertise and opinion in coming to their eventual decisions.

This present ground of challenge shows that those exercising statutory powers must steer a proper course between the process, voluntary or mandatory, of consultation and the requirement that the ultimate power of decision must remain in their hands. A context in which consultation is, perhaps, most likely to drift into dictation is where there is consultation of one organ of government by another. See, *e.g. Lavender* v. *Minister of Housing and Local Government* (below, p. 287) where it could be said that the respondent minister had acted under the dictation of the Minister of Agriculture.

3. In some instances legislation may expressly empower one body to issue "guidance" to another as to the exercise of the latter's powers. In *Laker Airways* v. *Department of Trade* [1977] Q.B. 643, the Court of Appeal considered the provisions of the Civil Aviation Act 1971 under which the Secretary of State was empowered to give "guidance" to the Civil Aviation Authority as to the exercise of its functions, and the CAA was, in turn, obliged to "perform those functions in such manner as it considers is in accordance with" such guidance (1971 Act, s.3(2)). Construing the scope of this power to issue guidance, the Court of Appeal held that it did not cover guidance which contradicted the general policy objectives which were expressly stated in the 1971 Act itself. The power to issue guidance was restricted to power to explain, amplify or supplement those objectives. As regards the CAA's duty to follow guidance given under the Act, Lord Denning M.R. explained (at p. 699):

> "So long as the 'guidance' given by the Secretary of State keeps within the due bounds of guidance, the Authority is under a duty to follow his guidance. Even

so, the Authority is allowed some degree of flexibility. It is to perform its functions 'in such manner as it considers is in accordance with the guidance.' So, whilst it is obliged to follow the guidance, the manner of doing so is for the Authority itself. . . ."

Note that a power, in the 1971 Act, under which the Secretary of State could give "directions" to the CAA was interpreted as denoting power to give orders which had to be obeyed by the CAA and which could, unlike the guidance, be contrary to the Act's general objectives.

In determining the extent to which a body is obliged to follow statutory guidance the particular terms of the legislation must be considered. For example, an Act may use a formula under which a body exercising powers is required simply to take guidance into account, without being obliged to follow the guidance. Such was the case in *R.* v. *Police Complaints Board ex p. Madden* [1983] 1 W.L.R. 447. The Police Complaints Board was required by the Police Act 1976 to "have regard to" certain guidance given to it by the Secretary of State. The Board adopted a policy of following the guidance given. McNeill J. held that the Board had thereby failed properly to exercise its own discretion as to the exercise of its powers. It had erred in regarding its obligation to "have regard to" the guidance as an obligation to "comply with" the guidance. Rather the Board, "as an independent body, ought to [have been] asserting its independence" (p. 470). Certainly it was obliged to take the guidance into account in reaching its own decisions. It fell into error in regarding the legislation as conferring a power of dictation on the Minister.

4. A local education authority may not use its power to dismiss school governors as a means of imposing its views on educational matters on the governors; it is the policy of the Education Act 1944 that the governors and the authority should have different spheres of responsibility: *R.* v. *Inner London Education Authority, ex p. Brunyate* [1989] 1 W.L.R. 542, H.L.; *R.* v. *Trustee of the Roman Catholic Diocese of Westminster, ex p. Andrews, The Times*, August 18, 1989. On the other hand, a decision that all council-appointed governors should face reappointment and replacement in order to ensure that the number of governors appointed by each political party continued to be in proportion with party representation on the council was held to be lawful in *R.* v. *Warwickshire County Council, ex p. Dill-Russell* (1990) 89 L.G.R. 640, D.C. and C.A.; and a local council can change the membership of one of its committees, which is not an independent body, in order to ensure that council policy is followed in committee: *R.* v. *Greenwich London Borough Council, ex p. Lovelace* [1991] 1 W.L.R. 506. (These cases might now be subject to the restrictions imposed on council appointments by the Local Government and Housing Act 1989, ss.15–17, which requires a political balance on committees and certain other bodies.)

5. The extent to which a decision by a councillor to vote in accordance with the "party line" can fall foul of the rule against the fettering of discretion was considered in the following case. In *R.* v. *Waltham Forest London Borough Council, ex p. Baxter* [1988] Q.B. 419, members of the majority group on the council held a private, party meeting where they discussed what the policy of the group would be as to the setting of the rate at the forthcoming council meeting. After discussion, the group agreed to support a rate increase of 62 per cent. for the domestic rate and 56.6 per cent. for the non-domestic rate. The group's standing orders provided that members were required to refrain from voting in opposition to group decisions, the sanction being withdrawal of the party whip. A number of members who voted against this level of increase at the group meeting voted in favour at the council meeting, at which a resolution to increase the rate by the previously agreed amounts was passed by 31 votes to 26. A number of ratepayers sought judicial review on a variety of grounds. The Divisional Court rejected

arguments to the effect (1) that the councillors had fettered their discretion by regarding themselves as bound by the terms of their election manifesto to undertake expenditure which rendered such a rate inevitable: (2) that the resolution was "irrational" or "*Wednesbury* unreasonable"; (3) that there was no genuine or adequate consultation with representatives of commerce and industry; and (4) that six or seven councillors had voted contrary to their personal views. The Court of Appeal dismissed an appeal confined to issue (4). The court held that had the councillors in question voted for the resolution not because they were in favour of it but because their discretion had been fettered by the vote at the group meeting, then the councillors would have been in breach of their duty to make up their own minds as to what rate was appropriate. However, that was not established on the facts. The councillors were entitled to take account of party loyalty and party policy as relevant considerations provided that they did not dominate so as to exclude other considerations. The court noted that the sanction was only withdrawal of the party whip: there was nothing to prevent a councillor who voted against the party line continuing as an independent member. Furthermore, these procedures were widely adopted by political groups throughout the country and this had not been regarded by the Widdicombe Committee on the Conduct of Local Authority Business (Cmnd. 9797, 1986) as a matter for concern.

(B) Unauthorised Delegation of Power

This ground of challenge reflects a presumption of statutory interpretation known as the principle *delegatus non potest delegare*—the principle that where a function has been entrusted by statute to body "X," the function should be performed by "X" and not delegated by "X" for performance by body "Y." The theory is that the legislature has delegated power to "X" and that a delegate does not itself have power further to delegate such power.

It is convenient to consider this ground of challenge here. Body "X" may be said in these circumstances to have failed properly to exercise its discretion by having delegated its power of decision to another body. Alternatively, we could have considered this topic in the context of "want of jurisdiction" (see above pp. 200 ff). The purported exercise of power by the body to whom there has been an unlawful delegation is challengeable as an act beyond the powers of that body.

This principle, taken to an extreme, could operate as a severe restraint on administrative decision-making. The materials which follow demonstrate not only the operation of the principle, but also important legislative and case-law limits. Thus we shall note that:

(i) the principle does not prevent the exercise by civil servants of powers entrusted by legislation to the ministerial head of a Department or entrusted to the Department itself—the *Carltona* principle (below p. 277);

(ii) Parliament may provide express authority to a body, on whom it has conferred powers, to delegate, and even for that delegate to subdelegate, those powers. The maxim *delegatus non potest delegare* is a presumption of interpretation which must give way to clear contrary legislative intention. Where a power of delegation does exist, the courts may still, of course, be called upon to consider whether the delegate has acted within or beyond the scope of the powers delegated. An important legislative provision of this kind, permitting wide powers of delegation in the context of the exercise of functions conferred on local authorities, is the Local Government Act 1972, s.101 (below p. 282);

(iii) The rule against delegation has been interpreted as requiring that the ultimate power of decision as to the whether and how a discretionary power is to be exercised should be retained by the designated statutory body. It does not preclude that body from delegating to another body some preliminary tasks leading up to that final decision. In so doing the appointed body is adopting a procedure by which it seeks assistance in reaching what can still be regarded as its own decision on the matter. Thus a body may delegate certain fact-finding tasks to, and even seek recommendations from, another body (or its own sub-committee). It must, however, retain to itself the power of final decision—it must not allow itself to be dictated to by the delegate, not can it confer power to make any binding decision (as distinct from non-binding recommendation) on the delegate. In truth this is no exception to the principle stated above—it is simply a situation where a court may hold that no delegation of the power of decision has in fact occurred. As we shall see the courts have been more tolerant of such decision-making arrangements in relation to the exercise of administrative functions than in relation to the exercise of judicial powers. See, generally, below pp. 272–277.

Note

On delegation, see generally J. Willis, "Delegatus Non Potest Delegare" (1943) 21 Can. Bar Rev. 257; *Allen*, pp. 177–195; P. H. Thorp, (1972) 2 Auck.U.L.J. 85.

HUTH v. CLARKE

(1890) 25 Q.B.D. 391; 59 L.J.Q.B. 559; 63 L.T. 348; 6 T.L.R. 373; 55 J.P. 86; [1886–1890] All E.R. Rep. 542 (Queen's Bench Division)

By Schedule 6 to the Contagious Diseases (Animals) Act 1878 a county council had power to appoint an executive committee with all the council's powers under the Act. In turn, the executive committee could appoint a sub-committee and delegate all or any of the committee's powers to it. A delegation could be revoked or altered from time to time. In 1889, West Sussex County Council appointed an executive committee. On October 9, 1889, the executive committee appointed local sub-committees, and authorised them to exercise certain powers, including power under the Rabies Order 1887, to make regulations for the muzzling of dogs. No such regulations were in fact made by the local sub-committee, but on March 21, 1890, the executive committee made an order under the Rabies Order that no dog should be at large within the district of Chichester local sub-committee unless it was effectively muzzled or kept under proper control. The appellant was summoned for a breach of this order. He argued in his defence that the order was *ultra vires*, on the ground that it could only be made by the Chichester sub-committee. The justices stated a case for the opinion of the High Court.

LORD COLERIDGE C.J.: . . . [W]e . . . have a regulation in force in the district made by the proper authority and dealing with a subject-matter with which they were competent to deal. It is suggested, however, that, because there was another authority which might (had it chosen) have violated good sense by making an inconsistent order, the executive committee had no power to make the regulation in question. But delegation does not imply a denudation of power and authority; the 6th schedule of the Act provides that the delegation may be revoked or altered and the powers resumed by the executive committee. The word "delegation" implies that powers are committed to another person or body which are as a rule always subject to resumption by the power delegating, and many examples of this might be given. Unless, therefore, it is controlled by statute, the delegating power can at any time resume its authority. Here the executive committee has exercised the power which the sub-committee might have exercised—but did not—and no question of conflict of jurisdiction arises. I think, therefore, that the justices came to a perfectly right conclusion, and the conviction must be upheld.

WILLS J. delivered a concurring judgment.

Notes

1. In holding that delegation does not mean parting with authority altogether, this case conflicts with *Blackpool Corporation* v. *Locker* [1948] 1 K.B. 349. It is suggested that *Huth* v. *Clarke* is correct on this point (see *de Smith*, p. 302) and that *Blackpool Corporation* v. *Locker* must be read in the light of its special facts. (See generally on this case *Allen*, pp. 187 *et seq.*; C. K. Allen, *Law and Disorders*, p. 87 "Squaring the Circular," 11 M.L.R. 338; 12 M.L.R. 37; 64 L.Q.R. 306; 66 L.Q.R. 14.)

2. A principal may at any time revoke authority which it has given to a delegate. The revocation of authority will, however, be of prospective effect only—it will not affect the validity of any acts already done under delegated authority: see *Battelley* v. *Finsbury Borough Council* (1958) 56 L.G.R. 165. Note also, that acts of an *unauthorised* body may be ratified or adopted by a body which *has* authority in the matter. This adoption will, however, be of prospective effect only—it does not give retrospective validity to the acts of the unauthorised body: see *Firth* v. *Staines* [1897] 2 Q.B. 70; *Warwick RDC* v. *Miller-Mead* [1962] Ch. 441, [1962] 1 All E.R. 212; *Stoke-on-Trent City Council* v. *B&Q. Retail Ltd.* [1984] Ch. 1, discussed in *Cross*, paras. 4–75–4–84.

BARNARD AND OTHERS v. NATIONAL DOCK LABOUR BOARD AND OTHERS

[1953] 2 Q.B. 18; [1953] 2 W.L.R. 995; 97 S.J. 331; [1953] 1 All E.R. 1113; [1953] 1 Lloyd's Rep. 371 (Court of Appeal)

The Dock Workers (Regulation of Employment) Order 1947 set up a scheme to ensure greater regularity of employment for dock workers, and to secure an adequate number of dock workers available for the efficient performance of dock work. The National Dock Labour Board was established by the Order to administer the scheme. It was required by the Order to delegate to local boards all appropriate functions. These included the operation of a disciplinary code. Under Clause 16 the local board could suspend for seven days a registered dock worker who failed to comply with any of the provisions of the scheme. One of the local boards, the London Dock Labour Board, passed a resolution which had the effect of leaving the power of suspension to the London port manager, Mr. Hogger. As the result of a dispute, Mr. Hogger suspended the plaintiffs. They exercised their rights of appeal to an appeal tribunal set up under the Order, which only had power to revise penalties imposed by the local board. Their appeals were dismissed. Further industrial action followed. Eventually the plaintiffs applied to the High Court for declarations that their suspensions had been wrongful in the light of the facts of the dispute. At the discovery of documents stage, the plaintiffs learned for the first time that they had been suspended, not by the local board, but by the port manager. They amended their pleadings and claimed a further declaration that the original notices of suspension were *ultra vires* and invalid. Counsel for the Board argued that the disciplining of dock workers was an administrative function, which could be delegated.

McNair J. held that the local board had power to delegate its disciplinary functions to the port manager.

The Court of Appeal reversed McNair J. on this point.

DENNING L.J.: . . . It was urged on us that the local board had power to delegate their functions to the port manager on the ground that the power of suspension was an administrative and not a judicial function. It was suggested that the action of the local board in suspending a man was similar in character to the action of an employer in dismissing him. I do not accept this view. Under the provisions of the scheme, so far from the board being in the position of an employer, the board are put in a judicial position between the men and the employers; they are to receive reports from the employers and investigate them; they have to inquire whether the man has been guilty of misconduct, such as failing to comply with a lawful order, or failing to comply with the provisions of the scheme; and if they find against him they can suspend him without pay, or can even dismiss him summarily. In those circumstances they are exercising a judicial function just as much as the tribunals which were considered by this court in the corn-porters' case, *Abbott* v. *Sullivan* [1952] 1 K.B. 189 and in *Lee* v. *Showmen's Guild of Great Britain* [1952] 2 Q.B. 329 the only difference being that those were domestic tribunals, and this is a statutory one. The board, by their procedure, recognize that before they suspend a man they must give him notice of the charge and an opportunity of making an explanation. That is entirely consonant with the view that they exercise a judicial function and not an administrative one, and we should, I think, so hold.

While an administrative function can often be delegated, a judicial function rarely can be. No judicial tribunal can delegate its functions unless it is enabled to do so expressly or by necessary implication. In *Local Government Board* v. *Arlidge* [1915] A.C. 120 the power to delegate was given by necessary implication; but there is nothing in this scheme authorizing the board to delegate this function, and it cannot be implied. It was suggested that it would be impracticable for the board to sit as a board to decide all these cases; but I see nothing impracticable at all; they have only to fix their quorum at two members and arrange for two members, one from each side, employers and workers, to be responsible for a week at a time: probably each pair would only have to sit on one day during their week.

Next, it was suggested that even if the board could not delegate their functions, at any rate they could ratify the actions of the port manager; but if the board have no power to delegate their functions to the port manager, they can have no power to ratify what he has done. The effect of ratification is to make it equal to a prior command; but just as a prior command, in the shape of a delegation, would be useless, so also is a ratification. . . .

We have to consider here two decisions: first, the decision to suspend the men; second, the decision of the appeal tribunal. So far as the decision to suspend is concerned, as I see it, . . . we are asked to interfere with the position of a usurper. The port manager (if he will forgive my saying so) is a usurper, or, at any rate, is in the position of a usurper. I do not mean this unkindly, because I know that he acted in good faith on the authority of the board; nevertheless, he has assumed a mantle which was not his, but that of another. This is not a case of a tribunal which has a lawful jurisdiction and exercises it; it is a case of a man acting as a tribunal when he has no right to do so. These courts have always had jurisdiction to deal with such a case. . . . We can declare that the suspension ordered by the port manager was unlawful and void. We can declare it to be the nullity which in law it was.

So far as the decision of the appeal tribunal is concerned, it seems to me that, once the port manager's order is found to be a nullity it follows that the order of the appeal tribunal is also a nullity. The appeal tribunal has no original jurisdiction of its own; it cannot itself make a suspension order; it can only affirm or disaffirm a suspension order which has already been made. If none has been made because it is a nullity, the tribunal can do nothing. It cannot make something out of nothing any more than anybody else can: see *Toronto Railway Co.* v. *Corporation of the City of Toronto* [1904] A.C. 809, 815. . . .

SINGLETON and ROMER L.JJ. delivered concurring judgments.

Notes

1. See case notes at 69 L.Q.R. 451; 16 M.L.R. 506.

2. As regards the issue of the power to delegate administrative, as distinct from judicial, functions compare the statements of Denning L.J. in *Barnard* with the decision of the House of Lords in *Vine* v. *National Dock Labour Board* [1957] A.C. 488, where the facts were similar. The plaintiff, a registered dockworker, was dismissed by a disciplinary committee appointed by the South Coast Local Dock Labour Board. Ormerod J. awarded him £250 damages and granted a declaration that the purported dismissal was *ultra vires*. His judgment was upheld in the House of Lords. Their Lordships were agreed that delegation was not permissible in the circumstances—the matter was "too important to delegate" (Lord Kilmuir L.C. at p. 499), and "of a judicial character" (Lord Morton at p. 502). Lord Cohen (at p. 505) doubted "whether the mere fact that it was an administrative act would be conclusive of the matter," but did not explore the point as he was satisfied that the local board as acting "in a judicial capacity." Lord Somervell (at p. 512) said:

> "In deciding whether a 'person' has power to delegate one has to consider the nature of the duty and the character of the person. Judicial authority normally cannot, of course, be delegated, though no one doubted in *Arlidge's* case that the Local Government Board, which consisted of the President, the Lord President of the Council, the Secretaries of State, the Lord Privy Seal and the Chancellor of the Exchequer (Local Government Board Act 1871), could act by officials duly deputed for the purpose, whether or not the act to be done had

judicial ingredients. There are, on the other hand, many administrative duties which cannot be delegated. Appointment to an office or position is plainly an administrative act. If under a statute a duty to appoint is placed on the holder of an office, whether under the Crown or not, he would, normally, have no authority to delegate. He could take advice, of course, but he could not by a minute authorize someone else to make the appointment without further reference to him. I do not, therefore, find it necessary to consider what judicial requirements might be held implicit in the local board's proceedings under clause 16. I am, however, clear that the disciplinary powers, whether 'judicial' or not, cannot be delegated. The non-entitlement to pay, the suspension, the notice or the dismissal must be a step taken by the board and not by a delegate. The penalities, in some cases, may be slight but, in some cases, very great. A man who has worked all his life in the docks may find himself precluded altogether from doing so. Today it may be easy for him to get other work, but that has not always been so. The constitution of the board also supports the conclusion. It is clearly constituted so as to inspire confidence and weigh fairly the interests of employers and employed. The purported delegation in the present case was to a representative of each side, but it is impossible to imply a limited right of delegation. *Osgood* v. *Nelson* (1872) L.R. 5 H.L. 636 (below, p. 272) decides that in somewhat similar circumstances the appointment of a committee to take evidence and report is not in itself a delegation of authority. If there are administrative difficulties, this may be an answer to them."

See note by E. C. S. Wade, [1957] C.L.J. 6.

3. Denning L.J. held that the board's decision could not retrospectively validate the decision of the unauthorised port manager. Compare the approach of the courts to the "curative" effect of appeal proceedings where the decision appealed from is tainted by failure to have complied with the principles of natural justice. See below, p. 561.

OSGOOD v. NELSON

(1872) L.R. 5 H.L. 636; 41 L.J.Q.B. 329 (House of Lords)

From 1856 to 1867, Mr. Osgood held the office of Registrar of the Sheriff's Court of the City of London. He was appointed by resolution of the Court of Common Council of the City. In August 1866 allegations of neglect in the performance of his duties were made against the plaintiff. These were referred by the Council to their "Officers and Clerks' Committee." Mr. Osgood appeared before the committee and had access to the relevant documents. The committee took evidence, and reported that in their opinion irregularities had occurred, such as seriously interfered with the proper conduct of public business. The matter was considered by the Council on May 2, 1867. Mr. Osgood was present, represented by counsel (Mr. Serjeant Tindal Atkinson). The council had before them the committee's report and a transcript of the notes of evidence. The council resolved to dismiss Mr. Osgood, and appoint Mr. Nelson in his place. The plaintiff brought an action in the Court of Queen's Bench to recover the fees of his office, in order to challenge the validity of the dismissal. The Court of Queen's Bench gave judgment for the defendant, and this was upheld in the Court of Exchequer Chamber. The case was then taken to the House of Lords on Error.

One issue was whether there had been an unlawful delegation to the committee.

MR. BARON MARTIN, speaking in the name of the Judges present said: . . . In our opinion there was no delegation at all. What was done was, that a complaint having been made to the body which had control in the matter, *viz.*, the Mayor, Aldermen, and Commons of the City of London, as to the conduct of Mr. Osgood, it was referred by them to a committee, which seems to have been long used in the Corporation of London, known as the "Officer and Clerk's Committee"; and what they were directed to do was to make inquiry with reference to the alleged complaint, to take evidence, and to ascertain the truth of it, not for the purpose of that committee coming to any judgment or decision themselves, but for the purpose of their report being submitted to the Mayor, Aldermen, and Commons in order that they might come to a judgment upon it. The argument of the learned counsel is erroneous in point of fact. That has not taken place which they allege to have taken place, and therefore there was no delegation.

. . . [W]e are of opinion, that in the proceedings before the committee in the first place, every possible opportunity that could be given to any man was given to Mr. Osgood in this matter. He was allowed to cross-examine witnesses, and he was permitted also to call as many witnesses as he pleased. He was repeatedly asked whether he had any farther evidence to produce, and he was permitted to address the Court himself, and to state his view of the matter, and to comment on the evidence. These proceedings having occupied four days, it was on March 21, that the committee came to a decision upon the matter. Therefore, as it seems to us, so far as the proceedings before this committee are concerned, it is impossible that any one can have had a fuller and fairer opportunity than Mr. Osgood had of bringing forward his case, with any evidence he might have to support it.

It was on March 21, that the report of the committee was presented to the Court of Common Council. The Common Council permitted a period of more than six weeks to elapse before proceeding to discuss it. It was then discussed, and Mr. Serjeant Tindal Atkinson, who was counsel on the part of Mr. Osgood, then repeated what Mr. Osgood had before said, and stated that he did not require any farther particularity in the charge. He was content to take the case as it then stood. He was requested by the Recorder to state whether or not he desired to offer any farther evidence than that which appeared on the shorthand writer's notes, and he stated that he did not, and then proceeded to address the Court at considerable length in regard to this matter. Throughout the whole of the proceedings Mr. Osgood had the presence either of the Recorder or of the Common Serjeant for the purpose of assisting the Committee and the Common Council. Therefore, it does seem to us that it is impossible for any man to have had what I may call a fairer trial than Mr. *Osgood* had with reference to this matter. . . .

LORD COLONSAY: . . . I quite agree with the observation made by the learned Baron, that there was no violation of the rule against delegation in this case. The mode adopted was the mode in which such inquiries are ordinarily conducted, and necessarily conducted, by such a tribunal. What was the course which [counsel for Mr. Osgood] stated to have been requisite? It was that after this committee had made their report, if they did make such a report, there should have been an assembling of the Common Council, there should have been a prosecutor appointed, and there should have been a new trial, with all the formalities of a criminal trial, before they could have arrived at a conclusion. But the committee appointed to inquire into this matter having made the inquiry in the ordinary way, having collected the evidence in the ordinary way, and allowed the party, who had been present at the collecting of that evidence, to state his case by counsel, I cannot conceive a more fair mode of proceedings. . . .

Notes

1. In *Jeffs and others* v. *New Zealand Dairy Production and Marketing Board* [1967] 1 A.C. 551, the Board had power to define zones from which particular factories could get cream and milk. The Board set up a committee of three of its members to investigate the question of supply to two factory-owning dairy companies. The committee, acting on its own initiative, held a public hearing at which farmers and other interested parties gave evidence and made oral and written submissions. The farmers opposed zoning. The committee made a written report, and recommended certain zonings, which were accepted by the Board without alteration. The report did not record, even in a summary form, the evidence given at the hearing, but did state the submissions that had been made. The Board conceded that it was under a duty to act judicially in determining zoning questions affecting the rights of individuals. The Privy Council held that the Board acted in breach of natural justice in failing to hear the interested parties, but that they would have complied with natural justice had the evidence and submissions been fully summarised. The appointment of a person or persons to hear evidence and submissions was appropriate where the credibility of witnesses was not involved. See K. J. Keith, (1968) 31 M.L.R. 87.

2. In *R.* v. *Race Relations Board, ex p. Selvarajan* [1975] 1 W.L.R. 1686, C.A., S.'s complaint of unlawful discrimination was investigated by a conciliation committee appointed under section 15(2)(*a*) of the Race Relations Act 1968, and then re-investigated by the Board under section 15(5). The Board had power under section 14(4) to act by a group of members selected by the chairman, and the re-investigation was undertaken by the Board's employment committee of seven. Each committee member was given a copy of the conciliation committee's report of over 100 pages and some other notes. Further information was collected by one of the Board's conciliation officers. When the employment committee met to consider the matter only three of the members had seen the full papers. The other four only had the officer's summary of the results of her inquiries. The committee decided that there had been no unlawful discrimination. Lord Denning M.R. inferred that the four "were not in a position to form an opinion of their own. They must have gone by the opinion of the other three. . . . If this had been a judicial body, I do not think this would be right. Every member of a judicial body must have access to all the evidence and papers in the case, he must have heard all the arguments, and he must come to his own conclusion. The maxim *delegatus non potest delegare* applies strictly to judicial functions. But it is different with a body which is exercising administrative functions or which is making an investigation or conducting preliminary inquiries, especially when it is a numerous body"

([1975] 1 W.L.R. 1686 at p. 1695). Lord Denning distinguished *Jeffs* v. *New Zealand Dairy Board* on the ground that the Dairy Board, unlike the Race Relations Board, had no power to delegate its functions.

3. In *Attorney-General ex rel. McWhirter* v. *Independent Broadcasting Authority* [1973] 1 Q.B. 629 the Court of Appeal considered the duty imposed by statute on the IBA to "satisfy themselves that, so far as possible . . . nothing is included in . . . programmes which offends against good taste or decency or is likely . . . to be offensive to public feeling. . . ." Discussing the extent to which the IBA could delegate this function, Lord Denning M.R. explained (at pp. 650–652):

"Such being the statutory requirements, Parliament puts a duty on the Independent Broadcasting Authority to "satisfy themselves" that they are complied with "so far as possible." This does not mean, of course, that the members of the authority are themselves to see every programme or go through it. They can and must leave a great deal to the staff. They are entitled in the ordinary way to accept the advice of their staff on the programmes in general, and on any programme in particular: see *Lewisham Metropolitan Borough and Town Clerk* v. *Roberts* [1949] 2 K.B. 608, 621, 629. It is only in a most exceptional case that they may be expected to see a programme for themselves in order to be "satisfied." But there are such exceptional cases, just as there are exceptional cases when a Minister must satisfy himself personally. It depends how serious is the case: see *Liversidge* v. *Anderson* [1942] A.C. 206, 223, 224.

Was this film a programme which they ought to have seen for themselves? Let me state the circumstances. (i) The programme was prepared by one of the programme companies called ATV Network Ltd. In its original form, the staff of the Independent Broadcasting Authority were so unhappy about it that they thought that the programme should be seen by the authority itself. (ii) ATV Network Ltd. thereupon deleted some of the material and introduced the film with a warning that "some people may find Warhol's views unusual and possible offensive." (iii) In the light of those modifications, the Director-General and staff of the Independent Broadcasting Authority felt able to recommend that the programme be transmitted as the usual network documentary on Tuesday, January 16, 1973, at 10.30 p.m. They made an intervention report to that effect. The Independent Broadcasting Authority accepted that recommendation but did not see the film themselves. (iv) On January 12 or 13, journalists were invited to a preview of the film. (v) On Sunday, January 14, and Monday, January 15, some of the journalists in their papers made severe criticisms of the film. If their accounts were correct, it included incidents which were indecent and likely to be offensive to public feeling. The News of the World, in particular, said that "Millions of viewers will find its frankness offensive." (vi) On reading those newspaper reports, the chairman and directors of one of the channels, Anglia Television, determined to have the film screened privately for them to see. They came to the unanimous conclusion that the programme, if broadcast, was likely to be offensive to public feeling. They announced that they were not going to supply it for broadcasting. (vii) The Independent Broadcasting Authority, however, did not see it. Some of them had an informal discussion with the senior staff, and, on their assurances, were prepared to let it be broadcast.

The question is: did the Independent Broadcasting Authority do what was sufficient or ought they not to have seen the film for themselves. . . .

In the circumstances I think that the Independent Broadcasting Authority ought to have seen the film for themselves on the Monday or Tuesday before passing it. Since that time they have done so. So have the General Advisory Council. The members of the General Council are drawn from a broad cross-section of the people, and are as representative and responsible a body as you could find anywhere. The General Council, by a majority of 17 to one, passed this resolution: "The Council felt that the staff were right to advise the Authority that the film which they had seen was suitable to be shown at the suggested time." The members of the Independent Broadcasting Authority are likewise most representative and responsible. Ten out of the 11 saw the film and unanimously reaffirmed the decision:

> "that the programme is suitable for transmission in the 10.30 p.m. documentary slot, and that it is satisfied that the programme complies with the requirements of Section 3(1)(*a*) of the Television Act 1964."

If those decisions are to be accepted as valid, they are decisive. The Independent Broadcasting Authority are the people who matter. They are the censors. The courts have no right whatever—and I may add no desire whatever—to interfere with their decisions so long as they reach them in accordance with law. . . ."

4. In *Mills* v. *London County Council* [1925] 1 K.B. 213, the L.C.C. had granted a licence to Mills, a cinema proprietor, subject to the following condition: "That no film . . . which has not been passed for universal exhibition by the British Board of Film Censors shall be exhibited in the premises without the express consent of the Council during the time that any child under . . . the age of 16 is therein." Mills contended that the condition was *ultra vires* because it involved delegation by the Council of that body's functions under the Cinematograph Act 1909 to another body, the B.B.F.C. The Divisional Court upheld the condition. Lord Hewart C.J. said (at pp. 220–221):

> "It is said, first of all, that this condition is bad, because it means that the London County Council have delegated, or transferred, to the British Board of Film Censors no small part of the duties of the London County Council under the Act, and reference is made to *Ellis* v. *Dubowski* [1921] 3 K.B. 621. In that case the condition which was attached to the licence was in these terms: "That no film be shewn . . . which has not been certified for public exhibition by the British Board of Film Censors." It was held with some doubt that that condition was unreasonable and *ultra vires*. . . . But one thing was made very plain by that Court, both in the course of the argument and also in the judgment, that different considerations would have applied if the condition had been so framed as to make the certificate or the decision of the British Board of Film Censors not final, but subject to review. . . . In the present case that mischief is avoided. This condition with which we are now concerned provides an exception where the express consent of the Council is given. In other words, there is an appeal in the matter from the decision of the British Board of Film Censors to the Council itself. In my opinion, therefore, the first objection fails. . . ."

In *R.* v. *Greater London Council ex p. Blackburn* [1976] 1 W.L.R. 550, the Court of Appeal unanimously upheld the decision in *Mills*. Lord Denning M.R. explained (at pp. 554–555):

> "I do not think the county councils can delegate the whole of their responsibilities to the board . . .; but they can treat the board as an advisory body whose views they can accept or reject, provided that the final decision—aye or nay—rests with the county council. If the exhibitor—or any member of the public—brings the film up before the county council, they ought themselves to review the decision of the British Board of Film Censors and exercise their own

judgment on it. That is, I think, the right way to interpret *Mills* v. *London County Council*. When the board issues a certificate permitting the exhibition of a film—and the county council take no objection to it—that is equivalent to a permission by the county council themselves. When the board refuses a certificate, the exhibitor can appeal to the county council. The county council can then give their consent to the exhibition, and from their decision there is no appeal.

The upshot of it all is this. The county council are in law the body which has the power to censor films for exhibition in cinemas, but in practice it is the board which carries out the censorship, subject to review by the county council."

5. In *R.* v. *Chester Borough Council, ex p. Quietlynn Ltd.* (1985) 83 L.G.R. 308, the Court of Appeal considered the practice of the local authority in handling applications for licences to operate sex shops, under the Local Government (Miscellaneous Provisions) Act 1982. The local authority had delegated its power to grant or refuse such licences to its Environmental Services Committee. There was clear statutory authority for this delegation (Local Government Act 1972, s.101, below p. 282). That committee set up a licensing panel to consider applications and to make recommendations to the committee. The panel consisted of five of the members of the committee. The panel held a hearing at which the applicants appeared, and then made a recommendation to the Environmental Services Committee that the application be refused. Refusal was on grounds relating to the character of the locality, the uses to which premises in the vicinity were being put, and that it considered that the appropriate number of sex establishments in the area should be nil. This recommendation was put before a meeting of the committee, at which 13 members (including the five panel members) were present. At this meeting some detailed discussion first took place in connection with another application, that application eventually being granted. When the applicants' application came up for consideration there was no report made and no discussion—simply a vote taken, which refused the application. The applicants argued that there had been a failure to comply with the statutory obligation, under the 1982 Act, that the committee or subcommittee should afford a hearing to an applicant before refusing a licence; and that this obligation had not, in the circumstances, been satisfied by the hearing before the panel. The local authority argued that as the members of the panel had been present at the committee meeting and therefore were available to have given any information about the hearing had any such information been requested by the other members; and because the panel decision, based on "character of locality," was based on information within the knowledge of all the members, it was not necessary for there to have been anything by way of full report to the committee. The Court of Appeal upheld the applicants' contentions. Stephen Brown L.J. noted (at p. 316) that "no report of any kind was made to the decision-making committee. It may be that a report could have been a very short report indeed, but . . . it is a requisite of the [legislation] that the applicants' representations should be considered by the committee making the decision." The decision of the authority was therefore quashed.

CARLTONA LTD. v. COMMISSIONERS OF WORKS AND OTHERS

[1943] 2 All E.R. 560 (Court of Appeal)

The appellants were manufacturers of food products, and on November 4, 1942, their factory was requisitioned by the Commissioners of Works under regulation 51(1) of the Defence (General) Regulations, 1939:

"A competent authority, if it appears to that authority to be necessary or expedient so to do in the interests of the public safety, the defence of the realm or the efficient prosecution of the war, or for maintaining supplies and services essential to the life of the community, may take possession of any land, and may give such directions as appear to the competent authority to be necessary or expedient in connection with the taking of possession of that land."

The notice of November 4, was signed by a Mr. Morse for and on behalf of the Commissioners of Works. The letter said in part:

"I have to inform you that the department have come to the conclusion that it is essential, in the national interest, to take possession of the above premises occupied by you."

The functions of the Commissioners of Works were made exercisable by the First Commissioner of Works, by the Crown Lands Act 1851 and 1852. Under the Minister of Works and Planning Act 1942 the functions of the First Commissioner were made exercisable by that minister. The appellants sought *inter alia* a declaration that the requisitioning notice was invalid, and an injunction restraining any action based on the notice. The action was dismissed by Hilbery J. Carltona Ltd. appealed to the Court of Appeal.

LORD GREENE M.R.: [stated the facts and continued:] . . . The next point which was taken was that the requisition itself was bad quite apart from the notice because the persons constituting the requisitioning authority never brought their minds to bear on the question. That argument is based, as it seems to me—and I say this without the slightest disrespect to the argument—upon a complete misapprehension as to the facts. It appears to have been thought at the time of the trial that the proper persons to take into consideration the question of exercising the power under this regulation were the Commissioners of Works themselves, a body which, as I have said, never meets. If that idea ever was put forward, and I am not quite sure whether it was or not, a moment's consideration will show that the argument cannot be supported for the very simple reasons, first, that the person who has the statutory power to act for the Commissioners of Works is the First Commissioner, and, secondly, that the person acting for the First Commissioner in this matter was the assistant secretary. There is no point in the argument at all that the Commissioners of Works as such did not take the matter into consideration, nor is there, in my opinion, any substance in the argument that, at any rate, the First Commissioner did not personally direct his mind to the matter.

In the administration of government in this country the functions which are given to ministers (and constitutionally properly given to ministers because they are constitutionally responsible) are functions so multifarious that no minister could ever personally attend to them. To take the example of the present case no doubt there have been thousands of requisitions in this country by individual ministries. It cannot be supposed that this regulation meant that, in each case, the minister in person should direct his mind to the matter. The duties imposed upon ministers and the powers given to ministers are normally exercised under the authority of the ministers by responsible officials of the department. Public business could not be carried on if that were not the case. Constitutionally, the decision of such an official is, of course, the decision of the minister. The minister is responsible. It is he who must answer before Parliament for anything that his officials have done under his authority, and, if for an important matter he selected an official of such junior standing that he could not be expected competently to perform the work, the minister would have to answer for that in Parliament. The whole system of departmental organisation and administration is based on the view that ministers, being responsible to Parliament, will see that important duties are committed to experienced officials. If they do not do that, Parliament is the place where complaint must be made against them.

In the present case the assistant secretary, a high official of the Ministry, was the person entrusted with the work of looking after this particular matter . . . The appeal must be dismissed. . . .

GODDARD and DU PARCQ L.JJ. agreed.

Notes

1. In *Local Government Board* v. *Arlidge* [1915] A.C. 120, Arlidge sought certiorari to quash an order made by the Board. The Board's order had rejected A's appeal against his local authority's decision not to terminate a closure order it had made in respect of his house, which it considered to be unfit for human habitation. One of the grounds on which certiorari was sought was that neither the Board, nor anyone lawfully authorised to act for them, had in fact determined the appeal. The matter had been investigated by one of the Board's housing inspectors, who had held an inquiry at which A had been represented. The inspector had submitted his report to the Board, together with a shorthand note of the speeches. The order of the Board did not indicate which officer of the Board had taken the final decision on the matter. In the House of Lords, Viscount Haldane L.C. said (at p. 133):

> "The Minister at the head of the Board is directly responsible to Parliament like other Ministers. He is responsible not only for what he himself does but for all that is done in his department. The volume of work entrusted to him is very great and he cannot do the great bulk of it himself. He is expected to obtain his materials vicariously through his officials, and he has discharged his duty if he sees that they obtain these materials for him properly. To try to extend his duty beyond this and to insist that he and other members of the Board should do everything personally would be to impair his efficiency. Unlike a judge in a court he is not only at liberty but is compelled to rely on the assistance of his staff. When, therefore, the Board is directed to dispose of an appeal that does not mean that any particular official of the Board is to dispose of it."

Lord Shaw of Dunfermline said (at p. 136):

> ". . . My Lords, how can the judiciary be blind to the well-known facts applicable not only to the constitution but to the working of such branches of the Executive? The department is represented in Parliament by its responsible

head. On the one hand he manages its affairs with such assistance as the Treasury sanctions, and on the other he becomes answerable in Parliament for every departmental act. His Board—that is, all the members of it together—may never meet, or they may only be convened on some question of policy; but a determination, signed and sealed and issued in correct form, stands as the deliverance of the Board as such, for which determination the President becomes answerable to Parliament. This is the general rule, acknowledged and familiar, of departmental action and responsibility. . . ."

2. The *Arlidge* and *Carltona* cases were each decided in wartime. They illustrate a degree of judicial self-restraint which is, perhaps, not surprising in such circumstances. Compare *Liversidge* v. *Sir John Anderson* [1942] A.C. 206, and below, p. 406, n. 2. The English courts have not, however, in the years since the decision in *Carltona* been anxious to impose limits to the scope of that decision.

Thus, in *R.* v. *Skinner* [1968] 2 Q.B. 700, the Court of Appeal held that approval of the "Alcotest" breath-testing device by the Home Secretary required by section 7(1) of the Road Safety Act 1967 (which was a necessary precondition to a conviction for an offence under the breathalyser legislation), could be expressed by an assistant secretary in the police department of the Home Office, acting in the name of the Home Secretary. The court applied the *Carltona* case, and dicta in *Lewisham B.C.* v. *Roberts* [1949] 2 K.B. 608. The personal approval of the Home Secretary was not necessary even though this was an isolated matter unlike the thousands of requisitioning cases that arose during the war which no Minister could have considered personally. Widgery L.J. emphasised (at p. 707) that: "It is not strictly a matter of delegation; it is that the official acts as the Minister himself and the official's decision is the Minister's decision."

Then, in *Re Golden Chemical Products Ltd.* [1976] Ch. 300, Brightman J. considered the exercise of powers contained in section 35 of the Companies Act 1967. This section empowered the Secretary of State to present a petition to the High Court for the winding-up of a company where "it appears [to the Secretary of State] . . . that it is expedient in the public interest that the body be wound up. . . ." His Lordship held that the functions of the Secretary of State under section 35 need not be exercised by the Secretary of State personally. His Lordship rejected the argument of counsel for the company, that unless a statute conferring a power on a Minister to do an act if it appears to him expedient provided otherwise, the initial decision-making process could be performed by someone other than the Minister only if it led to no serious invasion of the freedom or property rights of the subject. This argument ran counter to the *Carltona, Lewisham* and *Skinner* cases, and would result in a distinction which would be "impossibly vague" (*per* Brightman J. at p. 310). His Lordship accepted that the relationship between the Minister and his official was not one of delegation.

By way of contrast, some willingness by the courts to review the exercise by a Minister of his *Carltona* power to devolve decision-making has been indicated by the courts in the, more recent, case of *R.* v. *Secretary of State for the Home Department, ex p. Oladehinde* [1991] 2 A.C. 254. This concerned the lawfulness of a practice by which the Home Secretary had "delegated" to immigration inspectors (officials in the civil service who are equivalent in grade to senior executive officers, and who have considerable experience in immigration matters) his powers under the Immigration Act 1971 to authorise service of notices of intention to deport persons from the United Kingdom. The inspectors reached their decisions in the light of reports compiled by immigration officers. Following the service of such notices a right of appeal in certain cases might lie to an independent immigration adjudicator or to the Immigration Appeal Tribunal. However, such appeals, by "overstayers" served with notices of intention to deport, were severely restricted by the Immigration Act 1988. Following an unsuccessful appeal, or in the absence of an appeal, the deportation department at the Home Office reviewed each case before a final decision as to the making of a deportation order was made by the Secretary of State, acting on the advice of his department and his Minister of State.

In the Divisional Court ([1991] 2 A.C. at 258) certiorari was granted to quash decisions of immigration inspectors. Woolf L.J. referred to the *Carltona* principle and stated that the principle should be "regarded as an implication which is read into a statute in the absence of any clear contrary indication by Parliament that the implication is not to apply" (pp. 264–265). Such implications might be express (see, *e.g.* 1971 Act, ss.13(5), 14(3), and 15(3) and (4)—requiring certain decisions to be taken by the Secretary of State personally) or implied. In determining whether the principle was impliedly excluded, a number of matters were of relevance. Woolf L.J. noted that the scheme of the legislation was, somewhat unusually, to divide responsibilities and to assign specific functions to the Secretary of State and to particular categories of official. In such circumstances an implication was appropriate that the Secretary of State could not, under the *Carltona* principle, devolve to those officials the powers which had been conferred on himself. In addition to the "structure" of the legislative allocation of power, Woolf L.J. paid regard to the nature of the power devolved, noting the serious consequences for the individuals affected which might follow from the making of a deportation order. Pill J. analysed the *Carltona* principle in similar terms and agreed that "Parliament did not intend the relevant powers given to the Secretary of State with respect to deportation to be exercised on his behalf by members of the immigration service" (p. 270).

In the Court of Appeal ([1991] 2 A.C. at 278), Lord Donaldson M.R., giving the judgment of the court, stated (at p. 282) that the *Carltona* power to devolve decision-making was a "common law constitutional power, but one which is capable of being negatived or confined by . . . clearly necessary implication." In this connection his Lordship said that such challenge would normally be on the basis that the decision to devolve was *Wednesbury* unreasonable—*i.e.* not an arrangement for the exercise of the function which any reasonable Minister could have chosen to adopt. The Court of Appeal differed, however, from the Divisional Court in its view as to whether in this case these limitations to the *Carltona* power to devolve applied. It stressed that in its view:

> "there are clear advantages and no unfairness in the (provisional) decision to deport, which does not of itself affect the status of the immigrant . . ., being taken by civil servants who are readily available and have considerable experience and expertise in immigration matters."

The House of Lords affirmed the decision of the Court of Appeal. On the issue of the ambit of the *Carltona* principle, Lord Griffiths noted that the 1971 Act contained three explicit limitations on the Secretary of State's power to devolve—see sections referred to above. In these circumstances a court should be "very slow to read into the statute a further implicit limitation." His Lordship continued (at p. 303):

> "The immigration service is comprised of Home Office civil servants for whom the Home Secretary is responsible and I can see no reason why he should not authorise members of that service to take decisions under the *Carltona* principle *providing they do not conflict with or embarrass them in the discharge of their specific statutory duties under the Act and that the decisions are suitable to their grading and experience*" (emphasis added).

By way of example of a situation which would fall within the conflict/embarrassment limitation Lord Griffiths said (at p. 303): "it would not be right to authorise an inspector to take a decision . . . in any case in which he had been engaged as an immigration officer, for to do so would be too much like asking a prosecutor to be judge in the same cause." Lords Keith, Templeman, Brandon and Ackner concurred with Lord Griffiths.

3. The *Carltona* principle applies to the devolution of functions to civil servants within a department of central government. Outside this context, it has been held not to be applicable simply because administrative convenience may be served by such a practice. Thus, in *Nelms* v. *Roe* [1969] 3 All E.R. 1379, a police inspector sought information from R. under section 232(2)(*a*) of the Road Traffic Act 1960 as to the identity of the driver of R.'s car on an occasion when a traffic offence was allegedly committed. Under the section such information could be required "by or on behalf of a chief officer of police . . ." but there was no written authority from the Metropolitan Police Commissioner either to the inspector or to the inspector's superior officer, the superintendent in charge of Croydon sub-division. The superintendent claimed that he had implied authority by virtue of his office, and stated that he had given the inspector verbal authority to act under section 232. The court held (1) that the *alter ego* doctrine applicable to Ministers and civil servants could not be applied to the superintendent *vis-à-vis* the commissioner (*per* Lord Parker C.J. at p. 1382: "It is not, I think, sufficient to say that it is a principle which is applicable whenever it is difficult or impracticable for a person to act himself . . ."); but (2) that there was an implied delegation to the superintendent, which included power for the superintendent to sub-delegate to "a person in his unit in a responsible position."

4. See generally on the *Carltona* principle, D. Lanham, "Delegation and the *Alter Ego* Principle" (1984) 100 L.Q.R. 587.

LOCAL GOVERNMENT ACT 1972

Part VI

DISCHARGE OF FUNCTIONS

Arrangements for discharge of functions by local authorities

101.—(1) Subject to any express provision contained in this Act or any Act passed after this Act, a local authority may arrange for the discharge of any of their functions—

(*a*) by a committee, a sub-committee or an officer of the authority; or
(*b*) by any other local authority.

(2) Where by virtue of this section any functions of a local authority may be discharged by a committee of theirs, then, unless the local authority otherwise direct, the committee may arrange for the discharge of any of those functions by a sub-committee or an officer of the authority and where by virtue of this section any functions of a local authority may be discharged by a sub-committee of the authority, then, unless the local authority or the committee otherwise direct, the sub-committee may arrange for the discharge of any of those functions by an officer of the authority.

(3) Where arrangements are in force under this section for the discharge

of any functions of a local authority by another local authority, then, subject to the terms of the arrangements, that other authority may arrange for the discharge of those functions by a committee, sub-committee or officer of theirs and subsection (2) above shall apply in relation to those functions as it applies in relation to the functions of that other authority.

(4) Any arrangements made by a local authority or committee under this section for the discharge of any functions by a committee, sub-committee, officer or local authority shall not prevent the authority or committee by whom the arrangements are made from exercising those functions.

(5) Two or more local authorities may discharge any of their functions jointly and, where arrangements are in force for them to do so,—

(*a*) they may also arrange for the discharge of those functions by a joint committee of theirs or by an officer of one of them and subsection (2) above shall apply in relation to those functions as it applies in relation to the functions of the individual authorities; and

(*b*) any enactment relating to those functions or the authorities by whom or the areas in respect of which they are to be discharged shall have effect subject to all necessary modifications in its application in relation to those functions and the authorities by whom and the areas in respect of which (whether in pursuance of the arrangements or otherwise) they are to be discharged.

(6) A local authority's functions with respect to levying, or issuing a precept for, a rate [. . .] shall be discharged only by the authority . . .

Notes

1. This section gives very wide powers of delegation to local authorities. The general power of delegation to officers was new in the 1972 Act. Section 101(1) does not authorise the delegation of functions to a single member: *R.* v. *Secretary of State for Education and Science, ex p. Birmingham District Council* (1984) 83 L.G.R. 79, where it was held that a proposal by a local education authority to close a school had not been lawfully made where the date of closure had been fixed not by the authority but by its chairman. This view was confirmed by Woolf J. and the Court of Appeal in *R.* v. *Secretary of State for the Environment, ex p. Hillingdon London Borough Council* [1986] 1 W.L.R. 192 and 867, in respect of the issue of enforcement notices. The word "committee" in the 1972 Act did not extend to a committee of one. Woolf J. recognised, however, that the difficulties could be circumvented by delegating a power to an officer acting *in consultation* with a member. This would enable urgent action to be taken between meetings of the relevant committee or sub-committee. Where it is arranged for decisions to be made by an officer in consultation with a councillor the ultimate decision must be the officer's: if the dominant role is taken by the councillor, the decision will be *ultra vires*: *R.* v. *Port Talbot Borough Council, ex p. Jones* [1988] 2 All E.R. 207. On the other hand, there is no objection to standing orders requiring the officer to obtain the approval of a member of the council, such as a committee chairman, before exercising the delegated power: *Fraser* v. *Secretary of State for the Environment* (1987) 56 P. & C.R. 386. The difference appears to be that, in the former case, the officer would not

have made the positive decision in question had it not been for the intervention of the councillor. In the latter, the officer made a provisional decision independently, but was then required to obtain approval from a committee chairman before it could be made effective. The former situation was unlawful, the latter arrangement was lawful.

2. For indications that something analogous to the *Carltona* principle may have some limited operation in the context of *local* government decision-making, see *Provident Mutual Life Assurance Association* v. *Derby City Council* (1981) 79 L.G.R. 297, H.L., (enabling "administrative matters" in connection with rate collection to be dealt with by members of the treasurer's staff where power had been delegated to the treasurer), applied in *Cheshire County Council* v. *Secretary of State for the Environment* [1988] J.P.L. 30 and *Fitzpatrick* v. *Secretary of State for the Environment, The Times*, December 29, 1988. In *Fitzpatrick*, however, the member of the district secretary's staff was merely implementing an instruction by the council to the district secretary to issue an enforcement notice; as neither the member of staff nor the district secretary was exercising any independent discretion the problem of the delegation of power did not strictly arise. See also *R.* v. *Southwark London Borough Council, ex p. Bannerman* (1990) 22 H.L.R. 459.

(C) Over-Rigid Adherence to Self-Created Rules of Policy

The cases which follow demonstrate the balance which has been struck by the courts between:

(i) applying the presumption, often stated, that statutes conferring discretionary powers should be interpreted as intending that decisions as to whether and how that power is to be exercised should be taken in the light of individual consideration of the merits of each particular case; and,

(ii) appreciation that such individualised, case-by-case, decision-making may be less conducive to good and fair administration than an approach under which discretionary decisions are taken in the light of, though not unduly constrained by, previously determined (and perhaps promulgated) rules or principles of policy.

Individual justice is important. But decision-makers should also have regard to the "administrative justice" which is associated with consistency and predictability in decision-making.

In any case where a decision has been taken in accordance with a self-created rule of policy the following matters must be considered:

(i) is the policy intrinsically flawed? For example, does it require the decision-maker to take into account irrelevant considerations? Does it seek to operate the powers for an improper purpose? Is the policy "unreasonable"? These grounds of challenge are considered in the next chapter;

(ii) assuming that there is nothing intrinsically objectionable about the policy, has the policy been applied over-rigidly and to the exclusion of the genuine exercise of discretion in the particular case? The tests applied by the courts in determining this question appear from the cases which follow.

Note

See generally H. L. Molot, (1972) 18 McGill L.J. 310; D. J. Galligan, [1976] P.L. 332.

R. v. PORT OF LONDON AUTHORITY, ex p. KYNOCH LTD.

[1919] 1 K.B. 176; 88 L.J.K.B. 553; 120 L.T. 177; 35 T.L.R. 103; 83 J.P. 41; 16 L.G.R. 937 (Court of Appeal)

Kynoch Ltd. owned land at Canvey Island on the north bank of the Thames. They applied to the Port of London Authority for a licence (under the Port of London Act 1908, s.7, and the Thames Conservancy Act 1894, s.109) to construct a deep-water wharf and other works. In November 1917 the Authority rejected the application "on the ground that the accommodation applied for, is of the character of that which Parliament has charged the Authority with the duty of providing in the port." Under the Port of London Act 1908, s.2(1), the Authority was under a duty "to take into consideration the state of the river and the accommodation and facilities afforded in the Port of London, and, subject to the provisions of this Act to take such steps as they may consider necessary for the improvement thereof." Under section 2(2) they had power (*inter alia*) to "construct, equip, maintain, or manage any docks, quays, wharves and other works in connection therewith. . . ." In April 1918 Kynoch Ltd. gave notice of appeal to the Board of Trade under the 1908 Act. In September 1918 they withdrew this appeal and applied instead for mandamus to compel the Authority to exercise their discretion according to law. An affidavit from the Secretary to the Authority made it clear that the merits of the application had been fully considered by two committees and the Authority itself.

The Divisional Court refused to grant mandamus. Kynoch Ltd. appealed to the Court of Appeal.

BANKES L.J.: . . . The main ground [upon which the appellants sought mandamus] was that the Port authority had not heard and determined the application of June 8, 1917, for permission to carry out works of a very important character with a very extensive frontage to the river. . . .

Every case must depend on its own particular circumstances; but decided cases furnish some rules which ought to govern the court in the exercise of its discretion to grant or refuse the prerogative writ of mandamus. There must be something in the nature of a refusal to exercise jurisdiction by the tribunal or authority to whom the writ is to be directed. A refusal may be conveyed in one of two ways: there may be an absolute refusal in terms, or there may be conduct amounting to a refusal. In the latter case it is often difficult to draw the line between those cases where the tribunal or authority has heard and determined erroneously upon grounds which it was entitled to take into consideration and those cases where it has heard and determined upon grounds outside and beyond its jurisdiction; but this conclusion may be drawn from decided cases, that there is no refusal to hear and determine unless the tribunal or authority has in substance shut its ears to the application which was made to it, and has determined upon an application which was not made to it. On this point I would refer to the words of Farwell L.J. in *R.* v. *Board of Education* [1910] 2 K.B. 165, 179: "If the tribunal has exercised the discretion entrusted to it *bona fide*, not influenced by extraneous or irrelevant considerations, and not arbitrally or illegally, the courts cannot interfere; they are not a Court of Appeal from the tribunal, but they have power to prevent the intentional usurpation or mistaken assumption of a jurisdiction beyond that given to the tribunal by law, and also the refusal of their true jurisdiction by the adoption of extraneous considerations in arriving at their conclusion or deciding a point other than that brought before them, in which cases the courts have regarded them as declining jurisdiction." Again, in *R.* v. *Bowman* [1898] 1 Q.B. 663, 667, where licensing justices had allowed their decision to be influenced by extraneous considerations, Wills J. said: "There has been no real hearing, and the mandamus must therefore go." Those two cases furnish a rough test for deciding when a tribunal, in considering matters outside its jurisdiction, has refused to exercise its true and proper jurisdiction.

In the present case there is another matter to be borne in mind. There are on the one hand cases where a tribunal in the honest exercise of its discretion has adopted a policy, and, without refusing to hear an applicant, intimates to him what its policy is, and that after hearing him it will in accordance with its policy decide against him, unless there is something exceptional in his case. I think counsel for the applicants would admit that, if the policy has been adopted for reasons which the tribunal may legitimately entertain, no objection could be taken to such a course. On the other hand there are cases where a tribunal has passed a rule, or come to a determination, not to hear any application of a particular character by whomsoever made. There is a wide distinction to be drawn between these two classes. . . . [His Lordship referred to *R.* v. *Sylvester*, 31 L.J.(M.C.) 93, and *R.* v. *L.C.C.* [1918] 1 K.B. 68.]

Now to apply these principles to the facts of this case. There is the letter of November 2 written on behalf of the Port authority by their secretary . . . and there is his affidavit. It negatives the suggestion that the only matter considered by the Port authority was that specified in the letter. We must decide this case upon the affidavit. Read carefully and fairly it amounts to a statement that the Port authority did nothing which could be properly described as a refusal to hear and determine. But I go a step further. Even assuming that the letter contains the only ground on which the application was refused, I think, considering the position of the Port authority, that the matters involved in that decision were rightly and properly considered by them, and warrant the adoption of a general policy in granting licences for works of this particular class. Therefore on the main point the rule must be discharged. . . .

WARRINGTON L.J. agreed.

SCRUTTON L.J. delivered a concurring judgment.

Note

In *R.* v. *London County Council, ex p. Corrie* [1918] 1 K.B. 68, the local authority had made a by-law prohibiting, without its written consent, the selling of any article in the parks, gardens and open spaces under its control. After having granted permissions in some cases to sell literature at meetings in certain parks the local authority changed its policy. It revoked existing permits and resolved that no further consents should be granted for such sales. The applicant then sought permission to sell a pamphlet, "The British Blind," at meetings to be held by the National League of the Blind. She was refused permission. The letter of refusal included the following statement: "... the Council has decided that no permits for the sale of literature ... are to be issued. I regret that it is not possible to make an exception to this rule even in a most deserving case...." The King's Bench Division granted mandamus to the applicant, requiring that the Council should hear her application on its merits. Avory J., agreeing with Darling and Sankey JJ., stated (at p. 74):

> "I have come to the same conclusion, though somewhat reluctantly, because I doubt whether the [grant of mandamus] will be of any effective service to the [applicant], inasmuch as, when the application for permission is considered, the Council will probably refuse to give it.... I ... do not assent to the submission ... that the ... Council must give their consent unless they determine that the pamphlet is an improper one to be sold in parks.... No such duty is cast upon them by the by-laws. They may refuse their consent although, as an article, no exception can be taken to the pamphlet which it is proposed to sell."

LAVENDER (H.) & SON LTD. v. MINISTER OF HOUSING AND LOCAL GOVERNMENT

[1970] 1 W.L.R. 1231; 114 S.J. 636; [1970] 3 All E.R. 871; (1969) 68 L.G.R. 408

The company applied for planning permission to extract sand, gravel and ballast from part of Rivernook Farm, Walton-on-Thames. Most of the site was within an area of high quality agricultural land reserved for that purpose in accordance with the Waters Report on Sand and Gravel, 1948–53. The planning authority refused planning permission, and the company appealed to the Minister. The only substantial objection to the development came from the Ministry of Agriculture, which wished to see the land maintained as agricultural land. There was evidence that the company would be able to restore the land to a high standard of fertility after excavation. The inspector who conducted the public inquiry could find no reason to refuse planning permission apart from the objection of the Ministry of Agriculture. The Minister dismissed the appeal. His decision letter included the two sentences:

> "It is the Minister's present policy that land in the reservations should not be released for mineral working unless the Minister of Agriculture, Fisheries and Food is not opposed to working. In the present case the agricultural objection has not been waived, and the Minister has therefore decided not to grant planning permission for the working of the appeal site."

The company applied to the High Court under section 179 of the Town and Country Planning Act 1962 (now section 288 of the 1990 Act) for the Minister's decision to be quashed.

WILLIS J.: ... It is those last two sentences in the decision letter which lie at the heart of the matter in issue; and it is submitted, first of all, by counsel for the applicants, that they show, in this case, that the Minister had so fettered his own discretion to decide the appeal by the policy which he had adopted that the decisive matter was not the exercise of his own discretion on a consideration of the report and other material considerations, but the sustained objection of the Minister of Agriculture. In effect, he says that the decision was not that of the Minister of Housing and Local Government, the tribunal entrusted with the duty to decide, but the Minister of Agriculture, who had no status save perhaps in a consultative capacity and certainly no status to make the effective decision....

... In general support of his main submission, counsel for the applicants has referred me to Professor de Smith's well-known work *Judicial Review of Administrative Action* ((2nd ed., 1968), pp. 292–297) and to certain of the cases cited therein. He really puts his argument in two ways: (1) that the Minister has fettered his discretion by a self-created rule of policy; and (2) that the Minister, who has a duty to exercise his own discretion in determining an appeal, has in this case delegated that duty to the Minister of Agriculture, who has no such duty and is, statutorily, a stranger to any decision. It is, of course, common ground that the Minister is entitled to have a policy and to decide an appeal in the context of that policy. He can also differ from the inspector on any question of fact, and disagree with the inspector's conclusion and recommendations. He can, and no doubt should, reject any recommendation of an inspector which runs counter to his policy, since, as counsel for the Minister points out, it is of the very essence of the duties laid on the Minister by section 1 of the Minister of Town and Country Planning Act 1943 that he should secure consistency and continuity in the framing and execution of a national policy with respect to the use and development of land.

The courts have no authority to interfere with the way in which the Minister carries out his planning policy (see *per* Lord Denning M.R., *Lord Luke of Pavenham* v. *Minister of Housing and Local Government* [1968] 1 Q.B. 172 at p. 192). There is also no question but that the Minister, before making a decision whether or not to allow an appeal, may obtain the views of other government departments (see *Darlassis* v. *Minister of Education* (1954) 52 L.G.R. 304 at p. 318, *per* Barry J.). The duties of the Minister and their extent in relation to a matter such as the appeal in the present case, comprising in a hybrid form both administrative and quasi-judicial functions, were enunciated by Lord Greene M.R. in a well-known passage in *B. Johnson & Co. (Builders) Ltd.* v. *Minister of Health* [1947] 2 All E.R. 395, at pp. 397 and 399:

> "The duty placed on the Minister with regard to objections is to consider them before confirming the order. He is also to consider the report of the person who held the inquiry. Having done that, his functions are laid down by the last words of the paragraph (*i.e.* para. 4 of Sched. 1 to the Housing Act 1936), *viz.*, 'and may then confirm the order either with or without modification.' Those words are important, because they make it clear that it is to the Minister that Parliament has commit-

> ted the decision whether he will or will not confirm the order after he has done all that the statute requires him to do. There is nothing in that paragraph, or anywhere else in the Act, which imposes on the Minister any obligation with regard to the objections, save the obligation to consider them. He is not bound to base his decision on any conclusion that he comes to with regard to the objections, and that must be so when one gives a moment's thought to the situation. The decision whether to confirm or not must be made in relation to questions of policy, and the Minister, in deciding whether to confirm or not, will, like every Minister entrusted with administrative duties, weigh up the considerations which are to affect his mind, the preponderating factor in many, if not all, cases being that of public policy, having regard to all the facts of the case.... That decision must be an administrative decision, because it is not to be based purely on the view that he forms of the objections, *vis-à-vis* the desires of the local authority, but is to be guided by his view as to the policy which in the circumstances he ought to pursue."

Can there, nevertheless, come a point in this hybrid process when the court can interfere with a Ministerial decision which, *ex facie*, proceeds on a consideration of the inspector's report and concludes by applying Ministerial policy?

Counsel for the applicants submits that such a point can be reached and has been reached in this case. It is reached, he says, adopting the words of Professor de Smith (see p. 294), if a tribunal, entrusted with a discretion as the Minister was in the present case, disables itself from exercising that discretion in a particular case by the prior adoption of a general policy. In *R.* v. *Port of London Authority, ex p. Kynoch Ltd.*, Bankes L.J. said: ... [His Lordship cited the passage "In the present case ... by whomsoever made" (above, p. 286)]

In another licensing case, *R.* v. *County Licensing (Stage Plays) Committee of Flint County Council, ex p. Barrett* [1957] 1 All E.R. 112 at p. 122, where the decision was given in the interests of consistency, Jenkins L.J. said:

> "Then they went on ... to conclude ... that the Queen's Theatre licence must follow the fate of the Pavilion Theatre licence, because it was essential that the same rule should be applied in all cases or, in other words, that the committee should be consistent. I cannot think that that method of approach fulfils the requirement that the matter should be heard and determined according to law.... It seems to me that it wrongly pursues consistency at the expense of the merits of individual cases."

I have referred to these two cases since they were relied on by counsel for the applicants, but I am inclined to agree with counsel for the Minister that the considerations applicable to licensing cases are not of much assistance when considering the scope of a Minister's duties within a statutory framework. . . .

It is, of course, clear that if the Minister has prejudged any genuine consideration of the matter before him, or has failed to give genuine consideration to (*inter alia*) the inspector's report, he has failed to carry out his statutory duties properly (see *Franklin* v. *Minister of Town and Country Planning* [1948] A.C. 87 [below, p. 569]).

In the present case counsel for the applicants does not shrink from submitting that the decision letter shows that no genuine consideration was given to the question whether planning permission could, in the circumstances, be granted. I have carefully considered the authorities cited by counsel, but I have not found any clear guide to what my decision should be in this case. I have said enough to make it clear that I recognise that in the field of policy, and in relation to Ministerial decisions coloured or dictated by policy, the courts will interfere only within a strictly circumscribed field (see *per* Lord Greene M.R. in *Associated Provincial Picture Houses Ltd.* v. *Wednesbury Corpn.* [see below, p. 395]). It is also clear, and is conceded by counsel for the Minister, that where a Minister is entrusted by Parliament with the decision of any particular case he must keep that actual decision in the last resort in his own hands (see *R.* v. *Minister of Transport, ex p. Grey Coaches* (1933) 77 S.J. 301). I return, therefore, to the words used by the Minister. It seems to me that he has said in language which admits of no doubt that his decision to refuse permission was solely in pursuance of a policy not to permit minerals in the Waters agricultural reserves to be worked unless the Minister of Agriculture was not opposed to their working. Counsel for the Minister submits that, read as a whole, the decision letter should be taken as implying some such words as "I have gone through the exercise of taking all material considerations into account, but you have not persuaded me that this is such an exceptional case as would justify me in relaxing my policy; therefore I stick to it and apply it." If that were the right construction perhaps counsel for the Minister would be justified in saying that there was no error in law. But in my judgment the language used is not open to any such such implication. There is no indication that this might be an exceptional case such as would or could induce the Minister to change his policy. It is common ground that the Minister must be open to persuasion that the land should not remain in the Waters reservation. How can his mind be open to persuasion, how can an applicant establish an "exceptional case" in the case of an inflexible attitude by the Minister of Agriculture? That attitude was well known before the inquiry, it was maintained during the inquiry, and presumably thereafter. The inquiry was no doubt, in a sense, into the Minister of Agriculture's objection, since, apart from that objection, it might well have been that no inquiry would have been necessary, but I do not think that the Minister, after the inquiry, can be said in any real sense to have given genuine consideration to whether, on planning (including agricultural) grounds, this land could be worked. It seems to me that by adopting and applying his stated policy he has in effect inhibited himself from exercising a proper discretion (which would of course be guided by policy considerations) in any case where the Minister of Agriculture has made and maintained an objection to mineral working in an agricultural reservation. Everything else might point to the desirability of granting permission, but by applying and acting on his stated policy I think that the Minister has fettered himself in such a way that in this case it was not he who made the decision for which Parliament made him responsible. It was the decision of the Minister of Agriculture not to waive his objection which was decisive in this case, and while that might properly prove to be the decisive factor for the Minister when taking into account all material considerations, it seems to me quite wrong for a policy to be applied which in reality eliminates all the material considerations save only the consideration, when that is the case, that the Minister of Agriculture objects. That means, as I think, that the Minister has by his stated policy delegated to the Minister of Agriculture the effective decision on any appeal within the agricultural reservations where the latter objects to the working . . .

If the Minister was intending to follow his stated policy, I think that it was very undesirable that it should not have been made known in advance. It is possible to imagine great hardship falling on appellants who, all unawares, embark on an expensive appeal foredoomed to failure by reason of a strict though unannounced policy. However, I agree with counsel for the Minister that the failure to publicise the policy is not a ground for questioning the decision . . .

On the main ground on which this case has been argued, however, I am satisfied that the applicants should succeed. I think that the Minister failed to exercise a proper or indeed any discretion by reason of the fetter which he imposed on its exercise in acting solely in accordance with his stated policy; and further that on the true construction of the Minister's letter the decision to dismiss the appeal, while purporting to be that of the Minister, was in fact, and improperly, that of the Minister of Agriculture.

Questions

1. Was *ex p. Kynoch* applied in this case, or was some different rule adopted? See Galligan, *op. cit.*, pp. 348–350.

2. When may it be desirable for a decision-maker to evaluate "the weight of at least some factors that may be relevant to an exercise of discretion *in the future*"? (our question mark) (Galligan, *op. cit.*, p. 350, emphasis added).

Notes

1. See case note by D. G. T. Williams, [1971] C.L.J. 6. Other cases in which there has been successful challenge on this ground include: *R.* v. *Windsor Licensing Justices, ex p. Hodes* [1983] 1 W.L.R. 685 (justices failed to consider merits of particular application for liquor licence—applied their "store within store" supermarket policy over-rigidly); *R.* v. *Hampshire Education Authority, ex p. J.* (1985) 84 L.G.R. 547 (over-rigid policy in respect of exercise of discretion to pay independent school fees); *R.* v. *Canterbury City Council, ex p. Gillespie* (1986) 19 H.L.R. 7

(over-rigid application of policy as to allocation of council accommodation); *R.* v. *Secretary of State for Transport, ex p. Sherriff and Sons Ltd., The Times,* December 18, 1986 (revocation of discretionary grant based on over-rigid wording of Ministry's Memorandum of Explanation as to the availability of grants; see A. W. Bradley, [1987] P.L. 141 and [1989] P.L. 197).

2. *Stringer* v. *Minister of Housing and Local Government* [1970] 1 W.L.R. 1281 concerned (*inter alia*) the long-standing policy of the Ministry to discourage development which would interfere with the efficient operation of the Jodrell Bank radio telescope. Cooke J. held that the Minister was entitled to rely on this policy in refusing an appeal on application for planning permission, stating at p. 1298:

> "It seems to me that the general effect of the many relevant authorities is that a Minister charged with the duty of making individual administrative decisions in a fair and impartial manner may nevertheless have a general policy in regard to matters which are relevant to those decisions, provided that the existence of that general policy does not preclude him from fairly judging all the issues which are relevant to each individual case as it comes up for decision.
>
> I think that in this case the Minister was entitled to have a policy in regard to Jodrell Bank, and I think that his policy is not such as to preclude him from fairly considering a planning appeal on its merits. I do not think that it precluded him from fairly considering Mr. Stringer's appeal. I do not think that the Minister has prejudged the case, or tied his own hands, or abdicated any of his functions."

Further aspects of *Stringer* are considered below, p. 304.

BRITISH OXYGEN CO. LTD. v. MINISTER OF TECHNOLOGY

[1971] A.C. 610; [1970] 3 W.L.R. 488; [1970] T.R. 143; 114 S.J. 682; [1970] 3 All E.R. 165 (House of Lords)

The company manufactured, sold and delivered industrial and medical gases, which had to be kept in special containers of various kinds. One general class of container included individual cylinders of different sizes. The company bought a large number of these over three years, their total expenditure exceeding £4 million. They cost on average £20 each. The Board of Trade had a discretion to award investment grants under the Industrial Development Act 1966 in respect of new "plant." They had a rule of practice not to approve for grant expenditure on items which cost individually less than £25, however great the number of such individual items purchased at any one time. The company applied for a declaration that the Board of Trade was not entitled to decline to make a grant on the sole ground that each cylinder cost less than £25. Buckley J. ([1969] 1 Ch. 57) granted the declaration, saying that this "would not be an exercise of the discretion but an abrogation of it . . . every genuine and reasonable application . . . must be considered on its merits. Refusals to consider an application merely on the ground of the low cost of the individual equipment provided involves ignoring whatever characteristics the application has meriting approval." The Court of Appeal allowed an appeal ([1969] 2 Ch. 174, *sub nom. British Oxygen Co. Ltd.* v. *Board of Trade*). There was a further appeal to the House of Lords.

LORD REID: . . . [I]t is necessary to consider what is the duty of the respondent in administering the Act and what rights, if any, the Act confers on those eligible for grants.

Section 1 of the Act provides that the Board of Trade "may" make grants. . . . But how were the Board intended to operate that discretion? Does the Act read as a whole indicate any policy which the Board is to follow or even give any guidance to the Board? If it does then the Board must exercise its discretion in accordance with such policy or guidance (*Padfield* v. *Minister of Agriculture, Fisheries and Food* [below, p. 343]). One generally expects to find that Parliament has given some indication as to how public money is to be distributed. In this Act Parliament has clearly laid down the conditions for eligibility for grants and it has clearly given to the Board a discretion so that the Board is not bound to pay to every person who is eligible to receive a grant. But I can find nothing to guide the Board as to the circumstances in which they should pay or the circumstances in which they should not pay grants to such persons.

[His Lordship referred to the long title, section 1(6) and sections 2 to 8 of the 1966 Act.]

Sections 11 and 12 are perhaps more relevant. Section 11 provides for the appointment of committees to advise the Board on the administration of the Act and it could be taken as an indication that otherwise the Board's discretion is unlimited. Section 12 provides for an annual report to Parliament so that Parliament can *ex post facto* consider the way in which this discretion has been exercised. . . .

I cannot find that these provisions give any right to any person to get a grant. It was argued that the object of the Act is to promote the modernisation of machinery and plant and that the Board were bound to pay grants to all who are eligible unless, in their view, particular eligible expenditure would not promote that object. That might be good advice for an advisory committee to give but I find nothing in the Act to require the Board to act in that way. If the Minister who now administers the Act, acting on behalf of the Government, should decide not to give grants in respect of certain kinds of expenditure, I can find nothing to prevent him. . . . [I]f the Minister thinks that policy or good administration requires the operation of some limiting rule, I find nothing to stop him.

[His Lordship cited *R.* v. *Port of London Authority, ex p. Kynoch,* in particular the passage from the judgment of Bankes L.J. beginning— "There are on the one hand . . .," and ending—"between these two classes."]

I see nothing wrong with that. But the circumstances in which discretions are exercised vary enormously and that passage cannot be applied literally in every case. The general rule is that anyone who has to exercise a statutory discretion must not "shut his ears to an application" (to adapt from Bankes L.J.). I do not think there is any great difference between a policy and a rule. There may be cases where an officer or authority ought to listen to a substantial argument reasonably presented urging a change of policy. What the authority must not do is to refuse to listen at all. But a Ministry or large authority may have had to deal already with a multitude of similar applications and then they will almost certainly have evolved a policy so precise that it could well be called a rule. There can be no objection to that, provided the authority is always willing to listen to anyone with something new to say—of course I do not mean to say that there need be an oral hearing. In the present case the respondent's officers have carefully considered all that the appellants have had to say and I have no doubt that they will continue to do so. . . .

VISCOUNT DILHORNE: . . . [His Lordship read the passage from *ex p. Kynoch* quoted by Lord Reid above.]

Bankes L.J. clearly meant that in the latter case there is a refusal to exercise the discretion entrusted to the authority or tribunal but the distinction between a policy decision and a rule may not be easy to draw. In this case it was not challenged that it was within the power of the Board to adopt a policy not to make a grant in respect of such an item. That policy might equally well be described as a rule. It was both reasonable and right that the Board should make known to those interested the policy it was going to follow. By doing so fruitless applications involving expense and expenditure of time might be avoided. The Board says that it has not refused to consider any application. It considered the appellants'. In these circumstances it is not necessary to decide in this case whether, if it had refused to consider an application on the ground that it related to an item costing less than £25, it would have acted wrongly.

I must confess that I feel some doubt whether the words used by Bankes L.J. in the passage cited above are really applicable to a case of this kind. It seems somewhat pointless and a waste of time that the Board should have to consider applications which are bound as a result of its policy decision to fail. Representations could of course be made that the policy should be changed.

I cannot see any ground on which it could be said that it was *ultra vires* of the Board to decide not to make grants on items costing less that £25 . . . In my opinion, this appeal should be dismissed.

LORD MORRIS OF BORTH-Y-GEST, LORD WILBERFORCE and LORD DIPLOCK concurred with LORD REID.

Notes

1. Consider the views on the question of policy fetters expressed by the Court of Appeal in *Sagnata Investments Ltd.* v. *Norwich Corporation* [1971] 2 Q.B. 614, below, pp. 613–622.

Sagnata raises the question whether a power to license an activity may, by the adoption of a policy of "no licences," be used by an authority to prohibit all such activity? To prevent authorities going beyond what Parliament may have intended the courts may hold either that the policy goes beyond what the legislation authorises as a legitimate exercise of power, or that the authority has been unwilling to consider the merits of individual applications and has operated the policy in an inflexible way.

Parliament has, on occasions, made clear by the wording of legislation that such "blanket" policies are permissible. See, *e.g.* Local Government (Miscellaneous Provisions) Act 1982—local authority may reject an application to operate a "sex establishment" on the ground, *inter alia*, that there are already an appropriate number of such establishments in the area; express provision that the local authority may take the view that the appropriate number is "nil."

It has been held that legislation authorising such "blanket" policy decisions should be construed narrowly—see *Walker* v. *Leeds City Council* [1976] 3 All E.R. 709, H.L.

2. In *R.* v. *Secretary of State for the Environment, ex p. Brent London Borough Council* [1982] Q.B. 593, the Secretary of State had exercised powers to reduce the rate support grant payable to the applicant local authority. In so doing the Secretary of State had acted in accordance with a policy earlier formulated to deal with "overspending" authorities. He had refused to meet representatives of the local authority to discuss any alteration or amendment of the policy, regarding his policy on the matter as "settled." In the words of Ackner L.J. (at p. 644): ". . . the Secretary . . . clearly decided to turn a deaf ear to any and all representations to change the policy. . . ." In so acting the Secretary of State was held by the Court of Appeal to have erred. Again in the words of Ackner L.J. (*ibid.*): "In our judgment [he] was obliged to listen to any objector who showed that he might have something new to say; putting it negatively, he was obliged not to declare his unwillingness to listen. . . . We accept that to be entitled to be heard it was for the objector to show that he had, or might have, something new to say. . . ." The Secretary of State's decision was, accordingly, quashed. The court rejected the Secretary of State's argument that the "fettering" principle applied only to cases where a discretionary power conferred was of a general nature, to be exercised on more than one occasion and in relation to applications for the grant of some right which the person holding the power can confer, such as a permission or licence: see [1982] Q.B. at pp. 640–642. See S. H. Bailey, [1983] P.L. 8.

3. Note how this ground of challenge overlaps with others. To fail to give proper consideration to the merits of an individual matter may at one and the same time be to apply a policy over-rigidly and to fail to take into account a relevant consideration (see below, p. 362). Equally, to defend successfully a decision taken in accordance with a policy it may be necessary to show that one has "acted fairly" in the sense of having given notice of the policy which was to be followed, and having indicated that representations that an exception should be made or that the policy should be changed would be considered (see further on the "duty to act fairly," below, p. 498 ff). The need to make the policy known to those who may be affected by it would seem to follow from the obligation to be receptive to representations. This obligation is only of substance if those affected are aware of the policy in respect of which they may raise arguments.

(D) Fettering Discretion by Contractual or Similar Undertakings

The cases which follow demonstrate the line which the courts have sought to draw between, on the one hand, contracts or other binding undertakings which they have upheld as having been entered into in the valid exercise of discretionary power (or valid performance of public duty), and, on the other hand, purported contractual or other commitments which the courts have held to be invalid as unduly infringing the requirement that bodies in whom discretionary powers have been vested should retain freedom as to the exercise of those discretionary powers. The cases show how the courts have acknowledged the fact that public authorities will commonly need to enter into binding commitments with "outsiders" in order that they may perform their various statutory functions. Express provision to such effect may appear in legislation, or may appropriately be implied therefrom. At the same time, the courts have had regard to the principle that, notwithstanding an authority's possession of a power to enter into binding commitments, the authority's discretionary powers have been conferred on it to be exercised as the public interest may from time to time require. "Commitments" which seem unduly to restrict an authority from acting in the exercise of its powers as the public interest may in due course require will therefore be held invalid; and for a public body to regard itself as unable, because of "commitments" entered into, to exercise its powers as it may consider the public interest to require may involve that body in having failed to have retained sufficiently the broad scope of its discretionary power.

The following cases illustrate (i) the general principles applied by the courts as regards the performance/fettering of statutory powers; and (ii), the operation of the same, or at least a very similar, principle in respect of the capacity of the Crown to enter into binding commitments.

Note

See generally J. D. B. Mitchell, *The Contracts of Public Authorities* (1954), Chap. 2, esp. pp. 57–65; C. Turpin, *Government Contracts* (1972), pp. 19–25; P. W. Hogg, (1970) 44 A.L.J. 154; E. Campbell, (1971) 45 A.L.J. 338; P. Rogerson, [1971] P.L. 288.

(i) The General Principles

BIRKDALE DISTRICT ELECTRIC SUPPLY CO. LTD. v. SOUTHPORT CORPORATION

[1926] A.C. 355; 95 L.J.Ch. 587; 134 L.T. 673; 42 T.L.R. 303; 90 J.P. 77; 24 L.G.R. 157 (House of Lords)

In 1901 the appellants, an electricity company, took over, under an Electric Lighting Order (made under the Electric Lighting Acts), the local electricity supply undertaking from Birkdale U.D.C. Under a Supplemental Deed to the Main Deed of Transfer, it was agreed that the prices to be charged by the appellants to private consumers should not exceed those charged in the adjoining borough of Southport by Southport Corporation, which also operated an electricity supply undertaking. In 1911 Southport Corporation "took over" Birkdale U.D.C. The appellants continued to supply the Birkdale area. In 1923, the Corporation applied for an injunction to restrain the appellants from charging prices in excess of the Southport prices (as had been done since 1921). The appellants argued that the 1901 agreement was an *ultra vires* fetter on their own power to fix the price (subject to statutory maxima) of electricity supplied by them. In the future they might be faced with a difficult situation, and need to raise their prices above those in Southport. The Corporation argued that the 1901 agreement was a business agreement which was not incompatible with the proper performance by the appellants of their statutory functions. The question of incompatibility had to be judged at the date of the agreement. The fact that the agreement might be improvident, and lead to lower profits, was a matter between the appellant company and their shareholders, but did not render the agreement *ultra vires*. Astbury J. dismissed the action ([1925] 1 Ch. 63), but was reversed by the Court of Appeal ([1925] 1 Ch. 794). The company appealed to the House of Lords.

LORD SUMNER: ... Are ... [the agreements] void at common law as being *ultra vires* the appellants, a trading company, incorporated to exercise statutory powers vested in them in the public interest under the authority of the Legislature? This is a doctrine, which it may be unwise to circumscribe within the limits of an inelastic definition. We have, however, a long series of decisions, extending over nearly a century, and at any rate illustrating the cases to which the rule has been understood to extend. With the exception of *York Corporation* v. *Henry Leetham & Sons* [1924] 1 Ch. 557 no case has been cited, in which a contract by a trading company to compound with a customer without limit of time for the price to be paid for services rendered to him, has been declared to be *ultra vires*, and we were told that the diligence of counsel had failed to find any other case. Certainly I have been able to go no further.

Hitherto the question has mainly arisen, where servitudes have been claimed over the property, which the alleged servient owner acquired under statutory authority and for the purposes of a public undertaking. In *R.* v. *Inhabitants of Leake* (1833) 5 B. & Ad. 469 a public right of way was alleged to exist over the bank of a drain constructed by statutory Commissioners and reparable as such by the inhabitants of Leake. In *Staffordshire and Worcestershire Canal Navigation* v. *Birmingham Canal Navigations* (1866) L.R. 1 H.L. 254 a right was claimed to have water discharged from the respondents' canal into the canal of the appellants at the bottom of a flight of locks connecting the two navigations, ... The right in these cases ... was rested on prescription and not on express grant, but the argument, which prevailed, was that the theory of dedication to the public use rests on an implied grant but none could be implied, since even an express grant would have been void as being *ultra vires*.

Parallel with these decisions there is a line of cases, in which the servitude claimed has been upheld on the ground that a dedication would not under the circumstances have been incompatible with full observance of the terms and full attainment of the purposes for which the statutory powers had been granted. This principle is stated as early as *R.* v. *Inhabitants of Leake*, in which the dedication was upheld, and was acted on in *Grand Junction Canal Co.* v. *Petty* (1888) 21 Q.B.D. 273, a case of a public right of walking on a towpath, and in *Greenwich Board of Works* v. *Maudslay* (1870) L.R. 5 Q.B. 397, a case of a footpath along a sea wall, ... Parke J. says, in the *Leake* case, that, if the bank was vested in the Commissioners by statute, so that they were thereby bound to use it for some special purpose, incompatible with a public right of walking along it, they must be deemed to have been incapable in law of thus dedicating their property; otherwise they were in that regard in the same position as other landowners.... In the *Grand Junction* case Lindley L.J. says, that such incompatibility is a matter of evidence, and, in practice, evidence has regularly been given and considered for the purpose of testing the question.

My Lords, I do not think that these cases assist the appellants in any way, but in most respects are against them, for they show that, in default of proof of incompatibility in the present case, some other consideration of a cogent kind must be found. The incompetence of the company is only an incompetence *sub modo*, beyond which the powers necessary to its operation may be freely exercised.

Ayr Harbour Trustees v. *Oswald* (1883) 8 App.Cas. 323 introduces a new matter and is nearer to the present case. Harbour trustees, whose statutory power and duty were to acquire land, to be used as need might arise for the construction of works on the coast line of the harbour, sought to save money in respect of severance on the compulsory acquisition of a particular owner's land by offering him a perpetual covenant not to construct their works on the land acquired, so as to cut him off from access to the waters of the harbour, or otherwise to affect him injuriously in respect of land not taken but from which the acquired land was severed. It was held that such a covenant was *ultra vires*. Lord Blackburn's words should be quoted. "I think," he says, "that where the legislature confer powers on any body to take land compulsorily for a particular purpose, it is on the ground that the using of that land for that purpose will be for the public good. Whether that body be one which is seeking to make a profit for shareholders, or, as in the present case, a body of trustees acting solely for the public good . . . a contract, purporting to bind them and their successors not to use those powers, is void."

Founding on this case, Russell J. held in *York Corporation* v. *Henry Leetham & Sons* [1924] 1 Ch. 557 that a contract, terminable only by the customer, to carry his traffic at a fixed annual sum was equally *ultra vires*. Just as the covenant in the *Ayr Harbour* case tied the hands of the successors to the then trustees, and prevented them from constructing works on the land acquired, however necessary they might have become for the proper management of the undertaking, so he held that the corresponding contracts with Leetham fettered the free management of the canal in perpetuity, no matter how urgent it might be to increase the revenues of the undertaking.

My Lords, I do not think that there is a true analogy between these cases. On examining the facts in the *Ayr Harbour* case it is plain that, in effect, the trustees did not merely propose to covenant in a manner that committed the business of the harbour to restricted lines in the future; they were to forbear, once and for all, to acquire all that the statute intended them to acquire, for, though technically they acquired the whole of the land, they were to sterilize part of their acquisition, so far as the statutory purpose of their undertaking was concerned. This is some distance from a mere contract entered into with regard to trading profits. The land itself was affected in favour of the former owner in the *Ayr* case just as a towpath is affected in favour of the owner of a dominant tenement, if he is given a personal right of walking along it. If the Ayr trustees had reduced the acquisition price by covenanting with the respondent for a perpetual right to moor his barges, free of tolls, at any wharf they might construct on the water front of the land acquired, the decision might, and I think would, have been different.

There is, however, another aspect of the *Ayr Harbour* case which ought to be loyally recognized. It is certainly some ground for saying that there may be cases where the question of competence to contract does not depend on a proved incompatibility between the statutory purposes and the user, which is granted or renounced, but is established by the very nature of the grants or the contract itself. It was not proved in the *Ayr* case that there was any actual incompatibility between the general purposes of the undertaking and the arrangement by which the particular proprietor was to be spared a particular interference with the amenities or the advantages of his back land. I think the case was supposed to speak for itself and that, in effect, the trustees were held to have renounced a part of their statutory birthright. The appellants, however, contend, and Russell J. appears to have thought, that your Lordships' House extended other principles, namely, those applicable to servitudes over land acquired, to mere contracts restricting the undertakers' future freedom of action in respect to the business management of their undertaking. This point of view ought therefore to be examined.

The appellants, as I understand them, say that the doctrine is not confined to the creation of servitudes or other derogations by grant from plenary ownership, but extends also to such covenants in perpetuity as may, in events not actually impossible, starve their undertaking and spell its ruin. Southport, they say, now standing in the shoes of the Birkdale Council as well as in its own (if I may somewhat distort their metaphor), has behind it the pockets of the ratepayers of both areas, and though these may be no more inexhaustible than their patience, at least they may prove deeper and more enduring than the paid-up or uncalled capital of the appellant company, or its shareholders' willingness to subscribe to new issues of debentures or of preference stock. The thing speaks for itself. The covenant is fraught with potential suicide for the covenantors, and so is *ultra vires*.

My Lords, this hypothesis is conceivable, though neither from the evidence nor the argument have I gathered why these machinations should be attributed to the respondents or be tolerated by their outraged ratepayers. Municipal finance is capable of much curious development, but I think that among ordinary ratepayers a passion to supply current below cost price to private consumers is purely academic. If it exists at Southport, I think it should be proved by testimony.

The argument must be either that it is one of the direct statutory objects of the Electric Lighting Order that the undertakers should make a profit or at least not suffer any loss, or else that this is an indirect statutory object, since, if the undertakers make no profit, they will either pursue the undertaking without zeal or will drop it, so soon as this imaginary rate-war exhausts their resources.

My Lords, I am afraid this is beyond me. It may be the policy of the Electric Lighting Acts to get trading companies to take up and work Electric Lighting Orders in hope of gain, but I cannot see that it is any part of the direct purposes of the Order, that money should be made or dividends distributed. The primary object of the Electric Lighting Order was to get a supply of electric energy for the area in question, a thing only feasible at the time by getting a trading company to undertake the business. It was not to secure that certain charges should be made or that certain results should be shown upon a profit and loss account. As for the indirect effect, which will follow if no money is made or enough money is lost, the Order itself imposes a maximum price for the current and conceivably, therefore, might itself lead to the exhaustion of the company's funds. How, then, can it be part of the legal objects of the grant of these powers, that they should never result in financial disaster? The Order is really as little concerned with the company's ultimate ability to continue the undertaking as with its earning of a profit. The latter is the company's own affair; the former will simply lead to the revocation of the Order and the grant of a more favourable one to someone else. If this is so, there is a wide and more than sufficient difference between the contract of the Ayr Harbour Trustees not to acquire all that they were intended to acquire, and that of the appellants to obtain the transfer of the Order by convenanting among other considerations for something, which obviously is not and may never be, incompatible with the fulfilment of all the purposes of the Order and most of the purposes of the company's trading as well.

In *York Corporation* v. *Henry Leetham & Sons* there were two navigations, both vested in the Corporation of York, which appear to have differed somewhat in their incidents, the Ouse Navigation and the Foss Navigation. The original Act of 1726, which authorized the former, empowered trustees to levy tolls on craft using the navigation when completed, and, for the purpose of constructing the navigation, authorized them to mortgage these prospective tolls and so to raise the necessary capital. The resources of the trustees were therefore of a character wholly different from those of a limited liability company. A later Act, that of 1732, fixed a schedule of rates and provided that all commodities carried "shall" bear them, and that it should be lawful for the trustees to take the rates "by this Act directed and no others," though, if the full revenue derived from these rates proved to be more than was required to maintain the undertaking, there was power to moderate them. The Act, which authorized the latter navigation, provided for the incorporation of a company having a capital of 25,400*l.* in 100*l.* shares and borrowing powers up to 10,000*l.* No distinction appears, from the judgment of Russell J., to have been drawn in argument between these two undertakings, but it is possible that the agreement in dispute, by which the undertakers compounded the rate with a particular customer, might be regarded as a direct breach of the mandatory charging clause of the Ouse Act of 1732, and consequently *ultra vires*. The same view could not arise on the Foss Act. The *ratio decidendi* of the judgment, however, proceeds entirely on the analogy of the *Ayr Harbour* case.

My Lords, with all respect to the learned judge, I am unable to adopt this reasoning. As I have said, it is no part of the intention of the Legislature that the appellants should make a profit or avoid a loss. If, again, the agreement is to be *ultra vires* at all, it must be *ultra vires* all through. In cases like the *Ayr Harbour* case the land acquired under statutory powers was fettered in the undertakers' hands from the time the agreement was made. In the present case the company's activities have not yet been and may never be impaired by the agreement at all. So far it may have been and probably has been safe and beneficial. How then, can it have been *ultra vires* hitherto? There is further, in my opinion, a wide distinction between the position of the appellants and of such undertakers as the Ayr Harbour Trustees. The scheme here is that a limited liability company, not deprived of its right, as such, to go into voluntary liquidation or otherwise to terminate its enterprise, obtained the Order with the Board of Trade's consent and with the like consent may part with it. In other words, the Board of Trade is here the constituted authority, by whose discretionary intervention the supply of electricity may be secured in the interest of the locality. This is a very different scheme from a constitution of undertakers, which under the same statute establishes their existence, confers their powers, and defines their purposes.

It appears to me that no line can be drawn between the agreement now in question and any ordinary trading contract, if the appellants are right in testing the validity of the contract by its ultimate and theoretic possibility of bringing upon them a crippling loss. I do not think that a speculation as to the possible effect of what they have done is a legitimate ground for relieving them from their bargain, and it seems to me that the appeal should be dismissed.

THE EARL OF BIRKENHEAD, LORD ATKINSON, LORD WRENBURY and LORD CARSON concurred.

Notes

1. The Earl of Birkenhead (at p. 364) formulated the basic principle as:

> "a well established principle of law, that if a person or public body is entrusted by the Legislature with certain powers and duties expressly or impliedly for public purposes, those persons or bodies cannot divest themselves of these powers and duties. They cannot enter into any contract or take any action incompatible with the due exercise of their powers or the discharge of their duties."

2. The leading modern case on the implied dedication of rights of way by statutory corporation is *British Transport Commission* v. *Westmorland C.C.* [1958] A.C. 126. The House of Lords emphasised that the validity of express or implied dedications depends on the question of fact whether such dedication is incompatible with the corporation's statutory powers. Their Lordships rejected the Commission's argument that there could only be compatibility if it could be proved that in no conceivable circumstances could the proposed user at any future time and in any way possibly interfere with the statutory purpose for which the land was acquired. *Per* Viscount Simonds at p. 144:

> "to give to incompatibility such an extended meaning is in effect to reduce the principle to a nullity. For a jury, invited to say that in no conceivable circumstances and at no distance of time could an event possibly happen, could only fold their hands and reply that it was not for them to prophesy what an inscrutable Providence might in all the years to come disclose. I do not disguise from myself that it is difficult to formulate with precision what direction should be given to a jury. But, after all, we live in a world in which our actions are constantly guided by a consideration of reasonable probabilities of risks that can reasonably be foreseen and guarded against, and by a disregard of events of which, even if we think of them as possible, we can fairly say that they are not at all likely to happen. And it is, in my opinion, by such considerations as these, imprecise though they may be, that a tribunal of fact must be guided in determining whether a proposed user of land will interfere with the statutory purpose for which it was acquired."

Lord Radcliffe (at pp. 155–156) referred to Lord Sumner's description of the *Ayr* case as an example of an attempt to renounce a part of the "statutory birthright" of the trustees:

> "Striking as the phrase is, it does not seem to me to offer much help in deciding which are the cases in which the principle of *Paterson's* case (1880–1881) 6 App.Cas. 833 and *Oswald's* case is to be applied, where, as he says, 'the very nature of the grants or the contract itself' provides the answer, and which are those many other cases in which the test to be applied is the humbler one of incompatibility proved by evidence. The birthright of a statutory corporation includes all those powers and rights with which it is thought proper to invest it at its creation: and I do not think it easy for a court of law to decide merely by the nature of the thing which of those powers are inalienably entailed and which can be disentailed and disposed of by ordinary grant.
>
> In my opinion, we are bound to recognize that the principle of these two cases cannot be applied in all circumstances and on all occasions to all statutory corporations and public bodies. That, indeed, has already been recognized by the decision of this House in the *Birkdale* case, in which the electric supply company had certainly made a contract which deprived themselves and their successors of power at any future time to raise the charges for their supply beyond a fixed limit, however much the needs of their undertaking might require it. It is of some importance to remember, when searching for a dividing line, that the two cases which 'spoke for themselves' were both concerned with defined areas of land of no great extent, and the possible consequence of renouncing powers over such areas could be stated as a matter of practical observation. But nothing like the same observation can be brought to bear when the factors of the problem are, on the one hand, all the general powers derived by a railway company from the Railway Clauses Consolidation Act, 1845, and, on the other hand, many miles of railway lines covering great varieties of

setting. In such cases what I have called the pragmatic test is, I think, to be preferred. . . ."

3. In *Stourcliffe Estates Co. Ltd.* v. *Bournemouth Corporation* [1910] 2 Ch. 12 C.A., the defendant corporation purchased some land from the plaintiff to be used as a public park, and entered into a covenant not to erect any building except "such structures as summer houses a band stand or shelters." The corporation had power under the Bournemouth Improvement Act 1892 to build public conveniences on any of their public parks. The plaintiff was granted an injunction to restrain the corporation from erecting public conveniences on the land they had sold. The corporation's argument that the covenant was *ultra vires* was rejected. *Per* Cozens-Hardy M.R. at pp. 18–19:

> "That . . . is a proposition which seems to me to be startling. If the deed is wholly *ultra vires* I can understand it, but to suppose that the corporation could be allowed to retain the land and to repudiate the consideration or part of the consideration for it is a proposition to which certainly I could not give my adhesion."

His Lordship distinguished the *Ayr* case on the ground that in that case:

> ". . . the Act of Parliament, for public purposes and in the public interest, declared that certain land should be purchased by the undertakers, who were given compulsory powers for the purpose. That land included Mr. Oswald's land. Not only were they to make the harbour and a quay, but they had power—it was obviously part of the essence of the undertaking—to make over any part of the land so purchased, certain warehouses facing a certain road. . . . Here the corporation have general powers to purchase land for, *inter alia*, the purposes of a public park. They may go anywhere they like and may make a contract with anybody who is willing to enter into a contract with them for these purposes, and to say that a vendor under those circumstances cannot rely upon a restrictive covenant entered into by the purchaser would really be to render it practically impossible for a municipal corporation ever to enter into a contract with a landowner for purposes of this kind."

Buckley L.J. pointed out (at p. 22) that the corporation "must acquire not for all and every purpose for which they can acquire land anywhere, but for some definite purpose, some one of the purposes in respect of which they are entitled to acquire land. . . ." His Lordship saw no reason why the corporation should not take the land while binding themselves not to put a urinal there:

> "It is said that that is divesting themselves of some power, because under s.85 of their Act of 1892 they could have put a urinal there. That section means that it is not an improper expenditure of money by the corporation to, amongst other things, erect urinals in proper places, but it is not necessary that the corporation should with every piece of land which they buy acquire also the right to put a urinal there."

4. In *William Cory & Son Ltd.* v. *London Corporation* [1951] 2 K.B. 476 C.A., the corporation as sanitary authority entered a contract with Cory's for the removal by Cory's barges of refuse from the City of London. Subsequently, the corporation as port health authority made new by-laws with requirements as to coamings and coverings that were more stringent than the terms of the contract. Compliance with the by-laws would have been onerous, requiring expenditure of over £400

per barge, and preventing the use of the barges for carrying coal on the return journey. The company purported to treat the making of the by-laws as repudiation by anticipatory breach, to accept the repudiation, and to claim rescission. They claimed that there was an implied term in the contract to the effect that the corporation should not use their powers to make by-laws to impose more onerous burdens than those provided by the contract. The Court of Appeal, affirming Lord Goddard C.J. ([1951] 1 K.B. 8) held that in general an implied term might be read into a contract that one party should not act so as to prevent the other from being able to perform its obligations. However, the court held that, given the statutory responsibilities of the sanitary authority, there was in this case no such implied term, and therefore no repudiation. In the words of Lord Asquith of Bishopstone at pp. 484–485:

> "I consider that such a term, whether implied or even express, could not be valid. The language of section 84(1)(*a*) of the Public Health (London) Act, 1936, is mandatory. The provision is as follows: '(1) Every sanitary authority shall make by-laws (*a*) for the prevention of nuisances arising from snow, ice, salt, dust, ashes, rubbish, offal, carrion, fish or filth or other matter or thing in any street.' If the suggested term were express, it would have to take some such form as this: 'True we are charged by Parliament with the duty of making such by-laws with reference to refuse as may be called for from time to time by considerations of public health. But even if these considerations call, and call peremptorily, for a provision not less stringent than that made by the 1948 by-laws, even if a second plague of London is likely to occur, unless such provision is made, we undertake in such an event to neglect or violate our statutory duty so far as the requirement of such a by-law may exceed the requirements imposed by cl. 1 of our contract with the claimants.' Such a contractual provision would seem to be plainly invalid. . . ."

His Lordship relied on the point that the corporation was not "a body trading for profit," unlike the body executing statutory duties in *Southport Corporation* v. *Birkdale District Electric Supply Co.*, and like the trustees in the *Ayr* case. Thus "the considerations which were thought relevant in the *Southport* case (so far as that decision threw doubt in (*sic*) the *York* case) have no application here."

It was accepted, however, that the contract had been frustrated from the date the by-laws came into effect.

5. In March 1967, Cheshire County Council and Congleton Rural District Council entered into an agreement with Manchester University, whereby the councils undertook to discourage development "within the limits of their powers" in a zone within the rural district. The aim was to protect the Jodrell Bank radio telescope, which was operated by a department of the University. The rural district council dealt with applications for planning permission as agents for the county council (the local planning authority).

In *Stringer* v. *Minister of Housing and Local Government* [1970] 1 W.L.R. 1281, Cooke J. held that this agreement was *ultra vires* as inconsistent with the proper performance of the duties of a planning authority under the Town and Country Planning Act 1962, s.17(1). This required the authority to have regard to the provisions of the development plan, and to any other material considerations. It was admitted that after the agreement was signed the local planning authority did not override the Jodrell Bank objections to development, and the judge held that the intention of the agreement was to bind the authority to disregard considerations to which, under section 17(1), they were required to have regard. The judge held, further, that in refusing S.'s application for planning permission for 23 houses, the rural district council had intended to honour this agreement, it being immaterial whether or not it was legally binding, and so had failed to comply with section 17(1). The Rural District Council's determination was therefore void.

Nevertheless, Cooke J. ultimately decided against S. S. had appealed to the Minister against the Rural District Council's determination. The Minister had dismissed the appeal on the ground that the development would give rise to a very serious danger to the continued operation of the telescope. S. was now applying under s.179(1) of the 1962 Act for an order to quash the Minister's decision on the ground that it was not within the powers of the Act (see now s.288 of the 1990 Act and below, pp. 624–625). Cooke J. held that as the Minister had power to deal with appeals *de novo* (under s.23(4) of the 1962 Act; now, s.79(1) of the 1990 Act), he could entertain an appeal in this case even though the Rural District Council's determination was void. On the facts, the Minister had not been influenced by the 1967 agreement, and had not applied rigidly his policy to protect the telescope (see above, p. 292). S.'s application was dismissed.

Questions

1. Do public authorities need the protection of legal incapacity to enter "fettering" contracts? Should they be allowed to override express terms in contracts into which they enter freely without payment of compensation? Should they not be bound by the kinds of terms implied into contracts between private parties for their mutual protection? See P. Hogg, *Liability of the Crown* (pp. 134 *et seq*).

2. How satisfactorily is the *Ayr* case distinguished in the *Stourcliffe* case? Would the *Stourcliffe* case have been decided differently had the corporation been able to show that there was no other appropriate site for lavatories on the pleasure ground? Or in that part of Bournemouth?

3. How satisfactory is any distinction between a corporation acting solely for the public good and one trading for profit (*Cory*)? See Mitchell, *op. cit.*, p. 62.

DOWTY BOULTON PAUL LTD. v. WOLVERHAMPTON CORPORATION

[1971] 1 W.L.R. 204; (1970) 115 S.J. 76; [1971] 2 All E.R. 277; 69 L.G.R. 192 (Chancery Division, Pennycuick V.-C.)

[The facts are stated above at pp. 222–224 in relation to the sequel to this application.]

By notice of motion dated September 23, 1970, the company sought an interlocutory injunction that the corporation should ". . . do nothing which would cause the Board of Trade [later the Department of Trade and Industry] to determine the existing licence enabling Pendeford Aerodrome, Wrottesley, Wolverhampton to be used as a licensed airfield and shall do nothing to prevent the company from using the airfield for their lawful purposes."

PENNYCUICK V.-C.: . . . The first issue which has arisen upon the hearing of this motion is whether under the terms of the 1936 conveyance or under the general law the corporation is entitled to override the rights conferred upon the company under the 1936 conveyance. If it is so entitled that would be the end of the matter: the corporation will do no wrong to the company if it does nullify those rights by developing the airfield as a housing estate and the company will have no remedy whether by way of injunction or damages or otherwise.

Mr. Bagnall for the company was content to rely on the plain terms of the 1936 conveyance. . . .

Mr. Newsom's [main] contention, . . . was that, under the general law regarding the exercise of statutory powers, the corporation is at any time entitled to override this licence, if it requires to use the airfield for any of its statutory purposes. These, of course, include its powers as a housing authority. Mr. Newsom accepted that the grant of the licence under the 1936 conveyance was within the powers of the corporation. . . .

Mr. Newsom based his contention on the principle that a body entrusted with statutory powers cannot by contract fetter the exercise of those powers. He referred to a number of cases which establish beyond all doubt that principle. I refer shortly to three of those authorities.

[His Lordship referred to the *Ayr* case, *York Corporation* v. *H. Leetham* and *Southend-on-Sea Corporation* v. *Hodgson* [1962] 1 Q.B. 416 at p. 424.]

. . . That seems to me, however, a principle wholly inapplicable to the present case. What has happened here is that the corporation has made what is admittedly a valid disposition in respect of its land for a term of years. What is, in effect, contended by Mr. Newsom is that such a disposition—and, indeed, any other possible disposition of property by a corporation for a term of years, for example, an ordinary lease—must be read as subject to an implied condition enabling the corporation to determine it should it see fit to put the property to some other use in the exercise of any of its statutory powers. Nothing in the cases cited supports this startling proposition. The cases are concerned with attempts to fetter in advance the future exercise of statutory powers otherwise than by the valid exercise of a statutory power. The cases are not concerned with the position which arises after a statutory power has been validly exercised. Obviously, where a power is exercised in such a manner as to create a right extending over a term of years, the existence of that right *pro tanto* excludes the exercise of other statutory powers in respect of the same subject-matter, but there is no authority and I can see no principle upon which that sort of exercise could be held to be invalid as a fetter upon the future exercise of powers. . . .

[His Lordship referred to *Stourcliffe Ltd.* v. *Bournemouth Corporation* (above, p. 303) which had not been cited by counsel.]

I conclude for the purpose of this motion that the company has made out a *prima facie* case that it is entitled to this right and that the corporation is not entitled to override that right either under the terms of the 1936 conveyance or in exercise of its statutory power.

I turn now to consider the remedy available to the company should the corporation persevere in its intention to appropriate this land for housing. It seems to me that the remedy of the company must lie in damages only and that the company is not now entitled, and will not be entitled at the hearing of the action, if it is then otherwise successful, to any relief by way of injunction or mandatory order.

The right vested in the company necessarily involves the maintenance of the airfield as a going concern. That involves continuing acts of management, including the upkeep of runways and buildings, the employment of staff, compliance with the Civil Aviation Act 1949 and so forth, *i.e.* in effect the carrying on of a business. That is nonetheless so by reason that so far the corporation has elected to engage Don Everall Aviation Ltd. to manage the airfield on its behalf. It is very well established that the court will not order specific performance of an obligation to carry on a business or, indeed, any comparable series of activities: see in this connection *Halsbury's Laws of England*, 3rd ed. (1961) Vol. 36, pp. 267 to 269:

> "The court does not enforce the performance of contracts which involve continuous acts and require the watching and supervision of the court."

... The principle is established, I should have thought, beyond argument. For this purpose there is no difference between an order for specific performance of the contract and a mandatory injunction to perform the party's obligation under the contract. In the present case the notice of motion is expressed as one for a negative injunction, but one has only to look at it to see that it does involve a mandatory order upon the corporation to maintain the airfield. In order that the corporation could continue to allow the company to use the airfield, it is essential that the corporation should maintain the airfield. It would be quite impossible for the company to use the airfield if the corporation did not maintain it. So an injunction in the terms asked would put upon the corporation a duty, to be observed for something over 60 years, to maintain the airfield.

I conclude therefore in the first place, always so far as this interlocutory motion is concerned, that the company has made out a *prima facie* case that it is entitled to the right conferred by the 1936 conveyance, and the corporation will do an actionable wrong if it prevents the company from exercising that right. I conclude further that the remedy and the only remedy of the company lies in damages, with the consequence that I must make no order on this motion.

Questions

1. Could the corporation's liability to pay damages for breach of covenant properly be regarded as a fetter on the exercise of their statutory housing powers? Are those powers among the primary powers of the local authority (*cf.* the *Stourcliffe* case, above, p. 303)?

See J. M. Evans, (1972) 35 M.L.R. 88, who argues that the terms of the conveyance should have been construed as ineffective to prevent the corporation from exercising their powers of compulsory acquisition, but that the company's rights would have had to be acquired compulsorily, subject to the payment of compensation.

2. If the corporation had covenanted not to build dwelling-houses on the airport site, and such a covenant would have been binding on a private covenantor, should an injunction have been granted?

R. v. HAMMERSMITH AND FULHAM LONDON BOROUGH COUNCIL, ex p. BEDDOWES

[1987] 1 Q.B. 1050; [1987] 1 All E.R. 369 (Court of Appeal)

The council was the owner of an estate, Fulham Court, consisting of blocks of rented flats. All the blocks were in a very bad state of repair, much in need of renovation and improvement. The Conservative majority on the council favoured selling the blocks for development for owner-occupation. Labour councillors opposed this policy, regarding the loss of a considerable number of council rented flats as unacceptable.

In March 1986, the council's Housing Policy Committee resolved that a start be made in the implementation of the policy by means of the sale of one of the blocks to a private developer, Barratts. The sale was to be subject to the council committing itself to certain covenants as regards the, as yet unsold, blocks. The aim of the covenants was to provide assurance to the developers that the sale of the first block would be followed by similar sale for renovation of the other blocks, the developer wanting to avoid the danger of the council deciding to discontinue the policy of "sales," with the developer being left in possession of a renovated block amidst other unmodernised blocks. The applicant, a resident of the estate, sought to challenge the committee's resolution. In the Court of Appeal the principal argument was that the covenants imposed an unlawful fetter on the council's powers as a housing authority.

FOX L.J.: . . . The problem with which the council was faced was the modernisation of an estate laid out in blocks. The estate was 50 years old and in bad repair. It was no longer possible to limp along with day-to-day repairs which were not cost-effective, or indeed adequate. A major programme of modernisation was necessary, and the cost was high. It was estimated in November 1983 to be about £8 million, and was an amount which the council felt was too large for its own finances to sustain. The council, therefore, over a period developed a policy for dealing with the problem. The essential features of that policy in their final form were as follows:

(1) All the blocks should be sold to a developer for modernisation.

(2) The blocks, when modernised, should then be sold off as flats to the ultimate purchasers. The whole of Blocks A–G would eventually pass into the hands of owner-occupiers in this way.

(3) The preferred developers would be non-profit organisations, but the use of commercial developers was left open.

(4) The first block to be dealt with would be Block A, because it was different from the others in that it faced the Fulham Road, and it included a number of shops and it had a very ugly rear elevation which needed improvement for the benefit of the other blocks. In general, its attractive renovation was a matter of some importance in relation to the saleability of the other blocks.

(5) The council formed the view that persons buying owner-occupier flats in Block A (and in the other blocks as the development proceeded) should have a guarantee as to the user of the rest of the estate for owner-occupation. The individual purchasers of flats would be expending a substantial capital sum by way of premium, and would want binding assurances as to the user of the rest of the estate, since that would materially affect their own dwellings. . . . In the absence of certainty as to the development of the whole estate, marketing might be difficult and the whole project might flop. Although the flats were being sold at comparatively modest prices, for most purchasers the acquisition would be an important financial step.

(6) The council would not have to spend its own overstretched resources, and would indeed receive substantial capital sums which could be applied to housing purposes.

That, it seems to me, is a coherent policy which is not manifestly unreasonable. I appreciate that there may be sharp differences of opinion as to the respective merits of owner occupation and municipally rented housing, but the council's policy, as formulated, could not, I think, be struck down as "unreasonable" within the *Wednesbury* principles: *Associated Provincial Picture Houses Ltd.* v. *Wednesbury Corporation* [1948] 1 K.B. 223. . . .

The attack as developed on the appeal is, as I have indicated, really based upon the contention that the covenants fetter the council's discretion to deal with the retained land and are bad accordingly.

The first question, I think, in relation to that contention is whether the council is entitled to impose on its retained land covenants which were restrictive of its user of that land. In my opinion it is. . . .

A restrictive covenant does not operate merely in contract. It is an equitable interest in the burdened land. Section 104(1) of the Act of 1957 and section 32 of the Act of 1985 authorise a local authority to dispose of "land" held for housing purposes. Under Schedule 1 to the Interpretation Act 1978 " 'land' includes . . . any estate, interest, easement, servitude or right in or over land." It seems to me, therefore, that a local authority could, with the consent of the Minister, create restrictive covenants over its Part V (of the Act of 1957) and Part II (of the Act of 1985) land. The nature of a restrictive covenant was referred to in argument, but no question of absence of necessary consents has been raised in this case. Subject to consent, it seems to me that the council had power to create restrictive covenants under section 104(1) and (2) of the Act of 1957.

In general, I do not understand it to be disputed that there was power in the council (as the judge held) to create restrictive covenants under the Housing Acts, or otherwise. Power to create restrictive covenants does not, however, resolve the question whether the covenants constitute an unlawful fetter. There might, possibly, be an argument that if the Minister gave consent to the covenants under section 104 of the Act of 1957 or section 32 of the Act of 1985, and a contract was made accordingly, that is a complete and lawful disposition under the Housing Act itself, and no further question could arise as to its enforceability, but the point has not been investigated before us, and I disregard it altogether.

It is clear that a local authority cannot, in general, make declarations of policy which are binding in future on the council for the time being. A council cannot extinguish statutory powers in that way. But it may be able to do so by the valid exercise of other statutory powers. If a statutory power is lawfully exercised so as to create legal rights and obligations between the council and third parties, the result will be that the council for the time being is bound, even though that hinders or prevents the exercise of other statutory powers. . . . [His Lordship referred to *Dowty Boulton Paul Ltd.* v. *Wolverhampton Corporation* [1971] 1 W.L.R. 204: . . . [See above, p. 305].]

Stourcliffe Estates Co. Ltd. v. *Bournemouth Corporation* [1910] 2 Ch. 12 is an example of the same principle [see above, p. 303].

What we are concerned with in the present case are overlapping or conflicting powers. There is a power to create covenants restrictive of the use of the retained land; and there are powers in relation to the user of the retained land for housing purposes. In these circumstances, it is necessary to ascertain for what purpose the retained land is held. All other powers are subordinate to the main power to carry out the primary purpose: see *Blake* v. *Hendon Corporation* [1962] 1 Q.B. 283, 302.

Now the purpose for which the Fulham Court estate is held by the council must be the provision of housing accommodation in the district. The council's policy in relation to the estate, as I have set it out above, seems to me to be consistent with that purpose. The estate is in bad repair, and the policy is aimed at providing accommodation in the borough of higher quality than at present by means of a scheme of maintenance and refurbishment. The policy, it is true, is designed to produce owner-occupancy and not rented accommodation. Historically, local authority housing has been rented. But a substantial inroad upon that was made by Part I of the Housing Act 1980, which gave municipal tenants the right to purchase their dwellings. In the circumstances it does not seem to me that a policy which is designed to produce good accommodation for owner-occupiers is now any less within the purposes of the Housing Acts than the provision of rented housing. We are not dealing with a policy for providing highly expensive housing, but of owner accommodation at apparently reasonable prices. . . .

It seems to me that if the purpose for which the power to create restrictive covenants is being exercised can reasonably be regarded as the furtherance of the statutory object, then the creation of the covenants is not an unlawful fetter. All the powers are exercisable for the achieving of the statutory objects in relation to the land, and the honest and reasonable exercise of a power for that purpose cannot properly be regarded as a fetter upon another power given for the same purpose.

We were referred to the decision in *Ayr Harbour Trustees* v. *Oswald* (1883) 8 App.Cas. 623. But that was a case where the trustees simply "renounced part of their statutory birthright." There was an incompatibility between what they were proposing to do and the actual statutory purpose. In the present case, as it seems to me, the purpose of the contract is the same as the statutory purpose. . . .

I can see that there is something to be said for the view that so long as the council retains Part V land it should retain all the powers which the statute gives in relation to that land. That is simple and logical. But I think it is too inflexible and takes insufficient account of the practical difficulties of administering such an estate as Fulham Court. To bring it up to standard, money has to be found and compromises have to be made. It is not practicable to sell the whole estate at once. . . .

I should add that it is not suggested that there was bad faith in the timing of the scheme, as to implementation or otherwise. The idea of assurances of continuity was not new. In 1984 the council's officers had formed the view that the council would have to furnish guarantees on the future of the remainder of the estate. And in July 1985 the letter to the Housing Corporation stated that Block A would be sold in conjunction with an agreement "safeguarding the developers and investment alike."

In general, it seems to me that we are concerned with a rational scheme which the council could reasonably say that it was entitled to adopt as part of the housing policy of the borough. In saying that, I do not mean that a scheme for rented housing would have been irrational. Either could be defensible. But it is the function of politicians to choose policies. The court is not concerned with their merits but their legality.

. . . [T]he restrictions imposed by the covenants are, in effect, the following.

(i) The restriction of new lettings to long leases. That is central to the policy which the council had adopted in order to resolve the problems of this estate. For the reasons which I have indicated it seems to me a rational policy which a reasonable council could properly adopt. I appreciate that if the remaining blocks failed to sell, the council would be left with property which it could only put to a restricted use, *i.e.* direct owner/occupier sales. But there is nothing to indicate that such property, in London, will fail to sell.

(ii) It produces some degree of inflexibility in providing accommodation for tenants who do not wish to leave the estate, or to leave quickly, but would be prepared to move to another block so as to free their own block for the modernisation works. The council's hands are tied. That may be an inconvenience, but if the scheme generally is an effectuation of the Part V* purposes, I cannot see that it invalidates the whole.

* *i.e.* provision of housing accommodation purposes (Ed.).

(iii) Flats are left empty while the decanting is taking place and loss of revenue results. But that is inherent in the policy and it is clear that the question of voids was raised on a number of occasions at both committee and council meetings, including the housing policy committee meetings in June 1984 and February 1985. It was accepted because of what was regarded, not unreasonably, as the wider benefits of the scheme.

On the wider aspects of the matter, it was suggested on behalf of the applicant that if this scheme was valid, a council could, on the sale of a single flat, tie the hands of its successors by covenants in relation to the rest of a large estate. I do not think that is a valid argument. We are dealing with a long considered and rational scheme which was substantially advanced in its operation so that half the flats were vacant. It bears no resemblance to artificial devices based upon single flats.

For the reasons which I have indicated, I would reject the argument based on fetters. . . .

KERR L.J. I have come to a different conclusion on that part of the arguments which were presented under the heading "unlawful fettering." . . .

The relevant history concerning the policy for Fulham Court shows opposing political views within the housing policy committee and the council which were held throughout with passionate intensity. These clearly increased with the approach of the local elections on May 8, 1986, which were expected to result, as they did, in a change of the governing majority on the committee and council. The fact that this was in the mind of everyone concerned at the time of the meeting of the committee on March 19, 1986, when the decision was taken to sell Block A to Barratts subject to the . . . covenants, is clear from the affidavits which were sworn immediately thereafter in support of and opposition to the application for judicial review. That the date of May 8, 1986, was critical is also apparent from the fact, as we were told, that the hearing was thereupon expedited so that Schiemann J. was able to deliver his extempore judgment—a tour de force in the circumstances and by any standard—on the afternoon of Wednesday May 7. In the light of his decision the contract between the council and Barratts was then signed on the following day, subject to the outcome of any appeal. By that evening the political control of the council had changed.

Against that background, which represents only the final part of the history, it seems to me that the court must consider with the greatest care whether the decisions of the committee and council—evidently taken by a majority of a single vote or so throughout—were actuated by policy reasons based upon the proper discharge of the authority's powers and functions as a housing authority, or by extraneous motives. In saying this, I am of course not suggesting that political considerations must not affect the decisions of local authorities, which would plainly be absurd.

The point in the present case, however, is that it concerns a decision which, consciously and indeed in my view quite deliberately, fettered the freedom of action for the future of whoever might command a majority on the committee and council in relation to Fulham Court as a whole. That this was the intention is not really open to doubt, for the reasons explained hereafter. However, in saying this I am of course not questioning the sincerity of the opposing convictions held on both sides. Nor am I in the least concerned with their respective merits. The court is solely concerned with the question whether the decision under review was influenced by irrelevant considerations which ought to have been excluded under the principles stated by Lord Greene M.R. in the well known passage in *Associated Provincial Picture Houses Ltd.* v. *Wednesbury Corporation* [1948] 1 K.B. 223, 229 [below, p. 395]. In the present case I have reluctantly come to the conclusion that the decision to sell Block A to Barratts subject to the second schedule covenants was so influenced by political considerations designed to fetter the council's future policy that it should not be allowed to stand. . . .

[His Lordship quoted, with approval, a passage from *Wade's Administrative Law*, 5th ed. (1982), which included the following statement—"Since most contracts fetter freedom of action in some way, there may be difficult questions of degree in determining how far the authority may legally commit itself for the future." His Lordship considered the evidence in the case and stated that it had led him to the conclusion:]

. . . that the ultimate outcome, in the form of the committee's decision on March 19, 1986, was predominantly influenced by the political motive of fettering the political aspects of the future housing policy for Fulham Court rather than by any immediately necessary or relevant policy considerations. . . .

In saying this, I would like to emphasise . . . that in my view the overall proposals for Fulham Court favoured by the bare majority of the committee and council are not in themselves open to the slightest criticism from the point of view of a proper development policy for adoption by a housing authority. Indeed, this was never challenged by Mr. Arden on behalf of the applicant. But policies are liable to be reviewed, as the result of events or political changes or both. They should remain open to review under our democratic institutions, save to the extent that an immediate policy decision renders it reasonably necessary to fetter future policy decisions. I can see no such necessity for the second schedule covenants in the history of the present case. . . .

In the upshot, I am left with the following clear conclusions on the evidence. (i) The housing policies and aims for the development of Fulham Court as a whole pursued by the majorities on the committee and council were in themselves perfectly proper and open to no criticism whatever. (ii) But from about November 1985 onwards these policies were deliberately underpinned by the scheme of the second schedule covenants with the predominant motive of seeking to ensure the continuation and irrevocable maintenance of these policies in the event of a political change in the administration of the borough after the elections in May 1986.

On that basis I feel bound to conclude that the decision to contract with Barratts for the development of Block A on March 19, 1986, subject to these covenants, was an unreasonable and impermissible exercise of the powers and functions of a housing authority in the *Wednesbury* sense. Its predominant motivation was to fetter the political aspects of the future housing policy for Fulham Court, and not the implementation of the then (already modified) housing policy for reasons which were reasonably necessary at the time. It follows that in my view the decision of March 19, 1986, and the recent history which had preceded it, were predominantly motivated by purely political considerations designed to fetter future policies and not by any presently required contractual fetters. Accordingly, I would quash the decision of March 19, 1986, and the consequent contract with Barratts and allow this appeal.

SIR DENYS BUCKLEY [agreed with FOX L.J. In the course of his judgment he explained]: [I]f a statutory authority acting in good faith in the proper and reasonable exercise of its statutory powers undertakes some binding obligation, the fact that such obligation may thereafter preclude the authority from exercising some other statutory power, or from exercising its statutory powers in some other way, cannot constitute an impermissible fetter on its powers. Any other view would involve that the doctrine against fettering would itself involve a fetter on the authority's capacity to exercise its powers properly and reasonably as it thinks fit from time to time. So, in my view, the decision of the present case depends primarily upon whether the council was acting properly and reasonably in proposing to covenant with Barratts in the terms of the second schedule covenants. For the reasons indicated by Fox L.J., I think this was so.

Note

See case note by S. Tromans, [1987] C.L.J. 377.

(ii) The Crown

REDERIAKTIEBOLAGET AMPHITRITE v. THE KING

[1921] 3 K.B. 500; 91 L.J.K.B. 75; 126 L.T. 63; 37 T.L.R. 985; [1921] All E.R.Rep. 542 (Rowlatt J.)

(Petition of Right)

ROWLATT J. In this case the suppliants are a Swedish shipowning company who sue the Crown by petition of right for damages for breach of contract, the breach being that the ship *Amphitrite* was refused a clearance to enable her to leave this country, when she had entered a British port under an arrangement whereby she was promised that she should be given that clearance. Now undoubtedly the suppliants desired to get the clearest and most binding assurance that was possible. Their vessel was free; they might have employed her elsewhere; and they had experience of the difficulties encountered by foreign ships in getting away from this country when once they had come here. Accordingly they wrote on March 8, 1918, to the British Legation at Stockholm and asked whether, in the event of the vessel being put in trade between Sweden and England, the Legation could give them a guarantee that she would be allowed free passage without being detained in Great Britain. The Legation replied that they were "instructed to say that the S.S. *Amphitrite* will earn her own release and be given a coal cargo if she proceed to the United Kingdom with a full cargo consisting of a least 60% approved goods." That reply was given by the British Legation after consulting the proper authorities, and I must take it that it was given with the highest authority with which it could be given on behalf of His Majesty's Government. And the British Government thereby undertook that if the ship traded to this country she should not be subjected to the delays which were sometimes imposed. The letters in which that undertaking was contained were written with reference to an earlier voyage which was allowed to go through, the undertaking being on that occasion observed. But the undertaking was renewed with respect to the voyage in connection with which the present complaint arises by a letter from the British Legation, in which it was stated that "the S.S. *Amphitrite* will be allowed to release herself in her next voyage to the United Kingdom"—that is to say, upon the same terms as before. Now under those circumstances what I have to consider is whether this was a contract at all. I have not to consider whether there was anything of which complaint might be made outside a Court, whether that is to say what the Government did was morally wrong or arbitrary; that would be altogether outside my province. All I have got to say is whether there was an enforceable contract, and I am of opinion that there was not. No doubt the Government can bind itself through its officers by a commercial contract, and if it does so it must perform it like anybody else or pay damages for the breach. But this was not a commercial contract; it was an arrangement whereby the Government purported to give an assurance as to what its executive action would be in the future in relation to a particular ship in the event of her coming to this country with a particular kind of cargo. And that is, to my mind, not a contract for the breach of which damages can be sued for in a Court of law. It was merely an expression of intention to act in a particular way in a certain event. My main reason for so thinking is that it is not competent for the Government to fetter its future executive action, which must necessarily be determined by the needs of the community when the question arises. It cannot by contract hamper its freedom of action in matters which concern the welfare of the State. Thus in the case of the employment of public servants, which is a less strong case than the present, it has been laid down that, except under an Act of Parliament, no one acting on behalf of the Crown has authority to employ any person except upon the terms that he is dismissible at the Crown's pleasure; the reason being that it is in the interests of the community that the ministers for the time being advising the Crown should be able to dispense with the services of its employees if they think it desirable. Again suppose that a man accepts an office which he is perfectly at liberty to refuse, and does so on the express terms that he is to have certain leave of absence, and that when the time arrives the leave is refused in circumstances of the greatest hardship to his family or business, as the case may be. Can it be conceived that a petition of right would lie for damages? I should think not. I am of opinion that this petition must fail and there must be judgment for the Crown.

Judgment for the Crown.

Note

This brief judgment is the source of the so-called "doctrine of executive necessity," under which the Crown may apparently plead executive necessity as a defence to an action for breach of contract. See P. W. Hogg, *Liability of the Crown* (2nd ed., 1989) pp. 169–172; J. D. B. Mitchell, *The Contracts of Public Authorities*, pp. 27–32, 52–57 and Chap. V; C. Turpin, *Government Contracts*, pp. 19–25.

COMMISSIONERS OF CROWN LANDS v. PAGE

[1960] 2 Q.B. 274; [1960] 3 W.L.R. 446; 104 S.J. 642; [1960] 2 All E.R. 726 (Court of Appeal)

The Minister of Works, acting on behalf of the Crown, requisitioned in 1945 premises which had been demised in 1937 by the Commissioner of Crown Lands for a term of 25 years. There was no express covenant of quiet enjoyment. The premises were derequisitioned in 1955. The Commissioners claimed the arrears of rent. It was conceded that the Crown was one and indivisible as lessor and requisitioning authority. The lessee claimed that she had been "evicted," but the court held that there had been no "eviction," merely the requisitioning of the lessee's right of occupation (for which compensation was payable to the lessee). One point was whether the re-entry was "wrongful" as in breach of an *implied* covenant of quiet enjoyment. The Crown argued *inter alia* that the requisitioning was not done in the capacity of landlord, but as the Executive responsible for the government of the country.

DEVLIN L.J.: . . . Has the Crown committed a fundamental breach of the covenant? To answer that question one must consider the true scope and object of the covenant in such a lease as this where the Crown is the grantor. On the face of it, and if the covenant is taken as read without any limitation, there has been a breach. The Crown has deprived the defendant of the enjoyment of the demised premises for a long and indefinite period, and has done so deliberately, and (if one ignores the compulsion of public duty) has done so of its own free will; its act was authorised, but was not required by the statute. But, it is said by the Crown, it is not an act done as landlord, and it lacks other necessary constituents of the act of eviction.

I think that it may well be that the covenant of quiet enjoyment is limited to acts that are done by the landlord in supposed assertion of his rights as landlord, and that other trespasses, however grave, are outside the covenant. But because the landlord in this case is also the Crown, I have found it on the whole simpler to answer the question in the case not by reference to any special limitation on the covenant of quiet enjoyment affecting all landlords, but by reference to the general limitation that affects all contracts or covenants entered into by the Crown, or for that matter by any other public authority.

When the Crown, or any other person, is entrusted, whether by virtue of the prerogative or by statute, with discretionary powers to be exercised for the public good, it does not, when making a private contract in general terms, undertake (and it may be that it could not even with the use of specific language validly undertake) to fetter itself in the use of those powers, and in the exercise of its discretion. This principle has been accepted in a number of authorities; it is sufficient to mention *Ayr Harbour Trustees* v. *Oswald* (1883) 8 App.Cas. 623; *Rederiaktiebolaget Amphitrite* v. *The King* [1921] 3 K.B. 500; *Board of Trade* v. *Temperley Steam Shipping Co. Ltd.* (1926) 26 Ll.L.R. 76; affirmed (1927) 27 Ll.L.R. 230, C.A. and *William Cory & Sons Ltd.* v. *City of London Corporation* [1951] 2 K.B. 476 C.A.

The covenant for quiet enjoyment in the present case is implied, and is not dissimilar to the contractual provision considered in the two cases last cited, which were both concerned with the implied obligation on one party to a contract not to interfere with the performance by the other party of his obligations under it. In *Board of Trade* v. *Temperley Steam Shipping Co. Ltd.*, the Board were the charterers of the defendant's ship, and it was contended that they had prevented the defendants from making their ship efficient for her service under the charterparty because one of the Board's surveyors had refused a licence to do certain repairs. . . . [His Lordship summarised the *Cory* case, above, p. 303 (note).]

I do not, however, rest my decision in the present case simply on the fact that the covenant for quiet enjoyment has to be implied. For reasons which I think will appear sufficient in the next paragraph, I should reach the same conclusion if the ordinary covenant was expressed.

In some of the cases in which public authorities have been defendants, the judgments have been put on the ground that it would be *ultra vires* for them to bind themselves not to exercise their powers; and it has also been said that a promise to do so would be contrary to public policy. It may perhaps be difficult to apply this reasoning to the Crown, but it seems to me to be unnecessary to delve into the constitutional position. When the Crown, in dealing with one of its subjects, is dealing as if it too were a private person, and is granting leases or buying and selling as ordinary persons do, it is absurd to suppose that it is making any promise about the way in which it will conduct the affairs of the nation. No one can imagine, for example, that when the Crown makes a contract which could not be fulfilled in time of war, it is pledging itself not to declare war for so long as the contract lasts. Even if, therefore, there was an express promise by the Crown that it would not do any act which might hinder the other party to the contract in the performance of his obligations, the covenant or promise must by necessary implication be read to exclude those measures affecting the nation as a whole which the Crown takes for the public good.

During the last war the Ministries of War Transport, Food and Supply were trading on a vast scale, and were also issuing orders under their statutory powers which quite frequently frustrated their own contracts, or those made by some other government department. The Minister of Supply, for example, might be found prohibiting all importation of a commodity of a sort which he had contracted to buy; or the Ministry of War Transport might fail to make cargo space available for another department's purchases. So far as I am aware, there is no case in which it has been contended that because of such action, the Crown was in breach of contract. That shows the general understanding under which such business was done. If at the time of making any such contract the "officious bystander" had asked whether it was clear that the Crown was not undertaking to limit the use of its general executive powers, I think that there could have been only one answer. That is the proper basis for a necessary implication. I need not examine the question whether, if the Crown sought to fetter its future action in express and specific terms, it could effectively do so. It is most unlikely that in a contract with the subject, it would ever make the attempt. For the purpose of this case it is unnecessary to go further than to say that in making a lease or other contract with its subjects, the Crown does not (at least in the absence of specific words) promise to refrain from exercising its general powers under a statute or under the prerogative, or to exercise them in any particular way. That does not mean that the Crown can escape from any contract which it finds disadvantageous by saying that it never promised to act otherwise than for the public good. The distinction was clearly put by Roche J. in *Board of Trade* v. *Temperley Steam Shipping Co. Ltd.*, 26 Ll.L.R. 76 at p. 78, where he said: "I think and I hold that in this charterparty it is to be implied that the Crown should do nothing in connection with and in relation to and in the carrying out of the contract contained in the charterparty to prevent the shipowners from keeping the vessel seaworthy and to prevent them earning their hire. But I am utterly unable to imply in the charterparty a term or condition that the Crown should do nothing by virtue of some general legislation or by virtue of some executive action entirely remote from the charterparty and done by persons not connected with the performance of the contract directly or indirectly to bring about the results in question." That is a different thing from saying that the Crown can never bind itself in its dealings with the subject in case it might turn out that the fulfilment of the contract was not advantageous. The observations of Denning J. in *Robertson* v. *Minister of Pensions* [1949] 1 K.B. 227, 231, on the doctrine of "executive necessity" were, I think, directed to a case of that sort. Here we are dealing with an act done for a general executive purpose, and not an act done for the purpose of achieving a particular result under the contract in question.

I agree that the appeal should be dismissed.

[LORD EVERSHED M.R. and ORMEROD L.J. expressed no opinion on the effect of an express covenant, but agreed that an implied covenant of quiet enjoyment could not "extend to prevent the future exercise by the Crown of powers and duties imposed upon it in its executive capacity by statute" (*per* Lord Evershed M.R., at p. 287) or "be taken to go so far as to imply an undertaking by the Crown to refrain from exercising statutory powers in respect of the demised premises which the Crown may properly deem necessary" (*per* Ormerod L.J., at p. 289).]

Questions

1. Is the *Amphitrite* principle the same as that applied in *Ayr Harbour Trustees* v. *Oswald* and the other cases cited in the previous section (pp. 296–314)?

2. What limitations did Rowlatt J. place on the principle he applied? Are they sufficiently precise? Are they workable?

3. If the *Amphitrite* principle is not the *Ayr* principle in disguise, should any of the latter's limitations (*e.g.* the test of incompatibility) be applied to the Crown? See Turpin, *op. cit.*, p. 24.

4. Does the Crown need the protection of the *Amphitrite* principle? An injunction, or an order for specific performance cannot be awarded against the Crown (see s.21 of the Crown Proceedings Act 1947), and so the Crown in relying on this principle would merely be avoiding the payment of damages. See Hogg, *op. cit.*, p. 171, who suggests that the *Amphitrite* was wrongly decided, and Mitchell, *op. cit.* who accepts the statements of Rowlatt J. "as containing a sound general principle of law" (p. 222) but argues that compensation should be payable wherever contractual obligations are overridden in the public interest.

5. What would the position have been had the Crown covenanted expressly not to exercise any existing or future powers of entry under any legislation? Would that situation be strictly analogous with the *Amphitrite* case?

(E) FETTERING DISCRETION BY ESTOPPEL

The cases which follow raise the following questions:

(i) Whether a body which has held itself out as having greater powers than in fact it possesses will, in any subsequent legal proceedings, be prevented, "estopped," from relying on its lack of power in the matter in question? As we shall see, (the *Rhyl* case, below p. 320) the courts have noted that to apply the doctrine of estoppel in such circumstances would be to allow an agency *by its own actions* to extend the ambit of the legal powers conferred on it by Parliament. The principle has therefore been clearly stated that no agency may extend its legal powers by the process of estoppel.

(ii) Whether a body may by process of estoppel disentitle itself from performance of a legal duty imposed on it? Again, it has been held (*Maritime Electric* case, below p. 323), and for the same reason as in (i) above, that estoppel does not operate in public law to such effect.

(iii) Whether a body (the "principal") which possesses certain powers is bound by a *purported* exercise of those powers by an "agent"/"delegate" acting without strict legal authority to bind the "principal"? Here the courts have, over the years adopted a less clear and consistent approach. The judges have been torn between, on the one hand, sympathy for an applicant who may quite reasonably have relied on the apparent "authority" of an official employed by the body in question, or the apparent authority of one of its committees, as regards an (in fact) unauthorised assurance given or decision taken; and, on the other hand, their desire not to allow the notion of estoppel to undermine the fundamentals of the *ultra vires* doctrine. Critical questions which need to be asked in this context are:

(a) is the *substance* of the power in question *intra vires* the respondent body itself?;
(b) had that body chosen to have done so, would it have had *power to delegate the exercise of the power in question to the person/committee* which has purported to exercise that power?;
(c) was the assertion of authority of the "agent"/"delegate" assertion by the *respondent agency itself* as to the powers of its apparent "agent"/"delegate"; or was the assertion of authority that of the "agent"/"delegate" alone?

See on these issues, below, pp. 324–338.

We shall see that, after some equivocation, the courts have been reluctant to utilise the concept of estoppel for the benefit of applicants for review. Instead they have developed a doctrine under which bodies possessing discretionary powers may be held to have "abused" those powers if, having by their conduct engendered legitimate expectations as to how the powers will be exercised, they then exercise those powers, without good reason, in a way which defeats those expectations. We shall consider this developing doctrine when we look at the various grounds of review for abuse of discretion—see below p. 419. For the moment we should just note that this emerging ground of challenge may involve some potential for inconsistency with the oft-stated obligation of bodies to retain an unfettered discretion as to the manner of exercise of their powers. The reconciliation may lie in limits to the new doctrine. The new doctrine says, in effect—"Don't defeat expectations you have created unless there are good reasons in the public interest for so doing"; the retention of discretion principle requires discretion to be retained *in order that* bodies may through the course of time exercise their powers as the public interest may be considered to require.

Note

See generally J. A. Andrews, "Estoppels against Statutes" (1966) 29 M.L.R. 1; G. Ganz, [1965] P.L. 237; M. A. Fazal, [1972] P.L. 43; P. P. Craig, (1977) 93 L.Q.R. 398 and *Craig*, Chap. 16; A. W. Bradley, "Administrative Justice and the Binding Effect of Official Acts" (1981) C.L.P. 1.

(i) No Enlargement of Powers by Estoppel

RHYL URBAN DISTRICT COUNCIL v. RHYL AMUSEMENTS LTD.

[1959] 1 W.L.R. 465, [1959] 1 All E.R. 257, 57 L.G.R. 19 (Harman J.)

Rhyl U.D.C. sought a declaration that a 31-year lease which they had in 1932 granted to the defendant company was void. The only power under which the lease might have been granted was contained in section 177 of the Public Health Act 1875. This required the consent of the Minister of Health to have been obtained. No such consent had been obtained.

HARMAN J: It was . . . argued by the defendants, and so pleaded, that the plaintiffs are now estopped from denying the validity of the lease. The plea is based on the fact that the relations of the parties have been regulated by it ever since 1932 and that in that year the defendants changed their position by surrendering their 1921 lease on a promise to grant the new one. The representation so acted on must have been that the plaintiffs had power to grant a valid new lease. If the plaintiffs were private people this would be a strong plea, but in my judgment a plea of estoppel cannot prevail as an answer to a claim that something done by a statutory body is *ultra vires*: see *Minister of Agriculture and Fisheries* v. *Hulkin* (1948), an unreported case alluded to by Cassels J. in *Minister of Agriculture and Fisheries* v. *Matthews* [1950] 1 K.B. 148, where he said (at p. 153): "If, therefore, the Minister does something which is an *ultra vires* act, it is not the act of the Minister at all. In the unreported case of *Minister of Agriculture and Fisheries* v. *Hulkin* the present plaintiff was suing for the possession of a cottage and garden which was in the possession of the defendant. The action was brought in the county court and the county court judge took the view that under the relevant defence regulations it was competent for the County Agricultural Committee, acting under the authority of the Minister, and as the delegate of the Minister's own powers, to create a relationship of landlord and tenant between the Minister and the defendant.

The case went to the Court of Appeal and the appeal of the plaintiff was allowed. The first point which called for consideration was the finding of the county court judge that under the regulation the Minister had power to create a tenancy and that, by the document relied on in that case, he had in fact done so. In the Court of Appeal the defendant's counsel disclaimed any intention of attempting to support the county court judge's judgment on that point. He contended, however, that the Minister having done what he had done in that case was estopped from denying that the document, under which the defendant was in possession, created a tenancy.

In dealing with that contention, Lord Greene M.R. said: 'He (the defendant's counsel) suggested, first of all, that even assuming, as he conceded, that the regulations gave no power to the Minister to create a tenancy, nevertheless the Minister was estopped from denying that the document in question did create a tenancy and, accordingly, the relationship must be regarded as one of landlord and tenant. There is, I think, a very short answer to that. Accepting the view which Mr. Bailleu (the defendant's counsel) accepts, that the Minister had no power under the regulations to grant a tenancy, it is perfectly manifest to my mind that he could not by estoppel give himself such power. The power given to an authority under a statute is limited to the four corners of the power given. It would entirely destroy the whole doctrine of *ultra vires* if it was possible for the donee of a statutory power to extend his power by creating an estoppel. That point, I think, can be shortly disposed of.' " If I may say so with respect, this seems as good sense as it is good law.

It was ingeniously argued that the present was not a case of the plaintiff council having no power, but that they had a power if they obtained the necessary consent and that the doctrine does not apply except where no power exists, so that the plaintiffs might be estopped from denying that they obtained consent. If this be not, as I suspect, a quibble, a like answer could be made that it would destroy the necessity of ever obtaining consent if a statutory body omitting to obtain it could thereafter be held estopped. Such a body could by these means confer on itself a power which it had not got, and the *ultra vires* doctrine would be reduced to a nullity.

Declaration granted

Notes

1. In *Vestry of the Parish of St. Mary, Islington* v. *Hornsey U.D.C.* [1900] 1 Ch. 695, C.A., the plaintiffs allowed certain Hornsey landowners to use the plaintiffs' sewer. These "rights" were acquired by the defendants, and the plaintiffs allowed the defendants to use the sewer for over 30 years. By 1900, heavy use of the sewer by the defendants caused a serious nuisance in Islington. The Court of Appeal held, first, that the plaintiffs could not grant anything more than a revocable licence. A contract, or the grant of an easement, for the discharge of sewage through the plaintiffs' sewer would have been *ultra vires* as the Metropolis Management Acts only authorised persons within the metropolitan district to use metropolitan sewers. Islington was within, and Hornsey outside the metropolitan district. Secondly, the court held that the plaintiffs were not estopped or debarred by laches or acquiescence from revoking the licence. The only concession to the defendants' argument that disconnection would cause a public nuisance in Hornsey was that they were given 12 months to make alternative arrangements, with the plaintiffs given leave to apply for an injunction at the end of that time.

2. In *Yabbicom* v. *King* [1899] 1 Q.B. 444 D.C., Mr. King deposited plans for a house with the urban district council which revealed that when built it would not comply with by-laws made by the Council under the Public Health Act 1875, s.157. The plans were nevertheless approved by the council. This approval was held to be no defence to a prosecution subsequently brought for breach of the by-laws by the council's successor, Bristol Corporation. *Per* Day J. at p. 488 "The district council could not control the law, and by-laws properly made have the effect of laws; a public body cannot any more than private persons dispense with laws . . . they have no dispensing power whatever."

(ii) No Release of Duty by Estoppel

MARITIME ELECTRIC CO. LTD. v. GENERAL DAIRIES LTD.

[1937] A.C. 610; 53 T.L.R. 391; [1937] 1 All E.R. 748 (Privy Council: Lords Atkin, Thankerton, Russell of Killowen, Alness and Maugham)

The plaintiffs, although a private electricity supply company, were under a statutory duty to furnish reasonably adequate service and facilities, and were strictly limited as to the charges they could make, which had to be in exact accordance with filed schedules open to public inspection. To determine the amount of electricity supplied it was necessary to multiply the meter dial reading by 10. Through the plaintiffs' error this was not done over 28 months in relation to the defendants, a dairy company, who as a result, were charged for only one-tenth of the electricity supplied in this period. The plaintiffs sought to recover the balance of nine-tenths. The defendants had relied on the accuracy of the sums actually charged them for electricity in fixing the amounts they paid to the farmers who supplied them, and in fixing the prices they charged their customers.

LORD MAUGHAM: . . . The sections of the Public Utilities Act which are here in question are sections enacted for the benefit of a section of the public, that is, on grounds of public policy in a general sense. In such a case—and their Lordships do not propose to express any opinion as to statutes which are not within this category—where, as here, the statute imposes a duty of a positive kind, not avoidable by the performance of any formality, for the doing of the very act which the plaintiff seeks to do, it is not open to the defendant to set up an estoppel to prevent it. This conclusion must follow from the circumstance that an estoppel is only a rule of evidence which under certain special circumstances can be invoked by a party to an action; it cannot therefore avail in such a case to release the plaintiff from an obligation to obey such a statute, nor can it enable the defendant to escape from a statutory obligation of such a kind on his part. It is immaterial whether the obligation is onerous or otherwise to the party suing. The duty of each part is to obey the law. . . .

A similar conclusion will be reached if the question put by the learned judge is looked at from a somewhat different angle. It cannot be doubted that if the appellants, with every possible formality, had purported to release their right to sue for the sums remaining due according to the schedules, such a release would be null and void. A contract to do a thing which cannot be done without a violation of the law is clearly void. It may be asked with force why, if a voluntary release will not put an end to the obligation of the respondents, an inadvertent mistake by the appellants acted upon by the respondents can have the result of absolving the appellants from their duty of collecting and receiving payment in accordance with the law. . . . Their Lordships are unable to see how the Court can admit an estoppel which would have the effect *pro tanto* and in the particular case of repealing the statute.

(iii) Estoppel, Agency and Delegation

WESTERN FISH PRODUCTS LTD. v. PENWITH DISTRICT COUNCIL

[1981] 2 All E.R. 204; (1978) 38 P. & C.R. 7; (1978) 77 L.G.R. 185 (Court of Appeal)

In April 1976 W.F.P. bought an industrial site at Stable Hobba which included the buildings of a disused factory. The factory had previously been used for the production of fertiliser from fish and fishmeal. This use had ceased in 1975. W.F.P. wanted to use the site for the manufacture of fish oil and fishmeal, and for the preparation and packaging of fresh fish for human consumption. The company intended to spend considerable sums of money, demolishing some of the old buildings, repairing others, and building new buildings. On April 7, 1976, a meeting took place between the Chairman of W.P.F. (Mr. de Savary) and an official (Mr. Giddens) of the district council, deputy to and representing the council's chief planning officer. De S. asserted that because of the previous factory use of the site there existed an "established user right" which entitled his company to carry on their intended processes without needing to obtain planning permission from the council. G. said that W.F.P. should satisfy him of such entitlement in writing; and that if he was so satisfied, the council would do everything they could to assist the project.

W.F.P. then wrote two letters supplying G. with information. G. replied, on behalf of the chief planning officer. This letter included a statement which "confirmed that the limits of the various component parts of the commercial undertaking as now existing appear to be established." On the strength of this letter, which W.F.P. later stated they regarded as confirmation that planning permission for their proposed use of the land was not needed, the company began to demolish, renovate, repair, build, and install equipment. This work was carried out to the knowledge of the council's officials. Then, on July 6, G. contacted W.F.P. and asked that it submit applications for planning permission in respect of the building operations, and for an "established use certificate" under section 94 of the Town and Country Planning Act 1971. G. explained that the application for this certificate was purely a formality.

W.F.P. submitted applications for planning permission and for the certificate. On August 26 a full meeting of the council refused all the applications, and authorised the service of enforcement and stop notices in respect of the work in progress. In September the enforcement notices were issued and all work at the site stopped.

W.F.P. brought an action seeking declarations that they were entitled to existing use rights entitling them to use the factory for their intended purpose, or that they were entitled to be treated as having planning permission for that purpose. W.F.P. also claimed injunctions to prevent the enforcement of the notices, and damages. Walton J. dismissed the claims. The company appealed to the Court of Appeal.

MEGAW L.J. delivered the judgment of the Court (MEGAW, LAWTON and BROWNE L.JJ):

Outline of issues

This appeal raises points which may, very broadly, be stated as follows.

(A) Did the defendant council make representations to the plaintiffs as to what the plaintiffs were permitted to do on the Stable Hobba site in such circumstances that the defendant council became estopped from making decisions contrary to the representations, and so that, the defendant council having made or purported to make such decisions, the plaintiffs are entitled to damages and other relief?

(B) Did the defendant council make any determination under s.53 [see below, p. 331] or s.94 of the Town and Country Planning Act 1971, and, if so, what is the effect?

(C) Did the defendant council act in abuse of their statutory powers, or act negligently, so as to give the plaintiffs the right by action in a court of law to claim damages or any other remedy?

[His Lordship considered whether the company had existing use rights in respect of its proposed processes, and, concluding that it did not, held that planning permission was therefore required for such development. His Lordship then addressed the question whether by process of estoppel the company should be treated as having been given such permission:]

... Here arise various issues which we shall consider later, such as whether any oral statements which were made could be treated as giving rise to an estoppel, and if so, an estoppel as to what, whether the letter of April 26, 1976, from Mr. Giddens constitutes a relevant representation of anything, and if so, what, and whether the plaintiffs did rely on any representation which may be contained, or which they thought was contained, in that letter. . . .

Was the letter of April 26, a representation and, if so, of what?

... We are unable to accept that a person familiar with the relevant facts known to both the writer and the recipient of the letter, reading the letter with reasonable care, could reasonably have read it as giving the plaintiffs confirmation that there was an existing use right which would cover the uses contemplated by the plaintiffs' scheme without the necessity for planning permission in respect of use. Whether Mr. de Savary's belief that the letter contained that confirmation was because he was so firmly convinced of the "incontrovertible right" that he did not read the letter with due care, or whether it was for some other reason, we are unable to see how, taking full account of the relevant circumstances and of the context of the letter itself and of the letters and conversations which had led up to it, the words "Accordingly it is confirmed that the limits of the component parts of the commercial undertaking as now existing appear to be established" could reasonably be understood to be a confirmation of that which the plaintiffs allege it did confirm.

At the most the letter means that Mr. Giddens on behalf of the defendant council was satisfied that the buildings on the site had been used previously for the purposes written on the plan and that the dimensions of the respective buildings used for those various purposes were correctly shown. If and in so far as it could be interpreted as confirming any use right, it was no more than a use right for the purposes for which the site had previously been used.

It follows that no relevant estoppel, "proprietary" or otherwise, can be founded on any representation contained in that letter.

Did the plaintiffs rely on such representation as they allege?

Even if it were to be construed as having the meaning which the plaintiffs placed on it, it would still, in our judgment, not avail the plaintiffs as an estoppel. They did not act on it to their detriment.

The judge, as we understand his judgment, has held that the plaintiffs, through Mr. de Savary, did rely on what he understood to be the representation. "I think," says the judge, "he acted on that assurance, by going ahead with his projects as a whole"; and again, "He regarded it as all important, and considered that, having obtained that confirmation, all his troubles were over. . . ."

We regard the evidence provided by the contemporary documents and by Mr. de Savary himself in the witness box as being overwhelmingly in support of the conclusion that, if the plaintiffs had not received the letter of April 26, or had not construed it as they did, they would have gone ahead with their planned project as they did go ahead with it, both in timing and other respects. Mr. de Savary's absolute conviction of the incontrovertible status of his user rights in respect of his planned operations was such that he would not have been deterred by the absence of a confirmation from Mr. Giddens. . . .

Even if we had been satisfied that the defendant council through their officers had represented to the plaintiffs that all they wanted to do on the Stable Hobba site could be done because of the existing uses, planning permission being required only for new buildings and structures, and that they had acted to their detriment to the knowledge of the defendant council because of their representations, their claim would still have failed. There are two reasons for this: first, because they did not have the equitable right which has come to be called proprietary estoppel; and, second, because in law the defendant council could not be estopped from performing their statutory duties under the 1971 Act.

[His Lordship considered the doctrine of *proprietary estoppel*: "when A to the knowledge of B acts to his detriment in relation to his own land in the expectation, encouraged by B, of acquiring a right over B's land, such expectation arising from what B has said or done, the court will order B to grant A that right on such terms as may be just." His Lordship noted that "there was no question of [W.F.P.] acquiring any rights in relation to any other person's land, which is what proprietary estoppel is concerned with," and so held this argument inapplicable. His Lordship then proceeded to explain why the argument that the council could be estopped from the performance of its statutory duties failed:]

. . . The defendant council's officers, even when acting within the apparent scope of their authority, could not do what the 1971 Act required the defendant council to do; and if their officers did or said anything which purported to determine in advance what the defendant council themselves would have to determine in pursuance of their statutory duties, they would not be inhibited from doing what they had to do. An estoppel cannot be raised to prevent the exercise of a statutory discretion or to prevent or excuse the performance of a statutory duty (see *Spencer Bower and Turner on Estoppel by Representation* (3rd ed., 1977, p. 141) and the cases there cited). The application of this principle can be illustrated on the facts of this case: under section 29 of the 1971 Act the defendant council as the planning authority had to determine applications for planning permission, and when doing so had to have regard to the provision of the development plan and "to any other material considerations." The plaintiffs made an application for planning permission to erect a tall chimney on the site. When considering this application the defendant council had to "take into account any representations relating to that application" which were received by them following the publishing and posting of notices: see sections 26 and 29(2). This requirement was in the interests of the public generally. If any representations made by the defendant council's officers before the publication or posting of notices bound the council to act in a particular way, the statutory provision which gave the public opportunities of making representations would have been thwarted and the defendant council would have been dispensed from their statutory obligation of taking into account any representation made to them. The officers were appointed by the defendant council but the council's members were elected by the inhabitants of their area. Parliament by the 1971 Act entrusted the defendant council, acting through their elected members, not their officers, to perform various statutory duties. If their officers were allowed to determine that which Parliament had enacted the defendant council should determine there would be no need for elected members to consider planning applications. This cannot be. Under section 101(1) of the Local Government Act 1972 (which repealed section 4 of the 1971 Act, which re-enacted in an amended form section 64 of the Town and Country Planning Act 1968), a local authority may arrange for the discharge of any of their functions by an officer of the authority. This has to be done formally by the authority acting as such. In this case the defendant council issued standing orders authorising designated officers to perform specified functions including those arising under sections 53 and 94 of the 1971 Act. Their officers had no authority to make any other determinations under the 1971 Act. We can see no reason why Mr. de Savary, acting on behalf of the plaintiffs, and having available the advice of lawyers and architects, should have assumed, if he ever did, that Mr. Giddens could bind the defendant council generally by anything he wrote or said.

Counsel for the plaintiffs submitted that, notwithstanding the general principle that a statutory body could not be estopped from performing its statutory duties, there are exceptions recognised by this court. This case, he asserted, came within the exceptions.

There seem to be two kinds of exceptions. If a planning authority, acting as such, delegates to its officers powers to determine specific questions, such as applications under sections 53 and 94 of the 1971 Act, any decisions they make cannot be revoked. This kind of estoppel, if it be estoppel at all, is akin to *res judicata*. Counsel for the Department of the Environment accepted that there was this exception, as did counsel for the defendant council in his final submissions. *Lever (Finance) Ltd.* v. *Westminster Corpn.* [1970] 3 All E.R. 496, [1971] 1 Q.B. 222 can, we think, be considered as an application of this exception. The trial judge had found that it was a common practice amongst planning authorities, including the defendants, for planning officers to sanction immaterial modifications to plans sent with successful applications for planning permission. This is what one of the defendants' planning officers thought he was doing when he agreed with the plaintiffs' architect that they could make a modification to the plans of some houses which were being erected; but Lord Denning M.R. thought that what he had agreed to was not an immaterial modification: it was a material one. He should have told the plaintiffs that they required planning permission to make it. When the defendants found out what had happened as a result of complaints made by members of the public who were likely to be affected by the modification, they suggested to the plaintiffs that they should apply for planning permission. They did; and their application was refused. This court affirmed the declaration made by the trial judge that there was a valid planning permission for the modification. The members of this court gave different reasons for finding as they did. Sachs L.J. stated that the combined effect of the past practice, taken with the powers of delegation under section 64 of the 1968 Act, was that the oral agreement made between the plaintiffs' architect and the defendants' planning officer operated as if all the formalities of section 43 of the Town and Country Planning Act 1962 (now section 53 of the 1971 Act) had been complied with. The other members of the court (Lord Denning M.R. and Megaw L.J.) made no mention of this reasoning. It follows that it was not the *ratio decidendi* of the judgment. We do not agree with it, as appears later in this judgment. Lord Denning M.R. rested his judgment on estoppel and delegation. After referring to the authorities setting out the general rule that planning authorities cannot be estopped from doing their public duty, he went on as follows ([1970] 3 All E.R. 496 at 500, [1971] 1 Q.B. 222 at 230):

> "But those statements must now be taken with considerable reserve. There are many matters which public authorities can now delegate to their officers. If an officer, acting within the scope of his ostensible authority, makes a representation on which another acts, then a public authority may be bound by it, just as much as a private concern would be."

He went on to refer by way of illustration to *Wells* v. *Minister of Housing and Local Government* [1967] 2 All E.R. 1041, [1967] 1 W.L.R. 1000, which was concerned with what this court adjudged to be an informal application made under section 43 of the 1962 Act. It is pertinent to note too that Lord Denning M.R. used the words "may be bound." Megaw L.J. said that he agreed with the reasons for judgment given by Lord Denning M.R. This case, of course, binds us unless there is in the reasoning an element which can be said to be "*per incuriam.*" In our judgment it is not an authority for the proposition that every representation made by a planning officer within his ostensible authority binds the planning authority which employs him. For an estoppel to arise there must be some evidence justifying the person dealing with the planning officer for thinking that what the officer said would bind the planning authority. Holding an office, however senior, cannot, in our judgment, be enough by itself. In the *Lever (Finance) Ltd.* case there was evidence of a widespread practice amongst planning authorities of allowing their planning officers to make immaterial modifications to the plans produced when planning permission was given. Lever (Finance) Ltd.'s architect presumably knew of this practice and was entitled to assume that the practice had been authorised by the planning authorities in whose areas it was followed. The need for some evidence of delegation of authority can be illustrated in this way. Had Lever (Finance) Ltd.'s architect produced plans showing material and substantial modifications to the planning permission for a large development in Piccadilly Circus already granted, he could not sensibly have assumed that the planning officer with whom he was dealing had authority to approve the proposed modifications without putting them before the planning authority. Whether anyone dealing with a planning officer can safely assume that the officer can bind his authority by anything he says must depend on all the circumstances. In the *Lever (Finance) Ltd.* case [1970] 3 All E.R. 496 at 501, [1971] 1 Q.B. 222 at 231 Lord Denning M.R. said: "Any person dealing with them (*i.e.* officers of a planning authority] is entitled to assume that all necessary resolutions have been passed." This statement was not necessary for the conclusion he had reached and purported to be an addendum. We consider it to be *obiter*; with all respect, it stated the law too widely.

In this case there was no evidence of any relevant delegations of authority save in relation to applications under sections 53 and 94. We deal later in this judgment with the plaintiffs' submissions about the operation of those sections.

We can deal with the second exception shortly. If a planning authority waives a procedural requirement relating to any application made to it for the exercise of its statutory powers, it may be estopped from relying on lack of formality. Much, however, will turn on the construction of any statutory provisions setting out what the procedure is to be. *Wells* v. *Minister of Housing and Local Government* is an example of the exception. Both counsel for the Department of the Environment and counsel for the defendant council submitted that this case was wrongly decided. Counsel for the Department of the Environment said that the dissenting judgment of Russel L.J. was to be preferred and both he and counsel for the defendant council reserved the right to argue this point elsewhere. Save in relation to the plaintiffs' submissions as to the operation of sections 53 and 94 on the facts of this case, this exception cannot have any application to this case.

The extension of the concept of estoppel beyond these two exceptions, in our judgment, would not be justified. A further extension would erode the general principle as set out in a long line of cases of which the decision of the Privy Council in *Maritime Electric Co. Ltd.* v. *General Dairies Ltd.* [1937] 1 All E.R. 748, [1937] A.C. 610 and the judgment of the Divisional Court in *Southend-on-Sea Corpn.* v. *Hodgson (Wickford) Ltd.* [1961] 2 All E.R. 46, [1962] 1 Q.B. 416 are not notable examples. Parliament has given those who are aggrieved by refusals of planning permission or the serving of enforcement notices a right of appeal to the Secretary of State: see sections 36 and 88 of the 1971 Act. He can hear evidence as to the merits and take into account policy considerations. The courts can do neither. The application of the concept of estoppel because of what a planning officer had represented could result in a court adjudging that a planning authority was bound to allow a development which flouted its planning policy, with which the courts are not concerned.

There is another objection to any extension of the concept of estoppel which is illustrated by the facts of the *Lever (Finance) Ltd.* case. If the modifications which were permitted by the planning officer in that case had been properly to be regarded as immaterial, no problem of general principle would arise. But the court regarded itself as competent to decide as to the materiality and, despite the submission to the contrary by the successful plaintiffs, held that the modifications were material. On what basis of evidence or judicial notice the court reached that conclusion, we need not stay to consider. We assume both that the court had jurisdiction to decide that question, and that, on the facts of that case, their decision as to materiality was right. But then comes the difficulty, and the real danger of injustice. To permit the estoppel no doubt avoided an injustice to the plaintiffs. But it also may fairly be regarded as having caused an injustice to one or more members of the public, the owners of adjacent houses who would be adversely affected by this wrong and careless decision of the planning officer that the modifications were not material. Yet they were not, and it would seem could not, be heard. How, in their absence, could the court balance the respective injustices according as the court did or did not hold that there was an estoppel in favour of the plaintiffs? What "equity" is there in holding, if such be the effect of the decision, that the potential injustice to a third party, as a result of the granting of the estoppel is irrelevant? At least it can be said that the less frequently this situation arises the better for justice.

In *Brooks and Burton Ltd.* v. *Secretary of State for the Environment* (1976) 75

L.G.R. 285 at 296 Lord Widgery C.J. adverted to extending the concept of estoppel. He said:

> "There has been some advance in recent years of this doctrine of estoppel as applied to local authorities through their officers, and the most advanced case is the one referred to by the inspector, namely *Lever Finance Ltd.* v. *Westminster (City) London Borough Council.* I do not propose to read it. It no doubt is correct on its facts, but I would deprecate any attempt to expand this doctrine because it seems to me, as I said a few minutes ago, extremely important that local government officers should feel free to help applicants who come and ask them questions without all the time having the shadow of estoppel hanging over them and without the possibility of their immobilising their authorities by some careless remark which produces such an estoppel."

We agree with what he said.

The statutory position

We turn now to "the statutory position." Counsel for the plaintiffs submits that besides their claims based on estoppel the plaintiffs have rights and remedies arising from the planning legislation and the decisions of the courts as to the exercise by statutory authorities of their powers and duties. The consideration of these rights and remedies overlaps at one point with the estoppel claim, but the plaintiffs could succeed on the "statutory position" even if they fail on estoppel. The essence of this part of the plaintiffs' case is that the decisions made by the defendant council on August 26, were invalid, a "nullity," an "abuse of their powers" and "unlawful." We have already said that there was no fraud or malice on the part of the defendant council or their officers. In this part of the case, therefore, the phrase "abuse of powers" means no more than that the defendant council have mistakenly acted in a way which was not permitted by their powers.

Sections 53 and 94 of the 1971 Act

In addition or in the alternative to their contention that the letter of April 26, is the foundation of an estoppel, the plaintiffs contend that it was a "determination" under section 53 of the 1971 Act, or alternatively an "established use certificate" under section 94 of that Act. Counsel for the defendant council accepts that if it was such a determination or certificate the council would be bound by it; under their standing orders the power to make such decisions is delegated to their officers.

Section 53(1) provides as follows:

> "If any person who proposes to carry out any operations on land, or to make any change in the use of land, wishes to have it determined whether the carrying out of those operations, or the making of that

change, would constitute or involve development of the land, and, if so, whether an application for planning permission in respect thereof is required under this Part of this Act, having regard to the provisions of the development order, he may, either as part of an application for planning permission, or without any such application, apply to the local planning authority to determine that question."

Section 53(2) applies in relation to applications and determinations under this section a number of other provisions of the 1971 Act, relating to development orders (ss.24 and 31(1)), determinations by local planning authorities (s.29(1)), the power of the Secretary of State to give directions to local planning authorities (s.31(1)), the keeping of registers of applications which are open for inspection by the public (s.34(1) and (3)), the powers of the Secretary of State to call in applications (s.35) and the right of appeal to the Secretary of State (ss.35 and 36).

The Town and Country Planning General Development Order 1973 . . . makes provision for the procedure to be followed on section 53 applications and determinations. Articles 6(2) and 7(2), (3) and (4) provide for the steps to be taken, the provision in each case being governed by the word "shall."

. . . Counsel for the plaintiffs does not contend that the letter of April 26, amounted to a determination that no planning permission was required in respect of the plaintiffs' building operations, but he contends that it was a determination either that the user contemplated by the plaintiffs' project did not constitute development or that no planning permission was required for such development.

It seems to us that section 53(2) of the 1971 Act and articles 6(2) and 7(2), (3) and (4) of the 1973 order contemplate a considerable degree of formality in applications and determinations under section 53. But counsel for the plaintiffs relied on the decision of the majority of this court in *Wells* v. *Minister of Housing and Local Government* [1967] 2 All E.R. 1041, [1967] 1 W.L.R. 1000 and on the judgment of Sachs L.J. in *Lever (Finance) Ltd.* v. *Westminster Corpn.* [1970] 3 All E.R. 496, [1971] 1 Q.B. 222 as establishing that no particular formalities are required.

In the *Wells* case the plaintiffs had applied for planning permission for the erection of a concrete batching plant 27′ 6″ in height. The council engineer and surveyor replied by letter saying: "I am now instructed to inform you that the works proposed can be regarded as 'permitted development' under Class VIII of the . . . Development Order . . . and it is therefore not proposed to take any further action on your application." The plaintiffs then changed their minds and decided to build a plant 48′ high. Their architect assumed that this new proposal would be covered by the council's letter in respect of the 27′ 6″ plant and applied for byelaw consent in respect of the 48′ plant. The council granted byelaw consent on a form which contained the words: "No action should be taken hereunder till the approval of the town planning and licensing authority have been obtained" (*sic*); these words had been struck out but were still legible. The majority of the court (Lord Denning M.R. and Davies L.J., Russell L.J. dissenting) held that there had been a valid application and determination under section 43 of the 1962 Act (now s.53) that planning permission was not required for the 27′ 6″ plant, but the court held unanimously that there had been no application for planning permission, nor any application or determination under section 43 in respect of the 48′ plant.

In the *Lever (Finance) Ltd.* case (the facts of which have already been stated) Sachs L.J. took the view that what had happened could and should be treated as a valid application and determination under section 43 of the 1962 Act that no further planning permission was needed for the change in the position of the house (see [1970] 3 All E.R. 496 at 503–504, [1971] 1 Q.B. 222 at 234). But the majority of the court (Lord Denning M.R. and Megaw L.J.) put their decision on different grounds, which have been considered earlier in this judgment.

This court is, of course, bound by the ratio of the decision of the majority in the *Wells* case, though if we may respectfully say so we find the dissenting judgment of Russell L.J. very powerful. In our view, the ratio on which Lord Denning M.R. and Davies L.J. were agreed was that a formal written application for a determination under section 43 (now s.53) was not necessary and that an application for planning permission impliedly contains an invitation to determine under section 43 that planning permission is not required (see [1967] 2 All E.R. 1041 at 1045, 1046, [1967] 1 W.L.R. 1000 at 1008, 1010, *per* Lord Denning M.R. and Davies L.J.). But all three members of the court held that there was no application or determination under section 43 in respect of the 48′ plant, Lord Denning M.R. saying ([1967] 2 All E.R. 1041 at 1045, [1967] 1 W.L.R. 1000 at 1008):

> "Ready as I am to waive irregularities and procedural defects, I think that to satisfy section 43 there must be at least a positive statement in writing by or on behalf of the planning authority that no planning permission is necessary."

If we are right in our understanding of the ratio of the majority in the *Wells* case, it does not bind us to hold that there was in the present case an application under section 53: there was in April 1976 no application for planning permission. Although the judgment of Sachs L.J. in the *Lever (Finance) Ltd.* case would, we think, greatly extend beyond the *Wells* case the permitted degree of informality in applications and determinations under section 53, it is, as we have already said, not binding on this court. In our judgment, the decision of the majority in the *Wells* case as to the 27′ 6″ plant should not be extended beyond cases in which there has been an application for planning permission; we feel supported in this view by the unanimous decision as to the 48′ plant.

But even if this is wrong, and some communications from a proposed developer to a planning authority other than an application for planning permission can constitute an application under section 53, we should find it impossible to hold as a matter of construction of the letters of April 8 and 26, that they constituted an application or a determination under section 53. . . .

We also reject the alternative contention that the letter of April 26, was an established use certificate under section 94 of the 1971 Act. . . . The purpose and effect of a section 94 certificate is that it is conclusive evidence "as respects any matters stated therein" for the purposes of an appeal to the Secretary of State against an enforcement notice served in respect of any land to which it relates (s.94(7)); the benefit of the certificate runs with the land. One would therefore expect that it would be required to be a formal document, and Sched. 14 to the 1971 Act and Article 18 of the Town and Country Planning General Development Order 1973 contain provisions to that effect as to the application and the certificate. We do not think we need refer to them in detail. But they include provisions that an application "shall not be entertained" unless it is accompanied by a certificate containing the prescribed particulars (see para. 3(1) of Sched. 14 and art. 18(2)), which the letter of April 26, was not, and that established use certificates "shall be issued" in the form set out in Part II of Schedule 6 to the 1973 order, which of course does not bear the slightest resemblance to the letter of April 26. Even if these formal defects are not in themselves a complete answer to this contention, as in our view they are, we think it is impossible to construe the letter of April 26, as a certificate under section 94. We cannot see that it is capable of being conclusive evidence of anything. . . .

Appeal dismissed.

Notes

1. Contrast the judgment of the Court of Appeal in *Western Fish* with the following statements of Lord Denning M.R. in earlier cases. In *Robertson* v. *Minister of Pensions* [1949] 1 K.B. 227, 232:

> ". . . In my opinion if a government department in its dealings with a subject takes it upon itself to assume authority upon a matter with which he is concerned, he is entitled to rely upon it having the authority which it assumes. He does not know, and cannot be expected to know, the limits of its authority."

In *Howell* v. *Falmouth Boat Construction Co.* [1950] 2 K.B. 16, 26:

> ". . . The principle is this: whenever government officers, in their dealings with a subject, take on themselves to assume authority in a matter with which he is concerned, the subject is entitled to rely on their having the authority which they assume. He does not know and cannot be expected to know the limits of their authority, and ought not to suffer if they exceed it. That was the principle which I applied in *Robertson*. . . ."

And in *Wells* v. *Minister of Housing and Local Government* [1967] 1 W.L.R. 1000, 1007:

"... Now I know that a public authority cannot be estopped from doing its public duty, but I do think it can be estopped from relying on technicalities; and this is a technicality, to be sure. We were told that for many years the planning authorities . . . have written letters on the same lines as [this] letter. . . . It has been their practice to tell applicants that no planning permission is necessary. Are they now to be allowed to say that this practice was all wrong and their letters were of no effect? I do not think so. I take the law to be that a defect in the procedure can be cured, and an irregularity be waived, even by a public authority, so as to render valid that which would otherwise be invalid. Thus in *Robertson* . . . an assurance (that Colonel Robertson's disability was accepted as attributable to war service) was held binding on the Crown, even though it was given independently by the War Office instead of the Ministry of Pensions. . . ."

Note that Lord Denning's statement of principle in *Howell* was disapproved, obiter, when the House of Lords considered the case on appeal. Lord Simonds stated that "the illegality of an act is the same whether or not the actor has been misled by an assumption of authority on the part of a government officer however high or low in the hierarchy" [1951] A.C. 837, 845.

In due course Lord Denning M.R. appeared to have relented. In *Co-operative Retail Services Ltd.* v. *Taff-Ely B.C.* (1980) 39 P. & C.R. 1, he said in respect of a purported grant of planning permission by an unauthorised town clerk:

"... The protection of the public [*i.e.* as regards decisions as to planning permission] is entrusted to the representative bodies and to the minister. It would be quite wrong that it should be preempted by a mistaken issue by a clerk of a written form—without any authority in that behalf."

2. In *Norfolk County Council* v. *Secretary of State for the Environment* [1973] 1 W.L.R. 1400, the council resolved to refuse planning permission for a factory extension. By mistake, the planning officer sent a notice which contained all the details of a grant of planning permission to the applicants. The applicants ordered some machinery. Eleven days later the council told the applicant of the mistake and sent them the refusal of permission. The applicant cancelled the machinery order without penalty, but claimed that the first communication constituted a grant of permission, and made a token start on the extension. The council's enforcement notice was quashed by the Secretary of State who held that there was a valid grant. The notice contained no apparent defect and it was acted on in good faith by the applicants. The Divisional Court allowed the council's appeal. The officer "had no authority himself to make such a decision, [*i.e.* to grant permission]. His ostensible authority . . . only went to his authority to transmit the decision which had been made . . ." (*per* Lord Widgery C.J. at p. 1404). Therefore there was no planning permission. Moreover, the council was not estopped from denying that there was a grant of permission.

3. In *Rootkin* v. *Kent County Council* [1981] 1 W.L.R. 1186, the plaintiff's daughter was allocated a place at a school measured by the authority to be over three miles from her home. On that basis, the authority was under a duty either to provide transport or to reimburse travelling expenses, under section 39(2) of the Education Act 1944. It chose the latter course, and issued a bus pass, in the exercise of the discretionary power under section 55(2) of the 1944 Act. Shortly after, the authority made a more precise measurement and found the distance to be less than three miles. It then withdrew the bus pass. The plaintiff argued (1) that the authority was not entitled to rescind its determination that a bus pass should be issued, and (2) that the authority was estopped from revoking its decision. The Court of Appeal held that the authority was entitled to withdraw the pass. On the

first point it was stated that "if a citizen is entitled to payment in certain circumstances and a local authority is given the duty of deciding whether the circumstances exist and if they do exist of making the payment, then there is a determination which the local authority cannot rescind. That was established in *Livingston* v. *Westminster Corpn.* [1904] 2 K.B. 109. But that line of authority does not apply . . . to a case where the citizen has no right to a determination on certain facts being established, but only to the benefit of the exercise of a discretion by the local authority (*per* Lawton L.J. at p. 1195; *cf.* Eveleigh L.J. at p. 1197 and Sir Stanley Rees at p. 1200). On the second point, it was held that an estoppel could not arise where that would prevent the exercise of a statutory discretion (*Southend-on-Sea Corporation* v. *Hodgson (Wickford) Ltd.* [1961] 1 Q.B. 416), that there was here no exceptional situation of a kind contemplated in the *Western Fish* case, *supra*, and that in any event the plaintiff had not altered her position so as to entitle her to rely on the doctrine of estoppel (see Lawton L.J. at p. 1196; Sir Stanley Rees expressed his agreement with these reasons at p. 1200).

4. On the *Lever Finance* case, see J. M. Evans, (1971) 34 M.L.R. 335; J. E. Alder, [1974] J.P.L. 447; B. C. Gould, (1971) 87 L.Q.R. 15; A. W. Bradley, [1971] C.L.J. 3.

On the *Western Fish* case, see D. G. T. Williams, [1981] C.L.J. 198; A. W. Bradley, (1981) 34 C.L.P. 1; C. Crawford, (1982) 45 M.L.R. 87.

5. Consider Craig's argument (*Craig*, Chap. 16) that it would be preferable if instead of adopting a general rule (either applying the estoppel principle to public authorities, or denying its applicability) the courts were to develop a balancing approach in which the court would enquire on the facts of the case whether:

> "the disadvantages to the public interest by allowing estoppel to be pleaded really do outweigh the injustice to the individual." (p. 481).

6. It is clear from the *Western Fish* case and cases decided since then that it is only in exceptional circumstances that a public authority will be bound by an estoppel arising out of informal undertakings or representations made by itself or on its behalf, so as to preclude it altogether from making a decision inconsistent with that undertaking or representation. Instead, the courts have developed alternative mechanisms for reconciling the interests of public authorities with the legitimate interests and expectations of others arising from such informal undertakings or representations. Accordingly, an authority's subsequent failure to take account of such an undertaking or representation may constitute failure to take account of a relevant consideration, and thus an abuse of discretion (see pp. 362–394. A decision to act inconsistently with a previous undertaking or representation may be held to be irrational or unreasonable in the *Wednesbury* sense (see pp. 394–437). The undertaking or representation may give rise to a legitimate expectation entitling the person affected to an opportunity to make representations before the authority can lawfully decide to act inconsistently (see pp. 502–521).

7. One issue raised in each of the *Wells*, *Western Fish* and *Rootkin* cases was whether the authority in question had made a formal "determination" which the authority had no power to revoke. This issue also arose in *Re 56 Denton Road, Twickenham* [1953] Ch. 51. The plaintiff's house was partly demolished by enemy action, and the local authority subsequently pulled down what was left. The War Damage Act 1943 provided that compensation was payable to cover the cost of works in repairing damage, unless the damage involved total loss in which case a "value payment" was payable, unless the War Damage Commission exercised its power to make a cost of works payment instead. For the plaintiff, a "value payment" would be much lower than "cost of works payment." The Commission initially made a "preliminary classification" of total loss, then told the plaintiff by letter dated November 12, 1945, that it had been "reclassified" as not a total loss, with a cost of works payment accordingly becoming payable. The Commission

purported subsequently to change its mind again and revert to the original classification. Vaisey J. granted a declaration that the November 1945 letter constituted a final determination that the damage was one for which a cost of works payment ought to be awarded. His Lordship accepted the following proposition of the plaintiff's counsel:

> "that where Parliament confers upon a body such as the War Damage Commission the duty of deciding or determining any question, the deciding or determining of which affects the rights of the subject, such decision or determination made and communicated in terms which are not expressly preliminary or provision is final and conclusive, and cannot in the absence of express statutory power or the consent of the person or persons affected be altered or withdrawn by that body. I accept that proposition as well-founded, and applicable to the present case. It is, I think, supported by *Livingstone* v. *Westminster Corporation* [1904] 2 K.B. 109 and *Robertson* v. *Minister of Pensions* [1949] 1 K.B. 227.
>
> I think that the letter of November 12, 1945, was one upon which the plaintiff was invited to rely and was and is entitled to rely. It is, I think, admitted that if she had altered her position in reliance upon it, a case of estoppel would have been raised against the defendants. But I really cannot see that it ought to be denied its proper force and effect, quite apart from such a case.
>
> I think that the contrary view would introduce a lamentable measure of uncertainty, and so much disturbance in the minds of those unfortunate persons who have suffered war damage that the Act cannot have contemplated the possibility of such vacillations as are claimed to be permissible in such a case as the present."

See case notes at 214 L.T. 291; 69 L.Q.R. 13 (R.E.M.).

Compare this case with *R.* v. *Secretary of State for Education and Science, ex p. Hardy, The Times*, July 28, 1988. Proposals for the reorganisation of Ilkeston School were placed before the Parliamentary Under-Secretary for approval under section 12(6) of the Education Act 1980. He gave approval by ticking the word "Approve." Following a misunderstanding, an officer in the department informed the authority in confidence that the proposals had been approved. The Secretary of State subsequently decided that the proposals should be rejected. McNeill J. held that compliance with section 12(6) only occurred when there was a formal, precise and published decision. The initial approval was accordingly not an irrevocable decision, and could not be made so by a leak from the minister's private office.

See generally G. Ganz, "Estoppel and *Res Judicata* in Administrative law" [1965] P.L. 237; M. B. Akehurst, "Revocation of administrative decisions" [1082] P.L. 613; D. C. Stanley, "*Res judicata* in administrative law" (1983) 32 U.N.B. Law Journal 221.

Vaisey J. accepted in *Re 56 Denton Road* that a final decision could be reconsidered with the consent of the person affected. In *R.* v. *Hertfordshire County Council, ex p. Cheung, The Times*, April 4, 1986, the council in 1978 had refused C. a student grant on the ground that he was not "ordinarily resident" in the U.K. The test applied was shown to be erroneous by the House of Lords in *R.* v. *Barnet London Borough Council, ex p. Shah* [1982] 2 A.C. 309. Leave to challenge the 1978 decision was refused. The council refused C.'s request to reconsider the matter. McNeill J. at first instance held that the council did have power to reconsider the matter in the light of C.'s request; the Court of Appeal simply asserted that there was a discretion to reconsider. (The Court of Appeal held that C.'s case should have been reconsidered for the 1978/79 academic year so as to be consistent with one of the students in the *Shah* case.) See C. Lewis, [1987] P.L. 21, noting that the Court of Appeal had offered no guidance on the extent of the implied discretion to reconsider.

A decision on a planning appeal may give rise to issue estoppel (*Thrasyvoulou* v. *Secretary of State of the Environment* [1990] 2 A.C. 273; C. Crawford, (1990) 53 M.L.R. 814).

(F) Error of Law in Construing the Scope of a Discretion

R. v. VESTRY OF ST. PANCRAS

(1890) 24 Q.B.D. 371 (Court of Appeal)

Mr. R. Westbrook was appointed to the office of Collector of Rates for the parish of St. Pancras in 1858. In 1888, he wished to retire on health grounds, "upon such superannuation allowance as the vestry are empowered to grant for long services." The Superannuation (Metropolis) Act 1866, s.1, provided that the vestry might "at their discretion, grant . . . an annual allowance, not exceeding in any case two-thirds of his then salary, regard being had to the scale of allowances hereinafter contained. . . ." The scale indicated that a man with W.'s length of service would receive £230 per annum. The vestry thought that they only had discretion as to whether the full allowance suggested by the statute should or should not be paid, and as they did not think W. should have so large an allowance, they resolved to pay nothing. W. sought mandamus to compel the vestry to consider his application in accordance with the statute.

Lord Esher M.R.: . . . I have no doubt that the vestry should take his application into their fair consideration, and do what they think fair to the man under the circumstances, and if they do this, I have equally no doubt that the legislature has entrusted the sole discretion to them, and that no mandamus could go to them to alter their decision. But they must fairly consider the application and exercise their discretion on it fairly, and not take into account any reason for their decision which is not a legal one. If people who have to exercise a public duty by exercising their discretion take into account matters which the Courts consider not to be proper for the guidance of their discretion, then in the eye of the law they have not exercised their discretion. . . .

[T]he vestry of any parish and certain other bodies may in their discretion grant to any officer who satisfies the conditions an annual allowance. If the matter had stopped there, and in a subsequent part of the statute there had been found a fixed amount which was to be given, I should have thought that the discretion was limited to the question whether there should be an allowance or not. But the section goes on, "an annual allowance not exceeding two-thirds of his then salary." This by necessary implication involves that they may give less than the two-thirds. . . . Then there are the words in section 1, "regard being had to the scale of allowance hereinafter contained." That scale is set out in section 4, and is a rising scale according to the number of years' service. They are therefore, to look at the scale to see the number of years' service, but that does not affect the power given by section 1 or the necessary implication from the words, "not exceeding," used in that section. It seems to me, therefore, that they have a discretion as to the amount though they cannot go beyond that set out in the scale. This interpretation takes away all difficulty in considering the meaning of section 4, for the word "shall" only applies to the use of the scale to ascertain the maximum, and not otherwise to the question of amount; and further it gives a reasonable, fair and sufficiently elastic power to the vestry, instead of a hard and fast rule which may work injustice in some cases. . . .

The result in this case seems to me to be that . . . the vestry did not bring their minds to the question which they had to decide, and took into accound circumstances which they ought not to have taken into account, and so did not properly exercise their discretion. . . .

FRY L.J. delivered a concurring judgment.

CHAPTER 8

ABUSE OF DISCRETION

IN this chapter we shall consider various grounds upon which it may be alleged that the manner of exercise of a discretionary power amounts to an abuse of power. In this context the courts have consistently stated that their function is not to act as a "court of appeal" on the merits of the discretionary decision—their function is to intervene only if one or more of the established grounds of review, considered below, has been infringed. Consider, in reading the cases which follow, whether this distinction between "merits" and "legality" is tenable, and whether in all of the cases the courts have indeed been influenced only by the latter and not the former consideration.

The material which follows is divided into the following sections:

(i) Use of Powers for an Improper Purpose;
(ii) Taking into Account Irrelevant Considerations; Failure to Take into Account Relevant Considerations;
(iii) Unreasonableness;
(iv) Inconsistency.

There then follows a section on "proportionality"—a ground of challenge which exists in the administrative law of a number of European countries and of the EEC, but which does not, at least as yet, appear to constitute a discrete ground of challenge under English law.

(A) USE OF POWERS FOR AN IMPROPER PURPOSE

A statutory power must only be used for the purposes expressed in, or to be implied from, the relevant statute. The *Municipal Council of Sydney* case (below, p. 340) provides an example of successful challenge where the statute expressly stated the purpose(s) for which the power had been conferred.

Where purposes are not explicitly stated, the courts look to the legislation as a whole and consider what "purpose limitations" are implicit. See *Padfield* (below, p. 343) and *Congreve* (below, p. 361).

In some cases it may appear that a decision has been motivated by a mixture of legitimate and illegitimate purposes. This issue will be considered after review for "relevant/irrelevant considerations" has been covered (see below).

MUNICIPAL COUNCIL OF SYDNEY v. CAMPBELL AND OTHERS

[1925] A.C. 338; 94 L.J.P.C. 65; 133 L.T. 63 (Privy Council: Viscount Cave, Lord Blanesborough, Duff J., Sir Adrian Knox)

(Appeal from the Supreme Court of New South Wales)

By section 16 of the Sydney Corporation Amendment Act 1905, the council was empowered to purchase compulsorily any land required for "carrying out improvements in or remodelling any portion of the city." The council resolved that certain land including the property of the respondents should be purchased. Their object was to get the benefit of the increase in the value of this land which would result from the proposed extension of a highway by the council. No plan for improvement or remodelling was at any time proposed to, or considered by, the council. The Chief Judge in Equity granted injunctions restraining the council from acting on their resolution (24 S.R. (N.S.W.) 179). The council appealed to the Privy Council. The opinion of their Lordships was delivered by Duff J.

DUFF J.: . . . Their Lordships think it not reasonably disputable that at the time of the passing of the resolution in June, the council conceived it to be within its powers to resume lands not needed for the extension itself, but solely for the purpose of appropriating the betterments arising from the extension; and that, as Street C.J.E. found, the council had not at that time applied itself to the consideration of any other object in connection with the resumption of the residual lands. . . .

The legal principles governing the execution of such powers as that conferred by section 16, in so far as presently relevant, are not at all in controversy. A body such as the Municipal Council of Sydney, authorized to take land compulsorily for specified purposes, will not be permitted to exercise its powers for different purposes, and if it attempts to do so, the courts will interfere. As Lord Loreburn said, in *Marquess of Clanricarde* v. *Congested Districts Board* (1914) 79 J.P. 481: "Whether it does so or not is a question of fact." Where the proceedings of the council are attacked upon this ground, the party impeaching those proceedings must, of course, prove that the council, though professing to exercise its powers for the statutory purpose, is in fact employing them in furtherance of some ulterior object.

Their Lordships think that the conclusion of the learned Chief Judge in Equity upon this question of fact is fully sustained by the evidence.

Notes

1. The principles were stated more fully by the House of Lords in *Marquess of Clanricarde* v. *Congested Districts Board for Ireland* (1914) 79 J.P. 481. The Marquess claimed that the Board were exercising their powers of compulsory purchase (*inter alia*) for the reinstatement of evicted tenants, and not for the lawful purpose of the amalgamation or enlargement of smallholdings. The House held that there was no evidence to support the plaintiff's claims.

Per Earl Loreburn at p. 481:

> "In form their [*i.e.* the Board's] proceedings were regular, but in substance, so the appellant contended, they were proceeding *ultra vires*. . . . I believe the law is as follows. When an administrative body is authorised by statute to take land compulsorily for specified purposes, the court will interfere if it uses those powers for different purposes. Whether it does so or not is a question of fact. The administrative body must really intend to act for a statutory purpose, and the land they seek to take must be land which is capable of being made use of for a statutory purpose, by which I mean that, looking at the land as a whole, a man might in reason think the purchase could be utilised for any of the statutory purposes. That also is a question of fact. But anyone who objects to what is done

on either of these grounds must prove his objection. In the one case he must prove that there was not such a purpose, and in the other case he must prove that the land was quite incapable of being so used. And the court will not interfere with the discretion or revise the opinion of the administrative body if there was anything on which it could in reason come to the conclusion it reached. Of course fraud or dishonesty stands on quite a different footing. A court will always defeat that under any shape, and quite regardless of all form. But when a board is set up with such compulsory powers as are possessed by the Congested Districts Boards, it is not intended that courts of law shall do what we have been invited to do, namely, dog its footsteps and peer into its minutes as if they were to be suspected of meaning more than they say, or trip it up upon the ground that it has not acted judiciously or has not kept proper minutes, or upon any other ground, dishonesty apart, than that it has in fact exceeded its powers."

2. One problem which has arisen is that a development scheme may be delayed for so long, and so varied in accordance with the changing policies of a local council, that the eventual scheme bears little relation to the original plan. In *Grice* v. *Dudley Corporation* [1958] Ch. 329, a compulsory purchase order made in 1937 was confirmed by the Minister in 1938 for the purposes stated in the order of road widening and building a market hall. By 1956, the plans had changed several times so that what was envisaged was general redevelopment with neither road widening nor a market hall. Upjohn J. granted a declaration that the council could not rely on the 1937 order to purchase the plaintiff's property. Any purchase of the property would have to be at current and not pre-war prices, as the council would have to commence negotiations afresh.

This case may be compared with *Simpsons Motor Sales (London) Ltd.* v. *Hendon Corporation* [1964] A.C. 1088. Here, the House of Lords held that in spite of a six-year delay after the making of a compulsory purchase order, and the abandonment of the original plan for flats on the site, the corporation still intended to use the site for the original purpose of providing housing accommodation within Part V of the Housing Act 1936. Thus the order was still operative. See also *R.* v. *Carmarthen District Council, ex p. Blewin Trust Ltd.* (1989) 59 P. & C.R. 379.

3. In *Westminster Bank* v. *Beverley Borough Council* [1971] A.C. 509 the House of Lords held that the council as local planning authority could refuse planning permission for an extension to a bank on the ground that it "might prejudice the future widening" of the street, even though as highways authority the council could have prescribed an improvement line under the Highways Act 1959 to preserve a strip of land for the scheme. The improvement line procedure did, but refusal of planning permission did not, involve payment of compensation. It was held that it was not an "excess of power" to refuse planning permission on this ground. Section 118(1) of the Town and Country Planning Act 1947 provided "that the provisions of this Act . . . apply . . . in relation to any land notwithstanding that provision is made by any enactment in force at the passing of this Act . . . for . . . regulating any development of the land." The relevant Highways Act provisions were re-enacted from pre-1947 legislation. On the question as to whether there was an "abuse of power" in choosing the procedure where no compensation was payable:

Per Lord Reid (at p. 530):

"Parliament has chosen to set up two different ways of preventing development which would interfere with schemes for street widening. It must have been aware that one involved paying compensation but the other did not. Nevertheless it expressed no preference, and imposed no limit on the use of either. No doubt there might be special circumstances which make it unreasonable or an abuse of power to use one of these methods but here there were none. Even if the appellants' view of the facts is right, the authority had to choose whether to leave the appellants without compensation or to impose a burden on its ratepayers. One may think that it would be most equitable that the burden should be shared. But the Minister of Transport had made it clear in a circular sent to local authorities in 1954 that there would be no grant if a local authority proceeded in such a way that compensation would be payable, and there is nothing to indicate any disapproval of this policy by Parliament and nothing in any of the legislation to indicate that Parliament disapproved of depriving the subject of compensation. I cannot in these circumstances find any abuse of power in the local authority deciding that the appellants and not its ratepayers should bear the burden. . . ."

Cf. Asher v. *Secretary of State for the Environment* (above, p. 110); *Hoveringham Gravels Ltd.* v. *Secretary of State for the Environment* [1975] Q.B. 754; *R.* v. *Exeter City Council, ex p. J.L. Thomas & Co. Ltd.* [1991] 1 Q.B. 471.

PADFIELD AND OTHERS v. MINISTER OF AGRICULTURE, FISHERIES AND FOOD AND OTHERS

[1968] A.C. 997; [1968] 2 W.L.R. 924; 112 S.J. 171; [1968] 1 All E.R. 694 (House of Lords)

The Agricultural Marketing Act 1958 contained (*inter alia*) provisions relating to the milk marketing scheme. By section 19:

"(3) A committee of investigation shall— . . . (*b*) be charged with the duty, if the Minister in any case so directs, of considering, and reporting to the Minister on, any . . . complaint made to the Minister as to the operation of any scheme which, in the opinion of the Minister, could not be considered by a consumers' committee . . .

(6) If a committee of investigation report to the Minister that any provision of a scheme or any act or omission of a board administering a scheme is contrary to the interests of consumers of the regulated product, or is contrary to the interests of any persons affected by the scheme and is not in the public interest, the Minister, if he thinks fit to do so after considering the report—(*a*) may by order make such amendments in the scheme as he considers necessary or expedient for the purpose of rectifying the matter; (*b*) may by order revoke the scheme; (*c*) in the event of the matter being one which it is within the power of the board to rectify, may by order direct the board to take such steps to rectify the matter as may be specified in the order . . ."

Under the scheme, producers had to sell their milk to the Milk Marketing Board, which fixed the different prices paid to the producers for milk in each of the 11 regions into which England and Wales were divided. The differentials reflected (*inter alia*) the varying costs of transporting milk from the producers to the consumers.

Had there been no controls, the profits of the South-Eastern producers would have been the largest, as they were near to a very large market, and their transport costs would have been the lowest in the country. Under the scheme, transport costs were borne by the Board. Had a fixed price been paid to all producers, those in the South-East would have been treated unfairly. The current differentials had been fixed several years previously, when transport costs were much lower. For about 10 years, the South-Eastern producers had unsuccessfully been urging the

Board to increase the differentials. The differential between the South-East Region and the Far-West (where the lowest price was paid) was 1·19d. per gallon, and the South-Eastern producers wanted this increased to 3½d. Since the total sum available to the Board to pay for milk bought in all regions was fixed each year, giving effect to this claim would mean that the South-Eastern producers and perhaps those in some other regions would get higher prices, but producers in the Far-West and several other regions would get less.

The Board was constituted in such a way that the South-Eastern producers could not hope to get a majority for their proposals. The present appellants, who were office bearers of the South East regional committee, asked the Minister to appoint a committee of investigation under section 19. On May 1, 1964, they had been informed by letter that:

> "3. In considering how to exercise his discretion the Minister would, amongst other things, address his mind to the possibility that if a complaint were so referred and the committee were to uphold it, he in turn would be expected to make a statutory order to give effect to the committee's recommendations. It is this consideration, rather than the formal eligibility of the complaint as a subject for investigation, that the Minister would have in mind in determining whether your particular complaint is a suitable one for reference to the committee. We were unable to hold out any prospect that the Minister would be prepared to regard it as suitable.
>
> "4. The reasons which led us to this conclusion were explained to you as follows: (*a*) The guarantee given to milk producers under the Agriculture Acts is a guarantee given to the board on behalf of all producers. The Minister owes no duty to producers in any particular region, and this is a principle that would be seriously called into question by the making of an Order concerned with a regional price; (*b*) Such action would also bring into question the status of the Milk Marketing Scheme as an instrument for the self-government of the industry and such doubt would also, by extension, affect the other Marketing Schemes as well; and (*c*) It is by no means clear that the Minister could make an Order pertaining to the price of milk in the south-east without determining at least one of the major factors governing prices in the other regions, and he would therefore be assuming an inappropriate degree of responsibility for determining the structure of regional prices through England and Wales."

On March 23, 1965, the private secretary to the Minister wrote to inform the appellants that the Minister had decided not to refer the matter to the committee. The following reasons were given:

> "The Minister's main duty in considering this complaint has been to decide its suitability for investigation by means of a particular procedure. He has come to the conclusion that it would not be suitable. The complaint is of course one that raises wide issues going beyond the immediate concern of your clients, which is presumably the prices they themselves receive. It would also affect the interests of other regions and involve the regional price structure as a whole. In any event the Minister considers that the issue is of a kind which properly falls to be resolved through the arrangements available to producers and the board within the framework of the scheme itself."

The appellants' solicitor by a letter of November 4, 1965, asked the Minister if he had excluded from his mind the considerations set out in the 1964 letter. The Minister did not give a direct answer to this question, merely stating: "I considered that the issue . . . was one which in all the circumstances should be dealt with by the board rather than the committee of investigation."

In 1966, the Divisional Court granted an order of mandamus commanding the Minister (1) to refer the complaint to the committee or (2) to deal effectively with the complaints on relevant considerations only to the exclusion of irrelevant considerations (*The Times*, February 4, 1966). The Minister appealed successfully to the Court of Appeal (Diplock and Russell L.JJ., Lord Denning M.R. dissenting: [1968] A.C. 1003E–1015). The applicants appealed to the House of Lords.

LORD REID: ... The respondent contends that his only duty is to consider a complaint fairly and that he is given an unfettered discretion with regard to every complaint either to refer it or not to refer it to the committee as he may think fit. The appellants contend that it is his duty to refer every genuine and substantial complaint, or alternatively that his discretion is not unfettered and that in this case he failed to exercise his discretion according to law because his refusal was caused or influenced by his having misdirected himself in law or by his having taken into account extraneous or irrelevant considerations.

In my view, the appellants' first contention goes too far. There are a number of reasons which would justify the Minister in refusing to refer a complaint. For example, he might consider it more suitable for arbitration, or he might consider that in an earlier case the committee of investigation had already rejected a substantially similar complaint, or he might think the complaint to be frivolous or vexatious. So he must have at least some measure of discretion. But is it unfettered?

It is implicit in the argument for the Minister that there are only two possible interpretations of this provision—either he must refer every complaint or he has an unfettered discretion to refuse to refer in any case. I do not think that is right. Parliament must have conferred the discretion with the intention that it should be used to promote the policy and objects of the Act; the policy and objects of the Act must be determined by construing the Act as a whole and construction is always a matter of law for the court. In a matter of this kind it is not possible to draw a hard and fast line, but if the Minister, by reason of his having misconstrued the Act or for any other reason, so uses his discretion as to thwart or run counter to the policy and objects of the Act, then our law would be very defective if persons aggrieved were not entitled to the protection of the court. So it is necessary first to construe the Act.

When these provisions were first enacted in 1931 it was unusual for Parliament to compel people to sell their commodities in a way to which they objected and it was easily foreseeable that any such scheme would cause loss to some producers. Moreover, if the operation of the scheme was put in the hands of the majority of the producers, it was obvious that they might use their power to the detriment of consumers, distributors or a minority of the producers. So it is not surprising that Parliament enacted safeguards.

The approval of Parliament shows that this scheme was thought to be in the public interest, and in so far as it necessarily involved detriment to some persons, it must have been thought to be in the public interest that they should suffer it. But in sections 19 and 20 Parliament drew a line. They provide machinery for investigating and determining whether the scheme is operating or the board is acting in a manner contrary to the public interest.

The effect of these sections is that if, but only if, the Minister and the committee of investigation concur in the view that something is being done contrary to the public interest the Minister can step in. Section 20 enables the Minister to take the initiative. Section 19 deals with complaints by individuals who are aggrieved. I need not deal with the provisions which apply to consumers. We are concerned with other persons who may be distributors or producers. If the Minister directs that a complaint by any of them shall be referred to the committee of investigation, that committee will make a report which must be published. If they report that any provision of this scheme or any act or omission of the board is contrary to the interests of the complainers *and* is not in the public interest, then the Minister is empowered to take action, but not otherwise. He may disagree with the view of the committee as to public interest, and, if he thinks that there are other public interests which outweigh the public interest that justice should be done to the complainers, he would be not only entitled but bound to refuse to take action. Whether he takes action or not, he may be criticised and held accountable in Parliament but the court cannot interfere.

I must now examine the Minister's reasons for refusing to refer the appellants' complaint to the committee. I have already set out the letters of March 23 and May 3, 1965. I think it is right also to refer to a letter sent from the Ministry on May 1, 1964, because in his affidavit the Minister says he has read this letter and there is no indication that he disagrees with any part of it. It is as follows: [His Lordship read the letter and continued:]

The first reason which the Minister gave in his letter of March 23, 1965, was that this complaint was unsuitable for investigation because it raised wide issues. Here it appears to me that the Minister has clearly misdirected himself. Section 19(6) contemplates the raising of issues so wide that it may be necessary for the Minister to amend a scheme or even to revoke it. Narrower issues may be suitable for arbitration but section 19 affords the only method of investigating wide issues. In my view it is plainly the intention of the Act that even the widest issues should be investigated if the complaint is genuine and substantial, as this complaint certainly is.

Then it is said that this issue should be "resolved through the arrangements available to producers and the board within the framework of the scheme itself." This restates in a condensed form the reasons given in paragraph 4 of the letter of May 1, 1964, where it is said "the Minister owes no duty to producers in any particular region," and reference is made to the "status of the Milk Marketing Scheme as an instrument for the self-government of the industry," and to the Minister "assuming an inappropriate degree of responsibility." But, as I have already pointed out, the Act imposes on the Minister a responsibility whenever there is a relevant and substantial complaint that the board are acting in a manner inconsistent with the public interest, and that has been relevantly alleged in this case. I can find nothing in the Act to limit this responsibility or to justify the statement that the Minister owes no duty to producers in a particular region. The Minister is, I think, correct in saying that the board is an instrument for the self-government of the industry. So long as it does not act contrary to the public interest the Minister cannot interfere. But if it does act contrary to what both the committee of investigation and the Minister hold to be the public interest the Minister has a duty to act. And if a complaint relevantly alleges that the board has so acted, as this complaint does, then it appears to me that the Act does impose a duty on the Minister to have it investigated. If he does not do that he is rendering nugatory a safeguard provided by the Act and depriving complainers of a remedy which I am satisfied that Parliament intended them to have.

Paragraph 3 of the letter of May 1, 1964, refers to the possibility that, if the complaint were referred and the committee were to uphold it, the Minister "would be expected to make a statutory Order to give effect to the committee's recommendations." If this means that he is entitled to refuse to refer a complaint because, if he did so, he might later find himself in an embarrassing situation, that would plainly be a bad reason. I can see an argument to the effect that if, on receipt of a complaint, the Minister can satisfy himself from information in his possession as to the merits of the complaint, and he then chooses to say that, whatever the committee might recommend, he would hold it to be contrary to the public interest to take any action, it would be a waste of time and money to refer the complaint to the committee. I do not intend to express any opinion about that because that is not this case. In the first place it appears that the Minister has come to no decision as to the merits of the appellants' case and, secondly, the Minister has carefully avoided saying what he would do if the committee were to uphold the complaint.

It was argued that the Minister is not bound to give any reasons for refusing to refer a complaint to the committee, that if he gives no reasons his decision cannot be questioned, and that it would be very unfortunate if giving reasons were to put him in a worse position. But I do not agree that a decision cannot be questioned if no reasons are given. If it is the Minister's duty not to act so as to frustrate the policy and objects of the Act, and if it were to appear from all the circumstances of the case that that has been the effect of the Minister's refusal, then it appears to me that the court must be entitled to act. . . .

I have found no authority to support the unreasonable proposition that it must be all or nothing—either no discretion at all or an unfettered discretion. Here the words "if the Minister in any case so directs" are sufficient to show that he has some discretion but they give no guide as to its nature or extent. That must be inferred from a construction of the Act read as a whole, and for the reasons I have given I would infer that the discretion is not unlimited, and that it has been used by the Minister in a manner which is not in accord with the intention of the statute which conferred it.

As the Minister's discretion has never been properly exercised according to law, I would allow this appeal.

LORD HODSON: . . . The reasons disclosed are not, in my opinion, good reasons for refusing to refer the complaint seeing that they leave out of account altogether the merits of the complaint itself. The complaint is, as the Lord Chief Justice pointed out, made by persons affected by the scheme and is not one for the consumer committee as opposed to the committee of investigation and it was eligible for reference to the latter. It has never been suggested that the complaint was not a genuine one. It is no objection to the exercise of the discretion to refer that wide issues will be raised and the interests of other regions and the regional price structure as a whole would be affected. It is likely that the removal of a grievance will, in any event, have a wide effect and the Minister cannot lawfully say in advance that he will not refer the matter to the committee to ascertain the facts because, as he says in effect, although not in so many words, "I would not regard it as right to give effect to the report if it were favourable to the appellants."

It has been suggested that the reasons given by the Minister need not and should not be examined closely for he need give no reason at all in the exercise of his discretion. True it is that the Minister is not bound to give his reasons for refusing to exercise his discretion in a particular manner, but when, as here, the circumstances indicate a genuine complaint for which the appropriate remedy is provided, if the Minister in the case in question so directs, he would not escape from the possibility of control by mandamus through adopting a negative attitude without explanation. As the guardian of the public interest he has a duty to protect the interests of those who claim to have been treated contrary to the public interest.

I would allow the appeal accordingly. . . .

LORD PEARCE: . . . It is quite clear from the Act in question that the Minister is intended to have *some* duty in the matter. It is conceded that he must properly consider the complaint. He cannot throw it unread into the waste-paper basket. He cannot simply say (albeit honestly) "I think that in general the investigation of complaints has a disruptive effect on the scheme and leads to more trouble than (on balance) it is worth; I shall therefore never refer anything to the committee of investigation." To allow him to do so would be to give him power to set aside for his period as Minister the obvious intention of Parliament, namely, that an independent committee set up for the purpose should investigate grievances and that their report should be available to Parliament. This was clearly never intended by the Act. Nor was it intended that he could silently thwart its intention by failing to carry out its purposes. I do not regard a Minister's failure or refusal to give any reasons as a sufficient exclusion of the court's surveillance. If all the *prima facie* reasons seem to point in favour of his taking a certain course to carry out the intentions of Parliament in respect of a power which it has given him in that regard, and he gives no reason whatever for taking a contrary course, the court may infer that he has no good reason and that he is not using the power given by Parliament to carry out its intentions. In the present case, however, the Minister has given reasons which show that he was not exercising his discretion in accordance with the intentions of the Act. . . .

LORD UPJOHN: . . . My Lords, I would only add this: that without throwing any doubt upon what are well known as the club expulsion cases, where the absence of reasons has not proved fatal to the decision of expulsion by a club committee, a decision of the Minister stands on quite a different basis; he is a public officer charged by Parliament with the discharge of a public discretion affecting Her Majesty's subjects; if he does not give any reason for his decision it may be, if circumstances warrant it, that a court may be at liberty to come to the conclusion that he had no good reason for reaching that conclusion and order a prerogative writ to issue accordingly.

The Minister in my opinion has not given a single valid reason for refusing to order an inquiry into the legitimate complaint (be it well founded or not) of the South-Eastern Region; all his disclosed reasons for refusing to do so are bad in law.

LORD MORRIS OF BORTH-Y-GEST dissented.

Appeal allowed.

The House of Lords ordered that the cause be remitted to the Divisional Court of the Queen's Bench Division to require the respondent, the Minister of Agriculture, Fisheries and Food, to consider the complaint of the appellants according to law.

Notes

1. After the House of Lords decision, the Minister "decided to refer the complaint to the Committee of Investigation."[1] The Committee reported on January 7, 1969, "that the acts and/or omissions of the Board in prescribing the terms on, and the prices at which, milk should be sold to the Board were contrary to the reasonable interests of the complainants and were not in the public interest."[2] The Minister (Mr. Cledwyn Hughes having by then succeeded Mr. Fred Peart), announced his decision in a written answer in the House of Commons[3]:

[1] Report on Agricultural Marketing Schemes for 1966–67, p. 10 ([1967–68] H.C.P. 423).
[2] Report for 1967–68, p. 12 ([1968–69] H.C.P. 445).
[3] 780 H.C. Deb., cols. 46–47 (March 31, 1969).

"... I have carefully considered the Committee's findings. I am satisfied that even if its recommendations were implemented within the framework of the regional pricing structure of the Milk Marketing Scheme, they would have a profound effect on incomes of milk producers in different parts of the country. Many of them, particularly those in the West of the country, would suffer significant losses. Moreover, if the principle that each and every producer should be paid according to his proximity to a liquid market were pursued to its logical conclusion, it would bring to an end the present system for the organised marketing of milk which has been so successful.

The Committee recognised that the wider questions of agricultural, economic and social policy involved in this matter were beyond the scope of its inquiry. These must, however, in my view be given full weight. After considering with great care all the issues involved, and the very wide implications of the Committee's recommendations, I have concluded that it would not be in the public interest for me to direct the Board to implement the Committee's conclusions."

The Minister's decision was welcomed by dairy farmers in other parts of Britain, and by *The Times*, which pointed out in a leading article (April 1, 1969) that implementation of the Committee's recommendations could "easily reduce large tracts of the country, now relatively prosperous, to a condition where they were farmed on the 'dog-and-stick' methods of the inter-war years."

2. See case notes by J. F. Garner, (1968) 31 M.L.R. 446; H. W. R. Wade, (1968) 84 L.Q.R. 166; J. A. Farmer (and P. J. Evans), [1970] N.Z.L.J. 184. Note also the criticisms expressed by R. C. Austin, (1975) C.L.P. 150, 167–173.

3. This case can be regarded as an example of the Minister taking irrelevant considerations into account (see following section) as well as a failure to exercise a power in accordance with the purpose for which the power was given.

4. *Cf. British Oxygen Co. Ltd.* v. *Minister of Technology* (above, p. 292) where it was held that Parliament had not given any guidance as to how the Ministry's power to give grants to eligible applicants was to be exercised.

5. In *Secretary of State for Employment* v. *A.S.L.E.F. (No. 2)* [1972] 2 Q.B. 443, C.A., the Secretary of State could apply to the N.I.R.C. for a secret ballot order where it appeared to him (*inter alia*) that there were "reasons for doubting" whether workers would be taking part in industrial action in accordance with their wishes, and whether they had had an adequate opportunity of indicating their wishes. The Minister gave no reasons for his decision to apply for such an order. Lord Denning M.R. stated at pp. 493–494:

"We have been referred to several recent cases, of which *Padfield* v. *Minister of Agriculture, Fisheries and Food* [1968] A.C. 997 is the best example, in which the courts have stressed that in the ordinary way a Minister should give reasons, and if he gives none the court may infer that he had no good reasons. Whilst I would apply that proposition completely in most cases, and particularly in cases which affect life, liberty or property, I do not think that it applies in all cases. Here we are concerned with a ballot to ascertain the wishes of 170,000 men. The executive committees of the unions consist, we are told, of 60 men. These 60 are, no doubt, fully convinced that the whole 170,000 will support them. It is the honourable tradition of the men to support their leaders. There are many messages and telegrams which have told of support from the branches. Yet there are times when even their leaders, in touch as they are, may be mistaken.

The Solicitor-General suggested to us some reasons for doubting whether the wishes of the individual men were behind this. The Minister, he suggested, might think that, as the dispute has been discussed and debated, before a chairman agreed by both sides, many of the workers would wish to accept his award rather than take part in industrial action. The Minister also had asked the leaders of the unions earnestly to consider holding a ballot of the workers so as to ascertain their wishes. The leaders were quite sure, and are quite sure, that the men are wholly in support of this industrial action. If so, there would seem to be no good reason why they should in any way not be content for a ballot to be held. I do not say that those reasons are right, but they are such as a reasonable Minister might entertain; and, if they are such—if the Minister could on reasonable grounds form the view and opinion that he did—as I read the law and the statute this court has no jurisdiction or power to interfere with his decision."

Per Roskill L.J. at p. 511:

"It has often been said that there must be a strong case before the court will interfere. The court will, I apprehend, interfere in a case where there could in the nature of things be no evidence upon which a reasonable Secretary of State could have formed the reasons for the doubt claimed to exist and to justify an application. In my judgment, this point was effectively answered by the Solicitor-General yesterday afternoon. He was not giving the Secretary of State's actual reasons. Whether or not the Secretary of State gives those reasons is, as Buckley L.J. said, a matter of policy for him. It may be wise in some cases to give them, it may be unwise not to give them. That is not a matter with which this court is concerned. The Solicitor-General put forward, not as the Secretary of State's actual reasons, but as evidence before the court which was also available to the Secretary of State, evidence on which a reasonable Secretary of State could have formed the view that there were reasons to doubt whether the workers who were taking, or who were expected to take, part were or would be taking part in accordance with their wishes."

6. The *Padfield* dicta concerning the inferring of bad reasons for silence were applied in *R.* v. *Penwith District Council, ex p. May* (unreported, November 22, 1985). From about 1981, the Penzance and District Campaign for Nuclear Disarmament sold and distributed literature, badges and similar material in a pedestrian precinct in Penzance. The District Council resolved that as from April 1, 1984, Schedule 4 to the Local Government (Miscellaneous Provisions) Act 1982 would be applied in respect of this precinct and other streets. Accordingly, C.N.D.'s activities in selling material now required street trading consent. The council refused consent, without giving reasons. (Schedule 4 did not impose a requirement to give reasons.) There had been no objections to C.N.D.'s activities over the years, no objections to their application for consent and the Environmental Services Committee had recommended that consent be given. Taylor J. held, applying the *Padfield* dicta, that he was prepared to infer that the council had no good reasons for refusal and granted certiorari to quash the refusal of consent.
The limits to this aspect of *Padfield* were brought out in the following case.

R. v. SECRETARY OF STATE FOR TRADE AND INDUSTRY ex p. LONRHO plc.

[1989] 1 W.L.R. 525; [1989] 2 All E.R. 609 (House of Lords)

In March 1985 A.I.T. plc (which subsequently changed its name to House of Fraser plc ("Holdings")) acquired a majority of the share capital in House of Fraser plc, a company which owned a large number of department stores including Harrods. On March 14, 1985, before the acquisition had been completed, the Secretary of State for Trade and Industry announced that he had decided not to refer the proposed acquisition to the Monopolies and Mergers Commission. In April 1987 the Secretary of State appointed inspectors pursuant to section 432(2) of the Companies Act 1985 to investigate the affairs of Holdings in particular in relation to the acquisition of House of Fraser. The inspectors spent some 15 months pursuing their investigations and compiling their report, and during that time they received lengthy submissions from, *inter alios*, Lonrho plc, which had for several years been attempting to obtain a controlling interest in Harrods. On July 23, 1988 the inspectors submitted their report to the Secretary of State who by section 437 of the Act of 1985 had power to publish such a report "if he thinks fit." He did not publish it immediately upon receipt, but chose to submit the report to the Serious Fraud Office which was done by the end of July 1988. In August 1988 the Secretary of State also sent a copy of the report to the Director General of Fair Trading asking him to consider and to advise on whether the report disclosed the existence of material new facts and, if so, whether the merger of A.I.T. plc and House of Fraser plc should be referred to the Monopolies and Mergers Commission pursuant to section 64(4)(*b*) of the Fair Trading Act 1973, which empowered the Secretary of State to make such a reference if it appeared to him that there were new material facts about the merger and a reference was made within six months of the emergence of those facts. During that period, the Secretary of State received lengthy submissions from Lonrho urging him to publish the report. He indicated that his intention was to do so, and that the only question was the appropriate date for publication. On September 29, 1988, the Department of Trade and Industry issued a Press notice stating again the fact that the Secretary of State intended to publish the report. It added that he would not do so while the Serious Fraud Office was considering it. On November 25, 1988 the department reiterated that the report would not be published while the prosecution authorities were conducting their inquiries. It also announced that although the report did indicate the existence of previously undisclosed material the Secretary of State had decided, in accordance with the advice of the Director General of Fair Trading, that a reference was not appropriate.

On applications by Lonrho for judicial review of both decisions, the Divisional Court of the Queen's Bench Division ((1989) 5 B.C.C. 266) granted the applications and held (a) that the decision to delay publication of the report was *ultra vires* and unlawful and that mandamus should issue requiring reconsideration of the matter; (b) that the decision not to refer the 1984 and 1985 acquisition of the House of Fraser to the Monopolies and Mergers Commission was *ultra vires* and mandamus was issued requiring the Secretary of State to make that reference. On appeal by the Secretary of State, the Court of Appeal ((1989) 5 B.C.C. 284) allowed the appeal. Lonrho appealed to the House of Lords.

LORD KEITH OF KINKEL: [held, first, that the challenge to the decision not to publish the report failed: on the facts, the Secretary of State had not delegated (unlawfully) the exercise of his discretion whether to publish to the S.F.O.; he had not acted on incorrect advice; and his decision was neither perverse nor irrational: he was entitled to take the view that early publication might be prejudicial to the S.F.O. and to a fair trial. His Lordship continued:]

It is true that the Divisional Court took a different view of the effect of early publication but the members of the Divisional Court had not read the report and knew nothing of the investigations of the S.F.O. The Divisional Court was also confident of the ability of a jury on the instructions of a judge to forget everything they had read and seen before the trial. But the Secretary of State who had read the report and was advised by the S.F.O. and officials and counsel of the D.T.I., who had also read the report, was obliged to consider the possible risks stemming from the early publication of this particular report relating to a notorious controversy which was bound to continue between Mr. Rowland and the Al Fayed brothers.

The judgments of the Divisional Court illustrate the danger of judges wrongly though unconsciously substituting their own views for the views of the decision-maker who alone is charged and authorised by Parliament to exercise a discretion. The question is not whether the Secretary of State came to a correct solution or to a conclusion which meets with the approval of the Divisional Court but whether the discretion was properly exercised. The Secretary of State considered the advice he received from the S.F.O. about the effect of early publication and the contrary advice of counsel for Lonrho. The Secretary of State also considered the disadvantages urged by Lonrho of postponing publication. No fault can be found with the decision-making process of the Secretary of State and he was entitled and bound to make up his own mind to publish or postpone publication in the public interest. Any attack on the good faith of the Secretary of State was expressly disclaimed by counsel for Lonrho. The correspondence and memoranda of the negotiations between the D.T.I. and Lonrho show a scrupulous anxiety on the part of the D.T.I. to act fairly and to give proper consideration to the problems posed by the contents of the report.

The appeal in respect of the publication decision therefore fails.

The reference to the Monopolies and Mergers Commission

... Before arriving at [the decision not to make a reference to the Commission] the Secretary of State had not only received the inspectors' report and the advice of the director but had also had representations made to him on behalf of Lonrho by a legal team and by Mr. Rowland personally at meetings with both the Secretary of State himself and with the officials of his department. The Secretary of State must have received a unique amount of advice upon the issue of whether or not he should exercise his discretion to refer the matter to the M.M.C.

Despite the fact that the Secretary of State has acted in accordance with the advice which Parliament has directed that he should receive from the director, Lonrho assert that he has acted unlawfully and in breach of his statutory duty under the Act. It is said that in following the advice of the director not to refer the bid to the M.M.C., the Secretary of State has acted so irrationally that his decision should be quashed and he should be ordered to make a reference. Irrationality is the sole ground upon which the Secretary of State's decision was challenged; there is no suggestion that the decision was taken in bad faith or for any improper reason such as a cover-up of political or departmental ineptitude.

The Divisional Court found in Lonrho's favour on this issue because they regarded it as the policy of the Act that there should be a reference to the M.M.C. on the ground that "when a merger situation is complicated by factors which are best understood by men rich in experience of the business world, their powers of investigation should be enlisted and their advice invited." I cannot accept this interpretation of the Act. The Act vests a discretion in the Secretary of State to decide whether to seek the advice of the M.M.C. which is one of the three statutory bodies created by the Act to give advice to the Secretary of State. The approach of the Divisional Court is to convert this discretion into a duty and it also ignores the expertise of the Director of Fair Trading and his department who are also rich in experience of merger situations and under a duty to give advice whether or not to make a reference to the M.M.C. If every complicated merger that qualified for a reference under section 64 and which potentially affected the public interest had to be referred to the M.M.C. the whole system would break down under the weight of the work. In 1988, 260 merger situations were considered in the office of the director of which only 11 were ultimately referred to the M.M.C. If all 260 mergers had been referred, the M.M.C. could not possibly have carried out their statutory duty to investigate and report within the time limit of six months required by the Act. The Secretary of State must exercise his discretion to decide which mergers to refer and it is clearly the policy of the Act that his discretion should be guided, although not fettered, by the advice of the director.

Padfield v. *Minister of Agriculture, Fisheries and Food* [1968] A.C. 997 was relied upon by Lonrho to support two limbs of their argument. First it was said to support a construction of the Act that imposed a duty on the Secretary of State to make a reference to the M.M.C., and secondly, the fact that the Secretary of State had given no reason for his decision not to make a reference led to the conclusion that no rational reason existed for his decision. In my view that case does not support either limb of the argument. The decision in *Padfield* turned on the construction of the Agricultural Marketing Act 1958.

[See above, pp. 343–349. His Lordship read the headnote, and continued:]

The Minister gave among his reasons for refusing to appoint a committee of investigation that the complaint was unsuitable for investigation because it raised "wide issues" and that the Minister owed no duty to producers in any particular region. It was held that these were bad reasons for refusing to appoint a committee and showed that the Minister had misunderstood the policy and intention of the Act which was that genuine and substantial complaints of this nature should be investigated by a committee of investigation. I can find no parallel between the appointment of a committee to investigate a specific complaint that individuals are suffering injustice and a reference to the M.M.C. to enable a wide-ranging inquiry to determine whether a commercial situation is or may be operating against the public interest. The two situations are entirely different and the construction placed upon the Agricultural Marketing Act 1958 throws no light on the construction of the Fair Trading Act 1973.

Turning now to the question of reasons, Sir Dingle Foot Q.C., instructed on behalf of the Minister, submitted in the course of his argument that the Minister can refuse to act on a complaint without giving any reasons and in such a case a complainant would have no remedy and his decision cannot be questioned. Not surprisingly this submission was rejected. Lord Pearce said, at pp. 1053–1054:

> "I do not regard a Minister's failure or refusal to give any reasons as a sufficient exclusion of the court's surveillance. If all the prima facie reasons seem to point in favour of his taking a certain course to carry out the intentions of Parliament in respect of a power which it has given him in that regard and he gives no reason whatever for taking a contrary course, the court may infer that he has no good reason and that he is not using the power given by Parliament to carry out its intentions. In the present case, however, the Minister has given reasons which show that he was not exercising his discretion in accordance with the intentions of the Act."

See passages to the like effect in the speeches of Lord Reid, at p. 1032, Lord Hodson, at p. 1049 and Lord Upjohn, at p. 1061.

Although reference was made to the judgment of Sir John Donaldson M.R. in *R.* v. *Lancashire County Council, ex p. Huddleston* [1986] 2 All E.R. 941 in which he referred to the desirability of proceedings for judicial review being conducted with the cards face up on the table, it was not submitted to your Lordships that there was any general duty to give reasons for a decision in all cases, nor was it submitted that this Act imposed a particular duty on the Secretary of State to give reasons for his refusal to make a reference to the M.M.C.; and it is not the practice of the Secretary of State to give reasons when he decides not to make a reference to the M.M.C.

The absence of reasons for a decision where there is no duty to give them cannot of itself provide any support for the suggested irrationality of the decision. The only significance of the absence of reasons is that if all other known facts and circumstances appear to point overwhelmingly in favour of a different decision, the decision-maker who has given no reasons cannot complain if the court draws the inference that he had no rational reason for his decision.

It is difficult to see what useful purpose would have been achieved by a reference to the M.M.C. other than as a step towards enabling the Secretary of State to exercise his powers under Schedule 8 to order Holdings to divest themselves of their shares in Fraser, in other words, to take Harrods away from the Al Fayed brothers which is, of course, Lonrho's principal objective in these proceedings. No competition or consumer issues are involved in the present situation and there is no indication that the particular expertise of the M.M.C. is required to advise the Secretary of State on any aspect of the public interest. It can of course be said that it is contrary to the public interest in its widest sense that the Director and the Secretary of State should be deceived during the investigation of a merger and that there is a public interest in pursuing and punishing those who do so. But on this aspect of the public interest the Secretary of State has already received the inspectors' report and further public resources are being committed in the investigation by the S.F.O. and the D.P.P. The Secretary of State does not need the assistance of the M.M.C. to clarify these aspects of the public interest about which he is already fully informed.

The measures that the Secretary of State can take under Schedule 8 pursuant to a finding by the M.M.C. that a merger is contrary to the public interest are designed to prevent or correct damage to the economy as a consequence of an undesirable merger rather than as punitive measures against individuals. If the director and the Secretary of State who has acted on his advice take the view that in the present circumstances it is unnecessary to take the power to order Holdings to divest themselves of their shares in Fraser and therefore unnecessary to have a reference to the M.M.C., I can see nothing irrational in such a decision. If the current investigation should warrant proceedings for serious fraud no doubt the criminal law will take its course. Furthermore, there are extensive powers available under the Company Directors Disqualification Act 1986 which would, if circumstances justified it, enable the Al Fayed brothers to be removed from control of Fraser. Looking at the matter from the point of view of the overall health of the economy, which is the manifest purpose for which the Secretary of State is given his powers under the Act of 1973, I find it impossible to say that it was irrational to decide not to launch the M.M.C. on an inquiry that would cover ground already investigated by the inspectors and which is being further investigated by the S.F.O. and the D.P.P. I . . . reach, without hesitation, the conclusion that Lonrho has not made a case that no reasonable Secretary of State could have refused to make a reference to the Monopolies and Mergers Commission.

For these reasons I would dismiss the appeal. . . .

LORDS TEMPLEMAN, GRIFFITHS, ACKNER and LOWRY agreed.

Notes

1. See D. G. T. Williams, [1989] C.L.J. 161. The significance of the *Lonrho* case in the context of merger control is considered by S. Weatherill, "The Changing Law and Practice of U.K. and E.E.C. Merger Control" (1991) 11 O.J.L.S. 520. Weatherill argues that the imposition of a duty to give reasons would be helpful in the particular context of merger control. This:

"would not disturb the allocation of responsibility to Parliament for decisions taken by the Minister, yet it would create a climate conducive to informed and open discussion. It would be at least more likely that the debate would proceed on the basis of competition policy. It would not be governed so easily by the narrower interests, governmental contacts and financial might of the firms concerned" (p. 527).

The House of Lords rejection of this step in *Lonrho*: "leaves the system at the mercy of media manipulation" (p. 526).

2. The *Lonrho* litigation also gave rise to important contempt proceedings. See *Re Lonrho plc* [1990] 2 A.C. 154, H.L.

3. The inspectors' report was published in March 1990 (*House of Fraser Holdings plc*, H.M.S.O.), and concluded that the Fayeds had "won Government sanction of their £850 million bid for House of Fraser through the simple expedient of lying about their background and resources" (1990) 140 N.L.J. 349. The Government informed "an incredulous and angry House of Commons" that the available sanctions, which included prosecutions for obtaining by deception or perjury, or disqualification from holding directorships should not be invoked (*ibid.*). The Attorney-General said in the House of Commons that the evidence against the Fayeds was insufficient and hearsay (*The Independent*, March 13, 1990). The Divisional Court subsequently dismissed an application for judicial review of the decision not to apply to the court for an order under the Company Directors Disqualification Act 1986, s.8, disqualifying the Fayeds from being company directors (*R.* v. *Secretary of State for Trade and Industry, ex p. Lonrho plc, The Independent*, October 22, 1991). There were no grounds for saying that the Secretary of State had taken immaterial matters into account, or that his decision was perverse.

4. The reluctance of the courts to infer bad reasons from silence was confirmed in the context of dealings involving the Inland Revenue in *R.* v. *Inland Revenue Commissioners, ex p. T.C. Coombs & Co.* [1991] 2 A.C. 283, H.L., reversing the Court of Appeal. Lord Lowry said (at p. 301) that if "a strong case" was made for quashing a notice under the Taxes Management Act 1970, s.20(3) (requiring the production of documents), "it may be the duty of the revenue to meet that case with something more cogent than silence, however understandable or justifiable."

5. The *Lonrho* case confirms that there is no general common law duty to give reasons for a decision. In *R.* v. *Civil Service Appeal Board* v. *ex p. Cunningham* [1991] 4 All E.R. 310, Lord Donaldson M.R. stated that the contrary was "unarguable" (p. 317), citing the decision of the High Court of Australia in *Public Service Board of New South Wales* v. *Osmond* (1986) 63 A.L.R. 559).

Such a duty may be imposed by statute (see *e.g.* below, p. 659, n. 5). Moreover, in certain circumstances, the courts will infer that a discretion has been abused (*cf.* the comments on *Padfield* in *Lonrho*) or fettered (see *Sagnata Investments Ltd.* v. *Norwich Corporation*, below, pp. 613–621) unless reasons are forthcoming. Natural justice or the duty to act fairly may require the decision-maker to give prior notice and an opportunity to make representations before a decision is made, and this may require adequate disclosure of the evidence (see the discussion in *R.* v. *Gaming Board*, above, p. 525); moreover, a judicial tribunal may be required by the requirements of natural justice to give reasons (see p. 565).

It has often been argued that there *should* be a general duty to give reasons. Strong support for this position was given by the JUSTICE—All Souls Review of Administrative Law in the United Kingdom, *Administrative Justice: Some Necessary Reforms* (1988), Ch. 3. The duty should be imposed by legislation; would arise on a demand being made; would make it incumbent to state not only the reasons but also the findings on material questions of fact with reference to the evidence or other material on which such findings were based; and could be subject to exemptions for specified catagories of decision. Sir Harry Woolf has expressed the view that such a development would be "the most beneficial improvement which could be made to English administrative law" (*Protection of the Public—A New Challenge* (1990), p. 92).

6. Sir Harry Woolf has noted that once leave to apply for judicial review has been granted in respect of a decision of central government, it is the usual practice:

> "for the department to set out frankly in an affidavit the matters which were taken into account in reaching a decision. The decision-making process is fully disclosed."

(*Protection of the Public—A New Challenge* (1990), pp. 16–17, 92–97.) Indeed, he states that "most public bodies" adopt a "cards face up on the table" approach (*ibid.* p. 97). This enables the court in most cases to dispense with any order for discovery and cross-examination on affidavits.

WHEELER v. LEICESTER CITY COUNCIL

[1985] A.C. 1054; [1985] 3 W.L.R. 335, [1985] 2 All E.R. 1106 (House of Lords)

The local authority purported to terminate the use which Leicester [Rugby] Football Club made of a recreation ground owned by the council. This action was taken following the club's refusal to comply fully with a number of requirements made of it by the local authority. The requirements were the council's response to the decision of three of the club's players to take part in a rugby tour of South Africa. The club was willing to condemn the tour but was not willing, and indeed doubted its powers, to put pressure on the players to induce them not to take part in the tour. The club applied for certiorari to quash the council's decision. In the proceedings the council argued that its policy was in accordance with its obligations under section 71 of the Race Relations Act 1976—"it shall be the duty of every local authority to make appropriate arrangements with a view to securing their various functions are carried out with due regard to the need—(*a*) to eliminate unlawful racial discrimination; and (*b*) to promote equality of opportunity, and good relations, between persons of different racial groups." The council was acting, it argued, in the interests of its local population, which consisted of 25 per cent. persons of Asian or Afro-Caribbean origin.

The club was unsuccessful at first instance and in the Court of Appeal ([1985] 2 All E.R. 151). It then appealed to the House of Lords.

LORD ROSKILL: None of the judges in the courts below have felt able to hold that the action of the club was unreasonable or perverse in the *Wednesbury* sense. They do not appear to have been invited to consider whether those actions, even if not unreasonable on *Wednesbury* principles, were assailable on the grounds of procedural impropriety or unfairness by the council in the manner in which . . . they took their decision to suspend for 12 months the use by the club of the Welford Road recreation ground.

I would greatly hesitate to differ from four learned judges on the *Wednesbury* issue but for myself I would have been disposed respectfully to do this and to say that the actions of the council were unreasonable in the *Wednesbury* sense. But even if I am wrong in this view, I am clearly of the opinion that the manner in which the council took that decision was in all the circumstances unfair within the third of the principles stated in *Council of Civil Service Unions* v. *Minister for the Civil Service*. [Ed. *i.e.* "procedural impropriety."] The council formulated those four questions in the manner of which I have spoken and indicated that only such affirmative answers would be acceptable. They received reasoned and reasonable answers which went a long way in support of the policy which the council had accepted and desired to see accepted. The views expressed in these reasoned and reasonable answers were lawful views and the views which, as the evidence shows, many people sincerely hold and believe to be correct. If the club had adopted a different and hostile attitude, different considerations might well have arisen. But the club did not adopt any such attitude.

In my view, therefore, this is a case in which the court should interfere because of the unfair manner in which the council set about obtaining its objective. I would not, with profound respect, rest my decision upon the somewhat wider ground which appealed to Browne-Wilkinson L.J. in his dissenting judgment.

Since preparing this speech I have had the advantage of reading in draft the speech of my noble and learned friend Lord Templeman with which I find myself in complete agreement. . . .

LORD TEMPLEMAN. My Lords, in my opinion the Leicester City Council were not entitled to withdraw from the Leicester Football Club the facilities for training and playing enjoyed by the club for many years on the council's recreation ground for one simple and good reason. The club could not be punished because the club had done nothing wrong.

The 1984 Rugby Tour of South Africa was organised by the Rugby Football Union which invited individuals, including three members of the club, to join the tour. There were two views about the tour amongst the opponents of apartheid. The view taken by the council, a view which I share, was that the tour would endorse the racist policies of the South African Government. The opposite view was expressed by Mr. Dodge, who was one of the three members of the club who participated in the tour and who gave sworn evidence in these proceedings as follows:

> "I personally deplore apartheid as being morally wrong. It is nevertheless my genuine belief that maintaining sporting links with South Africa does help break down the evil social barriers of apartheid, a personal belief which has been strengthened by observing in 1984 the improvement since 1980."

The council agreed that this belief was sincerely held not only by Mr. Dodge but by other opponents of apartheid. The Government had subscribed to the Gleneagles agreement but did not take steps to ban the tour, leaving the decision to each individual invited to take part. The club does not practise racial discrimination, does not support apartheid, has not been guilty of any infringement of the Race Relations Act 1976, did not support the decision of the three members to join the tour and sought to discourage them from joining the tour by sending them copies of the reasoned memorandum published by the opponents of the tour. The council does not contend that the club should have threatened or punished the three club members who participated in the tour or that the club could properly have done so. Nevertheless, the club has been punished by the council according to Mr. Soulsby for "failing to condemn the tour and to discourage its members from playing." My Lords, the laws of this country are not like the laws of Nazi Germany. A private individual or a private organisation cannot be obliged to display zeal in the pursuit of an object sought by a public authority and cannot be obliged to publish views dictated by a public authority.

The club having committed no wrong, the council could not use their statutory powers in the management of their property or any other statutory powers in order to punish the club. There is no doubt that the council intended to punish and have punished the club. When the club were presented by the council with four questions it was made clear that the club's response would only be acceptable if, in effect, all four questions were answered in the affirmative. . . .

. . . In my opinion, this use by the council of its statutory powers was a misuse of power. The council could not properly seek to use its statutory powers of management or any other statutory powers for the purposes of punishing the club when the club had done no wrong.

In *Congreve* v. *Home Office* [1976] Q.B. 629, the Home Secretary had a statutory power to revoke television licences. In exercise of that statutory power he revoked the television licences of individuals who had lawfully surrendered an existing licence and taken out a new licence before an increase in the licence fee was due to take effect. Lord Denning M.R. said, at p. 651:

"If the licence is to be revoked—and his money forfeited—the Minister would have to give good reasons to justify it. Of course, if the licensee had done anything wrong—if he had given a cheque for £12 which was dishonoured, or if he had broken the conditions of the licence—the Minister could revoke it. But when the licensee has done nothing wrong at all, I do not think the Minister can lawfully revoke the licence, at any rate, not without offering him his money back, and not even then except for good cause. If he should revoke it without giving reasons, or for no good reason, the courts can set aside his revocation and restore the licence. It would be a misuse of the power conferred on him by Parliament: and these courts have the authority—and, I would add, the duty—to correct a misuse of power by a Minister or his department, no matter how much he may resent it or warn us of the consequences if we do."

Similar considerations apply, in my opinion, to the present case. Of course this does not mean that the council is bound to allow its property to be used by a racist organisation or by any organisation which, by its actions or its words, infringes the letter or the spirit of the Race Relations Act 1976. But the attitude of the club and of the committee of the club was a perfectly proper attitude, caught as they were in a political controversy which was not of their making.

For these reasons and the reasons given by my noble and learned friend Lord Roskill, I would allow the appeal.

LORDS BRIDGE, BRIGHTMAN and GRIFFITHS expressed their agreement with both LORD ROSKILL and LORD TEMPLEMAN.

Notes

1. For *Wednesbury* unreasonableness as a ground of challenge, see below, p. 395. For challenge for "procedural impropriety" see below on procedural *ultra vires*, the *audi alteram partem* rule of natural justice, and the duty to "act fairly" (pp. 448–469, 469–565, and 494–521).

2. Do you agree with Lord Roskill's approach, basing his decision on unfair procedure?

3. Browne-Wilkinson L.J.'s dissent in the Court of Appeal was based on the view that the council's action was a violation of the fundamental right of free speech that Parliament could not have intended to authorise by section 71 of the 1976 Act.

4. For comments on *Wheeler*, see C. Turpin, [1985] C.L.J. 333; T. R. S. Allan, (1985) 48 M.L.R. 448 (on the Court of Appeal decision) and (1986) 49 M.L.R. 121 (expressing a preference for the judgment of Browne-Wilkinson L.J. in the Court of Appeal).

5. In *Congreve* v. *The Home Office* [1976] 1 Q.B. 629, Mr. Congreve was one of over 20,000 people who took out a second colour television licence before the expiry of an existing one, in anticipation of an increase in the licence fee, from £12 to £18, as from April 1, 1975. By section 1(2) of the Wireless Telegraphy Act 1949 "A licence . . . may be issued subject to such terms, provisions and limitations as the [Minister] may think fit." Section 1(4) provided that a licence "may be revoked . . . by a notice in writing served on the holder. . . ." There were no other limitations expressed in the statute. The Home Office feared that a substantial part of the anticipated revenue from the issue of licences would be lost in view of the large estimated number of "overlappers." They initially demanded an extra £6 from each "overlapper" under threat of revocation, and subsequently modified their policy to one of revocation after eight months (£12 worth at an annual rate of £18). The Court of Appeal granted a declaration that the purported revocation of the plaintiff's licence was unlawful, invalid and of no effect. Lord Denning's somewhat extravagant reasoning, including the passage cited by Lord Templeman in *Wheeler*, was not echoed by the other judges in *Congreve*. Geoffrey Lane L.J., for example, put the matter more simply (p. 662):

". . . The licence was a valid one at the time of its issue. At that time the new regulation increasing the fee to £18 had not come into operation and therefore did not in law exist. There was no power to demand the extra £6 nor to receive it.... [The revocation] is illegal for two reasons. First, it is coupled with an illegal demand which taints the revocation and makes that illegal too. Secondly, or possibly putting the same matter in a different way, it is an improper exercise of a discretionary power to use a threat to exercise that power as a means of extracting money which Parliament has given the executive no mandate to demand: see *Attorney-General* v. *Wilts United Dairies* (1922) 91 L.J.K.B. 897...."

The Parliamentary Commissioner for Administration concluded that many members of the public had been caused needless distress and confusion through maladministration by the Home Office and their agents, the Television Licence Records Office, mainly in failing to make their policy officially and openly clear to the public (see his conclusions at para. 38 of his Report: the Seventh Report of the P.C.A. for Session 1974–75, H.C.P. 680). However, on the assumption that it was lawful, he "found no ground for questioning the principle behind the arrangements" (para. 42).

The decision of the Court of Appeal was celebrated by Mr. Bernard Levin in *The Times* of December 5, 1975: ("Blow the loud trumpets of victory for Us over Them in the T.V. licence war"). It was also welcomed by H. W. R. Wade, (1976) 92 L.Q.R. 331. G. Ganz, however, was unenthusiastic ([1976] P.L. 14–15): "To elevate tax avoidance into a liberty of the subject protected by the Bill of Rights is a complete inversion of moral values.... The case epitomises the dangers of allowing the courts more scope to impose their values in this area of law as advocated by Scarman L.J. in *English Law—The New Dimension*. Their values have become fossilised so that they still see the individual battling against a hostile Executive once embodied in an autocratic King. They do not see the issue as one between the plaintiff and other taxpayers who will pay more whilst he pays less and that their judgment leads to an unequal sharing of burdens by the many for the benefit of a few."

6. In *R.* v. *Derbyshire County Council, ex p. The Times Supplements Ltd.* (1990) 3 Admin.L.R. 241, the council resolved to remove all its advertising from newspapers owned by Mr. Rupert Murdoch. Shortly before, the *Sunday Times* had published articles about the council which had led to the institution of libel proceedings by Councillor Bookbinder, the council leader. The decision involved switching advertising for teaching posts from *The Times Educational Supplement* to *The Guardian* notwithstanding that the cost was greater and the likely readership among teachers much smaller. The Divisional Court granted certiorari to quash the decision. The court was satisfied on the evidence (some councillors were cross-examined on their affidavits) that there was no educational ground for the decision (contrary to the claims of councillors) and that the majority Labour group on the council had been activated by bad faith or vindictiveness. The decision was "an abuse of power contrary to the public good" (Watkins L.J. at p. 253). Had it been necessary to do so his Lordship was sure that the decision would have been held to be perverse, as having no sensible or justifiable basis (*ibid.*).

(B) Taking into Account Irrelevant Considerations; Failure to have Regard to Relevant Considerations

Logically, this ground of challenge is wide enough to cover situations where powers are exercised for an improper purpose, given that desire to achieve that purpose will inevitably constitute the taking into consideration of an irrelevant consideration. However, the case law shows that a distinction between these grounds of challenge is commonly drawn.

As with "improper purposes," statutes sometimes are explicit as to the considerations which are to be taken into consideration in coming to a decision as to the exercise of a power; more usually, it is for the courts to determine what is implicit from the terms of the legislation as regards the relevance/irrelevance of particular matters. Even where a statute states certain matters which must be taken into consideration, it will be a matter of construction for the courts as to whether these are exhaustive of relevant considerations.

ROBERTS v. HOPWOOD AND OTHERS

[1925] A.C. 578; 94 L.J.K.B. 542; 133 L.T. 289; 41 T.L.R. 436; 89 J.P. 105; 69 S.J. 475; [1925] All E.R.Rep. 24; 23 L.G.R. 337 (House of Lords)

Poplar Borough Council had power under section 62 of the Metropolis Management Act 1855 to pay to their employees "such salaries and wages as . . . [the council] may think fit." In 1914, the minimum wage for the lowest grade of worker was 30s. per week for men, and 22s. 6d. for women, these being in line with wages paid by the other metropolitan councils. By 1920, these figures had risen to 64s. and 49s. 9d. respectively. When auditing the 1920–21 accounts the district auditor, Mr. Carson Roberts, noted an increase to 80s. as the minimum for both men and women from May 1, 1920. He did not then raise any objection as the cost of living had greatly increased since 1914. In 1923, the auditor found that the rate of 80s. per week was still being maintained, although the cost of living had materially reduced. Indeed, he found that the total of the wage payments made by the council in 1921–22 exceeded by about £17,000 the total amount that would have been paid if the trade union rates had been applicable; that wage increases since 1914 exceeded cost-of-living increases by between 85 per cent. and 200 per cent. depending upon the grade of worker; that working hours were considerably shorter in 1922 than in 1914; and that in the lower grades the new minimum rate varied from nearly three times to over four times the rate paid per hour in 1914.

The auditor heard representations from the Socialist councillors who controlled the council, led by George Lansbury, to the effect that they regarded themselves as bound to maintain these wage levels by a "mandate of the electors." He decided that the council had not paid due regard to the interests of the ratepayers, and had made payments far in excess of those necessary to obtain the service required and to maintain a high standard of efficiency, which were thus in reality gifts to their employees in addition to remuneration for their services. He was under a duty under section 247(7) of the Public Health Act 1875 to "disallow every item of account contrary to law, and surcharge the same on the person making or authorising the making of the illegal payment." Acting under this section he disallowed £5,000 and surcharged it on the councillors concerned.

The councillors applied for certiorari under the Public Health Act to quash the disallowance and surcharge. Section 247(8) enabled a person aggrieved to apply for a writ of certiorari to remove the disallowance to the King's Bench Division. As interpreted in earlier cases, *e.g. R.* v. *Roberts* [1908] 1 K.B. 407, this was regarded as giving in effect a right to appeal on fact and/or law.

The Divisional Court (Lord Hewart C.J., Sankey and Salter JJ.) rejected their application ([1924] 1 K.B. 514: *sub nom. R.* v. *Roberts, ex p. Scurr*).

The councillors appealed successfully to the Court of Appeal ([1924] 2 K.B. 695). The House of Lords unanimously allowed the auditor's appeal.

LORD BUCKMASTER: . . . [T]he general rule applicable is that the council shall pay such wages as they may think fit, the discretion as to the reasonable nature of the wages being with them. The discretion thus imposed is a very wide one, and I agree with the principle enunciated by

Lord Russell in the case of *Kruse* v. *Johnson* [1899] 2 Q.B. 91, 99 [below, p. 914], that when such a discretion is conferred upon a local authority the court ought to show great reluctance before they attempt to determine how, in their opinion, the discretion ought to be exercised.

Turning to what the borough council have done, the reason for their action is to be found in the affidavit sworn by Mr. Scurr, Mr. Key, Mr. Lansbury and Mr. Sumner. In para. 6 of that affidavit they make the following statement: "The council and its predecessors the district board of works have always paid such a minimum wage to its employees as they have believed to be fair and reasonable without being bound by any particular external method of fixing wages, whether ascertainable by Trade Union rate, cost of living, payments by other local or national authorities or otherwise." And if the matter ended there it would be my opinion that a decision so reached could not be impeached until it were shown that it was not *bona fide*, and absence of *bona fides* is not alleged in the present proceedings. Para. 9, however, of the same affidavit puts the matter in a different form. It is there said: "9. . . . The Council did not and does not take the view that wages paid should be exclusively related to the cost of living. They have from time to time carefully considered the question of the wages and are of the opinion, as a matter of policy, that a public authority should be a model employer and that a minimum rate of 4*l*. is the least wage which ought to be paid to an adult having regard to the efficiency of their workpeople, the duty of a public authority both to the ratepayers and to its employees, the purchasing power of the wages and other considerations which are relevant to their decisions as to wages."

Now it appears that on August 31, 1921, a resolution was passed by the borough council to the effect that no reduction of wage or bonus should be made during the ensuing four months, and this was acted upon for the following 12 months. It was, I think, well within their power to fix wages for a reasonable time in advance, and there are cogent reasons why this should be done, but that decision should be made in relation to existing facts, which they appear to have ignored. In August 1921, the cost of living had been continuously falling since November of the previous year, and it continued to fall, so that it is difficult to understand how, if the cost of living was taken into account in fixing the wages for adult workers at a minimum basis of 4*l*., the sharp decline in this important factor should have been wholly disregarded by the borough council. But the affidavit contains another statement, which I think is most serious for the council's case. It states that 4*l*. a week was to be the minimum wage for adult labour, that is without the least regard to what that labour might be. It standardised men and women not according to the duties they performed, but according to the fact that they were adults. It is this that leads me to think that their action cannot be supported, and that in fact they have not determined the payment as wages, for they have eliminated the consideration both of the work to be done and of the purchasing power of the sums paid, which they themselves appear to regard as a relevant though not the dominant factor. Had they stated that they determined as a borough council to pay the same wage for the same work without regard to the sex or condition of the person who performed it, I should have found it difficult to say that that was not a proper exercise of their discretion. It was indeed argued that that is what they did, but I find it impossible to extract that from the statement contained in the affidavit. It appears to me, for the reasons I have given, that they cannot have brought into account the considerations which they say influenced them, and that they did not base their decision upon the ground that the reward for work is the value of the work reasonably and even generously measured, but that they took an arbitrary principle and fixed an arbitrary sum, which was not a real exercise of the discretion imposed upon them by the statute.

It is for these reasons that I think the appeal should succeed.

LORD ATKINSON: . . . It is but right and natural that the rate of wages should rise if the cost of living rises, because this tends directly to keep the purchasing power of the labourer's wage at what it was before the cost of living increased. The principle apparently adopted by the council, however, is that wages should rise if the cost of living rises, but should never go down if the cost of living goes down. . . .

In the sixth paragraph of Mr. Scurr's affidavit he states that "the Council have always paid such a minimum wage as they have believed to be fair and reasonable without being bound by any particular external method of fixing wages, whether by trade union rates, cost of living, payments of other local or national authorities or otherwise." Nobody has contended that the council should be bound by any of these things, but it is only what justice and common sense demand that, when dealing with funds contributed by the whole body of the ratepayers, they should take each and every one of these enumerated things into consideration in order to help them to determine what was a fair, just and reasonable wage to pay their employees for the services the latter rendered. The council would, in my view, fail in their duty if, in administering funds which did not belong to their members alone, they put aside all these aids to the ascertainment of what was just and reasonable remuneration to give for the services rendered to them, and allowed themselves to be guided in preference by some eccentric principles of socialist philanthropy, or by a feminist ambition to secure the equality of the sexes in the matter of wages in the world of labour.

In para. 9 of Mr. Scurr's affidavit he is good enough to disclose what the council did take into consideration in fixing the minimum rate of wages to be paid to their employees. . . .

This system of procedure might possibly be admirably philanthropic, if the funds of the council at the time that they were thus administered belonged to the existing members of that body. These members would then be generous at their own expense. . . . A body charged with the administration for definite purposes of funds contributed in whole or in part by persons other than the members of that body, owes, in my view, a duty to those latter persons to conduct the administration in a fairly businesslike manner with reasonable care, skill and caution, and with a due and alert regard to the interest of those contributors who are not members of the body. Towards these latter persons the body stands somewhat in the position of trustees or managers of the property of others.

This duty is, I think, a legal duty as well as a moral one, and acts done in flagrant violation of it should, in my view, be properly held to have been done "contrary to law" within the meaning of section 247(7) of the Public Health Act of 1875. . . . It was strongly pressed in argument that the auditor believed the council acted *bona fide*; but what in this connection do the words "*bona fide*" mean? Do they mean, as apparently this gentleman thought, that no matter how excessive or illegal their scale of wages might be, they were bound to put it into force because their constituents gave them a mandate so to do, or again, do the words mean that as the payment of wages was a subject with which they had legally power to deal, the amount of their funds which they devoted to that purpose was their own concern which no auditor had jurisdiction to revise, or in reference to which he could surcharge anything? The whole system of audit to which the Legislature has subjected every municipal corporation or council is a most emphatic protest against such opinions as these. . . .

[A]s wages are remuneration for services, the words "think fit" must, I think, be construed to mean "as the employer shall think fitting and proper" for the services rendered. It cannot, in my view, mean that the employer, especially an employer dealing with moneys not entirely his own, may pay to his employee wages of any amount he pleases. Still less does it mean that he can pay gratuities or gifts to his employees disguised under the name of wages. . . .

What is a reasonable wage at any time must depend, of course, on the circumstances which then exist in the labour market. I do not say there must be any cheeseparing or that the datum line, as I have called it, must never be exceeded to any extent, or that employees may not be generously treated. But it does not appear to me that there is any rational proportion between the rates of wages at which the labour of these women is paid and the rates at which they would be reasonably remunerated for their services to the council.

I concur with the auditor in thinking that what has been given to the women as wages is really to a great extent gifts and gratuities disguised as wages, and is therefore illegal. The council have evidently been betrayed into the course they have followed by taking into consideration the several matters mentioned in Mr. Scurr's affidavit, which they ought not properly to have taken into their consideration at all, and consequently did not properly exercise the discretion placed in them, but acted contrary to law: see *R.* v. *Adamson* (1875) 1 Q.B.D. 201; *R.* v. *St. Pancras Vestry*, 24 Q.B.D. 371 [above, p. 338]; *R.* v. *Board of Education* [1910] 2 K.B. 165 at p. 179.

I think the appeal succeeds.

LORD SUMNER: . . . The respondents conceded that for wages fixed *mala fide* no exemption from review could be claimed and that the mere magnitude of the wages paid, relatively to the wages for which the same service was procurable, might be enough in itself to establish bad faith. This admission, I am sure, was rightly made, but it leads to two conclusions. First, the final words of the section are not absolute, but are subject to an implied qualification of good faith—"as the board may *bona fide* think fit." Is the implication of good faith all? That is a qualification drawn from the general legal doctrine, that persons who hold public office have a legal responsibility towards those whom they represent—not merely towards those who vote for them—to the discharge of which they must honestly apply their minds. *Bona fide* here cannot simply mean that they are not making a profit out of their office or acting in it from private spite, nor is *bona fide* a short way of saying that the council has acted within the ambit of its powers and therefore not contrary to law. It must mean that they are giving their minds to the comprehension and their wills to the discharge of their duty towards that public, whose money and local business they administer.

The purpose, however, of the whole audit is to ensure wise and prudent administration and to recover for the council's funds money that should not have been taken out of them. If, having examined the expenditure and found clear proof of bad faith, which admittedly would open the account, the auditor further found that the councillors' evil minds had missed their mark, and the expenditure itself was right, then the expenditure itself would not be "contrary to law" and could not be disallowed. Bad faith admittedly vitiates the council's purported exercise of its discretion, but the auditor is not confined to asking, if the discretion, such as it may be, has been honestly exercised. He has to restrain expenditure within proper limits. His mission is to inquire if there is any excess over what is reasonable. I do not find any words limiting his functions merely to the case of bad faith, or obliging him to leave the ratepayers unprotected from the effects on their pockets of honest stupidity or unpractical idealism. The breach in the words "as they may think fit," which the admitted implication as to bad faith makes, is wide enough to make the necessary implication one both of honesty and of reasonableness. It might be otherwise if the express words were to be read as absolute and unqualified, but if they are to be read as subject to some qualification, I think that qualification must be derived from the purpose of the statutory audit, which is the protection of the ratepayers' pockets and not the immunity of spend-thrift administration. Next, in the case and for the purpose assumed, the auditor, when he reviews the accounts, is entitled and bound to use his own judgment as to the wages that would be reasonable under the circumstances. He must do so, in order to measure from that datum the excess of the wages paid, and to decide if the excess is so great as to evidence *mala fides*. So it will be also with the courts of law on appeal. If in the case of bad faith the auditor is capable of finding a reasonable amount and is bound to proceed to do so, I find no words in the section which, on a sound construction, preclude him from doing the same thing when good faith is present, and I think that in both cases the reasonableness of the amounts is a subject for his review. . . . I can find nothing in the Acts empowering bodies to which the Metropolis Management Act 1855 applies which authorizes them to be guided by their personal opinions on political, economic or social questions in administering the funds which they derive from levying rates.

Much was said at the Bar about the wide discretion conferred by the Local Government Acts on local authorities. In a sense this is true, but the meaning of the term needs careful examination. What has been said in cases which lie outside the provisions as to audit altogether is not necessarily applicable to matters which are concerned with the expenditure of public money. There are many matters which the courts are indisposed to question. Though they are the ultimate judges of what is lawful and what is unlawful to borough councils, they often accept the decisions of the local authority simply because they are themselves ill equipped to weigh the merits of one solution of a practical question as against another. This, however, is not a recognition of the absolute character of the local authority's discretion, but of the limits within which it is practicable to question it. There is nothing about a borough council that corresponds to autonomy. It has great responsibilities, but the limits of its powers and of its independence are such as the law, mostly statutory, may have laid down, and there is no presumption against the accountability of the authority. Everything depends on the construction of the sections applicable. In the present case, I think that the auditor was entitled to inquire into all the items of expenditure in question, to ask whether in incurring them the council had been guided by aims and objects not open to them or had disregarded considerations by which they should have been guided, and to the extent to which they had in consequence exceeded a reasonable expenditure, it was his duty to disallow the items.

LORD WRENBURY: . . . The cardinal word upon which emphasis is principally to be laid is the word "wages." Wages are the pecuniary return for services rendered. To determine the proper or true amount which in a given state of facts has been paid or is payable for services rendered is far from easy. It can never be determined with exactness. It is impossible to name in any particular case an amount which if diminished by 1*s*. a week would be too small, and if increased by 1*s*. a week would be too large. But it is possible to name an amount which would certainly be too large—as, for instance, if a charwoman were paid 2*l*. a day. Using my best endeavour to state the matter in general terms, I express it thus:

Wages in a particular service are such sum as a reasonable person, guiding himself by an investigation of the current rate in fact found to be paid in the particular industry, and acting upon the principle that efficient service is better commanded by paying an efficient wage, would find to be the proper sum. The figure to be sought is not the lowest figure at which the service could be obtained, nor is it the highest figure which a generous employer might, upon grounds of philanthropy or generosity, pay out of his own pocket. It is a figure which is not to be based upon or increased by motives of philanthropy nor even of generosity stripped of commercial considerations. It is such figure as is the reasonable pecuniary equivalent of the service rendered. Anything beyond this is not wages. It is an addition to wages, and is a gratuity. The authority is to pay not such sum but such wages as they think fit.

I pass from the word "wages" to the words "as [they] may think fit." We have heard argument upon the question whether these words are or are not to be understood as if the word "reasonable" or "reasonably" were inserted, so that the sentence would run "as they reasonably think fit" or "such reasonable wages as they may think fit." Is the verb "think" equivalent to "reasonably think"? My Lords, to my mind there is no difference in the meaning, whether the word "reasonably" or "reasonable" is in or out. . . . I rest my opinion upon higher grounds. A person in whom is vested a discretion must exercise his discretion upon reasonable grounds. A discretion does not empower a man to do what he likes merely because he is minded to do so—he must in the exercise of his discretion do not what he likes but what he ought. In other words, he must, by the use of his reason, ascertain and follow the course which reason directs. He must act reasonably.

Thirdly, and lastly, I point to the word "fit." That word means, I think, "fitting" or "suitable." The words "as they think fit" do not mean "as they choose." The measure is not the volition of the person vested with the discretion, it is the suitability or adequacy or fitness of the amount in the reasonable judgment of the person vested with the discretion.

[LORD CARSON delivered a short speech, concurring with some hesitancy. He held that it was "open to the auditor, upon coming to the conclusions as stated in his affidavit, to draw the inference that the council were not engaged in merely fixing a rate of wages, but were affected by considerations which could not be held to come within the ambit of the discretion entrusted to them."]

Appeal allowed.

Notes and questions

1. One of the problems of interpretation considered by the House was that while the power under section 62 of the 1855 Act was a general power to employ

officers and servants and to pay "such salaries and wages" as the authority "may think fit," other statutes which conferred on local authorities powers to employ persons for the purposes of the relevant statute often gave power to pay "reasonable" wages. Lord Buckmaster (p. 588) regarded section 62 as the dominant section. Lord Atkinson thought that "in each and every case the payment of all salaries and wages must be 'reasonable.' I see no difficulty in so construing the words of section 62" (p. 599). Lord Wrenbury thought that "there is no difference in the meaning, whether the word 'reasonably' or 'reasonable' is in or out" (p. 613). Nevertheless his Lordship did not rely on the presence of "reasonable" in some statutes—it was not obvious which provisions should give way. Lord Sumner and Lord Carson did not deal with the problem.

2. *Roberts* v. *Hopwood* also settled that the district auditor's power to disallow an "item" contrary to law was not limited to the situation where a complete item of account was *ultra vires* (as it would have been, for example, if the council had had no power to employ and pay any servants at all), but could be used in *excessive* expenditure on an otherwise lawful item—the excess only being *ultra vires*. See further on local authority audit, above, p. 28.

3. Note the attitude of the majority in the Court of Appeal ([1924] 2 K.B. 695) who were willing to defer to the views of elected representatives of the people in such a matter as this, except in a clear case. Is the decision of the House of Lords correct, leaving aside the purple passages? Would the case have been decided differently had there been no stress on the quasi-fiduciary duty owed by local authorities to ratepayers? Can any general propositions of law concerning "reasonableness" in the exercise of discretions be derived from this case?

4. The leaders of Poplar Borough Council had recently been in conflict with central government on another issue: the payment of outdoor relief to the able-bodied poor. The story of "Poplarism" is told by B. Keith-Lucas, [1962] P.L. 52, and further background information is given by G. W. Jones, [1973] P.L. 11 ("Herbert Morrison and Poplarism" and N. Branson, *Poplarism* (1979)). See also *Roberts* v. *Cunningham* (1925) 42 T.L.R. 162 and *Woolwich Corporation* v. *Roberts* (1927) 96 L.J.K.B. 757, where two other councils which paid "model" wages took their cases to the House of Lords.

5. At one stage in the events at Poplar, the councillors were imprisoned for their contempt of court in disobeying a writ of mandamus issued by the King's Bench Divisional Court. Some marched off to prison headed by the town band (at the cost of £10 which was subsequently disallowed by the District Auditor). Their imprisonment was a considerable political embarrassment for the Minister of Health.

6. In *Prescott* v. *Birmingham Corporation* [1955] 1 Ch. 210, the corporation, which had power to charge "such fares as they may think fit" on their public transport services resolved to introduce a scheme for free bus travel for old people. The corporation sought the consent of the traffic commissioners as required by the Road Traffic Act 1930. Consent was given, subject to the payment of £90,000 from the general rate fund to the account of the transport undertaking. A ratepayer brought an action for a declaration that the scheme was *ultra vires*. Vaisey J. and the Court of Appeal granted the declaration. Jenkins L.J. stated at pp. 235–238 that if a trustee running a bus service allowed a class of persons whom he considered badly-off to travel free or at reduced fares:

> "it may be that passengers charged the full fare could not object on that account. But we apprehend that the *cestuis que trustent* certainly could. . . .
>
> Local authorities are not, of course, trustees for their ratepayers, but they do, we think, owe an analogous fiduciary duty to their ratepayers in relation to the application of funds contributed by the latter. Thus local authorities running an omnibus undertaking at the risk of their ratepayers, in the sense that any deficiencies must be met by an addition to the rates are not, in our view,

entitled, merely on the strength of a general power, to charge different fares to different passengers or classes of passengers, to make a gift to a particular class of persons of rights of free travel on their vehicles, simply because the local authority concerned are of opinion that the favoured class of persons ought, on benevolent or philanthropic grounds, to be accorded that benefit. In other words, they are not, in our view, entitled to use their discriminatory power as proprietors of the transport undertaking in order to confer out of rates a special benefit on some particular class of inhabitants whom they, as the local authority for the town or district in question, may think deserving of such assistance. In the absence of clear statutory authority, for such a proceeding (which to our mind a mere general power to charge differential fares certainly is not) we would, for our part, regard it as illegal, on the ground that, to put the matter bluntly, it would amount simply to the making of a gift or present in money's worth to a particular section of the local community at the expense of the general body of ratepayers. . . .

We are not persuaded by Mr. Rowe's argument to the effect that the relevant legislation would allow the defendants to charge no fares at all to anyone and to finance their transport undertaking entirely out of the rates. We think it is clearly implicit in the legislation, that while it was left to the defendants to decide what fares should be charged within any prescribed statutory maxima for the time being in force, the undertaking was to be run as a business venture, or, in other words, that fares fixed by the defendants at their discretion, in accordance with ordinary business principles, were to be charged. That is not to say that in operating their transport undertaking the defendants should be guided by considerations of profit to the exclusion of all other considerations. They should, no doubt, aim at providing an efficient service of omnibuses at reasonable cost, and it may be that this objective is impossible of attainment without some degree of loss. But it by no means follows that they should go out of their way to make losses by giving away rights of free travel.

As to the instances of legitimate discrimination given by Mr. Rowe, the concession in favour of workmen is enjoined by statute, and therefore does not advance his argument. The concessions in favour of children (who travel free or at half-fares according to age) are of a kind commonly, if not universally, accorded by transport undertakings, and, we should have thought, readily justifiable on business principles. The practice of allowing free travel to blind and disabled persons may, or may not, be strictly justifiable, but may perhaps be classed as a minor act of elementary charity to which no reasonable ratepayer would be likely to object.

In our opinion the scheme now in question goes beyond anything which can reasonably be regarded as authorized by the discretionary power of fixing fares and differentiation in the fares charged to different passengers or classes of passengers possessed by the defendants under the relevant legislation, and is, accordingly, *ultra vires* the defendants.

. . . [T]he scheme fares no better if its adoption is considered as a purported exercise by the defendants of their discretion in a matter not, on the face of it, necessarily outside the general ambit of the discretionary power of differentiation of fares conferred on them by the relevant legislation. . . . If we are right in thinking that, after all allowance is made for their special position as a local authority, the defendants owe a duty to their ratepayers to operate their transport undertaking substantially on business lines, we think it must necessarily follow that, in adopting the scheme, the defendants misapprehended the nature and scope of the discretion conferred on them, and mistakenly supposed that it enabled them to confer benefits, in the shape of rights of free travel, on any class or classes of the local inhabitants appearing to them to be deserving of such benefits by reason of their advanced age and limited means. Accordingly, if the case is to be regarded as turning upon the question whether the decision to adopt the scheme was a proper exercise of a discretion conferred on the defendants with respect to the differential treatment of passengers in the matter of fares, the answer, in our opinion, must be that it was not a proper exercise of such discretion. We think some support for this view is to be derived from the speeches in the House of Lords in *Roberts* v. *Hopwood* [1925] A.C. 578." [See above, pp. 363–369.]

See case notes at 72 L.Q.R. 237; 18 M.L.R. 159; [1955] C.L.J. 135. Parliament intervened to validate existing concessions by the Public Service Vehicles (Travel Concessions) Act 1955, and to give general powers to make such concessions by the Travel Concessions Act 1964. See now the Transport Act 1985, ss.93–105.

7. Consider the implications of Lord Sumner's suggestion that where bad faith is proved but the amount of expenditure is reasonable, the courts cannot interfere. See *Re Walker's Decision* [1944] K.B. 644; *Robins* v. *Minister of Health* [1939] 1 K.B. 520 at pp. 537–538; *de Smith*, pp. 328–329.

8. A modern analysis of *Roberts* v. *Hopwood* is provided by P. Fennell, "Roberts v. Hopwood: the Rule against Socialism" (1986) 13 J.L.S. 401. He comments (p. 419):

"In *Roberts* v. *Hopwood* the conduct of the councillors was stigmatised as unreasonable, irrational, arbitrary and eccentric. In subsequent cases the courts have ruled that to policies which require expenditure of the rates is attached the requirement that the interests of the ratepayers must be considered at every turn. The connection between socialism and irresponsibility is never made as explicitly as it was in Lord Atkinson's judgment, because it is neither politic nor necessary to do so. A party elected on a policy of reducing rates and charging for services is already doing its legal duty; a party elected on a policy of increasing welfare services has it yet to do."

See also A. Bradney, "Facade: The Poplar Case" (1983) 43 N.I.L.Q. 1, who examines the political background of the judges who heard the case.

9. *Roberts* v. *Hopwood* was distinguished by the Divisional Court in *Pickwell* v. *Camden London Borough Council* [1983] 1 Q.B. 962, above, p. 28.

10. The notion of a "fiduciary duty" owed to ratepayers (now also chargepayers/council tax-payers) was one of a number of grounds upon which the House of Lords ruled against the Greater London Council's introduction of its new "Fares Fair" public transport subsidy policy in 1981: *Bromley London Borough Council* v. *Greater London Council* [1982] 1 A.C. 768. As the extracts below show, the case is also an example of successful challenge on grounds (i) that the GLC intended to exercise its statutory power to make grants for purposes beyond those implicit in the legislation; and (ii) that the GLC had failed properly to retain discretion because the majority Labour group regarded itself as bound by its election manifesto to go ahead with the promised policy once elected.

BROMLEY LONDON BOROUGH COUNCIL v. GREATER LONDON COUNCIL

[1982] 1 A.C. 768; [1982] 2 W.L.R. 92; [1982] 1 All E.R. 129 (House of Lords)

The facts are given by Lord Wilberforce in his speech.

LORD WILBERFORCE: My Lords, this case concerns the validity of a supplementary precept issued by the Greater London Council to the

London Borough of Bromley for the levying of a rate of 6·1p in the pound in respect of the period October 1, 1981, to March 31, 1982. The precept was issued pursuant to a resolution of the G.L.C. dated July 21, 1981. This resolution, in turn, was passed by way of implementation of a commitment, contained in an election manifesto for the election in May 1979, upon which the present majority in the G.L.C. was elected.

The supplementary precept went to all London boroughs. Bromley applied to the High Court for judicial review of the action of the G.L.C. by way of certiorari. They failed in the High Court but the Court of Appeal granted their application, quashed the supplementary precept and declared that it was *ultra vires*, null, void and of no effect.

The London Transport Executive is a party to the proceedings because the precept was issued in order to enable the G.L.C. to finance, by grant to the L.T.E., the cost of reducing L.T.E. fares overall by 25 per cent. and of introducing a simplified zonal system. If the precept is set aside, the L.T.E. will not be able to maintain these changes, and to reverse them will cause considerable dislocation.

The precept is attacked on two main grounds: (1) That it is beyond the powers of the G.L.C. as defined by the Transport (London) Act 1969. (2) That even if the G.L.C. has the necessary statutory powers, the issuance of the precept was an invalid exercise of its discretion under the Act. This ground itself may be divisible into two contentions (a) that the exercise of the G.L.C.'s discretion was unreasonable, or (b) that the G.L.C. when deciding to issue the precept did not take relevant considerations into account, or did take into account irrelevant considerations or misdirected itself as to the law.

Both of these grounds depend upon the fact, which it is right to emphasise at the start, that the G.L.C., though a powerful body, with an electorate larger and a budget more considerable than those of many nation states, is the creation of statute and only has powers given to it by statute. The courts will give full recognition to the wide discretion conferred upon the council by Parliament and will not lightly interfere with its exercise. But its actions, unlike those of Parliament, are examinable by the courts, whether on grounds of vires, or on principles of administrative law (those two may overlap). It makes no difference on the question of legality (as opposed to reasonableness—see *Secretary of State for Education and Science* v. *Tameside Metropolitan Borough Council* [1977] A.C. 1014), whether the impugned action was or was not submitted to or approved by the relevant electorate: that cannot confer validity upon *ultra vires* action. Indeed, it forms part of Bromley's argument, that the G.L.C. in so far as it considered that it has a commitment to bring about the reduction in fares, regardless of other considerations, misdirected itself in law.

The first ground of attack involves a question of construction of the Act of 1969. . . .

The general duty of the G.L.C. is stated, in section 1, as being to develop and encourage measures which will promote the provision of "integrated, efficient and economic transport facilities and services for Greater London."

There has been a good deal of argument as to the meaning of these words, particularly of "economic": no doubt they are vague, possibly with design. It has been strongly argued that the word means something like "on business principles" but for present purposes I will take it to mean "cost-effective," or "making the most effective use of resources in the context of an integrated system"—the meaning most favourable to the G.L.C.

Section 3 gives the G.L.C. power to make grants to the L.T.E. "for any purpose" and no doubt these words are wide enough to cover grants to revenue as well as for capital purposes. The section cannot, however, be read in isolation, and it is necessary to examine the rest of the Act in order to ascertain the framework in which this power is exercisable. Its extent and the manner in which it is to be exercised must be controlled by the fact that the G.L.C. owes a duty to two different classes. First, under its responsibility for meeting the needs of Greater London, it must provide for transport users: these include not only the residents of London, but persons travelling to and in London from outside (*e.g.* commuters) and tourists. Most of these will not pay rates to the G.L.C. Secondly, it owes a duty of a fiduciary character to its ratepayers who have to provide the money. These, it is said, represent 40 per cent. only of the electorate and probably a smaller proportion of the travelling public: they would themselves, most likely, also be travellers. Most of the rates (62 per cent.) have to be found from commercial ratepayers. For the extent of this fiduciary duty see *Prescott* v. *Birmingham Corporation* [1955] Ch. 210, a decision which remains valid in principle although free travel for selected categories has since been authorised by statute.

These duties must be fairly balanced one against the other: see *Roberts* v. *Hopwood* [1925] A.C. 578 and *Luby* v. *Newcastle-under-Lyme Corporation* [1964] 2 Q.B. 64, 72. *Roberts* v. *Hopwood*, which also remains authoritative as to principle although social considerations may have changed since 1925, was concerned with a case where there had been an election which, it was claimed, gave a mandate to the council to pay the wages in question, but Lord Atkinson at p. 596, emphatically rejected the proposition that however excessive or illegal their scale of wages might be, they were bound to put it into force—against the interests of ratepayers—because their constituents gave them a mandate so to do: see also *per* Lord Sumner, at pp. 607, 609 and Lord Wrenbury at p. 613.

Part II of this Act, containing sections 4–15 is headed "The London Transport Executive." The executive is set up by section 4 "For the purpose of implementing the policies which it is the duty of the council under section 1 to develop." Sections 5 and 7 are critical for present purposes so I quote the relevant parts:

"5—(1). Subject always to the requirements of section 7(3) of this Act, it shall be the general duty of the executive to exercise and perform their functions, in accordance with principles from time to time laid down or approved by the council, in such manner as, in conjunction with the railways board and the bus company, and with due regard to efficiency, economy and safety of operation, to provide or secure the provision of such public passenger transport services as best meet the needs for the time being of Greater London."

Here we find another triad of words with "economy" instead of "economic." Again, much fine argument has been given to them. If it makes any difference, I would read the words "of operation" as related only to "safety," but in any case I think that the triad must be taken as a whole. They seem to me to point rather more clearly than does section 1 in the direction of running on businesslike or commercial lines, but it would be reading "economy" too narrowly to treat it as requiring the executive to make, or try to make a profit. It does, on the other hand, prevent the L.T.E. from conducting its undertakings on other than economic considerations. . . .

[His Lordship set out the terms of s.7, and the rival arguments and continued:]

In my opinion there are two clear provisions in the Act. The first is in section 7(3)(*b*). This states the obligation of the London Transport Executive to make good a deficit in the year following a deficit year. This is an obligation, the meeting of which the executive is to ensure as far as practicable. In my opinion this points to the taking of action which it is in the power of the executive to take. On the other hand, though I feel less confident about this . . . I am willing to accept that, subject to the executive discharging the responsibilities cast upon it, it may make provision in its revenue account for grants in aid of revenue, actual or assumed. The corresponding provision as regards the G.L.C. is section 7(6) which dovetails with section 7(3). This recognises that the duty stated in section 7(3)(*b*) (to make up a deficit in year two) is one which "falls to be complied with by the executive," and then obliges the council in performing its functions to have regard to that duty and take action which will enable the executive to comply with those requirements. Such actions might take several forms: the council might direct fares to be raised or services to be adjusted. Or the council could decide to make a grant. But it can only do that after it has "had regard" to the executive's duty under section 7(3). The respective statutory obligations of the G.L.C. and London Transport Executive fit in with one another: the London Transport Executive must carry out its duty as defined in section 7(3): the G.L.C. cannot exercise its powers unless and until the London Transport Executive carries out that duty and must then do so with proper regard to its fiduciary duty to its ratepayers. If these constraints were not to exist, there would be no limit upon the power of the G.L.C. to make grants in aid of revenue, since the Act provides for no governmental control. I find it impossible, in the light of the previous history and of the far from definite language used, to accept that Parliament could have intended that this should be so. To say this is not to impose upon the London Transport Executive a rigid obligation to balance its accounts every year, nor, as it was at one time put in argument, to maximise fares. There is flexibility in the words "so far as practicable," and the obligatory establishment of a reserve gives room for manoeuvre (as indeed the London Transport Executive accounts from 1970 onwards show). But, given this, it appears to me clear that neither the executive in making its proposals, nor the G.L.C. in accepting them, could have power totally to disregard any responsibility for ensuring, so far as practicable, that outgoings are met by revenue, and that the London Transport Executive runs its business on economic lines. . . .

This, then, being, as I interpret them, the effect of the applicable statutory provisions, it remains to ask whether the council and the executive acted in accordance with them. In my opinion they plainly did not. The L.T.E., as regards the year 1980, was running a deficit. Acting, as I am willing to accept, in accordance with their obligations under the Act of 1969, it submitted to the G.L.C., in November 1980, proposals to achieve a break-even by a possible increase in fare revenue, increased productivity, and an assumed G.L.C. grant of £80 million. Its budget contains a careful review of the measures taken, by way of economy and better fare collection, to keep the deficit down as far as practicable. Obviously this was not the only possible budget at the time, but in its preparation and structure it represents a serious attempt to comply with the Act. If a radical departure is made from that budget, that seems to suggest, strongly, that it is made outside the Act.

After the change in control in May 1981, the new leader of the G.L.C. immediately intimated to the L.T.E. that it should submit proposals involving a general reduction in fares of 25 per cent., proposals which would inevitably and greatly (to the extent of about £69m.) increase the operating deficit. This increased deficit would have to be borne by the G.L.C. ratepayers, and, as it soon appeared, would automatically bring about a loss of rate support grant (under central government legislation) involving an additional heavy burden on the ratepayers of an amount (approximately £50m., attributable to the fare reduction) not far short of the whole cost of the 25 per cent. reduction itself.

The L.T.E. submitted proposals, including in them a new zoning scheme. (This, in itself, may well be advantageous but is wholly ancillary to the 25 per cent. reduction.) The G.L.C. approved them. In my opinion, both the G.L.C. and L.T.E. were in breach of their duties under the Act. The L.T.E. was, in its own words, meeting the G.L.C. requirement: it was not, and could not have thought that it was complying with its obligations under sections 5 and 7 of the Act of 1969. The G.L.C. could not have considered (as it was obliged to do before it could make a grant to revenue) that the L.T.E. was complying with its obligation under section 7(3). Furthermore, in deciding to proceed to make a grant to support the fare reduction, once it became apparent that the ratepayers' burden would be approximately doubled, it acted in breach of its fiduciary duty as defined above. It failed to hold the balance between the transport users and the ratepayers as it should have done.

I am therefore clearly of opinion that the actions of the G.L.C. and of the L.T.E. were *ultra vires* the Act of 1969. . . .

LORD DIPLOCK: It cannot be too emphatically stated that your Lordships in this appeal are not concerned with the wisdom or, indeed, the fairness of the G.L.C.'s decision to reduce by 25 per cent. the fares charged in Greater London by the London Transport Executive ("L.T.E.") which made it necessary to issue the supplementary precept, or the greater part of it. All that your Lordships are concerned with is the legality of that decision: was it within the limited powers that Parliament has conferred by statute upon the G.L.C.? . . .

[Lord Diplock reviewed the relevant statutory provisions and concluded:]

So I conclude that the mere fact that a grant on revenue account is made by the G.L.C. to the L.T.E. to enable it to comply with a direction to reduce fares to a level at which, in the absence of the grant, its revenue account could not be maintained in balance, is not *of itself* sufficient to render *ultra vires* either the grant or a precept issued by the G.L.C. to raise the money for the grant from rates.

This brings me back to the crucial section of the Act, section 1, to see what limitations (if any) it imposes upon the choice of policy by the G.L.C. as to the relative proportions in which the cost of running the passenger transport undertaking of the L.T.E. is to be met out of the fares paid by passengers or out of rates paid by ratepayers. Central to this question is the legal structure of the G.L.C. and the categories of persons to whom its duties, both generally and in particular in relation to public passenger transport, are owed.

When a statute speaks, as section 1 does, of a "duty" of a local authority composed of democractically elected members, it is speaking of the collective legal duty of all those members acting through the ordinary procedure of debate and resolution, to make choices of policy and of action that they believe to be in the best interests (weighing, where necessary, one against the other) of all those categories of persons to whom their collective duty is owed. This will involve identifying the persons to whom the particular duty is owed and in the event of a conflict of interest between one category and another deciding where the balance ought to lie. In the case of public passenger transport in Greater London those categories are: (1) potential passengers by bus and train in Greater London whether resident there or not; (2) residents in Greater London, who may be assumed to derive benefit from the general mobility of people living in or within commuting distance of Greater London resulting from the availability of a public passenger transport system, even though the particular resident may happen to make little or no use of it himself; and (3) ratepayers in Greater London, to the extent that they are required to contribute to the cost of the system. These three categories overlap but do not coincide. Most persons in category (2) will also be in category (1), and it will be convenient to refer to these as "passengers," but, as mentioned earlier, there is no such coincidence between either of these two categories and category (3), the ratepayers. They constitute only 40 per cent. of residents and that 40 per cent. bears only 38 per cent. of the total burden borne by all ratepayers. The conflict of interest lies between passengers and the ratepayers.

I have left out electors as such, as constituting a separate category. A council member once elected is not the delegate of those who voted in his favour only; he is the representative of all the electors (*i.e.* adult residents) in his ward. If he fought the election on the basis of policies for the future put forward in the election manifesto of a particular political party, he presumably himself considered that in the circumstances contemplated in the manifesto those policies were in the best interest of the electors in his ward, and, if the democratic system as at present practised in local government is to survive, the fact that he received a majority of votes of those electors who took enough interest in the future policies to be adopted by the G.L.C. to cause them to cast their votes, is a factor to which considerable weight ought to be given by him when participating in the collective duty of the G.L.C. to decide whether to implement those policies in the circumstances that exist at the time that the decision falls to be made. That this may properly be regarded as a weighty factor is implicit in the speeches in the House in *Secretary of State for Education and Science* v. *Tameside Metropolitan Borough Council* [1977] A.C. 1014; although the issues dealt with in that case were very different from those arising in the present appeals. In this respect, I see no difference between those members of the G.L.C. who are members of what as a result of the election becomes the majority party and those who are members of a minority party. In neither case when the time comes to play their part in performing the collective duty of the G.L.C. to make choices of policy or action on particular matters, must members treat themselves as irrevocably bound to carry out pre-announced policies contained in election manifestos even though, by that time, changes of circumstances have occurred that were unforeseen when those policies were announced and would add significantly to the disadvantages that would result from carrying them out.

My Lords, the conflicting interests with the G.L.C. had to balance in deciding whether or not to go ahead with the 25 per cent. reduction in fares, notwithstanding the loss of grant from central government funds that this would entail, were those of passengers and the ratepayers. It is well established by the authorities to which my noble and learned friend,

Lord Wilberforce, has already referred, that a local authority owes a fiduciary duty to the ratepayers from whom it obtains moneys needed to carry out its statutory functions, and that this includes a duty not to expend those moneys thriftlessly but to deploy the full financial resources available to it to the best advantage; the financial resources of the G.L.C. that are relevant to the present appeals being the rate fund obtained by issuing precepts and the grants from central government respectively. The existence of this duty throws light upon the true construction of the much-debated phrase in section 1(1) "integrated, efficient and economic transport facilities and services." "Economic" in this context must I think mean in the economic interests of passengers and the ratepayers looked at together, *i.e.* keeping to a minimum the total financial burden that the persons in these two categories have to share between them for the provision by the L.T.E. in conjunction with the railways board and the bus company of an integrated and efficient public passenger transport system for Greater London. As I have already indicated I think that the G.L.C. had a discretion as to the proportions in which that total financial burden should be allocated between passengers and the ratepayers. What are the limits of that discretion and whether those limits would have been exceeded if the only effect of the G.L.C.'s decision to instruct the L.T.E. to lower its fares by 25 per cent. had been to transfer to the ratepayers the cost (amounting to some £69m.) of the financial relief that was afforded to the passengers by the lowering of the fares is a difficult question on which the arguments for and against are by no means all one way. Fortunately I do not find it necessary to decide that question in the present appeals. It does not, in my view, arise, because the G.L.C.'s decision was not simply about allocating a total financial burden between passengers and the ratepayers, it was also a decision to increase that total burden so as nearly to double it and to place the whole of the increase on the ratepayers. For, as the G.L.C. well knew when it took the decision to reduce the fares, it would entail a loss of rate grant from central government funds amounting to some £50 million, which would have to be made good by the ratepayers as a result of the G.L.C.'s decision. So the total financial burden to be shared by passengers and the ratepayers for the provision of an integrated and efficient public passenger transport system was to be increased by an extra £50 million as a result of the decision, without any equivalent improvement in the efficiency of the system, and the whole of the extra £50 million was to be recovered from the ratepayers. That would, in my view, clearly be a thriftless use of moneys obtained by the G.L.C. from ratepayers and a deliberate failure to deploy to the best advantage the full financial resources available to it by avoiding any action that would involve forfeiting grants from central government funds. It was thus a breach of the fiduciary duty owed by the G.L.C. to the ratepayers. I accordingly agree with your Lordships that the precept issued pursuant to the decision was *ultra vires* and therefore void.

I would also have held the decision and the precept to be void upon another ground . . . the members of the majority party by whose votes the effective resolutions were passed, acted upon an erroneous view . . . that from first to last they regarded the G.L.C. irrevocably committed to carry out the reduction, whatever might be the additional cost to the rate-payers, because a reduction of that amount had been pre-announced in the election manifesto issued by the political party whose candidates formed a majority of the members elected. . . .

LORD KEITH OF KINKEL: . . . In my opinion the starting point for the consideration of this issue must be *Prescott* v. *Birmingham Corporation* [1955] Ch. 210. [His Lordship summarised this case, see above, p. 370, emphasising the requirement that fares be fixed "in accordance with ordinary business principles" and continued:]

The effect of the decision has been reversed by statute in relation to free travel for certain selected categories of persons, including the old (see section 138 of the Transport Act 1968, and, as regards London, section 40 of the Act of 1969), but the general principle laid down remains valid.

I turn to an examination of the Act of 1969 in order to determine whether that general principle has been statutorily departed from as regards London Transport. . . .

[Lord Keith considered the terms of the legislation and concluded:]

. . . I have reached the conclusion that both the London Transport Executive and the G.L.C. acted *ultra vires* in relation to the proposed reduction of fares. It must follow that the supplementary precept issued for the purpose of financing the reduction was also *ultra vires* and must be quashed.

In these circumstances it is unnecessary to consider the second issue arising in the appeal, namely, whether the G.L.C., while not acting outwith its statutory powers, nevertheless exercised its discretion in a manner which was unreasonable and otherwise contrary to the principles laid down in *Associated Provincial Picture Houses Ltd.* v. *Wednesbury Corporation* [1948] 1 K.B. 223. . . .

LORD SCARMAN: [considered the statutory provisions and concluded:]

I conclude, therefore, that the G.L.C. may make grants to provide not only for past, but for anticipated losses. It follows that the G.L.C. and the executive are entitled to anticipate a trading loss and to bring into their accounts grant to offset the resulting deficit.

It is the next step in the appellants' argument which I think is not authorised by the Act. They say that it follows that deficit on trading account is acceptable, even if it be, wholly or to some degree, avoidable, provided the G.L.C. judges it is justifiable on the ground of transport need. But, though revenue account may include grant income, it by no means follows that the Act entitles the G.L.C. and the executive to accept as an objective of policy a deficit upon trading account merely because it best meets what they regard as the interests of the travelling public and "transport need." So to interpret section 7(3) is, in my judgment, to disregard the duty owed to the ratepayers. The subsection is, however, capable of another interpretation which is consistent with that duty. This interpretation, which I accept, is that, while permitting advance budgeting, it, nevertheless requires the executive so to provide its services as to ensure, so far as practicable, that deficit is avoided. Though the executive may be compelled by circumstances to budget for a loss which will have to be made good by grant, the subsection requires them to avoid it, if they can. Their principal weapon is fares income. The subsection, though it envisages budgeting for a deficit, permits it not as an object of social or transport policy, but as a course of action which it may not be practicable or possible to avoid. Loss may be unavoidable: but it does not thereby become an acceptable object of policy.

To conclude . . . I find nothing in section 7 which cuts down or modifies the fiduciary duty of the G.L.C. to its ratepayers—a duty which requires it to see that the services of this instrument, the executive, are provided on business principles so as to ensure, so far as practicable, that no avoidable loss falls on the ratepayers.

LORD BRANDON OF OAKBROOK [considered the statutory provisions and concluded:]

. . . I am of opinion that it was beyond the powers of the L.T.E. to submit to the G.L.C. for their approval, and beyond the powers of the G.L.C. to approve proposals for an overall reduction of 25 per cent. in the level of fares charged by the L.T.E. for the carriage of passengers in trains and buses operated by them.

It follows that I would dismiss these two appeals on that ground alone.

My Lords, as I indicated earlier, if the G.L.C. and the L.T.E. fail on the question of powers, as I consider for the reasons which I have given that they do, it is not necessary to go on to examine the further question of discretion. In case I am wrong about the question of powers, however, I propose to deal shortly also with the question of discretion.

In considering that question it is necessary to assume, contrary to the opinion which I have expressed above, that it is the intention of the Act that the provision by the L.T.E. of proper passenger services for Greater London is to be financed partly by fares paid by passengers and partly by income grants from the G.L.C. derived ultimately from rates levied on the ratepayers of the London boroughs; and further that the extent to which such provision is financed from the one source or the other is a matter for the administrative discretion of the G.L.C.

On those two assumptions the question is whether the G.L.C., in approving the mix of somewhat under 70 per cent. and somewhat over 30 per cent., which they did approve, exercised their administrative discretion lawfully.

In my view it is plain for two reasons that the G.L.C. did not exercise their discretion lawfully. The first reason is that, if and in so far as they exercised their discretion at all, they considered themselves bound to exercise it in the way they did because they had promised to do so in their election manifesto. It is, of course, entirely appropriate for a council, the majority of whose members have been elected after setting out a particular policy in their election manifesto, to take into account, and give considerable weight to, that circumstance when exercising their discretion in relation to that policy after they have been elected and come to power. It is, however, entirely wrong for such a majority to regard themselves as bound to exercise their discretion in relation to that policy in accordance with their election promises, whatever the cost and other countervailing considerations may turn out to be. In my view it is an inevitable inference from the evidence taken as a whole that the majority on the G.L.C., when they approved the proposals for a 25 per cent. overall reduction in fares, were motivated solely for the belief that, because they had promised such a reduction before their election, they were completely and irrevocably bound to implement it after being elected.

The second reason why I consider that the G.L.C. did not exercise their discretion lawfully is that they persisted in implementing their pre-election policy even after it had become apparent to them that, because of the withdrawal by central government of a large amount of block grant which they had expected to be available to them, the cost to the ratepayers of the London boroughs of their doing so, already very large, was going to be nearly doubled. On the assumptions made, it was the duty of the G.L.C. to balance fairly against each other the interests of the travelling public on the one hand and those of the ratepayers in the London boroughs on the other. In my view the decision of the G.L.C. to persist in the implementation of their election policy on public transport, after it had become apparent that the originally contemplated cost to the ratepayers of the London boroughs would be nearly doubled, was not a decision which the council, directing themselves properly in law, could reasonably have made. . . .

Notes

1. The *Bromley* speeches adopted such a wide variety of reasoning that it is difficult, if not impossible, to extract a *ratio. Bromley* was distinguished in two subsequent cases in the Divisional Court. In *R.* v. *Merseyside County Council, ex p. Great Universal Stress Ltd.* (1982) 80 L.G.R. 639, Woolf J. rejected a challenge to the validity of the council's policy of subsidising bus fares from the rates. Distinguishing factors included the point that the Transport Act 1968 required the county council to promote the provision of a "properly integrated and efficient" public passenger transport system with due regard, *inter alia*, to "economy and safety of operation," whereas the Transport (London) Act 1969 required the

G.L.C. to promote the provision of "integrated, efficient *and economic*" transport facilities; there was no question of an automatic loss of rate support grant; the council's policies were in accordance with the Merseyside Structure plan; and the proposal had been considered afresh after the elections.

There was also a sequel to the *Bromley* case in London: *R.* v. *London Transport Executive, ex p. Greater London Council* [1983] Q.B. 484. Following the *Bromley* decision, fares were approximately doubled. Subsequently, the Divisional Court upheld the validity of a revised plan for London Transport fares, involving a reduction of about 25 per cent. in the new fares and an increase in the deficit on the L.T.E.'s revenue account of about 17 per cent., to be made good by a grant from the G.L.C. The G.L.C. was held to be entitled to make grants to the L.T.E. to meet continuing losses, provided there was no breach of the principles laid down in the *Wednesbury* and *Prescott* cases. Kerr L.J. expressed broad agreement with the submission on behalf of the G.L.C. that the references in *Bromley* and *Prescott* to the requirement to conduct a transport system on business principles were primarily intended to exclude philanthropic considerations and to emphasise the need for the proper and cost-effective use of resources; they did not mean that fare revenue had to be maximised on ordinary business principles of profit and loss (see pp. 497, 499). The court granted declarations to the effect that the revised plan was within the powers of the G.L.C. and the L.T.E. on the true construction of the Transport (London) Act 1969. It did not decide whether there was any breach of the *Wednesbury* and *Prescott* principles: both parties were agreed that there was no such breach and Kerr L.J. said that "nothing has emerged in the evidence and argument presented to us which has led us to think the contrary" (p. 497).

2. The *Bromley* case is analysed critically by J. Dignan, "Policy-Making, Local Authorities and the Courts: the 'G.L.C. Fares' Case" (1983) 99 L.Q.R. 605. He concludes (p. 643) that:

> "It is strongly arguable that all the appellate judges in the 'G.L.C. Fares' case failed fully to appreciate the scale of the changes brought about in the sphere of public transport administration by the related Acts of 1968 and 1969. The new financial and administrative infrastructure set up under these Acts vested in local authorities greatly enlarged discretionary powers in order to discharge their weighty responsibilities for planning and policy making across a broad range of local transport issues, which extended far beyond the traditional parochial concerns of running municipal bus services on ordinary business principles. Both the need to protect the ratepayers' interests, and the presumption in favour of private property which was reflected in this, and in the retention of the notion of ordinary business principles, look anachronistic in the light of more recent conceptions of the role of the local state, as reflected in these two Acts."

See also J. L. Yelland, [1982] P.L. 171; M. Loughlin, *Local Government in the Modern State* (1986), pp. 68–81; J. A. G. Griffith, "Judicial Decision-Making in Public Law" [1985] P.L. 564, 575–579. The opinion of counsel for Bromley, Harry Sales, is reproduced at [1991] P.L. 499. The impact of *Bromley* on local authorities was the subject of an interdisciplinary study: L. Bridges *et al.*, *Legality and Local Politics* (1987).

3. Compare the attitude of Lord Diplock and Lord Brandon on the significance to be attached to election manifesto commitments with that of the House of Lords in the *Tameside* case, below, p. 408.

In the cases so far considered in this chapter the question raised has been whether the purpose for which a power was exercised was a proper one, whether all relevant considerations were taken into account, or whether all irrelevant considerations were excluded from attention.

It may well be, however, that the issue is not so straightforward. What should be the position where a body is shown to have acted for a *plurality of purposes*, some of which are proper and some improper? Does the *mere fact* of having taken into consideration an irrelevant consideration taint the decision reached? Does failure to have taken into consideration *every one of a number of relevant factors* have that invalidating effect?

The cases which follow address these various issues.

WESTMINSTER CORPORATION v. LONDON AND NORTH-WESTERN RAILWAY CO.

[1905] A.C. 426; 74 L.J.Ch. 629; 93 L.T. 143; 69 J.P. 425; 3 L.G.R. 1120 (House of Lords)

The Corporation, a sanitary authority, constructed public lavatories underground in the middle of Parliament Street. In the words of Lord Macnaghten:

> "The plan of the construction is this: On each aside of the roadway there is an entrance, five feet nine inches wide, protected by railings and leading by a staircase of the same width to a passage or subway, ten feet wide and eight feet high, which runs the whole way across on a level with the underground conveniences. Out of this subway there are openings—two for men and one for women—into spacious chambers, where the usual accommodation (politely described as lavatories and cloak-rooms) is provided on a large and liberal scale. All the arrangements seem to have been designed and carried out with due regard to decency, and with every possible consideration for the comfort of wayfarers in need of such accommodation."

The Railway Company owned a large block of buildings on the east side of Parliament Street. They objected to the sanitary works, and sought to have them removed, basing their claim alternatively on trespass, or obstruction to the highway causing special damage. The Corporation relied on their powers under the Public Health (London) Act 1891 to provide, make and maintain public lavatories and sanitary conveniences. The Company pointed out that both the Corporation and its predecessor, the Vestry of St. Margaret's, Westminster, had exhibited a wish to have a subway constructed at that site. In September 1900 the Vestry's surveyor wrote to the Company referring to the construction of a "subway," and making no mention of the construction of the convenience. In December the acting town clerk of Westminster wrote that "the intention is the construction of a subway to facilitate pedestrians crossing . . . a thoroughfare of great width and very considerable traffic. . . . Admission to the conveniences, which will be accessible from the subways, could otherwise have been provided from refuges above them."

The railway company claimed an injunction to prevent the corporation from continuing to trespass on their premises and to obstruct the footway opposite the premises and damages. When the parties came to trial, it was found that owing to some mistake, the corporation's works had encroached upon the footway. The trial judge, Joyce J. ([1902] 1 Ch. 269), ordered the corporation to remove the encroachment. On appeal, the Court of Appeal (Vaughan Williams, Stirling and Cozens-Hardy L.JJ. [1904] 1 Ch. 759) ordered the corporation to "pull down and remove the whole of the staircase, railings, and other works placed by the defendants upon the lands of the plaintiffs other than the conveniences in the pleadings mentioned, and such further portion of the construction as the court [might], upon application, sanction as a proper approach to the said conveniences." The order was suspended pending an appeal to the House of Lords. On appeal the corporation acquiesced in the order of Joyce J. but contended that the order of the Court of Appeal was wrong.

LORD MACNAGHTEN: . . . There can be no question as to the law applicable to the case. It is well settled that a public body invested with statutory powers such as those conferred upon the corporation must take care not to exceed or abuse its powers. It must keep within the limits of the authority committed to it. It must act in good faith. And it must act reasonably. The last proposition is involved in the second, if not in the first. But in the present case I think it will be convenient to take it separately.

Now, looking merely at what has been done—at the work as designed and actually constructed—it seems to me that, apart from the encroachment on the footway, it is impossible to contend that the work is in excess of what was authorized by the Act of 1891. The conveniences themselves, extensive as the accommodation is, have not been condemned by the Court of Appeal or even attacked in the evidence.

[His Lordship then held that the entrance from the roadway was not excessively wide.]

Then I come to the question of want of good faith. That is a very serious charge. It is not enough to shew that the corporation contemplated that the public might use the subway as a means of crossing the street. That was an obvious possibility. It cannot be otherwise if you have an entrance on each side and the communication is not interrupted by a wall or a barrier of some sort. In order to make out a case of bad faith it must be shewn that the corporation constructed this subway as a means of crossing the street under colour and pretence of providing public conveniences which were not really wanted at that particular place. That was the view of their conduct taken by the Court of Appeal. "In my judgment," says Vaughan Williams L.J., "it is not true to say that the corporation have taken this land which they have taken with the object of using it for the purposes authorized by the Legislature." "You are acting *mala fide*," he added, "if you are seeking to acquire and acquiring lands for a purpose not authorized by the Act of Parliament." So you are; there can be no doubt of that. The other learned Lord Justices seem to take the same view of the conduct of the corporation. Now this, as I have said, is a very serious charge. A gross breach of public duty, and all for a mere fad! The learned judge who tried the case had before him the chairman of the works committee. That gentleman declared that his committee considered with very great care for a couple of years or more the question of these conveniences in Parliament Street. He asserted on oath that "the primary object of the committee was to provide these conveniences."

Why is this gentleman not to be believed? The learned judge who saw and heard him believed his statement. The learned judges of the Court of Appeal have discredited his testimony, mainly, if not entirely, on the ground of two letters about which he was not asked a single question. . . . The letter of the surveyor was a foolish letter, which the writer seems to have thought clever. The letter of the temporary representative of the acting town clerk, if you compare the two letters, seems to have derived its inspiration from the same source. I cannot conceive why the solemn statement of the chairman of the committee should be discredited on such a ground. I do not think there is anything in the minutes tending to disprove his testimony. I entirely agree with Joyce J. that the primary object of the council was the construction of the conveniences with the requisite and proper means of approach thereto and exit therefrom. . . .

LORD JAMES (dissenting): . . . [T]he question to be solved seems to be thus formulated: Was the so-called tunnel an approach to the conveniences only, or was it something more? (1) Was it a subway distinct from the approach, or (2) was it a subway in combination with the approach used for two distinct purposes?

In my judgment the construction in question comes within one or other of the two latter alternatives. Possibly within the first, certainly within the second.

If this finding on the facts is correct, the works, so far as they constitute the subway, are constructed without legal authority. The Legislature has not thought it right to confer on local bodies the power to compulsorily take land or impose rates for the purpose of constructing subways. In this case some land has been taken which would not have been required if the approach had not been enlarged into a subway, and an unauthorized burthen has been imposed upon the ratepayers in consequence of this enlargement.

Thus it is, in my opinion, that the appellants have acted beyond their powers and without justification.

THE EARL OF HALSBURY L.C. and LORD LINDLEY delivered speeches in favour of dismissing the appeal.

R. v. INNER LONDON EDUCATION AUTHORITY, ex p. WESTMINSTER CITY COUNCIL

[1986] 1 W.L.R. 28; [1986] 1 All E.R. 19 (Glidewell J.)

The I.L.E.A., being opposed to central government public expenditure limitation policies, commenced a programme by which they sought to raise public awareness of those policies and of their implications. Under section 142(2) of the Local Government Act 1972 the I.L.E.A. had power to incur expenditure on publishing within its area "information on matters relating to local government." In July 1984 a sub-committee of the I.L.E.A. resolved to retain an advertising agency to mount a media and poster campaign, at a cost of some £651,000. The I.L.E.A. acknowledged that the purpose of the campaign was both to "inform" the public about government proposals and their effects (a lawful purpose) and to "persuade" the public to support the I.L.E.A.'s stance on this matter (an unlawful purpose). The applicant council argued that the resolution was *ultra vires* the power in section 142(2), *inter alia,* because of the unlawful purpose and because the I.L.E.A. had taken into account an irrelevant consideration—its desire to persuade the public to oppose government policy.

GLIDEWELL J. outlined the facts, reviewed the terms of section 142(2), and continued:] . . . [T]he decision of July 23, 1984, was made with the two purposes of informing and persuading.

Two purposes

This brings me to what I regard as being the most difficult point in the case, namely: if a local authority resolves to expend its ratepayers' money in order to achieve two purposes, one of which it is authorised to achieve by statute but for the other of which it has no authority, is that decision invalid?

I was referred to the following authorities.

(i) *Westminster Corp.* v. *London and North Western Rly. Co.* [1905] A.C. 426. . . .

[His Lordship summarised this decision and concluded:] . . . this suggests that a test for answering the question is, if the authorised purpose is the primary purpose, the resolution is within the power.

(ii) *Sydney Municipal Council* v. *Campbell* [1925] A.C. 338. This . . . decision of the Privy Council . . . does not really deal with the question that confronts me of a resolution passed with two purposes in mind.

(iii) More recently in *Hanks* v. *Minister of Housing and Local Government* [1963] 1 Q.B. 999, Megaw J. did have to deal with a case in which it was alleged that a compulsory purchase order had been made for two purposes, one of which did not fall within the empowering Act. At p. 1019, he quoted part of the dissenting judgment of Denning L.J. in *Earl Fitzwilliam's Wentworth Estates Co. Ltd.* v. *Minister of Town and Country Planning* [1951] 2 K.B. 284, 307:

> "If Parliament grants to a government department a power to be used for an authorised purpose, then the power is only validly exercised when it is used by the department genuinely for that purpose as its dominant purpose. If that purpose is not the main purpose, but is subordinated to some other purpose which is not authorised by law, then the department exceeds its powers and the action is invalid."

It had been submitted to Megaw J. that, although Denning L.J. had dissented from the decision of the majority, this passage in his judgment did not differ from the view of the majority.

Megaw J. went on [1963] 1 Q.B. 999, 1020):

"I confess that I think confusion can arise from the multiplicity of words which have been used in this case as suggested criteria for the testing of the validity of the exercise of a statutory power. The words used have included 'objects,' 'purposes,' 'motives,' 'motivation,' 'reasons,' 'grounds' and 'considerations.' In the end, it seems to me, the simplest and clearest way to state the matter is by reference to 'considerations.' A 'consideration,' I apprehend, is something which one takes into account as a factor in arriving at a decision. I am prepared to assume, for the purposes of this case, that, if it be shown that an authority exercising a power has taken into account as a relevant factor something which it could not properly take into account in deciding whether or not to exercise the power, then the exercise of the power, normally at least, is bad. Similarly, if the authority fails to take into account as a relevant factor something which is relevant, and which is or ought to be known to it, and which it ought to have taken into account, the exercise of the power is normally bad. I say 'normally,' because I can conceive that there may be cases where the factor wrongly taken into account, or omitted, is insignificant, or where the wrong taking-into-account, or omission, actually operated in favour of the person who later claims to be aggrieved by the decision. . . ."

I have considered also the views of the learned authors of textbooks on this. Professor Wade in *Administrative Law* (5th edn., 1982) p. 388 under the heading "Duality of Purpose" says:

"Sometimes an act may serve two or more purposes, some authorised and some not, and it may be a question whether the public authority may kill two birds with one stone. The general rule is that its action will be lawful provided the permitted purpose is the true and dominant purpose behind the act, even though some secondary or incidental advantage may be gained for some purpose which is outside the authority's powers."

Professor Evans, in *de Smith's Judicial Review of Administrative Action* (4th ed., 1980) pp. 329–332, comforts me by describing the general problem of plurality of purpose as "a legal porcupine which bristles with difficulties as soon as it is touched." He distils from the decisions of the courts five different tests on which reliance has been placed at one time or another, including—

"(1) What was the *true purpose* for which the power was exercised? If the actor has in truth used his power for the purposes for which it was conferred, it is immaterial that he was thus enabled to achieve a subsidiary object. . . . (5) Was any of the purposes pursued an unauthorised purpose? If so, and if the unauthorised purpose has materially influenced the actor's conduct, the power had been invalidly exercised because irrelevant considerations have been taken into account."

These two tests, and Professor Evans' comment on them, seem to me to achieve much the same result and to be similar to that put forward by Megaw J. in *Hanks* v. *Minister of Housing and Local Government* [1963] 1 Q.B. 999 in the first paragraph of the passage I have quoted from his judgment. That is the part that includes the sentence: "In the end, it seems to me, the simplest and clearest way to state the matter is by reference to 'considerations.' " I gratefully adopt the guidance of Megaw J., and the two tests I have referred to from *de Smith*.

It thus becomes a question of fact for me to decide, on the material before me, whether, in reaching its decision of July 23, 1984, the staff and general sub-committee of I.L.E.A. was pursuing an unauthorised purpose, namely that of persuasion, which has materially influenced the making of its decision. I have already said that I find that one of the sub-committee's purposes was the giving of information. But I also find that it had the purpose of seeking to persuade members of the public to a view identical with that of the authority itself, and indeed I believe that this was a, if not the, major purpose of the decision. . . .

Adopting the test referred to above, I thus hold that I.L.E.A.'s sub-committee did, when making its decision of July 23, 1984, take into account an irrelevant consideration, and thus that decision was not validly reached.

If I am wrong on this, there would remain for consideration the last two arguments advanced by counsel for the city council. I will deal with these shortly. As to the alleged breach of fiduciary duty to the ratepayers, it is true that the cost of employing AMV was very substantially greater than the sums which I.L.E.A. had already authorised to be expended on the "campaign." But this is a matter of discretion for the authority, which was advised that it had to take into account its duty to the ratepayers. It would be for Westminster City Council to show, if they could, that I.L.E.A. had disregarded that duty. In my view, Westminster City Council have failed to do this. Similarly, I cannot say on the material before me that I.L.E.A.'s decision was so unreasonable as to be perverse. If therefore the matter depended on either of these two grounds, Westminster City Council's challenge would fail.

Declaration granted.

R. v. BROADCASTING COMPLAINTS COMMISSION, ex p. OWEN

[1985] Q.B. 1153; [1985] 2 All E.R. 522 (D.C. (Q.B.D.))

Under section 54 of the Broadcasting Act 1981 the B.C.C. had a statutory duty (subject to the terms of section 55(4)—discretion not to hear a complaint where, *inter alia*, "inappropriate") to consider and adjudicate upon complaints of, *inter alia*, "unjust or unfair treatment" in radio or television programmes. The applicant, Dr. David Owen, was the leader of the Social Democratic Party. That party had entered into an alliance with the Liberal Party. Together these two parties had obtained only 2 per cent. less of the votes at the 1983 election than had the main opposition party, the Labour Party. The number of seats won by alliance candidates was, however, very much smaller than those won by Labour. In June 1984, Dr. Owen wrote to the B.C.C. complaining of unjust and unfair treatment in that as a matter of policy the broadcasting organisations were giving considerably more attention in news and current affairs broadcasts to the views of the Labour Party than to the views of the alliance. In reply, the B.C.C. stated that (i) it had no jurisdiction to consider a complaint of such nature, and (ii) that, even if it had such jurisdiction, it would have declined to entertain the complaint for a variety of stated reasons.

May L.J. and Taylor J. held that the B.C.C. was wrong to have thought that it had no jurisdiction to have considered such a complaint. On the issue of whether it had properly exercised its discretion (under section 55(4)) to decline to hear complaints within jurisdiction:

MAY L.J.: . . . I turn therefore to the commission's decision contained in their letter of November 13, 1984 that even if they did have jurisdiction to entertain the applicant's complaint under section 54 it would be inappropriate for them to do so under section 55(4) for the reasons they gave. I bear well in mind [the submission of counsel for Dr. Owen] based on the decision in *Padfield's* case [1968] A.C. 997, that the discretion given to the commission to entertain or to refuse to entertain a complaint should be exercised to comply with the policy and objects of the Act of 1981. Nevertheless, the wording of section 55(4) is as wide as it could be. . . .

On the general principles of law laid down in the cases to which I have referred the commission would of course not be entitled to decline to entertain or proceed with the consideration of the applicant's complaint merely at their own whim. They must be able to show that their declinature was founded upon what I can briefly describe as a relevant reason or reasons within the *Wednesbury* principles and they must be able to repel any suggestion that they have failed to take into account any other relevant reason which they ought to have done.

[His Lordship stated that he had heard argument upon each of the reasons given for the B.C.C.'s decision, and continued:]

In the end I am quite satisfied that there is no sufficient justification for the applicant's criticism of [certain of the] reasons in the commission's letter. . . . The essence of the applicant's complaint is political and within it lies the thorny problem whether the voting system of this country should be changed so as to introduce some form of proportional representation. In these circumstances I think that the stance taken by the commission as indicated by those reasons in their letter . . . is that the applicant's complaint was to the effect that the broadcasting authorities have, as a matter of editorial policy, taken a decision about how they will treat the Alliance in comparison with the Labour Party. The complaint would, in effect, require the commission to decide whether its editorial policy, if it exists, is fair and just. But by what criteria? They would have to express a view about a fundamental issue of British politics, not merely about alleged unjust or unfair treatment in a broadcast or television programme about which there are quite clearly strongly different views held by both the Conservative and Labour Parties.

The applicant's real concern is not to have the broadcasting authorities required to publish a comment on the commission on past programmes but to achieve a change of what he contends is editorial policy on the part of the broadcasting authorities in the future. That is not the type of relief that the commission is empowered to grant.

In these circumstances, and on the above grounds, I think that [those] reasons ... given by the commission in their letter and the underlying thinking which they demonstrate were wholly justified in law and constituted an entirely relevant stance for the commission to take which cannot validly be criticised on, for instance, *Padfield's* principles....

In my opinion, however, reason 3 in their letter in support of their contention that to entertain the applicant's complaint was inappropriate cannot be justified in law. The mere fact that a task which it is their duty to carry out may be burdensome and require perhaps the employment of additional staff is not, I think, a sufficient reason to conclude that it would be inappropriate for them to proceed.

Contemplating the possibility that the court might reach the conclusion which I have, namely, that although four of the reasons given by the commission were valid in law, nevertheless the remaining fifth reason was not, [counsel for Dr. Owen] referred us to the decision of Forbes J. in *R.* v. *Rochdale Metropolitan Borough Council, ex p. Cromer Ring Mill Ltd.* [1982] 3 All E.R. 761, particularly the passage beginning at the foot of p. 768. Having considered a passage from *de Smith's Judicial Review of Administrative Action*, 4th ed. (1980), pp. 339–340, and then the judgment of Denning L.J. in *Earl Fitzwilliam's Wentworth Estates Co. Ltd.* v. *Minister of Town and Country Planning* [1951] 2 K.B. 284, 307 and of Megaw J. in *Hanks* v. *Minister of Housing and Local Government* [1963] 1 Q.B. 999, 1018–9, Forbes J. said, at pp. 769–770:

> "Although it is fair to say that *Hanks'* case is not binding on me, it is a very persuasive authority and I would undoubtedly follow it, and do. It seems to me Megaw J. is there saying, having been apprised of the argument about dominant purpose, that the exercise of a power is bad if it is shown that an authority exercising that power has taken an irrelevant factor into account, one of many factors, as long as that irrelevant factor is not insignificant or insubstantial. To that extent, it seems to me, that that case wholly supports the formulation in Professor de Smith's book: 'If the influence of irrelevant factors is established, it does not appear to be necessary to prove that they were the sole or even the dominant influence; it seems to be enough to prove that their influence was substantial.' "

On this authority [counsel for Dr. Owen] submitted that the invalidity of even only one of the reasons given by the commission invalidated their decision that it would be inappropriate for them to entertain or consider the applicant's complaint. In reply [counsel for B.C.C.] accepted that where reasons given by a statutory body are mixed and impossible to disentangle, as indeed was the situation in the *Rochdale* case, then the invalidity of one is sufficient to vitiate the whole of the decision based upon such reasons even if many of them are valid. He, nevertheless, submitted that where the reasons given are separate and alternative, then the mere fact that one can be criticised is not sufficient to vitiate a decision to which the statutory body would in any event have come had they left the invalid reason out of account.

For my part, I cannot accept [counsel for B.C.C.'s] entire submission on this point as he stated it. I respectfully agree that the material law is as was stated by Forbes J. but with one qualification. . . . Where the reasons given by a statutory body for taking or not taking a particular course of action are not mixed and can clearly be disentangled, but where the court is quite satisfied that even though one reason may be bad in law, nevertheless the statutory body would have reached precisely the same decision on the other valid reasons, then this court will not interfere by way of judicial review. In such a case, looked at realistically and with justice, such a decision of such a body ought not to be disturbed.

I am quite satisfied in this case on all the material before us that the commission would still have concluded that it would be inappropriate to entertain or consider the applicant's complaint if they had never thought about reason 3 in their letter of November 13, 1984.

Another approach to the same problem in such circumstances, which really reflects the same thinking is this: the grant of what may be the appropriate remedies in an application for judicial review is a matter for the discretion of this court. Where one is satisfied that although a reason relied on by a statutory body may not properly be described as insubstantial, nevertheless even without it the statutory body would have been bound to come to precisely the same conclusion on valid grounds, then it would be wrong for this court to exercise its discretion to strike down, in one way or another, that body's conclusion. . . .

[TAYLOR J. delivered a concurring judgment in which he expressed his agreement with May L.J., but did not deal specifically with the issues considered above.]

Notes

1. See H. F. Rawlings, (1985) 48 M.L.R. 584. *Cf. R.* v. *London Borough of Lewisham, ex p. Shell U.K. Ltd.* [1988] 1 All E.R. 938, where the council passed a resolution to boycott Shell products. The Divisional Court found that it had two purposes: (1) a lawful purpose to promote good race relations in the borough in accordance with its duty under section 71 of the Race Relations Act 1976; and (2) an unlawful purpose to put pressure on Shell to withdraw from South Africa. The court held that where two reasons or purposes could not be disentangled, and one was bad, or, where they could be disentangled the bad reason demonstrably exerted the substantial influence, the court could interfere to quash the decision. Here, the

two purposes were inextricably mixed up and the unlawful purpose had the effect of vitiating the decision as a whole. See T. R. S. Allan, [1988] C.L.J. 334.

2. As *ex p. Owen* illustrates, the courts may be called upon to determine whether a particular consideration is or is not "relevant." It may be that the background legislation provides sufficient pointers to enable the courts to perform this task with some confidence. However, there is a danger that the courts become too ready to spell out relevant and irrelevant considerations based not so much on the statute as on their view as to what is and is not appropriate. Consider, for example, *Bristol District Council* v. *Clark* [1975] 1 W.L.R. 1443, where the Court of Appeal identified a number of factors as relevant to decisions to evict council tenants, which were found not in the statute but in a Department of the Environment circular: see the criticism of this approach by R. J. Buxton, (1976) 39 M.L.R. 470; and *cf. Cannock Chase District Council* v. *Kelly* [1978] 1 W.L.R. 1. *Cf.* the "fiduciary duty" considered in *Roberts* v. *Hopwood* and *Bromley*, above, pp. 363–384.

In *R.* v. *Secretary of State for the Environment, ex p. Bolton Metropolitan Borough Council* [1991] J.P.L. 32, Hodgson J. rejected an argument that unless a decision-maker was expressly required to take into account some matter (*cf.* n. 3, below), he was only "impliedly" required by law to take the matter into account if it was one which no reasonable decision-maker would fail to do so: his Lordship regarded this conflation of *Wednesbury* principles as illegitimate. The Court of Appeal dismissed an appeal on other grounds.

3. The specific considerations that are relevant to an exercise of discretion may of course be set out expressly in the statute. For example, the Housing Act 1985, s.604(1), lists matters to which regard shall be had in determining whether a house is unfit for human habitation; the Education Act 1944, s.76, provides that the Secretary of State and local education authorities:

> "shall have regard to the general principle that, so far as is compatible with the provision of efficient instruction and training and the avoidance of unreasonable public expenditure, pupils are to be educated in accordance with the wishes of their parents."

and the Town and County Planning Act 1990, s.70(2), provides that in dealing with an application for planning permission, the authority:

> "shall have regard to the provisions of the development plan, so far as material to the application, and to any other material considerations."

In applying these provisions, the courts have emphasised that the public authority is not obliged to regard the consideration as decisive. Thus, a local education authority is not under a *duty* to comply with parental wishes (*Watt* v. *Kesteven County Council* [1955] 1 Q.B. 408; *Cummings* v. *Birkenhead Corporation* [1972] Ch. 12; *Harvey* v. *Strathclyde Regional Council* 1989 S.L.T. 612). A local planning authority was not required by section 70(2) to adhere "slavishly" to the plan (*Simpson* v. *Edinburgh Corporation* 1960 S.C. 313; *Enfield London Borough Council* v. *Secretary of State for the Environment* [1975] 233 E.G. 53; *Niarchos (London) Ltd.* v. *Secretary of State for the Environment* (1977) 35 P. & C.R. 259), although the Planning and Compensation Act 1991, s.26 (inserting s.54A in the 1990 Act) now provides that a determination:

> "shall be made in accordance with the plan unless material considerations indicate otherwise."

4. In some contexts, the courts have shown a disinclination to apply the considerations test. For example, it has been suggested that where the amount of

expenditure by a local authority on a particular item is not unreasonable, the fact that irrelevant considerations may have been taken into account may not render the expenditure unlawful (*per* Lord Sumner in *Roberts* v. *Hopwood*, above, p. 363; *Re Walker's Decision* [1944] 1 K.B. 644). In *Pickwell* v. *Camden London Borough Council* [1983] 1 Q.B. 962, Ormrod L.J. held that a failure to take into account relevant matters, or the taking into account of irrelevant matters were in effect only evidence that the authority might have acted *ultra vires* (*cf.* the approach of Forbes J. who simply held that a breach of the *Wednesbury* principles was not established on the evidence). See above, p. 28.

The suggestion of the Court of Appeal that the full *Wednesbury* principles might not apply in relation to purely administrative decisions not affecting rights (*R.* v. *Barnet and Camden Rent Tribunal, ex p. Frey Investments Ltd.* [1972] 2 Q.B. 342) has not found favour (see *Wade*, p. 422). In *R.* v. *Commission for Racial Equality, ex p. Hillingdon London Borough Council*, Griffiths L.J. in the Court of Appeal ([1982] Q.B. 276, 298–300) and Lord Diplock in the House of Lords ([1982] A.C. 779, 792) expressly affirmed that the *Wednesbury* principles apply to administrative functions.

It may be that suggestions that the considerations test does not apply in a particular context are simply a reflection of the point that there is no breach of the test where an authority considers but is not influenced by a particular legally irrelevant matter, or the same decision would have been reached by reference to other considerations (*ex p. Owen, supra*).

(C) Unreasonableness

The grounds of challenge considered in sections A and B, above, require evidence and proof of the purpose(s) of the body challenged, or the considerations which were or were not taken into account. In other words attention focuses in such cases on the "thought-processes" of the challenged body in exercising its discretionary power. Evidence of this may appear from any reasons, or explanation, it may give (or may be required to give) for its decision; or from affidavits (or, in exceptional cases, cross-examination) in the course of the legal challenge itself.

Challenge on the ground of "unreasonableness" proceeds on a rather different footing. It invites the court to hold that notwithstanding that there may be no firm evidence of improper purpose or relevant/irrelevant considerations, nevertheless the court should intervene on the basis that the decision as to the exercise of power is in substance one which no reasonable body, properly conversant with its legal obligations, could have come to.

The courts have consistently stated that in considering challenges on this ground they must preserve the distinction between review on the "merits" (is this the decision I would have come to?) and review of "legality" (is this a decision which a reasonable person could have come to?). The former may be appropriate in appeal proceedings, where such exist and permit the appellate body such a wide power of review; but is regarded by the judges as going beyond their proper remit in proceedings for judicial review. "Unreasonableness" is justified as a ground of review of legality on the basis that although Parliament may have intended to authorise a variety of, not unreasonable, ways in which a power might be exercised, and have intended to leave such choice to the body in question rather than to the judges, it can be assumed that Parliament had not intended its grant of that power to cover its unreasonable exercise.

(i) Wednesbury unreasonableness

ASSOCIATED PROVINCIAL PICTURE HOUSES LTD. v. WEDNESBURY CORPORATION

[1948] 1 K.B. 223; 177 L.T. 641; 63 T.L.R. 623; 112 J.P. 55; 92 S.J. 26; [1947] 2 All E.R. 680; 45 L.G.R. 635; [1948] L.J.R. 190 (Court of Appeal)

The plaintiff company, the owners and licensees of the Gaumont Cinema, Wednesbury, Staffordshire, were granted by the defendants who were the licensing authority for that borough under the Cinematograph Act 1909, a licence to give performances on Sunday under section 1(1) of the Sunday Entertainments Act 1932; but the licence was granted subject to a condition that "no children under the age of 15 years shall be admitted to any entertainment whether accompanied by an adult or not." In these circumstances the plaintiffs brought an action for a declaration that the condition was *ultra vires* and unreasonable.

Henn Collins J. ([1947] L.J.R. 678) dismissed the action, and the plaintiffs appealed to the Court of Appeal. Section 1(1) of the 1932 Act provided that the authority might attach to a licence "such conditions as the authority think fit to impose. . . ."

LORD GREENE M.R.: . . . Mr. Gallop, for the plaintiffs, argued that it was not competent for the Wednesbury Corporation to impose any such condition and he said that if they were entitled to impose a condition prohibiting the admission of children, they should at least have limited it to cases where the children were not accompanied by their parents or a guardian or some adult. His argument was that the imposition of that condition was unreasonable and that in consequence it was *ultra vires* the corporation. The plaintiffs' contention is based, in my opinion, on a misconception as to the effect of this Act in granting this discretionary power to local authorities. The courts must always, I think, remember this: first, we are dealing with not a judicial act, but an executive act; secondly, the conditions which, under the exercise of that executive act, may be imposed are in terms, so far as language goes, put within the discretion of the local authority without limitation. Thirdly, the statute provides no appeal from the decision of the local authority.

What, then, is the power of the courts? They can only interfere with an act of executive authority if it be shown that the authority has contravened the law. It is for those who assert that the local authority has contravened the law to establish that proposition. On the face of it, a condition of the kind imposed in this case is perfectly lawful. It is not to be assumed prima facie that responsible bodies, like the local authority in this case will exceed their powers; but the court, whenever it is alleged that the local authority have contravened the law, must not substitute itself for that authority. It is only concerned with seeing whether or not the proposition is made good. When an executive discretion is entrusted by Parliament to a body such as the local authority in this case, what appears to be an exercise of that discretion can only be challenged in the courts in a strictly limited class of case. As I have said, it must always be remembered that the court is not a court of appeal. When discretion of this kind is granted the law recognizes certain principles upon which that discretion must be exercised, but within the four corners of those principles the discretion, in my opinion, is an absolute one and cannot be questioned in any court of law. What then are those principles? They are well understood. They are principles which the court looks to in considering any question of discretion of this kind. The exercise of such a discretion must be a real exercise of discretion. If, in the statute conferring the discretion, there is to be found expressly or by implication matters which the authority exercising the discretion ought to have regard to, then in exercising the discretion it must have regard to those matters. Conversely, if the nature of the subject-matter and the general interpretation of the Act make it clear that certain matters would not be germane to the matter in question, the authority must disregard those irrelevant collateral matters. There have been in the cases expressions used relating to the sort of thing that authorities must not do, not merely in cases under the Cinematograph Act but, generally speaking, under the other cases where the powers of local authorities came to be considered. I am not sure myself whether the permissible grounds of attack cannot be defined under a single head. It has been perhaps a little bit confusing to find a series of grounds set out. Bad faith, dishonesty—those of course, stand by themselves—unreasonableness, attention given to extraneous circumstances, disregard of public policy and things like that have all been referred to, according to the facts of individual cases, as being matters which are relevant to the question. If they cannot all be confined under one head, they at any rate, I think, overlap to a very great extent. For instance, we have heard in this case a great deal about the meaning of the word "unreasonable."

It is true the discretion must be exercised reasonably. Now what does that mean? Lawyers familiar with the phraseology commonly used in relation to exercise of statutory discretions often use the word "unreasonable" in a rather comprehensive sense. It has frequently been used and is frequently used as a general description of the things that must not be done. For instance, a person entrusted with a discretion must, so to speak, direct himself properly in law. He must call his own attention to the matters which he is bound to consider. He must exclude from his consideration matters which are irrelevant to what he has to consider. If he does not obey those rules, he may truly be said, and often is said, to be acting "unreasonably." Similarly, there may be something so absurd that no sensible person could ever dream that it lay within the powers of the authority. Warrington L.J. in *Short* v. *Poole Corporation* [1926] Ch. 66, 90, 91, gave the example of the red-haired teacher, dismissed because she had red hair. That is unreasonable in one sense. In another sense it is taking into consideration extraneous matters. It is so unreasonable that it might almost be described as being done in bad faith; and, in fact, all these things run into one another.

In the present case, it is said by Mr. Gallop that the authority acted unreasonably in imposing this condition. It appears to me quite clear that the matter dealt with by this condition was a matter which a reasonable authority would be justified in considering when they were making up their mind what condition should be attached to the grant of this licence. Nobody, at this time of day, could say that the well-being and the physical and moral health of children is not a matter which a local authority, in exercising their powers, can properly have in mind when those questions are germane to what they have to consider. Here Mr. Gallop did not, I think, suggest that the council were directing their mind to a purely extraneous and irrelevant matter, but he based his argument on the word "unreasonable," which he treated as an independent ground for attacking the decision of the authority; but once it is conceded, as it must be conceded in this case, that the particular subject-matter dealt with by this condition was one which it was competent for the authority to consider, there, in my opinion, is an end of the case. Once that is granted, Mr. Gallop is bound to say that the decision of the authority is wrong because it is unreasonable, and in saying that he is really saying that the ultimate arbiter of what is and is not reasonable is the court and not the local authority. It is just there, it seems to me, that the argument breaks down. It is clear that the local authority are entrusted by Parliament with the decision on a matter which the knowledge and experience of that authority can best be trusted to deal with. The subject-matter with which the condition deals is one relevant for its consideration. They have considered it and come to a decision upon it. It is true to say that, if a decision on a competent matter is so unreasonable that no reasonable authority could ever have come to it, then the courts can interfere. That I think, is quite right; but to prove a case of that kind would require something overwhelming, and, in this case, the facts do not come anywhere near anything of that kind. I think Mr. Gallop in the end agreed that his proposition that the decision of the local authority can be upset if it is proved to be unreasonable, really meant that it must be proved to be unreasonable in the sense that the court considers it to be a decision that no reasonable body could have come to. It is not what the court considers unreasonable, a different thing altogether. If it is what the court considers unreasonable, the court may very well have different views to that of a local authority on matters of high public policy of this kind. Some courts might think that no children ought to be admitted on Sundays at all, some courts might think the reverse, and all over the country I have no doubt on a thing of that sort honest and sincere people hold different views. The effect of the legislation is not to set up the court as an arbiter of the correctness of one view over another. It is the local authority that are set in that position and, provided they act, as they have acted, within the four corners of their jurisdiction, this court, in my opinion, cannot interfere.

This case, in my opinion, does not really require reference to authority when once the simple and well known principles are understood on which alone a court can interfere with something prima facie within the powers of the executive authority, but reference has been made to a number of cases. . . . [His Lordship referred to *Harman* v. *Butt* [1944] K.B. 491; *R.* v. *Burnley JJ.*, 85 L.J. (K.B.) 1565; and *Ellis* v. *Dubowski* [1921] 3 K.B. 621, the latter two being cases of unlawful delegation of powers.] Another case on which Mr. Gallop relied is *Roberts* v. *Hopwood* [1925] A.C. 578, [above, p. 363]. That was a totally different class of case. The district auditor had surcharged the members of a council who had made payments of a minimum wage of 4*l*. a week to their lowest grade of workers. That particular sum had been fixed by the local authority not by reference to any of the factors which go to determine a scale of wages, but by reference to some other principle altogether, and the substance of the decision was that they had not fixed 4*l*. a week as wages at all and that they had acted unreasonably. When the case is examined, the word "unreasonable" is found to be used rather in the sense that I mentioned a short while ago, namely, that in fixing 4*l*. they had fixed it by reference to a matter which they ought not to have taken into account and to the exclusion of those elements which they ought to have taken into consideration in fixing a sum which could fairly be called a wage. That is no authority whatsoever to support the proposition that the court has power, a sort of overriding power, to decide what is reasonable and what is unreasonable. The court has nothing of the kind. . . .

In the result, this appeal must be dismissed. I do not wish to repeat myself but I will summarize once again the principle applicable. The court is entitled to investigate the action of the local authority with a view to seeing whether they have taken into account matters which they ought not to take into account, or, conversely, have refused to take into account or neglected to take into account matters which they ought to take into account. Once that question is answered in favour of the local authority, it may still be possible to say that, although the local authority have kept within the four corners of the matters which they ought to consider, they have nevertheless come to a conclusion so unreasonable that no reasonable authority could ever have come to it. In such a case, again, I think the court can interfere. The power of the court to interfere in each case is not as an appellate authority to override a decision of the local authority, but as a judicial authority which is concerned, and concerned only, to see whether the local authority have contravened the law by acting in excess of the powers which Parliament has confided in them. The appeal must be dismissed with costs.

SOMERVELL L.J. and SINGLETON L.J. agreed.

Appeal dismissed.

Notes

1. In addition to the regularly quoted words of Lord Greene M.R. a number of other formulations of this test of "unreasonableness" have been suggested. In

each case the courts have been concerned to stress the distinction between review on this ground and reconsideration on the merits.

Thus, in *R.* v. *Greenwich London Borough Council, ex p. Cedar Holdings* [1983] R.A. 173, Griffiths L.J. warned that a court might "all to easily [be] lure[d] . . . into substituting its own view of the way in which the . . . council should have exercised its discretion for that of the council itself." This temptation was, at all costs, to be avoided: "Only in a case where the decision of the council had been so outrageous that no right thinking person could support it would it be right to interfere. . . ."

In *Council of Civil Service Unions* v. *Minister for the Civil Service* [1985] A.C. 374, 410, Lord Diplock, having described the basis of this challenge as challenge for "irrationality," commented: "It applies to a decision which is so outrageous in its defiance of logic or of accepted moral standards that no sensible person who had applied his mind to the question to be decided could have arrived at it." See further on this case, above p. 199 and below, pp. 514–519.

In *Nottinghamshire County Council* v. *Secretary of State for the Environment* [1986] A.C. 240, 247, Lord Scarman explained that for this ground of challenge to succeed a decision must be so absurd that the decision-maker "must have taken leave of his senses."

This ground of challenge has been argued, and referred to by the courts, on many occasions. Very often the courts have adverted to the test to be applied only then to hold that on the facts the test has not been satisfied. In other words, reference to the *Wednesbury* principle has commonly been in order to emphasise the limits to the functions of a court of *review* as distinct from *appeal*. See, *e.g. Re Lamplugh* (1968) 19 P. & C.R. 125; *Manchester Corporation* v. *Connolly* [1970] 1 Ch. 420. Concern that the principle might, if stated in overly extreme terms, prove "awkward" for courts to apply even in appropriate cases led Lord Donaldson to express a preference for the expression *Wednesbury unreasonable* rather than the term *irrational*. In a situation where a usually reliable body has in a particular instance taken an unjustifiable decision, His Lordship felt that courts would feel more willing to intervene, and would cast less in the way of unnecessary aspersion, applying the former label than the latter: see *R.* v. *Devon County Council, ex p. G.* [1989] A.C. 573 at 577.

For a general survey, see G. L. Peiris, "*Wednesbury* unreasonableness: the Expanding Canvas" [1987] C.L.J. 53.

2. Notwithstanding the frequency with which the courts have noted this ground of challenge only to hold that, on the facts, the challenge did not succeed, there have been cases where this principle *has* formed the basis (sometimes together with other grounds) of successful challenge. Thus, in *Backhouse* v. *Lambeth London Borough Council, The Times*, October 14, 1972, the Labour-controlled council resolved to increase the rent of a three-bedroomed council house (unoccupied since May 1972 because of deficiencies in the damp course) from some £7 to £18,000 per week. Section 62(1) of the Housing Finance Act 1972 provided that: "Every local authority shall . . . make the increases [*i.e.* towards fair rents] required by sections 63 and 64. . . ." Section 63(1) provided that such increases should not be made "If the authority made a general rent increase in the first half of 1972–73 which produces £26 or more per dwelling in 1972–73. . . ." The council hoped to avoid a general rent increase of 55p per week by putting all the increase contemplated by section 63(1) on one house. Any tenant would get an "enormous" rebate. B., the leader of the council tenants, sought a declaration that the resolution was valid. Melford Stevenson J., however, held that it was *ultra vires*. His Lordship held that this was a resolution at which no reasonable local authority could have arrived. It was admittedly designed and only designed to avoid or evade obligations cast on the council by the 1972 Act.

[Counsel for the Secretary of State for the Environment, who defended the case instead of the council, also submitted that the council had obviously ignored all relevant considerations.]

In *West Glamorgan County Council* v. *Rafferty* [1987] 1 W.L.R. 457, the Court of Appeal held that the council had acted unreasonably in the *Wednesbury* sense in seeking an order for possession against gypsies occupying a council-owned site and causing a nuisance. The council had for over 10 years been in breach of its duty under section 6 of the Caravan Sites Act 1968 to provide adequate accommodation for gypsies in its area, and had not on this occasion made any arrangements for alternative accommodation. Ralph Gibson L.J. said (at p. 477):

> "The court is not, as I understand the law, precluded from finding a decision to be void for unreasonableness merely because there are admissible factors on both sides of the question. If the weight of the factors against eviction must be recognised by a reasonable council, properly aware of its duties and its powers, to be overwhelming, then a decision the other way cannot be upheld if challenged. The decision upon eviction was a decision which required the weighing of the factors according to the personal judgment of the councillors but the law does not permit complete freedom of choice or assessment because legal duty must be given proper weight."

This decision was distinguished by Rose J. in *R.* v. *Avon County Council, ex p. Rexworthy* (1988) 87 L.G.R. 470, where the council was held not to have acted unlawfully in seeking to evict gypsies from an encampment on a public highway where there was evidence of substantial obstruction and danger on and damage to the highway. The council was aware of its shortcomings in providing sites, and had not abandoned the search for alternative sites and had to balance its responsibilities to gypsies against its duties to highway users. *West Glamorgan County Council* v. *Rafferty* was also distinguished in *R.* v. *London Borough of Camden, ex p. Maugham and McDonagh* [1990] C.O.D. 390, where Otton J. refused to quash the council's decision to seek possession of two areas of land where gypsies were residing: the applicants were trespassers, there was a manifest nuisance, the council was not under a statutory duty towards them and, on the facts, the applicants had no legitimate expectation of an opportunity to make representations.

Given that there were "admissible factors on both sides of the question" in *Rafferty*, can it be said that the council "must have taken leave of its senses" in coming to its decision? If not, the case suggests that the test for unreasonableness is not in practice as extreme as the dicta cited in n.1 suggests.

For comments on *Rafferty*, see R. Ward, [1987] C.L.J. 374.

For further examples of successful challenge on *Wednesbury* grounds, see, *e.g. Niarchos (London) Ltd.* v. *Secretary of State for the Environment and Westminster City Council (No. 2)* (1981) 79 L.G.R. 264; *R.* v. *London Borough of Haringey, ex p. Barrs* [1983] J.P.L. 54; *R.* v. *Immigration Appeal Tribunal, ex p. Manshoora Begum* [1986] Imm. A.R. 385; *R.* v. *Bolton Metropolitan Borough, ex p. B.* [1985] F.L.R. 343; *R.* v. *Lewisham London Borough Council, ex p. p.* [1991] 1 W.L.R. 308. The ground was also a part of the reasoning in the speeches of Lord Brandon in the *Bromley* case (above, p. 381) and of Lord Roskill in the *Wheeler* case (above p. 358).

3. Note that the *Wednesbury* formula is also used by the courts for certain other purposes in the context of judicial review and appeals. See, *e.g.* the "no evidence" rule (below, p. 651), and the scope of review of the exercise of powers conferred in "subjective" form (below, p. 408).

4. "Unreasonableness" constitutes a ground upon which the validity of byelaws may be challenged—see *Kruse* v. *Johnson* [1898] 2 Q.B. 91 (below, p. 914).

5. It has been held that "irrationality" is not available as a ground of challenge where the decision has been approved by one or both Houses of Parliament. This

point has arisen in cases where the Secretary of State for the Environment has sought to "cap" the expenditure of designated local authorities. The most recent decision is *R.* v. *Secretary of State for the Environment, ex p. Hammersmith and Fulham London Borough Council* [1991] 1 A.C. 521, where the House of Lords rejected challenges by 19 of 21 designated authorities to the Secretary of State's decisions under the Local Government Finance Act 1988, s.100, to impose maximum budgets. (This would in turn require each authority to set a lower level of community charge.) Lord Bridge, having rejected arguments based on illegality, continued (at pp. 594–597):

"The remaining grounds of challenge fall under the heads of irrationality or procedural impropriety. Before turning to these grounds it is appropriate to consider whether any limitations upon the scope of judicial review are imposed by the subject-matter of the legislation. In this we are not without authoritative guidance.

In *Reg.* v. *Secretary of State for the Environment, ex p. Nottinghamshire County Council* [1986] A.C. 240, the House had to consider an earlier challenge to the action of the Secretary of State under the Local Government, Planning and Land Act 1980 which had this in common with the action here in question that the "expenditure guidance" which the Secretary of State had there issued to local authorities and which the authorities sought to challenge had a directly restraining effect on the authorities' conduct of their financial affairs but before it could take effect required the approval by resolution of the House of Commons. The appellant authorities in that case had challenged the Secretary of State's statutory expenditure guidance on the ground, *inter alia,* that it was unreasonable as contravening the principles expounded in the judgment of Lord Greene M.R. in *Associated Provincial Picture Houses Ltd.* v. *Wednesbury Corporation* [1948] 1 K.B. 223, 229, which is the classic statement of the basis for a challenge to an administrative decision on the ground of irrationality. Adverting to this challenge in the *Nottinghamshire* case [1986] A.C. 240, 247, Lord Scarman said:

"The submission raises an important question as to the limits of judicial review. We are in the field of public financial administration and we are being asked to review the exercise by the Secretary of State of an administrative discretion which inevitably requires a political judgment on his part and which cannot lead to action by him against a local authority unless that action is first approved by the House of Commons. . . . I cannot accept that it is constitutionally appropriate, save in very exceptional circumstances, for the courts to intervene on the ground of 'unreasonableness' to quash guidance framed by the Secretary of State and by necessary implication approved by the House of Commons, the guidance being concerned with the limits of public expenditure by local authorities and the incidence of the tax burden as between taxpayers and ratepayers. Unless and until a statute provides otherwise, or it is established that the Secretary of State has abused his power, these are matters of political judgment for him and for the House of Commons. They are not for the judges or your Lordships' House in its judicial capacity. For myself, I refuse in this case to examine the detail of the guidance or its consequences. My reasons are these. Such an examination by a court would be justified only if a prima facie case were to be shown for holding that the Secretary of State had acted in bad faith, or for an improper motive, or that the consequences of his guidance were so absurd that he must have taken leave of his senses."

Later he added, at pp. 250–251:

> "To sum it up, the levels of public expenditure and the incidence and distribution of taxation are matters for Parliament, and, within Parliament, especially for the House of Commons. If Parliament legislates, the courts have their interpretative role: they must, if called upon to do so, construe the statute. If a minister exercises a power conferred on him by the legislation, the courts can investigate whether he has abused his power. But if, as in this case, effect cannot be given to the Secretary of State's determination without the consent of the House of Commons and the House of Commons has consented, it is not open to the courts to intervene unless the minister and the House must have misconstrued the statute or the minister has—to put it bluntly—deceived the House. The courts can properly rule that a minister has acted unlawfully if he has erred in law as to the limits of his power even when his action has the approval of the House of Commons, itself acting not legislatively but within the limits set by a statute. But, if a statute, as in this case, requires the House of Commons to approve a minister's decision before he can lawfully enforce it, and if the action proposed complies with the terms of the statute (as your Lordships, I understand, are convinced that it does in the present case), it is not for the judges to say that the action has such unreasonable consequences that the guidance upon which the action is based and of which the House of Commons had notice was perverse and must be set aside. For that is a question of policy for the minister and the Commons, unless there has been bad faith or misconduct by the minister. Where Parliament has legislated that the action to be taken by the Secretary of State must, before it is taken, be approved by the House of Commons, it is no part of the judges' role to declare that the action proposed is unfair, unless it constitutes an abuse of power in the sense which I have explained; for Parliament has enacted that one of its Houses is responsible. Judicial review is a great weapon in the hands of the judges: but the judges must observe the constitutional limits set by our parliamentary system upon the exercise of this beneficent power."

Lord Scarman's speech commanded the agreement of all members of the Appellate Committee participating in the decision, of whom I was one. I regard the opinions expressed in the passages quoted as an accurate formulation of an important restriction on the scope of judicial review which is precisely in point in the instant case. There is here no suggestion that the Secretary of State acted in bad faith or for an improper motive or that his decisions to designate the appellant authorities or the maximum amounts to which he decided to limit their budgets were so absurd that he must have taken leave of his senses. Short of such an extreme challenge, and provided always that the Secretary of State has acted within the four corners of the Act, I do not believe there is any room for an attack on the rationality of the Secretary of State's exercise of his powers under Part VII of the Act.

This accords with the view expressed by the Divisional Court, though they went on to examine on their merits and to reject the grounds relied on by the applicant authorities including those challenging the rationality of the Secretary of State's decisions and orders. The Court of Appeal expressed a somewhat different view. Referring to irrationality as a ground for judicial review of the exercise of a statutory discretion they said, *ante*, p. 935D-E:

> "This head is relevant if it is alleged that the decision taker has had regard to matters which are legally irrelevant or has failed to have regard to matters which are legally relevant or that his decision would frustrate the policy of the Act upon which he relies for his authority: see *Padfield* v. *Minister of Agriculture, Fisheries and Food* [1968] A.C. 997. There is nothing in the judgments in

the *Nottinghamshire* case [1986] A.C. 240 to suggest that this aspect of the jurisdictional head of 'irrationality' has no application to decisions concerning public financial administration, whether or not they are also subject to review by one or both Houses of Parliament and no principle dictates that this should be the case."

I think there is a danger of confusion in terminology here. If the court concludes, as the House did in the *Padfield* case [1986] A.C. 997, that a minister's exercise of a statutory discretion has been such as to frustrate the policy of the statute, that conclusion rests upon the view taken by the court of the true construction of the statute which the exercise of the discretion in question is then held to have contravened. The administrative action or inaction is then condemned on the ground of illegality. Similarly, if there are matters which, on the true construction of the statute conferring discretion, the person exercising the discretion must take into account and others which he may not take into account, disregard of those legally relevant matters or regard of those legally irrelevant matters will lay the decision open to review on the ground of illegality.

The restriction on which the *Nottinghamshire* case [1986] A.C. 240 imposes on the scope of judicial review operates only when the court has first determined that the ministerial action in question does not contravene the requirements of the statute, whether express or implied, and only then declares that, since the statute has conferred a power on the Secretary of State which involves the formulation and the implementation of national economic policy and which can only take effect with the approval of the House of Commons, it is not open to challenge on the grounds of irrationality short of the extremes of bad faith, improper motive or manifest absurdity. Both the constitutional propriety and the good sense of this restriction seem to me to be clear enough. The formulation and the implementation of national economic policy are matters depending essentially on political judgment. The decisions which shape them are for politicians to take and it is in the political forum of the House of Commons that they are properly to be debated and approved or disapproved on their merits. If the decisions have been taken in good faith within the four corners of the Act, the merits of the policy underlying the decisions are not susceptible to review by the courts and the courts would be exceeding their proper function if they resumed to condemn the policy as unreasonable."

[His Lordship concluded that an argument that the determination was *Wednesbury* unreasonable, which he rejected on its merits (in agreement with the Court of Appeal) was in any event "inadmissible."]

This restriction has been the subject of academic criticism: see *Wade*, pp. 29, 410–411, 868; C. M. G. Himsworth, 1985 S.L.T. 369 and [1986] P.L. 139, and A. I. L. Campbell, 1986 S.L.T. 101 (on the similar approach of the Court of Session in the context of statutory instruments in *City of Edinburgh District Council* v. *Secretary of State for Scotland* 1985 S.L.T. 551, *cf.* below, p. 911, n. 3); Himsworth, [1986] P.L. 347; R. Ward, (1986) 49 M.L.R. 645 (on the *Nottinghamshire* decision) and [1991] P.L. 76 (on the *Hammersmith* decision). On the other hand, the point can be made that it is difficult to see what grounds of challenge are actually excluded by the terms of Lord Bridge's speech, given that a challenge to the *merits* of a "capping" decision would not in any event fall within the *ultra vires* doctrine.

Note the differences between the Court of Appeal and the House of Lords on the scope of the "irrationality" concept.

6. J. Jowell and A. Lester ("Beyond *Wednesbury*: Substantive Principles of Administrative Law" [1987] P.L. 368) argue persuasively that as a concept "*Wednesbury* unreasonableness" is unsatisfactory (pp. 372–374). It is "inadequate," providing insufficient justification for judicial intervention:

"Intellectual honesty requires a further and better explanation as to *why* the act is unreasonable. The reluctance to articulate a principled justification naturally encourages suspicion that prejudice or policy considerations may be hiding underneath *Wednesbury's* ample cloak."

It is "unrealistic," the courts in practice being:

> "willing to impugn decisions that are far from absurd and are indeed often coldly rational."

It is "confusing, because it is tautologous."

Instead, the courts should develop substantive principles of review, that prohibit decisions that are " 'irrational' in the accepted sense of that term" or arbitrary; that violate accepted standards of administrative probity, (*e.g.* fraudulent decisions or decisions in bad faith) or good administrative practice, (*e.g.* decisions that are unjustifiably inconsistent or disproportionate); or that violate fundamental rights and freedoms.

The courts have in recent years developed the concept of unjustifiable inconsistency (below, pp. 419–437). However, in the *Brind* case (below, pp. 438–445) the House of Lords has limited the extent to which administrators are to be required to take account of the European Convention on Human Rights, and has put the brakes on any development of "proportionality" as an independent ground of challenge.

(ii) Express requirements of reasonableness

In some instances a grant of discretionary power may expressly provide that the power is only to be exercisable "reasonably," or is only to be exercisable where the body in question has "reasonable" grounds to consider that certain defined circumstances exist. In such cases the courts may consider whether the positive requirement of reasonableness has been satisfied. They will not be restricted to a consideration of whether the decision on the relevant issue is "so unreasonable. . . ." The extent to which a reviewing court will be willing to substitute its own judgment of reasonableness for that of the statutorily designated body may depend on context. Compare the decisions in *Nakkuda Ali* and *Luby* (below).

NAKKUDA ALI v. JAYARATNE

[1951] A.C. 66; 66 T.L.R. (Pt. 2) 214; 94 S.J. 516 *sub nom. Ali* v. *Jayaratne*
(Privy Council on appeal from the Supreme Court of Ceylon)

The respondent, the Controller of Textiles in Ceylon, exercised his power to cancel a textile dealer's licence "where the Controller has reasonable grounds to believe that any dealer is unfit to be allowed to continue as a dealer" in respect of the appellant's licence. The appellant sought a mandate in the nature of certiorari to quash the cancellation on the ground of breach of natural justice. The Privy Council held that there had been no breach, but that in any event certiorari would not lie as the Controller was not acting judicially but taking executive action to withdraw a privilege. This general aspect of the case is discussed by Lord Reid in *Ridge* v. *Baldwin* (below, p. 475). One specific point dealt with by the Privy Council was whether the requirement that the Controller have "reasonable grounds" indicated that he was acting judicially, which was the view of the Supreme Court.

LORD RADCLIFFE delivered the opinion of the Privy Council (LORDS PORTER, OAKSEY and RADCLIFFE, SIR JOHN BEAUMONT and SIR LIONEL LEACH): . . . It would be impossible to consider the significance of such words as "Where the Controller has reasonable grounds to believe . . ." without taking account of the decision of the House of Lords in *Liversidge* v. *Sir John Anderson* [1942] A.C. 206. That decision related to a claim for damages for false imprisonment, the imprisonment having been brought about by an order made by the Home Secretary under the Defence (General) Regulations, 1939, reg. 18B, of the United Kingdom. It was not a case that had any direct bearing on the court's power to issue a writ of certiorari to the Home Secretary in respect of action taken under that regulation: but it did directly involve a question as to the meaning of the words "If the Secretary of State has reasonable cause to believe any person to be of hostile origin or associations . . ." which appeared at the opening of the regulation in question. And the decision of the majority of the House did lay down that those words in that context meant no more than that the Secretary of State had honestly to suppose that he had reasonable cause to believe the required thing. On that basis, granted good faith, the maker of the order appears to be the only possible judge of the conditions of his own jurisdiction.

Their Lordships do not adopt a similar construction of the words in reg. 62 which are now before them. Indeed, it would be a very unfortunate thing if the decision of *Liversidge's* case came to be regarded as laying down any general rule as to the construction of such phrases when they appear in statutory enactments. It is an authority for the proposition that the words "if A.B. has reasonable cause to believe" are capable of meaning "if A.B. honestly thinks that he has reasonable cause to believe" and that in the context and attendant circumstances of Defence Regulation 18B they did in fact mean just that. But the elaborate consideration which the majority of the House gave to the context and circumstances before adopting that construction itself shows that there is no general principle that such words are to be so understood; and the dissenting speech of Lord Atkin at least serves as a reminder of the many occasions when they have been treated as meaning "if there is in fact reasonable cause for A.B. so to believe." After all, words such as these are commonly found when a legislature or law-making authority confers powers on a minister or official. However read, they must be intended to serve in some sense as a condition limiting the exercise of an otherwise arbitrary power. But if the question whether the condition has been satisfied is to be conclusively decided by the man who yields the power the value of the intended restraint is in effect nothing. No doubt he must not exercise the power in bad faith: but the field in which this kind of question arises is such that the reservation for the case of bad faith is hardly more than a formality. Their Lordships therefore treat the words in reg. 62, "where the Controller has reasonable grounds to believe that any dealer is unfit to be allowed to continue as a dealer" as imposing a condition that there must in fact exist such reasonable grounds, known to the Controller, before he can validly exercise the power of cancellation. . . .

Notes

1. This aspect of *Nakkuda Ali* v. *Jayaratne* is generally accepted as correct. See Lord Reid in *Ridge* v. *Baldwin*, below p. 475, and *I.R.C.* v. *Rossminster Ltd.* [1980] A.C. 952—concession by I.R.C. on this point. *Liversidge* v. *Anderson* was not relied upon by the Solicitor-General in *Secretary of State for Employment* v. *A.S.L.E.F. (No. 2)* [1972] 2 Q.B. 443.

2. *Liversidge* v. *Anderson* [1942] A.C. 206 is a notorious case, but highly exceptional. For discussion, see *Garner*, pp. 162–164; *de Smith*, pp. 306–307; R. F. V. Heuston, *Essays in Constitutional Law*, pp. 171–177; *Allen*, pp. 256, 297 and Appendix 1; G. W. Keeton: (1942) 5 M.L.R. 162; (1942) 58 L.Q.R. 1 (W. S. Holdsworth), 3, 9, 243 (A.L.G.), 232, 462 (C. K. Allen); R. F. V. Heuston, "*Liversidge* v. *Anderson* in Retrospect" (1970) 86 L.Q.R. 33, and "*Liversidge* v. *Anderson*, Two Footnotes" (1971) 87 L.Q.R. 161.

LUBY v. NEWCASTLE-UNDER-LYME CORPORATION

[1965] 1 Q.B. 214; [1964] 3 W.L.R. 500; 128 J.P. 536; 108 S.J. 541; [1964] 3 All E.R. 169; 62 L.G.R. 622; [1964] R.V.R. 708, C.A.; *affirming* [1964] 2 Q.B. 64; [1964] 2 W.L.R. 475; 128 J.P. 138; 107 S.J. 983; [1964] 1 All E.R. 84; 62 L.G.R. 140 (Diplock L.J. and the Court of Appeal)

The plaintiff sought a declaration that the resolution of the defendant corporation to increase all their council house rents was *ultra vires*, on the ground that the corporation had not taken into account the individual personal circumstances of their tenants. The corporation did not operate a rent rebate or differential rent scheme, and the plaintiff claimed that the rent charged to him was unreasonable.

DIPLOCK L.J. [at first instance]: . . . I turn therefore to the relevant provisions of the Housing Act 1957, under which the defendants are empowered to make charges for the tenancy or occupation of houses provided by them under Part V of the Act. The leading section is section 111, subsection (1) of which reads as follows: "The general management, regulation and control of houses provided by a local authority under this Part of this Act shall be vested in and exercised by the authority, and the authority may make such reasonable charges for the tenancy or occupation of the houses as they may determine.

This subsection gives to the local authority a complete discretion as to the rents which they will charge, subject only to the requirement that they shall be "reasonable." I doubt whether the addition of the adjective "reasonable" has the effect of narrowing the wide discretion which the local authority would have if that word were not present, since (see *Roberts* v. *Hopwood* [1925] A.C. 578 [above, p. 363]) where a local authority is exercising a discretion conferred upon it by Parliament it must in any event exercise it "reasonably" in the sense in which that ambiguous word was used by Lord Russell in the leading case of *Kruse* v. *Johnson* [1898] 2 Q.B. 91 at p. 99.

[His Lordship cited the passage: "Notwithstanding what Cockburn C.J. said ... unreasonable and *ultra vires*" (see below, p. 916), and then the passages from Lord Greene's judgment in the *Wednesbury* case [1948] 1 K.B. 223 at p. 229, above, p. 396, "It is true that the discretion must be exercised reasonably ... run into one another" and "Here Mr. Gallop ... not the local authority."]

It is just there, it seems to me that the argument breaks down. It is clear that the local authority is entrusted by Parliament with the decision of a matter with which the knowledge and experience of that authority can best be trusted to deal. "Reasonable" in this context in which it appears in section 111(1) of the Housing Act 1957, is in my view to be construed as the converse of "unreasonable" in the sense in which it is used by Lord Greene M.R., and in the sense in which "reasonable" was construed by Lord Russell in the earlier case of *Kruse* v. *Johnson*.

The court's control over the exercise by a local authority of a discretion conferred upon it by Parliament is limited to ensuring that the local authority has acted within the powers conferred. It is not for the court to substitute its own view of what is a desirable policy in relation to the subject-matter of the discretion so conferred. It is only if it is exercised in a manner which no reasonable man could consider justifiable that the court is entitled to interfere.

In determining the rent structure to be applied to houses provided by a local authority the local authority is applying what is, in effect, a social policy upon which reasonable men may hold different views. Since any deficit in the housing revenue account has to be made good from the general rate fund, the choice of rent structure involves weighing the interests of the tenants as a whole and of individual impoverished tenants against those of the general body of ratepayers. Since the passing of the National Assistance Act 1948, and the making of the National Assistance (Determination of Need) Regulations 1948, which provide that the matters to be taken into consideration in assessing the relief to be granted to applicants shall include the net rent payable or such a part thereof as is reasonable in the circumstances, there is also involved a choice as to whether the individual impoverished tenant should be assisted at the expense of the general body of ratepayers by a reduction in the rent or at the expense of the general body of tax-payers by way of National Assistance.

The evidence shows that the defendant corporation has directed its mind to this problem and to the desirability or otherwise of applying a differential rent scheme. It has determined that the burden of assisting individual tenants who cannot afford to pay the rents which the corporation has fixed as appropriate for the type of house which they occupy ought to fall upon the general body of tax-payers and not upon the general body of ratepayers in their district. It is in my view quite impossible for this court to say that this choice, which is one of social policy, is one which no reasonable man could have made, and is therefore *ultra vires*, any more than it could be said that the opposite choice would have been *ultra vires*. The policy which the defendant corporation has adopted was, I think, within the discretion conferred upon them by section 111(1) of the Housing Act 1957. . . .

[The Court of Appeal dismissed an appeal agreeing with the reasoning of Diplock L.J. at first instance.]

Notes

1. This case is the converse of *Roberts* v. *Hopwood* (above, p. 363). Here the presence of "reasonable" in the statute added nothing to the scope of judicial review. There the absence of "reasonable" from the relevant statute did not prevent its implication by the courts.

2. *Cf. Backhouse* v. *Lambeth London Borough Council*, above, p. 399.

(iii) Reasonableness and subjective powers

The next issue to consider is the scope of review in situations where the grant of power is in "subjective" form—*i.e.* where it is power to act in circumstances where required circumstances are "believed" to prevail, or to do such things as are considered appropriate in the judgment of the donee of the power, (*e.g.* to impose such conditions as a body thinks fit). It might be argued that the intention of the legislation is, here, to exclude judicial review, or at least to restrict it to issues of "good faith" and actual honest belief. In fact the courts have been unwilling to accept such a limited power of review and have utilised the *Wednesbury* formula to strike down decisions based on honest but unreasonable subjective belief. This matter is considered fully in the extracts from the *Tameside* case (below).

SECRETARY OF STATE FOR EDUCATION AND SCIENCE v. METROPOLITAN BOROUGH OF TAMESIDE

[1977] A.C. 1014; [1976] 3 All E.R. 665; [1976] 3 W.L.R. 641 (Court of Appeal; House of Lords)

In March 1975, the defendant local education authority, then Labour controlled, submitted a scheme to the Secretary of State under section 13 of the Education Act 1944, for the introduction of comprehensive education in schools in their area; these proposals were approved by the Secretary of State. In May 1976, the balance of political power was changed at the local government elections, and the authority came under the control of the Conservative party, who had promised in their election propaganda to reconsider the question of comprehensive education. The authority decided to modify the decision made in 1975 and to retain five grammar schools, at least for the school year commencing September, 1976, although arrangements to convert them to "comprehensives" were already in hand. The Secretary of State formed the opinion that the authority were acting unreasonably in so deciding, and accordingly he gave them a formal direction under section 68 of the Education Act 1944 (see below) to the effect that they were required to implement the 1975 scheme. The defendant authority refused to accept this, and the Secretary of State applied for an order of mandamus against the authority requiring them to comply with his direction. An order of mandamus was granted by the Divisional Court on July 12, 1976, but this order was quashed by the Court of Appeal (Lord Denning M.R., Scarman and Geoffrey Lane L.JJ.) on July 26, 1976, and the Court of Appeal's decision was upheld by the House of Lords on August 2, 1976.

Section 68 of the Education Act 1944 provides as follows:

> "If the Secretary of State is satisfied, either on complaint by any person or otherwise, that any local education authority . . . have acted or are proposing to act unreasonably with respect to the exercise of any power conferred or the performance of any duty imposed by or under this Act, he may . . . give such directions as to the exercise of the power or the performance of the duty as appear to him to be expedient."

[In the Court of Appeal]

LORD DENNING M.R.: . . . It was suggested in one place in the papers—on June 21, 1976 by the chief officers of the council—that once the Secretary of State said he was "satisfied," his decision could not be challenged in the courts unless it was shown to be made in bad faith. We were referred by counsel for the Secretary of State to *Liversidge* v. *Anderson* ([1942] A.C. 206, at p. 233) where Lord Atkin drew attention to cases where the Defence Regulations required the Secretary of State to be "satisfied" of something or other. Lord Atkin said: "In all these cases, it is plain that unlimited discretion is given to the Secretary of State assuming, as everyone does, that he acts in good faith" to which I would add a similar passage by Somervell L.J. in *Robinson* v. *Minister of Town and Country Planning* ([1947] K.B. 702, at p. 721). Those statements were made, however, in regard to regulations in war time or immediately after the war when the decisions of the executive had to be implemented speedily and without question. That was pointed out by Lord Radcliffe in *Nakkuda Ali* v. *M. F. de S. Jayaratne* ([1951] A.C. 66, at p. 77) and by Lord Reid in *Ridge* v. *Baldwin* ([1964] A.C. 40, at p. 73). Those statements do not apply today. Much depends on the matter about which the Secretary of State has to be satisfied. If he is to be satisfied on the matter of opinion, that is one thing. But if he has to be satisfied that someone has been guilty of some discreditable or unworthy or unreasonable conduct, that is another. To my mind, if a statute gives a Minister power to take drastic action if he is satisfied that a local authority have acted or are proposing to act improperly or unreasonably, then the Minister should obey all the elementary rules of fairness before he finds that the local authority are guilty or before he takes drastic action overruling them. He should give the party affected notice of the charge of impropriety or unreasonableness and a fair opportunity of dealing with it. I am glad to see that the Secretary of State did so in this case. He had before him the written proposals of the new council and he met their leaders. In addition, however, the Minister must direct himself properly in law. He must call his own attention to the matters he is bound to consider. He must exclude from his consideration matters which are irrelevant to that which he has to consider. And the decision to which he comes must be one which is reasonable in this sense, that it is, or can be, supported with good reasons or at any rate be a decision which a reasonable person might reasonably reach. Such is, I think, plain from *Padfield* v. *Minister of Agriculture, Fisheries and Food* ([1968] A.C. 997), which is a landmark in our administrative law and which we had in mind in *Secretary of State for Employment* v. *Associated Society of Locomotive Engineers and Firemen* (*No.* 2) ([1972] 2 Q.B. 455). So much for the requirements if the Minister is to be "satisfied." . . .

[His Lordship held that the Secretary of State must have misdirected himself on the interpretation of "unreasonableness," and that there was no evidence on which the Secretary of State could declare himself satisfied that the council were proposing to act unreasonably.]

SCARMAN L.J. [delivered a concurring judgment, which included the following passage]: . . . I do not accept that the scope of judicial review is limited to quite the extent suggested by counsel for Secretary of State [*i.e.* to bad faith, misdirection in law, taking account of irrelevant matters, omitting to consider relevant matters, taking a view that no reasonable man could take]. I would add a further situation to those specified by him; misunderstanding or ignorance of an established and relevant fact. Let me give two examples. The fact may be either physical, something which existed or occurred or did not, or it may be mental, an opinion. Suppose that, contrary to the Secretary of State's belief, it was the fact that there was in the area of the authority adequate school accommodation for the pupils to be educated, and the Secretary of State acted under the section believing that there was not. If it were plainly established that the Secretary of State were mistaken, I do not think that he could substantiate the lawfulness of his direction under this section. Now, more closely to the facts of this case, taking a matter of expert professional opinion. Suppose that, contrary to the understanding of the Secretary of State, there does in fact exist a respectable body of professional or expert opinion to the effect that the selection procedures for school entry proposed are adequate and acceptable. If that body of opinion be proved to exist, and if that body of opinion proves to be available both to the authority and to the Secretary of State, then again I would have thought it quite impossible for the Secretary of State to invoke his powers under section 68. By adding this situation to situations more commonly described as occasions for judicial review, I can find no objection in principle.

Lord Denning M.R. has briefly referred to some of the case law on the matter; and in the short time available I have looked to see if there is authority which would belie what I believe to be the law, and there is none.

GEOFFREY LANE L.J. delivered a concurring judgment.

[In the House of Lords]

LORD WILBERFORCE: . . . This section (s.68 of the Education Act 1944) does not say what the consequences of the giving of directions are to be, but I accept, for the purposes of the appeal, that the consequences are to impose on the authority a statutory duty to comply with them which can be enforced by an order of mandamus.

Analysis of the section brings out three cardinal points. 1. The matters with which the section is concerned are primarily matters of educational administration. The action, which the Secretary of State is entitled to stop, is unreasonable action with respect to the exercise of a power or the performance of a duty; the power and the duty of the authority are presupposed and cannot be interfered with. Local education authorities are entitled under the 1944 Act to have a policy, and this section does not enable the Secretary of State to require them to abandon or reverse a policy just because the Secretary of State disagrees with it. Specifically, the Secretary of State cannot use power under this section to impose a general policy of comprehensive education on a local education authority which does not agree with the policy. He cannot direct it to bring in a scheme for total comprehensive education in its area, and if it has done so he cannot direct it to implement it. If he tries to use a direction under section 68 for this purpose, his direction would be clearly invalid. A direction under section 68 must be justified on the ground of unreasonable action in doing what under the 1944 Act the local authority is entitled to do, and under the Act it has a freedom of choice. I do not think that there is any controversy on these propositions.

The critical question in this case, and it is not an easy one, is whether, on a matter which appears to be one of educational administration, namely whether the change of course proposed by the authority in May 1976 would lead to educational chaos or undue disruption, the Secretary of State's judgment can be challenged.

2. The section is framed in a subjective form—if the Secretary of State "is satisfied." This form of section is quite well known, and at first sight might seem to exclude judicial review. Sections in this form may, no doubt, exclude judicial review on what is or has become a matter of pure judgment. But I do not think that they go further than that. If a judgment requires, before it can be made, the existence of some facts, then, although the evaluation of those facts is for the Secretary of State alone, the court must enquire whether those facts exist, and have been taken into account, whether the judgment has been made on a proper self direction as to those facts, whether the judgment has not been made on other facts which ought not to have been taken into account. If these requirements are not met, then the exercise of judgment, however bona fide it may be, becomes capable of challenge: see *Secretary of State for Employment* v. *Associated Society of Locomotive Engineers and Firemen* (No. 2) ([1972] 2 Q.B. 455, at p. 493), *per* Lord Denning M.R.

3. The section has to be considered within the structure of the 1944 Act. In many statutes a Minister or other authority is given a discretionary power and in these cases the court's power to review any exercise of the discretion, though still real, is limited. In these cases it is said that the

courts cannot substitute their opinion for that of the Minister; they can interfere on such grounds as that the Minister has acted right outside his powers or outside the purpose of the Act, or unfairly, or on an incorrect basis of fact. But there is no universal rule as to the principles on which the exercise of a discretion may be reviewed: each statute or type of statute must be individually looked at. This Act of 1944, is quite different from those which simply create a ministerial discretion. The Secretary of State, under section 68, is not merely exercising a discretion; he is reviewing the action of another public body which itself has discretionary powers and duties. He, by contrast with the courts in the normal case, may substitute his opinion for that of the authority: this is what the section allows, but he must take account of what the authority, under the statute, is entitled to do. The authority—this is vital—is itself elected, and is given specific powers as to the kind of schools it wants in its area. Therefore two situations may arise. One is that there may be a difference of policy between the Secretary of State (under Parliament) and the local authority: the section gives no power to the Secretary of State to make his policy prevail. The other is that, owing to the democratic process involving periodic elections, abrupt reversals of policy make take place, particularly where there are only two parties and the winner takes all. Any reversal of policy if at all substantial must cause some administrative disruption; this was as true of the 1975 proposals as of those of Tameside. So the mere possibility, or probability, of disruption cannot be a ground for issuing a direction to abandon the policy. What the Secretary of State is entitled, by a direction if necessary, to ensure is that such disruptions are not "unreasonable," *i.e.* greater than a body, elected to carry out a new programme, with which the Secretary of State may disagree, ought to impose on those for whom it is responsible. After all, those who voted for the new programme, involving a change of course, must also be taken to have accepted some degree of disruption in implementing it.

The ultimate question in this case, in my opinion, is whether the Secretary of State has given sufficient, or any, weight to this particular factor in the exercise of the judgment.

I must now enquire what were the facts on which the Secretary of State expressed himself as satisfied that the council were acting or proposing to act unreasonably. The Secretary of State did not give oral evidence in the courts, and the facts on which he acted must be taken from the department's letters at the relevant time—*i.e.* on or about June 11, 1976—and from affidavits sworn by its officers. These documents are to be read fairly and in *bonam partem*, if reasons are given in general terms, the court should not exclude reasons which fairly fall within them: allowance must be fairly made for difficulties in expression. The Secretary of State must be given credit for having the background to this actual situation well in mind, and must be taken to be properly and professionally informed as to education practices used in the area and as to resources available to the local education authority. His opinion based as it must be on that of a strong and expert department, is not to be lightly overridden.

On June 11 the direction under section 68 was given in a letter of that date. The letter stated that the Secretary of State was satisfied that the authority was proposing to act unreasonably according to the formula used in section 68. A change of plan designed to come into effect in less than three months must, in the opinion of the Secretary of State, give rise to "considerable difficulties." It pointed out that over 3,000 pupils transferring from primary schools had already been allocated and allotted places. Then followed this paragraph (which I shall call "para. A"):

> "The Authority's revised proposals *confront* the parents of children due to transfer in September *with the dilemma* of either adhering to secondary school allocations for their children which they may no longer regard as appropriate, or else *submitting* to an improvised selection procedure (the precise form of which the Secretary of State understands, has even now not been settled) carried out in circumstances and under a timetable which raise substantial doubts about its educational validity."

A further objection was taken to the proposed possible reallocation during or after the first year.... The change of plan at this time in the educational year threatened to give rise to practical difficulties in relation to the appointments of staff already made and the construction of buildings for the new comprehensive schools and to create a degree of confusion and uncertainty which could impair the efficient working of the schools.

These arguments were re-stated and expanded in the affidavit sworn on behalf of the Secretary of State in support of the application for mandamus. The affidavit stated three points. Point (i): that 653 of the 802 transfers, promotions and other appointments (of teachers) required to implement the reorganisation had been made. Point (ii): that contracts had been entered into for building work directly related to the change in character of two of the schools and work had started under the contracts. In the case of a third school, the authority had entered into commitments for such building work. Point (iii): that preparations were made for courses on the basis that the proposals communicated to the Secretary of State would be put into effect.

These points (i), (ii) and (iii) were dealt with fully by the authority and I need say no more about them than that they were completely exploded. They were held to have no substance in them by five of the six learned judges who have considered this matter: the sixth indicated general agreement without specific discussion and indeed point (ii) was criticised with some severity by one of the learned Lords Justices in the Court of Appeal.

Some attempt was made to rehabilitate these points in this House, but learned counsel decided, no doubt wisely, to concentrate on the allocation issue. But these three points cannot just be discarded as if they had never been made. They form part of a composite set of facts relied on as showing unreasonable conduct, and I am not at all sure that the disappearance of so many planks does not fatally weaken the stability of the platform. At the least—and I will give the department the benefit of this assumption—the remaining factual basis would need to be strong and clear if it alone were to be the basis for the Secretary of State's "satisfaction" as to unreasonable conduct.

So I come to the question of allocation, which was at the centre of the case as argued and it can best be approached via "para. A" above, a paragraph which I regard as revealing. It shows a very strange attitude toward the decision taken by the authority. After the electorate, including no doubt a large number of parents, had voted the new authority into office on the platform that some selective basis would be preserved, to say that this created "a dilemma" for the parents, with the undertone that this was something unreasonable, appears to me curious and paradoxical. Parents desired to have a chance of selective places. The new authority were giving it them. If they did not want selective places, they had no need and no obligation to apply for them. Unless the creation of freedom of choice, where no such freedom existed previously, is intrinsically an evil, it seems hard to understand how this so-called dilemma could be something unreasonably created. The impression which it gives of upsetting 3,000 places is entirely a false one since over 90 per cent. of these would remain unaltered. Then, to refer to "submitting to an improvised selection procedure" hardly does justice to the authority's plan. Some selection procedure was inherent in what the electorate had voted for, a choice which, if it meant anything, must involve some change in allocation for the forthcoming school year and, unless exactly 240 parents applied for the 240 places, some selection. It would seem likely that in voting for this change in May 1976 the electors must have accepted, if not favoured, some degree of improvisation. The whole paragraph forces the conclusion that the Secretary of State was operating under a misconception as to what would be reasonable for a newly elected council to do, and that he failed to take into account that it was entitled—indeed in a sense bound—to carry out the policy on which it was elected, and failed to give weight to the fact that the limited degree of selection (for 240 places out of some 3,000), which was involved, though less than perfect, was something which a reasonable authority might accept and which the parents concerned clearly did accept.

What the Secretary of State was entitled to do, under his residual powers, was to say something to the effect that: "the election has taken place; the new authority may be entitled to postpone the comprehensive scheme: this may involve some degree of selection and apparently the parents desire it. Nevertheless from an educational point of view, whatever some parents may think, I am satisfied that in the time available this, or some part of it, cannot be carried out, and that no reasonable authority would attempt to carry it out." Let us judge him by this test, though I do not think that this was the test he himself applied. Was the procedure to be followed for choosing which of the applicants were to be allotted the 240 selective places such that no reasonable authority could adopt it? The authority's letter of June 7 said that selection would be by "a combination of reports, records and interviews." They had about three months in which to carry it out. The plan was lacking in specification, but it must have conveyed sufficient to the experts at the department to enable them to understand what was proposed. Selection by 11 plus examination was not the only selection procedure available. Lancashire, part of which was taken over by Tameside, had evolved and operated a method of selection by head teacher recommendation, ranking of pupils, reports and records, and standardised verbal reasoning tests. The Tameside authority had set up in May a panel of selection to operate a procedure of this kind, the chairman of which was experienced in the Lancashire method. He was, as he deposed in an affidavit before the Court of Appeal, of opinion that even though a verbal reasoning test might not be practicable in the time there would be no difficulty in selecting the number of places required. There were other opinions, expressed with varying degrees of confidence by experts, and no doubt the procedure could not be said to be perfect, but I do not think that such defects as there were could possibly, in the circumstances, having regard to the comparatively small number of places involved, enable it to be said that the whole of the authority's programme of which this was a part was such that no reasonable authority would carry it out.

But there is a further complication. The authority's selection plans were opposed by a number of the teachers' unions, and there was the likelihood of non-cooperation by some of the head teachers in the primary schools in production of records and reports. The department letters and affidavits do not rely on this matter, for understandable reasons, but they must be assumed to have had it in mind. Is this a fact on which the Secretary of State might legitimately form the judgment that the authority were acting unreasonably?

To rephrase the question: on June 11, 1976 (this is the date of the direction, and we are not entitled to see what happened thereafter) could it be said that the authority were acting unreasonably in proceeding with the selection procedure which was otherwise workable, in face of the possibility of persistent opposition by teachers' unions and individual teachers, or would *the only* (not "the more") reasonable course have been for the authority to abandon their plans? This is I think the ultimate factual question in the case. And I think that it must be answered in the negative, *i.e.* that it could not be unreasonable, in June 1976, and assuming that the Secretary of State did not interfere, for the authority to put forward a plan to act on their approved procedure. The teachers, after all, are public servants, with responsibility for their pupils. They were under a duty to produce reports. These reports and the records in the primary schools are public property. I do not think that it could be unreasonable (not "was unreasonable") for the authority to take the view that if the Secretary of State did not intervene under his statutory power, the teachers would cooperate in working the authority's procedure—a procedure which had, in similar form, been operated in part of this very area.

On the whole case, I come to the conclusion that the Secretary of State, real though his difficulties were, fundamentally misconceived and misdirected himself as to the proper manner in which to regard the proposed action of the authority after the local election of May 1976; that if he had exercised his judgment on the basis of the factual situation in which this newly elected authority were placed—with a policy approved by their electorate, and massively supported by the parents—there was no ground, however much he might disagree with the new policy, and regret such administrative dislocation as was brought about by the change, on which he could find that the authority were acting or proposing to act unreasonably. In my opinion, the judgments in the Court of Appeal were right and the appeal must be dismissed.

LORD DIPLOCK: . . . A relevant question to which the Secretary of State should have directed his mind was the extent to which head teachers would be likely to persist in a policy of non-cooperation if he himself was known to have declined to stop the council from proceeding with their plan. There is no suggestion in the letter, nor in either of the affidavits sworn on his behalf by Mr. Jenkins, that the Secretary of State ever directed his mind to this particular question or formed any view about it. Indeed, it is not until the second affidavit that it is disclosed that the teachers' trade unions had been writing directly to the department on the matter at all. It is not for a court of law to speculate how the Secretary of State would have answered that question had he directed his mind to it, although like others of your Lordships and members of the Court of Appeal, I find it difficult to believe that responsible head teachers, regardful of the interests of their pupils, would have persisted in a refusal to do their best to make the selection procedure work fairly and effectively if the Secretary of State had made it clear to them by his decision that he was not prepared himself to interfere with the council's proceeding with its plans. Assuming, however, that he had formed the view that cooperation by head teachers was likely to be only partial so that the selection process would be liable to greater possibility of error than where full cooperation could be obtained, the Secretary of State would have to consider whether the existence of such a degree of imperfection in the selection system as he thought would be involved was so great as to make it unreasonable conduct for the council to attempt to fulfil the mandate which they had so recently received from the electors. Again, there is no indication that the Secretary of State weighed these two considerations against one another.

Like all your Lordships, I would dismiss this appeal, although I prefer to put it on the ground that, in my view, the council have succeeded in establishing in these proceedings that the Secretary of State did not direct his mind to the right question: and so, since his good faith is not in question, he cannot have directed himself properly in law.

LORD SALMON: . . . In my opinion, section 68, on its true construction, means that before the Secretary of State could lawfully issue directions under it, he must satisfy himself not only that he does not agree with the way in which the authority have acted or are proposing to act nor even that the authority are mistaken or wrong; the question he must ask himself is, could any reasonable local authority act in the way in which this authority have acted or are proposing to act? If, but only if, he is satisfied on any material capable of satisfying a reasonable man that the answer to the crucial question is No, he may lawfully issue directions under section 68. . . .

I find it impossible . . . to accept that any reasonable man could be satisfied that no reasonable authority on the evidence could take the view that a satisfactory selection of candidates for the 240 places in the grammar schools could have been made between June 11 and September 1, 1976. Therefore, either the Secretary of State must have erred in law by misconstruing s.68 and failing to ask himself the right question, or he asked himself that question and answered it No without any valid ground for doing so.

VISCOUNT DILHORNE and LORD RUSSELL OF KILLOWEN delivered concurring speeches.

Appeal dismissed.

Notes

1. See case notes by H. W. R. W[ade], (1977) 93 L.Q.R. 4 and D. G. T. Williams, [1977] C.L.J. 1. *The Tameside* case was the subject of a talk by A. W. Bradley in the Radio 3 "Law in Action" series. See *The Listener*, May 5, 1977. The factual background is re-examined by D. Bull, "*Tameside* Revisited" (1987) 50 M.L.R. 307, noting inadequacies in the courts' appreciation of the schools admissions process.

2. In 1944, the following clause was added at the committee stage of the Education Bill, as clause 92(2):

> "(2) Where the performance of any duty imposed by or for the purposes of this Act on a local education authority or on the managers or governors of any county school or auxiliary school is thereby made contingent upon the opinion of the authority or of the managers or governors, the Minister may nevertheless require the authority managers or governors to perform that duty if in his opinion the circumstances are such as to require the performance thereof."

This clause was withdrawn after objections were raised in the House of Lords (H.L. Deb., cols. 540–552, June 29, 1944). It was replaced by what became section 68 (H.L. Deb., cols. 862–864, July 12, 1944); (cols. 954–966 (July 18, 1944)). The Lord Chancellor (Viscount Simon) explained that the Minister would be able to act under section 68 to prevent "monstrous abuses" of discretion, or a "completely" or "utterly" unreasonable exercise of discretion, where mandamus would not be an appropriate remedy. The Earl of Selborne (who was in charge of the Bill in the House of Lords) stated that section 68 could be used to reverse an "unwise or unfortunate" decision. "The real purpose of the clause is to provide some court of appeal in cases where local authorities or managers have acted unreasonably" (col. 960).

3. The view taken by the ministry of their powers under section 68, as revealed in investigations by the P.C.A., is considered by D. Foulkes in "Tameside and the Education Act, 1944" (1976) 126 N.L.J. 649.

4. The *Tameside* case was discussed in the House of Commons on December 8, 1976. See H.C. Debates, Vol. 922, cols. 590–598 1976/77. The new Secretary of State (Mrs. Shirley Williams) stated that the Department was advised in 1948 that "unreasonableness" in section 68 involved an element of perversity: indeed the judgments in the House of Lords contained nothing surprising on the interpretation of "unreasonable." However, the courts had "made judgments on issues and findings of fact . . . in relation to matters which, as the law was previously understood, were regarded as entirely within the province of the Minister or Secretary of State," and some of the judgments and findings were "surprising" (col. 595). Overall, section 68 was used sparingly by successive Secretaries of State, almost invariably in relation to the allocation to schools of individual pupils or small groups of pupils.

Questions

1. Section 1 of the Education Act 1944 imposes on the Secretary of State the duty—

> "to promote the education of the people of England and Wales and the progressive development of institutions devoted to that purpose, and to secure the effective execution by local authorities, under his control and direction, of the national policy for providing a varied and comprehensive educational service in every area."

Do you think that sufficient weight was given to this section?

2. Lord Wilberforce states that under section 68 the Secretary of State "by contrast with the courts in the normal case, may substitute his opinion for that of the authority." How far is this borne out in the *Tameside* case?

3. Where the Secretary of State considers an education authority to be acting unreasonably in what ways (if any) is the section 68 procedure more useful for the minister than an application to the High Court for one of the general administrative law remedies?

4. There was general agreement that matters had to be judged as at June 11, 1976. Lord Russell of Killowen did not "subscribe to the view that facts subsequently brought forward as then existing can be relied on as showing that the proposals were not unreasonable, unless those facts are of such a character that they can be taken to be within the knowledge of the department." Should "new evidence" of this sort be generally admissible?

5. Is this case authority for the proposition that a decision is *ultra vires* if it is unsupported by any evidence? (See below, pp. 651 *et seq.*) Was the Secretary of State's decision that the authority were proposing to act unreasonably one of *jurisdictional* fact? (See above, pp. 210 *et seq.*)

(D) INCONSISTENCY

In the previous chapter we noted the unwillingness of the courts to utilise notions of estoppel in favour of applications for review who claim to have been misled by a public body as to the scope of its powers, or by an official or a committee as to the extent of his or its authority. See, above pp. 319–338. The concern of the courts in these cases has been an unwillingness to allow the concept of estoppel to result in the enlargement of the powers actually conferred by the terms of the legislation, or of the powers actually delegable, or delegated, by the respondent body.

We now turn to consider a series of cases in which the applicants are making complaints broadly similar to those in the estoppel cases, (*i.e.* that the respondent body has led them to expect something different from the course of action or decision actually taken, and that they have suffered loss or harm in consequence of relying on what they had been led to expect), but where conflict with the basic *ultra vires* doctrine is less apparent. In these cases there is no question of the courts being asked to "commit" a body to a decision which it had no power to make. The issue is whether in a situation where a body had a discretion to act in a variety of ways (or not to act at all) it may "commit" itself to a particular course of action because it had previously acted so as to engender in the applicant a legitimate expectation that it would exercise its discretion in that way. In other words, will the body be held no longer to retain its choice of alternatives, but be obliged to act so as to fulfil the expectations which its behaviour has aroused? It will be apparent that, just as in the "estoppel" cases, there are difficulties reconciling any such doctrine with the obligation (noted above, p. 263) that bodies possessing discretionary powers should retain an unencumbered discretion to exercise those powers as and how the public interest may from time to time require. In developing a doctrine of "unjustifiable inconsistency" we shall see that the courts have sought to achieve a compromise between this duty, and the notion that for a body to exercise discretionary power in a way which confounds expectations resulting from its own prior behaviour may itself be considered an abuse of the discretionary power.

RE PRESTON

[1985] A.C. 835; [1985] 2 All E.R. 327 (House of Lords)

In May 1978 an inspector of the Inland Revenue sought a meeting with the applicant taxpayer, to discuss his tax returns for the years 1975–76 to 1976–77, and in particular to discuss certain claims for reliefs in respect of losses and certain share transactions. The inspector requested full details of the share transactions. Bare details were furnished by the applicant. There followed an exchange of correspondence. In due course the applicant offered to withdraw his claim to reliefs if the Inland Revenue would settle his tax affairs for these years and raise no further questions about the share transactions. In July 1978 the inspector wrote to the applicant agreeing to this proposal. The taxpayer withdrew the claims and paid capital gains tax in respect of the shares. In October 1979 the Inland Revenue received information which led them to believe that the sale of the shares had been part of a tax avoidance scheme, thereby giving the applicant a "tax advantage." In July 1982, by which time it was too late for the applicant to make his claims for relief, the Inland Revenue issued a notice under section 465 of the Income and Corporation Taxes Act 1970 requiring the applicant to furnish information about the sale of the shares. The applicant supplied such information. The Inland Revenue, in September 1982, issued a further notice, under section 460 of the 1970 Act, cancelling the tax advantage gained by the applicant.

At first instance, Woolf J. held that the Revenue had failed to consider facts (*i.e.* the 1978 agreement) which were relevant to its exercise of discretion to issue the section 460 notice, and that it had in the circumstances exercised its discretion unreasonably ([1983] 2 All E.R. 300). The Court of Appeal allowed the Revenue's appeal, differing from the trial judge as to whether the Revenue had acted unreasonably. On appeal to the House of Lords:

LORD TEMPLEMAN: . . . The court can only intervene by judicial review to direct the commissioners to abstain from performing their statutory duties or from exercising their statutory powers if the court is satisfied that "the unfairness" of which the applicant complains renders the insistence by the commissioners on performing their duties or exercising their powers an abuse of power by the commissioners.

In most cases in which the court has granted judicial review on grounds of "unfairness" amounting to abuse of power there has been some proven element of improper motive. In the leading case of *Padfield* v. *Minister of Agriculture, Fisheries and Food* [1968] A.C. 997 the Minister abstained from exercising his statutory discretion to order an investigation because he feared the consequences of the investigation might be politically embarrassing. In *Congreve* v. *Home Office* [1976] Q.B. 629 the Minister exercised his power to revoke television licences because he disapproved of the conduct of the licence holders, albeit they had acted lawfully. In *Laker Airways Ltd.* v. *Department of Trade* [1977] Q.B. 643 the Minister exercised his statutory discretion to give directions with regard to civil airways with the ulterior motive of making it impossible for one of the airlines to pursue a course of which the Minister disapproved. In these case judicial review was granted because the Ministers acted "unfairly" when they abused their powers by exercising or declining to exercise those powers in order to achieve objectives which were not the objectives for which the powers had been conferred. The question of "fairness" was considered in *H.T.V. Ltd.* v. *Price Commission* [1976] I.C.R. 170.

In that case the Price Commission misconstrued the counter inflation price code and changed its mind as to the treatment of exchequer levy as an item in the costs of television companies allowable for the purpose of increasing their advertising charges within the limits prescribed by the code. The effect of the change of mind of the Price Commission was to deprive the companies of an increase of advertising charges which they were plainly intended to enjoy and which they badly needed in order to remain financially viable. Lord Denning M.R. said, at pp. 185–186:

> "It has been often said, I know, that a public body, which is entrusted by Parliament with the exercise of powers for the public good, cannot fetter itself in the exercise of them. It cannot be estopped from doing its public duty. But that is subject to the qualification that it must not misuse its powers: and it is a misuse of power for it to act unfairly or unjustly towards a private citizen when there is no overriding public interest to warrant it. . . ."

In the *H.T.V.* case [1976] I.C.R. 170 my noble and learned friend, then Scarman L.J., . . . after considering the Price Commission's change of mind, said, at p. 192, that "the commission's inconsistency has already resulted in unfairness, and, unless corrected, could cause further injustice. Firstly, it gives rise to a real possibility of an erosion of profit margin . . ." Next, if, as the Price Commission contended, the Exchequer levy was excluded in 1976 but included in 1973 then the television companies would be unable to obtain a fair increase in advertising charges corresponding to increases in costs between 1973 and 1976:

> "The commission, to avoid being unfair, must either include or exclude Exchequer levy as a cost upon both sides of the comparison. Since it has made clear that, in the absence of a ruling to the contrary, it intends to exclude it when calculating current profit margins, the commission must also exclude it when calculating the profit margin at April 30, 1973. I am not completely sure that it intends so to do if it succeeds in this litigation. . . . The commission has acted inconsistently and unfairly; and on this ground, were it necessary, I would think H.T.V. are also entitled to declaratory relief."

In the *H.T.V.* case [1976] I.C.R. 170, the "unfairness" of the decision was due not to improper motive on the part of the Price Commission but to an error of law whereby the Price Commission misconstrued the code they were intending to enforce. If the Price Commission had not misconstrued the code, they would not have acted "inconsistently and unfairly." Of course the inconsistent and unfair results to which Scarman L.J. drew attention were themselves powerful support for the contention that the Price Commission must have misconstrued the code.

In the present case, the appellant does not allege that the commissioners invoked section 460 for improper purposes or motives or that the commissioners misconstrued their powers and duties. However, the *H.T.V.* case and the authorities there cited suggest that the commissioners are guilty of "unfairness" amounting to an abuse of power if by taking action under section 460 their conduct would, in the case of an authority other than Crown authority, entitle the appellant to an injunction or damages based on breach of contract or estoppel by representation. In principle I see no reason why the appellant should not be entitled to judicial review of a decision taken by the commissioners if that decision is unfair to the appellant because the conduct of the commissioners is equivalent to a breach of contract or a breach of representation. Such a decision falls within the ambit of an abuse of power for which in the present case judicial review is the sole remedy and an appropriate remedy. There may be cases in which conduct which savours of breach of conduct or breach of representation does not constitute an abuse of power; there may be circumstances in which the court in its discretion might not grant relief by judicial review notwithstanding conduct which savours of breach of contract or breach of representation. In the present case, however, I consider that the appellant is entitled to relief by way of judicial review for "unfairness' amounting to abuse of power if the commissioners have been guilty of conduct equivalent to a breach of contract or breach of representations on their part.

[His Lordship reviewed the facts of the case and concluded that there had been no abuse of power in the above sense. In particular, the correspondence did not support the applicant's contention that the Revenue had agreed that there would be no further inquiries into the share transactions even on the Revenue becoming aware that the assessments, made in the light of the incomplete information supplied by the applicant, did not represent his full tax liability.]

LORD SCARMAN, agreeing with the reasons given by LORD TEMPLEMAN, said:

"It was the appellant's case that upon the true construction of the correspondence in 1978 . . . the commissioners purported to contract or to represent that they would not thereafter re-open the tax assessments . . . if he withdrew his claims for interest relief and capital loss. Had he made good this case, I do not doubt that he would have been entitled to relief by way of judicial review for unfairness amounting to abuse of the power. . . . But he failed upon the construction of the correspondence. . . ."

LORDS EDMUND-DAVIES, KEITH OF KINKEL and BRIGHTMAN also agreed with the reasons given by LORD TEMPLEMAN.

Note

See case note by C. Lewis, (1986) 49 M.L.R. 251, and the articles cited below at p. 437, n. 6.

R. v. SECRETARY OF STATE FOR THE HOME DEPARTMENT, ex p. ASIF MAHMOOD KHAN

[1984] 1 W.L.R. 1337; [1985] 1 All E.R. 40 (Court of Appeal)

A Home Office circular letter stated that although the Immigration Rules did not permit a foreign child subject to immigration control to enter the UK for the purposes of adoption, the Secretary of State would permit such entry provided certain specified criteria were met. The criteria involved the adoption being genuine and not merely a device for obtaining entry, that the child's welfare in this country be assured, that the courts here would be likely to grant an adoption order, and that one of the intending adopters be domiciled in the UK. The letter then stated the procedure to be followed by would-be adopters. This was to obtain an entry clearance from an entry clearance officer abroad. That officer would have to be satisfied of the child's wishes and the wishes of the natural parents. The applicant and his wife wished to adopt a relative's child, living with its natural mother in Pakistan. Application for an entry clearance was made in Islamabad. All the various criteria listed above appeared to have been satisfied. However, in due course, following referral of the matter to the Home Office, entry clearance was refused. This was on the ground that there were no "serious and compelling family and other considerations" making refusal of permission to enter undesirable. The entry clearance officer's report to the Home Office had made clear the fact that the child in question was living in good conditions with his natural mother. The applicant appealed against the decision of Stephen Brown J., dismissing his application for judicial review to quash the decision to refuse clearance.

PARKER L.J.: [His Lordship noted the policy actually applied by the Home Office in coming to its decision, and continued:]

If this was the policy, the "guidance" given in the Home Office letter is grossly misleading, as was frankly accepted by counsel on behalf of the Secretary of State. There is not a word [in the circular letter] to suggest that in exercising his discretion the Secretary of State requires to be satisfied that the natural parents are incapable of looking after the prospective adoptee, or even that their ability or inability to do so was considered relevant. Furthermore, there is no evidence that entry clearance officers were instructed to inquire as to this matter, which of course does not depend only on the standard of living enjoyed in the natural home. The whole tenor of the letter is that, if the application was genuine, if the child's welfare was assured, if a court would be likely to grant an order and if the natural parents gave a real consent, the child would be let in and its ultimate fate left to the court here. If an adoption order was made it would remain. If an order was refused it would be returned.

The applicant relies on three authorities on the basis of which he contends that the refusal of entry clearance should be quashed. The first of these cases is *R. v. Liverpool Corporation, ex p. Liverpool Taxi Fleet Operators' Association* [1972] 2 Q.B. 299. [See further, below p. 502. His Lordship considered this decision and continued:]

In that case there was a specific undertaking, whereas here there is not; the corporation had a statutory power, whereas here the power of the Secretary of State is a common law power; and the matter complained of was a positive act, whereas here the complaint is a refusal to act. There can, however, be no doubt that the Secretary of State has a duty to exercise his common law discretion fairly. Furthermore, just as, in the case cited, the corporation was held not to be entitled to resile from an undertaking and change its policy without giving a fair hearing so, in principle, the Secretary of State, if he undertakes to allow in persons if certain conditions are satisfied, should not in my view be entitled to resile from that undertaking without affording interested persons a hearing and then only if the overriding public interest demands it.

The second of the authorities relied on by the applicant is *O'Reilly* v. *Mackman* [1983] 2 A.C. 237. The case is relied on solely for a statement of principle in the speech of Lord Diplock with which Lord Fraser of Tullybelton, Lord Keith of Kinkel, Lord Bridge of Harwich and Lord Brightman agreed. It is therefore necessary to state the facts only to the limited extent necessary to render that statement understandable. Four prisoners had been awarded forfeiture of remission by the board of visitors. They sought to challenge the decision of the board on the ground that there had been a failure to observe the rules of natural justice, the relief sought being declaratory only. [His Lordship set out the passage:

> "It is not, and it could not be, contended that the decision of the board awarding him forfeiture of remission . . . which means no more than to act fairly towards him in carrying out their decision-making process, and I prefer so to put it," below p. 723).]

Here it is contended that the applicant, by virtue of the terms of the Home Office letter, had a legitimate expectation that the procedures set out in the letter would be followed and that such legitimate expectation gave him sufficient interest to challenge the admitted failure of the Secretary of State to observe such procedures. I agree and the contrary was not suggested by [counsel for the Secretary of State]. But to have a sufficient interest to afford a *locus standi* to challenge is a long way from being entitled to succeed in such challenge.

The applicant, however, contends that on the basis of the third authority on which he relies, coupled with his first which I have already considered, he is so entitled. That authority is a Privy Council case, *Att.-Gen. of Hong Kong* v. *Ng Yuen Shiu* [1983] 2 A.C. 629, which at the time of the hearing before the judge had been reported only in *The Times* newspaper. The advice of their Lordships were delivered by Lord Fraser of Tullybelton. The other members of the Judicial Committee were Lord Scarman, Lord Bridge of Harwich, Lord Brandon of Oakbrook and Sir John Megaw. For some years prior to October 23, 1980, the government of Hong Kong had adopted a policy under which illegal immigrants from China were not repatriated if they managed to reach the urban areas without being arrested. This was known as the "reached base" policy. On October 23, 1980, the government announced that this policy would be discontinued forthwith and at the same time issued a new ordinance which, inter alia, gave the Director of Immigration power to make removal orders in respect of illegal immigrants. There was no statutory provision for a hearing or inquiry before a removal order was made. Subsequent to the change of policy there were a series of television announcements stating that all illegal immigrants from China would be liable to be repatriated. Mr. Ng, like many others in the colony, although they had entered illegally from Macau, was of Chinese origin. They were accordingly worried and on October 28, 1980, a group, not including Mr. Ng, went to Government House and submitted a petition.

There, there were read out a series of questions and answers prepared in the office of the Secretary for Security which dealt with the position of such persons and the action they should take. One of such questions, with its answer, was:

> "*Q.* Will we be given identity cards? *A.* Those illegal immigrants from Macau will be treated in accordance with procedures for illegal immigrants from anywhere other than China. They will be interviewed in due course. No guarantee can be given that you may not subsequently be removed. Each case will be treated on its merits."

Although Mr. Ng was not present he did see a television programme on the subject on the evening of the same day.

On October 31 a removal order was made against him. This he challenged and eventually on May 13, 1981, the Court of Appeal of Hong Kong made an order of prohibition prohibiting the Director of Immigration from executing the removal order before an opportunity had been given to Mr. Ng of putting all the circumstances of his case before the director. The Attorney-General appealed to the Privy Council.

The High Court and the Court of Appeal in Hong Kong had both held that Mr. Ng had no general right to a fair hearing before a removal order was made against him and the Judicial Committee assumed, without deciding, that they had rightly so decided. It was concerned only with the narrow question whether what had been said outside Government House entitled Mr. Ng to such a hearing. It is necessary to cite four passages from Lord Fraser's judgment:

> (1) " 'Legitimate expectations' in this context are capable of including expectations which go beyond enforceable legal rights, *provided they have some reasonable basis*." (p. 636E–F)
>
> (2) "The expectations may be based on some *statement* or undertaking by, or on behalf of, the public authority which has the duty of making the decision, if the authority has, through its officers, acted *in a way that would make it unfair or inconsistent with good administration for him to be denied such* an inquiry." (p. 637C–D)
>
> (3) "Their Lordships see no reason why the principle should not be applicable when the person who will be affected by the decision is an alien, just as much as when he is a British subject. The justification for it is primarily that, *when a public authority has promised to follow a certain procedure, it is in the interest of good administration that it should act fairly and should implement its promise, so long as implementation does not interfere with its statutory duty*. The principle is also justified by the further consideration that, when the promise was made, *the authority must have considered that it would be assisted in discharging its duty fairly* by any representations from interested parties and as a general rule that is correct. In the opinion of their Lordships the principle that a public authority is bound by its undertakings as to the procedure it will follow, provided they do not conflict with its duty, is applicable to the undertaking given by the government of Hong Kong to the respondent, along with other illegal immigrants from Macau, in the announcement outside Government House on October 28, 1980, that each case would

> be considered on its merits. The only ground on which it was argued before the Board that the undertaking had not been implemented was that the respondent had not been given an opportunity to put his case for an exercise of discretion, which the director undoubtedly possesses, in his favour before a decision was reached." (p. 638E–H)
>
> (4) "Their Lordships consider that this is a very narrow case on its facts, but they are not disposed to differ from the view expressed by both the courts below, to the effect that the government's promise to the respondent has not been implemented. Accordingly the appeal ought to be dismissed. But in the circumstances their Lordships are of opinion that the order made by the Court of Appeal should be varied. The appropriate remedy is not the conditional order of prohibition made by the Court of Appeal, but an order of certiorari to quash the removal order made by the director on October 31, against the respondent. That order of certiorari is of course entirely without prejudice to the making of a fresh removal order by the Director of Immigration after a fair inquiry has been held at which the respondent has been given an opportunity to make such representations as he may see fit as to why he should not be removed." (p. 639E–F)

The emphasis in each case is mine.

That case is, of course, not binding on this court but is of high persuasive authority. In my view it correctly sets out the law of England and should be applied.

I have no doubt that the Home Office letter afforded the applicant a reasonable expectation that the procedures it set out, which were just as certain in their terms as the question and answer in Mr. Ng's case, would be followed, that if the result of the implementation of those procedures satisfied the Secretary of State of the four matters mentioned a temporary entry clearance certificate would be granted and that the ultimate fate of the child would then be decided by the adoption court of this country. I have equally no doubt that it was considered by the department at the time the letter was sent out that if those procedures were fully implemented they would be sufficient to safeguard the public interest. The letter can mean nothing else. This is not surprising. The adoption court will apply the law of this country and will thus protect all the interests which the law of this country considers should be protected. The Secretary of State is, of course, at liberty to change the policy but in my view, vis-à-vis the recipient of such a letter, a new policy can only be implemented after such recipient has been given a full and serious consideration whether there is some overriding public interest which justifies a departure from the procedures stated in the letter. . . .

I would allow the appeal and quash the refusal of entry clearance. This will leave the Secretary of State free either to proceed on the basis of the letter or, if he considers it desirable to operate the new policy, to afford the applicant a full opportunity to make representations why, in his case, it should not be followed.

I would only add this. If the new policy is to continue in operation, the sooner the Home Office letter is redrafted and false hopes cease to be raised in those who may have a deep emotional need to adopt, the better it will be. To leave it in its present form is not only bad and grossly unfair administration but, in some instances at any rate, positively cruel.

[Dunn L.J. also delivered a judgment allowing the appeal. He took the view that "although the circular letter did not create an estoppel" it had indicated what were the relevant considerations as regards the exercise of this discretionary power, and the Secretary of State had therefore taken into account an *irrelevant* consideration. In so doing he had "misdirected himself according to his own criteria and acted unreasonably." Watkins L.J. dissented, taking the view that, properly construed, the circular letter only indicated factors which if not satisfied would certainly lead to refusal of clearance; it did not indicate that compliance with those factors would itself lead to grant of permission. The letter said that the Secretary "may exercise his discretion and exceptionally allow. . . ." Parker L.J. had noted this formula, and had taken the view that a reader would have inferred that, provided the conditions were satisfied, permission to enter "would be the likely result."]

Appeal allowed

Notes

1. See case notes by C. Lewis, (1986) 49 M.L.R. 251 and A. R. Mowbray, [1985] P.L. 558.

2. Although Dunn L.J. says that he is not applying an estoppel, the proposition that considerations other than the published criteria were legally irrelevant seems to come to the same thing (see P. Elias in J. Jowell and D. Oliver (eds.), *New Directions in Judicial Review* (1988), p. 48).

3. Mr. Khan's application was subsequently re-considered in accordance with the circular letter, and the letter was redrafted for the future, referring expressly to the policy requirement that the original parents must be incapable of looking after the child, but also stating that:

> ". . . the Home Secretary may exceptionally exercise discretion to allow a child to come here for (adoption) if he is satisfied that this is appropriate in all the circumstances of the case."

Thus the Home Office had reacted "by reducing the specificity and precision of its administrative guidance" (see A. R. Mowbray, [1985] P.L. 558 at p. 563).

4. *Cf. Oloniluyi* v. *Secretary of State for the Home Department* [1989] Imm.A.R. 135, as explained in *R.* v. *Secretary of State for the Home Department, ex p. Mowla* [1991] Imm.A.R. 210.

R. v. INLAND REVENUE COMMISSIONERS, ex p. MFK UNDERWRITING AGENTS LTD.

[1990] 1 W.L.R. 1545; [1990] 1 All E.R. 90 (D.C. (Q.B.D.))

The applicants were Lloyd's underwriting agents. Under Lloyd's rule premiums had to be retained in trust funds for a period of two years after the close of an underwriting year. In order to produce a yield which was taxable as capital gain rather than as income Lloyd's syndicates invested in index-linked gilts or similar securities. Lloyd's rules also required that premiums paid in US/Canadian dollars be invested US/Canadian dollar accounts or securities. Until 1986 there were no index-linked dollar securities available in which to invest. A number of US banks therefore proposed to issue such securities for the Lloyd's market. The banks and their solicitors and accountants each made approaches to the Revenue seeking assurances that the index-linked element payable on redemption would be regarded as capital and not income. The Revenue gave this assurance. Between April 1986 and October 1988 the applicants bought such bonds. In October 1988 the Revenue decided to tax the index-linked element as income. The applicants sought judicial review of this decision.

BINGHAM L.J.: . . . C. The contentions of the parties . . . [Counsel for the applicants] submitted that decisions of the Revenue are subject to judicial review on the same grounds as those of any other public authority. These grounds include abuse or excess of power. The overriding criterion for deciding whether there has been an excess of abuse of power is to decide whether the authority's (here the Revenue's) conduct has been unfair. The Revenue's conduct was *prima facie* unfair if it conflicted with an undertaking or assurance of the Revenue which would (were the Revenue not a public body) give rise to an estoppel or breach of contract. If a public authority has a policy which it makes known or announces it may not act inconsistently with the policy without sufficient notice, and then not retrospectively. This rule applies even where, in private law, there might be no estoppel. It is a principle of public law that decisions of public bodies may not be internally inconsistent. A public body must recognise and give effect to the legitimate expectations of those who deal with it, in matters both of procedure and decision. For these propositions of law [counsel for the applicants] relied in particular on *R.* v. *Inland Revenue Commissioners, ex p. National Federation of Self-Employed and Small Businesses Ltd.* [1982] A.C. 617 ("the *Fleet Street Casuals* case"), *R.* v. *Inland Revenue Commissioners, ex p. Preston* [1985] A.C. 835, *H.T.V. Ltd.* v. *Price Commission* [1976] I.C.R. 170, *Att.-Gen. of Hong Kong* v. *Ng Yuen Shiu* [1983] 2 A.C. 629, *R.* v. *Secretary of State for the Home Department, ex p. Khan* [1984] 1 W.L.R. 1337 and *R.* v. *Secretary of State for the Home Department, ex p. Ruddock* [1987] 1 W.L.R. 1482.

On the facts [counsel for the applicants] submitted that the policy of the Revenue before March 1988 plainly was not to challenge as disguised interest the indexation uplift on bonds of this kind provided that the bonds paid a commercial rate of interest in addition to the indexation uplift. This policy was made known to potential investors and their advisers by answering the same sort of questions in the same way. The circumstances in which the answers were given were such that it was highly probable the answers would be passed to investors. On any view of the evidence the Revenue's statements were an effective inducement to these applicants to buy bonds.

The thrust of the applicants' argument was thus very simple. The Revenue had repeatedly made known its view of these bonds. It need not have done so, but it did. It would be grossly unfair to these applicants, and so an abuse of the Revenue's statutory powers, if the Revenue were now free to alter its position with retrospective effect to the prejudice of the applicants.

[Counsel for the Crown] accepted that his client was not immune from judicial review. . . . [Counsel] further accepted that unfairness might in principle amount to an abuse of power and that there could be an exceptional case where it would be unfair for the Revenue to resile from a representation made or undertaking given when the making of the representation or giving of the undertaking involved no breach of the Revenue's statutory duty. Judicial review could not, however, lie to oblige the Revenue to act contrary to its statutory duty. Such would be the case if these applications succeeded. It is for Parliament, and Parliament alone, to decide what taxes shall be paid. It is for the Inland Revenue to collect the tax Parliament has ordained. The Revenue has no general discretion to remit taxes Parliament has imposed: *Vestey* v. *Inland Revenue Commissioners* (*Nos 1 and 2*) [1980] A.C. 1148). While the Revenue has under the Inland Revenue Regulation Act 1890 and the Taxes Management Act 1970:

> "a wide managerial discretion as to the best means of obtaining for the national exchequer from the taxes committed to their charge, the highest net return that is practicable having regard to the staff available to them and the cost of collection"

(per Lord Diplock in the *Fleet Street Casuals* case [1982] A.C. 617, 636G), this was a discretion which could only lawfully be exercised for the better, more efficient and more economical collection of tax and not otherwise. The taxing Acts provided for inspectors to make assessments on individual taxpayers year by year. One inspector could not bind another, nor one inspector bind himself from one year to another. When an assessment was disputed, a familiar and well-lubricated machinery existed to resolve the dispute. Special or General Commissioners, or on questions of law the courts, were the ultimate arbiters. The Revenue could not without breach of statutory duty agree or indicate in advance that it would not collect tax which, on a proper construction of the relevant legislation, was lawfully due.

In any event, [counsel for the Crown] argued, the Revenue had here done no such thing. Even if the Revenue might in principle be bound by clear and unqualified answers to questions put with reference to specific and fully detailed transactions, it could not be bound by general and qualified statements of its current thinking given in relation to different transactions. Such, he submitted, was the material on which the applicants relied. In contrast with *Att.-Gen. of Hong Kong* v. *Ng Yuen Shiu*, *ex p. Khan* and *ex p. Ruddock* the statements relied on fell far short of any statement of official policy.

[Counsel for the applicants] in reply accepted that the Revenue could not bind itself to act in conflict with its statutory duty. If its statutory duty left the Revenue no choice but to collect taxes then there was no scope for any binding representation. But the representations here were made in pursuance of the Revenue's duty to collect tax and fell within its reasonable area of managerial discretion. . . .

D. *The correct approach in law*

I take as my starting point the following passage from Lord Templeman's speech in *ex p. Preston* [1985] A.C. 835, 866, expressly adopted by the other members of the House . . . [His Lordships cited the passage "However, the *H.T.V.* case and the authorities there cited . . . conduct equivalent to a breach of contract or breach of representations on their part."]

It was not suggested in *ex p. Preston* that the bargain allegedly made, if made, would have been a breach of the Revenue's statutory duty, but the applicants here accept that they must fail if the Revenue could not lawfully make the statements or representations which (it is said) it did. So if, in a case involving no breach of statutory duty, the Revenue makes an agreement or representation from which it cannot withdraw without substantial unfairness to the taxpayer who has relied on it, that may found a successful application for judicial review.

I cannot for my part accept that the Revenue's discretion is as limited as counsel for the Crown submitted. In the *Fleet Street Casuals* case the revenue agreed to cut past (irrecoverable) losses in order to facilitate collection of tax in future. In *ex p. Preston* the Revenue cut short an argument with the taxpayer to obtain an immediate payment of tax. In both cases the revenue acted within its managerial discretion. The present case is less obvious. But the Revenue's judgment on the best way of collecting tax should not lightly be cast aside. The Revenue might stick to the letter of its statutory duty, declining to answer any question when not statutorily obliged to do so (as it sometimes is: see, *e.g.* sections 464 and 488(11) of the Income and Corporation Taxes Act 1970) and maintaining a strictly arm's length relationship with the taxpayer. It is, however, understandable if the Revenue has not in practice found this to be the best way of facilitating collection of the public revenue. That this has been the Revenue's experience is, I think, made clear by Mr. Beighton, who, having described the machinery for assessment and appeal, continues:

> "6. Notwithstanding this general approach in administering the tax system, the Board see it as a proper part of their function and contributing to the achievement of their primary role of assessing and collecting

> the proper amounts of tax and to detect and deter evasion, that they should when possible advise the public of their rights as well as their duties, and generally encourage co-operation between the Inland Revenue and the public."

I do not think that we, sitting in this court, have any reason to dissent from this judgment. It follows that I do not think the assurances the Revenue are here said to have given are in themselves inconsistent with the Revenue's statutory duty.

I am, however, of opinion that in assessing the meaning, weight and effect reasonably to be given to statements of the Revenue the factual context, including the position of the Revenue itself, is all important. Every ordinarily sophisicated taxpayer knows that the Revenue is a tax-collecting agency, not a tax-imposing authority. The taxpayers' only legitimate expectation is, prima facie, that he will be taxed according to statute, not concession or a wrong view of the law (see *R.* v. *Attorney-General, ex p. Imperial Chemical Industries plc* (1986) 60 T.C. 1, 64 *per* Lord Oliver). Such taxpayers would appreciate, if they could not so pithily express, the truth of the aphorism of "One should be taxed by law, and not be untaxed by concession:" see *Vestey* v. *Inland Revenue Commissioners per* Walton J. [1979] Ch. 177, 197. No doubt a statement formally published by the Revenue to the world might safely be regarded as binding, subject to its terms, in any case falling clearly within them. But where the approach to the Revenue is of a less formal nature a more detailed inquiry is, in my view, necessary. If it is to be successfully said that as a result of such an approach the Revenue has agreed to forgo, or has represented that it will forgo, tax which might arguably be payable on a proper construction of the relevant legislation it would in my judgment, be ordinarily necessary for the taxpayer to show that certain conditions had been fulfilled. I say "ordinarily" to allow for the exceptional case where different rules might be appopriate, but the necessity in my view exists here. First, it is necessary that the taxpayer should have put all his cards face upwards on the table. This means that he must give full details of the specific transaction on which he seeks the Revenue's ruling, unless it is the same as an earlier transaction on which a ruling has already been given. It means that he must indicate to the Revenue the ruling sought. It is one thing to ask an official of the Revenue whether he shares the taxpayer's view of a legislative provision, quite another to ask whether the Revenue will forgo any claim to tax on any other basis. It means that the taxpayer must make plain that a fully considered ruling is sought. It means, I think, that the taxpayer should indicate the use he intends to make of any ruling given. This is not because the Revenue would wish to favour one class of taxpayers at the expense of another but because knowledge that a ruling is to be publicised in a large and important market could affect the person by whom and the level at which a problem is considered and, indeed, whether it is appropriate to give a ruling at all.

Second, it is necessary that the ruling or statement relied on should be clear, unambiguous and devoid of relevant qualification.

In so stating these requirements I do not, I hope, diminish or emasculate the valuable developing doctrine of legitimate expectation. If a public authority so conducts itself as to create a legitimate expectation that a certain course will be followed it would often be unfair if the authority were permitted to follow a different course to the detriment of one who entertained the expectation, particularly if he acted on it. If in private law a body would be in breach of contract in so acting or estopped from so acting a public authority should generally be in no better position. The doctrine of legitimate expectation is rooted in fairness. But fairness is not a one-way street. It imports the notion of equitableness, of fair and open dealing, to which the authority is as much entitled as the citizen. The Revenue's discretion, while it exists, is limited. Fairness requires that its exercise should be on a basis of full disclosure. Counsel for the applicants accepted that it would not be reasonable for a representee to rely on an unclear or equivocal representation. Nor, I think, on facts such as the present, would it be fair to hold the Revenue bound by anything less than a clear, unambiguous and unqualified representation.

E. *Conclusions*

Against that legal background I return to the representations relied on here to consider whether they meet the conditions specified. . . .

[Bingham L.J. considered the correspondence in detail and concluded:]

The materials before us in this case make plain how strongly the applicants feel that the Revenue's conduct, in taxing the indexation uplift on these bonds as income, is unfair. I do not, however, think that in the disputed cases the Revenue has promised to follow or indicated that it would follow a certain course so as to render any departure from that course unfair. I do not accordingly find any abuse of power. I would therefore refuse relief. Had I found that there was unfairness, significant enough to be an abuse of power, I would not exercise my discretion to refuse relief.

JUDGE J.: . . . In the present case the Revenue promulgated a number of guidelines and answered questions by or on behalf of taxpayers about the likely approach to a number of given problems. The Revenue is not bound to give any guidance at all. If however the taxpayer approaches the Revenue with clear and precise proposals about the future conduct of his fiscal affairs and receives an unequivocal statement about how they will be treated for tax purposes if implemented, the Revenue should in my judgment be subject to judicial review on grounds of unfair abuse of power if it peremptorily decides that it will not be bound by such statements when the taxpayer has relied on them. The same principle should apply to revenue statements of policy. In those cases where the taxpayer has approached the Revenue for guidance the court will be unlikely to grant judicial review unless it is satisfied that the taxpayer has treated the revenue with complete frankness about his proposals. Applying private law tests the situation calls for utmost good faith on the part of the taxpayer. He should make full disclosure of all the material facts known to him.

For the reasons given by Bingham L.J. the evidence in the present case does not establish abuse of power by the Revenue. Accordingly, I agree that these applications should be refused.

Notes

1. See A. R. Mowbray, (1990) 106 L.Q.R. 568; S. Tidball, [1991] B.T.R. 48 and W. Hinds, "Estopping the Taxman" [1991] B.T.R. 191.

2. The concept of "legitimate expectation" is at the heart of this developing ground of challenge for "inconsistency." This concept emerged first as a factor relevant to the question whether the *audi alteram partem* rule of natural justice applied in a particular context. To defeat a person's legitimate expectation was to do to that person an act which should in ordinary circumstances be preceded by warning and the giving of an opportunity to make representations. A stock example of such a situation is the person who, having had the benefit of a licence or permission seeks its renewal. See further, below p. 507.

Subsequently, the notion of legitimate expectation was utilised to assist an applicant who complained—(i) that he had been adversely affected by a decision or action taken, (ii) that although in ordinary circumstances this was not a situation in which he was entitled to any "hearing" under the *audi alteram partem* rule, (iii) on the facts he had been given a legitimate expectation to expect such a "hearing" prior to the decision or action being taken. Such expectation might arise either from a settled practice of affording such opportunities or from statements or assurances given. Where such complaints have been substantiated the courts have been willing to quash decisions taken without the expected procedure being complied with. See further, below p. 519.

Both these applications of the notion of legitimate expectation relate to procedural obligations prior to taking decisions. The cases considered above have used the concept of legitimate expectation to impose restrictions on the substance of decisions or action that a body may take.

3. An important issue is whether the doctrine of inconsistency—(i) prohibits any decision being taken which confounds the expectation which the body in question has engendered; or (ii) prohibits such decisions except where some countervailing facet of the public so requires, this being judged in the light of the harm being done to the applicant; or (iii) prohibits such decisions except in the circumstances referred to in (ii) above, but with the added requirement that the affected individual be notified of the intended change of policy, and be given an opportunity to offer his thoughts against the new policy and/or its application to himself. On this issue see the various statements of principle in the cases extracted above, and note also in the *Laker* case (below).

In *Laker Airways Ltd.* v. *Department of Trade* [1977] Q.B. 643 C.A. (the *Skytrain* case) the plaintiffs were granted a licence by the Civil Aviation Authority in 1972 for a cheap passenger air service between London and New York, a licence confirmed on appeal by the (Conservative) Secretary of State. The government also "designated" the plaintiffs under the Bermuda Agreement of 1946 between the United Kingdom and the United States of America, with the result under the Agreement that the United States government were under a duty to grant a permit for operations over United States territory "without undue delay," provided the plaintiffs came up to the required standards. The government worked closely with the plaintiffs in exerting pressure on the United States authorities. The plaintiffs, with the active help and encouragement of the government, spent over £6 million on the project. In 1975, the Labour government reversed its predecessor's policy, and decided that not more than one United Kingdom airline should be licensed for any given long-haul route. The Secretary of State instructed the Civil Aviation Authority to revoke the plaintiff's licence (see above, p. 265) and withdrew the "designation." Mocatta J. ([1976] 3 W.L.R. 537) held, *inter alia*, that the government were estopped by their previous conduct from withdrawing the designation, but was reversed on this point by the Court of Appeal.

Lawton L.J. said, at p. 271:

> "Whatever representations the Secretary of State in office between 1972 and 1974 may have made to Laker Airways Ltd. he made them pursuant to his public duty and in good faith. If in 1976 his successor was of the opinion that the public interest required him to go back on those representations, he was in duty bound to go back on them. The fact that Laker Airways Ltd. suffered loss as a result of the change is unfortunate: they have been the victims of a change of government policy. This often happens. Estoppel cannot be allowed to hinder the formation of government policy."

Roskill L.J. stated, at p. 254, that the doctrine of estoppel cannot be allowed to hinder the constitutional result of a general election.

Lord Denning M.R. said, (at p. 252):

> "The underlying principle is that the Crown cannot be estopped from exercising its powers, whether given in a statute or by common law, when it is doing so in the proper exercise of its duty to act for the public good, even though this may work some injustice or unfairness to a private individual: see *Maritime Electric Co. Ltd.* v. *General Dairies Ltd.* [above p. 323] where the Privy Council, unfortunately, I think, reversed the Supreme Court of Canada [1935] S.C.R. 519. It can, however, be estopped when it is not properly exercising its powers, but is misusing them; and it does misuse them if it exercises them in circumstances which work injustice or unfairness to the individual without any countervailing benefit for the public. . . ."

Applying this principle Lord Denning M.R. took the view that the claim of "estoppel" had not been made out.

4. A further authority that supports the view that a legitimate expectation can give rise to substantive as well as procedural rights is *R.* v. *Secretary of State for the Home Department, ex p. Ruddock and others* [1987] 2 All E.R. 518. One of the three applicants, John Cox, a Vice-President of the Campaign for Nuclear Disarmament, sought judicial review of a warrant issued by the Secretary of State authorising the tapping of his telephone, alleging that the intercept fell outside the criteria for the interception of communications, which required, *inter alia*, that there was reasonable cause to believe that major subversive activity was being carried out, and that interception was not to be used for party political purposes. These criteria had been published and successive Secretaries of State had acknowledged their binding effect. The Secretary of State argued that the doctrine of legitimate expectation related only to cases where the applicant's expectation was of being consulted or given the opportunity to make representations before a certain decision adverse to him was made, and that as here there could be no question of his being consulted or heard before a warrant was issued, the legiti-

mate expectation doctrine could not reply. Taylor J. considered *Schmidt* v. *Home Secretary*, the *CCSU*, *Ng Yuen Shiu*, *Findlay* and *ex p. Khan* cases, concluded that while most of the cases concerned the right to be heard, the doctrine could not be so confined:

> "Indeed, in a case where ex hypothesi there is no right to be heard, it may be thought the more important to fair dealing that a promise or undertaking by the minister as to how he will proceed should be kept. Of course such promise or undertaking must not conflict with his statutory duty or his duty, as here, in the exercise of a prerogative power. I accept . . . that the respondent cannot fetter his discretion. By declaring a policy he does not preclude any possible need to change it. But then if the practice has been to publish the current policy, it would be incumbent on him in dealing fairly to publish the new policy, unless again that would conflict with his duties" (p. 531).

Here a legitimate expectation that the published criteria would be applied arose from both an express promise and a regular practice. The Secretary of State did not argue that the criteria had been changed or that an exception had been made for security reasons; his contention was that the intercept fell within the published criteria. Taylor J. concluded on the evidence that the Secretary of State had not deliberately flouted the criteria and that his decision that the warrant fell within them was not irrational.

5. *Ex p. Ruddock* can be compared with two cases where legitimate expectations could not prevent changes in policy. In *Re Findlay* [1985] A.C. 318, the Secretary of State for the Home Department announced changes of parole policy in respect of certain categories of prisoners. Prisoners sentenced for the murder of police or prison officers, terrorist offences, sexual or sadistic murder of children, or murder by a firearm in the course of robbery would henceforth normally serve at least 20 years; prisoners serving determinate sentences of over five years for offences of violence of drug trafficking would, save in exceptional circumstances, be granted parole only when release under supervision for a few months before the end of their sentence was likely to reduce the long-term risk to the public. Four prisoners who were affected by the changes sought judicial review on a variety of grounds. One ground in respect of the two life sentence prisoners was that they had good reason under the old policy to expect release much earlier than was likely under the new policy. Lord Scarman commented (at p. 338):

> "The doctrine of legitimate expectation has an important place in the developing law of judicial review. It is however, not necessary to explore the doctrine in this case, it is enough merely to note that a legitimate expectation can provide a sufficient interest to enable one who cannot point to the existence of a substantive right to obtain the leave of the court to apply for judicial review. These two appellants obtained leave. But their submission goes further. It is said that the refusal to except them from the new policy was an unlawful act on the part of the Secretary of State in that his decision frustrated their expectation. But what was their *legitimate* expectation? Given the substance and purpose of the legislative provisions governing parole, the most that a convicted prisoner can legitimately expect is that his case will be examined individually in the light of whatever policy the Secretary of State sees fit to adopt provided always that the adopted policy is a lawful exercise of the discretion conferred upon him by the statute. Any other view would entail the conclusion that the unfettered discretion conferred by the statute upon the minister can in some cases be restricted so as to hamper, or even prevent, changes of policy. Bearing in mind the complexity of the issues which the Secretary of State has to consider and the

importance of the public interest in the administration of parole I cannot think that Parliament intended the discretion to be restricted in this way."

Then, in *R.* v. *Secretary of State for Health, ex p. United States Tobacco International Inc.* [1992] 1 Q.B. 353 the Divisional Court considered a challenge to the Secretary of State's change of policy in deciding to make regulations banning oral snuff (a smokeless tobacco product). The applicants marketed "Skoal Bandits," porous sachets containing oral snuff. In 1984 they had discussed with various government departments the possibility of opening a factory in Scotland to manufacture their product. On the advice of a committee that advised the Secretary of State for Health, the government negotiated an agreement whereby the applicants undertook not to market oral snuff to persons under 18. The applicants opened their factory in 1985, with the help of a government grant. The agreement was revised in 1986 and subsequently extended to April 1988. In June 1986, however, the committee advised the Secretary of State to ban oral snuff; in February 1988, the Secretary of State announced a proposal for such a ban. The Divisional Court quashed the regulations on the ground of a lack of consultation with the applicants (see below, p. 460). However, the court rejected an argument based on legitimate expectation. Taylor L.J. (as he now was) noted that the:

"applicants are understandably aggrieved that after leading them on, the government should then strike them a mortal blow by totally banning their products" (p. 368).

They contended that they had

"a legitimate expectation that, provided they continued to perform their obligations under the voluntary agreement and absent the emergence of stronger evidence as to the risk to health, their operators would be permitted to continue" (*ibid.*).

This was not based on any express promise, but was implied by the course of conduct. Taylor L.J. cited, *inter alia*, the passages from Lord Scarman's judgment in *Re Findlay* and his own judgment in *ex p. Ruddock* set out above. He then said (p. 369):

"In the present case, if the Secretary of State concluded on rational grounds that a policy change was required and oral snuff should be banned in the public interest, his discretion could not be fettered by moral obligations to the applicants deriving from his earlier favourable treatment of them. It would be absurd to suggest that some moral commitment to a single company should prevail over the public interest."

Morland J. said (at p. 372):

"The applicants were entitled to expect that their commercial operations would be allowed to continue and expand subject to their compliance with the voluntary agreement unless there were good and substantial reasons for a change in Government policy. However, they must have been aware that their expectations could never fetter the Secretary of State's duty to promote and safeguard the health of the public. That is a duty which must . . . override private commercial expectations and interests. The right of government to change its policy in the field of health must be unfettered. This is so even if the basic scientific evidence remains unchanged or substantially unchanged. Reconsideration and re-evaluation of that evidence may call for a change of policy."

See B. Schwehr and P. Brown, [1991] P.L. 163, who criticise the decision on this aspect of the case as diluting an "otherwise healthy and beneficial doctrine" (p. 167). In holding that there was no legitimate expectation, the court had conflated two distinct issues, first, whether there was a legitimate expectation and, secondly, if there was, whether there was good ground for it to be overridden in the public interest:

> "The relevant question for the court is not, 'is there a legitimate expectation?' but, 'has the minister shown a good reason for changing his mind?' " (p. 166).

The court had failed to address the second question directly (although the answer might still have been in the affirmative). See, to similar effect, P. P. Craig, (1992) 108 L.Q.R. 79, 97. *Cf.* Lord Donaldson M.R. in *R.* v. *Independent Television Commissions, ex p. Television South West, The Times,* February 7, 1992, expressing concern lest *Preston* and *MFK* be regarded as importing private law principles into public law. The text was basically one of fairness.

6. The legitimate expectation concept, in both its procedural and substantive aspects, has given rise to a considerable literature. See G. Ganz, "Legitimate expectation: A confusion of concepts" in C. Harlow (ed.), *Public Law and Politics* (1986), Ch. 8; R. Baldwin and D. Horne, "Expectations in a joyless landscape" (1986) 49 M.L.R. 685; P. Elias, "Legitimate expectation and judicial review" in J. Jowell and D. Oliver (eds.), *New Directions in Judicial Review* (1988), pp. 37–50; C. F. Forsyth, "The Provenance and Protection of Legitimate Expectations" [1988] C.L.J. 238; B. Hadfield, "Judicial review and the concept of legitimate expectation" (1988) 39 N.I.L.Q. 103; P. P. Craig, "Legitimate expectations: a conceptual analysis" (1992) 108 L.Q.R. 79. Some commentators are sceptical of the soundness of the substantive dimension to the concept, arguing that it can lead to conflict with the rule against the fettering of discretion, (*e.g.* Ganz); others have welcomed the development, (*e.g.* Forsyth, Craig).

(E) Note on "Proportionality" as a Ground of Review

In this chapter, and in the one which preceded it, we have considered the case law depicting the scope of review of discretionary powers. We have done so on the basis of categories and subdivisions which have, over the last three decades, partly as a result of the language of the judges and partly as a result of the rationalisations of commentators, acquired a familiarity and consistency of usage. This had had beneficial consequences in terms of the development and refinement of doctrine.

It does not follow, however, that the various categories are mutually exclusive as to their operation—indeed we have had cause to note areas of overlap and actual or potential conflict. Moreover, it does not follow that the categories are exhaustive of the ways in which a body may fail to retain or may abuse its discretionary powers.

In this latter regard there has been, and remains, some uncertainty as to the extent to which the notion of "proportionality" may or should be considered to be a ground of review. This concept is a common feature of the jurisprudence of civil law countries, and has become a regularly used tool of legal reasoning in the European Court of Justice and the European Court of Human Rights. In essence the doctrine provides that a court of review may intervene if it considers that the harms attendant upon a particular exercise of power are disproportionate to the benefits sought to be achieved.

It will be evident that in many cases where a plea of disproportionality might succeed the applicant would succeed also under one of the established grounds of challenge—for example, improper purpose or relevant/irrelevant considerations or unreasonableness. To this extent incorporation of proportionality as an accepted ground of review would add little beyond new vocabulary to the language of review.

Proponents of the doctrine would argue that it would, in fact, permit the courts a scope of review which goes beyond the existing categories, whilst still preserving the important distinction between review of legality and appeal on merits. These issues as to the scope of review (if any) on grounds of disproportionality was recently considered by the House of Lords in the *Brind* case (below).

R. v. SECRETARY OF STATE FOR THE HOME DEPARTMENT, ex p. BRIND

[1991] 1 A.C. 696; [1991] 2 W.L.R. 588; [1991] 1 All E.R. 721 (House of Lords)

In October 1988 the Home Secretary, exercising powers under the Broadcasting Act 1981 (in respect of independent broadcasting) and the BBC's licence and agreement (in respect of that body), issued a directive prohibiting the broadcasting of "words spoken" by any person representing or purporting to represent certain organisations. The organisations were those proscribed under the Northern Ireland (Emergency Provisions) Act 1978, the Prevention of Terrorism (Temporary Provisions) Act 1984, and Sinn Féin, Republican Sinn Féin and the Ulster Defence Association.

The powers under the 1981 Act and the licence/agreement authorised the Home Secretary to require the broadcasting authorities to "refrain from broadcasting any matter or classes of matter specified in the notice."

The applicants, who were journalists, sought judicial review of the Home Secretary's decision. They were unsuccessful in the Divisional Court and the Court of Appeal ([1990] 1 A.C. 700). On appeal to the House of Lords:

LORD BRIDGE OF HARWICH. My Lords, this appeal has been argued primarily on the basis that the power of the Secretary of State . . . to impose restrictions . . . may only be lawfully exercised in accordance with art. 10 of the European Convention on Human Rights. . . . Any exercise by the Secretary of State of the power in question necessarily imposes some restriction on freedom of expression. The obligations of the United Kingdom, as a party to the convention, are to secure to every one within its jurisdiction the rights which the convention defines, including both the right to freedom of expression under art. 10 and the right under art. 13 to "an effective remedy before a national authority" for any violation of the other rights secured by the convention. It is accepted, of course, by the appellants that, like any other treaty obligations which have not been embodied in the law by statute, the convention is not part of the domestic law, that the courts accordingly have no power to enforce convention rights directly and that, if domestic legislation conflicts with the convention, the courts must nevertheless enforce it. But it is already well settled that, in construing any provision in domestic legislation which is ambiguous in the sense that it is capable of a meaning which either conforms to or conflicts with the convention, the courts will presume that Parliament intended to legislate in conformity with the convention, not in conflict with it. Hence, it is submitted, when a statute confers upon an administrative authority a discretion capable of being exercised in a way which infringes any basic human right protected by the convention, it may similarly be presumed that the legislative intention was that the discretion should be exercised within the limitations which the convention imposes. I confess that I found considerable persuasive force in this submission. But in the end I have been convinced that the logic of it is flawed. When confronted with a simple choice between two possible interpretations of some specific statutory provision, the presumption whereby the courts prefer that which avoids conflict between our domestic legislation and our international treaty obligations is a mere canon of construction which involves no importation of international law into the domestic field. But where Parliament has conferred on the executive an administrative discretion without indicating the precise limits within which it must be exercised, to presume that it must be exercised within convention limits would be to go far beyond the resolution of an ambiguity. It would be to impute to Parliament an intention not only that the executive should exercise the discretion in conformity with the convention, but also that the domestic courts should enforce that conformity by the importation into domestic administrative law of the text of the convention and the jurisprudence of the European Court of Human Rights in the interpretation and application of it. If such a presumption is to apply to the statutory discretion exercised by the Secretary of State . . . in the instant case, it must also apply to any other statutory discretion exercised by the executive which is capable of involving an infringement of convention rights. When Parliament has been content for so long to leave those who complain that their convention rights have been infringed to seek their remedy in Strasbourg, it would be surprising suddenly to find that the judiciary had, without Parliament's aid, the means to incorporate the convention into such an important area of domestic law and I cannot escape the conclusion that this would be a judicial usurpation of the legislative function.

But I do not accept that this conclusion means that the courts are powerless to prevent the exercise by the executive of administrative discretions, even when conferred, as in the instant case, in terms which are on their face unlimited, in a way which infringes fundamental human rights. Most of the rights spelled out in terms in the convention, including the right to freedom of expression, are less than absolute and must in some cases yield to the claims of competing public interests. Thus, art. 10(2) of the convention spells out and categorises the competing public interests by reference to which the right to freedom of expression may have to be curtailed. In exercising the power of judicial review we have neither the advantages nor the disadvantages of any comparable code to which we may refer or by which we are bound. But again, this surely does not mean that in deciding whether the Secretary of State, in the exercise of his discretion, could reasonably impose the restriction he has imposed on the broadcasting organisations, we are not perfectly entitled to start from the premise that any restriction of the right to freedom of expression requires to be justified and that nothing less than an important competing public interest will be sufficient to justify it. The primary judgment as to whether the particular competing public interest justifies the particular restriction imposed falls to be made by the Secretary of State to whom Parliament has entrusted the discretion. But we are entitled to exercise a secondary judgment by asking whether a reasonable Secretary of State, on the material before him, could reasonably make that primary judgment.

Applying these principles to the circumstances of the case. . . . I find it impossible to say that the Secretary of State exceeded the limits of his discretion. In any civilised and law-abiding society the defeat of the terrorist is a public interest of the first importance. That some restriction on the freedom of the terrorist and his supporters to propagate his cause may well be justified in support of that public interest is a proposition which I apprehend the appellants hardly dispute. Their real case is that they, in the exercise of their editorial judgment, may and must be trusted to ensure that the broadcasting media are not used in such a way as will afford any encouragement or support to terrorism and that any interference with that editorial judgment is necessarily an unjustifiable restriction on the right to freedom of expression. Accepting, as I do, their complete good faith, I nevertheless cannot accept this proposition. The Secretary of State, for the reasons he made so clear in Parliament, decided that it was necessary to deny to the terrorist and his supporters the opportunity to speak directly to the public through the most influential of all the media of communication and that this justified some interference with editorial freedom. I do not see how this judgment can be categorised as unreasonable. What is perhaps surprising is that the restriction imposed is of such limited scope. There is no restriction at all on the matter which may be broadcast, only on the manner of its presentation. The viewer may see the terrorist's face and hear his words provided only that they are not spoken in his own voice. I well understand the broadcast journalist's complaint that to put him to the trouble of dubbing the voice of the speaker he has interviewed before the television camera is an irritant which the difference in effect between the speaker's voice and the actor's voice hardly justifies. I well understand the political complaint that the restriction may be counter-productive in the sense that the adverse criticism it provokes outweighs any benefit it achieves. But these complaints fall very far short of demonstrating that a reasonable Secretary of State could not reasonably conclude that the restriction was justified by the important public interest of combating terrorism. I should add that I do not see how reliance on the doctrine of "proportionality" can here advance the appellants' case. But I agree with what my noble and learned friend, Lord Roskill, says in his speech about the possible future development of the law in that respect.

I would dismiss the appeal.

LORD TEMPLEMAN: . . . The English courts must, in conformity with the *Wednesbury* principles . . . consider whether the Home Secretary has taken into account all relevant matters and has ignored irrelevant matters. These conditions are satisfied by the evidence in this case, including evidence by the Home Secretary that he took the convention into account. If these conditions are satisfied, then it is said on *Wednesbury* principles the court can only interfere by way of judicial review if the decision of the Home Secretary is "irrational" or "perverse."

The subject-matter and date of the *Wednesbury* principles cannot in my opinion make it either necessary or appropriate for the courts to judge the validity of an interference with human rights by asking themselves whether the Home Secretary has acted irrationally or perversely. It seems to me that the courts cannot escape from asking themselves only whether a reasonable Secretary of State, on the material before him, could reasonably conclude that the interference with freedom of expression which he determined to impose was justifiable. In terms of the convention, as construed by the European Court of Human Rights, the interference with freedom of expression must be necessary and proportionate to the damage which the restriction is designed to prevent.

My Lords, applying these principles I do not consider that the court can conclude that the Home Secretary has abused or exceeded his powers. The broadcasting authorities and journalists are naturally resentful of any limitation on their right to present a programme in such manner as they think fit. But the interference with freedom of expression is minimal and the reasons given by the Home Secretary are compelling.

I, too, would dismiss this appeal.

LORD ACKNER: . . . The Secretary of State's reasons for taking the action complained of are set out in the Hansard Reports of those debates and were before your Lordships. The four matters which influenced the Secretary of State were . . . (1) offence had been caused to viewers and listeners by the appearance of the apologists for terrorism, particularly after a terrorist outrage; (2) such appearances had afforded terrorists undeserved publicity which was contrary to the public interest; (3) these appearances had tended to increase the standing of terrorist organisations and to create a false impression that support for terrorism is itself a legitimate political opinion; (4) broadcast statements were intended to have, and did in some cases have, the effect of intimidating some of those at whom they were directed.

The challenge

I now turn to the bases upon which it is contended that the Secretary of State exceeded his statutory powers.

(1) . . .

(2) *The directives were unlawful on "Wednesbury" grounds*

Save only in one respect, namely the European Convention for the Protection of Human Rights and Fundamental Freedoms . . . which is the subject-matter of a later heading, it is not suggested that the minister failed to call his attention to matters which he was bound to consider, nor that he included in his considerations matters which were irrelevant. In neither of those senses can it be said that the minister acted unreasonably. The failure to mount such a challenge in this appeal is important. In a field which concerns a fundamental human right, namely that of free speech, close scrutiny must be given to the reasons provided as justification for interference with that right. Your Lordships' attention was drawn to *R. v. Secretary of State for Transport, ex p. de Rothschild* [1989] 1 All E.R. 933, a case which concerned compulsory purchase and therefore involved, albeit somewhat indirectly, another fundamental human right—the peaceful enjoyment of one's possessions: see art. 1 of the First Protocol to the Convention. In that case Slade L.J. said, at p. 939:

> "Given the obvious importance and value to land owners of their property rights, the abrogation of those rights in the exercise of his discretionary power to confirm a compulsory purchase order would, in the absence of what he perceived to be a sufficient justification on the merits, be a course which surely no reasonable Secretary of State would take."

Slade L.J. was in no sense increasing the severity of the *Wednesbury* test. . . . He was applying that part of it which requires the decision-maker to call his attention to matters that he is obliged to consider. He was emphasising the Secretary of State's obligation to identify the factors which had motivated his decision so as to ensure that he had overlooked none which a reasonable Secretary of State should have considered.

There remains however the potential criticism under the *Wednesbury* grounds . . . that the conclusion was "so unreasonable that no reasonable authority could ever have come to it." This standard of unreasonableness, often referred to as "the irrationality test," has been criticised as being too high. But it has to be expressed in terms that confine the jurisdiction exercised by the judiciary to a supervisory, as opposed to an appellate, jurisdiction. Where Parliament has given to a minister or other person or body a discretion, the court's jurisdiction is limited, in the absence of a statutory right of appeal, to the supervision of the exercise of that discretionary power, so as to ensure that it has been exercised lawfully. It would be a wrongful usurpation of power by the judiciary to substitute its view, the judicial view, on the merits and on that basis to quash the decision. If no reasonable minister properly directing himself would have reached the impugned decision, the minister has exceeded his powers and thus acted unlawfully and the court, in the exercise of its supervisory role, will quash that decision. Such a decision is correctly, though unattractively, described as a "perverse" decision. To seek the court's intervention on the basis that the correct or objectively reasonable decision is other than the decision which the minister has made, is to invite the court to adjudicate as if Parliament had provided a right of appeal against the decision, that is to invite an abuse of power by the judiciary.

So far as the facts of this case are concerned it is only necessary to read the speeches in the Houses of Parliament, . . . to reach the conclusion, that whether the Secretary of State was right or wrong to decide to issue the directives, there was clearly material which would justify a reasonable minister making the same decision. In the words of Lord Diplock in *Secretary of State for Education and Science* v. *Tameside Metropolitan Borough* [1977] A.C. 1014, 1064:

> "The very concept of administrative discretion involves a right to choose between more than one possible course of action on which there is room for reasonable people to hold differing opinions as to which is to be preferred."

. . . I entirely agree with McCowan L.J. [in the Court of Appeal] when he said that he found it quite impossible to hold that the Secretary of State's political judgment that the appearance of terrorists on programmes increases their standing and lends them political legitimacy is one that no reasonable Home Secretary could hold. . . .

Mr. Lester has contended that in issuing these directives the Secretary of State has used a sledgehammer to crack a nut. Of course that is a picturesque way of describing the *Wednesbury* "irrational" test. The Secretary of State has in my judgment used no sledgehammer. Quite the contrary is the case.

I agree with Lord Donaldson M.R. who, when commenting on how limited the restrictions were, said in his judgment . . . :

> "They have no application in the circumstances mentioned in para. 3 (proceedings in the United Kingdom Parliament and elections) and, by allowing reported speech either verbatim or in paraphrase, in effect put those affected in no worse a position than they would be if they had access to newspaper publicity with a circulation equal to the listening and viewing audiences of the programmes concerned. Furthermore, on the applicants' own evidence, if the directives had been in force during the previous 12 months, the effect would have been minimal in terms of air time. Thus, [ITN] say that 8 minutes 20 seconds (including repeats) out of 1,200 hours, or 0·01%, of air time would have been affected. Furthermore, it would not have been necessary to omit these items. They could have been recast into a form which complied with the directives."

Thus the extent of the interference with the right to freedom of speech is a very modest one. . . .

(3) *The minister failed to have proper regard to the European Convention for the Protection of Human Rights and Fundamental Freedoms and in particular art. 10*
Article 10 reads as follows:

> "(1) Everyone has the right to freedom of expression. This right shall include freedom to hold opinions and to receive and impart information and ideas without interference by public authority and regardless of frontiers. This Article shall not prevent States from requiring the licensing of broadcasting, television or cinema enterprises.
> (2) The exercise of these freedoms, since it carries with it duties and responsibilities, may be subject to such formalities, conditions, restrictions or penalties as are prescribed by law and are necessary in a democratic society, in the interests of national security, territorial integrity or public safety, for the prevention of disorder or crime, for the protection of health or morals, for the protection of the reputation or rights of others, for preventing the disclosure of information received in confidence, or for maintaining the authority and impartiality of the judiciary."

[His Lordship noted that the Convention is a treaty to which the United Kingdom is a party but which has not been incorporated by legislation into English domestic law. He also noted that the terms of a treaty may be used to resolve an ambiguity in an Act, but held that there was no such ambiguity in the terms of the 1981 Act. He then referred to a further argument of counsel for the applicants, and continued:]

. . . Mr. Lester . . . claims that the Secretary of State before issuing his directives should have considered not only the convention (it is accepted that he in fact did so) but that he should have properly construed it and correctly taken it into consideration. It was therefore a relevant, indeed a vital, factor to which he was obliged to have proper regard pursuant to the *Wednesbury* doctrine, with the result that his failure to do so rendered his decision unlawful. The fallacy of this submission is, however, plain. If the Secretary of State was obliged to have proper regard to the convention, *i.e.* to conform with art. 10, this inevitably would result in incorporating the convention into English domestic law by the back door. It would oblige the courts to police the operation of the convention and to ask itself in each case, where there was a challenge, whether the restrictions were "necessary in a democratic society . . ." applying the principles enunciated in the decisions of the European Court of Human Rights. The treaty, not having been incorporated in English law, cannot be a source of rights and obligations and the question—did the Secretary of State act in breach of art. 10?—does not therefore arise. . . .

(4) *The Secretary of State has acted ultra vires because he has acted "in a disproportionate manner"*

This attack is not a repetition of the *Wednesbury* "irrational" test under another guise. Clearly a decision by a minister which suffers from a total lack of proportionality will qualify for the "*Wednesbury* unreasonable" epithet. It is, ex hypothesi, a decision which no reasonable minister could make. This is, however, a different and severer test.

Mr. Lester is asking your Lordships to adopt a different principle: the principle of "proportionality" which is recognised in the administrative law of several members of the European Economic Community. What is urged is a further development in English administrative law, which Lord Diplock viewed as a possibility in *Council of Civil Service Unions* v. *Minister for the Civil Service* [1985] A.C. 374, 410.

In his written submissions, Mr. Lester was at pains to record "that there is a clear distinction between an appeal on the merits and a review based on whether the principle of proportionality has been satisfied." He was prepared to accept that to stray into the realms of appellate jurisdiction involves the courts in a wrongful usurpation of power. Yet in order to invest the proportionality test with a higher status than the *Wednesbury* test, an inquiry into and a decision upon the merits cannot be avoided. Mr. Pannick's (Mr. Lester's junior) formulation—could the minister reasonably conclude that his direction was necessary?—must involve balancing the reasons, pro and con, for his decision, albeit allowing him "a margin of appreciation" to use the European concept of the tolerance accorded to the decision-maker in whom a discretion has been vested. The European test of "whether the 'interference' complained of corresponds to a 'pressing social need' " (*The Sunday Times* v. *United Kingdom* (1979) 2 E.H.R.R. 245 at 277) must ultimately result in the question—is the particular decision acceptable?—and this must involve a review of the merits of the decision. Unless and until Parliament incorporates the convention into domestic law, a course which it is well known has a strong body of support, there appears to me to be at present no basis upon which the proportionality doctrine applied by the European Court can be followed by the courts of this country.

I would accordingly dismiss this appeal. . . .

Appeal dismissed.

Notes

1. Lord Roskill agreed with the reasons given by Lord Bridge. On the issue of proportionality he referred to Lord Diplock's statement in the *Council of Civil Service Unions* case about the "possible adoption in future" of this principle of review, and noted Lord Diplock's view that any such development would be on a case by case basis. Lord Roskill continued (p. 750):

> "I am clearly of the view that the present is not a case in which the first step can be taken for the reason that to apply the principle in the present case would be for the court to substitute its own judgment of what was needed to achieve a particular objective for the judgment of the Secretary of State upon whom that

duty has been laid by Parliament. But so to hold in the present case is not to exclude the possible future development of the law in this respect . . ."

Lord Lowry agreed with Lord Ackner. On the issue of "proportionality" as a ground of challenge, he said (pp. 766–767):

"In my opinion proportionality and the other phrases are simply intended to move the focus of discussion away from the hitherto accepted criteria for deciding whether the decision-maker has abused his power and into an area in which the court will feel more at liberty to interfere.

The first observation I would make is that there is *no* authority for saying that proportionality in the sense in which the appellants have used it is part of the English common law and a great deal of authority the other way. This, so far as I am concerned, is not a cause for regret for several reasons. (1) The decision-makers, very often elected, are those to whom Parliament has entrusted the discretion and to interfere with that discretion beyond the limits as hitherto defined would itself be an abuse of the judges' supervisory jurisdiction. (2) The judges are not, generally speaking, equipped by training or experience, or furnished with the requisite knowledge and advice, to decide the answer to an administrative problem where the scales are evenly balanced, but they have a much better chance of reaching the right answer where the question is put in a *Wednesbury* form. The same applies if the judges' decision is appealed. (3) Stability and relative certainty would be jeopardised if the new doctrine held sway, because there is nearly always something to be said against any administrative decision and parties who felt aggrieved would be even more likely than at present to try their luck with a judicial review application both at first instance and on appeal. (4) The increase in applications for judicial review of administrative action (inevitable if the threshold of unreasonableness is lowered) will lead to the expenditure of time and money by litigants, not to speak of the prolongation of uncertainty for all concerned with the decisions in question, and the taking up of court time which could otherwise be devoted to other matters. The losers in this respect will be members of the public, for whom the courts provide a service.

1(1) *Halsbury's Laws of England* (4th ed., vol. 1(1) reissue) (1989) recognises proportionality in the context of administrative law as follows:

'78. Proportionality. The courts will quash exercise of discretionary powers in which there is not a reasonable relationship between the objective which is sought to be achieved and the means used to that end, or where punishments imposed by administrative bodies or inferior courts are wholly out of proportion to the relevant misconduct. The principle of proportionality is well established in European law, and will be applied by English courts where European law is enforceable in the domestic courts. The principle of proportionality is still at a stage of development in English law; lack of proportionality is not usually treated as a separate ground of review in English law, but is regarded as one indication of manifest unreasonableness.'

(The High Court's decision in the instant case (see *The Times*, May 30, 1989) is cited in the copious footnotes to this paragraph as the authority for the concluding statement.)

It finally occurs to me that there can be very little room for judges to operate an independent judicial review proportionality doctrine in the space which is left between the conventional judicial review doctrine and the admittedly forbidden appellate approach. To introduce an intermediate area of deliberation for the court seems scarcely a practical idea, quite apart from the other disadvantages by which, in my opinion, such a course would be attended."

2. See comments by C. Lewis, [1991] C.L.J. 211; B. Thompson, [1989] P.L. 527 (on *Brind* in the Divisional Court) and [1991] P.L. 346; J. Jowell, [1990] P.L. 149 (on *Brind* in the Court of Appeal); and M. Halliwell, (1991) 42 N.I.L.Q. 246.

3. As mentioned in the extract from *Halsbury's Laws* cited by Lord Lowry, proportionality is well established as a ground of review in European Community Law, with its origins in continental administrative law: see D. Wyatt and A. Dashwood, *The Substantive Law of the E.E.C.* (2nd ed., 1987), pp. 60–61; and T. C. Hartley, *The Foundations of European Community Law* (2nd ed., 1988), pp. 145–147. In Case 181/84, *R.* v. *Intervention Board for Agricultural Produce, ex p. E.D. & F. Man (Sugar) Ltd.* [1986] 2 All E.R. 115, the Court of Justice of the European Communities stated that "in order to establish whether a provision of Community law is in conformity with the principle of proportionality it is necessary to ascertain whether the means which it employs are appropriate and necessary to attain the objective sought" (p. 124). Where a question of Community law arises for consideration in an English court, the court may be required to give effect to the proportionality principle as it is understood in Community law: see, *e.g. Thomas* v. *Adjudication Officer* [1991] 3 All E.R. 315; *cf.* Hoffman J. in *Stoke-on-Trent* v. *B.&Q. plc* [1991] 4 All E.R. 221. (Note, however, the argument of A. Arnull, (1991) 16 E.L.Rev. 112) that Hoffman J.'s formulation of the proportionality test in community law was incorrect. Hoffman J., in reviewing the proportionality of the Sunday trading legislation, was prepared only to inquire whether the "compromise adopted by the United Kingdom Parliament" was "one which a reasonable legislative could have reached" (p. 235); his Lordship refused to carry out a balancing exercise himself or to form his own view on whether the legislative objective (the arrangement of working hours "so as to accord with national or regional socio-cultural characteristics": Case 145/88, *Torfaen Borough Council* v. *B.&Q. plc* [1990] 2 Q.B. 19) could be achieved by other means. Arnull argues that Community law requires the latter approach to be adopted.

Chapter 9

ERRORS OF PROCEDURE

(A) Procedural Ultra Vires

ACTION taken by a government agency may be void if it offends against procedural rules laid down, expressly or by necessary implication, in the enabling statute. This principle may be applied in a variety of situations, including the methods by which a decision is taken and the identity of the persons taking the decision. In the latter instance, there may be a breach of the rule *delegatus non potest delegare* (above, pp. 267 *et seq.*), or a court or tribunal may be found to have been improperly constituted (above, pp. 235–236).

A distinction has traditionally been drawn in the case law between procedural requirements which are *mandatory*, breach of which renders the ultimate decision *ultra vires*, and those which are *directory*. In the latter case, the requirements should be observed, but if they are not there is at most a mere *intra vires* error. "[I]n each case you must look to the subject-matter; consider the importance of the provision that has been disregarded, and the relation of that provision to the general object intended to be secured by the Act; . . ." (*per* Lord Penzance in *Howard* v. *Bodington* (1877) 2 P.D. 203, 211). There are also authorities that support a more flexible approach (see pp. 461–468).

Natural justice also could be classified as a procedural requirement, the breach of which amounts to *ultra vires* action (see *Cooper* v. *Wandsworth Board of Works*, below, p. 470), but this is such a considerable subject that it merits separate treatment (below, pp. 468–592).

See generally J. Evans, "Mandatory and directory rules" (1981) 1 L.S. 227.

HOWARD v. SECRETARY OF STATE FOR THE ENVIRONMENT

[1975] Q.B. 235; [1974] 2 W.L.R. 459; 117 S.J. 853; [1974] 1 All E.R. 644; 72 L.G.R. 325; (1973) 27 P. & C.R. 131 (Court of Appeal)

Section 16 of the Town and Country Planning Act 1968 gave a right of appeal against an enforcement notice issued by the local planning authority to remedy a breach of planning control. The seven possible grounds of appeal were set out. Subsection 2 provided that: "An appeal under this section shall be made by notice in writing to the Minister, which shall indicate the grounds of appeal and state the facts on which it is based; . . ." A notice was of no effect pending the final determination or the withdrawal of the appeal (s.16(3)). In 1970, the local planning authority (the London Borough of Havering) was of the opinion that the plaintiff was using some land as a transport contractor's depot without the requisite planning permission. It served an enforcement notice requiring discontinuance of that use within one month. The notice was to take effect after 42 days (on November 18), unless an appeal was lodged under section 16.

On November 6 the plaintiff's solicitors wrote to what soon became the Department of the Environment:

"We have been instructed by our client, Mr. H. Howard, of 6 Birkbeck Road, Romford, regarding the enforcement notice herein dated October 7, 1970, received from the London Borough of Havering, and would ask you kindly to accept this letter as formal notice of appeal on his behalf."

The Department replied on November 10:

"You have not indicated which of the grounds of appeal listed in section 16(1) of the Act you consider apply to your case. Nor have you stated the facts on which the appeal is based, as required by section 16(2). Unless this information is provided, the Minister will be unable to entertain your appeal. The grounds of appeal and statement of facts must be sent to the Minister before the date on which the enforcement notice is to take effect."

This form of letter was in common use, and had been reproduced in multiple form. The plaintiff's solicitors wrote on November 16 giving the necessary information but, owing to an office error, the letter was not posted until after November 18, and reached the Department on November 24. The Department replied that they could take no action as the appeal had been made out of time, there being no power to extend the time. The plaintiffs now sought a declaration that either the letter of November 6 or that letter with the one of the 16th constituted a valid notice of appeal. Bristow J. refused a declaration ([1972] 3 All E.R. 310). The plaintiffs appealed.

LORD DENNING M.R.: [stated the facts, referred to the judgment of Lord Penzance in *Howard* v. *Bodington* (1877) 2 P.D. 203 at p. 210, and continued]: In applying that distinction [*i.e.* between imperative and directory provisions] . . . I must draw attention to a case which was decided on section 33 of the Caravan Sites and Control of Development Act 1960. That section was the predecessor to section 16 of the Act of 1968. It said [in subsection (4)] that an appeal shall be "by a written notice which shall indicate the grounds on which the appeal is brought." The case was *Chelmsford Rural District Council* v. *Powell* [1963] 1 W.L.R. 123. A written notice of appeal was given in due time. It set out two grounds of appeal. Neither ground was substantiated. But, before the hearing, the appellant (long after the time for appeal had expired) submitted a further ground of appeal. The minister allowed this ground to be raised and he allowed the appeal. The local planning authority urged that the Minister ought not to have considered this further ground. They said that the section was imperative. But the Divisional Court ruled that it was not imperative, but only informative, that is, directory. So it was open to the appellant to go further into the further ground although it was out of time and had not been contained in the original notice.

I think that decision was perfectly correct. It is common practice in these appeals to allow new grounds of appeal to be added, and new facts to be stated. Very often the true facts do not emerge until the hearing by the inspector, and justice requires that new ground be added and new facts stated.

Although the decision is plain enough, Lord Parker C.J. made an observation which was not at all necessary for the decision. He said, at p. 131:

> "I think it is quite clear that before the Minister can have any jurisdiction in the matter there must be an appeal. That appeal must be in writing, and it must indicate at any rate one of the grounds set out in paragraphs (*a*) to (*g*) of section 33(1). That, I think, is undoubtedly true."

I am afraid that Lord Parker C.J. there made a mistake. The section is no doubt imperative in that notice of appeal must be in writing and must be made within the specified time. But I think it is only directory as to the contents. Take first the requirement as to the "grounds" of appeal. The section is either imperative in requiring "the grounds" to be indicated, or it is not. That must mean all or none. I cannot see any justification for the view that it is imperative as to *one* ground and not imperative as to the rest. If *one* was all that was necessary, an appellant would only have to put in one frivolous or hopeless ground and then amend later to add his real grounds. That would be a futile exercise. Then as to "stating the facts." It cannot be supposed that the appellant must at all costs state all the facts on which he bases his appeal. He has to state the facts, not the evidence: and the facts may depend on evidence yet to be obtained, and may not be fully or sufficiently known at the time when the notice of appeal is given.

All things considered, it seems to me that the section, in so far as the "grounds" and "facts" are concerned, must be construed as directory only: that is, as desiring information to be given about them. It is not to be supposed that an appeal should fail altogether simply because the grounds are not indicated, or the facts stated. Even if it is wanting in not giving them, it is not fatal. The defects can be remedied later, either before or at the hearing of the appeal, so long as an opportunity is afforded of dealing with them.

I may observe that there are other provisions in these Planning Acts which have been held to be directory only, so that a failure to observe them does not make the whole thing void: see *Brayhead (Ascot) Ltd.* v. *Berkshire County Council* [1964] 2 Q.B. 303, 314 by Winn J. and *James* v. *Minister of Housing and Local Government* [1966] 1 W.L.R. 135, 142 by Lord Denning M.R. and [1968] A.C. 409, 456 by Lord Wilberforce.

I hold, therefore, that an appeal is good so long as it is made in writing and within the specified time. The grounds of appeal, and the facts, can be stated later so long as a fair opportunity (by adjournment or otherwise) is given of dealing with them. I hold that the letter of November 6, 1970, was a good appeal. I would allow this appeal, accordingly.

STAMP L.J.: . . . The purpose of requiring that the notice shall indicate the ground of the appeal and the facts on which it is based, is, as it appears to me, quite clearly to give information to the Minister for the purposes of the appeal; and, that being the purpose, I have come to the conclusion that those requirements are directory and do not go to the jurisdiction. . . . The purpose of imposing a limitation of time in section 16(1) is, as I see it, quite different: it is to prevent steps to enforce the enforcement notice being carried out before the time fixed has expired. The machinery of the enforcement provisions and the appeal therefrom simply would not work unless there was some fixed time put in section 16(1) to limit the time in which an appeal is to be brought. That provision is therefore imperative or mandatory and a failure to appeal within the time there limited clearly goes to the jurisdiction.

ROSKILL L.J. delivered a concurring judgment.

Appeal allowed.
Declaration granted.

Notes

1. The courts have been unable to develop clear guidelines on whether a particular step is to be regarded as mandatory or directory. A step is likely to be held to be mandatory if it provides an important safeguard to individual interests such as a requirement to give prior notice of a decision or a hearing (*Bradbury* v. *Enfield London Borough Council* [1967] 1 W.L.R. 1311; *Lee* v. *Department of Education and Science* (1967) 66 L.G.R. 211); or to give notice of rights of appeal (*London & Clydeside Estates Ltd.* v. *Aberdeen District Council*, below, p. 461); or to give notice of a right to make objections (*R.* v. *Lambeth London Borough Council, ex p. Sharp*, below p. 467); or to give the prescribed period of notice of the implementation of a licensing scheme by a council resolution (*R.* v. *Swansea City Council, ex p. Quietlynn Ltd., The Times*, October 19, 1983; *R.* v. *Birmingham City Council, ex p. Quietlynn Ltd.* (1985) 83 L.G.R. 461, 471–479, 512–514); or to consult appropriate bodies (*Agricultural etc. Training Board* v. *Aylesbury Mushrooms Ltd.*, below, p. 454). It may also be held to be mandatory where the requirement reflects the need for justice to be seen to be done (*Noble* v. *Inner London Education Authority* (1983) 82 L.G.R. 291, in respect of regulations prohibiting (*inter alia*) a teacher-governor of a school participating in the consideration of the transfer, promotion or retirement of a teacher where that would result in a vacant post for which he or she could be a candidate).

2. Trivial deviations from procedural requirements will not normally invalidate the whole process. Thus in *R.* v. *Dacorum Gaming Licensing Committee, ex p. E.M.I. Cinemas and Leisure Ltd.* [1971] 3 All E.R. 666, the Divisional Court held that a misprint in the public notice in a newspaper of an application for a bingo club licence (describing the club as the "A.B.E. Social Club" rather than the "A.B.C. Social Club") did not render the notice ineffective so as to deprive the gaming committee of jurisdiction to entertain the licence application. This was:

> "a trifling typographical error . . . which was not in any sense the fault of the applicants and which cannot possibly have misled anybody"

(*per* Lord Widgery C.J. at p. 668).

3. If substantial public inconvenience would be caused by classifying a requirement as mandatory, the courts may incline towards holding it to be directory. In *Simpson* v. *Attorney-General* [1955] N.Z.L.R. 271, the Governor General of New Zealand in 1946 issued his warrant for the holding of a general election 26 days after the last day of the previous Parliament, instead of within 7 days. (There had

been a misunderstanding about what was the last day of the Parliament). The New Zealand Court of Appeal held that the 7-day requirement was directory rather than mandatory, and rejected the argument that the general election (and the legislation subsequently passed by the new Parliament) was invalid.

4. The courts may also be inclined to hold a requirement to be directory if non-compliance causes no substantial prejudice. The question of notices under section 13 of the Education Act 1944 in relation to the establishment or closure of a school, as prescribed by the County and Voluntary Schools (Notices) Regulations 1968 (S.I. 1968 No. 615), was considered in *Coney* v. *Choyce and others* [1975] 1 All E.R. 979. The regulations required notice to be given in a local newspaper, in some conspicuous place or places, at or near any main entrance to the school, and in such other manner as appeared to be desirable for giving publicity to the notice. In the case of two schools no notice was posted at or near the main entrance. Templeman J. held that the main object of the regulations were "that notice should be published in a manner designed to show a representative number of people what their rights are." The specific requirements were therefore to be regarded as directory. The notices were in fact well publicised apart from these omissions, and so no substantial prejudice was suffered by those for whose benefit the requirements had been introduced.

Cf. R. v. *Liverpool City Council*, above, p. 38.

In *Secretary of State for Trade and Industry* v. *Langridge* [1991] Ch. 402, the Court of Appeal had to consider the effect of the Secretary of State's failure to give ten clear days' notice of his intention to apply for an order disqualifying L. from being a company director, as required by section 16(1) of the Company Directors Disqualification Act 1986. A letter giving notice was served on April 11, 1989, and the application was brought on April 21, 1989 (the last day within the relevant two-year limitation period). The court (Balcombe and Leggatt L.JJ., Nourse L.J. dissenting) held that the requirement was directory and not mandatory. The majority had regard to the considerations that the purpose of the 1986 Act was to protect the public, and that the object of the notice period was simply to inform the person concerned that an application was to be made rather than to protect his rights. The requirement offered only limited advantage to the person concerned given its short span, the fact that the grounds of the intended application did not have to be specified, and the point that in certain circumstances a disqualification order could be made without any formal notice being given. There was no suggestion that L. had been prejudiced by the fact that the notice served on him was one day short, and there was no suggestion that there had been anything other than a genuine mistake.

See also *Re T (A Minor) (Adoption: Validity of Order)* [1986] Fam. 160, C.A.

5. There is some authority for the proposition that failure to comply with a directory requirement will only be excused where there has been "substantial compliance." Thus, in *Cullimore* v. *Lyme Regis Corporation* [1962] 1 Q.B. 718, the borough council prepared a works scheme under the Coastal Protection Act 1949, whereby charges were to be levied for certain coast protection works. The scheme required the council within six months of completion of the work to determine the interests in the land benefited by reference to which charges were to be levied, and the amount of such charges. The council determined these matters almost two years after completion. Edmund Davies J. held that the charges were *ultra vires* and void on the grounds that either (1) the six month time limit was mandatory requirement, or (2) even if it were a directory requirement, there had been nothing approaching substantial compliance.

Cf. Lord Hailsham's remarks on this point in the *London and Clydeside* case, below, p. 461.

The following is a typical example of an express provision setting out a procedural requirement.

TOWN AND COUNTRY PLANNING ACT 1990

Service of notices

329.—(1) Any notice or other document required or authorised to be served or given under this Act may be served or given either—

(*a*) by delivering it to the person on whom it is to be served or to whom it is to be given; or

(*b*) by leaving it at the usual or last known place of abode of that person, or, in a case where an address for service has been given by that person, at that address; or

(*c*) by sending it in a prepaid registered letter, or by the recorded delivery service, addressed to that person at his usual or last known place of abode, or, in a case where an address for service has been given by that person, at that address; or

(*d*) in the case of an incorporated company or body, by delivering it to the secretary or clerk of the company or body at their registered or principal office, or sending it in a prepaid registered letter, or by the recorded delivery service, addressed to the secretary or clerk of the company or body at that office.

(2) Where the notice or document is required or authorised to be served on any person as having an interest in premises, and the name of that person cannot be ascertained after reasonable inquiry, or where the notice or document is required or authorised to be served on any person as an occupier of premises, the notice or document shall be taken to be duly served if—

(*a*) it is addressed to him either by name or by the description of "the owner" or as the case may be, "the occupier" of the premises (describing them) and is delivered or sent in the manner specified in subsection (1)(*a*), (*b*) or (*c*); or

(*b*) it is so addressed and is marked in such a manner as may be prescribed for securing that it is plainly identifiable as a communication of importance and—

(i) it is sent to the premises in a prepaid registered letter or by the recorded delivery service and is not returned to the authority sending it, or

(ii) it is delivered to some person on those premises, or is affixed conspicuously to some object on those premises.

(3) Where—

(*a*) the notice or other document is required to be served on or given to all persons who have interests in or are occupiers of premises comprised in any land, and

(*b*) it appears to the authority required or authorised to serve or give the notice or other document that any part of that land is unoccupied, the notice or document shall be taken to be duly served on all persons having interests in, and on any occupiers of, premises comprised in that part of the land (other than a person who has given to that authority an address for the service of the notice or document on him) if it is addressed to "the owners and any occupiers" of that part of the land (describing it) and is affixed conspicuously to some object on the land.

Notes

1. Section 7 of the Interpretation Act 1978 states:

"Where an Act authorises or requires any document to be served by post, (whether the expression 'serve,' or the expression 'give' or 'send' or any other expression is used) then, unless the contrary intention appears, the service is deemed to be effected by properly addressing, prepaying, and posting a letter containing the document and, unless the contrary is proved, to have been effected at the time at which the letter would be delivered in the ordinary course of post."

In *Hewitt* v. *Leicester Corporation* (1969) 20 P. & C.R. 629, the Court of Appeal held that where a notice sent through the post was returned through the post marked "gone away" it had not been served on the addressee.

2. In *Maltglade* v. *St. Albans R.D.C.* [1972] 1 W.L.R. 1230, the appellants were convicted by justices of the offence of demolishing a building subject to a building preservation notice. They appealed on the ground that the notice had not come into force as it had not been "served on both the owner and the occupier of the building to which it related," the precondition required by section 48(3) of the Town and Country Planning Act 1968. The copy of the notice sent to the owners, Maltglade Ltd., was posted by recorded delivery to an address previously given to the planning authority in connection with other planning matters affecting this land on another occasion. The letter was never delivered as the postman could find no sign that Maltglade Ltd. used that address. The council relied on the Town and Country Planning Act 1962, s.214(1)(*c*) and (*d*) [now s.329(1)(*c*) and (*d*) of the 1990 Act], and section 26 of the Interpretation Act 1889. The Divisional Court held that the notice had not been served. They applied *R.* v. *London County Quarter Sessions Appeals Committee, ex p. Rossi* [1956] 1 Q.B. 682, in drawing a distinction between the first and the second half of section 26, and holding that where the *time* of service is of importance (the situation envisaged by the second half), the "contrary" may be proved. Here the time of service was important as it had to be received "before the bulldozer came in."

This led to amending legislation in the Town and Country Planning (Amendment) Act 1972, s.7, which enabled the local planning authority in an emergency to "affix the notice conspicuously to some object on the building" instead of serving notice on owner and occupier. (The governing sections are now sections 3 and 4 of the Planning (Listed Buildings and Conservation Areas) Act 1990.

AGRICULTURAL, HORTICULTURAL AND FORESTRY INDUSTRY TRAINING BOARD v. AYLESBURY MUSHROOMS LTD.

[1972] 1 W.L.R. 190; (1971) 116 S.J. 57; [1972] 1 All E.R. 280; [1972] I.T.R. 16 (Donaldson J.)

The Industrial Training Act 1964 provided for the establishment by Order of industrial training boards. Each board arranged training for those employed in the industries concerned, and was supported by levies imposed on the employers in those industries. Section 1(4) of the Act provided:

> "Before making an industrial training order the Minister shall consult any organisation or association of organisations appearing to him to be representative of substantial numbers of employers engaging in the activities concerned and any organisation or association of organisations appearing to him to be representative of substantial numbers of persons employed in those activities; and if those activities are carried on to a substantial extent by a body established for the purpose of carrying on under national ownership any industry or part of an industry or undertaking, shall consult that body."

In 1965, the Ministry of Labour was minded to set up the plaintiff board. Consultations were held between Ministry officials and the largest representative body concerned, the National Farmers' Union. By April 1966 a draft Order had been prepared. An advance copy of the schedule to the Order, which defined the industry to which the order related, was sent to the National Farmers' Union on April 15, 1966. On April 26, 1966, copies of this document were circulated to a large number of addresses, including the Mushroom Growers' Association, inviting comments. Simultaneously there was a press notice summarising the activities which it was proposed should be covered by the new board and advising any organisation which considered that it had an interest in the draft schedule and which had not received a copy to apply to the Ministry of Labour. No comments were received from the Mushroom Growers' Association and no application was made by them for a copy of the schedule.

The Order was made on August 2, 1966, laid before Parliament on August 11, and came into operation on August 15. The Mushroom Growers' Association applied in May 1968 for complete exemption from the Order on various grounds. They had never received a copy of the draft schedule, and had no knowledge of the consultations between the Ministry and the National Farmers' Union, or of the press notice. The Mushroom Growers' Association was a specialist branch of the National Farmers' Union, although largely autonomous. It represented about 85 per cent. of all mushroom growers in England and Wales, who were responsible for about 80 per cent. of mushroom production.

The Board sought a determination as to whether the Minister had complied with his duty of consultation, and if not, what were the consequences. The real defendants were the Mushroom Growers' Association, but as that was an unincorporated association, it was thought more convenient that the nominal defendants should be Aylesbury Mushrooms Ltd., who were representative of the Mushroom Growers' Association membership.

DONALDSON J.: ... Both parties are agreed that under the terms of section 1(4) of the Act, some consultation by the Minister is mandatory and that in the absence of any particular consultation which is so required, the persons who should have been but were not consulted are not bound by the Order, although the Order remains effective in relation to all others who were in fact consulted or whom there was no need to consult. Both parties are further agreed that if consultation with the Mushroom Growers' Association was mandatory and there was no sufficient consultation the Order takes effect according to its terms subject to a rider that it does not apply to the growing of mushrooms or to persons engaged in this activity solely by reason of their being so engaged. They may, of course, come within the scope of the Order in some other capacity.

Both parties are also agreed that the organisations required to be consulted are those which appear to the Minister, or to his alter ago who in this case was a Mr. Devey, to be representative of substantial numbers of employers engaging in the activities concerned or persons employed therein and nationalised industries which engage in those activities to a substantial extent. Thus whether any particular organisation has to be consulted depends upon a subjective test, subject always to *bona fides* and reasonableness which are not in question.

Against this background Mr. Bradburn, for the association, submits that the court must see what organisations appeared to the Minister to fall into the specified categories, and that the Minister clearly sought to consult the Mushroom Growers' Association thereby showing that he regarded it as being within the class of organisation which had to be consulted. It follows, as he submits, that neither the board nor the Minister can now turn round and say that consultation with the National Farmers' Union constituted a sufficient discharge of his duties. Mr. Bradburn goes on to submit that there can be no consultation without at least unilateral communication and that no such communication occurred.

Mr. Gettleson for the board submitted that "any" in the phrase "the Minister shall consult any organisation" imposed a duty to consult not more than one organisation, that posting the letter of April 26, 1966, constituted consultation with the Mushroom Growers' Association despite the fact that it was never received, that the Mushroom Growers' Association was not an organisation which had to be consulted and that consultation with the National Farmers' Union involved consultation with all its branches including the Mushroom Growers' Association.

I have no doubt that Mr. Gettleson's first point is without foundation. "Any" must mean "every" in the context of section 1(4). There is a little more to be said for his submission that the mere sending of the letter of April 26, 1966, constituted consultation in that the Shorter Oxford English Dictionary gives as one definition of the verb "to consult" "to ask advice of, seek counsel from; to have recourse to for instruction or professional advice." However, in truth the mere sending of a letter constitutes but an attempt to consult and this does not suffice. The essence of consultation is the communication of a genuine invitation, extended with a receptive mind, to give advice: see *per* Bucknill L.J. approving a dictum of Morris J. in *Rollo* v. *Minister of Town and Country Planning* [1948] 1 All E.R. 13, 17. If the invitation is once received, it matters not that it is not accepted and no advice is proffered. Were it otherwise organisations with a right to be consulted could, in effect, veto the making of any order by simply failing to respond to the invitation. But without communication and the consequent opportunity of responding, there can be no consultation.

This leaves only the related questions of whether the Mushroom Growers' Association did in fact appear to the Minister to be an organisation falling within the categories set out in section 1(4) with the consequence that he was under an obligation to consult them and whether in any event his consultations with the National Farmers' Union constituted consultation with the Mushroom Growers' Association as a branch of the N.F.U. This is the heart of the problem.

Mr. Devey has deposed in paragraph 5 of his affidavit:

> "In accordance with practice the circulation of the draft schedule was not restricted to organisations that appeared to me to be representative of substantial numbers of employers engaging in activities specified in the draft schedule. This will appear sufficiently from a persual of the document. In particular the Mushroom Growers' Association was listed, although it was, and remains, a specialist branch of the National Farmer's Union. The listed address of the association is the same as that of the union which is Agriculture House, Knightsbridge, London, S.W.1."

In each case he sent a covering letter in one of three forms. The addresses on the first list, such as the National Farmers' Union, the Trades Union Congress, the Confederation of British Industry, and major government departments received special letters from Mr. Devey. Those on the second list received letters which were in standard form but were sent personally to named officials of the organisation concerned. These included the Local Government Examinations Board which clearly is an organisation which should have been consulted, but not one which in the terms of the Act had to be consulted. Those on the third list, including the Mushroom Growers' Association, received or should have received letters in standard form addressed to the organisation impersonally. I can find no clue in the form of the covering letter to whether any particular addressee appeared to the Minister to be a section 1(4) organisation and examples can be found in each list of organisations which plainly fall outside this category. I am thus thrown back on Mr. Devey's affidavit coupled with a letter dated January 20, 1969, signed by a Mr. Thomson of the Department of Employment and Productivity which states that a copy of the draft schedule was sent to the National Farmers' Union of which it is understood that the Mushroom Growers' Association is a specialist branch "and also as a matter of courtesy to that association." Bearing in mind the importance which attaches to consultation in the scheme of the Industrial Training Act 1964, which seems to be based upon the healthy principle of "no taxation without consultation," and the fact that Mr. Devey has not in terms said that the association did not appear to him to fall within the scope of section 1(4), I feel obliged to conclude that it was an organisation which had to be consulted, although its small membership in the context of the number of persons employed in agriculture, horticulture and forestry, and the specialised nature of their activities could well have led the Minister to take a different view.

This only leaves the question of whether it was consulted vicariously, and it may be accidentally, by means of the consultations with the National Farmers' Union. This is a nice point. *Prima facie* consultation with the parent body undoubtedly constitutes consultation with its constituent parts, but I think that this general rule is subject to an exception where, as here, the Minister has also attempted and intended direct consultation with a branch. The association's complaint has very little merit, because it seems to have been completely blind to all that was going on around it. Nevertheless it is important that statutory powers which involve taxation shall strictly construed and, so construed, I consider that the association should have been consulted and was not consulted.

I therefore answer the questions in the originating summons as follows: "Whether before making an order establishing a training board for the agricultural, horticultural and forestry industry, the Minister was under a duty to consult the Mushroom Growers' Association"—yes.

"Whether the consultations held by the Minister with the National Farmers' Union constituted a sufficient consultation with an organisation or association of organisations representative of those engaged in the activity of horticulture"—no.

"If it be held that the Minister was under a duty to consult the Mushroom Growers' Association, whether on the facts such consultation took place"—no.

"If it be held that the Minister was under a duty to consult the Mushroom Growers' Association and failed to do so, what effect such failure had upon the provisions of the Industrial Training (Agricultural, Horticultural and Forestry Board) Order 1966 (S.I. 1966 No. 969)"—the Order has no application to mushroom growers as such.

Order accordingly.

Notes

1. See case note by D. Foulkes, (1972) 35 M.L.R. 647.

2. In *Agricultural etc. Training Board* v. *Kent* [1970] 1 All E.R. 304, C.A., levy assessment notices were sent out to certain employers without indicating the recipients' rights of appeal and without stating the board's address for the service of a notice of appeal as required by the relevant legislation. The Court of Appeal held that this was a breach of a mandatory procedural requirement. Lord Denning M.R. stated that he regarded "the right of appeal as being of the first importance."

3. The question of consultation was raised in *R.* v. *Secretary of State for the Environment, ex p. Association of Metropolitan Authorities* [1986] 1 W.L.R. 1. The Secretary had power under the Housing Benefits Act 1982 to make regulations constituting the housing benefit scheme. Section 36(1) of the Act provided that before making regulations (including amending regulations) "the Secretary of State shall consult with organisations appearing to him to be representative of the authorities concerned" (*i.e.* local authorities). The Secretary of State habitually consulted the local authority associations, including the AMA, before making regulations, and it was common ground that the AMA was one of the organisations contemplated by s.36(1). On November 16 1984, the DHSS wrote to the AMA requesting their views on proposals to make certain amendments to the

regulations designed to close a "loophole." The letter was received on November 22 and a response was sought by November 30. The AMA requested an extension of time but no answer was forthcoming. Further proposed amendments were summarised in a letter of December 4, which sought a response by December 12. No draft of the proposed amendments was enclosed, and no mention was made of a material feature (which would require local authorities to investigate the background to the creation of joint tenancies by claimants so as to satisfy themselves that the tenancies had not been contrived to take advantage of the housing benefit scheme). The AMA replied on December 13 with brief comments. The amending regulations were made on December 17 and became law on December 19. Webster J. granted a declaration that the Secretary of State had failed to comply with s.36(1), but refused, in the exercise of his discretion, to quash the regulations. Webster J. said (at pp. 4–5):

> "There is no general principle to be extracted from the case law as to what kind or amount of consultation is required before delegated legislation, of which consultation is a precondition, can validly be made. But in any context the essence of consultation is the communication of a genuine invitation to give advice and a genuine receipt of that advice. In my view it must go without saying that to achieve consultation sufficient information must be supplied by the consulting to the consulted party to enable it to tender helpful advice. Sufficient time must be given by the consulting to the consulted party to enable it do to that, and sufficient time must be available for such advice to be considered by the consulting party. Sufficient, in that context, does not mean ample, but at least enough to enable the relevant purpose to be fulfilled. By helpful advice, in this context, I mean sufficiently informed and considered information or advice about aspects of the form or substance of the proposals, or their implications for the consulted party, being aspects material to the implementation of the proposal as to which the Secretary of State might not be fully informed or advised and as to which the party consulted might have relevant information or advice to offer.
>
> These propositions, as it seems to me, can partly be derived from, and are wholly consistent with, the decisions and various dicta, which I need not enumerate, in *Rollo* v. *Minister of Town and Country Planning* [1948] 1 All E.R. 13 and *Port Louis Corporation* v. *Attorney-General of Mauritius* [1965] A.C. 1111."

Webster J. noted that as the day-to-day administration of the scheme was in the hands of local authorities, who bore 10 per cent. of the scheme's cost, the obligation to consult was mandatory and not directory. In considering whether the consultation required by s.36(1) was in substance carried out, the court:

> "should have regard not so much to the actual facts which preceded the making of the regulations as to the material before the Secretary of State when he made the regulations, that material including facts or information as it appeared or must have appeared to him acting in good faith, and any judgments made or opinions expressed to him before the making of the regulations about those facts which appeared to could have appeared to him to be reasonable."

The effect of this approach was:

> "to give a certain flexibility to the notions of sufficiency, sufficient information, sufficient time and sufficiently informed and consider information and advice in my homespun attempt to define proper consultation. Thus, it can have the effect that what would be sufficient information or time in one case might be more or less than sufficient in another, depending on the relative degrees of

urgency and the nature of the proposed regulation. There is no degree of urgency, however, which absolves the Secretary of State from the obligation to consult at all."

His Lordship concluded that while the department was entitled to expect a quick response, the urgency of the situation was not such as to justify requiring views within such a short period that they might be insufficiently informed or considered.

However, the regulations were not quashed. Only one of six local authority associations had challenged the regulations; authorities would by then have adapted to the difficulties created by the regulations; revocation would mean that applicants refused benefit under the amended regulations would be entitled to make fresh claims, but this advantage would only last for six months as the challenged regulations had subsequently been consolidated in the Housing Benefits Regulations 1985, and the consolidation was not challenged.

4. In *R.* v. *Secretary of State for Health, ex p. United States Tobacco International Inc.* [1992] 1 Q.B. 353 (the "Skoal Bandits" case, above, p. 436), the regulations were quashed on the ground of inadequate consultation. Section 11(5)(*a*) of the Consumer Protection Act 1987 provided that before making safety regulations the Secretary of State was under a duty to consult "such organisations as appear to him to be representative of interests substantially affected by the proposal." Taylor L.J. stated (at pp. 369–372) that there were three reasons why consultation under s.11(5)(*a*) in the present case "required a high degree of fairness and candour to be shown by the Secretary of State." First, the history.

"Although the applicants cannot successfully rely on the doctrine of legitimate expectation, the fact is that they were led up the garden path."

Secondly, although the regulations were of general application, they impinged almost exclusively on the applicants as the sole manufacturers and packagers of oral snuff in the United Kingdom. Thirdly, the effect of the regulations was likely to be catastrophic to the applicants' United Kingdom business. Accordingly:

"it was important that the Secretary of State . . . should give the applicants a full opportunity to know and respond to the material and evaluations which led him to such a striking change of policy."

The Secretary of State was not obliged to let the applicants see the 300 other representations received given his undertaking to apprise the applicants of any fresh point arising from them to which he was minded to have regard (this point had already been settled in *R.* v. *Secretary of State for Social Security, ex p. United States Tobacco International Inc.*, Unreported, July 21, 1988). However, his refusal to disclose the text of the professional advice received from his advisory committee could not be justified. His claim that otherwise committee members might feel inhibited in expressing their views was "unconvincing." The committee members were "scientific experts of integrity and standing. . . . I cannot believe that they would be affected by the suggested inhibitions."

"One cannot help feeling that the denial of the applicants' request was due to an inbuilt reluctance to give reasons or disclose advice lest it give opponents fuel for argument. . . . To conceal from them the scientific advice which directly led to the ban was . . . unfair and unlawful."

LONDON & CLYDESIDE ESTATES LTD. v. ABERDEEN DISTRICT COUNCIL

[1980] 1 W.L.R. 182; [1979] 3 All E.R. 876 (House of Lords)

By virtue of section 25 of the Land Compensation (Scotland) Act 1963 a person whose interest in land was proposed to be acquired by an authority with powers of compulsory purchase might apply to the local planning authority for a certificate of alternative development as to the nature of the development for which planning permission might reasonably have been expected to be granted if the land was not to be compulsorily acquired for another purpose. A certificate was relevant to the amount of compensation.

By article 3(2) of the Town and Country Planning (General Purposes) (Scotland) Order 1959 the time prescribed for the issue of a certificate was two months. By article 3(3), if the local planning authority issued such a certificate:

> "they shall in that certificate include a statement in writing . . . of the rights of appeal to the Secretary of State given by section 6 [section 26 of the Act of 1963] and this Order."

By article 4(1) the time prescribed for appeal was one month.

The appellant company owning land which the respondent council proposed to acquire compulsorily for educational purposes applied for a certificate of alternative development, submitting that an appropriate class of redevelopment would be residential. The certificate issued stated that planning permission could not reasonably be expected for purposes other than educational. It did not mention the right of appeal. The company having appealed more than one month after the date of the certificate, its appeal was rejected as incompetent.

The company raised an action for (a) reduction of the certificate and (b) declaration that the council was bound to issue a new certificate. The Lord Ordinary granted both. The Second Division of the Court of Session granted the reduction but refused the declaration.

The House of Lords allowed an appeal by the company and dismissed an appeal by the council. The following extracts concern the validity of the certificate.

LORD HAILSHAM OF ST. MARYLEBONE: . . . On this basis, the first question for consideration is the consequence of what was admitted to be a defect in the purported certificate of October 22, 1974, namely the failure by the predecessors of the respondents to include in the certificate information in writing as to the appellants' rights of appeal to the Secretary of State. Was this requirement, which has the authority of Parliament behind it, mandatory or was it in some sense directory only? I have no doubt that it was mandatory, and that the failure to include this information was fatal to the certificate. In the course of argument counsel for the respondents candidly conceded that the only purpose of the requirement was to inform the applicant of his rights of appeal, including the time limit within which they should be exercised. The present appellants aver that they were misled by this defect and that it was as a result of this that their appeal was out of time. The averment has never been put to the proof, and one of the respondents' alternative arguments was that, in the event of otherwise total failure, the appellants should be put to the proof of this.

But in my view this argument is without foundation. The validity of the certificate itself is in question, and if, as I believe, the requirement is mandatory, the certificate falls independently of whether the appellants were in fact misled. I find it impossible to accept that a requirement by an instrument of statutory force designed for the very purpose of compelling a public authority to inform the subject of his legal rights can be treated as simply regulatory if the requirement is not complied with. If I required authority for this proposition I would refer to *Agricultural, Horticultural and Forestry Industry Training Board* v. *Kent* [1970] 2 Q.B. 19, *Rayner* v. *Stepney Corporation*[1911] 2 Ch. 312, and *Brayhead (Ascot) Ltd.* v. *Berkshire County Council* [1964] 2 Q.B. 303, notwithstanding that it relied on *Edwick* v. *Sunbury-on-Thames Urban District Council* [1962] 1 Q.B. 229 which was disapproved in *James* v. *Minister of Housing and Local Government* [1968] A.C. 409, which was decided on an argument irrelevant to the present appeal. However I am content to assert a general principle to the effect that where Parliament prescribes that an authority with compulsory powers should inform the subject of his right to question those powers, *prima facie* the requirement must be treated as mandatory. For the reasons which follow, however, this does not dispose the matter in the appellants' favour.

If the requirement that the subject should be informed of his legal rights was mandatory, what follows? The respondents attempted, as I thought, at one time, to argue that it thereupon became a nullity, and that therefore a decree of reduction was inappropriate because there was nothing upon which it could operate. But I do not accept this argument. The certificate was effective until it was struck down by a competent authority (*cf. Brayhead (Ascot) Ltd.* v. *Berkshire County Council* [1962] 1 Q.B. 229; *James* v. *Minister of Housing and Local Government* [1968] A.C. 409). In the course of argument I ventured to draw attention to the passage at p. 763 of the opinion of the Judicial Committee in *Calvin* v. *Carr* [1979] 2 W.L.R. 755, in which Lord Wilberforce says of a contention that a decision of the stewards of the Australian Jockey Club was void for breach of natural justice:

> "This argument led necessarily into the difficult area of what is void and what is voidable, as to which some confusion exists in the authorities. Their Lordships' opinion would be, if it became necessary to fix on one or other of these expressions, that a decision made contrary to natural justice is void, but that, until it is so declared by a competent body or court, it may have some effect, or existence, in law. This condition might be better expressed by saying that the decision is invalid or vitiated. In the present context, where the question is whether an appeal lies, the impugned decision cannot be considered as totally void, in the sense of being legally non-existent. So to hold would be wholly unreal."

The subject-matter of that case was wholly different from the present, but my opinion is that the thinking behind it is applicable. The certificate was vitiated in the sense that it failed to comply with a mandatory requirement. But the subject could not safely disregard it as not having been issued. Had he done so, he might well have fallen into the very trap of losing his right to complain of the vitiating factor which has caught other subjects in the reported decisions, and, in my view, he was not only wise but bound to seek a decree of reduction or some other appropriate remedy striking down the offending certificate.

A similar line of reasoning disposes of the next contention of the respondents, also rejected in the Second Division, to the effect that, if the certificate is vitiated, the position is the same as if no certificate had been issued and that section 26(4) of the Land Compensation (Scotland) Act 1963 then operates in such a way that, no certificate having been issued under section 25, the preceding provisions of the section as to appeals should apply at the expiry of the prescribed period "as if" the local planning authority had issued a certificate "containing such a statement as is mentioned in" section 25(4)(*b*) of the Act. The effect of this read with articles 3 and 4 of the Order would have put the appellants out of time for appeal on the expiry of one month after the expiry of the prescribed (2 months) for the due issue of the certificate by the respondents. The fallacy in this argument lies in the assumption (for it is no more) that the issue by an authority of a certificate vitiated by failure to comply with a mandatory requirement is the same thing as the failure by that authority to issue any purported certificate at all.

At this stage I should notice a contention on the part of the Respondents, which, though, as will be seen, I partly agree with it, does not seem to me to be relevant to the disposal of the cross-appeal.

The contention was that in the categorisation of statutory requirements into "mandatory" and "directory," there was a subdivision of the category "directory" into two classes composed (i) of those directory requirements "substantial compliance" with which satisfied the requirement to the point at which a minor defect of trivial irregularity could be ignored by the court and (ii) those requirements so purely regulatory in character that failure to comply could in no circumstances affect the validity of what was done. The contention of the respondents was that, even on the assumption against themselves that the requirement of the Order that the certificate should include a notification of the appellants' rights to appeal to the Secretary of State, the rest of the certificate was so exactly in accordance with the provisions of the Order that the remaining defect could be safely ignored.

I do not consider that this argument assists the respondents in the present appeal. I have already held that the requirement relating to notification of the appellants' rights of appeal was mandatory and not directory in either sense contended for by the respondents. But on the assumption that I am wrong about this, a total failure to comply with a significant part of a requirement cannot in any circumstances be regarded as "substantial compliance" with the total requirement in such a way as to bring the respondents' contention into effect.

Nevertheless I wish to examine the contention itself. In this appeal we are in the field of the rapidly developing jurisprudence of administrative law, and we are considering the effect of non-compliance by a statutory authority with the statutory requirements affecting the discharge of one of its functions. In the reported decisions there is much language presupposing the existence of stark categories such as "mandatory" and "directory," "void" and "voidable," a "nullity," and "purely regulatory."

Such language is useful; indeed, in the course of this opinion I have used some of it myself. But I wish to say that I am not at all clear that the language itself may not be misleading in so far as it may be supposed to present a court with the necessity of fitting a particular case into one or other of mutually exclusive and starkly contrasted compartments, compartments which in some cases (*e.g.* "void" and "voidable") are borrowed from the language of contract or status, and are not easily fitted to the requirements of administrative law.

When Parliament lays down a statutory requirement for the exercise of legal authority it expects its authority to be obeyed down to the minutest detail. But what the courts have to decide in a particular case is the legal consequence of non-compliance on the rights of the subject viewed in the light of a concrete state of facts and a continuing chain of events. It may be that what the courts are faced with is not so much a stark choice of alternatives but a spectrum of possibilities in which one compartment or description fades gradually into another. At one end of this spectrum there may be cases in which a fundamental obligation may have been so outrageously and flagrantly ignored or defied that the subject may safely ignore what has been done and treat it as having no legal consequences upon himself. In such a case if the defaulting authority seeks to rely on its action it may be that the subject is entitled to use the defect in procedure simply as a shield or defence without having taken any positive action of his own. At the other end of the spectrum the defect in procedure may be so nugatory or trivial that the authority can safely proceed without remedial action, confident that, if the subject is so misguided as to rely on the fault, the courts will decline to listen to his complaint. But in a very great number of cases, it may be in a majority of them, it may be necessary for a subject, in order to safeguard himself, to go to the court for declaration of his rights, the grant of which may well be discretionary, and by the like token it may be wise for an authority (as it certainly would have been here) to do everything in its power to remedy the fault in its procedure so as not to deprive the subject of his due or themselves of their power to act. In such cases, though language like "mandatory," "directory," "void," "voidable," "nullity" and so forth may be helpful in argument, it may be misleading in effect if relied on to show that the courts, in deciding the consequences of a defect in the exercise of power, are necessarily bound to fit the facts of a particular case and a developing chain of events into rigid legal categories or to stretch or cramp them on a bed of Procrustes invented by lawyers for the purposes of convenient exposition. As I have said, the case does not really arise here, since we are in the presence of total non-compliance with a requirement which I have held to be mandatory. Nevertheless I do not wish to be understood in the field of administrative law and in the domain where the courts apply a supervisory jurisdiction over the acts of subordinate authority purporting to exercise statutory powers, to encourage the use of rigid legal classifications. The jurisdiction is inherently discretionary and the court is frequently in the presence of differences of degree which merge almost imperceptibly into differences of kind.

There was only one other argument for the respondents on their cross-appeal that I need notice. This was that the requirement not complied with was separable from the rest of the requirements as to the certificate. I do not read it as such. It was an integral part of the requirement that the certificate should "include" a written notification of the rights of appeal.

[On the appeal, his lordship held that; on a proper construction of s.25, the authority's duty to issue a certificate was a continuing duty, which was not terminated by non-compliance with art.3(2) in tone. Accordingly, the court could order the issue of a new certificate. His lordship also expressed his agreement with LORD FRASER and LORD KEITH.]

LORD KEITH OF KINKEL: . . . [I]t was contended that article 3(3) was not intended to be mandatory or imperative, but merely directory and procedural in effect. It was said that any applicant for a certificate of appropriate alternative development must have read the Order of 1959 for the purpose of finding out how to make application. . . .

The word "shall" used in article 3(3) is normally to be interpreted as connoting a mandatory provision, meaning that what is thereby enjoined is not merely desired to be done but must be done. In many instances failure to obtemper a mandatory provision has the consequence that the proceedings with which the failure is connected are rendered invalid. But that is not necessarily so. As is shown by the case of *Brayhead (Ascot) Ltd. v. Berkshire County Council* [1964] 2 Q.B. 303 something may turn upon the importance of the provision in relation to the statutory purpose which the provision is directed to achieving, and whether any opportunity exists of later putting right the failure. I have no doubt that in the present case the provision under consideration is intended to be mandatory and is of such a character that failure to comply with it renders the certificate invalid. Where Parliament, albeit through subordinate legislation, has enacted that a person is to be informed of the rights of appeal conferred upon him by statute in relation to a particular subject-matter whereby his rights may be very materially affected, it will not do to say that failure to comply with the enactment has no legal result whatever. The matter is of great importance and has been shown to have been so regarded by Parliament. Failure to comply may deprive the person concerned of his rights of appeal with no opportunity of rectifying the situation. While it is indeed curious that no provision is made for acquainting an applicant for a certificate with his rights of appeal where no certificate is issued within the prescribed time, I regard that omission as inadvertent, and not serving in any way to indicate an intention that the provisions of article 3(3) about notification of rights of appeal should be merely directory. I note that authority in favour of the view that a provision of this nature is mandatory in the sense that failure to comply renders the proceedings invalid is to be found in *Agricultural, Horticultural and Forestry Industry Training Board* v. *Kent* [1970] 2 Q.B. 19. . . .

The final argument for the respondents on this branch of the case turned on the terms of section 26(4) of the Act of 1963. . . . In my opinion this argument also is unsound. In the first place it is to be observed that the argument is elided if decree is to be granted not only reducing the certificate actually issued but also ordaining the respondents to issue a new certificate in proper form. It is not an argument in favour of the validity of the certificate issued. Indeed, it requires that the certificate should have been totally void *ab initio* and that the respondents should be treated as having done nothing at all in response to the appellants' application. That would, in my opinion, be totally unrealistic. The respondents did issue a certificate, but it contained a defect enabling it to be successfully attacked as invalid. I do not consider that section 26(4) applies to that situation. It applies where after the expiry of the time prescribed "no certificate has been issued." Here a certificate was issued which, though defective, was not a complete nullity. In this context use of the expressions "void" and "voidable," which have a recognised significance and importance in certain fields of the law of contract, is to be avoided as inappropriate and apt to confuse. A decision or other act of a more or less formal character may be invalid and subject to being so declared in court of law and yet have some legal effect or existence prior to such declaration. In particular, it may be capable of being submitted to an appeal (*cf. Calvin* v. *Carr* [1979] 2 W.L.R. 755, 763, *per* Lord Wilberforce). In my opinion the certificate issued in the present case was of that character. It had some legal effect unless and until reduced, and in particular it might, in my view, have been the proper subject of a timeous appeal to the Secretary of State. . . .

LORD WILBERFORCE agreed with the speeches of LORD HAILSHAM and LORD KEITH. LORD FRASER OF TULLYBELTON delivered a concurring speech. LORD RUSSELL OF KILLOWEN agreed with LORD KEITH.

Notes

1. The dicta in Lord Hailsham's speech in favour of a more flexible approach than the traditional mandatory/directory dichotomy have found favour with

some judges in later cases. In *Main* v. *Swansea City Council* (1984) 49 P. & C.R. 26, the Court of Appeal held that in principle the grant of outline planning permission for the residential development of certain land was vitiated: first, the necessary certificate that all the other owners of the land had been notified was incorrect, in that a small part of the land was in fact owned by a third party whose identity was known; secondly, as the land included land within 67 metres of the middle of a highway, the Secretary of State should have been given notice of the application under art. 11 of the Town and Country Planning General Development Order 1973. The Court of Appeal cited the *London and Clydeside* case both on the point that an invalid certificate could nevertheless have some legal effect, and on Lord Hailsham's preference for a flexible approach. Parker L.J. said (at p. 37):

> "In our judgment, the most significant observation in Lord Hailsham's speech, indeed in the whole of the *Clydesdale* [*sic*] case, is that the court must consider the consequences in the light of a concrete state of facts and a continuing chain of events. This recognises that the court looks not only at the nature of the failure but also at such matters as the identity of the applicant for relief, the lapse of time, the effect on other parties and on the public and so on."

The court, however, declined to quash the permission, in the exercise of its discretion. The outline permission had been granted in 1977; reserved matters were approved in 1980, and during this period no objections had been made to the outline permission; the actual development would not take place on the land owned by the unidentified person; and the Secretary of State had for a very long time been aware of the position and had not sought relief.

In *R.* v. *London Borough of Lambeth, ex p. Sharp* (1986) 55 P. & C.R. 232, notice of a proposed development published in a local newspaper failed to specify the period during which objections should be made, and failed to state that objections should be in writing. The Court of Appeal upheld the trial judge's decision to quash the subsequent grant of planning permission. Stephen Brown L.J. said (at p. 238):

> "It seems to me that it is not necessary to consider whether these requirements are 'mandatory' or 'directory,' or whether they go to powers or duties. One has to look at the terms of the regulations, and a breach of them, in my judgment, clearly provides a basis upon which the court can be seized of an application for judicial review. It is of course material to consider the nature of such a breach—that is to say, its gravity and relevance—when considering whether relief shall be granted. For my part, I am satisfied that the breach in question, which I find the judge was right to hold established, was fundamental, bearing in mind that it is a provision which requires notification of proposed development to members of the public. This was in a conservation area and is obviously a matter of general local public interest. Public notification of the proposed grant of planning permission must accordingly be of fundamental public importance. I would hold that this is not a mere procedural technicality but rather it is a requirement fundamental to the operation of this particular planning procedure."

His Lordship also rejected an argument that the court should decline to quash the permission on the basis that there had been substantial compliance with the requirement of the regulation as a whole, and that no one had been prejudiced. This was a fundamental flaw; it was impossible to say that the applicant had not been prejudiced (he had not seen the site notice); and it was a matter of intense public interest in the locality.

Woolf L.J. said (at pp. 239–240):

> "The regulations are but an example of the numerous different statutory regulations which lay down procedures which have to be followed by public authorities in carrying out their functions. When the provisions of such regulations are contravened, almost invariably it is unhelpful to consider what are the consequences of non-compliance with the regulations by classifying them as containing mandatory or directory provisions, or as containing a condition precedent, or as containing a provision which renders a decision void or voidable, or by considering whether they contain a provision which goes to jurisdiction. What has to be considered is: what is the particular provision designed to achieve? If, as here, it is designed to give the public an opportunity to make objections to what is proposed, then the court is bound to attach considerable importance to any failure to comply with the requirements.
>
> However, the breach of the requirements cannot be considered alone. It has to be considered in the context of the particular circumstances in relation to which the matter comes before the court."

(His Lordship stated that he adopted the approach of Parker L.J. in *Main* v. *Swansea City Council*, which in turn was based upon Lord Hailsham's speech in the *London and Clydeside* case.)

> "In adopting that approach to the circumstances in this case, I would come to the same conclusion as the learned judge and my Lord, Stephen Brown L.J. I appreciate that it may be said that this approach introduces an element of uncertainty as to what will be the consequences of a breach of regulations of this nature. However, while accepting that this may be the position, I observe that the attempts which have been made in the past to categorise breaches, and therefore their consequences, have not in fact achieved any degree of continuity and, indeed, have in themselves been a source of considerable litigation as to the particular category in relation to which a particular breach could be said to fall."

Sir John Donaldson M.R. agreed with both judgments.

For further examples of the adoption of the flexible approach, see Woolf J. in *R.* v. *Chester City Council, ex p. Quietlynn Ltd., The Times*, October 19, 1983, and *R.* v. *Secretary of State for the Environment, ex p. Leicester City Council* (1985) 25 R.V.R. 31; Schiemann J. in *R.* v. *Doncaster Metropolitan Borough Council* [1987] J.P.L. 444 and M. T. Pill Q.C. in *Robbins* v. *Secretary of State for the Environment* (1987) 56 P. & C.R. 416 and *Porritt* v. *Secretary of State for the Environment* [1988] J.P.L. 414.

2. On the point that the court retains a discretion whether to quash even where there has been a breach of a mandatory requirement, see also *R.* v. *Greenwich London Borough Council, ex p. Patel* (1985) 84 L.G.R. 241; *Porritt, supra*; and *Mayes* v. *Secretary of State for the Environment, The Independent*, January 26, 1989.

3. On the effect of non-compliance with a procedural requirement in the context of statutory applications to quash, see below pp. 622–639.

4. The language of the mandatory/directory distinction has not been eradicated. See, *e.g.* Lord Keith in *Inverclyde District Council* v. *Lord Advocate* [1982] J.P.L. 313, 314; and the Court of Appeal in *Secretary of State for Trade and Industry* v. *Langridge* [1991] Ch. 402 (above p. 452, n. 4).

(B) NATURAL JUSTICE: THE DUTY TO ACT FAIRLY

In administrative law the "rules of natural justice" have traditionally been regarded as comprising the rules *audi alteram partem* and *nemo judex in causa sua.*

Respectively, these apply to require the maker of a decision to give prior notice of the decision to persons affected by it, and an opportunity for those persons to make representations; and also to disqualify the decision-maker from acting if he or she has a direct pecuniary or proprietary interest, or he or she might otherwise be biased. The rules are historically closely tied to judicial decision-making in the courts, but they have been extended to apply to administrative authorities and to administrative decision-making, and it is here that the main difficulties have arisen. It is not clear how far the rules of natural justice apply to decisions which do not have a significant judicial element. Here, the courts have sometimes prescribed a basis duty to act fairly, which may include some aspects of "natural justice," but which may simply amount to a duty to refrain from any abuse of discretion.

In the case of each of the twin rules of natural justice two basic issues are involved:

(a) Does the rule apply to the particular situation; and
(b) if so, what is the precise content of the rule in that situation?

Finally, of course, if it applies, has the rule been observed?

See generally, P. Jackson, *Natural Justice* (2nd ed., 1979); G. A. Flick, *Natural Justice* (2nd ed., 1984).

(i) Audi Alteram Partem

In the twentieth century, the application of this rule has been considered by the House of Lords in a series of cases including *Board of Education* v. *Rice* [1911] A.C. 179, *Local Government Board* v. *Arlidge* [1915] A.C. 120, *Ridge* v. *Baldwin* (1963) (below, p. 475), *Bushell* v. *Secretary of State for the Environment* (1980) (below, p. 550), *Lloyd* v. *McMahon* (1987) (below, p. 541), *R.* v. *Board of Visitors of H.M. Prison, The Maze, ex p. Hone* (1988) (below, p. 545) and *Al-Mehdawi* v. *Secretary of State for the Home Department* (1990) (below, p. 533). The pivotal decision is that of *Ridge* v. *Baldwin*. This removed some restrictions on the rule's application that had developed since 1914 in lower courts, and led to an "explosion" of natural justice cases.

Briefly stated, the traditional basic principle is that the *audi alteram partem* rule must be observed by anyone who is making a judicial or quasi-judicial, as distinct from an administrative, decision. Since *Ridge* v. *Baldwin*, a wider variety of decisions have been regarded as "judicial" or "quasi-judicial" for this purpose (note the discussion of these categories in Chapter 1 above, p. 1). In turn this has led some judges to argue that it is no longer necessary to distinguish between the "judicial" or "quasi-judicial" and the "administrative," (*e.g.* Lord Denning in *Schmidt* v. *Secretary of State for Home Affairs* [1969] 2 Ch. 149). If a decision seriously affects individual interests, natural justice or fairness must be observed irrespective of the label applicable to that decision, all the legal argument being about the appropriate content of the rule in the particular situation. Another approach that has been taken is to require observation of "natural justice" in the making of judicial or quasi-judicial decisions, and of a "duty to act fairly" in the making of administrative decisions (*e.g.* Lord Parker C.J. in *Re H.K. (An Infant)* (1967), below, p. 494). This will usually lead to the same result as the previous approach, but it preserves the need to label decisions, a task that properly should be redundant.

Each of these approaches may be contrasted with the previous situation where judges adopted an "analytical" approach, denying the relevance of natural justice to non-judicial decisions. This led either to injustice, where natural justice was held not to apply to decisions that substantially prejudiced individual interests (as in *Nakkuda Ali* v. *Jayaratne* [1951] A.C. 66 (discussed in *Ridge* v. *Baldwin*), where a decision to revoke a trader's licence and thereby to deprive him of his livelihood was held to be non-judicial), or strained analysis, where clearly administrative decisions were classified as "judicial" (as in *Cooper* v. *Wandsworth Board of Works*, below p. 470).

In the following subsections we consider (1) the types of decision-making which have been subject to some form of fair hearing obligations, (2) factors which have induced the judiciary to limit the application of the right to a fair hearing, and (3) the content of the right to a fair hearing in particular decision-making contexts.

(a) When does the "Right to a Fair Hearing" Apply?

COOPER v. THE BOARD OF WORKS FOR THE WANDSWORTH DISTRICT

(1863) 14 C.B.(N.S.) 180; 32 L.J.C.P. 185; 8 L.T. 278; 2 New Rep. 31; 9 Jur.(N.S.) 1155; 11 W.R. 646; 143 E.R. 414 (Court of Common Pleas)

The Metropolis Local Management Act 1855, s.76, provided that: "before beginning to lay or dig out the foundation of any new house or building . . . seven days notice in writing shall be given to the . . . board by the person intending to build . . . such house or building. . . ." This ensured that the board had opportunity to give directions under the Act as to the drains. Section 76 also provided that "in default of such notice . . . it shall be lawful for . . . the board to cause such house or building to be demolished or altered . . . and to recover the expenses thereof from the owner. . . ." The plaintiff, a builder, was employed to build a house in Wandsworth. He claimed that he sent a notice under section 76 to the board, but this was denied. He admitted, however, that he had commenced digging out the foundations within five days of the day on which he claimed to have sent the notice. The house had reached the second storey when the board, without giving any notice, sent round their surveyor and a number of workmen at a late hour in the evening. The men razed the house to the ground.

The plaintiff sued for damages for trespass. Willes J. found for the plaintiff. The defendants obtained a rule nisi for a nonsuit. They argued (*inter alia*) (1) that "the great safeguard against abuses . . . is that the members of which these boards are composed are elected by the rate-payers of the district." (2) "What necessity can there be for giving the party notice, when he well knows that he is doing an illegal act, and that the board have power to prostrate his house?" (3) "It is not like the case where a judicial discretion is to be exercised. An arbitrary power is conferred upon the board, which is necessarily to be exercised without any control."

ERLE C.J.: . . . The contention on the part of the plaintiff has been, that, although the words of the statute, taken in their literal sense, without any qualification at all, would create a justification for the act which the district board has done, the powers granted by that statute are subject to a qualification which has been repeatedly recognised, that no man is to be deprived of his property without his having an opportunity of being heard. . . . I think that the power which is granted by the 76th section is subject to the qualification suggested. It is a power carrying with it enormous consequences. The house in question was built only to a certain extent. But the power claimed would apply to a complete house. It would apply to a house of any value, and completed to any extent; and it seems to me to be a power which may be exercised most perniciously, and that the limitation which we are going to put upon it is one which ought, according to the decided cases, to be put upon it, and one which is required by a due consideration for the public interest. I think the board ought to have given notice to the plaintiff, and to have allowed him to be heard. The default in sending notice to the board of the intention to build, is a default which may be explained. There may be a great many excuses for the apparent default. The party may have intended to conform to the law. He may have actually conformed to all the regulations which they would wish to impose, though by accident his notice may have miscarried; and, under those circumstances, if he explained how it stood, the proceeding to demolish, merely because they had ill-will against the party, is a power that the legislature never intended to confer. I cannot conceive any harm that could happen to the district board from hearing the party before they subjected him to a loss so serious as the demolition of his house; but I can conceive a great many advantages which might arise in the way of public order, in the way of doing substantial justice, and in the way of fulfilling the purposes of the statute, by the restriction which we put upon them, that they should hear the party before they inflict upon him such a heavy loss. I fully agree that the legislature intended to give the district board very large powers indeed: but the qualification I speak of is one which has been recognised to the full extent. It has been said that the principle that no man shall be deprived of his property without an opportunity of being heard, is limited to a judicial proceeding, and that a district board ordering a house to be pulled down cannot be said to be doing a judicial act. I do not quite agree with that; neither do I undertake to rest my judgment solely upon the ground that the district board is a court exercising judicial discretion upon the point: but the law, I think, has been applied to many exercises of power which in common understanding would not be at all more a judicial proceeding than would be the act of the district board in ordering a house to be pulled down. The case of the corporation of the University of Cambridge, who turned out Dr. Bentley, in the exercise of their assumed power of depriving a member of the University of his rights, and a number of other cases which are collected in the Hammersmith Rent-Charge Case, 4 Exch. 96, in the judgment of Parke B., show that the principle has been very widely applied. The district board must do the thing legally; there must be a resolution; and, if there be a board, and a resolution of that board, I have not heard a word to show that it would not be salutary that they should hear the man who is to suffer from their judgment before they proceed to make the order under which they attempt to justify their act. It is said that an appeal from the district board to the metropolitan board (under s.211) would be the mode of redress. But, if the district board have the power to do what is here stated, I am not at all clear that there would be a right of redress in that way. The metropolitan board may not have a right to give redress for that which was done under the provisions of the statute. I think the appeal clause would evidently indicate that many exercises of the power of a district board would be in the nature of judicial proceedings; because, certainly when they are appealed from, the appellant and the respondent are to be heard as parties, and the matter is to be decided at least according to judicial forms. I take that to be a principle of very wide application, and applicable to the present case; and I think this board was not justified under the statute, because they have not qualified themselves for the exercise of their power by hearing the party to be affected by their decision.

WILLES J.: I am of the same opinion. I apprehend that a tribunal which is by law invested with power to affect the property of one of Her Majesty's subjects, is bound to give such subject an opportunity of being heard before it proceeds: and that that rule is of universal application, and founded upon the plainest principles of justice. Now, is the board in the present case such a tribunal? I apprehend it clearly is, whether we consider it with reference to the discretion which is vested in it, or whether we look at the analogy which exists between it and other recognised tribunals (and no one ever doubted that such tribunals are bound by the rules which a court of justice is bound by), or whether you look at it with reference to the estimation in which it is held by the legislature, as appears from the language used in the statute. . . .

. . . With respect to nuisances, the board exercises the power of a criminal court of high jurisdiction, because it has a discretion as to whether it will abate that which is a nuisance altogether, or whether it will simply direct that there shall be a modification of the works which in its opinion are necessary for the health of the neighbourhood. I apprehend it is clear that the powers thus exercised by the board under the Act are powers which have always been considered judicial, and which could not be exercised without giving notice to the party who is to be proceeded against. In this very section, 76, the legislature speaks of coming "under the jurisdiction of the vestry or board"; and it is clear that these boards do exercise judicial powers. The power here is one that, probably more than any, requires that the party to be affected by it should be heard, because of its extent, and because the board may be satisfied with a modification of that which has been done. . . .

[His Lordship summarised section 76.]

The matter to be considered by the board before they make that order [*i.e.* an order giving directions] is, first of all, has any notice been given? And then the party clearly ought to be allowed to show, either that he has given a notice which may have been overlooked, or, if the notice has not been received by the board, to show that he did his best towards doing so, in order to induce them to look on the case favourably—not to demolish the house, but to seen whether any and what qualification is necessary for the purpose of bringing it within what should be done if the notice had been regularly served. In either of those cases, I apprehend, it is clear that it would be the right of the party to be heard. But there is a third case; and that is where, by wilfully disregarding the order, or by the act of some third person, whom he did his best to control, the owner of the house may have subjected his house to demolition by the board, or to be dealt with severely by reason of its defects. That is a case in which judicial power is to be exercised, and in which clearly the party sought to be affected should be heard. Then, as to the appeal section, 211, what light does that throw upon the matter? There is an appeal from the district board, not to any judicial tribunal in the sense of any tribunal more judicial in its form than the local board of works, but to the metropolitan board of works, which is just as much and just as little judicial in its acts as the board whose conduct we are now considering. What is to take place upon such appeal? "And all such appeals shall stand referred to the committee appointed by such board for hearing appeals, as herein provided; and such committee shall *hear and determine* all such appeals." Nothing can be more clear than that the legislature thought that the matters which might come before the board upon appeal, that is, the same matters which came before the local board of works in the first instance, were proper, not only to be determined, but also to be heard; and, if fit to be heard upon an appeal, a *fortiori* fit to be heard in the first instance, before a wrongful decision can make an appeal lie. . . .

. . . There is another remark to be made with reference to these parties' proceedings. The board are not only to do the work of demolishing the house, if they think proper, or modifying it, but they are to charge the expenses on the person who has erred against the Act. His property is affected and his purse is further affected. What happens upon that? and how is the money to be got? That is a proceeding under the 225th section, which is a section giving jurisdiction to the justices before whom the costs are to be ascertained and recovered; and it is clear that under that section the justices could not proceed without having before them the person against whom the expenses are to be adjudged. And it does seem an absurdity to say, that, in determining the amount of expenses, the party shall be heard, but that, in determining whether proceedings should be taken, his mouth should be closed. I cannot help thinking that a board exercising this large power should follow the ordinary rule, that the party sought to be affected should be heard; and I think that the verdict for the plaintiff ought to stand.

BYLES J.: I am of the same opinion. This is a case in which the Wandsworth district board have taken upon themselves to pull down a house, and to saddle the owner with the expenses of demolition, without notice of any sort. There are two sorts of notice which may possibly be required, and neither of them has been given: one, a notice of a hearing, that the party may be heard if he has anything to say against the demolition; the other is a notice of the order, that he may consider whether he can mitigate the wrath of the board, or in any way modify the execution of the order. Here they have given him neither opportunity. It seems to me that the board are wrong whether they acted judicially or ministerially. I conceive they acted judicially, because they had to determine the offence, and they had to apportion the punishment as well as the remedy. That being so, a long course of decisions, beginning with Dr. Bentley's case,[1] and ending with some very recent cases, establish, that, although there are no positive words in a statute requiring that the party shall be heard, yet the justice of the common law will supply the omission of the legislature. The judgment of Mr. Justice Fortescue, in Dr. Bentley's case, is somewhat quaint, but it is very applicable, and has been the law from that time to the present. He says, "The objection for want of notice can never be got over. The laws of God and man both give the party an opportunity to make his defence, if he has any. I remember to have heard it observed by a very learned man, upon such an occasion, that even God himself did not pass sentence upon Adam before he was called upon to make his defence. 'Adam' (says God), 'where art thou? Hast thou not eaten of the tree whereof I commanded thee that thou shouldest not eat?' And the same question was put to Eve also." If, therefore, the board acted judicially, although there are no words in the statute to that effect, it is plain they acted wrongly. But suppose they acted ministerially—then it may be they were not bound to give the first sort of notice, *viz.* the notice of the hearing; but they were clearly bound, as it seems to me, by the words of the statute, to give notice of their order before they proceeded to execute it. Section 76 contains these words: "The vestry or district board shall make their order in relation to the matters aforesaid, and cause the same to be notified" (observe what follows) "to the person from whom such notice was received, within seven days after the receipt of the notice." The plain construction of those words, as it seems to me, is this: the order is to be notified, and, in the case of a person who has given a notice, that notification is to be conveyed to him within seven days from the date of his notice. That has not been done. There has been neither notice of the one sort nor of the other; and it seems to me, therefore, that, whether the board acted judicially or ministerially, they have acted against the whole current of authorities, and have omitted to do that which justice requires, and contravened the words of the statute. I entirely agree with what my Brother Willes has said about section 211, which clearly shows, that, if the board acted ministerially, they ought to give notice of the latter character. I cannot entertain any doubt that in this case the board have exercised their power wrongfully.

KEATING J. delivered a concurring judgment.

Rule discharged.

[1] *The King* v. *The Chancellor, &c., of Cambridge,* 1 Stra. 557; 2 Ld.Raym. 1334; 8 Mod. 148; Fortescue 202.

Notes

1. A wide variety of arguments are advanced by the judges; note in particular their avowed aim of promoting good administration. They do not simply incant "no man shall be deprived of his property without a hearing."

2. Note the willingness of Byles J. to read words requiring a hearing into the statute. Compare the views of the Privy Council in *Furnell* v. *Whangarei School Board* [1973] 1 All E.R. 400, P.C. The majority (Lords Morris of Borth-y-Gest, Simon of Glaisdale and Kilbrandon) were of the opinion that where a detailed and elaborate disciplinary code was prescribed by statutory regulations, as it was for the investigation of complaints against teachers in New Zealand, it was "not lightly to be affirmed" that it was unfair "when it has been made on the advice of the responsible Minister and on the joint recommendation of organisations representing teachers employed and those employing. Nor is it the function of the court to redraft the code" (p. 411). The approach of the minority (Viscount Dilhorne and Lord Reid) was to ask first whether the nature of the powers exercised gave rise to a presumption that they were to be exercised only after the person affected had been given a fair hearing. If a fair hearing was necessary but had not been given, the burden shifted to the authority to establish that the regulations "clearly show an intention to exclude that which natural justice would otherwise require" (p. 417). Which approach is preferable? See casenote by J. M. Evans, (1973) 36 M.L.R. 439 and article by J. F. Northey, [1972] N.Z.L.J. 307.

RIDGE v. BALDWIN AND OTHERS

[1964] A.C. 40; [1963] 2 W.L.R. 935; 127 J.P. 295; 107 S.J. 313; [1963] 2 All E.R. 66; 61 L.G.R. 369 (House of Lords)

The Municipal Corporations Act 1882 provided by section 191: "(4) The Watch Committee, . . . may at any time dismiss, any borough constable whom they think negligent in the discharge of his duty, or otherwise unfit for the same." The Police Act 1919 provided by section 4(1): "It shall be lawful for the Secretary of State to make regulations as to the . . . conditions of service of the members of all police forces within England and Wales, and every police authority shall comply with the regulations so made."It was accepted that the 1919 Act did not impliedly repeal the relevant provisions of the 1882 Act. The relevant regulations contained detailed provisions as to the procedure to be followed where a report or allegation was received by the police authority from which it appeared that a chief constable might have committed an offence against the "Discipline Code" (set out in the regulations).

According to the regulations, the detailed procedure, which involved a formal hearing before a specially constituted tribunal, could only be dispensed with if the chief constable admitted that he had committed an offence against the code.

Charles Ridge was appointed chief constable of the County Borough of Brighton in 1956. The appointment was "subject to the Police Act and Regulations." In 1957, Ridge, two police officers and two others were indicted for conspiracy to obstruct the course of justice between 1949 and 1957. Ridge was acquitted, but the other two police officers were convicted. On February 28, in passing sentence, the trial judge, Donovan J., made certain observations as to the chief constable's conduct. In the words of Lord Evershed: "As I understand the language of Donovan J. . . . the appellant had been shown not to possess a sense of probity or of responsibility sufficient for the office which he held, and so had been unable to provide the essential leadership and example to the police force under his control which his office properly required." On March 6, no evidence was offered against R. on a further charge of corruption. Here Donovan J. referred to the police force's need for a leader "who will be a new influence and who will set a different example from that which has lately obtained." The following day, the Watch Committee, purporting to act under section 191(4) of the 1882 Act summarily dismissed R. on the ground that in their opinion he had been negligent in the discharge of his duty, and was unfit for the same. He was given neither any notice of the meeting, nor any opportunity to make representations. The regulations were in no way operated. On March 18, the committee heard representations from R.'s solicitor, but gave no further particulars of the case against him. On July 5, the Home Secretary dismissed R.'s appeal under the Police (Appeals) Act 1927 (as amended), holding "that there was sufficient material on which the Watch Committee could properly exercise their power of dismissal under section 191 (4)." The appeal had been made expressly without prejudice to any rights to contend that the purported dismissal was bad in law as being contrary to natural justice and not in accordance with the regulations.

R. then brought an action in the High Court for a declaration that the dismissal was illegal, *ultra vires* and void, and for damages. His main purpose was to obtain the opportunity to resign voluntarily, his pension rights thus being preserved.

Eight significant issues arose:

1. Did the regulations apply? If they did, there had been a clear non-compliance.
2. If they did not, did the *audi alteram partem* rule of natural justice nevertheless apply?
3. If it applied, was it complied with?
4. If the decision to dismiss was bad under either of the foregoing heads, was it void or voidable?
5. If the initial dismissal was bad, was it cured by the second meeting of the committee on March 18?
6. Did the exercise of the right of appeal cure any invalidity?
7. Was the invalidity cured by the Police (Appeals) Act 1927, s.2(3), which stated that the Secretary of State's decision should be final and binding on all parties?
8. Should the invalidity be ignored, on the ground that the case was "as plain as a pikestaff?"

Streatfeild J. at first instance ([1961] 2 W.L.R. 1054), held that natural justice had to be observed, and that the Watch Committee had done so. The Court of Appeal ([1963] 1 Q.B. 539) held that natural justice did not have to be observed as the action of the committee was "administrative" or "executive." They were not deciding a question between two contending parties. Ridge's appeal to the House of Lords was allowed. The leading speeches were those of Lord Reid, who dealt mainly with natural justice at common law, and Lord Morris of Borth-y-Gest, who dealt mainly with the regulations. Lord Hodson came to the same conclusions as both Lord Reid and Lord Morris. Lord Devlin's speech was based solely on the regulations. Lord Evershed dissented.

LORD REID: . . . The appellant's case is that in proceeding under the Act of 1882 the watch committee were bound to observe what are commonly called the principles of natural justice. Before attempting to reach any decision they were bound to inform him of the grounds on which they proposed to act and give him a fair opportunity of being heard in his own defence. The authorities on the applicability of the principles of natural justice are in some confusion, and so I find it necessary to examine this matter in some detail. The principle *audi alteram partem* goes back many centuries in our law and appears in a multitude of judgments of judges of the highest authority. In modern time opinions have sometimes been expressed to the effect that natural justice is so vague as to be practically meaningless. But I would regard these as tainted by the perennial fallacy that because something cannot be cut and dried or nicely weighed or measured therefore it does not exist. The idea of negligence is equally insusceptible to exact definition, but what a reasonable man would regard as fair procedure in particular circumstances and what he would regard as negligence in particular circumstances are equally capable of serving as tests in law, and natural justice as it has been interpreted in the courts is much more definite than that. It appears to me that one reason why the authorities on natural justice have been found difficult to reconcile is that insufficient attention has been paid to the great difference between various kinds of cases in which it has been sought to apply the principle. What a minister ought to do in considering objections to a scheme may be very different from what a watch committee ought to do in considering whether to dismiss a chief constable. So I shall deal first with cases of dismissal. These appear to fall into three classes: dismissal of a servant by his master, dismissal from an office held during pleasure, and dismissal from an office where there must be something against a man to warrant his dismissal.

The law regarding master and servant is not in doubt. There cannot be specific performance of a contract of service, and the master can terminate the contract with his servant at any time and for any reason or for none. But if he does so in a manner not warranted by the contract he must pay damages for breach of contract. So the question in a pure case of master and servant does not at all depend on whether the master has heard the servant in his own defence: it depends on whether the facts emerging at the trial prove breach of contract. But this kind of case can resemble dismissal from an office where the body employing the man is under some statutory or other restriction as to the kind of contract which it can make with its servants, or the grounds on which it can dismiss them. The present case does not fall within this class because a chief constable is not the servant of the watch committee or indeed of anyone else.

Then there are many cases where a man holds an office at pleasure. Apart from judges and others whose tenure of office is governed by statute, all servants and officers of the Crown hold office at pleasure, and this has been held even to apply to a colonial judge (*Terrell* v. *Secretary of State for the Colonies* [1953] 2 Q.B. 482). It has always been held, I think rightly, that such an officer has no right to be heard before he is dismissed, and the reason is clear. As a person having the power of dismissal need not have anything against the officer, he need not give any reason. That was stated as long ago as 1670 in *R.* v. *Stratford-on-Avon Corporation* (1809) 11 East 176 where the corporation dismissed a town clerk who held office *durante bene placito*. The leading case on this matter appears to be

R. v. *Darlington School Governors* (1844) 6 Q.B. 682 although that decision was doubted by Lord Hatherley L.C. in *Dean* v. *Bennett* (1870) L.R. 6 Ch. 489 and distinguished on narrow grounds in *Willis* v. *Childe* (1851) 13 Beav. 117. I fully accept that where an office is simply held at pleasure the person having power of dismissal cannot be bound to disclose his reasons. No doubt he would in many cases tell the officer and hear his explanation before deciding to dismiss him. But if he is not bound to disclose his reason and does not do so, then, if the court cannot require him to do so, it cannot determine whether it would be fair to hear the officer's case before taking action. But again that is not this case. In this case the Act of 1882 only permits the watch committee to take action on the grounds of negligence or unfitness. Let me illustrate the difference by supposing that a watch committee who had no complaint against their present chief constable heard of a man with quite outstanding qualifications who would like to be appointed. They might think it in the public interest to make the change, but they would have no right to do it. But there could be no legal objection to dismissal of an officer holding office at pleasure in order to put a better man in his place.

So I come to the third class, which includes the present case. There I find an unbroken line of authority to the effect that an officer cannot lawfully be dismissed without first telling him what is alleged against him and hearing his defence or explanation. An early example is *Bagg's Case* (1615) 11 Co.Rep. 93b though it is more properly deprivation of the privilege of being a burgess of Plymouth. *R.* v. *Gaskin* (1799) 8 Term Rep. 209 arose out of the dismissal of a parish clerk, and Lord Kenyon C.J. referred to *audi alteram partem* as one of the first principles of justice. *R.* v. *Smith* (1844) 5 Q.B. 614 was another case of dismissal of a parish clerk, and Lord Denman C.J. held that even personal knowledge of the offence was no substitute for hearing the officer: his explanation might disprove criminal motive or intent and bring forward other facts in mitigation, and in any event delaying to hear him would prevent yielding too hastily to first impressions. *Ex parte Ramshay* (1852) 18 Q.B. 173 is important. It dealt with the removal from office of a county court judge, and the form of the legislation which authorised the Lord Chancellor to act is hardly distinguishable from the form of section 191, which confers powers on the watch committee. The Lord Chancellor was empowered if he should think fit to remove on the ground of inability or misbehaviour, but Lord Campbell C.J. said (*ibid.* 190) that this was "only on the implied condition prescribed by the principles of eternal justice." In *Osgood* v. *Nelson* (1872) L.R. 5 H.L. 636 at p. 649, H.L., objection was taken to the way in which the Corporation of the City of London had removed the clerk to the Sheriff's Court, and Lord Hatherley L.C. said: "I apprehend, my Lords, that, as has been stated by the learned Baron who has delivered, in the name of the judges, their unanimous opinion, the Court of Queen's Bench has always considered that it has been open to that court, as in this case it appears to have considered, to correct any court, or tribunal, or body of men who may have a power of this description, a power of removing from office, if it should be found that such persons have disregarded any of the essentials of justice in the course of their inquiry, before making that removal, or if it should be found that in the place of reasonable cause those persons have acted obviously upon mere individual caprice."

That citation of authority might seem sufficient, but I had better proceed further. In *Fisher* v. *Jackson* [1891] 2 Ch. 84 three vicars had power to remove the master of an endowed school. But, unlike the *Darlington* case, 6 Q.B. 682 the trust deed set out the grounds on which he could be removed—briefly, inefficiency or failing to set a good example. So it was held that they could not remove him without affording him an opportunity of being heard in his own defence. Only two other cases of this class were cited in argument, *Cooper* v. *Wilson* [1937] 2 K.B. 309 and *Hogg* v. *Scott* [1947] K.B. 759. Both dealt with the dismissal of police officers and both were complicated by consideration of regulations made under the Police Acts. In the former the majority at least recognised that the principles of natural justice applied, and in deciding the latter Cassels J. in deciding that a chief constable could dismiss without hearing him an officer who had been convicted of felony, appears to have proceeded on a construction of the regulations. Of course, if the regulations authorised him to do that and were *intra vires* in doing so, there would be no more to be said. I do not think it necessary to consider whether the learned judge rightly construed the regulations, for he did not expressly or, I think, by implication question the general principle that a man is not to be dismissed for misconduct without being heard.

Stopping there, I would think that authority was wholly in favour of the appellant, but the respondent's argument was mainly based on what has been said in a number of fairly recent cases dealing with different subject-matter. Those cases deal with decisions by ministers, officials and bodies of various kinds which adversely affected property rights or privileges of persons who had had no opportunity or no proper opportunity of presenting their cases before the decisions were given. And it is necessary to examine those cases for another reason. The question which was or ought to have been considered by the watch committee on March 7, 1958, was not a simple question whether or not the appellant should be dismissed. There were three possible courses open to the watch committee—reinstating the appellant as chief constable, dismissing him, or requiring him to resign. The difference between the latter two is that dismissal involved forfeiture of pension rights, whereas requiring him to resign did not. Indeed, it is now clear that the appellant's real interest in this appeal is to try to save his pension rights.

It may be convenient at this point to deal with an argument that, even if as a general rule a watch committee must hear a constable in his own defence before dismissing him, that case was so clear that nothing that the appellant could have said could have made any difference. It is at least very doubtful whether that could be accepted as an excuse. But, even if it could, the respondents would, in my view, fail on the facts. It may well be that no reasonable body of men could have reinstated the appellant. But as between the other two courses open to the watch committee the case is not so clear. Certainly on the facts, as we know them, the watch committee could reasonably have decided to forfeit the appellant's pension rights, but I could not hold that they would have acted wrongly or wholly unreasonably if they had in the exercise of their discretion decided to take a more lenient course.

I would start an examination of the authorities dealing with property rights and privileges with *Cooper* v. *Wandsworth Board of Works* (1863) 14 C.B.(N.S.) 180.

[His Lordship summarised this case, and *Hopkins* v. *Smethwick Local Board of Health* (1890) 24 Q.B.D. 712; *Smith* v. *The Queen* (1878) L.R. 3 App.Cas. 614, P.C.; and *De Verteuil* v. *Knaggs* [1918] A.C. 557.]

I shall now turn to a different class of case—deprivation of membership of a professional or social body. In *Wood* v. *Woad* (1874) L.R. 9 Ex. 190 the committee purported to expel a member of a mutual insurance society without hearing him, and it was held that their action was void, and so he was still a member. Kelly C.B. said of *audi alteram partem* (*ibid.* 196): "This rule is not confined to the conduct of strictly legal tribunals, but is applicable to every tribunal or body of persons invested with authority to adjudicate upon matters involving civil consequences to individuals." This was expressly approved by Lord Macnaghten giving the judgment of the Board in *Lapointe* v. *L'Association de Bienfaisance et de Retraite de la Police de Montréal* [1906] A.C. 535, P.C. In that case the board of directors of the association had to decide whether to give a pension to a dismissed constable—the very point the watch committee had to decide in this case—and it was held (*ibid.* p. 539) that they had to observe "the elementary principles of justice."

Then there are the club cases, *Fisher* v. *Keane* (1878) 11 Ch.D. 353 and *Dawkins* v. *Antrobus* (1879) 17 Ch.D. 615 (C.A.). In the former, Jessel M.R. said of the committee, 11 Ch.D. 353 at pp. 362–363: "They ought not, as I understand it, according to the ordinary rules by which justice should be administered by committees of clubs, or by any other body of persons who decide upon the conduct of others, to blast a man's reputation for ever—perhaps to ruin his prospects for life, without giving him an opportunity of either defending or palliating his conduct." In the latter case it was held that nothing had been done contrary to natural justice. In *Weinberger* v. *Inglis* [1919] A.C. 606, H.L., a member of enemy birth was excluded from the Stock Exchange, and it was held that the committee had heard him before acting. Lord Birkenhead L.C. said (*ibid.* at p. 616): ". . . if I took the view that the appellant was condemmed upon grounds never brought to his notice, I should not assent to the legality of this course, unless compelled by authority." He said this although the rule under which the committee acted was in the widest possible terms—that the committee should each year re-elect such members as they should deem eligible as members of the Stock Exchange.

I shall not at present advert to the various trade union cases because I am deliberately considering the state of the law before difficulties were introduced by statements in various fairly recent cases. It appears to me that if the present case had arisen 30 or 40 years ago the courts would have had no difficulty in deciding this issue in favour of the appellant on the authorities which I have cited. So far as I am aware none of these authorities has ever been disapproved or even doubted. Yet the Court of Appeal have decided this issue against the appellant on more recent authorities which apparently justify that result. How has this come about?

At least three things appear to me to have contributed. In the first place there have been many cases where it has been sought to apply the principles of natural justice to the wider duties imposed on Ministers and other organs of government by modern legislation. For reasons which I shall attempt to state in a moment, it has been held that those principles have a limited application in such cases and those limitations have tended to be reflected in other decisions on matters to which in principle they do not appear to me to apply. Secondly, again for reasons which I shall attempt to state, those principles have been held to have a limited application in cases arising out of war-time legislation; and again such limitations have tended to be reflected in other cases. And, thirdly, there has, I think, been a misunderstanding of the judgment of Atkin L.J. in *R.* v. *Electricity Commissioners, ex p. London Electricity Joint Committee Co.* [1924] 1 K.B. 171.

In cases of the kind I have been dealing with the Board of Works or the Governor or the club committee was dealing with a single isolated case. It was not deciding, like a judge in a lawsuit, what were the rights of the person before it. But it was deciding how he should be treated—something analogous to a judge's duty in imposing a penalty. No doubt policy would play some part in the decision—but so it might when a judge is imposing a sentence. So it was easy to say that such a body is performing a quasi-judicial task in considering and deciding such a matter, and to require it to observe the essentials of all proceedings of a judicial character—the principles of natural justice.

Sometimes the functions of a minister or department may also be of that character, and then the rules of natural justice can apply in much the same way. But more often their functions are of a very different character. If a minister is considering whether to make a scheme for, say, an important new road, his primary concern will not be with the damage which its construction will do to the rights of individual owners of land. He will have to consider all manner of questions of public interest and, it may be, a number of alternative schemes. He cannot be prevented from attaching more importance to the fulfilment of his policy than to the fate of individual objectors, and it would be quite wrong for the courts to say that the minister should or could act in the same kind of way as a board of works deciding whether a house should be pulled down. And there is another important difference. As explained in *Local Government Board* v. *Arlidge* [1915] A.C. 120 a minister cannot do everything himself. His officers will have to gather and sift all the facts, including objections by individuals, and no individual can complain if the ordinary accepted methods of carrying on public business do not give him as good protection as would be given by the principles of natural justice in a different kind of case.

We do not have a developed system of administrative law—perhaps because until fairly recently we did not need it. So it is not surprising that in dealing with new types of cases the courts have had to grope for solutions, and have found that old powers, rules and procedure are largely inapplicable to cases which they were never designed or intended to deal with. But I see nothing in that to justify our thinking that our old methods are any less applicable today than ever they were to the older types of case. And if there are any dicta in modern authorities which point in that direction, then, in my judgment, they should not be followed.

And now I must say something regarding war-time legislation. The older authorities clearly show how the courts engrafted the principles of natural justice on to a host of provisions authorising administrative interference with private rights. Parliament knew quite well that the courts had an inveterate habit of doing that and must therefore be held to have authorised them to do it unless a particular Act showed a contrary intention. And such an intention could appear as a reasonable inference as well as from express words. It seems to me to be a reasonable and almost an inevitable inference from the circumstances in which Defence Regulations were made and from their subject-matter that, at least in many cases, the intention must have been to exclude the principles of natural justice. War-time secrecy alone would often require that, and the need for speed and general pressure of work were other factors. But it was not to be expected that anyone would state in so many words that a temporary abandonment of the rules of natural justice was one of the sacrifices which war conditions required—that would have been almost calculated to create the alarm and despondency against which one of the regulations was specifically directed. And I would draw the same conclusion from another fact. In many regulations there was set out an alternative safeguard more practicable in war time—the objective test that the officer must have reasonable cause to believe whatever was the crucial matter. (I leave out of account the very peculiar decision of this House in *Liversidge* v. *Anderson* [1942] A.C. 206.) So I would not think that any decision that the rules of natural justice were excluded from war-time legislation should be regarded as of any great weight in dealing with a case such as this case, which is of the older type, and which involves the interpretation of an Act passed long before modern modifications of the principles of natural justice became necessary, and at a time when, as Parliament was well aware, the courts habitually applied the principles of natural justice to provisions like section 191(4) of the Act of 1882.

The matter has been further complicated by what I believe to be a misunderstanding of a much-quoted passage in the judgment of Atkin L.J. in *R.* v. *Electricity Commissioners, ex p. London Electricity Joint Committee Co.* [1924] 1 K.B. 171 at p. 205. He said: "... the operation of the writs [of prohibition and certiorari] has extended to control the proceedings of bodies which do not claim to be, and would not be recognised as, courts of justice. Wherever any body of persons having legal authority to determine questions affecting the rights of subjects, and having the duty to act judicially, act in excess of their legal authority, they are subject to the controlling jurisdiction of the King's Bench Division exercised in these writs."

A gloss was put on this by Lord Hewart C.J. in *R.* v. *Legislative Committee of the Church Assembly, ex p. Haynes-Smith* [1928] 1 K.B. 411. There it was sought to prohibit the Assembly from proceeding further with the Prayer Book Measure 1927. That seems to me to have no resemblance to a question whether a person should be deprived of his rights or privileges, and the case was decided on the ground that this was a deliberative or legislative body and not a judicial body. Salter J. put it in a few lines (*ibid.* at p. 419): "The person or body to whom these writs are to go must be a judicial body in this sense, that it has power to determine and to decide; and the power carries with it, of necessity, the duty to act judicially. I think that the Church Assembly has no such power, and therefore no such duty." But Lord Hewart said (*ibid.* at p. 415) having quoted the passage from Atkin L.J.'s judgment: "The question, therefore, which we have to ask ourselves in this case is whether it is true to say in this matter, either of the Church Assembly as a whole, or of the Legislative Committee of the Church Assembly, that it is a body of persons having legal authority to determine questions affecting the rights of subjects, and having the duty to act judicially. It is to be observed that in the last sentence which I have quoted from the judgment of Atkin L.J. the word is not 'or,' but 'and.' In order that a body may satisfy the required test it is not enough that it should have legal authority to determine questions affecting the rights of subjects; there must be superadded to that characteristic the further characteristic that the body has the duty to act judicially. The duty to act judicially is an ingredient which, if the test is to be satisfied, must be present. As these writs in the earlier days were issued only to bodies which without any harshness of construction could be called, and naturally would be called courts, so also today these writs do not issue except to bodies which act or are under the duty to act in a judicial capacity."

I have quoted the whole of this passage because it is typical of what has been said in several subsequent cases. If Lord Hewart meant that it is never enough that a body simply has a duty to determine what the rights of an individual should be, but that there must always be something more to impose on it a duty to act judicially before it can be found to observe the principles of natural justice, then that appears to me impossible to reconcile with the earlier authorities. ... And, as I shall try to show, it cannot be what Atkin L.J. meant.

In *R.* v. *Electricity Commissioners, ex p. London Electricity Joint Committee Co.* [1924] 1 K.B. 171, the commissioners had a statutory duty to make schemes with regard to electricity districts and to hold local inquiries before making them. They made a draft scheme which in effect allocated duties to one body which the Act required should be allocated to a different kind of body. This was held to be *ultra vires*, and the question was whether prohibition would lie. It was argued that the proceedings of the commissioners were purely executive and controllable by Parliament alone. Bankes L.J. said (*ibid.* at p. 198): "On principle and on authority it is in my opinion open to this court to hold, and I consider that it should hold, that powers so far-reaching, affecting as they do individuals as well as property, are powers to be exercised judicially, and not ministerially or merely, to use the language of Palles C.B., as proceedings towards legislation." So he inferred the judicial element from the nature of the power. And I think that Atkin L.J. did the same. Immediately after the passage which I said has been misunderstood, he cited a variety of cases and in most of them I can see nothing "superadded" (to use Lord Hewart's word) to the duty itself. Certainly Atkin L.J. did not say that anything was superadded. And a later passage in his judgment convinces me that he, like Bankes L.J., inferred the judicial character of the duty from the nature of the duty itself. Although it is long I am afraid I must quote it [1924] 1 K.B. 171 at pp. 206–207: "In the present case the Electricity Commissioners have to decide whether they will constitute a joint authority in a district in accordance with law, and with what powers they will invest that body. The question necessarily involves the withdrawal from existing bodies of undertakers of some of their existing rights, and imposing upon them of new duties, including their subjection to the control of the new body, and new financial obligations. It also provides in the new body a person to whom may be transferred rights of purchase which at present are vested in another authority. The commissioners are proposing to create such a new body in violation of the Act of Parliament, and are proposing to hold a possibly long and expensive inquiry into the expediency of such a scheme, in respect of which they have the power to compel representatives of the prosecutors at attend and produce papers. I think that in deciding upon the scheme, and in holding the inquiry, they are acting judicially in the sense of the authorities I have cited."

There is not a word in Atkin L.J.'s judgment to suggest disapproval of the earlier line of authority which I have cited. On the contrary, he goes further than those authorities. I have already stated my view that it is more difficult for the courts to control an exercise of power on a large scale where the treatment to be meted out to a particular individual is only one of many matters to be considered. This was a case of that kind, and, if Atkin L.J. was prepared to infer a judicial element from the nature of the power in this case, he could hardly disapprove such an inference when the power relates solely to the treatment of a particular individual.

The authority chiefly relied on by the Court of Appeal in holding that the watch committee were not bound to observe the principles of natural justice was *Nakkuda Ali* v. *Jayaratne* [1951] A.C. 66. In that case the Controller of Textiles in Ceylon made an order cancelling the appellant's licence to act as a dealer, and the appellant sought to have that order quashed. The controller acted under a Defence Regulation which empowered him to cancel a licence "where the controller has reasonable grounds to believe that any dealer is unfit to be allowed to continue as a dealer."

The Privy Council regarded that (*ibid.* at p. 77) as "imposing a condition that there must in fact exist such reasonable grounds, known to the controller, before he can validly exercise the power of cancellation." But according to their judgment certiorari did not lie, and no other means was suggested whereby the appellant or anyone else in his position could obtain redress even if the controller acted without a shred of evidence. It is quite true that the judgment went on, admittedly unnecessarily, to find that the controller had reasonable grounds and did observe the principles of natural justice, but the result would have been just the same if he had not. This House is not bound by decisions of the Privy Council, and for my own part nothing short of a decision of this House directly in point would induce me to accept the position that, although an enactment expressly requires an official to have reasonable grounds for his decision, our law is so defective that a subject cannot bring up such a decision for review however seriously he may be affected and however obvious it may be that the official acted in breach of his statutory obligation.

The judgment proceeds: "But it does not seem to follow necessarily from this that the controller must be acting judicially in exercising the power. Can one not act reasonably without acting judicially? It is not difficult to think of circumstances in which the controller might, in any ordinary sense of the words, have reasonable grounds of belief without having ever confronted the licence holder with the information which is the source of his belief. It is a long step in the argument to say that because a man is enjoined that he must not take action unless he has reasonable ground for believing something he can only arrive at that belief by a course of conduct analogous to the judicial process. And yet, unless that proposition is valid, there is really no ground for holding that the controller is acting judicially or quasi-judicially when he acts under this regulation. If he is not under a duty so to act then it would not be according to law that his decision should be amenable to review and, if necessary, to avoidance by the procedure of certiorari."

I would agree that in this and other Defence Regulation cases the legislature has submitted an obligation not to act without reasonable grounds for the ordinary obligation to afford to the person affected an opportunity to submit his defence. It is not necessary in this case to consider whether by so doing he has deprived the courts of the power to intervene if the officer acts contrary to his duty. The question in the present case is not whether Parliament substituted a different safeguard for that afforded by natural justice, but whether in the Act of 1882 it excluded the safeguard of natural justice and put nothing in its place.

So far there is nothing in the judgment of the Privy Council directly relevant to the present case. It is the next paragraph which causes the difficulty and I must quote the crucial passage (*ibid.* at p. 78): "But the basis of the jurisdiction of the courts by way of certiorari has been so exhaustively analysed in recent years that individual instances are now only of importance as illustrating a general principle that is beyond dispute. That principle is most precisely stated in the words of Atkin L.J. in *R.* v. *Electricity Commissioners, ex p. London Electricity Joint Committee Co.* [1924] 1 K.B. 171 at p. 205"—and then follows the passage with which I have already dealt at length. And then there follows the quotation from Lord Hewart, which I have already commented on, ending with the words—"there must be superadded to that characteristic the further characteristic that the body has the duty to act judicially." And then it is pointed out: "It is that characteristic that the controller lacks in acting under regulation 62."

Of course, if it were right to say that Lord Hewart's gloss of Atkin L.J. stated "a general principle that is beyond dispute," the rest would follow. But I have given my reasons for holding that it does no such thing, and in my judgment the older cases certainly do not "illustrate" any such general principle—they contradict it. No case older than 1911 was cited in *Nakkuda's* case on this question, and this question was only one of several difficult questions which were argued and decided. So I am forced to the conclusion that this part of the judgment in *Nakkuda's* case was given under a serious misapprehension of the effect of the older authorities and therefore cannot be regarded as authoritative.

I would sum up my opinion in this way. Between 1882 and the making of police regulations in 1920 section 191(4) had to be applied to every kind of case. The respondents' contention is that, even where there was a doubtful question whether a constable was guilty of a particular act of misconduct, the watch committee were under no obligation to hear his defence before dismissing him. In my judgment it is abundantly clear from the authorities I have quoted that at that time the courts would have rejected any such contention. In later cases dealing with different subject-matter, opinions have been expressed in wide terms so as to appear to conflict with those earlier authorities. But learned judges who expressed those opinions generally had no power to overrule those authorities, and in any event it is a salutary rule that a judge is not to be assumed to have intended to overrule or disapprove of an authority which has not been cited to him and which he does not even mention. So I would hold that the power of dismissal in the Act of 1882 could not then have been exercised and cannot now be exercised until the watch committee have informed the constable of the grounds on which they propose to proceed and have given him a proper opportunity to present his case in defence.

Next comes the question whether the respondents' failure to follow the rules of natural justice on March 7 was made good by the meeting on March 18. I do not doubt that if an officer or body realises that it has acted hastily and reconsiders the whole matter afresh, after affording to the person affected a proper opportunity to present his case, then its later decision will be valid. An example is *De Verteuil's* case. But here the appellant's solicitor was not fully informed of the charges against the appellant and the watch committee did not annul the decision which they had already published and proceed to make a new decision. In my judgment, what was done on that day was a very inadequate substitute for a full rehearing. Even so, three members of the committee changed their minds, and it is impossible to say what the decision of the committee would have been if there had been a full hearing after disclosure to the appellant of the whole case against him. I agree with those of your Lordships who hold that this meeting of March 18 cannot affect the result of this appeal.

The other ground on which some of your Lordships prefer to proceed is the respondents' failure to act in accordance with the Police Regulations. I have had an opportunity of reading the speech about to be delivered by my noble and learned friend, Lord Morris of Borth-y-Gest, and I agree with his view about this.

Then there was considerable argument whether in the result the watch committee's decision is void or merely voidable. Time and again in the cases I have cited it has been stated that a decision given without regard to the principles of natural justice is void, and that was expressly decided in *Wood* v. *Woad*. I see no reason to doubt these authorities. The body with the power to decide cannot lawfully proceed to make a decision until it has afforded to the person affected a proper opportunity to state his case.

Finally, there is the question whether by appealing to the Secretary of State the appellant is in some way prevented from now asserting the nullity of the respondents' decision. A person may be prevented from asserting the truth by estoppel, but it is not seriously argued that that doctrine applies here. Then it is said that the appellant elected to go to the Secretary of State and thereby waived his right to come to the court. That appears to me to be an attempt to set up what is in effect estoppel where the essential elements for estoppel are not present. There are many cases where two remedies are open to an aggrieved person, but there is no general rule that by going to some other tribunal he puts it out of his power thereafter to assert his right in court; and there was no express waiver because in appealing to the Secretary of State the appellant reserved his right to maintain that the decision was a nullity.

But then it was argued that this case is special because by statute the decision of the Secretary of State is made final and binding. I need not consider what the result would have been if the Secretary of State had heard the case for the appellant and then given his own independent decision that the appellant should be dismissed. But the Secretary of State did not do that. He merely decided "that there was sufficient material on which the watch committee could properly exercise their power of dismissal under section 191(4)." So the only operative decision is that of the watch committee, and, if it was a nullity, I do not see how this statement by the Secretary of State can make it valid.

Accordingly, in my judgment, this appeal must be allowed. There appears to have been no discussion in the courts below as to remedies which may now be open to the appellant, and I do not think that this House should do more than declare that the dismissal of the appellant is null and void and remit the case to the Queen's Bench Division for further procedure. But it is right to put on record that the appellant does not seek to be reinstated as chief constable: his whole concern is to avoid the serious financial consequences involved in dismissal as against being required or allowed to resign.

[LORD EVERSHED (dissenting) held that:

(1) "the shortcomings of the appellant as chief constable" did not fall within the Discipline Code;
(2) therefore, the Watch Committee were entitled to exercise their residual powers under section 191(4) of the 1882 Act without observing the regulations;
(3) there was no "report or allegation" before the Watch Committee. Those words suggested "something in the nature of an accusation as distinct from a conclusion reached after proper inquiry" (*i.e.* Donovan J.'s conclusion);
(4) that "this was a special and entirely exceptional case outside the scope of the regulations, and, as a matter of public notoriety, requiring instant action by the Watch Committee";
(5) that if natural justice ought to have been observed, a decision in breach of natural justice would normally be voidable, not void, in that the body would be "acting within its jurisdiction." A decision would only be void if based on "frivolous or futile" grounds or if there had been "a real substantial miscarriage of justice";
(6) that apart from the prejudice to pension rights, the Watch Committee need not have given the plaintiff any opportunity to state points he had already made before Donovan J. The committee also had to act urgently. However, his Lordship was prepared to assume that the plaintiff should have had an opportunity to state his case for being allowed to resign;
(7) that justice had been done as representations had been made to the Watch Committee on March 18;
(8) that if he (his Lordship) was wrong on the last point, any defect was cured by the appeal to the Secretary of State, whose decision was rendered "final and binding" by section 2(3) of the Police (Appeals) Act 1927.

Therefore his Lordship would have dismissed the appeal.

LORD MORRIS OF BORTH-Y-GEST held that:

(1) there was a "report or allegation" before the Watch Committee. There were, for example, a transcript of the judge's remarks, and "certain statements made . . . by members of the committee and the town clerk";
(2) the regulations should have been applied. As there was no admission of the commission of an offence, the regulations required a hearing;
(3) as the regulations had been ignored, the dismissal was void. (*Andrews* v. *Mitchell* [1905] A.C. 78, *Lapointe* v. *L'Association de Bienfaisance et de Retraite de la Police de Montréal* [1906] A.C. 535, and *Annamunthodo* v. *Oilfield Workers' Trade Union* [1961] A.C. 945 applied);
(4) the defect was not cured by the second hearing on March 18, as the plaintiff was never given notice of the allegations against him;
(5) the defect was not cured by the appeal to the Secretary of State as the original decision was a nullity, and the plaintiff so maintained during the appeal;
(6) apart from the regulations, natural justice should have been observed. The dismissal was not an "executive or administrative act" as it was based on a "suggestion of neglect of duty";
(7) a decision in breach of natural justice was void not voidable.

LORD HODSON delivered a speech concurring substantially with LORD REID and LORD MORRIS.

LORD DEVLIN held that the regulations applied and should have been observed. Any decision in breach of the regulations would be voidable unless any regulation laid down a "condition precedent to the conferment of authority on the committee which had not been fulfilled." Article 11(1) of the 1882 regulations allowed the police authority to act only on receipt of a report from the tribunal set up under the regulations to hear the evidence and make recommendations. The committee's decision was therefore void *ab initio*.

His Lordship held that a decision in breach of natural justice was voidable only.]

Appeal allowed.

Notes

1. There are many points of interest, including the scope of natural justice, the ways in which defective decisions may or may not be cured, whether such decisions are void or voidable, the application of statutory procedural requirements, and the proper approach that should be taken to cases decided in wartime.

The case has been followed and cited in many subsequent cases. See case notes and articles by A. W. Bradley, [1964] C.L.J. 83; G. H. L. Fridman, (1963) 113 L.J. 716; A. L. Goodhart, (1964) 80 L.Q.R. 105; (1963) 26 M.L.R. 543; D. G. Benjafield and H. Whitmore, (1963) 37 A.L.J. 140; D. Paterson, [1966] N.Z.L.J. 107; P. Brett, 16 Malaya L.R. 100; K. J. Keith, "*Ridge* v. *Baldwin*—twenty years on" (1983) 13 V.U.W.L.R. 239. The distinction between the "void" and the "voidable" is developed in Chapter 14.

2. The dismissal of police officers is now regulated by the Police Act 1964, and regulations made thereunder.

3. In *Durayappah* v. *Fernando* [1967] 2 A.C. 337, a minister had power to order the dissolution of a municipal council if it appeared to him that it "is not competent to perform, or persistently makes default in the performance of, any duty or duties imposed upon it, or persistently refuse or neglects to comply with any provision of law. . . ." Such an order was made in respect of Jaffna Municipal Council, and challenged by the mayor on the ground that no hearing had been given. The Privy Council rejected the view of the Supreme Court of Ceylon, that the subjective wording automatically excluded a duty to act judicially. They pointed out that words could be implied into a statute, as in *Cooper* v. *Wandsworth Board of Works*, and that if the law were otherwise, *Capel* v. *Child* (1832) 2 Cromp. & Jer. 558 would have been decided differently. It would be wrong to attempt to give an exhaustive classification of the cases where the *audi alteram partem* principle should be applied. *Per* Lord Upjohn at p. 349:

> "Outside the well-known classes of cases, no general rule can be laid down as to the application of the general principle in addition to the language of the provision. In their Lordships' opinion there are three matters which must always be borne in mind when considering whether the principle should be applied or not. These three matters are: first, what is the nature of the property, the office held, status enjoyed or services to be performed by the complainant of injustice. Secondly, in what circumstances or upon what occasions is the person claiming to be entitled to exercise the measure of control entitled to intervene. Thirdly, when a right to intervene is proved, what sanctions in fact is the latter entitled to impose upon the other. It is only upon a consideration of all these matters that the question of the application of the principle can properly be determined."

These matters were considered in turn. First, the Council was by statute a public corporation entrusted with the administration of a large area and the discharge of important duties. It enjoyed a considerable measure of independence from the central government. The responsibility of the Minister to the legislature did not exclude the possibility of "responsibility to the courts under the principle *audi alteram partem*." Secondly, it was a most serious charge to allege persistent default or refusal or neglect to comply with a provision of law. It was not possible to distinguish these from the ground actually alleged here, namely, incompetence. It would not be right to hold that whether or not natural justice had to be observed depended on the ground on which the order was eventually made. Thirdly, the sanction was "as complete as could be imagined," the dissolution of the Council and the confiscation of all its properties. The Council owned large areas of land, had a municipal fund, and levied rates. So, on the principle of *Cooper* v. *Wandsworth Board of Works* "that no man is to be deprived of his property without a hearing," in addition to the other grounds, the Minister should have observed natural justice.

Nevertheless, the Mayor of Jaffna was refused a remedy, on the grounds that he had insufficient *locus standi*. See below, p. 840.

See J. M. Eekelaar, (1967) 30 M.L.R. 701; G. Nettheim, (1967) 2 Federal L.R. 215.

4. Subsequently, in *Chief Constable of North Wales* v. *Evans* [1982] 1 W.L.R. 1155, the House of Lords held that a Chief Constable is subject to the rules of natural justice when exercising his statutory powers to discharge a probationer constable. In that case inaccurate rumours regarding the private life of probationary Constable Evans were conveyed to senior officers. The Chief Constable briefly interviewed Constable Evans and gave him the opportunity or resigning or being dismissed. Evans resigned and sought judicial review of the Chief Constable's actions. Lord Brightman (with whom the other Law Lords agreed) referred to *Ridge* and then concluded:

> "it was the duty of the Chief Constable to deal fairly with the respondent in relation to the adverse factors upon which he was proposing to act. The Chief Constable failed in his performance of that duty because these supposedly adverse factors were never put to the respondent. He was given no opportunity to offer one word of explanation. . . . The decision-making process was therefore defective" (p. 1174).

Their Lordships granted a declaration to the effect that the Chief Constable had acted unlawfully in threatening to dismiss Evans unless he resigned, but they did not order his reinstatement as to have done so would have "usurped" the powers of the Chief Constable.

Sir William Wade believes, "[Evans'] correct remedy, it would appear, was an action for damages for the tort of intimidation, having been forced to act to his detriment under threat of unlawful injury" (1983) 99 L.Q.R. 171 at p. 172. See also J. McMullen, (1984) 47 M.L.R. 234.

5. The tri-partite classification of employment relationships articulated by Lord Reid in *Ridge* was further refined by his Lordship in *Malloch* v. *Aberdeen Corporation* [1971] 1 W.L.R. 1578. In that case Mr. Malloch was a teacher employed by the corporation. Regulations made under the Education (Scotland) Act 1946, required all teachers employed by education authorities to register with a new statutory body—the General Teaching Council for Scotland. Malloch was entitled to be registered with the Teaching Council, but he refused on a point of principle. Aberdeen Corporation were advised that they could no longer employ Malloch and they informed him (as they were obliged to do under the Education (Scotland) Act 1962) that the education committee would be meeting to pass a resolution for his dismissal. Malloch was permitted to attend the committee's meeting, but he was not allowed to address the meeting. The committee resolved to dismiss him. Malloch then sought judicial review of that decision arguing that it had been made in breach of the rules of natural justice. In the House of Lords, Lord Reid stated (at p. 1582):

> "An elected public body is in a very different position from a private employer. Many of its servants in the lower grades are in the same position as servants of a private employer. But many in higher grades or "offices" are given special statutory status or protection. The right of a man to be heard in his own defence is the most elementary protection of all and, where a statutory form of protection would be less effective if it did not carry with it a right to be heard, I would not find it difficult to imply this right."

His Lordship then went on to find that despite Malloch's employment status, as an office holder dismissable at pleasure, legislation had impliedly given him a right to be heard before being dismissed. Therefore, the Corporation had acted unlawfully (Lords Guest and Morris and Borth-y-Gest dissented).

During the 1980s the courts displayed a reluctance to allow employment disputes to be litigated through the judicial review procedure of R.S.C. Ord. 53, see the example the Court of Appeal's decision in *R.* v. *East Berkshire Health Authority, ex p. Walsh* [1985] Q.B. 152 (below, p. 705).

Today employees who are categorised as "servants" may be able to take proceedings against their employer (before an Industrial Tribunal) for unfair dismissal if, *inter alia*, they have not been accorded a fair procedure before being dismissed (see the Employment Protection (Consolidation) Act 1978).

Moreover, the courts are now more prepared to hold that an obligation to observe natural justice is to be implied into the contract of employment, and more willing to grant the remedies of a declaration or injunction. See *Stevenson* v. *United Road Transport Union* [1977] I.C.R. 893 (trade union official); *R.* v. *British Broadcasting Corporation, ex p. Lavelle* [1983] 1 W.L.R. 23 (B.B.C. employee); F. P. Davidson, "Judicial review of decisions to dismiss" (1984) 35 N.I.L.Q. 121.

6. Note Lord Reid's dismissal of the argument that nothing the chief constable could have said would have made any difference. The same point arose in *Malloch* v. *Aberdeen Corporation* (above, n. 5). The Corporation argued that a hearing was unnecessary as they were bound by the regulations to dismiss Mr. Malloch. Lord Wilberforce said (at p. 1595):

> "The appellant has first to show that his position was such that he had, in principle, a right to make representations before a decision against him was taken. But to show this is not necessarily enough, unless he can also show that if admitted to state his case he had a case of substance to make. A breach of procedure, whether called a failure of natural justice, or an essential administrative fault, cannot give him a remedy in the courts, unless behind it there is something of substance which has been lost by the failure. The court does not act in vain."

His Lordship accepted Lord Reid's view that something of substance was at stake. Lord Reid said (at pp. 1582–1583):

> "Then it was argued that to have afforded a hearing to the appellant before dismissing him would have been a useless formality because whatever he might have said could have made no difference. If that could be clearly demonstrated it might be a good answer. But I need not decide that because there was here, I think, a substantial possibility that a sufficient number of the committee might have been persuaded not to vote for the appellant's dismissal. The motion for dismissal had to be carried by a two-thirds majority of those present, and at the previous meeting of the committee there was not a sufficient majority to carry a similar motion. Between these meetings the committee had received a strong letter from the Secretary of State urging them to dismiss the teachers who refused to register. And it appears that they had received some advice which might have been taken by them to mean that those who failed to vote for dismissal might incur personal liability. The appellant might have been able to persuade them that they need not have any such fear.
>
> Then the appellant might have argued that on their true construction the regulations did not require the committee to dismiss him and that, if they did require that, they were *ultra vires*. The question of *ultra vires* was not argued before us and on that I shall say no more than that it is not obvious that the Secretary of State had power under any statute to make regulations requiring the dismissal of teachers who failed to acquire and pay for a new qualification such as registration. But the question of the proper construction of the regulations was argued and there I think that the appellant had at least an arguable case. . . ."

These speeches accordingly both recognised the possibility that the court might not have intervened if a hearing would have made no difference, and rejected the argument on the facts.

Two possibilities should be noted. The law could be that as a matter of substance there is no *breach* of natural justice unless something of substance has been lost (D. H. Clark, [1975] P.L. 27, 48, argues that this is what Lord Wilberforce meant in *Malloch*). Alternatively, this factor could simply be considered by the court in deciding, in the exercise of its discretion, whether to grant a remedy. This approach is illustrated by the following case. In *Glynn* v. *Keele University* [1971] 1 W.L.R. 487, Pennycuick V.-C. held that the university vice-chancellor was "acting in a quasi-judicial capacity" in exercising his disciplinary power to suspend a student who had "appeared naked" on the campus. This could not be regarded as a matter merely of "internal discipline" (which would not "lie within the purview of the court in its control over quasi-judicial acts") because it was "so fundamental to the position of the student in the university" (p. 495). The student had been given no prior notice of the decision, and no opportunity to make representations, and his Lordship held this to be a clear breach of natural justice. Nevertheless, an injunction was refused in the exercise of the court's discretion:

> "I recognise that this particular discretion should be very sparingly exercised in that sense where there has been some failure in natural justice. On the other hand, it certainly should be exercised in that sense in an appropriate case, and I think this is such a case. There is no question of fact involved, as I have already said. I must plainly proceed on the footing that the plaintiff was one of the individuals concerned. There is no doubt that the offence was one of a kind which merited a severe penalty according to any standards current even today. I have no doubt that the sentence of exclusion of residence in the campus was a proper penalty in respect of that offence. Nor has the plaintiff in his evidence put forward any specific justification for what he did. So the position would have been that if the vice-chancellor had accorded him a hearing before making his decision, all that he, or anyone on his behalf, could have done would have been to put forward some plea by way of mitigation. I do not disregard the importance of such a plea in an appropriate case, but I do not think the mere fact he was deprived of throwing himself on the mercy of the vice-chancellor in that way is sufficient to justify setting aside a decision which was intrinsically a perfectly proper one.
>
> In all the circumstances, I have come to the conclusion that the plaintiff has suffered no injustice. . . ."

(See case notes by M. H. Matthews, [1971] C.L.J. 181; H. W. R. W[ade], (1971) 37 L.Q.R. 320.)

In either form, the argument needs to be viewed with caution. Where, *ex hypothesi*, the adjudicating body has failed to observe natural justice, *its* protestations that a hearing would have made no difference must be in principle viewed with scepticism (see further D. H. Clark, [1975] P.L. 27, 43–60). In *John* v. *Rees* [1970] Ch. 345, Megarry J. said (at p. 402):

> "As everybody who has anything to do with the law well knows, the path of the law is strewn with examples of open and shut cases which, somehow, were not; of unanswerable charges which, in the event, were completely answered; of inexplicable conduct which was fully explained; of fixed and unalterable determinations that, by discussion suffered a change."

For further examples of cases where this argument has been rejected on the facts, see *R.* v. *Secretary of State for the Environment, ex p. Brent London Borough Council* [1982] Q.B. 593, 645–646 (in respect of the discretion to refuse a remedy) and *Lloyd* v. *McMahon* [1987] A.C. 625, 669, where Woolf L.J. (in the Court of Appeal) said in respect of the submission that the result would have inevitably been the same even if there had not been such a defect in procedure:

> "I recognise that there can be cases where such a submission will have to be considered by the court. However, I regard the authorities on which [counsel] relies, including *George* v. *Secretary of State for the Environment* [see *infra*] and *Malloch* v. *Aberdeen Corporation* . . . as having application in very limited circumstances, and certainly I would not regard them as applying here."

(On the House of Lords decision, see below, p. 541.)

Lord Denning has also doubted the validity of this kind of argument. In *Annamunthodo* v. *Oilfield Workers Trade Union* [1961] A.C. 945, he said (at p. 956):

> "Mr. Lazarus did suggest that a man could not complain of a failure of natural justice unless he could show that he had been prejudiced by it. Their Lordships cannot accept this suggestion. . . . It is a prejudice to any man to be denied justice. . . . [H]e can always ask for the decision to be set aside."

Then, in *Kanda* v. *Government of Malaya* [1962] A.C. 322, he said (at p. 337):

> "The court will not go into the likelihood of prejudice. The risk of it is enough."

However, in *George* v. *Secretary of State for the Environment* (1979) 77 L.G.R. 689, Lord Denning M.R. stated, equally firmly, in the context of a statutory application to quash (see below, pp. 622–639), that:

> ". . . there is no such thing as a technical breach of natural justice . . . the position under the first limb is almost indistinguishable from that under the second limb. You should not find a breach of natural justice unless there has been substantial prejudice to the applicant as a result of the mistake or error which has been made" (p. 695).

[Under the second limb, the ground of challenge was that the applicant had been substantially prejudiced by a failure to comply with a (procedural) requirement.] On the facts, the court seemed justified in holding that Mrs. George was not prejudiced where the council failed to serve her with notice of a compulsory purchase order: the council mistakenly thought that Mr. George was the sole owner (whereas they were joint owners); Mr. George had been served, had appeared at the local public inquiry, and "took every objection that was open to either of them. . . . She was not prejudiced, either substantially or at all" (*per* Lord Denning M.R. at p. 694). (*Cf. Cheall* v. *A.P.E.X.* [1983] 2 A.C. 180 and Brandon L.J. in *Cinnamond* v. *British Airports Authority*, below p. 520.)

The question cannot, accordingly, be regarded as wholly settled.

Re H. K. (AN INFANT)

[1967] 2 Q.B. 617; [1967] 2 W.L.R. 962; 111 S.J. 296; *sub nom. Re K. (H.) (An Infant)* [1967] 1 All E.R. 226 D.C. (Queen's Bench Division)

Until the Commonwealth Immigrants Act 1962 came into force, Commonwealth subjects were entitled as of right to come to the United Kingdom. Thereafter, under section 2(1) of that Act, an immigration officer had a discretion to refuse admission to Commonwealth citizens, or to admit them subject to conditions. However, under section 2(2), that discretion could not be exercised in respect of "any person who satisfies an immigration officer that he . . . (*a*) is ordinarily resident in the United Kingdom or was so resident at any time within the past two years; or (*b*) is the . . . child under 16 years of age, of a Commonwealth citizen who is resident in the United Kingdom . . ." Paragraph 2(4) of Schedule 1 to that Act gave an immigration officer power to cancel a notice refusing a person admission.

Abdul Rehman Khan, a native of Pakistan, settled in Bradford in 1961. He claimed that he had left in Pakistan a wife and five children. In 1966, he went to Pakistan and returned with H. K., whom he said was his son aged 15½. On arrival at London Airport they were interviewed by an immigration officer. Abdul Rehman appeared to be within s.2(2)(*a*). However, the officer's suspicions were aroused because H. K. appeared to be well over 15. The officer sent H. K. to the port medical officer, who estimated the boy's age at "17 years." The officer then interviewed A. R. and H. K. separately, with the aid of interpreters. His suspicions were increased, and he referred the matter to the Chief Immigration Officer, Mr. Collison. As a result of further interviews Mr. Collison made up his mind that he was not satisfied that H. K. was under 16, and a notice refusing admission was served on November 21. H. K. was to be removed at noon on the following day. The following morning, further inquiries were made concerning a school certificate which gave as a date of birth February 29, 1951 (a non-existent date). Abdul Rehman applied for a writ of habeas corpus, and H. K.'s departure was delayed. During the course of the hearing by the Divisional Court he was given leave to move also for an order of certiorari to quash the decision to refuse H. K. admission.

LORD PARKER C.J.: . . . Mr. Gratiaen [counsel] submits that in deciding whether or not he is satisfied as to the matter set out in the subsection—in this case whether he is satisfied that the boy is under 16—an immigration officer is acting in a judicial or quasi-judicial capacity and must conform to the rules of natural justice. Subject to there being due compliance with those rules, Mr. Gratiaen admits that the decision of the immigration officer cannot be challenged and that this court could not interfere. He does, however, maintain that the rules of natural justice require that before reaching his decision the immigration officer must give the immigrant an opportunity to satisfy him and if, as in this case, he has formed an impression that the immigrant is 16 or more, he must give the immigrant an opportunity to remove that impression. He claims that if that opportunity had been given, evidence would have been provided such as has been produced before us in these proceedings and that such evidence would have satisfied the officer. Having regard to the course which these proceedings have taken, it is unnecessary and, I think, indeed inadvisable to comment on that further evidence. . . . One thing I myself am quite clear on and that is that even if an immigration officer is required to act judicially or quasi-judicially, even if that is so, he is not under any duty to hold a full-scale inquiry or to adopt judicial process and procedure. The burden here under the Act is on the immigrant to satisfy the immigration officer and the provisions of the Schedule to which I have referred quite clearly show that it is impossible and therefore not contemplated that an immigration officer should hold any inquiry of that sort. . . . I doubt whether it can be said that the immigration authorities are acting in a judicial or quasi-judicial capacity as those terms are generally understood. But at the same time, I myself think that even if an immigration officer is not in a judicial or quasi-judicial capacity, he must at any rate give the immigrant an opportunity of satisfying him of the matters in the subsection, and for that purpose let the immigrant know what his immediate impression is so that the immigrant can disabuse him. That is not, as I see it, a question of acting or being required to act judicially, but of being required to act fairly. Good administration and an honest or bona fide decision must, as it seems to me, require not merely impartiality, nor merely bringing one's mind to bear on the problem, but acting fairly; and to the limited extent that the circumstances of any particular case allow, and within the legislative framework under which the administrator is working, only to that limited extent do the so-called rules of natural justice apply, which in a case such as this is merely a duty to act fairly. I appreciate that in saying that it may be said that one is going further than is permitted on the decided cases because heretofore at any rate the decisions of the courts do seem to have drawn a strict line in these matters according to whether there is or is not a duty to act judicially or quasi-judicially. It has sometimes been said that if there is no duty to act judicially or quasi-judicially there is no power in the court whatever to interfere. I observe that in the well-known case of *Nakkuda Ali* v. *M. F. de S. Jayaratne* [1951] A.C. 66 again a decision of the Privy Council, the court were considering this kind of case. There the Controller of Textiles in Ceylon was empowered to revoke licences where the controller had reasonable grounds to believe that any dealer was unfit to be allowed to continue as a dealer. Those were the words to be considered in that case which are of course different in the present case. But Lord Radcliffe, when giving the advice of the Judicial Committee, began by distinguishing that case from the well-known case of *Liversidge* [1942] A.C. 206 and went on to consider the position of the controller in law. He said [1951] A.C. 66 at p. 78:

> "In truth, when he cancels a licence he is not determining a question: he is taking executive action to withdraw a privilege because he believes, and has reasonable grounds to believe, that the holder is unfit to retain it."

He goes on to say that:

> "the power conferred on the controller . . . stands by itself on the bare words of the regulation and, if the mere requirement that the controller must have reasonable grounds of belief is insufficient to oblige him to act judicially, there is nothing else in the context or conditions of his jurisdiction that suggests that he must regulate his action by analogy to judicial rules."

Having come to that decision, Lord Radcliffe then went on in effect to deal with the position if that was wrong, and if the controller was acting in a judicial capacity. He said (*ibid.* at p. 81):

> "It is impossible to see in this any departure from natural justice. The respondent had before him ample material that would warrant a belief that the appellant had been instrumental in getting the interpolations made and securing for himself a larger credit at the bank than he was entitled to. Nor did the procedure adopted fail to give the appellant the essentials that justice would require, assuming the respondent to have been under a duty to act judicially."

That might be understood as saying that if there was no duty to act judicially, then it would be impossible to interfere, even if the applicant had not been given the essentials that justice requires. I very much doubt, however, whether it was intended to say any more than that there is no duty to invoke judicial process unless there is a duty to act judicially. I do not understand him to be saying that if there is no duty to act judicially, then there is no duty even to be fair.

When, however, that has been said, it seems to me impossible in the present case to say that the decision made on the evening of November 21, 1966, was not arrived at, as I put it, fairly. It is impossible to believe other than that both father and son knew full well of what they had to satisfy the authorities. They were, as it seems to me, given ample opportunity to do so, and the fact that the officer was not satisfied is not, as is admitted, a matter for this court.

[His Lordship then held that any question as to whether the authorities should have taken any further steps in the light of evidence adduced after the decision had been taken was not a matter for certiorari or habeas corpus. Furthermore the matter was now having the personal attention of the Home Secretary. "Accordingly, it seems to me that Mr. Gratiaen has had even more that he hoped for, and that there is no reason why this court should retain any further control over it. . . . I would dismiss both the application for habeas corpus and the application for certiorari."]

SALMON L.J.: . . . I have no doubt at all that . . . the immigration officer is obliged to act in accordance with the principles of natural justice. That does not of course mean that he has to adopt judicial procedures or hold a formal inquiry, still less than he has to hold anything in the nature of a trial, but he must act, as Lord Parker C.J. has said, fairly in accordance with the ordinary principles of natural justice. If, for example, and this I am sure would never arise, it could be shown that when he made an order refusing admission he was biased or had acted capriciously or dishonestly, this court would have power to intervene by the prerogative writ. There are, as my Lord has said, a good many cases in which the view has been expressed that unless a person exercising a power is acting in a judicial or quasi-judicial capacity the courts cannot intervene. Of course, an immigration officer is acting in an administrative rather than in a judicial capacity. What, however, is a quasi-judicial capacity has, so far as I know, never been exhaustively defined. It seems to me to cover at any rate a case where the circumstances in which a person who is called upon to exercise a statutory power and make a decision affecting basic rights of others are such that the law impliedly imposes upon him a duty to act fairly. When Parliament passed the Commonwealth Immigrants Act 1962, it deprived Commonwealth citizens of their right of unrestricted entry into the United Kingdom. It laid down conditions under which they might enter and left it to the immigration officers to decide whether such conditions existed. Their decision is of vital importance to the immigrants since their whole future may depend upon it. In my judgment it is implicit in the statute that the authorities in exercising these powers and making decisions must act in accordance with the principles of natural justice.

Mr. Gratiaen has not suggested, nor would it be possible to suggest on the evidence before this court, that when on November 21, 1966, the immigration officer refused admission to H. K. to enter the United Kingdom, he acted otherwise than in accordance with the rules of natural justice. It is quite plain that no one could say that on the material then before him as a fair man he must have been satisfied that this boy was under 16 years of age. The material before him did not satisfy him and I for one am not at all surprised. Therefore the refusal made and the notice served on November 21, 1966, are unimpeachable. It follows that the boy's detention pending his removal abroad was lawful.

Accordingly, the application in this case is quite hopeless.

BLAIN J.: . . . I would only say that an immigration officer having assumed the jurisdiction granted by those provisions [*i.e.* to cancel a notice refusing admission, under Sched. 1, para. 2(4)] is in a position where it is his duty to exercise that assumed jurisdiction, whether it be administrative, executive or quasi-judicial, fairly, by which I mean applying his mind dispassionately to a fair analysis of the particular problem and the information available to him in analysing it. If in any hypothetical case, and in any real case, this court was satisfied that an immigration officer was not so doing, then in my view mandamus would lie. That is not the position in this case, nor indeed is the court in this case moved for leave to issue a writ of mandamus.

I need say no more other than that I agree with what has fallen from my Lords.

Applications refused.

Notes

1. The modern "duty to act fairly" is sometimes said to originate in this case. There are no authorities cited to support such a duty. There are dicta in earlier cases which indicate that certain decisions by administrative authorities must be

taken "fairly." In *L.G.B.* v. *Arlidge* [1915] A.C. 120, Viscount Haldane L.C. said (at p. 133) that the board should act "judicially and fairly" although they need not observe the procedures of a court. Lord Shaw said that they must "do their best to act justly, and to reach just ends by just means." In *Board of Education* v. *Rice*, Lord Loreburn L.C. indicated that the Board was "under a duty to act in good faith, and to listen fairly to both sides." Many other judgments stress that natural justice does not require the scrupulous procedures of courts to be imposed on administrative authorities. The concepts of "fairness," "just means," "substantial justice" are indistinguishable, and require elaboration in decided cases to be properly understood.

2. The "duty to act fairly" has been implied by the courts in many cases outside immigration law. See, for example, *R.* v. *Birmingham City Justice, ex p. Chris Foreign Foods (Wholesalers) Ltd.*, [1970] 1 W.L.R. 1428 (proceedings for the condemnation of unfit food); *Cinnamond* v. *British Airports Authority* [1980] 1 W.L.R. 582 (exercise of the power to ban specific persons from Heathrow airport; see below, p. 520); and *Bushell* v. *Secretary of State for the Environment* (below p. 550) (public inquiry proceedings). For further discussions of "fairness" see, D. J. Mullan, "Fairness: The New Natural Justice?" (1975) 25 U.T.L.J. 281, the response by M. Loughlin at (1978) 28 U.T.L.J. 215 and D. J. Mullan, "Natural Justice and Fairness—Substantive as well as Procedural Standards for the Review of Administrative Decision-Making?" (1982) 27 McGill L.J. 250.

3. The modern approach was summarised as follows by Taylor L.J. in *R.* v. *Army Board of the Defence Council, ex p. Anderson* [1992] 1 Q.B. 169. A., the only black soldier in his platoon, went absent without leave after various incidents of racial harassment and abuse. He was subsequently arrested and returned to his unit. His commanding officer called in the Special Investigation Branch of the Royal Military Police to inquire into his allegations of racial discrimination. A copy of the SIB's report was not made available to A. despite his request. A. pleaded guilty at his court-martial to going AWOL, and was sentenced to detention. After the court-martial, the Ministry of Defence gave him a summary of the SIB report, which stated that his complaints of verbal abuse, but not assault, had been borne out by the admissions of other soldiers, but also alleged that A. had sought to exploit the racial issue. A. made a formal complaint of racial discrimination, which under the Race Relations Act 1976 was referred to his C.O. rather than an industrial tribunal. The C.O. rejected the complaint and informed him that disciplinary action had been taken against two soldiers who had admitted racial abuse. A. then complained to the Army Board. His requests for disclosure of the SIB report and other documents and for an oral hearing were rejected. The complaint was dealt with by two members of the board, who considered the papers separately and reached their individual conclusions without meeting to discuss the matter. The board stated that appropriate action had been taken against those responsible for the abuse, but refused compensation or apology and gave no reasons for that refusal.

The Court of Appeal quashed the board's decision. On the question of what procedural requirements were necessary, Taylor L.J. said (at pp. 185–186):

"What procedural requirements are necessary to achieve fairness when the Army Board considers a complaint of this kind? In addressing this issue, counsel made much of the distinction between judicial and administrative functions. Were it necessary to decide in those terms the functions of the Army Board when considering a race discrimination complaint, I would characterise it as judicial rather than administrative. The board is required to adjudicate on an alleged breach of a soldier's rights under the 1976 Act and, if it be proved, to take any necessary steps by way of redress. It is accepted that the board has the power, *inter alia*, to award compensation. A body required to consider and adjudicate upon an alleged breach of statutory rights and to grant redress when necessary seems to me to be exercising an essentially judicial function. It matters not that the body has other functions which are non-judicial: see *R.* v. *Secretary of State for the Home Dept., ex p. Tarrant* [1985] Q.B. 251, 268.

However, to label the board's function either 'judicial' or 'administrative' for the purpose of determining the appropriate procedural regime is to adopt too inflexible an approach. We were referred to many decided cases, but the principles laid down in *Ridge* v. *Baldwin* [1964] A.C. 40 are well summarised by Sir William Wade in his *Administrative Law* (6th edn., 1988) pp. 518–519 as follows:

> '[Lord Reid] attacked the problem at its root by demonstrating how the term "judicial" had been misinterpreted as requiring some superadded characteristic over and above the characteristic that the power affected some person's rights. The mere fact that the power affects rights or interests is what makes it "judicial," and so subject to the procedures required by natural justice. In other words, a power which affects rights must be exercised "judicially," *i.e.* fairly, and the fact that the power is administrative does not make it any the less "judicial" for this purpose. Lord Hodson put his point very clearly [1964] A.C. 40 at 130): "... the answer in a given case is not provided by the statement that the giver of the decision is acting in an executive or administrative capacity as if that were the antithesis of a judicial capacity. The cases seem to me to show that persons acting in a capacity which is not on the face of it judicial but rather executive or administrative have been held by the Courts to be subject to the principles of natural justice." '

This approach was echoed by Lord Lane C.J. in *R.* v. *Commission for Racial Equality, ex p. Cottrell & Rothon* [1980] 1 W.L.R. 1580, 1587. He said:

> 'It seems to me that there are degrees of judicial hearing, and those degrees run from the borders of pure administration to the borders of the full hearing of a criminal cause or matter in the Crown Court. It does not profit one to try to pigeon-hole the particular set of circumstances either into the administrative pigeon-hole or into the judicial pigeon-hole. Each case will inevitably differ, and one must ask oneself what is the basic nature of the proceeding which was going on here.' "

His Lordship also referred to *Lloyd* v. *McMahon*, below, p. 541. He accepted the arguments of counsel for the board that by deliberately excluding soldiers' complaints from industrial tribunals, it could not be axiomatic that all the tribunal's procedures had to be made available by the board. On the other hand, he rejected the argument that the board's duty of fairness required no more than that it should act *bona fide*, not capriciously or in a biased manner, and that it should afford the complainant a chance to respond to the basic points put against him. This did not go far enough:

> "The Army Board as the forum of last resort, dealing with an individual's fundamental statutory rights, must by its procedures achieve a high standard of fairness."

The requirements were:

(1) There must be a proper hearing "in the sense that the board must consider, as a single adjudicating body, all the relevant evidence and contentions before reaching its conclusions": accordingly, the board should meet.

(2) The hearing did not necessarily have to be an oral hearing in all cases:

"Whether an oral hearing is necessary will depend upon the subject matter and circumstances of the particular case and upon the nature of the decision to be made. It will also depend upon whether there are substantial issues of fact which cannot be satisfactorily resolved on the available written evidence. This does not mean that, whenever there is a conflict of evidence in the statements taken, an oral hearing must be held to resolve it. Sometimes such a conflict can be resolved merely by the inherent unlikelihood of one version or the other. Sometimes the conflict is not central to the issue for determination and would not justify an oral hearing. Even when such a hearing is necessary, it may only require one or two witnesses to be called and cross-examined."

There did not have to be oral hearings in all discrimination cases. On the other hand the board here had fettered its discretion by having an inflexible policy never to hold oral hearings.

(3) The board had a discretion whether to have the evidence tested by cross-examination.

(4) "Whether oral or not, there must be what amounts to a hearing of any complaint under the 1976 Act. This means that the Army Board must have such a complaint investigated, consider all the material gathered in the investigation, give the complainant an opportunity to respond to it and consider his response.

But what is the board obliged to disclose to the complainant to obtain his response? Is it sufficient to indicate the gist of any material adverse to his case or should he be shown all the material seen by the board? Mr. Pannick submits that there is no obligation to show all to the complainant. He relies upon three authorities, *R.* v. *Secretary of State for the Home Department, ex p. Mughal* [1974] Q.B. 313; *R.* v. *Secretary of State for the Home Department, ex p. Santillo* [1981] Q.B. 778 and *R.* v. *Monopolies and Mergers Commission, ex p. Matthew Brown plc* [1987] 1 W.L.R. 1235. However, in each of those cases, the function of the decision-making body was towards the administrative end of the spectrum. Because of the nature of the Army Board's function pursuant to the Race Relations Act 1976, already analysed above, I consider that a soldier complainant under that Act should be shown all the material seen by the board, apart from any documents for which public interest immunity can properly be claimed. The board is not simply making an administrative decision requiring it to consult interested parties and hear their representations. It has a duty to adjudicate on a specific complaint of breach of a statutory right. Except where public interest immunity is established, I see no reason why on such an adjudication the board should consider material withheld from the complainant."

Here, A.s' response had been hampered by the lack of full information.

On point (2), see also *R.* v. *Department of Health, ex p. Gandhi* [1991] 4 All E.R. 547 (Secretary of State not obliged to hold an oral hearing when dealing with an appeal against a decision of a Medical Practices Committee raising a complaint of racial discrimination).

R. v. LIVERPOOL CORPORATION, ex p. LIVERPOOL TAXI FLEET OPERATORS' ASSOCIATION

[1972] 2 Q.B. 299; [1972] 2 W.L.R. 1262; 116 S.J. 201; 71 L.G.R. 387; *sub nom. Re Liverpool Taxi Owners' Association* [1972] 2 All E.R. 589 (Court of Appeal)

From 1948 onwards, Liverpool Corporation, in the exercise of its powers under section 37, of the Town Police Clauses Act 1847, to "license . . . such number of hackney coaches or carriages . . . as they think fit" in their area, limited the number of taxi cabs to 300. In 1970 and 1971 there were many private cars operating for hire in Liverpool. These did not have to be licensed. To meet this competition, the taxi cab drivers wanted the number of licenses increased. The taxi cab owners wanted the number to remain at 300. All the 300 existing owners were represented by two associations, the Liverpool Taxi Fleet Operators' Association and the Liverpool Taxi Owners' Association. On July 24, 1970, the town clerk wrote to the associations, saying:

> "No decision has been taken on the number of hackney carriage plates and, before any such decision was taken, you have my assurance that interested parties would be fully consulted."

That was reaffirmed on October 28, 1970, when the town clerk wrote:

> "I have no doubt that your clients will be given an opportunity to make representations, at the appropriate time, should they wish to do so."

In July 1971 the matter was considered by a sub-committee of the corporation. The taxicab owners were represented by counsel. The sub-committee recommended an increase above 300, to the extent that there should be 50 more in the year beginning in January 1972 (making 350) and a further 100 in the year beginning January 1973 (making 450), and thereafter an unlimited number.

On August 4, 1971, that recommendation came up for consideration by the city council itself. The minutes were approved subject to some matters being sent back. In addition the chairman of the committee, Alderman Craine, gave an undertaking (which was put into writing by the town clerk in a letter on August 11, 1971):

> "The chairman of the committee gave an undertaking in council that no plates in addition to the existing 300 would be issued until proposed legislation had been enacted and had come into force."

After the meeting on August 4 the alderman came out to the representatives of the taxicab proprietors. The treasurer of the association asked:

> "It is right, Alderman Craine, that no licenses will be issued until legislation controlling private hire vehicles is in force?" The alderman replied: "I have just stated that publicly. I have just made an announcement to that effect."

At that time it was expected that the Bill promoted by the corporation would be introduced towards the end of 1971, passed in 1972, and in force early in 1973.

The corporation was then advised that the undertaking was not lawful and that they ought not to hold themselves bound by it. Without informing the owners or their associations, a sub-committee met on November 16, 1971. They rescinded the earlier resolution and put forward a new recommendation, namely, that from January 1, 1972, a further 50 licences would be issued bringing the total to 350: and that from July 1, 1972, a further 50, bringing the total to 400; and no limit from January 1, 1973.

The taxicab owners indirectly got to hear of that recommendation. (They were never told officially). So their solicitors asked for a further hearing. They asked if there were any new facts and requested that their clients should be given an opportunity of making further representations. On December 7, 1971, the town clerk replied:

> "There are no new important material facts. if there are any new material facts of which you have become aware, please let me have details of them by return."

The meeting was to be on the next day, December 8. It was impossible for the owners to make any reply by return.

The sub-committee recommendation was confirmed at the committee meeting on December 8, and at a meeting of the city council on December 22. The associations applied to the Divisional Court of the Queen's Bench Division (Lord Widgery C.J., Phillimore L.J. and Lawson J.) for leave to apply for:

(1) an order of prohibition prohibiting the corporation from issuing more than 300 licences:
(2) an order of mandamus requiring the corporation to hear and determine in their discretion the question whether or not the 300 limit should be increased;
(3) an order of certiorari to quash the city council's resolution of December 22, and the sub-committee's resolution of November 16.

They were refused leave, and then appealed to the Court of Appeal, who heard full argument on whether the orders should be granted.

LORD DENNING M.R.: ... That Act was explained by Lord Goddard C.J., in *R.* v. *Weymouth Borough Council, ex p. Teletax (Weymouth) Ltd.* [1947] K.B. 583, 589:

> "It also seems reasonably clear that what Parliament had in mind was that it was desirable that the commissioners should be able to control the number of carriages which applied for hire in a given area, and should also be entitled to prescribe the kind and the description of the carriages. . . . I have no doubt they . . . certainly could take into consideration the number of cabs which were already licensed, so that there would not be an undue number or, on the other hand, if they found there were not enough for the reasonable requirements of the public, they would be able to license more from time to time as they thought fit."

The licence is a licence for the vehicle. It is not a licence for the owner or the driver. Accordingly the owner of a vehicle can transfer his vehicle during the year to a buyer. The buyer can use it under the licence for the rest of the year. When the owner applies for the licence to be renewed for another year, the corporation can take into consideration not only the then proprietor, but also any new applicant. We were referred to an unreported case on that point: *R.* v. *Southampton Corporation, ex p. Lankford* on October 27, 1960. . . .

First I would say this: when the corporation consider applications for licences under the Town Police Clauses Act 1847, they are under a duty to act fairly. This means that they should be ready to hear not only the particular applicant but also any other persons or bodies whose interests are affected. In *R.* v. *Brighton Corporation, ex p. Thomas Tilling Ltd.* (1916) 85 L.J.K.B. 1552, 1555, Sankey J. said:

> "Persons who are called upon to exercise the functions of granting licences for carriages and omnibuses are, to a great extent, exercising judicial functions; and although they are not bound by the strict rules of evidence and procedure observed in a court of law, they are bound to act judicially. It is their duty to hear and determine according to law, and they must bring to that task a fair and unbiased mind."

It is perhaps putting it a little high to say they are exercising judicial functions. They may be said to be exercising an administrative function. But even so, in our modern approach, they must act fairly: and the court will see that they do so.

To apply that principle here: suppose the corporation proposed to reduce the number of taxicabs from 300 to 200, it would be their duty to hear the taxicab owners' association: because their members would be greatly affected. They would certainly be persons aggrieved. Likewise suppose the corporation propose to increase the number of taxicabs from 300 to 350 or 400 or more: it is the duty of the corporation to hear those affected before coming to a decision adverse to their interests. The Town Clerk of Liverpool was quite aware of this and acted accordingly. His letters of July 24, 1970, and October 28, 1970, were perfectly proper.

The other thing I say is that the corporation were not at liberty to disregard their undertaking. They were bound by it so long as it was not in conflict with their statutory duty.

It is said that a corporation cannot contract itself out of its statutory duties. In *Birkdale District Electric Supply Co. Ltd.* v. *Southport Corporation* [1926] A.C. 355 Lord Birkenhead said, at p. 364, that it was

> "a well established principle of law, that if a person or public body is entrusted by the legislature with certain powers and duties expressly or impliedly for public purposes, those persons or bodies cannot divest themselves of these powers and duties. They cannot enter into any contract or take any action incompatible with the due exercise of their powers or the discharge of their duties."

But that principle does not mean that a corporation can give an undertaking and break it as they please. So long as the performance of the undertaking is compatible with their public duty, they must honour it. And I should have thought that this undertaking was so compatible. At any rate they ought not to depart from it except after the most serious consideration and hearing what the other party has to say: and then only if they are satisfied that the overriding public interest requires it. The public interest may be better served by honouring their undertaking than by breaking it. This is just such a case. It is better to hold the corporation to their undertaking than to allow them to break it. Just as it was in *Robertson* v. *Minister of Pensions* [1949] 1 K.B. 227 and *Lever Finance Ltd.* v. *Westminster (City) London Borough Council* [1971] 1 Q.B. 222.

Applying these principles, it seems to me that the corporation acted wrongly at their meetings in November and December 1971. In the first place, they took decisions without giving the owners' association an opportunity of being heard. In the second place, they broke their undertaking without any sufficient cause or excuse.

The taxicab owners' association here have certainly a locus standi to apply for relief.

We have considered what the actual relief should be. On the whole we think it is sufficient in this case to let prohibition issue. The order should prohibit the corporation or their committee or sub-committee from acting on the resolutions of November 16, 1971, December 8, 1971, and December 22, 1971; in particular, from granting any further number of licences pursuant to section 37 of the Town Police Clauses Act 1847 over and above the 300 currently existing, without first hearing any representations which may be made by or on behalf of any persons interested therein, including the applicants in this case and any other matters relevant thereto, including the undertaking recorded in the town clerk's letter of August 11. If prohibition goes in those terms, it means that the relevant committee, sub-committee and the corporation themselves can look at the matter afresh. They will hear all those interested and come to a right conclusion as to what is to be done about the number of taxicabs on the streets of Liverpool. . . .

RUSSELL L.J.: . . . I do not think this court is under any duty to protect the interests of either rival group of licensees or would-be licensees. Its duty is to see that in dealing with the conflicting interests the council acts fairly between them. It is for the council and not for this court to determine what the future policy should be in relation to the number of taxi licences which are to be issued in the City of Liverpool. . . . This court is concerned to see that whatever policy the corporation adopts is adopted after due and fair regard to all the conflicting interests. The power of the court to intervene is not limited, as once was thought, to those cases where the function in question is judicial or quasi-judicial. The modern cases show that this court will intervene more widely than in the past. Even where the function is said to be administrative, the court will not hesitate to intervene in a suitable case if it is necessary in order to secure fairness. It has been said by Mr. Morland that there is no precedent for this court to intervene and enforce an undertaking which he claims to be of no legal effect and thus prevent the council giving effect to delegated legislation of the validity of which there is not doubt. For my part, I am not prepared to be deterred by the absence of precedent if in principle the case is one in which the court should interfere.

If I thought that the effect of granting to the applicants the relief sought was to prevent the council validly using those powers which Parliament has conferred upon it, I would refuse relief. But that is not the present case. It seems to me that the relief claimed will in the end, as Mr. Morland in effect ultimately conceded, assist the council to perform rather than inhibit the performance of its statutory duties. Lord Denning M.R. has referred to *Birkdale District Electric Supply Co. Ltd.* v. *Southport Corporation* [1926] A.C. 355. The decision of this court in *William Cory & Son Ltd.* v. *London Corporation* [1951] 2 K.B. 476, shows that a local authority such as the council cannot contractually fetter the performance of its statutory duties. But the present case is not such a case. The principle applicable is plain. In matters of this kind, such as the granting of licences for hackney carriages, the local authority concerned is required to act fairly, as well as, as Lord Denning M.R. has said, in a quasi-judicial capacity. It has been said that the council and its relevant committee and sub-committee were never under any duty to hear any representations from the applicants. That may or may not be correct. In the light of what has happened, I do not think it necessary to express any opinion upon that question. The relevant sub-committee had the advantage of hearing representations made on behalf of the applicants. Subsequently, having heard those representations, they made the recommendation which led up to the resolution of August 4, 1971, as well as, of course, to the undertaking of the breach of which complaint is made. It seems to me, therefore, that now to allow the council to resile from that undertaking without notice to and representations from the applicants is to condone unfairness in a case where the duty was to act fairly. To stop temporarily action on the resolution of December 22, 1971, is not in any way to perpetuate that undertkaing; nor should it embarrass the council in carrying out its statutory duties. The council must make up its own mind what policy it wishes to follow; but before doing so it must act fairly to all concerned, to present licensees and to would-be licensees and to others also who may be interested. In the end it may adhere to its present policy or it may not; but in my view this court should not allow the undertaking given by Alderman Craine on August 4 and repeated by the town clerk with the council's authority in the letter of August 11 to be set at naught. The council can at some future date, if it wishes, depart from that undertaking; but if it does so, it must do so after due and proper consideration of the representations of all those interested. I am not persuaded that any such due and proper consideration has yet been given. On the contrary, the evidence before this court shows that the passing of the resolution of December 22 was—as I have said—a flagrant breach of the undertaking. . . .

SIR GORDON WILLMER delivered a concurring judgment.

Application for prohibition granted.
Applications for certiorari and mandamus refused.

Notes

1. See case note by J. M. Evans, (1973) 36 M.L.R. 93.
2. See above, Ch. 7 on undertakings and estoppel.
3. Note that neither Russell L.J. (nor Sir Gordon Willmer) was prepared to go as far as Lord Denning M.R. so as to hold the authority bound by the assurance unless it was satisfied that the overriding public interest required departure from it. All the judges were agreed that in the light of the assurance, fairness required that the Association be given a further opportunity to make representations (note the form of the relief granted). Lord Denning's broader view has, however, helped form the basis of a development whereby assurances can in certain circumstances give rise to substantive effects (see above, pp. 419–437).
4. Which "undertaking" is the real foundation of this case: the undertakings that the association would be consulted or the undertkaing that the limit on licences would not be raised above 300 until the proposed private legislation was in force? Does it matter?
5. Compare the cases on legitimate expectations (below, pp. 514–521). Although the expression "legitimate expectation" is not used in the judgments, could it have been?
6. *Cf. R.* v. *Gravesham Borough Council, ex p. Gravesham Association of Licensed Hackney Carriage Owners, The Independent*, January 14, 1987, where Hodgson J. held that taxi drivers had no legitimate expectation to be consulted before the council decided to adopt a policy of placing no numerical ceiling on the number of hackney carriage licences which it issued under section 16 of the Transport Act 1985. There had been no promise of consultation, no prior consultation with them and no right of theirs was being infringed.

McINNES v. ONSLOW-FANE AND ANOTHER

[1978] 1 W.L.R. 1520; [1978] 3 All E.R. 211 (Chancery Division, Megarry V.-C.)

The plaintiff had held a promoter's licence for boxing matches issued in the 1950s by the British Boxing Board of Control (a voluntary self-regulatory organisation). In 1971 the board granted him a trainer's licence and in 1973 a master of ceremonies' licence. After an incident at a boxing match in 1973, the Board withdrew all the plaintiff's licences. Subsequently, he applied to the Board for a manager's licence on 5 occasions, but his applications were rejected. The plaintiff sought a declaration against the Board (represented by two of its members) that it had acted contrary to the rules of natural justice/or unfairly by (1) failing to inform the plaintiff of the case against him so that he could answer those concerns and (2) by not granting him an oral hearing prior to rejecting his last licence application.

MEGARRY V.-C.: . . . It was common ground between Mr. Beloff [counsel for the plaintiff] and Mr. Moses [counsel for the defendants] that the point before me was the subject of no direct authority: although expulsion from clubs and other bodies is the subject of an ample range of authorities, the refusal of applications for membership is much less richly endowed. It was also accepted that the point is of considerable general importance. There are many bodies which, though not established or operating under the authority of statute, exercise control, often on a national scale, over many activities which are important to many people, both as providing a means of livelihood and for other reasons. Sometimes that control is exercised, as by the board, by means of a system of granting or refusing licences, and sometimes it is operated by means of accepting or rejecting applications for membership. One particular aspect of this is membership of a trade union, without which it is impossible to obtain many important forms of work. In such cases it is plainly important, both to the body and the applicant, for them to know whether, before the application is rejected, the applicant is entitled to prior notice of any case against granting him a licence or admitting him to membership, and whether he is entitled to an oral hearing.

I think that I should take the matter by stages. First, there is the question of whether the grant or refusal of a licence by the board is subject to any requirements of natural justice or fairness which will be enforced by the courts. The question is not one that is governed by statute or contract, with questions of their true construction or the implication of terms; for there is no statute, and there is no contract between the plaintiff and the board. Nevertheless, in recent years there has been a marked expansion of the ambit of the requirements of natural justice and fairness reaching beyond statute and contract. A striking example is *Nagle* v. *Feilden* [1966] 2 Q.B. 633. There, a woman sought a declaration and injunctions against the Jockey Club to enforce her claim that she ought not to be refused a trainer's licence for horse-racing merely because she was a woman. At first instance her claim had been struck out, but the Court of Appeal reversed this decision. Lord Denning M.R. accepted that social clubs could refuse to admit an applicant for membership as they wished; but the Jockey Club exercised "a virtual monopoly in an important field of human activity," and what gave the courts jurisdiction was "a man's right to work": see pp. 644, 646. In reaching his conclusion, Lord Denning M.R. observed that being a jockey could be regarded as being an unsuitable occupation for a woman, whereas being a trainer could not: see p. 647.

. . . [W]here the court is entitled to intervene, I think it must be considered what type of decision is in question. I do not suggest that there is any clear or exhaustive classification; but I think that at least three categories may be discerned. First, there are what may be called the forfeiture cases. In these, there is a decision which takes away some existing right or position, as where a member of an organisation is expelled or a licence is revoked. Second, at the other extreme there are what may be called the application cases. These are cases where the decision merely refuses to grant the applicant the right or position that he seeks, such as membership of the organisation, or a licence to do certain acts. Third, there is an intermediate category, which may be called the expectation cases, which differ from the application cases only in that the applicant has some legitimate expectation from what has already happened that his application will be granted. This head includes cases where an existing licence-holder applies for a renewal of his licence, or a person already elected or appointed to some position seeks confirmation from some confirming authority: see, for instance, *Weinberger* v. *Inglis* [1919] A.C. 606; *Breen* v. *Amalgamated Engineering Union* [1971] 2 Q.B. 175; and see *Schmidt* v. *Secretary of State for Home Affairs* [1969] 2 Ch. 149, 170, 173 and *R.* v. *Barnsley Metropolitan Borough Council, ex p. Hook* [1976] 1 W.L.R. 1052, 1058.

It seems plain that there is a substantial distinction between the forfeiture cases and the application cases. In the forfeiture cases, there is a threat to take something away for some reason: and in such cases, the right to an unbiased tribunal, the right to notice of the charges and the right to be heard in answer to the charges (which in *Ridge* v. *Baldwin* [1964] A.C. 40, 132, Lord Hodson said were three features of natural justice which stood out) are plainly apt. In the application cases, on the other hand, nothing is being taken away, and in all normal circumstances there are no charges, and so no requirement of an opportunity of being heard in answer to the charges. Instead, there is the far wider and less defined question of the general suitability of the applicant for membership or a licence. The distinction is well-recognised, for in general it is clear that the courts will require natural justice to be observed for expulsion from a social club, but not on an application for admission to it. The intermediate category, that of the expectation cases, may at least in some respects be regarded as being more akin to the forefeiture cases than the application cases; for although in form there is no forfeiture but merely an attempt at acquisition that fails, the legitimate expectation of a renewal of the licence or confirmation of the membership is one which raises the question of what it is that has happened to make the applicant unsuitable for the membership or licence for which he was previously thought suitable.

I pause there. I do not think that I need pursue the expectation cases, for in the present case I can see nothing that would bring the plaintiff within them. . . .

. . . In my judgment, the case is plainly an application case in which the plaintiff is seeking to obtain a licence that he has never held and had no legitimate expectation of holding; he had only the hope (which may be confident or faint or anything between) which any applicant for anything may always have.

. . . [T]here is the question of the requirements of natural justice or fairness that have to be applied in an application case such as this. What are the requirements where there are no provisions of any statute or contract either conferring a right to the licence in certain circumstances, or laying down the procedure to be observed, and the applicant is seeking from an unofficial body the grant of a type of licence that he has never held before, and, though hoping to obtain it, has no legitimate expectation of receiving?

I do not think that much help is to be obtained from discussing whether "natural justice" or "fairness" is the more appropriate term. It one accepts that "natural justice" is a flexible term which imposes different requirements in different cases, it is capable of applying appropriately to the whole range of situations indicated by terms such as "judicial," "quasi-judicial" and "administrative." Nevertheless, the further the situation is away from anything that resembles a judicial or quasi-judicial situation, and the further the question is removed from what may reasonably be called a justiciable question, the more appropriate it is to reject an expression which includes the word "justice" and to use instead terms such as "fairness," or "the duty to act fairly": see *In re H. K. (An Infant)* [1967] 2 Q.B. 617, 630, *per* Lord Parker C.J.; *In re Pergamon Press Ltd.* [1971] Ch. 388, 399, *per* Lord Denning M.R.; *Breen's* case [1971] 2 Q.B. 175, 195, *per* Edmund Davies L.J. ("fairly exercised"); *Pearlberg* v. *Varty* [1972] 1 W.L.R. 534, 545, *per* Viscount Dilhorne, and at p. 547, *per* Lord Pearson. The suitability of the term "fairness" in such cases is increased by the curiosities of the expression "natural justice." Justice is far from being a "natural" concept. The closer one goes to a state of nature, the less justice does one find. Justice, and with it "natural justice," is in truth an elaborate and artificial product of civilisation which varies with different civilisations: see *Maclean* v. *Workers' Union* [1929] 1 Ch. 602, 624, *per* Maugham J. To Black J., "natural justice" understandably meant no more than "justice" without the adjective: see *Green* v. *Blake* [1948] I.R. 242, 268. However, be that as it may, the question before me is that of the content of "the duty to act fairly" (or of "natural justice") in this particular case. What does it entail? In particular, does it require the board to afford the plaintiff not only information of the "case against him" but also an oral hearing? . . .

I think it is clear that there is no general obligation to give reasons for a decision. Certainly in an application case, where there are no statutory or contractual requirements but a simple discretion in the licensing body, there is no obligation on that body to give their reasons. . . .

As I have said, Mr. Moses accepted that the board were under a duty to reach an honest conclusion without bias and not in pursuance of any capricious policy. That, I think, is right: and if the plaintiff showed that any of these requirements had not been complied with, I think the court would intervene. Mr. Beloff accepted that the burden of proof would have been on him if any such questions had arisen. But assume a board acting honestly and without bias or caprice: why should a duty to act fairly require them to tell an applicant the gist of the reasons (which may vary from member to member) why they think he ought not to be given a licence? Is a college or university, when selecting candidates for admission or awarding scholarships, or a charity when making grants to the needy, acting 'unfairly" when it gives no reason to the unsuccessful? Are editors and publishers "unfair" when they send out unreasoned rejection slips? Assume that they are under no enforceable duty to act fairly, and it may still be a matter of concern to them if they are to be told that they are acting "unfairly" in not giving the gist of their reasons to the rejected. Again, do judges act unfairly when, without any indication of their reasons, they refuse leave to appeal, or decide questions of costs? . . .

Looking at the case as whole, in my judgment there is no obligation on the board to give the plaintiff even the gist of the reasons why they refused his application, or proposed to do so. This is not a case in which there has been any suggestion of the board considering any alleged dishonesty or morally culpable conduct of the plaintiff. A man free from any moral blemish may nevertheless be wholly unsuitable for a particular type of work. The refusal of the plaintiff's application by no means necessarily puts any slur on his character, nor does it deprive him of any statutory right. There is no mere narrow issue as to his character, but the wide and general issue whether it is right to grant this licence to this applicant. In such circumstances, in the absence of anything to suggest that the board have been affected by dishonesty or bias or caprice, or that there is any other impropriety, I think that the board are fully entitled to give no reasons for their decision, and to decide the application without any preliminary indication to the plaintiff of those reasons. The board are the best judges of the desirability of granting the licence, and in the absence of any impropriety the court ought not to interfere.

There is a more general consideration. I think that the courts must be slow to allow any implied obligation to be fair to be used as a means of bringing before the courts for review honest decisions of bodies exercising jurisdiction over sporting and other activities which those bodies are far better fitted to judge than the courts. This is so even where those bodies are concerned with the means of livelihood of those who take part in those activities. The concepts of natural justice and the duty to be fair must not be allowed to discredit themselves by making unreasonable requirements and imposing undue burdens. Bodies such as the board which promote a public interest by seeking to maintain high standards in a field of activity which otherwise might easily become degraded and corrupt ought not to be hampered in their work without good cause. Such bodies should not be tempted or coerced into granting licences that otherwise they would refuse by reason of the courts having imposed on them a procedure for refusal which facilitates litigation against them. As Lord Denning M.R. said in *In re Pergamon Press Ltd.* [1971] Ch. 388, 400, "No one likes to have an action brought against him, however unfounded." The individual must indeed be protected against impropriety; but any claim of his for anything more must be balanced against what the public interest requires.

That brings me to the fifth point, the contention that the board are obliged to afford the plaintiff a hearing. This, I think, has in large part been disposed of by what I have said in rejecting the contention that the plaintiff has a right to be told the gist of the reasons for proposing to reject his application. The contention that the plaintiff ought to be given a hearing seems to have been put forward mainly as an ancillary to the alleged obligation to inform him of the gist of the reasons for provisionally deciding not to grant him the licence, and so as to enable him to meet what is said. However, if one treats the right to a hearing as an independent requirement, I would say that I cannot see how the obligation to be fair can be said in a case of this type to require a hearing. I do not see why the board should not be fully capable of dealing fairly with the plaintiff's application without any hearing. The case is not an expulsion case where natural justice confers the right to know the charge and to have an opportunity of meeting it at a hearing. I cannot think that there is or should be any rule that an application for a licence of this sort cannot properly be refused without giving the applicant the opportunity of a hearing, however hopeless the application, and whether it is the first or the fifth or the fiftieth application that he has made. Certainly Mr. Beloff has not referred me to any authority which appears to me to give any real support to such a proposition in a case such as this. I therefore reject the contention that the board should be required to give the plaintiff a hearing or interview.

In my judgment, therefore, the plaintiff's claim fails. It is easy to understand a very natural curiosity and, doubtless, anxiety on his part to know what it is that stands between him and the grant of the licence that he seeks. He may wonder whether it is something that endeavour on his part may put right, or whether it is something beyond cure. It may be that it would be considerate of the board if they were to give him at least some indication of what stands in his way. I for one would not be surprised if his previous career as a licence-holder had played a substantial part in this, although no details of the various episodes have been put before me. At the same time, I can well see that the board would be reluctant to adopt a more elaborate and time-consuming procedure for determining applications for licences, and even more reluctant to be required to give reasons (whether in full or in outline) which might provide ammunition for litigation against the board. The board's regulations seem to me to make fair and reasonable provisions for disciplinary cases which may lead to the suspension or withdrawal of a licence and so on, and the distinction under the regulations between such cases and applications for the grant of licences seems to me to be proper and generally in accordance with the law. Furthermore, the offer of a hearing made by the board's solicitors after the originating summons had been issued seems to me to have been reasonable and benign; I regret that the plaintiff's solicitors should have been insistent upon the board paying the plaintiff's costs. My duty, however, is simply to apply the law as I understand it; and for the reasons that I have given, I hold that on the questions that are before me the plaintiff's claims fail and will be dismissed.

Summons dismissed.

Notes

1. Eleven years after the above decision, Michael Beloff Q.C. (who had been counsel for Mr. McInnes) expressed the following view regarding the judicial attitude towards legal actions brought against the governing bodies of different sports: "no less than three Vice-Chancellors of different generations and jurisdictions have taken the view that the courts should abstain where possible from interfering with the decisions of bodies controlling sporting spheres. . . . It is, I suspect, the floodgates argument that is the unspoken premise of the Vice-Chancellarial observations, the fear that limited court time will be absorbed by a new and elastic category of case with much scope for abusive or captious litigation. It is an argument which intellectually has little to commend it, and pragmatically is usually shown to be ill-founded. For it is often the case that, once the courts have shown the willingness to intervene, the standards of the bodies at risk of their intervention tend to improve. The threat of litigation averts its actuality" "(Pitch, Pool, Rink, . . . Court? Judicial Review in the Sporting World" [1989] P.L. 95 at pp. 109–110). See also E. Grayson, *Sport and the Law* (1988).

2. Where licensing decisions under statutory powers do have an effect on livelihood, the court have generally been willing to imply procedural standards. In *R.* v. *Huntingdon District Council, ex p. Cowan* [1984] 1 W.L.R. 501., Glidewell J. held that when dealing with an application for an entertainment licence under Part I of the Local Government (Miscellaneous Provisions) Act 1982 a local authority must inform the applicant of the substance of any objection or representation in the nature of an objection (not necessarily the whole of it, nor to say necessarily who has made it); and give the applicant an opportunity to make representations in reply. (See also *R.* v. *Preston Borough Council, ex p. Quietlynn Ltd.* and other cases (1984) 83 L.G.R. 308, C.A.). In *R.* v. *Bristol City Council, ex p. Pearce* (1984) 83 L.G.R. 711, the same judge held that when considering an application for a street trading consent under para. 7 of Schedule 4 to the Local Government (Miscellaneous Provisions) Act 1982, a local authority was obliged to tell the applicants of the content of any objection (other than from its own officers or the police) and to give them some opportunity to comment. However, an oral hearing need not be held, and reasons need not be given. (His Lordship held that the applicant here did not have a legitimate expectation, but that nevertheless some procedural standards were applicable.) In *R.* v. *Wear Valley District Council, ex p. Binks* [1985] 2 All E.R. 699, the council decided to terminate the applicant's contractual licence to station a caravan on the council's land (in a market place). The applicant used the caravan to earn her living by selling take away food. Taylor J. held that the council was obliged to give notice of and the reasons for the proposed termination, and an opportunity to be heard, notwithstanding that the licence was contractual and not statutory.

Question

Is Megarry V.-C.'s explanation of the relationship between natural justice and procedural fairness convincing?

COUNCIL OF CIVIL SERVICE UNIONS v. MINISTER FOR THE CIVIL SERVICE

[1985] A.C. 374; [1985] I.C.R. 14; [1984] 3 W.L.R. 1174; [1984] 3 All E.R. 935 (House of Lords)

The main functions of Government Communications Headquarters ("GCHQ") were to ensure the security of military and official communications and to provide the Government with signals intelligence; they involved the handling of secret information vital to national security. Since 1947, staff employed at GCHQ had been permitted to belong to national trade unions, and most had done so. There was a well-established practice of consultation between the official and trade union sides about important alterations in the terms and conditions of service of the staff. On December 22, 1983, the Minister for the Civil Service gave an instruction, purportedly under article 4 of the Civil Service Order in Council 1982, for the immediate variation of the terms and conditions of service of the staff with the effect that they would no longer be permitted to belong to national trade unions. There had been no consultation with the trade unions or with the staff at GCHQ prior to the issuing of that instruction. The applicants, a trade union and six individuals, sought judicial review of the minister's instruction on the ground that she had been under a duty to act fairly by consulting those concerned before issuing it. In an affidavit, the Secretary to the Cabinet deposed to disruptive industrial action in support of national trade unions that had taken place at GCHQ as part of a national campaign by the unions designed to damage government agencies and that it had been considered that prior consultation about the minister's instruction would have involved a risk of precipitating further disruption and would moreover have indicated vulnerable areas of GCHQ's operations. Glidewell J. granted the applicants a declaration that the instruction was invalid and of no effect. The Court of Appeal allowed an appeal by the minister, and a further appeal was dismissed.

The House of Lords held (1) that the government's action was not immune from judicial review merely because it was in pursuance of a common law or a prerogative power; (2) that the applicants would apart from national security considerations have had a legitimate expectation that unions and employees would have been consulted before the instruction was issued; but (3) that the Minister had shown that her decision had in fact been based on considerations of national security that outweighed the applicant's legitimate expectation.

The following extracts concern the second issue:

LORD FRASER OF TULLYBELTON: . . .

The duty to consult

Mr. Blom-Cooper submitted that the Minister had a duty to consult the CCSU, on behalf of employees at GCHQ, before giving the instruction on December 22, 1983, for making an important change in their conditions of service. His main reason for so submitting was that the employees had a legitimate, or reasonable, expectation that there would be such prior consultation before any important change was made in their conditions.

It is clear that the employees did not have legal right to prior consultation. The Order in Council confers no such right, and article 4 makes no reference at all to consultation. The Civil Service handbook (*Handbook for the new civil servant*, 1973 ed. as amended 1983) which explains the normal method of consultation through the departmental Whitley Council, does not suggest that there is any legal right to consultation; indeed it is careful to recognise that, in the operational field, considerations of urgency may make prior consultation impracticable. The Civil Service Pay and Conditions of Service Code expressly states:

> "The following terms and conditions also apply to your appointment in the Civil Service. It should be understood, however, that in consequence of the constitutional position of the Crown, the Crown has the right to change its employees' conditions of service at any time, and that they hold their appointments at the pleasure of the Crown."

But even where a person claiming some benefit or privilege has no legal right to it, as a matter of private law, he may have a legitimate expectation of receiving the benefit or privilege, and, if so, the courts will protect his expectation of judicial review as a matter of public law. This subject has been fully explained by my noble and learned friend, Lord Diplock, in *O'Reilly* v. *Mackman* [1983] 2 A.C. 237 and I need not repeat what he has so recently said. Legitimate, or reasonable, expectation may arise either from an express promise given on behalf of a public authority or from the existence of a regular practice which the claimant can reasonably expect to continue. Examples of the former type of expectation are *R.* v. *Liverpool Corporation, ex p. Liverpool Taxi Fleet Operators' Association* [1972] 2 Q.B. 299 and *Attorney-General of Hong Kong* v. *Ng Yuen Shiu* [1983] 2 A.C. 629. (I agree with Lord Diplock's view, expressed in the speech in this appeal, that "legitimate" is to be preferred to "reasonable" in this context. I was responsible for using the word "reasonable" for the reason explained in *Ng Yuen Shiu*, but it was intended only to be exegetical of "legitimate.") An example of the latter is *R.* v. *Board of Visitors of Hull Prison, ex p. St. Germain* [1979] Q.B. 425 approved by this House in *O'Reilly*, at p. 274D. The submission on behalf of the appellants is that the present case is of the latter type. The test of that is whether the practice of prior consultation of the staff on significant changes in their conditions of service was so well established by 1983 that it would be unfair or inconsistent with good administration for the Government to depart from the practice in this case. Legitimate expectations such as are now under consideration will always relate to a benefit or privilege to which the claimant has no right in private law, and it may even be to one which conflicts with his private law rights. In the present case the evidence shows that, ever since GCHQ began in 1947, prior consultation has been the invariable rule when conditions of service were to be significantly altered. Accordingly in my opinion if there had been no question of national security involved, the appellants would have had a legitimate expectation that the minister would consult them before issuing the instruction of December 22, 1983.

LORD DIPLOCK: . . . Judicial review, now regulated by R.S.C., Ord. 53, provides the means by which judicial control of administrative action is exercised. The subject-matter of every judicial review is a decision made by some person (or body of persons) whom I will call the "decision-maker" or else a refusal by him to make a decision.

To qualify as a subject for judicial review the decision must have consequences which affect some person (or body of persons) other than the decision-maker, although it may affect him too. It must affect such other person either:

(a) by altering rights or obligations of that person which are enforceable by or against him in private law; or

(b) by depriving him of some benefit or advantage which either (i) he had in the past been permitted by the decision-maker to enjoy and which he can legitimately expect to be permitted to continue to do until there has been communicated to him some rational grounds for withdrawing it on which he has been given an opportunity to comment; or (ii) he has received assurance from the decision-maker will not be withdrawn without giving him first an opportunity of advancing reasons for contending that they should not be withdrawn. (I prefer to continue to call the kind of expectation that qualifies a decision for inclusion in class (b) a "legitimate expectation" rather than a "reasonable expectation," in order thereby to indicate that it has consequences to which effect will be given in public law, whereas an expectation or hope that some benefit or advantage would continue to be enjoyed, although it might well be entertained by a "reasonable" man, would not necessarily have such consequences. The recent decision of this House in *In re Findlay* [1985] A.C. 318 presents an example of the latter kind of expectation. "Reasonable" furthermore bears different meanings according to whether the context in which it is being used is that of private law or of public law. To eliminate confusion it is best avoided in the latter.)

For a decision to be susceptible to judicial review the decision-maker must be empowered by public law (and not merely, as in arbitration, by agreement between private parties) to make decisions that, if validly made, will lead to administrative action or abstention from action by an authority endowed by law with executive powers, which have one or other of the consequences mentioned in the preceding paragraph. The ultimate source of the decision-making power is nearly always nowadays a statute or subordinate legislation made under the statute; but in the absence of any statute regulating the subject-matter of the decision the source of the decision-making power may still be the common law itself, *i.e.* that part of the common law that is given by lawyers the label of "the prerogative." Where this is the source of decision-making power, the power is confined to executive officers of central as distinct from local government and in constitutional practice is generally exercised by those holding ministerial rank.

It was the prerogative that was relied on as the source of the power of the Minister for the Civil Service in reaching her decision of December 22,

1983, that membership of national trade unions should in future be barred to all members of the home civil service employed at GCHQ. . . .

My Lords, I see no reason why simply because a decision-making power is derived from a common law and not a statutory source, it should *for that reason only* be immune from judicial review. Judicial review has I think developed to a stage today when without reiterating any analysis of the steps by which the development has come about, one can conveniently classify under three heads the grounds upon which administrative action is subject to control by judicial review. The first ground I would call "illegality," the second "irrationality" and the third "procedural impropriety." That is not to say that further development on a case by case basis may not in course of time add further grounds. I have in mind particularly the possible adoption in the future of the principle of "proportionality" which is recognised in the administrative law of several of our fellow members of the European Economic Community; but to dispose of the instant case the three already well-established heads that I have mentioned will suffice.

By "illegality" as a ground for judicial review I mean that the decision-maker must understand correctly the law that regulates his decision-making power and must give effect to it. Whether he has or not is par excellence a justiciable question to be decided, in the event of dispute, by those persons, the judges, by whom the judicial power of the state is exercisable.

By "irrationality" I mean what can by now be succinctly referred to as "*Wednesbury* unreasonableness" (*Associated Provincial Picture Houses Ltd.* v. *Wednesbury Corporation* [1948] 1 K.B. 223). It applies to a decision which is so outrageous in its defiance of logic or of accepted moral standards that no sensible person who had applied his mind to the question to be decided could have arrived at it. Whether a decision falls within this category is a question that judges by their training and experience should be well equipped to answer, or else there would be something badly wrong with our judicial system. To justify the court's exercise of this role, resort I think is today no longer needed to Viscount Radcliffe's ingenious explanation in *Edwards* v. *Bairstow* [1956] A.C. 14 of irrationality as a ground for a court's reversal of a decision by ascribing it to an inferred though unidentifiable mistake of law by the decision-maker. "Irrationality" by now can stand upon its own feet as an accepted ground on which a decision may be attacked by judicial review.

I have described the third head as "procedural impropriety" rather than failure to observe basic rules of natural justice or failure to act with procedural fairness towards the person who will be affected by the decision. This is because susceptibility to judicial review under this head covers also failure by an administrative tribunal to observe procedural rules that are expressly laid down in the legislative instrument by which its jurisdiction is conferred, even where such failure does not involve any denial of natural justice. But the instant case is not concerned with the proceedings of an administrative tribunal at all. . . .

[His Lordship concluded that it was well established that decisions whose ultimate source of power was the common law (whether or not labelled as "the prerogative") could be the subject of judicial review on the grounds of illegality or procedural impropriety. There was no *a priori* reason to rule out challenge on the ground of irrationality, he found it difficult to envisage cases where such a challenge would be justifiable.]

Prima facie . . . civil servants employed at GCHQ who were members of national trade unions had, at best, in December 1983, a legitimate expectation that they would continue to enjoy the benefits of such membership and of representation by those trade unions in any consultations and negotiations with representatives of the management of that government department as to changes in any term of their employment. So, but again *prima facie* only, they were entitled, as a matter of public law under the head of "procedural propriety," before administrative action was taken on a decision to withdraw that benefit, to have communicated to the national trade unions by which they had theretofore been represented the reason for such withdrawal, and for such unions to be given an opportunity to comment on it. . . .

LORD ROSKILL: . . . The particular manifestation of the duty to act fairly which is presently involved is that part of the recent evolution of our administrative law which may enable an aggrieved party to evoke judicial review if he can show that he has "a reasonable expectation" of some occurrence or action preceding the decision complained of and that that "reasonable expectation" was not in the event fulfilled.

The introduction of the phrase "reasonable expectation" into this branch of our administrative law appears to show its origin to Lord Denning M.R. in *Schmidt* v. *Secretary of State for Home Affairs* [1969] 2 Ch. 149, 170 (when he used the phrase "legitimate expectation"). Its judicial evolution is traced in the opinion of the Judicial Committee delivered by my noble and learned friend, Lord Fraser of Tullybelton, in *Attorney-General of Hong Kong* v. *Ng Yuen Shiu* [1983] 2 A.C. 629, 636–638. Though the two phrases can. I think, now safely be treated as synonymous for the reasons there given by my noble and learned friend, I prefer the use of the adjective "legitimate" in this context and use it in this speech even though in argument it was the adjective "reasonable" which was generally used. The principle may now be said to be firmly entrenched in this branch of the law. As the cases show, the principle is closely connected with "a right to be heard." Such an expectation may take many forms. One may be an expectation of prior consultation. Another may be an expectation of being allowed time to make representations especially where the aggrieved party is seeking to persuade an authority to depart from a lawfully established policy adopted in connection with the exercise of a particular power because of some suggested exceptional reasons justifying such a departure. . . .

My Lords, if no question of national security were involved I cannot doubt that the evidence and the whole history of the relationship between management and staff since 1919 shows that there was a legitimate expectation of consultation before important alterations in the conditions of service of civil servants were made. No doubt in strict theory civil servants are dismissible at will and the various documents shown to your Lordships seek to preserve the strict constitutional position. But in reality the management-staff relationship is governed by an elaborate code to which it is unnecessary to refer in detail. I have little doubt that were management to seek to alter without prior consultation the terms and conditions of civil servants in a field which had no connection whatever with national security or perhaps, though the matter does not arise in this appeal, with urgent fiscal emergency, such action would in principle be amenable to judicial review.

LORDS SCARMAN and BRIGHTMAN delivered concurring speeches.

Notes

1. The important decision in *Attorney-General of Hong Kong* v. *Ng Yeun Shui* [1983] 2 A.C. 629 is summarised in *R.* v. *Secretary of State for the Home Department, ex p. Khan,* above p. 422. Although cited by Lord Fraser, the *Liverpool Taxi* case (above p. 502) does not actually use the term "legitimate expectation."

2. The literature on legitimate expectations is listed above at p. 437, n. 6. The argument that a legitimate expectation gives rise to procedural rights is less controversial than the notion it can also place substantive restrictions on the powers of the decision-maker (see above, p. 419–437).

3. It is now clear that a "legitimate expectation" may be the legitimate expectation of some advantage being accorded to the applicant (see *Schmidt* v. *Secretary of State for Home Affairs* [1969] 2 Ch. 149; *McInnes* v. *Onslow Fane* (above p. 507); *R.* v. *Secretary of State for the Home Department, ex p. Khan,* above p. 422; *R.* v. *Brent London Borough Council, ex p. MacDonagh* (1989) 21 H.L.R. 494); or a legitimate expectation of being afforded a hearing (*Att.-Gen. of Hong Kong* v. *Ng Yuen Shui,* above, p. 424; the *C.C.S.U.* case, above). This has been termed a "crucial ambiguity" (*Cane,* p. 112).

4. A legitimate expectation of being consulted may arise simply from the nature of the applicant's interests, as distinct from past practice or an express undertaking. In *R.* v. *Brent London Borough Council, ex p. Gunning* (1985) 84 L.G.R. 168, Hodgson J. held that while there was no statutory duty placed upon local education authorities to consult parents of pupils before making proposals for the closure or amalgamation of schools, parents nevertheless had a legitimate expectation that they would be consulted. "The interest of parents in the educational arrangements in the area in which they lived is self-evident. It is explicitly recognised in the legislation (see, *e.g.* section 6 of the Education Act 1980). The legislation places clear duties upon parents, backed by draconian criminal sanctions." Local authorities (including Brent) habitually consulted on these matters, and were exhorted to do so by the Secretary of State. On the facts here, the consultative document was wholly inadequate and misleading as to the cost of the proposals and the period allowed for consultation was unreasonably short. Furthermore, as the proposals ultimately adopted were materially different from

those on which consultation had taken place, the parents of school children in the area should have been given a further opportunity to be consulted. The authority's decision to make the proposals was quashed.

(Hodgson J. stated (at p. 187) that their legitimate expectation gave them the same right as if it had been specifically given by statute. In *R.* v. *Gwent County Council, ex p. Bryant, The Independent*, April 19, 1988, his Lordship stated that he had gone too far in equating a legitimate expectation with a statutory right. In the former case, a defect in consultation could be rectified by the Secretary of State, in the latter, it could not; *R.* v. *Northampton County Council, ex p. Tebbutt*, unreported, June 26, 1986, applied. See also *R.* v. *Haberdashers' Aske's Hatcham School Governors, ex p. Inner London Education Authority, The Times*, March 7, 1989.) See P. Meredith, [1988] P.L. 4.

5. There is some authority than a person's misconduct may deprive him or her of a *legitimate* expectation. In *Cinnamond* v. *British Airports Authority* [1980] 1 W.L.R. 582, the authority exercised its power under byelaws to prohibit six car-hire drivers from entering Heathrow airport (save as a *bona fide* passenger), until further notice. Each of the six had many convictions under the byelaws for loitering and offering services to passengers, and all had unpaid fines outstanding. The authority had received many complaints that car hire drivers charged exorbitant fares in comparison with the licensed taxis. The drivers sought a declaration that the notices were invalid. One ground was that they had not been given an opportunity to make representations. Lord Denning M.R. said (at pp. 590–591) that the drivers had no legitimate expectation:

> "... suppose that these car-hire drivers were of good character and had for years been coming into the airport under an implied licence to do so. If in that case there was suddenly a prohibition order preventing them from entering, then it would seem only fair that they should be given a hearing and a chance to put their case. But that is not this case. These men have a long record of convictions. They have large fines outstanding. They are continuing to engage in conduct which they must know is unlawful and contrary to the byelaws. When they were summonsed for past offences, they put their case, no doubt, to the justices and to the Crown Court. Now when the patience of the authority is exhausted, it seems to me that the authority can properly suspend them until further notice—just like the police officer I mentioned. In the circumstances they had no legitimate expectation of being heard. It is not a necessary preliminary that they should have a hearing or be given a further chance to explain. Remembering always this: that it must have been apparent to them why the prohibition was ordered: and equally apparent that, if they had a change of heart and were ready to comply with the rules, no doubt the prohibition would be withdrawn. They could have made representations immediately, if they wished, in answer to the prohibition order. That they did not do."

Shaw L.J. said (at p. 592):

> "As to the suggestion of unfairness in that the drivers were not given an opportunity of making representations, it is clear on the history of this matter that the drivers put themselves so far outside the limits of tolerable conduct as to disentitle themselves to expect that any further representations on their part could have any influence or relevance. The long history of contraventions, of flouting the regulations, and of totally disregarding the penalties demonstrate that in this particular case there was no effective deterrent. The only way of dealing with the situation was by excluding them altogether.
>
> It does not follow that the attitude of the authority may not change if they can

be persuaded by representations on behalf of the drivers that they are minded in future to comply with the regulations."

Brandon L.J. agreed with Lord Denning and Shaw L.J. on the natural justice point, and then said (p. 593):

"If I am wrong in thinking that some opportunity should have been given, then it seems to me that no prejudice was suffered by the minicab drivers as a result of not being given that opportunity. It is quite evident that they were not prepared then, and are not even prepared now, to give any satisfactory undertakings about their future conduct. Only if they were would representations be of any use. I would rely on what was said in *Malloch* v. *Aberdeen Corporation* [1971] 1 W.L.R. 1578, first *per* Lord Reid at p. 1582 and secondly *per* Lord Wilberforce at p. 1595. [See above, p. 491.] The effect of what Lord Wilberforce said is that no one can complain of not being given an opportunity to make representations if such an opportunity would have availed him nothing."

B. L. Jones comments (*Garner*, p. 188) that Lord Denning's statement that the drivers had no legitimate expectation of being heard:

"should not be construed literally but be regarded as a short-hand for 'They had no legitimate expectation (because of their past conduct) of not being barred totally from entry and *therefore* they had no right to be heard before the action was taken'."

Cf. Cane, p. 113:

"This is an objectionable use of the concept of legitimate expectation, because it enables the court, in the name of procedural fairness, to judge the merits of the case."

See also I. R. Ward, (1981) 44 M.L.R. 103.

(b) Limitations on the Right to a Fair Hearing

(i) National Security

R v. SECRETARY OF STATE FOR HOME AFFAIRS, ex p. HOSENBALL

[1977] 1 W.L.R. 766; [1977] 3 All E.R. 452. (Court of Appeal)

The appellant was a United States citizen who worked as a journalist in the United Kingdom. At first he worked for the weekly journal "Time Out" and was responsible for an article entitled "The Eavesdroppers" about communications monitoring by the government, which appeared in May 1976. During July 1976, Hosenball moved to the "Evening Standard" as a general news reporter. In November 1976, he was informed that the Home Secretary had decided to deport him on the grounds that Hosenball's "departure from the United Kingdom would be conducive to the public good as being in the interests of national security." The Home Secretary considered that Hosenball had sought and obtained for publication information harmful to the security of the United Kingdom and prejudicial to the safety of Crown servants. Hosenball had no right of appeal against the decision under the terms of the Immigration Act 1971. However, he was given a non-statutory hearing before "three advisers" (appointed by the Home Secretary) who reported back in confidence to the Secretary of State. The Home Secretary later made a deportation against Hosenball. Hosenball then applied for an order of certiorari to quash the deportation order on the ground, *inter alia*, that the principle of *audi alteram partem* had been breached by the failure to supply him with details of the case against him prior to his appearance before the "three advisers." The High Court dismissed Hosenball's application and he then appealed to the Court of Appeal.

LORD DENNING M.R.: . . . Now I would like to say at once that if this were a case in which the ordinary rules of natural justice were to be observed, some criticism could be directed upon it. For one thing, the Home Secretary himself, and I expect the advisory panel also, had a good deal of confidential information before them of which Mr. Hosenball knew nothing and was told nothing: and which he had no opportunity of correcting or contradicting; or of testing by cross-examination. In addition, he was not given sufficient information of the charges against him so as to be able effectively to deal with them or answer them. All this could be urged as a ground for upsetting any ordinary decision of a court of law or of any tribunal, statutory or domestic: see *Kanda* v. *Government of Malaya* [1962] A.C. 322, 337.

But this is no ordinary case. It is a case in which national security is involved: and our history shows that, when the state itself is endangered, our cherished freedoms may have to take second place. Even natural justice itself may suffer a set-back. Time after time Parliament has so enacted and the courts have loyalty followed. In the first world war in *R.* v. *Halliday* [1917] A.C. 260, 270 Lord Finlay L.C. said: "The danger of espionage and of damage by secret agents . . . had to be guarded against." In the second world war in *Liversidge* v. *Sir John Anderson* [1942] A.C. 206, 219 Lord Maugham said:

> ". . . there may be certain persons against whom no offence is proved nor any charge formulated, but as regards whom it may be expedient to authorise the Secretary of State to make an order for detention."

That was said in time of war. But times of peace hold their dangers too. Spies, subverters and saboteurs may be mingling amongst us, putting on a most innocent exterior. They may be endangering the lives of the men in our secret service, as Mr. Hosenball is said to do.

If they are British subjects, we must deal with them here. If they are foreigners, they can be deported. The rules of natural justice have to be modified in regard to foreigners here who prove themselves unwelcome and ought to be deported. . . .

So it seems to me that when the national security is at stake even the rules of natural justice may have to be modified to meet the position. I would refer in this regard to the speech of Lord Reid in *R.* v. *Lewes JJ., ex p. Secretary of State for Home Department* [1973] A.C. 388, 402. . . .

The information supplied to the Home Secretary by the Security Service is, and must be, highly confidential. The public interest in the security of the realm is so great that the sources of the information must not be disclosed—nor should the nature of the information itself be disclosed—if there is any risk that it would lead to the sources being discovered. The reason is because, in this very secretive field, our enemies might try to eliminate the sources of information. So the sources must not be disclosed. Not even to the House of Commons. Nor to any tribunal or court of inquiry or body of advisers, statutory or non-statutory. Save to the extent that the Home Secretary thinks safe. Great as is the public interest in the freedom of the individual and the doing of justice to him, nevertheless in the last resort it must take second place to the security of the country itself. . . .

There is a conflict here between the interests of national security on the one hand and the freedom of the individual on the other. The balance between these two is not for a court of law. It is for the Home Secretary. He is the person entrusted by Parliament with the task. In some parts of the world national security has on occasions been used as an excuse for all sorts of infringements of individual liberty. But not in England. Both during the wars and after them, successive ministers have discharged their duties to the complete satisfaction of the people at large. They have set up advisory committees to help them, usually with a chairman who has done everything he can to ensure that justice is done. They have never interfered with the liberty or the freedom of movement of any individual except where it is absolutely necessary for the safety of the state. In this case we are assured that the Home Secretary himself gave it his personal consideration, and I have no reason whatever to doubt the care with which he considered the whole matter. He is answerable to Parliament as to the way in which he did it and not to the courts here.

I would dismiss the appeal.

Geoffrey Lane L.J.: There are occasions, though they are rare, when what are more generally the rights of an individual must be subordinated to the protection of the realm. When an alien visitor to this country is believed to have used the hospitality extended to him so as to present a danger to security, the Secretary of State has the right and, in many cases, has the duty of ensuring that the alien no longer remains here to threaten our security. It may be that the alien has been in the country for many years. It may be that he has built a career here in this country, and that consequently a deportation order made against him may result in great hardship to him. It may be that he protests that he has done nothing wrong so far as this country's security is concerned. It may be that he protests that he cannot understand why any action of this sort is being taken against him. In ordinary circumstances common fairness—you can call it natural justice if you wish—would demand that he be given particulars of the charges made against him; that he be given the names of the witnesses who are prepared to testify against him and, indeed, probably the nature of the evidence which those witnesses are prepared to give should also be delivered to him. But there are counter-balancing factors. . . .

It may well be that if an alien is told with particularity what it is said he has done it will become quite obvious to him from whence that information has been received. The only person who can judge whether such a result is likely is the person who has in his possession all the information available. That, in this case, is the Secretary of State himself. If he comes to the conclusion that for reasons such as those which I have just endeavoured to outline he cannot afford to give the alien more than the general charge against him, there one has the dilemma. The alien certainly has inadequate information upon which to prepare or direct his defence to the various charges which are made against him, and the only way that could be remedied would be to disclose information to him which might probably have an adverse effect on the national security. The choice is regrettably clear: the alien must suffer, if suffering there be, and this is so on whichever basis of argument one chooses. . . .

Different principles and strict principles apply where matters of the safety of the realm are at stake. What is fair cannot be decided in a vacuum: it has to be determined against the whole background of any particular case. The advisory panel system is an effort to ensure fairness as far as possible in these difficult circumstances, but in the end it is the Secretary of State who must in those circumstances be trusted to speak the last word. . . .

I would dismiss the appeal.

CUMMING-BRUCE L.J. I agree with all that has fallen from Lord Denning M.R. and Geoffrey Lane L.J. . . .

Appeal dismissed.

Notes

1. After the above legal action Hosenball returned to the United States from where he contributed to the "Sunday Times."

2. The general public became aware of the existence of Government Communications Headquarters ("G.C.H.Q.") in Cheltenham during January 1984, when the Government announced that its employees would no longer be able to join national trade unions. This action led to the famous *C.C.S.U.* case, see above (p. 514).

3. Lord Denning's contented view of the relationship between the legitimate needs of national security and individual liberty has not been endorsed by either the European Commission of Human Rights or the Committee of Ministers of the Council of Europe. In the case of *Hewitt and Harman and N.* v. *U.K.* (1989), the Commission reached the opinion that the Security Service had violated the applicants' right to privacy (under Article 8 of the European Convention on Human Rights) by means of secret surveillance and information gathering

directed at the applicants. As a consequence of this case the Government secured the passage of the Security Service Act 1989, which places the Service on a statutory basis and creates a Tribunal to deal with complaints against the organisation.

4. During the Gulf War of early 1991, the Home Secretary decided to deport a number of Iraqis and other Arab persons living in the United Kingdom, on the grounds that their continued presence was not conducive to national security. In one instance a Lebanese citizen, who had lived in the United Kingdom for 15 years, sought judicial review of the Home Secretary's decision arguing, *inter alia*, that the denial of legal representation before the three advisers and the provision of less than full particulars of the allegations against him violated natural justice. Lord Donaldson M.R. emphasised the limited role of the courts in reviewing matters of national security: "... the responsibility is exclusively that of the government of the day, but its powers are limited by statute and the courts will intervene if it is shown that the minister responsible has acted otherwise than in good faith or has in any way overstepped the limitations upon his authority which are imposed by the law" (p. 334). His Lordship rejected the appellant's contentions by noting that, "... natural justice has to take account of realities and something which would otherwise constitute a breach is not to be so considered if it is unavoidable" (p. 335): *R.* v. *Secretary of State for the Home Department, ex p. Cheblak* [1991] 2 All E.R. 319. See I. Leigh, [1991] P.L. 331.

(ii) Withholding of Confidential Information

R. v. GAMING BOARD FOR GREAT BRITAIN, ex p. BENAIM AND KHAIDA

[1970] 2 Q.B. 417; [1970] 2 W.L.R. 1009; 114 S.J. 266; [1970] 2 All E.R. 528 (Court of Appeal)

The Gaming Act 1968 prohibited gaming except in premises licensed for this purpose by the justices. Before any person could apply for a licence he had to obtain a "certificate of consent" from the Gaming Board, a body set up by the 1968 Act. The present applicants, the joint managing directors of Crockford's gaming club, applied unsuccessfully for a certificate. The board declined to give reasons for the refusal. In particular they refused to specify the matters which troubled them. The applicants sought certiorari to quash the refusal, and mandamus to compel the board to give sufficient information to enable them to answer the case against them.

LORD DENNING M.R.: ... To what extent are the board bound by the rules of natural justice? That is the root question before us. Their jurisdiction is country wide. They have to keep under review the extent and character of gaming in Great Britain: see s.10(3). Their particular task in regard to Crockford's is to see if the applicants are fit to run a gaming club: and if so, to give a certificate of consent.

Their duty is set out in Schedule 2, para. 4(5) and (6):

> "... (5) ... the board shall have regard only to the question whether, in their opinion, the applicant is likely to be capable of, and diligent in, securing that the provisions of this Act and of any regulations made

> under it will be complied with, that gaming on those premises will be fairly and properly conducted, and that the premises will be conducted without disorder or disturbance.
>
> "(6) For the purposes of sub-paragraph (5) . . . the board shall in particular take into consideration the character, reputation and financial standing—(*a*) of the applicant, and (*b*) of any person (other than the applicant) by whom . . . the club . . . would be managed, or for whose benefit . . . that club would be carried on, but may also take into consideration any other circumstances appearing to them to be relevant in determining whether the applicant is likely to be capable of, and diligent in, securing the matters mentioned in that sub-paragraph."

Note also that Schedule 1, paragraph 7, gives the board power to regulate their own procedure. Accordingly the board have laid down an outline procedure which they put before us. It is too long to read in full. So I will just summarise it. It says that the board will give the applicant an opportunity of making representations to the board, and will give him the best indications possible of the matters that are troubling them. Then there are these two important sentences:

> "In cases where the *source* or *content* of this *information* is *confidential*, the board accept that they are obliged to withhold particulars of the disclosure of which would be a breach of confidence inconsistent with their statutory duty and the public interest. . . ."
>
> "In the course of the interview the applicant will be made aware, to the greatest extent to which this is consistent with the board's statutory duty and the public interest, of the matters that are troubling the board."

Mr. Quintin Hogg criticised that outline procedure severely. He spoke as if Crockford's were being deprived of a right of property or of a right to make a living. He read his client's affidavit saying that "Crockford's has been established for over a century and is a gaming club with a worldwide reputation for integrity and respectability," with assets and goodwill valued at £185,000. He said that they ought not to be deprived of this business without knowing the case they had to meet. He criticised especially the way in which the board proposed to keep that confidential information. He relied on some words of mine in *Kanda* v. *Government of Malaya* [1962] A.C. 322, 337, when I said "that the judge or whoever has to adjudicate must not hear evidence or receive representations from one side behind the back of the other."

Mr. Hogg put his case, I think, too high. It is an error to regard Crockford's as having any right of which they are being deprived. They have not had in the past, and they have not now, any right to play these games of chance—roulette, chemin-de-fer, baccarat and the like—for their own profit. What they are really seeking is a privilege—almost, I might say, a franchise—to carry on gaming for profit, a thing never hitherto allowed in this country. It is for them to show that they are fit to be trusted with it.

If Mr. Hogg went too far on his side, I think Mr. Kidwell went too far on the other. He submitted that the Gaming Board are free to grant or refuse a certificate as they please. They are not bound, he says, to obey the rules of natural justice any more than any other executive body, such as, I suppose, the Board of Trade, which grant industrial development certificates, or the Television Authority, which awards television programme contracts. I cannot accept this view. I think the Gaming Board are bound to observe the rules of natural justice. The question is: What are those rules?

It is not possible to lay down rigid rules as to when the principles of natural justice are to apply: nor as to their scope and extent. Everything depends on the subject-matter: see what Tucker L.J. said in *Russell* v. *Norfolk (Duke of)* [1949] 1 All E.R. 109, 118 and Lord Upjohn in *Durayappah* v. *Fernando* [1967] 2 A.C. 337, 349. At one time it was said that the principles only apply to judicial proceedings and not to administrative proceedings. That heresy was scotched in *Ridge* v. *Baldwin* [1964] A.C. 40. At another time it was said that the principles do not apply to the grant or revocation of licences. That too is wrong. *R.* v. *Metropolitan Police Commissioner, ex p. Parker* [1953] 1 W.L.R. 1150 and *Nakkuda Ali* v. *Jayaratne* [1951] A.C. 66 are no longer authority for any such proposition. See what Lord Reid and Lord Hodson said about them in *Ridge* v. *Baldwin* [1964] A.C. 40, 77–79, 133.

So let us sheer away from those distinctions and consider the task of this Gaming Board and what they should do. The best guidance is, I think, to be found by reference to the cases of immigrants. They have no right to come in, but they have a right to be heard. The principle in that regard was well laid down by Lord Parker C.J. in *In re H. K. (An Infant)* [1967] 2 Q.B. 617. He said, at p. 630:

> "... even if an immigration officer is not in a judicial or quasi-judicial capacity, he must at any rate give the immigrant an opportunity of satisfying him of the matters in the subsection, and for that purpose let the immigrant know what his immediate impression is so that the immigrant can disabuse him. That is not, as I see it, a question of acting or being required to act judicially, but of being required to act fairly."

Those words seem to me to apply to the Gaming Board. The statute says in terms that in determining whether to grant a certificate, the board "shall have regard only" to the matters specified. It follows, I think, that the board have a duty to act fairly. They must give the applicant an opportunity of satisfying them of the matters specified in the subsection. They must let him know what their impressions are so that he can disabuse them. But I do not think that they need quote chapter and verse against him as if they were dismissing him from an office, as in *Ridge* v. *Baldwin* [1964] A.C. 40; or depriving him of his property, as in *Cooper* v. *Wandsworth Board of Works* (1863) 14 C.B.N.S. 180. After all, they are not charging him with doing anything wrong. They are simply inquiring as to his capability and diligence and are having regard to his character, reputation and financial standing. They are there to protect the public interest, to see that persons running the gaming clubs are fit to be trusted.

Seeing the evils that have led to this legislation, the board can and should investigate the credentials of those who make application to them. They can and should receive information from the police in this country or abroad who know something of them. They can, and should, receive information from any other reliable source. Much of it will be confidential. But that does not mean that the applicants are not to be given a chance of answering it. They must be given the chance, subject to this qualification: I do not think they need tell the applicant the source of their information, if that would put their informant in peril or otherwise be contrary to the public interest. Even in a criminal trial, a witness cannot be asked who is his informer. The reason was well given by Lord Eyre C.J. in *Hardy's* case [*R.* v. *Hardy*] 24 State Trials 199, 808:

> "... there is a rule which has universally obtained on account of its importance to the public for the detection of crimes, that those persons who are the channel by means of which that detection is made, should not be unnecessarily disclosed."

And Buller J. added, at p. 818: "... if you call for the name of the informer in such cases, no man will make a discovery, and public justice will be defeated." That rule was emphatically reaffirmed in *Attorney-General* v. *Briant* (1846) 15 M. & W. 169 and *Marks* v. *Beyfus* (1890) 25 Q.B.D. 494. That reasoning applies with equal force to the inquiries made by the Gaming Board. That board was set up by Parliament to cope with disreputable gaming clubs and to bring them under control. By bitter experience it was learned that these clubs had a close connection with organised crime, often violent crime, with protection rackets and with strong-arm methods. If the Gaming Board were bound to disclose their sources of information, no one would "tell" on those clubs, for fear of reprisals. Likewise with the details of the information. If the board were bound to disclose every detail, that might itself give the informer away and put him in peril. But, without disclosing every detail, I should have thought that the board ought in every case to be able to give to the applicant sufficient indication of the objections raised against him such as to enable him to answer them. That is only fair. And the board must at all costs be fair. If they are not, these courts will not hesitate to interfere.

Accepting that the board ought to do all this when they come to give their decision, the question arises, are they bound to give their reasons? I think not. Magistrates are not bound to give reasons for their decisions:

see *R.* v. *Northumberland Compensation Appeal Tribunal, ex p. Shaw* [1952] 1 K.B. 338, at p. 352. Nor should the Gaming Board be bound. After all, the only thing that they have to give is their *opinion* as to the capability and diligence of the applicant. If they were asked by the applicant to give their reasons, they could answer quite sufficiently: "In our opinion, you are not likely to be capable of or diligent in the respects required of you." Their opinion would be an end of the matter.

Tested by those rules, applying them to this case, I think that the Gaming Board acted with complete fairness. They put before the applicants all the information which led them to doubt their suitability. They kept the sources secret, but disclosed all the information. Sir Stanley Raymond said so in his affidavit: and it was not challenged to any effect. The board gave the applicants full opportunity to deal with the information. And they came to their decision. There was nothing whatever at fault with their decision of January 9, 1970. They did not give their reasons. But they were not bound to do so.

But then complaint is made as to what happened afterwards. It was said that the board did not pin-point the matters on which they thought the explanations were not satisfactory. They did not say which of the matters (a) to (e) they were not satisfied about. But I do not see anything unfair in that respect. It is not as if they were making any charges against the applicants. They were only saying they were not satisfied. They were not bound to give any reasons for their misgivings. And when they did give some reasons, they were not bound to submit to cross-examination on them.

Finally, complaint was made that the board refused to consider a new or amended application in respect of these premises of Crockford's in the current round. They refused to consider applications in other names or in new names. But here again I see nothing unfair. Crockford's had full opportunity of putting their application in the first instance. If there had been a technical defect in it, I feel sure that the board would have allowed an amendment. But if the application fails in matters of substance, that should be the end of it. There must be an end to the claim to "cut and come again."

In all the circumstances I think that all the criticisms of the board's conduct fail, and in my opinion the application should be dismissed.

LORD WILBERFORCE and PHILLIMORE L.J. agreed.

Application dismissed.

Notes

1. The doctrine of Public Interest Immunity may also be invoked by bodies performing some public function to justify the withholding of confidential information during the course of legal proceedings. For an account of this doctrine see, de Smith and Brazier, *Constitutional and Administrative Law*, 6th ed. (1989), p. 636,

and for the application of this doctrine to the work of the Gaming Board see *R.* v. *Lewes JJ., ex p. Secretary of State for Home Department* [1973] A.C. 388.

2. See comments by H. W. R. Wade, (1970) 86 L.Q.R. 309, and S. A. de Smith, [1970] C.L.J. 177. The decision was applied by Glidewell J. in *R.* v. *Bristol City Council, ex p. Pearce*, above, p. 513.

(iii) Emergency Action

R. v. SECRETARY OF STATE FOR TRANSPORT, ex p. PEGASUS HOLDINGS (LONDON) LTD. AND ANOTHER

[1988] 1 W.L.R. 990; [1989] 2 All E.R. 481 (Schiemann J.)

The applicant companies provided foreign holidays from the United Kingdom and used aircraft chartered from a Romanian organisation and flown by a Romanian crew. In order for the Romanian aircraft and crew to be allowed to operate such holiday flights from the United Kingdom they had received a permit from the Secretary of State granted under the authority of the Air Navigation Order 1985, Article 83. Article 62 of the Order empowered the Transport Secretary to provisionally suspend permits if he thought fit, pending a full investigation of the matter. During the middle of July 1987, five Romanian pilots voluntarily undertook flying tests conducted by the British Civil Aviation Authority; all these pilots failed the test (four displayed an inability to manoeuvre the aircraft). On July 29 at midday, the Department of Transport received a letter from the C.A.A., informing them of these test results. During the ensuing afternoon the Department alerted the applicants to the concerns of the C.A.A. On July 30 the Secretary of State signed provisional suspension orders (made under Article 62) regarding the Romanians' permit to operate the holiday charter flights from the United Kingdom. This decision caused the applicant package holiday company great difficulties in transporting its customers. The applicants sought a judicial review of the decision of the Transport Secretary, claiming, *inter alia*, that the suspension orders had been made in breach of the requirements of natural justice.

SCHIEMANN J.: . . . So far as the law is concerned, I do not think that there is anything between the parties as to the principles to be applied. These are conveniently set out in the leading case of *Wiseman* v. *Borneman* [1971] A.C. 297, where Lord Guest, at p. 311, cites an earlier judgment by Tucker L.J. in *Russell* v. *Duke of Norfolk* [1949] 1 All E.R. 109, 118 in which Tucker L.J. opined:

> "There are, in my view, no words which are of universal application to every kind of inquiry and every kind of domestic tribunal. The requirements of natural justice must depend on the circumstances of the case, the nature of the inquiry, the rules under which the tribunal is acting, the subject-matter that is being dealt with, and so forth. Accordingly, I do not derive much assistance from the definitions of natural justice which have been from time to time used, but, whatever standard is adopted, one essential is that the person concerned should have a reasonable opportunity of presenting his case."

Mr. Flint accepts that the opportunity to state a case can in certain circumstances be excluded in relation to such provisional matters as those with which I am concerned but says that they should not be excluded unless the situation genuinely demands it.

Mr. Pannick referred me to a Court of Appeal case, *Lewis* v. *Heffer* [1978] 1 W.L.R. 1061, where there are discussions in the various unreserved judgments delivered by the court that are not precisely to the same effect in what they say. In particular, he drew my attention to the following comments of Lord Denning M.R., at p. 1073. After having quoted Megarry J. in *John* v. *Rees* [1970] Ch. 345 where he had said, at p. 397:

> "suspension is merely expulsion *pro tanto*. Each is penal, and each deprives the member concerned of the enjoyment of his rights of membership or office. Accordingly, in my judgment the rules of natural justice *prima facie* apply to any such process of suspension in the same way that they apply to expulsion."

Lord Denning M.R. went on to say:

> "Those words apply, no doubt, to suspensions which are inflicted by way of punishment: as for instance when a member of the Bar is suspended from practice for six months, or when a solicitor is suspended from practice. But they do not apply to suspensions which are made, as a holding operation, pending inquiries. Very often irregularities are disclosed in a government department or in a business house: and a man may be suspended on full pay pending inquiries. Suspicion may rest on him: and so he is suspended until he is cleared of it. No one, so far as I know, has ever questioned such a suspension on the ground that it could not be done unless he is given notice of the charge and an opportunity of defending himself and so forth. The suspension in such a case is merely done by way of good administration. A situation has arisen in which something must be done at once. The work of the department or the office is being affected by rumours and suspicions. The others will not trust the man. In order to get back to proper work, the man is suspended. At that stage the rules of natural justice do not apply: . . ."

It is right to point out that the other Lords Justices tend not to go quite as far as Lord Denning M.R. in that formulation.

In the present case, I am content to proceed on the basis that the rules of natural justice do apply but that, in the words chosen by Mr. Pannick, in such an emergency as the present, with a provisional suspension being all that one is concerned with, one is at the low end of the duties of fairness. Mr. Pannick referred me in the course of his submissions on this point to *R.* v. *Civil Aviation Authority, ex p. Northern Air Taxis Ltd.* [1976] 1 Lloyd's Rep. 344. That case, which was a Divisional Court case, was concerned with matters not dissimilar in some ways to the present. Natural justice as such was not argued; the matters were dealt with on the basis of the statutory requirements, but undoubtedly the result does lend some support to the view that, when one is dealing with this type of situation, not much is required of the Secretary of State in order to act fairly.

The way the case is put by Mr. Flint is this. He says that in the present case the Secretary of State could not reasonably decline to afford Tarom[1] a short period to put its case as to why the permit should not be suspended, having regard to a number of matters that Mr. Flint identified. One of these is the lack of action on the letter of July 14, which I have read. As I have indicated, I regard that letter as irrelevant. A second matter to which Mr. Flint drew my attention in this context was the time that the C.A.A. took to refer the matter, which he said was some indication as to its view of the urgency. I have set out the relevant dates. It is clear that the failing of the tests took place on July 17, and the Secretary of State was not informed until July 29. That may or may not be a legitimate criticism of the C.A.A., but in my judgment, so far as the action of the Secretary of State is concerned, it cannot be regarded as unfair in the circumstances of this case that he acted in the speedy way in which he did act. One has in the context of unfairness to bear in mind, on the one hand, the no doubt substantial economic damage to the applicants and perhaps the irritation and inconvenience that I do not doubt the passengers suffered. On the other hand, one has to bear in mind the magnitude of the risk, by which I mean not so much the high percentage chance of it happening but the disastrous consequences of what would happen if something did happen. It is the old problem that one has with installations of nuclear power, or vehicles such as aeroplanes carrying a large number of people, that, if something goes wrong, then very many lives will be lost. While I do not doubt that different people, and maybe different Secretaries of State, would react differently to the same basic material, I am not prepared to say that the failure of the Secretary of State to permit more by way of representations than I have indicated took place was a breach of the rules of natural justice. . . .

Application dismissed.

Note

Apart from the need to take emergency action, another factor present in the above case was the nature of the decision being taken,—*i.e.* to suspend *provisionally* the Romanians' permit. Other cases indicate that where the challenged decision is a preliminary determination, which will be subject to a more detailed later consideration, then the full rigour of the *audi alteram partem* principle may not be invoked against the procedures leading up to the preliminary decision. For example in *Pearlberg* v. *Varty* [1972] 1 W.L.R. 534, a taxpayer asserted that the Inland Revenue were obliged to give him a fair hearing prior to seeking to make tax assessments on him. The House of Lords rejected his claims and Lord Hailsham L.C. stated:

[1] The Romanian organisation which owned and operated the aircraft.

"the third factor which affects my mind is the consideration that the decision, once made, does not make any final determination of the rights of the taxpayer. It simply enables the inspector to raise an assessment, by satisfying the commissioner that there are reasonable grounds for suspecting loss of tax resulting from neglect, fraud, or wilful default, that is that there is a *prima facie* probability that there has been neglect, etc., and that the Crown may have lost by it. When the assessment is made, the taxpayer can appeal against it, and, on the appeal, may raise any question, (*inter alia*) which would have been relevant on the application for leave, except that the leave given should be discharged."

Question

In what other decision-making contexts should emergency action be permitted to limit the right to a fair hearing?

(iv) Failings of the Individual's Legal Advisers

AL-MEHDAWI v. SECRETARY OF STATE FOR THE HOME DEPARTMENT

[1990] 1 A.C. 876; [1989] 3 All E.R. 843 (House of Lords)

The respondent was an Iraqi citizen who was refused a further extension of his leave to remain in the United Kingdom during May 1984. In March 1985 the respondent was notified that the Home Secretary had decided to make a deportation order against him. The respondent instructed solicitors to appeal against the deportation decision. The solicitors were notified of the hearing date for the appeal before an immigration adjudicator; however, neither they nor the respondent attended the appeal. Consequently, the adjudicator determined the appeal on the basis of the documents before him and dismissed the appeal. There was no appeal lodged against the adjudicator's decision within the statutory time limits. Subsequently, it emerged that the respondent's solicitors had sent notice of the hearing date and the Adjudicator's decision to a previous address of the respondent (even though they knew his current one) with the result that he had received no information regarding the appellate proceedings. The respondent sought judicial review of the Adjudicator's decision on the ground that there had been a breach of the rules of natural justice in that he had been denied a hearing. The High Court granted his application and the Court of Appeal affirmed that decision. The Home Secretary appealed to the House of Lords.

LORD BRIDGE OF HARWICH: . . . The appeal raises a question of great importance with respect to the scope of the remedy by order of certiorari to quash the decision of an inferior tribunal. Does certiorari lie to quash a decision given without hearing the applicant for certiorari when the tribunal giving the decision has acted correctly in the procedure adopted but the applicant was deprived of the opportunity to put his case by the negligence of his own legal advisers or otherwise without personal fault on the part of the applicant. This question had been considered once before by the Court of Appeal in *R. v. Diggines, ex p. Rahmani* [1985] 1 Q.B. 1109. That was another case relating to the decision of an adjudicator under the Act of 1971 who was mistakenly informed by the United Kingdom Immigrants Advisory Service ("U.K.I.A.S."), acting for the appellant, that they had no instructions. The Court of Appeal quashed the decision on the ground of a denial of natural justice to the appellant arising from the fault of the U.K.I.A.S. The Court of Appeal proceeded on the assumption that there had been no error of procedure by the adjudicator. However, when *ex p. Rahmani* came before your Lordships' House on appeal the House held that the question decided by the Court of Appeal did not arise and dismissed the appeal on the ground that the adjudicator had erred in determining the appeal without a hearing in reliance on rule 12(*c*) of the Immigration Appeals (Procedure) Rules 1972 (S.I. 1972 No. 1684), the rules then in force, since there was no material before the adjudicator which justified him in finding under that sub-rule that no person was authorised to represent the appellant at the hearing. In the instant case, by contrast, no criticism is, nor could be, made of the procedure adopted by the adjudicator in hearing and determining the appeal in the absence of the appellant in the exercise of the express discretion conferred on him by rule 34(2) of the Rules of 1984. . . .

The central submission made by Mr. Laws, for the Secretary of State, is that the so-called rules of natural justice are concerned solely with the propriety of the procedure adopted by the decision maker. In particular, the rule expressed in the Latin maxim *audi alteram partem* requires no more than that the decision maker should afford to any party to a dispute an opportunity to present his case. This view certainly receives support from many classic statements of the doctrine. The duty "fairly to hear both sides" is described by Lord Loreburn L.C. in *Board of Education* v. *Rice* [1911] A.C. 179, 182 as "a duty lying upon every one who decides anything." In *Ridge* v. *Baldwin* [1964] A.C. 41, 64, Lord Reid said of the watch committee who had dismissed the chief constable without a hearing:

> "Before attempting to reach any decision they were bound to inform him of the grounds on which they proposed to act and give him a fair opportunity of being heard in his own defence."

. . . Mr. Laws submits that the very concept of impropriety in the procedure by which a decision is reached necessarily connotes an irregularity in the conduct of the proceedings by the decision maker. Conversely, a failure by the legal adviser or any other agent to whom a party to any proceedings has entrusted the conduct of his case, being beyond the knowledge and control of the decision maker, cannot involve either any procedural impropriety or the breach of any duty which the decision maker owes to that party.

However, the authority on which Sir Charles Fletcher-Cooke [counsel for the respondent] relies, and which persuaded the Court of Appeal that the procedural impropriety involved in a breach of the rules of natural justice could not be confined to errors on the part of the decision-making body, is *R.* v. *Leyland Justices, ex p. Hawthorn* [1979] Q.B. 283. In that case the driver of one of two cars involved in a collision had been prosecuted and convicted for driving without due care and attention. The police had taken statements from two witnesses of the accident, but these witnesses were not called by the prosecution and their existence was not disclosed to the defence. The driver successfully applied for an order of certiorari to quash the conviction. Delivering the first judgment Lord Widgery C.J. said, at p. 286:

> "There is no doubt that an application can be made by certiorari to set aside an order on the basis that the tribunal failed to observe the rules of natural justice. Certainly if it were the fault of the justices that this additional evidentiary information was not passed on, no difficulty would arise. But the problem—and one can put it in a sentence—is that certiorari in respect of breach of the rules of natural justice is primarily a remedy sought on account of an error of the tribunal, and here, of course, we are not concerned with an error of the tribunal; we are concerned with an error of the police prosecutors. Consequently, amongst the arguments to which we have listened an argument has been that this is not a certiorari case at all on any of the accepted grounds.
>
> "We have given this careful thought over the short adjournment because it is a difficult case in that the consequences of the decision either way have their unattractive features. However, if fraud, collusion, perjury and such-like matters not affecting the tribunal themselves justify an application for certiorari to quash the conviction, if all those matters are to have that effect, then we cannot say that the failure of the prosecution which in this case has prevented the tribunal from giving the defendant a fair trial should not rank in the same category.
>
> "We have come to the conclusion that there was here a clear denial of natural justice. Fully recognising the fact that the blame falls on the prosecutor and not on the tribunal, we think that it is a matter which should result in the conviction being quashed. In my judgment, that is the result to which we should adhere."

This decision was followed in *R.* v. *Blundeston Prison Board of Visitors, ex p. Fox-Taylor* [1982] 1 All E.R. 646.

Though I do not question the correctness of the decision in *Ex p. Hawthorn* [1979] Q.B. 283, I do question whether it is correctly classified as a case depending on either procedural impropriety or a breach of the rules of natural justice. Certainly there was unfairness in the conduct of the proceedings, but this was because of a failure by the prosecutor, in breach of a duty owed to the court and to the defence, to disclose the existence of witnesses who could have given evidence favourable to the defence. Although no dishonesty was suggested, it was this *suppressio veri* which had the same effect as a *suggestio falsi* in distorting and vitiating the process leading to conviction, and it was, in my opinion, the analogy which Lord Widgery C.J. drew between the case before him and the cases of fraud, collusion and perjury which had been relied on in counsel's argument, which identified the true principle on which the decision could be justified.

In any event, *Ex p. Hawthorn*, if it is relied on as an authority to support the conclusion of the Court of Appeal in *Ex p. Rahmani* [1985] Q.B. 1109 and the instant case, proves too much. If unfairness resulting from a failure by the prosecutor to disclose the names of witnesses, so that the defence is deprived of their evidence, is taken as a precedent for allowing certiorari on the ground of a failure in the conduct of proceedings by the defendant's own legal advisers, the logic of the argument would lead to the conclusion that a negligent failure by the defendant's own legal advisers to secure the attendance of necessary defence witnesses would entitle the defendant to have his conviction quashed if he was personally free of blame for the failure. But this was a conclusion which Sir Charles Fletcher-Cooke rightly declined to support. . . .

But there are many familiar situations where one party to litigation will effectively lose the opportunity to have his case heard through the failure of his own legal advisers, but will be left with no remedy at all except against those legal advisers. I need only instance judgments signed in default, actions dismissed for want of a prosecution and claims which are not made within a fixed time limit which the tribunal has no power to extend. In each of these situations a litigant who wishes his case to be heard and who has fully instructed his solicitor to take the necessary steps may never in fact be heard because of his solicitor's neglect and through no fault of his own. But in any of these cases it would surely be fanciful to say that there had been a breach of the *audi alteram partem* rule. Again, take the case of a county court action where a litigant fails to appear at the hearing because his solicitor has neglected to inform him of the date and consequently judgment is given against him. He can at best invite the court in its discretion to set aside the judgment and it is likely to do so only on the terms that he should pay the costs thrown away. Yet, if it can be said that he has been denied natural justice, he ought in principle to be able to apply for certiorari to quash the judgment which, if he is personally blameless, should be granted as a matter of course.

These considerations lead me to the conclusion that a party to a dispute who has lost the opportunity to have his case heard through the default of his own advisers to whom he has entrusted the conduct of the dispute on his behalf cannot complain that he has been the victim of a procedural impropriety or that natural justice has been denied to him, at all events when the subject-matter of the dispute raises issues of private law between citizens. Is there any principle which can be invoked to lead to a different conclusion where the issue is one of public law and where the decision taken is of an administrative character rather than the resolution of a *lis inter partes*? I cannot discover any such principle and none has been suggested in the course of argument. . . .

But I would add that, if once unfairness suffered by one party to a dispute in consequence of some failure by his own advisers in relation to the conduct of the relevant proceedings was admitted as a ground on which the High Court in the exercise of its supervisory jurisdiction over inferior tribunals could quash the relevant decision, I can discern no principle which could be invoked to distinguish between a "fundamental unfairness," which would justify the exercise of the jurisdiction, and a less than fundamental unfairness, which would not. Indeed, Sir Charles Fletcher-Cooke was constrained to rest on the proposition that, in the last analysis, it was all a matter of discretion and the court could be trusted only to exercise its discretion in extreme cases where justice demanded a remedy. I am of the opinion that the decision of the Court of Appeal can only be supported at the cost of opening such a wide door which would indeed seriously undermine the principle of finality in decision making.

The effect of this conclusion in a deportation case may appear harsh, though no harsher than the perhaps more common case when an immigrant's solicitor fails to give notice of appeal under section 15 within the time limited by rule 4 of the Rules of 1984. But it is perhaps worth pointing out that in neither case is the immigrant left wholly without a remedy. In the case of a notice of appeal served out of time, the Secretary of State has a discretion under rule 5 to extend the time "if he is of the opinion that, by reason of special circumstances, it is just and right so to do." In the case where the immigrant has failed to attend the hearing of his appeal to the adjudicator and the appeal has been heard and dismissed in his absence, the Secretary of State has the discretion conferred on him by section 21 of the Act whereby he "may at any time refer for consideration under this section any matter relating to the case which was not before the adjudicator." If such a reference is made, the adjudicator is required by section 21(2) to "consider the matter which is the subject of the reference and report to the Secretary of State the opinion of the adjudicator . . . thereon." It would, as it seems to me, certainly be open to the Secretary of State, if persuaded that the merits of a case required it, to invite an adjudicator to hear the oral evidence of an appellant whose appeal had, through no fault of his own, been dismissed in his absence, and to report his opinion whether this evidence would have affected the outcome of the appeal.

I would allow the appeal, set aside the orders of MacPherson J. and the Court of Appeal and restore the determination of the adjudicator.

LORDS ROSKILL, BRANDON OF OAKBROOK, OLIVER OF AYLMERTON and GOFF OF CHIEVELEY agreed with the speech given by LORD BRIDGE.

Appeal allowed.

Notes

1. The above decision has been criticised for unduly circumscribing the application of the *audi alteram partem* principle. One critic has suggested the following approach:

"By drawing on the theory that natural justice—and judicial review as a whole—is vitally concerned with setting standards for public authorities and structuring the exercise of public power, it is suggested that the House of Lords should have held that certiorari for breach of natural justice could lie although a tribunal was not responsible for the defect, but only where responsibility for the procedural impropriety can be attributed to a body exercising public authority: either the prosecutor (in a criminal case) or a party to an adversarial process with a public law function (for example, the Home Office in proceedings before the immigration adjudicator). Such a view recognises the strong argument in favour of finality of litigation, but holds that finality should not override the importance of natural justice in "policing" public power . . ."

(J. Herberg, "The Right to a Hearing: Breach Without Fault?" [1990] P.L. 467 at pp. 474–475)

2. *Ex p. Hawthorn* was applied, and *Al-Mehdawi* distinguished, in *R.* v. *Bolton JJ., ex p. Scally* [1991] 2 All E.R. 619, where the Divisional Court quashed convictions for driving with excess alcohol based on scientific evidence subsequently shown to be flawed. There had been no dishonesty, but the prosecutor had "corrupted the process leading to conviction in a manner which was unfair."

(v) The Making of Legislation

BATES v. LORD HAILSHAM OF ST. MARYLEBONE AND OTHERS

[1972] 1 W.L.R. 1373; 116 S.J. 584; [1972] 2 All E.R. 1019 (Megarry J.)

Mr. Bates was a solicitor and a leading member of the British Legal Association, to which about 2,900 of the 26,000 solicitors with practising certificates belonged. On May 1, 1972, the Lord Chancellor announced at a Press conference that the scale fees for conveyancing work prescribed under Schedule 1 to the Solicitors' Remuneration Order 1883, would be replaced by a *quantum meruit* system. The British Legal Association sent a circular to all solicitors opposing the changes. The Law Society received a draft order for the implementation of the changes from the Lord Chancellor's department as required by the Solicitors' Act 1957, s.58(3). A period of one month was prescribed by section 56 for observations to be submitted to the statutory committee which would make the new order. The date of the meeting of the committee was fixed for July 19, at 4.30 p.m. On June 21, the draft order was published in the Law Society's Gazette. The British Legal Association sent submissions and letters to the committee on July 11 and 14, requesting postponement of the changes "for perhaps two months," and further consultations. On July 18, the Lord Chancellor wrote to the British Legal Association refusing their requests. The plaintiff the same day served a writ against the members of the committee. He contended that the draft order had been prepared by the Lord Chancellor's department and had not been considered by the committee. He claimed: (i) a declaration that any order made by the committee under section 56 would be *ultra vires* and void unless the draft had been considered by the committee and an opportunity had been given for representations on the order to be made by the British Legal Association and others; (ii) an injunction restraining the committee from making an order until these steps had been taken. At 2.00 p.m. on July 19, the plaintiff moved *ex parte* for an injunction to stop the committee making an order at its 4.30 p.m. meeting.

MEGARRY J.: . . . His [*i.e.* Counsel for the plaintiff's] two main points were, first, that if the order was made at the meeting of the committee, the committee would not be complying with its duty to act fairly. The committee, he said, would be exercising not judicial or quasi-judicial functions, but administrative functions; and where, as here, so vast a change was going to be made as the overturn of the entire basis of charging in conveyancing transactions, a basis that had lasted for nearly 90 years and affected a profession of some 26,000 spread throughout the country, it was not fair to make it without a substantially longer period for consultation and representations. His second point was one which he accepted as being technical; but in effect he said that it was advanced in a good cause. It was that it was implicit in section 56(3) that the draft of the order which was to be sent to the council of the Law Society must be a draft prepared or approved by the committee, and not, as appeared to be the case here, a draft prepared by or on behalf of the Lord Chancellor's department, without previous consultation with the committee.

On the first point, Mr. Nicholls relied on *R.* v. *Liverpool Corporation, ex p. Liverpool Taxi Fleet Operators' Association* [1972] 2 Q.B. 299 [above, p. 502]; and he read me some passages from the judgments of Lord Denning M.R. and Roskill L.J. It cannot often happen that words uttered by a judge in his judicial capacity will, within six months, be cited against him in his personal capacity as defendant; yet that is the position here. The case was far removed from the present case. It concerned the exercise by a city council of its powers to license hackney carriages, and a public undertaking given by the chairman of the relevant committee which the council soon proceeded to ignore. The case supports propositions relating to the duty of a body to act fairly when exercising administrative functions under a statutory power: see at pp. 307, 308 and 310. Accordingly, in deciding the policy to be applied as to the number of licences to grant, there was a duty to hear those who would be likely to be affected. It is plain that no legislation was involved: the question was one of the policy to be adopted in the exercise of a statutory power to grant licences.

In the present case, the committee in question has an entirely different function: it is legislative rather than administrative or executive. The function of the committee is to make or refuse to make a legislative instrument under delegated powers. The order, when made, will lay down the remuneration for solicitors generally; and the terms of the order will have to be considered and construed and applied in numberless cases in the future. Let me accept that in the sphere of the so-called quasi-judicial the rules of natural justice run, and that in the administrative or executive field there is a general duty of fairness. Nevertheless, these considerations do not seem to me to affect the process of legislation, whether primary or delegated. Many of those affected by delegated legislation, and affected very substantially, are never consulted in the process of enacting that legislation; and yet they have no remedy. Of course, the informal consultation of representative bodies by the legislative authority is a commonplace; but although a few statutes have specifically provided for a general process of publishing draft delegated legislation and considering objections (see, for example, the Factories Act 1961, Schedule 4), I do not know of any implied right to be consulted or make objections, or any principle upon which the courts may enjoin the legislative process at the suit of those who contend that insufficient time for consultation and consideration has been given. I accept that the fact that the order will take the form of a statutory instrument does not *per se* make it immune from attack, whether by injunction or otherwise; but what is important is not its form but its nature, which is plainly legislative.

There is a further point. The power in question in the *Liverpool Corporation* case [1972] 2 Q.B. 299 was a general power to "license . . . such number of hackney coaches or carriages . . . as they think fit" under section 37 of the Town Police Clauses Act 1847, with no special procedure laid down for the process of licensing. Here, Parliament has laid down the procedure to be followed. *Expressum facit cessare tacitum*. It is easier to imply procedural safeguards when Parliament has provided none than where Parliament has laid down a procedure, however inadequate its critics may consider it to be. Parliament has here provided that the committee must, before making any order, consider any observations in writing submitted to it by the council of the Law Society within one month of the draft having been sent to the council. What in effect the plaintiff is seeking to do is to add by implication a further requirement that if the draft will make momentous changes, more than a month must be allowed, and opportunities must be given for representations to be made by bodies other than the council of the Law Society. Mr. Nicholls understandably shrank from asserting that the process of consultation need go beyond any substantial organised body of solicitors, or that the committee need accede to a request for further time from any other body or persons. My difficulty is to see how even the organised bodies that he postulated can be implied into the subsection or imposed upon it. If the procedure laid down by Parliament is fairly and substantially followed, I cannot see that the committee need do more; and I see nothing in the evidence to suggest that the committee has not fully and fairly complied with the statutory requirements. . . .

[His Lordship then rejected the plaintiff's second point.]

Notes

1. The unwillingness of the judiciary to place common law procedural obligations upon legislative processes has been alluded to by the House of Lords. In a case involving the disciplinary powers of prison governors, Lord Oliver stated:

> "it is a public function which affects the liberty and, to a degree, the status of the persons affected by it. As such it must, as it seems to me, be subject to the

general common law principle which imposes a duty of procedural fairness when a public authority makes a decision *not of a legislative nature* affecting the rights, privileges and interests of individuals"

(emphasis added): *Leech* v. *Parkhurst Prison Deputy Governor* [1988] 1 All E.R. 485 at p. 509.

2. On consultation and delegated legislation see J. F. Garner, [1976] P.L. 307 and A. Jergesen, [1978] P.L. 290. More generally see the Chapter on delegated legislation below, p. 887, and above, p. 454 *et seq*.

3. Similarly, a local authority need not give an opportunity for persons to be heard before making a decision that is universal in its application such as the fixing by the authority of the rates for the year (now the level of community charge) or the scale on which fees are to be charged (*R.* v. *Greater London Council, ex p. The Rank Organisation Ltd., The Times*, February 19, 1982).

(c) Specific Aspects of the Right to a Fair Hearing in Particular Decision-Making Contexts

(i) Oral or Written Representations?

LLOYD AND OTHERS v. McMAHON

[1987] 1 A.C. 625; [1987] 1 All E.R. 1118 (House of Lords)

During 1984 Liverpool Council had delayed making a rate until July of that year. In April of 1985 the district auditor sent a report to the council expressing concern that a rate had not yet been made for 1985. On May 21 the district auditor sent a further report to the council in which he stated that unless a rate was made by the end of May he would commence action under the Local Government Act 1982, s.20, to recover any financial losses occasioned by the failure to make a rate from the members responsible for incurring them. On June 6 the Audit Commission ordered that an extraordinary audit of the council be carried out. The council made a rate on June 14. On June 26 the district auditor sent a notice to 42 councillors (who by their voting or absence might have failed to discharge their duties as councillors) stating that he had to consider whether to certify the sum of £106,103 as lost by their wilful misconduct. The individual councillors were informed that they could make written representations to the district auditor before he reached a decision. The councillors (assisted by the chief executive of the council) made a collective written response to the district auditor. They did not seek an oral hearing before the district auditor. In September 1985 the district auditor certified that the named councillors were jointly and severally liable for the above sum. The councillors appealed to the High Court (under section 20(3) of the Act) against the district auditor's decision. The High Court dismissed their appeal and that decision was confirmed by the Court of Appeal. The councillors then appealed to the House of Lords.

LORD KEITH OF KINKEL: . . . The argument by counsel for the appellants did not invite your Lordships to enter deeply into the merits of the question whether or not they had been guilty of wilful misconduct, nor was attention drawn to any details of the affidavits and other material placed before the Divisional Court. The substance of the argument was that the district auditor's decision had been vitiated by his failure to offer the appellants an oral hearing before reaching it, and should therefore have been quashed. The argument was supported by an examination of earlier legislation in regard to local government audits, starting with the Poor Law Amendment Act 1844 (7 & 8 Vict. c. 101), where oral hearings were the order of the day, and by reference to the Code of Local Government Audit Practice for England and Wales, made under section 14 of the Act of 1982 and approved by resolution of both Houses of Parliament. The code, by paragraphs 16 to 20, contemplates that an oral hearing will be held where the auditor is dealing with a notice of objection given under section 17(3) of the Act of 1982, which itself refers to the objector attending before the auditor. The code does not deal with the procedure to be followed where the auditor takes action under section 20(1). Counsel produced a list of all instances since 1972 where a district auditor had occasion to consider an issue of wilful misconduct, indicating that in all but one of them an oral hearing had been offered. This had the effect, so it was maintained, of creating a legitimate expectation on the part of the appellants that they would be offered an oral hearing before the district auditor arrived at his decision.

My Lords, if the district auditor had reached a decision adverse to the appellants without giving them any opportunity at all of making representations to him, there can be no doubt that his procedure would have been contrary to the rules of natural justice and that, subject to the question whether the defect was capable of being cured on appeal to the Divisional Court, the decision would fall to be quashed. In the event, written representations alone were asked for. These were duly furnished, in very considerable detail, and an oral hearing was not requested, though that could very easily have been done, and there is no reason to suppose that the request would not have been granted. None of the appellants stated, in his or her affidavit before the Divisional Court, that they had an expectation that an oral hearing, though not asked for, would be offered. The true question is whether the district auditor acted fairly in all the circumstances. It is easy to envisage cases where an oral hearing would clearly be essential in the interests of fairness, for example where an objector states that he has personal knowledge of some facts indicative of wilful misconduct on the part of a councillor. In that situation justice would demand that the councillor be given an opportunity to depone to his own version of the facts. In the present case the district auditor had arrived at his provisional view upon the basis of the contents of documents, minutes of meetings and reports submitted to the council from the auditor's department and their own officers. All these documents were appended to or referred to in the notice of June 26 sent by the district auditor to the appellants. Their response referred to other documents, which were duly considered by the district auditor, as is shown by his statement of reasons dated September 6, 1985. No facts contradictory of or supplementary to the contents of the documents were or are relied on by either side. If the appellants had attended an oral hearing they would no doubt have reiterated the sincerity of their motives from the point of view of advancing the interests of the inhabitants of Liverpool. It seems unlikely, having regard to the position adopted by their counsel on this matter before the Divisional Court, that they would have been willing to reveal or answer questions about the proceedings of their political caucus. The sincerity of the appellants' motives is not something capable of justifying or excusing failure to carry out a statutory duty, or of making reasonable what is otherwise an unreasonable delay in carrying out such a duty. In all the circumstances I am of opinion that the district auditor did not act unfairly, and that the procedure which he followed did not involve any prejudice to the appellants. . . .

Upon the view which I take, that the district auditor's decision was not vitiated by procedural unfairness, the question whether such unfairness, had it existed, was capable of being cured by the appeal to the High Court does not arise directly for decision. It is, however, my opinion that the particular appeal mechanism provided for by section 20(3) of the Act of 1982, considered in its context, is apt to enable the court, notwithstanding that it finds some procedural defect in the conduct of an audit which has resulted in a certificate based on wilful misconduct, to inquire into the merits of the case and arrive at its own decision thereon. Section 20(3)(*b*) empowers the court to "confirm the decision or quash it and give any certificate which the auditor could have given." The relevant rules of court enable a rehearing of the broadest possible scope to take place. Evidence may be given on oath, which is not possible before the auditor, and there is no limit to the further material which may be introduced so as to enable the whole merits to be fully examined. There is no question of the court being confined to a review of the evidence which was available to the auditor. . . .

I may add that I agree entirely with all that is said upon this aspect of the appeal in the speech of my noble and learned friend Lord Bridge of Harwich.

LORD BRIDGE OF HARWICH: My Lords, the so-called rules of natural justice are not engraved on tablets of stone. To use the phrase which better expresses the underlying concept, what the requirements of fairness demand when any body, domestic, administrative or judicial, has to make a decision which will affect the rights of individuals depends on the character of the decision-making body, the kind of decision it has to make and the statutory or other framework in which it operates. In particular, it is well-established that when a statute has conferred on any body the power to make decisions affecting individuals, the courts will not only require the procedure prescribed by the statute to be followed, but will readily imply so much and no more to be introduced by way of additional procedural safeguards as will ensure the attainment of fairness. . . .

I followed with interest Mr. Blom-Cooper's [counsel for the appellants] carefully researched review of the history of local government audit legislation, but I did not find that it threw any light on what, in particular, is required to provide such an opportunity in the circumstances of any particular case under the statute presently in force. Still less do I attach any significance to the fact that since 1972, when provisions substantially to the like effect as those which we find in the Act of 1982 first reached the Statute Book, auditors have, as a matter of practice, always invited oral representations from members of local authorities before certifying the amount of any loss or deficiency as due from them. When a single individual is thought to have failed to bring a sum into account or by his wilful misconduct to have caused a loss or deficiency, it is no doubt a very appropriate practice to invite his explanation orally. But I fail to understand how that practice can constrain the courts to construe the statute as requiring an auditor proposing to act under section 20 to invite oral representations as a matter of law in every case. . . .

The proposition that it was, *per se*, in breach of the rules of natural justice not to invite oral representations in this case is quite untenable. . . .

These conclusions would be sufficient to dispose of the appeals. But I return to the question of more general importance whether, if there had been any unfairness in the procedure followed by the auditor, this would necessarily have led, as the Divisional Court thought, to the quashing of the certificate or whether, as the Court of Appeal concluded, the full hearing of the appeal to the court on the merits was in law able to make good any deficiency in the auditor's procedure. It was in order to set this question in its proper context that I thought it necessary, earlier in this opinion, to set out the relevant statutory provisions *in extenso*. The question how far in domestic and administrative two-tier adjudicatory systems a procedural failure at the level of the first tier can be remedied at the level of the second tier was considered by the Privy Council in *Calvin* v. *Carr* [1980] A.C. 574 in which all the relevant previous authorities on the subject are reviewed. I do not find it necessary in this case to examine the general principles there discussed, nor would I think it appropriate in this case to seek to lay down any principles of general application. This is because the question arising in the instant case must be answered by considering the particular statutory provisions here applicable which establish an adjudicatory system in many respects quite unlike any that has come under examination in any of the decided cases to which we were referred. We are concerned with a point of statutory construction and nothing else. . . .

In every case it must be for the court, as a matter of discretion, to decide how in all the circumstances its jurisdiction under section 20(3) can best be exercised to meet the justice of the case. But I am clearly of opinion that when the court has, as here, in fact conducted a full hearing on the merits and reached a conclusion that the issue of a certificate was justified, it would be an erroneous exercise of discretion nevertheless to quash the certificate on the ground that, before the matter reached the court, there had been some defect in the procedure followed.

LORDS BRANDON and GRIFFITHS agreed. LORD TEMPLEMAN delivered a concurring speech.

Appeal dismissed.

Notes

1. The background to the process of district audit is considered in Chapter 2, above, p. 28.

2. A local fund was established to raise the moneys needed to discharge the councillors' legal liabilities. By 1990 the fund had collected such an amount.

3. The second limb of their Lordships' decision concerned the issue of "curative appeals" which is examined below (pp. 561–565) in the case of *Calvin* v. *Carr*.

4. On the oral hearing point see also *R.* v. *Army Board of the Defence Council, ex p. Anderson*, above, p. 499, applied in *R.* v. *Secretary of State for Health, ex p. Gandhi* [1991] 4 All E.R. 547, 556–577.

Question

How significant was it that none of the councillors asked for an oral hearing before the district auditor?

(ii) A Right to Legal Representation?

R. v. BOARD OF VISITORS OF H.M. PRISON, THE MAZE, ex p. HONE

[1988] 1 A.C. 379; [1988] 1 All E.R. 321 (House of Lords)

The appellant was a prisoner serving a life sentence in Northern Ireland. He was charged with an offence against discipline of assaulting a prison officer contrary to rule 31(5) of the Prison Rules (Northern Ireland) 1982. Because of the seriousness of the charge it was referred to the board of visitors for determination. The board found the charge proved (the appellant had pleaded not guilty) and sentenced him to 30 days' cellular confinement and a concurrent loss of privileges for 60 days. The appellant sought judicial review of the board's decision arguing, *inter alia*, that it was unlawful as he had been denied the right to legal representation before the board. The High Court dismissed the application and this decision was confirmed by the Court of Appeal. The appellant then appealed to the House of Lords.

This case was dealt with as a consolidated appeal together with a similar action brought by another prisoner, McCartan.

LORD GOFF OF CHIEVELEY: . . . Before your Lordships' House, the submissions on behalf of the appellants were as follows. The basic submission was that a convicted prisoner retains all his civil rights, except those which are taken away from him expressly or by necessary implication; and that an ordinary citizen charged with a criminal offence is entitled to legal representation before the tribunal which hears the charge against him. It was, however, accepted that, on an inquiry by the governor of a prison, a prisoner has no right to legal representation; such a right, it was submitted, applied only to hearings before boards of visitors, when the prisoner is charged with a criminal offence or the equivalent of a criminal offence.

... The first of the authorities is the decision of the Court of Appeal in *R.* v. *Assessment Committee of St. Mary Abbotts, Kensington* [1891] 1 Q.B. 378. In that case it was held that a householder who objected to a valuation list and wished his objection to be advanced before the assessment committee need not appear in person before the committee but could depute another person to do so on his behalf. This decision has been invoked on subsequent occasions in support of the proposition that any person appearing before a disciplinary tribunal is entitled to legal representation. The decision of the Court of Appeal in *Pett* v. *Greyhound Racing Association Ltd.* [1969] 1 Q.B. 125 appeared, at first sight, to give some credence to that proposition. In that case the plaintiff claimed the right to legal representation at an inquiry by the association into a disciplinary matter, concerned with a serious charge against the plaintiff relating to the circumstances in which a greyhound of his was withdrawn from a race, it being alleged that traces of barbiturates were found in the dog's urine. On an interlocutory appeal Lord Denning M.R., in holding that natural justice required that in matters affecting a man's reputation or livelihood or any matters of serious purport he should, if he wished, be legally represented, relied upon the *St. Mary Abbotts* case; and Russell L.J., at p. 135, referred to his "common law right" to be so represented. However, on the substantive hearing (*Pett* v. *Greyhound Racing Association Ltd. (No. 2)* [1970] 1 Q.B. 46), Lyell J. concluded that the only duty on the association was to observe the rules of natural justice, and distinguished the *St. Mary Abbotts* case as being concerned not with legal representation before a tribunal but with a man employing an agent to communicate with a body performing an administrative act. He said, at p. 63:

> "It appears to me that the Court of Appeal regarded the overseers as performing an administrative act in preparing the valuation lists ... It has, so far as I am aware, never been suggested that the valuation officer in considering such objections is acting otherwise than in an administrative capacity. In view of the many authorities that domestic tribunals are subject only to the duty of observing what are called the rules of natural justice and any procedure laid down or necessarily to be implied from the instrument that confers their power, I am unable to follow the views expressed by the Court of Appeal, that the plaintiff is entitled to appear by an agent unless such right was expressly negatived by the rules of the club."

Subsequent cases have proceeded on the same basis. Thus in *Enderby Town Football Club Ltd.* v. *Football Association Ltd.* [1971] Ch. 591, Lord Denning M.R. rejected the suggestion that a man who is charged before a domestic tribunal is entitled as of right to be legally represented; on the contrary, he regarded that matter as being within the discretion of the tribunal. A similar suggestion was rejected by the Court of Appeal in *Fraser* v. *Mudge* [1975] 1 W.L.R. 1132, which is very much in point in the present case. There a prisoner asked for an injunction to restrain a board of visitors from inquiring into a charge against him of assaulting a prison officer unless he was represented by a solicitor and counsel of his choice. The case therefore raised the question whether, in such circumstances, the prisoner was entitled to legal representation as of right. Chapman J. refused to grant the injunction, and his decision was affirmed by the Court of Appeal. Roskill L.J. said, at p. 1134:

> "The argument of Mr. Sedley, as I follow it, really involves that justice cannot be done or cannot at least be seen to be done by the defendants, the visitors, in this case unless there is legal representation of the plaintiff. I wish to make it plain that I do not subscribe to the view that in every type of case, irrespective of the nature or jurisdiction of the body in question, justice can neither be done nor be seen to be done without legal representation of the party or parties appearing before that body. Such a proposition to my mind is untenable. There are many bodies before which a party or parties can be required to appear but who can do justice and can be seen to do justice without the party against whom complaint is made being legally represented. Further, as Lord Denning M.R. has said, if the argument in relation to rule 49(2) of the Prison Rules 1964 were well founded, it would equally apply to complaints heard by the governor to which the same language applies, a proposition which I think is also untenable. One looks to see what are the broad principles underlying these rules. They are to maintain discipline in prison by proper, swift and speedy decisions, whether by the governor or the visitors; and it seems to me that the requirements of natural justice do not make it necessary that a person against whom disciplinary proceedings are pending should as of right be entitled to be represented by solicitors or counsel or both."

Subsequently, in *R.* v. *Secretary of State for the Home Department, ex p. Tarrant* [1985] Q.B. 251, a Divisional Court (consisting of Kerr L.J. and Webster J.) accepted *Fraser* v. *Mudge* as binding authority that, before a board of visitors, a prisoner charged with a disciplinary offence has no right to legal representation, though it was held that a board of visitors has a discretion to grant representation; and, in his full and careful judgment, Webster J. referred to considerations which he considered that every board of visitors should take into account when exercising its discretion whether to allow legal representation, or indeed the assistance of a friend or adviser, to a prisoner appearing before it on a disciplinary charge. . . .

In advancing his submissions for the appellants in the present case before your Lordships' House, Mr. Hill had of necessity to submit that the decision of the Court of Appeal in *Fraser* v. *Mudge* was wrong. In support of his submissions, which I have already summarised, he relied upon rule 30(2) of the Rules of 1982, which provides that at an inquiry into a charge against a prisoner he shall be given a full opportunity of presenting his own case. He stressed that a hearing before a board of visitors is a sophisticated hearing. In particular, he submitted, there is an oral hearing; a formal plea is entered; cross-examination is allowed and witnesses are called; the onus and standard of proof are the same as in a criminal trial; free legal aid is available; punishments are imposed; a plea in mitigation can be entered; and the board has greater powers of punishment than those exercised by magistrates' courts. He also, like others before him, invoked the *St. Mary Abbotts* case [1891] 1 Q.B. 378 as authority for the proposition that each appellant had a common law right to appoint a lawyer as his agent to appear before the board of visitors on his behalf.

I am unable to accept these submissions. I would first of all reject the argument founded upon the *St. Mary Abbotts* case as misconceived, for the very reasons given by Lyell J. in *Pett* v. *Greyhound Racing Association Ltd. (No. 2)* [1970] 1 Q.B. 46, 63, quoted above, that the case is not in point since it was concerned only with the making of a communication to an administrative body. But, so far as Mr. Hill's wider submissions are concerned, I am unable to accept his second proposition that any person charged with a crime (or the equivalent thereof) and liable to punishment is entitled as a matter of natural justice to legal representation. No doubt it is true that a man charged with a crime before a criminal court is entitled to legal representation—both before the Crown Court and (as a matter of statute) before a magistrates' court: see section 122 of the Magistrates' Courts Act 1980. . . . No doubt it is also correct that a board of visitors is bound to give effect to the rules of natural justice. But it does not follow that, simply because a charge before a disciplinary tribunal such as a board of visitors relates to facts which in law constitute a crime, the rules of natural justice require the tribunal to grant legal representation. Indeed, if this were the case, then, as Roskill L.J. pointed out in *Fraser* v. *Mudge* [1975] 1 W.L.R. 1132, exactly the same submission could be made in respect of disciplinary proceedings before the governor of a prison. Mr. Hill was at pains to escape from this conclusion by attempting to distinguish between a governor and a board of visitors, on the basis that there was no right of legal representation before the governor but an absolute right to legal representation before the board of visitors. I for my part am unable to accept this distinction. Each, both governor and board of visitors, is exercising a disciplinary jurisdiction; and, as the Rules of 1982 clearly demonstrate, each may do so in respect of offences against discipline which could in law constitute criminal offences. Each must also be bound by the rules of natural justice. The difference between them is not so much a legal as a practical difference. The jurisdiction exercised by the governor is of a more summary nature, and should properly be exercised with great expedition; furthermore the punishments which he can award are limited to those set out in rule 32 of the Rules of 1982, though he can refer the matter to the Secretary of State (and, through him, to a board of visitors) under rule 33(1)(*e*) if he considers that it may be desirable that a more severe punishment should be awarded. In the nature of things, it is difficult to imagine that the rules of natural justice would ever require legal representation before the governor. But though the rules of natural justice may require legal representation before a board of visitors, I can see no basis for Mr. Hill's submission that they should do so in every case as of right. Everything must depend on the circumstances of the particular case, as is amply demonstrated by the circumstances so carefully listed by Webster J. in *R.* v. *Secretary of State for the Home Department, ex p. Tarrant* [1985] Q.B. 251 as matters which boards of visitors should take into account. But it is easy to envisage circumstances in which the rules of natural justice do not call for representation, even though the disciplinary charge relates to a matter which constitutes in law a crime, as may well happen in the case of a simple assault where no question of law arises, and where the prisoner charged is capable of presenting his own case. To hold otherwise would result in wholly unnecessary delays in many cases, to the detriment of all concerned including the prisoner charged, and to wholly unnecessary waste of time and money, contrary to the public interest. Indeed, to hold otherwise would not only cause injustice to prisoners; it would also lead to an adventitious distinction being drawn between disciplinary offences which happen also to be crimes and those which happen not to be so, for the punishments liable to be imposed do not depend upon any such distinction. . . .

LORD MACKAY OF CLASHFERN L.C., LORD BRIDGE OF HARWICH, LORD ACKNER and LORD OLIVER OF AYLMERTON agreed with the above speech.

Appeals dismissed.

Notes

1. The criteria articulated by Webster J. in *R.* v. *Secretary of State for the Home Department, ex p. Tarrant* [1985] Q.B. 251, were the following:

- (a) The seriousness of the charge and of the potential penalty;
- (b) Whether any points of law are likely to arise in the proceedings;
- (c) The capacity of the prisoner to present his/her own case (*i.e.* their intellectual and educational abilities);
- (d) Procedural difficulties (*e.g.* whether the prisoner has been able to interview relevant witnesses prior to the hearing);
- (e) The need for reasonable speed in making an adjudication;
- (f) The need for fairness between prisoners and between prisoners/prison officers.

2. In *Tarrant* it was reported that nationally boards of visitors reached approximately 3,000 adjudications per year. In his report *Prison Disturbances* (Cm. 1456) (examining the Strangeways and subsequent other prison riots), Woolf L.J. recommended the abolition of the disciplinary powers of boards of visitors. The

Report favoured increasing the role of the ordinary criminal courts in dealing with serious misbehaviour inside prisons. See generally, S. H. Bailey, D. J. Harris and B. L. Jones, *Civil Liberties: Cases and Materials* (3rd ed., 1991), pp. 715–745.

3. For further discussion of the role of administrative law and the rights of prisoners see Chapter 3(*e*), above, p. 102.

4. M. J. Dixon is critical of Lord Goff's speech in *Hone* because:

> "It is unfortunate that the House of Lords in *Hone* did not seize the opportunity to examine the whole matter in closer detail. As it is, they were content to rely on general propositions about the flexible nature of natural justice and on previous decisions which are not altogether satisfactory. The jurisdiction of a board of visitors is non-voluntary, and it is not enough to rely on cases that deny the right of legal representation before tribunals whose jurisdiction depends wholly on the consent of the parties . . . However, not only has the decision in *Hone* extinguished any possibility of a prisoner being entitled to legal representation as of right, Lord Goff's emphasis on administrative efficiency may encourage visitors to exercise that discretion against a prisoner in all but the most extreme cases" ((1989) 40 N.I.L.Q. 71 at p. 77).

Question

To what extent can the reasoning in *Tarrant* and *Hone* be applied outside the context of adjudications by boards of visitors?

(iii) A Right to Cross-examine Opponents?

BUSHELL AND ANOTHER v. SECRETARY OF STATE FOR THE ENVIRONMENT

[1981] A.C. 75; [1980] 3 W.L.R. 22; [1980] 2 All E.R. 608; (1980) 78 L.G.R. 269 (House of Lords)

The department had proposed the construction of two adjoining stretches of motorway in the West Midlands. Local residents, and other amenity groups, objected to the proposals. Under the terms of the Highways Act 1959, the Secretary of State was obliged to hold a local public inquiry into such objections. One local inquiry was convened to hear the above objections (100 different parties were present at the inquiry which lasted for 100 working days). The respondents were objectors who sought to challenge the statistical methods used by the department to predict future traffic needs. The inspector allowed the respondents to criticise the department's methodology (contained in the "Red Book") and to call expert witnesses to support their criticisms, but he would not permit them to cross-examine the department's representatives upon this matter. The inspector noted the respondents' criticisms in his report which was generally favourable to the department's proposals. The Secretary of State accepted the inspector's recommendations and made schemes for the construction of these sections of motorway. The respondents applied, under Schedule 2 to the 1959 Act, to the High Court to quash the schemes on the ground, *inter alia*, that the inspector had been wrong in law to disallow them from cross-examining departmental representatives on the "Red Book." The High Court dismissed their application, but the Court of Appeal (Templeman L.J. dissenting) allowed their appeal. The Secretary of State appealed to the House of Lords.

LORD DIPLOCK: The provision and improvement of a national system of routes for through traffic for which a government department and not a local authority should be the highway authority has formed a part of national transport policy since the passing of the Trunk Roads Act in 1936. As part of this national network, or superimposed upon it, there have been constructed by stages during the course of the last 30 years special roads familiarly known as motorways which were first authorised by the Special Roads Act 1949. The construction of motorways is a lengthy and expensive process and it has been the policy of successive governments, which would in any event have been dictated by necessity, to construct the network by stages. The order in which the various portions of the network are to be constructed thus becomes as much a matter of government transport policy as the total extent and configuration of the motorway network itself. It also has the consequence that schemes for the provision of special roads which the Minister proposes to make under section 11 of the Highways Act 1959 deal with comparatively short stretches in a particular locality of what, when the other stretches are completed, will be integral parts of the national network. It follows, therefore, that there will be a whole series of schemes relating to successive stretches of the national network of motorways each of which may be the subject of separate local inquiries under Schedule 1, paragraph 9, to the Act.

. . . So from the publication of the draft scheme to the actual construction of the stretch of motorway which is authorised the process is necessarily a long one in the course of which circumstances may alter and even government policy may change.

Where it is proposed that land should be acquired by a government department or local authority and works constructed on it for the benefit of the public either as a whole or in a particular locality, the holding of a public inquiry before the acquisition of the land and the construction of the works are authorised has formed a familiar part of the administrative process ever since authorisation by ministerial order of compulsory acquisition of land for public purposes began to be used to replace parliamentary authorisation by Private Bill procedure in the nineteenth century. The essential characteristics of a "local inquiry," an expression which when appearing in a statute has by now acquired a special meaning as a term of legal art, are that it is held in public in the locality in which the works that are the subject of the proposed scheme are situated by a person appointed by the Minister upon whom the statute has conferred the power in his administrative discretion to decide whether to confirm the scheme. The subject-matter of the inquiry is the objections to the proposed scheme that have been received by the Minister from local authorities and from private persons in the vicinity of the proposed stretch of motorway whose interests may be adversely affected, and in consequence of which he is required by Schedule 1, paragraph 9, to hold the inquiry. The purpose of the inquiry is to provide the Minister with as much information about those objections as will ensure that in reaching his decision he will have weighed the harm to local interests and private persons who may be adversely affected by the scheme against the public benefit which the scheme is likely to achieve and will not have failed to take into consideration any matters which he ought to have taken into consideration.

. . . The Highways Act 1959 being itself silent as to the procedure to be followed at the inquiry, that procedure, within such limits as are necessarily imposed by its qualifying for the description "local inquiry," must necessarily be left to the discretion of the Minister or the inspector appointed by him to hold the inquiry on his behalf, or partly to one and partly to the other. In exercising that discretion, as in exercising any other administrative function, they owe a constitutional duty to perform it fairly and honestly and to the best of their ability, as Lord Greene M.R. pointed out in his neglected but luminous analysis of the quasi-judicial and administrative functions of a Minister as confirming authority of a compulsory purchase order made by a local authority, which is to be found in *B. Johnson & Co. (Builders) Ltd.* v. *Minister of Health* [1947] 2 All E.R. 395, 399–400. That judgment contains a salutary warning against applying to procedures involved in the making of administrative decisions concepts that are appropriate to the conduct of ordinary civil litigation between private parties. So rather than use such phrases as "natural justice" which may suggest that the prototype is only to be found in procedures followed by English courts of law, I prefer to put it that in the absence of any rules made under the Tribunals and Inquiries Act 1971, the only requirement of the Highways Act 1959, as to the procedure to be followed at a local inquiry held pursuant to Schedule 1, paragraph 9, is that it must be fair to all those who have an interest in the decision that will follow it whether they have been represented at the inquiry or not. What is a fair procedure to be adopted at a particular inquiry will depend upon the nature of its subject-matter.

What is fair procedure is to be judged not in the light of constitutional fictions as to the relationship between the Minister and the other servants of the Crown who serve in the government department of which he is the head, but in the light of the practical realities as to the way in which administrative decisions involving forming judgments based on technical considerations are reached. To treat the Minister in his decision-making capacity as someone separate and distinct from the department of government of which he is the political head and for whose actions he alone in constitutional theory is accountable to Parliament is to ignore not only practical realities but also Parliament's intention. Ministers come and go; departments, though their names may change from time to time, remain. Discretion in making administrative decisions is conferred upon a Minister not as an individual but as the holder of an office in which he will have available to him in arriving at his decision the collective knowledge, experience and expertise of all those who serve the Crown in the department of which, for the time being, he is the political head. The collective knowledge, technical as well as factual, of the civil servants in the department and their collective expertise is to be treated as the Minister's own knowledge, his own expertise. It is they who in reality will have prepared the draft scheme for his approval; it is they who will in the first instance consider the objections to the scheme and the report of the inspector by whom any local inquiry has been held and it is they who will give to the Minister the benefit of their combined experience, technical knowledge and expert opinion on all matters raised in the objections and the report. This is an integral part of the decision-making process itself; it is not to be equiparated with the Minister receiving evidence, expert opinion or advice from sources outside the department after the local inquiry has been closed. . . .

It is evident that an inquiry of this kind and magnitude is quite unlike any civil litigation and that the inspector conducting it must have a wide discretion as to the procedure to be followed in order to achieve its objectives. These are to enable him to ascertain the facts that are relevant to each of the objections, to understand the arguments for and against them and, if he feels qualified to do so, to weigh their respective merits, so that he may provide the Minister with a fair, accurate and adequate report on these matters.

Proceedings at a local inquiry at which many parties wish to make representations without incurring the expense of legal representation and cannot attend the inquiry throughout its length ought to be as informal as is consistent with achieving those objectives. To "over-judicialise" the inquiry by insisting on observance of the procedures of a court of justice which professional lawyers alone are competent to operate effectively in the interests of their clients would not be fair. It would, in my view, be quite fallacious to suppose that at an inquiry of this kind the only fair way of ascertaining matters of fact and expert opinion is by the oral testimony of witnesses who are subjected to cross-examination on behalf of parties who disagree with what they have said. Such procedure is peculiar to litigation conducted in courts that follow the common law system of procedure; it plays no part in the procedure of courts of justice under legal systems based upon the civil law, including the majority of our fellow Member States of the European Community; even in our own Admiralty Court it is not availed of for the purpose of ascertaining expert opinion on questions of navigation—the judge acquires information about this by private inquiry from assessors who are not subject to cross-examination by the parties. So refusal by an inspector to allow a party to cross-examine orally at a local inquiry a person who has made statements of facts or has expressed expert opinions is not unfair *per se*.

Whether fairness requires an inspector to permit a person who has made statements on matters of fact or opinion, whether expert or otherwise, to be cross-examined by a party to the inquiry who wishes to dispute a particular statement must depend on all the circumstances. In the instant case, the question arises in connection with expert opinion upon a technical matter. Here the relevant circumstances in considering whether fairness requires that cross-examination should be allowed include the nature of the topic upon which the opinion is expressed, the qualifications of the maker of the statement to deal with that topic, the forensic competence of the proposed cross-examiner, and, most important, the inspector's own views as to whether the likelihood that cross-examination will enable him to make a report which will be more useful to the Minister in reaching his decision than it otherwise would be is sufficient to justify any expense and inconvenience to other parties to the inquiry which would be caused by any resulting prolongation of it.

The circumstances in which the question of cross-examination arose in the instant case were the following. Before the inquiry opened each objector had received a document containing a statement of the Minister's reasons for proposing the draft scheme. It was itself a long and detailed document, and was accompanied by an even longer and more detailed one called "Strategic Studies Information," which gave an account of various traffic studies that had been undertaken between 1964 and 1973 in the area to be served by M42 Bromsgrove and M40 Warwick, the methodology used for those studies and the conclusions reached. The second paragraph of the Minister's statement of reasons said: "The Government's policy to build these new motorways" (*sc.* for which the two schemes provided) "will not be open to debate at the forthcoming inquiries [*sic*]: the Secretary of State is answerable to Parliament for this policy."

"Policy" as descriptive of departmental decisions to pursue a particular course of conduct is a protean word and much confusion in the instant case has, in my view, been caused by a failure to define the sense in which it can properly be used to describe a topic which is unsuitable to be the subject of an investigation as to its merits at an inquiry at which only persons with local interests affected by the scheme are entitled to be represented. A decision to construct a nationwide network of motorways is clearly one of government policy in the widest sense of the term. Any proposal to alter it is appropriate to be the subject of debate in Parliament, not of separate investigations in each of scores of local inquiries before individual inspectors up and down the country upon whatever material happens to be presented to them at the particular inquiry over which they preside. So much the respondents readily concede.

At the other extreme the selection of the exact line to be followed through a particular locality by a motorway designed to carry traffic between the destinations that it is intended to serve would not be described as involving government policy in the ordinary sense of that term. It affects particular local interests only and normally does not affect the interests of any wider section of the public, unless a suggested variation of the line would involve exorbitant expenditure of money raised by taxation. It is an appropriate subject for full investigation at a local inquiry and is one on which the inspector by whom the investigation is to be conducted can form a judgment on which to base a recommendation which deserves to carry weight with the Minister in reaching a final decision as to the line the motorway should follow.

Between the black and white of these two extremes, however, there is what my noble and learned friend, Lord Lane, in the course of the hearing described as a "grey area." Because of the time that must elapse between the preparation of any scheme and the completion of the stretch of motorway that it authorises, the department, in deciding in what order new stretches of the national network ought to be constructed, has adopted a uniform practice throughout the country of making a major factor in its decision the likelihood that there will be a traffic need for that particular stretch of motorway in 15 years from the date when the scheme was prepared. This is known as the "design year" of the scheme. Priorities as between one stretch of motorway and another have got to be determined somehow. Semasiologists may argue whether the adoption by the department of a uniform practice for doing this is most appropriately described as government policy or as something else. But the propriety of adopting it is clearly a matter fit to be debated in a wider forum and with the assistance of a wider range of relevant material than any investigation at an individual local inquiry is likely to provide; and in that sense at least, which is the relevant sense for present purposes, its adoption forms part of government policy.

The "need" for a new road to carry traffic between given destinations is an imprecise concept. If it is to be used as an important factor in comparing one situation with another for the purpose of determining priorities, there must be uniform criteria by which that need in each locality is to be measured. The test of future needs in the design year which the department has adopted is: whether, if the new stretch of motorway is not constructed, there will be undue congestion of traffic on existing roads, either in the locality or forming other parts of the national network of motorways, for which the new stretch of motorway would provide an alternative route. To apply this test of need to a design year 15 years ahead involves, among other things, estimating (1) the amount of traffic that the existing roads in the locality are capable of bearing without becoming so congested as to involve unacceptable delays; and (2) the amount of traffic that in the absence of the new stretch of motorway would in the design year be using those existing roads which the motorway is intended to relieve.

The methods used by the department for arriving at these estimates are very complicated. So far as I am capable of understanding them as one who is by now (I hope) a reasonably well-informed layman, it is obvious to me that no one who is not an expert in this esoteric subject could form a useful judgment as to their merits. The methods used are kept under periodical review by the department's own experts as a result of which they are revised from time to time. They are described in published documents. One which it will be necessary to mention dealt with the capacity of rural roads; but that which is most relevant to the respondents' complaint about refusal to permit cross-examination in the instant case has been referred to as the "Red Book." It was published in 1968 under the title *Traffic Prediction for Rural Roads (Advisory Manual on)* and described the method that had been used for predicting the growth of traffic up to the design year on the roads which the M42 Bromsgrove and M40 Warwick were intended to relieve. Important features of the method set out in the Red Book for predicting traffic that will be using the roads in a particular locality are the assumptions (1) that in general, traffic on rural roads throughout the country will grow at the same rate in all areas, except where exceptional changes can be foreseen as likely to take place in a particular locality; and (2) that the annual rate of growth will fall off as vehicle ownership in the country approaches saturation point; and that the best way of predicting what the growth will have been up to a particular design year is by assuming that it can be graphically represented by a curve that is asymptotic (*i.e.* broadly "S"-shaped) and whose shape where it represents future years can be extrapolated (*i.e.* predicted) from the shape of the curve which represents the observed annual increase in vehicle registrations over past years. It was recognised that predictions as applied to individual roads could only be very approximate and were subject to margins of error as high as 10 per cent. to 20 per cent.

The decisions to make these two assumptions for the purpose of calculating and comparing what traffic needs will be in all localities throughout the country in which it is proposed to construct future stretches of the national network of motorway might not, in a general context, be most naturally described as being government policy; but if a decision to determine priorities in the construction of future stretches of the national network of motorways by reference to their respective traffic needs in a design year 15 years ahead can properly be described as government policy, as I think it can, the definition of "traffic needs" to be used for the purposes of applying the policy, *viz.* traffic needs as assessed by methods described in the Red Book and the departmental publication on the capacity of rural roads, may well be regarded as an essential element in the policy. But whether the uniform adoption of particular methods of assessment is described as policy or methodology, the merits of the methods adopted are, in my view, clearly not appropriate for investigation at individual local inquiries by an inspector whose consideration of the matter is necessarily limited by the material which happens to be presented to him at the particular inquiry which he is holding. It would be a rash inspector who based on that kind of material a positive recommendation to the Minister that the method of predicting traffic needs throughout the country should be changed and it would be an unwise Minister who acted in reliance on it.

At the local inquiry into the M42 Bromsgrove and the M40 Warwick, objectors including the respondents, whose property would be affected by the scheme, and the M42 Action Committee, a "pressure group" which supported them primarily upon environmental grounds, had studied in advance the Minister's reasons for the schemes, the "Strategic Studies Information" and the Red Book. They came to the inquiry prepared to criticise the methods used to predict the traffic needs in the design year on local roads in the localities of the M42 Bromsgrove and M40 Warwick and to call evidence of witnesses with professional qualifications to testify to their unreliability. The circumstances in which the inspector was induced to give an early ruling as to what evidence he would admit and what cross-examination he would allow are recounted in the speeches of my noble and learned friends. In the result—and when one is considering natural justice it is the result that matters—the objectors were allowed to voice their criticisms of the methods used to predict traffic needs for the purposes of the two schemes and to call such expert evidence as they wanted to in support of their criticisms. What they were not allowed to do was to cross-examine the department's representatives upon the reliability and statistical validity of the methods of traffic prediction described in the Red Book and applied by the department for the purpose of calculating and comparing traffic needs in all localities throughout the country. This is the only matter in relation to the conduct of the inquiry by the inspector of which complaint is made.

Was this unfair to the objectors? For the reasons I have already given and in full agreement with the minority judgment of Templeman L.J. in the Court of Appeal, I do not think it was. I think that the inspector was right in saying that the use of the concept of traffic needs in the design year *assessed by a particular method* as the yardstick by which to determine the order in which particular stretches of the national network of motorways should be constructed was government policy in the relevant sense of being a topic unsuitable for investigation by individual inspectors upon whatever material happens to be presented to them at local inquiries held throughout the country. . . .

VISCOUNT DILHORNE: . . . It is clear that the objectors at this inquiry had every opportunity of putting forward their case. An inspector at an inquiry has a wide discretion as to its conduct. He may, in my view, properly disallow a particular line of cross-examination if it is not likely to serve any useful purpose. An admission or expression of view in the course of cross-examination at a trial may well affect the result, but the views of departmental witnesses as to the comparative merits of different methods of forecasting traffic elicited in the course of cross-examination are not likely to affect the ultimate outcome.

In the lengthy and detailed report of the inspector the evidence of the expert witnesses called by objectors was faithfully recorded. It was there for the Secretary of State to see and consider, no doubt in the light of advice he received from the civil servants in his department. I cannot think that the expression of views at the inquiry by civil servants as to methods of forecasting traffic would have assisted him or have served any useful purpose.

In my opinion the inspector was fully entitled in the exercise of his discretion to refuse to allow that cross-examination and only if one treats proceedings at an inquiry as a trial—which they are not—can any ground be found for saying that in disallowing this cross-examination there was a denial of natural justice or unfairness. In my opinion there was not. . . .

LORD EDMUND-DAVIES (dissenting): . . . My Lords, for the present I defer considering whether the outcome of the inquiry would, or might have been, different had cross-examination been allowed. The topic now under consideration relates solely to the propriety of its refusal. I have natural diffidence in differing from your Lordships in regarding that refusal as clearly wrong, but such is my considered view. It is beyond doubt that the inspector could—and should—disallow questions relating to the merits of government policy. But matters of policy are matters which involve the exercise of political judgment, and matters of fact and expertise do not become "policy" merely because a department of government relies on them. And, as the Franks committee had put it in 1957: "We see no reason why the factual basis for a departmental view should not be explained and its validity tested in cross-examination." (*Report of the Committee on Administrative Tribunals and Inquiries* (Cmnd. 218), para. 316.)

Then, if the Red Book is not "government policy," on what basis can the cross-examination of departmental witnesses relying on its methodology be properly refused? Sir Douglas Frank Q.C. surprisingly asserted, 76 L.G.R. 460, 472–473 (a) that its *authors* "were the only persons competent to answer questions on it," and (b) that "it seems to me necessarily to follow that the inspector was entitled to disallow cross-examination on it of a person who had had nothing to do with its preparation." But expert witnesses frequently quote and rely upon the publications of others and are regularly cross-examined upon the works so relied upon even though they played no part in their preparation. Nor, my Lords, is it right to assume, as was suggested in the course of the inquiry and as some of your Lordships appear to accept, that Mr. Brooks, the highly qualified and experienced traffic engineer, would have been incompetent to deal in cross-examination with questions directed to establishing the unreliability of the Red Book methodology upon which he himself heavily relied, albeit not without some emendations. Indeed, in paragraph 567 of this report the inspector described the witness as "thoroughly competent."

Pausing there, I conclude that the grounds hitherto considered for refusing cross-examination are unacceptable. But is it the case that, in an inquiry such as that with which this House is presently concerned, some special rule prevails which renders regular a procedure which in other circumstances would undoubtedly have been condemned as irregular? The general law may, I think, be summarised in this way: (a) In holding an administrative inquiry (such as that presently being considered), the inspector was performing quasi-judicial duties. (b) He must therefore discharge them in accordance with the rules of natural justice. (c) Natural justice requires that objectors (no less than departmental representatives) be allowed to cross-examine witnesses called for the other side on all relevant matters, be they matters of fact or matters of expert opinion. (d) In the exercise of jurisdiction outside the field of criminal law, the only restrictions on cross-examination are those general and well-defined exclusionary rules which govern the admissibility of relevant evidence (as to which reference may conveniently be had to *Cross on Evidence*, 5th ed. (1979), p. 17); beyond those restrictions there is *no* discretion on the civil side to exclude cross-examination on relevant matters.

There is ample authority for the view that, as Professor H. W. R. Wade Q.C. puts it (*Administrative Law*, 4th ed. (1977), p. 418): ". . . it is once again quite clear that the principles of natural justice apply to administrative acts generally." And there is a massive body of accepted decisions establishing that natural justice requires that a party be given an opportunity of challenging by cross-examination witnesses called by another party on relevant issues; see, for example, *Marriott* v. *Minister of Health* (1935) 52 T.L.R. 63, *per* Swift J., at p. 67—compulsory purchase orders inquiry; *Errington* v. *Minister of Health* [1935] 1 K.B. 249, *per* Maugham L.J., at p. 272—clearance order; *R.* v. *Deputy Industrial Injuries Commissioner, ex p. Moore* [1965] 1 Q.B. 465, *per* Diplock L.J., at pp. 488A, 490E–G; and *Wednesbury Corporation* v. *Ministry of Housing and Local Government (No. 2)* [1966] 2 Q.B. 275, *per* Diplock L.J., at pp. 302G–303A—local government inquiry.

Then is there any reason why those general rules should have been departed from in the present case? We have already seen that the parameters of the inquiry, as agreed to by the department representatives, embraced *need* as a topic relevant to be canvassed and reported upon. We have already considered the unacceptable submission that the Red Book was "government policy." And, while I am alive to the inconvenience of different inspectors arriving at different conclusions regarding different sections of a proposed trunk road, the risk of that happening cannot, in my judgment, have any bearing upon the question whether justice was done at this particular inquiry, which I have already explained was, in an important respect, unique of its kind.

There remains to be considered the wholly novel suggestion, which has found favour with your Lordships, that there is a "grey area"—existing, as I understand, somewhere between government policy (which admittedly may not be subjected to cross-examination) and the exact "line" of a section of a motorway (which may be)—and that in relation to topics falling within the "grey area" cross-examination is a matter of discretion. I find that suggestion to be too nebulous to be grasped. Furthermore, *why* such an area should exist has not been demonstrated—certainly not to my satisfaction—nor have its boundaries been defined, unlike those existing restrictions on cross-examination to which I have already referred. And I confess to abhorrence of the notion that any such area exists. For the present case demonstrates that its adoption is capable of resulting in an individual citizen denied justice nevertheless finding himself with no remedy to right the wrong done to him.

My Lords, it is for the foregoing reasons that I find myself driven to the conclusion that the refusal in the instant case to permit cross-examination on what, by common agreement, was evidence of cardinal importance was indefensible and unfair and, as such, a denial of natural justice. . . .

LORD LANE: . . . The objectors submit that by depriving them of the opportunity of cross-examining the department's witnesses as to how they came to the conclusion that the motorway was necessary the inspector in short did not accord them a fair hearing.

There can be no doubt that the obligation to hold an inquiry comprises the requirement that the inquiry should be fair. If the inquiry is not fair then there has been a "failure to comply" within the terms of paragraph 3 of Schedule 2 to the Act of 1959. If that failure has resulted in the objectors' interests being substantially prejudiced, then the court may quash the order. . . .

It is clear that all the material was before the Secretary of State and his staff. The only things missing were the replies which Mr. Brooks might have made to questions put to him by the objectors and their representatives. I find it difficult to see how in the circumstances the inability to cross-examine can be described as unfair. There are some occasions when cross-examination may be vital, for example, when at trial a witness's accuracy of recollection or observation is in question. But this was not a trial, nor was the witness's accuracy being challenged. It was a local inquiry convened because there had been objections to proposals in respect of one stretch of a proposed motorway. The obligation on the Secretary of State under paragraph 10 of Schedule 1 to the Act of 1959 was simply to consider any objections which were not withdrawn and to consider the report of the person holding the inquiry before coming to his conclusion about the scheme. To say, as the objectors do, that because cross-examination would have been allowed at a trial it was wrong to disallow it here is to misunderstand the nature of the inquiry. The refusal of cross-examination did not *ipso facto* result in unfairness. If cross-examination had been permitted, the result would have been, as is apparent from the extract from the report I have quoted, an even lengthier hearing without any appreciable advantage. . . .

Appeal allowed.

Questions

How does Lord Diplock's elaboration of the concept of "policy" differ from that articulated by Lord Edmund-Davies? Is it significant that Lord Diplock subjects local inquiries to the requirements of "fairness," whereas Lord Edmund-Davies applies the rules of natural justice to the holding of such inquiries?

Notes

1. For a fuller consideration of inquiries see above, Chapter 3(*d*).

2. The statutory provisions regulating highway inquiries are now contained in the Highways Act 1980 and the Highways (Inquiries Procedure) Rules 1976, S.I. 1976 No. 721.

3. Professor Jackson concludes:

> "Dicta abound for, and against the view that natural justice (or fairness) requires a right to cross-examine. To take them out of context as authority for an absolute rule is misleading. *Bushell* demonstrates, in an unusually full discussion of the problem, that the answer depends on a number of factors including the purpose of the hearing, the issue involved, the nature of the evidence" ((1980) 96 L.Q.R. 497).

4. Giving the opinion of the Privy Council, Lord Diplock stated that in the context of a New Zealand Royal Commission (a body analogous to a Tribunal of Inquiry in the United Kingdom):

> "The technical rules of evidence applicable to civil or criminal litigation form no part of the rules of natural justice. What is required . . . is that the decision to make the finding must be based upon *some* material that tends logically to show the existence of facts consistent with the finding and that the reasoning supportive of the finding, if it be disclosed, is not logically self-contradictory" (*Mahon* v. *Air New Zealand Ltd. and Others* [1984] A.C. 808 at p. 821).

(iv) Can a Breach of the Audi Alteram Partem Principle be Cured by a Later Rehearing or Appeal?

CALVIN v. CARR AND OTHERS

[1980] A.C. 574; [1979] 2 All E.R. 440 (Privy Council)

The appellant was the part-owner of a racehorse which competed in a race organised under the auspices of the Australian Jockey Club. The horse did not run as well as expected and his performance was subject to a stewards' inquiry. The stewards interviewed, *inter alios*, the jockey, the trainer and the appellant. They also saw film of the horse running in other races. Thirteen days after the race, the stewards determined that the jockey was guilty of an offence under the Club's Rules of Racing (namely not running a horse on its merits) and that the appellant was a party to that breach. They disqualified the appellant from membership of the Club for one year, which prevented him from entering any horse in a race organised by the Club for that period. The appellant exercised his right, under the Rules, to appeal against the stewards' decision to a committee of the Club. Before the committee he was represented by counsel and had full opportunity to call witnesses and subject others to cross-examination. The committee dismissed his appeal. The appellant then brought an action in the Supreme Court of New South Wales for a declaration that his disqualification from the Club was unlawful and an injunction to restrain the Club from acting on the purported disqualification. The major argument advanced by the appellant was that the stewards had acted in breach of the right to a fair hearing, consequently their decision was invalid, and this defect could not be cured by a lawful hearing before the appellate committee. The action was dismissed by the Australian court, so the appellant brought this appeal before the Privy Council.

LORD WILBERFORCE: . . . The plaintiff's second argument can be stated, for purposes of description, as being that such defects of natural justice as may have existed as regards the proceedings before the stewards were not capable of being cured by the appeal proceedings before the committee, even though, as was not contested before this Board, these were correctly and fairly conducted. The defendants contend the contrary. This part of the argument involved consideration of a wide range of authorities of this Board, and in Australia, Canada, England and New Zealand. As regards decisions of this Board a conflict was said to exist between *Annamunthodo* v. *Oilfields Workers' Trade Union* [1961] A.C. 945 and *Pillai* v. *Singapore City Council* [1968] 1 W.L.R. 1278, each of which has been followed by other decisions. There was also said to be a conflict between *Annamunthodo's* case, and the High Court in *Australian Workers' Union* v. *Bowen (No. 2)*, 77 C.L.R. 601, a conflict giving rise to difficulties for Australian state courts. Other individual decisions were cited which it appears difficult to reconcile.

Although, as will appear, some of the suggested inconsistencies of decisions disappear, or at least diminish, on analysis, their Lordships recognise and indeed assert that no clear and absolute rule can be laid down on the question whether defects in natural justice appearing at an original hearing, whether administrative or quasi-judicial, can be "cured" through appeal proceedings. The situations in which this issue arises are too diverse, and the rules by which they are governed so various, that this must be so. There are, however, a number of typical situations as to which some general principle can be stated. First there are cases where the rules provide for a rehearing by the original body, or some fuller or enlarged form of it. This situation may be found in relation to social clubs. It is not difficult in such cases to reach the conclusion that the first hearing is superseded by the second, or, putting it in contractual terms, the parties are taken to have agreed to accept the decision of the hearing body, whether original or adjourned. Examples of this are *De Verteuil* v. *Knaggs* [1918] A.C. 557, 563; *Posluns* v. *Toronto Stock Exchange and Gardiner* (1965) 53 D.L.R. (2d) 193; *In re Clark and Ontario Securities Commission* (1966) 56 D.L.R. (2d) 585; *In re Chromex Nickel Mines Ltd.* (1970) 16 D.L.R. (3d) 273; and see also *Ridge* v. *Baldwin* [1964] A.C. 40, 79, *per* Lord Reid.

At the other extreme are cases, where, after examination of the whole hearing structure, in the context of the particular activity to which it relates (trade union membership, planning, employment, etc.) the conclusion is reached that a complainant has the right to nothing less than a fair hearing both at the original and at the appeal stage. This was the result reached by Megarry J. in *Leary* v. *National Union of Vehicle Builders* [1971] Ch. 34. In his judgment in that case the judge seems to have elevated the conclusion thought proper in that case into a rule of general application. In an eloquent passage he said, at p. 49:

"If the rules and the law combine to give the member the right to a fair trial and the right of appeal, why should he be told that he ought to be

> satisfied with an unjust trial and a fair appeal? . . . As a general rule . . . I hold that a failure of natural justice in the trial body cannot be cured by a sufficiency of natural justice in an appellate body."

In their Lordships' opinion this is too broadly stated. It affirms a principle which may be found correct in a category of cases: these may very well include trade union cases, where movement solidarity and dislike of the rebel, or renegade, may make it difficult for appeals to be conducted in an atmosphere of detached impartiality and so make a fair trial at the first—probably branch—level an essential condition of justice. But to seek to apply it generally overlooks, in their Lordships' respectful opinion, both the existence of the first category, and the possibility that, intermediately, the conclusion to be reached, on the rules and on the contractual context, is that those who have joined in an organisation, or contract, should be taken to have agreed to accept what in the end is a fair decision, notwithstanding some initial defect.

In their Lordship's judgment such intermediate cases exist. In them it is for the court, in the light of the agreements made, and in addition having regard to the course of proceedings, to decide whether, at the end of the day, there has been a fair result, reached by fair methods, such as the parties should fairly be taken to have accepted when they joined the association. Naturally there may be instances when the defect is so flagrant, the consequences so severe, that the most perfect of appeals or rehearings will not be sufficient to produce a just result. Many rules (including those now in question) anticipate that such a situation may arise by giving power to remit for a new hearing. There may also be cases when the appeal process is itself less than perfect: it may be vitiated by the same defect as the original proceedings: or short of that there may be doubts whether the appeal body embarked on its task without predisposition or whether it had the means to make a fair and full inquiry, for example where it has no material but a transcript of what was before the original body. In such cases it would no doubt be right to quash the original decision. These are all matters (and no doubt there are others) which the court must consider. Whether these intermediate cases are to be regarded as exceptions from a general rule, as stated by Megarry J., or as a parallel category covered by a rule of equal status, is not in their Lordships' judgment necessary to state, or indeed a matter of great importance. What is important is the recognition that such cases exist, and that it is undesirable in many cases of domestic disputes, particularly in which an inquiry and appeal process has been established, to introduce too great a measure of formal judicialisation. While flagrant cases of injustice, including corruption or bias, must always be firmly dealt with by the courts, the tendency in their Lordships' opinion in matters of domestic disputes should be to leave these to be settled by the agreed methods without requiring the formalities of judicial processes to be introduced. . . .

It remains to apply the principles above stated to the facts of the present case. In the first place, their Lordships are clearly of the view that the proceedings before the committee were in the nature of an appeal, not by way of an invocation, or use, of whatever original jurisdiction the committee may have had. . . .

In addition to these formal requirements, a reviewing court must take account of the reality behind them. Races are run at short intervals; bets must be disposed of according to the result. Stewards are there in order to take rapid decisions as to such matters as the running of horses, being entitled to use the evidence of their eyes and their experience. As well as acting inquisitorally at the stage of deciding the result of a race, they may have to consider disciplinary action: at this point rules of natural justice become relevant. These require, at the least, that persons should be formally charged, heard in their own defence, and know the evidence against them. These essentials must always be observed but it is inevitable, and must be taken to be accepted, that there may not be time for procedural refinements. It is in order to enable decisions reached in this way to be reviewed at leisure that the appeal procedure exists. Those concerned know that they are entitled to a full hearing with opportunities to bring evidence and have it heard. But they know also that this appeal hearing is governed by the Rules of Racing, and that it remains an essentially domestic proceeding, in which experience and opinions as to what is in the interest of racing as a whole play a large part, and in which the standards are those which have come to be accepted over the history of this sporting activity. All those who partake in it have accepted the Rules of Racing, and the standards which lie behind them: they must also have accepted to be bound by the decisions of the bodies set up under those rules so long as when the process of reaching these decisions has been terminated, they can be said, by an objective observer, to have had fair treatment and consideration of their case on its merits.

In their Lordships' opinion precisely this can, indeed must, be said of the present case. The plaintiff's case has received, overall, full and fair consideration, and a decision, possibly a hard one, reached against him. There is no basis on which the court ought to interfere, and his appeal must fail. . . .

Appeal dismissed.

Notes

1. Elliott considers that the most significant aspect of this judgment was "the way it eschews statements of abstract principle." Instead, he approves of Lord Wilberforce's pragmatic attitude towards the tailoring of procedural obligations to different decision-making contexts. But, Elliott wonders whether, "an administrative law adversarial action before judges with necessarily limited knowledge may not be the best place to assess the procedures that particular situations

require . . .": M. Elliott, "Appeals, Principles and Pragmatism in Natural Justice" (1980) 43 M.L.R. 66.

Do the views of Elliott represent a fundamental attack upon the process of procedural review undertaken by the courts? What other institutions might be better suited to this task?

2. Although *Calvin* v. *Carr* concerns the decision of a sporting body, it is clear that the principles stated by Lord Wilberforce may apply to administrative bodies exercising statutory powers. See *R.* v. *Oxfordshire Local Valuation Panel, ex p. Oxford City Council* (1981) 79 L.G.R. 432; the Court of Appeal decision in *Lloyd* v. *McMahon* [1987] A.C. at pp. 655, 669 (above, p. 541); *cf. R.* v. *Brent London Borough Council, ex p. Gunning* (1985) 84 L.G.R. 168 (above, p. 519). In *ex p. Gunning* it was argued that any defects in the local council's consultation process could be cured by the procedure in the Education Act 1980, s.12(3), (4) and (6), under which objections could be made to the Secretary of State. Hodgson J. doubted whether the principles of fairness "developed in the quasi-judicial field of domestic disciplinary proceedings," could apply to "purely administrative procedures of the sort with which we are concerned." If he was wrong on that, he expressed a preference for the approach of Megarry J. in *Leary* v. *National Union of Vehicle Builders* [1971] Ch. 34, 49 (cited by Lord Wilberforce in *Calvin* v. *Carr*, above, p. 562), and the approach of the Privy Council in *Calvin* v. *Carr* itself (see pp. 192–193). Here:

> "in any event, in the circumstances of this case, the statutory procedures are themselves fatally flawed by the inadequacies of the previous consultation." (p. 193).

(v) Does Natural Justice Require the Adjudicator to Give Reasons?

There is no general common law duty to give reasons (above, p. 357). However, the Court of Appeal has held that a "fully judicial body" is required by natural justice to give "sufficient reasons for its decision to enable the parties to know the issues to which it addressed its mind and acted lawfully" (*R.* v. *Civil Service Appeal Board, ex p. Cunningham* [1991] 4 All E.R. 310, *per* Lord Donaldson M.R. at pp. 318, 320). See J. Herberg, [1991] P.L. 340.

(ii) The Rule "Nemo Judex in Causa Sua Potest"

Most of the large number of cases involving natural justice reported since *Ridge* v. *Baldwin* (1964) have raised the *audi alteram partem* rule. That rule has been applied in situations where previously it had not been thought relevant. Some cases proceeded on a wider view of what was a "judicial" decision, others on a denial that the decision had to be capable of being analysed as "judicial." Traditionally, the rule against bias or interest applied only to "judicial" decisions. It has not been established how far the recent developments in the *audi alteram partem* rule apply to the other branch of natural justice.

The *nemo judex* rule is clearly applicable to the decisions of judges and magistrates in courts of law. Other clear examples include members of tribunals and Ministers exercising judicial functions, such as the hearing of appeals. The problem is how far the rule should apply to decisions with both administrative and judicial elements, and to purely administrative decisions (see below, p. 585). It must be remembered that this rule is concerned with appearances. The courts do not look for actual bias; they ask whether there was a real likelihood or reasonable suspicion of bias. They take no account of the fact that a person with a direct pecuniary interest did not allow himself to be influenced by it in any way: the direct pecuniary interest disqualifies automatically. Thus the *nemo judex* rule can be seen as additional to other aspects of the *ultra vires* principle which apply to all decisions, whether judicial or administrative, made by virtue of statute. It is always easier to establish an improper appearance than actual impropriety.

Another consequence of the rule's stress on appearances is that the arguments used for extending the *audi alteram partem* rule to new situations do not necessarily apply with the same force here. The content of the *audi alteram partem* rule is variable, the requirement becoming less as the judicial element in a decision becomes less. The *nemo judex* rule is not so flexible. The result of its application is to disqualify a particular adjudicator altogether, not as with the other branch of natural justice, to require him to observe certain appropriate procedural steps. The only real scope for flexibility is where it is alleged that an adjudicator is "biased" because of his open adherence to a particular policy. The courts recognise that it may be part of the adjudicator's general functions to formulate and have regard to an overall policy. The difference lies between on the one hand the justice who has previously expressed peculiarly strong views against Welshmen trying a Welshman for a criminal offence, and on the other, the Minister of Planning who has regard to general departmental policy when hearing planning appeals, or indeed local justices who have established general principles to guide them in the allocation of liquor licences.

The cases raise several principal questions: when does the rule apply, what are the differences between the rule against "interest" and the rule against "bias" and how are statutory formulations of the *nemo judex* principle applied?

(a) When Does the "Nemo Judex" Rule Apply?

R. v. KENT POLICE AUTHORITY, ex p. GODDEN

[1971] 2 Q.B. 662; [1971] 3 W.L.R. 416; 115 S.J. 640; 69 L.G.R. 533; *sub nom. Re Godden* [1971] 3 All E.R. 20 (Court of Appeal)

In 1969 the applicant, a police chief inspector, was transferred to administrative duties. He made accusations of unjust treatment against his superiors. A chief constable held an inquiry and reported in May 1970 that there was no evidence of malpractice. The applicant was told the result of the inquiry but was not shown the report.

On July 4, 1970, the applicant's desk was searched by a senior officer. Erotic documents including a draft letter said to be in the applicant's handwriting were removed. The applicant denied knowledge of the documents. It was arranged for the applicant to be seen by the chief medical officer of the force, who was supplied with a copy of the report of May 1970 and the documents. He saw the applicant and on July 23, 1970, reported that after reading the reports he formed the opinion that the applicant was "suffering from a mental disorder of paranoid type." On July 31, 1970, he certified that the applicant was unfit for police duty on the same ground. The applicant was put on sick leave.

The applicant saw his own doctor, who sent him to a consultant psychiatrist. The consultant psychiatrist reported on August 18, 1970, that the applicant was "psychiatrically completely normal" and on May 17, 1971, that in his opinion he was "normal psychiatrically and in good mental and physical health." The police would not allow the consultant psychiatrist to see the report of May 1970.

The police authority took steps compulsorily to retire the applicant. On January 22, 1971, they notified the applicant that they had selected the same chief medical officer as their "duly qualified practitioner" to determine whether the applicant was "permanently disabled" under regulation 70(2) of the Police Pensions Regulations 1971.

The applicant sought orders of prohibition and mandamus. The Divisional Court dismissed the applications. The applicant appealed.

LORD DENNING M.R.: . . . I am clearly of opinion that the decisions leading to compulsory retirement are of a judicial character and must conform to the rules of natural justice. They are, first, decision by the medical practitioner or on appeal by the medical referee, and, secondly, the inquiry by the police authority themselves. We have been referred to two cases where medical certificates were required which affected the rights of individuals. One is *R.* v. *Postmaster-General, ex p. Carmichael* [1928] 1 K.B. 291. The other is *R.* v. *Boycott, ex p. Keasley* [1939] 2 K.B. 641. In each of those cases certiorari was granted.

When a medical practitioner is making a decision which may lead to a man being compulsorily retired, he must act fairly. He is not acting simply as doctor to patient. He is not diagnosing illness or prescribing treatment. He is not saying merely whether a man is fit or unfit for duty. He is doing something which affects the man's whole future. He must beyond doubt act fairly. Take this very case. A man's mental state is at issue. It affects not only his pension rights and payments to him. It affects his standing in the community, his ability to get other work and the like. It is quite plain to me that the person concerned is entitled to have a fair opportunity of correcting or contradicting any statements made to his prejudice, and a fair opportunity of calling in his own medical consultant and getting him to give his opinion to the deciding person. His own medical consultant should be entitled to have before him all material which the other doctors have.

That brings me to the first question: was it proper for the Kent police authorities to refer for decision this question to Dr. Crosbie Brown? I must say I think it was not. Dr. Crosbie Brown was disqualified from acting. He had already expressed an opinion adverse to Chief Inspector Godden. As early as July 23, 1970, Dr. Crosbie Brown had said that the chief inspector was suffering from a mental disorder. Dr. Crosbie Brown acted on that opinion by putting him on sick leave. He has put his opinion on affidavit. He has committed himself to a view in advance of the inquiry. I think it would be impossible for Dr. Crosbie Brown—who is just a general medical practitioner and not a consultant—to bring a completely impartial mind to bear upon the matter. In any event, to the person affected by it, Chief Inspector Godden, it must inevitably appear that Dr. Crosbie Brown cannot bring an impartial judgment to bear upon the matter. If he was to decide the matter justice would not be seen to be done. In view of the additional material before us (which was not before the Divisional Court) I hold that Dr. Crosbie Brown is disqualified. For that reason in my opinion the first request for prohibition should go "to prohibit Dr. Crosbie Brown from determining whether Chief Inspector Godden was permanently disabled within the police pensions regulations for the time being in force."

If the police authority determine further to consider the matter, they should refer it for decision to somebody else. I would suggest that it would be better to have someone quite outside this case altogether—not even any of the names which have been mentioned, such as Dr. Pollitt or Dr. Hierons—but some duly qualified medical practitioner who has had no part in the case hitherto. Then the question arises, what material may or should be put before such a person? Is it to include the Pratt report and all such other matters? I am inclined to think it should. Whoever is entrusted with the decision should have before him all material relative to the state of mind of Chief Inspector Godden, whether it is for him or against him.

The next question is whether Chief Inspector Godden's own medical advisers should see the material. In my opinion they should. Dr. Hordern (or whatever medical consultant Chief Inspector Godden engages) should have the selfsame material before him upon which to give his opinion as that which is placed before any other doctor who is considering the matter.

One word more. Although the medical advisers on each side should be fully informed, I do not see that justice requires that Chief Inspector Godden should himself be able to roam through this Pratt report. One does not want to keep anything back from him, but in a matter of this kind it seems to me that justice can well be done by his own consultant seeing it. No doubt his own consultant will have to ask him many questions on it, and he is bound to get to know a good deal about it. But for myself I do not see that justice requires that Chief Inspector Godden should see it all himself. I do not suggest that he would use it as a basis for an action for libel, but it would be most deplorable if it were used for that purpose. Rather than risk such a thing, it seems to me justice can fairly be done by letting his medical consultant see everything that any other doctor sees on the matter and give his advice accordingly. I would therefore issue an order of mandamus to the police authority telling them that, if at any time consideration is given as to whether Chief Inspector Godden is permanently disabled within the police pensions regulations, they should supply to the medical consultant of Chief Inspector Godden all letters and other material which is placed by them before any duly qualified practitioner selected by them under police pensions regulation 70. I would therefore allow the appeal and let prohibition and mandamus issue in the terms which I have stated.

SALMON L.J.: . . . It seems to me that the duly qualified medical practitioner selected by the authority to give a decision as to whether a police officer is disabled, and, if so, whether the disablement is likely to be permanent, is undoubtedly performing a quasi-judicial function in reaching that decision. The relationship between him and the officer concerned is not an ordinary relationship of patient and doctor. Now, when I say he is exercising a quasi-judicial function, I certainly do not mean that he should conduct anything in the nature of a trial or hear the officer's legal advisers; nor that he is bound by the rules of evidence. He must, however, act fairly. . . .

KARMINSKI L.J. delivered a concurring judgment.

Appeal allowed.

FRANKLIN AND OTHERS v. MINISTER OF TOWN AND COUNTRY PLANNING

[1948] A.C. 87; [1947] L.J.R. 1440; 63 T.L.R. 446; 111 J.P. 497; [1947] 2 All E.R. 289; 45 L.G.R. 581 (House of Lords)

In January 1946, a committee appointed in 1945 by the Minister and the Secretary of State for Scotland (the "Reith Committee") made an interim report (Cmd. 6759) which pointed out that Stevenage was suggested in the Greater London Plan 1944 as one of the new towns in the outer ring round London. The committee had been informed that this development was urgently needed, and they recommended that a government-sponsored corporation should be established in advance of legislation. The Minister, Lewis Silkin, introduced the New Towns Bill in the House of Commons in April.

On May 6, 1946, Mr. Silkin spoke at a public meeting in Stevenage Town Hall, called to consider a proposal for the designation of land near Stevenage as the site of a new town. The meeting was lively. Mr. Silkin explained the plans for the development of new towns to relieve London's population density. His speech included the following passages:

> "In anticipation of the passage of the Bill—and I have no doubt that it will go through—certain preliminary steps have been taken regarding Stevenage by way of discussion with some of the local authorities concerned—(*Voice*: There has been no discussion with the Stevenage Local Authority)—and the preparation of a plan, and the giving of notices for the acquisition of land under powers which I already have in pursuance of the Town and Country Planning Act, 1932 . . . I think you will agree that if we are to carry out our policy of creating a number of new towns to relieve congestion in London we could hardly have chosen for the site of one of them a better place than Stevenage. Now I know that many objections have been raised by the inhabitants of Stevenage, perhaps not unnaturally. . . . The project will go forward. It will do so more smoothly and more successfully with your help and co-operation. Stevenage will in a short time become world famous—(*Laughter*). . . . In answer to a question as to whether the rates would be increased by the development, the respondent said: No, in due course Stevenage will gain. Local authorities will be consulted all the way through. But we have a duty to perform, and I am not going to be deterred from that duty. While I will consult as far as possible all the local authorities, at the end, if people are fractious and unreasonable, I shall have to carry out my duty—(*Voice*: Gestapo!)."

The New Towns Bill received the Royal Assent on August 1, 1946. On August 3, the Minister prepared the draft Stevenage New Town (Designation) Order 1946 under paragraph 1 of Schedule 1 to the Act. The draft order was publicised as required by the Act. Objections to the designation were received from the appellants and others. A public local inquiry was held on behalf of the Minister in

October. The inspector's report to the Minister summarised the objector's submissions and evidence.

In November, the Minister wrote to the objectors that he had decided to make the order, "after giving careful consideration to the various submissions made to him. . . ." He dealt with the main objections raised. The order was made on November 11. The following month, the present appellants who owned houses and land in the area, applied to the High Court to have the order quashed on the grounds that: (1) The order was not within the powers of the Act, or alternatively that the Act's requirements had not been complied with to the substantial prejudice of the appellants' interests, in that—(a) before considering the objections the Minister stated that he would make the order and was thereby biased in any consideration of the order; and (b) the Minister did not before making the order cause a public local inquiry to be held with respect thereto; and (2) That the Act impliedly required that the appellants' objections should be fairly and properly considered by the Minister and that the Minister should give fair and proper effect to the result of such consideration in deciding whether the order should be made, and that such implied requirements were not complied with.

The Minister swore an affidavit which was not challenged, stating (*inter alia*): "Before causing the said order to be made, I personally carefully considered all the objections made by the objectors including the present [appellants] together with the submissions made and evidence given on their behalf as appearing in the said transcript" (of the inquiry proceedings). He also stated that he carefully considered the inspector's report.

Henn Collins J. (63 T.L.R. 143) held that the Minister had not fulfilled his duty to act judicially in considering the objections.

The Court of Appeal (63 T.L.R. 187) reversed this decision, holding that the appellants had not discharged the onus of proving that the Minister was biased when he made the order.

The appellants appealed to the House of Lords.

LORD THANKERTON: [stated the facts, expressed agreement with the Court of Appeal's views that the appellant had not proved that the Minister was biased, and continued:] My Lords, I agree with the decision of the Court of Appeal, but I am of opinion that an incorrect view of the law applicable in this case was taken by the learned judge, and I feel bound, despite the assumption of its correctness by the Court of Appeal, to examine the correctness of the learned judge's view as to the proper inference from the respondent's speech of May 6, 1946. While the fact that the speech was made just before the second reading of the Bill, and some months before the statutory duties as to designation of new towns was imposed on the respondent has some bearing on the fair construction of the speech, I am prepared to assume in favour of the appellants that, under the Bill as introduced, it was proposed to impose these duties on the respondent, as Minister of Town and Country Planning, and that these duties presented no material difference from those contained in the Bill when passed into law. It could hardly be suggested that, prior to its enactment, he was subject to any higher duty than is to be found in the statute. In my opinion, no judicial, or quasi-judicial, duty was imposed on the respondent, and any reference to judicial duty, or bias, is irrelevant in the present case. The respondent's duties under section 1 of the Act and Sch. I thereto are, in my opinion, purely administrative, but the Act prescribes certain methods of or steps in, discharge of that duty. It is obvious that, before making the draft order, which must contain a definite proposal to designate the area concerned as the site of a new town, the respondent must have made elaborate inquiry into the matter and have consulted any local authorities who appear to him to be concerned, and obviously other departments of the Government, such as the Minister of Health, would naturally require to be consulted. It would seem, accordingly, that the respondent was required to satisfy himself that it was a sound scheme before he took the serious step of issuing a draft order. It seems clear also, that the purpose of inviting objections, and, where they are not withdrawn, of having a public inquiry, to be held by someone other than the respondent, to whom that person reports, was for the further information of the respondent, in order to the final consideration of the soundness of the scheme of the designation; and it is important to note that the development of the site, after the order is made, is primarily the duty of the development corporation established under section 2 of the Act. I am of opinion that no judicial duty is laid on the respondent in discharge of these statutory duties, and that the only question is whether he has complied with the statutory directions to appoint a person to hold the public inquiry, and to consider that person's report. On this contention of the appellants no suggestion is made that the public inquiry was not properly conducted, nor is there any criticism of the report by Mr. Morris. In such a case the only ground of challenge must be either that the respondent did not in fact consider the report and the objections, of which there is here no evidence, or that his mind was so foreclosed that he gave no genuine consideration to them, which is the case made by the appellants. Although I am unable to agree exactly with the view of the respondent's duty expressed by the learned judge, or with some of the expressions used by the Court of Appeal in regard to that matter, it does appear to me that the issue was treated in both courts as being whether the respondent had genuinely considered the objections and the report, as directed by the Act.

My Lords, I could wish that the use of the word "bias" should be confined to its proper sphere. Its proper significance, in my opinion, is to denote a departure from the standard of even-handed justice which the law requires from those who occupy judicial office, or those who are commonly regarded as holding a quasi-judicial office, such as an arbitrator. The reason for this clearly is that, having to adjudicate as between two or more parties, he must come to his adjudication with an independent mind, without any inclination or bias towards one side or other in the dispute. . . . But, in the present case, the respondent having no judicial duty, the only question is what the respondent actually did, that is, whether in fact he did genuinely consider the report and the objections.

Coming now to the inference of the learned judge from the respondent's speech on May 6, that he had not then a mind open to conviction, the learned judge states it thus (1947) 176 L.T. 200 at p. 203: "If I am to judge by what he said at the public meeting which was held very shortly before the Bill, then published, became an Act of Parliament, I could have no doubt but that any issue raised by objectors was forejudged. The Minister's language leaves no doubt about that. He was not only saying there must and shall be satellite towns, but he was saying that Stevenage was to be the first of them." It seems probable that the learned judge's mind was influenced by his having already held that the respondent's function was quasi-judicial, which would raise the question of bias, but, in my view, I am clearly of opinion that nothing said by the respondent was inconsistent with the discharge of his statutory duty, when subsequently objections were lodged, and the local public inquiry took place, followed by the report of that inquiry, genuinely to consider the report and the objections. . . .

[His Lordship referred to the contentious passages from the Minister's speech.]

My Lords, these passages in a speech, which was of a political nature, and of the kind familiar in a speech on second reading, demonstrate (1) the speaker's view that the Bill would become law, that Stevenage was a most suitable site and should be the first scheme in the operation, and that the Stevenage project would go forward, and (2) the speaker's reaction to the hostile interruptions of a section of the audience. In my opinion, these passages are not inconsistent with an intention to carry out any statutory duty imposed on him by Parliament, although he intended to press for the enactment of the Bill, and thereafter to carry out the duties thereby involved, including the consideration of objections which were neither fractious nor unreasonable. I am, therefore of opinion that the first contention of the appellants fails, in that they have not established either that in the respondent's speech he had forejudged any genuine consideration of the objections or that he had not genuinely considered the objections at the later stage when they were submitted to him. . . .

[His Lordship went on to hold that the Act did not require evidence to be led at the public inquiry in support of the order. Paragraph 3 of Schedule 1 to the 1946 Act required that, if objections were made, "the Minister shall, before making the order, cause a public local inquiry to be held with respect thereto. . . . The last three words were held to mean "with respect to the objections." Thus the inquiry was properly held.]

LORDS PORTER, UTHWATT, DU PARCQ AND NORMAND concurred.

Appeal dismissed.

Notes and questions

1. This case was decided at a time when the courts tied the label "judicial" only to *lis inter partes* situations. In the context of planning, a minister was held to be acting in a judicial capacity only after objections had been received and an inquiry was necessary. See *Errington* v. *Minister of Health* [1935] 1 K.B. 249.

2. Assuming that it is irrelevant whether the Minister is acting judicially or administratively, should the order had been quashed for bias on these facts?

3. The decision of the Court of Appeal is a little unsatisfactory in so far as it turned on the failure of the appellant to "prove" bias.

4. Should administrative bias as here demonstrated have the same effect as the "interest" of such cases as *Dimes* v. *Grand Junction Canal* (below).

5. *Cf.* the cases on the applicability of the *nemo judex* principle to the planning decisions of local authorities below, p. 585, n. 1.

6. Other cases in which the rule against bias has been held not to apply include the following. In *R.* v. *Secretary of State for Trade, ex p. Perestrello* [1981] Q.B. 19, Woolf J. held that the rule did not apply to inspectors conducting an investigation of a company under the Companies Act 1967, s.109, although they were under a duty to act fairly in the sense of a duty not to exceed or abuse their discretion. The inspectors were acting in a "policing role"; it was "wholly inappropriate for the case to be approached in the same way as one would approach a person performing a normal judicial or quasi-judicial role; a situation where the person is making a determination" (p. 35).

Then, in *R.* v. *Reading Borough Council, ex p. Quietlynn Ltd.* (1986) 85 L.G.R. 387, Kennedy J. held that a panel appointed by the council to consider and determine applications for sex establishment licences was not a judicial body so as to be subject to the rule against bias. The panel's composition could only be impugned for bias if it was clear that the panel could not exercise a proper discretion (the test applied in *R.* v. *Sevenoaks District Council, ex p. Terry*, below, p. 586). It was not sufficient to invalidate the panel's decisions that a councillor who held strong views on the grant of such licences, and who was a member of a political group which was not in favour of such establishment, was appointed to the panel.

(b) The Rule Against Interest

An adjudicator with a direct pecuniary or other personal interest is disqualified from acting. The existence of such an interest is equivalent to a conclusive presumption of a real likelihood or reasonable suspicion of bias. The arguments in favour of applying the *nemo judex* rule to administrative decisions are strongest here. Admittedly, if an administrative decision is influenced by the financial interest of the person taking the decision, it is likely to be an *ultra vires* abuse of power in that an irrelevant consideration has been taken into account. Why should it have to be proved that the interest influenced the decision merely because the decision is analytically administrative?

DIMES v. GRAND JUNCTION CANAL PROPRIETORS

(1852) 3 H.L.Cas. 759; 8 State Tr. N.S. 85; 19 L.T.O.S. 317; 17 Jur. 73; 10 E.R. 301 (House of Lords)

In 1796, the canal proprietors, a company incorporated under statute, purchased some land, part of which was used for the canal and tow-path. This land was the subject of litigation between the proprietors and Dimes, an attorney who was the Lord of the Manor, which dragged on from 1831 to 1852. In 1838, 1848 and 1850 Lord Chancellor Cottenham affirmed decrees made by the Vice-Chancellor in favour of the proprietors, including an injunction to restrain Dimes from obstructing the canal (for example, by throwing bricks into it), and an order subsequently committing him to prison for contempt in disobeying the injunction. In 1849, Dimes discovered that the Lord Chancellor had for over 10 years held several thousand pounds worth of shares in the canal company, some in his own right and the others as trustee. The Lord Chancellor continued to hear matters concerned with the litigation, relying on the advice of the Master of the Rolls with whom he sat. Dimes appealed to the House of Lords against all the decrees and orders made in the litigation. He was represented by the Solicitor-General and other counsel, who argued that the whole proceedings were void in that the Lord Chancellor was disqualified by interest, and that his incompetency affected his deputy, the Vice-Chancellor. On the other hand, it was accepted that the formal act of enrolling the order to enable an appeal to be brought to the House of Lords had to be performed by the Lord Chancellor: "The enrolment of this order is a matter of necessity, but it is also a matter of form, and is not an act which decides the case, but only enables the party to make the decision the subject of an appeal. The House cannot say to an appealing party who complains of the wrongful exercise of an unwarranted jurisdiction, that he cannot come here to make the complaint without getting the Lord Chancellor's signature, and yet, when he gets it, that he thereby admits the jurisdiction. That would be to make the wrong itself a reason for refusing the remedy." This was not to say that it was necessary for the Lord Chancellor to hear the main issues. "There might have been a bill of complaint addressed to the Sovereign in the High Court of Chancery, and it would have been referred to the Master of the Rolls. . . ." (3 H.L.Cas. at p. 770.)

The House of Lords took the advice of the Judges:

MR. BARON PARKE: In answer to the first question proposed by your Lordships, I have to state the unanimous opinion of the Judges, that, in the case suggested, the order or decree of the Lord Chancellor was not absolutely *void*, on account of his interest, but *voidable* only.

If this had been a proceeding in an inferior court, one to which a prohibition might go from a court in Westminster Hall, such a prohibition would be granted, pending the proceedings, upon an allegation that the presiding Judge of the court was interested in the suit: whether a prohibition could go to the Court of Chancery, it is unnecessary to consider.

If no prohibition should be applied for, and in cases where it could not be granted, the proper mode of taking the objection to the interest of the Judge would be, in courts of common law, by bringing a writ of error. . . .

The former course was stated to be proper in the case of *Brooks* v. *Earl of Rivers* (Hardr. 503), it being suggested that the Earl of Derby, who was Chamberlain of Chester, had an interest in the suit; and the Court held that, where the Judge had an interest, neither he nor *his deputy* can determine a cause or sit in court; and if he does, a prohibition lies.

The latter course was adopted in the case of *The Company of Mercers and Ironmongers of Chester* v. *Bowker* (1 Stra. 639), where it was assigned for error in fact, on the record of a judgment for the Company of Mercers in the Mayor's Court at Chester, that after verdict, and before judgment, one of the Company of Mercers became mayor; and for that reason the judgment was reversed in the Court of Quarter Sessions, and that judgment of reversal affirmed in the King's Bench.

In neither of these cases was the judgment held to be absolutely void. Till prohibition had been granted in one case, or judgment reversed in the other, we think that the proceedings were valid, and the persons acting under the authority of the Court would not be liable to be treated as trespassers.

The many cases in which the Court of King's Bench has interfered (and may have gone to a great length), where interested parties have acted as magistrates, and quashed the orders made by the Court of which they formed part, afford an analogy.

None of these orders is absolutely void; it would create great confusion and inconsequence if it was. The objection might be one of which the parties acting under these orders might be totally ignorant till the moment of the trial of an action of trespass for the act done (see, with relation to this point, the observations of the Lord Chancellor in the case of *Scadding* v. *Lorant*, *ante*, p. 447); but these orders may be quashed after being removed by *certiorari*, and the Court shall do complete justice in that respect.

We think that the order of the Chancellor is not void; but we are of opinion, that as he had an interest which would have disqualified a witness under the old law, he was disqualified as a Judge; that it was a voidable order, and might be questioned and set aside by appeal or some application to the Court of Chancery, if a prohibition would not lie.

[The Judges also advised that the Vice-Chancellor was not the mere deputy of the Lord Chancellor, but exercised an independent jurisdiction; that his decrees took effect unaffected by the Lord Chancellor's disqualification; and that as the latter's signature was required by statute for the enrolment of the decrees the disqualification did not affect that act.]

For this is a case of necessity, and where that occurs the objection of interest cannot prevail. Of this the case in the Year Book (Year Book, 8 Hen. 6, 19; 2 Roll. Abr. 93) is an instance, where it was held that it was no objection to the jurisdiction of the Common Pleas that an action was brought against all the Judges of the Common Pleas, in a case in doubt which could only be brought in that court. . . .

[Their Lordships then heard arguments on the merits, in form acting as if on an appeal directly from the Vice-Chancellor. At its conclusion, their Lordships expressed their views on the disqualification issue.]

LORD ST. LEONARDS L.C. and LORD BROUGHAM concurred in the opinion of the Judges, and said that it was proper to reverse the orders of Lord Cottenham L.C.

LORD CAMPBELL: I take exactly the same view of this case as do my noble and learned friends, and I have very little to add to their observations. With respect to the point upon which the learned Judges were consulted, I must say that I entirely concur in the advice which they have given to your Lordships. No one can suppose that Lord Cottenham could be, in the remotest degree, influenced by the interest that he had in this concern; but, my Lords, it is of the last importance that the maxim that no man is to be a judge in his own cause should be held sacred. And that is not to be confined to a cause in which he is a party, but applies to a cause in which he has an interest. Since I have had the honour to be Chief Justice of the Court of Queen's Bench, we have again and again set aside proceedings in inferior tribunals because an individual, who had an interest in a cause, took a part in the decision. And it will have a most salutary influence on these tribunals when it is known that this high Court of last resort, in a case in which the Lord Chancellor of England had an interest, considered that his decree was on that account a decree not according to law, and was set aside. This will be a lesson to all inferior tribunals to take care not only that in their decrees they are not influenced by their personal interest, but to avoid the appearance of labouring under such an influence. . . .

[The Vice-Chancellor's decrees and orders were upheld on the merits.]

Notes

1. See further, pp. 837 *et seq.*, on the distinction between "void" and "voidable" acts.

2. A pecuniary interest in order to disqualify may be trivial in amount, but it must not be "too remote." In *R.* v. *Rand* (1866) L.R. 1 Q.B. 230, Bradford Corporation were empowered by statute to take water flowing into Harden Beck. They could do so without the consent of the millowners on that beck, if they obtained first a justices' certificate that a certain reservoir was completed, of a given capacity, and filled with water. Two of the justices who granted this certificate were trustees of institutions which held Bradford corporation bonds. The Court of Queen's Bench held that these justices were not disqualified by interest, even though "the security of their *cestui qui trusts* would be improved by anything improving the borough fund, and anything improving the waterworks . . . would produce that effect." The two justices might have been disqualified by interest had they been "liable to costs, or to other pecuniary loss or gain" in consequence of being trustees (*per* Blackburn J. at p. 232). The court also held that there was no "real likelihood of bias" (see below). See also *Metropolitan Properties* v. *Lannon* (below).

3. One man may not act both as "prosecutor" and "judge." See *Taylor* v. *N.U.S.* [1967] 1 W.L.R. 532; *R.* v. *L.C.C., ex p. Akkersdyk* [1892] 1 Q.B. 190; *R.* v. *Barnsley M.B.C., ex p. Hook* [1976] 1 W.L.R. 1052, C.A. In the *Hook* case, a complaint was made about the behaviour of Hook, a stallholder, to the manager of Barnsley market. At a subsequent hearing before a council sub-committee, the manager was present throughout, gave evidence in the absence of Hook and his representatives, and acted as "prosecutor." The decision to revoke Hook's licence to hold a stall in the market was quashed by certiorari. *Cf. R.* v. *Chief Constable of South Wales, ex p. Thornhill, The Times,* June 1, 1987, where the chief constable's decision in disciplinary proceedings was not quashed, notwithstanding a private visit to him by his deputy, the prosecutor, during an adjournment to deal with other matters.

(c) The Rule Against Bias

Where there is no personal or financial interest, the facts may nevertheless give the appearance that the adjudicator might be biased. The problem is how far the courts should insist on the maintenance of appearances. The key issues are: at what time are the appearances to be judged?; by whom are they to be judged, a reasonable man on the outside, or the judges who have inquired into all the circumstances? Two formulations that have been adopted in the cases are: "Was there a real likelihood of bias?"; "Was there a reasonable suspicion of bias?" In most, possibly all, cases each test would lead to the same result. See F. A. Trinidade (1965) 7 Malaya Law Rev. 170; F. Alexis, "Reasonableness in the establishment of bias" [1979] P.L. 143 and Stocker J. in *R.* v. *St Edmundsbury B.C., ex p. Investors in Industry Commercial Properties Ltd.* [1985] 3 All E.R. 235 at p. 255.

METROPOLITAN PROPERTIES CO. (F.G.C.) LTD. v. LANNON AND OTHERS; R. v. LONDON RENT ASSESSMENT PANEL COMMITTEE, ex p. METROPOLITAN PROPERTIES CO. (F.G.C.) LTD.

[1969] 1 Q.B. 577; [1968] 3 W.L.R. 694; 112 S.J. 585; [1968] 3 All E.R. 304; 19 P. & C.R. 856; [1968] R.V.R. 490 (Court of Appeal)

The tenants in a block of flats in Oakwood Court, Kensington Gardens, applied under the Rent Act 1965 for a fair rent for each of the flats to be determined by a rent officer. The landlords objected to the officer's determination, and the matter was referred to the rent assessment committee. The committee fixed the rent at amounts below both those put forward by experts called on behalf of the landlords, and those put forward by the rent officer. Mr. Lannon, a solicitor, was the chairman of the committee. He lived with his father, who was a tenant of a flat at Regency Lodge. His father's landlord was an associate company belonging to the same group (the "Freshwater Group") as the landlords of Oakwood Court. Mr. Lannon's firm had acted for other tenants in Regency Lodge, who were in dispute with their landlord on matters similar to those before the committee. Mr. Lannon himself had assisted his father in the latter's dispute with the Regency Lodge landlords. The Oakwood Court landlords appealed to the Queen's Bench Division under the Tribunals and Inquiries Act 1958, arguing, *inter alia*, that Mr. Lannon was disqualified from hearing the case on the ground that there were reasonable grounds for the landlords to believe that he could not give them an unbiased hearing. The Divisional Court found against the landlords ([1968] 1 W.L.R. 815). The landlords appealed to the Court of Appeal, and now sought an order of certiorari.

LORD DENNING M.R.: . . . A man may be disqualified from sitting in a judicial capacity on one of two grounds. First, a "direct pecuniary interest" in the subject-matter. Second, "bias" in favour of one side or against the other.

So far as "pecuniary interest" is concerned, I agree with the Divisional Court that there is no evidence that Mr. John Lannon had any direct pecuniary interest in the suit. He had no interest in any of the flats in Oakwood Court. The only possible interest was his father's interest in having the rent of 55 Regency Lodge reduced. It was put in this way: if the committee reduced the rents of Oakwood Court, those rents would be used as "comparable" for Regency Lodge, and might influence their being put lower than they otherwise would be. Even if we identify the son's interest with the father's, I think this is too remote. It is neither direct nor certain. It is indirect and uncertain.

So far as bias is concerned, it was acknowledged that there was no actual bias on the part of Mr. Lannon, and no want of good faith. But it was said that there was, albeit unconscious, a real likelihood of bias. This is a matter on which the law is not altogether clear: but I start with the oft-repeated saying of Lord Hewart C.J. in *R.* v. *Sussex Justices, ex p. McCarthy* [1924] 1 K.B. 256 at p. 259: "It is not merely of some importance, but is of fundamental importance that justice should not only be done, but should manifestly and undoubtedly be seen to be done."

In *R.* v. *Barnsley Licensing Justices, ex p. Barnsley and District Licensed Victuallers' Association* [1960] 2 Q.B. 167, at p. 187 Devlin J. appears to have limited that principle considerably, but I would stand by it. It brings home this point: in considering whether there was a real likelihood of bias, the court does not look at the mind of the justice himself or at the mind of the chairman of the tribunal, or whoever it may be, who sits in a judicial capacity. It does not look to see if there was a real likelihood that he would, or did, in fact favour one side at the expense of the other. The court looks at the impression which would be given to other people. Even if he was as impartial as could be, nevertheless if right-minded persons would think that, in the circumstances, there was a real likelihood of bias on his part, then he should not sit. And if he does sit, his decision cannot stand: see *R.* v. *Huggins* [1895] 1 Q.B. 563; and *R.* v. *Sunderland Justices* [1901] 2 K.B. 357 (C.A.) *per* Vaughan Williams L.J. (*ibid.* at p. 373). Nevertheless there must appear to be a real likelihood of bias. Surmise or conjecture is not enough: see *R.* v. *Camborne Justices, ex p. Pearce* [1955] 1 Q.B. 41 at pp. 48–51 and *R.* v. *Nailsworth Licensing Justices, ex p. Bird* [1953] 1 W.L.R. 1046. There must be circumstances from which a reasonable man would think it likely or probable that the justice, or chairman, as the case may be, would, or did, favour one side unfairly at the expense of the other. The court will not inquire whether he did, in fact, favour one side unfairly. Suffice it that reasonable people might think he did. The reason is plain enough. Justice must be rooted in confidence: and confidence is destroyed when right-minded people go away thinking: "The judge was biased."

Applying these principles, I ask myself: Ought Mr. John Lannon to have sat? I think not. If he was himself a tenant in difference with his landlord about the rent of his flat, he clearly ought not to sit on a case against the selfsame landlord, also about the rent of a flat, albeit another flat. In this case he was not a tenant, but the son of a tenant. But that makes no difference. No reasonable man would draw any distinction between him and his father, seeing he was living with him and assisting him with his case.

Test it quite simply: if Mr. John Lannon were to have asked any of his friends: "I have been asked to preside in a case about the rents charged by the Freshwater Group of Companies at Oakwood Court. But I am already assisting my father in his case against them, about the rent of his flat in Regency Lodge, where I am living with him. Do you think I can properly sit?" The answer of any of his good friends would surely have been: "No, you should not sit. You are already acting, or as good as acting, against them. You should not, at the same time, sit in judgment on them."

No man can be an advocate for or against a party in one proceeding, and at the same time sit as a judge of that party in another proceeding. Everyone would agree that a judge, or a barrister or solicitor (when he sits ad hoc as a member of a tribunal) should not sit on a case to which a near relative or a close friend is a party. So also a barrister or solicitors should not sit on a case to which one of his clients is a party. Nor on a case where he is already acting against one of the parties, Inevitably people would think he would be biased.

I hold, therefore, that Mr. John Lannon ought not to have sat on this rent assessment committee. The decision is voidable on that account and should be avoided. . . .

DANCKWERTS L.J.: . . . What would a normal judicial person do in [these] circumstances? . . . I think that such a person would feel that either he ought not to act in the matter as a member of the committee, or, at least, he should mention these matters at the hearing and inquire whether the parties objected before going on with the hearing. Nothing was said in fact. A person subsequently hearing of these matters might reasonably feel doubts, I think, of the chairman's impartiality, and the results reached in the committee's decision, and the form of the affidavits would, I think, increase any suspicion of bias or inability to be impartial by the chairman that might have been present in the mind of a party.

Of course, I am not saying that the mere fact that a solicitor has acted for or advised tenants should disqualify him from sitting. But the facts of this case display some lack of appreciation of the rules of conduct by Mr. Lannon, and my conclusion is that it was not wise of Mr. Lannon to act as chairman of the committee in the circumstances. Accordingly, I would allow the appeal.

EDMUND DAVIES L.J.: . . . The appellants submit that the Divisional Court "misdirected itself in holding that on the facts proved or admitted there were no sufficient grounds for the appellant-applicants to believe that the said John Lannon"—that is, the chairman of the committee—"could not give them an unbiased hearing." Not until a late stage in the hearing of this appeal was that matter touched upon. What had chiefly been contested was whether such complaint (be it well founded or not) poses the correct question in law. Mr. Slynn submits that it does not. Resting himself upon such decisions as *R.* v. *Camborne Justices* and *R.* v. *Barnsley Licensing Justices* he propounds the correct test as being: Was there a *real likelihood* that the chairman was biased in his participation in the committee's decision? He submits that the *possibility* of bias is insufficient, and so is the suspicion thereof, even though reasonably held by right-thinking people.

It cannot be made too clear that the appellants expressly disclaim *actual* bias in the chairman. But if Mr. Slynn be right, what becomes of the principle which remains transcendent despite its enshrinement in the excessively quoted words of Lord Hewart in *R.* v. *Sussex Justices* [1924] 1 K.B. 256 at p. 259 that "justice should not only be done, but should manifestly and undoubtedly be seen to be done"? As Professor de Smith has written (*Judicial Review of Administrative Action* (1959), p. 150):

> "The courts have often quashed decisions on the strength of the reasonable suspicions of the party aggrieved, without having made any finding that a real likelihood of bias in fact existed."

But, after referring to *R.* v. *Camborne Justices* [1955] 1 Q.B. 41, the writer continues—

> "In so far as the 'real likelihood' and 'reasonable suspicion' tests are inconsistent with each other, it is submitted that the former is to be preferred; the reviewing court should make an objective decision, on the basis of the whole evidence before it, whether there was a real likelihood that the inferior tribunal would be biased. That members of an independent tribunal are likely to have been biased is a serious allegation. The public interest will not be served by relaxing the conditions under which it may be successfully made."

Nor in my judgment will the public interest be served if, in the light of all the circumstances as they finally emerge, it appears to right-thinking people that there are solid grounds for suspecting that a member of the tribunal responsible for the decision may (however unconsciously) have been biased.

But it must be conceded that the tide of judicial opinion is to some extent in favour of the professor. Thus, in *Healey* v. *Rauhina* [1958] N.Z.L.R. 945 Hutchinson J., after reviewing the cases, said (*ibid.* at p. 951): ". . . the weight of authority now is that the test to be applied is that of real likelihood of bias, and that reasonable suspicion of bias is insufficient."

And in *R.* v. *Barnsley Licensing Justices* [1960] 2 Q.B. 167 referring to the dissenting judgment of Salmon J. in the Divisional Court ([1959] 2 Q.B. 276) Devlin L.J. said ([1960] 2 Q.B. 167 at p. 187):

> "I am not quite sure what test Salmon J. applied. If he applied the test based on the principle that justice must not only be done but manifestly be seen to be done, I think he came to the right conclusion on that test. . . . But . . . it is *not* the test. *We have not to enquire what impression might be left on the minds of the present applicants or on the minds of the public generally.* We have to satisfy ourselves that there was a real likelihood of bias—*not* merely satisfy ourselves that that was the sort of impression that might reasonably get abroad. The term 'real likelihood of bias' is not used, in my opinion, to import the principle in *R.* v. *Sussex Justices* to

which Salmon J. referred ([1959] 2 Q.B. 276 at p. 286). It is used to show that it is *not* necessary that actual bias should be proved. It is unnecessary . . . to investigate the state of mind of each individual justice. '*Real likelihood' depends on the impression which the court gets from the circumstances in which the justices were sitting*. Do they give rise to a real likelihood that the justices might be biased? The court might come to the conclusion that there was such a likelihood, without impugning the affidavit of a justice that he was not in fact biased. Bias is or may be an unconscious thing. . . . The matter must be determined upon the probabilities to be inferred from the circumstances in which the justices sat."

With profound respect to those who have propounded the "real likelihood" test, I take the view that the requirement that justice must manifestly be done operates with undiminished force in cases where bias is alleged and that any development of the law which appears to emasculate that requirement should be strongly resisted. That the different tests, even when applied to the same facts, may lead to different results is illustrated by *R.* v. *Barnsley Licensing Justices* itself, as Devlin L.J. made clear in the passage I have quoted. But I cannot bring myself to hold that a decision may properly be allowed to stand even although there is *reasonable* suspicion of bias on the part of one or more members of the adjudicating body.

Adopting that approach in relation to the facts of the present case, the circumstances already adverted to by my Lords are such that I regard it as most unfortunate that this particular chairman sat to try these appeals. The reality of the situation emerges clearly from the record of the committee itself, for when it sat on January 19, 1967, its clerk began his notes of the hearing by transcribing as the landlords of the Oakwood Court flats *not* "Metropolitan Properties Co. (F.G.C.) Ltd." but "The Freshwater Group of Companies," to that same group belonged the Swiss Cottage flat tenanted by Mr. Lannon senior, on whose behalf his son had written to the rent officer only six days before the hearing in terms critical of the landlords. It is indeed difficult to see how the chairman could have failed to be aware of the ambiguous position in which he was placing himself by so soon thereafter proceeding to adjudicate on the Oakwood Court applications. Be that as it may, the result of his having sat is highly unfortunate. It is conceivable that, although "startling," the decisions of the committee were nevertheless correct—that remains to be seen. But it is not manifest that they were just, and they therefore ought not to be allowed to stand. I concur with my Lords in holding that they should be quashed.

Appeal allowed. Decision of committee quashed by certiorari. Case remitted to committee to hear. No order on section 9 appeal.

HANNAM v. BRADFORD CORPORATION

[1970] 1 W.L.R. 937; 114 S.J. 414; 68 L.G.R. 498; *sub nom. Hannam* v. *Bradford City Council* [1970] 2 All E.R. 690 (Court of Appeal)

From November 1962 to October 1967 H. taught physics at St. Bede's Grammar School, Bradford. The school was an aided voluntary school maintained by the corporation (the local education authority). On October 6, H. absented himself from his duties without leave, and refused to return. On December 19, the school governors met and terminated his employment, giving him the full period of notice required by the contract of employment. Under the Education Act 1944, s.24(2)(*a*), the local education authority had power to prohibit the dismissal, and this power was included in the school's articles of government (made pursuant to s.24 of the 1944 Act) and in the relevant conditions of service of teachers. On January 18, 1968, the corporation's staff sub-committee met and held an inquiry (as required by the articles) whether the corporation should exercise their power to prohibit the dismissal. The chairman and two members of the sub-committee were also members of the school's governing body. The sub-committee recommended that the power should not be exercised, and that decision was affirmed by the full council. The dismissal took effect on April 30.

The plaintiff sued for damages in the county court. One ground was that for a number of reasons, there had been a breach by the corporation of their contractual obligation to ensure that the inquiry of the staff sub-committee was conducted in accordance with natural justice, and by persons who were not liable to bias. Eight grounds were put forward by the plaintiff to support this claim of which one was upheld by the judge. This was that the sub-committee included three members likely to be biased. The corporation appealed, alleging that there was no contract at all between them and the plaintiff touching such an inquiry; that if there was such a contract, it did not apply to a termination of employment by due notice; and that in any event there was no breach of contract as regards the composition of the staff sub-committee.

SACHS L.J.: [stated the facts, and continued:] It should be noted that there was an explicit finding by the county court judge that that decision was reached honestly and in good faith and that none of these three governors was actuated by bias. . . .

[Counsel for the council] rightly conceded that the staff subcommittee were exercising a quasi-judicial function at such a hearing. He submitted, however, that the presence of the three governors as members of the subcommittee of ten—the quorum was three—did not invalidate the proceedings. His case was that there was "no real likelihood" of bias on their part, and he prayed in aid the fact that none of them attended the meeting of the governors on December 19, 1967, at which it was determined to dismiss the plaintiff.

At this point it is convenient to note the ground for dismissal of the plaintiff. These were that as from October 6, 1967, he had consistently absented himself without leave from his duties because of what he referred to as slanderous statements touching his professional capacity made by one member of the staff in the presence of other members of the staff, but not in the presence of the headmaster. He had refused, in a high-handed manner (to which later reference will be made), to return to his duties unless the headmaster dealt with the matter in a particular way upon which he insisted. At the staff subcommittee meeting it was thus the exercise of the governors' discretion in dismissing the plaintiff in such circumstances that was in issue.

The county court judge applied the test as to whether "a reasonable man would say that a real danger of bias existed." Mr. Duncan asserted that that test was erroneous and that, anyway, no real danger existed. This court was referred to the well-known series of authorities, not all of which had been cited to the county court judge, ranging from *R.* v. *Rand* (1866) L.R. 1 Q.B. 230, through the case of *R.* v. *Camborne Justices, ex p. Pearce* [1954] 1 Q.B. 41 to *Metropolitan Properties Co.* (*F.G.C.*) *Ltd.* v. *Lannon* [1969] 1 Q.B. 577, a recent decision of this court. . . .

[His Lordship cited passages from the last case.]

Those judgments involve, in effect, somewhat of a swing back towards the principle enunciated in the *Sussex Justices'* case [1924] 1 K.B. 256, which had to some account been discounted in some previous decisions. For my part, I doubt whether in practice materially different results are produced by the "real likelihood of bias" test urged by Mr. Duncan or that adopted by the county court judge. If there is such a difference, I uphold the latter and respectfully adhere to the school of thought adopted in *Lannon's* case [1969] 1 Q.B. 577, for the reasons there given by Lord Denning M.R. I agree, too, that the county court judge applied the test correctly to the facts.

I would, however, add that there is a slightly different ground on which it was abundantly clear that the staff subcommittee decision could not stand. No man can be a judge of his own cause. The governors did not, upon donning their subcommittee hats, cease to be an integral part of the body whose action was being impugned, and it made no difference that they did not personally attend the governors' meeting of December 19. The fallacy of any contrary view is exemplified by considering what the position would be if there had been a quorum meeting of three members of the subcommittee, all of whom had been governors. To say that a decision of such a trio could stand would be to produce an absurdity. There thus fails the argument that was put in the forefront of his case by Mr. Duncan in his attack on the decision on liability made at first instance by the county court judge. . . .

[His Lordship went on to hold that s.24(2)(*a*) applied to all dismissals including those with due notice, that there was a contract between the plaintiff and the council, and that therefore he was "not limited to such rights as he might be able to enforce either by certiorari or mandamus or by obtaining an injunction against the school for acting without the proper procedure having been implemented." However, damages would be nominal as it was "not conceivable that any properly constituted staff subcommittee of the council could have decided to prohibit the dismissal."]

WIDGERY L.J.: [stated that he was content to accept the concession that the functions of the staff subcommittee were quasi-judicial, and continued:] "So far as bias is concerned, I, like my Lord [Sachs L.J.], am satisfied that there was a real likelihood of bias in this case. I do not wish to add to the somewhat confusing welter of authority on what is meant by "bias" in this connection by attempting any further definition myself, because I think that whichever of the tests adumbrated in *Metropolitan Properties Co. (F.G.C.) Ltd.* v. *Lannon* [1969] 1 Q.B. 577 is properly to be applied in this case, the plaintiff had made out his allegation. I am much impressed by the fact that when the subcommittee sat down to consider what the plaintiff would regard as an appeal, the chairman was a member of the governors against whose decision this so-called appeal was being brought. I think that if it had been disclosed at the outset that no less a person than the chairman of the subcommittee was a member of the governors in question, the immediate reaction of everyone would have been that some real likelihood of bias existed. I say that with every respect to the distinguished gentleman who chaired the subcommittee on this occasion; but when one is used to working with other people in a group or on a committee, there must be a built-in tendency to support the decision of that committee, even though one tries to fight against it, and this is so even though the chairman was not sitting on the occasion when the decision complained about was reached.

I, therefore, would find that the trial judge below was right on both those points, namely, that the functions were quasi-judicial and that a real likelihood of bias existed. Accordingly, it seems to me that if the plaintiff had been minded promptly to move for mandamus, he might, in theory at any rate, have had an opportunity of having a rehearing of his complaint. I think in fact that such considerations are now academic, not only because over two years has expired since the decision complained of, but because the discretionary remedy of mandamus would not, I think, have been afforded to the plaintiff in this case when it is so abundantly clear, as my Lord has demonstrated, that no committee of the council faced with this question could have reached a conclusion other than that which was reached in this case. I think that in those circumstances, if application for a mandamus had been made, it would have failed on the basis of its being a discretionary remedy unjustified in the circumstances; and the matter is a fortiori when one finds oneself in March, 1970, with no action of this kind being taken.

[His Lordship held, disagreeing with SACHS L.J., that there was no contractual relationship between the plaintiff and the council, the right to a hearing being contained solely in the statute-based articles of government.]

CROSS L.J.: [agreed with the judgment of SACHS L.J. on all points except that the plaintiff was in contractual relations with the council. On that point he agreed with WIDGERY L.J.] I would just add a few words on the question of bias. To my mind, there really is little (if any) difference between the two tests which are propounded in the cases which have been cited to us. If a reasonable person who has no knowledge of the matter beyond knowledge of the relationship which subsists between some members of the tribunal and one of the parties would think that there might well be bias, then there is in his opinion a real likelihood of bias. Of course, someone else with inside knowledge of the characters of the members in question might say: "Although things don't look very well, in fact there is no real likelihood of bias." That, however, would be beside the point, because the question is not whether the tribunal will in fact be biased, but whether a reasonable man with no inside knowledge might well think that it might be biased.

I agree with Widgery L.J. in thinking that this appeal should be allowed and the action dismissed.

Appeal allowed.

Notes

1. Over recent years the lower courts have expressed divergent views as to the extent to which the rule against bias applies to the decision-making of local planning authorities. In *Steeples* v. *Derbyshire County Council* [1985] 1 W.L.R. 256, the council owned an area of parkland and entered into an agreement with a company to jointly develop the site. The agreement provided that the council would take reasonable steps to obtain planning permission for the proposed development. The planning committee of the council considered the application and granted permission for the development. A member of a local amenity group sought a declaration that the permission was unlawful having been made in breach of the rule against bias. Webster J. sought to judge the legality of the council's actions according to a modified version of the *Lannon* test:

> "In conclusion . . . it is probable that a reasonable man, not having been present at the meeting when the decision was made, and not knowing of my conclusion as to the actual fairness of it, knowing of the existence and of all the terms of the contract (but without regard to the question whether they would in law have been enforceable), would think that there was a real likelihood that those provisions in the contract which require the county council, and for that matter the joint venture committee, to use their best endeavours to obtain planning permission, and the contract as a whole in the light of its provision to which I have referred, had had a material and significant effect on the planning committee's decision to grant the permission; and accordingly, on that ground, I hold that that decision was either voidable or void" (at p. 288).

Whereas, in *R.* v. *Amber Valley District Council, ex p. Jackson* [1985] 1 W.L.R. 298, Woolf J. doubted the applicability of the *Lannon* principle to administrative decisions of planning committees. This case was a sequel to *Steeples* in that subsequently the development company applied to the local district council (Amber Valley), whose area covered the parkland, for planning permission to develop the site. Prior to Amber Valley's planning committee considering the application, the majority Labour party group on the council resolved to support the development (this policy was in accordance with the views of the Labour controlled Derbyshire County Council). A member of the local amenity group opposed to the development sought an order of prohibition against Amber Valley District Council to prevent the council considering the planning application on the grounds that any determination was likely to be biased in the light of the earlier policy decision of the controlling Labour group. The learned judge considered:

"The rules of fairness or natural justice cannot be regarded as being rigid. They must alter in accordance with the context. Thus in the case of highways, the department can be both the promoting authority and the determining authority. When this happens, of course any reasonable man would regard the department as being pre-disposed towards the outcome of the inquiry. The department is under an obligation to be fair and carefully to consider the evidence given before the inquiry but the fact that it has a policy in the matter does not entitle a court to intervene. So in this case I do not consider the fact that there is a declaration of policy by the majority group can disqualify a district council from adjudicating on a planning application" (pp. 307–308).

Consequently, the application for an order of prohibition was dismissed.

In *R.* v. *Sevenoaks District Council, ex p. Terry* [1985] 3 All E.R. 226, the High Court disagreed with the *Steeples* test for bias and proposed its own formula. The case concerned a piece of land owned by the council. In the summer of 1981 the council accepted an offer from a development company to lease the site in order to construct a supermarket. Then in early 1982 the council granted the developers planning permission to develop the site. A local ratepayer sought an order of certiorari to quash the planning grant on the ground that the council was biased in favour of the application because of its previous dealings with the developers. Glidewell J. determined that the *Lannon* principle did not apply to this decision-making function:

"Of course, the council must act honestly and fairly, but it is not uncommon for a local authority to be obliged to make a decision relating to land or other property in which it has an interest. In such a situation, the application of the rule designed to ensure that a judicial officer does not appear to be biased would, in my view, often produce an administrative impasse. . . . the correct test to be applied in the present case is for the court to pose to itself the question: had the district council before [determining the planning application] acted in such a way that it is clear that, when the committee came to consider [the developers'] application for planning permission, it could not exercise proper discretion? Of course, in asking that question, it may appear that the answer is Yes, even though an individual councillor says quite genuinely and honestly that he personally was able to approach the decision without bias. But, if the answer to the question is No, it is in my judgment neither necessary nor desirable for the court to go further and consider what the opinion of a reasonable man would be. In so far as this formulation differs from that adopted by Webster J. in *Steeples* v. *Derbyshire C.C.*, I respectfully disagree with him" (p. 233).

Applying this test the learned judge found that the council had not unlawfully fettered the exercise of its discretion to grant or refuse planning permission for the site in January 1982; therefore, he dismissed the application. This test was also endorsed and applied by Stocker J. in *R.* v. *St Edmundsbury Borough Council, ex p. Investors in Industry Commercial Properties Ltd.* [1985] 3 All E.R. 234.

The above cases demonstrate that there is clearly a need for the appellate courts to clarify the law in this area of administrative decision-making.

2. There are many cases applying the *nemo judex* principle to justices. See, *e.g. R.* v. *Altrincham JJ., ex p. Pennington* [1975] Q.B. 549; *R.* v. *Smethwick JJ., ex p. Hands*, *The Times*, December 4, 1980 (decision on allegation of statutory nuisance against local authority quashed because one of the justices was the wife of the former

chairman of the housing committee); *R.* v. *Liverpool City JJ., ex p. Topping* [1983] 1 W.L.R. 119 (justices have a discretion whether to continue to hear a charge they are about to try where they become aware of other unrelated charges against the defendant; the test to be applied is "would a reasonable and fair-minded person sitting in court and knowing all the relevant facts have a reasonable suspicion that a fair trial for the applicant was not possible?"); *R.* v. *Weston-super-Mare JJ., ex p. Shaw* [1987] Q.B. 640; *R.* v. *Mulvihill* [1990] 1 All E.R. 436 (applying the *Topping* test to a Crown Court judge who held 1,650 shares in one of a number of banks and building societies the appellant was said to have robbed; appeal dismissed).

3. Some difficulty is caused by the competing formulations of the bias test, "reasonable suspicion" or "real likelihood." Note the helpful comments in *Craig*, pp. 236–237, stressing the importance of distinguishing two issues. The first is "from which or whose perspective is the court viewing the issue of bias?" The *Lannon* decision makes it clear that the issue is to be considered from the perspective of the "reasonable man" (and not the mind of the justice (or other challenged individuals); the individual affected; or *ex post facto* by the reviewing court). The second issue is "What must the reasonable man be perceiving?" Lord Denning M.R. in *Lannon* (and in effect the court in *Hannam*) state that it must be a "real likelihood" of bias, and not merely a "reasonable suspicion." This is not, however, *overall*, the real likelihood test of the *Camborne JJ.* and *Barnsley* cases, where the matter is judged from the perspective of the reviewing court.

For an argument that the choice of test should depend on the context, see H. F. Rawlings, [1980] P.L. 122; *cf.* Webster J. in *Steeples*, above, n. 1.

4. Is a "judge" who holds a fixed or firm view on, *e.g.*, teetotalism, vivisection of animals, blood sports etc., an offender against the *nemo judex* rule if he or she adjudicates in a case where such questions are involved?

5. Distinguish the *nemo judex* rule from the rule prohibiting an administrative agency from exercising a discretion in accordance with a preconceived fixed policy (above, p. 284).

6. The bias principle may be excluded or modified by an express statutory provision (see *Wilkinson* v. *Barking Corporation* [1948] 1 K.B. 721) or by necessity, where all available adjudicators would otherwise be disqualified (see the *Dimes* case, above, p. 573; R. R. S. Tracey, [1982] P.L. 628).

7. Where a breach of the *nemo judex* principle is alleged it is not necessary for the applicant to show that he or she has been prejudiced by it (*R. (Snaith)* v. *The Ulster Polytechnic* [1981] N.I. 28); (*cf.* the position under the *audi alteram partem* rule, above. p. 490).

(d) Statutory Formulations of the Nemo Judex Rule

Note

See *Rands* v. *Oldroyd* (above, p. 34), applying the provisions of the Local Government Acts (see now ss.94–97 of the Local Government Act 1972) relating to the declaration of "interest" by members of local authorities.

LOCAL GOVERNMENT ACT 1972

Disability of members of authorities for voting on account of interest in contracts, etc.

94.—(1) Subject to the provisions of section 97 below, if a member of a local authority has any pecuniary interest, direct or indirect, in any contract, proposed contract or other matter, and is present at a meeting of the local authority at which the contract or other matter is the subject of consideration, he shall at the meeting and as soon as practicable after its commencement disclose the fact and shall not take part in the consideration or discussion of the contract or other matter or vote on any question with respect to it.

(2) If any person fails to comply with the provisions of subsection (1) above he shall for each offence be liable on summary conviction to a fine not exceeding [level 4 on the standard scale] unless he proves that he did not know that the contract, proposed contract or other matter in which he had a pecuniary interest was the subject of consideration at that meeting.

(3) A prosecution for an offence under this section shall not be instituted except by or on behalf of the Director of Public Prosecutions.

(4) A local authority may by standing orders provide for the exclusion of a member of the authority from a meeting of the authority while any contract, proposed contract or other matter in which he has a pecuniary interest, direct or indirect, is under consideration.

(5) The following, that is to say—

(*a*) the receipt by the chairman, vice-chairman or deputy chairman of a principal council of an allowance to meet the expenses of his office or his right to receive, or the possibility of his receiving, such an allowance;

(*b*) the receipt by a member of a local authority of an allowance or other payment under any provision of sections 173 to 176 below [or under any scheme made by virtue of s.18 of the Local Government and Housing Act 1989] or his right to receive, or the possibility of his receiving, any such payment; shall not be treated as a pecuniary interest for the purposes of this section.

Pecuniary interests for purposes of section 94

95.—(1) For the purposes of section 94 above a person shall be treated, subject to the following provisions of this section and to section 97 below, as having indirectly a pecuniary interest in a contract, proposed contract or other matter, if—

(*a*) he or any nominee of his is a member of a company or other body with which the contract was made or is proposed to be made or which has a direct pecuniary interest in the other matter under consideration; or

(*b*) he is a partner, or is in the employment, of a person with whom the contract was made or is proposed to be made or who has a direct pecuniary interest in the other matter under consideration.

(2) Subsection (1) above does not apply to membership of or employment under any public body, and a member of a company or other body

shall not by reason only of his membership be treated as having an interest in any contract, proposed contract or other matter if he has no beneficial interest in any securities of that company or other body.

(3) In the case of married persons living together the interest of one spouse shall, if known to the other, be deemed for the purpose of section 94 above to be also an interest of the other.

General notices and recording of disclosures for purposes of section 94

94.—(1) A general notice given in writing to the proper officer of the authority by a member thereof to the effect that he or his spouse is a member or in the employment of a specified company or other body, or that he or his spouse is a partner or in the employment of a specified person, or that he or his spouse is the tenant of any premises owned by the authority, shall, unless and until the notice is withdrawn, be deemed to be a sufficient disclosure of his interest in any contract, proposed contract or other matter relating to that company or other body or to that person or to those premises which may be the subject of consideration after the date of the notice.

(2) The proper officers of the authority shall record in a book to be kept for the purpose particulars of any disclosure made under section 94 above and of any notice given under this section, and the book shall be open at all reasonable hours to the inspection of any member of the local authority.

Removal or exclusion of disability, etc.

97.—(1) The district council, as respects a member of a parish or community council, and the Secretary of State, as respects a member of any other local authority, may, subject to such conditions as the district council or the Secretary of State may think fit to impose, remove any disability imposed by section 94 above in any case in which the members of the local authority disabled by that section at any one time would be so great a proportion of the whole as to impede the transaction of business, or in any other case in which it appears to the district council or the Secretary of State in the interests of the inhabitants of the area that the disability should be removed.

(2) The power of a district council and of the Secretary of State under subsection (1) above includes power to remove, either indefinitely or for any period, any such disability which would otherwise attach to any member (or, in the case of the power of the Secretary of State, any member or any class or description of members) by reason of such interests, and in respect of such matters, as may be specified by the council or the Secretary of State.

(3) Nothing in section 94 above precludes any person from taking part in the consideration or discussion of, or voting on, any question whether

an application should be made to a district council or the Secretary of State for exercise of the powers conferred by subsections (1) and (2) above.

(4) Section 94 above does not apply to an interest in a contract, proposed contract or other matter which a member of a local authority has as [a person who is liable under the local Government Finance Act 1988 to pay an amount in respect of any community charge or under any enactment or as] a ratepayer or inhabitant of the area or as an ordinary consumer of water, or to an interest in any matter relating to the terms on which the right to participate in any service, including the supply of goods, is offered to the public.

(5) For the purposes of section 94 above a member shall not be treated as having a pecuniary interest in any contract, proposed contract or other matter by reason only of an interest of his or of any company, body or person with which he is connected as mentioned in section 95(1) above which is so remote or insignificant that it cannot reasonably be regarded as likely to influence a member in the consideration or discussion of, or in voting on, any question with respect to that contract or matter.

(6) Where a member of a local authority has an indirect pecuniary interest in a contract, proposed contract or other matter by reason only of a beneficial interest in securities of a company or other body, and the total nominal value of those securities does not exceed [£5,000] or one-hundredth of the total nominal value of the issued share capital of the company or body, whichever is the less, and if the share capital is of more than one class, the total nominal value of shares of any one class in which he has a beneficial interest does not exceed one-hundredth of the total issued share capital of that class, section 94 above shall not prohibit him from taking part in the consideration or discussion of the contract or other matter or from voting on any question with respect to it, without prejudice, however, to his duty to disclose his interest.

Note

Analogous provisions apply to school governors by virtue of the Education (School Government) Regulations 1989 (S.I. 1989 No. 1503). These are regarded as mandatory: see *Noble* v. *Inner London Education Authority* (1984) L.G.R. 291; *Bostock* v. *Kay* (1989) 87 L.G.R. 583; *R.* v. *Governors of Small Heath School, ex p. Birmingham City Council* [1990] C.O.D. 23; *R.* v. *Governors of John Bacon School, ex p. Inner London Education Authority* [1990] C.O.D. 414.

LICENSING ACT 1964

Part XIV

Supplemental

Disqualification of justices

193.—(1) No justice shall act for any purpose under this Act in any county, . . . or be capable of being appointed or being a member of any committee therein for any such purpose, who is, or is in partnership with, a brewer, distiller, maker of malt for sale or retailer of malt or of any intoxicating liquor, in that county. . . .

(2) No justice who holds any share or stock in a company which is such a brewer, distiller, maker of malt or retailer as aforesaid in any county, . . . shall be capable of being appointed or being a member of a licensing committee . . . in that county . . . unless before his appointment as a member thereof he has disclosed to the justices appointing him the fact that he holds the share or stock; but where a member of any such committee . . . is disqualified for being a member thereof by acquiring any such share or stock he may be re-appointed if before his re-appointment he has disclosed to the justices re-appointing him the fact that he has acquired the share or stock.

(3) A person who is the beneficial owner of any such share or stock as aforesaid held by him (whether his beneficial ownership extends to the whole holding or to a part of it or an interest in it only) shall not be appointed or re-appointed a member of any such committee . . . as aforesaid unless the justices appointing or re-appointing him are satisfied that the extent to which the company in question carries on or is interested in the business of brewing, distilling, making of malt for sale or retailing of malt or of any intoxicating liquor is so small in comparison with its whole business that the fact that the said person is interested in the company affords no reasonable ground for suggesting that he is not a proper person to be a member of the committee. . . .

(4) Subject to subsection (5) of this section, no justice shall act for any purpose under this Act in a case that concerns any premises in the profits of which he is interested, or of which he is wholly or partly the owner, lessee, or occupier, or for the owner, lessee, or occupier of which he is manager or agent; but a justice shall not be disqualified under this provision by reason of his having vested in him a legal interest only, and not a beneficial interest, in the premises concerned or the profits of them.

(5) A justice having an interest in the profits of any premises shall not be thereby disqualified under subsection (4) of this section or otherwise from acting under this Act, if he would not fall to be treated as having such an interest but for the fact that he has a beneficial interest in shares of a company or other body having an interest in those profits, and if his beneficial interest in the shares of the company or body does not extend to shares of a total nominal value greater than twenty-five pounds, or to more than one-hundredth in nominal value of its issued share capital or of any class of its issued share capital.

In this subsection "share" includes stock, and "share capital" shall be construed accordingly.

(6) No act done by any justice disqualified by this section shall be invalid by reason only of that disqualification, and no act done by any justice who by virtue of this section has ceased to be a member of any licensing committee . . . shall be invalid by reason only of the cessation of membership.

(7) If any justice, knowing that the circumstances are such that under this Act he is disqualified for acting for any of the purposes of this Act, acts as a justice for that purpose he shall be liable to a penalty not exceeding one hundred pounds, to be recovered by action in the High Court; but a justice proceeded against for more than one contravention of this section committed before the institution of the proceedings shall not be liable in respect of all such contraventions to an aggregate penalty exceeding one hundred pounds.

(8) No objection shall be allowed to any justices' licence on the ground that it was granted by justices not qualified to grant it.

Note

A leading case on this section is *R.* v. *Barnsley County Borough Licensing Justices, ex p. Barnsley and District Licensed Victuallers Association* [1960] 2 Q.B. 167. Six of seven justices who were sitting when the Barnsley Co-operative Society were granted a spirits licence were members of the society. The husband of the seventh justice was also a member. Members were entitled to a "dividend" according to the amount of their purchases. The Court of Appeal held:

(1) that the reference to any premises "in the profits of which he is interested" in section 48(4) of the Licensing Act 1953 (now s.193(4) of the 1964 Act) meant in its context, "interested in the profits of the trade or business carried on upon the premises," and not interested in the profit such as the rental of the premises themselves;

(2) that the justices were so "interested" under section 48(4);

(3) that section 48(5), (now s.193(5) replaced the common law rule that an adjudicator with a direct pecuniary interest was disqualified from acting, where the interest was of the nature set out in section 48(4);

(4) that the justices' act was therefore not vitiated by their pecuniary interest;

(5) that their act would have been vitiated had there been a "real likelihood of bias," or a kind of direct pecuniary interest other than that contemplated by section 48(4); and

(6) that there was on the facts no real likelihood of bias, and no other pecuniary interest.

See S. A. de Smith, (1959) 22 M.L.R. 669; A. W. Bradley, [1961] C.L.J. 8; and H. F. Rawlings, [1980] P.L. 122, 125–126.

CHAPTER 10

ERROR OF LAW ON THE FACE OF THE RECORD

IN 1951, the Court of Appeal held in the *Northumberland* case (below) that the Divisional Court of the King's Bench Division retained power to grant certiorari to quash a decision of an inferior tribunal on the ground that the record of the proceedings revealed an error of law. The historical background was discussed at length by Lord Goddard C.J. in the Divisional Court, and by Denning L.J. (as he then was), and see the Privy Council in *R.* v. *Nat Bell Liquors Ltd.* [1922] 2 A.C. 128. Since then, there have been applications for certiorari on this ground in several different contexts, although not in many cases. The usefulness of this remedy has varied from context to context. It is well established as a method for reviewing decisions of the Criminal Injuries Compensation Board and Immigration Appeal Tribunals and has been used in respect of other tribunals until the creation of a statutory right of appeal. It has been granted to quash an invalid planning permission (see the *Royco Homes* case, below, p. 772). It was also unclear how useful the remedy was to ensure observance of the law by Supplementary Benefit Appeal Tribunals (see *R.* v. *Preston S.B.A.T., ex p. Moore*, below, p. 601).

The efficacy of this remedy depends in any particular case on the nature of the "record" of proceedings. Section 10 of the Tribunals and Inquiries Act 1958 (s. 10 of the 1992 Act, above, p. 76) considerably extended the obligations of tribunals and Ministers to give reasons for decisions. These reasons are deemed to be part of the record (s. 10(6)). Where there is a statutory right to appeal on a point of law to the High Court (below, p. 639), certiorari for error on the face is superfluous.

On the limited availability of a declaration in relation to non-jurisdictional error, see references given below, at p. 788.

R. v. NORTHUMBERLAND COMPENSATION APPEAL TRIBUNAL, ex p. SHAW

[1952] 1 K.B. 338; [1952] 1 T.L.R. 161; 116 J.P. 54; 96 S.J. 29; [1952] 1 All E.R. 122; 50 L.G.R. 193; 2 P. & C.R. 361 (Court of Appeal)

By the passing of the National Health Service Act 1946, the applicant lost his employment as clerk to the West Northumberland Joint Hospital Board. Aggrieved by the amount of compensation awarded to him by the compensating authority, the Gosforth Urban District Council, he referred the matter to the tribunal designated by the National Health Service (Transfer of Offices and Compensation) Regulations 1948. It became the duty of the tribunal to consider the matter so referred "in accordance with the provisions" of the regulations and "to determine accordingly whether any and, if so, what compensation ought to be awarded to the claimant" (see regulation 12). The tribunal therefore were bound by the definition of "service" contained in the regulations.

The order of the tribunal set out the period of the applicant's service with the hospital board as being from October 7, 1936, to March 31, 1949. It set out the contention of the compensating authority that the compensation payable should be based on that period of service with the hospital board, and the tribunal stated that they agreed that this service was the only service to be taken into account. The decision did not set out the contention of the applicant, who was clerk to the

Gosforth Urban District Council, that the whole of his local government service should be taken into account. And the tribunal dismissed the appeal from the decision of the compensating authority.

Thereupon the applicant applied to the Divisional Court for an order of certiorari to remove the decision of the tribunal into the King's Bench Division that it might be quashed. Before the Divisional Court it was admitted by counsel for the tribunal that there was error on the face of the decision given by the tribunal, but he contended that certiorari would lie to such a statutory tribunal only in the case of want or excess of jurisdiction. The Divisional Court granted the order for certiorari ([1951] 1 K.B. 711) and the tribunal appealed. The Gosforth Urban District Council did not appeal.

Counsel for the tribunal contended: (1) that certiorari could not be granted in respect of a decision of a statutory tribunal of the ground of error on the face of the record; and (2) that in any event there was no error on the face of the record.

DENNING L.J. The question in this case is whether the Court of King's Bench can intervene to correct the decision of a statutory tribunal which is erroneous in point of law. No one has ever doubted that the Court of King's Bench can intervene to prevent a statutory tribunal from exceeding the jurisdiction which Parliament has conferred on it; but it is quite another thing to say that the King's Bench can intervene when a tribunal makes a mistake of law. A tribunal may often decide a point of law wrongly whilst keeping well within its jurisdiction. If it does so, can the King's Bench intervene?

There is a formidable argument against any intervention on the part of the King's Bench at all. The statutory tribunals, like this one here, are often made the judges both of fact and law, with no appeal to the High Court. If, then, the King's Bench should interfere when a tribunal makes a mistake of law, the King's Bench may well be said to be exceeding its own jurisdiction. It would be usurping to itself an appellate jurisdiction which has not been given to it. The answer to this argument, however, is that the Court of King's Bench has an inherent jurisdiction to control all inferior tribunals, not in an appellate capacity, but in a supervisory capacity. This control extends not only to seeing that the inferior tribunals keep within their jurisdiction, but also to seeing that they observe the law. The control is exercised by means of a power to quash any determination by the tribunal which, on the face of it, offends against the law. The King's Bench does not substitute its own views for those of the tribunal, as a Court of Appeal would do. It leaves it to the tribunal to hear the case again, and in a proper case may command it to do so. When the King's Bench exercises its control over tribunals in this way, it is not usurping a jurisdiction which does not belong to it. It is only exercising a jurisdiction which it has always had.

The origin of this controlling power was the writ of certiorari, by which the King commanded the judges of any inferior Court of Record to certify the record of any matter in their court with all things touching the same, and to send it to the King's Court to be examined. The wording of the writ was for many centuries as follows, being originally in Latin and afterwards in English: "We being willing for certain reasons that all and singular orders made by you (as is said) be sent by you before us, do command that you do send forthwith before us all and singular the said orders with all things touching the same, as fully and perfectly as they have been made by you and now remain in your custody or power, together with this our writ, that we may cause further to be done thereon what of right and according to the law and custom of England we shall see fit to be done."

I would pause for a moment to notice the amplitude of this writ. The record of the inferior court is to be sent up so that the King's Bench may cause to be done thereon "what of right and according to the law and custom of England" ought to be done. The width of these words is only matched by the width of the words used by the great masters of the law in speaking of certiorari. Thus Joseph Chitty in his book on practice written in 1833, Vol. 2, at p. 353, said: "As an essential mode of exercising a control over all inferior courts, the Court of King's Bench has a most extensive power to bring before it their proceedings and fully to inform itself upon *every subject essential to decide upon the propriety of the proceedings below*. This is effected by a writ called certiorari. The writ issues in civil as well as criminal cases. . . ." Thus such a writ was ordered to be issued to the judge of an inferior jurisdiction to return and certify the practice of his court: see *Williams* v. *Bagot* (1824) 4 D. & R. 315. Ninety years later Lord Sumner used words of equal width: the supervision by certiorari "goes to two points: one is the area of the inferior jurisdiction and the qualifications and conditions of its exercise; the other is the observance of the law in the courts of its exercise:" see *R.* v. *Nat Bell Liquors Ltd.* [1922] 2 A.C. 128, 156.

Of recent years the scope of certiorari seems to have been somewhat forgotten. It has been supposed to be confined to the correction of excess of jurisdiction, and not to extend to the correction of errors of law; and several judges have said as much. But the Lord Chief Justice has, in the present case, restored certiorari to its rightful position and shown that it can be used to correct errors of law which appear on the face of the record, even though they do not go to jurisdiction. I have looked into the history of the matter, and find that the old cases fully support all that the Lord Chief Justice said. Until about 100 years ago, certiorari was regularly used to correct errors of law on the face of the record. It is only within the last century that it has fallen into disuse, and that is only because there has, until recently, been little occasion for its exercise. Now, with the advent of many new tribunals, and the plain need for supervision over them, recourse must once again be had to this well-tried means of control. I will endeavour to show how the writ of certiorari was used in former times, so that we can take advantage of the experience of the past to help us in the problems of the present.

Let me start with convictions by magistrates in summary proceedings under Acts of Parliament. Ever since the days of Holt C.J. the Court of

King's Bench has been extremely strict to see that all was in order. Everything necessary to support the conviction had to appear on the face of the record. The conviction had to recite the information in its precise terms. It had to set out the evidence of each witness as nearly as possible in his actual words. It had to state the adjudication with complete certainty. It had to show that the case was brought within the terms of the Act of Parliament creating the offence. If there was any defect in point of form, or any error in point of law, appearing on the face of the record, the conviction would be moved in to the King's Bench by certiorari and quashed. Nothing could be supplied by argument or intendment. The principles on which the court acted will be found well stated by Holt C.J. in *R.* v. *Chandler* (1703) 1 Salk. 378 and by Bayley and Holroyd JJ. in *R.* v. *Daman* (1819) 1 Chit. 147. An entertaining illustration will be found in *R.* v. *Barnaby* (1704) 1 Salk. 181 and specimen convictions in 1 Chitty's Reports, at p. 158, and in *R.* v. *Marsh* (1824) 4 D. & R. 260 where the conviction was drawn up by counsel on both sides so as to raise the point of law.

The result of all this strictness, however, was that many convictions were quashed for defects of form and not of substance. The legislature therefore intervened in 1848 to make the record of a conviction much more simple. Instead of a detailed speaking record, there was provided an unspeaking common form, which rarely disclosed any error. Thenceforward there was not so much room for certiorari in the case of convictions, but the fundamental principles remained untouched: see *R.* v. *Nat Bell Liquors Ltd.* [1922] 2 A.C. 128, 159, *per* Lord Sumner.

Next I will turn to the orders of justices in civil matters. The Court of King's Bench was never so strict about these as it was about convictions. It did not require a detailed speaking record to be sent up to them. The record had to contain everything necessary to show that the justices had jurisdiction to deal with the matter, and it had to set out their adjudication; but it was not necessary to set out either the evidence or the reasons. If a point of law arose, however, on which either party desired the ruling of the King's Bench, he could ask the justices to make a speaking order, that is, to make a special entry upon the record of the reasons for their judgment. The justices were not bound to do this, but they usually did so if they entertained a doubt about the point. When their reasons thus appeared on the record, the Court of King's Bench would on certiorari inquire into their correctness, and, if the reasons were wrong, would quash the decision. Sometimes the justices would find the facts and state them specially as part of the record so as to enable the Court of King's Bench to say whether their judgment on those facts was in law right or wrong. It was then known as a case stated, and the King's Bench would again on certiorari determine whether the decision was correct or not. The principles on which the court acted will be found well stated by Holt C.J. in *R.* v. *Inhabitants of Audly* (1701) 2 Salk. 526 and *Parish of Ricelip* v. *Parish of Henden* (1698) 5 Mod. 417 and in the argument before Abbott C.J. and his colleagues in *R.* v. *Justices of Devon* (1819) 1 Chit. 34 and by Lord Cairns L.C. in *Walsall Overseers* v. *London and North Eastern Railway Co.*, 4 App-.Cas. 30, 39–42. Interesting illustrations will be found in *R.* v. *Dobbyn* (1696) 2 Salk. 474, *R.* v. *London* (1703) 3 Salk. 261, *Ditton's* case (1701) 2 Salk. 490 and *Inter The Inhabitants of Talbury and the Hamlet of Fostin in Scropton* (1691) 2 Salk. 475. The procedure in these cases was, however, simplified in 1857 when the legislature intervened to enable justices to state a case for the opinion of the court without the record being removed by a writ of certiorari: see section 10 of the Summary Jurisdiction Act 1857. Thenceforward there was not so much room for certiorari in the case of orders of justices, but again the fundamental principles remained untouched.

So far I have considered only the convictions or orders of justices, which were by far the most numerous cases in which certiorari was used. I now come to the orders of statutory tribunals. The Court of King's Bench has from very early times exercised control over the orders of statutory tribunals, just as it has done over the orders of justices. The earliest instances that I have found are the orders of the Commissioners of Sewers, who were set up by statute in 1532 to see to the repairs of sea walls and so forth. The Court of King's Bench used on certiorari to quash the orders of the commissioners for errors on the face of them, such as when they failed to set out the facts necessary to show that they had jurisdiction in the matter, or when they contained some error in point of law. It is recorded that on one celebrated occasion the commissioners refused to obey a certiorari issued out of the King's Bench, and for this the whole body of them were "laid by the heels." The control thus exercised over the Commissioners of Sewers was used by Holt C.J. as a precedent to control by certiorari the orders of any tribunal set up by Parliament, such as the College of Physicians and the Commissioners for the repair of Cardiff Bridge. Since that time it has never been doubted that certiorari will lie to any statutory tribunal. It was suggested before us on behalf of the Crown that, in the case of these statutory tribunals, the Court of King's Bench only interfered by certiorari to keep them within their jurisdiction, and not to correct their errors of law. There are, however, many cases in the books where certiorari was used to correct errors of law on the face of the record. A striking instance was where the Commissioners of Sewers imposed an excessive fine, and it was quashed by the Court of King's Bench on the ground that in law their fines ought to be reasonable. Other instances are the numerous cases where certiorari was used to determine the validity of a sewer's rate imposed by the Commissioners of Sewers. There are several cases where an auditor's certificate has been quashed for error of law on the face of it. And I have no doubt that many more instances could be found throughout the books. The principles on which the court acted in the case of the Commissioners of Sewers will be found set out in *Cummins* v. *Massam* (1643) March 196 (ed. 1675), 202 (ed. 1685). See *Callis on Sewers* (4th ed., 1823), pp. 203–204, 342–344; and

Chitty's Practice, Vol. II, at p. 370. The decisions of Holt C.J. are *Groenwelt* v. *Burwell* (1700) 1 Salk. 144; 1 Ld.Raym. 451–469 and the case of *Cardiff Bridge* (1699) 1 Salk. 146; 1 Ld.Raym. 580. The case of an auditor's certificate is *R.* v. *White* (1883–84) 11 Q.B.D. 309; 14 Q.B.D. 358.

Leaving now the statutory tribunals, I turn to the awards of arbitrators. The Court of King's Bench never interfered by certiorari with the award of an arbitrator, because it was a private tribunal and not subject to the prerogative writs. If the award was not made a rule of court, the only course available to an aggrieved party was to resist an action on the award or to file a bill in equity. If the award was made a rule of court, a motion could be made to the court to set it aside for misconduct of the arbitrator on the ground that it was procured by corruption or other undue means: see 9 & 10 Will. 3, c. 15. At one time an award could not be upset on the ground of error of law by the arbitrator, because that could not be said to be misconduct or undue means; but ultimately it was held in *Kent* v. *Elstob* (1802) 3 East 18 that an award could be set aside for error of law on the face of it. This was regretted by Williams J. in *Hodgkinson* v. *Fernie* (1857) 3 C.B.N.S. 189 but is now well established. This remedy by motion to set aside is, however, confined to arbitrators. It does not extend to statutory tribunals: see *Racecourse Betting Control Board* v. *Secretary for Air* [1944] Ch. 114. I look upon that decision as merely a decision as to the scope of the remedy of setting aside on motion. It is not a decision on substantive law. It does not take away or diminish the inherent jurisdiction of the Court of King's Bench to interfere by certiorari.

It will have been seen that throughout all the cases there is one governing rule: certiorari is only available to quash a decision for error of law if the error appears on the face of the record. What, then, is the record? It has been said to consist of all those documents which are kept by the tribunal for a permanent memorial and testimony of their proceedings: see *Blackstone's Commentaries*, Vol. III, at p. 24. But it must be noted that, whenever there was any question as to what should, or should not be, included in the record of any tribunal, the Court of King's Bench used to determine it. It did it in this way: when the tribunal sent their record to the King's Bench in answer to the writ of certiorari, this return was examined, and if it was defective or incomplete it was quashed: see *Apsley's* case (1648) Style 85, *R.* v. *Levermore* (1701) 1 Salk. 146 and *Ashley's* case (1698) 2 Salk. 479, or, alternatively, the tribunal might be ordered to complete it: *Williams* v. *Bagot*, 4 D. & R. 315 and *R.* v. *Warnford* (1825) 5 D. & R. 489. It appears that the Court of King's Bench always insisted that the record should contain, or recite, the document or information which initiated the proceedings and thus gave the tribunal its jurisdiction; and also the document which contained their adjudication. Thus in the old days the record sent up by the justices had, in the case of a conviction, to recite the information in its precise terms; and in the case of an order which had been decided by quarter sessions by way of appeal, the record had to set out the order appealed from: see *Anon* (1697) 2 Salk. 479. The record had also to set out the adjudication, but it was never necessary to set out the reasons (see *South Cadbury* (*Inhabitants*) v. *Braddon, Somerset* (*Inhabitants*) (1710) 2 Salk. 607), nor the evidence, save in the case of convictions. Following these cases, I think the record must contain at least the document which initiates the proceedings; the pleadings, if any; and the adjudication; but not the evidence, nor the reasons, unless the tribunal chooses to incorporate them. If the tribunal does state its reasons, and those reasons are wrong in law, certiorari lies to quash the decision.

The next question which arises is whether affidavit evidence is admissible on an application for certiorari. When certiorari is granted on the ground of want of jurisdiction, or bias, or fraud, affidavit evidence is not only admissible, but it is, as a rule, necessary. When it is granted on the ground of error of law on the face of the record, affidavit evidence is not, as a rule, admissible, for the simple reason that the error must appear on the record itself: see *R.* v. *Nat Bell Liquors Ltd.* [1922] A.C. 123, 156. Affidavits were, however, always admissible to show that the record was incomplete, as, for instance, that a conviction omitted the evidence of one of the witnesses (see *Chitty's Practice*, Vol. 2, at p. 222, note (*d*)), or did not set out the fact that the justices had refused to hear a competent witness for the defence (see *R.* v. *Anon.* (1816) 2 Chit. 137), whereupon the court would either order the record to be completed, or it might quash the conviction at once.

Notwithstanding the strictness of the rule that the error of law must appear on the face of the record, the parties could always by agreement overcome this difficulty. If they both desired a ruling of the Court of King's Bench on a point of law which had been decided by the tribunal, but which had not been entered on the record, the parties could agree that the question should be argued and determined as if it were expressed in the order. The first case I have found in which this was done was in 1792, *R.* v. *Essex* (1792) 4 T.R. 591, but thereafter it was quite common. It became a regular practice for parties to supplement the record by affidavits disclosing the points of law that had been decided by the tribunal. This course was only taken if no one objected. It seems to have been adopted by litigants as a convenient alternative to asking the tribunal to make a speaking order. Thus, in the numerous cases on the validity of a sewer's rate, it was the regular course of proceeding for affidavits to be lodged stating the objections in law to the rate; and the case was decided on the objections stated in the affidavits: see, for instance, *R.* v. *Tower Hamlets* (1829) 9 B. & C. 517. Recent cases such as *R.* v. *West Riding of Yorkshire Justices* [1910] 2 K.B. 192 and *General Medical Council* v. *Spackman* [1942] 2 K.B. 261; [1943] A.C. 627 show that the practice continues today. The explanation of all these cases is, I think, that the affidavits are treated by consent as if they were part of the record and make it into a speaking order.

Apart from these consent cases, it is often a very nice question whether an error which does not appear on the record is one which goes to jurisdiction or is only an error of law within the jurisdiction. If it goes to jurisdiction, affidavits are admissible, but otherwise not. I do not venture on a discussion of what does, or does not, go to jurisdiction, because it does not arise in this case. Nor do I venture on a discussion of the cases where Parliament has intervened to restrict the use of certiorari except to say that those restrictions can often be overcome by consent: *R.* v. *Dickenson* (1857) 7 E. & B. 831. No such restriction appears in this case.

We have here a simple case of error of law by a tribunal, an error which they frankly acknowledge. It is an error which deprives Mr. Shaw of the compensation to which he is by law entitled. So long as the erroneous decision stands, the compensating authority dare not pay Mr. Shaw the money to which he is entitled lest the auditor should surcharge them. It would be quite intolerable if in such case there were no means of correcting the error. The authorities to which I have referred amply show that the King's Bench can correct it by certiorari. It is true that the record which has been sent up to the court does not distinctly disclose the error, but that is only because the record itself is incomplete. The tribunal has sent up its decision, but it has not sent up the claim lodged with the compensating authority or the order made by them on it or the notice of appeal to the tribunal. Those documents would, I think, properly be part of the record. They would, I understand, have disclosed the error. If it had been necessary, the court could have ordered the record to be completed. But that is unnecessary, having regard to the fact that it was admitted in open court by all concerned that the decision was erroneous. I am clearly of opinion that an error admitted openly in the face of the court can be corrected by certiorari as well as an error that appears on the face of the record. The decision must be quashed, and the tribunal will then be able to hear the case again and give the correct decision.

In my opinion the appeal should be dismissed.

MORRIS L.J. [also held that certiorari was available to quash for error of law on the fact of the record]: In my judgment the second submission is not open to the tribunal. It was conceded before the Divisional Court that the decision of the tribunal was a "speaking order," and that error was apparent on the face of it. The matter proceeded before the Divisional Court on that basis. There was, in my view, scope for argument as to whether (if the metaphor of a "speaking order" is adopted) the decision "spoke" its error of law. While the mere admission of counsel cannot convert a document into something different from what it is, I consider that as in the present case those appearing for Mr. Shaw desired to press before the Divisional Court a submission that the decision "spoke" its error, and as this submission was acceded to and was conceded on behalf of the tribunal it would not now be fitting to allow, on appeal, the reclaiming of that which was jettisoned. I entertain no laments for this result, inasmuch as though it was sought to be argued on appeal that the face of the decision was not sufficiently self-revealing, yet it was expressly admitted that in fact the decision was only reached by treading the paths of legal error.

SINGLETON L.J. [held that certiorari could be granted on the ground of error of law on the face of the record, agreeing with the reasoning of the Lord Chief Justice in the Divisional Court. Furthermore, the error was apparent on the face of the tribunal's decision: "it is a 'speaking order'; read alongside the regulations, it shows that the tribunal declined to consider any service other than service with the hospital board," notwithstanding the fact that the decision did not say expressly that the local government service had been ignored.]

Notes and questions

1. See case notes by S. A. de Smith, 14 M.L.R. 207, 15 M.L.R. 217; D. Gordon, 67 L.Q.R. 452.
2. The Divisional Court and Court of Appeal in this case declined to follow the decision of the Court of Appeal in *Racecourse Betting Control Board* v. *Secretary for Air* [1944] Ch. 114, where it was held that certiorari did not lie for non-jurisdictional error. This decision was held to conflict with views expressed by the House of Lords in *Walsall Overseers* v. *L.N.W. Ry. Co.* (1878) 4 App.Cas. 30, and by the Privy Council in *R.* v. *Nat Bell Liquors Ltd.* [1922] 2 A.C. 128. These views had not been cited (see Singleton L.J. [1952] 1 K.B. 338 at pp. 343–344 and Morris L.J. at p. 357).
3. The assertions of Denning L.J. that the court may order a tribunal to complete its record, and that the parties can by consent bring disputed points of law to the attention of the court even though they do not appear on the record, have been doubted (see *de Smith*, p. 406).
4. How can *ex p. Shaw* be reconciled with the *Anisminic* case (above, p. 237)?
5. The principles which should guide the courts when invited to quash determinations of Supplementary Benefit Appeal Tribunals were stated by Lord Denning M.R. in *R.* v. *Preston S.B.A.T., ex p. Moore; R.* v. *Sheffield S.B.A.T., ex p. Shine* [1975] 1 W.L.R. 624 at pp. 631–632:

> "It is plain that Parliament intended that the Supplementary Benefit Act 1966 should be administered with as little technicality as possible. It should not become the happy hunting ground for lawyers. The courts should hesitate long before interfering by certiorari with the decisions of the appeal tribunals. Otherwise the courts would become engulfed with streams of cases just as they did under the old Workmen's Compensation Acts: see *R.* v. *Industrial Injuries Commissioner, ex p. Amalgamated Engineering Union (No. 2)* [1966] 2 Q.B. 31, 45. The courts should not enter into a meticulous discussion of the meaning of this or that word in the Act. They should leave the tribunals to interpret the Act in a broad reasonable way, according to the spirit and not to the letter: especially as Parliament has given them a way of alleviating any hardship. The courts should only interfere when the decision of the tribunal is unreasonable in the sense that no tribunal acquainted with the ordinary use of language could reasonably reach that decision: see *Cozens* v. *Brutus* [1973] A.C. 854, 861. Nevertheless, it must be realised that the Act has to be applied daily by thousands of officers of the commission: and by 120 appeal tribunals. It is most important that cases raising the same points should be decided in the same way. There should be uniformity of decision. Otherwise grievances are bound to arise. In order to ensure this, the courts should be ready to consider points of law of general application. Take these two cases. In Moore's case, Mr. Blom-Cooper raised an

important point on the meaning of the word "resources." Did it mean actual resources, or notional resources? It applied to all students seeking educational grants. It was very right for the High Court to give a ruling upon it. In Shine's case, Mr. Langan raised an important point on the meaning of "householder" when there were two or more joint tenants. It applied to all students sharing a flat when all were directly responsible for expenses. Were all entitled to the householder's allowance? Or only one? Or none? It is very desirable for this point to be authoritatively decided. So we have decided it. But so far as Mr. Shine's £50 grant is concerned, that is of small importance, though of general application. So the High Court should not be troubled with it. And Mr. Langan did not press it before us.

In short, the court should be ready to lay down the broad guide-lines for tribunals. But no further. The courts should not be used as if there was an appeal to them. Individual cases of particular application must be left to the tribunals.

And, of course, the courts will always be ready to interfere if the tribunals have exceeded their jurisdiction or acted contrary to natural justice. That goes without saying."

The points in issue were these:

(a) Moore's resources were calculated so as to include sums which notionally he had because his student's grant covered the period for which he claimed benefit. In fact he had spent all the grant, so that these were not "actual" resources. Lord Denning M.R. held that there were "many indications" that the relevant Act referred to notional resources.

(b) Shine received the minimum student's grant of £50. The local education authority and the Supplementary Benefits Commission regarded this as a grant to help him in the vacation, and so £46 was regarded as his vacation allowance, that sum being the allowance on a full grant. The challenge on this point was not pressed.

(c) Shine was one of four joint tenants of a flat, paying a quarter of the rent and expenses. A higher rate of benefit was payable to a "person living alone or householder . . . who is directly responsible for household necessities and rent (if any)." The Supplementary Benefits Commission and Supplementary Benefit Appeal Tribunal rejected S.'s claim that he was a "householder." Lord Denning M.R. held that there was much in his contention "if this were to be regarded as a strict point of law . . ." Under the Interpretation Act 1889, singular included plural, and so all four were householders. However:

"[t]his seems to me a good instance where the High Court should not interfere with the tribunal's decision, even though it may be said to be erroneous in point of law. It cannot be supposed that each one of these four should each have the full allowance as if he was responsible for the whole. Nor even that one of them—Mr. Fairbairn—should have the full allowance. The better way of administering the Act is to hold that none of the four gets the allowance as being the householder: but that each should be regarded as a lodger contributing towards a householder's commitments. Each should get an allowance in respect of his contribution to the rent: see paragraph 13; and each may be granted a special addition under paragraph 4(1)(*a*) to take account of the exceptional circumstances. That is what the tribunal allowed to Mr. Shine. It was a reasonable way of administering the Act on a point which was not covered by the Schedule."

This approach was criticised by Professor Street, *L.A.G. Bulletin*, May 1975, p. 118; Chris Smith (1975) 2 *British Journal of Law and Society* 217; Henry Hodge,

Justice, Discretion and Poverty (ed. by Adler and Bradley), pp. 74–75; N. Lewis, *ibid.* p. 87, n. 12.

The Divisional Court, notwithstanding *Moore* (which was cited in both cases), quashed the Supplementary Benefit Appeal Tribunal's decisions in *R.* v. *West London S.B.A.T., ex p. Clarke* [1975] 1 W.L.R. 1396; and *ibid., ex p. Taylor* [1975] 1 W.L.R. 1048. It is difficult to see that the point raised in *Taylor* was one of general importance—but the tribunal's decision was clearly erroneous, and quite rightly quashed. *Cf. R.* v. *Barnsley S.B.A.T., ex p. Atkinson* [1976] 2 All E.R. 686 D.C., C.A.

From January 1978, there was a right to appeal on a point of law from an S.B.A.T. to the High Court (S.I. 1977 No. 1735). This was replaced by a right to appeal on a point of law to the (renamed) Social Security Commissioners (Supplementary Benefits Act 1976, s.15A, inserted by the Social Security Act 1979, s.6), with a further appeal on a point of law to the Court of Appeal (Social Security Act 1980, s.14). This structure was maintained when S.B.A.T.s were merged with N.I.L.T.s to form Social Security Appeal Tribunals in 1983. Applications for judicial review are, accordingly, no longer necessary or appropriate. In theory, the appeal on a point of law is wider than judicial review for jurisdictional error or error of law on the face of the record. In practice, however, "the judicial approach has not changed fundamentally" (A. Ogus and E. Barendt, *The Law of Social Security* (3rd ed., 1988), p. 587). See generally, R. Sainsbury, "Social Security Appeals: in Need of Review" in W. Finnie, *et al.* (eds.), *Edinburgh Essays on Public Law* (1991).

6. In *Baldwin & Francis Ltd.* v. *Patents Appeal Tribunal* [1959] A.C. 663, H.L., Lord Denning stated that the "record" of proceedings before an inferior tribunal includes the formal record, if that is kept, and where a tribunal does not keep a formal record "there must be brought before the Queen's Bench not only the formal order of the tribunal but also, as the old writ said, 'all things touching the same'; and this includes the reasons for the decision when the tribunal gives them." In addition where certiorari lay to an appellate tribunal, the decision at first instance was to be brought before the High Court:

> "Now turning to modern cases, it will be seen that, in our day, too, the courts have proceeded on the footing that there should be included in the record, not only the formal order, but all those documents which appear therefrom to be the basis of the decision—that on which it is grounded. Such as the claim for compensation in the *Northumberland* case, the report of the medical specialist in *Gilmore's* case [1957] 1 Q.B. 574 and the medical certificates in *R.* v. *Head* [1958] 1 Q.B. 132, 138. It is really to be supposed that the Crown in those cases made concessions which it was not bound to make and could have successfully resisted the issue of certiorari?" (*per* Lord Denning at p. 690).

Applying these principles, Lord Denning held that the record of proceedings in the present case included the decision of the superintending examiner (at first instance), and the patent specifications, as well as the decision of the appeal tribunal.

The other members of the House of Lords did not express any concluded opinion on what constituted the "record," as on the assumption that it included the items mentioned, it disclosed no error of law. Furthermore, Lord Denning was of the opinion that certiorari should not issue in the exercise of the court's discretion, even though there was an error of law.

Lord Denning's views on the content of the record were accepted by the Divisional Court in *R.* v. *Patents Appeal Tribunal, ex p. Swift & Co.* [1962] 2 Q.B. 647. See further Lord Denning's remarks in *ex p. Shaw* (above, p. 600) and in *ex p. Gilmore* (below, p. 867); and see *R.* v. *Southampton JJ., ex p. Green* [1976] Q.B. 11, C.A., where affidavit evidence was admitted in the Court of Appeal to establish that the justices had failed to take into account a relevant consideration, and had taken into account an irrelevant consideration. Browne L.J. accepted that these affidavits were part of the record on the ground that they were admitted by consent, and held that certiorari was available to quash for error of law on the face of the record. Lord Denning M.R. and Brightman J. agreed, but also thought that these were jurisdictional errors, it being clear that such errors could be established by affidavit evidence external to the record. *Cf. R.* v. *Southampton JJ., ex p. Corker, The Times*, February 11, 1976. The content of the "record" is discussed at length by Abel [1963] 15 U. of Toronto L.J. 108–122; Fitzgerald and Elliott [1964] Melb.U.L.Rev. 564–579.

On the question whether an oral decision can be quashed for error of law on the face of the record see *R.* v. *Chertsey JJ., ex p. Franks* [1961] 2 Q.B. 152, where the Divisional Court stated that certiorari would so lie (but see R. E. Megarry (1962) 77 L.Q.R. 157; D. M. Gordon *ibid.* 322; *de Smith*, p. 580; *Griffith and Street*, p. 217).

Moreover, in *R.* v. *Knightsbridge Crown Court, ex p. International Sporting Club (London) Ltd.* [1982] Q.B. 304 the Divisional Court held that the "record" of proceedings in the Crown Court included the reasons contained in a transcript of the oral judgment of the court, notwithstanding that the reasons were not formally incorporated in the court's order.

In this, and other recent cases, it has been stated that a liberal view should be taken of what constitutes the "record." In *R.* v. *Knightsbridge Crown Court, ex p. Aspinall Curzon Ltd., The Times*, December 16, 1982, the applicants sought certiorari to quash a decision of the Crown Court allowing an appeal by the Gaming Board against the grant by a Gaming Licensing Committee of a gaming licence to them. They relied upon an affidavit sworn by their solicitors which set out the history of the matter. They claimed that the court had failed to take a certain matter into account. Woolf J. stated that it was only when one considered the affidavit that it was possible to see the basis on which the case was put forward. The restrictions which led to the court confirming certiorari to errors on the face of the record were largely to be explained by the procedural history relating to the ancient writ of certiorari. Under the new procedure in Order 53, in cases where it was necessary for the court, in order to be able to determine an issue which was appropriate to be decided on judicial review, and even though the remedy sought was not certiorari, the court could look at evidence which enabled it to deal with the issue, albeit that the evidence was not technically part of the record, and could not have been examined before the introduction of the new Order 53. Woolf J.'s view was endorsed by Glidewell J. in *R.* v. *South Western JJ., ex p. London Borough of Wandsworth, The Times*, January 20, 1983. It is submitted, however, that the *Aspinall Curzon* case can be analysed as an allegation of jurisdictional error, in which event the applicant would not have been restricted to the record even prior to the introduction of the new Order 53. The *South Western JJ.* case was treated by Glidewell J. as involving error of law on the face of the record.

7. The use of certiorari to quash an excessive fine imposed by the Commissioner of Sewers was relied on by Lord Denning M.R. in *R.* v. *Barnsley M.B.C., ex p. Hook* [1976] 3 All E.R. 452. His Lordship held that the decision to deprive H. of his livelihood by revoking his stallholder's licence, following a "trifling incident," was "altogether excessive and out of proportion to the occasion" (p. 456). H. had urinated in a side street near the market shortly after the market had been closed for the night, and had abused a council security officer who reprimanded him. Sir John Pennycuick held that H.'s licence could only be revoked for good cause, and this incident was "manifestly not a good cause. . . ." Scarman L.J. based his judgment solely on breach of natural justice (above, p. 576 (note)). See further above, p. 437.

CHAPTER 11

APPEALS

IN law, an appeal against a decision is possible only if it has been established by statute. In the context of administrative law Parliament has not been consistent in the creation of rights of appeal. There are considerable variations in the type of decision appealable, the possible grounds of appeal, and the body to which an appeal may be made. In this chapter we show how appeals were viewed by the Franks Committee, and we give examples of different kinds of appeal.

Because appeals depend on a statutory, as distinct from a common law, origin, the grounds of appeal will be confined to those specified in, or to be deduced from, the statute. These appeals must be distinguished from *review* by the courts under their common law powers.

See *de Smith C.A.*, pp. 542–544; D. Price, *Appeals* (1982); *Lewis*, Ch. 13.

(A) WHEN SHOULD AN APPEAL BE AVAILABLE?

REPORT OF THE FRANKS COMMITTEE ON ADMINISTRATIVE TRIBUNALS AND ENQUIRIES 1957

(H.M.S.O. Cmnd. 218)

Part II: **Tribunals in General**

103. Most of the evidence which we have received has stressed the desirability of some form of appeal from tribunals of first instance, and many witnesses have advocated that at some stage there should be an appeal to the courts.

The merits of a right of appeal

104. The existence of a right of appeal is salutary and makes for right adjudication. Provision for appeal is also important if decisions are to show reasonable consistency. Finally, the system of adjudication can hardly fail to appear fair to the applicant if he knows that he will normally be allowed two attempts to convince independent bodies of the soundness of his case.

An appeal structure for tribunals

105. The first question is the extent to which appeals should lie to the courts or to further appellate tribunals. An appeal to the courts on matters of fact would not, we think, be desirable since it would constitute an

appeal from a body expert in the particular subject to a relatively inexpert body. In the absence of special consideration we consider that the ideal appeal structure for tribunals should take the form of a general appeal from a tribunal of first instance to a second or appellate tribunal. By a general appeal we mean an appeal on fact, law or merits. We do not think that it is necessary for appeals to the second or appellate tribunal always to be heard orally. As a matter of general principle we consider that appeal should not lie from a tribunal to a Minister.

106. It is not essential to set up an appellate tribunal when the tribunal of first instance is so exceptionally strong and well qualified that an appellate tribunal would be no better qualified to review its decisions. Thus, for example, we see no need to provide for appeal to a further tribunal from decisions of Pensions Appeal Tribunals or the General Claims Tribunal. The evidence indicates no dissatisfaction with the absence of such appeal in these cases.

Appeals to the courts on points of law

107. We are firmly of the opinion that all decisions of tribunals should be subject to review by the courts on points of law. This review could be obtained either by proceedings for certiorari or by appeal. If, as we recommend, tribunals are compelled to give full reasons for their decisions any error of law in such a decision would subject the decision to quashing by order of certiorari in England, and it is now clear that the fact that the decision of the tribunal may be expressed in the statute as "final" does not oust this jurisdiction. The courts in Scotland do not, however, exercise this jurisdiction to quash a decision for error of law on the face of the record. Moreover, an application to quash a decision on this ground is quite different from an appeal on a point of law. In the former case the court can only quash the decision, while in the latter case the court may substitute, or in effect substitute, its own decision. Again, in the former case, the court must find the error, if it can, on the face of the record, for example in the notice of decision mentioned in the preceding Chapter; it cannot look at anything else. In the latter case the court can in addition look at the notes of the evidence given before the tribunal if the point of law is whether there was evidence on which the tribunal could in law have arrived at its decision. An appeal on a point of law is therefore wider in scope. For all these reasons we recommend that review by the courts of decisions of tribunals should in general be provided by making the decisions subject to appeal on points of law. We think, however, that special considerations arise in connection with the National Insurance Commissioner, the Industrial Injuries Commissioner and National Assistance Appeal Tribunals. . . .

109. The reasons which lead us to think that appeals on merits from National Assistance Appeal Tribunals are unnecessary (see paragraph 182) apply equally to appeals on points of law from these Tribunals.

Accordingly we think that an exception to the general rule should also be made in the case of these Tribunals, leaving any review by the courts to be exercised by certiorari. . . .

115. There remains the question of the court to which appeals on points of law should lie. The possible alternatives are the Court of Appeal, the Divisional Court of the Queen's Bench Division, a nominated judge of the High Court or the County Court. We think that there would be some advantage in concentrating appeals in the Divisional Court. . . . Nevertheless we think that it would be wrong to lay down a hard and fast rule. In the case of the Lands Tribunal and the Transport Tribunal there seems no cogent reason for disturbing the present practice by which appeals lie to the Court of Appeal. In certain cases it may, as the Law Society suggests, be cheaper and simpler for appeals to lie to County Courts. Where a number of new tribunals is set up and there is likely to be a large volume of appeals on technical matters there is much to be said in favour of the appeals being decided by a nominated judge, as are appeals from Pensions Appeal Tribunals.

116. We do not necessarily intend that in every case there should be unrestricted recourse through the Supreme Court and up to the House of Lords. To permit this would in many cases be inconsistent, by reason of the expense and delay involved, with the purposes for which tribunals are established. We suggest that in each case there should be one further appeal on law, by leave, and no more.

Notes

1. See section 11 of the Tribunals and Inquiries Act 1992, above, p. 77.

2. Paragraph 182, in relation to National Assistance Appeal Tribunals stated: "182. Although in form [National Assistance Appeal] Tribunals hear and determine appeals against decisions of local officers of the National Assistance Board and therefore exercise adjudicating functions, in practice their task much resembles that of an assessment or case committee, taking a further look at the facts and in some cases arriving at a fresh decision on the extent of need. For this reason and also because by their very nature questions of assistance require to be finally determined as quickly as possible, we do not think that the provision of a further appeal on merits from the Tribunals is appropriate. We have already recommended, in paragraph 109, that decisions of these Tribunals should be subject to review by certiorari but not subject to appeal on points of law."

This recommendation is discussed by A. W. Bradley in *Justice, Discretion and Poverty* (ed. by Adler and Bradley), pp. 45–46. There were many suggestions that there should be a right of further appeal from the decisions of these tribunals, subsequently renamed Supplementary Benefit Appeal Tribunals. See Ruth Lister (*ibid.* p. 181); H. Calvert (*ibid.* Chap. xiv); and Adler and Bradley (*ibid.* pp. 213–216). See now above, p. 603 (note 5).

Controversially, on the replacement of supplementary budget by income support and payments from the social fund, under Part III of the Social Security Act 1986, appeals were only established in respect of income support. Payments from the cash-limited social fund (replacing single payments and urgent needs payment under the supplementary benefit legislation), mostly in the form of loans, are made by social fund officers appointed by the Secretary of State. These are in theory discretionary payments, but the detailed directions given to the officers by the Secretary of State operate very much in the manner of regulations. Instead of an appeal, there is provision for internal review by social fund inspectors, who are DSS officials appointed as inspectors by the Social Fund Commissioner. The Commissioner is appointed by the Secretary of State. The lack of a proper appeal to an independent tribunal was criticised (to no avail) by the Council on Tribunals: Special Report, *Social Security—Abolition of independent appeals under the proposed social fund* (Cmnd. 9722, 1986), above, p. 134. See H. Bolderson, (1988) 15 J.L.S. 279; R. Drabble and T. Lynes, [1989] P.L. 297.

The Council has also long pressed for the introduction of a right of appeal from the Immigration Appeal Tribunal to the courts, on a point of law, replacing applications for judicial review (Annual Report, 1990–91 (1991–92 H.C. 97), pp. 8–9).

3. Sir Harry Woolf has argued cogently that order needs to be introduced into the chaos of appeals to the High Court and Court of Appeal from inferior tribunals and other judicial and quasi-judicial bodies ("A Hotchpotch of Appeals—The Need for a Blender" (1988) 7 C.J.Q. 44). Appeals from a court should go to the Court of Appeal direct, normally with a requirement of leave, and with the same time limits applying to all appeals. Appeals from other bodies should only lie to the Court of Appeal if the sole issue turns on the construction of a statute or document or involves a conflict between previous decisions of the court; or the appeal is from an appellate body such as the E.A.T. Otherwise, the sole method of application should be by way of an application for judicial review.

Part IV: **Administrative Procedures Involving an Inquiry or Hearing—General Questions**

355. Under present legislation the Minister's decision in the various procedures relating to land is final, subject in most cases to a right of appeal to the High Court, exercisable generally within six weeks of the decision, on the ground that the order in question (the compulsory purchase order, clearance order, etc.) is *ultra vires* or that the prescribed procedure has not been followed. It is provided that the decision shall not otherwise be questioned in any legal proceedings whatsoever. This right of appeal thus replaces any remedy by way of an order of certiorari. Where this right of appeal is not given, for example in the case of decisions on planning appeals, the action of the Minister could presumably be challenged in certiorari proceedings.

Appeal on fact or merits

356. Several proposals have been submitted to us, particularly by organisations representing members of the legal profession, for extending the scope of recourse to the courts against the Minister's decision. We do not propose to describe them in detail; it is fair to say that for the most part their broad effect would be to enable appeals to be brought additionally on the ground either that the inspector's report or the Minister's letter of decision contained errors of fact or that, in one respect or another, the Minister's decision was not "reasonably" based upon the evidence at the inquiry and the facts found by the inspector.

357. Many of these proposals, particularly those which seek to apply a

test of "reasonableness" to the basis of the Minister's decision, would have the effect of introducing an appeal on merits against the decision. We cannot regard such an appeal as appropriate. If, as we have already recommended, the parties are enabled to propose corrections to the inspector's findings of fact and the Minister is required to submit new factual evidence to the parties, there seems no need for an appeal beyond the Minister on fact.

358. Most of the witnesses who in their memoranda of evidence had proposed a wider scope of appeal to the courts agreed in oral evidence that, provided that the findings of fact were properly open to challenge before the decision and that the procedure was improved in other respects—notably by making inspectors independent of the deciding Minister and by requiring from the Minister, whenever possible, a statement of policy before the inquiry and full reasons for his eventual decision—then appeals to the courts against the Minister's decision could be restricted, as at present, to the two grounds of *ultra vires* and procedural defect.

Appeal on law

359. There remains the question of an appeal on law. It is difficult to see how any question of law could arise other than a question of jurisdiction or procedure. The present form of appeal, covering these two matters, seems to us adequate, particularly since the scope for bringing appeals on grounds of alleged procedural irregularity will be wider if the various recommendations which we have made for strengthening and improving the procedure are adopted and, where appropriate, given statutory effect. This form of appeal should, however, be applied to decisions on planning appeals in the same way as it applies to decisions in other cases relating to land. We think that it would be reasonable to reduce, for example from six to four weeks, the limit of time for lodging appeals to the courts if a period of 14 days were allowed at an earlier stage for challenging the inspector's findings of fact. It is for consideration whether, following the lines of our suggestions concerning tribunals, all such appeals could not with advantage be made to the Divisional Court. There should then be one further appeal, by leave.

Note

See further pp. 622 *et seq*. below, on the form of appeal described in paragraph 355.

(B) Examples of Appeals on Questions of Fact or Merits

HOUSING ACT 1985, s.191

[Part VI of this Act concerns Repair Notices. Where the local housing authority is satisfied that a dwelling house or a house in multiple occupation is unfit for human habitation it must serve a repair notice on the person in control, if satisfied that this is the most satisfactory course of action (s.189). There is also a discretionary power to serve a repair notice where a house is in disrepair but not unfit (s.190). The notice specifies the works to be done. If the notice is not complied with, the works may be done by the authority at the owner's expense. Section 191 sets out the right of appeal.]

Appeals against repair notices

191.—(1) A person aggrieved by a repair notice may within 21 days after the date of service of the notice, appeal to the county court.

[(1A) Without prejudice to the generality of subsection (1), it shall be a ground of appeal that some person other than the appellant, being a person who is an owner in relation to the dwelling-house [[house in multiple occupation]] or part of the building concerned, ought to execute the works or pay the whole or part of the cost of executing them.]

[(1B) Without prejudice to the generality of subsection (1), it shall be a ground of appeal, in the case of a repair notice under section 189, that making a closing order under section 264 or a demolition order under section 265 is the most satisfactory course of action; and, where the grounds on which an appeal is brought are or include that specified in this subsection, the court, on the hearing of the appeal, shall have regard to any guidance given to the local housing authority under section 604A.]

(2) On an appeal the court may make such order either confirming, quashing or varying the notice as it thinks fit.

(3) Where the appeal is allowed against a repair notice under section 189 [[and the reason or one of the reasons for allowing the appeal is that making a closing order under section 264 or a demolition order under section 265 is the most satisfactory course of action, the judge shall, if requested to do so by the appellant or the local housing authority, include in his judgement a finding to that effect.

[(3A) Where the grounds on which an appeal is brought are or include that specified in subsection (1A), the appellant shall serve a copy of his notice of appeal on each other person referred to; and on the hearing of the appeal the court may—

(*a*) vary the repair notice so as to require the works to be executed by any such other person; or

(*b*) make such order as it thinks fit with respect to the payment to be made by any such other person to the appellant or, where the works are executed by the local housing authority, to the authority.

(3B) In the exercise of its powers under subsection (3A), the court shall take into account, as between the appellant and any such other person as is referred to in that subsection—

(*a*) their relative interests in the dwelling-house [[or house in multiple occupation]] or part of the building concerned (considering both the nature of the interests and the rights and obligations arising under or by virtue of them);

(*b*) their relative responsibility for the state of the dwelling-house [[or house in multiple occupation]] or building which gives rise to the need for the execution of the works; and

(*c*) the relative degree of benefit to be derived from the execution of the works.

(3C) If, by virtue of the exercise of the court's powers under subsection (3A), a person other than the appellant is required to execute the works specified in a repair notice, then, so long as that other person continues to be an owner in relation to the premises to which the notice relates, he shall be regarded as the person having control of those premises for the purposes of the following provisions of this Part.]

(4) If an appeal is brought the notice does not become operative until—

(*a*) a decision on the appeal confirming the notice (with or without variation) is given and the period within which an appeal to the Court of Appeal may be brought expires without any such appeal having been brought, or

(*b*) if a further appeal to the Court of Appeal is brought, a decision on that appeal is given confirming the notice (with or without variation);

and for this purpose the withdrawal of an appeal has the same effect as a decision confirming the notice or decision appealed against.

Notes

1. The section is set out as amended by the Housing Act 1988, Sched. 15, para. 3 and the Local Government and Housing Act 1989, Sched. 9, para. 4.

2. Note that apart from subsections (1A) and (1B) no grounds of appeal are specified. An appeal can raise a question as to the validity of the notice itself (*Elliott* v. *Brighton Borough Council* (1980) 79 L.G.R. 506), although such a question can be raised on an application for judicial review (*R.* v. *London Borough of Southwark, ex p. Lewis Levy Ltd.* (1983) 8 H.L.R. 1). (*Cf.* below, p. 661.)

An appeal can also raise a question as to the merits of the notice, as illustrated by the following case, decided under a forerunner of s.191.

COCHRANE v. CHANCTONBURY RURAL DISTRICT COUNCIL

[1950] 2 All E.R. 1134; 115 J.P. 17 (Court of Appeal)

The Rural District Council served on the owner of a house a notice under section 9(1) of the Housing Act 1936 requiring her to execute certain works to render her house fit for habitation. The owner appealed to the county court against the notice on the ground that the work was unnecessary. At the hearing she admitted that some of the work was necessary and reasonable, and she undertook to execute it. The council did not ask that, having regard to the admissions of the owner, the order should be varied and not quashed. The appeal was allowed and the notice quashed in its entirety. The council appealed to the Court of Appeal.

DENNING L.J.: I do not wish it to be supposed that the courts are not anxious to see defective houses repaired, but it is very important to keep the right balance between the local authority and the owner. Since 1936 the county courts have been entrusted with the task of keeping the balance. They must see that defects are made good, but they must also protect the owner from undue burdens. There is one point which I must mention at once. In serving a notice the local authority are not bound to specify the particular respects in which they say the house is unfit for human habitation. They are only bound to specify the works which they require the owner to execute. That is what the local authority have done in this case, leaving the owner to find out for herself what the defects are. This method of giving notice is, no doubt, valid and, indeed, necessary, but it may have the consequence that, even if defects exist, the notice may be bad because the works required may be more than is reasonably necessary. Much less work may be sufficient to make good the defects without going to the expense which the notice involves. If a local authority requires work to be done which is altogether excessive, the judge is not bound to amend the notice, in their favour, so as to specify less work which would make it good. He may, if he thinks fit, quash it and leave the authority to serve a fresh notice specifying more limited work.

In this case the local authority required the owner to "take up and remove all decayed and dry rot affected floor timbers, excavate and remove earth to a suitable depth, and provide and lay four inches of cement concrete over the whole of the site, construct a new floor employing new timbers adequately supported, provide efficient means of sub-floor ventilation." The owner's surveyor took a different view about this room. He said: "Floor requires repair, but what is required is unreasonable. Some boards require renewing. New boards will make all as good as the existing good ones, which have probably been there for fifty years." There was, therefore, a difference as to what was reasonably necessary. The local authority required concrete over the whole of the site and a new floor, whereas the owner's surveyor said that new boards where necessary, would suffice. That was a question of fact which the judge decided in favour of the owner. The requirements of the local authority in that respect, therefore, could not stand. Some of the other requirements were reasonable and were not disputed by the owner. She said she would do them, but that does not mean that in point of law the judge was bound to confirm the notice. He had, no doubt, power under the Act to vary the notice and to confirm it subject to variations, but he was not bound to do so. He was entitled to look at the notice as a whole, and if he thought the major requirements were altogether excessive, he might decide not to confirm it, even with variations, but to quash it altogether. That is what he chose to do, and I do not think we can say that in point of law he was wrong in so doing. I agree that the appeal should be dismissed.

SOMERVELL L.J. and LLOYD-JACOB J. delivered concurring judgments.

Appeal dismissed.

SAGNATA INVESTMENTS LTD. v. NORWICH CORPORATION

[1971] 2 Q.B. 614; [1971] 3 W.L.R. 133; [1971] 2 All E.R. 1441; 69 L.G.R. 471 (Court of Appeal)

The Betting, Gaming and Lotteries Act 1963, Sched. 6, para. 2 provided that the grant of a permit for amusements with prizes should be "at the discretion of the local authority." Schedule 6, para. 6, provided that where a local authority refused an application for a permit, the applicant could "appeal in accordance with the provisions of the Quarter Sessions Act 1849" to quarter sessions. Section 1 of the 1849 Act provided that "In every case of appeal . . . to any court of quarter sessions 14 clear days' notice of appeal . . . shall be given . . . and such notice of appeal shall be in writing, . . . and the grounds of appeal shall be specified in every such notice: Provided always, that it shall not be lawful for the appellant or appellants, on the trial of any such appeal, to go into or give evidence of any other ground of appeal besides those set forth in such notice."

In March 1969, Sagnata Investments Ltd. applied under the Act of 1963 for a permit for amusements with prizes at an amusement arcade to be built at a site known as Old Post Office Court in Norwich. That application was in due course refused by the Fire Service and Licensing Committee of Norwich Corporation, and their written grounds of refusal were in the following terms:

> "(a) The use of these premises as an amusement place would be likely to have undesirable social effects on the young people expected to frequent them; (b) the making available of gaming facilities in Norwich which could be used by children was something which the committee are not prepared to permit; (c) the number of amusements with prizes machines legally available elsewhere in Norwich for the use of adults was sufficient to meet all reasonable needs."

The unsuccessful applicants appealed from that refusal to Norwich City Quarter Sessions, their stated ground of appeal being, "that the decision . . . was unreasonable, having regard to the information available to the committee and contrary to natural justice."

The recorder, Michael Havers Q.C., found the following facts to be either proved or admitted: that no objection was made to the company, the premises or the site, the last named being particularly suitable; that the council as a whole had by an overwhelming majority of 41 to 1 taken a general policy decision not to grant permits for amusements with prizes for any such amusement places in Norwich and that decision had been applied to the application by the committee; that whilst it was likely that a certain number of children and young people would use the amusement arcade there was no evidence either way as to whether or not they would do so to a considerable extent and/or whether or not such a use would be socially undesirable. In that respect evidence was called before the recorder in the form of the committee chairman—a Norwich city councillor since 1934 and a former Lord Mayor who expressed his fears in that matter. Whilst accepting his evidence the recorder did not find that it amounted to anything more than the expression of a realistic and honest opinion; that the committee's decision was reached fairly and honestly with a genuine belief in the socially harmful result of setting up such an amusement arcade; that there were not sufficient facilities of that nature in Norwich at the present time.

The recorder was of the opinion that the committee had so fettered its discretion by following the policy decisions of the council that no application for such a permit could succeed before it and the committee had therefore failed to exercise its discretion at all; that it was for the corporation to prove that the provision of an amusement arcade would be socially undesirable; that having regard to the exclusion of amusement places from section 3 of the Betting, Gaming and Lotteries Act 1964 neither the committee nor quarter sessions were entitled to take into consideration the fact that by reason of the purpose for which or the persons by whom the premises were to be used it was undesirable that such a permit be granted; that the obiter dictum of Lord Parker C.J. in *R.* v. *Essex Quarter Sessions, ex p. Thomas* [1966] 1 W.L.R. 359, 362, that:

> "Speaking for myself, I would hesitate, and I would expect any chairman of quarter sessions to hesitate, long before differing from the local justices who had dealt with the matter in their locality with the greatest care,"

had no bearing on such an appeal as the recorder was hearing. In the result the recorder felt he had no alternative but to allow the appeal.

The corporation appealed unsuccessfully to the Divisional Court, and then to the Court of Appeal. The grounds of appeal were that the recorder (1) misdirected himself that his appellate discretion was absolute and unfettered, with the result that he substituted his own discretion for that of the Fire Service and Licensing Committee notwithstanding the fact that the committee were not shown to have erred in fact or law; (2) misdirected himself in holding as a matter of law and/or fact that the committee had fettered its own discretion by implementing a general policy decision of the whole council; (3) misdirected himself in holding that the views of the councillors who sat on the committee were irrelevant and/or of no evidential value to him as appellate tribunal in deciding the issue as to the desirability and need for the provision of such an amusement arcade; (4) failed to take into consideration the evidence of the chairman of the committee; (5) erred in fact and in law in holding that there was no sufficient evidence before him to establish that the provision of such facilities in the locality was socially undesirable or harmful; (6) failed to deal adequately or at all with the third and final ground on which the committee based its refusal, namely, that such new facilities were not required since there were adequate amusement with prizes machines already available elsewhere in Norwich.

LORD DENNING M.R.: (dissenting) [His Lordship summarised the facts, the legislative history and the relevant statutory provisions, and continued:]

4. *The Hearing by the Local Authority*

On May 2, 1969, the licensing committee of the City of Norwich heard the application. The applicants were represented by a solicitor, who put their case fully. The committee asked pertinent questions which the solicitor answered. At the end of the committee thanked him for presenting a clear case and he, in his turn, thanked the committee for listening to him. We were given a note of the proceedings before the committee. I append it herewith (post, p. 628G). It shows that the committee acted with the utmost fairness and discretion. They explored questions of policy and of detail, and, at the end, reserved their decision. . . .

5. *The Appeal to the Recorder*

[His Lordship summarised the reasons of the recorder in allowing the appeal, and pointed out that no evidence was given in support of the stated ground of appeal.] The recorder was not even told of the "information available to the committee." And I see no possible justification for the assertion that the decision was "unreasonable" or "contrary to natural justice. . . ."

6. *The General Policy Decision*

There has been much discussion lately on the right of a licensing body to lay down for itself a general policy to guide its decisions. In the past, recourse has been had to the words of Bankes L.J. in *R.* v. *Port of London Authority, ex p. Kynoch Ltd.* [1919] 1 K.B. 176, 182–186, and to the judgment of Lord Goddard C.J. in *R.* v. *Torquay Licensing Justices, ex p. Brockman* [1951] 2 K.B. 784, 788–792; but these cases have now to be read in the light of the decisions of Cooke J. in *Stringer* v. *Minister of Housing and Local Government* [1970] 1 W.L.R. 1281, 1297–1298 and of the House of Lords in *British Oxygen Co. Ltd.* v. *Board of Trade* [1971] A.C. 610, and of this court in *Cumings* v. *Birkenhead Corporation* [1971] 2 W.L.R. 1458. I take it to be perfectly clear now that an administrative body, including a licensing body, which may have to consider numerous applications of a similar kind, is entitled to lay down a general policy which it proposes to follow in coming to its individual decisions, provided always that it is a reasonable policy which it is fair and just to apply. Once laid down, the administrative body is entitled to apply the policy in the individual cases which come before it. The only qualification is that the administrative body must not apply the policy so rigidly as to reject an applicant without hearing what he has to say. It must not "shut its ears to an application": see [1971] A.C. 610, 625, *per* Lord Reid. The applicant is entitled to put forward reasons urging that the policy should be changed, or saying that in any case it should not be applied to him. But, so long as the administrative body is ready to hear him and consider what he has to say, it is entitled to apply its general policy to him as to others.

The local authority at Norwich fulfilled every one of these requirements. If you read the note of the proceedings before the committee, it is apparent that, although the city council laid down a general policy, the licensing committee did not regard that policy as inflexible or as binding on them: that they listened to everything that the applicants had to say: and yet decided against them.

The recorder seems to have thought that the local authority were not entitled to have a general policy at all: or, at any rate, not to be able to apply it in any individual case. He said:

> "I have sympathy with the committee who feel that the well-being and protection of the young people of this city is part of their general responsibility, and I am absolutely certain that they have acted fairly, honestly and fearlessly in forming their policy. It may be that their policy is right, but unless and until Parliament provides for a local

authority in this type of application the right to make the kind of policy rule that does exist in respect of other premises, each application must be treated on its merits. . . ."

I think that, in these words, the recorder misdirected himself in law. By his very words, he acknowledges that the policy was fairly and honestly formed and was a reasonable policy. If so, the local authority were entitled to have the policy and to apply it in this individual case, provided that they listened to all the applicant had to say—which they most clearly did.

7. *Evidence de Novo*

The recorder said:

". . . this being an appeal to quarter sessions, I must consider the matter de novo. . . . I must now approach the matter afresh with a complete and unfettered discretion. What is the evidence? As I have said, no objection is taken to the applicant, the premises or the site. The objection for which I have some sympathy is really the risk of providing easily accessible gambling facilities to children and young persons. On the facts there seems to be very little evidence of this; . . . I would require some evidence not only that such a place would be used to a considerable extent by young people, but also that such a use would be socially undesirable."

Those were the grounds of the recorder's judgment.

Mr. Boreham Q.C. [counsel for the company] supported this view. He submitted that the recorder ought to hear the evidence afresh, and exercise his own discretion, quite uninfluenced by what the local authority had done. He relied on *Godfrey* v. *Bournemouth Corporation* [1969] 1 W.L.R. 47, 52. I do not think this is correct. It is plain from the Act of 1849 that the recorder must hear evidence on all matters raised by the notice of appeal: and is not to travel outside on to other matters, because that might prejudice the respondent. It is also plain that the recorder ought to give great weight to the decision of the local authority. Lord Parker C.J. said so in *R.* v. *Essex Quarter Sessions, ex p. Thomas* [1966] 1 W.L.R. 359, 361–362, and repeated it in this very case.

In this case the local authority formed the opinion that it was socially undesirable to have amusement arcades in Norwich. That is why they laid down their general policy. But the recorder put their views on one side. He was not prepared, he said, to act on "unproved general principles of social undesirability and potential danger to young people," but wanted evidence on it.

I think that, in so holding, the recorder misdirected himself in law. Seeing that Parliament has entrusted the discretion to the local authority, it must intend then that their views should carry great weight. They are elected by the people to do all things proper to be done for the good administration of their city. They know their locality. They know its needs. They respond to the feelings of the citizens. If they think that an amusement arcade is socially undesirable, they are entitled to say so. They do not require evidence for the purpose. It is a matter of opinion on which their views are worth as much as those of any other person: and, indeed, worth more than those of a stranger. In any case, their views coincide with those of the Churches' Committee on Gambling: and that goes a long way. Their views should not be pushed on one side by the courts as worth nothing. Just as with their power to make by-laws, so also with their power to grant licences for amusement arcades. Their decision "ought to be supported if possible": see *Kruse* v. *Johnson* [1898] 2 Q.B. 91, 99, *per* Lord Russell C.J. In rejecting their views, the recorder was in error.

8. *Conclusion*

In my opinion the recorder erred in law in the two respects which I have stated. I would therefore allow the appeal and uphold the decision of the local authority.

My brethren disagree. Together with the recorder, and all the other judges, they hold that the views of the citizens of Norwich must be overruled. They must grant the freedom of their city to this amusement arcade, even though they believe it to be socially undesirable. I do not think this is right. This, in my opinion, is a matter for local self-government. Parliament intentionally made this a matter for the discretion of the local authority and there is no good reason for overruling their decision.

EDMUND DAVIES L.J.: . . . This litigation is said to raise in an acute form the question as to the nature of appeals to quarter sessions in such cases as the present. At one stage, Lord Denning M.R. summarised the issue in this way:

> "Is the hearing to be treated as a new trial to be determined on evidence de novo, without being influenced by what the local authority has done? Or is the hearing to be treated as an appeal proper, in which the local authority's decision is to be regarded as of considerable weight, and is not to be reversed unless their decision is shown to be wrong?"

With profound respect, however, I do not think that this is the proper antithesis, and I shall seek to show that there is a half-way house between these two approaches.

It is well established that no right of appeal exists apart from statute. As already observed, the only statutory provision relevant to the present case is that "the applicant may appeal in accordance with the provisions of the Quarter Sessions Act 1849." In *Drover* v. *Rugman* [1951] 1 K.B. 380, dealing with a case stated by quarter sessions on an appeal from the juvenile court, Lord Goddard C.J. said, at p. 382:

> "When a case goes to a quarter sessions it is reheard; the person seeking an order proves his case over again. That only means that quarter sessions are taking the place, as it may be expressed, of petty sessions; but the proceedings are none the less an appeal."

This, he explained, was due to the fact that there was no formal record of proceedings before justices, an observation equally true of proceedings before the licensing committee of this local authority, which (as Lord Denning M.R. has observed) are wholly dissimilar to those conducted by a body exercising judicial functions.

For my part, I cannot see how it is practicable in cases such as the present for an appeal to quarter sessions to be other than by way of a complete rehearing. Having no record before him of what transpired before the local authority, how could the recorder otherwise begin to judge the cogency of the written reasons placed before him? . . .

As it appears to me, Mr. Tapp [counsel for the corporation] has attached excessive weight to the fact that the granting or renewal of a permit under the Act of 1963 is expressed to be "at the discretion of the local authority" when he concludes therefrom that quarter sessions are bound by the decision of the local authority and its stated reasons unless it can be demonstrated that they were wrong. A similar contention was raised—and rejected—in *Stepney Borough Council* v. *Joffe* [1949] 1 K.B. 599, where street traders' licences to trade were revoked by the borough council. This they had done pursuant to a statutory provision where "the applicant or licensee is on account of misconduct or for any other sufficient reason in their opinion unsuitable to hold such licence. . . ." Section 25(1) of the London County Council (General Powers) Act 1947 provided that persons aggrieved by such refusal "may appeal to a petty sessional court and on any such appeal the court may confirm, reverse or vary the decision of the borough council. . . ." The traders accordingly appealed to a magistrate, whereupon the council contended (1) that the magistrate was not entitled to substitute his own opinion as to the suitability of the traders to hold licences for that of the council; (2) that he was not empowered to review the merits; and (3) that his jurisdiction was limited to considering whether or not there was any material on which the council could reasonably have arrived at their decisions to revoke the licences. (One may note, in parenthesis, the close similarity of those submissions to that advanced by the present appellant.) But the magistrate would have none of this. He held that he was bound to consider the whole matter de novo, and he allowed the appeals. Upholding that decision in the Divisional Court, and referring to the submission that the magistrate had not been entitled to substitute his opinion for that of the borough council and that all he could decide was whether there was evidence upon which the council could arrive at their conclusion, Lord Goddard C.J. said, at p. 602:

"If that argument be right, the right of appeal, ... would be purely illusory. Such an appeal would ... really be only an appeal on the question of law whether there was any evidence upon which the borough council could have formed an opinion. If their decision were a mere matter of opinion and that opinion were to be conclusive, I do not know that the borough council would be obliged to have any evidence. They could simply say: 'In our opinion this person is unsuitable to hold a licence.' It is true that they must give a sufficient reason, but they could give any reason they liked and say: 'That is sufficient in our opinion.' I do not know how a court could then say on appeal that that was not a sufficient reason. If the reason need only be one which is sufficient in the opinion of the borough council, it is difficult to see how any court of appeal could set aside their decision. It seems to me that [section 25(1)] gives an unrestricted right of appeal, and if there is an unrestricted right of appeal, it is for the court of appeal to substitute its opinion for the opinion of the borough council."

I would apply those words in full measure to the present case. The provision for an appeal to quarter sessions seems to me largely, if not entirely, "illusory" if the contention of the appellant council is right. If it is, I am at a loss to follow how the recorder would set about discharging his appellate function. Lacking all information as to what had happened before the local authority, save the bare knowledge that they had refused the application and their written grounds for refusal, he would be powerless, as I think, to make any effective examination of the validity of those reasons. Furthermore, unless he is free to embark on a complete consideration of all the relevant material presented to him, how can he in due course proceed to state a case for the Divisional Court if called upon to do so? The customary (and preferable) way of doing this is *inter alia* to set out in separate paragraphs those facts found by the lower court to have been "proved or admitted," and indeed we were shown a copy of the draft case prepared (but ultimately not used) by the local authority in the present case which was in that form. But how could the recorder proceed to state what *his* findings of fact were if he was not free to receive evidence and assess it? No satisfactory answer to this question has, in my judgment, been advanced, and for this reason, among others, I am forced to the conclusion that the appellants are wrong in their main contention. I hold that the proceedings before this recorder were by way of a complete rehearing.

But, contrary to what has been contended, this conclusion does *not* involve that the views earlier formed by the local authority have to be entirely disregarded by quarter sessions. It is true that in *Godfrey* v. *Bournemouth Corporation* [1969] 1 W.L.R. 47, after observing that an appeal to quarter sessions under Schedule 6 to this same Act was by way of a complete rehearing. Lord Parker C.J. said, at p. 52, "the discretion is a discretion which the recorder in the present case had to arrive at himself uninfluenced by what the local authority had done." But with respect, I do not accept this. It went much too far, it was in direct conflict with the view which Lord Parker C.J. had earlier expressed in *R.* v. *Essex Quarter Sessions, ex p. Thomas* [1966] 1 W.L.R. 359, 363, it was contrary to the approach adopted both by the recorder and by Lord Parker C.J. himself in the instant case, and it was, with deference, an uncalled-for observation. Here again, *Stepney Borough Council* v. *Joffe* [1949] 1 K.B. 599 establishes what I regard as the proper approach, for, having made the point that there was in that case an unrestricted appeal, Lord Goddard C.J. continued, at pp. 602, 603:

> "That does not mean to say that the court of appeal, in this case the metropolitan magistrate, ought not to pay great attention to the fact that the duly constituted and elected local authority have come to an opinion on the matter, and ought not lightly, of course, to reverse their opinion. It is constantly said (although I am not sure that it is always sufficiently remembered) that the function of a court of appeal is to exercise its powers when it is satisfied that the judgment below is wrong, not merely because it is not satisfied that the judgment was right."

I find no reason for thinking that the recorder in the present case failed in any degree to pay proper regard to the decision arrived at by an overwhelming majority of the local authority. On the contrary, he manifestly entertained considerable sympathy with their attitude. But, as he said, he was ultimately obliged to act on the totality of the material placed before him, balancing that called for the appellants against that presented by the local authority and paying due regard to the existing decision being appealed from. Having done so, he concluded that the appellants had made out their case, the Divisional Court in its turn have upheld him, and for my part I have to say that it was not established to my satisfaction that either erred in law. I therefore find myself compelled to hold that this appeal should be dismissed and that the order of the recorder granting the permit be upheld.

PHILLIMORE L.J.: . . . [T]here is no need for authority for the proposition that a council and its committees are entitled to agree on a policy provided always that they do not impose it inflexibly. In this case, however, we were told that the chairman of the committee—a former Mayor of Norwich—gave evidence before the recorder to the effect that they had rejected the application solely on the basis of the policy decision taken by the General Purposes Committee. . . .

[The recorder said:]

> "I am forced to the conclusion that in this case, where the application met with all the ordinary requirements as to suitability of site, premises

and management, the general policy must have been applied. In other words, no application to the local authority, however suitable, would succeed."

In other words the council had *not* exercised any form of discretion. They had simply dismissed this application after going through the necessary motions without regard to its individual merits or demerits. I take this to be a finding of fact with which this court is in no position to interfere.

Incidentally, I cannot see that the recorder could avoid this decision. Apparently no evidence was called to support either ground (a) or ground (b). Nobody came forward to say that this sort of arcade had resulted in disastrous damage to the morality of the young in Great Yarmouth or any other seaside place or was likely to prove particularly harmful to the young of Norwich. Indeed, as I think, the Act of 1964 by section 3 tends to suggest that in regard to premises such as this it is wrong to refuse a licence on the ground that some particular class such as young persons may be injuriously affected. . . .

I think that the recorder was clearly right and that his judgment should not be disturbed. This is a case where he was satisfied that the council's committee had failed to keep an open mind and had applied their policy without regard to the facts of the individual case.

[His Lordship agreed with EDMUND DAVIES L.J. that the appeal to Quarter Sessions was by way of rehearing.]

Appeal dismissed.

Notes and Questions

1. See case note by J. Prophet, [1971] P.L. 162.

2. The recorder said: "In my view . . . the licensing committee have decided that they will not grant a permit for *any* amusement place with prizes in the City of Norwich, and the reasons they give for *this* refusal would apply to *any* application." (Italics added by Edmund Davies L.J.). What are the implications of this view?

3. Where should the right to decide such a question as that raised in *Sagnata* lie, with the courts or with the local authority?

4. Appeals which formerly lay to quarter sessions now lie to the Crown Court: the Courts Act 1971, ss.8, 9, Scheds. 1, 9; I. R. Scott, *The Crown Court*, paras. 204–233.

5. The grant of permits in respect of the provision of amusements with prizes is now governed by Part III of the Gaming Act 1968 (gaming by means of machines) and the Lotteries and Amusements Act 1976 (see C. Milner Smith and S. P. Monkcom, *The Law of Betting, Gaming and Lotteries* (1987), Chaps. 10 and 11.

The *Sagnata* approach applies also to appeals to the Crown Court concerning general gaming club licences (*i.e.* casino and bingo club licences) (*R.* v. *Crown Court at Knightsbridge, ex p. Aspinall Curzon Ltd.*, *The Times*, December 16, 1982 (see above, p. 604; Smith and Monkcom, *op. cit.*, pp. 218–220).

6. In certain situations, local authorities have express statutory power to pass "blanket" resolutions that would otherwise be impermissible under the rule against the fettering of discretion. A local authority is empowered by the Gaming Act 1968, Sched. 9, para. 3, to resolve not to grant or renew permits under Part III in respect of "a class of premises specified in the resolution." However, the power

cannot apply to premises used or to be used wholly or mainly for the provision of amusements by means of machines to which Part III applies (para. 4), thus requiring applications in respect of amusement centres, arcades and the like to be considered on their merits. The policy behind this power was:

> "parliament's view that local consideration should be given considerable weight in determining in which types of premises amusements with prizes generally, and machines in particular, should be available to the general public for gaming. A particular factor which influenced parliament . . . was the availability of such machines to persons under the age of 18" (Smith and Monkcom, *op. cit.*, p. 325.

It is uncertain whether a local authority's resolution not to grant or renew permits in respect of *all* premises in its area other than those exempted by para. 4 would be *intra vires* (see Smith and Monkcom, *op. cit.*, pp. 326–328, noting the view of Woolf J. in *Westminster City Council* v. *Lunepalm Ltd.*, *The Times*, December 10, 1985, that it would be, but dicta to the contrary in *Walker* v. *Leeds City Council* [1978] A.C. 403, 421, 422, *per* Lords Simon and Kilbrandon).

Similarly, the Lotteries and Amusements Act 1976, Sched. 3, para. 2 enables a local authority to pass a resolution that it will not grant, or will neither grant nor renew, any permits for the commercial provision of amusements with prizes in respect of premises of a class specified in the resolution. By para. 3, such a resolution may not be passed in respect of premises used or to be used wholly or mainly for the purposes of a pleasure fair consisting wholly or mainly of amusements. These provisions, which formerly appeared in the Betting, Gaming and Lotteries Act 1963, Sched. 6 (as amended), were considered in *R.* v. *Herrod, ex p. Leeds City Council* [1976] Q.B. 540 C.A.; affirmed, *sub nom. Walker* v. *Leeds County Council* [1978] A.C. 403, H.L. The Court of Appeal emphasised that the courts should construe the power to pass "blanket" resolutions strictly, as the refusal or non-renewal of a licence without a hearing seemed contrary to natural justice and a non-renewal might cause serious economic loss (see Lord Denning M.R. at p. 560, James L.J. at p. 566 and Shaw L.J. at p. 570–71). Accordingly, the term "pleasure fair" in the para. 3 exemption was to be given a wide meaning as including premises used for the purposes of playing prize bingo. An appeal to the House of Lords was dismissed. Lord Wilberforce stated at p. 417 that if the term "pleasure fair" was to be interpreted restrictively as meaning "fun fair," bingo hall owners in areas where the appropriate "blanket" resolutions were passed would be "unable even to present a case on the merits to the local authorities. They are automatically resolved out of business. This, in relation to a comparatively innocuous form of activity, seems rather draconian, and at least justifies the courts looking to see whether there is possible alternative."

(C) Statutory Ultra Vires

ACQUISITION OF LAND ACT 1981

Part IV Validity and Date of Operation of Orders and Certificates

Grounds for application to High Court

23.—(1) If any person aggrieved by a compulsory purchase order desires to question the validity thereof, or of any provision contained therein, on the ground that the authorisation of a compulsory purchase thereby granted is not empowered to be granted under this Act or any such enactment as is mentioned in section 1(1) of this Act, he may make an application to the High Court.

(2) If any person aggrieved by—

(*a*) a compulsory purchase order, or

(*b*) a certificate under Part III of, or Schedule 3 to, this Act.

desires to question the validity thereof on the ground that any relevant requirement has not been complied with in relation to the order or certificate he may make an application to the High Court.

(3) In subsection (2) above, "relevant requirement" means—

(*a*) any requirement of this Act, or of any regulation under section 7(2) above, or

(*b*) any requirement of the Tribunals and Inquiries Act 1971 or of any rules made, or having effect as if made, under that Act.

(4) An application to the High Court under this section shall be made within six weeks.

(*a*) in the case of a compulsory purchase order to which the Statutory Orders (Special Procedure) Act 1945 applies (and which is not excluded by section 27 below), from the date on which the order becomes operative under that Act,

(*b*) in the case of a compulsory purchase order to which the said Act of 1945 does not apply, from the date on which notice of the confirmation or making of the order is first published in accordance with this Act,

(*c*) in the case of a certificate, the date on which notice of the giving of the certificate is first published in accordance with this Act.

Powers of the court

24.—(1) On an application under section 23 above the court may by interim order suspend the operation of the compulsory purchase order or any provision contained therein, or of the certificate, either generally or in so far as it effects any property of the applicant, until the final determination of the proceedings.

(2) If on the application the court is satisfied that—

(*a*) the authorisation granted by the compulsory purchase order is not empowered to be granted under this Act or any such enactment as is mentioned in section 1(1) of this Act, or

(*b*) the interests of the applicant have been substantially prejudiced by any relevant requirement (as defined in section 23(3) above) not having been complied with,

the court may quash the compulsory purchase order or any provision contained therein, or the certificate, either generally or in so far as it affects any property of the applicant.

Restriction on other court proceedings

25. Subject to the preceding provisions of this Part of this Act, a compulsory purchase order, or a certificate under Part III of, or Schedule 3 to, this Act, shall not, either before or after it has been confirmed, made or given, be questioned in any legal proceedings whatsoever.

Date of operation

26.—(1) Subject to section 24 above, a compulsory purchase order, other than one to which the Statutory Orders (Special Procedure) Act 1945 applies, shall become operative on the date on which notice of the confirmation or making of the order is first published in accordance with this Act.

(2) Subject to section 24 above, a certificate under Part III of, or Schedule 3 to, this Act shall become operative on the date on which notice of the giving of the certificate is first published in accordance with this Act.

Exclusion of orders confirmed by Act of Parliament

27. This Part of this Act shall not apply to an order which is confirmed by Act of Parliament under section 6 of the Statutory Orders (Special Procedure) Act 1945.

Notes

1. An appeal provision in this form was first introduced in section 11 of the Housing Act 1930, which Act gave greater slum clearance powers to local authorities. The limitations both as to the grounds and the period allowed for appeals were thought necessary in view of the chaos that had been caused by the availability of the prerogative writs to challenge improvement schemes under earlier legislation. In *R.* v. *Minister of Health, ex p. Davis*,[1] the Divisional Court had granted a writ of prohibition to restrain the Minister from confirming a scheme for a site in the centre of Derby. The scheme was held to be *ultra vires* on the ground that some of the land was to be purchased compulsorily for the purpose of resale, and not for any purpose of rearrangement or reconstruction as authorised by the Act. It was alleged that no scheme confirmed by the Minister up to 1929 was valid.[2] Counsel for the property owners in the *Davis* case said that he had examined about 100 schemes, all of which were invalid.[3] As a result new schemes and schemes in progress were held up[4]; "and . . . it was decided that the whole purpose of the Act had been frustrated by the slum landlords and the Court, and that nothing substantial could be done until new legislation was passed."[5]

From 1930, provisions similar to section 11 of the Housing Act 1930 were included in many statutes, perhaps too often as a matter of course.[6] The need for

[1] [1929] 1 K.B. 619.

[2] Sir John Lorden, *Minutes of Evidence of the Donoughmore Committee*, p. 68, para. 1010.

[3] Mr. H. A. Hill, *ibid.* p. 72, para. 1027.

[4] The Minister of Health (Mr. Arthur Greenwood): oral answer, H.C.Deb., Vol. 234, col. 1164 (January 30, 1930); Second Reading of the Housing Bill, H.C.Deb., Vol. 237, cols. 1805–1807 (April 7, 1930).

[5] W. I. Jennings, "Local Government Law" (1935) 51 L.Q.R. 180, at p. 193.

[6] B. Schwartz lists 18 examples from 1930 to 1948 in *Law and the Executive in Britain* (1949), p. 209, n. 138.

finality is rarely as compelling as it is for large scale slum clearance schemes, compulsory purchase orders and the like. The main examples of "statutory *ultra vires*" clauses are: the Acquisition of Land Act 1981, Part IV, (compulsory purchase orders: see *Smith* v. *East Elloe R.D.C.* below, p. 871); the New Towns Act 1981, Sched. 1 (orders designating the site of a new town: see *Franklin* v. *Minister of Town and Country Planning*, above, p. 569); the Highways Act 1980, Sched. 2 (orders designating a highway as a trunk road, motorway schemes, etc.); *ibid.* Sched. 7 (public path creation extinguishment and diversion orders); the Town and Country Planning Act 1990, s.287 (structure or local plans, etc.); *ibid.* s.288 (a large variety of planning matters including decisions of the Secretary of State on appeals against a refusal of planning permission; *cf.* section 289 of the 1990 Act which give rights of appeal on a point of law to the High Court, against decisions of the Secretary of State (*inter alia*) to uphold an enforcement notice.

"Statutory *ultra vires*" clauses were considered by Swift J. in cases under the Housing Act 1930 (*e.g. Re Bowman*, below). In more recent times the attitude the courts should take to these clauses has been restated by Lord Denning M.R. (in the *Ashbridge* and *Coleen* cases, below, pp. 627 and 634). Other examples of challenges under these procedures given in this book are *Lavender* v. *M.H.L.G.* (p. 287); *Stringer* v. *M.H.L.G.* (p. 304 (note)); *Hanks* v. *M.H.L.G.* (p. 387) and *Franklin* v. *Minister of Town and Country Planning* (p. 569). The question of the exclusion of judicial review by procedures other than that laid down in the relevant clause are considered in *Smith* v. *East Elloe R.D.C.* (p. 871) an *ex p. Ostler* (p. 880).

2. The line between decisions and orders that are protected by a statutory *ultra vires* clause, and decisions that remain subject to judicial review can be complex, and depends on the exact wording of the clause in question. For example, the special appeal provisions apply to a decision by the Secretary of State to confirm a compulsory purchase order, but not a refusal to confirm an order, or a decision to exclude land from an order (*Islington London Borough Council* v. *Secretary of State for the Environment; Stockport Metropolitan Borough Council* v. *Secretary of State for the Environment* (1980) 43 P. & C.R. 300; *R.* v. *Secretary of State for the Environment, ex p. Melton Borough Council* [1986] J.P.L. 190); or a question whether implementation of an order would be unconscionable (*R.* v. *Carmarthenshire District Council, ex p. Blewin Trust* (1989) 59 P. & C.R. 379). On the position under the Town and Country Planning Act 1990, see annotations to section 284 in the *Encyclopedia of Planning Law and Practice.*

Re BOWMAN, SOUTH SHIELDS (THAMES STREET) CLEARANCE ORDER 1931

[1932] 2 K.B. 621; 101 L.J.K.B. 798; 147 L.T. 150; 48 T.L.R. 351; 96 J.P. 207; 30 L.G.R. 245; [1932] W.N. 91 (Swift J.)

In April 1931 South Shields county borough council made a clearance order in respect of the Thames Street area. The order included a number of houses belonging to Mr. Bowman. The order was confirmed by the Minister of Health, with modifications. The owner sought to have the order quashed under section 11 of the Housing Act 1930. The first point was that the order as made originally required most of the premises to be vacated within seven days. This was modified by the minister to 28 days, which was the period authorised by the statute. The owner argued that the original order was not effective as regards the houses subject to the seven-day period, and that the minister was not empowered to bring into the order houses not originally there (Sched. 1 para. 4). The second point was that the notice of the order served on the owners omitted a particular note which was included in the form prescribed by the minister.

SWIFT J.: . . . The Housing Act 1930, is one of a series of Acts which have from time to time been passed for the purpose of enabling local authorities to regulate the occupation, and indeed the existence of dwelling-houses in their districts. There have been Acts which have provided for dealing with particular insanitary houses, and Acts which have provided for schemes for the demolition of houses and the rebuilding of them or the securing of open spaces where the houses had hitherto been, and this Act of 1930 is the last of these Acts. It gives to local authorities, in my opinion, very much greater power than they have ever had before. It enables them, under proper limitations and observing due precautions, to order the owners of dwelling-houses to vacate them, to pull them down and not to erect any other buildings upon the sites save under the supervision of and subject to the conditions imposed by the local authority, and this is to be done entirely at the expense of the owner of the property and without any compensation being given to him for the loss of that which is certainly of pecuniary value to him at the time when the order is made. When an owner of property against whom an order has been made under the Act comes into this Court and complains that there has been some irregularity in the proceedings and that he is not liable to have his property taken away, it is right, I think, that his case should be entertained sympathetically and that a statute under which he is being deprived of his rights to property should be construed strictly against the local authority and favourably towards the interest of the applicant, inasmuch as he for the benefit of the community is undoubtedly suffering a substantial loss, which in my view must not be inflicted upon him unless it is quite clear that Parliament has intended that it shall. . . .

[His Lordship summarised section 11, and continued:] If . . . the order having been confirmed by the Minister of Health, any person feels himself aggrieved by it, he may apply to this Court under the Act on one or other or on both of two grounds, but on those grounds alone, one of the grounds being that the order as confirmed is not within the powers of the Act, and the other ground being that some requirement of the Act has not been complied with. He is not, in my view, entitled to come here and complain that the local authority have made a mistake in fact in making the order. He is not entitled to say that his house is not insanitary or unfit for human habitation, and that, therefore, the order should not have been made. These seem to me to be matters which are left by the Legislature entirely to the local authority subject to the confirmation of the Minister of Health. Section 1 of the Act begins by saying: "Where a local authority, upon consideration of an official representation or other information in their possession, are satisfied" that the houses in the area are unfit for human habitation, and when once the local authority say that they are satisfied as to that matter it does not seem to me that there is any power in any tribunal, unless it be the Minister of Health, to interfere with that finding of fact. There may some day arise a case, which is certainly not this case, in which it may be said that there was no material, no information and no representation before the local authority upon which they could, as reasonable people, possibly be satisfied that a clearance order ought to be made. When such a case as that arises it will be dealt with, but where, as in this case, there was obviously ample material before the local authority to justify them in making the clearance order if they thought fit to do so, it does not seem to me that this Court has any right to interfere. I do not think that this Court is authorized to retry or rehear the case, or to reconsider the matters with which the local authority has been intrusted, or to interfere in the decision at which they have arrived. On these grounds I declined at an earlier stage of the proceedings to accede to Mr. Montgomery's request that I should hear evidence on the question whether or not in regard to particular houses the order ought to have been made. Mr. Montgomery, . . . stated to me that he could not say that there was not evidence upon which the local authority might have come to the conclusion to which they did come and that the case was one in which there was no evidence to support the conclusion. In those circumstances I held that it was a matter for the local authority and not for this Court as a court of appeal sitting over them to determine the facts, and it being admitted that there was some evidence upon which they might act, I declined to interfere in that part of the case.

[His Lordship outlined the argument on the first point, and continued:] I cannot assent to that very seductive argument. I think that although the order improperly and inaccurately stated the period within which the houses were to be vacated, it nevertheless was an order applying to the houses. It may well be that it did not comply with the requirements of the Act and that it might have been found impossible to enforce it, but those houses were in it and the Minister was quite right in altering the period to twenty-eight days. That he had power to do this I am convinced. . . .

[On the second point, Swift J. held that although it was admitted that owing to the omission of the note a requirement of the Act had not been complied with, the applicant's interests had not been prejudiced in any way. He had been informed of his rights of appeal, had made objections to the order, and had appeared at the public inquiry.]

Application dismissed.

ASHBRIDGE INVESTMENTS LTD. v. MINISTER OF HOUSING AND LOCAL GOVERNMENT

(Re Stalybridge (Castle Hall No. 7) and (Acres Lane and Lawton Street) Compulsory Purchase Order 1963)

[1965] 1 W.L.R. 1320; 129 J.P. 580; 109 S.J. 595; [1965] 3 All E.R. 371; 63 L.G.R. 400 (Court of Appeal)

Stalybridge Borough Council declared an area to be a clearance area for the purposes of section 42(1) of the Housing Act 1957, on the ground that the houses therein were unfit for human habitation. This area included two adjoining terrace houses of similar appearance, numbers 17 and 19, Grosvenor Street, owned by the respondents. Subsequently the local authority made a compulsory purchase order in respect of the clearance area, which was coloured pink on the map of the order, and of certain adjoining land which was coloured grey on the map. The compensation payable in respect of the pink area (unfit houses) was less than that payable in the grey area. Following objections by the owners, a local inquiry was held. The minister confirmed the order with modifications. One modification was the transfer of number 19 from the pink area to the grey area on the ground that it had lost its identity as a dwelling, and so was not a "house." The owners applied under Schedule 4, para. 2, to the Housing Act 1957, for an order quashing the compulsory purchase order in so far as it affected number 17, on the ground that it was not a "house," or alternatively was not unfit for human habitation.

Mocatta J. (1965) 109 S.J. 474, held that the question whether number 17 was a "house" was a question going to the jurisdiction of the minister and that the court should receive evidence of the facts and reach its own conclusion thereon, and was not confined to the question whether the minister, on the evidence before him could properly conclude that number 17 was a house. The minister appealed.

LORD DENNING M.R.: [outlined the facts and continued:] Now the owners make application to the High Court asking for the order to be quashed in regard to No. 17. They say that the Minister has gone outside his jurisdiction because No. 17 is not a house. It is no more a house than No. 19. The owners say that the court should receive evidence afresh on this point and should come to its own conclusion as to whether or no No. 17 is a house or not.

The Minister objects. He says: "This is not a matter on which the court should receive fresh evidence at all, or go into the matter afresh. It is simply a case for the court to ask: Did the Minister have reasonable grounds or no for determining No. 17 to be a house?" The Minister concedes that, if he had no evidence before him such as to justify that finding, or if the materials before him were such that he could not reasonably come to the conclusion that it was a house then, of course, the court could interfere. The Minister also concedes that if he has erred in point of law the court can inquire into and quash his decision. But he says that this should be determined on the materials which he had before him, and not on fresh evidence. Mocatta J. has held that the court can look into the matter afresh and receive fresh evidence.

Section 42 of the Housing Act 1957, says: "(1) Where a local authority, upon consideration of an official representation or other information in their possession, are satisfied as respects any area in their district—(*a*) that the houses in that area are unfit for human habitation ... the authority shall cause that area to be defined on a map," and so on. It is apparent that the question "fit or unfit?" is essentially one for the inspector and the Minister, and the courts would not ordinarily admit fresh evidence on it. But the owners say that, on the question of "house or not a house," the court can and should look into the whole matter itself afresh.

In order to decide this question it is helpful to look at Schedule 3, para. 4(3). It says that "If the Minister is of opinion that any land included by the local authority in a clearance area should not have been so included, he shall . . . modify it so as to exclude that land for all purposes from the clearance area." It is clear, therefore, that the Minister can move the land from the pink into the grey if he thinks that it should not have been originally included in the pink area. It seems to me that, in order to determine this matter, the Minister must himself decide the question of "house or not a house," just as he must decide "fit or unfit." The legislature has entrusted it to the Minister for decision. If it is not unfit, he can remove it from the pink to the grey. If it is not a house, he can likewise remove it from the pink to the grey.

Seeing that that decision is entrusted to the Minister, we have to consider the power of the court to interfere with his decision. It is given in Schedule 4, para. 2. The court can only interfere on the ground that the Minister has gone outside the powers of the Act or that any requirement of the Act has not been complied with. Under this section it seems to me that the court can interfere with the Minister's decision if he has acted on no evidence; or if he has come to a conclusion to which on the evidence he could not reasonably come; or if he has given a wrong interpretation to the words of the statute; or if he has taken into consideration matters which he ought not to have taken into account, or vice versa; or has otherwise gone wrong in law. It is identical with the position when the court has power to interfere with the decision of a lower tribunal which has erred in point of law.

We have to apply this to the modern procedure whereby the inspector makes his report and the Minister gives his letter of decision, and they are made available to the parties. It seems to me that the court should look at the material which the inspector and the Minister had before them just as it looks at the material before an inferior court, and see whether on that material the Minister has gone wrong in law. We were referred to two cases: *In re Butler, Camberwell (Wingfield Mews) No. 2 Clearance Order, 1936* [1939] 1 K.B. 570 and *In re Ripon (Highfield) Housing Confirmation Order, 1938, White and Collins* v. *Minister of Health* [1939] 2 K.B. 838 [above, p. 210]. They were decided at a time when the report of the inspector was not open to the parties. There was no letter of decision. There was nothing but the formal order of the Minister. It was necessary, therefore, for affidavits to be received showing what was the material available before the Minister. They were received in those cases for that purpose. Nowadays, when the material is available, it seems to me that the court should limit itself to that material. Fresh evidence should not be admitted save in exceptional circumstances. It is not correct for the court to approach the case absolutely do novo as though the court was sitting to decide the matter in the first instance. The court can receive evidence to show what material was before the Minister; but it cannot receive evidence of the kind which was indicated in the present case so as to decide the whole matter afresh.

I think that the preliminary point taken on behalf of the Minister, namely, that this is not a matter for fresh evidence, ought to be upheld, and I would allow the appeal accordingly.

HARMAN L.J.: . . . The judge before whom this matter came was, I think, misled by the two cases to which we have been referred. In *In re Ripon*, which on the face of it looks the nearest to this one, the decision eventually was that there was no evidence on which the Minister could have come to his conclusion. The terms of the Act were that if the land in question was part of a park it could not be included; that was not a matter for the opinion of the Minister or the satisfaction of the local authority, but was a statutory prohibition.

Therefore, it was necessary to see on what grounds the Minister had come to this conclusion, and as he had not been bound to give any reasons, nor to publish the report of his inspector, it was absolutely necessary to have some evidence to show what must have been the materials on which he so decided. Once they came out, it was seen that this was in fact part of a park and could not have been anything else. Therefore, there was no evidence on which the Minister could reach the conclusion which he did, and the order was quashed.

Now that does not seem to me to be an authority which involves anything here. It is true that the headnote states that the Court of Appeal held that a motion of this sort was a new and independent proceeding, and not a rehearing or a retrial. That, of course, we accept. But the fact that it is a new and independent proceeding does not mean that everything is necessarily open to the court. Some of the matters are left to the Minister, some are not. It is left to his opinion to decide whether a house is a house or another building, and it is left to his opinion also to decide whether it is or is not unfit for human habitation. In both those matters he relies on his inspector's view, and it is quite clear from the inspector's report in this case that he did take both those matters into his consideration. . . . That being so, and it appearing from paragraph 4(3) of Schedule 3 that those matters are for the Minister's opinion, it would not be right for this court to substitute its opinion for that of the Minister; and I do not think there is any case which involves us in doing so. . . .

We can interfere if the decision of the Minister was perverse and could not have been properly arrived at on the facts which his inspector gathered for him, but otherwise it seems to me that the legislature has entrusted that part of it to him, and not to us, and we should not interfere. . . .

WINN L.J.: . . . The essential point in this case is whether or not any matter affecting the jurisdiction of the Minister to confirm the compulsory purchase order in question lies before this court, the High Court, for decision. By contrast with *In re Butler* and *In re Ripon*, there is in this case no suggestion that the compulsory purchase order in respect of No. 17, Grosvenor Street was made without jurisdiction. . . .

It is not contended by Mr. Drinkwater that there was no power to include No. 17 in that order. He says that, legally, it could only have been included in (b) and not in (a) of that order, and that the Minister was bound in law, when confirming this order—because the house so-called was not a house within the meaning of section 42(1)—to include No. 17 under (b) and not (a) of the confirmation, introducing in this, as well as in other, respects a modification of that order made by the council. . . .

The Minister, when deciding to confirm such an order as this, is given expressly, by the provisions to which my Lords have referred, power to take properties which have been submitted to him as included under (a) of such an order out of that sub-paragraph and to put them into (b), and so cause them to attract higher compensation.

It seems to me that, unless it can be postulated that the Minister's only power in relation to No. 17, Grosvenor Street was so to transfer it, and that he had no power to confirm the compulsory purchase order save after transfer of No. 17, the owners' contention must fail: by the statute itself that decision is left to the Minister and not to the court, because it is left to the Minister to decide whether or not to transfer and, therefore, to decide not to transfer.

Appeal allowed.

Notes

1. Clearance area compulsory purchase orders made under the Housing Act 1985, s.290, on or after April 1, 1990, are regulated by the Acquisition of Land Act 1981 (see above, p. 622 for the applicable appeal provisions).

2. The Minister has not in any reported case taken the point that the error of law alleged does not take him beyond his powers. See for example *Chelmsford Corporation* v. *Secretary of State for the Environment* (1971) 22 P. & C.R. 880 at p. 881 (Browne J.; a planning case). Lord Denning's *Ashbridge* formula has been applied in *Crabtree* v. *M.H.L.G.* (1965) 64 L.G.R. 104 (Paull J.; a planning case); *Howard* v. *M.H.L.G.* (1967) 65 L.G.R. 257 (John Stephenson J.; a housing case); the *Coleen* case (below, p. 634); *British Dredging (Services) Ltd.* v. *Secretary of State for Wales* [1975] 1 W.L.R. 687 (Park J.; a case under the Coast Protection Act 1949); *R.* v. *Medicines Commission, ex p. Organon Laboratories Ltd.* [1989] C.O.D. 479 (a case under the Medicines Act 1968, s.107); and *R.* v. *Secretary of State for Transport, ex p. de Rothschild* [1989] 1 All E.R. 933. In *Brookdene Investments Ltd.* v. *M.H.L.G.* (1970) 21 P. & C.R. 545, counsel for the Minister expressly reserved the point whether the court could intervene for a non-jurisdictional error of law. Fisher J. also thought that counsel would have conceded that if a non-jurisdictional error of law involved a failure to comply with a relevant requirement, and substantial prejudice were established, a decision could be quashed.

3. In *Re Lamplugh* (1968) 19 P. & C.R. 125, an order by Cornwall County Council under section 28 of the Town and Country Planning Act 1962 (now s.102 of the 1990 Act) requiring the removal from certain land of a disused coastguard station, was challenged under section 179 of the 1962 Act (s.280 of the 1990 Act). Roskill J. said at pp. 137–138:

> "[Counsel for the Minister submitted] that in all the cases and where the question of challenge to the exercise of executive powers has arisen in the courts, one finds the relevant statutory provisions falling broadly into two classes. First, he said, there is the class of case where, as a necessary condition

precedent to the exercise by the Minister or by some other executive authority of powers, there must exist, if I may use his phrase, the necessary substratum of fact. Secondly, he said, there is the class of case where the exercise of the power is not preconditioned by the existence of any such substratum of fact, but there is what he described as an executive discretion given to the authority concerned, be it a Minister or local authority, to exercise the powers given either by Parliament or by delegated legislation. . . .

It appears to me reasonably plain, without going through all the cases, that, while they may not fall precisely into two neat classes, they do broadly fall into those two classes. . . . Mr. Bridge pointed out, in my judgment rightly, that in the *Stalybridge* case [*i.e.* the *Ashbridge* case] Lord Denning M.R.'s observations were made in a case which fell into what he called 'the substratum of fact' class of case, and that that was why it was open to the court in that case, as in the *Ripon* case some thirty years before, to consider upon what evidence the Minister had acted. It has, as I understand the law, always been open to the court in "the substratum of fact" class of case to review the matter and to consider, though in the old days it was often difficult to find out on what material the point had been considered, on what material the decision had been reached. But, of course, as Lord Denning M.R. pointed out in the *Stalybridge* case, it is now very much easier to find out what the material was, for the Minister is required to hold an inquiry and to make the evidence available to the parties. Whilst it is true, therefore, that the *Stalybridge* case was a case which falls into what I will call, adopting Mr. Bridge's phrase, 'the substratum class,' nevertheless Lord Denning M.R. did not limit his observations when he was considering Schedule 4, para. 2, of the Housing Act 1957 (which gives virtually the same powers as appear in section 179 of the present Act) to "the substratum class" of case. Nor, if I may respectfully say so, do I think he intended to. I think that he was dealing in general with what the powers of the court now are where cases come up for review. . . ."

Roskill J. held that the present case was of the "executive discretion" kind, that Lord Denning's *Ashbridge* formula was applicable, and that there were no grounds to interfere with the exercise of discretion in this case.

The argument rejected by Roskill J. does, perhaps, throw some light on the nature of the minister's concession in *Ashbridge*, and has not as yet been considered by the Court of Appeal. If the argument were to be accepted, the scope of review under the statutory formula would be narrower than at common law in as much as a determination of "jurisdictional" fact could only be upset if unsupported by any evidence, or unreasonable, or erroneous in law and not merely because it was wrong. Moreover, in cases where there was no "factual pre-condition" the *Ashbridge* principles would not apply at all, and it would be necessary to determine on ordinary principles whether the decision was *ultra vires*. The limitation of the *Ashbridge* principles in this way would, however, enable the courts to draw a meaningful distinction between the scope of review under these statutory formulae and the scope of review on appeals limited to points of law (see *infra*).

4. In *Bradley* v. *Secretary of State for the Environment* (1982) 47 P. & C.R. 374 Glidewell J. stated (at p. 388) that in his view Lord Denning in the *Ashbridge* case was "expressing in somewhat different form exactly the same principles as those formulated by Lord Greene" in *Associated Provincial Picture Houses Ltd.* v. *Wednesbury Corporation* [1948] 1 K.B. 223. It is submitted that the wording of the *Ashbridge* case is on its face significantly wider: this being made clear by the equation with interference with decisions of an inferior tribunal for error of law. In *R.* v. *Secretary of State for Transport, ex p. de Rothschild* [1989] 1 All E.R. 933, Slade L.J. stated that the conventional grounds for challenging a compulsory purchase order were

those set out in the *Ashbridge* case taken together with those derived from *Wednesbury*, thus indicating that they are distinct.

5. Four further points may be noted. First, where a "requirement" of the Act is not fulfilled, and there is "substantial prejudice", then a decision may be quashed whether the error is jurisdictional or non-jurisdictional (*per* Fisher J., *obiter*, in *Brookdene Investments* v. *Minister of Housing and Local Government* (1970) 21 P. & C.R. 545, 553). Secondly, a literal interpretation of the statutory formula would limit the need to show "substantial prejudice" to cases of non-compliance with procedural requirements under the second limb of the statutory formula. Moreover, in some cases, such non-compliance would be so serious as to render the decision *ultra vires* and so open to attack under the first limb (see *Wade*, pp. 740–741, where it is suggested that the second limb may well be intended to cover cases of non-compliance with directory procedural requirements: see pp. 448–468). It has been suggested, however, that it is necessary to establish "substantial prejudice" under both limbs of the statutory formula (*Re Manchester (Ringway Airport) Compulsory Purchase Order* (1935) 153 L.T. 219, Branson J.) although this view is difficult to reconcile with the terms of the relevant provisions (*cf.* Forbes J. in *Seddon Properties* v. *Secretary of State for the Environment* (1978) 248 E.G. 950, (1978) 42 P. & C.R. 26 (Note) and in *Bell and Colvill Ltd.* v. *Secretary of State for the Environment* [1980] J.P.L. 823, 828). Establishing that there has been a breach of the rules does not *per se* discharge the onus of showing substantial prejudice (*Bell and Colvill, supra.*).

Thirdly, the view has been taken that the provision under the statutory formula that the court "may" quash an order on one or other of the stated grounds gives the court a discretion whether to intervene even where one of the grounds is clearly established (*Errington* v. *Minister of Health* [1935] 1 K.B. 249, 279 *per* Maugham L.J.; *Miller* v. *Weymouth and Melcombe Regis Corporation* (1974) 27 P. & C.R. 468, 478–480, Kerr J: criticised by J. E. Alder, (1975) 91 L.Q.R. 10; *Preston Borough Council* v. *Secretary of State for the Environment* [1978] J.P.L. 548; *Peak Park Joint Planning Board* v. *Secretary of State for the Environment* (1979) 39 P. & C.R. 361; *London Borough of Richmond upon Thames* v. *Secretary of State for the Environment* [1984] J.P.L. 24).

In the *Peak Park* case, Sir Douglas Frank said that the discretion not to quash should in general only be exercised if the point is technical and there is no possible detriment to the applicant (p. 385). In the *Richmond* case, Glidewell J. declined to quash a grant of planning permission by an inspector, where the inspector was wrong to hold that a policy in the development plan had been overridden, but where there had been other considerable advantages in the proposed development, and where it would be a waste of time to send the matter back to the Secretary of State.

Fourthly, affidavit evidence may be received if designed to establish "no evidence" on a point in issue (*H. Sabey & Co.* v. *Secretary of State for the Environment* [1978] 1 All E.R. 586); or to establish that proper procedures have not been complied with or that a particular matter of real importance had been left out of the inspector's report (*East Hampshire District Council* v. *Secretary of State for the Environment* [1978] J.P.L. 182).

6. "Statutory *ultra vires*" clauses are discussed by J. Alder, (1975) 38 M.L.R. 274; H. Donovan, *Law Society's Gazette*, June 9, 1976, p. 476; Sir Frederick Corfield and R. J. A. Carnwath, *Compulsory Acquisition and Compensation* (1978), pp. 52–66; M. Grant, *Urban Planning Law* (1982), pp. 633–644, and annotations to the Town and Country Planning Act 1990, ss.284–288, in the *Encyclopedia of Planning Law and Practice*; *Wade*; pp. 733–747; M. Purdue, E. Young and J. Rowan-Robinson, *Planning Law and Procedure* (1989), pp. 564–581.

Questions

Lord Denning M.R. equates the catalogue of errors which cause a Minister to act outside his powers "with the position when the court has power to interfere with the decision of a tribunal which has erred in point of law."

1. How obvious is it that the concept of "not within the powers of the Act" is the same as that of "error of law"?

2. Can Lord Denning's judgment be reconciled with that of Swift J. in *Re Bowman*?

3. If Lord Denning is right, is there any point in Parliament's drawing a distinction between appeals on points of law, and applications to quash as under Schedule 2 to the Housing Act? Compare sections 287 and 288 of the Town and Country Planning Act 1990 (applications to quash structure plans, etc.) with section 289 (appeals on points of law against enforcement notices, etc.).

4. How far do the other members of the Court of Appeal agree with Lord Denning?

5. Is the "catalogue" part of Lord Denning's judgment part of the *ratio decidendi*?

6. Compare Lord Denning's views with those expressed in the House of Lords in the *Anismінic* case (above, p. 237).

COLEEN PROPERTIES LTD. v. MINISTER OF HOUSING AND LOCAL GOVERNMENT

[1971] 1 W.L.R. 433; 115 S.J. 112; [1971] 1 All E.R. 1049; 69 L.G.R. 175; 22 P. & C.R. 417 (Court of Appeal)

Tower Hamlets London Borough Council declared two rows of houses, on Clark Street and Sidney Street, to be clearance areas under the Housing Act 1957. By section 43(2) of that Act they had power to purchase compulsorily "any adjoining land the acquisition of which is reasonably necessary for the satisfactory development or use of the cleared area." They wished to exercise this power in respect of Clark House, a good property owned by Coleen Properties Ltd. and situated on the corner of the two streets. The owners objected, and an inspector held a public local inquiry and inspected the properties. The council called witnesses (the Medical Officer of Health, Housing Officer, and Public Health Housing Inspector) to show that the old houses in the clearance areas were in a bad condition. They did not call any witnesses as to the planning merits, in particular to show that it was necessary to acquire Clark House. They merely asserted, through the mouth of their advocate, the Deputy Town Clerk, that:

> "the acquisition of such properties (*i.e.* the added lands including Clark House) is reasonably necessary for the purpose of the satisfactory development or use of the clearance areas (*i.e.* the old houses)."

The objectors called a qualified surveyor and architect to give evidence on the planning merits.

The inspector reported to the Minister as to Clark House:

> "This is a first class property and I am of the opinion that its acquisition by the council is not reasonably necessary for the satisfactory development or use of the cleared area."

However, his recommendation that Clark House be excluded from the compulsory purchase order was rejected by the Minister:

> "The Minister disagrees with the inspector's recommendation with regard to Reference No. 13 (*i.e.* Clark House). It appears to him that by the very nature of

its position, the exclusion of this property must seriously inhibit the future redevelopment of the rectangular block of land between Sidney Street and Damien Street in which it stands. He has decided, therefore, that the acquisition of Reference 13 (Clark House) is reasonably necessary for the satisfactory development or use of the cleared area. . . ."

The owners applied to the High Court for the order to be quashed in so far as it affected Clark House under Schedule 4, para. 2 to the Housing Act 1957.

LORD DENNING M.R.: . . . [referred to his statement in the *Ashbridge* case (above, p. 629) . . . "the court can interfere . . . lower tribunal which has erred in point of law."] . . .

In my opinion the Minister was in error in reversing the inspector's recommendation. The Minister had before him only the report of the inspector. He did not see the premises himself. To my mind there was no material on which the Minister could properly overrule the inspector's recommendation. Clark House is a first class new property. It has shops with flats over. In order to acquire it compulsorily, the local authority must show that the acquisition "is reasonably necessary for the satisfactory development or use of the cleared area." In order to show it, they ought to have produced some evidence to the inspector as to what kind of development would be a "satisfactory development" of the area, and to show how the acquisition of Clark House is "reasonably necessary." I do not say that they ought to have produced a detailed plan of the proposed development. I realise well enough that in many cases that may not be practicable. For instance, when an area is to be developed for industrial purposes, you cannot go into details until you have the businessmen wanting the factories. But, when an area is to be developed for residential purposes—for the council's own housing plans—it ought to be possible to give an outline plan of the proposed development. I cannot myself see that the council could get any more dwellings on to the site of Clark House than the six flats which are already there. The council may desire to make a neat and tidy development of these two streets, including Clark House, but this may well be possible whilst leaving Clark House standing. At any rate, I am quite clear that the mere *ipse dixit* of the local council is not sufficient. There must be some evidence to support their assertion. And here there was none.

Then there is the report of the inspector. He was clearly of opinion that the acquisition of Clark House was not reasonably necessary. I can see no possible justification for the Minister in overruling the inspector. There was no material whatever on which he could so do. I know that on matters of planning policy the Minister can overrule the inspector, and need not send it back to him, as happened in *Luke* v. *Minister of Housing and Local Government* [1968] 1 Q.B. 172. But the question of what is "reasonably necessary" is not planning policy. It is an inference of fact on which the Minister should not overrule the inspector's recommendation unless there is material sufficient for the purpose. There was none here. In my judgment the Minister was wrong and this court should intervene and overrule him. . . .

SACHS L.J.: . . . [Counsel's] submission raised the question as to whether there was any evidence before the Minister upon which he could properly come to a conclusion which would enable him to exercise the powers that stem from the provisions of Part III of the Act of 1957—clearance and redevelopment: was he entitled to reverse the finding contained in paragraph 37 of the inspector's report to the effect that it was not reasonably necessary for the satisfactory development or use of the cleared area to acquire the property at the corner known as Clark House? The need for evidence to be available to a Minister before he can act has been the subject of earlier decisions. The question before him was not, to my mind, one of policy: it was in essence a question of fact that had to be established as a condition precedent to the exercise of the powers to take away the subject's property. It was no less a question of fact because it involved forming a judgment on matters on which expert opinion can and indeed ought to be given. (I rather doubt whether there is much material difference between the view I have just expressed and that of Mr. Slynn who has argued that the question was simply a matter of planning judgment which had to be based on evidence.) As long ago as the *Sheffield* case (*Sheffield Burgesses* v. *Minister of Health* (1935) 52 T.L.R. 171 at p. 173) Swift J. said:

> ". . . it is for the court, if the matter is brought before it, to say whether there is any material on which the Minister could have come to the conclusion that it was reasonably necessary. If the court comes to the conclusion that there is no such material, then it will not hesitate to quash the Minister's order."

That passage coincides with those passages in the judgment of Lord Denning M.R. in the *Ashbridge* case [1965] 1 W.L.R. 320 to which he has referred.

The Minister, therefore, cannot come to a conclusion of fact contrary to that which the inspector found in this case unless there was evidence before the latter on which he (the Minister) could form that contrary conclusion. Upon the inquiry, an inspector is, of course, entitled to use the evidence of his own eyes, evidence which he as an expert, in this case he was an architect, can accept. The Minister, on the other hand, can only look at what is on the record. He cannot, as against the subject, avail himself of other expert evidence from within the Ministry—at any rate, without informing the subject and giving him an opportunity to deal with that evidence on the lines which are set out in regard to a parallel matter in the Compulsory Purchase by Local Authorities (Inquiries Procedure) Rules 1962.[7] Whilst the inspector, even if not an architect, may well be

[7] [S.I. 1962 No. 1424: see now S.I. 1990 No. 512.]

looked on as an expert for the purpose of forming an opinion of fact, the Minister is in a different position. It is by no means intended as a criticism to say with all respect that no Minister can personally be an expert on all matters of professional opinion with which his officers deal from day to day.

Before turning to the report and examining the evidence, there is a further observation to be made. When seeking to deprive a subject of his property and cause him to move himself, his belongings and perhaps his business to another area, the onus lies squarely on the local authority to show by clear and unambiguous evidence that the order sought for should be granted. What then is the state of the evidence here? Mr. Slynn has properly pressed us to look at plan B. . . . From that plan it is quite plain that when developing the rectangle it may well be convenient to have the corner site included in the development, so as perhaps to make it more homogeneous. It is plain that to get possession of it and include it in the development may well be "a tidy idea" according to the canons of Whitehall. It may be that it is better from the point of view of looks. But all that is not enough. It must be reasonably *necessary* for the satisfactory development or use under consideration.

The nature of the development or use under consideration in this case is to be found in paragraph 20 of the report, which refers to "the area zoned in the development plan for residential use" and again in the Minister's own phraseology in his letter of October 25: "The council proposed to redevelop the two clearance areas for housing purposes." That then is the object of the proposed development and use: but what materially serious obstacle to that objective is constituted by the existence of Clark House, a first class property reconstructed in 1956 at public expense and described in paragraphs 29 and 36 as containing, *inter alia*, six self-contained flats with four shops?

On the evidence, there is nothing on which to suggest that there was any material, far less a materially serious obstacle. There is no evidence that the demolition of Clark House would result in even a single extra family being housed. There is no evidence that any addition to the costs of the redevelopment scheme because Clark House was not acquired would approach or exceed the value of the buildings. There was no evidence that some amenity to the community to be housed on the redeveloped site would be lost: thus there was no question of any gardens of Clark House being needed to such purpose—so far as I can see, it had none. There is no suggestion that Clark House or any portion of the area it occupied was needed for road widening: indeed the contrary was established. Thus there was no evidence whatsoever establishing that Clark House fell within the ambit of section 43(2).

The architect inspector came to his conclusion after an inspection. His conclusions are certainly no help to the submission on behalf of the Minister that this site did fall within the subsection: on the contrary, on the facts of this particular case, one would have thought that his opinion—the only expert opinion—was almost conclusive the other way. Having already made plain that the Minister was not entitled in this case to find as a fact that the premises were reasonably necessary for the purpose mentioned except on evidence before the inspector, and it being clear that there was no such evidence, he had no power to make the order, and in my judgment the appeal should be allowed.

BUCKLEY L.J.: . . . The crucial consideration here I think is whether there was material before the Minister in this case which justified him in the course which he took . . . Mr. Slynn, appearing before us on behalf of the Minister, has submitted that that decision is a matter of planning judgment; but he concedes that the judgment must be based upon some evidence. That evidence must be, I take it, evidence of a kind which would justify a reasonable man in reaching the conclusion which the Minister reached. . . . As I think that the Minister had no sufficient material upon which to reach the decision which he did reach, it follows that he acted *ultra vires* the section and that his decision is one which should not be permitted to stand. I therefore agree that this appeal should be allowed.

Appeal allowed.

Notes

1. See case notes by J. M. Evans, (1971) 34 M.L.R. 561 and H.W.R.W[ade], (1971) 87 L.Q.R. 318.

2. In *Migdal Investments Ltd.* v. *Secretary of State for the Environment* [1976] J.P.L. 365, Bristow J. distinguished *Coleen* on the ground that evidence of fact and opinion given by a qualified expert (a Senior Planning Officer of the City of Manchester) was not the "mere *ipse dixit*" of the local authority. The statute did not require the authority to place before the Minister a plan of some degree of precision showing why the acquisition of neighbouring land was reasonably necessary for the satisfactory development or use of the relevant clearance areas. In *Banks Horticultural Products Ltd.* v. *Secretary of State for the Environment* (1979) 252 E.G. 811, Banks appealed against a refusal of permission to extract peat from certain land. At the inquiry, it became clear that the question turned on whether there were other reasonable sources of supply. By agreement, it was left to the Ministry of Agriculture's witness to supply written evidence on the point after the inquiry. This was done, and the appeal was rejected. Phillips J. held that this evidence provided a wholly insufficient basis for the inspector to reach a conclusion on this point, as it dealt only with the physical characteristics of the alternative supply of peat and not with such questions as availability, suitability and cost. There was either no evidence, or no evidence upon which the inspector could have properly have reached his conclusion.

3. In *R.* v. *Secretary of State for the Environment, ex p. Powis* [1981] 1 W.L.R. 584, the applicant challenged the decision of the Secretary of State to certify under section 57(1) of the Landlord and Tenant Act 1954 that land held by a county council as landlord was requisite for the purposes of the authority, and that its use or occupation be changed. One ground was that the only evidence before the Minister was the bald assertion of the council that no alternative sites were available for its purposes, and that therefore there was no evidence upon which the Secretary of State was entitled to rely, under the *Coleen* principle. The Court of

Appeal rejected this argument. Unlike the situation in *Coleen*, section 57 did not envisage a hearing or inquiry. As there was no public hearing, it was for the Minister to weigh the statements submitted to him, and reach a conclusion based on that material.

Question

Is the *Coleen* case an example of judicial review for lack of evidence to support a finding of jurisdictional fact (*cf. White & Collins* v. *Minister of Health*, above, p. 210, and *Re Lamplugh*, above, p. 631 (note)), or is it authority for a general proposition that all determinations unsupported by any evidence are *ultra vires* (*contra R.* v. *Nat Bell Liquors Ltd.* [1922] 2 A.C. 128, below, p. 652)?

(D) Appeals on Questions of Law

This is the typical ground upon which Parliament has granted rights of appeal to the High Court. See for example section 289 of the Town and Country Planning Act 1990, and note the extension of rights of appeal from the decisions of tribunals by section 9 of the Tribunals and Inquiries Act 1958 (now s.11 of the 1992 Act, above, p. 77), following recommendations of the Franks Committee (above, p. 606).

(E) The Distinction Between Questions of Law and Questions of Fact[8]

It is necessary to draw this distinction where an appeal is limited to a question of law and where there is an application for certiorari to quash for error of law on the face of the record. The distinction may also be relevant where there is an allegation of jurisdictional error, as the courts are less likely to find that there has been an error of fact than an error of law.[9]

The line between law and fact has been drawn differently in different contexts. The distinction has generated much case law, but the courts have generally been unwilling to adopt a consistent approach. Areas of administrative law which have been particularly fertile include revenue law,[10] workmen's compensation,[11] national insurance,[12] town and country planning[13] and rating.[14] In the wider

[8] See W. A. Wilson, "A Note on Fact and Law" (1963) 26 M.L.R. 609; W. A. Wilson, "Questions of Degree" (1969) 32 M.L.R. 361; C. Morris, "Law and Fact" (1941–42) 55 Harv.L.R. 1303; L. B. Jaffe, "Judicial Review—Questions of Law" (1955–56) 69 Harv.L.R. 239; H. W. R. W[ade] (1969) 85 L.Q.R. 18–20; H. Whitmore [1967] 2 *Federal Law Review* 159; *de Smith*, pp. 126–139; E. Mureinik, "The Application of Rules: Law or Fact" (1982) 98 L.Q.R. 587; J. Beatson, "The Scope of Judicial Review for Error of Law" (1984) 4 O.J.L.S. 22; *Emery and Smythe*, Chap. 3 (based on (1984) 100 L.Q.R. 612); G. J. Pitt, "Law, Fact and Casual Workers" (1985) 101 L.Q.R. 217.

[9] See *ex p. Honig* and *ex p. Zerek*, above, pp. 232 and 234.

[10] "The issue, upon cases stated by the Commissioners . . . has been *directly* before the courts in well over two hundred cases." A. Farnsworth, (1946) 62 L.Q.R. at p. 248. See *Simon's Taxes*, paras. A3.711–712.

[11] See *Willis's Workmen's Compensation* (notes to s.1(1)–(3) of the Workmen's Compensation Act 1925).

[12] See, *e.g.* the *Global Plant* case (below, p. 644) and *R.* v. *National Insurance Commissioner, ex p. Secretary of State* (below, p. 648).

[13] See, *e.g. Bendles Ltd.* v. *Bristol Corporation* (below, p. 641); *Encyclopedia of Planning Law and Practice*, notes to s.289 of the Town and Country Planning Act 1990.

[14] See *Ryde on Rating and the Community Charge* (1991), paras. F410–F415.

context, the distinction has been before the courts in connection with magisterial law (particularly appeals by way of case stated to the Divisional Court from decisions of the justices[15]), and appeals to the Court of Appeal on a point of law from decisions of county court judges.[16]

It is clear that an issue is one of fact where its resolution depends on the reliability or credibility (but not the admissibility in law) of direct evidence such as a witness's testimony. A finding based on an admission is equivalent to a fact proved by direct evidence. An issue whose resolution depends on probabilities, for example on an inference from circumstantial evidence, is also one of fact. An issue which depends on whether the facts found fall within a statutory description does not fall clearly into either category of fact or law. In different contexts such an issue has been characterised as one of "law," "fact," "mixed law and fact," "fact and degree," "degree," or as *sui generis*.[17] Which view is taken seems to depend on how much control an appellate court wishes to exercise over an inferior court or tribunal, rather than by reference to principle. There may occasionally be a tendency for an appellate court to classify an issue as one of law merely because it thinks the decision below wrong or unjust. Other factors which may be influential include whether the word or phrase in the statute can be said to be an "ordinary English expression" (see *R.* v. *National Insurance Commissioner, ex p. Secretary of State*, below, p. 648), or a "question of degree" (see the *Bendles* case, below, p. 641).

BRITISH LAUNDERERS' ASSOCIATION v. BOROUGH OF HENDON RATING AUTHORITY

[1949] 1 K.B 462; [1949] L.J.R. 416; 65 T.L.R. 103; 93 S.J. 58; *sub nom. British Launderers' Research Association* v. *Central Middlesex Assessment Committee and Hendon Rating Authority*, 113 J.P. 72; [1949] 1 All E.R. 21; 47 L.G.R. 113; 41 R. & I.T. 564 (Court of Appeal)

The Association was established to promote research and other scientific work in connection with the laundry and cleaning trades. It owned a site in Hendon with a laboratory block, an experimental laundry, a boiler house and other buildings. The rating authority demanded rates in respect of the site in 1946 for the first time in 20 years. The Association claimed they were exempt from rates by reason of section 1 of the Scientific Societies Act 1843. They appealed successfully on this point to quarter sessions. The Divisional Court reversed the decision of quarter sessions, on an appeal by case stated on a point of law, holding that the Association was not instituted "for the purposes of science . . . exclusively," as required by section 1, but also for commercial purposes which were not merely incidental to the purposes of science. The Association argued that this was a question of fact from which there was no appeal to the Divisional Court.

DENNING L.J.: . . . Mr. Rowe says, however, that quarter sessions came to a conclusion of fact in his favour with which the Divisional Court should not have interfered. On this point it is important to distinguish between primary facts and the conclusions from them. Primary facts are

[15] See the Magistrates' Courts Act 1980, s.111.

[16] See *Halsbury's Laws of England* (4th ed.), Vol. 10, "County Courts," para. 658; *The County Court Practice* 1991, pp. 68–72.

[17] See Whitmore, *op. cit.* pp. 170–177. As a matter of *theory* it is difficult to resist the conclusion that this is really a question of law: Mureinik, *op. cit.*; *Wade*, pp. 939–940.

facts which are observed by witnesses and proved by oral testimony or facts proved by the production of a thing itself, such as original documents. Their determination is essentially a question of fact for the tribunal of fact, and the only question of law that can arise on them is whether there was any evidence to support the finding. The conclusions from primary facts are, however, inferences deduced by a process of reasoning from them. If, and in so far as, those conclusions can as well be drawn by a layman (properly instructed on the law) as by a lawyer, they are conclusions of fact for the tribunal of fact: and the only questions of law which can arise on them are whether there was a proper direction in point of law; and whether the conclusion is one which could reasonably be drawn from the primary facts: see *Bracegirdle* v. *Oxley* [1947] K.B. 349 at p. 358. If, and in so far, however, as the correct conclusion to be drawn from primary facts requires, for its correctness, determination by a trained lawyer—as, for instance, because it involves the interpretation of documents or because the law and the facts cannot be separated, or because the law on the point cannot properly be understood or applied except by a trained lawyer—the conclusion is a conclusion of law on which an appellate tribunal is as competent to form an opinion as the tribunal of first instance.

... The question is whether the association was instituted for the purposes of science exclusively. That is, a conclusion of law to be drawn from the primary facts, particularly, but not exclusively, from the memorandum and articles of association, and involves questions of interpretation of those documents and of the Act. The Divisional Court were able, and indeed bound, to form their own opinion as to the proper conclusion to be drawn from those primary facts, and I find myself in entire agreement with them....

BUCKNILL L.J. and JENKINS J. agreed.

Appeal dismissed.

BENDLES MOTORS LTD. v. BRISTOL CORPORATION AND ANOTHER

[1963] 1 W.L.R. 247; 127 J.P. 203; 107 S.J. 77; [1963] 1 All E.R. 578; 14 P. & C.R. 128; 61 L.G.R. 205 D.C. (Queen's Bench Division)

Bendles Ltd. permitted the installation by one J. Allcock, a veterinary surgeon and poultry farmer, of an egg-vending machine, free-standing on a base two feet seven inches square, on their garage and petrol filling station forecourt, which had a frontage of 120 feet and a depth of 15 feet. The local planning authority served an enforcement notice stating that it appeared that development had been carried out without permission and the site-owners appealed to the Minister of Housing and Local Government who ordered an inquiry. The Minister considered the evidence and arguments on the issues of law put forward at the inquiry, and concluded that the stationing on the site involved a change of use of the land on which the machine stood; that, while a petrol filling station was not a shop, the machine standing in part of the forecourt of the petrol filling station was of the nature of shop use; and, being satisfied on the facts that the introduction of the machine involved a material change of use, dismissed the appeal and upheld the enforcement notice.

Bendles Ltd. appealed to the Divisional Court on a point of law.

Section 12(1) of the Town and Country Planning Act 1962 (now s.55(1) of the 1990 Act) provided that development (for which planning permission was required) "means the carrying out of building, engineering, mining or other operations in, on, over or under land, or the making of any material change in the use of any buildings or other land. . . ."

LORD PARKER C.J.: . . . In his report [the inspector] said: "33. While in the case at issue the existence of this free-standing machine is not visually offensive and, although on the forecourt of a petrol filling station, is somewhat incongruous, it is inconspicuous and it is noted that the Authority conceded the degree of danger to be insignificant. 34. I cannot but feel however that with the arrival of the egg-vending machine, it should be contained within its fundamental retail sales category of a shopping use; it follows that such use in a residential area is of itself bad and if it is decided by the Minister that what is assumed in the enforcement notices to be development did constitute development for the purposes of Part III of the Town and Country Planning Act 1947, then I recommend that permission be not granted for the development to which the enforcement notices relate."

It is to be observed from that that the inspector himself made no finding that there had been a material change in use which would constitute development. The Minister in his decision of August 31, 1962, recited the relevant parts of the inspector's report, and went on: "3. The Minister has considered the evidence and the arguments put forward at the inquiry on the issues of law. He notes that the machine is not attached to the freehold and is movable, though it is of substantial size and construction and is not normally intended to be moved about the site. It appears to the Minister that its stationing on the site involves a change of use of the land on which it stands. It is now necessary to consider whether the change of use is material."

In the next paragraph he says: "As to this it is to be observed that a petrol filling station is excepted from the definition of 'shop' in the Town and Country Planning (Use Classes) Order 1950, by article 2(2) of the Order. The machine stands in part of the forecourt of the petrol filling station and is of the nature of a 'shop' use. Moreover, although the space occupied by the machine is small in comparison with the total area of the forecourt, it attracts customers not necessarily concerned with the motoring service provided by the establishment and introduces a noticeably different element of use of the premises. The Minister is satisfied, on the facts, that the introduction of the machine on the site involves a material change of use of the land, for which the grant of planning permission is required."

As this court has said on more than one occasion, the question of whether a change of use is a material change of use is largely a matter of degree and fact. In *East Barnet Urban District Council* v. *British Transport Commission* [1962] 2 Q.B. 484 after referring to this matter, I said (*ibid.* at p. 492): "It is a question of fact and degree in every case and, when the matter comes before this court by way of case stated, the court is unable to interfere with a finding of the justices on such a matter unless it must be said that they could not properly have reached that conclusion." That was dealing with a case stated from justices, but in my judgment the same is true of an appeal from the Minister himself. This court can only interfere if satisfied that it is a conclusion that he could not, properly directing himself as to the law, have reached.

That being so, one has to examine his decision with some care. Counsel for the site-owners has stated first that there is a fatal error at the very outset in that the Minister is only considering the nine square feet, or whatever it may be, upon which the machine stands. Quite clearly, if one is looking at those nine square feet alone, there would be a change of use and undoubtedly a material change of use. Counsel says, and in my judgment rightly, that that is the wrong approach, and that in considering materiality one ought to consider the premises as a whole. It seems to me, however, that that is exactly what the Minister has done. It is true that he was referring to the fact that the stationing of this machine involves a change of use of the land upon which this machine stands, but he then goes on to deal with the matter of whether it is a material change, and for the purposes of deciding the material change it is clear that he is going beyond the nine square feet upon which the machine stands and is considering, if not the whole of the premises, at any rate the forecourt because he says in the next paragraph: "Moreover, although the space occupied by the machine is small in comparison with the total area of the forecourt, it attracts customers not necessarily concerned with the motoring service" and so on.

The Minister having, therefore, properly directed himself on the law, this court could in my judgment only interfere if satisfied that the judgment was perverse in the sense that the evidence could not support it. That is going a very long way when one is dealing with planning considerations. I confess that at first sight, and indeed at last sight, I am somewhat surprised that it can be said that the placing of this small machine on this large forecourt can be said to change the use of these premises in a material sense from that of a garage and petrol filling station by the addition of a further use. It is surprising, and it may be, if it was a matter for my own personal judgment, that I should feel inclined to say that the egg-vending machine was *de minimis*; but it is not a question of what my opinion is on that matter, it is for the Minister to decide.

I cannot say that he was wrong in law in holding that the undoubted change of use of part of the premises did not amount to a material change of use of the whole. The Minister, in this case, has given a very careful decision, to which I find it unnecessary to refer in detail, but it is quite clear that with this type of machine coming on to the market it may well be that premises like garage premises may become used as shopping centres. The Minister in this case has not considered this as a case of *de minimis* and, that being so, I find it impossible to interfere. I would dismiss the appeal.

ASHWORTH and LYELL JJ. agreed.

Appeal dismissed.

Notes

1. *Bendles* may be compared with *Birmingham Corporation* v. *M.H.L.G. and Habib Ullah* [1964] 1 Q.B. 178 where the Divisional Court held that the Minister had erred in law in holding that the intensification of a use of land could not constitute a material change of use, and remitted the case to him to determine whether on the facts there had been such a change.

2. See further on the meaning of "development": Sir Desmond Heap, *An Outline of Planning Law* (10th ed., 1991), Ch. 7; A. E. Telling, *Planning Law and Procedure* (8th ed., 1990), Ch. 5; M. Purdue, E. Young and J. Rowan-Robinson, *Planning Law and Procedure* (1989), Ch. 5.

GLOBAL PLANT LTD. v. SECRETARY OF STATE FOR SOCIAL SERVICES

[1972] 1 Q.B. 139; [1971] 3 W.L.R. 269; 115 S.J. 506; [1971] 3 All E.R. 385 (Lord Widgery C.J.)

The company employed two drivers for earth-moving machines. Some factors of the employment indicated that there were contracts of service, other factors that there were contracts for services. The Secretary of State determined that they were the former, and that the company as a consequence were liable to pay employer's contributions under the National Insurance Act 1965. The company appealed to the High Court by case stated on a point of law.

LORD WIDGERY C.J.: . . . There is no doubt whatever that the only right of appeal to this court is a right of appeal on a point of law, and some difficulty may arise in the application of that rule because the question "contract of service or no?" is inevitably a mixed question of law and fact. The question of whether it is a matter primarily of law or fact has been considered before. Indeed as far back as the days of the Workmen's Compensation Act 1906 one finds in *Simmons* v. *Heath Laundry Co.* [1910] 1 K.B. 543 that Cozens-Hardy M.R., in relation to this very issue which the Minister had to decide in the present case, said, at p. 548:

> "In such a case there may be a contract for services, but there is not a contract of service. In any particular case it will be for the arbitrator, after considering all the circumstances, to decide whether the injured professional person is or is not a 'workman.' This is not a question of law, but a question of fact. . . ."

That is echoed in the same case by Buckley L.J. who said, at p. 553:

"The question in this case then resolves itself into this: Was there such evidence before the learned judge as that he upon those principles could and did find as a matter of fact that this girl in giving lessons upon the pianoforte was contracting to use her skill to achieve the result of instructing the child in playing the piano, or was she placing herself in the position of owing the duty of obeying the mother's orders as to how she should give her lessons?"

Buckley L.J. treated it as a matter of fact....

[His Lordship referred to *Phipps* v. *Minister of National Insurance* (unreported) November 30, 1951 where Parker J. did not express a final view on the same problem.]

But Diplock J. in *Terrar* v. *Minister of Pensions and National Insurance* (unreported) July 13, 1960 goes very much further. Dealing with the same problem, when speaking of a determination made by the Minister in that case, he said:

"In order to set aside that determination, limited as I am to setting aside determinations which are erroneous in law, Mr. Turner-Samuels must satisfy me either that there was no evidence upon which the Minister could reach the decision that he did that the appellant was an independent contractor—and I do not think Mr. Turner-Samuels contends that there was no evidence of that; if he does so contend, I certainly do not accept that contention—or, alternatively it seems to me that he must fall back upon the principle which is applied from time to time by appellate courts when they dislike the opinion of the tribunal of fact. That is set out perhaps most clearly in *Edwards* v. *Bairstow* [1956] A.C. 14. Either one can reach the same result by talking about primary facts and secondary facts—and by that I mean inferences from primary facts—on which the appellate court is entitled to intervene, or else one can do it rather more simply, as appears in Lord Radcliffe's speech where he said, at p. 36: 'If the case contains anything *ex facie* which is bad law and which bears upon the determination, it is, obviously, erroneous in point of law. But, without any such misconception appearing *ex facie*, it may be that the facts are such that no person acting judicially and properly instructed as to the relevant law could have come to the determination under appeal....' "

In my judgment that is the proper approach for me to take in the present case, and I say that notwithstanding certain dicta of Lord Parker C.J. in *Morren* v. *Swinton and Pendlebury Borough Council* [1965] 1 W.L.R. 576. That was a case in which the issue of contract of service or no had to be determined substantially from a written contract. The terms of service therefore were a matter of construction of the contract, and in connection with the construction of the contract Lord Parker C.J., and the other members of the court of whom I was one agreed, said, at p. 583:

> "Mr. Threlfall has pressed upon the court that the question of what is the legal quality of the contract is a question of fact, and being a question of fact it is for the Minister and not for this court to determine, provided that there is any evidence which would justify the Minister in arriving at this conclusion. I am quite unable to accept that. The terms of the contract of course are fact, and to that extent the determination depends upon fact, but it seems to me perfectly clear that once the primary facts are found, then it is a pure question of law as to what is the reasonable inference based on the legal interpretation of the contract. In my judgment the only inference that could reasonably be drawn by someone properly directing his mind as to the law in the present case is that the appellant was an employee in the sense that he was employed by the respondents under a contract of service."

At first sight it looks as though Lord Parker C.J. is saying that the conclusion to be drawn from the primary facts on the issue with which I am concerned is a conclusion drawn as a matter of law, and in so far as he is dealing with the construction of a written agreement he would, if I may say so with respect, obviously be right. I do not think that *Morren's* case in any way destroys the validity of the approach of Diplock J. to the question which I have to decide, that approach being the one in *Terrar's* case (unreported) to which I have referred.

It seems to me, therefore, that I must first examine the Minister's decision to see whether it contains a false proposition of law *ex facie*. It does not; neither counsel has suggested that it might.

It is next relevant to consider whether the decision reached by the Minister is one which was supported by no evidence, in which event of course his decision would be wrong in law. That is not a conclusion open to me in this case because there clearly was some evidence upon which the conclusion could be supported.

Then finally I must consider, in the words of Lord Radcliffe in *Edwards* v. *Bairstow* [1956] A.C. 14, 36 quoted in the judgment of Diplock J. in *Terrar's* case, whether the facts found are such that no person acting judicially and properly instructed as to the relevant law could have come to the determination under appeal. It is not, as I see it, for me to balance again the arguments pro and con the decision which the Minister has reached, giving the separate factors the weight which I think they should or should not have. That balancing operation is a matter for the Minister. All that I have to ask myself is whether the conclusion which he has reached is one that no person acting judicially and properly instructed as to the relevant law could have come to in this determination. I am perfectly satisfied that although there were pointers either way, it would be quite out of the question to suggest that the Minister's decision was one open to attack on the ground to which I have last referred.

In the end, therefore, it seems to me that the company have failed to establish an error of law in the present appeal, and that the appeal must be dismissed.

Appeal dismissed.

Notes

1. *Edwards* v. *Bairstow* [1956] A.C. 14 is a leading revenue law case on the distinction between "law" and "fact," and on the grounds on which a decision of the Inland Revenue Commissioners may be reversed on appeal to the courts on a point of law. Viscount Simonds stated at p. 29:

> "... in my opinion, whatever test is adopted, that is, whether the finding that the transaction was not an adventure in the nature of trade is to be regarded as a pure finding of fact or as the determination of a question of law or of mixed law and fact, the same result is reached in this case. The determination cannot stand: this appeal must be allowed and the assessments must be confirmed. For it is universally conceded that, though it is a pure finding of fact, it may be set on grounds which have been stated in various ways but are, I think, fairly summarized by saying that the court should take that course if it appears that the commissioners have acted without any evidence or upon a view of the facts which could not reasonably be entertained.... The primary facts, as they are sometimes called, do not, in my opinion, justify the inference or conclusion which the commissioners have drawn: not only do they not justify it but they lead irresistibly to the opposite inference or conclusion. It is therefore a case in which, whether it be said of the commissioners that their finding is perverse or that they have misdirected themselves in law by a misunderstanding of the statutory language or otherwise, their determination cannot stand...."

Lord Radcliffe stated at p. 33:

> "My Lords, I think that it is a question of law what meaning is to be given to the words of the Income Tax Act 'trade, manufacture, adventure or concern in the nature of trade' and for that matter what constitute 'profits or gains' arising from it. Here we have a statutory phrase involving a charge of tax, and it is for the courts to interpret its meaning, having regard to the context in which it occurs and to the principles which they bring to bear upon the meaning of income. But, that being said, the law does not supply a precise definition of the word 'trade': much less does it prescribe a detailed or exhaustive set of rules for application to any particular set of circumstances. In effect it lays down the limits within which it would be permissible to say that a 'trade' as interpreted by section 237 of the Act does or does not exist.
>
> But the field so marked out is a wide one and there are many combinations of circumstances in which it could not be said to be wrong to arrive at a conclusion one way or the other. If the facts of any particular case are fairly capable of being so described, it seems to me that it necessarily follows that the determination of the Commissioners, Special or General, to the effect that a trade does or does not exist is not 'erroneous in point of law'; and, if a determination cannot be shown to be erroneous in point of law, the statute does not admit of its being upset by the court on appeal. I except the occasions when the commissioners, although dealing with a set of facts which would warrant a decision either way,

show by some reason they give or statement they make in the body of the case that they have misunderstood the law in some relevant particular.

All these cases in which the facts warrant a determination either way can be described as questions of degree and therefore as questions of fact. . . ."

This approach has been adopted in many other cases in administrative law. See *Emery and Smythe*, pp. 114–121, citing, *inter alia*, *R.* v. *Industrial Injuries Commissioner, ex p. A.E.U. (No. 2)* [1966] 2 Q.B. 31, where the Court of Appeal, including Lord Denning M.R., considered the question whether an employee was injured "in the course of employment" (note Lord Denning's comments on this case in *R.* v. *Preston S.B.A.T., ex p. Moore*, above, p. 601); *O'Kelly* v. *Trusthouse Forte plc* [1984] Q.B. 90 (question whether a contract was "for services" or "of service" held not to be a pure question of law); *I.R.C.* v. *Scottish and Newcastle Breweries Ltd.* [1982] 1 W.L.R. 322 (application of the term "plant" for income tax purposes); and *A.C.T. Construction Ltd.* v. *Customs and Excise Commissioners* [1982] 1 All E.R. 84 (below, n. 4). For a defence of the approach against charges of uncertainty (Beatson, (1984) 4 O.J.L.S. 22) and that it "smacks of abdication of responsibility" and fails to take rights seriously (Pitt, (1985) 101 L.Q.R. 217, 233), see *Emery and Smythe*, pp. 121–127.

2. See *R.* v. *National Insurance Commissioner, ex p. Secretary of State for Social Services* [1974] 1 W.L.R. 1290, D.C., where the court held the question whether the functions related to going to bed were attributable to the "night" or the "day," for the purposes of entitlement to attendance allowance, was a question of fact for the attendance allowance board (an expert board of medical practitioners). The national insurance commissioner, hearing an appeal limited to points of law, could only interfere with the board's decision that these functions were attributable to the day "if the construction of the statute drove one to the conclusion that preparations for bed were necessarily part of the night," or "if the conclusion of the board is so unreasonable that no properly instructed board could have reached it" (*per* Lord Widgery C.J. at p. 1295). Neither of these alternatives was established, and so the court granted certiorari to quash the commissioner's decision to allow an appeal from the board. The court also gave some guidance on the proper construction of "night" and "day" in this context (which settled a divergence of view among the commissioners: see Sir Robert Mickelthwait, *The National Insurance Commissioners* (1976), pp. 136, 146 (notes 40, 41)). In this Lord Widgery noted the words of Lord Reid in *Cozens* v. *Brutus* [1973] A.C. 854 at p. 861, to the effect that the giving of a meaning to an ordinary English word is not a question of law at all, although the construction of a statute is a question of law. "However, though 'night' is one of the commonest English words in its ordinary usage, it does have different shades of meaning and the decision of the correct shade of meaning to give to the word in a particular context requires consideration of the context, and thus becomes a matter of construction and therefore a matter of law" (p. 1296). His Lordship thought that in this context "night" meant "the coming of night according to the domestic routine of the household."

3. In *Cozens* v. *Brutus* [1973] A.C. 854, Lord Reid stated at p. 861 (in relation to the meaning of "insulting" in section 5 of the Public Order Act 1936):

"The meaning of an ordinary word of the English language is not a question of law. The proper construction of a statute is a question of law. If the context shows that a word is used in an unusual sense the court will determine in other words what that unusual sense is. But here there is in my opinion no question of the word 'insulting' being used in any unusual sense. It appears to me, for reasons which I shall give later, to be intended to have its ordinary meaning. It is for the tribunal which decides the case to consider, not as law but as fact, whether in the whole circumstances the words of the statute do or do not as a matter of ordinary usage of the English language cover or apply to the facts which have been proved. If it is alleged that the tribunal has reached a wrong decision then there can be a question of law but only of a limited character. The question would normally be whether their decision was unreasonable in the sense that no tribunal acquainted with the ordinary use of language could reasonably reach that decision.

Were it otherwise we should reach an impossible position. When considering the meaning of a word one often goes to a dictionary. There one finds other words set out. And if one wants to pursue the matter and find the meaning of those other words the dictionary will give the meaning of those other words in still further words which often include the word for whose meaning one is searching.

No doubt the court could act as a dictionary. It could direct the tribunal to take some word or phrase other than the word in the statute and consider whether that word or phrase applied to or covered the facts proved. But we have been warned time and again not to substitute other words for the words of a statute. And there is very good reason for that. Few words have exact synonyms. The overtones are almost always different.

Or the court could frame a definition. But then again the tribunal would be left with words to consider. No doubt a statute may contain a definition—which incidentally often creates more problems than it solves—but the purpose of a definition is to limit or modify the ordinary meaning of a word and the court is not entitled to do that."

Cf. Lord Denning's remarks in the *British Launderers' Association* case, above, p. 640. Do you think this approach results in the classification of too many matters as questions of fact? *Cf.* the discussion in the criminal law context by Glanville Williams, [1976] Crim.L.R. 472 and 532. The "ordinary English word" argument has in the criminal law context been ignored more often in practice than applied: D. W. Elliott, "*Brutus* v. *Cozens*: Decline and Fall" [1989] Crim.L.R. 323.

4. Lord Denning was not always consistent on this question. In *A.C.T. Construction Ltd.* v. *Customs and Excise Commissioners* [1981] 1 All E.R. 324, the question was whether work done in underpinning a house with inadequate foundations constituted "maintenance." If it did, the work was positive-rated for VAT; if not the work was zero-rated. Lord Denning said (at pp. 327–328):

"The great contest in the case is whether it is 'maintenance' or not. Counsel for the Crown said that the question whether a particular work is 'maintenance' or not is a matter on which two opinions can easily be held without either being unreasonable at all. Quite reasonably one person might say that underpinning is 'maintenance.' Another person might equally reasonably say that it is not 'maintenance.' So he said there is a band in which either view is reasonable. He said that in such a case the courts should not interfere with the decision of a tribunal, whichever way it decided. He said the courts should not interfere with the decision of a tribunal unless it was right outside the band of reasonableness, so unreasonable that no reasonable man could come to that conclusion. He sought to find some support for this argument in some observations of Lord Diplock in the recent case of *Re Racal Communications Ltd.* [1980] 2 All E.R. 634 at 639, [1980] 3 W.L.R. 181 at 187–188. But I cannot accept that submission. Once you have the primary facts established, as you have here, about the underpinning, then the question whether the work comes within the word 'maintenance' or not is a question of law for the judges to decide. Brandon and Ackner L.JJ. pointed out that in hundreds of arbitrations in the City of London the arbitrators state their findings of fact and then ask the court whether on the true construction of the document (the charterparty or whatever it may be) they came to the right conclusion. In everyday practice, once the primary facts are found, the interpretation of a word is a question of law for the judges to decide.

Many a time we have expressly so held. We so held in a value added tax case, *British Railways Board* v. *Customs and Excise Comrs.* [1977] 2 All E.R. 873, [1977] S.T.C. 221; and we so held in an analogous case not involving value added tax but structural alterations, *Pearlman* v. *Keepers and Governors of Harrow School* [1979] 1 All E.R. 365, [1979] Q.B. 56. With regard to the latter case, I would say that the whole court were unanimous in thinking that the county court judge below was wrong in his construction of the words 'structural alterations,' and that accordingly he had made a mistake of law. The only ground on which Geoffrey Lane L.J. dissented was that he thought it was an error within their jurisdiction which was not subject to correction. But, on whether it was a point of law, Geoffrey Lane L.J. agreed with the rest of us.

I would add that this is especially important in work which is repetitive, and frequently arising, as in this case of underpinning. Throughout the industry it is essential that the contractors and their employers should know whether the work is to be positive-rated or zero-rated. It would be intolerable if one tribunal were to give one view and another tribunal were to give another view, and that no one could decide between them. You would have different rulings in relation to similar work in different parts of the country, according to which tribunal happened to be hearing the case. That cannot be right. I would ask: if there are two tribunals giving different decisions, what are the commissioners to do? Are they to be the arbitrators between the differing views? I hope not. Tax gatherers should not be judges in their own cases. Surely not. When a definite ruling is needed for the guidance of builders and customers everywhere, it must be for the courts of law to give a definite and final ruling as to the meaning of a word such as 'maintenance.' "

Brandon L.J. stated that the question of law was whether the work was "capable of coming within the expression 'maintenance' " (p. 329). Ackner L.J. said that:

"To my mind this appeal raises a short question of law, *viz.* whether on the true construction of the relevant section of and schedule to the Finance Act 1972, as applied to the undisputed facts in this case, there was a zero-rated supply of service" (p. 330).

(To what extent are these formulations different ways of saying the same thing?)

All three members of the Court of Appeal were agreed that the underpinning was a work of alteration and not maintenance. The decision was affirmed by the House of Lords ([1982] 1 All E.R. 84). The sole speech was delivered by Lord Roskill, who regarded the case as raising "a single short point of construction" (p. 87), and endorsed Brandon L.J.'s approach (p. 88). He concluded:

"My Lords, I decline to attempt to define 'repair or maintenance' when the 1972 Act and the 1972 order do not do so, but leave those ordinary words which are in common use to be given their ordinary meaning. In some cases, there may be room for dispute which side of the line particular work falls. If so, that would be a question of fact or degree for the tribunal of fact concerned to determine. The problem should not prove difficult of solution if their task is approached by applying the facts as that tribunal finds them to the relevant statutory provisions interpreted as I have endeavoured to state" (p. 88).

This seems to endorse the *Edwards* v. *Bairstow* approach rather than Lord Denning's (see *Emery and Smythe*, pp. 120–121).

5. The approach adopted in distinguishing questions of law from questions of

fact becomes crucial if it is accepted that all errors *of law* go to jurisdiction (above, pp. 237–262). The adoption of Lord Denning's approach in the *A.C.T.* case would give the courts a wide power to intervene; the adoption of the *Edwards* v. *Bairstow* approach (or that of Lord Denning himself in *ex p. A.E.U. (No. 2)*), a narrower power. This point is made forcefully by J. Beatson at (1984) 4 O.J.L.S. 22, 39–45, noting that Lord Diplock in *Re Racal Communications* seemed to prefer the *Edwards* v. *Bairstow* approach (see above, p. 258).

(F) Error of Law

The courts have used many different phrases to describe errors of law, and it is usually possible to describe a particular error in more than one of these ways. Examples include "misinterpreting a statute" (*e.g.* the *Northumberland* case, above, p. 593); "taking irrelevant considerations into account" (*e.g. R.* v. *Southampton JJ., ex p. Green* [1976] Q.B. 11, above, p. 603 (note); *cf.* pp. 362–394 on abuse of discretion); "applying the wrong legal test" (*e.g.* in determining the "planning unit" relevant to the question whether there has been a material change of use under s.55 of the Town and Country Planning Act 1990: see *Burdle* v. *Secretary of State for the Environment* [1972] 1 W.L.R. 1207; M. Purdue, E. Young and J. Rowan-Robinson, *Planning Law and Procedure* (1989), pp. 94–101. Note that Lord Denning equates the grounds for statutory applications to quash with error of law in the *Ashbridge* case (above, p. 629).

Three particularly important problems are (a) whether lack of evidence for a decision renders it erroneous in point of law (below), (b) whether failure to give reasons constitutes error of law (below, p. 653) and (c) whether a point as to *vires* may be raised on an appeal on a point of law (below, p. 661).

(i) Lack of Evidence

[See *de Smith*, pp. 133, 137; J. M. Evans, (1971) 34 M.L.R. 561 (case note on *Coleen Properties Ltd.* v. *M.H.L.G.*); R. R. S. Tracey, (1976) 50 A.L.J. 568.]

Notes and questions

1. The following cases illustrate the rule that a decision based on "no evidence" is erroneous in law: *Bendles Ltd.* v. *Bristol Corporation* (above, p. 641); *Global Plant Ltd.* v. *Secretary of State* (above, p. 644); *Ashbridge Investments Ltd.* v. *M.H.L.G.* (above, p. 627); *Coleen Properties Ltd.* v. *M.H.L.G.* (above, p. 634).

2. The powers of the Divisional Court in dealing with appeals by way of case stated on a point of law from decisions of magistrates' courts were summarised as follows by Lord Goddard C.J. in *Bracegirdle* v. *Oxley* [1947] 1 K.B. 349, at p. 353:

> "... [Counsel] concedes that if magistrates come to a decision to which no reasonable bench of magistrates, applying their minds to proper considerations and giving themselves proper directions, could come, then this court can interfere, because the position is exactly the same as if the magistrates had come to a decision of fact without evidence to support it. Sometimes it has been said of the verdict of a jury given in those circumstances, that it is perverse, and I should have no hesitation in applying that term to the decisions of magistrates which are arrived at without evidence to support them."

Humphreys J. stated at p. 357:

> "... [F]or a very great number of years, whenever justices have found facts from which only one conclusion can be drawn by reasonable persons honestly

applying their minds to the question, and have refused to draw that only conclusion, this court has invariably upset the decision of the justices in the appropriate manner."

Denning J. (as he then was) stated at p. 358:

"In a case under s.11 of the Road Traffic Act 1930, the question whether a speed is dangerous is a question of degree and a conclusion on a question of degree is a conclusion of fact. The court will only interfere if the conclusion cannot reasonably be drawn from the primary facts, but that is the case here. In my opinion, the conclusion drawn by these justices from the primary facts was not one that could reasonably be drawn from them."

Will these formulations invariably lead to the same result? Which of them are used in the cases cited in note 1?

3. Does the "no evidence" rule apply in the same way to (i) a primary finding of fact; (ii) the application of a statutory description to facts where this is regarded as a question of fact; and (iii) the final determination in a case of all the relevant questions of law and fact?

4. If a body acts on "no evidence" has it "failed to take into account relevant considerations"?

5. Is a decision unsupported by any evidence *ultra vires*?

In *R. v. Nat Bell Liquors Ltd.* [1922] 2 A.C. 128, P.C., the defendant firm was convicted of selling liquor contrary to the Liquor Act 1916. The only evidence of the fact of sale was furnished by a police *agent provocateur*. The firm sought certiorari to quash the conviction (*inter alia*) on the ground of lack of evidence.

Per Lord Sumner at pp. 143–144, 151–152:

"[Their Lordships] . . . have not been referred to any decisive authority which applies to certiorari the same considerations as apply to testing a jury's verdict, when challenged on a motion for a new trial or on an appeal; nor, apart from a few expressions, here and there, not very carefully considered, can any judicial dicta be found to support it. Whether the verdict was one which 12 reasonable men could have found, whether the evidence was such that 12 reasonable men could find on it otherwise than in one way, whether the evidence was such that a jury could safely confict upon it, and whether it was such that a court of criminal appeal should refuse to interfere with the conviction, are questions which, though fully argued, have no relation to the functions of a superior court on certiorari. They all imply that there was evidence, but not much; they all ask whether that little evidence was enough; they are all applied to a body of men who are not the absolute judges of fact, but only judges whose decision may, though rarely, be disturbed. On certiorari, so far as the presence or absence of evidence becomes material, the question can at most be whether any evidence at all was given on the essential point referred to. Its weight is entirely for the inferior court. . . .

It has been said that the matter may be regarded as a question of jurisdiction, and that a justice who convicts without evidence is acting without jurisdiction to do so. Accordingly, want of essential evidence, if ascertained somehow, is on the same footing as want of qualification in the magistrate, and goes to the question of his right to enter on the case at all. Want of evidence on which to convict is the same as want of jurisdiction to take evidence at all. This, clearly, is erroneous. A justice who convicts without evidence is doing something that he ought not to do, but he is doing it as a judge, and if his jurisdiction to entertain the charge is not open to impeachment, his subsequent error, however grave, is a wrong exercise of a jurisdiction which he has, and not a usurpation of a jurisdiction which he has not. How a magistrate, who has acted within his jurisdiction up to the point at which the missing evidence should have been, but was not given, can, thereafter, be said by a kind of relation back to have had no jurisdiction over the charge at all, it is hard to see. It cannot be said that his conviction is void, and may be disregarded as a nullity, or that the whole proceeding was *coram non judice*. To say that there is no jurisdiction to convict without evidence is the same thing as saying that there is jurisdiction if the decision is right, and none if it is wrong; or that jurisdiction at the outset of a case continues so long as the decision stands, but that, if it is set aside, the real conclusion is that there never was any jurisdiction at all."

Can this be reconciled with *Coleen Properties Ltd.* v. *M.H.L.G.*? Consider Lord Sumner's reasoning in the light of the *Anisminic* case, above, p. 237.

6. A finding of a preliminary or jurisdictional fact which is unsupported by any evidence will presumably cause the decision on the main question to be *ultra vires*. See above, pp. 210–236. Was *Re Ripon; White and Collins* v. *Minister of Health* (above, p. 210) decided on this ground? (See *Ashbridge Investments Ltd.* v. *M.H.L.G.*, above, p. 627; and *Re Lamplugh*, above, p. 631 (note).) Is this the proper explanation of *R.* v. *Secretary of State for the Home Department, ex p. Zamir* (above, p. 213).

7. Wade argues (*Administrative Law* (6th ed.), pp. 319–326), that "this ground of review ought now to be regarded as established on a general basis." It is recognised in habeas corpus cases (see *Wade*, pp. 622–624); in cases under the Housing Acts (*e.g.* the *Coleen* case, *supra*); in jurisdictional fact cases (see n. 6); and by Lord Diplock as an aspect of natural justice (see p. 561).

8. The equivalent rule in the United States allows a "reviewing court to determine whether an administrative determination made after a formal hearing is supported by substantial evidence on the record taken as a whole" (*Schwartz and Wade*, p. 228, referring to s.10(*e*)(B)5 of the Federal Administrative Procedure Act 1946,[18] and Article 78 of the New York Civil Practice Law and Rules, which are based on case law).

The rule is useful in relation to formal decision-making processes where there is a full record of the proceedings, including the evidence, and it enables the courts to exercise a greater measure of control than the British "no evidence" rule. While a much smaller proportion of decisions in this country are supported by a full record than in the United States, that does not mean that the "substantial evidence" rule should not be applied where a full record is available, for example, in planning appeals with the inspector's report, and Minister's letter.

(ii) Failure to Give Adequate Reasons

MOUNTVIEW COURT PROPERTIES LTD. v. DEVLIN AND OTHERS

(1970) 21 P. & C.R. 689; 114 S.J. 474; [1971] J.P.L. 113 D.C. (Q.B.D.)

Landlords appealed against a decision of a rent assessment committee of the London Rent Assessment Panel in 1969, whereby they fixed the fair rent of three flats (Nos. 43, 55 and 73) at roughly the same figure as the fair rent fixed for a comparable flat (No. 64) in the same block in 1966. The landlords expected higher figures, to account for inflation between 1966 and 1969. In addition an expert had

[18] See further, *de Smith*, p. 139; H. Whitmore, (1967) 2 *Federal Law Review* 159, 163–170.

given evidence that he valued market rents of the flats at higher figures than those fixed by the committee. The committee stated their reasons in this form: they referred in the first instance to a minor defect with regard to the flat number 43 (which accounted for a difference of £5 between the fair rents fixed for that and the otherwise comparable number 73); they then stated that they had considered the evidence adduced, the 1966 decision in respect of number 64, and their inspection. They first dealt with costs in respect of services which they put at £19 for each flat, and then stated the amounts fixed as the fair rents. They did not deal with the landlords' argument based on inflation since the 1966 decision. An *ex parte* application for certiorari by the landlords was adjourned for the committee to supply further particulars. These dealt with points such as the dampness in number 43, the fact that the building showed signs of neglect and the fact that, while the landlords said that they were going to spend some £4,000 on the building, that had not been commenced; the rents could be reviewed on completion. The committee concluded:

> "The committee, therefore, using its own knowledge of the level of rents in the area, and applying that knowledge to the facts, and having carefully considered the evidence adduced and the evidence of their own inspection, saw no reason to vary the rent officer's determination except to add £5 to the rent of each flat for additional cost of services, a schedule of which is annexed to the decision as Appendix I."

The landlords appealed to the Divisional Court on a point of law.

LORD PARKER C.J.: . . . [T]he first point, as I see it, is whether the reasons given in the decision as supplemented, as they were, in January of this year, are, even now, sufficient, or, in other words, whether the committee have fulfilled their duty under section 12 of the Tribunals and Inquiries Act 1958 [now s.10 of the 1992 Act, above, p. 76] which provides that "It shall be the duty"—now of the committee (Tribunals and Inquiries (Rent Assessment Committees) Order 1965, art. 3)—

> "to furnish a statement, either written or oral, of the reasons for the decision if requested, on or before the giving or notification of the decision, to state the reasons: . . ."

What reasons are sufficient in any particular case must, of course, depend upon the facts of the case. I approach the matter in this way: that reasons are not deficient merely because every process of reasoning is not set out. I further think that reasons are not insufficient merely because they fail to deal with every point raised before the committee at the hearing. Indeed, I would adopt the words used by Megaw J. in *Re Poyser and Mills' Arbitration* [1964] 2 Q.B. 467. That was dealing with an arbitrator's award, but Megaw J. said (*ibid.* pp. 477–478):

> "The whole purpose of section 12 of the Tribunals and Inquiries Act 1958 was to enable persons whose property, or whose interests, were being affected by some administrative decision or some statutory arbitration to know, if the decision was against them, what the reasons for

it were. Up to then, people's property and other interests might be gravely affected by a decision of some official. The decision might be perfectly right, but the person against whom it was made was left with the real grievance that he was not told why the decision had been made. The purpose of section 12 was to remedy that, and to remedy it in relation to arbitrations under this Act. Parliament provided that reasons shall be given, and in my view that must be read as meaning that proper, adequate reasons must be given. The reasons that are set out must be reasons which will not only be intelligible, but which deal with the substantial points that have been raised."

A little further down, he said (*ibid.* p. 478):

"I do not say that any minor or trivial error, or failure to give reasons in relation to every particular point that has been raised at the hearing"

—and he was dealing with an error of law on the face of an award—"would be sufficient ground for invoking the jurisdiction of this court."

Here, as it seems to me, whilst the tribunal had before them evidence of comparable flats in the vicinity, they had in addition a schedule of all the contractual rents and past histories including fair rents fixed by the rent officer and by the committee itself with regard to other flats in Mountview Court, yet the striking bit of evidence which they had before them was No. 64, and, beyond their saying, in the first reasons which they gave, that they had, to use their own words, "considered the evidence adduced," the decision in objection No. LON/31/551 [the 1966 decision] and their inspection, there is no explanation at all to show why they rejected what one would think would have to be a greater market value, a greater fair rent in respect, at any rate, of the two larger flats, Nos. 43 and 73. In my judgment, that failure does result in the fact that they have here given insufficient reasons; they have not complied fully with their duty under section 12 of the Tribunals and Inquiries Act 1958.

Accordingly, the next question is what flows from that. There is, in my judgment, undoubtedly power to compel any tribunal to which section 12 of the Act applies to give sufficient reasons; they could be ordered by mandamus to do so; in an appeal they could be required to do so by remission of the case to them. Indeed, as Lord Denning M.R. said in *Iveagh (Earl)* v. *Minister of Housing and Local Government* [1964] 1 Q.B. 395, 410: "The whole purpose of the enactment is to enable the parties and the courts to see what matters he"—and that was the Minister of Housing in that case—

"has taken into consideration and what view he has reached on the points of fact and law which arise. If he does not deal with the points that arise, he fails in his duty: and the court can order him to make good the omission."

It was in the light of that that, in the last case of this kind which came before this court, *Cubes Ltd.* v. *Heaps* (unreported; January 28, 29 and June 9, 1970, D.C.) the court kept seisin of it but adjourned it, remitting the decision to the committee for them to amplify their reasons so as to make those reasons sufficient. When that had been done, the case came back to this court.

That, as I see it, is the proper and normal procedure in such a case. However, Mr. Bernstein goes further and has contended, in the first instance, that the mere failure to give reasons is itself an error in law and that, as this is an appeal on a point of law, he is entitled to have the decision quashed and to have a rehearing before a differently constituted committee. This submission is based on two cases to which this court has been referred; the more recent of the two, with which it is convenient to deal first, is *Givaudan & Co. Ltd.* v. *Minister of Housing and Local Government* [1967] 1 W.L.R. 250. That was, again, a case in which insufficient reasons had been given—indeed, reasons which were thought to be almost unintelligible—and there is no doubt that the Minister's decision was quashed. It is, however, I think, important to realise that the motion then before the court was one under section 179 of the Town and Country Planning Act 1962, which gives a remedy in lieu of certiorari in respect of decisions which are beyond the powers of the Minister or in respect of which it is alleged that there has been a failure to comply with the relevant requirements. One of the relevant requirements in that case was rule 11(1) of the Town and Country Planning Inquiries (Procedure) Rules 1962, which provided for the giving of reasons. It, again, was a decision of Megaw J., and it is quite true that, in the last four lines of his judgment, he said (*ibid.* p. 263):

> "... since in my judgment the reasons given by the Minister for his decision are not proper and adequate reasons, there is a failure to comply with the important requirements of rule 11(1) of the rules, and the decision must therefore be quashed."

If one reads, for rule 11(1) of the Rules of 1962, section 12 of the Tribunals and Inquiries Act 1958, then it would be right to say that a failure *per se* to give reasons was being held to be grounds for quashing the decision. It is quite clear when one looks at the report as a whole, however, that, as I have said, that was a proceeding to have the decision quashed under section 179 of the Town and Country Planning Act 1962—that the failure to comply with the rule providing for the giving of reasons did amount to a failure to comply with the relevant requirements for the purposes of section 179. Quite apart from that, as I understand it, it was in that case really conceded that the decision must be quashed.

What is really relied on here is, again, *Re Poyser and Mills' Arbitration* to which I have already referred, where Megaw J. did, apparently, hold that the failure to give reasons constituted an error of law. That was in relation to an arbitration under the Agricultural Holdings Act 1948, and what Megaw J. was concerned with was an error of law on the face of the award, whereas what this court is concerned with in the present case is an appeal under section 9(1) of the Tribunals and Inquiries Act 1958, which provides that:

> "If any party to proceedings before any such tribunal . . . is dissatisfied in point of law with a decision of the tribunal given on or after the appointed day he may, according as rules of court may provide, either appeal therefrom to the High Court or require the tribunal to state and sign a case for the opinion of the High Court."

For my part, I find it impossible to say that a failure to provide sufficient reasons of itself gives rise to the right of this court on an appeal to quash the decision of the committee. Secondly, it is to be observed that, quite apart from that, *Re Poyser and Mills' Arbitration* was really a case where, on the reasons stated, the proper inference was that there had been an error of law and that the arbitrator had misdirected himself. Of course, if the very insufficiency of the reason gives rise to a proper inference that there has been an error of law in arriving at the decision, then clearly it would be a case for quashing the decision.

Accordingly, Mr. Bernstein goes on in the present case to submit that this really is that sort of case, and that the only proper inference, as he would say, in particular after the committee have had, as it were, two bites at stating their reasons, is that they have not addressed their minds to the landlords' point with regard to flat No. 64 or, alternatively, that they have not asked themselves whether there were good grounds for rejecting the contention based on flat No. 64. I confess that I would have been more willing to accept Mr. Bernstein's submission in this regard if the letter asking for further reasons had pin-pointed the argument concerning flat No. 64. As I said earlier in my judgment, I think that it was unfortunate that that was not done. It not having been done and the tribunal not having had their mind directed specifically to the argument concerning flat No. 64, I am quite unable to say that the proper inference here is that they have misdirected themselves in some way.

In those circumstances, I do not think that this is a case in which there is any power to quash the decision, and I for my part would do what was done in the previous case of *Cubes Ltd.* (unreported) namely, adjourn this appeal, remit the matter to the committee with the opinion of this court and ask them to give further reasons on the point at issue.

COOKE J. agreed.

BRIDGE J. [delivered a concurring judgment: . . . [The] language [of s.9 of the Tribunals and Inquiries Act 1958], and, indeed, any analogous language found in the statutes giving a right of appeal on a point of law, to my mind connotes that a successful appellant must demonstrate that the decision with which he is dissatisfied is itself vitiated by reason of the fact that it has been reached by an erroneous process of legal reasoning. . . . I agree with the order proposed that the case should go back to the committee with a direction to state their reasons fully and adequately.

Order accordingly.

Notes

1. The whole question of the giving of reasons is discussed by M. B. Akehurst, (1970) 33 M.L.R. 154. See also *de Smith*, pp. 148–151; G. Richardson, [1986] P.L. 437.

Cf. R. v. *Gaming Board* above, p. 525; and the *Padfield* case [1968] A.C. above, p. 343 on the obligation to supply reasons apart from statutory requirements.

2. In *Crake* v. *Supplementary Benefits Commission* [1982] 1 All E.R. 498, Woolf J. considered the reasons given by a S.B.A.T. for deciding that a man and woman were living together as husband and wife. (The tribunal was under a duty to give reasons by virtue of both the Supplementary Benefit (Appeal Tribunal) Rules 1971, r. 12(1), and the Tribunals and Inquiries Act 1971, s.12.) The tribunal did not make any findings of fact, but merely summarised the history of the case and the parties' submissions; and gave as its reasons that most of the criteria specified in a supplementary benefits handbook had been satisfied. Woolf J. said at pp. 507–508:

"I would therefore still regard the *Mountview* case as being the main authority to be applied. However, it has to be applied in the light of the 10 years which have elapsed since that case was decided. Over that period of 10 years the approach of the courts with regard to the giving of reasons has been much more definite than they were at that time and courts are now much more ready to infer that because of inadequate reasons there has been an error of law, than perhaps they were prepared to at the time that the *Mountview* case was decided.

In other spheres there are numerous cases which have been before the courts where tribunals of all sorts have had to reconsider their decisions because the reasoning was inadequate. Therefore in practice I think that there will be few cases where it will not be possible, where the reasons are inadequate, to say one way or another whether the tribunal has gone wrong in law. In some cases the absence of any reasons would indicate that the tribunal had never properly considered the matter (and it must be part of the obligation in law to consider the matter properly) and that the proper thought processes have not been gone through.

In other cases it will be seen from the reasons given that there has been a failure to take into account something which should have been taken into account or that something which should not have been taken into account has in fact been taken into account. Again, in that situation, there will be an error of law which will justify this court interfering on an appeal on a point of law.

In the rare case where it is not possible to decide either way whether or not there is an error of law, then, in my view, this court has got a jurisdiction, as was indicated in the *Mountview* case, to remit the matter to the tribunal for reconsideration. That power arises because of the very wide terms of s.13 of the Tribunals and Inquiries Act 1971, which is the Act which brings the matter before this court; and also because of the wording of R.S.C., Ord. 55, r. 7. There are great practical disadvantages in that course, as was stressed in argument before me, in relation to tribunals of this nature, because tribunals of this nature are informal bodies which cannot readily be reconvened and, indeed, if they are reconvened, may well have no recollection of the case which they heard; and so obviously the situations where it will be necessary to remit the matter will be limited. They can be limited if it is borne in mind that, as I have already stressed, this sort of tribunal cannot be expected to give the fullest and most detailed reasons, and a short and succinct statement is all that is required."

Here, the tribunal's reasons were inadequate, as they suggested that the tribunal was acting only as a review body. However, the decision was not quashed as the chairman's notes showed that in fact the tribunal had treated the matter, correctly, as an appeal on the merits. *Crake* was followed in respect of reasons given by a rent assessment committee in *R.* v. *London Rent Assessment Committee, ex p. St. George's Court Ltd.* (1983) 265 E.G. 984, and the same approach has been adopted in the contexts of road transport licences (*R.* v. *Secretary of State for Transport, ex p. Cumbria County Council* [1983] R.T.R. 88) and immigration appeals (*R.* v. *Immigration Appeal Tribunal, ex p. Khan* [1983] Q.B. 790).

3. There are, by contrast, a number of situations where a failure to give adequate reasons will be regarded as an error of law leading to the quashing of the decision in question. Examples include the decisions of the National Industrial Regulations Court and the Employment Appeal Tribunal (*Alexander Machinery (Dudley) Ltd.* v. *Crabtree* [1974] I.C.R. 120; *Levy* v. *Marrable & Co.* [1984] I.C.R. 583; and decisions of mental health review tribunals (*R.* v. *Mental Health Review Tribunal, ex p. Pickering* [1986] 1 All E.R. 99).

It is difficult to discern a principled basis for the distinction between these cases and those summarised in the preceding note: see G. Richardson, [1986] P.L. 437, 447–469.

5. In planning cases, by the Town and Country Planning (Inquiries Procedure) Rules 1988, r. 17(1), the Secretary of State is required to give reasons for his decisions in determining appeals. The same duty applies where an appeal is determined by an inspector. A failure to give adequate and intelligible reasons may lead to the decision being quashed under section 288 of the Town and Country Planning Act 1990 on the ground that the applicant's interests have been substantially prejudiced by a failure to comply with a relevant requirement. The reasons must be proper, adequate and intelligible and deal with the substantial points raised (*In re Poyser and Mills' Arbitration* [1964] 2 Q.B. 467, 478, approved by the House of Lords in *Westminster City Council* v. *Great Portland Estates plc* [1985] 661, 673) and enable

"the appellant to understand on what grounds the appeal has been decided and be in sufficient detail to enable him to know what conclusions the inspector has reached on the principal important controversial issues"

(*per* Phillips J. in *Hope* v. *Secretary of State for the Environment* (1975) 31 P. & C.R. 120, 123, approved by Lord Bridge for the House of Lords in *Save Britain's Heritage* v. *Number 1 Poultry Ltd.* [1991] 1 W.L.R. 153, 165). Decision letters should not be construed as statutes and should be read as a whole (*ibid.*). However, Lord Bridge in the *Save Britain's Heritage* case emphasised that the courts could not set a general standard as to the adequacy of reasons. Commenting on a passage from Woolf L.J.'s judgment in the Court of Appeal (60 P. & C.R. 539, 545), he said (at pp. 166–167):

"I certainly accept that the reasons should enable a person who is entitled to contest the decision to make a proper assessment as to whether the decision should be challenged. But I emphatically reject the proposition that in planning decisions the 'standard,' 'threshhold' or 'quality' of the reasons required to satisfy the statutory requirement varies according to who is making the decision, how much time he has to reflect upon it, and whether or not he had legal assistance, or depends upon the degree of importance which attaches to the matter falling to be decided. The obligation, being imposed on the Secretary of State and his inspectors in identical terms, must be construed in the same sense.

The three criteria suggested in the dictum of Megaw J. in *In re Poyser and Mills' Arbitration* [1964] 2 Q.B. 467, 478 are that the reasons should be proper, intelligible and adequate. The application of the first two of these presents no problem. If the reasons given are improper they will reveal some flaw in the decision-making process which will be open to challenge on some ground other than the failure to give reasons. If the reasons given are unintelligible, this will be equivalent to giving no reasons at all. The difficulty arises in determining whether the reasons given are adequate, whether, in the words of Megaw J., they deal with the substantial points that have been raised or, in the words of Phillips J. in *Hope* v. *Secretary of State for the Environment*, 31 P. & C.R. 120, 123, enable the reader to know what conclusion the decision-maker has reached on the principal controversial issues. What degree of particularity is required? It is tempting to think that the Court of Appeal or your Lordships' House would be giving helpful guidance by offering a general answer to this question and thereby "setting the standard" but I feel no doubt that the temptation should be resisted, precisely because the court has no authority to put a gloss on the words of the statute, only to construe them. I do not think one can safely say more in general terms than that the degree of particularity required will depend entirely on the nature of the issues falling for decision.

Whatever may be the position in any other legislative context, under the planning legislation, when it comes to deciding in any particular case whether the reasons given are deficient, the question is not to be answered *in vacuo*. The alleged deficiency will only afford a ground for quashing the decision if the court is satisfied that the interests of the applicant have been substantially prejudiced by it. This reinforces the view I have already expressed that the adequacy of reasons is not to be judged by reference to some abstract standard. There are in truth not two separate questions: (1) were the reasons adequate? (2) if not, were the interests of the applicant substantially prejudiced thereby? The single indivisible question, in my opinion, which the court must ask itself whenever a planning decision is challenged on the ground of a failure to give reasons is whether the interests of the applicant have been substantially prejudiced by the deficiency of the reasons given. Here again, I disclaim any intention to put a gloss on the statutory provisions by attempting to define or delimit the circumstances in which deficiency of reasons will be capable of causing substantial prejudice, but I should expect that normally such prejudice will arise from one of three causes. First, there will be substantial prejudice to a developer whose application for permission has been refused or to an opponent of development when permission has been granted where the reasons for the decision are so inadequately or obscurely expressed as to raise a substantial doubt whether the decision was taken within the powers of the Act. Secondly, a developer whose application for permission is refused may be substantially prejudiced where the planning considerations on which the decision is based are not explained sufficiently clearly to enable him reasonably to assess the prospects of succeeding in an application for some alternative form of development. Thirdly, an opponent of development, whether the local planning authority or some unofficial body like Save, may be substantially prejudiced by a decision to grant permission in which the planning considerations on which the decision is based, particularly if they relate to planning policy, are not explained sufficiently clearly to indicate what, if any, impact they may have in relation to the decision of future applications."

(The House held, reversing the Court of Appeal, that the reasons given by the Secretary of State in granting planning permission for the demolition of listed buildings and their replacement by a modern building were adequate. See above, p. 100 and Sir Desmond Heap and M. Thomas, [1991] J.P.L. 207.)

6. In *French Kier Developments Ltd.* v. *Secretary of State for the Environment* [1977] 1 All E.R. 296, Willis J. quashed the minister's decision to dismiss an appeal against a refusal of planning permission. One ground was that the minister had not given a clear and intelligible statement of the reasons for his decision. The inspector had recommended that the appeal be allowed. The minister agreed with all his findings of fact, but expressed "some disagreement with him about the degree of emphasis which he has put" on certain factors. *Per* Willis J. at p. 304: "One is entitled to ask, where has he gone wrong? What is the nature of the disagreement? Where should the emphasis have been put? Nothing could be vaguer on these matters than the decision letter."

This approach may be compared with that of the Divisional Court in *Guppys (Bridport) Ltd.* v. *Sandoe* (1975) 30 P. & C.R. 69. Here, a rent assessment committee decided to assess the fair rent for a house on the basis suggested by the tenant, and not on any of the bases suggested by the landlord. In the statement of reasons required by the Tribunals and Inquiries Act 1971, the committee explained *which* basis they adopted, but not *why* they rejected those suggested by the landlord. The court held that the committee had complied with their duty to give reasons. Lord Widgery C.J. (at pp. 74–75) stated that where a judge has two conflicting opinions put before him in evidence, it is not possible to explain why one is preferable to the other. "Such explanations are not possible. They are matters of judgment, impression and sometimes even instinct, and it is quite impossible to give detailed reasons to explain how the system of decision has worked, and so with a rent assessment committee."

Cf. Metropolitan Property Holdings Ltd. v. *Laufer* (1974) 29 P. & C.R. 172.

7. The nature of reasons given by Supplementary Benefit Appeal Tribunals was discussed in the Annual Report of the Council on Tribunals for 1972–73, paras. 70–73. The Council's views were expressed to all tribunal chairmen in a letter reproduced in Appendix B to their Report.

(iii) Questions of *vires*

Notes

There are a number of authorities that suggest or hold that a question of *vires* cannot be raised on an appeal on a point of law. In some, this has been on the doubtful basis that if a decision is *ultra vires* and void there is nothing to appeal against (*Metropolitan Properties Co. (F.G.C.) Ltd.* v. *Lannon* [1968] 1 W.L.R. 815, D.C., and *Chapman* v. *Earl* [1968] 1 W.L.R. 1315, D.C., below, p. 838). In *Henry Moss Ltd.* v. *Customs and Excise Commissioners* [1981] 2 All E.R. 86, where Lord Denning M.R. stated (at p. 90) that the proper way to challenge the validity of regulations and administrative directions made under the authority of a statute was by way of an application for judicial review under Order 53, and not by an appeal on a point of law. The other members of the Court of Appeal did not mention the point expressly. Each of them prefaced his judgment by the words "I agree" but it is possible that these words merely indicated agreement with the order allowing the appeal, and not necessarily with all the reasons given in the judgment of Lord Denning M.R. Counsel for the Commissioners invited the court to deal with the case as if there had been an application for judicial review, and the court acceded to that invitation. This approach was criticised as unduly restrictive by A. W. Bradley, [1981] P.L. 476, as apparently regarding the introduction of Order 53 outlawing collateral review.

In *Chief Adjudication Officer* v. *Foster* [1992] 1 Q.B. 31, the Court of Appeal held that a question as to the validity of income support regulations could not be raised through the statutory appellate structure. The Social Security Commissioner held on an appeal from a social security appeal tribunal under the Social Security Act 1975, s.101, on the ground that its decision was "erroneous in point of law," that the relevant regulations were *ultra vires*. The court held that it could not have been Parliament's intention that this should be possible:

> "The distinction between an appellate and a judicial review jurisdiction is well known and the latter is strictly confined to the High Court. It is not, therefore, to be expected that a judicial review jurisdiction would be conferred upon those exercising a 'closed' statutory appeals jurisdiction in the absence of clear words" (*per* Lord Donaldson M.R. at p. 48).

Considerations pointing to this conclusion included that if the Commissioners had this power, then so would have the "relatively junior adjudication officers" and the tribunals; and that it could not be the case that the Secretary of State's power to review one of his own decisions under section 96(1) of the 1975 Act on the ground that it was "erroneous in point of law" enabled him "to consider, and still more to decide, whether his own exercise of a regulation-making power was *intra vires*" (*per* Lord Donaldson M.R. at p. 48). On the other hand, the court held that on the appeal "on a question of law" from the Commissioner to the Court of Appeal under section 14 of the Social Security Act 1980, the court "undoubtedly" had "jurisdiction to decide upon the limits of the commissioner's jurisdiction" (*per* Lord Donaldson M.R. at p. 49). This suggests that the question of whether a question of *vires* can be raised on an appeal on a point of law depends on the interpretation of the right of appeal in question.

There are certainly other authorities which accept that a question of *vires can* be raised on an appeal. See, *e.g. Elliott* v. *Brighton Borough Council* (above, p. 611: a general right to "appeal"); *Nolan* v. *Leeds City Council* (1990) 23 H.L.R. 135 (Housing Act 1985, ss.353 and 367, 362 and 371, which, respectively, provided for an appeal on the ground of an "informality, defect or error in or in connection with the notice," no specified ground, and that "the making of the order was unnecessary"). In *R.* v. *Inland Revenue Commissioners, ex p. Preston* [1985] A.C. 835, Lord Templeman stated at p. 862 that on an appeal by case stated on a point of law from the General or Special Commissioners to the High Court, the court:

> "can . . . correct all kinds of errors of law including errors which might otherwise be the subject of judicial review proceedings: see *Edwards (Inspector of Taxes)* v. *Bairstow* [1956] A.C. 14."

Writing extra-judicially, Sir Harry Woolf has said that on an appeal on a point of law:

> "what could on an application for judicial review be put forward as being a *Wednesbury* point can normally be passed off without much difficulty as a point of law"

("A Hotchpotch of Appeals—The Need for a Blender" (1988) 7 C.J.Q. 44, 48).

It is certainly arguable that this broader approach is convenient as it enables cases which raise points of *vires* as well as legality or (if appropriate) merits to be fully disposed of on appeal: *Wade*, p. 946.

These cases strictly concern the *jurisdiction* of the appellate court to consider questions of *vires*. The relationship between appeals and judicial review is further complicated by the separate principles (1) that it may be held to be an abuse of process for a point as to *vires* to be raised other than on an application for judicial review (*O'Reilly* v. *Mackman*, below, pp. 722–744); and (2) that judicial review will not lie, as a matter of discretion, if there is another more appropriate remedy, such as an appeal (below, pp. 772–773). It will be noted that these principles pull in different directions. The former was considered in *R.* v. *Oxford Crown Court, ex p. Smith, The Independent*, January 19, 1990, where Simon Brown J. held that it was not an abuse of process for a point as to *vires* to be raised on an appeal to the Crown Court against a clearance notice served under section 65 of the Town and Country Planning Act 1971 (now s.215 of the 1990 Act); his Lordship dealt with the matter as raising the *O'Reilly* v. *Mackman* principle rather than as a question of the proper interpretation of the statutory grounds of appeal. Similarly, in *Nolan* v. *Leeds City Council* (1990) 23 H.L.R. 135, the Court of Appeal held that it was not an abuse of process to raise a matter of *vires* on appeals under the Housing Act 1985. The latter principle was emphasised by Lord Templeman in *Preston* (*supra*), although in that case the allegation was that the conduct of the commissioners in initiating proceedings was unlawful, in which case the relevant appeal procedure could not begin to operate.

Finally, it may be noted that Parliament may expressly provide that certain matters shall not be challenged *except* by judicial review: see, *e.g.* the Local Government Finance Act 1988, s.138, in respect of the setting of community charges and related matters.

(G) "Persons Aggrieved"

Many appeals established by statute may only be brought by a "person aggrieved." This term has been considered by the courts on many occasions. The view most commonly relied on as to its meaning is that expressed by James L.J. in *ex p. Sidebotham* (1880) 14 Ch.D. 458 at p. 465:

> "... [T]he words 'person aggrieved' do not really mean a man who is disappointed of a benefit which he might have received if some other order had been made. A 'person aggrieved' must be a man who has suffered a legal grievance, a man against whom a decision has been pronounced which has wrongfully deprived him of something, or wrongfully refused him something, or wrongfully affected his title to something."

The attitude of the court has, however, varied according to the context.

In many areas of local government law, a local authority is empowered to serve a notice requiring a private person to have works done on his property, and a person aggrieved by the notice may appeal to a court. That private person is a "person aggrieved" by the notice, and by a decision of a court upholding a notice. Is the local authority a "person aggrieved" by a decision of the justices against them? A series of decisions of the Divisional Court established that it was not, unless a legal burden was placed upon them as a result of the decision. This was clear where the justices' decision threw a financial burden on the authority (beyond the costs of the magistrates' court proceedings), as in *Phillips* v. *Berkshire County Council* [1967] 2 Q.B. 991, where justices decided that a street was not a private street, and thus was maintainable at the public expense. Where the authority was seeking to enforce a restriction on activities, it was unlikely that they would be placed under a burden if the private person appealed successfully to the court. The cases where it was held that a local authority was not a "person aggrieved" by the quashing of an enforcement notice served by the authority had to be overruled by statute (see now s.289 of the Town and Country Planning Act

1990, and *cf.* s.288(2) (*ibid.*)). The obligation to pay costs was in some cases held to be sufficient to render the authority a "person aggrieved" (*e.g.* under section 301 of the Public Health Act 1936: *R.* v. *Surrey Quarter Sessions, ex p. Lilley* [1951] 2 K.B. 749, applied in *Cook* v. *Southend Borough Council* (1987) 151 J.P. 641, D.C.), but not in others (*e.g. R.* v. *Dorset Quarter Sessions Appeals Committee, ex p. Weymouth Corporation* [1960] 2 Q.B. 230, in relation to the Town and Country Planning Act 1947, s.23).

Another common situation was where the local authority could grant a licence for an activity. A person refused a licence was a "person aggrieved" for the purposes of an appeal (*e.g. Stepney B.C.* v. *Joffe* [1949] 1 K.B. 599); but it was held that the local authority might not be a "person aggrieved" by the reversal of their decision (*e.g. R.* v. *London Q.S., ex p. Westminster Corporation* [1951] 2 K.B. 508, applied in *R.* v. *Southwark London Borough Council, ex p. Watts* (1989) 88 L.G.R. 86; but *cf. Penwith District Council* v. *McCartan-Mooney, The Times,* October 20, 1984).

The courts showed a less rigid attitude where the question concerned persons affected by the decisions of public authorities (*Turner* v. *Secretary of State for the Environment,* below). The cases concerning public authorities as "persons aggrieved" were reconsidered by the Court of Appeal in *Cook* v. *Southend Borough Council,* below, p. 672.

TURNER AND ANOTHER v. SECRETARY OF STATE FOR THE ENVIRONMENT AND OTHERS

(1973) 72 L.G.R. 380; 28 P. & C.R. 123; 228 E.G. 335 (Ackner J.)

In February 1967 the local planning authority gave outline planning permission, with details reserved, for the erection of two houses in the grounds of Rutland Lodge, Petersham. In October 1967 they gave permission on a detailed application to carry out that development (two two-storey houses). Further alternative applications were made to erect two larger houses on the land. The Secretary of State decided to hold a local inquiry to consider whether he should exercise his default powers under section 207 of the Town and Country Planning Act 1962 (now s.100 of the 1992 Act) in respect of the first two permissions. He "called in" the second two applications under section 22 (now s.77) for his own determination and these too were considered at the inquiry. In July 1971, after the inquiry, the Secretary of State refused permission on the second two applications, and gave notice of his intention to revoke the original permissions (*inter alia*) because of the detrimental effect the development would have on the view from Richmond Hill.

In August 1971 the landowner applied for permission to erect two single-storey houses on the land. The local planning authority regarded this as a fresh application. The Secretary of State called this application in for consideration in conjunction with the proposed revocation order. In June 1972 a second inquiry was held. The inspector exercised his discretion to allow certain opponents of any grant of planning permission in relation to the land to be represented at the inquiry. These were the Petersham Society (a local preservation society), and other amenity societies. At the inquiry the landowner maintained, and the local council did not contest, that the August 1971 application was not a fresh application, but an application for approval of the details reserved in the February 1967 outline permission. If this contention were correct, the only relevant considerations would concern whether the detailed design was acceptable, and not whether development was acceptable in principle. The inspector recommended that if the landowner's contention were correct, permission should be granted, as the proposed design was reasonable, and compensation would be payable for revocation of permission. On the other hand, if the proper view were that this was a fresh application, permission should be refused, as a wider range of considerations could properly be considered. The Secretary of State accepted the landowner's view of the legal status of the application, and approved the plan to erect two single-storey houses. The October 1967 detailed permission [*i.e.* for two two-storey houses] was revoked.

The Petersham Society sought to have this decision quashed under section 245(1)(*b*) of the 1971 Act [see now s.288 of the 1990 Act]. They pointed out that the site of the August 1971 application overlapped and exceeded the area subject to the February 1967 outline permission. Counsel for the Secretary of State, and for the landowner, argued that Ackner J. had no jurisdiction to hear the appeal, on the ground that the Society was not a "person aggrieved."

ACKNER J.: . . . The first point taken by Mr. Frank and Mr. Rich is the familiar one, that the applicants are not persons aggrieved by any action on the part of the Secretary of State. Both counsel rely, essentially, on the decision of this court in *Buxton* v. *Minister of Housing and Local Government* [1961] 1 Q.B. 278; 59 L.G.R. 45, a decision of Salmon J. In that case the owners and occupiers of certain land (the operators) applied under section 14 of the Town and Country Planning Act 1947, to the local planning authority for permission to develop their land by digging chalk. The local planning authority refused the application, and the operators appealed to the Minister of Housing and Local Government pursuant to section 16 of the Act of 1947. The Minister caused a local inquiry to be held by an inspector appointed by him under sections 15 and 16 of the Act into the refusal of permission by the local planning authority. Amongst those who appeared at the inquiry, called evidence and were heard were the operators, the local authority, and the applicants, four substantial landowners whose land was adjacent to that of the operators and was being used for agricultural and residential purposes. The inspector in his report recommended that the operators' appeal should be dismissed. The Minister rejected the inspector's report and allowed the appeal; hence, the application by the landowners against the decision. The preliminary point was taken on behalf of the Minister that the landowners were not persons aggrieved within the meaning of section 31 of the Act, which was in identical terms to section 245 of the Act of 1971 so far as is relevant to this case. In his judgment the judge stated that the case raised the perennial question as to what the legislature meant when it used the words "aggrieved person." . . .

Later in his judgment Salmon J. said, at pp. 283 and 47:

"Superficially, there is much to be said for the view that the applicants are aggrieved by the Minister's action. For example, Mr. Buxton, one of the applicants, as the inspector's report shows, has an estate of about 250 acres adjoining the operators' land. He is interested in landscape gardening and ornithology and has spent large sums of money for these purposes on his land. Moreover, he has a herd of pedigree pigs and some breeding mares very close indeed to the site from which the

> chalk is to be won. I can well understand his annoyance at the Minister's decision to reject recommendations which the Minister's inspector has made after a thorough inspection of the site and careful investigation of a considerable body of evidence. If I could approach this problem free from authority, without regard to the scheme of the Town and Country Planning legislation and its historical background, the arguments in favour of the applicants on the preliminary point would be most persuasive, if not compelling, for in the widest sense of the word the applicants are undoubtedly aggrieved. In my judgment, however, I am compelled to restrict the meaning of the words 'person aggrieved' to a person with a legal grievance."

He then dealt in some detail with the legislation and ended by saying, at pp. 285 and 48:

> "The Minister's action which these applicants seek to challenge infringed none of their common law rights. They have no rights as individuals under the statutes. Accordingly, in my judgment, none of their legal rights has been infringed, and in these circumstances it could not, in my view, have been the intention of the legislature to enable them to challenge the Minister's decision in the courts. Ever since the judgment of James L.J. in the well-known case of *In re Sidebotham* (1880) 14 Ch.D. 458, it has been generally accepted that the words 'person aggrieved' in a statute connote the person with a legal grievance, that is to say, someone whose legal rights have been infringed. James L.J. said: 'the words "person aggrieved" do not really mean a man who is disappointed of a benefit which he might have received if some other order had been made. A "person aggrieved" must be a man who has suffered a legal grievance, a man against whom a decision has been pronounced which has wrongfully deprived him of something, or wrongfully refused him something, or wrongfully affected his title to something.' "

Salmon J. considered that the guiding principle was that laid down by James L.J. in that case, and which, as far as he knew, had never been challenged.

At the time when that decision was made, July 1960, there was not then in existence the Town and Country Planning (Inquiries Procedure) Rules 1962, which have been re-enacted with various amendments until they are now to be found in the Town and Country Planning (Inquiries Procedure) Rules 1969. The Rules of 1962, as continued to be provided, made provision for appearances at the inquiry and in their present form they are to be found in rule 5 which deals with notification of inquiry, and rule 7 with appearances at the inquiry. Rule 7 provides:

> "(1) The persons entitled to appear at the inquiry shall be"—and then it sets out obvious categories such as the applicant and the local planning

authority, and ends with—"(*g*) any persons on whom the Minister has required notice to be served under rule 5(2)(*b*). (2) Any other person may appear at the inquiry at the discretion of the appointed person."

The part of the judgment in *Buxton's* case (*supra*) upon which the respondents, including, of course, the owner, relied is found on pp. 285 and 48 and reads:

"In my judgment, anyone given a statutory right to have his representations considered by the Minister impliedly has the right that the Minister, in considering those representations, shall act within the powers conferred upon him by the statute and shall comply with the relevant requirements of the statute."

It is accepted by Mr. Frank and Mr. Rich that a rule 7(1)(*g*) person is a person given a statutory right to have his representations considered by the Minister and is covered by what follows in that part of the judgment, but they each contend that a rule 7(2) person, a person who appears at the inquiry at the discretion of the appointed person, is a "second-class citizen" for the purpose of rights of appeal from which it must follow that Salmon J.'s judgment should be adopted in regard to them to read as follows:

"In my judgment, anyone given a right to appear at the inquiry at the discretion of the appointed person has impliedly no right that the Minister in considering his representations shall act within the powers conferred upon him by the statute and shall comply with the relevant requirements of the statute."

I must say that I find that a particularly unattractive proposition and I am sure Salmon J. would have felt the same if that submission had been made to him. In further support of the proposition that the rule 7(2) person has no entitlement to appeal my attention was drawn to the decision of Paull J. in *Gregory* v. *Camden London Borough Council* [1966] 1 W.L.R. 899; 64 L.G.R. 215. . . .

A number of cases were referred to in argument and in the judgment, and there was a reference to the decision of Salmon J. The decision in *Buxton's* case (*supra*) was on the fringe of the issues there being decided because there the issue was the right to bring an action for a declaration direct against the owner and did not raise the question as to what were the statutory rights of appeal given against the decision of the Minister following an inquiry held at his instance and at which parties seeking to appeal had been allowed to appear and make representations. I do not, therefore, find it of any assistance in this case and, significantly, neither of the extremely experienced counsel who appeared and who were praised for their interesting and detailed arguments thought fit to invite the judge's attention to two recent authorities which clearly have a direct bearing upon the extent to which Salmon J.'s decision should now be followed. Those two cases are, first, *Attorney-General of the Gambia* v. *N'Jie* [1961] A.C. 617, a decision of the Privy Council. In that case section 7 of the Supreme Court Ordinance of the Gambia provided:

> "... it shall be lawful for the Governor to appoint a deputy judge to represent the judge of the Supreme Court of the Colony of the Gambia [the Chief Justice] in the exercise of his judicial powers..."

and Order IX, r. 7 of the Rules of the Supreme Court of the Gambia provided:

> "The judge shall have power, for reasonable cause, to suspend any barrister or solicitor from practising within the jurisdiction of the court ... or order his name to be struck off the Roll of Court."

The name of the respondent, a member of the English Bar who had been admitted to practise as a barrister and solicitor of the Supreme Court of the Gambia, was, after due inquiry into allegations of professional misconduct by a deputy judge appointed under section 7 of the Supreme Court Ordinance, ordered by him to be struck off the roll of the Supreme Court of the Gambia. On his appeal, the West African Court of Appeal set aside the deputy judge's order on the ground that he had only jurisdiction to represent the Chief Justice "in the exercise of his judicial powers," and that the power to strike a legal practitioner off the roll was not a judicial power. On appeal by the Attorney-General of the Gambia by special leave the Privy Council held:

> "... that the Attorney-General, representing the Crown as guardian of the public interest, was a 'person aggrieved'—words of wide import—by the decision of the West African Court of Appeal within the meaning of section 31 of the West African (Appeal to Privy Council) Order in Council, 1949, and accordingly had a *locus standi* to petition for special leave to appeal."

In that case Lord Denning in giving the opinion of the Board made a specific reference to James L.J.'s judgment in *In re Sidebotham* (*supra*) which was much relied upon by Salmon J. in the manner in which I have already indicated. Lord Denning said at p. 634:

> "If this definition were to be regarded as exhaustive, it would mean that the only person who could be aggrieved would be a person who was a party to a *lis*, a controversy *inter partes*, and had had a decision given against him. The Attorney-General does not come within this defini-

tion, because, as their Lordships have already pointed out, in these disciplinary proceedings there is no suit between parties, but only action taken by the judge, *ex mero motu* or at the instance of the Attorney-General or someone else, against a delinquent practitioner. But the definition of James L.J. is not to be regarded as exhaustive. Lord Esher M.R. points that out in *ex p. Official Receiver, In re Reed, Bowen & Co.* (1887) 19 Q.B.D. 174 at p. 178. The words 'person aggrieved' are of wide import and should not be subjected to a restrictive interpretation. They do not include, of course, a mere busybody who is interfering in things which do not concern him; but they do include a person who has a genuine grievance because an order has been made which prejudicially affects his interests."

That case was referred to in a decision of the Court of Appeal in *Maurice* v. *London County Council* [1964] 2 Q.B. 362; 62 L.G.R. 241. The owner of premises situated within 100 yards of a proposed block of flats more than 100 feet high appealed under section 52(2)(*a*) of the London Building Act 1930, as a person who deemed herself aggrieved, against a consent granted by the London County Council under section 51 of the Act of 1930 as amended by section 5 of the London County Council (General Powers) Act 1954. In the course of his judgment Lord Denning M.R. said, on the subject of "person aggrieved," at pp. 377–378 and 243–244:

"Miss Maurice now appeals to this court. The first point argued before us is whether she can complain of loss of amenity. On this point I am afraid I have come to a decision different from that of the Divisional Court. The material words in section 52(2)(*a*) give a right of appeal 'to the owner or lessee of any land within 100 yards who may deem himself aggrieved' by the grant of consent. It is quite clear that the person must be aggrieved in respect of his interest in a building or land within 100 yards. But there is no limitation whatever as to the kind of grievance. I can see no reason whatever for excluding loss of amenities. I know that at one time the words 'person aggrieved' (which I regard as the same as 'person who shall deem himself aggrieved') were given in these courts a very narrow and restricted interpretation. It was said that the words 'person aggrieved' in a statute only meant a person who had suffered a legal grievance. Indeed in *Buxton* v. *Minister of Housing and Local Government (supra)*, which I mentioned in the course of the argument, Salmon J. declined to go into the question of loss of amenities. But that narrow view should now be rejected. In the more recent case of *Attorney-General of the Gambia* v. *N'Jie (supra)*, the Privy Council had to consider these words 'person aggrieved' once again. On behalf of the Board, I ventured to say there"—he then sets out that part of the opinion of the Board which I have cited—"so here in this case they do include a person who has a genuine grievance because a consent has been given which prejudicially affects his interests. His interests may be prejudicially affected, not only in regard to light and air, but in regard to amenities also. The one requisite must be that his grievance must be in respect of his interest as an owner or lessee of a building within 100 yards."

Pearson L.J. agreed with Lord Denning M.R. He said, at pp. 381 and 246:

> "It is clear that in order to qualify for appealing under section 52(2)(*a*) the appellant must be the owner or lessee of a building or land within 100 yards of the site of the intended building, and must also deem herself to be aggrieved by the grant of the consent. Evidently the word 'deem' is used because, when she launches her appeal, she can only have an opinion that she is aggrieved. In my view (and Mr. Megarry does not dispute this) there is an implication that the appellant, in order to establish a prima facie case in her appeal, must prove that she is, by reason of the height of the intended building, likely to suffer damage in her capacity as owner or lessee of her property."

Wilberforce J. said, at pp. 384 and 248: "I entirely agree with the judgments which have been delivered." . . .

There is a firm, fixed, immutable time limit provided in the appeal provisions. The appeal can only be based on very limited and restricted grounds, as the section clearly reveals. I see no merit in the proposition that a person who has merely been given notice of the existence of the inquiry at the request of and not by the requirement of the Secretary of State and whose right to attend and make his representations has resulted from the exercise of the inspector's discretion, should be obliged to sit by and accept the decision which, *ex hypothesi*, is bad in law. I can see no compelling matter of policy which requires this form of silence to be imposed upon a person who has, again *ex hypothesi*, a clear grievance in law. On the other hand, I see good reason, so long as the grounds of appeal are so restricted, for ensuring that any person who, in the ordinary sense of the word, is aggrieved by the decision, and certainly any person who has attended and made representations at the inquiry, should have the right to establish in the courts that the decision is bad in law because it is *ultra vires* or for some other good reason. It is true that the would-be developer may be held up while the appeal is made but, as the dates in this case indicate, the procedure is a reasonably expeditious one, and I have no doubt that an application for special expedition, where justified, would be listened to sympathetically by the court.

In his report the inspector classifies the applicants, *inter alios*, as "interested persons," a classification which is clearly justified by the facts. They were persons whom the appointed person in his discretion had allowed to appear at the inquiry and make representations in relation to the subject-matter of the inquiry, which representations had to be recorded by the inspector and transmitted with the inspector's findings of fact and conclusions to the Secretary of State with a view to the Secretary of State accepting or rejecting those findings of fact and conclusions. Such persons have, in my judgment, impliedly the right that the Secretary of State, in considering those representations, shall act within the powers conferred upon him by the statute and shall comply with the relevant requirements of the statute, in just the same way (as is conceded to be the case) as a person who makes representations at the inquiry being a person on whom the Secretary of State has required notice of the inquiry to be served. I thus conclude that no valid differentiation can be made between a person who appears at an inquiry and makes his representations having had notice of the inquiry at the insistence of the Secretary of State and a person who appears and makes his representations by permission of the appointed person. This question was not before Salmon J. in *Buxton's* case (*supra*), the Inquiry Procedure Rules of 1962 having not then been passed. Moreover, I derive from the recommendation of the Court of Appeal that the narrow construction should now be rejected, just sufficient fortitude for not following the decision in the *Buxton* case so reluctantly reached by the judge. I therefore reject the first proposition that there is no jurisdiction in this court because I am obliged to impose a very restricted meaning upon the words "aggrieved person. . . ."

[His Lordship nevertheless held that he had no jurisdiction, on the ground that sections 242(3) and 245(3) of the 1971 Act gave a right of appeal against "any decision of the Secretary of State on an application for planning permission referred to him under section 35 of this Act," and not against a decision on an application for approval of reserved details.]

Notes

1. See articles by J. E. Trice, [1973] J.P.L. 580 (written before *Turner's* case was reported); and H. M. Purdue and Trice, [1974] J.P.L. 20 (on *Turner's* case); W. Parkes, [1978] J.P.L. 739; B. Hough, [1992] J.P.L. 319.

2. Full materials on the *Chalkpit* affair, of which *Buxton's* case was a part, are given in J. A. G. Griffith and H. Street, *A Casebook of Administrative Law*. See also [1961] P.L. 121; [1962] P.L. 362.

3. *Turner* has been followed in *Bizony* v. *Secretary of State for the Environment* [1976] J.P.L. 306; *Hollis* v. *Secretary of State for the Environment* (1982) 47 P. & C.R. 351; and approved by the Court of Appeal in *Times Investment Ltd.* v. *Secretary of State for the Environment* [1991] J.P.L. 67, where it was held that a successor in title to land subject to a planning appeal can be a person aggrieved.

Questions

1. How satisfactory is the reasoning of Ackner J. (1) on the general approach to *locus standi*; (2) on the question whether the present applicants were "persons aggrieved" on the assumption that the narrow approach of Salmon J. in *Buxton* is not followed?

2. Compare this decision with the case law on applications for judicial review (below, pp. 744–764).

COOK v. SOUTHEND BOROUGH COUNCIL

[1990] 2 Q.B. 1; [1990] 2 W.L.R. 61; [1990] 1 All E.R. 243; (1990) 88 L.G.R. 408 (Court of Appeal) (Pet. dis., [1990] 1 W.L.R. 1, H.L.

C.'s hackney carriage vehicle and driver's licences were revoked by the council under sections 60 and 61 of the Local Government (Miscellaneous Provisions) Act 1976. C. successfully appealed to the magistrates' court, which made an order for costs against the council. The council appealed to the Crown Court, claiming to be a "person aggrieved" and therefore entitled to appeal by virtue of section 77(1) of the 1976 Act and section 301 of the Public Health Act 1936. The Crown Court allowed the appeal. C. appealed by case stated to the High Court, and the judge dismissed the appeal, holding that he was constrained by authority to hold that the council was a person aggrieved on the ground that an order for costs had been made against it by the magistrates. The Court of Appeal dismissed C.'s appeal, but was free to reconsider the basis of the council's standing.

WOOLF L.J.: . . . The question of who is "a person aggrieved" for the purpose of giving a right to make an application to a court or other judicial or quasi-judicial body has been the subject of a great many reported decisions of the courts going back from the present day to the nineteenth century. However, the majority of the decisions are at first instance and not binding on this court. They draw arbitrary and unsatisfactory distinctions between different statutes and situations and lead to needless highly technical arguments as to *locus standi*.

In these circumstances it is, I hope, useful if I set out certain general propositions which I would expect to apply where the expression "a person aggrieved" is used in relation to a right of appeal in the absence of a clear contrary intention in a particular statutory context. (1) A body corporate including a local authority is just as capable of being a person aggrieved as an individual. (2) Any person who has a decision decided against him (particularly in adversarial proceedings) will be a person aggrieved for the purposes of appealing against that decision unless the decision amounts to an acquittal of a purely criminal offence. In the latter case the statutory context will be all-important. (3) The fact that the decision against which the person wishes to appeal reverses a decision which was originally taken by that person and does not otherwise adversely affect that person does not prevent that person being a person aggrieved. On the contrary it indicates that he is a person aggrieved who is entitled to exercise the right of appeal in order to have the original decision restored.

Turning to the circumstances giving rise to this appeal, in the absence of authority I would have no hesitation in coming to the conclusion that irrespective of whether or not the justices had made an order for costs, the council had a right of appeal under section 301. The purpose of entrusting the council with the power of granting licences to drivers of hackney carriages and in respect of hackney carriages is so that the public in the locality will be provided with a suitable taxi service. This involves proper standards being maintained as to drivers and vehicle licence holders. Although there is an appeal to justices, and that appeal is a rehearing, the justices are entitled to take into account the policy of the council. As Lord Goddard C.J. said in *Stepney Borough Council* v. *Joffe* [1949] 1 K.B. 599, 602–603:

> "if there is an unrestricted right of appeal, it is for the court of appeal to substitute its opinion for the opinion of the borough council. That does not mean to say that the court of appeal, in this case the metropolitan magistrate, ought not to pay great attention to the fact that the duly constituted and elected local authority have come to an opinion on the matter, and it ought not lightly, of course, to reverse their opinion."

Where, as for example here, the justices have departed from a policy which the council has in relation to who is an appropriate person to hold a licence, I consider the council can justifiably feel aggrieved. Furthermore, the council would, in the context of the statutory provisions here being considered, clearly be a "person" because of the application of the Interpretation Act 1978 (previously the Interpretation Act 1889) which provides [by section 5 and Schedule 1] that unless a contrary intention appears " 'person' includes a body of persons corporate or unincorporate." There is nothing in the context of section 301 or the other provisions of the Act of 1936 which indicates a contrary intention, and the contrast between the language of section 301 of the Act of 1936 and sections 60(3) and 61(3) of the Act of 1976 which have to be treated as part of the Act of 1936, referring as they do specifically to a "driver" and "proprietor," emphasise that this is the position.

However, there are the authorities, to which I must now turn, the majority of which indicate that in the past the courts have adopted an unduly restrictive approach to who is a person aggrieved, unlike the approach on an application for judicial review under R.S.C., Ord. 53, where the test is whether the applicant "has a sufficient interest in the matter to which the application relates" (see Ord. 53, r. 3(7)), a test which was deliberately substituted for that of a person aggrieved, which was the test which applied to applications for the prerogative orders prior to the introduction of judicial review in 1977.

[His Lordship reviewed the authorities (see above, pp. 663–664), which fell into three groups: pre-1951 (the *Westminster* case, *supra*); 1951–1960 (the *Weymouth* case, *supra*); and the post-1960 cases.]

Normally when there has been the number of decisions which there has been as to who is a person aggrieved, by the Divisional Court, I consider this court should pause long before interfering although the decisions are not strictly binding on the Court of Appeal. This is especially the situation where as here the cases were decided by a Divisional Court presided over by the Lord Chief Justice of the day who had great experience of administrative law. It is for this reason that I have felt it necessary to set out in detail so many of the relevant authorities. However, having analysed those authorities against the background of the first and last groups of decisions to which I have referred, I am quite satisfied that the Divisional Court took a wrong turning in the *Westminster Corporation* case both in relation to the question as to whether the council was a "person" and as to whether it was "aggrieved." This wrong turn has resulted in the decisions which have occurred since that time deviating from the right road.

As the present case illustrates, the question of who is a "person aggrieved" is still very much alive in many statutory situations. It therefore appears to me to be important for this court to intervene so that in future the decisions in the 1950s will not continue to cause the courts unduly to restrict the right of local authorities to appeal. I have therefore come to the conclusion that *R.* v. *London Quarter Sessions, ex p. Westminster Corporation* [1951] 2 K.B. 508 should be regarded as having been wrongly decided and should no longer be followed. There is no need for a legal burden to be placed on a party to proceedings to give a right of appeal. A decision against the party suffices. Furthermore, all the later cases in which the *Westminster Corporation* case has been followed should be treated with considerable reserve and re-examined. Whether or not they are correctly decided will depend upon their individual circumstances. However, I suggest that, except for criminal cases which come within a special category, and where the decision against which a local authority seeks to appeal can be regarded as being an acquittal, the normal result of that re-examination should be that a public authority which has an adverse decision made against it in an area where it is required to perform public duties, is entitled to be treated as a person aggrieved. As to whether a local authority is in this context a "person," the Interpretation Act 1978 will normally be decisive. It should not be forgotten that frequently the body against which the public authority will take action will itself be a body corporate and if this body is a person there are difficulties in treating a public authority in a different way.

In *R.* v. *Dorset Quarter Sessions Appeal Committee, ex p. Weymouth Corporation* [1960] 2 Q.B. 230, Lord Parker C.J. regarded the question as being by no means easy and he was clearly influenced in coming to his conclusion by the absurd result which would follow if the planning authority was "a person aggrieved" only because of the order for costs. In the ordinary situation, where the special considerations which apply to criminal proceedings do not exist, it is clearly in the public interest that if a wrong decision has been made against a public authority, that public authority should be entitled to seek to have the position remedied in a higher court. Its interest in the issues is much greater than those of an ordinary member of the public, as was made clear in *Stepney Borough Council* v. *Joffe* [1949] 1

K.B. 599. Those interests justify the public authority in that situation being regarded as a person aggrieved.

The desirability of this approach is in my view emphasised by the fact that many of the statutory provisions which give a right of appeal to a person aggrieved are doing little more than giving a statutory right to judicial review. The approach of the courts on the appeal is the same: see, for example, section 245 of the Town and Country Planning Act 1971. In the case of such a statutory provision, it would be nonsense to regard the public authority as not being a person aggrieved since it would in any event be entitled to obtain the same relief by applying for judicial review. In the case of the present appeal provision the position is not the same. While the council would be entitled to apply for judicial review if it had no right to appeal, the court's powers on the appeal are much more extensive than they would be on an application for judicial review since the appeal is a rehearing. In general, if Parliament intends the person against whom action is taken by the public authority to have a right of appeal, I cannot see any reason why Parliament should not also intend that the public authority should have a right of appeal.

I would therefore dismiss this appeal on the basis that the council was a person aggrieved by the decision of the Southend justices quite apart from the order for costs which was made against the council. However, even if this is not the position, the effect of the order for costs is to make this case indistinguishable from the decision of the House of Lords in *Jennings* v. *Kelly* [1940] A.C. 206.

It follows that in my view this appeal must be dismissed.

SIR JOHN MEGAW and DILLON L.J. agreed.

Appeal dismissed.

CHAPTER 12

REMEDIES

THE position as to remedies in administrative law was materially affected by the introduction of the "application for judicial review," with effect from January 11, 1978, by a revised version of R.S.C. Order 53. Prior to that date, the position was as follows.

There was a series of prerogative remedies available against public authorities: *Certiorari* lay to quash a decision that was ultra vires or in breach of natural justice, that was affected by an error of law that was apparent on the face of the record or that was procured by fraud. *Prohibition* lay to prevent action or continuing action in excess of jurisdiction or contrary to natural justice. *Mandamus* lay to compel performance of a public duty. Certiorari and prohibition traditionally lay:

> "wherever any body of persons having legal authority to determine questions affecting the rights of subjects, and having the duty to act judicially, act in excess of their legal authority. . . ." (*per* Atkin L.J. in *R.* v. *Electricity Commissioners, ex p. London Electricity Joint Committee Co.* [1924] 1 K.B. 411, 415.)

Mandamus was never limited to judicial or quasi-judicial functions. The remedies originally took the form of prerogative writs but, by virtue of the Administration of Justice (Miscellaneous Provisions) Act 1938, they had become prerogative orders.

Apart from these public law remedies, from the 1950s in particular, increasing use had been made against public authorities of the private law remedies of *injunction* and *declaration*.

> "An injunction is an order of a court addressed to a party to proceedings before it and requiring him to refrain from doing, or to do, a particular act" (*de Smith*, p. 434).

A prohibitory injunction might be granted to restrain the performance of *ultra vires* acts. A mandatory injunction might (rarely) be available to compel performance of a public duty. A declaration would simply declare authoritatively the law on a disputed point.

Other remedies that might be available when appropriate included *damages*, where a public authority was held liable in contract or tort, and the prerogative writ of *habeas corpus*, available to test the legality of the actions of the respondent (whether or not a public authority) in holding a person in detention.

Applications for certiorari, prohibition and mandamus were governed by the unreformed R.S.C. Order 53 and were heard in the Divisional Court of the Queen's Bench Division, usually by a court presided over by the Lord Chief Justice. Proceedings for a declaration or injunction were ordinary civil proceedings in the High Court, and could be commenced in the Queen's Bench Division or the Chancery Division, in practice according to the preference of counsel for the plaintiff.

The remedies were discretionary, and there were particular rules governing not only the kinds of decisions or acts that could be reached by each remedy, but also such matters as *locus standi*, whether interlocutory relief was available and the grounds on which the remedy could be refused. Some of these rules were by no means settled.

The Law Commission in its Report on Remedies in Administrative Law (Cmnd. 6407, 1976, Law Com. 73) highlighted the defects in the existing arrangements (below). The revised version of R.S.C. Order 53 (below p. 680) was largely based on this report. Express statutory authority for the application for judicial review was subsequently enshrined in the Supreme Court Act 1981, s.31 (see below, p. 685).

Under the new Order 53, any of the remedies summarised above (except *habeas corpus*, which is governed by R.S.C. Ord. 52), may be granted on an application for judicial review. This is indeed the exclusive procedure by which one of the prerogative orders may be obtained. An injunction or declaration may still be obtained against a public authority in ordinary proceedings, but the House of Lords in *O'Reilly* v. *Mackman* (below, p. 722) held that in certain circumstances it will be an abuse of process to attempt to secure an injunction or declaration against a public authority other than on an application for judicial review.

(A) The Law Commission Report

THE LAW COMMISSION REPORT ON REMEDIES IN ADMINISTRATIVE LAW

(Law Com. 73, Cmnd. 6407, March 1976)

Part III: **The Procedure of Judicial Control Critically Examined . . .**

5. The dilemma of the litigant seeking judicial review

31. It will have been seen from the foregoing survey of the methods by which a litigant may obtain judicial review of the acts or omissions of public authorities that he may find himself in a dilemma. The scope and procedural particularities of one remedy may suit one case except in one respect; but another remedy which is not deficient in this respect may well be unsatisfactory from other points of view; and to add to his difficulties he may not be able to apply for both remedies in one proceeding. We may summarize the deficiencies of the present system of remedies as follows:

(*a*) The declaration may be obtained in respect of the legality of a very wide range of acts, or proposed acts, or omissions of public authorities (including the Crown), and proceedings for a declaration may be initiated without leave, with no fixed limit of time and with the advantages of full discovery. It also enables a litigant to include with his application for a declaratory order a claim for damages or relief by way of an injunction.

(*b*) On the other hand, the declaration only states the legal position; it does not order or prohibit any action, and it cannot quash a decision which a body has made within its jurisdiction. Furthermore, there is considerable doubt as to the standing which a person requires in order to bring an action for a declaration. The declaration also suffers from what may be a disadvantage in proceedings against the Crown in that it cannot be obtained in a provisional form in order to preserve the *status quo* pending final determination of the issue.

(*c*) If a litigant seeks to avoid the disadvantages of the declaration summarized under (*b*) above by resorting to a prerogative order, he may lose some of the advantages of the declaration set out in (*a*) above. Thus, an application for certiorari may be made to quash a decision, even given within the jurisdiction of a deciding authority. The Court may direct that action on the decision in question be stayed pending the conclusion of the final hearing of the application for the order; and a wide range of applicants may apply for leave to bring proceedings for such an order. But leave to apply is necessary, discovery will not in practice be available and, in the case of certiorari, the application must be made within six months of the decision impugned. Moreover, it will not be possible to join to the application for certiorari a claim for damages or relief by way of injunction. Similarly, mandamus and prohibition (where a public body is failing to carry out a duty or is about to act in excess of jurisdiction or contrary to the rules of natural justice) will lie to order or to prohibit action (except against the Crown), but, in respect of leave and discovery, they are subject to the same conditions as certiorari.

(*d*) The litigant, desiring to avoid the particular disadvantages of the declaration that it does not order or prohibit action on the part of a public authority, may, however, have resort to an injunction. This remedy will give him the same advantages as the declaration in respect of absence of leave to apply, discovery and joinder of claims for damages or for a declaration; in addition, in proceedings for an injunction the *status quo* pending final determination of the issue can be preserved by means of an interim injunction. But an injunction does not lie against the Crown, and in a case against the Crown the litigant will have to be content with asking for a declaration with its attendant limitations, as set out in (*b*) above.

32. The unsatisfactory nature of the present position has been succinctly stated by the late Professor S. A. de Smith in his evidence to the Franks Committee:

"Until the Legislature intervenes, therefore, we shall continue to have two sets of remedies against the usurpation or abuse of power by administrative tribunals—remedies which overlap but do not coincide, which must be sought in wholly distinct forms of proceedings, which are overlaid with technicalities and fine distinctions, but which would conjointly cover a very substantial area of the existing field of judicial control. This state of affairs bears a striking resemblance to that which obtained when English civil procedure was still bedevilled by the old forms of action."

33. Although a considerable variety of views was expressed in consultation on Working Paper No. 40 there was a general consensus among those whom we consulted, including members of the judiciary, on the desirability of remedying the procedural defects in administrative law to which we have referred above. . . .

Part VI: **Summary of Conclusions and Recommendations**

1. Matters not covered by this report

56. The substantive law and institutional arrangements relating to the judicial control of administrative authorities are outside our terms of reference, and we have not considered them. Nor, for the same reason, have we considered clauses excluding judicial review of administrative acts or omissions, special statutory limitation periods for judicial review or a new remedy in damages for loss arising from illegal administrative acts or omissions . . .

2. Defects in the present procedure of judicial review

57. The five methods by which judicial review of the acts or omissions of public authorities may be obtained (*i.e.* the prerogative orders of certiorari, prohibition and mandamus and actions for a declaration or an injunction) each have their characteristic procedural advantages and disadvantages from the standpoint of the litigant. There is, however, no single procedure of review available which preserves the advantages of some of these remedies, while eliminating, or at least reducing, the disadvantages of the other remedies; furthermore, it is not even possible to obtain in a single proceeding a declaration or injunction as an alternative to a prerogative order. Nor is it possible to join with an application for a prerogative order a claim for damages for loss arising from the illegal acts or omissions in respect of which the prerogative order is being sought . . .

3. Proposals for reform not adopted in this report

58. We are not in this report recommending—

(*a*) that the new procedure we envisage in respect of applications to the Divisional Court for judicial review should be exclusive in the sense that it would become the only way by which public law issues relating to the legality of the acts or omissions of persons or bodies could be decided; where such issues arise in ordinary actions or criminal proceedings they would not have to be referred to the Divisional Court but would continue to be dealt with as at present by the Court seized of the case (paragraph 34);

(*b*) that the procedure applicable to prerogative order proceedings be assimilated to that of ordinary actions; nor are we recommending that the new procedure we are recommending for judicial review should be obtainable without leave; . . .

Notes

1. The Law Commission had originally proposed a broader inquiry into administrative law, extending beyond remedies, to cover the *scope* of remedies in administrative law, the availability of damages as a remedy, whether special principles should govern the liability of the administration in contract and tort, and how far change should be made in the organisation and personnel of the courts in which proceedings might be brought against the administration. The Labour government did not think that this was the "right time" to undertake the wider inquiry (see Law Com. 73 paras. 1–3). For comments on the Report, see H.W.R. W[ade], (1976) 92 L.Q.R. 334.

2. The rules introducing the "application for judicial review" (the new Order 53) largely followed the Law Commission's detailed recommendations. One exception was the lack of any provision for interim declaratory relief against the Crown (see below, p. 719).

(B) R.S.C. Order 53; Supreme Court Act 1981, ss.29–31

R.S.C. ORDER 53: APPLICATIONS FOR JUDICIAL REVIEW

(As amended by S.I. 1980 No. 2000, and S.I. 1982 No. 1111)

Cases appropriate for application for judicial review

1.—(1) An application for—

(*a*) an order of mandamus, prohibition or certiorari, or
(*b*) an injunction under Section [30 of the Act][1] restraining a person from acting in any office in which he is not entitled to act,

shall be made by way of an application for judicial review in accordance with the provisions of this Order.

(2) An application for a declaration or an injunction (not being an injunction mentioned in paragraph (1)(*b*)) may be made by way of an application for judicial review, and on such an application the Court may grant the declaration or injunction claimed if it considers that, having regard to—

[1] (Ed.) *i.e.* the Supreme Court Act 1981.

(*a*) the nature of the matters in respect of which relief may be granted by way of an order of mandamus, prohibition or certiorari,
(*b*) the nature of the persons and bodies against whom relief may be granted by way of such an order, and
(*c*) all the circumstances of the case,

it would be just and convenient for the declaration or injunction to be granted on an application for judicial review.

Joinder of claims for relief

2. On an application for judicial review any relief mentioned in rule 1(1) or (2) may be claimed as an alternative or in addition to any other relief so mentioned if it arises out of or relates to or is connected with the same matter.

Grant of leave to apply for judicial review

3.—(1) No application for judicial review shall be made unless the leave of the Court has been obtained in accordance with this rule.

[(2) An application for leave must be made *ex parte* to a judge by filing in the Crown Office—

(*a*) a notice in Form No. 86A containing a statement of
  (i) the name and description of the applicant,
  (ii) the relief sought and the grounds upon which it is sought,
  (iii) the name and address of the applicant's solicitors (if any), and
  (iv) the applicant's address for service; and
(*b*) an affidavit verifying the facts relied on.

(3) The judge may determine the application without a hearing, unless a hearing is requested in the notice of application, and need not sit in open court; in any case, the Crown Office shall serve a copy of the judge's order on the applicant.

(4) Where the application for leave is refused by the judge, or is granted on terms, the applicant may renew it by applying—

(*a*) in any criminal cause or matter, to a Divisional Court of the Queen's Bench Division;
(*b*) in any other case, to a single judge sitting in open court or, if the Court so directs, to a Divisional Court of the Queen's Bench Division:

Provided that no application for leave may be renewed in any non-criminal cause or matter in which the judge has refused leave under paragraph (3) after a hearing.

(5) In order to renew his application for leave the applicant must, within 10 days of being served with notice of the judge's refusal, lodge in the Crown Office notice of his intention in Form No. 86B.]

(6) Without prejudice to its powers under Order 20, rule 8, the Court hearing an application for leave may allow the applicant's statement to be amended, whether by specifying different or additional grounds or relief or otherwise, on such terms, if any, as it thinks fit.

(7) The Court shall not grant leave unless it considers that the applicant has a sufficient interest in the matter to which the application relates.

(8) Where leave is sought to apply for an order of certiorari to remove for the purpose of its being quashed any judgment, order, conviction or other proceeding which is subject to appeal and a time is limited for the bringing of the appeal, the Court may adjourn the application for leave until the appeal is determined or the time for appealing has expired.

(9) If the Court grants leave, it may impose such terms as to costs and as to giving security as it thinks fit.

(10) Where leave to apply for judicial review is granted, then—

(*a*) if the relief sought is an order of prohibition or certiorari and the Court so directs, the grant shall operate as a stay of the proceedings to which the application relates until the determination of the application or until the Court otherwise orders;

(*b*) if any other relief is sought, the Court may at any time grant in the proceedings such interim relief as could be granted in an action begun by writ.

[4.—(1) An application for judicial review shall be made promptly and in any event within three months from the date when grounds for the application first arose unless the Court considers that there is good reason for extending the period within which the application shall be made.

(2) Where the relief sought is an order of certiorari in respect of any judgment, order, conviction or other proceeding, the date when grounds for the application first arose shall be taken to be the date of that judgment, order, conviction or proceeding.

(3) Paragraph (1) is without prejudice to any statutory provision which has the effect of limiting the time within which an application for judicial review may be made.]

Mode of applying for judicial review

5.—[(1) In any criminal cause or matter where leave has been granted to make an application for judicial review, the application shall be made by originating motion to a Divisional Court of the Queen's Bench Division.

(2) In any other such cause or matter, the application shall be made by originating motion to a judge sitting in open court, unless the Court directs that it shall be made—

(*a*) by originating summons to a judge in chambers; or

(*b*) by originating motion to a Divisional Court of the Queen's Bench Division.

Any direction under sub-paragraph (*a*) shall be without prejudice to the judge's powers under Order 32, rule 13.]

(3) The notice of motion or summons must be served on all persons directly affected and where it relates to any proceedings in or before a court and the object of the application is either to compel the court or an officer of the court to do any act in relation to the proceedings or to quash them or any order made therein, the notice or summons must also be served on the clerk or registrar of the court and, where any objection to the conduct of the judge is to be made, on the judge.

(4) Unless the Court granting leave has otherwise directed, there must be at least 10 days between the service of the notice of motion or summons and . . . the hearing.

(5) A motion must be entered for hearing within 14 days after the grant of leave.

(6) An affidavit giving the names and addresses of, and the places and dates of service on, all persons who have been served with the notice of motion or summons must be filed before the motion or summons is entered for hearing and, if any person who ought to be served under this rule has not been served, the affidavit must state that fact and the reason for it; and the affidavit shall be before the Court on the hearing of the motion or summons.

(7) If on the hearing of the motion or summons the Court is of opinion that any person who ought, whether under this rule or otherwise, to have been served has not been served, the Court may adjourn the hearing on such terms (if any) as it may direct in order that the notice or summons may be served on that person.

Statements and affidavits

6.—(1) Copies of the statement in support of an application for leave under rule 3 must be served with the notice of motion or summons and, subject to paragraph (2), no grounds shall be relied upon or any relief sought at the hearing except the grounds and relief set out in the statement.

(2) The Court may on the hearing of the motion or summons allow the applicant to amend his statement, whether by specifying different or additional grounds or relief or otherwise, on such terms, if any, as it thinks fit and may allow further affidavits to be used if they deal with new matters arising out of an affidavit of any other party to the application.

(3) Where the applicant intends to ask to be allowed to amend his statement or to use further affidavits, he shall give notice of his intention and of any proposed amendment to every other party.

[(4) Any respondent who intends to use an affidavit at the hearing shall file it in the Crown Office, and give notice thereof to the applicant, as soon as practicable and in any event, unless the Court otherwise directs, within 21 days after the service upon him of the documents required to be served by paragraph (1).]

(5) Each party to the application must supply to every other party on demand and on payment of the proper charges copies of every affidavit which he proposes to use at the hearing including, in the case of the applicant, the affidavit in support of the application for leave under rule 3.

Claim for damages

7.—(1) On an application for judicial review the Court may, subject to paragraph (2), award damages to the applicant if—

(*a*) he has included in the statement in support of his application for leave under rule 3 a claim for damages arising from any matter to which the application relates, and

(*b*) the Court is satisfied that, if the claim had been made in an action begun by the applicant at the time of making his application, he could have been awarded damages.

(2) Order 18, rule 12, shall apply to a statement relating to a claim for damages as it applies to a pleading.

Application for discovery, interrogatories, cross-examination, etc.

8.—(1) Unless the Court otherwise directs, any interlocutory application in proceedings on an application for judicial review may be made to any judge or a master of the Queen's Bench Division, notwithstanding that the application for judicial review has been made by motion and is to be heard by a Divisional Court.

In this paragraph "interlocutory application" includes an application for an order under Order 24 or 26 or Order 38, rule 2(3), or for an order dismissing the proceedings by consent of the parties.

(2) In relation to an order made by a master pursuant to paragraph (1), Order 58, rule 1, shall, where the application for judicial review is to be heard by a Divisional Court, have effect as if a reference to that Court were substituted for the reference to a judge in chambers.

(3) This rule is without prejudice to any statutory provision or rule of law restricting the making of an order against the Crown.

Hearing of application for judicial review

9.—(1) On the hearing of any motion or summons under rule 5, any person who desires to be heard in opposition to the motion or summons, and appears to the Court to be a proper person to be heard, shall be heard, notwithstanding that he has not been served with notice of the motion or the summons.

(2) Where the relief sought is or includes an order of certiorari to remove any proceedings for the purpose of quashing them, the applicant may not question the validity of any order, warrant, commitment, conviction, inquisition or record unless before the hearing of the motion or summons he has lodged in the Crown Office a copy thereof verified by affidavit or

accounts for his failure to do so to the satisfaction of the Court hearing the motion or summons.

(3) Where an order of certiorari is made in any such case as is referred to in paragraph (2), the order shall, subject to paragraph (4), direct that the proceedings shall be quashed forthwith on their removal into the Queen's Bench Division.

(4) Where the relief sought is an order of certiorari and the Court is satisfied that there are grounds for quashing the decision to which the application relates, the Court may, in addition to quashing it, remit the matter to the court, tribunal or authority concerned with a direction to reconsider it and reach a decision in accordance with the findings of the Court.

(5) Where the relief sought is a declaration, an injunction or damages and the Court considers that it should not be granted on an application for judicial review but might have been granted if it had been sought in an action begun by writ by the applicant at the time of making his application, the Court may, instead of refusing the application, order the proceedings to continue as if they had been begun by writ; and Order 28, rule 8, shall apply as if, in the case of an application made by motion, it had been made by summons.

Saving for person acting in obedience to mandamus

10. No action or proceeding shall be begun or prosecuted against any person in respect of anything done in obedience to an order of mandamus. . . .

[*Appeal from judge's order*

13. No appeal shall lie from an order made under paragraph (3) of rule 3 on an application for leave which may be renewed under paragraph (4) of that rule.]

Meaning of "Court"

14. In relation to the hearing by a judge of an application for leave under rule 3 or of an application for judicial review, any reference in this Order to "the Court" shall, unless the context otherwise requires, be construed as a reference to the judge."

SUPREME COURT ACT 1981

Orders of mandamus, prohibition and certiorari

29.—(1) The High Court shall have jurisdiction to make orders of mandamus, prohibition and certiorari in those classes of cases in which it had power to do so immediately before the commencement of this Act.

(2) Every such order shall be final, subject to any right of appeal therefrom.

(3) In relation to the jurisdiction of the Crown Court, other than its jurisdiction in matters relating to trial on indictment, the High Court shall have all such jurisdiction to make orders of mandamus, prohibition or certiorari as the High Court possesses in relation to the jurisdiction of an inferior court.

(4) The power of the High Court under any enactment to require justices of the peace or a judge or officer of a county court to do any act relating to the duties of their respective offices, or to require a magistrates' court to state a case for the opinion of the High Court, in any case where the High Court formerly had by virtue of any enactment jurisdiction to make a rule absolute, or an order, for any of those purposes, shall be exercisable by order of mandamus.

(5) In any enactment—

(*a*) references to a writ of mandamus, of prohibition or of certiorari shall be read as references to the corresponding order; and
(*b*) references to the issue or award of any such writ shall be read as references to the making of the corresponding order.

Injunctions to restrain persons from acting in offices in which they are not entitled to act

30.—(1) Where a person not entitled to do so acts in an office to which this section applies, the High Court may—

(*a*) grant an injunction restraining him from so acting; and
(*b*) if the case so requires, declare the office to be vacant.

(2) This section applies to any substantive office of a public nature and permanent character which is held under the Crown or which has been created by any statutory provision or royal charter.

Application for judicial review

31.—(1) An application to the High Court for one or more of the following forms of relief, namely—

(*a*) an order of mandamus, prohibition or certiorari;
(*b*) a declaration or injunction under subsection (2); or
(*c*) an injunction under section 30 restraining a person not entitled to do so from acting in an office to which that section applies,

shall be made in accordance with rules of court by a procedure to be known as an application for judicial review.

(2) A declaration may be made or an injunction granted under this subsection in any case where an application for judicial review, seeking

that relief, has been made and the High Court considers that, having regard to—

(*a*) the nature of the matters in respect of which relief may be granted by orders of mandamus, prohibition or certiorari;
(*b*) the nature of the persons and bodies against whom relief may be granted by such orders; and
(*c*) all the circumstances of the case,

it would be just and convenient for the declaration to be made or the injunction to be granted, as the case may be.

(3) No application for judicial review shall be made unless the leave of the High Court has been obtained in accordance with rules of court; and the court shall not grant leave to make such an application unless it considers that the applicant has a sufficient interest in the matter to which the application relates.

(4) On an application for judicial review the High Court may award damages to the applicant if—

(*a*) he has joined with his application a claim for damages arising from any matter to which the application relates; and
(*b*) the court is satisfied that, if the claim had been made in an action begun by the applicant at the time of making his application, he would have been awarded damages.

(5) If, on an application for judicial review seeking an order of certiorari, the High Court quashes the decision to which the application relates, the High Court may remit the matter to the court, tribunal or authority concerned, with a direction to reconsider it and reach a decision in accordance with the findings of the High Court.

(6) Where the High Court considers that there has been undue delay in making an application for judicial review, the court may refuse to grant—

(*a*) leave for the making of the application; or
(*b*) any relief sought on the application,

if it considers that the granting of the relief sought would be likely to cause substantial hardship to, or substantially prejudice the rights of, any person or would be detrimental to good administration.

(7) Subsection (6) is without prejudice to any enactment or rule of court which has the effect of limiting the time within which an application for judicial review may be made.

Note

For comments on the introduction of the new Order 53, see J. F. Garner, (1982) 1 C.J.Q. 292; V. Moore, [1980] P.L. 349 and [1981] P.L. 28; J. Beatson and M. Matthews, (1978) 41 M.L.R. 419; L. Blom-Cooper, [1982] P.L. 250.

(C) Scope of the Application for Judicial Review

Traditionally judicial review remedies have been available against public bodies, established by statute or under the royal prerogative. The decision of the Court of Appeal in the following case showed that the application for judicial review can extend to all bodies exercising public functions.

R. v. PANEL ON TAKE-OVERS AND MERGERS, ex p. DATAFIN plc AND ANOTHER

[1987] Q.B. 815; [1987] 2 W.L.R. 699; [1987] 1 All E.R. 564
(Court of Appeal)

The applicants, Datafin plc and Prudential Bache Securities Inc., who were bidding in competition with Norton Opax plc to take over another company, McCorquodale plc, complained to the Panel of Take-overs and Mergers that N. Plc. had acted in concert with other parties in breach of the City Code on Take-overs and Mergers. The panel dismissed the complaint and the applicants applied to the High Court for leave to apply for judicial review by way, *inter alia*, of certiorari to quash the panel's decision and of mandamus to compel the panel to reconsider the complaint. Hodgson J. refused leave on the ground that the panel's decision was not susceptible to judicial review.

On the renewed application before the Court of Appeal, the court granted leave in order itself to consider both the substantive application and the question of jurisdiction.

Sir John Donaldson M.R. The Panel on Take-overs and Mergers is a truly remarkable body. Perched on the 20th floor of the Stock Exchange building in the City of London, both literally and metaphorically it oversees and regulates a very important part of the United Kingdom financial market. Yet it performs this function without visible means of legal support.

The panel is an unincorporated association without legal personality and, so far as can be seen, has only about twelve members. But those members are appointed by and represent the Accepting Houses Committee, the Association of Investment Trust Companies, the Association of British Insurers, the Committee of London and Scottish Bankers, the Confederation of British Industry, the Council of the Stock Exchange, the Institute of Chartered Accountants in England and Wales, the Issuing Houses Association, the National Association of Pension Funds, the Financial Intermediaries Managers and Brokers Regulatory Association, and the Unit Trust Association; the chairman and deputy chairman being appointed by the Bank of England. Furthermore, the panel is supported by the Foreign Bankers in London, the Foreign Brokers in London and the Consultative Committee of Accountancy Bodies.

It has no statutory, prerogative or common law powers and it is not in contractual relationship with the financial market or with those who deal in that market. According to the introduction to the City Code on Take-overs and Mergers, which it promulgates:

"The code has not, and does not seek to have, the force of law, but those who wish to take advantage of the facilities of the securities markets in the United Kingdom should conduct themselves in matters relating to take-overs according to the code. Those who do not so conduct themselves cannot expect to enjoy those facilities and may find that they are withheld. The provisions of the code fall into two categories. On the one hand, the code enunciates general principles of conduct to be observed in take-over transactions: these general principles are a codification of good standards of commercial behaviour and should have an obvious and universal application. On the other hand, the code lays down a series of rules, some of which are no more than examples of the application of the general principles whilst others are rules of procedure designed to govern specific forms of take-over. Some of the general principles, based as they are upon a concept of equity between one shareholder and another, while readily understandable in the City and by those concerned with the securities markets generally, would not easily lend themselves to legislation. The code is therefore framed in non-technical language and is, primarily as a measure of self-discipline, administered and enforced by the panel, a body representative of those using the securities markets and concerned with the observance of good business standards, rather than the enforcement of the law. As indicated above, the panel executive is always available to be consulted and where there is doubt this should be done in advance of any action. Taking legal or other professional advice on matters of interpretation under the code is not an appropriate alternative to obtaining a view or a ruling from the executive."

"Self-regulation" is an emotive term. It is also ambiguous. An individual who voluntarily regulates his life in accordance with stated principles, because he believes that this is morally right and also, perhaps, in his own long term interests, or a group of individuals who do so, are practising self-regulation. But it can mean something quite different. It can connote a system whereby a group of people, acting in concert, use their collective power to force themselves and others to comply with a code of conduct of their own devising. This is not necessarily morally wrong or contrary to the public interest, unlawful or even undesirable. But it is very different.

The panel is self-regulating body in the latter sense. Lacking any authority de jure, it exercises immense power de facto by devising, promulgating, amending and interpreting the City Code on Take-overs and Mergers, by waiving or modifying the application of the code in particular circumstances, by investigating and reporting upon alleged breaches of the code and by the application or threat of sanctions. These sanctions are no less effective because they are applied indirectly and lack a legally enforceable base. Thus, to quote again from the introduction to the code:

> "If there appears to have been a material breach of the code, the executive invites the person concerned to appear before the panel for a hearing. He is informed by letter of the nature of the alleged breach and of the matters which the director general will present. If any other matters are raised he is allowed to ask for an adjournment. If the panel finds that there has been a breach, it may have recourse to private reprimand or public censure or, in a more flagrant case, to further action designed to deprive the offender temporarily or permanently of his ability to enjoy the facilities of the securities markets. The panel may refer certain aspects of a case to the Department of Trade and Industry, the Stock Exchange or other appropriate body. No reprimand, censure or further action will take place without the person concerned having the opportunity to appeal to the appeal committee of the panel."

The unspoken assumption, which I do not doubt is a reality, is that the Department of Trade and Industry or, as the case may be, the Stock Exchange or other appropriate body would in fact exercise statutory or contractual powers to penalise the transgressors. Thus, for example, rules 22 to 24 of the Rules of the Stock Exchange (1984) provide for the severest penalties, up to and including expulsion, for acts of misconduct and by rule 23.1:

> "Acts of misconduct may consist of any of the following . . . (g) Any action which has been found by the Panel on Take-overs and Mergers (including where reference has been made to it, the appeal committee of the panel) to have been in breach of the City Code on Take-overs and Mergers. The findings of the panel, subject to any modification by the appeal committee of the panel, shall not be re-opened in proceedings taken under rules 22 to 24."

The principal issue in this appeal, and only issue which may matter in the longer term, is whether this remarkable body is above the law. Its respectability is beyond question. So is its *bona fides*. I do not doubt for one moment that it is intended to, and does, operate in the public interest and that the enormously wide discretion which it arrogates to itself is necessary if it is to function efficiently and effectively. Whilst not wishing to become involved in the political controversy on the relative merits of self-regulation and governmental or statutory regulation, I am content to assume for the purposes of this appeal that self-regulation is preferable in the public interest. But that said, what is to happen if the panel goes off the rails? Suppose, perish the thought, that it were to use its powers in a way which was manifestly unfair. What then? Mr. Alexander submits that the panel would lose the support of public opinion in the financial markets and would be unable to continue to operate. Further or alternatively, Parliament could and would intervene. Maybe, but how long would that take and who in the meantime could or would come to the assistance of those who were being oppressed by such conduct? . . .

It will be seen that there are three principal issues, *viz.*: (a) Are the decisions of the panel susceptible to judicial review? This is the "jurisdictional" issue. (b) If so, how in principle is that jurisdiction to be exercised given the nature of the panel's activities and the fact that it is an essential part of the machinery of a market in which time is money in a very real sense? This might be described as the "practical" issue. (c) If the jurisdictional issue is answered favourably to the applicants, is this a case in which relief should be granted and, if so, in what form?

As the new Norton Opax ordinary shares have been admitted to the Official Stock Exchange List and so can be traded, subject to allotment, any doubt as to the outcome of the present proceedings could affect the price at which these shares are or could be traded and thus the rights of those entitled to trade in them. Accordingly we thought it right to announce at the end of the argument that the application for judicial review would be refused. However, I propose to explain my reasons for reaching this conclusion by considering the three issues in the order in which I have set them out.

The jurisdictional issue

As I have said, the panel is a truly remarkable body, performing its function without visible means of legal support. But the operative word is "visible," although perhaps I should have used the word "direct." Invisible or indirect support there is in abundance. Not only is a breach of the code, so found by the panel, *ipso facto* an act of misconduct by a member of the Stock Exchange, and the same may be true of other bodies represented on the panel, but the admission of shares to the Official List may be withheld in the event of such a breach. This is interesting and significant for listing of securities is a statutory function performed by the Stock Exchange in pursuance of the Stock Exchange (Listing) Regulations 1984 (S.I. 1984 No. 716), enacted in implementation of E.E.C. directives. And the matter does not stop there, because in December 1983 the Department of Trade and Industry made a statement explaining why the Licensed Dealers (Conduct of Business) Rules 1983 (S.I. 1983 No. 585) contained no detailed provisions about take-overs. It said:

> "There are now no detailed provisions in these statutory rules about take-overs and the following paragraphs set out the provisions as regards public companies and private companies respectively. 2. As regards public companies (as well as private companies which have had some kind of public involvement in the ten years before the bid) the department considers it better to rely on the effectiveness and flexibility of the City Code on Take-overs and Mergers, which covers bids made for public companies and certain private companies which have had some past public involvement. The City code has the support of, and

can be enforced against, professional security dealers and accordingly the department expects, as a matter of course, that those making bids for public companies (and private companies covered by the code) to use the services of a dealer in securities authorised under the Prevention of Fraud (Investments) Act 1958 (such as a stockbroker, exempt dealer, licensed dealer, or a member of a recognised association), in which case the Secretary of State's permission for the distribution of take-over documents is not required. This is seen as an important safeguard for the shareholders of the public company (of which there may be several hundreds or thousands) and as a means of ensuring that such take-overs are conducted properly and fully in accordance with the provisions of the City code. It would only be in exceptional cases that the Secretary of State would consider removing this safeguard by granting permission under section 14(2) of the Act for the distribution of take-over documents in these circumstances."

The picture which emerges is clear. As an act of government it was decided that, in relation to take-overs, there should be a central self-regulatory body which would be supported and sustained by a periphery of statutory powers and penalties wherever non-statutory powers and penalties were insufficient or non-existent or where E.E.C. requirements called for statutory provisions.

No one could have been in the least surprised if the panel had been instituted and operated under the direct authority of statute law, since it operates wholly in the public domain. Its jurisdiction extends throughout the United Kingdom. Its code and rulings apply equally to all who wish to make take-over bids or promote mergers, whether or not they are members of bodies represented on the panel. Its lack of a direct statutory base is a complete anomaly, judged by the experience of other comparable markets world wide. The explanation is that it is an historical "happenstance," to borrow a happy term from across the Atlantic. Prior to the years leading up to the "Big Bang," the City of London prided itself upon being a village community, albeit of an unique kind, which could regulate itself by pressure of professional opinion. As government increasingly accepted the necessity for intervention to prevent fraud, it built on City institutions and mores, supplementing and reinforcing them as appeared necessary. It is a process which is likely to continue, but the position has already been reached in which central government has incorporated the panel into its own regulatory network built up under the Prevention of Fraud (Investments) Act 1958 and allied statutes, such as the Banking Act 1979.

The issue is thus whether the historic supervisory jurisdiction of the Queen's courts extends to such a body discharging such functions, including some which are quasi-judicial in their nature, as part of such a system. Mr. Alexander, for the panel, submits that it does not. He says that this jurisdiction only extends to bodies whose power is derived from legislation or the exercise of the prerogative. Mr. Lever for the applicants, submits that this is too narrow a view and that regard has to be had not only to the source of the body's power, but also to whether it operates as an integral part of a system which has a public law character, is supported by public law in that public law sanctions are applied if its edicts are ignored and performs what might be described as public law functions.

In *R. v. Criminal Injuries Compensation Board, ex p. Lain* [1967] 2 Q.B. 864, 882, Lord Parker C.J., who had unrivalled experience of the prerogative remedies both on the Bench and at the Bar, said that the exact limits of the ancient remedy of certiorari had never been and ought not to be specifically defined. I respectfully agree and will not attempt such an exercise. He continued, at p. 882:

> "They have varied from time to time being extended to meet changing conditions. At one time the writ only went to an inferior court. Later its ambit was extended to statutory tribunals determining a lis inter partes. Later again it extended to cases where there was no lis in the strict sense of the word but where immediate or subsequent rights of a citizen were affected. The only constant limits throughout were that it was performing a public duty. Private or domestic tribunals have always been outside the scope of certiorari since their authority is derived solely from contract, that is, from the agreement of the parties concerned. . . . We have as it seems to me reached the position when the ambit of certiorari can be said to cover every case in which a body of persons of a public as opposed to a purely private or domestic character has to determine matters affecting subjects provided always that it has a duty to act judicially. Looked at in this way the board in my judgment comes fairly and squarely within the jurisdiction of this court. It is, as Mr. Bridge said, 'a servant of the Crown charged by the Crown, by executive instruction, with the duty of distributing the bounty of the Crown.' It is clearly, therefore, performing public duties."

Diplock L.J., who later was to make administrative law almost his own, said, at pp. 884–885:

> "The jurisdiction of the High Court as successor of the Court of Queen's Bench to supervise the exercise of their jurisdiction by inferior tribunals has not in the past been dependent upon the source of the tribunal's authority to decide issues submitted to its determination, except where such authority is derived solely from agreement of parties to the determination. The latter case falls within the field of private contract and thus within the ordinary civil jurisdiction of the High Court supplemented where appropriate by its statutory jurisdiction under the Arbitration Acts. The earlier history of the writ of certiorari shows that it was issued to courts whose authority was derived from the prerogative, from Royal Charter, from franchise or custom as well as from Act of

Parliament. Its recent history shows that as new kinds of tribunals have been created, orders of certiorari have been extended to them too and to all persons who under authority of the Government have exercised quasi-judicial functions. True, since the victory of Parliament in the constitutional struggles of the 17th century, authority has been, generally if not invariably, conferred upon new kinds of tribunals by or under Act of Parliament and there has been no recent occasion for the High Court to exercise supervisory jurisdiction over persons whose ultimate authority to decide matters is derived from any other source. But I see no reason for holding that the ancient jurisdiction of the Court of Queen's Bench has been narrowed merely because there has been no occasion to exercise it. If new tribunals are established by acts of government, the supervisory jurisdiction of the High Court extends to them if they possess the essential characteristics upon which the subjection of inferior tribunals to the supervisory control of the High Court is based. What are these characteristics? It is plain on the authorities that the tribunal need not be one whose determinations give rise directly to any legally enforceable right or liability. Its determination may be subject to certiorari notwithstanding that it is merely one step in a process which may have the result of altering the legal rights or liabilities of a person to whom it relates. It is not even essential that the determination must have that result, for there may be some subsequent condition to be satisfied before the determination can have any effect upon such legal rights or liabilities. That subsequent condition may be a later determination by another tribunal (see *R.* v. *Postmaster-General, ex p. Carmichael* [1928] 1 K.B. 291; *R.* v. *Boycott, ex p. Keasley* [1939] 2 K.B. 651). Is there any reason in principle why certiorari should not lie in respect of a determination, where the subsequent condition which must be satisfied before it can affect any legal rights or liabilities of a person to whom it relates is the exercise in favour of that person of an executive discretion, as distinct from a discretion which is required to be exercised judicially?"

Ashworth J., who like Lord Parker C.J. had served as junior counsel to the Treasury and as such had vast experience in this field, said, at pp. 891–892:

"It is a truism to say that the law has to adjust itself to meet changing circumstances and although a tribunal, constituted as the board, has not been the subject of consideration or decision by this court in relation to an order of certiorari, I do not think that this court should shrink from entertaining this application merely because the board had no statutory origin. It cannot be suggested that the board had unlawfully usurped jurisdiction: it acts with lawful authority, albeit such authority is derived from the executive and not from an Act of Parliament. In the past this court has felt itself able to consider the conduct of a minister when he is acting judicially or quasi-judicially and while the present case may involve an extension of relief by way of certiorari I should not feel constrained to refuse such relief if the facts warranted it."

The Criminal Injuries Compensation Board, in the form which it then took, was an administrative novelty. Accordingly it would have been impossible to find a precedent for the exercise of the supervisory jurisdiction of the court which fitted the facts. Nevertheless the court not only asserted its jurisdiction, but further asserted that it was a jurisdiction which was adaptable thereafter. This process has since been taken further in *O'Reilly* v. *Mackman* [1983] 2 A.C. 237, 279 (*per* Lord Diplock) by deleting any requirement that the body should have a duty to act judicially; in *Council of Civil Service Unions* v. *Minister for the Civil Service* [1985] A.C. 374 by extending it to a person exercising purely prerogative power; and in *Gillick* v. *West Norfolk and Wisbech Area Health Authority* [1986] A.C. 112, where Lord Fraser of Tullybelton, at p. 163F and Lord Scarman, at p. 178F–H expressed the view obiter that judicial review would extend to guidance circulars issued by a department of state without any specific authority. In all the reports it is possible to find enumerations of factors giving rise to the jurisdiction, but it is a fatal error to regard the presence of all those factors as essential or as being exclusive of other factors. Possibly the only essential elements are what can be described as a public element, which can take many different forms, and the exclusion from the jurisdiction of bodies whose sole source of power is a consensual submission to its jurisdiction.

In fact, given its novelty, the panel fits surprisingly well into the format which this court had in mind in the *Criminal Injuries Compensation Board* case. It is without doubt performing a public duty and an important one. This is clear from the expressed willingness of the Secretary of State for Trade and Industry to limit legislation in the field of take-overs and mergers and to use the panel as the centrepiece of his regulation of that market. The rights of citizens are indirectly affected by its decisions, some, but by no means all of whom, may in a technical sense be said to have assented to this situation, *e.g.* the members of the Stock Exchange. At least in its determination of whether there has been a breach of the code, it has a duty to act judicially and it asserts that its raison d'etre is to do equity between one shareholder and another. Its source of power is only partly based upon moral persuasion and the assent of institutions and their members, the bottom line being the statutory powers exercised by the Department of Trade and Industry and the Bank of England. In this context I should be very disappointed if the courts could not recognise the realities of executive power and allowed their vision to be clouded by the subtlety and sometimes complexity of the way in which it can be exerted.

Given that it is really unthinkable that, in the absence of legislation such as affects trade unions, the panel should go on its way cocooned from the attention of the courts in defence of the citizenry, we sought to investigate whether it could conveniently be controlled by established forms of private law, *e.g.* torts such as actionable combinations in restraint of trade, and, to this end, pressed Mr. Lever to draft a writ. Suffice it to say that the result was wholly unconvincing and, not surprisingly, Mr. Alexander did not admit that it would be in the least effective. . . .

[His Lordship held on the *practical issue* that there were insufficient reasons for excluding judicial review altogether (see n. 1 below), and rejected the applicants' arguments on the substance of their claim].

LLOYD L.J.: . . . Mr. Alexander . . . argues (i) that the sole test whether the body of persons is subject to judicial review is the source of its power, and (ii) that there has been no case where that source has been other than legislation, including subordinate legislation, or the prerogative.

I do not agree that the source of the power is the sole test whether a body is subject to judicial review, nor do I so read Lord Diplock's speech. Of course the source of the power will often, perhaps usually, be decisive. If the source of power is a statute, or subordinate legislation under a statute, then clearly the body in question will be subject to judicial review. If, at the other end of the scale, the source of power is contractual, as in the case of private arbitration, then clearly the arbitrator is not subject to judicial review: see *R.* v. *National Joint Council for the Craft of Dental Technicians (Disputes Committee), ex p. Neate* [1953] 1 Q.B. 704.

But in between these extremes there is an area in which it is helpful to look not just at the source of the power but at the nature of the power. If the body in question is exercising public law functions, or if the exercise of its functions have public law consequences, then that may, as Mr. Lever submitted, be sufficient to bring the body within the reach of judicial review. It may be said that to refer to "public law" in this context is to beg the question. But I do not think it does. The essential distinction, which runs through all the cases to which we referred, is between a domestic or private tribunal on the one hand and a body of persons who are under some public duty on the other. Thus in *R.* v. *Criminal Injuries Compensation Board, ex p. Lain* [1967] 2 Q.B. 864 Lord Parker C.J., after tracing the development of certiorari from its earliest days, said, at p. 882:

> "The only constant limits throughout were that [the tribunal] was performing a public duty. Private or domestic tribunals have always been outside the scope of certiorari since their authority is derived solely from contract, that is, from the agreement of the parties concerned."

To the same effect is a passage from a speech of Lord Parker C.J. in an earlier case, to which we were not, I think, referred, *R.* v. *Industrial Court, ex p. A.S.S.E.T.* [1965] 1 Q.B. 377, 389:

> "It has been urged on us that really this arbitral tribunal is not a private arbitral tribunal but that in effect it is undertaking a public duty or a

quasi-public duty and as such is amenable to an order of mandamus. I am quite unable to come to that conclusion. It is abundantly clear that they had no duty to undertake the reference. If they refused to undertake the reference they could not be compelled to do so. I do not think that the position is in any way different once they have undertaken the reference. They are clearly doing something which they are not under any public duty to do and, in those circumstances, I see no jurisdiction in this court to issue an order of mandamus to the industrial court."

More recently, in *R.* v. *British Broadcasting Corporation, ex p. Lavelle* [1983] 1 W.L.R. 23, Woolf J. had to consider an application for judicial review where the relief sought was an injunction under R.S.C., Ord. 53, r. 1(2). The case was brought by an employee of the B.B.C. In refusing relief, Woolf J. said, at p. 31:

"Ord. 53, r. 1(2) does not strictly confine applications for judicial review to cases where an order for mandamus, prohibition or certiorari could be granted. It merely requires that the court should have regard to the nature of the matter in respect of which such relief may be granted. However, although applications for judicial review are not confined to those cases where relief could be granted by way of prerogative order, I regard the wording of Ord. 53, r. 1(2) and section 31(2) of the Act of 1981 as making it clear that the application for judicial review is confined to reviewing activities of a public nature as opposed to those of a purely private or domestic character. The disciplinary appeal procedure set up by the B.B.C. depends purely upon the contract of employment between the applicant and the B.B.C., and therefore it is a procedure of a purely private or domestic character."

So I would reject Mr. Alexander's argument that the sole test whether a body is subject to judicial review is the source of its power. So to hold would in my judgment impose an artificial limit on the developing law of judicial review. That artificiality is well illustrated in the present case by reference to the listing regulations issued by the Council of the Stock Exchange. As the foreword to the current edition makes clear, a new edition of the regulations became necessary as the result of the Stock Exchange (Listing) Regulations 1984. Those Regulations were made as the result of a requirement of an E.E.C. Council directive. Mr. Alexander conceded that the listing regulations are now the subject of public law remedies. By contrast (if his submission is correct) the code, which is the subject not of a Council directive, but of a Commission recommendation, is not.

I now turn to the second of Mr. Alexander's two arguments under this head. He submits that there has never been a case when the source of the power has been other than statutory or under the prerogative. There is a certain imprecision in the use of the term "prerogative" in this connection, as Professor Sir William Wade makes clear in another Child & Co. Oxford Lecture, "Procedure and Prerogative in Public Law" (1985) 101 L.Q.R. 180. Strictly the term "prerogative" should be confined to those powers which are unique to the Crown. As Professor Wade points out, there was nothing unique in the creation by the government, out of funds voted by Parliament, of a scheme for the compensation of victims of violent crime. Any foundation or trust, given sufficient money, could have done the same thing. Nor do I think that the distinction between the Criminal Injuries Compensation Board and a private foundation or trust for the same purposes lies in the source of the funds. The distinction must lie in the nature of the duty imposed, whether expressly or by implication. If the duty is a public duty, then the body in question is subject to public law.

So once again one comes back to what I regard as the true view, that it is not just the source of the power that matters, but also the nature of the duty. I can see nothing in *R.* v. *Criminal Injuries Compensation Board, ex p. Lain* [1967] 2 Q.B. 864 which contradicts that view, or compels us to decide that, in non-statutory cases, judicial review is confined to bodies created under the prerogative, whether in the strict sense, or in the wider sense in which that word has now come to be used. Indeed, the passage from Diplock L.J.'s judgment, at p. 884, which Sir John Donaldson M.R. has already read, points in the opposite direction.

But suppose I am wrong: suppose that the courts are indeed confined to looking at the source of the power, as Mr. Alexander submits. Then I would accept Mr. Lever's submission that the source of the power in the present case is indeed governmental, at least in part. Mr. Alexander argued that, so far from the source of the power being governmental, this is a case where the government has deliberately abstained from exercising power. I do not take that view. I agree with Mr. Lever when he says that there has been an implied devolution of power. Power exercised behind the scenes is power nonetheless. The express powers conferred on inferior tribunals were of critical importance in the early days when the sole or main ground for intervention by the courts was that the inferior tribunal had exceeded its powers. But those days are long since past. Having regard to the way in which the panel came to be established, the fact that the Governor of the Bank of England appoints both the chairman and the deputy chairman, and the other matters to which Sir John Donaldson M.R. has referred, I am persuaded that the panel was established "under authority of the Government," to use the language of Diplock L.J. in *Lain's* case. If in addition to looking at the source of the power we are entitled to look at the nature of the power, as I believe we are, then the case is all the stronger.

Before leaving Mr. Alexander's second argument, I should mention one last point. The jurisdiction of the court to grant relief by way of judicial review is now, of course, recognised by section 31 of the Supreme

Court Act 1981. Section 31(1)(*a*) refers specifically to the old prerogative writs, namely mandamus, prohibition and certiorari. Section 31(1)(*b*) and (2) provide that in an application for judicial review, the court may grant a declaration or injunction if it is just or convenient to do so, having regard to various matters. I have already referred to the passage in Woolf J.'s judgment in *R.* v. *British Broadcasting Corporation, ex p. Lavelle* [1983] 1 W.L.R. 23, 31, in which he says that applications for judicial review under R.S.C., Ord. 53, r. 1(2) are not confined to those cases where relief could be granted by way of prerogative order. As at present advised, I would agree with that observation. I would only add as a rider that section 31(1) of the Supreme Court Act 1981 should not be treated as having put a stop to all further development of the law relating to the prerogative remedies. I do not accept Mr. Alexander's submission that we are here extending the law. But if we were, I would not regard that as an insuperable objection. The prerogative writs have always been a flexible instrument for doing justice. In my judgment they should remain so.

NICHOLLS L.J. delivered a concurring judgment.

Notes

1. In relation to the *practical issue*, counsel for the panel argued that the court having and exercising jurisdiction to review the decisions of the panel would have disastrous consequences. Even unmeritorious applications for judicial review would dislocate the operation of the market during the pendency of proceedings; rulings by the panel were required to have speed and certainty.

In response, Sir John Donaldson noted (1) that a panel decision would remain effective unless set aside; (2) the court retained a discretion whether to grant a remedy; (3) the courts were aware of the need for speed; and (4) an applicant needed leave to make an application. The panel and those affected by its decisions should treat them as valid and binding, unless and until they were set aside.

There would be little scope for complaint that the panel had promulgated rules that were *ultra vires*, save in the unlikely eventuality that they violated the principle, proclaimed by the panel, of being based on the concept of doing equity between one shareholder and another. In interpreting the rules, considerable latitude would be given to the panel, both because they were the legislators, and because the rules laid down principles to be applied in spirit as much as in letter. Moreover, the court might well decline to quash an interpretative decision, instead granting a declaration as to the true meaning of the rule, and leaving it to the panel to promulgate a new rule accurately expressing its intentions.

As regards the panel's disciplinary function, the internal right of appeal should be exercised before the court could consider intervening. The only circumstances where the use of certiorari would be anticipated would be where there was a breach of natural justice.

Sir John Donaldson concluded that the limitations in practice to the scope of intervention by the courts would lead to "a workable and valuable partnership between the courts and the panel in the public interest and would avoid all of the perils to which Mr. Alexander alluded" (p. 842).

The Court of Appeal returned to some of these issues in *R.* v. *Panel on Take-overs and Mergers, ex p. Guinness plc* [1990] 1 Q.B. 146. Here the court rejected applications for declarations that the panel had acted unfairly in refusing to adjourn a hearing into allegations that Guinness, under its previous management, had acted "in concert" with a third party in purchasing shares in Distillers, a take-over target, this being contrary to the City Code. Lord Donaldson referred to the point he made in *Datafin* that he would expect the relationship between the panel and the court to be historic rather than contemporaneous (above, p. 699), said that this had been "misunderstood, at least by academic writers," and commented (pp. 158–159):

> "When the take-over is in progress the time scales involved are so short and the need of the markets and those dealing in them to be able to rely on the rulings of the panel so great, that contemporary intervention by the court will usually either be impossible or contrary to the public interest. Furthermore it is important that this should be known, as otherwise attempts would undoubtedly be made to undermine the authority of the panel by tactical applications for judicial review. On the other hand, once the immediate problem has been dealt with by the panel, no similar objections would apply to a retrospective review of its actions designed to avoid the repetition of error, if error there has been. And when it comes to disciplinary action by the panel, which necessarily will be taken in retrospect and with all due deliberation, the court will find itself in its traditional position of protecting the individual from any abuse of power."

As to the *grounds* of challenge,

> "Illegality would certainly apply if the panel acted in breach of the general law, but it is more difficult to apply in the context of an alleged misinterpretation of its own rules by a body which under the scheme is both legislator and interpreter. Irrationality, at least in the sense of failing to take account of relevant factors or taking account of irrelevant factors, is a difficult concept in the context of a body which is itself charged with the duty of making a judgment on what is and what is not relevant, although clearly a theoretical scenario could be constructed in which the panel acted on the basis of considerations which on any view must have been irrelevant or ignored something which on any view must have been relevant. And similar problems arise with procedural impropriety in the narrow sense of failing to follow accepted procedures, given the nature of the panel and of its functions and the lack of any statutory or other guidance as to its procedures which are intended to be of its own devising. Similarly, in the broad sense of breach of the rules of natural justice, what is or is not fair may depend on underlying value judgments by the panel as to the time scale which is appropriate for decision, the consequences of delay and matters of that kind. Approaching the problem on the basis of separate grounds for relief may at once bring several interlocking and mutually inconsistent considerations into play—were the underlying judgments tainted by illegality or irrationality? If not, accepting those judgments, was the action unfair? If the underlying judgments were so tainted, was the action unfair on the basis of judgments which might reasonably have been made? The permutations, if not endless, are considerable and confusing.
>
> It may be that the true view is that in the context of a body whose constitution, functions and powers are sui generis, the court should review the panel's acts and omissions more in the round than might otherwise be the case and, whilst basing its decision on familiar concepts, should eschew any formal categorisation."

(pp. 159–160).

On *Datafin*, see P. Cane, "Self Regulation and Judicial Review" (1987) 6 C.J.Q. 324; L. Hilliard, (1987) 50 M.L.R. 372; H. W. R. Wade, (1987) 103 L.Q.R. 323; C. F. Forsyth, [1987] P.L. 356; C. J. Kinsella, [1987] C.L.J. 200; J. Beatson, "The courts and the regulators" (1987) 3 P.N. 121. More generally on the Panel, see Lord Alexander of Weedon, "Judicial Review and City Regulators" (1989) 52 M.L.R. 640, J. Jowell, "The Take-over Panel: Autonomy, Flexibility and Legality" [1991] P.L. 149 and G. K. Morse "The City Code on Takeovers and Mergers—Self-Regulation or Self Protection" [1991] J.B.L. 509.

2. Prior to the establishment of the application for judicial review, the analogous issue to that considered in *Datafin* was the scope of the prerogative orders of prohibition and certiorari. It was held that these orders lay to bodies performing a public duty, such as inferior courts, (*e.g.* an election court: *R.* v. *Cripps, ex p. Muldoon* [1984] Q.B. 686), statutory tribunals, individuals exercising public functions, (*e.g. R.* v. *Kent Police Authority, ex p. Godden*: above, p. 566), ministers of the crown, government bodies and bodies established under the royal prerogative, (*e.g. R.* v. *Criminal Injuries Compensation Board, ex p. Lain*: considered in *Datafin*, above, p. 693). They did not lie against the Crown; to a body which had no legal authority (*Re Clifford and O'Sullivan* [1921] 2 A.C. 570: a military court acting under martial law, and not under statute law or the common law, which was to be regarded as a body of military officers advising the military commander); to a non-statutory arbitrator (*R.* v. *Disputes Committee of Dental Technicians* [1953] 1 Q.B. 704); to a legislative assembly (*R.* v. *Church Assembly, ex p. Haynes-Smith* [1928] 1 K.B. 411) or to a body exercising authority by virtue of a contract (*R.* v. *Post Office, ex p. Byrne* [1975] I.C.R. 221).

3. Initially, a similar approach was adopted as regards the scope of the application for judicial review. In particular, bodies exercising jurisdiction by virtue of a contract were held not to be subject to judicial review (*cf.* Lloyd L.J. in *Datafin*, above, p. 696). In *R.* v. *British Broadcasting Corporation, ex p. Lavelle* [1983] 1 W.L.R. 23, Miss Lavelle, a BBC employee, was charged with the theft of tapes from the BBC. Pending her trial at the Crown Court, the BBC instituted disciplinary proceedings against her, leading to a decision that she be dismissed. Only one hour's notice of the initial disciplinary interview was given, and she was unable to arrange to be accompanied by a union or other representative, as allowed by the BBC's disciplinary procedure. Although she still had the right to appeal to the Director General of the BBC, she applied for judicial review of the decision to dismiss. Woolf J. was clear that this procedure was inappropriate (see the passage cited in Lloyd L.J.'s judgment, above, p. 697). With the consent of the parties, Woolf J. proceeded, under Ord. 53 r. 9(5), to consider the case on the basis that the action had been begun by writ. He concluded (1) that the court did have jurisdiction to grant an injunction or declaration in an employment situation of the kind involved here; but (2) that on the facts, no relief would be granted (*cf.* above, p. 492).

Moreover, in *Law* v. *National Greyhound Racing Club Ltd.* [1983] 1 W.L.R. 1302, the Court of Appeal refused to strike out claims for declaration against the NGRC, a company limited by guarantee which acted as the judicial body for the discipline and conduct of greyhound racing in Great Britain. The stewards suspended the plaintiff's trainer's licence for six months because he had in his charge a greyhound that had been doped. The plaintiff issued an originating summons seeking declarations that this decision was ultra vires. The court rejected the NGRC's argument that the plaintiff should have applied for judicial review, holding that the NGRC was not in any event amenable to judicial review. The pre-1978 authorities such as *R.* v. *Criminal Injuries Compensation Board, ex p. Lain* [1967] 2 Q.B. 864, 882 and *R.* v. *Post Office, ex p. Byrne* [1975] I.C.R. 221 were clear that the prerogative orders did not lie to domestic tribunals. The position had not been changed by the new Order 53, and, in particular, the enactment of section 31 of the Supreme Court Act 1981.

per Lawton L.J. at p. 1308:

"The nature of the matters with which the plaintiff's originating summons deals is the alleged abuse of power by the stewards. Abuse of power, submitted Mr.

Henderson, was a matter with which prerogative orders dealt. The circumstances of the case involved the public interest because of the need to stamp out malpractices in greyhound racing. Although prerogative orders had not in the past been made against domestic tribunals, in this case 'it would be just and convenient' for the declarations asked for by the plaintiff to be made or refused. Mr. Henderson saw no difficulty in the fact that when the court had regard to 'the nature of the persons and bodies against whom relief may be granted by orders of mandamus, prohibition or certiorari,' it would find that domestic tribunals were not amongst them. All the subsection required the court to do was to have regard to this factor. If, despite its absence, the court was of the opinion that it was just and convenient to make the declaration it could do so.

I cannot accept this submission. The purpose of section 31 is to regulate procedure in relation to judicial reviews, not to extend the jurisdiction of the court. It puts into statutory language, with modifications, what is in Order 53 of the Rules of The Supreme Court. That Order 'introduced a most beneficent reform in the practice and procedure relating to administrative law': see the note 53/1–14/1 in *THE SUPREME COURT PRACTICE* 1982, vol. 1, p. 865. It did not purport to enlarge the jurisdiction of the court so as to enable it to review the decisions of domestic tribunals."

per Slade L.J. at pp. 1313–1315:

"... in my opinion, it is plain that, apart from any changes in law or procedure which may have been effected by section 31 of the Supreme Court Act 1981, the present is not a case where the process of judicial review would have been open to the plaintiff. Mr. Henderson, however, has submitted, as the main feature of his argument, that section 31 makes it not only possible, but obligatory, for the plaintiff to use the process of judicial review for the purpose of seeking the declarations and injunctions which he seeks by his originating summons.

Section 29(1) of the Act of 1981 provides:

> "the High Court shall have jurisdiction to make orders of mandamus, prohibition and certiorari in those classes of cases in which it had power to do so immediately before the commencement of this Act."

The wording of this subsection, in my opinion, shows that the Act was not intended to extend the jurisdiction of the court to make orders of mandamus, prohibition and certiorari, and I did not understand Mr. Henderson to contend otherwise. I therefore think it clear that the court would not have jurisdiction to make orders of this nature at the suit of the plaintiff in the present case.

Mr. Henderson, however, pointed out that, omitting immaterial words, section 31(1) of the Act of 1981 provides:

> "An application to the High Court for ... (*b*) a declaration or injunction under subsection (2) ... shall be made in accordance with rules of court by a procedure to be known as an application for judicial review."

The mandatory word "shall," which does not appear in the R.S.C. Ord. 53, in his submission, renders it obligatory to apply to the court by way of an application for judicial review in any case where the relief sought is a declaration or injunction falling within subsection (2). The provisions of subsection (2) are set out in the judgment of Lawton L.J.

In relation to paragraph (*a*) of that subsection Mr. Henderson submitted that the nature of the matters in respect of which relief might be granted by the three traditional prerogative orders included, *inter alia*, excess of jurisdiction, abuse of power, misconstruction of a relevant power-giving rule, denial of natural justice and bias. He referred us to certain rules of the N.G.R.C. (for example, rules 160(*e*) and 163) which, he submitted, indicated that their stewards' inquiries had all the hallmarks of a quasi-judicial inquiry. The nature of the plaintiff's complaint, he submitted, is such that proceedings for judicial review would undoubtedly be the appropriate procedure if the N.G.R.C. were a body created by statute, or statutory instrument or Royal Charter. It is important in the public interest that any questioning of the powers of the stewards of the N.G.R.C., or the exercise of such powers, should take place promptly. In all the circumstances of the case, he submitted, justice and convenience requires that the stewards should have the benefit of the protections available to persons and bodies against whom relief is sought by way of judicial review. In his submission such protections ought to be available, provided that the nature of the matter is such that relief might be granted by one of the traditional prerogative orders and all the circumstances render it just and convenient for the declaration sought to be made or the injunction sought to be granted. If this is so it matters not that the respondent to the application is a person or body against whom relief could not be granted by such traditional orders. Though the court must "have regard to" the matters mentioned in paragraph (*b*) of section 31(2), so it said, the paragraph does not absolutely preclude the court from granting relief by way of declaration or injunction on an application for judicial review, in an appropriate case, against such a respondent.

I accept that the wording of section 31(2) does not explicitly confine applications for injunctions or declarations by way of judicial review to cases where, on the particular facts, orders for mandamus, prohibition or certiorari could appropriately be granted. Nevertheless, paragraphs (*a*) and (*b*) of section 31(2) must, in my opinion, be read together with section 29(1) of the Act of 1981, which restricts the court, in making orders of mandamus, prohibition and certiorari, to "those classes of cases in which it had power to do so immediately before the commencement of this Act." It is thus, in my opinion, clear that even since the passing of the Act, on an application for judicial review, the court would have no jurisdiction to make an order in any of these three traditional forms in respect of a private law dispute arising out of a contractual relationship between the N.G.R.C. and one of its licence-holders, whether or not the court would have otherwise thought it just and convenient to grant such relief. In these circumstances it would be anomalous in the extreme if the effect of the Act was to confer on the court a new jurisdiction on an application for judicial review to grant an injunction or declaration in respect of a private law dispute of this nature. I do not think that section 31 compels, or indeed permits, such an interpretation. If the court in such a case where to grant relief by way of declaration or injunction in purported exercise of its powers under section 31(2), it would be acting not so much "having regard to" the factors mentioned in paragraphs (*a*) and (*b*) as in flagrant disregard of such factors."

Similarly, decisions of the Jockey Club and the Football Association have been held not to be amenable to judicial review (*R.* v. *Jockey Club, ex p. Massingberd-Mundy, The Times*, January 3, 1990, [1990] C.O.D. 260, and *R.* v. *Jockey Club, ex p. RAM Racecourses Ltd., The Times*, April 6, 1990, [1990] C.O.D. 346; *R.* v. *Football Association of Wales, ex p. Flint Town United Football Club* [1991] C.O.D. 44; *R.* v. *Football Association Ltd., ex p. The Football League Ltd., The Times*, August 22, 1991). In *ex p. Massingberd-Mundy*, the Divisional Court stated that if the matter had been free from authority it might (Neill L.J.) or would (Roch J.) have concluded that at least some decisions of the Jockey Club related to quasi-public functions amenable to judicial review; however, the point was concluded by the decision of the Court of Appeal in *Law*. In *R.* v. *Royal Life Saving Society, ex p. Heather Rose Mary Howe* [1990] C.O.D. 440, the Court of Appeal held that the decision of the Society not to conduct a formal inquiry into complaints against the applicant, one of its examiners, was not subject to judicial review. The fact that the Society had been incorporated by Royal Charter "was a factor of very little, if any, weight." The applicable grievance was a private grievance with no element of public law.

D. Pannick ([1992] P.L. 1) argues that the courts have taken an unduly restrictive approach to the scope of judicial review. The key question should be whether a body exercises monopolistic powers. If it does, judicial review should not be ruled out on the basis of a consensual submission to jurisdiction, as the individual in question has "no effective choice but to comply with their rules, regulations and decisions in order to operate in that area" (p. 3). Moreover, it should not be necessary to speculate as to what Parliament would do but for the existence of the body in question; the fact that powers are monopolistic is sufficient itself to justify the imposition of minimum standards on the substance and procedure of decision-making in that context (p. 6).

4. Outside the sporting field, it has been held that a decision of the Chief Rabbi in respect of the dismissal of a Rabbi was not subject to judicial review (*R.* v. *The Chief Rabbi, ex p. Watchmann* [1991] C.O.D. 309). To attract the court's supervisory jurisdiction there had to be not merely a public but potentially a governmental interest in the decision-making power in question. It could not be suggested that but for the office of the Chief Rabbi, the government would impose a statutory regime. By contrast, decisions of the Rabbinical Commission, chaired by the Chief Rabbi, in the exercise of statutory licensing functions under the Slaughterhouses Act 1974, Sched. 1, were subject to judicial review (*R.* v. *Rabbinical Commission, ex p. Cohen*, Unreported, December 14, 1987, C.A.). Similarly, in *R.* v. *Imam of Bury Park Jame Masjid, Luton, ex p. Sulaiman Ali, The Independent*, September 13, 1991, the Imam's decision that the applicants were not eligible to vote in the election of the executive committee of a mosque was held not to be subject to judicial review. It lacked the requisite public element, and involved matters intimate to a religious community.

5. The position is more difficult where the institution is a statutory body, which is clearly amenable to judicial review in respect of its statutory functions, but which is dealing with what is arguably a contractual matter. This situation was considered in *R.* v. *East Berkshire Health Authority, ex p. Walsh* (below, p. 705). Cases near the borderline where a public authority has been held to be performing a public function include *R.* v. *Secretary of State for the Home Department, ex p. Benwell* [1985] Q.B. 554, where the dismissal of a prison officer was held to be subject to judicial review; the officer had no private law rights that could be enforced in civil proceedings. (See M. Stokes, (1985) 14 I.L.J. 117 and Y. Cripps, [1985] C.L.J. 177.) However, in *McClaren* v. *Home Office* [1990] I.C.R. 824, the Court of Appeal held that it was at least arguable that the relationship between the Home Office and prison officers was a contractual one. See further, below, p. 710. Another example is *R.* v. *Kidderminster District Valuer, ex p. Powell, The Times*, July 23, 1991, where the Divisional Court held that the valuation by the district valuer of a particular house for the purpose of determining the maximum limit of rent allowance payable to a police officer under the Police Regulations 1987 (S.I. 1987 No. 851), reg. 49(4)(*b*), was a public function subject to judicial review. It was a function performed within the statutory framework of the regulations and had important public elements.

6. Other non-statutory bodies which have been held to be amenable to judicial review include the following: a hospital ethics committee (*R.* v. *Ethical Committee of St. Mary's Hospital, ex p. Harriott* [1988] 1 F.L.R. 512 (see A. Grubb and D. Pearl, [1988] C.L.J. 167)); the Civil Service Appeal Board, which is a non-statutory body established under the royal prerogative to hear appeals against the dismissal

of civil servants (*R.* v. *Civil Service Appeal Board, ex p. Bruce* [1979] I.C.R. 171); the Advertising Standards Authority, a non-statutory body that regulates advertisers (*R.* v. *Advertising Standards Authority Ltd., ex p. The Insurance Service plc* [1990] C.O.D. 42); the Professional Conduct Committee of the General Council of the Bar (*R.* v. *General Council of the Bar, ex p. Percival* [1991] 1 Q.B. 212); the Code of Practice Committee of the Association of the British Pharmaceutical Industry, a voluntary self-regulating body whose Code of Practice had emerged in its present form as a result of consultation with the Department of Health (*R.* v. *Code of Practice Committee of the Association of the British Pharmaceutical Industry, ex p. Professional Counselling Aids Ltd.* [1991] C.O.D. 228); LAUTRO (*R.* v. *Life Assurance Trust Regulatory Organisation, ex p. Ross* [1992] 1 All E.R. 422); FIMBRA (*R.* v. *Financial Intermediaries Managers and Brokers Regulatory Association, ex p. Cochrane* [1991] B.C.L.C. 106: concession by counsel for FIMBRA); and a university visitor (*R.* v. *Visitor of the University of Hull, ex p. Page* [1991] 1 W.L.R. 1277).

7. Where a function falls in general within the scope of judicial review, there must still be a *decision* in the exercise of that function if an application is to be entertained. In *R.* v. *London Waste Regulation Authority, ex p. Specialist Waste Management Ltd., The Times*, November 1, 1988, an expression of opinion, to a person using plant to dispose of "controlled waste" within the meaning of the Control of Pollution Act 1974, to the effect that he required a disposal licence, was held not to be amenable to judicial review. It was not a decision to which the applicant had to conform. Similarly, in *R.* v. *Devon County Council, ex p. L.* [1991] C.O.D. 205, Eastham J. held that a letter from the council responding to a request that social workers refrained from disseminating the belief that L. was a child sex abuser, in the absence of a case conference or other proceedings, was not a "decision" amenable to judicial review: the letter dealt solely with what had occurred in the past and did not deal with the assurance requested. *Cf. R.* v. *Secretary of State for the Environment, ex p. London Borough of Greenwich, The Times*, May 17, 1989 (decision to issue leaflet on the community charge potentially open to judicial review for abuse of discretion: see C. R. Munro, [1990] P.L. 1, 7–9); *R.* v. *Secretary of State for Employment, ex p. Equal Opportunities Commission* [1992] 1 All E.R. 545.

8. For general surveys of the scope of judicial review post-*Datafin*, see M. J. Beloff, "The Boundaries of Judicial Review"; D. Pannick, "What is a Public Authority for the Purposes of Judicial Review" in J. Jowell and D. Oliver, *New Directions in Judicial Review* (1988), pp. 5 and 23; and *Lewis*, Ch. 2.

R. v. EAST BERKSHIRE HEALTH AUTHORITY, ex p. WALSH

[1985] Q.B. 152; [1985] 3 W.L.R. 818; [1984] I.C.R. 743;
[1984] 3 All E.R. 425 (Court of Appeal) (pet. dis.,
[1984] 1 W.L.R. 1357, H.L.)

The applicant, a senior nursing officer employed by the health authority under a contract which incorporated the Whitley Council agreement on conditions of service in the health service, was dismissed by a district nursing officer for misconduct. He applied for judicial review under R.S.C., Ord. 53 for an order of certiorari to quash the dismissal on the grounds that the district nursing officer had no power to dismiss him and that there had been a breach of the rules of natural justice in the procedure which led up to his dismissal. The health authority raised the preliminary point whether the subject matter of the application entitled the applicant to apply for judicial review. The judge held that, although the public might have no interest in an ordinary master and servant case, the public was concerned to see that a great public service acted lawfully and fairly to its officers and the remedy of an order of certiorari would be an appropriate remedy. Alternatively, the judge held that it would be appropriate to allow the proceedings to continue under Ord. 53 r. 9(5), as if they had been begun by writ. The Court of Appeal allowed an appeal by the health authority.

SIR JOHN DONALDSON M.R.: . . . I now return to the main issue, namely whether the applicant's complaints give rise to any right to judicial review. They all relate to his employment by the health authority and the purported termination of his employment and of his contract of employment. Essentially they fall into two distinct categories. The first relates to Miss Cooper's power to act on behalf of the authority in dismissing him. The second relates to the extent to which there was any departure from the rules of natural justice in the procedures which led up to that dismissal. Both fall well within the jurisdiction of an industrial tribunal. The first goes to whether or not the applicant was dismissed at all within the meaning of section 55 of the Employment Protection (Consolidation) Act 1978. The second goes to whether the dismissal, if such there was, was unfair. Furthermore, both are issues which not uncommonly arise when the employer is a company or individual, as contrasted with a statutory authority. However, this only goes to the exercise of the court's discretion, whether or not to give leave to apply for and whether or not to grant judicial review. As the authority seek to have the proceedings dismissed in limine, if they are to succeed they can only do so on the basis that, accepting all the applicant's complaints as valid, the remedy of judicial review is nevertheless wholly inappropriate and the continuance of the application for judicial review would involve a misuse—the term "abuse" has offensive overtones—of the procedure of the court under R.S.C., Ord. 53.

The remedy of judicial review is only available where an issue of "public law" is involved, but, as Lord Wilberforce pointed out in *Davy* v. *Spelthorne Borough Council* [1984] A.C. 262, 276, the expressions "public law" and "private law" are recent immigrants and, whilst convenient for descriptive purposes, must be used with caution, since English law traditionally fastens not so much upon principles as upon remedies. On the other hand, to concentrate on remedies would in the present context involve a degree of circularity or levitation by traction applied to shoestrings, since the remedy of certiorari might well be available if the health authority is in breach of a "public law" obligation, but would not be if it is only in breach of a "private law" obligation.

The judge referred carefully and fully to *Vine* v. *National Dock Labour Board* [1957] A.C. 488; *Ridge* v. *Baldwin* [1964] A.C. 40 and *Malloch* v. *Aberdeen Corporation* [1971] 1 W.L.R. 1578. He seems to have accepted that there was no "public law" element in an "ordinary" relationship of master and servant and that accordingly in such a case judicial review would not be available. However, he held, on the basis of these three cases and, in particular, *Malloch's* case, that the applicant's relationship was not "ordinary." He said:

"The public may have no interest in the relationship between servant and master in an 'ordinary' case, but where the servant holds office in a great public service, the public is properly concerned to see that the authority employing him acts towards him lawfully and fairly. It is not a pure question of contract. The public is concerned that the nurses who serve the public should be treated lawfully and fairly by the public authority employing them.... It follows that if in the exercise of my discretion I conclude that the remedy of certiorari is appropriate, it can properly go against the respondent authority."

The judge then said that if he was wrong in this conclusion, it would be appropriate to allow the proceedings to continue as if they had been begun by writ: see R.S.C., Ord. 53, r. 9(5).

None of the three decisions of the House of Lords to which I have referred was directly concerned with the scope of judicial review under R.S.C., Ord. 53. Two, *Ridge* v. *Baldwin* [1964] A.C. 40 and *Malloch* v. *Aberdeen Corporation* [1971] 1 W.L.R. 1578, were concerned with whether or not the plaintiff had a right to be heard before being dismissed and the third, *Vine* v. *National Dock Labour Board* [1957] A.C. 488, with whether the body purporting to dismiss was acting ultra vires. *Vine's* case and *Ridge's* case were actions begun by writ. *Malloch's* case was a Scottish proceeding in which the remedy of "production and reduction" was claimed. This is indeed akin to certiorari, but it is available whether or not the claim involves "public" or "administrative" law. There are, however, dicta, particularly in the speech of Lord Wilberforce in *Malloch's* case, which may be thought to point the way in which we should go.

[His Lordship then considered passages by Lord Reid in *Ridge* v. *Baldwin* (above, p. 475), and by Lords Reid and Wilberforce in *Malloch* (above, p. 492.)]

In all three cases there was a special statutory provision bearing directly upon the right of a public authority to dismiss the plaintiff. In *Vine* v. *National Dock Labour Board* [1957] A.C. 488 the employment was under the statutory dock labour scheme and the issue concerned the statutory power to dismiss given by that scheme. In *Ridge* v. *Baldwin* [1964] A.C. 40 the power of dismissal was conferred by statute: section 191(4) of the Municipal Corporations Act 1882 (45 & 46 Vict. c. 50). In *Malloch* v. *Aberdeen Corporation* [1971] 1 W.L.R. 1578 again it was statutory: section 3 of the Public Schools (Scotland) Teachers Act 1882 (45 & 46 Vict. c. 18). As Lord Wilberforce said, at pp. 1595–1596, it is the existence of these statutory provisions which injects the element of public law necessary in this context to attract the remedies of administrative law. Employment by a public authority does not *per se* inject any element of public law. Nor does the fact that the employee is in a "higher grade" or is an "officer." This only makes it more likely that there will be special statutory restrictions upon dismissal, or other underpinning of his employment: see *per* Lord Reid in *Malloch* v. *Aberdeen Corporation*, at p. 1582. It will be this underpinning and not the seniority which injects the element of public law. Still less can I find any warrant for equating public law with the interest of the public. If the public through Parliament gives effect to that interest by means of statutory provisions, that is quite different, but the interest of the public *per se* is not sufficient.

I have therefore to consider whether and to what extent the applicant's complaints involve an element of public law sufficient to attract public law remedies, whether in the form of certiorari or a declaration. That he had the benefit of the general employment legislation is clear, but it was not contended that this was sufficient to attract administrative law remedies. What is relied upon are statutory restrictions upon the freedom of the authority to employ senior and other nursing officers on what terms it thought fit. This restriction is contained in the National Health Service (Remuneration and Conditions of Service) Regulations 1974 (S.I. 1974 No. 296), which provides by regulation 3(2):

> "Where conditions of service, other than conditions with respect to remuneration, of any class of officers have been the subject of negotiations by a negotiating body and have been approved by the Secretary of State after considering the result of those negotiations, the conditions of service of any officer belonging to that class shall include the conditions so approved."

The conditions of service of, *inter alios*, senior nursing officers were the subject of negotiations by a negotiating body, namely the Whitley Council for the Health Service (Great Britain) and the resulting agreement was approved by the Secretary of State. It follows, as I think, that if the applicant's conditions of service had differed from those approved conditions, he would have had an administrative law remedy by way of judicial review enabling him to require the authority to amend the terms of service contained in his contract of employment. But that is not the position. His notification of employment dated May 12, 1975, which is a memorandum of his contract of employment, expressly adopted the Whitley Council agreement on conditions of service.

When analysed, the applicant's complaint is different. It is that *under* those conditions of service Miss Cooper had no right to dismiss him and that *under* those conditions he was entitled to a bundle of rights which can be collectively classified as "natural justice." Thus he says, and I have to assume for present purposes that he is correct, that under section XXXIV of the Whitley Council's agreement on conditions of service, his position as a senior nursing officer is such that his employment can only be terminated by a decision of the full employing authority and that this power of dismissal cannot be delegated to any officer or committee of officers. I do not think that he relies upon any express provision of those conditions when claiming the right to natural justice, but if he has such a right, apart from the wider right not to be unfairly dismissed which includes the right to natural justice, it clearly arises out of those conditions and is implicit in them.

The ordinary employer is free to act in breach of his contracts of employment and if he does so his employee will acquire certain private law rights and remedies in damages for wrongful dismissal, compensation for unfair dismissal, an order for reinstatement or re-engagement and so on. Parliament can underpin the position of public authority employees by directly restricting the freedom of the public authority to dismiss, thus giving the employee "public law" rights and at least making him a potential candidate for administrative law remedies. Alternatively it can require the authority to contract with its employees on specified terms with a view to the employee acquiring "private law" rights under the terms of the contract of employment. If the authority fails or refuses to thus create "private law" rights for the employee, the employee will have "public law" rights to compel compliance, the remedy being mandamus requiring the authority so to contract or a declaration that the employee has those rights. If, however, the authority gives the employee the required contractual protection, a breach of that contract is not a matter of "public law" and gives rise to no administrative law remedies. . . .

I therefore conclude that there is no "public law" element in the applicant's complaints which could give rise to any entitlement to administrative law remedies. I confess that I am not sorry to have been led to this conclusion, since a contrary conclusion would have enabled *all* National Health Service employees to whom the Whitley Council agreement on conditions of service apply to seek judicial review. Whilst it is true that the judge seems to have thought that this right would be confined to senior employees, I see no grounds for any such restriction in principle. The most that can be said is that only senior employees could complain of having been dismissed in the exercise of delegated authority, because it is only senior employees who are protected from such dismissal. *All* employees would, however, have other rights based upon the fact that Parliament had intervened to specify and, on this view, protect those conditions of service as a matter of "public law."

In my judgment, this is not therefore a case for judicial review.

There remains the alternative of allowing the matter to proceed pursuant to R.S.C., Ord. 53, r. 9(5) as "if it had been sought in an action begun by writ." This is an anti-technicality rule. It is designed to preserve the position of an applicant for relief, who finds that the basis of *that relief* is private law rather than public law. It is not designed to allow him to amend and to claim different relief.

Only two species of relief are claimed by the notice of application, namely certiorari and prohibition. Prohibition is no longer sought and certiorari is a purely public law remedy. If R.S.C., Ord. 53, r. 9(5) is to be applied in the applicant's case, it can only be on the basis that the passing reference in his affidavit to "a declaration" is sufficient to justify the court in ordering the proceedings to continue as if a declaration had been sought in an action begun by writ. But if a declaration had been so sought, its terms would have been defined, if not in the writ, at least in the statement of claim. Yet in the 592 pages of documentation before Hodgson J. the terms of the declaration are never mentioned. Even in this court all that has been achieved, under pressure from the court, is a few lines indicating the type of declarations which might be sought if leave were given to amend to seek declarations. Furthermore, it seems likely that the applicant will want to claim damages, although there is no hint of that in the papers, and may also want to claim accrued wages, *i.e.* to have a judgment in debt, but that is outside the scope of R.S.C., Ord. 53. Accordingly I would not allow the applicant to continue the proceedings under R.S.C., Ord. 53, r. 9(5) and claim declaratory relief. I consider that costs will be saved and the issues emerge much more clearly if the applicant issues a writ and properly formulates what relief, if any, he is really seeking in addition or in the alternative to his claim for unfair dismissal. . . .

I would allow the appeal and order that the applicant's application for judicial review be dismissed.

MAY and PURCHAS L.JJ. delivered concurring speeches.

Appeal allowed.

Notes

1. See H. Collins, (1984) 13 I.L.J. 174; Y. Cripps, [1984] C.L.J. 214; K. D. Ewing and A. Grubb, (1987) 16 I.L.J. 145, 146–155; B. Walsh, [1989] P.L. 131; S. Fredman and G. S. Morris, [1988] P.L. 58, *The State as Employer* (1989), Chaps. 3 and 7, (1991) 107 L.Q.R. 298 and [1991] P.L. 485; M. R. Freedland, (1990) 19 I.L.J. 199 and (1991) 20 I.L.J. 72.

2. Note the fine distinction drawn between questions concerning the *incorporation* of Whitley Council conditions and the *application* of the approved conditions. Is this distinction workable? Is it perhaps explained by the variant of the familiar "floodgates" argument that appears later in Sir John Donaldson's judgment?

3. In *McClaren* v. *Home Office* [1990] I.C.R. 824, a prison officer was suspended without pay for refusing to work a new shift system. The officer brought a private law action claiming, *inter alia*, a declaration that he was still employed on the basis of the previous shift system and the payment of salary withheld. He contended that the new system was in breach of the Fresh Start collective agreement between the Home Office and the Prison Officers' Association and a local agreement, and that these agreements were incorporated into his contract or his conditions of service. The Court of Appeal refused to strike out the claim, rejecting the Home Office's argument that the officer could only apply for judicial review, and holding that it was at least arguable that the officer had a contractual claim. A helpful analysis was provided by Woolf L.J. (pp. 836–837):

"There are two issues on this appeal. (1) Is the plaintiff required to bring his claim against the Home Office by way of judicial review? (2) If he is not required to bring his proceedings by way of judicial review has he a reasonable cause of action or was his claim correctly struck out as being clearly unsustainable?

The first issue

In resolving this issue the following principles have to be borne in mind.
(1) In relation to his personal claims against an employer, an employee of a

public body is normally in exactly the same situation as other employees. If he has a cause of action and he wishes to assert or establish his rights in relation to his employment he can bring proceedings for damages, a declaration or an injunction (except in relation to the Crown) in the High Court or the county court in the ordinary way. The fact that a person is employed by the Crown may limit his rights against the Crown but otherwise his position is very much the same as any other employee. However, he may, instead of having an ordinary master and servant relationship with the Crown, hold office under the Crown and may have been appointed to that office as a result of the Crown exercising a prerogative power or, as in this case, a statutory power. If he holds such an appointment then it will almost invariably be terminable at will and may be subject to other limitations, but whatever rights the employee has will be enforceable normally by an ordinary action. Not only will it not be necessary for him to seek relief by way of judicial review, it will normally be inappropriate for him to do so: see *Kodeeswaran* v. *Attorney-General of Ceylon* [1970] A.C. 1111; *R.* v. *East Berkshire Health Authority, ex p. Walsh* [1984] I.C.R. 743 and *R.* v. *Derbyshire County Council, ex p. Noble* [1990] I.C.R. 808.

(2) There can however be situations where an employee of a public body can seek judicial review and obtain a remedy which would not be available to an employee in the private sector. This will arise where there exists some disciplinary or other body established under the prerogative or by statute to which the employer or the employee is entitled or required to refer disputes affecting their relationship. The procedure of judicial review can then be appropriate because it has always been part of the role of the court in public law proceedings to supervise inferior tribunals and the court in reviewing disciplinary proceedings is performing a similar role. As long as the 'tribunal' or other body has a sufficient public law element, which it almost invariably will have if the employer is the Crown, and it is not domestic or wholly informal, its proceedings and determination can be an appropriate subject for judicial review. An example is provided here by the decision of the Divisional Court in *R.* v. *Civil Service Appeal Board, ex p. Bruce* [1988] I.C.R. 649. If there had not been available the more effective alternative remedy before an industrial tribunal, the Divisional Court would have regarded the decision of the Civil Service Appeal Board in that case as reviewable upon judicial review. The decision of this court which has just been given in *R.* v. *Secretary of State for the Home Department, ex p. Attard, The Times*, March 14, 1990 [[1990] C.O.D. 261] is another example of the same situation. There what was being considered by this court were the powers of a prison governor in connection with disciplinary proceedings in respect of prison officers. The prison governor's disciplinary powers in relation to prisoners are reviewable only on judicial review (see *Leech* v. *Deputy Governor of Parkhurst Prison* [1988] A.C. 533) and they can also be reviewed on judicial review where they affect a prison officer on the application of that officer.

(3) In addition if an employee of the Crown or other public body is adversely affected by a decision of general application by his employer, but he contends that that decision is flawed on what I loosely describe as *Wednesbury* grounds (*Associated Provincial Picture Houses Ltd.* v. *Wednesbury Corporation* [1948] 1 K.B. 223), he can be entitled to challenge that decision by way of judicial review. Within this category comes *Council of Civil Service Unions* v. *Minister for the Civil Service* [1985] I.C.R. 14. In the House of Lords there was no dispute as to whether the case was appropriately brought by way of judicial review. The House of Lords assumed that it was and I would respectfully suggest that they were right to do so. The decision under challenge was one affecting employees at GCHQ generally. The action which was being challenged was the instruction by the Minister for the Civil Service in the interests of national security to vary the terms and conditions of service of the staff so that they would no longer be

permitted to belong to trade unions. Although the decision affected individual members of the staff, it was a decision which was taken as a matter of policy, not in relation to a particular member of staff, but in relation to staff in general and so it could be the subject of judicial review.

(4) There can be situations where although there are disciplinary procedures which are applicable they are of a purely domestic nature and therefore, albeit that their decisions might affect the public, the process of judicial review will not be available. However this does not mean that a particular employee who is adversely affected by those disciplinary proceedings will not have a remedy. The existence of the disciplinary proceedings may be highly material to indicate that the category of employee concerned, unlike an ordinary employee, is not limited to a claim for damages but can in the appropriate circumstances in an ordinary action seek a declaration or an injunction to ensure that the proceedings are conducted fairly. (As to dismissal see *Ridge* v. *Baldwin* [1964] A.C. 40, 65, *per* Lord Reid; *Law* v. *National Greyhound Racing Club Ltd.* [1983] 1 W.L.R. 1302 and *R.* v. *British Broadcasting Corporation, ex p. Lavelle* [1983] I.C.R. 99.)"

Woolf L.J. concluded that the proceedings here fell with the first of these categories, and that concluded the first issue in favour of the plaintiff. (See also his judgment in *R.* v. *Derbyshire County Council, ex p. Noble* [1990] I.C.R. 808. For comments on *McClaren* and *ex p. Noble,* see H. Carty, (1991) 54 M.C.R. 129.)

4. *Ex p. Walsh* has been applied by Macpherson J. in *R.* v. *Trent Regional Health Authority, ex p. Jones, The Times,* June 19, 1986 (refusal to appoint consultant surgeon not subject to judicial review; no statutory underpinning); by Russell J. in *R.* v. *South Glamorgan Health Authority, ex p. Phillips, The Times,* November 21, 1986 (disciplinary decision of the health authority declared to be of no effect as the disciplinary tribunal had applied the wrong standard of proof; the judge allowed an application for judicial review to be continued as if begun by writ under r. 9(5)); by the Court of Appeal in *R.* v. *Derbyshire County Council, ex p. Noble* [1990] I.C.R. 808 (termination of appointment as deputy police surgeon held not to have a sufficient public law element to attract judicial review) and by Otton J. in *R.* v. *Secretary of State for the Home Department, ex p. Hebron,* Unreported, January 18, 1991 (challenge to dismissal of prison officer held to be a private law matter; leave to apply for judicial review set aside). These seem to fall into Woolf L.J.'s category (1).

5. Other examples of Woolf L.J.'s category (3) include the following. In *R.* v. *Liverpool City Council, ex p. Ferguson, The Times,* November 20, 1985, the council's decision to dismiss all teachers in order to alleviate the consequences of its failure to set a rate sufficient to balance its budget was declared *ultra vires* as it (1) was the direct consequence of setting an illegal rate; (2) was not made for proper educational purposes; and (3) would lead to a breach of the council's duties under the Education Act 1944, s. 8, to secure the provision of sufficient schools (see G. Morris, (1986) 15 I.L.J. 194). In further proceedings involving most of the same parties, *R.* v. *Liverpool City Council, ex p. Ferguson and Ferguson* [1985] I.R.L.R. 501, the council's decision to refuse to pay teachers who presented themselves for work on a "day of action," but who were unable to work because of the actions of other trade unionists, was quashed on the grounds of unreasonableness. Mann J., applying a statement by Sir John Donaldson M.R. in *R.* v. *Herefordshire County Council, ex p. N.U.P.E.* [1985] I.R.L.R. 258, 260, held that the allegation of *Wednesbury* unreasonableness rendered the matter justiciable by way of judicial review. This broad approach is criticised by Bernadette Walsh at [1989] P.L. 131, 149–152, noting that this:

"puts the cart before the horse. The primary question is surely whether the public authority in the performance of a particular function is subject to judicial review. If it is subject to judicial review, then an applicant may challenge the performance of the particular function on the grounds of unreasonableness. The approach advocated by Donaldson M.R. is rather to ask whether the challenge is based on unreasonableness and, if it is, to conclude that the applicant is entitled to judicial review. . . . It is most unlikely that Donaldson M.R intended that the principles in *Walsh* should be subverted by the simple expedient of basing a challenge on this ground." (See also M. Stokes, (1985) 14 I.L.J. 117, 119–120.)

This comment is perhaps echoed by the Divisional Court in *R.* v. *London Borough of Hammersmith and Fulham, ex p. NALGO* [1990] I.R.L.R. 249, where Nolan L.J. stated (at p. 256):

> "I do not believe that Woolf L.J. was saying [in his category (3)] that every policy decision of a public authority affecting its employees as a whole is automatically justiciable as a matter of public law."

Nevertheless, he went on to hold that an allegation, as in the present case, that the adoption by a local authority of an employment or redeployment policy that was in breach of the Sex Discrimination Act or the Race Relations Act or was otherwise unlawful on *Wednesbury* grounds, could be challenged by way of judicial review. On the facts, it could not be shown that the policy as a whole was unlawful. The most that could be said was that the implementation of the policy might offend the law in individual cases, depending on how the implementation was carried out. This could only properly be tested on a case by case basis in pursuance of the applicants' private law remedies.

6. The question of the availability (and possible exclusivity) of judicial review has also arisen in cases concerning civil servants. Here, the long-standing view that civil servants are not employed under a contract of employment has come increasingly into question (see S. Fredman and G. S. Morris, *The State as Employer* (1989), pp. 61–71 and [1988] P.L. 58). It is no longer thought that there is any constitutional bar to the contractual employment of civil servants (*Kodeeswaren* v. *Attorney-General of Ceylon* [1970] A.C. 1111, P.C.), and in *R.* v. *Lord Chancellor's Department, ex p. Nangle* [1991] I.C.R. 743, the Divisional Court held that there could be, and was, the necessary intention to create legal relations (not following the decision to the contrary of the Divisional Court in *R.* v. *Civil Service Appeal Board, ex p. Bruce* [1988] I.C.R. 649). In *ex p. Nangle*, the court concluded that as the applicant was employed by the Crown under a contract of service, then, applying *ex p. Walsh*, he had no remedy in public law. Furthermore, the court concluded that if they were wrong on that point, and there was no contract between the Crown and the civil servant, there was still not a sufficient public law element to attract judicial review: the case arose out of "internal disciplinary proceedings" which were "of a domestic nature" and "informal." (The court seemed to doubt the decision in *R.* v. *Secretary of State for the Home Department, ex p. Benwell* [1985] Q.B. 554, above, p. 704.) (This is alarming. It is one thing to say that a person must pursue contractual remedies rather than judicial review (or vice versa); on this argument the applicant is left without any external remedy.) See S. Fredman and G. S. Morris, [1991] P.L. 485.

7. The recent spate of cases in this area is reviewed by S. Fredman and G. S. Morris, "Public or Private? State Employees and Judicial Review" (1991) 107 L.Q.R. 298. They argue that the state as employer:

> "has characteristics which mean that the exercise of its employment function cannot simply be regarded as a matter for regulation by private law" (p. 315).

These include (pp. 309–312) the source of its power to employ from statute or the prerogative; in the case of central government, its power to endow managerial decisions with the force of law; the exclusive power of the executive to decide issues of national security; the weak arrangements for political accountability to which the state is subject; and the fact that the government derives its revenue to pay employees primarily from taxation, rather than profits. These points require recognition of a public law dimension. However, they argue that current attempts to establish a clear dividing line between the private law and public law dimensions:

> "are haphazard, unpredictable and produce illogical results. . . . It is high time that the quest for the ephemeral dividing line was abandoned. Employment decisions relating to public employees should be considered in a single forum which would enable the public interest in good administration to be secured without prejudice to individual rights" (pp. 315–316).

8. Outside the field of employment, there are a number of cases where the commercial or business decisions of a public body have been held not to be subject to judicial review. In *R.* v. *National Coal Board, ex p. National Union of Mineworkers* [1986] I.C.R. 791, Macpherson J. held that the Board's decision to close a colliery contrary to a recommendation of an independent review body established by itself and the union, was not the subject of judicial review. This was:

> "an executive, or business, or management decision in exactly the same category as a decision in similar circumstances made by a public company" (p. 795).

It was not a decision in the exercise of powers or duties under the Coal Industry Nationalisation Act 1946, which would have been subject to judicial review. Similarly, in *R.* v. *Independent Broadcasting Authority, ex p. Rank Organisation plc, The Times*, March 14, 1986, Mann J. held that the IBA's decision not to permit Rank to exercise voting rights in respect of shares constituting in excess of 5 per cent. of the issued voting shares of Granada, was not subject to judicial review. The power arose under Granada's articles of association and not in the exercise of any function under the Broadcasting Act 1981.

In other contexts, the exercise of the contractual powers of public authorities has been held to be subject to judicial review principles. The courts have sometimes, but not always taken the view that this only follows where there is a public law element in the decision (*cf.* the *East Berkshire* case). See the survey by S. Arrowsmith, "Judicial Review and the Contractual Powers of Public Authorities" (1990) 106 L.Q.R. 277. Judicial review has been held to be applicable to the termination of market trader's licences (*R.* v. *Barnsley Metropolitan Borough Council, ex p. Hook* [1976] 1 W.L.R. 1052, above, p. 604: the council's powers were held to regulate the trader's common law rights to trade in the market; *R.* v. *Basildon District Council, ex p. Brown* (1981) 79 L.G.R. 655: Lord Denning M.R. here regarded all the council's powers as derived from statute and therefore reviewable, Templeman L.J. simply asserted that judicial review was applicable, Dunn L.J. disagreed on this point (see R. Ward, (1982) 45 M.L.R. 588); *R.* v. *Wear Valley District Council, ex p. Binks* [1985] 2 All E.R. 699, above, p. 513: Taylor J. found that there was a public law element as the public had access to the land (see P. Jackson, (1986) 102 L.Q.R. 24); *R.* v. *Durham City Council, ex p. Robinson, The Times*, January 31, 1992). Decisions of local authorities as landlords have been held to be subject to judicial review without the courts seeking to identify a public law element: *Cannock Chase District Council* v. *Kelly* [1978] 1 W.L.R. 1; *Sevenoaks District Council* v. *Emmett* (1979) 79 L.G.R. 346; *Wheeler* v. *Leicester City Council*, above, p. 358; as have procurement decisions: *R.* v. *Lewisham London Borough Council, ex p. Shell U.K.*

Ltd., above, p. 392; *R.* v. *Enfield London Borough Council, ex p. Unwin* [1989] C.O.D. 466.

Arrowsmith (*op. cit.*, p. 291) argues that the courts should "adopt the same approach to the judicial review of contractual powers as they do to the review of other activities of government"; review could be negated or limited by special policy factors, but there would be no need to identify a public law element. The *East Berkshire* case is the main obstacle to such a development. Can it be limited to employment cases?

(D) Procedure

Notes

The application for leave

1. The procedure on an application for judicial review is a two-stage process, modelled on the previous practice in relation to the prerogative orders. The application for leave is made *ex parte* to a judge, although it may be renewed to a Divisional Court (in a criminal case or, otherwise, if the court directs) or to a judge sitting in open court. A statement of the applicant's name and description, the relief sought, the grounds and certain other matters, and an affidavit verifying the facts relied on must be filed. The statement can be amended with the court's consent.

The courts require *uberrima fides* on the part of an applicant. If material facts are suppressed by the applicant in his affidavit, the court may dismiss the application without going into the merits (*R.* v. *Kensington Income Tax Commissioners, ex p. de Polignac* [1917] 1 K.B. 486 (prohibition); *R.* v. *Stevens, ex p. Callender* [1956] C.L.Y. 2160, *The Times*, October 26, 1956; *O'Reilly* v. *Mackman* [1983] 2 A.C. 237, 280; *R.* v. *Secretary of State for the Home Department, ex p. Nachatter Singh, The Times*, August 2, 1985; *R.* v. *British Coal Corporation and Roo Management Ltd., ex p. G.C. Whittaker (Properties) Ltd.* [1989] C.O.D. 528). All matters must be disclosed which are likely to affect the court in exercising its discretion to grant leave. R. 3(2)(*b*) is not limited only to facts of advantage to the applicant's case (*R.* v. *Greenwich JJ., ex p. Aikens, The Times*, July 3, 1982; *R.* v. *Secretary of State for the Home Department, ex p. Mannan, The Times*, March 29, 1984). Where an extension of time is granted on the basis of incomplete disclosure of the material facts the court on the *inter partes* application may reconsider the extension and dismiss the application (*R.* v. *British Railways Board, ex p. Great Yarmouth Borough Council, The Times*, March 15, 1983).

The grant of leave

2. Leave may be refused where the applicant has no reasonable case to put forward: *R.* v. *Hammersmith and Fulham Borough Council, ex p. People Before Profit Ltd.* (1981) 80 L.G.R. 322. In *Inland Revenue Commissioners* v. *National Federation of Self-Employed and Small Businesses Ltd.* [1982] A.C. 617, Lord Diplock suggested at p. 644 that it should be sufficient for an applicant to show that he has an "arguable case" for him to be given leave. Lord Scarman stated at p. 655 that the applicants in that case should have been granted leave had they been able to show reasonable grounds for believing that the board had abused its discretion "or that there was a case to that effect which merited investigation and examination by the court." In *R.* v. *Inspector of Taxes, ex p. Kissane* [1986] 2 All E.R. 37, Nolan J. said (at p. 39) that on an application for leave "it is not for me to delve too deeply into the arguments. I have to be satisfied, before giving leave, that there is at any rate an arguable case. The threshold, if one excludes obviously hopeless claims, is fairly low." In *R.* v. *Secretary of State for the Home Department, ex p. Swati* [1986] 1 W.L.R. 477, Sir John

Donaldson M.R. stated (at p. 485) that "an applicant must show more than that it is not impossible that grounds for judicial review exist. To say that he must show a prima facie case that such grounds do in fact exist may be putting it too high, but he must at least show that it is a real, as opposed to a theoretical, possibility. In other words, he must have an arguable case."

If on the papers in support of the *ex parte* application the judge remains uncertain whether there is an arguable case, he should invite the putative respondent to attend and make representations as to the grant or refusal of leave: only brief arguments should be submitted at such a hearing (*R.* v. *Secretary of State for the Home Department, ex p. Angur Begum* [1990] Imm.A.R. 1, C.A.).

The existence of the leave requirement has been controversial. The JUSTICE-All Souls Review of Administrative Law recommended that it should be abolished as a matter of principle:

> "The citizen does not require leave to sue a fellow citizen and we do not think that he should have to obtain leave in order to proceed against the state and administrative bodies"

(*Administrative Justice: Some Necessary Reforms* (1988), pp. 152–155). However, it has been defended by Sir Harry Woolf as a useful filter in respect of vexatious and frivolous applications, as being an inexpensive and simple procedure, and as it "enables a litigant expeditiously and cheaply to obtain the view of a High Court judge on the merits of his application" (*Protection of the Public—A New Challenge* (1990), pp. 19–23). A review of the law and practice of the leave requirement by A. P. Le Sueur and M. Sunkin ("Applications for Judicial Review: The Requirement of Leave" [1992] P.L. 102) concluded that the political reality seemed to be that the requirement would remain for the foreseeable future. However, there should be a presumption in favour of the grant of leave; "the exercise of judicial discretion at the leave stage should be more clearly confined, structured and checked"; the "arguability" test should be replaced by a test whether there is a "serious case to be tried"; and consideration should be given to a mechanism to dispense with the leave requirement where both parties agree there is a triable case.

Setting aside a grant of leave

3. An application may be made under the general inherent jurisdiction of the court (R.S.C., Ord. 32, r. 6) to set aside leave which has been granted *ex parte* (*R.* v. *Governor of Pentonville Prison, ex p. Herbage (No. 2)* [1987] Q.B. 1077; *R.* v. *District Auditor, No. 10 Audit District, ex p. Judge* [1989] C.O.D. 390; *R.* v. *Arthur Young (a firm), ex p. Thamesdown Borough Council* [1989] C.O.D. 392; *R.* v. *Secretary of State for the Home Department, ex p. Angur Begum* [1989] Imm.A.R. 302; *R.* v. *British Coal Corporation and Roo Management Ltd., ex p. G.G. Whittaker (Properties) Ltd.* [1989] C.O.D. 528). If the judge is satisfied that the substantive motion has no reasonable prospect of success and must accordingly fail, then the leave, whether granted by himself or another judge, must be set aside; otherwise he would be aiding and abetting a waste of time and money (*per* McCowan J. in *ex p. Angur Begum, supra*).

The Crown Office list

4. Applications for judicial review are entered in the Crown Office list, along with other public law matters, including proceedings for committal for contempt of court, applications for *habeas corpus* and a variety of statutory appeals. See *Practice Direction (Trials in London)* [1981] 1 W.L.R. 1296; *Practice Direction (Crown Office list)* [1987] 1 W.L.R. 232; *Practice Direction (Crown Office list) (No. 2)* [1991] 1 W.L.R. 280. There are 18 High Court judges nominated by the Lord Chief Justice to hear Crown Office proceedings, and the Deputy Chief Justice exercises partic-

ular responsibility in Crown Office matters (R. Gordon, *Crown Office Proceedings* (1990), para. A1–004).

Discovery

5. Order 53 r. 8(1) enables an application for discovery under Order 24 to be made in judicial review proceedings. There is no *right* to discovery; the matter lies in the discretion of the judge. In *I.R.C.* v. *National Federation of Self-Employed and Small Businesses Ltd.* [1982] A.C. 617, Lord Scarman said (at p. 654):

> "... Upon general principles, discovery should not be ordered unless and until the court is satisfied that the evidence reveals reasonable grounds for believing that there has been a breach of public duty; and it should be limited strictly to documents relevant to the issue which emerges from the affidavits."

However, this view may be too restrictive. In *O'Reilly* v. *Mackman* [1983] 2 A.C. 237, Lord Diplock stated simply that discovery should be ordered "whenever, and to the extent that, the justice of the case so requires" (below, p. 730).

These views were discussed by Hodgson J. in *R.* v. *Governor of Pentonville Prison, ex p. Herbage (No. 2), The Times*, May 29, 1986. Hodgson J. held that in deciding whether to grant discovery in judicial review proceedings the court should apply a standard no higher than that applied when considering whether or not leave to apply for judicial review should be granted (appeal dismissed: [1987] Q.B. 1077, *sub. nom. R.* v. *Secretary of State for the Home Department, ex p. Herbage (No. 2)*). See also Simon Brown J. in *R.* v. *Inland Revenue Commissioners, ex p. J. Rothschild Holdings* [1986] S.T.C. 410 (appeal dismissed: [1987] S.T.C. 163); *R.* v. *Secretary of State for the Home Department, ex p. Harrison, The Independent*, December 21, 1987, considered in *R.* v. *Inland Revenue Commissioners, ex p. Taylor* [1988] S.T.C. 832; *R.* v. *Parole Board, ex p. Bradley* [1990] C.O.D. 375; *R.* v. *Secretary of State for the Environment, ex p. Doncaster Borough Council* [1990] C.O.D. 441. Discovery will only be ordered to go behind the contents of an affidavit if there is some material before the court which suggests that the affidavits of the party are not accurate: *R.* v. *Secretary of State for the Environment, ex p. Doncaster Borough Council* [1990] C.O.D. 441; *R.* v. *Secretary of State for the Home Department, ex p. B.H. et al.* [1990] C.O.D. 445; *R.* v. *Secretary of State for the Environment, ex p. Islington London Borough Council, The Independent*, September 6, 1991; *R.* v. *Governors and Appeals Committee of Bishop Challenor R.C. Comprehensive School, ex p. C. and P.* (1991) 90 L.G.R. 1037. It will not be ordered merely "in the hope that something might turn up" (characterised by Henry J. in *Re CEMI Ltd.* (Unreported, February 18, 1987) as "contingent" or "Micawber" discovery): *ex p. Doncaster Borough Council, supra.*

Cross-examination on affidavits

6. Evidence in judicial review proceedings is normally given by way of affidavits.

Rule 8(1), by virtue of the express reference to Order 38, r. 1(3), makes it clear that cross-examination on affidavits may be allowed. Previously, cross-examination under Order 38, r. 2(3) on applications for a prerogative order was possible but permitted only in very exceptional circumstances (*R.* v. *Kent JJ, ex p. Smith* [1928] W.N. 137; *R.* v. *Stokesley, Yorkshire, JJ., ex p. Bartram* [1956] 1 W.L.R. 254). At first, at least, it seemed unlikely that the practice would be more liberal even though express provision had now been made (*George* v. *Secretary of State for the Environment* (1979) 77 L.G.R. 689: statutory application to quash; *R.* v. *Home Secretary, ex p. Zamir* [1980] A.C. 930, 949). In *R.* v. *Secretary of State for the Home Department, ex p. Khawaja* [1984] A.C. 74, Lord Bridge stated (at pp. 124–5): "It may be that the express discretion conferred on the court to permit cross-examination by the new procedure for judicial review under R.S.C. Ord. 53 has been too sparingly exercised when deponents could readily attend court. But, however that may be, the discretion to allow cross-examination should only be exercised when justice so demands." The House of Lords in *O'Reilly* v. *Mackman* [1983] 2 A.C. 237 made it clear that "the grant of leave to cross-examine deponents on applications for judicial review is governed by the same principles as it is in actions begun by originating summons; it should be allowed whenever the justice of the particular case so requires" (*per* Lord Diplock at pp. 282–283). See also *R.* v. *Board of Visitors, Nottingham Prison, ex p. Moseley, The Times*, January 23, 1981 (conflict of affidavit evidence resolved without recourse to cross-examination); *R.* v. *Secretary of State for the Environment, ex p. Manuel, The Times*, March 21, 1984 (cross-examination ordered on the application of the Secretary of State where the applicant, Manuel, had offered himself for cross-examination); *R.* v. *Waltham Forest London Borough Council, ex p. Baxter* [1988] Q.B. 419 (councillors cross-examined as to whether they had fettered their discretion in voting); *R.* v. *Derbyshire County Council, ex p. The Times Supplements, The Times*, July 19, 1990 (above, p. 362).

On cross-examination and discovery in judicial review, see M. Purdue, "The scope for fact finding in judicial review" in G. Hand and J. McBride (eds.), *Droit Sans Frontieres: Essays in Honour of L. Neville Brown* (1991), pp. 193–201.

Interim relief

7. Rule 3(10) provides for interim relief on an application for judicial review.

The normal principles on which an interim injunction may be awarded are set out by the House of Lords in *American Cyanamid Co.* v. *Ethicon Ltd.* [1975] A.C. 396. Lord Diplock stated at pp. 407–408 that the court should consider, first, whether there is "a serious question to be tried," and, if satisfied that there is, proceed to consider the "balance of convenience":

> "As to that, the governing principle is that the court should first consider whether, if the plaintiff were to succeed at the trial in establishing his right to a permanent injunction, he would be adequately compensated by an award of damages for the loss he would have sustained as a result of the defendant's continuing to do what was sought to be enjoined between the time of the application and the time of the trial. If damages in the measure recoverable at common law would be adequate remedy and the defendant would be in a financial position to pay them, no interlocutory injunction should normally be granted, however strong the plaintiff's claim appeared to be at that stage. If, on the other hand, damages would not provide an adequate remedy for the plaintiff in the event of his succeeding at the trial, the court should then consider whether, on the contrary hypothesis that the defendant were to succeed at the trial in establishing his right to do that which was sought to be enjoined, he would be adequately compensated under the plaintiff's undertaking as to damages for the loss he would have sustained by being prevented from doing so between the time of the application and the time of the trial. If damages in the measure recoverable under such an undertaking would be an adequate remedy and the plaintiff would be in a financial position to pay them, there would be no reason upon this ground to refuse an interlocutory injunction.
>
> It is where there is doubt as to the adequacy of the respective remedies in damages available to either party or to both, that the question of balance of convenience arises. It would be unwise to attempt even to list all the various matters which may need to be taken into consideration in deciding where the balance lies, let alone to suggest the relative weight to be attached to them. These will vary from case to case.

Where other factors appear to be evenly balanced it is a counsel of prudence to take such measures as are calculated to preserve the status quo."

Examples of the application of these principles include the following. In *Smith* v. *Inner London Education Authority* [1978] 1 All E.R. 411, the Court of Appeal discharged interlocutory injunctions restraining the authority from closing a grammar school: the applicants had "no real prospect of . . . succeeding at the trial" (*per* Lord Denning M.R. at p. 418). In *R.* v. *Westminster City Council, ex p. Sierbien, The Times*, March 30, 1987, the Court of Appeal approved the refusal of Otton J. to grant interlocutory injunctions to restrain the council from enforcing the Local Government (Miscellaneous Provisions) Act 1982. The applicants sought the injunctions pending the outcome of their application for judicial review of the council's refusal to grant them a licence to carry on a sex encounter establishment. The court held that the ordinary financial considerations in *American Cyanamid*, although relevant, had to be qualified by a recognition of the public interest. The grant of an injunction would have the effect of preventing a public body from carrying out its duty and of trespassing on a matter in the domain of the criminal law.

On the availability of a mandatory injunction on an interlocutory application see *De Falco* v. *Crawley Borough Council* [1980] Q.B. 460; *Locabail International Finance Ltd.* v. *Agroexport* [1986] 1 W.L.R. 657.

An application for interim relief can be made *ex parte* or on notice to the other side. Nevertheless, the giving of notice is an advisable step in all cases (see *R.* v. *Kensington and Chelsea Royal London Borough Council, ex p. Hammell* [1989] Q.B. 518, 539, *per* Parker L.J.).

On the question of undertakings in damages and interim relief, see below, pp. 780 and 842.

Interim declaratory relief

8. An interim declaration may not be granted (see *Underhill* v. *Minister of Food* [1950] 1 All E.R. 593, *International General Electric Co. of New York Ltd.* v. *Customs and Excise Commissioners* [1962] Ch. 784 and *R.* v. *Inland Revenue Commissioners, ex p. Rossminster Ltd.* [1980] A.C. 952).

A final declaration may exceptionally be awarded in interlocutory proceedings (see *Wallersteiner* v. *Moir* [1974] 1 W.L.R. 991, 1030; *Meade* v. *Haringey London Borough Council* [1979] 1 W.L.R. 637, 648–9, 657 (see below, p. 819); *Malone* v. *Metropolitan Police Commissioner* [1979] Ch. 344, 382; *Clarke* v. *Chadburn* [1985] 1 W.L.R. 78; *cf. Ashby* v. *Ebdon* [1984] 3 All E.R. 869, 872).

The general absence of interim declaratory relief causes particular difficulty in respect of proceedings against the Crown. Section 21(2) of the Crown Proceedings Act 1947 provides that "The court shall not in any civil proceedings grant any injunction or make any order against an officer of the Crown if the effect of granting the injunction or making the order would be to give any relief against the Crown which could not have been obtained in proceedings against the Crown." In *R.* v. *Secretary of State for the Home Department, ex p. Kirkwood* [1984] 2 All E.R. 390, Mann J. held that s.21 prevented the court ordering a stay on granting leave for an application for judicial review of a decision of the Secretary of State. However, in *R.* v. *Governor of Pentonville Prison, ex p. Herbage* [1987] Q.B. 872, Hodgson J. held that the court had jurisdiction under Ord. 53, r. 3(10)(*b*) to grant an interim injunction against an officer of the Crown. Section 21 of the Crown Proceedings Act 1947 referred to "civil proceedings" which term did not include proceedings on the Crown side of the Queen's Bench Division (*ibid.*, s.38). An injunction was however refused in the exercise of his Lordship's discretion. Hodgson J.'s view was endorsed by the majority of the Court of Appeal (Woolf and Taylor L.JJ., Dillon L.J. dissenting) in *R.* v. *Licensing Authority, ex p. Smith,*

Kline and French Laboratories Ltd. (*No.* 2) [1990] 1 Q.B. 54. Indeed, Woolf and Taylor L.JJ. stated that, since the enactment of the Supreme Court Act 1981, s.31, the court now had jurisdiction to award a final injunction against the Crown, and not merely an interim injunction. *Herbage* and *Smith, Kline* were, however, overruled on the interim injunction point by the House of Lords in *R.* v. *Secretary of State for Transport, ex p. Factortame Ltd.* [1990] 2 A.C. 85: section 31(2) could not be read as conferring a new jurisdiction on the court to grant interim injunctions against the Crown; such a change would have been by an express provision. On the other hand, the Court of Appeal has held that the court does have jurisdiction under r. 3(10)(*a*) to order a stay of the implementation of the decision of a minister: *R.* v. *Secretary of State for Education and Science, ex p. Avon County Council* [1991] 1 Q.B. 558.

There seems no good reason why interim declaratory relief should not be made available. The Law Commission so recommended in its Report on Remedies in Administrative Law (Law Com. No. 73), para. 51. This was supported by Lord Diplock in the *Rossminster* case ([1980] A.C. at p. 1015), but opposed by Lords Wilberforce, Dilhorne and Scarman in the same case (at pp. 1001, 1007, 1027). Lord Scarman said:

> "For myself, I find absurd the posture of a court declaring one day in interlocutory proceedings that an applicant has certain rights and upon a later day that he has not" (p. 1027).

On the other hand, it can be argued that it is not self-evidently absurd for a court at an interim stage to express a *provisional* or *prima facie* view, where that would be helpful for one or both of the parties.

The ruling on the interim injunction point by the House of Lords in *Factortame* has, moreover, been cogently criticised by Sir William Wade, (1991) 107 L.Q.R. 4. The principle that the courts cannot grant coercive remedies against the Crown should not apply to Crown servants (such as Ministers) exercising powers conferred on them in their own names and not upon the Crown.

The House of Lords has subsequently ruled that English courts may be required by European Community law to award interim relief against the Crown, where a point of Community law is involved: Case C 213/89, *R.* v. *Secretary of State for Transport, ex p. Factortame Ltd.* (*No.* 2) [1991] 1 A.C. 603, E.C.J. and H.L.

See generally on the *Factortame* litigation, N. P. Gravells, [1989] P.L. 568 and [1991] P.L. 180. For other comments on interim relief against the Crown, see J. Alder, (1987) 50 M.L.R. 10; M. Matthews, (1988) 8 O.J.L.S. 154.

The Crown and the Home Office are not, but ministers in a personal capacity are amenable to the contempt jurisdiction (*M.* v. *Home Office* [1992] 1 Q.B. 270, C.A.).

Availability of declarations

9. In *Inland Revenue Commissioners* v. *National Federation of Self-Employed and Small Businesses Ltd.* [1982] A.C. 617 Lord Diplock (at p. 639) and Lord Scarman (at p. 648) expressed the view that a declaration could only be granted under Order 53 in circumstances where one or other of the prerogative orders could issue. Otherwise, r. 1(2) would have been *ultra vires* in that it would have purported to effect a substantive and not merely a procedural change in the law. (See P. Cane, [1981] P.L. 322, 325–329.) The subsequent enactment of the basic features of Order 53 in the Supreme Court 1981 could be regarded as overcoming any such difficulty. Nevertheless, Lord Diplock's view was accepted by Fox and Slade L.JJ. in *Law* v. *National Greyhound Racing Club Ltd.* [1983] 1 W.L.R. 1302, 1310, 1313 (see further, above, p. 703); and the views of both Lords Diplock and Scarman were

accepted by Lord Wilberforce in *Davy* v. *Spelthorne Borough Council* [1984] A.C. 262, 277–278.

On the other hand, in *R.* v. *Bromley London Borough Council, ex p. Lambeth London Borough Council, The Times,* June 16, 1984, Hodgson J. held that the court had jurisdiction to grant a declaration that the proposed payment of a subscription to the Association of London Authorities would be *intra vires,* notwithstanding that there was as yet no judgment, order or decision to be reviewed, and that there was no claim in the application for one of the prerogative orders. His Lordship accepted the argument that the enactment of section 31 of the Supreme Court Act 1981 meant that it was no longer necessary to consider whether one of the prerogative orders would have been available on the facts. A similar view was expressed by Kennedy J. in *R.* v. *Secretary of State for the Environment, ex p. Nottinghamshire County Council, The Independent,* November 13, 1986 (but *cf.* McNeill J. in *R.* v. *Secretary of State for the Home Department, ex p. Dew* [1987] 1 W.L.R. 881).

In a number of cases, a declaration has been sought on an application for judicial review in respect of a legislative instrument; certiorari would not be available (see below, p. 775), but it has not been suggested that the procedure was inappropriate (see, *e.g. R.* v. *Inland Revenue Commissioners, ex p. Woolwich Equitable Building Society* [1990] 1 W.L.R. 1400).

Appeals

10. Rule 13 provides that no appeal lies from an order on an application for leave which may be renewed to a Divisional Court or judge sitting in open court under r. 3(4).

In a criminal cause or matter, the application is renewed to a Divisional Court (r. 3(4)(*a*)), and an appeal lies thereafter to the House of Lords under the Administration of Justice Act 1960, ss.1 and 19, Sched. 3. It is uncertain whether an appeal can lie to the House of Lords against a refusal of leave by the Divisional Court (see G. Aldous and J. Alder, *Applications for Judicial Review* (1985), pp. 159–160, who point out that such a refusal would be unlikely in practice to raise a point of law of general public importance). In other cases, the application may be renewed either to a judge in open court or to a Divisional Court (if the Court so directs) (r. 3(4)(*b*)) except that if the decision to refuse leave is made by a judge after hearing, the application for leave may not be renewed under r. 3(4) (see the proviso to r. 3(4) in conjunction with r. 13).

In a non-criminal cause or matter, where an application for leave may not be further renewed in the High Court, a renewed application may be made to the Court of Appeal (*R.* v. *Commissioner for the Special Purposes of the Income Tax Acts, ex p. Stipplechoice Ltd.* [1985] 2 All E.R. 465; *R.* v. *Secretary of State for the Home Department, ex p. Swati* [1986] 1 W.L.R. 477; *Re Dhillon, The Times,* January 28, 1987). This is not technically an appeal against the refusal of leave (*per* Sir John Donaldson M.R. in *Re Dhillon, supra*). Renewed applications made to the Court of Appeal are treated as a priority category (*In Re Bakole, The Times,* March 25, 1988). If the Court of Appeal grants leave it may hear the substantive motion (*R.* v. *Industrial Injuries Commissioner, ex p. A.E.U.* [1966] 2 Q.B. 21), but this will now not normally be done unless the court below is bound by authority or for some other reason an appeal to the Court of Appeal is inevitable (*Practice Direction (Judicial Review: Appeals)* [1982] 1 W.L.R. 1375): the application is normally to be heard by a single judge, unless a judge directs that the application is to be heard by a Divisional Court (*Practice Note* [1990] 1 W.L.R. 51). In *British Airways Board* v. *Laker Airways Ltd.* [1984] 1 Q.B. 142, the Court of Appeal, exceptionally, ordered the substantive application for judicial review to be made direct to the Court of Appeal after granting a renewed application for leave: this was to enable the matter to be considered in conjunction with other appeals pending before that court (see pp. 184–185). Similarly, in *R.* v. *Secretary of State for Education, ex p. Avon County Council (No. 2)* (1990) 88 L.G.R. 737, the hearing of a substantive application for judicial review was reserved to the Court of Appeal with the agreement of both parties: this was to secure the early hearing of a challenge to decisions rejecting proposals for the reorganisation of secondary education in Bath and approving the acquisition by one school of grant maintained status.

There is no further appeal, in respect of a refusal of leave, to the House of Lords (*In re Poh* [1983] 1 W.L.R. 2; *Practice Direction (House of Lords: Petitions: Judicial Review)* [1983] 1 W.L.R. 404).

Where in a civil case a full application has been heard in the High Court, further appeals may lie to the Court of Appeal and the House of Lords.

(E) Exclusivity of the Application for Judicial Review

O'REILLY AND OTHERS v. MACKMAN AND OTHERS

[1983] 2 A.C. 237; [1983] 3 W.L.R. 1096; [1982] 3 All E.R. 1124
(House of Lords)

The four plaintiffs, prisoners in Hull Prison, were charged with disciplinary offences before the board of visitors to the prison, arising out of riots in December 1976 (in the case of three of the plaintiffs) and 1979 (in the case of the fourth). In the case of each plaintiff the board held an inquiry, found the charges proved and imposed penalties. In 1980, three of the plaintiffs brought actions by writ in the Queen's Bench Division of the High Court against the board alleging that it had acted in breach of the Prison Rules and the rules of natural justice and claiming a declaration that the board's findings against them and the penalties awarded were void and of no effect. The fourth plaintiff started proceedings by originating summons in the Chancery Division against the Home Office and the board of visitors alleging bias by a member of the board and claiming a declaration that the board's adjudication was void for want of natural justice. In all four cases the defendants applied to strike out the proceedings. Peter Pain J. dismissed the applications. The Court of Appeal reversed that decision and struck out the proceedings on the ground that they were an abuse of the process of the court and that the plaintiffs' only proper remedy was by way of judicial review under R.S.C. Ord. 53. The House of Lords (Lords Diplock, Fraser, Keith, Bridge and Brightman) unanimously dismissed the plaintiffs' appeals. The leading speech was delivered by Lord Diplock.

Lord Diplock: . . . [N]o question arises as to the "jurisdiction" of the High Court to grant to each of the appellants relief by way of a declaration in the terms sought, if they succeeded in establishing the facts alleged in their respective statements of claim or originating summons and the court considered a declaration to be an appropriate remedy. All that is at issue in the instant appeal is the procedure by which such relief ought to be sought. Put in a single sentence the question for your Lordships is: whether in 1980 after R.S.C., Ord. 53 in its new form, adopted in 1977, had come into operation it was an abuse of the process of the court to apply for such declarations by using the procedure laid down in the Rules for proceedings begun by writ or by originating summons instead of using the procedure laid down by Order 53 for an application for judicial review of the awards of forfeiture of remission of sentence made against them by the board which the appellants are seeking to impugn?

In their respective actions, the appellants claim only declaratory relief. It is conceded on their behalf that, for reasons into which the concession makes it unnecessary to enter, no claim for damages would lie against the members of the board of visitors by whom the awards were made. The only claim was for a form of relief which it lies within the discretion of the court to grant or to withhold. So the first thing to be noted is that the relief sought in the action is discretionary only.

It is not, and it could not be, contended that the decision of the board awarding him forfeiture of remission had infringed or threatened to infringe any right of the appellant derived from private law, whether a common law right or one created by a statute. Under the Prison Rules remission of sentence is not a matter of right but of indulgence. So far as private law is concerned all that each appellant had was a legitimate expectation, based upon his knowledge of what is the general practice, that he would be granted the maximum remission, permitted by rule 5(2) of the Prison Rules, of one-third of his sentence if by that time no disciplinary award of forfeiture of remission had been made against him. So the second thing to be noted is that none of the appellants had any remedy in private law.

In public law, as distinguished from private law, however, such legitimate expectation gave to each appellant a sufficient interest to challenge the legality of the adverse disciplinary award made against him by the board on the ground that in one way or another the board in reaching its decision had acted outwith the powers conferred upon it by the legislation under which it was acting; and such grounds would include the board's failure to observe the rules of natural justice: which means no more than to act fairly towards him in carrying out their decision-making process, and I prefer so to put it.

The power of boards of visitors of a prison to make disciplinary awards is conferred upon them by subordinate legislation: the Prison Rules 1964 made by the Secretary of State under sections 6 and 47 of the Prison Act 1952. The charges against the appellants were of grave offences against discipline falling within rule 51. They were referred by the governor of the prison to the board under rule 51(1). It thereupon became the duty of the board under rule 51(3) to inquire into the charge and decide whether it was proved and if so to award what the board considered to be the appropriate punishment. Rule 49(2) is applicable to such inquiry by the board. It lays down expressly that the prisoner "shall be given a full opportunity of hearing what is alleged against him and of presenting his own case." In exercising their functions under rule 51 members of the board are acting as a statutory tribunal, as contrasted with a domestic tribunal upon which powers are conferred by contract between those who agree to submit to its jurisdiction. Where the legislation which confers upon a statutory tribunal its decision-making powers also provides expressly for the procedure it shall follow in the course of reaching its decision, it is a question of construction of the relevant legislation, to be decided by the court in which the decision is challenged, whether a particular procedural provision is mandatory, so that its non-observance in the process of reaching the decision makes the decision itself a nullity, or whether it is merely directory, so that the statutory tribunal has a discretion not to comply with it if, in its opinion, the exceptional circumstances of a particular case justify departing from it. But the requirement that a person who is charged with having done something which, if proved to the satisfaction of a statutory tribunal, has consequences that will, or may, affect him adversely, should be given a fair opportunity of hearing what is alleged against him and of presenting his own case, is so fundamental to any civilised legal system that it is to be presumed that Parliament intended that a failure to observe it should render null and void any decision reached in breach of this requirement. What is alleged by the appellants other than Millbanks would amount to an infringement of the express rule 49; but even if there were no such express provision a requirement to observe it would be a necessary implication from the nature of the disciplinary functions of the board. In the absence of express provision to the contrary Parliament, whenever it provides for the creation of a statutory tribunal, must be presumed not to have intended that the tribunal should be authorised to act in contravention of one of the fundamental rules of natural justice or fairness: *audi alteram partem*.

In Millbanks's case, there is no express provision in the Prison Rules that the members of the board who inquire into a disciplinary offence under rule 51 must be free from personal bias against the prisoner. It is another fundamental rule of natural justice or fairness, too obvious to call for express statement of it, that a tribunal exercising functions such as those exercised by the board in the case of Millbanks should be constituted of persons who enter upon the inquiry without any pre-conceived personal bias against the prisoner. Failure to comply with this implied requirement would likewise render the decision of the tribunal a nullity. So the third thing to be noted is that each of the appellants, if he established the facts alleged in his action, was entitled to a remedy in public law which would have the effect of preventing the decision of the board from having any adverse consequences upon him.

My Lords, the power of the High Court to make declaratory judgments is conferred by what is now R.S.C., Ord. 15, r. 16. The language of the rule which was first made in 1883 has never been altered, though the numbering of the rule has from time to time been changed. It provides:

> "No action or other proceeding shall be open to objection on the ground that a merely declaratory judgment or order is sought thereby, and the court may make binding declarations of right whether or not any consequential relief is or could be claimed."

This rule, which is in two parts separated by "and," has been very liberally interpreted in the course of its long history, wherever it appeared to the court that the justice of the case required the grant of declaratory relief in the particular action before it. Since "action" is defined so as to have included since 1938 an originating motion applying for prerogative orders, Ord. 15, r. 16 says nothing as to the appropriate procedure by which declarations of different kinds ought to be sought. Nor does it draw any distinction between declarations that relate to rights and obligations under private law and those that relate to rights and obligations under public law. Indeed the appreciation of the distinction in substantive law between what is private law and what is public law has itself been a latecomer to the English legal system. It is a consequence of the development that has taken place in the last 30 years of the procedures available for judicial control of administrative action. This development started with the expansion of the grounds upon which orders of certiorari could be obtained as a result of the decision of the Court of Appeal in *R.* v. *Northumberland Compensation Appeal Tribunal, ex p. Shaw* [1952] 1 K.B. 338; it was accelerated by the passing of the Tribunals and Inquiries Act 1958, and culminated in the substitution in 1977 of the new form of R.S.C., Ord. 53 which has since been given statutory confirmation in section 31 of the Supreme Court Act 1981.

[His Lordship referred to the re-discovery in *ex p. Shaw* of the power to grant certiorari to quash for error of law on the face of the record (above, pp. 593–604); and the provisions in the 1958 Act, now replaced by the 1971 Act, requiring most statutory tribunals to give reasons, and repealing most clauses purporting to exclude judicial review.]

[Section 14(1) of the Act (now s.12(1) of the 1992 Act, above, p. 78)] it is to be observed, says nothing about any right to bring civil actions for declarations of nullity of orders or determinations of statutory bodies where an earlier Act of Parliament contains a provision that such order or determination "shall not be called into question in any court." Since actions begun by writ seeking such declarations were already coming into common use in the High Court so as to provide an alternative remedy to orders of certiorari, the section suggests a parliamentary preference in favour of making the latter remedy available rather than the former. I will defer consideration of the reasons for this preference until later.

Fortunately for the development of public law in England, section 14(3) contained express provision that the section should not apply to any order or determination of the Foreign Compensation Commission, a statutory body established under the Foreign Compensation Act 1950, which Act provided by section 4(4) an express provision: "The determination by the commission of any application made to them under this Act shall not be called in question in any court of law." It was this provision that provided the occasion for the landmark decision of this House in *Anisminic Ltd.* v. *Foreign Compensation Commission* [1969] 2 A.C. 147, and particularly the leading speech of Lord Reid, which has liberated English public law from the fetters that the courts had theretofore imposed upon themselves so far as determinations of inferior courts and statutory tribunals were concerned, by drawing esoteric distinctions between errors of law committed by such tribunals that went to their jurisdiction, and errors of law committed by them within their jurisdiction. The breakthrough that the *Anisminic* case made was the recognition by the majority of this House that if a tribunal whose jurisdiction was limited by statute or subordinate legislation mistook the law applicable to the facts as it had found them, it must have asked itself the wrong question, *i.e.* one into which it was not empowered to inquire and so had no jurisdiction to determine. Its purported "determination," not being a "determination" within the meaning of the empowering legislation, was accordingly a nullity.

Anisminic Ltd. v. *Foreign Compensation Commission* was an action commenced by writ for a declaration, in which a minute of the commission's reasons for their determination adverse to the plaintiff company did not appear upon the face of their determination, and had in fact been obtained only upon discovery: but, as appears from the report of my own judgment when the *Anisminic* case was in the Court of Appeal ([1968] 2 Q.B. 862, 893), the case had been argued up to that stage as if it were an application for certiorari in which the minute of the commission's reasons formed part of the "record" upon which an error of law appeared. In the House of Lords the question of the propriety of suing by writ for a declaration instead of applying for certiorari and mandamus played no part in the main argument for the commission. It appears for the first time in the report of the commission's counsel's reply, where an argument that the court had no "jurisdiction" to make the declaration seems to have been put forward upon the narrow ground, special to the limited functions of the commission, alluded to at pp. 910–911 of my own judgment in the Court of Appeal that the House overruled; but I did not purport to decide the question because, in the view that I had (erroneously) taken of the effect of section 4(4) of the Act, it appeared to me to be unnecessary to do so.

My Lords, *Anisminic Ltd.* v. *Foreign Compensation Commission* [1969] 2 A.C. 147 was decided by this House before the alteration was made to R.S.C., Ord. 53 in 1977. The order of the Supreme Court dealing with applications for the prerogative orders of mandamus, certiorari and prohibition in force at the time of the *Anisminic* case was numbered Order 53 and had been made in 1965. It replaced, but in substance only repeated, the first 12 rules of what had been Order 59 and which had in 1938 itself replaced the former Crown Office Rules of 1906. The pre-1977 Order 53, like its predecessors, placed under considerable procedural disadvantage applicants who wished to challenge the lawfulness of a determination of a statutory tribunal or any other body of persons having legal authority to determine questions affecting the common law or statutory rights or obligations of other persons as individuals. It will be noted that I have broadened the much-cited description by Atkin L.J. in *R.* v. *Electricity Commissioners, ex p. London Electricity Joint Committee Co. (1920) Ltd.* [1924] 1 K.B. 171, 205 of bodies of persons subject to the supervisory jurisdiction of the High Court by prerogative remedies (which in 1924 then took the form of prerogative writs of mandamus, prohibition, certiorari, and quo warranto) by excluding Atkin L.J.'s limitation of the bodies of persons to whom the prerogative writs might issue, to those "having the duty to act judicially." For the next 40 years this phrase gave rise to many attempts, with varying success, to draw subtle distinctions between decisions that were quasi-judicial and those that were administrative only. But the relevance of arguments of this kind was destroyed by the decision of this House in *Ridge* v. *Baldwin* [1964] A.C. 40, where again the leading speech was given by Lord Reid. Wherever any person or body of persons has authority conferred by legislation to make decisions of the kind I have described, it is amenable to the remedy of an order to quash its decision either for error of law in reaching it or for failure to act fairly towards the person who will be adversely affected by the decision by failing to observe either one or other of the two fundamental rights accorded to him by the rules of natural justice or fairness, *viz.* to have afforded to him a reasonable opportunity of learning what is alleged against him and of putting forward his own case in answer to it, and to the absence of personal bias against him on the part of the person by whom the decision falls to be made. In *Ridge* v. *Baldwin* it is interesting to observe that Lord Reid said at p. 72 "We do not have a developed system of administrative law—perhaps because until fairly recently we did not need it." By 1977 the need had continued to grow apace and this reproach to English law had been removed. We did have by then a developed system of administrative law, to the development of which Lord Reid himself, by his speeches in cases which reached this House, had made an outstanding contribution. To the landmark cases of *Ridge* v. *Baldwin* and *Anisminic Ltd.* v. *Foreign Compensation Commission* [1969] 2 A.C. 147 I would add a third, *Padfield* v. *Minister of Agriculture, Fisheries and Food* [1968] A.C. 997, another case in which a too-timid judgment of my own in the Court of Appeal was (fortunately) overruled.

Although the availability of the remedy of orders to quash a decision by certiorari had in theory been widely extended by these developments, the procedural disadvantages under which applicants for this remedy laboured remained substantially unchanged until the alteration of Order 53 in 1977. Foremost among these was the absence of any provision for discovery. In the case of a decision which did not state the reasons for it, it was not possible to challenge its validity for error of law in the reasoning by which the decision had been reached. If it had been an application for certiorari those who were the plaintiffs in the *Anisminic* case would have failed; it was only because by pursuing an action by writ for a declaration of nullity that the plaintiffs were entitled to the discovery by which the minute of the commission's reasons which showed that they had asked themselves the wrong question, was obtained. Again under Order 53 evidence was required to be on affidavit. This in itself is not an unjust disadvantage; it is a common feature of many forms of procedure in the High Court, including originating summonses; but in the absence of any express provision for cross-examination of deponents, as your Lordships who are familiar with the pre-1977 procedure will be aware, even *applications* for leave to cross-examine were virtually unknown—let alone the grant of leave itself—save in very exceptional cases of which I believe none of your Lordships has ever had actual experience. Lord Goddard C.J., whose experience was at that time unrivalled, had so stated in *R.* v. *Stokesley, Yorkshire, Justices, ex p. Bartram* [1956] 1 W.L.R. 254, 257.

On the other hand as compared with an action for a declaration commenced by writ or originating summons, the procedure under Order 53 both before and after 1977 provided for the respondent decision-making statutory tribunal or public authority against which the remedy of certiorari was sought protection against claims which it was not in the public interest for courts of justice to entertain.

First, leave to apply for the order was required. The application for leave which was *ex parte* but could be, and in practice often was, adjourned in order to enable the proposed respondent to be represented, had to be supported by a statement setting out, *inter alia*, the grounds on which the relief was sought and by affidavits verifying the facts relied on: so that a knowingly false statement of fact would amount to the criminal offence of perjury. Such affidavit was also required to satisfy the requirement of *uberrima fides*, with the consequence that failure to make on oath a full and candid disclosure of material facts was of itself a ground for refusing the relief sought in the substantive application for which leave had been obtained on the strength of the affidavit. This was an important safeguard, which is preserved in the new Order 53 of 1977. The public interest in good administration requires that public authorities and third parties should not be kept in suspense as to the legal validity of a decision the authority has reached in purported exercise of decision-making powers for any longer period than is absolutely necessary in fairness to the person affected by the decision. In contrast, allegations made in a statement of claim or an indorsement of an originating summons are not on oath, so the requirement of a prior application for leave to be supported by full and candid affidavits verifying the facts relied on is an important safeguard against groundless or unmeritorious claims that a particular decision is a nullity. There was also power in the court on granting leave to impose terms as to costs or security.

Furthermore, as Order 53 was applied in practice, as soon as the application for leave had been made it provided a very speedy means, available in urgent cases within a matter of days rather than months, for determining whether a disputed decision was valid in law or not. A reduction of the period of suspense was also effected by the requirement that leave to apply for certiorari to quash a decision must be made within a limited period after the impugned decision was made, unless delay beyond that limited period was accounted for to the satisfaction of the judge. The period was six months under the pre-1977 Order 53; under the current Order 53 it is further reduced to three months.

My Lords, the exclusion of all right to discovery in application for certiorari under Order 53, particularly before the passing of the Tribunal and Inquiries Act 1958, was calculated to cause injustice to persons who had no means, if they adopted that procedure, of ascertaining whether a public body, which had made a decision adversely affecting them, had done so for reasons which were wrong in law and rendered their decision invalid. It will be within the knowledge of all of your Lordships that, at any rate from the 1950s onwards, actions for declarations of nullity of decisions affecting the rights of individuals under public law were widely entertained, in parallel to applications for certiorari to quash, as means of obtaining an effective alternative remedy. I will not weary your Lordships by reciting examples of cases where this practice received the express approval of the Court of Appeal, though I should point out that of those cases in this House in which this practice was approved, *Vine* v. *National Dock Labour Board* [1957] A.C. 488 and *Ridge* v. *Baldwin* [1964] A.C. 40 involved, as well as questions of public law, contracts of employment which gave rise to rights under private law. In *Anisminic Ltd.* v. *Foreign Compensation Commission* [1969] 2 A.C. 147 the procedural question was not seriously argued, while *Pyx Granite Ltd.* v. *Ministry of Housing and Local Government* [1960] A.C. 260, which is referred to in the notes to Order 19 appearing in the *Supreme Court Practice* (1982) as an instance of the approval by this House of the practice of suing for a declaration instead of applying for an order of certiorari, appears on analysis to have been concerned with declaring that the plaintiffs had a legal right to do what they were seeking to do without the need to obtain any decision from the Minister. Nevertheless I accept that having regard to disadvantages, particularly in relation to the absolute bar upon compelling discovery of documents by the respondent public authority to an applicant for an order of certiorari, and the almost invariable practice of refusing leave to allow cross-examination of deponents to affidavits lodged on its behalf, it could not be regarded as an abuse of the process of the court, before the amendments made to Order 53 in 1977, to proceed against the authority by an action for a declaration of nullity of the impugned decision with an injunction to prevent the authority from acting on it, instead of applying for an order of certiorari; and this despite the fact that, by adopting this course, the plaintiff evaded the safeguards imposed in the public interest against groundless, unmeritorious or tardy attacks upon the validity of decisions made by public authorities in the field of public law.

Those disadvantages, which formerly might have resulted in an applicant's being unable to obtain justice in an application for certiorari under Order 53, have all been removed by the new Order introduced in 1977. There is express provision in the new rule 8 for interlocutory applications for discovery of documents, the administration of interrogatories and the cross-examination of deponents to affidavits. Discovery of documents (which may often be a time-consuming process) is not automatic as in an action begun by writ, but otherwise Order 24 applies to it and discovery is obtainable upon application whenever, and to the extent that, the justice of the case requires; similarly Order 26 applies to applications for interrogatories; and to applications for cross-examination of deponents to affidavits Ord. 28, r. 2(3) applies. This is the rule that deals with evidence in actions begun by originating summons and permits oral cross-examination on affidavit evidence wherever the justice of the case requires. It may well be that for the reasons given by Lord Denning M.R. in *George* v. *Secretary of State for the Environment* (1979) 77 L.G.R. 689, it will only be upon rare occasions that the interests of justice will require that leave be given for cross-examination of deponents on their affidavits in applications for judicial review. This is because of the nature of the issues that normally arise upon judicial review. The facts, except where the claim that a decision was invalid on the ground that the statutory tribunal or public authority that made the decision failed to comply with the procedure prescribed by the legislation under which it was acting or failed to observe the fundamental rules of natural justice or fairness, can seldom be a matter of relevant dispute upon an application for judicial review, since the tribunal or authority's findings of fact, as distinguished from the legal consequences of the facts that they have found, are not open to review by the court in the exercise of its supervisory powers except on the principles laid down in *Edwards* v. *Bairstow* [1956] A.C. 14, 36; and to allow cross-examination presents the court with a temptation, not always easily resisted, to substitute its own view of the facts for that of the decision-making body upon whom the exclusive jurisdiction to determine facts has been conferred by Parliament. Nevertheless having regard to a possible misunderstanding of what was said by Geoffrey Lane L.J. in *R.* v. *Board of Visitors of Hull Prison, ex p. St. Germain (No. 2)* [1979] 1 W.L.R. 1401, 1410 your Lordships may think this an appropriate occasion on which to emphasise that whatever may have been the position before the rule was altered in 1977 in all proceedings for judicial review that have been started since that date the grant of leave to cross-examine deponents upon applications for judicial review is governed by the same principles as it is in actions begun by originating summons; it should be allowed whenever the justice of the particular case so requires.

Another handicap under which an applicant for a prerogative order under Order 53 formerly laboured (though it would not have affected the appellants in the instant cases even if they had brought their actions before the 1977 alteration to Order 53) was that a claim for damages for breach of a right in private law of the applicant resulting from an invalid decision of a public authority could not be made in an application under Order 53. Damages could only be claimed in a separate action begun by writ; whereas in an action so begun they could be claimed as additional relief as well as a declaration of nullity of the decision from which the damage claimed had flowed. Rule 7 of the new Order 53 permits the applicant for judicial review to include in the statement in support of his application for leave a claim for damages and empowers the court to award damages on the hearing of the application if satisfied that such damages could have been awarded to him in an action begun by him by writ at the time of the making of the application.

Finally rule 1 of the new Order 53 enables an application for a declaration or an injunction to be included in an application for judicial review. This was not previously the case; only prerogative orders could be obtained in proceedings under Order 53. Declarations or injunctions were obtainable only in actions begun by writ or originating summons. So a person seeking to challenge a decision had to make a choice of the remedy that he sought at the outset of the proceedings, although when the matter was examined more closely in the course of the proceedings it might appear that he was not entitled to that remedy but would have been entitled to some other remedy available only in the other kind of proceeding.

This reform may have lost some of its importance since there have come to be realised that the full consequences of the *Anisminic* case, in introducing the concept that if a statutory decision-making authority asks itself the wrong question it acts without jurisdiction, have been virtually to abolish the distinction between errors within jurisdiction that rendered voidable a decision that remained valid until quashed, and errors that went to jurisdiction and rendered a decision void *ab initio* provided that its validity was challenged timeously in the High Court by an appropriate procedure. Failing such challenge within the applicable time limit, public policy, expressed in the maxim *omnia praesumuntur rite esse acta*, requires that after the expiry of the time limit it should be given all the effects in law of a valid decision.

Nevertheless, there may still be cases where it turns out in the course of proceedings to challenge a decision of a statutory authority that a declaration of rights rather than certiorari is the appropriate remedy. *Pyx Granite Co. Ltd.* v. *Ministry of Housing and Local Government* [1960] A.C. 260 provides an example of such a case.

So Order 53 since 1977 has provided a procedure by which every type of remedy for infringement of the rights of individuals that are entitled to protection in public law can be obtained in one and the same proceeding by way of an application for judicial review, and whichever remedy is found to be the most appropriate in the light of what has emerged upon the hearing of the application, can be granted to him. If what should emerge is that his complaint is not of an infringement of any of his rights that are entitled to protection in public law, but may be an infringement of his rights in private law and thus not a proper subject for judicial review, the court has power under rule 9(5), instead of refusing the application, to order the proceedings to continue as if they had begun by writ. There is no such converse power under the R.S.C. to permit an action begun by writ to continue as if it were an application for judicial review; and I respectfully disagree with that part of the judgment of Lord Denning M.R. which suggests that such a power may exist; nor do I see the need to amend the rules in order to create one.

My Lords, at the outset of this speech, I drew attention to the fact that the remedy by way of declaration of nullity of the decisions of the board was discretionary—as are all the remedies available upon judicial review. Counsel for the plaintiffs accordingly conceded that the fact that by adopting the procedure of an action begun by writ or by originating summons instead of an application for judicial review under Order 53 (from which there have now been removed all those disadvantages to applicants that had previously led the courts to countenance actions for declarations and injunctions as an alternative procedure for obtaining a remedy for infringement of the rights of the individual that are entitled to protection in public law only) the plaintiffs had thereby been able to evade those protections against groundless, unmeritorious or tardy harassment that were afforded to statutory tribunals or decision-making public authorities by Order 53, and which might have resulted in the summary, and would in any event have resulted in the speedy disposition of the application, is among the matters fit to be taken into consideration by the judge in deciding whether to exercise his discretion by refusing to grant a declaration; but, it was contended, this he may only do at the conclusion of the trial.

So to delay the judge's decision as to how to exercise his discretion would defeat the public policy that underlies the grant of those protections: *viz.*, the need, in the interests of good administration and of third parties who may be indirectly affected by the decision, for speedy certainty as to whether it has the effect of a decision that is valid in public law. An action for a declaration or injunction need not be commenced until the very end of the limitation period; if begun by writ, discovery and interlocutory proceedings may be prolonged and the plaintiffs are not required to support their allegations by evidence on oath until the actual trial. The period of uncertainty as to the validity of a decision that has been challenged upon allegations that may eventually turn out to be baseless and unsupported by evidence on oath, may thus be strung out for a very lengthy period, as the actions of the first three appellants in the instant appeals show. Unless such an action can be struck out summarily at the outset as an abuse of the process of the court the whole purpose of the public policy to which the change in Order 53 was directed would be defeated.

My Lords, Order 53 does not expressly provide that procedure by application for judicial review shall be the exclusive procedure available by which the remedy of a declaration or injunction may be obtained for infringement of rights that are entitled to protection under public law; nor does section 31 of the Supreme Court Act 1981. There is great variation between individual cases that fall within Order 53 and the Rules Committee and subsequently the legislature were, I think, for this reason content to rely upon the express and the inherent power of the High Court, exercised upon a case to case basis, to prevent abuse of its process whatever might be the form taken by that abuse. Accordingly, I do not think that your Lordships would be wise to use this as an occasion to lay down categories of cases in which it would necessarily always be an abuse to seek in an action begun by writ or originating summons a remedy against infringement of rights of the individual that are entitled to protection in public law.

The position of applicants for judicial review has been drastically ameliorated by the new Order 53. It has removed all those disadvantages, particularly in relation to discovery, that were manifestly unfair to them and had, in many cases, made applications for prerogative orders an inadequate remedy if justice was to be done. This it was that justified the courts in not treating as an abuse of their powers resort to an alternative procedure by way of action for a declaration or injunction (not then obtainable on an application under Order 53), despite the fact that this procedure had the effect of depriving the defendants of the protection to statutory tribunals and public authorities for which for public policy reasons Order 53 provided.

Now that those disadvantages to applicants have been removed and all remedies for infringements of rights protected by public law can be obtained upon an application for judicial review, as can also remedies for infringements of rights under private law if such infringements should also be involved, it would in my view as a general rule be contrary to public policy, and as such an abuse of the process of the court, to permit a person seeking to establish that a decision of a public authority infringed rights to which he was entitled to protection under public law to proceed by way of an ordinary action and by this means to evade the provisions of Order 53 for the protection of such authorities.

My Lords, I have described this as a general rule; for though it may normally be appropriate to apply it by the summary process of striking out the action, there may be exceptions, particularly where the invalidity of the decision arises as a collateral issue in a claim for infringement of a right of the plaintiff arising under private law, or where none of the parties objects to the adoption of the procedure by writ or originating summons. Whether there should be other exceptions should, in my view, at this stage in the development of procedural public law, be left to be decided on a case to case basis—a process that your Lordships will be continuing in the next case in which judgment is to be delivered today [*Cocks* v. *Thanet District Council* [1983] 2 A.C. 286].

In the instant cases where the only relief sought is a declaration of nullity of the decisions of a statutory tribunal, the Board of Visitors of Hull Prison, as in any other case in which a similar declaration of nullity in public law is the only relief claimed, I have no hesitation, in agreement with the Court of Appeal, in holding that to allow the actions to proceed would be an abuse of the process of the court. They are blatant attempts to avoid the protections for the defendants for which Order 53 provides.

I would dismiss these appeals.

Notes

1. Lord Diplock makes it clear that this was not a case where the applicants had any claim to a remedy as a matter of private law. In the 1950s, 1960s and 1970s the courts had taken a generous view of the availability of private law remedies against public authorities. The orthodox view of the requirement of *locus standi* for an injunction or declaration was that, as private law remedies, they were only available to protect an applicant's private law rights, or where an applicant suffered special damage from interference with a public right. Occasionally, judges adopted this strict approach, (*e.g. Gregory* v. *Camden London Borough Council* [1966] 1 W.L.R. 899). More commonly, declarations and injunctions were awarded against public authorities in circumstances where it did not seem that the applicant's private law rights were at stake, or that he had suffered special damage, but where no point was taken by the public authority as to the plaintiff's standing on the availability of the remedy (see, *e.g. Prescott* v. *Birmingham Corporation* [1955] Ch. 210; *Lee* v. *Department of Education and Science* [1967] 66 L.G.R. 211).

The House of Lords in *Gouriet* v. *Union of Post Office Workers* [1978] A.C. 435, in a case where the plaintiff was seeking an injunction to restrain a threatened breach of the criminal law by the respondent trade union, reaffirmed that the proper test for *locus standi* was whether the plaintiff's legal rights were at stake, or he had suffered special damage. The position where the respondent was a public authority was not tested before the introduction of the new Order 53.

In the light of this, *O'Reilly* v. *Mackman* can be interpreted simply as repudiating the generous, but unsoundly based, approach to standing in injunction and declaration cases that was in any event under a cloud following *Gouriet*. What might have given rise to cause for concern would have been if the new approach had made it more difficult for plaintiffs to vindicate their private law rights where the defendant was a public authority. Subsequent case law has provided some reassurance on the point.

2. The decision of the House of Lords in *Cocks* v. *Thanet District Council* [1983] 2 A.C. 286 was delivered on the same day as that in *O'Reilly* v. *Mackman*. In this case, the plaintiff applied to the council, as the local housing authority, for permanent accommodation for himself and his family. The council provided temporary accommodation. The plaintiff commenced proceedings in the county court for a declaration that the council owed and was in breach of its duty under the Housing (Homeless Persons) Act 1977, for consequential mandatory injunctions and for damages. The matter was removed by consent into the High Court, where Milmo J. decided, as a preliminary question, that the plaintiff was entitled to proceed as he was doing, and not limited to proceeding by way of an application for judicial review. In this, the judge was bound by the decision of the Court of Appeal in *De Falco* v. *Crawley Borough Council* [1980] Q.B. 460. The council appealed directly to the House of Lords, and the House unanimously allowed the appeal. The council's duty to provide permanent accommodation under the housing legislation (the "full housing duty") arose where an applicant was (1) homeless or threatened with homelessness; (2) had a priority need; and (3) had not become homeless intentionally. The issue here was likely ultimately to turn on the question of intentional homelessness. The only speech was delivered by Lord Bridge, who stated that the functions of housing authorities under the legislation fell into two distinct categories (pp. 292–293):

"On the one hand, the housing authority are charged with decision-making functions. It is for the housing authority to decide whether they have reason to believe the matters which will give rise to the duty to inquire or to the temporary housing duty. It is for the housing authority, once the duty to inquire has arisen, to make the appropriate inquiries and to decide whether they are satisfied, or not satisfied as the case may be, of the matters which will give rise to the limited housing duty or the full housing duty. These are essentially public law functions. The power of decision being committed by the statute exclusively to the housing authority, their exercise of the power can only be challenged before the courts on the strictly limited grounds (i) that their decision was vitiated by bias or procedural unfairness; (ii) that they have reached a conclusion of fact which can be impugned on the principles set out in the speech of Lord Radcliffe in *Edwards* v. *Bairstow* [1956] A.C. 14; or (iii) that, in so far as they have exercised a discretion (as they may require to do in considering questions of reasonableness under section 17(1)(2) and (4) [of the 1977 Act]), the exercise can be impugned on the principles set out in the judgment of Lord Greene M.R. in *Associated Provincial Picture Houses Ltd.* v. *Wednesbury Corporation* [1948] 1 K.B. 223. All this is trite law and the contrary has, so far as I know, never been argued in any case which has come before the courts under the Act of 1977.

On the other hand, the housing authority are charged with executive functions. Once a decision has been reached by the housing authority which gives rise to the temporary, the limited or the full housing duty, rights and obligations are immediately created in the field of private law. Each of the duties referred to, once established, is capable of being enforced by injunction and the breach of it will give rise to a liability in damages. But it is inherent in the scheme of the Act that an appropriate public law decision of the housing authority is a condition precedent to the establishment of the private law duty."

The Court of Appeal in *De Falco* (of which Lord Bridge had been a member) had "failed to appreciate the significance" of this dichotomy of functions.

Lord Bridge then considered whether the *O'Reilly* v. *Mackman* principle was applicable:

"Does the same general rule apply, where the decision of the public authority which the litigant wishes to overturn is not one alleged to infringe any existing right but a decision which, being adverse to him, prevents him establishing a necessary condition precedent to the statutory private law right which he seeks to enforce? Any relevant decision of a housing authority under the Act of 1977 which an applicant for accommodation wants to challenge will be of that character. I have no doubt that the same general rule should apply to such a case. The safeguards built into the Order 53 procedure which protect from harassment public authorities on whom Parliament has imposed a duty to make public law decisions and the inherent advantages of that procedure over proceedings begun by writ or originating summons for the purposes of investigating whether such decisions are open to challenge are of no less importance in relation to this type of decision than to the type of decision your Lordships have just been considering in *O'Reilly* v. *Mackman*. I have in mind, in particular, the need to obtain leave to apply on the basis of sworn evidence which makes frank disclosure of all relevant facts known to the applicant; the court's discretionary control of both discovery and cross-examination; the capacity of the court to act with the utmost speed when necessary; and the avoidance of the temptation for the court to substitute its own decision of fact for that of the housing authority. Undue delay in seeking a remedy on the part of an aggrieved applicant for accommodation under the Act of 1977 is perhaps not often likely to present a problem, but since this appeal, unlike *O'Reilly* v. *Mackman*, arises from proceedings commenced after the coming into operation of the Supreme Court Act 1981, it is an appropriate occasion to observe both that section 31 of that Act removes any doubt there may have been as to the *vires* of the 1977 amendment of R.S.C., Ord. 53 and also that section 31(6), by expressly recognising that delay in seeking the public law remedies obtainable by application for judicial review may be detrimental to good administration, lends added weight to the consideration that the court, in the control of its own process, is fully justified in confining litigants to the use of procedural machinery which affords protection against such detrimental delay.

Even though nullification of a public law decision can, if necessary, be achieved by declaration as an alternative to an order of certiorari, certiorari to quash remains the primary and most appropriate remedy. Now that all public law remedies are available to be sought by the unified and simplified procedure of an application for judicial review, there can be no valid reason, where the quashing of a decision is the sole remedy sought, why it should be sought otherwise than by certiorari. But an unsuccessful applicant for accommodation under the Act of 1977, confronted by an adverse decision of the housing authority as to, say, the question of his intentional homelessness, may strictly need not only an order of certiorari to quash the adverse decision but also an order of mandamus to the housing authority to determine the question afresh according to law. I have said that the court has no power to substitute its own decision for that of the housing authority. That is strictly correct, though no doubt in practice there will be cases where the court's decision will effectively determine the issue, as for instance where on undisputed primary facts the court holds that no reasonable housing authority, correctly directing itself in law, could be satisfied that the applicant became homeless intentionally. But it will be otherwise where the housing authority's decision is successfully impugned on other grounds, as for instance that the applicant was not fairly heard or that irrelevant factors have been taken into account. In such cases certiorari to quash and mandamus to re-determine will, in strictness, be the appropriate remedies and the only appropriate remedies.

It follows from these considerations that proceedings in which an unsuccessful applicant for accommodation under the Act of 1977 sets out to challenge the decision of the housing authority against him will afford another application of Lord Diplock's general rule and will amount to an abuse of the process of the court if instituted otherwise than by an application for judicial review under R.S.C., Ord. 53.

. . . I think it appropriate to emphasise that the conclusion reached in this appeal arises from the English court's inherent jurisdiction to control its own process to prevent abuse, and has nothing to do with any limitation on the jurisdiction of the county court. As Lord Diplock has observed in *O'Reilly* v. *Mackman* [1983] 2 A.C. 237, the validity of a public law decision may come into question collaterally in an ordinary action. In such a case the issue would have to be decided by the High Court or the county court trying the action, as the case might be."

One interesting point is that while the decision in *Cocks* v. *Thanet District Council* was delivered *after* that in *O'Reilly* v. *Mackman*, argument had been heard in *Cocks* v. *Thanet District Council* first. Moreover, the plaintiff in that case did not appear and was not represented. The plaintiff *was* represented in *O'Reilly* v. *Mackman* but it seems that it was by then difficult to persuade the House to take a different view.

3. In *Davy* v. *Spelthorne Borough Council* (1983) 81 L.G.R. 580, the plaintiff was the owner of premises used to produce precast concrete. In November 1979, he entered an agreement with the defendant (the local planning authority) whereby

he undertook not to appeal against an enforcement notice in respect of the use of the premises provided that the notice was not enforced by the authority for a period of three years from the date of service of the notice. In October 1980, a notice was served as contemplated by the agreement, and, *inter alia*, required the removal of buildings. The plaintiff did not appeal against the notice and the time for appealing against it expired. In August 1982, the plaintiff brought an action in the Chancery Division claiming (1) an injunction restraining the council from implementing the enforcement notice, (2) damages for negligent advice alleged to have been given by the council resulting in a failure to appeal against the notice and (3) an order that the enforcement notice be set aside. The Court of Appeal held that claims (1) and (3) should be struck out as an abuse of process as in substance they involved an attack on the validity of the notice and were designed to have the same effect as would be obtained by an order of certiorari or a declaration under Order 53. However, the claim for damages should not be struck out as it was a claim at common law for a breach of duty owned in private law, notwithstanding that it related to the exercise of statutory functions and notwithstanding that in order to obtain a substantial award of damages, he would have to demonstrate that he had lost at least a chance of making out a good defence to the enforcement notice. While such a claim could be brought under Order 53, this would only be permitted at the discretion of the Queen's Bench Division. If there was a successful application out of time for judicial review, all the proceedings should continue in the Queen's Bench Division; otherwise, the action for damages should proceed in the Chancery Division. The local authority appealed against the refusal of the Court of Appeal to strike out the claim for damages. The House of Lords unanimously dismissed the appeal ([1984] A.C. 262). Lord Fraser of Tullybelton (with whose speech Lords Roskill, Brandon and Brightman agreed) stated that "[i]n the present case . . . the respondent does not impugn or wish to overturn the enforcement notice. His whole case on negligence depends on the fact that he has lost his chance to impugn it. In my opinion therefore the general rule stated in *O'Reilly* v. *Mackman* is inapplicable" (*ibid*. p. 274). The respondent's claim was concerned with the alleged infringement of his rights at common law. Other considerations were (1) that as the notice itself was not now challenged, no public authority or third party was being kept in suspense on that matter and there was accordingly no requirement for a speedy decision; (2) that in any event procedure under Order 53 would be "entirely inappropriate in this case" (*ibid.*, p. 274); (3) that if the claim were to be struck out, "the blow to the respondent's chances of recovering damages might well be mortal" (*ibid.*, p. 274): the court had no power to order the proceedings to continue as if they had been made under Order 53 and so the respondent would have to seek leave to start proceedings for judicial review, now long out of time; and (4) it was impossible to hold that the true purpose of the claim for damages was only to put pressure on the local authority not to enforce the notice. In his concurring speech, Lord Wilberforce emphasised the point that "[b]efore a proceeding at common law can be said to be an abuse of process, it must, at least, be shown (1) that the claim in question *could* be brought by way of judicial review (2) that it *should* be brought by way of judicial review" (*ibid.*, p. 751). In *O'Reilly* v. *Mackman, supra*, it was not argued that the prisoners would not have had a remedy by way of judicial review, and "indeed, as I understand the case, they would not have had a remedy in private law at all" (*ibid.*). The claim in the present case neither could nor should be brought by way of judicial review.

The case is of significance at two levels. First, the House of Lords' decision to refuse to strike out claim (2) made it clear that the courts would be reluctant to apply the principle of *O'Reilly* v. *Mackman* to interfere with what was one of the classic forms of a private right of action: an action for damages in tort. However, could it not also be said that the authority's decision to serve an enforcement notice involved at least a potential interference with private rights? If the plaintiff did not comply with the notice, he could be prosecuted for a criminal offence. Moreover, the local authority could have entered the land and itself undertaken the work necessary for compliance with the notice. Can it be argued that the Court of Appeal's decision in this case takes matters one step beyond *O'Reilly* v. *Mackman*? The decision of the House of Lords was echoed in *Roy* v. *Kensington and Chelsea and Westminster Family Practitioner Committee* [1992] 2 W.L.R. 239 where the House of Lords refused to strike out part of an action based on the plaintiff's private law rights. Lord Lowry (at pp. 264–265) expressed a preference for a "broad approach" under which *O'Reilly* v. *Mackman* "merely required the aggrieved person to proceed by judicial review only when private law rights were not at stake"; however, the case was decided on a "narrow approach," under which it was to be regarded as an exception to the principle. See I. Hare, [1992] C.L.J. 203; S. Fredman and G. Morris, (1992) 108 L.Q.R. 353; P. Cane, [1992] P.L. 193.

4. In *O'Reilly* v. *Mackman*, Lord Diplock stated (at p. 285) that an exception might be made "where the invalidity of the decision arises as a collateral issue in a claim for infringement of a right of the plaintiff arising under private law." Subsequent case law has shown that the *O'Reilly* v. *Mackman* principle does not apply to prevent the invalidity of a decision being raised as a defence to enforcement proceedings. The point has arisen in both civil and criminal cases.

The leading authority in civil cases in *Wandsworth London Borough Council* v. *Winder* [1985] A.C. 461. W. occupied a flat let by the council on a secure tenancy. In 1981 and 1982 the council, in exercise of its powers under the Housing Act 1957, resolved to increase council rents. On each occasion, W. regarded the increase as unreasonable and paid only such rent as he considered reasonable. The council took proceedings in the county court claiming arrears of rent, and also claiming possession of the premises on the ground that the rent lawfully due had not been paid. W. defended the action on the ground that the decisions increasing the rent were *ultra vires* and void as being unreasonable. He also counterclaimed for a declaration that the notices of increases of rent were *ultra vires* and void, and for a declaration that the rent payable was the old rent. The registrar dismissed the council's application to strike out the paragraphs of the defence and counterclaim that asserted that the decisions were void. The county court judge allowed the council's appeal, but stayed the proceedings to allow W. to seek leave to apply for judicial review out of time. (W.'s application for leave was refused.) The Court of Appeal (Robert Goff and Parker L.JJ., Ackner L.J. dissenting) then allowed W.'s appeal against the order of the county court judge. The council's further appeal to the House of Lords was dismissed.

The sole speech was delivered by Lord Fraser. His Lordship noted that there were two important differences between the facts of *O'Reilly* v. *Mackman* and the present case. First, the plaintiffs in *O'Reilly* v. *Mackman* "had not suffered any infringement of their rights in private law," whereas here "what the respondent complains of is the infringement of a contractual right in private law" (p. 507). Until April 6, 1981, W. "had a contractual right to occupy the flat, provided he paid the rent of £12.06 and complied with the other terms of the tenancy" (p. 505). The terms could only be varied by a notice that, *inter alia*, was not unreasonable in the *Wednesbury* sense. The second difference was that "in *O'Reilly* the prisoners had initiated the proceedings . . . while in the present case the respondent is the defendant" (p. 507). *Cocks* v. *Thanet District Council* was also distinguishable: the impugned decision in that case "did not deprive the plaintiff of a pre-existing private law right; it prevented him from establishing a new private law right," moreover "the party complaining of the decision was the plaintiff" (p. 508).

Lord Fraser did *not*, however, regard the case as falling with any of the exceptions mentioned by Lord Diplock in *O'Reilly* v. *Mackman*. In particular, the invalidity of the council's decision was not "truly collateral to the issue between the parties . . . [I]t is the whole basis of the respondent's defence and it is the central issue which has to be decided."

Nevertheless, the principle underlying *O'Reilly* v. *Mackman* and *Cocks* v. *Thanet District Council* was not applicable (pp. 510–511):

"The main argument urged on behalf of the appellants was that this is a typical case where there is a need for speedy certainty in the public interest. I accept, of course, that the decision in this appeal will indirectly affect many third parties including many of the appellants' tenants, and perhaps most if not all of their ratepayers because if the appellants' impugned decisions are held to be invalid, the basis of their financial administration since 1981 will be upset. That would be highly inconvenient from the point of view of the appellants, and of their ratepayers, and it would be a great advantage to them if persons such as the respondent who seek to challenge their decision were limited to doing so by procedure under Order 53. It may well be that such protection to public authorities tends to promote good administration. But there may be other ways of obtaining speedy decisions; for example in some cases it may be possible for a public authority itself to initiate proceedings for judicial review. In any event, the arguments for protecting public authorities against unmeritorious or dilatory challenges to their decisions have to be set against the arguments for preserving the ordinary rights of private citizens to defend themselves against unfounded claims.

It would in my opinion be a very strange use of language to describe the respondent's behaviour in relation to this litigation as an abuse or misuse by him of the process of the court. He did not select the procedure to be adopted. He is merely seeking to defend proceedings brought against him by the appellants. In so doing he is seeking only to exercise the ordinary right of any individual to defend an action against him on the ground that he is not liable for the whole sum claimed by the plaintiff. Moreover he puts forward his defence as a matter of right, whereas in an application for judicial review, success would require an exercise of the court's discretion in his favour. Apart from the provisions of Order 53 and section 31 of the Supreme Court Act 1981, he would certainly be entitled to defend the action on the ground that the plaintiff's claim arises from a resolution which (on his view) is invalid: see for example *Cannock Chase District Council* v. *Kelly* [1978] 1 W.L.R. 1, which was decided in July 1977, a few months before Order 53 came into force (as it did in December 1977). I find it impossible to accept that the right to challenge the decision of a local authority in course of defending an action for non-payment can have been swept away by Order 53, which was directed to introducing a procedural reform. As my noble and learned friend Lord Scarman said in *R.* v. *Inland Revenue Commissioners, ex p. Federation of Self Employed and Small Businesses Ltd.* [1982] A.C. 617, 647G 'The new R.S.C., Ord. 53 is a procedural reform of great importance in the field of public law, but it does not—indeed, cannot—either extend or diminish the substantive law. Its function is limited to ensuring "ubi jus, ibi remedium." ' Lord Wilberforce spoke to the same effect at p. 631A. Nor, in my opinion, did section 31 of the Supreme Court Act 1981 which refers only to "an application" for judicial review have the effect of limiting the rights of a defendant sub silentio. I would adopt the words of Viscount Simonds in *Pyx Granite Co. Ltd.* v. *Ministry of Housing and Local Government* [1960] A.C. 260, 286 as follows:

> 'It is a principle not by any means to be whittled down that the subject's recourse to Her Majesty's courts for the determination of his rights is not to be excluded except by clear words.'

The argument of the appellants in the present case would be directly in conflict with that observation.

If the public interest requires that persons should not be entitled to defend actions brought against them by public authorities, where the defence rests on a challenge to a decision by the public authority, then it is for Parliament to change the law."

(Having been allowed to raise it, Mr. Winder's defence was in the event unsuccessful: *Wandsworth London Borough Council* v. *Winder (No. 2)* (1987) 19 H.L.R. 204.)

Wandsworth London Borough Council v. *Winder* was distinguished by the Court of Appeal in *Avon County Council* v. *Buscott and others* [1988] 2 Q.B. 656. Here, the respondents to eviction proceedings brought by the council were held not to be entitled to resist them on the ground that the council's decision to institute them was unreasonable in the *Wednesbury* sense. The respondent conceded that they were trespassers and that they had no defence on the merits. Accordingly they were not seeking to protect their legal rights and it was this factor that distinguished the case from *Winder*. *Winder* was also distinguished in *Waverley Borough Council* v. *Hilden* [1988] 1 W.L.R. 246, where Scott J. held that where a defendant to proceedings for an injunction commenced by a local authority under section 222 of the Local Government Act 1972 sought to argue that the decision to proceed under section 222 was *ultra vires*, that challenge had to be by way of an application for judicial review. It did not amount to a substantive defence to the enforcement proceedings.

5. The principle of *O'Reilly* v. *Mackman, supra*, does not prevent the defendant in a criminal case relying on the *ultra vires* doctrine in conducting his defence. For example, in *R.* v. *Jenner* [1983] 1 W.L.R. 873 the Court of Appeal (Criminal Division) quashed the appellant's conviction for contravention of a stop notice issued under section 90 of the Town and Country Planning Act 1971 on the ground that he had not been permitted to argue in his defence that the stop notice was invalid. The court rejected the prosecution's argument that the only way by which the appellant could challenge the validity of the notice was by applying for judicial review. *Per* Watkins L.J. at p. 877:

"The process of judicial review, which rarely allows of the reception of oral evidence, is not suited to resolving the issues of fact involved in deciding whether activity said to be prohibited by it is caught by section 90. These issues could not possibly be decided upon the contents of affidavits which is the form of evidence usually received by the Divisional Court."

On the other hand, in *Plymouth City Council* v. *Quietlynn Ltd.* [1988] Q.B. 114, the Divisional Court held that the company was not entitled in defence to a prosecution before a magistrates' court for offences of using premises as a sex establishment without a licence to argue that the council's refusal to grant a licence under the Local Government (Miscellaneous Provisions) Act 1982 was *ultra vires*. If a *bona fide* challenge to the validity of the decision was raised, proceedings should be adjourned to enable an application for judicial review to be made and determined. Except where a decision was invalid on its face, every decision of the licensing authority under the Act was presumed to have been validly made and to continue in force unless and until it had been struck down by the High Court; and neither the justices nor the Crown Court had power to investigate or decide upon its validity (pet. dis., [1987] 1 W.L.R. 1090, H.L.; see J. Alder, (1988) 51 M.L.R. 109). The *Quietlynn* decision was distinguished in *R.* v. *Reading Crown Court, ex p. Hutchinson; R.* v. *Devizes JJ., ex p. Lee* [1988] Q.B. 384, where the Divisional Court held it was not to be taken to affect the long-established practice whereby magistrates rule on the validity of a by-law where that is raised by the defence as a collateral issue in a criminal prosecution for breach of the by-law (pet. dis., [1988] 1

W.L.R. 308). See also *Canterbury City Council* v. *Bern* (1981) 44 P. & C.R. 178, *Scarborough Borough Council* v. *Adams* (1983) 47 P. & C.R. 133 and *Warrington Borough Council* v. *David Garvey* [1989] J.P.L. 752.

6. Other cases decided after *O'Reilly* v. *Mackman*, where private actions have been struck out as an abuse of process include *Luxclose Ltd.* v. *London Borough of Hammersmith and Fulham* [1983] J.P.L. 662; *London Borough of Wandsworth* v. *Orakpo* (1986) 19 H.L.R. 57; *G.* v. *Hounslow London Borough Council* (1987) 86 L.G.R. 186; *Allen* v. *Chief Constable of Cheshire*, *The Times*, July 18, 1988 (injunction set aside by the Court of Appeal).

Cases where private actions have not been struck out include *An Bord Bainne Co-operative Ltd. (Irish Dairy Board)* v. *Milk Marketing Board* [1984] 1 C.M.L.R. 519 (decisions in the public law field alleged to constitute infringements of directly effective E.E.C. regulations which created direct rights in private law: these rights could be protected in the same way as an individual could in certain cases sue for breach of statutory duty) affirmed: [1984] 2 C.M.L.R. 584, C.A.; *Ettridge* v. *Morrell* (1986) 85 L.G.R. 100 (candidate's right to use of school room under s.96(1) of the Representation of the People Act 1983 enforceable in private law); *Doyle* v. *Northumbria Probation Committee* [1991] 4 All E.R. 294 (action for breach of contract not struck out where the respondent raised a public law defence at a time when the plaintiff was out of time to proceed by judicial review).

7. In *O'Reilly* v. *Mackman*, Lord Diplock indicated (above, p. 733) that ordinary proceedings might be brought by agreement. In *Inner London Education Authority* v. *Department of the Environment* (1983) 82 L.G.R. 322, Woolf J. heard proceedings for a declaration commenced by originating summons, in respect of the issue whether I.L.E.A. was a "local authority" for the purpose of Part III of the Local Government, Planning and Land Act 1980. No objection was taken to this course and the matter was set down in the Crown Office list. See also *Gillick* v. *West Norfolk and Wisbech Area Health Authority* [1986] A.C. 112, *per* Lord Scarman at pp. 177–178.

8. Academic reaction to the *O'Reilly* v. *Mackman* principle has generally been critical. There are several themes. On the assumption that both a civil action and an application for judicial review were technically available, for

> "a complainant, whether against a public authority or not, to find his complaint dismissed without an investigation of its merits, not on the ground that it is without substance . . . not even on the ground that he lacks *locus standi*, but purely and simply because he selected the wrong form of action is a singularly unfortunate step back to the technicalities of a bygone age."

(J. A. Jolowicz, [1983] C.L.J. 15, 18).

> "The overall picture is one of waste of time and money on litigation merely about procedure."

(H. W. R. Wade, (1985) 101 L.Q.R. 180, 187). See also the comment by Henry J. in *Doyle* v. *Northumbria Probation Committee* [1991] 4 All E.R. 294, 300.

The line between "public law" and "private law" is widely recognised as difficult to draw, the cases summarised in the previous notes failing to provide clear and convincing guidance. See the discussion by J. Beatson, " 'Public' and 'Private' in Administrative Law" (1987) 103 L.Q.R. 34; C. F. Forsyth, "Beyond *O'Reilly* v. *Mackman*: The Foundations and Nature of Procedural Exclusivity" [1985] C.L.J. 415; G. L. Peiris, "The Exclusivity of Judicial Review Procedure: The Growing Boundary Dispute" (1986) 15 Anglo-Am.L.R. 83; *Lewis*, Ch. 3. The point is well illustrated by the cases in the section on the scope of Order 53 (above, pp. 688–715).

A third line of criticism addresses the twin assumptions that underlie the present state of the law: (1) that public authorities need the special safeguards inherent in the Order 53 procedure; but (2) that the vindication of private rights ought not to be encumbered by the restrictions that apply in consequence to litigants. If the safeguards are really necessary in the public interest why should they not apply also to private actions against public authorities (*cf. Craig*, p. 423). Why should interests protected by public law be regarded as less important than private law rights?

"... [W]hen one considers the subject matter of some of the public law interests which have generated litigation (*e.g.* remission of sentence, obtaining council housing) this assumption appears absurd" (*Cane*, p. 170).

The present difficulties have been said to be the "inevitable" result of the recommendations of the Law Commission: a new procedure with safeguards for public authorities was to be set up, but was not to be exclusive (Wade, (1985) 101 L.Q.R. 180, 187; *Craig*, p. 425):

"The Law Commission's scheme had failed to remove the illogicalities inherent in the dual system of remedies, so that the force of Lord Denning's and Lord Diplock's arguments was, in the circumstances, irresistable" (Wade, *op. cit.*).

If the differences between public law and private law had been exaggerated the appropriate move would presumably be towards greater assimilation of public law and private law procedures. For Sir Harry Woolf, the move should be towards the greater procedural exclusivity of Order 53 ("Public Law—Private Law: Why the Divide? A Personal View" [1986] P.L. 220; *Protection of the Public—A New Challenge* (1990), pp. 19–32). He regards the House of Lords decision in *Wandsworth London Borough Council* v. *Winder* (above, p. 738) as an undesirable exception to *O'Reilly* v. *Mackman*:

"I am ... appalled that a situation should be able to arise where Mr. Winder would not succeed on an application for judicial review because the court would not exercise discretion in his favour but he could still succeed on the same facts as a defence and for the purposes of obtaining a declaration by way of counterclaim" (*Protection of the Public*, p. 31).

"... I have difficulty in understanding why Mr. Winder should be in a better position if he waits to be sued than if he takes the course of applying himself, as in my view he should have done, to challenge the decision of the local authority to increase rents at the proper time" ([1986] P.L. at p. 234).

Alternatively, provision should be made for such allegations in a counterclaim to be advanced only with the leave of the court, after (if they are in the County Court) being transferred to the Crown Office list of the High Court (*ibid.* at p. 235).

Others have argued that the proper approach would be:

"to fit the prerogative remedies into the mechanism of an ordinary action, so that there would be no dichotomy and no dilemma for the litigant" (Wade, (1985) 101 L.Q.R. 180, 189).

There would then be one single form of action covering both public and private law; there would be no leave requirement, but the respondent authority could apply for an expedited procedure incorporating the appropriate Order 53 safeguards, such as the time limits (Wade, *op. cit.* pp. 189–190; *cf. Craig*, pp. 425–426).

A variant of this is suggested by Cane. On the assumption that public bodies need special protection (which is itself questionable), every applicant for a remedy against a public body would need first to obtain leave. If no public law issues were raised, private law procedure would then be followed and the *litigant* would choose whether to proceed by writ (where there were substantial disputes of fact) or originating summons (otherwise). If public law issues were involved the *court* would choose which of two procedural tracks should apply, one suitable for cases raising substantial factual disputes, the other for cases where there were no such disputes (*Cane*, pp. 178–179).

For other comments see J. McBride, (1983) 2 C.J.Q. 268; M. Sunkin, (1983) 46 M.L.R. 645; H. W. R. Wade, (1983) 99 L.Q.R. 199; A. Grubb, [1983] P.L. 190; P. Cane, [1983] P.L. 202 (on *O'Reilly* and *Cocks*); A. Grubb, [1983] C.L.J. 16; P. Cane, [1984] P.L. 16 (on *Davy* v. *Spelthorne*); C. F. Forsyth, [1985] P.L. 355; A. Grubb, (1985) 101 L.Q.R. 486 (on *Winder*); C. T. Emery, [1992] C.L.J 308.

9. The JUSTICE—All Souls Review of Administrative Law in the United Kingdom (*Administrative Justice: Some Necessary Reforms* (1988), Chap. 6) concluded that *O'Reilly* v. *Mackman* was an unfortunate decision. "All" the disadvantages associated with the prerogative orders had not been removed; objectionable features survived (the need to obtain leave, the shortness of the time-limit, little change in the old attitudes unfavourable to discovery and cross-examination on affidavit evidence (see pp. 717–718)); a clear-cut distinction could not be drawn between public law and private law rights:

> "It should be left to Parliament to decide, after appropriate consultation, whether there are any circumstances in which a plaintiff should be obliged to use the Order 53 procedure and be debarred from proceeding by action on originating summons" (p. 166).

The Committee also recommended that the leave requirement should be abandoned; that the three-month time-limit should be repealed, and matter of delay left on the more general basis provided by the Supreme Court Act 1981, s.31(6) (above, p. 687, below, pp. 764–772); discovery of documents, interrogatories and cross-examination should be permitted more liberally; provision should be made enabling the court to order that proceedings wrongly commenced by writ should continue as if they were an application for judicial review.

The Law Commission's Fifth Programme includes an item on the procedures and forms of relief available by way of judicial review, including the effect of *O'Reilly* v. *Mackman*, time limits, interim relief, discovery, standing and certain other specific matters.

10. One of the arguments in favour of procedural exclusivity is that of the expertise of the judges who are nominated to take cases on the Crown Office list (see p. 716). This point was not made by Lord Diplock in *O'Reilly* v. *Mackman*, although it was by Lord Denning M.R. at the Court of Appeal stage ([1983] 2 A.C. 237, 259) and by Goulding J. in *Heywood* v. *Board of Visitors of Hull Prison* [1980] 1 W.L.R. 1386. Beatson comments that:

> ". . . if this is the case the administrative court should hear all cases brought by and against public authorities and not only those in which it is sought to quash administrative decisions or to compel the execution of a public duty. Furthermore, it does not follow that the way to promote expertise is by a procedural specialisation as opposed to a subject matter specialisation" ((1987) 103 L.Q.R. 34, 43).

The establishment of the scheme of nominated judges has taken the substance out of proposals for a new Administrative Division of the High Court (see the

JUSTICE—All Souls Review of Administrative Law, *Administrative Justice: Some Necessary Reforms* (1988), pp. 168–170).

(F) Standing

R. v. INLAND REVENUE COMMISSIONERS, ex p. NATIONAL FEDERATION OF SELF-EMPLOYED AND SMALL BUSINESSES LTD.

[1982] A.C. 617; [1981] 2 W.L.R. 722; [1981] 2 All E.R. 93
(House of Lords)

Some 6,000 casual workers in Fleet Street were nominated by their trade unions to work for newspapers on specified occasions. They were given call slips and then collected pay dockets to enable them to draw their pay from their employers but a substantial number of them gave false names and addresses (*e.g.* "Mickey Mouse of Sunset Boulevard" and "Sir Gordon Richards of Tattenham Corner") so that it was impossible for the Inland Revenue to collect the tax which was due from them. The consequent loss to the revenue was estimated at £1 million a year. In view of the frauds the Inland Revenue after discussions with the employers and the unions, introduced a special arrangement which would ensure that for the future tax would either be deducted at source or be properly assessed and made it clear that, if the arrangement were generally accepted, and subject to certain other conditions, investigation into tax lost in certain previous years would not be carried out. A federation representing the self-employed and small businesses, who contrasted the attitude taken by the revenue to the tax evasions of the Fleet Street casuals with that adopted by the revenue in other cases where tax evasions were suspected, applied for judicial review and claimed a declaration that the Inland Revenue acted unlawfully in granting the amnesty and an order of mandamus directed to the revenue to assess and collect income-tax from the casual workers.

The Divisional Court granted leave *ex parte*, but at the hearing *inter partes*, on the Inland Revenue's objection that the federation had no *locus standi*, the Divisional Court held that the federation had not "sufficient interest" within R.S.C., Ord. 53, r. 3(5), to claim the declaration and order sought.

On the federation's appeal, which proceeded on the assumption that the Inland Revenue had no power to grant such a tax "amnesty," the Court of Appeal (by a majority) allowed the appeal ([1980] Q.B. 407) holding that the body of taxpayers represented by the federation could reasonably assert that they had a genuine grievance in the alleged failure of the Inland Revenue to do its duty and the granting of an unlawful tax indulgence to the casual workers, and accordingly they had a "sufficient interest" within the meaning of R.S.C., Ord. 53, r. 3(5) to apply for judicial review under that order.

The Inland Revenue appealed to the House of Lords and the House unanimously allowed their appeal.

Lord Wilberforce: . . . [noted that the question of *locus standi* had been taken as a preliminary point of law, and continued:] I think that it is unfortunate that this course has been taken. There may be simple cases in which it can be seen at the earliest stage that the person applying for judicial review has no interest at all, or no sufficient interest to support the application: then it would be quite correct at the threshold to refuse him leave to apply. The right to do so is an important safeguard against the courts being flooded and public bodies harassed by irresponsible applications. But in other cases this will not be so. In these it will be necessary to consider the powers or the duties in law of those against whom the relief is asked, the position of the applicant in relation to those powers or duties, and to the breach of those said to have been committed. In other words, the question of sufficient interest can not, in such cases, be considered in the abstract, or as an isolated point: it must be taken together with the legal and factual context. The rule requires sufficient interest *in the matter to which the application relates*. This, in the present case, necessarily involves the whole question of the duties of the Inland Revenue and the breaches or failure of those duties of which the respondents complain.

Before proceeding to consideration of these matters, something more needs to be said about the threshold requirement of "sufficient interest." The courts in exercising the power to grant prerogative writs, or, since 1938, prerogative orders, have always reserved the right to be satisfied that the applicant had some genuine *locus standi* to appear before it. This they expressed in different ways. Sometimes it was said, usually in relation to certiorari, that the applicant must be a person aggrieved; or having a particular grievance (*R.* v. *Thames Magistrates' Court, ex p. Greenbaum* (1957) 55 L.G.R. 129); usually in relation to mandamus, that he must have a specific legal right (*R.* v. *Lewisham Union Guardians* [1897] 1 Q.B. 498 and *R.* v. *Russell, ex p. Beaverbrook Newspapers Ltd.* [1969] 1 Q.B. 342); sometimes that he must have a sufficient interest (*R.* v. *Cotham* [1898] 1 Q.B. 802, 804 (mandamus), *ex p. Stott* [1916] 1 K.B. 7 (certiorari)). By 1977, when R.S.C., Ord. 53 was introduced, the courts, guided by Lord Parker C.J., in cases where mandamus was sought, were moving away from the *Lewisham Union* test of specific legal right, to one of sufficient interest. In *R.* v. *Russell* Lord Parker had tentatively adhered to the test of legal specific right but in *R.* v. *Customs and Excise Commissioners, ex p. Cook* [1970] 1 W.L.R. 450 he had moved to sufficient interest. Shortly afterward the new rule (R.S.C., Ord. 53, r. 3) was drafted with these words.

R.S.C., Ord. 53 was, it is well known, introduced to simplify the procedure of applying for the relief formerly given by prerogative writ or order—so the old technical rules no longer apply. So far as the substantive law is concerned, this remained unchanged: the Administration of Justice (Miscellaneous Provisions) Act 1938 preserved the jurisdiction existing before the Act, and the same preservation is contemplated by legislation now pending. The Order, furthermore, did not remove the requirement to show *locus standi*. On the contrary, in rule 3, it stated this in the form of a threshold requirement to be found by the court. For all cases the test is expressed as one of sufficient interest in the matter to which the application relates. As to this I would state two negative propositions. First, it does not remove the whole—and vitally important—question of *locus standi* into the realm of pure discretion. The matter is one for decision, a mixed decision of fact and law, which the court must decide on legal principles. Secondly, the fact that the same words are used to cover all the forms of remedy allowed by the rule does not mean that the test is the same in all cases. When Lord Parker C.J. said that in cases of mandamus the test may well be stricter (sc. than in certiorari)—the *Beaverbrook Newspapers* case [1969] 1 Q.B. 342 and in *Cook's* case [1970] 1 W.L.R. 450, 455F, "on a very strict basis," he was not stating a technical rule—which can now be discarded—but a rule of common sense, reflecting the different character of the relief asked for. It would seem obvious enough that the interest of a person seeking to compel an authority to carry out a duty is different from that of a person complaining that a judicial or administrative body has, to his detriment, exceeded its powers. Whether one calls for a stricter rule than the other may be a linguistic point: they are certainly different and we should be unwise in our enthusiasm for liberation from procedural fetters to discard reasoned authorities which illustrate this. It is hardly necessary to add that recognition of the value of guiding authorities does not mean that the process of judicial review must stand still.

In the present case we are in the area of mandamus—an alleged failure to perform a duty. It was submitted by the Lord Advocate that in such cases we should be guided by the definition of the duty, in this case statutory, and inquire whether expressly, or by implication, this definition indicates—or the contrary—that the complaining applicant is within the scope or ambit of the duty. I think that this is at least a good working rule though perhaps not an exhaustive one.

The Inland Revenue Commissioners are a statutory body. Their duties are, relevantly, defined in the Inland Revenue Regulation Act 1890 and the Taxes Management Act 1970.

. . . [I]t is clear that the Inland Revenue Commissioners are not immune from the process of judicial review. They are an administrative body with statutory duties, which the courts, in principle, can supervise. They have indeed done so—see *R.* v. *Income Tax Special Commissioners* (1881) 21 Q.B.D. 313 (mandamus) and *Income Tax Special Commissioners* v. *Linsleys (Established 1894) Ltd.* [1958] A.C. 569, where it was not doubted that a mandamus could be issued if the facts had been right. It must follow from these cases and from principle that a taxpayer would not be excluded from seeking judicial review if he could show that the revenue had either failed in its statutory duty toward him or had been guilty of some action which was an abuse of their powers or outside their powers altogether. Such a collateral attack—as contrasted with a direct appeal on law to the courts—would no doubt be rare, but the possibility certainly exists.

The position of other taxpayers—other than the taxpayers whose assessment is in question—and their right to challenge the revenue's assessment or non-assessment of that taxpayer, must be judged according to whether, consistently with the legislation, they can be considered as having sufficient interest to complain of what has been done or omitted. I proceed thereto to examine the revenue's duties in that light.

These duties are expressed in very general terms and it is necessary to take account also of the framework of the income tax legislation. This establishes that the commissioners must assess each individual taxpayer in relation to his circumstances. Such assessments and all information regarding taxpayers' affairs are strictly confidential. There is no list or record of assessments which can be inspected by other taxpayers. Nor is there any common fund of the produce of income tax in which income taxpayers as a whole can be said to have any interest. The produce of income tax, together with that of other inland revenue taxes, is paid into the consolidated fund which is at the disposal of Parliament for any purposes that Parliament thinks fit.

The position of taxpayers is therefore very different from that of ratepayers. As explained in *Arsenal Football Club Ltd.* v. *Ende* [1979] A.C. 1, the amount of rates assessed upon ratepayers is ascertainable by the public through the valuation list. The produce of rates goes into a common fund applicable for the benefit of the ratepayers. Thus any ratepayer has an interest, direct and sufficient, in the rates levied upon other ratepayers; for this reason, his right as a "person aggrieved" to challenge assessments upon them has long been recognised and is so now in section 69 of the General Rate Act 1967. This right was given effect to in the *Arsenal* case.

The structure of the legislation relating to income tax, on the other hand, makes clear that no corresponding right is extended to be conferred upon taxpayers. Not only is there no express or implied provision in the legislation upon which such a right could be claimed, but to allow it would be subversive of the whole system, which involves that the commissioners' duties are to the Crown, and that matters relating to income tax are between the commissioners and the taxpayer concerned. No other person is given any right to make proposals about the tax payable by any individual: he cannot even inquire as to such tax. The total confidentiality of assessments and of negotiations between individuals and the revenue is a vital element in the working of the system. As a matter of general principle I would hold that one taxpayer has no sufficient interest in asking the court to investigate the tax affairs of another taxpayer or to complain that the latter has been under-assessed or over-assessed: indeed, there is a strong public interest that he should not. And this principle applies equally to groups of taxpayers: an aggregate of individuals each of whom has no interest cannot of itself have an interest.

That a case can never arise in which the acts or abstentions of the revenue can be brought before the court I am certainly not prepared to assert, nor that, in a case of sufficient gravity, the court might not be able to hold that another taxpayer or other taxpayers could challenge them. Whether this situation has been reached or not must depend upon an examination, upon evidence, of what breach of duty or illegality is alleged. Upon this, and relating it to the position of the complainant, the court has to make its decision.

[His Lordship examined the evidence and concluded that the arrangements in question had been entered by the Inland Revenue, acting genuinely in the care and management of the taxes, under the powers entrusted to them.]

Looking at the matter as a whole, I am of opinion that the Divisional Court, while justified on the *ex parte* application in granting leave, ought, having regard to the nature of "the matter" raised, to have held that the federation had shown no sufficient interest in that matter to justify its application for relief. I would therefore allow the appeal and order that the originating motion be dismissed.

LORD DIPLOCK: ... The whole purpose of requiring that leave should first be obtained to make the application for judicial review would be defeated if the court were to go into the matter in any depth at that stage. If, on a quick perusal of the material then available, the court thinks that it discloses what might on further consideration turn out to be an arguable case in favour of granting to the applicant the relief claimed, it ought, in the exercise of a judicial discretion, to give him leave to apply for that relief. The discretion that the court is exercising at this stage is not the same as that which it is called upon to exercise when all the evidence is in and the matter has been fully argued at the hearing of the application.

The analysis to which ... the relevant legislation has been subjected by some of your Lordships, ... mean that occasions will be very rare on which an individual taxpayer (or pressure group of taxpayers) will be able to show a sufficient interest to justify an application for judicial review of the way in which the revenue has dealt with the tax affairs of any taxpayer other than the applicant himself.

Rare though they may be, however, if, in the instant case, what at the threshold stage was suspicion only had been proved at the hearing of the application for judicial review to have been true in fact (instead of being utterly destroyed), I would have held that this was a matter in which the federation had a sufficient interest in obtaining an appropriate order, whether by way of declaration or mandamus, to require performance by the board of statutory duties which for reasons shown to be *ultra vires* it was failing to perform.

It would, in my view, be a grave lacuna in our system of public law if a pressure group, like the federation, or even a single public-spirited taxpayer, were prevented by outdated technical rules of *locus standi* from bringing the matter to the attention of the court to vindicate the rule of law and get the unlawful conduct stopped. The Attorney-General, although he occasionally applies for prerogative orders against public authorities that do not form part of central government, in practice never does so against government departments. It is not, in my view, a sufficient answer to say that judicial review of the actions of officers or departments of central government is unnecessary because they are accountable to

Parliament for the way in which they carry out their functions. They are accountable to Parliament for what they do so far as regards efficiency and policy, and of that Parliament is the only judge; they are responsible to a court of justice for the lawfulness of what they do, and of that the court is the only judge.

I would allow this appeal upon the ground upon which, in my view, the Divisional Court should have dismissed it when the application came to be heard, instead of singling out the lack of a sufficient interest on the part of the federation, *viz.* that the federation completely failed to show any conduct by the board that was *ultra vires* or unlawful.

LORD FRASER: . . . .I agree with the reasoning of Lord Wilberforce and Lord Roskill but I wish to explain my reasons in my own words. . . . The rules of court give no guidance as to what is a sufficient interest for this purpose. I respectfully accept from my noble and learned friends who are so much more familiar than I am with the history of the prerogative orders that little assistance as to the sufficiency of the interest can be derived from the older cases. But while the standard of sufficiency has been relaxed in recent years, the need to have an interest has remained and the fact that R.S.C., Ord. 53, r. 3 requires a sufficient interest undoubtedly shows that not every applicant is entitled to judicial review as of right.

The new Order 53, introduced in 1977, no doubt had the effect of removing technical and procedural differences between the prerogative orders, and of introducing a remedy by way of declaration or injunction in suitable cases, but I do not think it can have had the effect of throwing over all the older law and of leaving the grant of judicial review in the uncontrolled discretion of the court. On what principle, then, is the sufficiency of interest to be judged? All are agreed that a direct financial or legal interest is not now required, and that the requirement of a legal specific interest laid down in *R.* v. *Lewisham Union Guardians* [1897] 1 Q.B. 488 is no longer applicable. There is also general agreement that a mere busybody does not have a sufficient interest. The difficulty is, in between those extremes, to distinguish between the desire of the busybody to interfere in other people's affairs and the interest of the person affected by or having a reasonable concern with the matter to which the application relates. In the present case that matter is an alleged failure by the appellants to perform the duty imposed upon them by statute.

The correct approach in such a case is, in my opinion, to look at the statute under which the duty arises, and to see whether it gives any express or implied right to persons in the position of the applicant to complain of the alleged unlawful act or omission. On that approach it is easy to see that a ratepayer would have a sufficient interest to complain of unlawfulness by the authorities responsible for collecting the rates. . . . The position of the taxpayer is entirely different . . .

[I]f the class of persons with a sufficient interest is to include all taxpayers it must include practically every individual in the country who has his own income, because there must be few individuals, however frugal their requirements, who do not pay some indirect taxes including value added tax. It would, I think, be extravagant to suggest that every taxpayer who believes that the Inland Revenue or the Commissioners of Customs and Excise are giving unlawful preference to another taxpayer, and who feels aggrieved thereby, has a sufficient interest to obtain judicial review under Order 53. It may be that, if he was relying on some exceptionally grave or widespread illegality, he could succeed in establishing a sufficient interest, but such cases would be very rare indeed and this is not one of them.

LORD SCARMAN: . . . In your Lordships' House the Lord Advocate, who now appears for the appellants, the Inland Revenue Commissioners, . . . has put at the forefront of his argument a reasoned analysis of the statutory duties of the revenue, and has invited the House to hold that the statutory code neither recognises nor imposes upon the revenue a duty such as the federation alleges to the general body, or any group of taxpayers.

Before I consider this submission, it is necessary to deal with a subsidiary point taken by the Lord Advocate. He submitted that, notwithstanding the language of R.S.C., Ord. 53, r. 1(2), the court has no jurisdiction to grant to a private citizen a declaration save in respect of a private right or wrong: and he relied on the House's decision in *Gouriet* v. *Union of Post Office Workers* [1978] A.C. 435. Declaration is, of course, a remedy developed by the judges in the field of private law. *Gouriet's* case is authority for the proposition that a citizen may not issue a writ claiming a declaration or other relief against another for the redress of a public wrong unless he can persuade the Attorney-General, on his "relation," to bring the action. The case has nothing to do with the prerogative jurisdiction of the High Court; and it was decided before the introduction of the new Order 53, at a time when a declaration could not be obtained by a private citizen unless he could show (as in a claim for injunction) that a private right of his was threatened or infringed. The new Order has made the remedy available as an alternative, or an addition, to a prerogative order. Its availability has, therefore, been extended, but only in the field of public law where a prerogative order may be granted. I have already given my reasons for the view that this extension is purely a matter of procedural law, and so within the rule-making powers of the Rules Committee. I therefore reject this submission of the Lord Advocate.

I pass now to the two critical issues: (1) the character of the duty upon the revenue and the persons to whom it is owed. Is it legal, political, or merely moral? (2) The nature of the interest which the applicant has to show. It is an integral part of the Lord Advocate's argument that the existence of the duty is a significant factor in determining the sufficiency of an applicant's interest.

The duty

[His Lordship concluded:]

[A] legal duty of fairness is owed by the revenue to the general body of taxpayers. It is, however, subject to the duty of sound management of the tax which the statute places upon the revenue.

The interest

The sufficiency of the interest is, as I understand all your Lordships agree, a mixed question of law and fact. The legal element in the mixture is less than the matters of fact and degree: but it is important, as setting the limits within which, and the principles by which, the discretion is to be exercised. At one time heresy ruled the day. The decision of the Divisional Court in *R.* v. *Lewisham Union Guardians* [1897] 1 Q.B. 498 was accepted as establishing that an applicant must establish "a legal specific right to ask for the interference of the court" by order of mandamus: *per* Wright J. at p. 500. I agree with Lord Denning M.R. in thinking this was a deplorable decision. It was at total variance with the view of Lord Mansfield C.J. Yet its influence has lingered on, and is evident even in the decision of the Divisional Court in this case. But the tide of the developing law has now swept beyond it, as the Court of Appeal's decision in *R.* v. *Greater London Council, ex p. Blackburn* [1976] 1 W.L.R. 550 illustrates. In the present case the House can put down a marker buoy warning legal navigators of the danger of the decision. As Professor Wade pointed out in *Administrative Law*, 4th ed. (1977), p. 610, if the *Lewisham* case were correct, mandamus would lose its public law character, being no more than a remedy for a private wrong.

My Lords, I will not weary the House with citation of many authorities. Suffice it to refer to the judgment of Lord Parker C.J. in *R.* v. *Thames Magistrates' Court, ex p. Greenbaum*, 55 L.G.R. 129, a case of certiorari; and to words of Lord Wilberforce in *Gouriet* v. *Union of Post Office Workers* [1978] A.C. 435, 482, where he stated the modern position in relation to prerogative orders: "These are often applied for by individuals and the courts have allowed them liberal access under a generous conception of *locus standi.*" The one legal principle, which is implicit in the case law and accurately reflected in the rule of court, is that in determining the sufficiency of an applicant's interest it is necessary to consider the matter to which the application relates. It is wrong in law, as I understand the cases, for the court to attempt an assessment of the sufficiency of an applicant's interest without regard to the matter of his complaint. If he fails to show, when he applies for leave, a *prima facie* case, or reasonable grounds for believing that there has been a failure of public duty, the court would be in error if it granted leave. The curb represented by the need for an applicant to show, when he seeks leave to apply, that he has such a case is an essential protection against abuse of legal process. It enables the court to prevent abuse by busybodies, cranks, and other mischief-makers. I do not see any further purpose served by the requirement for leave.

But, that being said, the discretion belongs to the court: and, as my noble and learned friend, Lord Diplock, has already made clear, it is the function of the judges to determine the way in which it is to be exercised. Accordingly I think that the Divisional Court was right to grant leave *ex parte*. Mr. Payne's affidavit of March 20, 1979, revealed a prima facie case of failure by the Inland Revenue to discharge its duty to act fairly between taxpayer and taxpayer. But by the time the application reached the Divisional Court for a hearing, *inter partes*, of the preliminary issue, two very full affidavits had been filed by the revenue explaining the "management" reasons for the decision not to seek to collect the unpaid tax from the Fleet Street casuals. At this stage the matters of fact and degree upon which depends the exercise of the discretion whether to allow the application to proceed or not became clear. It was now possible to form a view as to the existence or otherwise of a case meriting examination by the court. And it was abundantly plain upon the evidence that the applicant could show no such case. But the Court of Appeal, misled into thinking that, at that stage and notwithstanding the evidence available, *locus standi* was to be dealt with as a preliminary issue, assumed illegality (where in my judgment none was shown) and, upon that assumption, held that the applicant had sufficient interest. Were the assumption justified, which on the evidence it was not, I would agree with the reasoning of Lord Denning M.R. and Ackner L.J. I think the majority of the Court of Appeal, in formulating a test of genuine grievance reasonably asserted, were doing no more than giving effect to the general principle which Lord Mansfield C.J. had stated in the early days on the remedy. Any more stringent test would, as *Wade, Administrative Law*, 4th ed., p. 612 observes, open up "a serious gap in the system of public law." . . .

LORD ROSKILL: . . . It is clear that the respondents are seeking to intervene in the affairs of individual taxpayers, the Fleet Street casual workers, and to require the appellants to assess and collect tax from them which the appellants have clearly agreed not to do. Theoretically, but one trusts only theoretically, it is possible to envisage a case when because of some grossly improper pressure or motive the appellants have failed to perform their statutory duty as respects a particular taxpayer or class of taxpayer. In such a case, which emphatically is not the present, judicial review might be available to other taxpayers. But it would require to be a most extreme case for I am clearly of the view, having regard to the nature of the appellants' statutory duty and the degree of confidentiality enjoined by statute which attaches to their performance, that in general it is not open to individual taxpayers or to a group of taxpayers to seek to interfere between the appellants and other taxpayers, whether those other taxpayers are honest or dishonest men, and that the court should, by refusing relief by way of judicial review, firmly discourage such attempted interference by other taxpayers. It follows that, in my view, taking all those matters into account, it cannot be said that the respondents had a "sufficient interest" to justify their seeking the relief claimed by way of judicial review....

[His Lordship also expressed agreement with LORD WILBERFORCE and LORD FRASER.]

Notes

1. For comments, see P. Cane, [1981] P.L. 322; D. Feldman, (1982) 45 M.L.R. 92; and *Lewis*, Ch. 10. The old law of standing was highly complex, varying according to the remedy sought, and with uncertainty if not conflicting authorities on many points. See generally S. M. Thio, *Locus Standi and Judicial Review*; P. Cane, "The Function of Standing Rules in Administrative Law" [1980] P.L. 303. In theory, the old law was not entirely swept away by the new Order 53 or the *Fleet Street Casuals* case. Nevertheless, references to the old authorities when points as to standing are considered are now unusual. Points that emerge from the *Fleet Street Casuals* case (also sometimes known as "Mickey Mouse" case) include (1) that the question of *locus standi* cannot be considered in isolation from the legal and factual context of the application; (2) that it is one of mixed law and fact to be decided on legal principles and not simply a matter of discretion; (3) that a decision that an applicant has sufficient interest to be granted leave does not preclude the matter being raised at the full hearing; (4) that the question is inappropriate to be taken on appeal as a preliminary issue; and (5), most significantly, that the courts should not take an unduly restrictive approach to questions of standing. There are a number of difficulties.

On point (1), their Lordships indicate that the court must consider both whether on the facts it is established that the decision is *ultra vires*, and, if so, the nature of the illegality. If this means that no person has standing without a good case on the merits and, conversely, that every person with a good case on the merits has standing, then standing has disappeared as a separate concept. Wade accepts that the "House of Lords' new criterion would seem virtually to abolish the requirement of standing "as a distinct concept" (*Administrative Law* (6th ed.), p. 703). However, this seems to put it too high. Schiemann J., writing extra-judicially, states that:

> "wherever someone is ... excluded by reason of *locus standi* rules, the law regards it as preferable that an illegality should continue than that the person excluded should have access to the courts" ([1990] P.L. at 342).

(*Cf.* his Lordship's comments in the *Rose Theatre* case, below, p. 758).

Too much cannot be read into point (2). While Lords Wilberforce, Scarman and Roskill make this point, it is clear from Lord Scarman's speech that the "legal element is less than the matters of fact and degree" (see above, p. 751). In other words the test of sufficient interest is so broadly expressed as to leave considerable leeways for choice on the part of the judges; whether this is to be labelled "law and fact" or "discretion" is of less significance. Only Lord Diplock was prepared to say that the court has an "unfettered discretion to decide what in its own good judgment it considers to be 'a sufficient interest' on the part of an applicant in the particular circumstances of the case before it" (at p. 642). Subsequent judges have used the term "discretion" (see, *e.g.* Watkins L.J. in *R.* v. *Felixstowe JJ., ex p. Leigh* [1987] Q.B. 582, 597; *cf.* Schiemann J. in the *Rose Theatre* case, below p. 759).

It is clear from point (3) that the question of standing arises at two stages. One difficulty is that the statutory test in Ord. 53, r. 3(7), and the Supreme Court Act 1981, s.31(3), refers expressly to the leave stage; the House of Lords acted on the assumption that this was also the appropriate test on the hearing of the full application. While *formally* the same test applies at both stages, its application differs in that at the leave stage the court is only forming a "provisional" or "*prima facie*" view on the question (see the extracts from Lord Diplock's and Lord Scarman's speeches (above, pp. 748 and 752)). A final view can only properly be expressed at the second stage, when the merits of the complaint can be considered. Accordingly, it is only in the clearest of cases that an application will be ruled out at the leave stage on the ground that the applicant lacks *locus*.

2. The House of Lords confirmed, *obiter*, that a ratepayer has *locus standi* to challenge rating decisions concerning other ratepayers in the same area (*cf. Arsenal Football Club Ltd.* v. *Ende* [1979] A.C. 1). It is likely that ratepayers and community charge payers will have standing to challenge decisions of local authorities that involve expenditure (and possibly other decisions or acts, though not necessarily all; a charge payer is unlikely, for example, automatically to have *locus standi* to challenge a decision in the field of child care).

The general principle that one taxpayer does not have *locus standi* to challenge decisions concerning other taxpayers is not an absolute rule. No member of the House of Lords was willing to say that a taxpayer would *never* have *locus standi* in such a case. Then, in *R.* v. *Attorney-General, ex p. Imperial Chemical Industries plc* [1985] 1 C.M.L.R. 588, Woolf J. held that I.C.I. had *locus standi* to challenge a valuation of ethane for the purposes of calculating Petroleum Revenue Tax that would be unduly favourable to its rivals, Esso, Shell and B.P. I.C.I.'s interests were adversely affected by the approach of the Revenue, and was the only body whose interests were likely to be so affected. They were not complaining about a particular assessment in relation to another taxpayer's affairs but about an approach which, but for the judicial review proceedings, would presumably have continued for a substantial time and was in certain respects wrong in law. Woolf J.'s judgment on this point was endorsed by the Court of Appeal [1987] 1 C.M.L.R. 72).

The position of a taxpayer is stronger when he wishes to challenge unlawful expenditure. In *R.* v. *H.M. Treasury, ex p. Smedley* [1985] 1 Q.B. 657, Slade L.J. said that he did not "feel much doubt" that Mr. Smedley, "if only in his capacity as a taxpayer" had sufficient interest to raise a "serious question" as to the *vires* of an Order in Council, which would have led to the expenditure of substantial sums from the Consolidated Fund for the purpose of the European Community budget.

3. Since the House of Lords' decision, *locus standi* has been accorded to persons and bodies such as amenity societies who oppose grants of planning permission. In *Covent Garden Community Association Ltd.* v. *Greater London Council* [1981] J.P.L. 183, Woolf J. held that the applicant company, formed to represent and safeguard the interests of Covent Garden residents, had *locus standi* to seek certiorari to quash a decision of the council to grant "deemed planning permission" in respect of premises in the Covent Garden area owned by the council. Certiorari was, however, refused on the merits. (*Cf. R.* v. *Sheffield City Council, ex p. Mansfield* (1979) 37 P. & C.R. 1 and *R.* v. *Stroud District Council, ex p. Goodenough* [1982] J.P.L. 246 (mandamus); *R.* v. *Royal County of Berkshire, ex p. Mangnall* [1985] J.P.L. 258; *R.* v. *Castle Point District Council, ex p. Brooks* [1985] J.P.L. 473.). In *R.* v. *Hammersmith and Fulham Borough Council, ex p. People Before Profit Ltd.* (1981) 80 L.G.R. 322, an unincorporated association of persons called "People Before Profit" took an active part at a public inquiry in objecting to the Hammersmith Local Plan. After the inquiry, but before the report came out, the planning policy committee of the borough council resolved to grant planning permission to London Transport in respect of a proposed development which was an aspect of the plan to which objections had been made. The subsequent report favoured the objectors. The association was formed into a company limited by guarantee and sought leave to bring an application for judicial review seeking an order quashing the resolution. Comyn J. held (1) that the organisation had *locus standi*: any person was entitled to object in a planning matter if he had a legitimate *bona fide* reason—he did not have

to be a ratepayer or a resident, but was not to be an officious bystander or busybody; (2) that the mere fact of a different legal entity was not alone sufficient to defeat them having fulfilled all the other qualifications as objectors; but (3) that they had no reasonable case to put forward. Leave to bring the application was accordingly refused. Then, in *R.* v. *Poole Borough Council, ex p. Beebee and others* [1991] C.O.D. 264, Schiemann J. held that the British Herpetological Society had *locus standi* to seek judicial review of the council's decision to grant planning permission to itself for the development of part of a heath. The Society had a long association with the site in connection with rare species found on it, and had been named in a condition attached to the permission. On the other hand, the World-wide Fund for Nature, which had made grants to the Society and had been involved in conservation of the Dorset heathlands for 15 years, would not in principle have had a sufficient interest, had there been no consent order to its being joined as an applicant after leave had been granted.

A person with a "legitimate expectation" protected by public law will have *locus standi* to seek judicial review (see Lord Diplock in *O'Reilly* v. *Mackman* (above, p. 723) and pp. 507–521).

Other cases indicative of a broad approach to questions of standing include the following. In *R.* v. *Secretary of State for the Environment, ex p. Ward* [1984] 1 W.L.R. 834, Woolf J. held that a gypsy had *locus* to challenge a decision of the Secretary of State not to exercise his powers under section 9 of the Caravan Sites Act 1968 to direct local authorities to provide caravan sites for gypsies. The same judge held that the Child Poverty Action Group (although not the Greater London Council) had *locus* to challenge the manner in which the Secretary of State was administering the law concerning social security payments (*R.* v. *Secretary of State for Social Services, ex p. Greater London Council, The Times*, August 16, 1984; appeal dismissed, *The Times*, August 8, 1985; *cf. R.* v. *Secretary of State for Social Services, ex p. Child Poverty Action Group* [1989] 1 All E.R. 1047). In *R.* v. *Liverpool City Corporation, ex p. Ferguson* [1985] I.R.L.R. 501, it was held that the secretary of a branch of a teachers' union (the branch having no corporate status) had *locus standi* to challenge the decision of a council sub-committee to refuse to pay teachers who presented themselves for work on a "day of action," but who were unable to work because of the actions of the other trade unionists.

In *R.* v. *Felixstowe JJ., ex p. Leigh* [1987] Q.B. 582, a journalist was granted a declaration that the justices had erred in law in deciding as a matter of policy that their identities should not be disclosed. The journalist had not been covering the case in respect of which the decision challenged had been made, but was a "public spirited citizen" acting as "guardian of the public interest in the maintenance and preservation of open justice in magistrates' courts, a matter of vital concern in the administration of justice." This was "a matter of national importance" as a policy of routine non-disclosure was being adopted by a growing number of justices elsewhere: "No one has contended that he has acted as a mere busybody in coming to this court to ask for the relief he seeks. The seriousness of his purpose is apparent. I think he has a sufficient interest..." (*per* Watkins L.J. at p. 598). However, he had insufficient standing to be granted mandamus to order disclosure in the case in question, as his aim "was not to report the case; it was to comment on various issues arising out of reports by others of the case" (*per* Watkins L.J. at p. 597). This reinforces Lord Wilberforce's point that the application of the test may *differ* according to the remedy sought, although Watkins L.J. was "inclined to think" that the test was not *stricter* for mandamus (p. 597).

Finally, in *R.* v. *Manchester City Council, ex p. Baragrove Properties Ltd.* (1991) 23 H.L.R. 337, the Divisional Court held that a property management company had *locus* to challenge the council's interpretation of a housing benefit regulation, which directly affected the rents receivable by the applicants; the company would not, however, have had *locus* to challenge a determination made in relation to the particular circumstances of a tenant.

4. Prior to the introduction of the application for judicial review, the issue of *locus standi* was considered separately in respect of each administrative law remedy, the courts generally being stricter in respect of the private law remedies of declaration or injunction (see above, p. 734). The orthodox approach in respect of private law remedies was set out in *Boyce* v. *Paddington Corporation* [1903] 1 Ch. 109. The plaintiff, shortly before the action, erected buildings on land abutting on an open space under the control of the borough council. The council resolved to erect a hoarding which would obstruct the access of light to the plaintiff's windows. The plaintiff brought an action to restrain the council from doing this. It was held that as the plaintiff was suing in respect of an alleged private right to the access of light, or in respect of an alleged interference with a public right from which he personally sustained special damage, he could sue without joining the Attorney-General as plaintiff, (see below, p. 779). The action failed on grounds unconnected with the right to sue. The House of Lords in *Gouriet* v. *Union of Post Office Workers* [1978] A.C. 435 affirmed that this was the correct approach in respect of a private action for an injunction to restrain a threatened breach of the criminal law by a trade union.

Different views have been expressed on the test for *locus standi* where a private action is brought against a public authority. In *Steeples* v. *Derbyshire County Council* [1985] 1 W.L.R. 256, Webster J. held that the plaintiff had the necessary *locus standi* to challenge the grant of planning permission by the council for two interrelated developments, which involved the establishment of a leisure complex at Shipley Park, near Ilkeston, Derbyshire. The plaintiff alleged, *inter alia*, breach of procedural requirements and the breach of the *nemo judex* principle of natural justice. Webster J. held that the plaintiff had the necessary *locus standi* under *Boyce* v. *Paddington Borough Council* [1903] 1 Ch. 109. As regards one of the two interrelated developments ("the ancillary development") the plaintiff's private right was affected as a small part of his land was to be taken for it. The other development ("the leisure development") would take place on land adjacent to his own and would result in his view being impaired, in the ambient noise level being increased, in some interference with his use of a lane which bisected land farmed by him and in a risk of his land being invaded by litter and possibly by vandals or trespassers. This would amount to special damage resulting from interference with a public right:

> "If the Plaintiff can show that a proprietary interest of his, reasonably and probably to be affected by the act in question, will probably be prejudiced by it then, even in the absence of authority, I would hold that he suffers in respect of that act damage under a head recognised by the law."

The judge also held that the plaintiff had *locus standi* in respect of the leisure development by virtue of his undoubted *locus* in respect of the ancillary development, as the two developments were closely connected.

The judge further stated that if it had been necessary to decide the point, he would have held that a person with sufficient interest for the purpose of an application for judicial review, and having thereby *locus standi* to apply for an injunction, would have a similar *locus standi* to seek an injunction in ordinary proceedings. Any difference in substance between the two forms of proceeding could, if necessary, be given effect to when the discretion of the court arose as to the relief to be given.

The *Gouriet* case was distinguished on the grounds that the plaintiff here was not attempting to enforce the criminal law but to challenge the decision of a public body which he said was wrongly made, and claimed to be threatened by damage special to himself resulting from that decision.

However, in *Barrs* v. *Bethell* [1982] Ch. 294, three ratepayers of Camden London Borough Council issued a writ and statement of claim in the Chancery Division against the members of the majority group on the council and the council itself claiming certain declarations and other orders. It was alleged that there had been various abuses of discretion, and that the councillors had breached the fiduciary duty owed to the ratepayers, *inter alia*, by failing to make cuts in services and to raise council house rents. Warner J. held that a ratepayer was not entitled to sue a local authority or its members, without the leave of the Attorney-General, unless he could show that he had *locus standi* under the rules laid down in *Boyce* v. *Paddington Borough Council* [1903] 1 Ch. 109. His Lordship disagreed with the view expressed by Webster J. in the *Steeples* case, *supra*, that a person with "sufficient interest" under Order 53 would have *locus standi* in ordinary proceedings.

5. As indicated by Lord Wilberforce, the old cases demonstrated a wide variety of approaches on the question of *locus standi* for mandamus. Lord Denning M.R. tended to take a broad view. In *R.* v. *Commissioner of Police of the Metropolis, ex p. Blackburn* [1968] 2 Q.B. 118, Raymond Blackburn sought an order of mandamus (*inter alia*) requiring the Commissioner to reverse a policy decision that the time of police officers would not be spent on enforcing the provisions of the Betting, Gaming and Lotteries Act 1963 against gaming clubs. The Court of Appeal held that the Commissioner was under a duty to enforce the law of the land, but as he had by then undertaken to reverse the policy decision, mandamus was no longer necessary. On the question of standing, Lord Denning stated that it was an "open question" whether he had a sufficient interest. "No doubt any person who was adversely affected by the action of the commissioner in making a mistaken policy decision would have such an interest. The difficulty is to see how Mr. Blackburn himself has been affected." Salmon and Edmund Davies L.JJ. were also doubtful (pp. 145, 149). Then in *R.* v. *Commissioner of Police of the Metropolis, ex p. Blackburn (No. 3)* [1973] Q.B. 241, Mr. Blackburn and his wife applied for mandamus directed to the Commissioner to enforce the laws against the publication and sale of pornography. The application was dismissed on the merits, the members of the Court of Appeal taking the opportunity to criticise the current state of the law as to obscenity. Mr. and Mrs. Blackburn appeared "out of concern . . . for their five children." Counsel for the Commissioner did not take any point as to the applicants' status, but reserved the question.

Subsequently, in *Att.-Gen.* v. *Independent Broadcasting Authority* [1973] Q.B. 629, 649, Lord Denning M.R., commenting on these cases said (at p. 649) that "Mr. Blackburn had a sufficient interest, even though it was shared with thousands of others. . . . His intervention was both timely and useful." Finally, in *R.* v. *Greater London Council, ex p. Blackburn* [1976] 1 W.L.R. 550, the Court of Appeal held that Mr. Blackburn had sufficient *locus standi* to obtain an order of prohibition restraining the council from censoring films according to the wrong (and too lenient) legal test. Lord Denning M.R. said that Mr. Blackburn fell within his broad test for standing (cited below, at p. 763):

> "Mr. Blackburn is a citizen of London. His wife is a ratepayer. He has children who may be harmed by the exhibition of pornographic films. If he has no sufficient interest, no other citizen has" (pp. 558–559).

How would the courts today deal with the question of standing in such cases as these?

R. v. SECRETARY OF STATE FOR THE ENVIRONMENT, ex p. ROSE THEATRE TRUST CO.

[1990] 1 Q.B. 504; [1990] 2 W.L.R. 186; [1990] 1 All E.R. 754 (Schiemann J.)

In the course of development of a site in central London, some remains of an historical theatre, the Rose Theatre, were discovered. A trust company was set up with the objects of preserving the remains and making them accessible to the public. The company applied to the Secretary of State for the Environment for the theatre to be listed in the Schedule of monuments made under section 1 of the Ancient Monuments and Archaeological Areas Act 1979. The Secretary of State, whilst accepting that the remains were of national importance, declined to list them and, in his decision letter, gave as reasons, *inter alia*, his view that the site was not under threat, that scheduling might give rise to claims for compensation, the need to balance the desirability of preservation against the need for a city to thrive, and the likelihood of co-operation by the developers. The company applied for judicial review. Schiemann J. held that the Secretary of State had lawfully exercised his discretion. His Lordship also considered the question of *locus standi*.

SCHIEMANN J.: . . . I turn now to consider the question of *locus standi*. It follows from the foregoing that I do not accept that the decision of the Secretary of State is flawed in law. I go on to consider what logically I ought perhaps to have considered first, namely, does the applicant have any standing to move for judicial review. I introduce this section of my judgment by pointing out something which may well surprise many laymen and some lawyers who do not practise in this branch of the law.

Inevitably, in the tide of human affairs decisions are from time to time reached which are unlawful, occasionally by someone who knows he is acting unlawfully but more usually by someone who does not know this. The law provides in general that even an unlawful decision is to be treated as lawful until such time as the court, at the suit of someone with a sufficient interest in the matter to which the application relates, allows an application to quash that decision. Often the law provides a time limit or other conditions which have to be complied with before the court is empowered to quash an admittedly unlawful decision. The reason for that, at first sight, surprising willingness of the law to treat the admittedly unlawful as lawful is that in many fields, if it were otherwise, uncertainty and, at times, complete chaos would result.

Suppose a decision to build a motorway turns out, once it has been built, to have been unlawful because the Secretary of State took into account something which he ought not to have done? If everyone could challenge an unlawfully granted planning permission for a house, what would be the position of the innocent first or subsequent purchaser? These are the types of problems with which the concept of standing is concerned.

The relevant general enactment made by Parliament is section 31(1) of the Supreme Court Act 1981. [His Lordship read s.31(1) and s.31(3) (see above, p. 687).] Note the indefinite article before the words "sufficient interest." R.S.C., Ord. 53, r. 3(7) is in similar terms.

In the present case leave was granted to apply for judicial review and one might have thought, unaided by authority, that the sufficiency of the interest point could not be taken at the stage of the substantive application unless there was at that same time an application to set aside the leave which had, on this hypothesis, been wrongly granted. However, it is common ground that the point can be taken at this stage without such a formal application and that there is a fair amount of case law to guide the court. There is no doubt that, in the early part of this decade, the High Court was fairly liberal in its interpretation of who had "a sufficient interest" to be able to apply for judicial review: see *Covent Garden Community Association Ltd.* v. *Greater London Council* [1981] J.P.L. 183, a decision of Woolf J. on April 2, 1980; *R.* v. *Stroud District Council, ex p. Goodenough* (1982) 43 P. & C.R. 59, a decision dated June 3, 1980, again with Woolf J. with whom Donaldson L.J. agreed; and *R.* v. *Hammersmith and Fulham London Borough Council, ex p. People Before Profit Ltd.* (1982) 80 L.G.R. 322, a decision of Comyn J. on May 20, 1981. . . .

The leading case on this branch of the law is *R.* v. *Inland Revenue Commissioners, ex p. National Federation of Self-Employed and Small Businesses Ltd.* [1982] A.C. 617. In that case, which concerned the right of the federation to apply for a declaration that the Inland Revenue had acted unlawfully in granting an amnesty to the Fleet Street casuals, five separate speeches were delivered by the five Law Lords who decided the case. I do not propose to lengthen this judgment by a close analysis of what each Law Lord said but I think the following propositions, to put it no higher, are not inconsistent with that case. 1. Once leave has been given to move for judicial review, the court which hears the application ought still to examine whether the applicant has a sufficient interest. 2. Whether an applicant has a sufficient interest is not purely a matter of discretion in the court. 3. Not every member of the public can complain of every breach of statutory duty by a person empowered to come to a decision by that statute. To rule otherwise would be to deprive the phrase "a sufficient interest" of all meaning. 4. However, a direct financial or legal interest is not required. 5. Where one is examining an alleged failure to perform a duty imposed by statute it is useful to look at the statute and see whether it gives an applicant a right enabling him to have that duty performed. 6. Merely to assert that one has an interest does not give one an interest. 7. The fact that some thousands of people join together and assert that they have an interest does not create an interest if the individuals did not have an interest. 8. The fact that those without an interest incorporate themselves and give the company in its memorandum power to pursue a particular object does not give the company an interest.

The applicant's argument on standing runs essentially like this. 1. When scheduled monument consent is sought anybody who wishes to make representations to the Secretary of State can do so and the Secretary of State must consider any such representations once made: see paragraph 3(3) of Schedule 1 to the Act of 1979. 2. Therefore Parliament recognised that everyone has an interest in the preservation of monuments considered by the Secretary of State to be of national importance and everyone has a legitimate expectation to be consulted on such a matter. 3. The Secretary of State considers the Rose Theatre to be a monument of national importance. 4. At the stage when he is considering whether or not to schedule a monument considered by him to be of national importance, the area of discretion left to the Secretary of State is a very small one and therefore it would be artificial to make a distinction so far as standing is concerned between the position at the scheduling stage and the position at the scheduled monument consent stage. (I interpose to point out—and it will be evident—that earlier on in this judgment I rejected this particular submission.) 5. Therefore, the court should recognise that everyone has a sufficient interest to challenge, by way of judicial review, the lawfulness of the Secretary of State's decision in deciding not to schedule. 6. Although as a matter of form the applicant is a company, as a matter of substance the company is merely the corporate expression of the wills and desires of persons of undoubted expertise and distinction in the fields of archaeology, the theatre, literature and other fields and includes local residents, the local Member of Parliament and so on. These are not mere busybodies. 7. The very fact that the Secretary of State has answered with care the representations made by those whose will the applicant embodies gives them a sufficient interest for the purpose of this application. 8. There is no evidence of any rival organisation which claims to represent the public in relation to the Rose Theatre and thus if this application is struck down for lack of standing then the legality of the Secretary of State's decision is unlikely to be tested in the courts. It was implicitly but not expressly suggested that the Attorney-General is unlikely to act *ex officio* and unlikely to give his fiat for a relator action which, however, in the present case has not been sought.

The history of how persons gathered together to try to preserve the remains of the Rose Theatre and how the applicant company came to be formed is set out in Mr. Grayling's affidavit. Mr. Goldsmith submitted that the applicant company had even less of a claim to standing than those who agreed that a company should be used as a vehicle for the campaign. This raises points of some difficulty. It was, I think, accepted on behalf of the applicant that the company could have no greater claim to standing than the members of the campaign had before the company was made into the campaign's vehicle. In any event I so hold. It would be absurd if two people, neither of whom had standing could, by an appropriately worded memorandum, incorporate themselves into a company which thereby obtained standing.

That being so, I propose first to examine the question of standing, leaving aside the fact of incorporation. I raised with Mr. Griffiths, who replied on behalf of the applicant, whether, if I found that no individual in the campaign has standing, he would submit that the agglomeration of individuals might have a standing which any one individual lacked. He replied that he did not so submit. I can therefore consider the question of standing by considering whether an individual of acknowledged distinction in the field of archaeology, of which the company has several amongst its members, has sufficient standing to move for judicial review of a decision not to schedule.

Applying the approach indicated in the propositions enumerated earlier on in this judgment it seems to me that the decision not to schedule is one of those governmental decisions in respect of which the ordinary citizen does not have a sufficient interest to entitle him to obtain leave to move for judicial review. Clearly a person cannot obtain a sufficient interest by writing a letter to the Secretary of State. I approach with reluctance the submission that because the Secretary of State sent a considered reply, that gives the recipient an interest which he would not have had if no reply had been sent beyond a formal acknowledgement. If the court were to sanction such an argument it might cause the decision makers to be less helpful to the general public. Further, what about the man who appears in the decision maker's office, the man who telephones the decision maker and so on?

None of these points are unanswerable but I hope my reluctance to go down this path is at least understandable. In any event, I do not consider that an interested member of the public who has written and received a reply in relation to a decision not to schedule a site as an ancient monument has sufficient interest in that decision to enable him to apply for judicial review.

Finally, I ought to say that I recognise the force of Mr. Sullivan's submission that since an unlawful decision in relation to scheduling either has been made (if the earlier part of my judgment be wrong) or may well be made in the future, my decision on standing may well leave an unlawful act by a minister unrebuked and indeed unrevealed since there will be those in the future who will not have the opportunity to ventilate—on this hypothesis—their well-founded complaints before the court.

This submission is clearly right. The answer to it is that the law does not see it as the function of the courts to be there for every individual who is interested in having the legality of an administrative action litigated. Parliament could have given such a wide right of access to the court but it has not done so. The challenger must show that he "has a sufficient interest in the matter to which the application relates." The court will look at the matter to which the application relates—in this case the non-scheduling of a monument of national importance—and the statute under which the decision was taken (in this case the Act of 1979) and decide whether that statute gives that individual expressly or impliedly a greater right or expectation than any other citizen of this country to have that decision taken lawfully. We all expect our decision makers to act lawfully. We are not all given by Parliament the right to apply for judicial review.

Since, in my judgment, no individual has the standing to move for judicial review it follows, from what I ruled earlier, that the company created by those individuals has no standing. In consequence I need not and I do not consider the effect of the interposition of the company in the present case.

Application dismissed.

Notes

1. This decision has been criticised as unduly restrictive by R. Gordon, *Crown Office Proceedings* (1990), para. C3–031; *cf.* P. Cane, [1991] P.L. 307, who criticises the reasoning rather than the result. Cane argues that possible problems of "uncertainty" and "chaos," and the possible effect on the willingness of officials to give advice, have "nothing to do with standing," being properly dealt with by the rules concerning time limits and the residual discretion to refuse a remedy:

> "Schiemann J.'s view about the function of standing rules perhaps reveals the (concealed) value judgment which he applied to the case, namely that the financial interests of the developers were, if possible, to be preferred to the historical and cultural concerns of the Rose Theatre Trust and its members" (p. 309).

However, the specification of the Historic Buildings and Monuments Commission as the only body the Secretary of State was expressly required to consult might alone have given grounds for Schiemann J.'s decision. Cane also argues that:

> "true liberalisation of standing rules requires not only that applicants be accorded standing to represent interests which they share with many others, but also that standing be accorded to genuine representatives of interested persons, even if the only interest of the representative is to further the interests of the represented" (p. 311).

(*Cf.* the *Felixstowe JJ.* and *C.P.A.G.* cases, above, p. 755).

2. The precise *purposes* of the requirement of standing in respect of public law remedies are rarely discussed by the judges, including the law lords in the *Fleet Street Casuals* case. Schiemann J. is an exception, both in the *Rose Theatre Trust* case and extra-judicially, [1990] P.L. 342, although the latter is more an exposition of the need for greater certainty on this question and an enumeration of relevant considerations than an attempt to state conclusions. The distinctions between standing for remedies in private law and in public law is explained as follows by Cane ([1980] P.L. 303):

> "In private law entitlement to a remedy and the right to apply for that remedy merge; the two issues are not treated separately—the former entails the latter" (p. 203).

For example, the law of tort limits the range of plaintiffs who may sue for economic loss:

> "By limiting entitlement to the remedy of damages, entitlement to institute proceedings is *ipso facto* also limited" (*ibid.*).

The position in public law is different:

> "... the public law litigant is required to show that the respondent public body has infringed one of the values embodied in the substantive heads of judicial review and *also* that some personal interest of his has been thereby infringed thus giving a reason why *he* should be allowed to complain in court of the abuse of power" (p. 304).

The literature generally is clearer on the purposes that are or should *not* be served by standing rules. For example, in discussing these rules in the context of American constitutional law, K.C. Davis wrote, in a passage cited by Cane:

> "The law of standing is the wrong tool to accomplish judicial objectives unrelated to the task of deciding whether a particular interest asserted is deserving of judicial protection. The courts should avoid hypothetical or remote questions—through the law of ripeness,[1] not through the law of standing. The courts should decline to enter political areas—through the law of political questions, not through the law of standing. The courts should limit themselves to issues 'appropriate for judicial determination'—through the law of case or controversy, but not through that part of the law of case or controversy pertaining to standing. The courts should avoid taking over functions of government that are committed to executives or administrators—through the law of scope of review, not through the law of standing. The courts should virtually stay away from some governmental activities, such as foreign affairs and military operations—through the law of unreviewability,[2] not through the law of standing. The courts should insist upon competent presentation of cases—through refusals to respond to inadequate presentations, not through the law of standing." (37 Univ. of Chicago L.R. 450, 469).

What is clear is that rules that confined access to judicial review to those whose private law rights were at stake would not be appropriate. One of the clear purposes of judicial review is to secure the public interest that governmental institutions act within the law, and this would not be served if standing rules were unduly restrictive. There is much to be said for Lord Denning's statement in *R.* v. *Greater London Council, ex p. Blackburn* [1976] 1 W.L.R. 550, 556:

> "I regard it as a matter of high constitutional principle that if there is good ground for supposing that a government department or a public authority is transgressing the law, or is about to transgress it, in a way which offends or injures thousands of Her Majesty's subjects, then any one of those offended or injured can draw it to the attention of the courts of law and seek to have the law enforced, and the courts in their discretion can grant whatever remedy is appropriate."

This was endorsed by Lord Diplock in the *Fleet Street Casuals* case (p. 641), but rejected by Lord Roskill (p. 661) and by Lord Wilberforce (in the context of relator actions) in the *Gouriet* case ([1978] A.C. 435, 483).

3. In *R.* v. *Tower Hamlets London Borough Council, ex p. Thrasyvoulou* (1990) 23 H.L.R. 30, Kennedy J. held that hotel owners did not have standing to challenge the council's decision to cease to use low grade hotels, including hotels owned by the applicants, as bed and breakfast accommodation for the homeless:

[1] (Ed.) *Cf.* below, p. 785.
[2] (Ed.) *Cf.* above, p. 199.

"At root, what is alleged is a failure by the respondents properly to perform the duty imposed on them by . . . the Housing Act 1985. . . . The Housing Act does not give any express or implied right to hoteliers to complain of an action which, it is conceded, was carried out for a proper motive in the best interests of the homeless and in no way contrary to the interests of the rate payers" (p. 47).

The *Rose Theatre Trust* case showed that *locus standi* "can still be an important consideration" (*ibid.*). The applicants' arguments were also dismissed on their merits. It is submitted that his Lordship's approach to *locus standi* is misconceived. The duty under the Housing Act is of course owed to the homeless and not the hoteliers, but the complaint here was that the council has fettered its discretion and acted in breach of natural justice in the way its discretion was exercised in the course of discharging its duty under the Act. Given that the applicants' interests were substantially prejudiced in fact by the decision, that should have been regarded as giving rise to a sufficient interest.

(G) Discretionary Refusal of a Remedy

(i) Delay

Delay was an established ground on which, prior to the introduction of the application for judicial review, the court might, in the exercise of its discretion, refuse one of the prerogative remedies or an injunction or declaration. The new Ord. 53 made express provision concerning delay. However, as the following case shows, there have been difficulties arising from the defective drafting of the relevant provisions.

R. v. DAIRY PRODUCE QUOTA TRIBUNAL, ex p. CASWELL

[1990] 2 A.C. 738; [1990] 2 W.L.R. 1320; [1990] 2 All E.R. 434
(House of Lords)

The applicants, Mr. and Mrs. Caswell, having failed to qualify for a wholesale quota in respect of milk production, claimed relief under the exceptional hardship provisions set out in the Dairy Produce Quotas Regulations 1984. In February 1985 the Dairy Produce Quota Tribunal, on their construction of the Regulations, dismissed the claim. Initially unaware of a remedy, the applicants took no step to challenge the tribunal's decision until 1987 when they applied for and obtained *ex parte* leave to move for judicial review. On the hearing of the substantive application the applicants conceded before the judge that there had been "undue delay" within the meaning of section 31(6) of the Supreme Court Act 1981 and R.S.C., Ord. 53, r. 4(1), but they resisted an assertion by the tribunal that since there had been a number of other unsuccessful applications to which the same provisions applied, the grant of relief would be detrimental to good administration. The judge held that the tribunal had erred in their construction of the Regulations but, accepting the tribunal's evidence, he declined to grant relief. The Court of Appeal and the House of Lords dismissed the applicants' appeal. In the House, the sole speech was delivered by Lord Goff.

LORD GOFF: . . . [stated the facts, read Ord. 53 r. 4 and s.31(6), (7), of the Supreme Court Act 1981 (above pp. 682, 687), and continued:]

When Order 53 was redrawn in 1977, rule 4(1) then provided that, where there had been undue delay in making an application for judicial review, the court might refuse to grant leave for the making of the application, or any relief sought on the application:

> "if, in the opinion of the court, the granting of the relief sought would be likely to cause substantial hardship to, or substantially prejudice the rights of, any person or would be detrimental to good administration."

Rule 4(2) then provided that, for an order of certiorari to remove any proceeding for the purpose of quashing it, the relevant period for the purpose of paragraph (1) was three months after the date of the relevant proceeding. In 1980, however, that rule was replaced by the present rule, save only that rule 4(1) referred to "An application for judicial review. . . ." Following critical comment by the Court of Appeal in *R.* v. *Stratford-on-Avon District Council, ex p. Jackson* [1985] 1 W.L.R. 1319, in which it was held that those words must be read as referring to an application for leave to apply for judicial review, the rule was amended to give express effect to that interpretation. Despite the change in Ord. 53, r. 4, made in 1980, section 31(6) of the Supreme Court Act 1981 mirrored the old rule 4, which had by then been replaced. In 1985, clause 43 of the Administration of Justice Bill of that year contained a provision which would have repealed section 31(6) of the Act of 1981; but the clause was abandoned for other reasons, and the proposed repeal fell with it.

In the result, the courts have been left with the task of giving effect to two provisions relating to delay, which at first sight are not easy to reconcile. First, in Ord. 53, r. 4(1), undue delay is defined, whereas in section 31(6) it is not. Secondly, rule 4(1) applies only to applications for leave to apply for judicial review, whereas section 31(6) applies both to applications for leave to apply and to applications for substantive relief. Thirdly, rule 4(1) looks to the existence of good reason for extending the specified period, whereas section 31(6) looks to certain effects of delay as grounds for refusing leave, or substantive relief, as the case may be. A further twist is provided by the fact that rule 4(1) and (2) are expressed to be without prejudice to any statutory provision which has the effect of limiting the time within which an application for judicial review may be made; and that section 31(6) is expressed to be without prejudice to any enactment or rule of court which had that effect. These two provisions were said by Lloyd L.J., in the Court of Appeal, to produce a *circulus inextricabilis*: [1989] 1 W.L.R. 1089, 1094F.

The relationship between Ord. 53, r. 4, and section 31(6) was considered by the Court of Appeal in *R.* v. *Stratford-on-Avon District Council, ex p. Jackson* [1985] 1 W.L.R. 1319 (to which I have already referred) with particular reference to the meaning of the expression "undue delay." It was there submitted that, where good reason had been held to exist for the failure to act promptly as required by Ord. 53, r. 4(1), and the time for applying for leave had therefore been extended, the effect of section 31(7) was that in such circumstances there was no power to refuse either leave to apply or substantive relief under section 31(6) on the ground of undue delay, because an extension of time under Ord. 53, r. 4, itself negatives the existence of undue delay. That submission was rejected by the Court of Appeal. Ackner L.J., who delivered the judgment of the court, said, at p. 1325:

> "This is not an easy point to resolve, but we have concluded that whenever there is a failure to act promptly or within three months there is 'undue delay.' Accordingly, even though the court may be satisfied in the light of all the circumstances, including the particular position of the applicant, that there is good reason for that failure, nevertheless the delay, viewed objectively, remains 'undue delay.' The court therefore still retains a discretion to refuse to grant leave for the making of the application or the relief sought on the substantive application on the grounds of undue delay if it considers that the granting of the relief sought would be likely to cause substantial hardship to, or substantially prejudice the rights of, any person or would be detrimental to good administration."

With this conclusion, I respectfully agree. First, when section 31(6) and (7) refer to "an application for judicial review," those words must be read as referring, where appropriate, to an application for leave to apply for judicial review. Next, as I read rule 4(1), the effect of *the rule* is to limit the time within which an application for leave to apply for judicial review may be made in accordance with its terms, *i.e.* promptly and in any event within three months. The court has, however, power to grant leave to apply despite the fact that an application is late, if it considers that there is good reason to exercise that power; this it does by extending the period. This, as I understand it, is the reasoning upon which the Court of Appeal reached its conclusion in *R.* v. *Stratford-on-Avon District Council, ex p. Jackson*. Furthermore, the combined effect of section 31(7) and of rule 4(1) is that there is undue delay for the purposes of section 31(6) whenever the application for leave to apply is not made promptly and in any event within three months from the relevant date.

It follows that, when an application for leave to apply is not made promptly and in any event within three months, the court may refuse leave on the ground of delay unless it considers that there is good reason for extending the period; but, even if it considers that there is such good reason, it may still refuse leave (or, where leave has been granted, substantive relief) if in its opinion the granting of the relief sought would be likely to cause hardship or prejudice (as specified in section 31(6)) or would be detrimental to good administration. I imagine that, on an *ex parte* application for leave to apply before a single judge, the question most likely to be considered by him, if there has been such delay, is whether there is good reason for extending the period under rule 4(1). Questions of hardship or prejudice, or detriment, under section 31(6) are, I imagine, unlikely to arise on an *ex parte* application, when the necessary material would in all probability not be available to the judge. Such questions could arise on a contested application for leave to apply, as indeed they did in *R.* v. *Stratford-on-Avon District Council, ex p. Jackson;* but even then, as in that case, it may be thought better to grant leave where there is considered to be good reason to extend the period under rule 4(1), leaving questions arising under section 31(6) to be explored in depth on the hearing of the substantive application.

In this way, I believe, sensible effect can be given to these two provisions, without doing violence to the language of either. Unlike the Court of Appeal, I do not consider that rule 4(3) and section 31(7) lead to a *circulus inextricabilis*, because 31(6) does not limit "the time within which an application for judicial review may be made" (the words used in rule 4(3)). Section 31(6) simply contains particular grounds for refusing leave or substantive relief, not referred to in rule 4(1), to which the court is bound to give effect, independently of any rule of court.

Accordingly, in the present case, the fact that the single judge had granted leave to the appellants to apply for judicial review despite the lapse (long before) of three months from the date when the ground for their application first arose, did not preclude the court from subsequently refusing substantive relief on the ground of undue delay in the exercise of its discretion under section 31(6). This was the approach adopted by both courts below, applying (as they were bound to do) the decision of the Court of Appeal in *R.* v. *Stratford-on-Avon District Council, ex p. Jackson* [1985] 1 W.L.R. 1319. Before your Lordships Mr. Gordon for the appellants submitted that the principles stated in *ex p. Jackson* were erroneous; but, for the reasons I have already given, I am unable to accept that submission.

It follows that there is no doubt that, in the present case, there was undue delay within section 31(6). No suggestion has been made that substantial hardship or substantial prejudice were likely to be caused by the grant of the relief sought. The only questions which remained on the appeal were (1) whether the Court of Appeal should reject the judge's conclusion that the grant of such relief would be detrimental to good administration; and (2) if not, whether it should interfere with the judge's exercise of his discretion to refuse such relief. The Court of Appeal decided against the appellants on both of these points.

On the question of detriment to good administration, the judge reviewed with care the evidence before him. This consisted of an affidavit sworn by Mr. Newton, who was secretary of D.P.Q.T. until September 1988, and two affidavits submitted by the appellants in answer to that affidavit, one sworn by Mr. May of the legal department of the National Farmers' Union, and the other by Mr. Collinson, a partner in the solicitors acting for the appellants. It appeared from the evidence that the essence of the quota system is that there is a finite amount of milk quota available, so that a quota given to one producer is not available to others. In fact, about 4,000 exceptional hardship appeals were heard by D.P.Q.T. Of these, about 600 were successful, additional quota being granted; so about 3,400 producers failed in their applications for additional quota on this ground. In a large number of these latter cases, the end of the final quota year was stated to be the major consideration. Next, the fact that judicial review was the remedy available to a milk producer aggrieved by a decision of D.P.Q.T. must have become well known at least after September 1985, when the first hearing of an application for judicial review in such a case received wide publicity in the dairy trade.* Consideration was given to the possibility of other producers seeking judicial review of adverse decisions of D.P.Q.T. if the appellants' application for substantive relief was successful. It was accepted that sufficient provision had been made to deal with the appellants' claim for extra quota. But, in Mr. Newton's opinion, a small but administratively substantial number of milk producers could be encouraged to make applications for judicial review relying on the same point as the appellants, or a variation of it; and that could mean re-opening the quota for the year 1984–85, and for each succeeding year. Further allocations of quota could only be made at the expense of all other producers whose quotas would have to be reduced accordingly. Mr. Collinson, in his affidavit, questioned whether other milk producers would be likely to follow the appellants' lead and seek judicial review or whether, if they did so, they would obtain leave to apply after such a long delay.

Having reviewed the evidence, the judge expressed his conclusion on this point in the following passage in his judgment:

> "It is obvious that if there are a number of applications the problem of re-opening these claims, going back now three years, is going to be very great. It arises out of events in 1985. The evidential problems are self-evident, leaving aside the question of being able fairly to deal with claims now in relation to matters in 1985. I think there is likely to be a very real problem in relation to a number of cases. I do not think the number of cases is de minimis. I have concluded that the fact that hitherto there have been only these two applications is not a matter which is of very great help in determining what the effect will be of the particular decision in this case. I have come to the clearest view that there will be a detriment to good administration if this application were granted."

The judge's conclusion, on the evidence before him, that there was likely to be a very real problem in relation to a number of cases, was a finding of fact with which I can see no reason to interfere. Once that

* *Reg.* v. *Dairy Produce Quota Tribunal for England and Wales, ex p. Atkinson* (unreported), September 25, 1985, Macpherson J.

conclusion was reached, it seems to me inevitable that to grant the relief sought in the present case would cause detriment to good administration. As Lloyd L.J. pointed out in his judgment [1989] 1 W.L.R. 1089, 1099, two things emerged from the evidence with sufficient clarity: first that, if the appellants' application for substantive relief were to be successful, there would be a significant number of further applications, and secondly that, if a significant number of applications were granted, then all previous years back to 1984 would have to be re-opened. These facts disclose, in my opinion, precisely the type of situation which Parliament was minded to exclude by the provision in section 31(6) relating to detriment to good administration. Lord Diplock pointed out in *O'Reilly* v. *Mackman* [1983] 2 A.C. 237, 280–281:

> "The public interest in good administration requires that public authorities and third parties should not be kept in suspense as to the legal validity of a decision the authority has reached in purported exercise of decision-making powers for any longer period than is absolutely necessary in fairness to the person affected by the decision."

I do not consider that it would be wise to attempt to formulate any precise definition or description of what constitutes detriment to good administration. This is because applications for judicial review may occur in many different situations, and the need for finality may be greater in one context than in another. But it is of importance to observe that section 31(6) recognises that there is an interest in good administration independently of hardship, or prejudice to the rights of third parties, and that the harm suffered by the applicant by reason of the decision which has been impugned is a matter which can be taken into account by the court when deciding whether or not to exercise its discretion under section 31(6) to refuse the relief sought by the applicant. In asking the question whether the grant of such relief would be detrimental to good administration, the court is at that stage looking at the interest in good administration independently of matters such as these. In the present context, that interest lies essentially in a regular flow of consistent decisions, made and published with reasonable dispatch; in citizens knowing where they stand, and how they can order their affairs in the light of the relevant decision. Matters of particular importance, apart from the length of time itself, will be the extent of the effect of the relevant decision, and the impact which would be felt if it were to be re-opened. In the present case, the court was concerned with a decision to allocate part of a finite amount of quota, and with circumstances in which a re-opening of the decision would lead to other applications to re-open similar decisions which, if successful, would lead to re-opening the allocation of quota over a number of years. To me it is plain, as it was to the judge and to the Court of Appeal, that to grant the appellants the relief they sought in the present case, after such a lapse of time had occurred, would be detrimental to good administration. It is, in my opinion, unnecessary to deal expressly with the detailed arguments advanced by Mr. Gordon on behalf of the appellants on this point. They were substantially the same as the arguments canvassed by him before the Court of Appeal, which considered and dismissed each argument seriatim. None of them, in my opinion, made any impact upon the essential matters, which I have identified.

Finally, I can, like the Court of Appeal, see no basis for interfering with the judge's exercise of his discretion. The judge took into account the relevant factors, including in particular the financial hardship suffered by the appellants by reason of the erroneous approach adopted by D.P.Q.T., and in particular the imposition upon them of substantial superlevy in the years 1986–87 and 1987–88. He then balanced the various factors and, as he said, came down firmly against the view of the appellants. I can perceive no error here which would justify interference with the judge's conclusion.

For these reasons, I would dismiss the appeal.

LORDS BRIDGE, GRIFFITHS, ACKNER and LOWRY agreed with LORD GOFF.

Appeal dismissed.

Notes

A number of points emerge from the relevant provisions, and their interpretation in *Caswell*:

- The three-month limit is not an *entitlement*; an application for leave must in any event be made promptly. In *Re Friends of the Earth Ltd.* (Unreported, July 6, 1987) an application for leave to apply for judicial review of the decision of the Secretary of State for Energy to grant consent for the construction of Sizewell B nuclear power station, made just within the three-month period, was rejected. Kennedy J. held that it had not been made promptly, there were no good reasons for the delay, and there would be considerable prejudice to good administration if leave were granted. The applicants had been aware that time was of the essence. This view was endorsed by the Court of Appeal in respect of two of the grounds: the others were unarguable: [1988] J.P.L. 93.
- A finding on an *inter partes* hearing of an application for leave that the application, brought within three months, has been made promptly, does not prevent the court at the substantive hearing finding that there has been undue delay, and exercising its discretion under section 31(6)(*b*) of the Supreme Court Act 1981 to refuse to grant any relief: *R.* v. *Swale Borough Council, ex p. Royal Society for the Protection of Birds* [1991] J.P.L. 39.
- The applicant must, in the application, give reasons for any delay (*Practice Direction* (*Crown Office List: Criminal Proceedings*) [1983] 1 W.L.R. 925, para. 3); *R.* v. *Elmbridge Borough Council, ex p. Health Care Corporation* (1991) 63 P.&C.R. 260, 264–265.
- The fact that a respondent to a hearing for judicial review indicates that no point will be taken on delay is no bar to the court considering the matter of its own motion (*R.* v. *Dairy Produce Quota Tribunal, ex p. Wynn Jones* (1987) 283 E.G. 463).

- An extension of time granted on an *ex parte* application for leave is not final, but is open to consideration on the *inter partes* application (*R.* v. *British Railways Board, ex p. Great Yarmouth Borough Council, The Times,* March 15, 1983; *R.* v. *Tavistock General Commissioners, ex p. Worth* [1985] S.T.C. 565.)

Moreover:

"If the consent of a proposed respondent to an extension of time has been obtained such consent should be submitted with the application. If a proposed respondent has not consented to an extension he shall on notice to the applicant have the right to apply promptly in open court to set aside any leave or direction which is given. Such an application to set aside will not always be necessary since in any event on the substantive hearing a respondent will be entitled to rely on delay in making the application as a ground for opposing the grant of relief." (*Practice Direction* (*Crown Office List: Criminal Proceedings*) [1983] 1 W.L.R. 925, para. 3.)

- Cases where an extension of time has been granted include the following.

R. v. *Stratford-on-Avon District Council, ex p. Jackson* [1985] 1 W.L.R. 1319 concerned a challenge to a grant of planning permission to a third party. Among the reasons for delay, which the court regarded as legitimate, were that time was taken in an attempt made, on the advice of counsel, to persuade the Secretary of State to "call in" the planning application, and that time was taken in obtaining legal aid. In *R.* v. *Hertfordshire County Council, ex p. Cheung; R.* v. *Sefton Metropolitan Borough Council, ex p. Pau, The Times,* April 4, 1986, Sir John Donaldson M.R. stated, *obiter,* that where a test case was in progress in the public law court, others in the same position as the applicant should not be expected themselves to begin proceedings in order to protect their positions. That would strain the resources of that court to breaking point. More importantly, it was a cardinal principle of good administration that all persons who were in a similar position should be treated similarly. Accordingly, they could assume that the result of the case would be applied to them without the need for proceedings, and if that did not occur, the court would regard that as a complete justification for a late application for judicial review. In *R.* v. *Port Talbot Borough Council, ex p. Jones, The Independent,* January 5, 1988, the applicant commenced proceedings on December 11 for judicial review of a decision, taken in April, to grant a divorced Councillor the tenancy of a house (rather than a flat). Nolan J. granted certiorari and a declaration, holding that the applicant could not reasonably be expected to come to court before an internal inquiry had been held by the council. There was therefore no culpable delay of any significance and there were good grounds for extending the time limit. In *R.* v. *Commissioner for Local Administration, ex p. Croydon London Borough Council* [1989] 1 All E.R. 1033, the Commissioner in October 1985 notified the council that a complaint against the council had been received, and sought further information. His jurisdiction was challenged by the council in November 1985, but he proceeded with the investigation and reported in October 1986. The council then applied for judicial review. The Divisional Court granted a declaration that the report was void, holding that there had been no undue delay: it had been reasonable for the council to wait until the report had been made. Woolf L.J. stated that r. 4 and s.31(6) of the 1981 Act "are not intended to be applied in a technical manner. As long as no prejudice is caused . . ., the courts will not rely on those provisions to deprive a litigant who has behaved sensibly and reasonably of relief to which he is otherwise entitled." (p. 1046). In *R.* v. *Chichester JJ. and another, ex p. Chichester District Council* (1990) 88 L.G.R. 707, the council sought judicial review of the decision of magistrates on November 30, 1988, to dismiss committal proceedings. The Divisional Court held that there had not been undue delay in applying: counsel's opinion had had to be obtained, then the authority of the appropriate committee; in addition, Christmas and New Year had intervened. No substantial hardship had been caused.

In many more cases, such as the *Caswell* case, applications are refused on the ground of delay.

- As *Caswell* shows, where an extension of time is granted, relief may still ultimately be refused on the ground of delay.
- Even where an application for leave is brought promptly, a delay before the hearing of the application for leave may give rise to an argument that the discretion to refuse relief under s.31(6) should be exercised (*R.* v. *South Hertfordshire District Council, ex p. Felton* [1991] J.P.L. 633, where the argument was rejected on the facts: the hearing of an application for leave to challenge a grant of planning permission was adjourned by agreement, while an alternative site was considered; there was no risk to good administration).

(ii) Effect of Alternative Remedies

It is well established that the court will not entertain an application for judicial review where there is some equally convenient and beneficial remedy, such as an appeal to a specialised tribunal, or to the High Court by case stated, or to a more appropriate Division of the High Court. For example, in *R.* v. *Hillingdon London Borough, ex p. Royco Homes Ltd.* [1974] 1 Q.B. 720, Lord Widgery C.J. held that a planning condition that was invalid in law on its face could be challenged directly by an application for certiorari, notwithstanding the existence of the statutory appeal structure; in such circumstances it might well be "more efficient, cheaper and quicker to proceed by certiorari." In *R.* v. *Paddington Valuation Officer, ex p. Peachey Property Ltd.* [1966] 1 Q.B. 380, Lord Denning M.R. stated (at p. 400) that where it was alleged that a whole valuation list was invalid, the statutory procedure for proposing alterations in a valuation list would be "nowhere near so convenient, beneficial and effectual as certiorari or mandamus." In *R.* v. *Huntingdon District Council, ex p. Cowan* [1984] 1 All E.R. 58, Glidewell J. stated that the question was which remedy was "the most effective and convenient in all the circumstances" (p. 63).

In *ex p. Waldron* [1986] Q.B. 824 Glidewell L.J. said (at p. 852):

> "Whether the alternative statutory remedy will resolve the question at issue fully and directly, whether the statutory procedure would be quicker or slower, than procedure by way of judicial review, whether the matter depends on some particular or technical knowledge which is more readily available to the alternative appellate body, these are amongst the matters which a court should take into account when deciding whether to grant relief by way of judicial review when an alternative remedy is available."

More recently, it has been emphasised that where there is a statutory remedy, the mere fact that an application for judicial review might be more convenient and effective may not be sufficient for the court to intervene by way of judicial review: judicial review in such circumstances will only be granted in exceptional cases. In *R.* v. *Chief Constable of the Merseyside Police, ex p. Calveley* [1986] Q.B. 424, complaints were made in 1981 against five police officers in respect of an incident in which the officers had arrested the complainants. An investigating officer was appointed, but the officers were not notified of the complaints until November 1983; the Police (Discipline) Regulations 1977 (S.I. 1977 No. 580), reg. 7, required this to be done "as soon as is practicable." In September 1984, following a disciplinary hearing, the chief constable found the offences proved, required three officers to resign and dismissed the others. The officers gave notice of appeal to an appeal tribunal constituted under the Police (Appeal) Rules 1977 (S.I. 1977 No. 759), but also sought certiorari to quash the chief constable's decisions, in particular on the ground that the non-compliance with reg. 7 had prejudiced the officers. The Court of Appeal granted certiorari, holding that the officers were not required to exhaust the appeal procedures first. Sir John Donaldson M.R. (with whom Glidewell L.J. agreed) stated that the court would only "very rarely" make judicial review available where there was an alternative remedy by way of appeal. Moreover, the appeal tribunal did possess specialist expertise, which the chief constable had argued rendered it better than a court to assess the prejudice. Nevertheless, here there had been "so serious a departure from the police disciplinary procedure" that judicial review should be granted.

In *R.* v. *Secretary of State for the Home Department, ex p. Swati* [1986] 1 W.L.R. 477, the Master of the Rolls stated that the *Calveley* case decided that:

> "the jurisdiction would not be exercised where there was an alternative remedy by way of appeal, save in exceptional circumstances" (p. 485).

Note that in this formulation there is no requirement that the alternative remedy be "equally convenient and beneficial." In *Calveley*, May L.J. expressly denied (pp. 436–437) that the judgment in the *Royco Homes* and *Peachey Properties* cases supported the view that judicial review would be granted merely because it might be more effective and convenient to do so. In *ex p. Swati* itself, a person refused leave to enter the United Kingdom was refused leave to apply for judicial review, and left to his statutory right of appeal. From the applicant's point of view the latter was certainly less "convenient" as it could only be exercised from outside the United Kingdom, but that consideration did not sway the court, Parker L.J. stating that this did not, even arguably, constitute an "exceptional circumstance." Sir John Donaldson M.R. stated that:

> ". . . where Parliament provides an appeal procedure, judicial review will have no place unless the applicant can distinguish his case from the type of case for which the appeal procedure was provided" (p. 485).

(Can this be right? If the point *cannot* be raised on the statutory appeal, then that ceases to be an "alternative remedy.") These new, restrictive, dicta are criticised by Wade (*Administrative Law* (6th ed.), pp. 714–716) who argues that:

> "if an applicant can show illegality, it is wrong in principle to require him to exercise a right of appeal. Illegal action should be stopped in its tracks as soon as it is shown" (p. 715).

Factors such as convenience and speed are in principle irrelevant. However, he also notes that "the established rule is . . . still working, but behind a camouflage of discouraging language" (p. 715), noting that there was nothing really exceptional in the *Calveley* case, and that the applicant in *ex p. Swati* had no arguable case. "When genuine grounds for judicial review are alleged, it is the refusal rather than the grant of review which is the exceptional course" (p. 716).

See generally N. Collar, (1991) 10 C.J.Q. 138; S. Juss, [1986] C.L.J. 372 (on *Swati*); and C. Lewis, "The Exhaustion of Alternative Remedies in Administrative Law" [1992] C.L.J. 138 and *Lewis*, pp. 297–309; and compare the cases where the courts have held that the courts supervisory jurisdiction is excluded by the existence of an alternative remedy (below, pp. 786–788).

(iii) Other Grounds

Even where an applicant for judicial review establishes one of the grounds for review, the court retains a discretion whether to grant a remedy. Relevant factors that have already been mentioned include the nature of the applicant's standing, any delay and the existence of alternative remedies. See *R.* v. *Secretary of State for Social Services, ex p. Association of Metropolitan Authorities* [1986] 1 W.L.R. 1, above, p. 458.

In *R.* v. *Monopolies and Mergers Commission, ex p. Argyll Group plc* [1986] 1 W.L.R. 763, Sir John Donaldson M.R. stated (at p. 774) that in exercising this discretion the court should approach its duties with a proper awareness of the needs of public administration. Among the factors relevant there were that good public administration is concerned with substance rather than form, and with the speed of decision, particularly in the financial field; it requires a proper consideration of the public interest and of the legitimate interest of individual citizens; and requires decisiveness and finality unless there are compelling reasons to the contrary. The court declined to quash a decision of the chairman of the commission to lay aside a reference of a take-over bid to the commission, which decision should have been made by a group of members and not by the chairman alone (see also Dillon L.J. at pp. 778–779 and Neill L.J. at pp. 782–783). In *R.* v. *Secretary of State for Education and Science, ex p. London Borough of Lewisham* [1990] C.O.D. 31, the Divisional Court declined to quash a decision of the Secretary of State to give leave to school governors to serve a notice discontinuing two schools as voluntary schools under Part II of the Education Act 1944, prior to their becoming City Technology Colleges; the Secretary of State's consultation process had been flawed, but the applications were not made with the promptness that the situation demanded, it was virtually certain that the Secretary of State would, after reconsideration, reach the same decision, and granting relief would merely lead to a further year's uncertainty which would be likely to cause substantial hardship to all concerned. (The last two cases were applied in *R.* v. *Warwickshire City Council, ex p. Boyden* [1991] C.O.D. 31.) In *Dorot Properties Ltd.* v. *London Borough of Brent* [1990] C.O.D. 378, the Court of Appeal declined to quash a flawed decision to refuse overpaid rates: the ratepayer had wrongfully delayed in paying rates it was obliged to pay, and the sum in question represented no more than fair compensation for the council's loss of interest.

In older cases, certiorari was refused where the applicant had behaved unreasonably. In *ex p. Fry* [1954] 1 W.L.R., a fireman disobeyed an order (to clean a superior officer's uniform) which he claimed was unlawful. He subsequently sought certiorari to quash the decision to caution him for a disciplinary offence, alleging breach of natural justice. Singleton L.J. thought his disobedience "extraordinarily foolish conduct." He should have obeyed the order and made a complaint later through the procedures laid down by regulations.

See generally, Sir Thomas Bingham, "Should Public Law Remedies be Discretionary?" [1991] P.L. 64; *Lewis*, Ch. 11.

H. Particular Remedies

(i) Certiorari and Prohibition

(a) Scope

An order of certiorari quashes a decision that had already been made. Prohibition restrains a body from acting unlawfully in the future or from completing an act already begun. The traditional view of the scope of these remedies was expressed by Atkin L.J. in *R.* v. *Electricity Commissioners* [1924] 1 K.B. 171, who stated that it lay:

> "whenever any body of persons having legal authority to determine questions affecting the rights of subjects, and having the duty to act judicially, act in excess of their legal authority. . . ."

Lord Reid in *Ridge* v. *Baldwin* [1964] A.C. 40 (above, p. 484) made it clear that the duty to act judicially could be inferred from the legal authority to determine questions affecting the rights of subjects, and that "rights" was not to be construed narrowly. Furthermore, it now seems that the remedy extends generally to administrative acts and is not limited to cases where there is a duty to act judicially (*R.* v. *Hillingdon London Borough Council, ex p. Royco Homes Ltd.* [1974] 1 Q.B. 720 (certiorari granted to quash a grant of planning permission); *O'Reilly* v. *Mackman* [1983] 2 A.C. 237, 279, *per* Lord Diplock (above, p. 727)). Certiorari has been granted, for example, to quash a decision to refuse a mandatory grant to a student (*R.* v. *Barnet London Borough Council ex p. Nilish Shah* [1983] 2 A.C. 309) and a decision to abolish corporal punishment in schools (*R.* v. *Manchester City Council, ex p. Fulford* (1982) 81 L.G.R. 292).

It still seems, however, that certiorari would not be available to quash an *ultra vires* act of a legislative assembly: *R.* v. *Legislative Committee of the Church Assembly, ex p. Haynes-Smith* [1928] 1 K.B. 411, D.C., cited by Lord Reid in *Ridge* v. *Baldwin* [1964] A.C. 40 at p. 74 (above, p. 483). Certiorari is probably not available in respect of any legislative acts. In *R.* v. *Hastings Board of Health* (1865) 6 B. & S. 401, 122 E.R. 1243, the court held that certiorari would not lie to quash a provisional order made by the Secretary of State for the compulsory purchase of land by the board under the Lands Clauses Consolidation Act 1845. The order was not valid until confirmed by Act of Parliament. If the Secretary of State had exceeded his jurisdiction in making the order, it would be "thrown out" by the select committee. On the other hand, modern compulsory purchase orders would be challengeable by prohibition or certiorari were it not for the provisions of the Acquisition of Land Act 1981. If the order were *ultra vires* as made, prohibition would lie to prevent confirmation by the Minister (*R.* v. *Minister of Health, ex p. Davis* [1929] 1 K.B. 619), and if the confirmed order were *ultra vires*, certiorari would lie (*R.* v. *Minister of Health, ex p. Yaffe* [1931] A.C. 494, where, however, the order was *intra vires*). There seems no good reason in principle why certiorari should not be available here (see *Craig*, p. 367). Legislative action can be challenged on an application for a declaration (see p. 721). See generally, *Lewis*, pp. 144–164.

(b) Grounds

Certiorari may be granted (i) if a decision is *ultra vires* or in breach of natural justice; (ii) if there is an error of law in the face of the record (above, p. 593); or (iii) if a decision has been procured by assertions shown clearly to be fraudulent or deliberately misleading. Ground (iii) is illustrated by *R.* v. *Ashford JJ.* [1956] 1 Q.B. 167; *R.* v. *Wolverhampton Crown Court, ex p. Crofts* [1983] 1 W.L.R. 204 (order quashing conviction procured by perjured evidence); *cf. R.* v. *Knightsbridge Crown Court, ex p. Goonatilleke* [1986] Q.B. 1 (conviction based on evidence of a witness who concealed his previous bad character quashed for breach of natural justice rather than fraud; it was not *certain* that the magistrate would have acquitted but for the fraud or perjury).

In *R.* v. *West Sussex Quarter Sessions, ex p. Albert and Maud Johnson Trust Ltd.* [1973] Q.B. 188, the Court of Appeal (Lord Denning M.R. dissenting) held that certiorari would not lie to quash a decision merely on the ground that fresh evidence, relevant to the issue in the case, had been discovered after the trial. Lord Denning suggested that as evidence was admissible by affidavit to prove fraud or collusion, then it should also be admissible to prove mistake, but the majority (Orr and Lawton L.JJ.) held that the limits of certiorari were well established, and did not extend beyond defects or irregularities at the trial.

Prohibition prevents action or continuing action in excess of jurisdiction or contrary to natural justice: see, *e.g. Dimes* v. *Grand Junction Canal Co.* (above, p. 573); *R.* v. *Kent Police Authority, ex p. Godden* (above, p. 566).

Disobedience to certiorari or prohibition may lead to proceedings for contempt of court (*cf.* below, p. 778).

(ii) Mandamus

(a) Scope

See A.J. Harding, *Public Duties and Public Law* (1989); *Lewis*, pp. 164–173.

Mandamus lies to compel the performance of a public duty, in the performance of which the applicant has a sufficient legal interest (*de Smith*, p. 540). There has never been any limitation of mandamus to judicial or quasi-judicial acts. Alternative methods of enforcing public or statutory duties include an action for damages (below, Chap. 13); for a mandatory injunction (below, p. 778); or for a declaration (below, p. 783); criminal prosecution or a statutory default power (above, p. 110).

As in the case of certiorari and prohibition, the line between public and private duties is difficult to draw. Statutory duties fall clearly into the former category, but duties imposed by the common law, custom or contract may be sufficiently public to be enforced by mandamus (see, for example, *R.* v. *Barnes B.C., ex p. Conlon*, above, p. 49). However, in *R.* v. *Industrial Court and others, ex p. A.S.S.E.T.* [1965] 1 Q.B. 377, the Divisional Court held that a particular reference to the Industrial Court established by the Industrial Courts Act 1919 was not made under the Act, but was in the nature of a reference to a private arbitral tribunal. Mandamus therefore did not lie to compel the court to hear the reference (see further, pp. 688–715).

(b) Statutory duties

A statutory duty must be couched in fairly precise terms if it is to be enforceable. For example, section 1(1) of the Education Act 1944 provides that: "[It shall be the duty of the Secretary of State for Education] to promote the education of the people of England and Wales and the progressive development of institutions devoted to that purpose, and to secure the effective execution by local authorities, under his control and direction, of the national policy for providing a varied and comprehensive educational service in every area." This is pitched at such a high level of generality that there is no question of its being a legally enforceable duty, although no doubt a failure to fulfil the "duty" will be the subject of political criticism. See also section 1(1)(*b*) of the Coal Industry Nationalisation Act 1946, discussed in *de Smith*, p. 535.

The most straightforward situation is where statute requires a specific act to be done, and it is not done. This may be because the person entrusted with the duty believes that the statute gives him a discretion whether or not to act, and so the main issue before the court is the proper interpretation of the statute.

Where the statute gives a discretion rather than imposes a duty, mandamus may still be available to compel the exercise of discretion according to law, for example, where a power is used for an improper purpose (*Padfield* v. *Minister of Agriculture*, above, p. 343); where irrelevant considerations are taken into account (see *R. v. P.L.A., ex p. Kynoch Ltd.*, above, p. 285, where mandamus was refused on the facts); where a discretion is fettered by reliance on a fixed rule of policy (*R. v. Torquay JJ., ex p. Brockman* [1951] 2 K.B. 784); or where there is an error of law in construing the scope of a discretion (*R. v. Vestry of St. Pancras*, above, p. 338). Indeed, mandamus is available wherever an inferior tribunal wrongfully declines to exercise a discretion or jurisdiction that in law it possesses. It would be unusual (although possible) for Parliament to entrust powers to a named body and at the same time to allow them to decline to *consider* whether those powers should be exercised. The courts emphasise in these circumstances that they do not seek to control the merits of an exercise of discretion or jurisdiction, but the circumstances may be such that the inferior tribunal is left with little alternative but to exercise the discretion, or their jurisdiction to determine a dispute, in a particular way (See *R. v. Justices of Kingston, ex p. Davey* (1902) 86 L.T. 589; and note the form of the order in *Padfield's* case, above, p. 349).

Notes

1. The following cases illustrate situations where mandamus lies. *R. v. Braintree District Council, ex p. Willingham* (1982) 81 L.G.R. 70 concerned section 71 of the Shops Act 1950, which provides that it is the duty of every local authority to enforce the Act. The council decided not to prosecute the operators of a Sunday Market for offences under the Act. The Divisional Court found that they had taken into account the expense of prosecuting and the fact that the market was popular in the locality. The court held that these were irrelevant considerations, and mandamus should go, requiring the council to perform its duty under section 71. The council had no general discretion not to enforce the Act; the only scope for discretion was whether any particular proceedings were necessary to secure observance, and, as an aspect of that, the council could take account of the likelihood of failure. Then, in *R. v. Camden London Borough Council, ex p. Gillan* (1988) 21 H.L.R. 114, the council was held to be in breach of its statutory duty to hear and adjudicate upon applications regarding homelessness under Part III of the Housing Act 1985 where the homeless persons unit was only open between 9.30 a.m. and 12.30 p.m. on weekdays. Furthermore, applications had to be made by telephone and not face-to-face. A shortage of money arising from rate capping was not an adequate excuse. Orders of mandamus and declarations were granted.

2. Compare the cases on tort liability for breach of statutory duty, below, pp. 817–826.

(c) Particular Grounds for the Refusal of Mandamus

• The defendant is the Crown; or a servant of the Crown who is being sued in respect of a duty owed to the Crown. See *de Smith*, pp. 553–555, *cf. R. v. Customs and Excise Commissioners, ex p. Cook* [1970] 1 W.L.R. 450.

• *Per* Scarman L.J. in *R. v. Bristol Corporation, ex p. Hendy* [1974] 1 W.L.R. 498, C.A., at p. 503: "I[f] there is evidence that a local authority is doing all that it honestly and honourably can to meet the statutory obligation, and that its failure, if there be failure, to meet that obligation arises really out of circumstances over which it has no control, then I would think it would be improper for the court to make an order of mandamus compelling it to do that which either it cannot do or which it can only do at the expense of other persons not before the court who may have equal rights with the applicant and some of whom would certainly have equal moral claims."

The court held that the local authority had complied with their duty under section 39(1) of the Land Compensation Act 1973 to secure that the applicant was provided with "suitable alternative residential accommodation on reasonable terms" after he had been displaced from his flat by a closing order under the

Housing Act 1957. They had offered him temporary accommodation until a council house was available. Section 39(1) was held not to require the authority to give the applicant priority over other persons on the housing list.

Cf. R. v. *Secretary of State for the Environment, ex p. Smith* [1988] C.O.D. 3.

• Where there is another equally convenient and beneficial remedy, such as a default power (*Pasmore* v. *Oswaldtwistle Urban District Council* [1898] A.C. 387; *cf. Meade* v. *Haringey London Borough Council*, below, pp. 819–826; and above, p. 772; J. G. Logie, "Enforcing Statutory Duties: The Courts and Default Powers" (1988) J.S.W.L. 185.

(d) Effect of disobedience

If a local authority disobeys an order of mandamus, whether derived from the prerogative writ or statute, proceedings for contempt of court may be taken against the council. Local councils in Northern Ireland which disobeyed orders of mandamus requiring the holding of meetings for the proper despatch of business have been fined: *Re Cook's Application* [1986] 3 N.I.J.B. 64 (Belfast City Council, £25,000); *Re Morrow's Application* [1987] 3 N.I.J.B. 16 (Castlereagh Borough Council, £10,000); *Re Cook's Application* [1987] 4 N.I.J.B. 42 (Belfast City Council, £25,000 fine reimposed). In addition, contempt proceedings may be taken against the individual councillors concerned: *R.* v. *Worcester Corporation* (1903) 68 J.P. 130; (1905) 69 J.P. 269; *R.* v. *Poplar Borough Council* (*No.* 2) [1922] 1 K.B. 95. In the latter case most of the Poplar councillors were imprisoned for a period for contempt: B. Keith-Lucas, "Poplarism" [1962] P.L. 52, 60–62.

(iii) Injunction

"An injunction is an order of a court addressed to a party to proceedings before it and requiring him to refrain from doing, or to do, a particular act" (*de Smith*, p. 434). A prohibitory injunction may be appropriate to restrain the performance of *ultra vires* acts. A mandatory injunction may (rarely) be available to compel performance of a public duty. See generally, *Lewis*, Ch. 8.

An action for an injunction may include an application for interlocutory relief to maintain the status quo pending trial of the main action. (See above, pp. 718–719.)

An injunction may be granted in one of several different forms. It may be expressed to last for a fixed period, or for ever, or indefinitely until some condition is fulfilled. It may be suspended to give reasonable time for compliance.

(a) Examples of the Use of Injunctions in Administrative Law

Mandatory Injunctions

An example of a case where a mandatory injunction was granted is *Att.-Gen.* v. *Bastow* [1957] 1 Q.B. 514 where the Attorney-General at the relation of a local planning authority obtained an order requiring (*inter alia*) the removal of caravans placed on land in breach of planning control. An example of a refusal of an injunction in the exercise of the court's discretion on grounds peculiar to the mandatory form is *Dowty Boulton Paul Ltd.* v. *Wolverhampton Corporation* (*No. 1*), above, p. 305; and see *Morris* v. *Redland Bricks* [1970] A.C. 652.

Prohibitory Injunctions

These may lie as follows:

- To restrain breaches of statutory duty (*e.g. Att.-Gen. ex rel. McWhirter* v. *I.B.A.* (The "Warhol" case) [1973] 1 Q.B. 629, see *de Smith*, Appendix.
- To restrain *ultra vires* acts (*e.g. Att.-Gen.* v. *Fulham Corporation*, above, p. 200; *Att.-Gen.* v. *Crayford U.D.C.*, above, p. 203; especially where the *ultra vires* act involves unlawful payments from public funds (*e.g. Att.-Gen.* v. *De Winton* [1906] 2 Ch. 106, and *cf.* the functions of the district auditor discussed above, pp. 28–33). See also *Municipal Council of Sydney* v. *Campbell*, above, p. 340.
- To restrain repeated breaches of the criminal law, such as breaches of planning control and disobedience to enforcement notices (see *Att.-Gen.* v. *Bastow, supra*). Compare *Att.-Gen.* v. *Harris* [1961] 1 Q.B. 74, where Mr. and Mrs. Harris were restrained by injunction from selling flowers outside Southern Cemetery, Manchester, contrary to the Manchester Police Regulation Act 1844. Mr. Harris had been convicted and fined for offences against the Act on 142 occasions, his wife on 95. Further proceedings were taken against them, subsequently, for contempt of court: see *The Times*, September 21, 1960; February 15 and 28, 1961. *Cf. Gouriet* v. *Union of Post Office Workers* [1978] A.C. 435, where the House of Lords refused to grant G. a declaration that it would be unlawful for the union to seek to interrupt mail between this country and South Africa, on the ground that G. lacked *locus standi*. See D. Feldman, "Injunctions and the Criminal Law" (1979) 42 M.L.R. 369; *Imperial Tobacco Ltd.* v. *Attorney-General* [1981] A.C. 718 and *Att.-Gen.* v. *Able* [1984] Q.B. 795 (declarations and the criminal law).
- To restrain a public nuisance (*e.g. Pride of Derby Angling Association* v. *British Celanese and others* [1953] Ch. 149).

(b) Locus Standi in Relation to Injunctions

Apart from on an application for judicial review (see above, pp. 744–764), an action for an injunction may be brought:

• by the Attorney-General, on behalf of the Crown as *parens patriae* for "the protection of public rights or public interests as opposed to matters of a private character" (*Thio*, p. 134). He may for example seek to restrain a public although not a private nuisance (*Att.-Gen.* v. *P.Y.A. Quarries* [1957] 2 Q.B. 169); to restrain public bodies from exceeding their powers; and to restrain repeated breaches of the criminal law;

• by a private individual "in two cases: first, where the interference with the public right is such that some private right of his is at the same time interfered with . . .; and, secondly, where no private right is interfered with, but the plaintiff, in respect of his public right, suffers special damage peculiar to himself from the interference with the public right" (*per* Buckley J. in *Boyce* v. *Paddington B.C.* [1903] 1 Ch. 109, 114). These principles were first established in private actions for public nuisance, but are of wider application, and it is normally a pre-condition for *locus standi* for an injunction for a plaintiff to be in a position to sue for damages for a tort or other wrong. If the execution of an *ultra vires* act would be an actionable tort, then the person affected clearly has *locus standi* to obtain an injunction (*e.g. Westminster Corporation* v. *L.N.W. Ry.*, above, p. 384). These principles were reaffirmed by the House of Lords in *Gouriet* v. *Union of Post Office Workers* [1978] A.C. 435 (see above, pp. 734 and 750–752).

• by the Attorney-General in a relator action. See *Att.-Gen.* v. *Crayford U.D.C.*, above, p. 203; *Att.-Gen.* v. *I.B.A.* [1973] Q.B. 629; below, p. 781.

• by a local authority:

"LOCAL GOVERNMENT ACT 1972

Power of local authorities to prosecute or defend legal proceedings

222.—(1) Where a local authority consider it expedient for the promotion or protection of the interests of the inhabitants of their area—

(*a*) they may prosecute or defend or appear in any legal proceedings and, in the case of civil proceedings, may institute them in their own name, and
(*b*) they may, in their own name, make representations in the interests of the inhabitants at any public inquiry held by or on behalf of any Minister or public body under any enactment."

Note

This has altered the previous rule that local authorities were subject to the same *locus standi* requirements as private individuals (*Thio*, pp. 206–215). Now authorities are able to commence *any* civil proceedings in their own name—not just actions for an injunction. Local authorities have frequently relied on section 222 to seek injunctions to restrain breaches of the tree preservation orders (*e.g. Kent County Council* v. *Batchelor (No. 2)* [1979] 1 W.L.R. 213); enforcement and stop notices (*e.g. Westminster City Council* v. *Jones* (1981) 80 L.G.R. 241; *Runnymede Borough Council* v. *Ball* [1986] 1 W.L.R. 353; see S. Tromans [1986] C.L.J. 374); unlicensed street trading (*Westminster City Council* v. *Freeman* (1985) 135 N.L.J. 1232); the operation of an unlicensed sex shop (*Portsmouth City Council* v. *Richards* [1989] 1 C.M.L.R. 673); breaches of a noise control notice (*City of London Corporation* v. *Bovis Construction Ltd.* (1988) 86 L.G.R. 660). Most difficulties have arisen in respect of injunctions to restrain breaches of the Sunday trading law, particularly on the question of the compatibility of that law with European Community law (see *Stoke-on-Trent City Council* v. *B. & Q. (Retail) Ltd.* [1984] A.C. 754; *Wychavon District Council* v. *Midland Enterprises (Special Events) Ltd.* (1987) 86 L.G.R. 83; Case 145/88, *Torfaen Borough Council* v. *B. & Q. plc* [1990] 2 Q.B. 19, E.C.J.; *W.H. Smith Do-It-All Ltd.* v. *Peterborough City Council* [1991] 1 Q.B. 304; *Stoke-on-Trent City Council* v. *B. & Q. plc* [1991] Ch. 48). See P. Diamond, "Dishonourable Defences: The Use of Injunctions and the E.E.C. Treaty—Case Study of the Shops Act 1950" (1991) 54 M.L.R. 72.

The local authority must consider whether the institution of civil proceedings is in the interests of the inhabitants of their area (*Stoke-on-Trent City Council* v. *B. & Q. (Retail) Ltd.* [1984] A.C. 754). After some uncertainty, the House of Lords has held that a local authority is not necessarily to be required to give an undertaking in damages (*Kirklees Metropolitan Borough Council* v. *Wickes Building Supplies Ltd.*, *The Times*, June 29, 1992, below, p. 843).

Apart from section 222, local authorities may be given specific powers to seek injunctions. Recent examples include the Environmental Protection Act 1990, s.81(5) (statutory nuisances); the Town and Country Planning Act 1990, s.187B (inserted by the Planning and Compensation Act 1991, s.3) (breaches of planning control): see M. Phillips, [1992] J.P.L. 407.

The enactment of section 222 of the Local Government Act 1972 and the extension of specific powers to seek injunctions means that local authorities are unlikely to have to use relator proceedings. See generally on section 222, B. Hough, "Local Authorities as Guardians of the Public Interest" [1992] P.L. 130.

(c) Relator actions

The role of the Attorney-General in relator actions was explained as follows by Lord Denning M.R. in *Att.-Gen.* (*ex rel. McWhirter*) v. *I.B.A.* [1973] Q.B. 629, pp. 646–648:

"*The role of the Attorney-General*

It is settled in our constitutional law that in matters which concern the public at large the Attorney-General is the guardian of the public interest. Although he is a member of the government of the day, it is his duty to represent the public interest with complete objectivity and detachment. He must act independently of any external pressure from whatever quarter it may come. As the guardian of the public interest, the Attorney-General has a special duty in regard to the enforcement of the law.

His duty has been thus stated by members of this court who, each in his turn, had held the office of Attorney-General. In 1879 Baggallay L.J. said:

> 'It is the interest of the public that the law should in all respects be respected and observed, and if the law is transgressed or threatened to be transgressed . . . it is the duty of the Attorney-General to take the necessary steps to enforce it, nor does it make any difference whether he sues ex officio, or at the instance of relators': see *Attorney-General* v. *Great Eastern Railway Co.* (1879) 11 Ch.D. 449, 500.

In 1924, Sir Ernest Pollock M.R. repeated those very words with approval: see *Attorney-General* v. *Westminster City Council* [1924] 2 Ch. 416, 420. To these I would add the words of Lord Abinger, who had himself been Attorney-General:

> '. . . it has been the practice, which I hope never will be discontinued, for the officers of the Crown to throw no difficulty in the way of any proceeding for the purpose of bringing matters before a court of justice, where any real point of difficulty that requires judicial decision has occurred': see *Deare* v. *Attorney-General* (1835) 1 Y. & C.Ex. 197, 208.

Before the Attorney-General gives leave, however, there are certain regulations which any private individual is required to observe. These regulations go back a long time and are set out in *Robertson's Civil Proceedings by and against the Crown* (1908), p. 835, and repeated in the *Supreme Court Practice* (1973) (notes to Ord. 15, r. 11). The member of the public must instruct solicitor and counsel. He must get them to prepare a writ and statement of claim. The counsel must certify that 'this writ and statement of claim are proper for the allowance of Her Majesty's Attorney-General.' The solicitor must certify that the relator is a proper person to be relator, and that he is competent to answer the costs of the proposed action.

It sounds to me that that would all take some time, as well as money, but the Attorney-General assured us that it could be, and had been, carried through, sometimes within minutes, and certainly within hours.

At any rate, when all that is done and the Attorney-General gives his consent, he virtually drops out of the proceedings. As Sir Jocelyn Simon, when he was a law officer, told the House of Commons, December 1, 1960: 'Although the Attorney-General is the nominal plaintiff in the action, in reality the action is brought by the complainant.' Once the consent of the Attorney-General is obtained, the actual conduct of the proceedings is entirely in the hands of the relator who is responsible for the costs of the action.

In all this, however, one thing is clear. In exercising his functions, the Attorney-General is not subject to the control of the courts. It was so laid down by Lord Halsbury L.C. in *London County Council* v. *Attorney-General* [1902] A.C. 165, 169, when he said:

'. . . but the initiation of the litigation, and the determination of the question whether it is a proper case for the Attorney-General to proceed in, is a matter entirely beyond the jurisdiction of this or any other court. It is a question which the law of this country has made to reside exclusively in the Attorney-General.' "

Notes

1. The House of Lords in *Gouriet* v. *Union of Post Office Workers* [1978] A.C. 435 confirmed that the refusal of the Attorney-General to grant his consent to relator proceedings was not subject to review by the courts; and rejected the dictum by Lord Denning M.R. in *Att.-Gen.* v. *I.B.A.* [1973] Q.B. 629 at p. 649 that an individual member of the public can apply for an injunction "if the Attorney-General refuses leave in a proper case, or improperly or unreasonably delays in giving leave, or his machinery works too slowly."

On *Gouriet*, see H. W. R. Wade, (1978) 94 L.Q.R. 4; D. G. T. Williams, [1977] C.L.J. 201 and [1977] Crim.L.R. 703; D. Lunny, (1978) 12 U.B.C. Law Rev. 320; D. Feldman, (1979) 42 M.L.R. 369.

2. For an argument that the House of Lords decision in the *C.C.S.U.* case extending the scope of judicial review in respect of prerogative powers (above, p. 199) should lead to a reconsideration of the Attorney-General's immunity to review, see B. Hough, "Judicial review where the Attorney General refuses to act: time for a change" (1988) 8 L.S. 189.

3. The continued value of the relator action as a mechanism for obtaining a remedy against a public authority is uncertain (see S. Nott, [1984] P.L. 22). The broader the approach to *locus standi* under Order 53 (see above, pp. 744–764), the less the need to seek the Attorney-General's consent to relator proceedings. One substantial limitation is that the Attorney in practice does not give consent where the proceedings are brought against a minister or a central government department (see *Wade*, p. 605). Relator proceedings have become something of a rarity (13 consents were given between 1983 and 1988: Sir Harry Woolf, *Protection of the Public—A New Challenge* (1990), p. 107).

For recent examples, see *Att.-Gen. ex rel. Tilley* v. *Wandsworth London Borough Council* [1981] 1 W.L.R. 854; *Att.-Gen. ex rel. Yorkshire Derwent Trust Ltd.* v. *Brotherton* [1992] 1 A.C. 270 (assertion of a public right of way). *Cf. Att.-Gen. ex rel. Scotland* v. *Barratt Manchester Ltd.* (1991) 63 P. & C.R. 179 (remedy refused as no public right was involved). Relator proceedings presumably constitute an exception to the principle of *O'Reilly* v. *Mackman* (above, pp. 722–744). See A. Grubb, [1983] P.L. 190, 200.

4. Sir Harry Woolf has argued the case for the establishment of an office of Director of Civil Proceedings. The D.C.P. would take over from the Attorney-General responsibility for instituting or intervening in proceedings in the public interest, having the advantage of being outside politics and holding office independently and irrespective of the government of the day. The Attorney would retain responsibility for advising, and instituting proceedings on behalf of, the government. The D.C.P. would also be able to authorise a member of the public to bring proceedings, his decision being subject to the supervision of the courts, and would have general responsibility for the development of the civil law and, in particular, public law. See "Public Law—Private Law: Why the Divide? A Personal View" [1986] P.L. 220, 236–238; *Protection of the Public—A New Challenge* (1990), pp. 103–113.

5. See generally on relator actions, *Wade*, pp. 603–612; J. LL. J. Edwards, *The Law Officers of the Crown* (1964), pp. 186–195, and *The Attorney-General, Politics and the Public Interest* (1984), pp. 129–153; The JUSTICE—All Souls Review of Administrative Law, *Administrative Justice: Some Necessary Reforms* (1988), pp. 186–190, 203–204.

(d) Grounds on Which an Injunction May be Refused

The injunction is an equitable remedy, and so, like the prerogative remedies, is discretionary. It may be refused in accordance with various recognised principles such as waiver, acquiescence, delay or unmeritorious conduct (see, *e.g. Bates* v. *Lord Hailsham*, above, p. 538; but *cf. Islington Vestry* v. *Hornsey U.D.C.*, above, p. 322 (note)). Similarly, an injunction may be refused if it is unnecessary in view of the availability of an alternative remedy, an undertaking by the defendant, or the triviality of the injury to the plaintiff (*cf. Glynn* v. *Keele University*, above, p. 493 (note)).

A court cannot grant an injunction or an order for specific performance against the Crown (Crown Proceedings Act 1947, s.21(1)(*a*)); or against an officer of the Crown "if the effect of granting the injunction or making the order would be to give any relief against the Crown which could not have been obtained in proceedings against the Crown" (*ibid.* s.21(2)). (See above, p. 719.)

(iv) Declaration

See I. Zamir, *The Declaratory Judgment* (1962) and (1977) C.L.P.; G. Borrie, (1955) 18 M.L.R. 138; P. W. Young, *Declaratory Orders* (2nd ed., 1984); *Lewis*, Ch. 7.

(a) General Principles

RULES OF THE SUPREME COURT

Declaratory Judgment (Ord. 15, r. 16)

16. No action or other proceeding shall be open to objection on the ground that a merely declaratory judgment or order is sought thereby, and the court may make binding declarations of right whether or not any consequential relief is or should be claimed.

Note

Cf. the procedure by way of originating summons under R.S.C. 1965, Ord. 5, r. 2, where a question arises on an instrument.

The declaration is the most useful of the remedies in administrative law in situations where a coercive order, disobedience of which constitutes a contempt, is not required, or where no wrongful act has as yet been committed. In some situations, for example in an action against the Crown, it is the only possible remedy (see above, p. 719). Where the defendant is a public authority, there is usually no question but that the law will be obeyed, once the precise legal position has been established authoritatively. Moreover, a declaratory order will be *res judicata* between the parties. For example, a planning condition declared to be *ultra vires* by a court can not be the subject of enforcement proceedings. There are additional advantages in the considerable flexibility in the form that a declaration may take, and the wide variety of situations in which a declaration may be made. A basic feature is that it is a discretionary remedy.

It is now available on an application for judicial review or in private law proceedings, subject to the principle of *O'Reilly* v. *Mackman* (see above).

(b) *Locus standi for a declaration*

Outside the application for judicial review, the principles applicable to injunctions are generally applicable also to declarations (see pp. 779–780).

Note

There have been cases that are difficult to fit within the traditional *locus standi* principles where the courts have given guidance on difficult and contentious issues of law in proceedings for a declaration. In *Royal College of Nursing* v. *Department of Health and Social Security* [1981] A.C. 800, the House of Lords (by 3–2) granted the College a declaration that advice in a D.H.S.S. circular that no offence was committed by nurses who terminated a pregnancy by medical induction if a doctor decided on the termination, initiated it, and remained responsible throughout for its overall conduct and control, did not involve the performance of unlawful acts by members of the college. Woolf J. at first instance noted that neither party desired to take any points as to the jurisdiction of the court to grant a declaration; stated that, nevertheless, questions of *locus standi* could not be overcome by consent of the parties; and concluded that he had jurisdiction, accepting the Solicitor General's argument that the case should be regarded as exceptional because of the college's special responsibilities in providing advice and insurance for its members, and the relationship between the department and the nurses, many of whom were employed by bodies acting under the department's supervision. It would, however, have been much better for proceedings to have been brought under Order 53. This aspect of the case was not mentioned by the Court of Appeal or the House of Lords.

Then, in *Gillick* v. *West Norfolk and Wisbech Area Health Authority* [1986] A.C. 112, the House of Lords held (by 3–2) that a D.H.S.S. memorandum of guidance, which stated that in exceptional cases it was a matter for the doctor's clinical judgment to decide whether to prescribe contraception for a child under 16 without the knowledge and consent of the parents, did not contain advice that was an infringement of parents' rights or was unlawful. As in the *RCN* case, it was not suggested that Mrs. Gillick was acting inappropriately in instituting proceedings for a declaration. The writ and statement of claim was issued three months before the decision in *O'Reilly* v. *Mackman* (above, pp. 722–744) (see Lord Fraser at p. 163). Lord Scarman stated (at p. 178) that Mrs. Gillick's action was "essentially to protect what she alleges to be her rights as a parent under private law." He did not see her claim "as falling under the embargo imposed by *O'Reilly's* case;" if he was wrong on that he would nevertheless think "that the private law content of her claim was so great as to make her case an exception to the general rule" (p. 178). Both the "collateral issue" and "consent" exceptions recognised by Lord Diplock in *O'Reilly* (above, p. 733) could be said to apply. Lord Fraser agreed with Lord Scarman (p. 163). Lord Bridge, in contrast, said that Mrs. Gillick "had no private right which she is in a position to assert" against the second respondent, the D.H.S.S. Nevertheless no objection had or could now be raised on the "procedural technicality that the proceedings were commenced by writ rather than by application for judicial review" (p. 192). Lords Brandon and Templeman did not discuss the procedural question. Lord Bridge expressed concern on another point. He did not agree with Lords Scarman and Fraser that the issue of a memorandum with guidance that would result in unlawful acts would be challengeable as an *ultra vires* abuse of discretion on *Wednesbury* grounds. "Here there is no specific statutory background by reference to which the appropriate *Wednes-*

bury questions would be formulated" (p. 192). Instead, it had to be recognised that the *RCN* case

"does effect a significant extension of the court's power of judicial review. We must now say that if a government department, in a field of administration in which it exercises responsibility, promulgates in a public document, albeit non-statutory in form, advice which is erroneous in law, then the court, in proceedings in appropriate form commenced by an applicant or plaintiff who possesses the necessary *locus standi*, has jurisdiction to correct the error of law by an appropriate declaration. Such an extended jurisdiction is no doubt a salutary and indeed a necessary one in certain circumstances, as the *Royal College of Nursing* case [1981] A.C. 800 itself well illustrates. But the occasions of a departmental non-statutory publication raising, as in that case, a clearly defined issue of law, unclouded by political, social or moral overtones, will be rare. In cases where any proposition of law implicit in a departmental advisory document is interwoven with questions of social and ethical controversy, the court should, in my opinion, exercise its jurisdiction with the utmost restraint, confine itself to deciding whether the proposition of law is erroneous and avoid either expressing *ex cathedra* opinions in areas of social and ethical controversy in which it has no claim to speak with authority or proferring answers to hypothetical questions of law which do not strictly arise for decision" (pp. 193–194).

Lord Templeman echoed Lord Bridge's warning "against the involvement of the courts in areas of social and ethical controversy or hypothetical questions. Nevertheless the questions raised by this appeal must now be answered" (p. 206).

The willingness of the House of Lords to entertain the case is strongly criticised by C. Harlow, (1986) 49 M.L.R. 768, who argues that Mrs. Gillick lacked *locus standi* to be granted a private law declaration, and that *O'Reilly* v. *Mackman* should have applied. See also H. W. R. Wade, (1986) 102 L.Q.R. 173; Sir Harry Woolf, *Protection of the Public—A New Challenge* (1990), pp. 43–44.

(c) Some Grounds on Which a Declaration May be Refused

The matter is non-justiciable, for example, because it is a question of morality rather than law (see *Cox* v. *Green* [1966] 1 Ch. 216: medical ethics); or because it is a question of the Crown's treaty-making power which the courts decline to consider for policy reasons (see *Blackburn* v. *Att.-Gen.* [1971] 1 W.L.R. 1037 and *McWhirter* v. *Att.-Gen.* [1972] C.M.L.R. 882); or because there is an attempt to challenge the validity of Parliamentary proceedings (see *British Railways Board* v. *Pickin* [1974] A.C. 765; *cf. R.* v. *H.M. Treasury, ex p. Smedley* [1985] Q.B. 657).

Moreover, there must be a real and not a hypothetical question in dispute between two parties (see Lord Sumner in *Russian Commercial and Industrial Bank* v. *British Bank for Foreign Trade Ltd.* [1921] 2 A.C. 438 at p. 452) J. Jaconelli, (1985) 101 L.Q.R. 587. In *Blackburn* v. *Att.-Gen.* [1971] 1 W.L.R. 1037, the Court of Appeal declined to make a declaration on the hypothetical question whether by signing the Treaty of Rome, Her Majesty's Government would irreversibly surrender in part the sovereignty of Parliament. In *R.* v. *Secretary of State for the Environment, ex p. Nottinghamshire County Council, The Independent*, November 13, 1986, declarations were refused where they related to determinations subsequently validated by retrospective legislation (*cf. R.* v. *Local Commissioner, ex p. Eastleigh Borough Council* (above, p. 176)). Then, in *R.* v. *Secretary of State for Education and Science, ex p. Birmingham City Council* (unreported, May 14, 1991), Brooke J. set aside the grant of leave to the council to seek a declaration that revised arrangements for its secondary schools would enable the council to comply with its obligations under the Sex Discrimination Act 1975. (In *Birmingham City Council* v. *Equal Opportunities Commission* [1989] A.C. 1155, the House of Lords had held the council to be in breach of its obligations under the 1975 Act). The Secretary of State had expressed no view on the question and was not a proper contradictor.

A point frequently litigated is whether the matter has been entrusted exclusively by Parliament to another tribunal. The general principle is that "where Parliament has created new rights and duties and by the same enactment has appointed a specific tribunal for their enforcement, recourse must be had to that tribunal alone" (*de Smith*, p. 500). See *Barraclough* v. *Brown* [1897] A.C. 615, distinguished in *Pyx Granite Co.* v. *M.H.L.G.*, below. The exclusive alternative remedy may be a ministerial default power. (See the descussion in *Meade* v. *Haringey L.B.C.*, below, p. 819.)

PYX GRANITE CO. LTD. v. MINISTRY OF HOUSING AND LOCAL GOVERNMENT AND ANOTHER

[1960] A.C. 260; [1959] 3 W.L.R. 346; 123 J.P. 429; 103 S.J. 633; [1959] 3 All E.R. 1; 10 P. & C.R. 319; 58 L.G.R. 1 (House of Lords)

A private Act of Parliament, the Malvern Hills Act 1924, promoted to preserve the amenities of the hills against depredation by quarrying, provided that "for the protection" of the plaintiff quarry company, various matters agreed between the company, the Malvern Hill Conservators, and Malvern Council, should be binding on the parties. Under this agreement, the company gave up their rights to quarry many areas of land, in return for a promise by the Conservators that the company's rights to quarry two areas of land should remain undisturbed. The Town and Country Planning General Development Order 1950, made under the 1947 Act, provided that "development authorised by any local or private Act of Parliament" might be undertaken without planning permission. The company claimed declarations that the quarrying which they proposed to carry out on the two areas of land mentioned in the agreement, was "authorised" by the 1924 Act. The minister had previously determined that planning permission was required, and should be refused for some land so that the skyline would be preserved, and granted for other land subject to conditions. The company also sought a declaration that the conditions were invalid as restrictions on the continuance of an existing use which could only be imposed by a discontinuance notice subject to compensation. The defendants raised preliminary objections that the court had no jurisdiction to grant the declarations as (a) by sections 15 and 17 of the Town and Country Planning Act 1947 the decision of the minister on an application to determine whether permission was required "shall be final" and (b) the wide discretion conferred on the minister to impose such conditions as he thought fit disentitled the company from seeking a declaration that they were invalid. Lloyd Jacob J. held that he had jurisdiction and granted declarations in favour of the company. The Court of Appeal (a) (Hodson L.J. dissenting) held that the court had jurisdiction to grant declarations; (b) (Morris L.J. dissenting) held that planning permission was necessary; and (c) held that the conditions were valid ([1958] 1 Q.B. 554).

The company appealed to the House of Lords.

VISCOUNT SIMONDS: . . . The question is whether the statutory remedy is the only remedy and the right of the subject to have recourse to the courts of law is excluded. Obviously it cannot altogether be excluded; for, as Lord Denning has pointed out ([1958] 1 Q.B. 554, 566, 567) if the subject does what he has not permission to do and so-called enforcement proceedings are taken against him, he can apply to the court of summary jurisdiction under section 23 of the Act and ask for the enforcement notice to be quashed, and he can thence go to the High Court upon case stated. But I agree with Lord Denning and Morris L.J. in thinking that this circuity is not necessary. It is a principle not by any means to be whittled down that the subject's recourse to Her Majesty's courts for the determination of his rights is not to be excluded except by clear words. That is, as McNair J. called it in *Francis* v. *Yiewsley and West Drayton Urban District Council* [1957] 2 Q.B. 136, 148, a "fundamental rule" from which I would not for my part sanction any departure. It must be asked, then, what is there in the Act of 1947 which bars such recourse. The answer is that there is nothing except the fact that the Act provides him with another remedy. Is it, then, an alternative or an exclusive remedy? There is nothing in the Act to suggest that, while a new remedy, perhaps cheap and expeditious, is given, the old and, as we like to call it, the inalienable remedy of Her Majesty's subjects to seek redress in her courts is taken away. And it appears to me that the case would be unarguable but for the fact that in *Barraclough* v. *Brown* [1897] A.C. 615 upon a consideration of the statute there under review it was held that the new statutory remedy was exclusive. But that case differs vitally from the present case. There the statute gave to an aggrieved person the right in certain circumstances to recover certain costs and the expenses from a third party who was not otherwise liable in a court of summary jurisdiction. It was held that that was the only remedy open to the aggrieved person and that he could not recover such costs and expenses in the High Court. "I do not think," said Lord Herschell (*ibid.* at p. 620), "the appellant can claim to recover by virtue of the statute, and at the same time insist upon doing so by means other than those prescribed by the statute which alone confers the right." Or, as Lord Watson said (*ibid.* at p. 622): "The right and the remedy are given *uno flatu*, and the one cannot be dissociated from the other." The circumstances here are far different. The appellant company are given no new right of quarrying by the Act of 1947. Their right is a common law right and the only question is how far it has been taken away. They do not *uno flatu* claim under the Act and seek a remedy elsewhere. On the contrary, they deny that they come within its purview and seek a declaration to that effect. There is, in my opinion, nothing in*Barraclough* v. *Brown* which denies them that remedy, if it is otherwise appropriate.

The appropriateness of the remedy was the final point on this part of the case. It was urged that, even if the court had jurisdiction to make the declaration claimed, it was a discretionary jurisdiction which should not be exercised in this case. My Lords, this plea should not, in my opinion, prevail. It is surely proper that in a case like this involving, as many days of argument showed, difficult questions of construction of Acts of Parliament, a court of law should declare what are the rights of the subject who claims to have them determined. I do not dissent from the contention of the respondents that, where the administrative or the quasi-judicial powers of the Minister are concerned, declaratory judgments should not readily be given by the court. But here, if ever, was a case where the jurisdiction could properly by invoked. It might even be thought surprising that the Minister should not be glad to have such questions authoritatively determined. . . .

[His Lordship held that permission for development was not required.]

LORD GODDARD:. . . . [cited *Barraclough* v. *Brown*, and continued:] I agree with the majority in the Court of Appeal, who held that this decision had no application to the facts of this case and that there were no words in the statute which deprived the appellants of their right to obtain a declaration. It was also argued that if there was a remedy obtainable in the High Court it must be by way of certiorari. I know of no authority for saying that if an order or decision can be attacked by certiorari the court is debarred from granting a declaration in an appropriate case. The remedies are not mutually exclusive, though no doubt there are some orders, notably convictions before justices, where the only appropriate remedy is certiorari. . . .

[His Lordship agreed with the judgment of Morris L.J., and held that no planning permission was necessary. It was therefore unnecessary for him to consider the validity of the conditions.]

LORD OAKSEY agreed with LORD GODDARD.

LORD KEITH OF AVONHOLM agreed with LORD JENKINS, subject to a minor qualification. LORD JENKINS delivered a generally concurring speech.

Appeal allowed.

Notes

1. See case note by H. W. R. Wade, [1959] C.L.J. 143 and *Lewis*, pp. 309–315.

2. Note that *Barraclough* v. *Brown* was an attempt to invoke the courts *original* rather than *supervisory* jurisdiction; and the declaration granted in *Pyx Granite* was also a declaration of rights under the 1924 Act rather than a declaration that the minister's previous determination to the contrary was *ultra vires*. Where the supervisory jurisdiction is involved, the better view is that the existence of an alternative remedy does not exclude the *jurisdiction* to grant judicial review, but only gives rise to a *discretion* to refuse a remedy (above, pp. 772–773; *Leech* v. *Deputy Governor of Parkhurst Prison* [1988] A.C. 533, H.L.).

3. On the question whether a declaration is available in respect of an error of law within jurisdiction, see *Craig*, pp. 396–397; P. Cane, "A fresh look at Punton's Case" (1980) 43 M.L.R. 266. On the question whether declaratory relief may be prospective only, see C. Lewis, "Retrospective and Prospective Rulings in Administrative Law" [1988] P.L. 78.

I. Self-Help

STROUD v. BRADBURY

[1952] 2 All E.R. 76; 116 J.P. 386; 96 S.J. 397; 50 L.G.R. 452, D.C. (Q.B.D.)

On February 17, 1951, following the failure of the appellant's wife to carry out works for renewing a drain at her bungalow, in accordance with a notice served on her by Herne Bay U.D.C. under section 39(1) of the Public Health Act 1936, the respondent, the clerk to the council, wrote to her saying that the council intended to proceed under section 290(6) of the Act to carry out the works themselves. A builder, on the instructions of the council, visited the bungalow several times in May, 1951. With permission he measured the work, for which he had been invited to tender, and subsequently informed the appellant and his wife that he was coming to commence the work. On June 1, 1951, a sanitary inspector employed by the local authority, with the builder and his men, attended at the premises to carry out the work, but the appellant, the owner's husband, refused to allow them to proceed with it and threatened to assault them if any attempt were made to carry it out.

The appellant was convicted by the justices of wilfully obstructing the sanitary inspector when acting in the execution of the Public Health Act 1936, and was fined £4 and £1 costs. He appealed unsuccessfully to quarter sessions, and then by way of case stated to the Queen's Bench Division.

Lord Goddard C.J.: To be entitled to enter the premises to execute the works the employees of the council had to observe the provisions of the Public Health Act 1936, s.287(1), which gives them that right subject to their giving proper notice of their intention. When the sanitary inspector of the council arrived, the appellant obstructed him with all the rights of a free-born Englishman whose premises were being invaded and defied him with a clothes prop and a spade. He was entitled to do that unless the sanitary inspector had a right to enter. He was brought before the justices and fined, and quarter sessions upheld the conviction. In the opinion of this court, the appellant now succeeds because the sanitary inspector had not done that which the statute required him to do before he had a right of entry. It was very necessary that the inspector should enter the premises to do this work and it was very necessary that the work should be done, but before the inspector could enter the premises he must comply with the statute. The statute provides by the proviso to section 287(1):

> "... admission to any premises not being a factory, workshop or workplace, shall not be demanded as of right unless twenty-four hours' notice of the intended entry has been given to the occupier."

By section 283(1) of the Act the notice must be in writing. The only document relied on as a notice justifying this entry on June 1 was a letter which was written on February 17, 1951, more than three months before, saying:

> "This matter has now been held over for a considerable time since the appeal was dismissed by the quarter sessions committee, and, as you have not complied with the council's notice, it is intended to proceed under s.290(6) of the Public Health Act 1936."

Section 290(6) provides:

> "... if the person required by the notice to execute works fails to execute the works indicated within the time thereby limited, the local authority may themselves execute the works and recover from that person the expenses reasonably incurred by them in so doing and, without prejudice to their right to exercise that power, he shall be liable to a fine not exceeding £5, and to a further fine not exceeding 40s. for each day on which the default continues after conviction therefor."

It may be that the appellant's wife was liable to some penalties for not having done the work. It may be that the council are entitled to enter and do the work themselves, but before they do so they must give the proper notice. The contention that an expression of intention on February 17 to proceed under section 290(6) of the Act of 1936 on June 1 can possibly be a twenty-four hours' notice of the intended entry is quite untenable. Therefore, the appellant was not guilty of obstructing the sanitary inspector in the execution of his duty because the sanitary inspector had no right to enter the appellant's wife's premises when he did. The appellant was entitled to order him off and prevent him from entering. The result is that the appeal is allowed, the appellant's conviction is quashed, and he must have the costs here and the costs of the appeal before the appeal committee.

DEVLIN and GORMAN JJ. agreed.

Conviction quashed.

CHAPTER 13

CIVIL LIABILITY OF PUBLIC AUTHORITIES

(A) CONTRACT

SEE C. Turpin, *Government Procurement and Contracts* (1989); H. Street, *Governmental Liability* (1953), Chap. 3; J. D. B. Mitchell, *The Contracts of Public Authorities* (1954); M. Aronson and H. Whitmore, *Public Torts and Contracts* (1982); S. Arrowsmith, *Government Procurement and Judicial Review* (1988) and (1990) 10 L.S. 231; P. W. Hogg, *Liability of the Crown* (2nd ed., 1989), Ch. 8.

Powers to contract may be conferred specifically by statute (see *Cross*, pp. 10/1–10/3; Turpin, *op. cit.* p. 84), generally by such statutory provisions as section 111 of the Local Government Act 1972 (above, p. 207), and by the common law, such as the general contractual capacity of the Crown apart from statute (Turpin, *op. cit.* pp. 83–84). If an authority enters into a contract when it has no power to do so, the contract is null and void—neither party may sue on it (see *Rhyl U.D.C.* v. *Rhyl Amusements Ltd.*, above, p. 320), and the authority will not be estopped from denying its validity (*ibid.*). Moreover, a public authority may not disable itself by contract from discharging its primary purposes (see cases given above, at pp. 295 *et seq.*). This principle is closely related to, if not identical with, the doctrine of *The Amphitrite* (see Turpin, *op. cit.* pp. 85–90, above, p. 314). In general, the courts have shown some reluctance to apply judicial review principles to the exercise of contractual powers (see S. Arrowsmith, (1990) 106 L.Q.R. 277; (1990) 10 L.S. 231, arguing that "the contractual nature of a power should in itself generally be irrelevant to the scope of review" (p. 239)). See above, pp. 688–715 on the scope of the application for judicial review. The exercise of contractual powers is also normally excluded from review by the P.C.A. or the Local Government Ombudsman.

See *Cross*, pp. 10/3–10/8 on the formalities of the exercise of contractual powers. Since the passing of the Corporate Bodies Contracts Act 1960, these are comparatively unimportant. On the modern law and practice of the contracts of central government, see Turpin, *op. cit.*

Parliament has recently imposed express restrictions on the power of local authorities to take account of non-commercial considerations (see above, pp. 117–120); cf. the use of contracting powers by central government to achieve policy goals (above, pp. 114–117).

Public procurement is now increasingly regulated by European Community law. Public supply and works contracts with an estimated value above the prevailing threshold are subject to common advertising procedures and award criteria (Directives 77/62, as amended, and 71/305, as amended; DoE Circulars 6/89 and 16/90). Other Directives (70/32 and 71/304) require the abolition of discriminatory practices which might prevent contractors from other Member States from participating in public contracts on equal terms. The enforcement of these obligations has been left to the EC Commission to take action in the European Court against a Member State under Art. 169/EEC. Directive 89/665 introduced new requirements for the establishment of review procedures in national courts or tribunals in respect of alleged infringement of Community law in the field of public procurement or national rules implementing that law. See S. Weatherill, "National Remedies and Equal Access to Public Procurement" (1990) 10 Y.E.L.

243. The Public Supply Contracts Regulations 1991 (S.I. 1991 No. 2679) and the Public Works Contracts Regulations 1991 (S.I. 1991 No. 2680) enact the relevant EC procurement directives. They apply, respectively, to certain contracts for the supply of goods, and to certain building and engineering works, placed by "contracting authorities," a term that includes Ministers, government departments, local authorities and many other specified bodies. The regulations make provision in respect of technical specifications in contract documents, procedures leading to the award of contracts, the selection of suppliers or contractors, and the award of contracts. The obligation on a contracting authority to comply with the Regulations and any enforceable Community obligation in relation to the award of a contract is a duty owed to contractors and is actionable by "any contractor who, in consequence, suffers, or risks suffering, loss or damage." Proceedings may not be brought unless the contractor has notified the authority of the breach and of his intention to bring proceedings; and must be brought promptly and in any event within three months from the date when grounds for proceedings first arose unless the court considers there is good reason for extending the period. (*Cf.* the position on judicial review, above, pp. 764–772.) The court may by an interim order (which may include an injunction against the Crown; *cf.* above, p. 720) and may set aside a decision or action taken or award damages. If the contract has been entered into, the only remedy is damages. (For the enforcement provisions, see S.I. 1991 No. 2679, reg. 26 and S.I. 1991 No. 2680, reg. 31.)

(B) TORT

See A. Rubinstein, *Jurisdiction and Illegality* (1965), Chap. VI; G. E. Robinson, *Public Authorities and Legal Liability* (1925); H. Street, *Governmental Liability* (1953), Chap. 2; M. B. Cairns, *Law of Tort in Local Government* (2nd ed., 1969); P. W. Hogg, *Liability of the Crown* (2nd ed.), Chs. 5–7; B. C. Gould, "Damages as a remedy in administrative law" (1972) 5 N.Z.U.L.R. 105; C. Harlow, "Fault Liability in French and English Public Law" (1976) 39 M.L.R. 516 and *Compensation and Government Torts* (1982); M. Aronson and H. Whitmore, *Public Torts and Contracts* (1982); A. W. Bradley, (1989) 23 L.T. 109; T. Weir, [1989] P.L. 40; *Lewis*, pp. 374–414.

Public authorities may both sue and be sued in tort (see section 222 of the Local Government Act 1972, above, p. 780). The liability of public authorities in tort is of particular interest to administrative lawyers in so far as the ordinary principles of liability are modified, or should be modified, to take account of the special position of those authorities in law and society. In many respects a public authority is in no different position from that of any other plaintiff or defendant. For example, if a local authority steamroller is carelessly driven, and injury is caused, ordinary tort principles apply. (Did the driver fall below the standard of the reasonable steamroller driver? Was the driver in the course of his employment, or was he taking the steamroller on a frolic of his own?) It makes no difference that the steamroller was publicly rather than privately owned.

On the other hand, the position of public authorities is complicated by the facts that their powers and duties are usually derived from statute, and that they must act *intra vires*. Statutory authority may be pleaded as a defence to an action in tort. Conversely, the grounds of an action may be failure to perform a statutory power or duty, the negligent performance of a power or duty, or malicious performance of a power (the malicious performance of a duty presumably merely adds insult to "injury"). Difficult questions of statutory interpretation may arise. It is a matter of debate how far, if at all, the legitimate interests of public authorities can be sufficiently protected by the application of ordinary tort principles.

It should be noted that the particular officer who commits the tortious act is personally liable, in addition to the vicarious liability of the authority (see *Ministry of Housing and Local Government* v. *Sharp* [1970] 2 Q.B. 223). Moreover, exemplary damages may be awarded in cases of oppressive, arbitrary or unconstitutional action in the exercise of public powers (*Rookes* v. *Barnard* [1964] A.C. 1129 at p. 1226, *per* Lord Devlin; *Broome* v. *Cassell & Co.* [1972] A.C. 1027; *Bradford Metropolitan City Council* v. *Arora* [1991] 2 Q.B. 50) (exemplary damages awarded against council by industrial tribunal following finding of unlawful discrimination on the grounds of race and sex).

Outside the law of tort, a finding of maladministration by an ombudsman may commonly lead to an *ex gratia* award of compensation. See A. W. Bradley, (1989) 23 L.T. 109, 126–127.

(i) The Defence of Statutory Authority

See J. Fleming, *The Law of Torts* (7th ed.), pp. 408–409; *Cross*, pp. 10/15–10/19; G. Kodilinye, (1990) 19 Anglo-Am. L.R. 72.

It is a good defence to an action in tort that the act alleged to constitute, for example, nuisance or trespass is expressly or impliedly authorised by statute.

Where the act of a public authority would be a tort if committed by a private person, and it is *ultra vires* the authority, the defence obviously fails. For example, in *Smith* v. *East Elloe R.D.C. and John Champion & Son Ltd.* (1952) 160 E.G. 148 ([1952] C.P.L. 738; 103 L.J. 108) Devlin J. (sitting with a jury) gave judgment for the plaintiff for £850, as damages for trespass. The council had continued the requisition of the plaintiff's property although the lawful purposes of the requisition (to house evacuees, and then to help to relieve the consequences of the housing shortage) had ceased because of dilapidations (see the sequel, below, p. 871). Another example is *Cooper* v. *Wandsworth Board of Works* (above, p. 470 (trespass)). *A fortiori*, a public authority may not argue in its *defence* that the act alleged to be tortious was *ultra vires*, and therefore not one which they had a legal power to perform (*Campbell* v. *Paddington Corporation* [1911] 1 K.B. 869, where the corporation authorised its employees to erect a stand in the street opposite the plaintiff's house. This was held to be a public nuisance). Rather more difficult are those cases where it it not clear whether the statute authorises the specific act that has been done. There must be a power or duty to perform the specific act in the particular manner complained of (*Metropolitan Asylum District* v. *Hill* (1881) 6 App.Cas. 193). Alternatively the infringement of legal rights must be the inevitable or unavoidable result of authorised acts (*Hammersmith Ry.* v. *Brand* (1869) L.R. 4 H.L. 171). The key factor is the precision of the statutory authorisation, and not necessarily whether that authorisation is a power or a duty. Thus, on the assumption that the provision of a smallpox hospital can constitute a nuisance to neighbours (*cf. Metroplitan Asylum District* v. *Hill*), a duty to build such a hospital on a particular site negatives liability to the neighbours; a power to build on that site (*i.e.* a choice whether or not to build) presumably also negatives liability; a power to build with no site specified will not negative liability, unless it is impossible to build without infringing someone's rights. On the defence of statutory authority and the rule in *Rylands* v. *Fletcher*, see *Dunne* v. *N.W. Gas Board* [1964] 2 Q.B. 806, C.A.

Different again are cases where there is power to act for the public benefit as and when it is deemed necessary or expedient (see Jenkins L.J. in *Marriage* v. *E. Norfolk Rivers Catchment Board* [1950] 1 K.B. 284; and *cf. Home Office* v. *Dorset Yacht Co.* [1970] A.C. 1004, below, pp. 806–808 (note)).

Jenkins L.J. in the *Marriage* case summarised at pp. 304–305:

"the general principle that Acts of Parliament by which statutory powers are conferred should not be construed as absolving those invested with them from liability, enforceable by action in the courts, in respect of any avoidable injury to others occasioned by the exercise of the powers."

We were referred to a number of well-known authorities in which this principle has been enunciated and illustrated, and in particular to *Geddis* v. Proprietors of the Bann Reservoir, 3 App.Cas. 430, 450, where Lord Hatherley said: "I apprehend that the true construction of all such powers given to companies is this: You may carry out your work to its full extent, and in some cases you must carry it out to its fullest extent, in the manner provided by the Act, but in so doing you shall not create any needless injury; you shall use all those precautions against injury to others which you would use against injury to yourself in carrying on a similar work, and if we find that in carrying out your powers damage has been done by you, the law will say that the powers which you can exercise shall be exercised for the prevention of mischief." Lord Blackburn said (*ibid.* at p. 455): "For I take it, without citing cases, that it is now thoroughly well established that no action will lie for doing that which the legislature has authorized, if it be done without negligence, although it does occasion damage to anyone; but an action does lie for doing that which the legislature has authorized, if it be done negligently. And I think that if by a reasonable exercise of the powers, either given by statute to the promoters, or which they have at common law, the damage could be prevented, it is, within this rule, 'negligence' not to make such reasonable exercise of their powers. I do not think that it will be found that any of the cases (I do not cite them) are in conflict with that view of the law." The cases cited on this aspect of the matter also included *Manchester Corporation* v. *Farnworth*, where Lord Dunedin said [1930] A.C. 171, 183: "When Parliament has authorized a certain thing to be made or done in a certain place, there can be no action for nuisance caused by the making or doing of that thing if the nuisance is the inevitable result of the making or doing so authorized. The onus of proving that the result is inevitable is on those who wish to escape liability for nuisance, but the criterion of inevitability is not what is theoretically possible but what is possible, according to the state of scientific knowledge at the time, having also in view a certain common-sense appreciation which cannot be rigidly defined, of practical feasibility in view of situation and of expense." . . .

"The general principle is thus well settled, but its application in any particular case must depend on the object and terms of the statute conferring the powers in question (including the presence or absence of a clause providing for compensation and the scope of any such clause), the nature of the act giving rise to the injury complained of, and the nature of the resulting injury. I venture to think that the questions which arise in any given case of this kind are substantially these: first, was the act which occasioned the injury complained of authorized by the statute?; secondly, did the statute contemplate that the exercise of the powers conferred would or might cause injury to others?; thirdly, if so, was the injury complained of an injury of a kind contemplated by the statute?; and, fourthly, did the statute provide for compensation in respect of any injury of the kind complained of sustained through the exercise of the powers conferred? If the answers to all these questions are in the affirmative then, I think, it must follow that the party injured is deprived of his right of action and left to his remedy in the form of compensation under the statute. . . .

[On the question of whether the injury complained of was of the kind authorised by the statute:] There is, I think, an important distinction for this purpose between (A) statutory powers to execute some particular work or carry on some particular undertaking (for example, the construction and operation of the reservoir, in *Geddis* v. *Proprietors of Bann Reservoir*, 3 App.Cas. 430, the provision of hospitals, in *Metropolitan Asylum District Managers* v. *Hill*,

6 App.Cas. 193 . . .); and (B) statutory powers to execute a variety of works of specified descriptions in a given area (the works in question being of such a kind as necessarily to involve some degree of interference with the rights of others) as and when the body invested with the powers deems it necessary or expedient to do so in furtherance of a general duty imposed on it by the Act . . . [*e.g.* the powers of the catchment board to dredge a river and deposit spoil on the banks in order to comply with their duty of maintaining the river in a due state of efficiency].

In cases of the former class, the powers are, in the absence of clear provision to the contrary in the Act, limited to the doing of the particular things authorized without infringement of the rights of others, except in so far as any such infringement may be a demonstrably necessary consequence of doing what is authorized to be done. Thus, power to construct and operate a reservoir and pass water from it down a prescribed channel does not authorize the passing of water down the channel without keeping it in a fit condition to receive the water so as to avoid the flooding of adjoining lands: *Geddis's* case; power to provide hospitals does not authorize the provision of a fever hospital in a populous place in which it will be a nuisance to neighbouring inhabitants: *Hill's* case . . In cases of the latter class, such as the present, it is obvious that, if the powers are subjected to an implied limitation to the effect that they are not to be exercised so as to cause any avoidable infringement of the rights of others, the powers will in great measure be nullified and the manifest object of the Act will be largely frustrated. . . . The injury, or apprehended injury, would, moreover, always be avoidable by abandonment of the particular project, however beneficial that project might be to riparian owners other than the complainant, and the board would therefore never be able to defeat the complainant on the ground that the injury or apprehended injury was as an unavoidable consequence of the exercise of their statutory powers.

[His Lordship concluded] that the intention of the Land Drainage Act 1930 was to make the board, acting in good faith and within their powers, the sole judge of what was necessary or proper to be done in the way of drainage operations for the benefit of their catchment area as a whole and, within limits which I will endeavour to define below, to deprive persons injured by any exercise of the board's powers of their ordinary remedy by way of action, and substitute the remedy by way of compensation prescribed by s.34, subs. 3."

[His Lordship stated that ordinary rights of action would remain in respect of incidental acts of negligence, or the undertaking of an operation "which on the face of it is so capricious or unreasonable, or so fraught with manifest danger to others, that no catchment board acting *bona fide* and rationally, not recklessly, would ever have undertaken it."]

(ii) Negligent Exercise of Powers and Duties

Public authorities are clearly liable for the negligent exercise of powers and duties, as can be seen from the limits of the defence of statutory authority. Jenkins L.J. in *Marriage* v. *E. Norfolk Rivers Catchment Board* [1950] 1 K.B. 284 emphasised (at p. 309) that the defence would not apply to "some negligent act occurring in the course of some exercise of the board's powers but not in itself an act which the board are authorized to do," or to "some unintended occurrence brought about in the course of carrying out the work [*i.e.* the operation which the board intended to carry out] owing to negligence in carrying it out." The main difficulties have arisen in respect of some of the specialised activities of public authorities—in particular in determining whether a duty of care is owed (*Anns* v. *Merton London Borough Council*, below; *Jones* v. *Department of Employment*, below, p. 810).

ANNS AND OTHERS v. MERTON LONDON BOROUGH COUNCIL

[1978] A.C. 728; [1977] 2 W.L.R. 1024; *sub nom. Anns and Others* v. *London Borough of Merton* [1977] 2 All E.R. 492 (House of Lords)

The plaintiffs were lessees under long leases of seven flats or maisonettes in a two-storey block in Wimbledon. The owners of the block were the builders and after their completion in 1962 they granted long leases: only two of the plaintiffs were original lessees, the others having acquired their leases by assignment at dates in 1967 and 1968. On February 9, 1962, the then local authority passed building plans for the block which were deposited under the by-laws. Subsequently that authority was superseded by the defendant council which took over its predecessor's duties and liabilities. In February 1970, structural movements began to occur in the building and those resulted, *inter alia*, in cracks in the walls and sloping of floors. On February 21, 1972, writs were issued against both the builders and the council and later the separate proceedings were consolidated. The claims against the council were for damages for negligence in that the structural damage had been caused by the negligence of the council in allowing the builders to construct the block upon foundations which were only two feet six inches deep instead of three feet or deeper as required by the deposited plans, alternatively in failing to carry out the necessary inspections sufficiently carefully or at all, as a result of which the structural movement occurred.

The plaintiffs' actions were dismissed by an official referee on the ground that they were statute-barred. The plaintiffs' appeal to the Court of Appeal was allowed. The council appealed to the House of Lords. The House granted the council leave to argue the question whether in the circumstances the council were under any legal duty of care to the plaintiffs at all. The council wished to challenge the correctness of the decision in *Dutton* v. *Bognor Regis U.D.C.* [1972] 1 Q.B. 373, where the Court of Appeal had held that a duty of care was owed where foundations were negligently approved.

LORD WILBERFORCE: . . . This being a preliminary point of law, as was the argument on limitation, it has to be decided on the assumption that the facts are as pleaded. There is some difference between those facts and those on which *Dutton's* case was based, and in the present case the plaintiffs rely not only upon negligent inspection, but, in the alternative, upon a failure to make any inspections.

In these circumstances I take the questions in this appeal to be:

1. Whether the defendant council was under: (*a*) a duty of care to the plaintiffs to carry out an inspection of the foundations (which did not arise in *Dutton's* case); (*b*) a duty, if any inspection was made, to take reasonable care to see that the by-laws were complied with (as held in *Dutton's* case); (*c*) any other duty including a duty to ensure that the building was constructed in accordance with the plans, or not to allow the builder to construct the dwelling-house upon foundations which were only two feet six inches deep instead of three feet or deeper (as pleaded).

2. If the defendant council was under any such duty as alleged, and committed a breach of it, resulting in damage, at what date the cause of action of the plaintiffs arose for the purposes of the Limitation Act 1939. No question arises directly at this stage as to the damages which the

plaintiffs can recover and no doubt there will be issues at the trial as to causation and quantum which we cannot anticipate. But it will be necessary to give some general consideration to the kind of damages to which, if they succeed, the plaintiffs may become entitled. This matter was discussed in *Dutton's* case and is closely connected with that of the duty which may be owed and with the arising of the cause of action.

The duty of care

Through the trilogy of cases in this House—*Donoghue* v. *Stevenson* [1932] A.C. 562, *Hedley Byrne & Co. Ltd.* v. *Heller & Partners Ltd.* [1964] A.C. 465, and *Dorset Yacht Co. Ltd.* v. *Home Office* [1970] A.C. 1004, the position has now been reached that in order to establish that a duty of care arises in a particular situation, it is not necessary to bring the facts of that situation within those of previous situations in which a duty of care has been held to exist. Rather the question has to be approached in two stages. First one has to ask whether, as between the alleged wrongdoer and the person who has suffered damage there is a sufficient relationship of proximity or neighbourhood such that, in the reasonable contemplation of the former, carelessness on his part may be likely to cause damage to the latter—in which case a *prima facie* duty of care arises. Secondly, if the first question is answered affirmatively, it is necessary to consider whether there are any considerations which ought to negative, or to reduce or limit the scope of the duty or the class of person to whom it is owed or the damages to which a breach of it may give rise: see *Dorset Yacht* case [1970] A.C. 1004, *per* Lord Reid at p. 1027. Examples of this are *Hedley Byrne's* case [1964] A.C. 465 where the class of potential plaintiffs was reduced to those shown to have relied upon the correctness of statements made, and *Weller & Co.* v. *Foot and Mouth Disease Research Institute* [1966] 1 Q.B. 569; and (I cite these merely as illustrations, without discussion) cases about "economic loss" where, a duty having been held to exist, the nature of the recoverable damages was limited: see *S.C.M. (United Kingdom) Ltd.* v. *W. J. Whittall & Son Ltd.* [1971] 1 Q.B. 337 and *Spartan Steel & Alloys Ltd.* v. *Martin & Co. (Contractors) Ltd.* [1973] Q.B. 27.

The factual relationship between the council and owners and occupiers of new dwellings constructed in their area must be considered in the relevant statutory setting—under which the council acts. That was the Public Health Act 1936. I must refer to the relevant provisions. . . .

To summarise the statutory position. The Public Health Act 1936, in particular Part II, was enacted in order to provide for the health and safety of owners and occupiers of buildings, including dwelling-houses, by *inter alia* setting standards to be complied with in construction, and by enabling local authorities, through building by-laws, to supervise and control the operations of builders. One of the particular matters within the area of local authority supervision is the foundations of buildings—clearly a matter of vital importance, particularly because this part of the building comes to be covered up as building proceeds. Thus any weakness or inadequacy will create a hidden defect which whoever acquires the building has no means of discovering: in legal parlance there is no opportunity for intermediate inspection. So, by the by-laws, a definite standard is set for foundation work (see by-law 18(1)(*b*)): the builder is under a statutory (*sc*. by-law) duty to notify the local authority before covering up the foundations: the local authority has at this stage the right to inspect and to insist on any correction necessary to bring the work into conformity with the by-laws. It must be in the reasonable contemplation not only of the builder but also of the local authority that failure to comply with the by-laws' requirement as to foundations may give rise to a hidden defect which in the future may cause damage to the building affecting the safety and health of owners and occupiers. And as the building is intended to last, the class of owners and occupiers likely to be affected cannot be limited to those who go in immediately after construction.

What then is the extent of the local authority's duty towards these persons? Although, as I have suggested, a situation of "proximity" existed between the council and owners and occupiers of the houses, I do not think that a description of the council's duty can be based upon the "neighbourhood" principle alone or upon merely any such factual relationship as "control" as suggested by the Court of Appeal. So to base it would be to neglect an essential factor which is that the local authority is a public body, discharging functions under statute: its powers and duties are definable in terms of public not private law. The problem which this type of action creates, is to define the circumstances in which the law should impose, over and above, or perhaps alongside, these public law powers and duties, a duty in private law towards individuals such that they may sue for damages in a civil court. It is in this context that the distinction sought to be drawn between duties and mere powers has to be examined.

Most, indeed, probably all, statutes relating to public authorities or public bodies, contain in them a large area of policy. The courts call this "discretion" meaning that the decision is one for the authority or body to make, and not for the courts. Many statutes also prescribe or at least presuppose the practical execution of policy decisions: a convenient description of this is to say that in addition to the area of policy or discretion, there is an operational area. Although this distinction between the policy area and the operational area is convenient, and illuminating, it is probably a distinction of degree; many "operational" powers or duties have in them some element of "discretion." It can safely be said that the more "operational" a power or duty may be, the easier it is to superimpose upon it a common law duty of care.

I do not think that it is right to limit this to a duty to avoid causing extra or additional damage beyond what must be expected to arise from the exercise of the power or duty. That may be correct when the act done under the statute *inherently* must adversely *affect* the interest of individuals. But many other acts can be done without causing any harm to anyone—indeed may be directed to preventing harm from occurring. In these cases the duty is the normal one of taking care to avoid harm to those likely to be affected.

Let us examine the Public Health Act 1936 in the light of this. Undoubtedly it lays out a wide area of policy. It is for the local authority, a public and elected body, to decide upon the scale of resources which it can make available in order to carry out its functions under Part II of the Act—how many inspectors, with what expert qualifications, it should recruit, how often inspections are to be made, what tests are to be carried out, must be for its decision. It is no accident that the Act is drafted in terms of functions and powers rather than in terms of positive duty. As was well said, public authorities have to strike a balance between the claims of efficiency and thrift (du Parcq L.J. in *Kent* v. *East Suffolk Rivers Catchment Board* [1940] 1 K.B. 319, 338): whether they get the balance right can only be decided through the ballot box, not in the courts. It is said—there are reflections of this in the judgments in *Dutton* v. *Bognor Regis Urban District Council* [1972] 1 Q.B. 373—that the local authority is under no duty to inspect, and this is used as the foundation for an argument, also found in some of the cases, that if it need not inspect at all, it cannot be liable for negligent inspection: if it were to be held so liable, so it is said, councils would simply decide against inspection. I think that this is too crude an argument. It overlooks the fact that local authorities are public bodies operating under statute with a clear responsibility for public health in their area. They must, and in fact do, make their discretionary decisions responsibly and for reasons which accord with the statutory purpose; see *Ayr Harbour Trustees* v. *Oswald* (1883) 8 App.Cas. 623, 639, *per* Lord Watson:

> "the powers which [section 10] confers are discretionary. . . . But it is the plain import of the clause that the harbour trustees . . . shall be vested with, and shall avail themselves of, these discretionary powers, whenever and as often as they may be of opinion that the public interest will be promoted by their exercise."

If they do not exercise their discretion in this way they can be challenged in the courts. Thus, to say that councils are under no duty to inspect, is not a sufficient statement of the position. They are under a duty to give proper consideration to the question whether they should inspect or not. Their immunity from attack, in the event of failure to inspect, in other words, though great is not absolute. And because it is not absolute, the necessary premise for the proposition "if no duty to inspect, then no duty to take care in inspection" vanishes.

Passing then to the duty as regards inspection, if made. On principle there must surely be a duty to exercise reasonable care. The standard of care must be related to the duty to be performed—namely to ensure compliance with the by-laws. It must be related to the fact that the person responsible for construction in accordance with the by-laws is the builder, and that the inspector's function is supervisory. It must be related to the fact that once the inspector has passed the foundations they will be covered up, with no subsequent opportunity for inspection. But this duty, heavily operational though it may be, is still a duty arising under the statute. There may be a discretionary element in its exercise—discretionary as to the time and manner of inspection, and the techniques to be used. A plaintiff complaining of negligence must prove, the burden being on him, that action taken was not within the limits of a discretion *bona fide* exercised, before he can begin to rely upon a common law duty of care. But if he can do this, he should, in principle, be able to sue.

Is there, then, authority against the existence of any such duty or any reason to restrict it? It is said that there is an absolute distinction in the law between statutory duty and statutory power—the former giving rise to possible liability, the latter not, or at least not doing so unless the exercise of the power involves some positive act creating some fresh or additional damage.

My Lords, I do not believe that any such absolute rule exists: or perhaps, more accurately, that such rules as exist in relation to powers and duties existing under particular statutes, provide sufficient definition of the rights of individuals affected by their exercise, or indeed their non-exercise, unless they take account of the possibility that, parallel with public law duties there may coexist those duties which persons—private or public—are under at common law to avoid causing damage to others in sufficient proximity to them. This is, I think, the key to understanding of the main authority relied upon by the appellants—*East Suffolk Rivers Catchment Board* v. *Kent* [1941] A.C. 74.

The statutory provisions in that case were contained in the Land Drainage Act 1930 and were in the form of a power to repair drainage works including walls or banks. The facts are well known: there was a very high tide which burst the banks protecting the respondent's land. The Catchment Board, requested to take action, did so with an allocation of manpower and resources (graphically described by MacKinnon L.J. [1940] 1 K.B. 319, 330) which was hopelessly inadequate and which resulted in the respondent's land being flooded for much longer than it need have been. There was a considerable difference of judicial opinion. Hilbery J. [1939] 2 All E.R. 207 who tried the case, held the board liable for the damage caused by the extended flooding and his decision was upheld by a majority of the Court of Appeal [1940] 1 K.B. 319. This House, by majority of four to one, reached the opposite conclusion [1941] A.C. 74. The speeches of their Lordships contain discussion of earlier authorities, which well illustrate the different types of statutory enactment under which these cases may arise. There are private Acts conferring powers—necessarily—to interfere with the right of individuals: in such cases, an action in respect of damage caused by the exercise of the powers generally does not lie, but it may do so "for doing that which the legislature has authorised, if it be done negligently": see *Geddis* v. *Bann Reservoir Proprietors* (1878) 3 App.Cas. 430, 456, *per* Lord Blackburn. Then there are cases where a statutory power is conferred, but the scale on which it is exercised is left to a local authority: *Sheppard* v. *Glossop Corporation* [1921] 3 K.B. 132. That concerned a power to light streets and the corporation decided, for economy reasons, to extinguish the lighting on Christmas night. Clearly this was within the discretion of the authority but Scrutton L.J. in the Court of Appeal, at p. 146, contrasted this situation with one where "an option is given by statute to an authority to do or not to do a thing and it elects to do the thing and does it negligently." (Compare *Indian Towing Co. Inc.* v. *United States* (1955) 350 U.S. 61, which makes just this distinction between a discretion to provide a lighthouse, and at operational level, a duty, if one is provided, to use due care to keep the light in working order). Other illustrations are given.

My Lords, a number of reasons were suggested for distinguishing the *East Suffolk* case [1941] A.C. 74—apart from the relevant fact that it was concerned with a different Act, indeed type of Act. It was said to be a decision on causation: I think that this is true of at least two of their Lordships (Viscount Simon L.C. and Lord Thankerton). It was said that the damage was already there before the board came on the scene: so it was but the board's action or inaction undoubtedly prolonged it, and the action was in respect of the prolongation. I should not think it right to put the case aside on such arguments. To me the two significant points about the case are, first, that it is an example, and a good one, where operational activity—at the breach in the wall—was still well within a discretionary area, so that the plaintiff's task in contending for a duty of care was a difficult one. This is clearly the basis on which Lord Romer, whose speech is often quoted as a proposition of law, proceeded. Secondly, although the case was decided in 1940, only one of their Lordships considered it in relation to a duty of care at common law. It need cause no surprise that this was Lord Atkin. His speech starts with this passage, at p. 88:

> "On the first point" [*sc.* whether there was a duty owed to the plaintiff and what was its nature] "I cannot help thinking that the argument did not sufficiently distinguish between two kinds of duties: (1) A statutory duty to do or abstain from doing something. (2) A common law duty to conduct yourself with reasonable care so as not to injure persons liable to be affected by your conduct."

And later he refers to *Donoghue* v. *Stevenson* [1932] A.C. 562—the only one of their Lordships to do so—though I think it fair to say that Lord Thankerton (who decided the case on causation) in his formulation of the duty must have been thinking in terms of that case. My Lords, I believe that the conception of a general duty of care, not limited to particular accepted situations, but extending generally over all relations of sufficient proximity, and even pervading the sphere of statutory functions of public bodies, had not at that time become fully recognised. Indeed it may well be that full recognition of the impact of *Donoghue* v. *Stevenson* in the latter sphere only came with the decision of this House in *Dorset Yacht Co. Ltd.* v. *Home Office* [1970] A.C. 1004.

In that case the Borstal officers, for whose actions the Home Office was vicariously responsible, were acting, in their control of the boys, under statutory powers. But it was held that, nevertheless they were under a duty of care as regards persons who might suffer damage as the result of their carelessness—see, *per* Lord Reid, at pp. 1030–1031, Lord Morris of Borth-y-Gest, at p. 1036, Lord Pearson, at p. 1055: "The existence of the statutory duties does not exclude liability at common law for negligence in the performance of the statutory duties." Lord Diplock in his speech gives this topic extended consideration with a view to relating the officers' responsibility under public law to their liability in damages to members of the public under private civil law: see pp. 1064 *et seq*. My noble and learned friend points out that the accepted principles which are applicable to powers conferred by a private Act of Parliament, as laid down in *Geddis* v. *Bann Reservoir Proprietors*, 3 App.Cas. 430, cannot automatically be applied to public statutes which confer a large measure of discretion upon public authorities. As regards the latter, for a civil action based on negligence at common law to succeed, there must be acts or omissions taken outside the limits of the delegated discretion: in such a case "Its actionability falls to be determined by the civil law principles of negligence": see [1970] A.C. 1004, 1068.

It is for this reason that the law, as stated in some of the speeches in *East Suffolk Rivers Catchment Board* v. *Kent* [1941] A.C. 74, but not in those of Lord Atkin or Lord Thankerton, requires at the present time to be understood and applied with the recognition that, quite apart from such consequences as may flow from an examination of the duties laid down by the particular statute, there may be room, once one is outside the area of legitimate discretion or policy, for a duty of care at common law. It is irrelevant to the existence of this duty of care whether what is created by the statute is a duty or a power: the duty of care may exist in either case. The difference between the two lies in this, that, in the case of a power, liability cannot exist unless the act complained of lies outside the ambit of the power. In *Dorset Yacht Co. Ltd.* v. *Home Office* [1970] A.C. 1004 the officers may (on the assumed facts) have acted outside any discretion delegated to them and having disregarded their instructions as to the precautions which they should take to prevent the trainees from escaping: see, *per* Lord Diplock, at p. 1069). So in the present case, the allegations made are consistent with the council or its inspector having acted outside any delegated discretion either as to the making of an inspection, or as to the manner in which an inspection was made. Whether they did so must be determined at the trial. In the event of a positive determination, and only so, can a duty of care arise. I respectfully think that Lord Denning M.R. in *Dutton* v. *Bognor Regis Urban District Council* [1972] 1 Q.B. 373, 392 puts the duty too high.

To whom the duty is owed. There is, in my opinion, no difficulty about this. A reasonable man in the position of the inspector must realise that if the foundations are covered in without adequate depth or strength as required by the by-laws, injury to safety or health may be suffered by owners or occupiers of the house. The duty is owed to them—not of course to a negligent building owner, the source of his own loss. I would leave open the case of users, who might themselves have a remedy against the occupier under the Occupiers' Liability Act 1957. A right of action can only be conferred upon an owner or occupier, who is such when the damage occurs (see below). This disposes of the possible objection that an endless, indeterminate class of potential plaintiffs may be called into existence.

The nature of the duty. This must be related closely to the purpose for which powers of inspection are granted, namely, to secure compliance with the by-laws. The duty is to take reasonable care, no more, no less, to secure that the builder does not cover in foundations which do not comply with by-law requirements. The allegations in the statements of claim, in so far as they are based upon non-compliance with the plans, are misconceived. . . .

Conclusion. I would hold:

1. that *Dutton* v. *Bognor Regis Urban District Council* [1972] 1 Q.B. 373 was in the result rightly decided. The correct legal basis for the decision must be taken to be that established by your Lordships in this appeal;

2. that the question whether the defendant council by itself or its officers came under a duty of care toward the plaintiffs must be considered in relation to the powers, duties and discretions arising under the Public Health Act 1936;

3. that the defendant council would not be guilty of a breach of duty in not carrying out inspection of the foundations of the block unless it were shown (*a*) not properly to have exercised its discretion as to the making of inspections, and (*b*) to have failed to exercise reasonable care in its acts or omissions to secure that the by-laws applicable to the foundations of the block were complied with;

4. that the defendant council would be liable to the respondents for breach of duty if it were proved that its inspector, having assumed the duty of inspecting the foundations, and acting otherwise than in the *bona fide* exercise of any discretion under the statute, did not exercise reasonable care to ensure that the by-laws applicable to the foundations were complied with;

5. that on the facts as pleaded none of the actions are barred by the Limitation Act 1939.

And consequently that the appeal should be dismissed with costs.

LORDS DIPLOCK, SIMON OF GLAISDALE AND RUSSELL OF KILLOWEN agreed with LORD WILBERFORCE.

LORD SALMON held that the council was under no obligation to exercise its power to inspect the foundations before or after the building now occupied by the plaintiffs was constructed, but that if it did exercise such powers of inspection before the building was constructed, it was under a legal duty to the plaintiffs to use reasonable care and skill in making the inspection.

Appeal dismissed.

Notes

1. The *Anns* case gave rise to a mass of difficulties, which led ultimately to the decision of a seven-member House of Lords in *Murphy* v. *Brentwood District Council* [1991] 1 A.C. 398 that it should be overruled under the 1966 *Practice Statement*. However, *Murphy* does not necessarily lay all these difficulties to rest. They can be summarised as follows:

(a) The General Approach to the Duty of Care

Lord Wilberforce's "two-stage test" (p. 797) has increasingly come into disrepute. It has been reinterpreted so that the first stage is not necessarily satisfied by the existence of "reasonable contemplation of likely harm"; there has to be a sufficient relationship of "proximity" (*Yuen Kun-yeu* v. *Att.-Gen. of Hong Kong* [1988] A.C. 175, below, p. 811). A duty of care will only be imposed if that is "just and reasonable" (the *Peabody* case, below, p. 812). In *Caparo Industries plc* v. *Dickman* [1990] 2 A.C. 605, Lord Bridge said (at p. 618) that:

> "the law has now moved in the direction of attaching greater significance to the more traditional categorisation of distinct and recognisable situations as guides to the existence, the scope and the limits of the varied duties of care which the law imposes."

He approved the view expressed by Brennan J. in *Sutherland Shire Council* v. *Heyman* (1985) 60 A.L.R. 1, 43–44, that:

> "It is preferable . . . that the law should develop novel categories of negligence incrementally and by analogy with established categories. . . ."

(See, to similar effect, Lord Roskill at p. 628, and Lord Oliver at p. 635. Lord Ackner agreed with these speeches (p. 629).)

(b) Liability for Omission

Both the Court of Appeal in *Dutton* and the House of Lords in *Anns* failed fully (if at all) to appreciate that they were dealing essentially with the local authority's failure to protect the plaintiff from the negligence of the builder (whether or not an inspection was actually conducted). Liability for an omission is only imposed in the law of negligence in special circumstances (see M. Jones, *Textbook on Torts* (3rd ed., 1991), pp. 36–44), and there was no discussion of whether there were such special circumstances here. This point was recognised by the House of Lords in *Curran* v. *Northern Ireland Co-ownership Housing Assocation Ltd.* [1987] A.C. 718, where *Anns* was distinguished. In *Curran*, the plaintiffs purchased a house in Northern Ireland. A predecessor in title of the vendors had constructed an extension with the benefit of an improvement grant from the fourth defendant, the Northern Ireland Housing Executive, a statutory authority exercising housing functions. The construction of the extension was found to be so defective that it had to be completely rebuilt at great expense. The plaintiffs sued a number of defendants, including the Executive. A preliminary point of law arose as to whether the Executive owed a duty of care to the plaintiffs to ensure that the works were carried out in a manner free from defect. The House of Lords held that no such duty of care was owed. The only control over the building works open to the Executive was to withhold payment of the grant if the works were not carried out to its satisfaction. The purpose of this power was for the protection of the public revenue and not of the recipient of the grant or successors in title. The Executive had no powers of building control analogous to those on which the decision in *Anns* was based.

Lord Bridge noted that the *Anns* decision had been cogently criticised "particularly in its tendency to obscure the important distinction between misfeasance and nonfeasance" (p. 724). "[Y]our Lordships are, I think, entitled to be wary of effecting any extension in the principle of the *Anns* case whereby, although under no statutory duty, a statutory body may be held to owe a common law duty of care to exercise its statutory powers to control the activities of third parties in such a way as to save harmless those who may be adversely affected by those activities if they are not effectively controlled" (p. 726).

His Lordship identified three elements as fundamental to the ratio of *Anns*:

> "First, the statutory power which the authority is alleged to have negligently failed to exercise or to have exercised in a negligent way must be specifically directed to safeguarding the public, or some section of the public of which the plaintiff asserting the duty of care is a member, from the particular danger which has resulted; in the *Anns* case the danger of buildings being erected on inadequate foundations. Secondly, the power must have been such that its due exercise could have avoided the danger; if the defect in the foundations had been discovered before they were covered up, the authority had power under the statute to require that the defect be made good. Thirdly, the non-exercise or negligent exercise of the power must have created a hidden defect which cannot subsequently be discovered and remedied before damage results" (pp. 727–728).

The exact status of the House of Lords decision in *East Suffolk Catchment Board* v. *Kent* [1941] A.C. 74 is uncertain. It is submitted that it should be regarded as good law. There seems no good reason why the Board, a body with limited resources, should be liable in negligence to the plaintiffs for inefficiency in rescuing their land from the effects of flooding given that (1) the Board were under no duty to act; (2) that on the facts as found, neither the plaintiffs themselves nor any third party would have been in a position to do the necessary work; and (3) that the plaintiffs had not secured the Board's services under a contract (for which they would have provided consideration). See further Bowman and Bailey, [1984] P.L. 277.

If the Board's employees had through negligence caused additional physical damage to the plaintiffs' land, the Board would have been held liable on ordinary principles. In this situation, the Board's *actions* would have caused distinct damage.

(c) The Nature of the Loss

The main ground on which *Anns* was overruled in *Murphy* v. *Brentwood District Council* [1991] 1 A.C. 398 was that the loss suffered by the plaintiff in repairing a house that was inherently defective was properly characterised as pure economic loss, which is normally irrecoverable in negligence (see M. Jones, *op. cit.* pp. 55–93).

(d) The Policy-Operational Dichotomy

In considering as a matter of policy whether the local authority should owe a duty of care, Lord Wilberforce regarded a distinction between policy decisions and the operational implementation of policy as helpful (see p. 798). Where a plaintiff wished to sue for damages in respect of an aspect of a decision that could be characterised as a "policy" or "discretionary" matter, he would have to establish that the decision was *ultra vires* in public law as well as in breach of a duty of care at private law. A complaint concerning "operational" action would be regulated solely by private law principles. The distinction was loosely based on the position in American law, where the Federal Tort Claims Act 1946 establishes an immunity in respect of policy decisions (see P. Craig, (1978) 94 L.Q.R. 428, 442–447). It was also adverted to by Lord Diplock in *Home Office* v. *Dorset Yacht Co.* [1970] A.C. 1004, where the House of Lords decided that the Home Office owed a duty of care towards the owners of property damaged by escaping Borstal trainees. Lord Diplock discussed the relationship between negligence at common law and the *ultra vires* principle in the contexts of exercises of discretion (pp. 1066–1068):

> "If one accepted the principle laid down in relation to private Acts of Parliament in the passages already cited by your Lordships from *Geddis* v. *Proprietors of Bann Reservoir*, 3 App.Cas. 430, as a proposition of law of general application to modern statutes which confer upon government departments or public authorities a discretion as to the way in which a particular purpose is to be achieved, the courts would be required, at the suit of any plaintiff who had in fact sustained damage at the hands of a Borstal trainee who had been released, to review the Home Office decision to release him and to determine whether sufficient consideration had been given to the risk of his causing damage to the plaintiff.
>
> A private Act of Parliament in the nineteenth century, of which that under consideration in *Geddis* v. *Proprietors of Bann Reservoir* was typical, conferred upon statutory undertakers powers to construct and maintain works which interfered with the common law proprietary rights of other persons. The only conflict of interests to which the exercise of these powers could give rise was between the interests of the undertakers in achieving the physical result contemplated by the private Bill which they had promoted and the interests of those other persons whose common law proprietary rights would be affected by the exercise of the powers. In construing a statute of this kind it can be presumed that Parliament did not intend to authorise the undertakers to exercise the powers in such a way as to cause damage to the proprietary rights of private citizens which could be avoided by reasonable care without prejudicing the achievement of the contemplated result. In the context of proprietary rights, the concept of a duty of reasonable care was one with which the courts were familiar in the nineteenth century as constituting a cause of action in 'negligence.' The analogy between the careless exercise of statutory powers conferred by a private Act of this kind and the careless exercise of powers existing at common law in respect of property was close and the issues involved suitable for decision by a jury, upon evidence admissible and adduced in

accordance with the ordinary procedure of courts of law. There was no compelling reason to suppose that Parliament intended to deprive of any remedy at common law private citizens whose common law proprietary rights were injured by the careless, and therefore unauthorised, acts or omissions of the undertakers.

But the analogy between 'negligence' at common law and the careless exercise of statutory powers breaks down where the act or omission complained of is not of a kind which would itself give rise to a cause of action at common law if it were not authorised by the statute. To relinquish intentionally or inadvertently the custody and control of a person responsible in law for his own acts is not an act or omission which, independently of any statute, would give rise to a cause of action at common law against the custodian on the part of another person who subsequently sustained tortious damage at the hands of the person released. The instant case thus lacks a relevant characteristic which was present in the series of decisions from which the principle formulated in *Geddis* v. *Proprietors of Bann Reservoir* was derived. Furthermore, there is present in the instant case a characteristic which was lacking in *Geddis* v. *Proprietors of Bann Reservoir*. There the only conflicting interests involved were those on the one hand of the statutory undertakers responsible for the act or omission complained of and on the other hand of the person who sustained damage as a consequence of it. In the instant case, it is the interest of the Borstal trainee himself which is most directly affected by any decision to release him and by any system of relaxed control while he is still in custody that is intended to develop his sense of personal responsibility and so afford him an opportunity to escape. Directly affected also are the interests of other members of the community of trainees subject to the common system of control, and indirectly affected by the system of control while under detention and of release under supervision is the general public interest in the reformation of young offenders and the prevention of crime.

These interests, unlike those of a person who sustains damage to his property or person by the tortious act or omission of another, do not fall within any category of property or rights recognised in English law as entitled to protection by a civil action for damages. The conflicting interests of the various categories of persons likely to be affected by an act or omission of the custodian of a Borstal trainee which has as its consequence his release or his escape are thus of different kinds for which in law there is no common basis for comparison. If the reasonable man when directing his mind to the act or omission which has this consequence ought to have in contemplation persons in all the categories directly affected and also the general public interest in the reformation of young offenders, there is no criterion by which a court can assess where the balance lies between the weight to be given to one interest and that to be given to another. The material relevant to the assessment of the reformative effect upon trainees of release under supervision or of any relaxation of control while still under detention is not of a kind which can be satisfactorily elicited by the adversary procedure and rules of evidence adopted in English courts of law or of which judges (and juries) are suited by their training and experience to assess the probative value.

It is, I apprehend, for practical reasons of this kind that over the past century the public law concept of *ultra vires* has replaced the civil law concept of negligence as the test of the legality, and consequently of the actionability, of acts or omissions of government departments or public authorities done in the exercise of a discretion conferred upon them by Parliament as to the means by which they are to achieve a particular public purpose. According to this concept Parliament has entrusted to the department or authority charged with the administration of the statute the exclusive right to determine the particular means within the limits laid down by the statute by which its purpose can best be fulfilled. It is not the function of the court, for which it would be ill-suited, to substitute its own view of the appropriate means for that of the department or authority by granting a remedy by way of a civil action at law to a private citizen adversely affected by the way in which the discretion has been exercised. Its function is confined in the first instance to deciding whether the act or omission complained of fell within the statutory limits imposed upon the department's or authority's discretion. Only if it did not would the court have jurisdiction to determine whether or not the act or omission, not being justified by the statute, constituted an actionable infringement of the plaintiff's rights in civil law.

These considerations lead me to the conclusion that neither the intentional release of a Borstal trainee under supervision, nor the unintended escape of a Borstal trainee still under detention which was the consequence of the application of a system of relaxed control intentionally adopted by the Home Office as conducive to the reformation of trainees, can have been intended by Parliament to give rise to any cause of action on the part of any private citizen unless the system adopted was so unrelated to any purpose of reformation that no reasonable person could have reached a *bona fide* conclusion that it was conducive to that purpose. Only then would the decision to adopt it be *ultra vires* in public law. . . ."

[His Lordship went on to hold that a cause of action was capable of arising from failure by the custodian to take reasonable care to prevent the detainee from escaping, if his escape was the consequence of an act or omission of the custodian falling outside the limits of the discretion delegated to him under the statute.

"The allegations of negligence against the Borstal officers are consistent with their having acted outside any discretion delegated to them and having disregarded their instructions as to the precautions which they should take to prevent members of the working party of trainees from escaping from Brownsea Island. Whether they had or not could only be determined at the trial of the action."

His Lordship then held that a duty of care arose where there is "some relationship between the custodian and the person to whom the duty is owed which exposes that person to a particular risk of damage in consequence of that escape which is different in its incidence from the general risk of damage from criminal acts of others which he shares with all members of the public." There was material for consideration at the trial whether a duty was owed on the facts.]

See also Lord Reid's speech in this case, and Jenkins L.J. in *Marriage* v. *E. Norfolk Rivers Catchment Board* [1950] 1 K.B. 284. *N.B.* the other members of the House of Lords in *Home Office* v. *Dorset Yacht Co.* adopted different lines of reasoning. Lord Diplock's speech is analysed on this point by Bailey and Bowman, [1986] C.L.J. 430, 431–436.

The distinction between the "policy" and "operational" aspects of an authority's activities proved difficult to draw in practice (see, *e.g. Bird* v. *Pearce* [1978] R.T.R. 290 and [1979] R.T.R. 369; *Haydon* v. *Kent County Council* [1978] Q.B. 343; *Vicar of Writtle* v. *Essex County Council* (1979) 77 L.Q.R. 656, discussed by D. Oliver, (1980) 33 C.L.P. 269 and S. H. Bailey and M. J. Bowman, [1986] C.L.J. 430). Commentators were divided on the question whether the concept of "policy" or "discretion" would cover any situation where the authority had an element of choice, or whether it only applied where the issues involved were not suitable for consideration by a court of law (see M. Aronson and H. Whitmore, *Public Torts and Contracts* (1982), pp. 69–73; Bailey and Bowman, [1986] C.L.J. 430, 437–439).

They were also divided on the more fundamental question whether there was any justification for a special immunity for public authorities, or whether private law principles were sufficiently flexible to accommodate the legitimate interests of public authorities.

The Privy Council, in *Takaro Properties Ltd.* v. *Rowling* [1988] A.C. 473, recognised that the problem whether a duty of care is owed cannot be solved by a "simple reference" to the distinction:

> "They incline to the opinion, expressed in the literature, that this distinction does not provide a touchstone of liability, but rather is expressive of the need to exclude altogether those cases in which the decision under attack is of such a kind that a question whether it has been made negligently is unsuitable for judicial resolution, of which notable examples are discretionary decisions on the allocation of scarce resources or the distribution of risks: see especially the discussion in *Craig on Administrative Law* (1983), pp. 534–538. If this is right, classification of the relevant decision as a policy or planning decision in this sense may exclude liability; but a conclusion that it does not fall within that category does not, in their Lordships' opinion, mean that a duty of care will necessarily exist" (*per* Lord Keith of Kinkel at p. 501).

The courts generally have relied on a variety of policy arguments in rejecting duties of care (see notes (a) and (e)) and have not needed to rely on the policy-operational dichotomy. It was, however, regarded as potentially applicable by Sir Nicolas Browne-Wilkinson V.-C., in refusing to strike out a claim by Lonrho for damages for negligence against the Secretary of State and the DTI arising out their failure to release Lonrho from its undertaking not to acquire more than 30 per cent. of the House of Fraser's share capital, despite a report by the Monopolies and Mergers Commission that a takeover by Lonrho would not be contrary to the public interest. The timing of the release might properly be characterised as an operational rather than a policy decision, and it would be premature to strike the action out (*Lonrho plc* v. *Tebbit* [1991] 4 All E.R. 973).

(e) Policy Issues Concerning the Liability of Public Authorities

In recent cases concerning public authority defendants, the courts have tended to identify policy arguments against the imposition of a duty of care without needing to refer to the policy-operational dichotomy. See *Jones* v. *Department of Employment*, below. The courts have paid closer attention to the purposes for which a statutory power is conferred, (*cf.* the *Curran* case, above).

There is now an extensive body of literature on the negligence liability of public authorities—see, *e.g.* W. Friedmann (1944) 8 M.L.R. 31; H. Street, *Governmental Liability* (1953), pp. 40, 56–80; C. J. Hamson, [1969] C.L.J. 273 (on the Court of Appeal decision in *Home Office* v. *Dorset Yacht Co.*); G. Ganz, "Compensation for Negligent Administrative Action" [1973] P.L. 84; B. V. Slutsky, (1973) 36 M.L.R. 656; C. S. Phegan, (1976) 22 McGill L.J. 605; C. Harlow, "Fault Liability in French and English Public Law" (1976) 39 M.L.R. 516, (1980) 43 M.L.R. 241, and *Compensation and Government Torts* (1982); P. P. Craig, (1978) 94 L.Q.R. 428 and *Craig*, pp. 448–458; D. Oliver, (1980) 33 C.L.P. 269; M. J. Bowman and S. H. Bailey, [1984] P.L. 277; S. H. Bailey and M. J. Bowman, [1986] C.L.J. 430; S. Todd, "The Negligence Liability of Public Authorities: Divergence in the Common Law" (1986) 102 L.Q.R. 370 and "Public Authorities' Liability: The New Zealand Dimension" (1987) 103 L.Q.R. 19; P. W. Hogg, *Liability of the Crown* (2nd ed., 1989) Ch. 6.

JONES v. DEPARTMENT OF EMPLOYMENT

[1989] Q.B. 1, [1988] 2 W.L.R. 493, [1988] 1 All E.R. 725 (Court of Appeal)

The plaintiff's claim for unemployment benefit was disallowed by an adjudication officer but allowed on appeal by the social security tribunal. Thereafter the plaintiff began an action in negligence in the county court against the defendant, the Department of Employment, alleging that the adjudication officer, as its employee, had reached his decision negligently and that the defendant had failed to review the decision on receiving further evidence from the plaintiff's solicitor. The defendant applied to strike out the proceedings as disclosing no cause of action on the ground that the adjudication officer's duties were of a judicial nature attracting immunity from suit under section 2(5) of the Crown Proceedings Act 1947. The judge held that no such immunity applied and refused the application. The defendant appealed on grounds not advanced in the county court, namely (1) that section 117(1) of the Social Security Act 1975, as amended, in providing that apart from the appellate procedures set out in the Act the adjudication officer's decision on any claim was final, excluded any common law right of action in negligence relating to the making of a decision by an adjudication officer, and (2) that an adjudication officer owed no duty of care at common law to a person whose claim he was considering so as to found an action in negligence. The Court of Appeal agreed that the officer was not performing a judicial function for the purpose of the 1947 Act, s.2(5). On the other points:

GLIDEWELL L.J.: [held, first, that the claim was barred by section 117(1) of the 1975 Act (see now section 60 of the Social Security Administration Act 1992). His Lordship continued:]

However, Mr. Laws' second and broader proposition was argued before us and I think it right to express my view on this also. His argument on this ground goes somewhat as follows. Unlike, for example, the Factories Act, the Social Security Act 1975 gives no statutory right enforceable by action. It is not here suggested that the adjudication officer was guilty of a breach of statutory duty. The claim is framed in common law negligence. But the right to unemployment benefit derives from statute. It would be strange if a mistake which, temporarily, deprived a claimant of benefit to which he was entitled did not amount to a breach of statutory duty, but was a breach of a common law duty of care. He gives as examples an inspector of taxes who makes an assessment to income tax; a customs officer who levies a demand for VAT; or a planning officer of a local authority who advises his authority on an application for planning permission. The decision of each of these officers may be challenged by the statutory process of appeal but none of them, submits Mr. Laws, owes to the applicant a duty of care at common law the breach of which can give rise to an action.

Put another way, Mr. Laws' argument is that the duty of the adjudication officer lies in the field of public law, and is enforceable only by the statutory appeal procedure or by the public law remedy of judicial review. There is no remedy available to the applicant in private law as opposed to public law.

Mr. Hill-Smith submits that the relationship between the adjudication officer and the claimant to unemployment benefit is sufficiently close or proximate to give rise to a duty of care, within the meaning of the dicta in recent decisions which have extended the boundaries of the laws of negligence.

The question we therefore have to decide is whether such a duty of care can exist. In *Curran* v. *Northern Ireland Co-ownership Housing Association Ltd.* [1987] A.C. 718, 724, Lord Bridge of Harwich said:

> "My Lords, *Anns* v. *Merton London Borough Council* [1978] A.C. 728 may be said to represent the high-water mark of a trend in the development of the law of negligence by your Lordships' House towards the elevation of the 'neighbourhood' principle derived from the speech of Lord Atkin in *Donoghue* v. *Stevenson* [1932] A.C. 562 into one of general application from which a duty of care may always be derived unless there are clear countervailing considerations to exclude it."

In his speech in *Anns* v. *Merton London Borough Council* [1978] A.C. 728, 751–752, in a famous passage Lord Wilberforce said: [His Lordship cited the passage:

> "Through the trilogy of cases in this House—. . or the damages to which a breach of it may give rise: see *Dorset Yacht* case [1970] A.C. 1004, *per* Lord Reid at p. 1027" (above, p. 797).]

In more recent authorities a somewhat different approach has been adopted. In *Yuen Kun Yeu* v. *Attorney-General of Hong Kong* [1988] A.C. 175, Lord Keith of Kinkel commented on Lord Wilberforce's formulation. Lord Keith said, at p. 191:

> "Their Lordships venture to think that the two-stage test formulated by Lord Wilberforce for determining the existence of a duty of care in negligence has been elevated to a degree of importance greater than it merits, and greater perhaps than its author intended. Further, the expression of the first stage of the test carries with it a risk of misinterpretation. As Gibbs C.J. pointed out in *Council of the Shire of Sutherland* v. *Heyman*, 59 A.L.J.R. 564, 570, there are two possible views of what Lord Wilberforce meant. The first view, favoured in a number of cases mentioned by Gibbs C.J., is that he meant to test the sufficiency of proximity simply by the reasonable contemplation of likely harm. The second view, favoured by Gibbs C.J. himself, is that Lord Wilberforce meant the expression 'proximity or neighbourhood' to be a composite one, importing the whole concept of necessary relationship between plaintiff and defendant described by Lord Atkin in *Donoghue* v. *Stevenson* [1932] A.C. 562, 580. In their Lordships' opinion the second view is the correct one. As Lord Wilberforce himself observed in *McLoughlin* v.

O'Brian [1983] 1 A.C. 410, 420, it is clear that foreseeability does not of itself, and automatically, lead to a duty of care. There are many other statements to the same effect. The truth is that the trilogy of cases referred to by Lord Wilberforce in *Anns* v. *Merton London Borough Council* [1978] A.C. 728, 751, each demonstrate particular sets of circumstances, differing in character, which were adjudged to have the effect of bringing into being a relationship apt to give rise to a duty of care. Foreseeability of harm is a necessary ingredient of such a relationship, but it is not the only one. Otherwise there would be liability in negligence on the part of one who sees another about to walk over a cliff with his head in the air, and forbears to shout a warning."

In *Governors of the Peabody Donation Fund* v. *Sir Lindsay Parkinson & Co. Ltd.* [1985] A.C. 210 Lord Keith, having set out the passage quoted above from the speech of Lord Wilberforce in *Anns* v. *Merton London Borough Council* said, at pp. 240–241:

"There has been a tendency in some recent cases to treat these passages as being themselves of a definitive character. This is a temptation which should be resisted. The true question in each case is whether the particular defendant owed to the particular plaintiff a duty of care having the scope which is contended for, and whether he was in breach of that duty with consequent loss to the plaintiff. A relationship of proximity in Lord Atkin's sense must exist before any duty of care can arise, but the scope of the duty must depend on all the circumstances of the case. In *Dorset Yacht Co.* v. *Home Office* [1970] A.C. 1004, 1038, Lord Morris of Borth-y-Gest, after observing that at the conclusion of his speech in *Donoghue* v. *Stevenson* [1932] A.C. 562, Lord Atkin said that it was advantageous if the law 'is in accordance with sound common sense' and expressing the view that a special relation existed between the prison officers and the yacht company which gave rise to a duty on the former to control their charges so as to prevent them doing damage, continued, at p. 1039: 'Apart from this I would conclude that, in the situation stipulated in the present case, it would not only be fair and reasonable that a duty of care should exist but that it would be contrary to the fitness of things were it not so. I doubt whether it is necessary to say, in cases where the court is asked whether in a particular situation a duty existed, that the court is called upon to make a decision as to policy. Policy need not be invoked where reason and good sense will at once point the way. If the test as to whether in some particular situation a duty of care arises may in some cases have to be whether it is fair and reasonable that it should so arise, the court must not shrink from being the arbiter. As Lord Radcliffe said in his speech in *Davis Contractors Ltd.* v. *Fareham Urban District Council* [1956] A.C. 696, 728, the court is "the spokesman of the fair and reasonable man."' So in determining whether or not a duty of care of particular scope was incumbent upon a defendant it is material to take into consideration whether it is just and reasonable that it should be so."

The question thus is whether, taking all these circumstances into account, it is just and reasonable that the adjudication officer should be under a duty of care at common law to the claimant to benefit. Having regard to the non-judicial nature of the adjudication officer's responsibilities, and in particular to the fact that the statutory framework provides a right of appeal which, if a point of law arises, can eventually bring the matter to this court, it is my view that the adjudication officer is not under any common law duty of care. In other words, I agree with Mr. Laws that his decision is not susceptible of challenge at common law unless it be shown that he is guilty of misfeasance.

Indeed, in my view, it is a general principle that, if a government department or officer, charged with the making of decisions whether certain payments should be made, is subject to a statutory right of appeal against his decisions, he owes no duty of care in private law. Misfeasance apart, he is only susceptible in public law to judicial review or to the right of appeal provided by the statute under which he makes his decision.

Thus I agree with Mr. Laws's submissions on this broader head. For that reason also, as well as on the narrower argument related to section 117 of the Act 1975, I would allow the appeal . . . and strike out the particulars of claim in this action as disclosing no reasonable cause of action.

SLADE L.J.: . . . The categories of relationship which are capable of giving rise to a duty of care are not closed. A series of recent decisions has shown that in some circumstances it may be difficult to decide on which side of the line a particular relationship falls. However, it is a striking feature of the present appeal that Mr. Hill-Smith, on behalf of the plaintiff, has been able to cite no case in which it has ever been decided that a government officer or department, who or which is charged by statute with deciding whether or not certain payments should be made out of public funds, has been held liable to a recipient or potential recipient in negligence at common law because of his decision. He accepted that, if his submissions are correct, they could have far-reaching implications for many other government officers performing such functions in a variety of offices, as well as for adjudication officers. However, this does not by itself show that the submissions are ill-founded.

If, in deciding whether the adjudication officer, or the department, owes a duty to the claimant, it were right to apply the two-stage test adumbrated in the familiar passage from Lord Wilberforce's speech in *Anns* v. *Merton London Borough Council* [1978] A.C. 728, 751, I would be inclined to accept that the plaintiff would surmount the first stage. I would be inclined to accept Mr. Hill-Smith's submission that, as between the adjudication officer, or the department, and the plaintiff:

> "there is a sufficient relationship of proximity or neighbourhood such that, in the reasonable contemplation of the former, carelessness on his part may be likely to cause damage to the latter. . . ."

However, on this two-stage test it would still be necessary to consider whether "there are any considerations which ought to negative . . . the duty." For reasons which will appear later, I am of the clear opinion that, even on the application of this two-stage test, there would have been considerations negativing the existence of the duty in the present case.

However,

> "In view of the direction in which the law has since been developing, their Lordships consider that for the future it should be recognised that the two-stage test in *Anns* v. *Merton London Borough Council* [1978] A.C. 728, 751–752, is not to be regarded as in all circumstances a suitable guide to the existence of a duty of care": see *Yuen Kun Yeu* v. *Attorney-General of Hong Kong* [1988] A.C. 175, 194, *per* Lord Keith of Kinkel.

In the latter case the question was whether the Commissioner of Deposit-taking Companies in Hong Kong, who was charged under the Deposit-taking Companies Ordinance 1976 with various regulatory functions in relation to deposit-taking business in Hong Kong, including the power to register or revoke the registration of companies of this nature, owed a duty of care to potential depositors in exercising this power. Lord Keith said, at p. 194:

> "The primary and all-important matter for consideration, then, is whether in all the circumstances of this case there existed between the commissioner and would-be depositors with the company such close and direct relations as to place the commissioner, in the exercise of his functions under the Ordinance, under a duty of care towards would-be depositors."

Lord Keith, at pp. 194F–195D, then proceeded to refer to one of the purposes of the Ordinance and the methods thereby adopted for securing that object. He observed, at p. 194H that "mere foreseeability of harm does not create a duty." He referred to the potential consequences for other persons of deregistering a company, pointing out that the power is:

> "quasi-judicial in character, as is demonstrated by the right of appeal to the Governor in Council conferred upon companies by section 34 of the Ordinance, and the right to be heard by the commissioner conferred by section 47."

He pointed out that the Ordinance conferred no power to control the day-to-day management of a company. He concluded, at p. 195C:

"In these circumstances their Lordships are unable to discern any intention on the part of the legislature that in considering whether to register or deregister a company the commissioner should owe any statutory duty to potential depositors. It would be strange that a common law duty of care should be superimposed upon such a statutory framework."

Likewise, in *Governors of the Peabody Donation Fund* v. *Sir Lindsay Parkinson & Co. Ltd.* [1985] A.C. 210 Lord Keith concluded, at p. 242E–F, that the defendants owed no duty of care to the plaintiff because it could not have been the intention of the legislature, in conferring on a borough council power to enforce against a defaulting site owner requirements made by it in accordance with paragraph 13 of Part III of Schedule 9 to the London Government Act 1963 to protect such owner against damage which he himself might suffer through his own failure to comply with such requirements.

Following a similar process of thought, I feel no doubt that it was not the intention of the legislature, in imposing the relevant duties by the Act of 1975 on insurance officers (or adjudication officers as they are now called), to expose such insurance officers (or the department itself) to claims in negligence at common law by aggrieved claimants. Quite the contrary. For the protection of aggrieved claimants, sections 100 and 101 of the Act of 1975 as amended have specifically laid down the elaborate system of rights of appeal . . . by which aggrieved claimants may seek redress. This system has been extended by section 14 of the Social Security Act 1980. Section 117(1) of the Act of 1975 as amended provides in effect that, subject to those provisions of the Act of 1975 and section 14 of the Act of 1980, which specifically give a claimant the right to challenge a decision on a claim made in accordance with the Act, such decision shall be "final."

The plaintiff's right to receive unemployment benefit was simply that conferred by the Act of 1975. In my judgment, it would be contrary to both the wording of section 117(1) and the intention of the Act of 1975 as a whole to hold that an adjudication officer owes any duty of care at common law to a claimant such as is now alleged and that it is open to a claimant to challenge the correctness of his decision by bringing an action in negligence.

If in the present case it be necessary or appropriate to consider whether it is just and reasonable that the alleged duty of care should be held to exist (*cf. Peabody's* case, at p. 241C, *per* Lord Keith and *Curran* v. *Northern Ireland Co-ownership Housing Association Ltd.* [1987] A.C. 718, 729), I hold without hesitation that it would not be just and reasonable, if only for these reasons. First, as Mr. Hill-Smith more or less accepted, the appeal procedure provided for by the Act of 1975 and the Act of 1980 itself for practical purposes provides a disappointed claimant with a perfectly adequate remedy for recovery of unemployment benefit properly due to him though, it is true, without costs, interest and any general damages for anxiety and distress. Secondly, as Mr. Hill-Smith also accepted, one logically inevitable consequence of holding that a common law duty of care existed would be this. Immediately following an arguably negligent and erroneous decision of an adjudication officer, a claimant would have the right to pursue an action in negligence against the adjudication officer and/or the department without even pursuing his statutory rights of appeal (albeit at the risk of having any award of damages reduced, though not necessarily eliminated, on the grounds that he had not mitigated his damage by appealing). In the context of this legislation, under which there are likely to be many thousands of citizens who rightly or wrongly consider themselves aggrieved, it would seem to me to make no sense to hold that it is open to a disappointed citizen to challenge the decision in this particular manner.

In more general terms, I would agree that Glidewell L.J. that ordinarily, and subject of course to the particular provisions of the relevant statute, a government officer or department who or which is charged by statute with deciding whether certain payments should be made out of public funds and is subject to a statutory right of appeal against such decisions, will owe no duty of care to potential recipients in private law. Misfeasance apart, I would agree that ordinarily it or he will only be susceptible (in public law) to judicial review and also to the relevant rights of appeal.

However, on the narrower grounds which I have adumbrated, principally based on the particular statutory framework under which the adjudication officer and the department operate, I agree that the plaintiff's statement of claim discloses no reasonable cause of action and that this appeal should accordingly be allowed.

CAULFIELD J.: I agree with both the judgments delivered by Glidewell and Slade L.JJ.

Notes

1. See W. J. Swadling, [1988] P.L. 328; A. W. Bradley, [1989] P.L. 199.

2. Other cases where courts have held there to be no duty of care include the *Yuen Kun Yeu* and *Peabody* cases discussed in *Jones*. Others include the following:

In *Hill* v. *Chief Constable of West Yorkshire* [1989] A.C. 59, the House of Lords held that the police did not owe a duty of care to individual members of the public to identify and apprehend an unknown criminal, even though it was reasonably foreseeable that harm was likely to be caused. In *Calveley* v. *Chief Constable of the Merseyside Police* [1989] A.C. 1228, the House held that police investigating a possible crime did not owe a duty of care to the suspect:

> "... it would plainly be contrary to public policy, in my opinion, to prejudice the fearless and efficient discharge by police officers of their vitally important public duty of investigating crime by requiring them to act under the shadow of a potential action for damages for negligence by the suspect"

(*per* Lord Bridge at p. 1238). The fact that a police station receives information that traffic lights at a particular junction are malfunctioning is not sufficient to impose on the police a duty of care to every motorist who may thereafter use the junction (*Clough* v. *Bussan* (*West Yorkshire Police Authority*) (*Third Party*) [1990] 1 All E.R. 431). "[P]ublic policy requires that senior police officers should not generally be liable to their subordinates who may be injured by rioters or the like for on-the-spot operational decisions taken in the course of attempts to control serious public disorder" (May J. in *Hughes* v. *National Union of Mineworkers* [1991] 4 All E.R. 278, 288).

The courts have also been reluctant to impose duties of care upon regulatory authorities (the *Yuen Kun Yeu* case, above, p. 814); *Minories Finance Ltd.* v. *Arthur Young (a firm)* (*Bank of England, third party*) [1989] 2 All E.R. 105 (Bank of England held not to be under a legal obligation to an individual commercial bank to exercise reasonable care and skill in carrying out its function of supervising the operation of commercial banks); *Davies* v. *Radcliffe* [1990] 1 W.L.R. 821, P.C.). See H. McLean, "Negligent regulatory authorities and the duty of care" (1988) 8 O.J.L.S. 442.

3. A public authority may be liable where its negligent misstatement leads to economic loss under the principle of *Hedley Byrne & Co.* v. *Heller and Partners Ltd.* [1964] A.C. 465. See *Coats Patons (Retail) Ltd.* v. *Birmingham Corporation* (1971) 69 L.G.R. 356; *cf. Ministry of Housing and Local Government* v. *Sharp* [1970] 2 Q.B. 223; *L. Shaddock & Associates Pty Ltd.* v. *Parramatta City Council* (1981) 55 A.L.J.R. 713. (*Cf.* the cases on misleading assurances by officials, above, pp. 324–336).

(iii) Failure to Perform Duties

See *Winfield*, Chap. 8; *Salmond and Heuston of the Law of Torts* (19th ed.), Chap. 10; C. S. Phegan (1974) 8 U. of Queensland L.J. 158; R. A. Buckley, (1984) 100 L.Q.R. 204; K. M. Stanton, *Breach of Statutory Duty in Tort* (1986); M. A. Jones, *Textbook on Torts* (3rd ed., 1991), Chap. 9.

REFFELL v. SURREY COUNTY COUNCIL

[1964] 1 W.L.R. 358; 128 J.P. 261; 108 S.J. 119; [1964] 1 All E.R. 743; 62 L.G.R. 186 (Veale J.)

R., a girl pupil at Godalming Grammar School, was injured when a cloakroom door swung towards her and she put her hand through a glass panel. The panel consisted of ⅛-inch, non-toughened glass. R. brought an action against the education authority alleging breach of statutory duty under section 10 of the Education Act 1944 (which imposed a "duty" on the authority to secure that their school premises conformed to the standards prescribed by regulations) and regulation 51 of the Standards for School Premises Regulations 1959[1] (which prescribed that in all school buildings "the design, the construction . . . and the properties of the materials shall be such that the health and safety of the occupants . . . shall be reasonably assured") and common law negligence.

VEALE J.: . . . The question whether or not a private person has a right of action for the breach of a statutory duty is always a very difficult one. Reliance is placed by the plaintiff on cases such as *Groves* v. *Wimborne* [1898] 2 Q.B. 402 (C.A.) and on the observations of their Lordships in *Cutler* v. *Wandsworth Stadium* [1949] A.C. 398, 407, 413 (H.L.). It is said

[1] (S.I. 1959 No. 890) replaced by The Standards for School Premises Regulations, 1972 (S.I. 1972 No. 2051).

that there is a strong presumption that a private right of action can be enforced by a private individual in cases where the statute provides no penalty for the breach. That is the case here, because the Education Act 1944, by section 99, gives power to the Minister to issue directions to an education authority and, if necessary, an application can be made for mandamus.

I think that the best approach to this kind of question is that set out in *Charlesworth on Negligence* (4th ed., 1962), paragraph 963, at page 454: "It has been said, 'No universal rule can be formulated which will answer the question whether in any given case an individual can sue in respect of a breach of statutory duty.' In addition to the general rules set out in the preceding section, however, the most important matters to be taken into consideration appear to be: (a) Is the action brought in respect of the kind of harm which the statute was intended to prevent? (b) Is the person bringing the action one of the class which the statute desired to protect? (c) Is the special remedy provided by the statute adequate for the protection of the person injured? If the first two questions are answered in the affirmative and the third in the negative then, in most cases, the individual can sue. . . ."

I have come to the conclusion that the answers in this case to the three questions set out in the paragraph I have just read are "yes" to the first two and "no" to the third. Bearing in mind that no penalty is laid down by the statute for a breach, I think that an action does lie by a pupil or master at a school who can prove a breach of the regulation.

What then is the nature of the duty? Counsel for the plaintiff says that, if in fact that is a breach in the sense that premises are not reasonably safe or that safety is not reasonably assured, this statutory duty is wider than any duty at common law, because—so the argument runs—the test is objective; that is to say, it matters not what this authority or other authorities knew or did not know, did or did not do, or what the past experience was. . . .

In my judgment, the argument of the plaintiff on this point is right. . . . Put it another way, if safety is not reasonably assured in the premises in fact, then there is a breach. . . .

[His Lordship held further that the authority were also liable at common law.]

Question

Why should the test for breach of these statutory duties be stricter than the common law? Is Veale J.'s view correct?

Note

In *R.* v. *Deputy Governor of Parkhurst Prison, ex p. Hague* [1992] 1 A.C. 58, the House of Lords held that the fundamental question in breach of statutory duty cases was "Did the legislature intend to confer on the plaintiff a cause of action for breach of statutory duty?" This could not be transposed into "Did the legislature intend to confer on the plaintiff protection from damage of a kind for which, if the protection is not effectively provided, the common law will afford a monetary remedy?" although that might be a suitable approach where the statutory duty was imposed to protect a class of persons from the risk of personal injury (see Lord Bridge at pp. 157–161, Lord Jauncey at pp. 168–173). The House held that breach of the Prison Rules made under the Prison Act 1952 does not give rise to an action for breach of statutory duty.

MEADE v. HARINGEY LONDON BOROUGH COUNCIL

[1979] 1 W.L.R. 637; [1979] I.C.R. 494; [1979] 2 All E.R. 1016; 77 L.G.R. 577 (Court of Appeal)

On January 15, 1979, two trade unions notified the council's chief education officer that their members, who included school caretakers holding the keys to the borough schools and ancillary manual staff, would be taking strike action as from January 22 and that "all educational establishments" in the borough "will be closed from that date." The officer gave instructions to school heads and teachers, and specifically advised that "no one should attempt to open a school." On January 29 the local authority issued a leaflet which, while expressing support for the union's pay claim, regretted hardship to parents and children and added that they were doing everything possible, in negotiation with the unions with whom they had good relations, to lessen the impact of the strike on those hardest hit.

Some of the parents affected complained to the Secretary of State for Education (Mrs. Shirley Williams) under section 99(1) of the Education Act 1944 asking her to require the education authority to discharge their duty under section 8 of the Act to provide schools (including education); but she replied that on the information before her the authority had not failed to discharge their duty under section 8. After the schools had been closed for four weeks, the plaintiff, a parent, issued a writ on his own behalf and on behalf of other interested persons in the borough, asking for an injunction requiring the authority to fulfil their duty under section 8 by causing the schools to be opened and the pupils admitted; and for declarations that the authority had failed in their duty, *inter alia*, under section 8 and that the schools had been closed without lawful authority. On the same date he moved the court for an interim injunction in mandatory terms and declarations in the terms of the writ. On the day the hearing of the motion was begun the authority deposed on affidavit that in negotiations with the unions they had obtained a modification of the situation in that, though the strike continued, the unions had resolved that as from February 26 the schools would be open for four days a week on a rota basis.

Goulding J. dismissed the motion. The plaintiff appealed and, on the first day of the hearing of the expedited appeal, the authority deposed that by a union resolution of March 2, all striking members of the staff were resuming normal working and all the schools were opened.

LORD DENNING M.R.: . . .

The law

The point of law which arises is this: if the local education authority have failed to perform their duty (to keep open the schools), have the parents any remedy in the courts of law? There is a remedy given by the statute itself. It is to complain to the Secretary of State under section 99 of the Act. But that remedy has proved to be of no use to the parents. Can they now come to the courts? This depends on the true construction of the statute. Lord Simonds put it thus in *Cutler* v. *Wandsworth Stadium Ltd.* [1949] A.C. 398, 407:

> "It is . . . often a difficult question whether, where a statutory obligation is placed on A., B. who conceives himself to be damnified by A.'s breach of it has a right of action against him . . . the answer must depend on a consideration of the whole Act and the circumstances, including the pre-existing law, in which it was enacted."

Section 99(1) of the Education Act 1944 says:

> "If the Minister is satisfied, either upon complaint by any person interested or otherwise, that any local education authority . . . have failed to discharge any duty imposed upon them by or for the purposes of this Act, the Minister may make an order declaring the authority . . . to be in default in respect of that duty, and giving such directions for the purpose of enforcing the execution thereof as appear to the Minister to be expedient; and any such directions shall be enforceable, on an application made on behalf of the Minister, by mandamus."

Now although that section does give a remedy—by complaint to a Minister—it does not exclude any other remedy. To my mind it leaves open all the established remedies which the law provides in cases where a public authority fails to perform its statutory duty either by an act of commission or omission. Thus when a local education authority were put by the statute under a duty to secure that schools premises were up to prescribed standards, and they failed in that duty by letting them fall into disrepair—as a result of which a child was injured—it was held that there was a remedy by action in the courts for any person who was particularly damaged by the breach: see *Ching* v. *Surrey County Council* [1910] 1 K.B. 736 and *Reffell* v. *Surrey County Council* [1964] 1 W.L.R. 358. Again when a local education authority were under a duty to provide education free of charge and then they sought to exclude some children from that benefit, the parents were held entitled to sue for damages and, if need be, an injunction: see *Gateshead Union* v. *Durham County Council* [1918] 1 Ch. 146, where Scrutton L.J. said at p. 167:

> "A parent is a person specially injured by any authorised exclusion of his child from the free education to which he is entitled, and therefore a person entitled to sue for such a breach of statutory obligation."

Once again, where the local education authority were under a duty to "maintain" existing schools—or conversely were under a duty not to "cease to maintain" them—and they broke that duty in a fundamental respect, by changing the character of the school—from a senior school into an infants' school—or from a boys' school into a girls' school, it was held that the parents of the children affected could come to the courts for an injunction so as to ensure that the duty was performed: see *Wilford* v. *West Riding of Yorkshire County Council* [1908] 1 K.B. 685 and *Bradbury* v. *Enfield London Borough Council* [1967] 1 W.L.R. 1311.

So reviewing all the cases afresh, they seem to me to bear out the principle which I stated in *Cumings* v. *Birkenhead Corporation* [1972] Ch. 12, 36, that the local education authority are liable when:

> "They are acting beyond their powers, or, in Latin, *ultra vires*. If that were the case, then this court would interfere. The courts will always interfere if a Minister or local authority or any other body is acting beyond the powers conferred on it by the law."

That view was accepted by Brightman J. in *Herring* v. *Templeman* [1973] 2 All E.R. 581. Conversely, when the local education authority is acting within its powers, there is no recourse to the courts: see *Watt* v. *Kesteven County Council* [1955] 1 Q.B. 408 and *Smith* v. *Inner London Education Authority* [1978] 1 All E.R. 411.

This principle has received powerful support from the House of Lords. If a statute imposes a duty on a public authority—or entrusts it with a power—to do this or that in the public interest, but expresses it in general terms so that it leaves it open to the public authority to do it in one of several ways or by one of several means, then it is for the public authority to determine the particular way or the particular means by which the performance of the statute can best be fulfilled. If it honestly so determines—by a decision which is not entirely unreasonable—its action is then *intra vires* and the courts will not interfere with it: see especially by Lord Diplock in *Dorset Yacht Co. Ltd.* v. *Home Office* [1970] A.C. 1004, 1067–1068. But if the public authority flies in the face of the statute, by doing something which the statute expressly prohibits, or by failing to do something which the statute expressly enjoins, or otherwise so conducts itself—by omission or commission—as to frustrate or hinder the policy and objects of the Act, then it is doing what it ought not to do—it is going outside its jurisdiction—it is acting *ultra vires*. Any person who is particularly damnified thereby can bring an action in the courts for damages or an injunction, whichever be the most appropriate. . . .

This case

Applying these principles, I am clearly of opinion that if the borough council of Haringey, of their own free will, deliberately closed one school in their borough for one week—without just cause or excuse—it would be *ultra vires*: and each of the parents whose child suffered thereby would have an action for damages. All the more so if they closed it for five weeks or more. Or for all schools. No one can suppose that Parliament authorised the borough council to renounce their duties to such a extent as deliberately to close the schools without just cause or excuse. To use Lord

Reid's words, it was their duty "not to act so as to frustrate the policy and objects of the Act"; *Padfield* v. *Minister of Agriculture, Fisheries and Food* [1968] A.C. 997, 1032–1033.

Just cause or excuse

Now comes the great question in this case: had the borough council any just cause or excuse for closing the schools as they did? On the evidence as it stands, the borough council were acting under the influence of the trade unions and indeed in combination with them. And the trade unions and their secretaries were, as I see it, acting quite unlawfully. They were calling upon the local authority to break their statutory duty—to close the schools instead of keeping them open as they should have done. The trade unions had no right whatever to ask the borough council to close the schools. The borough council had no business whatever to agree to it. Instead they should have kept the schools open—and risked the consequences of the dispute escalating. Or they should have moved the court for an injunction to restrain the leaders of the trade unions from interfering with the due opening of the schools. I am confident that the people at large would have supported such a move and expect the trade union leaders to obey it; and they would have obeyed it. . . .

Locus standi

I ought to say a word about *locus standi*. The parents undoubtedly were in a position to sue. As Lord Fraser of Tullybelton said in *Gouriet* v. *Union of Post Office Workers* [1978] A.C. 435, 518:

> "The general rule is that a private person is only entitled to sue in respect of interference with a public right if either there is also interference with a private right of his or the interference with the public right will inflict special damage on him. . . ."

Declaration

Although Sir George Jessel M.R. once said that he had "constantly made declarations both on petition and on summons"—see *In re St. Nazaire Co.* (1879) 12 Ch.D. 88, 93–94, nevertheless the practice is not to do it: for the simple reason that it is final in its nature and is inappropriate on an interlocutory application which by definition is not final: see *International General Electric Co. of New York Ltd.* v. *Commissioners of Customs and Excise* [1962] Ch. 784, 789 by Upjohn L.J. and *Wallersteiner* v. *Moir* [1974] 1 W.L.R. 991, 1093 by Buckley L.J.

Conclusion

On the evidence as it stands before us, it appears that the trade unions were the dominating influence in requiring the schools to be closed—and not reopened: and the borough council closed them at the behest of the trade unions or in agreement with them. In so doing the borough council were breaking their statutory duty: and the trade unions' leaders were inducing them to break it. Such conduct was in my view unlawful: and the trade unions' leaders have no immunity in respect of it. It was open to the parents to come to the courts of law and to complain of it—and to ask the courts to restrain any further breach of the statutory duty. There remains the question whether the court should grant an injunction. That depends on the balance of convenience. If the strike had been still continuing, I should have been in favour of granting an injunction. But that is now unnecessary. The very imminence of an injunction seems to have brought everyone to their senses. During the hearing before us the strike was called off. The schools opened. The teachers went back. The pupils returned to their desks. All's well that ends well. But it must not happen again. The court should make no order except that the costs here and below be costs in the cause.

EVELEIGH L.J.: . . . What is said quite firmly is that the council, being politically sympathetic to the unions, decided to close the schools when they could avoid doing so because they were influenced by sympathy with the unions' claim. In such a case the council would be acting unlawfully, and a parent whose children are affected may sue. The same is true if the council decide not to open the school, and section 99 of the Education Act 1944 would be no bar; for, while it might be said that they would be failing to provide education under section 8 of the Act, and therefore section 99 applies, the true interpretation of their conduct would be that they were positively misusing their power of administration in the field of education for an improper purpose. It would be an abuse of power and a tort. The gravity of such conduct again makes it a conclusion that would not lightly be arrived at. . . .

It has been argued by the respondents that the plaintiff has no right to sue. If there is a single failure to comply with the duty under section 8, I could accept the argument in an appropriate case. Section 99 provides a procedure by complaint to the Minister. However, whether the conduct of the council is justifiable or not in this case, it is not a simple failure. We have a situation where educational facilities exist and are being used by all concerned when the council take a decision positively to stop production, as it were. Teachers who are in receipt of their salaries and under a duty to teach are discouraged from doing so. This is positive conduct bringing the system to a halt. I therefore do not think that section 99 can apply. . . .

We are no longer concerned with the question of an injunction, but I take the view on all the evidence in this case as it was before the judge that he was entitled to refuse it. Only a declaration would now be of any value to the plaintiff, and it is for this that he asks. Whether or not a declaration can ever be given in interlocutory proceedings, the issues of fact in this case are such that they must be decided by a proper trial before any declaration can be given.

SIR STANLEY REES: . . . There is of course a well-established general principle that where a statute expressly provides machinery for the enforcement of its provisions that is the only remedy. There are to be found dicta applying that principle to a failure to carry out the duty imposed by section 8 of the Education Act by Denning L.J. and by Parker L.J. in *Watt* v. *Kesteven County Council* [1955] 1 Q.B. 408 and by Lord Denning M.R. in *Bradbury* v. *Enfield London Borough Council* [1967] 1 W.L.R. 1311. It will, in my judgment, be sufficient if I quote a very brief passage from the judgment of Parker L.J. in the *Kesteven* case [1955] 1 Q.B. 408. Parker L.J. said, at pp. 429–430:

> "Finally, the point remains whether the breach of the obligation imposed by section 76 enables a parent who has suffered injury to bring a civil action. While it is plain that the breach of some provisions of the Act would not give rise to a cause of action, I am certainly not prepared to say that no breach of any obligation imposed by the Act affords a cause of action to a parent who has suffered damage. To do so would be to fly in the face of authority, and in particular in the face of the decision in *Gateshead Union* v. *Durham County Council* [1918] 1 Ch. 146, a decision of this court. It is necessary, I think, in every case to consider the duty in question and, where the allegation is that there has been a breach of section 76, to consider the duty in connection with which it is shown that the provisions of section 76 have not been observed. Assuming, contrary to the conclusion I have reached above, that there is an obligation to pay full tuition fees at an independent school of the parents' choice, it seems to me that the *Gateshead* case is directly in point and that an action would lie. On the other hand, if, as I think, the duty under section 8 is merely to secure that facilities are available, the only remedy for a breach of that duty would be by action by the Minister on complaint under section 99."

To that general principle there are well-established exceptions which enable an aggrieved person who has suffered damage as a result of a breach of statutory duty to seek a remedy in the courts notwithstanding that the relevant statute contains provisions for enforcement.

The first exception applies if it be established that the act complained of constitutes malfeasance and not mere nonfeasance. In this context Diplock L.J. said in *Bradbury* v. *Enfield London Borough Council* [1967] 1 W.L.R. 1311, 1326 these words:

> "That section"—he is referring to section 99 of the Education Act, which is relevant in this case—"follows closely the wording of section 299 of the Public Health Act 1875 which was considered by the House of Lords in *Pasmore* v. *Oswaldtwistle Urban Council* [1898] A.C. 387, where it was held that the effect of that section, in the case of nonfeasance by a

> local authority, was to deprive the subject aggrieved by that nonfeasance of a remedy in the courts by mandatory injunction and to substitute therefor as the sole remedy the exercise by the Minister of the powers given in cases of default. That, however, is confined to acts of nonfeasance—failure to perform a duty which is imposed upon the local education authority by the Act. It does not, in my view, and in the view of the judge [Goff J.], exclude a remedy by injunction at the suit of a person aggrieved where there is a direct prohibition in the Act of certain acts by a local education authority."

There are, of course, inescapable practical difficulties in distinguishing between an act which may be misfeasance or malfeasance from one which is mere nonfeasance. The difficulty of making the distinction between nonfeasance and misfeasance in the instant case is especially acute because the case against the defendants is that they did not comply with their statutory duty under section 8 to open the schools.

The second exception applies if it be established that the defendants have acted outside their powers or *ultra vires*. Again this exception presents difficulties of interpretation in the instant case. These difficulties, as well as those arising from the distinction to be made between nonfeasance and misfeasance, are impressively stated in Goulding J.'s judgment in this case.

The argument in the present case (as stated earlier in this judgment) is that the defendants acted *ultra vires* because their decision not to open the schools was (a) governed by political sympathy with the strikers' cause or (b) because they submitted to intimidation from the strikers or (c) because they entered into an unlawful agreement with the strikers not to open the schools.

[His Lordship considered *Padfield* v. *Minister of Agriculture, Fisheries and Food* [1968] A.C. 997, above, pp. 343–351.]

This authority, in my judgment, supports the view that, if in the instant case it were established by the evidence that the decision of the defendants was based wholly or partly upon any of the motives alleged, then their failure to take action to comply with their statutory duty to make schools available under section 8 would be enforceable in the courts at the suit of a person who had suffered damage.

[His Lordship agreed that this was not an appropriate case for the award of a declaration in interlocutory proceedings; that the judge had been right to refuse an interlocutory injunction in the exercise of his discretion; but that he had been wrong to hold that the plaintiff had failed to make out a clear *prima facie* case of breach of statutory duty in that the defendants had acted *ultra vires* and/or were guilty of misfeasance.]

Appeal dismissed.

Notes

See P. Cane, [1981] P.L. 11, who argues that in *Meade*, the court was "really concerned with a power and not a duty"; section 8 of the 1944 Act was to be regarded as:

> "imposing a duty to provide a minimum level of schooling coupled with a discretion to determine, consistently with the fulfilment of that duty and in accordance with the statutory guidelines, what the requirement of sufficient schools entails"

(p. 18) (*cf. Cumings* v. *Birkenhead Corporation* [1972] Ch. 12; *Smith* v. *Inner London Education Authority* [1978] 1 All E.R. 411). The reference to breach of statutory duty and the possibility of an action for damages indicated a "line of reasoning" that was "confused":

> "The fact that an authority has acted in *ultra vires* exercise of a power provides no reason to give a judicial remedy in tort for breach of statutory duty" (p. 18).

Moreover, loss caused by an *ultra vires* act is not necessarily actionable in tort (see the following section).

(iv) Misfeasance in a Public Office

BOURGOIN S.A. v. MINISTRY OF AGRICULTURE, FISHERIES AND FOOD

[1986] Q.B. 716; [1985] 3 W.L.R. 1027; [1985] 3 All E.R. 585 (Mann J. and C.A.)

The plaintiffs, who were variously concerned in the production in France of frozen turkeys and turkey parts and in their sale and distribution within the United Kingdom, imported frozen turkeys and turkeys parts into the United Kingdom under a general licence granted by the defendant. On September 1, 1981, the defendant, purporting to act in the interests of preventing the spread of Newcastle disease into the United Kingdom, revoked the licence and replaced it with one which had the effect of prohibiting the importation of turkeys and turkey parts from France. The European Court of Justice subsequently held that the withdrawal of the licence had constituted a contravention of Article 30 of the EEC Treaty and had therefore been *ultra vires*, and in consequence of that decision the defendant issued a licence which permitted the resumption of such importation from November 1982. The plaintiffs claimed damages, alleging (by paragraph 23 of the amended statement of claim) that the withdrawal of the licence and the defendant's refusal subsequently to permit turkeys or turkey parts to be imported into the United Kingdom from France had caused the plaintiffs substantial loss and damage; (by paragraph 24) that such loss and damage had been caused by the defendant's breach of his statutory duty under Article 30 and that such a breach sounded in damages; (by paragraph 25) that such loss and damage had been caused by the commission by the defendant of an innominate tort by so breaching Article 30, or acting contrary to its provisions, as to cause them injury; and (by paragraph 26) that the withdrawal of the licence had amounted to misfeasance in public office, in that the defendant had exercised its power to withdraw the licence for a purpose which, as it had known, was contrary to Article 30 and/or was calculated to, and did, damage unlawfully the plaintiffs and/or was not the purpose for which those powers had been conferred on the defendant.

On the trial of the preliminary issue whether paras. 23–26 disclosed any causes of action, Mann J. found for the plaintiffs, holding that since Article 30 of the Treaty had direct effect, it conferred on persons injured by a contravention, even though arising from a breach of statutory duty, a cause of action in damages and that the defendant was liable to the plaintiffs for any damage which had flowed from the withdrawal of the licence as pleaded in paragraphs 23 and 24, but, since the commission of an innominate tort as a formulation of a cause of action was obsolete, the claim in paragraphs 23 and 25 did not disclose any cause of action; that in order to establish the tort of misfeasance in public office it was not necessary to prove that the defendant had been actuated by malice towards the plaintiff or had acted in bad faith but it was sufficient to show that the officer knew that he had no power to do that which he did and that his action would injure the plaintiff and subsequently did injure him and that paragraphs 23 and 26 did disclose a cause of action.

The Court of Appeal allowed an appeal in part, holding (Oliver L.J. dissenting) that breach of Article 30 did not give rise to a cause of action in damages (although it would give rise to a right to judicial review). On the other points, the Court of Appeal agreed with Mann J.

OLIVER L.J.: . . .

The third way in which the case is formulated on the pleadings is as a claim for damages against the Minister for misfeasance in public office, a tort which was described by Lord Diplock in *Dunlop* v. *Woollahra Municipal Council* [1982] A.C. 158, 173E, as "well-established." That is not in dispute. The difference between the parties rests only in their respective appreciations of the essential ingredients of the tort. For the purposes only of the preliminary issue, it was accepted that the Minister's purpose in revoking the general licence was to protect English turkey producers, and that he knew at the time (i) that this involved a failure to perform the United Kingdom's obligations under Article 30; (ii) that the revocation would cause damage to the plaintiffs in their business; and (iii) that the protection of English producers from foreign competition was not one for the achievement of which powers were conferred on him by the enabling legislation or the Importation of Animal Products and Poultry Products Order 1980. The Solicitor-General's submission, however, was that it was an essential allegation, and one not made on the pleadings, that the Minister acted with the purpose of inflicting harm upon the plaintiffs. This has been referred to conveniently as an allegation of "targeted malice."

The court has been referred to a large number of cases both in this country and in Canada and Australia from which, it is said, the inference can be drawn that in order to constitute the tort it is necessary to show an improper motive specifically aimed at the plaintiff. The authorities were extensively reviewed by the judge and it would, I think, be a work of supererogation to repeat the exercise here. There are in certain of the older cases phrases in the judgments or pleadings which might be taken to suggest that "targeted malice" was regarded as essential. I say "might," because in my judgment they are entirely inconclusive. There are also strong indications in the other direction, particularly in the older election cases. For instance in *Cullen* v. *Morris* (1819) 2 Stark. 577, 587, Abbott C.J. observed:

> "On the part of the defendant it has been contended, that an action is not maintainable for merely refusing the vote of a person who appears afterwards to have really had a right to vote, unless it also appears that the refusal resulted from a malicious and improper motive, and that if the party act honestly and uprightly according to the best of his judgment, he is not amenable in an action for damages. I am of opinion, that the law, as it has been stated by the counsel for the defendant, is correct."

Again, he said, at p. 589:

> "If a vote be refused with a view to prejudice either the party entitled to vote, or the candidate for whom he tenders his vote, the notice is an improper one, and an action is maintainable."

Coming to more modern times there is the Privy Council case of *Dunlop* v. *Woollahra Municipal Council* [1982] A.C. 158, where the allegation was one of damage caused to the plaintiff by passing planning resolutions, which were in fact invalid, restricting the height of his proposed building. Paragraph 15A of the pleading was (so far as material) in these terms, at pp. 169–170:

> "the defendant was a public corporate body which occupied office and was incorporated by a public statute . . . and the defendant abused its said office and public duty under the said statute by purporting to pass each of the said resolutions with the consequence that damage was occasioned to the plaintiff."

In delivering the judgment of the Board, Lord Diplock said, at p. 172:

> "In pleading in paragraph 15A of the statement of claim that the council abused their public office and public duty the plaintiff was relying upon the well-established tort of misfeasance by a public officer in the discharge of his public duties . . . [Their Lordships] agree with [the trial judge's] conclusion that, in the absence of malice, passing without knowledge of its invalidity a resolution which is devoid of any legal effect is not conduct that of itself is capable of amounting to such 'misfeasance' as is a necessary element in this tort."

Of this case Wade in his book on *Administrative Law*, 5th ed. (1982), pp. 672–673, comments that the Privy Council held that the tort "required as a necessary element either malice or knowledge . . . of the invalidity" a view which is in line with that expressed by Smith J. in *Farrington* v.

Thomson and Bridgland [1959] V.R. 286, which was carefully considered by Mann J. in the course of his judgment in the instant case. Having concluded his review of the authorities, Mann J. concluded, *ante*, p. 740D–G:

> "I do not read any of the decisions to which I have been referred as precluding the commission of the tort of misfeasance in public office where the officer actually knew that he had no power to do that which he did, and that his act would injure the plaintiff as subsequently it does. I read the judgment in *Dunlop* v. *Woollahra Municipal Council* [1982] A.C. 158 in the sense that malice and knowledge are alternatives. There is no sensible reason why the common law should not afford a remedy to the injured party in circumstances such as are before me. There is no sensible distinction between the case where an officer performs an act which he has no power to perform with the object of injuring A (which the defendant accepts is actionable at the instance of A) and the case where an officer performs an act which he knows he has no power to perform with the object of conferring a benefit on B but which has the foreseeable and actual consequence of injury to A (which the defendant denies is actionable at the instance of A). In my judgment each case is actionable at the instance of A and, accordingly, I determine that paragraphs 23 and 36 of the amended statement of claim do disclose a cause of action."

For my part, I too can see no sensible distinction between the two cases which the judge mentions.

If it be shown that the Minister's motive was to further the interests of English turkey producers by keeping out the produce of French turkey producers—an act which must necessarily injure them—it seems to me entirely immaterial that the one purpose was dominant and the second merely a subsidiary purpose for giving effect to the dominant purpose. If an act is done deliberately and with knowledge of its consequences, I do not think that the actor can sensibly say that he did not 'intend" the consequences or that the act was not "aimed" at the person who, it is known, will suffer them. In my judgment, the judge was right in his conclusion also on this point.

PARKER and NOURSE L.JJ. agreed with OLIVER L.J. on this point.

Notes

1. On this tort, see A. Rubinstein, *Jurisdiction and Illegality* (1965), pp. 128–33; B. Gould, (1972) 5 N.Z.U.L.R. 105; J. McBride, [1979] C.L.J. 323; M. Aronson and H. Whitmore, *Public Torts and Contracts* (1982), pp. 120–131.

2. The earlier authorities were considered by Mann J. at first instance in *Bourgoin* in the following passages (pp. 736–740):

> "*Smith* v. *East Elloe Rural District Council* [1956] A.C. 736 concerned complaints by the plaintiff about a compulsory purchase order which had been made by the rural district council and confirmed by the Minister of Health. The

complaints were ventilated in three actions. The first was an action in trespass against the council. It was determined against the council and an award of damages was made: see *Smith* v. *East Elloe Rural District Council* [1955] 1 W.L.R. 380. The second was an action in conspiracy against the clerk of the council, Mr. J. C. Pywell, and an official of the Ministry of Health, Mr. L. E. Spicer. The third gave rise to the appeal to the House of Lords and was against the council and Mr. Pywell. Their Lordships had to decide, amongst other matters, whether a writ, which in so far as it alleged that Mr. Pywell had acted wrongfully and in bad faith in procuring the making and confirmation of the compulsory purchase order, should be struck out. Their Lordships unanimously held that the allegation should not be struck out. Viscount Simonds said, [1956] A.C. 736, 752:

> 'Here the appellant by her writ claims against the personal defendant a declaration that he knowingly acted wrongfully and in bad faith in procuring the order and its confirmation, and damages, and that is a claim which the court clearly has jurisdiction to entertain.'

The defendant drew my attention to the phrase 'and in bad faith' as an addition to the phrase 'knowingly acted wrongfully,' but Viscount Simonds was doing no more than reciting the endorsement on the writ: see [1956] A.C. 736, 738. What the pleader intended by that endorsement I cannot know. Eventually the third case was consolidated with the second and came for trial before Diplock J. as *Smith* v. *Pywell and Spicer* (1959) 173 E.G. 1009; *The Times*, April 28, 1959. The third case was, according to the report in the *Estates Gazette*, disposed of on the ground that Diplock J.:

> 'was not satisfied on the evidence that the first defendant had in fact known that he had no power to continue the requisition, or that he acted in bad faith. There was no suggestion whatever that he was actuated by notices of personal gain. He was actuated by excessive zeal for his employers—the council—and by "bumbledom." '

The report in *The Times* disposes of the action upon another, and presently immaterial, ground. I suspect that there were two grounds for the decision; one of which attracted one reporter, and the second of which attracted the other. It is to be observed that Mr. Pywell was separately acquitted of knowing that he had no power to continue a previous requisition of the subject property and of acting in bad faith. The separate acquittals suggest that a finding against Mr. Pywell in either head could have founded a liability, but I think that it would be dangerous to rely over much upon the reports of this case.

However, the proposition that either knowledge of lack of power or bad faith is sufficient to establish liability can, in my judgment, find support in the judgment of the Privy Council in *Dunlop* v. *Woollahra Municipal Council* [1982] A.C. 158, 172, where Lord Diplock said that their Lordships agreed with the conclusion of the Supreme Court of New South Wales:

> 'in the absence of malice, passing without knowledge of its invalidity a resolution which is devoid of any legal effect is not conduct that of itself is capable of amounting to such "misfeasance" as is a necessary element in this tort.'

Professor Wade in his *Administrative Law*, 5th ed., pp. 672–673 comments that the Privy Council held that the tort 'required as a necessary element either malice or knowledge . . . of the invalidity' and at p. 673, he cites *Farrington* v. *Thomson and Bridgland* [1959] V.R. 286 without adverse comment.

There are a number of English authorities to the effect that the tort of misfeasance in public office is committed where the officer's conduct is actuated by malice towards the plaintiff. I was taken back first to *Harman* v. *Tappenden* (1801) 1 East 555 (the report of which includes, at pp. 563–566, a note of *Drewe* v. *Coulton* (1787)). Lord Kenyon C.J. said at pp. 561–562:

> 'have you any precedent to show that an action of this sort will lie, without proof of malice in the defendants, or that the act of disfranchisement was done on purpose to deprive the plaintiff of the particular advantage which resulted to him from his corporate character? I believe this is a case of the first impression where an action of this kind has been brought upon a mere mistake or error in judgment.'

Lawrence J. said, at pp. 562–563:

> 'There is no instance of an action of this sort maintained for an act arising merely from error of judgment. Perhaps the action might have been maintained, if it had been proved that the defendants contriving and intending to injure and prejudice the plaintiff, and deprive him of the benefit of his profits from the fishery, which as a member of this body he was entitled to according to the custom, had *wilfully and maliciously* procured him to be disfranchised, in consequence of which he was deprived of such profits. But there was no evidence of any wilful and malicious intention to deprive the plaintiff of his profits, or that they had disfranchised him with that intent, which is necessary to maintain the action.'

It is to be observed that the case was one of mistake and that the defendants did not do that which they did knowing that they had no power to do it.

The second case is *Cullen* v. *Morris* (1819) 2 Stark. 577, which was an action against a returning officer for refusing a vote at a parliamentary election. Lord Abbott C.J. directed the jury in these terms, at p. 587:

> 'On the part of the defendant it has been contended, that an action is not maintainable for merely refusing the vote of a person who appears afterwards to have really had a right to vote, unless it also appears that the refusal resulted from a malicious and improper motive, and that if the party act honestly and uprightly according to the best of his judgment, he is not amenable in an action for damages.'

Again, it is to be observed that there seems to have been no suggestion that the defendant knew that he had no power to do that which he had done.

The third case is *Tozer* v. *Child* (1857) 7 El. & Bl. 377, where the remarks in earlier cases are recited in a context similar to that of *Cullen* v. *Morris*, 2 Stark. 577. Martin B. said, at p. 383: 'At any rate the officer cannot be liable for merely drawing a wrong conclusion of law.' See also Cresswell J. on p. 383.

The fourth case is the decision of the Privy Council in *David* v. *Abdul Cader* [1963] 1 W.L.R. 834, where Viscount Radcliffe, in delivering the judgment of their Lordships on an appeal from Ceylon, said, in regard to the decision of the Court of Appeal in *Davis* v. *Bromley Corporation* [1908] 1 K.B. 170, at pp. 839–840:

> 'In their Lordships' opinion it would not be correct today to treat it as establishing any wide general principle in this field; certainly it would not be correct to treat it as sufficient to found the proposition, as asserted here, that an applicant for a statutory licence can in no circumstances have a right to

damages if there has been a malicious misuse of the statutory power to grant the licence. Much must turn in such cases on what may prove to be the facts of the alleged misuse and in what the malice is found to consist. The presence of spite or ill-will may be insufficient in itself to render actionable a decision which has been based on unexceptionable grounds of consideration and has not been vitiated by the badness of the motive. But a "malicious" misuse of authority, such as is pleaded by the appellant in his plaint, may cover a set of circumstances which go beyond the mere presence of ill-will, and in their Lordships' view it is only after the facts of malice relied upon by a plaintiff have been properly ascertained that it is possible to say in a case of this sort whether or not there has been any actionable breach of duty.'

There are three Commonwealth authorities to which I must refer. The first is *Roncarelli* v. *Duplessis* (1959) 16 D.L.R. (2d) 689, which is a decision of the Supreme Court of Canada. It was a flagrant case of an officer performing an unlawful act with the object of injuring the plaintiff. Rand J., who was amongst the majority of the court, said, at pp. 705–706:

'To deny or revoke a permit because a citizen exercises an unchallengeable right totally irrelevant to the sale of liquor in a restaurant is equally beyond the scope of the discretion conferred. There was here not only revocation of the existing permit but a declaration of a future definitive disqualification of the appellant to obtain one: it was to be "forever." This purports to divest his citizenship status of its incident of membership in the class of those of the public to whom such a privilege could be extended. Under the statutory language here, that is not competent to the Commission and *a fortiori* to the government or the respondent: *McGillivray* v. *Kimber* (1915) 26 D.L.R. 164, 52 S.C.R. 146. There is here an administrative tribunal which, in certain respects, is to act in a judicial manner; and even on the view of the dissenting justices in *McGillivray*, there is liability: what could be more malicious than to punish this licensee for having done what he had an absolute right to do in a matter utterly irrelevant to the Alcoholic Liquor Act? Malice in the proper sense is simply acting for a reason and purpose knowingly foreign to the administration, to which was added here the element of intentional punishment by what was virtually vocation outlawry.'

Secondly, there is *Gershman* v. *Manitoba Vegetable Producers' Marketing Board* (1976) 69 D.L.R. (3d) 114, where the Manitoba Court of Appeal considered that decision. O'Sullivan J.A. said, at p. 123:

'The principle that public bodies must not use their powers for purposes incompatible with the purposes envisaged by the statutes under which they derive such powers cannot be in doubt in Canada since the landmark case of *Roncarelli* v. *Duplessis* (1959) 16 D.L.R. (2d) 689, [1959] S.C.R. 121. Since that case, it is clear that a citizen who suffers damages as a result of flagrant abuse of public power aimed at him has the right to an award of damages in a civil action in tort.'

The defendant emphasised the words 'aimed at him.' The words were wholly appropriate in the context of the disgraceful conduct of the respondent in *Roncarelli's* case but they do not preclude another path towards liability; that is to say, knowledge that an act is invalid coupled with foresight that its commission would damage the plaintiff.

Thirdly, there is the decision of the High Court of Australia in *Beaudesert Shire Council* v. *Smith* (1966) 120 C.L.R. 145, 156, that 'a person who suffers harm or loss as the inevitable consequence of the unlawful, intentional and positive acts of another is entitled to recover damages from that other.' There is apparently a decision of Hallett J. to the same effect: see *Wood* v. *Blair* (unreported), July 4, 1957, Court of Appeal Transcript No. 209 of 1957, p. 9. The tort described in *Beaudesert Shire Council* v. *Smith*, 120 C.L.R. 145 was said by Lord Diplock—with whom the other four members of the House agreed—in *Lonrho Ltd.* v. *Shell Petroleum Co. Ltd. (No. 2)* [1982] A.C. 173, 188, to be 'no part of the law of England.' The wrong described before me is not the wrong which was described before the High Court of Australia. The wrong described before me is that of an act performed by a public officer with actual knowledge that it is performed without power and is so performed with the known consequence that it would injure the plaintiffs.

I do not read any of the decisions to which I have been referred as precluding the commission of the tort of misfeasance in public office where the officer actually knew that he had no power to do that which he did, and that his act would injure the plaintiff as subsequently it does. I read the judgment in *Dunlop* v. *Woollahra Municipal Council* [1982] A.C. 158 in the sense that malice and knowledge are alternatives. There is no sensible reason why the common law should not afford a remedy to the injured party in circumstances such as are before me. There is no sensible distinction between the case where an officer performs an act which he has no power to perform with the object of injuring A (which the defendant accepts is actionable at the instance of A) and the case where an officer performs an act which he knows he has no power to perform with the object of conferring a benefit on B but which has the foreseeable and actual consequence of injury to A (which the defendant denies is actionable at the instance of A). In my judgment each case is actionable at the instance of A and, accordingly, I determine that paragraphs, 23 and 26 of the amended statement of claim do disclose a cause of action."

The parties in *Bourgoin* settled for £3.5M (Vol. 102, H.C. Deb., July 23, 1986, col. 116, written answer).

3. There is a considerable literature on the question whether the position in English law as regards compensation for unlawful administrative action is sufficient to comply with the Community law requirement that national remedies for breach of Community law be effective (Case 45/76, *Comet* v. *Produktschap* [1976] E.C.R. 204]; Case 33/76, *Rewe* v. *Landwirtschaftskammer* [1976] E.C.R. 1989); Case C–6/90 and C–9/90, *Francovich* v. *Republic of Italy* [1992] I.R.L.R. 84). See P. Oliver "Enforcing Community Rights in English Courts" (1987) 50 M.L.R. 881; J. Steiner, "How to make the action suit the case" (1987) 12 E.L.Rev. 102; A. Ward, "Government liability in the United Kingdom for breach of individual rights in European Community Law" (1990) 19 Anglo-Am. L.R. 1; S. Weatherill, "National remedies and equal access to public procurement" (1990) 10 Y.E.L. 243.

4. In *Wood* v. *Blair and the Helmsley R.D.C.*, *The Times*, July 3, 4, 5, 1957, [1956–57] Admin. L.R. 343, the manageress of the plaintiff's dairy farm was found to be suffering from typhoid. The plaintiff was ill in hospital at the same time, and had had typhoid in the past. The medical officer of health (B) served a notice under regulation 20 of the Milk and Dairies Regulations 1949[2] forbidding the sale of milk for human consumption. He later served a notice forbidding the sale of unpasteurised milk from the farm. The plaintiff obeyed the notices, and for six weeks poured the milk produced down the drain. His business as a retailer of bottled milk came to a standstill. The notices were subsequently held to be nullities. Hallett J. held that if the plaintiff could show that he had suffered damage by complying with the notices he had a good cause of action, but that he had not suffered any loss because he would have had to leave the farm anyway because of

[2] (S.I. 1949 No. 1588).

troubles with the landlords, and the cancellation of his registration as a dairy farmer and the revocation of his T.T. licence. On appeal, the Court of Appeal held that the plaintiff had not proved any of his claims for general or special damages, apart from one item in respect of a lost milk subsidy of £99 from the Milk Marketing Board. His claim for exemplary damages failed because the defendants acted from the highest motives.

5. The misfeasance tort is applicable in respect of the abuse of any powers exercisable by a public authority or officer, whether private powers or powers with a statutory or public origin (*Jones* v. *Swansea City Council* [1990] 1 W.L.R. 54: where the Court of Appeal held that the alleged abuse of a contractual power would give rise to the tort; the court left open whether it could in any event properly be regarded as a purely "private" power. This question was left open on appeal to the House of Lords: [1990] 1 W.L.R. 1453, 1458. In *Jones* v. *Swansea City Council* [1990] 1 W.L.R. 1453, the House of Lords upheld the decision of the trial judge to dismiss the plaintiff's claim for damages for misfeasance arising out of the council's decision as landlord to refuse consent for the change of use of certain premises leased by the plaintiff. The decision had been taken by 28 to 15, the majority being formed by Labour councillors. The plaintiff's husband was a political opponent of the Labour group. Lord Lowry stated that in such circumstances "generally speaking, if a plaintiff proves that a majority of the councillors present, having voted for a resolution, did so with the object of damaging the plaintiffs, he thereby proves against the council misfeasance in a public office" (pp. 1458–1459). This apparently would mean 22 out of the 43 councillors present (p. 1470). However, the plaintiff's pleadings alleged that all the 28 councillors had been infected by malice, and the judge had rightly found this not to be made out on the evidence.

(C) Restitution

The extent of the liability of a public authority to make restitution where there has been an unlawful demand for tax has recently been considered by the Court of Appeal in *Woolwich Building Society* v. *Inland Revenue Commissioners* (*No.* 2) [1991] 4 All E.R. 577. The Building Society paid some £57M in response to a Revenue demand. The demand was based on regulations subsequently held by the House of Lords to be *ultra vires* (*Woolwich Equitable Building Society* v. *Inland Revenue Commissioners* [1990] 1 W.L.R. 1400 (below, p. 865)). The Revenue had repaid the money when the judicial review proceedings had been decided against them at first instance. The Society now claimed the payment of interest on the capital from the date of payment until judgment was given at first instance. The Court of Appeal (Glidewell and Butler-Sloss L.JJ., Ralph Gibson L.J. dissenting) upheld the Society's claim. Glidewell L.J. said (at pp. 598–599, 602):

"SUMMARY OF ARGUMENTS

What then are the arguments in favour of there being a general restitutionary principle, *i.e.* a principle of law that, if a government body or officer makes a demand for the payment of a tax or duty which he has no legal power to require, and payment is made in response to the demand, there is a presumption of law that the payer has an immediate right to recover the payment? There is no doubt that such a presumption arises in the withholding cases, *i.e.* where there has been an actual or threatened seizure of the plaintiff's goods, or the withholding of a service he wishes to receive, as a sanction for the plaintiff complying with the demand made by the official. This concept, though it may not strictly amount to duress in the sense in which that word is understood in private law, nevertheless clearly bears a relationship to duress.

The argument for Woolwich in the present case is that it is illogical and unjust that the presumption should only arise in such circumstances. I summarise the arguments in favour of the wider presumption as follows. (i) The Bill of Rights (1688) point, *i.e.* that where there is no parliamentary authority for the imposition of a tax or duty, the taxing authority never was entitled to any money paid on an invalid demand, and thus must be obliged to repay. (ii) The taxing officer or body has powers conferred by statute to enforce his demand over and above the private citizen's right to bring an action at law. In addition, in some situations, of which this is one, the statutory provisions may put the taxpayer at a disadvantage if he does not make a payment which in the end it proves he was obliged to make as against his position if he does make a payment which he was not obliged to make. I refer here to what Nolan J. called 'the interest factor.' (iii) Such a general restitutionary principle must have underlain, though it was not expressly articulated in, the decisions in *Campbell* v. *Hall* (1774) 1 Cowp. 204, [1558–1774] All E.R. Rep. 252 (which expressly relied on the Bill of Rights ground), *Dew* v. *Parsons* (1819) 2 B. & Ald. 562, 106 E.R. 471, the judgment of Martin B. and that of Parke B., possibly *obiter*, in *Steele* v. *Williams* (1853) 8 Exch. 625, 155 E.R. 1502, and *Hooper* v. *Exeter Corp.* (1887) 56 L.J.Q.B. 457. (iv) It accords also with the general approach of the House of Lords in *Tower Hamlets London B.C.* v. *Chetnik Developments Ltd.* [1988] 1 All E.R. 961, [1988] A.C. 858. (v) It also accords with the judgments in Australia and America of O'Connor J. in *Sargood Bros.* v. *Commonwealth* (1910) 11 C.L.R. 258, Holmes J. in *Atchison Topeka and Santa Fe Rly. Co.* v. *O'Connor* (1912) 223 U.S. 280 and Dixon C.J. and Kitto J. in *Mason* v. *New South Wales* (1959) 102 C.L.R. 108. (vi) Not least, the principle is based on a general standard of fairness in the relations and dealings between officers and organs of government who require the payment of a tax or customs duty, and the taxpayer.

I am persuaded by these arguments. I am clearly of the view that there should, in the interests both of justice and good government, be such a general restitutionary principle as that for which Woolwich contends. The authorities I have quoted support the view that such a principle is part of the common law, though it is not always by any means articulated clearly in those decisions. I have therefore considered whether there are any authorities, binding on this court, which would compel us to adopt the contrary view.

[His Lordship considered a number of cases.] . . . [N]one of these authorities, even the decision of this court which is binding on us, impels us to the view that there is no general restitutionary principle. What they appear to show is that there are limitations on the application of such a principle, both in cases where it can properly be said that the payment was made in order to close the transaction, and in cases where the payment was made as a result of the payer being mistaken as to the proper interpretation of the relevant statute. It is arguable that it is illogical that a general restitutionary principle should be subject to these limitations. However, in the light of the authorities to which I have referred, it is not in my view open to us in this court to accept this argument. We are bound by this court's previous decisions in *Maskell* v. *Horner* [[1915] 3 K.B. 106] and *National Pari-Mutuel Association Ltd.* v. *R.* [(1930) 47 T.L.R. 110].

I therefore conclude that there is such a general principle as that for which Woolwich contends, but, at least in cases where the matter in issue is the interpretation of the statute, that principle is subject to the two limitations to which I have just referred, *i.e.* that the payment may not be recoverable if it was made to close the transaction or under a mistake of law. Whether these limitations apply in a situation where what is in issue is not the proper interpretation of the statute, but an *ultra vires* regulation, I doubt. But in the circumstances of this case I do not find it necessary to consider that matter further."

Notes

1. On restitution and public authorities, see P. Birks, (1980) 33 C.L.P. 191 and "Restitution from the Executive" in P. Finn (ed.), *Essays on Restitution* (1990); W. Cornish, [1987] J.M.C.L. 41; A. Burrows, "Public Authorities, *Ultra Vires* and Restitution" in Burrows (ed.), *Studies on the Law of Restitution* (1991); G. Jones, *Restitution in Public and Private Law* (1991).

2. The Court of Appeal rejected the view that a payment under a mistake of law could not be recovered where the demand was based on an *ultra vires* regulation; the court was bound by the Court of Appeal decision in *National Pari-Mutuel Association Ltd.* v. *R.* which held that money paid under a mistake of law as to the proper interpretation of a statute is irrecoverable. The Court of Appeal gave leave for an appeal to the House of Lords. On the *Woolwich* case in the Court of Appeal, see E. McKendrick, (1991) 107 L.Q.R. 526; G. Jones, [1992] C.L.J. 29.

3. The Law Commission is in the course of a review of the law in this area. See Law Commission Working Paper No. 120, *Restitution of Payments Made Under a Mistake of Law* (1991).

4. There are some statutory provisions which expressly authorise the repayment of overpaid taxes, etc. See *Tower Hamlets London Borough Council* v. *Chetnik Developments Ltd.* [1988] A.C. 858, considering the General Rate Act 1967, s.9.

CHAPTER 14

VALIDITY OF UNLAWFUL ADMINISTRATIVE ACTION

(A) THE PRINCIPLES

THE question has caused considerable academic controversy. See: H. W. R. Wade, (1967) 83 L.Q.R. 499 and (1968) 84 L.Q.R. 95; M. B. Akehurst, (1968) 31 M.L.R. 2, 138; *de Smith*, pp. 151–155, 240–246, 273–275; A. Rubinstein, *Jurisdiction and Illegality*; P. Cane, "A Fresh Look at Punton's Case" (1980) 43 M.L.R. 266; D. Oliver, (1981) C.L.P. 43; G. L. Peiris, [1983] P.L. 634; M. Taggart, "Rival Theories of Invalidity in Administrative Law" in Taggart (ed.), *Judicial Review of Administrative Action in the 1980s* (1986), pp. 70–103; *Craig*, pp. 323–341.

In principle, an *ultra vires* act should be regarded as null and void for all purposes ("void," "a nullity"). On the other hand, an act which may be set aside only on appeal, or on an application to quash for non-jurisdictional error of law on the face of the record, may be said to be voidable; it is valid until set aside. See *Wade*, p. 349. This formulation is, however, deceptively simple. Much of the difficulty in the case law has arisen through a failure fully to appreciate that "voidness" in administrative law is a *relative* and not an *absolute* concept. An *ultra vires* act is not totally devoid of legal effect:

(i) In some situations it can simply be ignored (see note (a) below). However, it will often be advisable, or even necessary, for the person affected to obtain a court ruling that the act is *ultra vires*. At this point, it must be remembered that the courts will not always be prepared to intervene. A direct challenge may only be brought by a person with the appropriate *locus standi* and within the relevant time limit. Even if the applicant makes out a good case as a matter of substance, the court may decline to grant a remedy in the exercise of its discretion. These matters are considered in Chapter 12. In consequence, if an act is not challenged by the only persons with *locus standi* to do so then the courts will treat it as valid. For example, only the Chief Constable in *Ridge* v. *Baldwin* would be regarded as having standing to challenge the lawfulness of his own dismissal (*cf.* the discussion of this point in *Durayappah* v. *Fernando*, below, p. 840). This point is also illustrated by the *Rose Theatre Trust* case (above, p. 758), on the assumption that English Heritage would have had standing to challenge the Secretary of State's decision (unlike the applicants in that case), but chose not to do so. Similarly, once a statutory time limit for challenging an act has expired, it may be regarded as valid (see *Smith* v. *East Elloe R.D.C.*, below, p. 871; *cf.* the cases on undue delay on an application for judicial review (above, pp. 764–772)).

(ii) If an act is not invalid on its face, the courts will act on the assumption that it is valid, unless and until it is set aside (see *F. Hoffman-La Roche* v. *Secretary of State for Trade and Industry*, below, p. 842).

However, if the court does rule that an act is *ultra vires*, the act is properly regarded as void *ab initio*; the ruling is *retrospective* in effect. It is this point that distinguishes the void from the voidable. If a court sets aside on appeal or quashes a voidable act (in the sense of voidable mentioned at the start of the chapter), the ruling is *prospective* in effect.

In some of the cases discussed in this chapter, judges have taken the view that the fact that an *ultra vires* act is not totally devoid of legal effects in the senses already discussed means that "voidable" is the only appropriate label. This assumes that "void" is only to be used in an *absolute* sense, and is misleading.

Where an act is *void*, in the relative sense in which the term is properly understood, several consequences follow:

(a) It may, if appropriate, be ignored by the person affected. If the public authority takes enforcement proceedings, the voidness of the act can be raised as a defence. See, for example, *Maltglade Ltd.* v. *St. Albans R.D.C.*, above, p. 454, *Allingham* v. *Minister of Agriculture* [1948] 1 All E.R. 780 (where a notice requiring farmers to grow sugar beet on certain fields was held to be invalid because the task of specifying the fields had been delegated unlawfully by a county agricultural committee to an officer). A person with the appropriate standing is normally permitted to raise a question as to *vires* as a collateral question, by way of an exception to the principle of *O'Reilly* v. *Mackman* (see pp. 738–741). In many situations, however, this will be of no use to the person affected. For example, where a decision refuses an applicant some licence or other benefit, he or she will normally have to take direct action to have the decision set aside.

(b) A statutory provision purporting to prohibit recourse to the courts to challenge the validity of an act will normally be interpreted as effective to prevent challenges to voidable acts only. A void act is not an "act," "order," or "decision" protected by the privative clause at all. See below, pp. 866 *et seq.* and *Anisminic Ltd.* v. *Foreign Compensation Commission* (above, p. 237).

(c) The courts may refuse to hear an appeal against a void decision, on the basis that there is nothing to appeal against. See *Metropolitan Properties Co. (F.G.C.) Ltd.* v. *Lannon* (above, p. 577), and *Chapman* v. *Earl* [1968] 1 W.L.R. 1315. In the latter case the Divisional Court, on an appeal on a point of law against the decision of a rent assessment committee, gave leave for the plaintiff to apply for certiorari on the ground that a mandatory procedural step had not been observed by the committee. Certiorari was granted, and the appeal dismissed.

Statute may expressly provide for an appeal on the ground that the act impugned is *ultra vires*: see above, pp. 622 *et seq.*; and the Magistrates' Courts Act 1980, s.111 (appeals by way of case stated).

(d) The exercise of a right of appeal to a higher administrative body will not necessarily cure the defect of a void act (*Ridge* v. *Baldwin*, above, p. 475). If the proceedings on appeal are by way of a complete rehearing, then the invalidity of the original decision may be irrelevant. The appellate body makes its own, independent, valid decision. (See *Stringer* v. *Minister of Housing and Local Government*, above, pp. 292 and 304; *Calvin* v. *Carr*, above, p. 561).

(e) There is a general rule that a void act cannot be validated by the consent, waiver or acquiescence of the person affected by it. In *Mayes* v. *Mayes* [1971] 1 W.L.R. 679, justices dismissed a wife's complaint of desertion after hearing her evidence, without giving her solicitor the opportunity of addressing them on her behalf. This was held to be a breach of natural justice, which was not cured by the fact that the right to address was not asserted at the time. Sir Jocelyn Simon P. stated at p. 684: "I am inclined to think that the general principle is that a rule of natural justice which goes to the very basis of judicature (as I think this does) cannot be waived. You cannot by waiver convert a nullity into a validity."

(B) Case Law

The authorities are in a state of confusion. de Smith refers to the "morass of inconsistent and often unconsidered judicial dicta," particularly "in cases where it was immaterial whether the defect was treated as making the impugned decision void or voidable" (*de Smith*, p. 152).

The general principle that an *ultra vires* act is void, and that a breach of natural justice renders an act void was stated unequivocally in *Anisminic Ltd.* v. *Foreign Compensation Commission* [1969] 2 A.C. 147 (above, p. 237), by Lord Reid at page 171 (p. 240), Lord Pearce at page 195 (p. 248) and Lord Wilberforce at pages 207–208. The speeches of Lord Morris and Lord Pearson contained nothing against that principle. The majority in *Ridge* v. *Baldwin* [1964] A.C. 40 similarly had held that breach of the *audi alteram partem* rule of natural justice rendered the decision void. See Lord Reid at page 80 (above, p. 487), Lord Morris at page 125 and Lord Hodson at page 136. Lord Morris at page 117, Lord Hodson at page 135 and Lord Devlin at page 139, expressly held that the decision was also void for breach of mandatory procedural requirements. Similarly, in *O'Reilly* v. *Mackman* (above, p. 724), Lord Diplock confirmed that breach of natural justice renders the decision void.

The main authorities for the proposition that an *ultra vires* act may be voidable only are found as follows:

(i) some cases on the effect of interest or bias on the validity of a decision (below);
(ii) the speeches of Lord Evershed and Lord Devlin in *Ridge* v. *Baldwin* [1964] A.C. 40 and the judgment of the Privy Council in *Durayappah* v. *Fernando* (below, p. 840);
(iii) the decision of the House of Lords in *F. Hoffman-La Roche & Co. A.G. and Others* v. *Secretary of State for Trade and Industry* [1975] A.C. 295 (below, p. 842).

When properly analysed, however, these authorities are not necessarily inconsistent with the principles already stated, commonly just revealing disagreement over terminology.

(i) The effect of interest or bias

The leading case for the view that the effect is that the decision is voidable, not void is *Dimes* v. *Grand Junction Canal Proprietors* (1852) 3 H.L.C. 759 at p. 786 (above, p. 573). The statement of Parke B. is criticised by H. W. R. Wade in (1968) 84 L.Q.R. 95 at pp. 107–108. He points out that the *Dimes* case concerned a decision of one of the superior courts of law—the Lord Chancellor in the Court of Chancery, and that the decrees were challenged by appeal to the House of Lords. So "voidable" was a perfectly proper synonym for "appealable." Moreover the authorities cited by Parke B. did not support his assertion. Professor Wade concludes: "It is surely time that Parke B.'s *obiter dicta* were retired to the museum of antiquities" (*cf. de Smith*, p. 275).

The view that a biased decision is voidable is reinforced by the point that a party may waive his objections to the qualification of the adjudicator(s). This normally is not possible in respect of *ultra vires* acts (above, p. 838). One answer to this is that the non-acquiescence of the party affected may be a condition built into the relevant branch of the *ultra vires* principle. Professor Wade at (1968) 84 L.Q.R. 109 suggests that the rule is that "no disqualified person shall adjudicate unless this is acceptable to the person concerned." Certainly it is difficult to see how there can be a "reasonable suspicion of bias," or a "real likelihood of bias" where the person affected, with knowledge of the possible disqualification, nevertheless accepts the adjudicator. See on this, *de Smith*, at pp. 275–276 and Akehurst, *op. cit.* at pp. 144–149.

An authority for the proposition that a decision tainted by bias or interest is void is *Cooper* v. *Wilson* [1937] 2 K.B. 309. Moreover, there seems little reason why a decision in breach of the *audi alteram partem* rule should be void, where one in breach of the *nemo judex* rule should be voidable. If the influence of actual bias is proved, then a decision is clearly *ultra vires* and void as being influenced by bad faith or irrelevant considerations (see above, pp. 362–394). In *Cooper* v. *Wilson* [1937] 2 K.B. 309, Cooper, a sergeant in the Liverpool police force, was purportedly dismissed by the Chief Constable 18 days after C. had handed in his resignation. He was charged with disciplinary offences. Subsequently, the Watch Committee, at a meeting at which the Chief Constable was present during the deliberations, purported to dismiss the sergeant's appeal from the Chief Constable's sentence of dismissal. The appellant sued the Chief Constable and the Watch Committee claiming declarations that he had duly resigned, and was therefore entitled to be repaid his accumulated pension contributions. The Court of Appeal held (*inter alia*) that the right to dismiss a constable was vested solely in the Watch Committee, but that in this case the Committee had no power to dismiss the appellant, who had already terminated his service by due notice of resignation. The court also held in the alternative that he was entitled to a declaration that the dismissal was void as contrary to natural justice: Greer L.J. at pp. 322–324, Scott L.J. at pp. 342–345, 348. Macnaghten J. dissented: on this point he held that as the Chief Constable took no more than a formal part in the hearing, and although he remained with the Committee during their deliberations in the appellant's absence, he took no part in them. The judge did not dissent on the basis that the decision was merely voidable. The *Dimes* case was not cited.

(ii) The Privy Council in Durayappah v. Fernando[1]

For the facts, see above, p. 490. Having held that natural justice should have been observed on the dissolution of Jaffna Municipal Council, the opinion continued (*per* Lord Upjohn at pp. 352 *et seq*.):

"Had the matter remained there their Lordships would have allowed the appeal and held the order of May 29, 1966, to have been inoperative. However, during the hearing of the appeal, their Lordships raised the question, not taken in the court below, whether the appellant was entitled to maintain this action and appeal. This question is of some general importance. The answer must depend essentially upon whether the order of the Minister was a complete nullity or whether it was an order voidable only at the election of the council. If the former, it must follow that the council is still in office and that, if any councillor, ratepayer or other person having a legitimate interest in the conduct of the council likes to take the point, they are entitled to ask the court to declare that the council is still the duly elected council with all the powers and duties conferred upon it by the Municipal Ordinance.

Apart altogether from authority their Lordships would be of opinion that this was a case where the Minister's order was voidable and not a nullity. Though the council should have been given the opportunity of being heard in its defence, if it deliberately chooses not to complain and takes no step to protest against its dissolution, there seems no reason why any other person should have the right to interfere. To take a simple example to which their Lordships will have to advert in some detail presently, if in *Ridge* v. *Baldwin* [1964] A.C. 40 the appellant Ridge, who had been wrongly dismissed because he was not given the opportunity of presenting his defence, had preferred to abandon the point and accept the view that he had been properly dismissed, their Lordships can see no reason why any other person, such, for example, as a ratepayer of Brighton should have any right to contend that Mr. Ridge was still the Chief Constable of Brighton. As a matter of ordinary common sense, with all respect

[1] [1967] 2 A.C. 337.

to other opinions that must have been expressed, if a person in the position of Mr. Ridge had not felt sufficiently aggrieved to take any action by reason of the failure to afford him his strict right to put forward a defence, the order of the watch committee should stand and no one else should have any right to complain. The matter is not free of authority, for it was much discussed in that case. Lord Reid (*ibid.* at p. 80) reached the conclusion that the committee's decision was void and not merely voidable and he relied on the decision in *Wood* v. *Woad* (1874) L.R. 9 Ex. 190. Their Lordships deprecate the use of the word void in distinction to the word voidable in the field of law with which their Lordships are concerned because, as Lord Evershed pointed out in *Ridge* v. *Baldwin* [1964] A.C. 40, 92, quoting from Sir Frederick Pollock, the words void and voidable are imprecise and apt to mislead. These words have well-understood meanings when dealing with questions of proprietary or contractual rights. It is better, in the field where the subject-matter of the discussion is whether some order which has been made or whether some step in some litigation or quasi-litigation is effective or not, to employ the verbal distinction between whether it is truly a 'nullity,' that is to all intents and purposes, of which any person having a legitimate interest in the matter can take advantage or whether it is 'voidable' only at the instance of the party affected. On the other hand the word 'nullity' would be quite inappropriate in questions of proprietary or contractual rights; such transactions may frequently be void but the result can seldom be described as a nullity. In the field now under consideration there are many cases illustrating the difference, see for example *Macfoy* v. *United Africa Co. Ltd.* [1962] A.C. 152 where it was held that a failure to comply with certain rules of the Supreme Court rendered the proceedings voidable and not a nullity. On the other side, is the very recent decision of their Lordships' board in *C. Devan Nair* v. *Yong Kuan Teik* [1967] 2 A.C. 31 (P.C.) where a failure to comply with a rule was held to make purported subsequent proceedings a nullity. Their Lordships understand Lord Reid to have used the word 'void' in the sense of being a nullity. In *Ridge* v. *Baldwin* [1964] A.C. 40, 135 Lord Hodson took the view that the decision of the watch committee was a nullity. On the other hand Lord Evershed (*ibid.* at pp. 88–90), though he differed on the main question as to whether the principle *audi alteram partem* applied, devoted a considerable part of his judgment to the question whether the decision was voidable or a nullity and with this part of his judgment Lord Devlin expressly stated his agreement. Lord Evershed examined the case of *Wood* v. *Woad* (1874) L.R. 9 Ex. 190 in some detail and he reached the conclusion that in *Wood* v. *Woad* the question whether the purported exclusion from the association by the committee was void or voidable was not essential or indeed material to the claim made in the action by the plaintiffs for damages against the members of the committee. He continued ([1964] A.C. 40, 90), speaking of that case:

> 'Certainly in my judgment it cannot be asserted that the judgments in the case cited or indeed any of them support or involve the proposition that where a body such as the watch committee in the present case, is invested by the express terms of a statute with a power of expulsion of any member of the police force and purports in good faith to exercise such power, a failure on their part to observe the principle of natural justice, *audi alteram partem*, has the result that the decision is not merely voidable by the court but is wholly void and a nullity.'

Lord Morris of Borth-y-Gest ([1964] A.C. 40, 119) also considered this question and reached the conclusion that the order of the watch committee was voidable and not a nullity. He examined the question as to the nature of the relief that the party aggrieved (Ridge) would apply for, which would be that the decision was invalid and of no effect and null and void. Their Lordships entirely agree with that and with the conclusions which he drew from it, namely, that if the decision is challenged by the person aggrieved on the grounds that the principle has not been obeyed, he is entitled to claim that as against him it is void *ab initio* and has never been of any effect. But it cannot possibly be right in the type of case which their Lordships are considering to suppose that if challenged successfully by the person entitled to avoid the order yet nevertheless it has some limited effect even against him until set aside by a court of competent jurisdiction. While in this case their Lordships have no doubt that in an action by the council the court should have held that the order was void *ab initio* and never had any effect, that is quite a different matter from saying that the order was a nullity of which advantage could be taken by any other person having a legitimate interest in the matter.

Their Lordships therefore are clearly of opinion that the order of the Minister on May 29, 1966, was voidable and not a nullity. Being voidable it was voidable only at the instance of the person against whom the order was made, that is the council. But the council have not complained. The appellant was no doubt mayor at the time of its dissolution but that does not give him any right to complain independently of the council. He must show that he is representing the council or suing on its behalf or that by reason of certain circumstances, such, for example, as that the council could not use its seal because it is in the possession of the Municipal Commissioner, or for other reasons it has been impracticable for the members of the council to meet to pass the necessary resolutions, the council cannot be the plaintiff. Had that been shown then there are well-known procedures whereby the plaintiff can sue on behalf of himself and the other corporators making the council a defendant and on pleading and proving the necessary facts may be able to establish in the action that he is entitled to assert the rights of the council. That, however, is not suggested in this case. The appellant sets up the case that as mayor he is entitled to complain but as such he plainly is not. If the council is dissolved, the office of mayor is dissolved with it and he has no independent right of complaint, because he holds no office that is independent of the council. If the mayor were to be heard individually he could only deal with complaints against the council which *ex hypothesi* the council itself did not wish to deal. So, accordingly, it seems to their Lordships that on this short ground the appellant cannot maintain this action.

For these reasons which differ entirely from those in the court below their Lordships have, therefore, humbly advised Her Majesty that the appeal should be dismissed."

Appeal dismissed.

Note

Craig comments (p. 324) that "both Lord Evershed in *Ridge* and the Privy Council in *Durayappah* are using void or nullity in the absolute sense." Note also the comments of Lord Diplock in the *Hoffman-La Roche* case (below, p. 850).

F. HOFFMANN-LA ROCHE & CO. A.G. AND OTHERS v. SECRETARY OF STATE FOR TRADE AND INDUSTRY

[1975] A.C. 295; [1974] 3 W.L.R. 104; 118 S.J. 500; [1974] 2 All E.R. 1128 (House of Lords)

Hoffmann-La Roche and some associated companies held a patent for two tranquillising drugs, "Librium" and "Valium." They were widely used in the United

Kingdom and most were paid for by the Department of Health and Social Security. The Department of Health and Social Security felt that the price charged was too high. The Secretary of State for Trade and Industry referred the matter to the Monopolies Commission for investigation and report under the Monopolies, etc. Act 1948. The Commission reported that the prices were excessive, and should be reduced substantially. The report was laid before Parliament as required by the Act. Under the 1948 Act, and the Monopolies and Mergers Act 1965, this reduction could be ordered by statutory instrument approved by both Houses of Parliament. An Order was made, and after debate, and investigation by a special orders committee of the House of Lords, the Order was approved by Parliament. The companies alleged that the Monopolies Commission report had been prepared in breach of natural justice and was therefore invalid. The power to make the statutory instrument depended on the existence of a valid report, and so the Order was invalid. They threatened to ignore the order and continue to charge the old prices. The Secretary of State then sought an injunction restraining the companies from charging prices in excess of the figures fixed by the Order. On a motion for an interim injunction, the Secretary of State refused to give an undertaking in damages so as to recompense the companies if at the trial of the action the Order was held to be invalid. On July 13, 1973, Walton J. refused to grant the interim injunction on the companies' undertaking to pay the difference between the prices being charged and those specified in the Order into a bank account in the joint names of the parties' solicitors. The Court of Appeal ([1975] A.C. 308) allowed the Secretary of State's appeal.

LORD DENNING M.R.: [held at pp. 318–319 that although there might be many situations where it would be proper for the Crown to give an undertaking in damages, as was the usual practice in the case of ordinary litigants, this was not a proper case for an undertaking as the Crown was coming to court "to enforce the law." On the plaintiff's submission that the report of the Monopolies Commission was void for breach of natural justice his Lordship stated:] . . . I will assume for present purposes that the Monopolies Commission did act contrary to the rules of natural justice—though I would not wish to imply that it was in fact the case. Mr. Yorke says that their report would be void. He referred us to passages from *Ridge* v. *Baldwin* [1964] A.C. 40, 80; *Durayappah* v. *Fernando* [1967] 2 A.C. 337, 355 and *Anisminic Ltd.* v. *Foreign Compensation Commission* [1969] 2 A.C. 147, 171.

I have always understood the word "void" to mean that the transaction in question is absolutely void—a nullity incapable of any legal consequences—not only bad but incurably bad—so much so that all the world can ignore it and that nothing can be founded on it: see *MacFoy* v. *United Africa Co. Ltd.* [1962] A.C. 152, 160.

If the word "void" is used in that sense, the report of the Monopolies Commission was certainly not void. A failure to observe the rules of natural justice does not render a decision or order or report absolutely void in the sense that it is a nullity. The legal consequences are best told by recounting the remedies available in respect of it. A person who has been unfairly treated (by reason of the breach of natural justice) can go to the courts and ask for the decision or order or report, or whatever it is, to be quashed, or for a declaration that it is invalid, that it has not and never has had any effect as against him. But it is a personal remedy, personal to him. If he does not choose himself to query it and seek a remedy, no one else can do so: see *Durayappah* v. *Fernando* [1967] 2 A.C. 337, 353. But it is within the discretion of the court whether to grant him such a remedy or not. He may be debarred from relief if he has acquiesced in the invalidity or has waived it. If he does not come with due diligence and ask for it to be set aside, he may be sent away with nothing: see *R.* v. *Aston University Senate, ex p. Roffey* [1969] 2 Q.B. 538. If his conduct has been disgraceful and he has in fact suffered no injustice, he may be refused relief: see *Glynn* v. *Keele University* [1971] 1 W.L.R. 487 and *Ward* v. *Bradford Corpn.* (1971) 70 L.G.R. 27. If it is a decision or order or report which affects many other persons besides him, the court may not think it right to declare it invalid at his instance alone: see *Maxwell* v. *Department of Trade and Industry* (unreported), December 20, 1972, a decision of Wien J., of which we were supplied with a transcript. Moreover, pending a decision by the courts as to its validity, other persons may be justified in acting on the footing that it is valid. If the decision or order or report is good on the face of it, and there is no good reason for supposing it to be invalid, other persons can treat it as valid. To it would apply the words of Lord Radcliffe in *Smith* v. *East Elloe Rural District Council* [1956] A.C. 736, 769–770:

> "An order, . . . is still an act capable of legal consequences. It bears no brand of invalidity upon its forehead. Unless the necessary proceedings are taken at law to establish the cause of invalidity and to get it quashed or otherwise upset, it will remain as effective for its ostensible purpose as the most impeccable of orders."

So here, the report of the Monopolies Commission, even if it was made in breach of the rules of natural justice, is still capable of legal consequence. The question, therefore, is of what legal consequences is it capable? In my opinion, when the Secretary of State received the report of the Monopolies Commission, he was entitled to treat it as valid and to act as he did on the faith of it. It was perfectly good on the face of it. Under the statute he was authorised to make an Order if it appeared to him "on the facts found by the commission as stated in the report" that the prices charged were such as "to operate, against the public interest": see section 3(4)(*c*) of the Act of 1965. Applying that provision, the Secretary of State was entitled to go by the facts stated in the report. He was entitled to make the statutory Order so as to compel the plaintiffs to reduce their prices. Likewise when the Secretary of State laid the Order before Parliament, each House was entitled to treat the Order as valid. . . .

BUCKLEY and LAWTON L.JJ. delivered concurring judgments.
The company appealed to the House of Lords.

LORD REID: . . . An interim injunction against a party to a litigation may cause him great loss if in the end he is successful. In the present case it is common ground that a long time—it may be years—will elapse before a decision can be given. During that period if an interim injunction is granted the appellants will only be able to make the charges permitted by the Order. So if in the end the Order is annulled that loss will be the difference between those charges and those which they could have made if the Order had never been made. And they may not be able to recover any part of that loss from anyone. It is said that the loss might amount to £8m. The appellants' case is that justice requires that such an injunction should not be granted without an undertaking by the respondent to make good that loss to them if they are ultimately successful.

The respondent's first answer is that when an interim injunction is granted to the Crown no undertaking can be required as a condition of granting it. It is not in doubt that in an ordinary litigation the general rule has long been that no interim injunction likely to cause loss to a party will be granted unless the party seeking the injunction undertakes to make good that loss if in the end it appears that the injunction was unwarranted. He cannot be compelled to give an undertaking but if he will not give it he will not get the injunction.

But there is much authority to show that the Crown was in a different position. In general no undertaking was required of it. But whatever justification there may have been for that before 1947 I agree with your Lordships that the old rule or practice cannot be justified since the passing of the Crown Proceedings Act of that year. So if this had been a case where the Crown were asserting a proprietary right I would hold that the ordinary rule should apply and there should be no interlocutory injunction unless the Crown chose to give the usual undertaking.

But this is a case in a different and novel field. No doubt it was thought that criminal penalties were inappropriate as a means of enforcing Orders of this kind, and the only method of enforcement is by injunction. Dealing with alleged breaches of the law is a function of the Crown (or of a department of the executive) entirely different in character from its function in protecting its proprietary right. It has more resemblance to the function of prosecuting those who are alleged to have committed an offence. A person who is prosecuted and found not guilty may have suffered serious loss by reason of the prosecution but in general he has no legal claim against the prosecutor. In the absence of special circumstances I see no reason why the Crown in seeking to enforce Orders of this kind should have to incur legal liability to the person alleged to be in breach of the Order.

It must be borne in mind that an Order made under statutory authority is as much the law of the land as an Act of Parliament unless and until it has been found to be *ultra vires*. No doubt procedure by way of injunction is more flexible than procedure by prosecution and there may well be cases when a court ought to refuse an interim injunction or only to grant it on terms. But I think that it is for the person against whom the interim injunction is sought to show special reason why justice requires that the injunction should not be granted or should only be granted on terms.

The present case has a special feature which requires anxious consideration. As I have already indicated, the Crown has a very large financial interest in obtaining an interim injunction. The Department of Health will reap a large immediate benefit from the lower prices set out in the Order at the expense of the appellants. If in the end it were decided that the order was *ultra vires* those prices ought never to have been enforced, the department ought never to have had that benefit and the appellants would have suffered a large loss. So why should the respondent not be required to give the undertaking which the appellants seek as a condition of getting the interim injunction?

But, on the other hand, the Order which the appellants seek to annul is the law at present and if an interim injunction is refused that means that the law is not to be enforced and the appellants are to be at liberty to disregard it by charging forbidden prices. And the matter does not stop there. Doctors will continue to prescribe these drugs. Chemists will have to pay the forbidden prices if the public are to be provided with drugs which doctors think they ought to have. And chemists cannot be expected to pay the appellants' prices unless the department is willing to reimburse them. So the department will have to acquiesce in and indeed aid and abet the appellants' breaches of the law if the medical profession and the public are to get what they are entitled to.

It is true that the appellants have proposed an ingenious scheme which they would undertake to operate if an interim injunction is refused. The effect of it would be that they would continue to charge the forbidden prices but that if the Order were ultimately held to be *intra vires* they would repay the difference between the forbidden charges which they had made and the lower charges which they ought to have made. The scheme would involve considerable practical difficulties and would probably not be fully effective, but I shall not discuss those difficulties because the serious objection would remain that the law laid down in the Order is to be disregarded until the case is decided.

My Lords, if I thought that the appellants had a strong case on the merits I would try to stretch a point in their favour to protect them from obvious injustice though I would find difficulty in doing so. It is true that although we heard a good deal of argument on the merits we are not in a position to express any firm opinion as to the appellants' prospects of success. But if it is for them to show us at this stage that their case is so strong that they are entitled to some special consideration, I can say that they have completely failed to convince me that they have a strong prima facie case.

I would therefore dismiss this appeal.

LORD WILBERFORCE: (dissenting) [stated that the discretion as exercised by Walton J.] seems to be well within the area permitted to the judge and should not be displaced except for some error in law. The result appears both "just and convenient." The contrary course, approved by the Court of Appeal, of granting an injunction *tout court* (as if the D.T.I. had already won the action) potentially creates a serious injustice.

The position so stated—and there is I believe no over-simplification about it—is for me decisive of this appeal: I think that the judge's approach was right.

[His Lordship added "brief observations" on some of the other arguments heard, holding first that an undertaking in damages could be required of the Crown. His Lordship continued:] 2. . . . I regard [the argument that the Crown was "enforcing the law"] as fallacious. To say that the Crown is enforcing the law is a *petitio principii*, since the very issue in the action is whether what is alleged to be law (and denied to be law by the appellants) is law or not. The answer given to this is, I understand, that there is a presumption of validity until the contrary is shown. The consequence drawn from this is that unconditional obedience must be required by the court: "obey first and argue afterwards" in Lord Denning M.R.'s graphic phrase [1973] 3 W.L.R. 805, 821. I think that there is a confusion here. It is true enough that a piece of subordinate legislation is presumed to be valid against persons who have no *locus standi* to challenge it—the puzzling case of *Durayappah* v. *Fernando* [1967] 2 A.C. 337 can be understood as exemplifying this. But it is quite another matter to say, and I know of no supporting authority, that such a presumption exists when the validity of the subordinate legislation is legitimately in question before a court and is challenged by a person who has *locus standi* to challenge it. Certainly no support for any such proposition is to be found in the passage, so often partially quoted, from the speech of Lord Radcliffe in *Smith* v. *East Elloe Rural District Council* [1956] A.C. 736. One has only to read what he said, at pp. 769–770:

> "At one time the argument was shaped into the form of saying that an order made in bad faith was in law a nullity and that, consequently, all references to compulsory purchase orders in paragraphs 15 and 16 must be treated as references to such orders only as had been made in good faith. But this argument is in reality a play on the meaning of the word nullity. An order, even if not made in good faith, is still an act capable of legal consequences. It bears no brand of invalidity upon its forehead. Unless the necessary proceedings are taken at law to establish the cause of invalidity and to get it quashed or otherwise upset, it will remain as effective for its ostensible purpose as the most impeccable of orders."

How this can be said to support an argument that when proceedings *are* taken at law the impugned Order must be given full legal effect against the challenger before the proceedings are decided I am unable to comprehend.

In any event the argument proves too much, for, if it were right, the court would have no discretion to refuse an injunction whatever the consequences, however irreparably disastrous, to the object. Such rigidity of power seems to be contrary to section 45 of the Supreme Court of Judicature (Consolidation) Act 1925. Further, if one considers some of the Orders which, under this same Act, can be made under section 3 the injustice of this can be easily perceived. And as an example in practice there is the case of *Post Office* v. *Estuary Radio Ltd.* [1967] 1 W.L.R. 847; [1968] 2 Q.B. 740 which I discuss below, a case where an interim injunction was refused—no doubt just because to grant it would cause irreparable damage. If, then, it is said that there must always remain a residual discretion the argument vanishes: we are back on discretion.

3. It is said that no undertaking should be insisted on unless the effect of the appellants' eventual success were to make the order "void *ab initio*"—the argument being that otherwise no injustice would result. Buckley L.J. ([1973] 3 W.L.R. 805, 827–828) made this the conclusion of a judgment with the rest of which I respectfully concur. The phrase "void *ab initio*" has engendered many learned distinctions and much confused thinking—unnecessarily, in my opinion. There can be no doubt in the first place that an *ultra vires* act is simply void—see in confirmation *Ridge* v. *Baldwin* [1964] A.C. 40. In truth when the court says that an act of administration is voidable or void but not *ab initio* this is simply a reflection of a conclusion, already reached on unexpressed grounds, that the court is not willing *in casu* to give compensation or other redress to the person who establishes the nullity. Underlying the use of the phrase in the present case, and I suspect underlying most of the reasoning in the Court of Appeal, is an unwillingness to accept that a subject should be indemnified for loss sustained by invalid administrative action. It is this which requires examination rather than some supposed visible quality of the order itself.

In more developed legal systems this particular difficulty does not arise. Such systems give indemnity to persons injured by illegal acts of the administration. Consequently, where the prospective loss which may be caused by an order is pecuniary, there is no need to suspend the impugned administrative act: it can take effect (in our language an injunction can be given) and at the end of the day the subject can, if necessary, be compensated. On the other hand, if the prospective loss is not pecuniary (in our language "irreparable") the act may be suspended pending decision—in our language, interim enforcement may be refused.

There is clearly an important principle here which has not been elucidated by English law, or even brought into the open. But there are traces of it in some areas. I have referred to *Post Office* v. *Estuary Radio Ltd.* [1967] 1 W.L.R. 847, [1968] 2 Q.B. 740, which arose upon a section in the Wireless Telegraphy Act 1949, similar to section 11 of the Act of 1968. In that case the Post Office applied for an injunction and also moved for interim relief; this was refused, no doubt partly for the reason that to grant it at the interim stage would cause the defendant irreparable damage. We are not bound by the decision, but I suggest that it is based on sound principle.

Secondly, there are instances of statutes which themselves provide for the interim suspension of impugned orders. One such is the Acquisition of Land (Authorisation Procedure) Act 1946, Schedule 1, Part IV. This provides that if any person desires to question the validity of a compulsory purchase order the court may *ad interim* suspend the effect of the order. These are examples of at least a partial recognition in our law that the subject requires protection against action taken against him or his property under administrative orders which may turn out to be invalid. How far this principle goes need not, and cannot, be decided in the present case. But what can be said is that the combination of section 11 of the Act of 1948 with section 45 of the Supreme Court of Judicature (Consolidation) Act 1925 gives to the court a practical instrument by which injustice to private individuals, faced with possibly invalid action, may be avoided. If this is not possible in every case, it should not be rejected in a case, however special, where justice to both sides can be done. . . .

LORD DIPLOCK: . . .

The legal status of the Order

Under our legal system . . . the courts as the judicial arm of government do not act on their own initiative. Their jurisdiction to determine that a statutory instrument is *ultra vires* does not arise until its validity is challenged in proceedings *inter partes* either brought by one party to enforce the law declared by the instrument against another party or brought by a party whose interests are affected by the law so declared sufficiently directly to give him *locus standi* to initiate proceedings to challenge the validity of the instrument. Unless there is such challenge and, if there is, until it has been upheld by a judgment of the court, the validity of the statutory instrument and the legality of acts done pursuant to the law declared by it are presumed. It would, however, be inconsistent with the doctrine of *ultra vires* as it has been developed in English law as a means of controlling abuse of power by the executive arm of government if the judgment of a court in proceedings properly constituted that a statutory instrument was *ultra vires* were to have any lesser consequence in law than to render the instrument incapable of ever having had any legal effect upon the rights or duties of the parties to the proceedings (*cf. Ridge* v. *Baldwin* [1964] A.C. 40). Although such a decision is directly binding only as between the parties to the proceedings in which it was made, the application of the doctrine of precedent has the consequence of enabling the benefit of it to accrue to all other persons whose legal rights have been interfered with in reliance on the law which the statutory instrument purported to declare.

The presumption of validity of the Order

My Lords, I think it leads to confusion to use such terms as "voidable," "voidable *ab initio*," "void" or "a nullity" as descriptive of the legal status of subordinate legislation alleged to be *ultra vires* for patent or for latent defects, before its validity has been pronounced on by a court of competent jurisdiction. These are concepts developed in the private law of contract which are ill-adapted to the field of public law. All that can usefully be said is that the presumption that subordinate legislation is *intra vires* prevails in the absence of rebuttal, and that it cannot be rebutted except by a party to legal proceedings in a court of competent jurisdiction who has *locus standi* to challenge the validity of the subordinate legislation in question.

All *locus standi* on the part of anyone to rebut the presumption of validity may be taken away completely or may be limited in point of time or otherwise by the express terms of the Act of Parliament which conferred the subordinate legislative power, though the courts lean heavily against a construction of the Act which would have this effect (*cf. Anisminic Ltd.* v. *Foreign Compensation Commission* [1969] 2 A.C. 147). Such was the case, however, in the view of the majority of this House in *Smith* v. *East Elloe Rural District Council* [1956] A.C. 736, at any rate as respects invalidity on the ground of latent defects, so the compulsory purchase order sought to be challenged in the action had legal effect notwithstanding its potential invalidity. Furthermore, apart from express provision in the governing statute, *locus standi* to challenge the validity of subordinate legislation may be restricted, under the court's inherent power to control its own procedure, to a particular category of persons affected by the subordinate legislation, and if none of these persons chooses to challenge it the presumption of validity prevails. Such was the case in *Durayappah* v. *Fernando* [1967] 2 A.C. 337 where on an appeal from Ceylon, although the Privy Council was of opinion that an order of the Minister was *ultra vires* owing to a latent defect in the procedure prior to its being made, they nevertheless treated it as having legal effect because the party who sought to challenge it had, in their view, no *locus standi* to do so.

The legal status of the Regulation of Prices (Tranquillising Drugs) (No. 3) Order 1973 which the appellants seek to challenge in the instant case is aptly stated in the words of Lord Radcliffe in *Smith* v. *East Elloe Rural District Council* [1956] A.C. 736, 769–770:

> "An order, . . ., is still an act capable of legal consequences. It bears no brand of invalidity upon its forehead. Unless the necessary proceedings are taken at law to establish the cause of invalidity and to get it quashed or otherwise upset, it will remain as effective for its ostensible purpose as the most impeccable of orders."

The instant case is not one where the appellants contend that what they are threatening to do would not be a contravention of the Order—as was the case in *Post Office* v. *Estuary Radio Ltd.* [1967] 1 W.L.R. 847, [1968] 2 Q.B. 740. Different considerations would apply to that. Their only answer to the application for an interim injunction to enforce the Order against them is that they intend to challenge its validity. It is not disputed that they have *locus standi* to do so, but this does not absolve them from their obligation to obey the Order while the presumption in favour of its validity prevails—as it must so long as there has been no final judgment in the action to the contrary.

So in this type of law enforcement action if the only defence is an attack on the validity of the statutory instrument sought to be enforced the ordinary position of the parties as respects the grant of interim injunctions is reversed. The duty of the Crown to see that the law declared by the statutory instrument is obeyed is not suspended by the commencement of proceedings in which the validity of the instrument is challenged. Prima facie the Crown is entitled as of right to an interim injunction to enforce obedience to it. To displace this right or to fetter it by the imposition of conditions it is for the defendant to show a strong prima facie case that the statutory instrument is *ultra vires*.

Even where a strong prima facie case of invalidity has been shown upon the application for an interim injunction it may still be inappropriate for the court to impose as a condition of the grant of the injunction a requirement that the Crown should enter into the usual undertaking as to damages. For if the undertaking falls to be implemented, the cost of implementing it will be met from public funds raised by taxation and the interests of members of the public who are not parties to the action may be affected by it. . . .

Accordingly, I agree with the majority of your Lordships that the Secretary of State is entitled to the interim injunction that he claimed without giving any undertaking as to damages unless the appellants have succeeded in showing a strong prima facie case that the Order sought to be enforced by the injunction is *ultra vires*. It is not for the Secretary of State to show that the appellant's case cannot possibly succeed as Walton J. thought it was. It is for the appellants to show that their defence of *ultra vires* is likely to be successful.

I agree with the majority of your Lordships that they have signally failed to do this. . . .

Lords Morris of Borth-y-Gest and Cross of Chelsea delivered speeches in favour of dismissing the appeal.

Appeal dismissed.

Notes

1. See the notes by H. W. R. W[ade], (1974) 90 L.Q.R. 436; P. Wallington, [1974] C.L.J. 26, 194.
2. Lord Denning's views on this question have varied over the years. His

statement in *Hoffman-La Roche* (above, p. 843) seems consistent with the principles stated at the start of the chapter, save for his preference for the use of the word "void" in the, inappropriate, absolute sense.

In *D.P.P.* v. *Head* [1959] A.C. 83, H. was convicted of having carnal knowledge of a mental defective, a Miss Henderson, contrary to the Mental Deficiency Act 1913. The Court of Criminal Appeal quashed the conviction on the ground that the prosecution had failed to establish that Miss Henderson had lawfully been made subject to the 1913 Act. This required an order of the Secretary of State, based on the certificates of two medical practitioners, but neither certificate fully complied with the relevant statutory provisions. On appeal to the House of Lords, Lord Denning stated (at p. 112) that the Secretary of State's order was voidable only:

> "The most that appears here is that the Secretary of State—acting within his jurisdiction—exercised that jurisdiction erroneously. . . . It is said that he made the order on no evidence or on insufficient materials. So be it. His error is a wrong exercise of a jurisdiction which he has, and not a usurpation of a jurisdiction which he has not. . . . If that error appears on the face of the record—as it is said to do here—it renders the order liable to be quashed on certiorari, but it does not make it a nullity. . . ."

Had the order been outside the jurisdiction altogether, it would have been void:

> "There would be no need for an order to quash it. It would be automatically null and void without more ado" (p. 111)

Lord Denning nevertheless concluded on another ground that it would be wrong to restore the conviction. Lord Somervell, however, expressed reservations. He was "not satisfied that the order was not void." In any event, he did not think that the question whether a man should go or not go to prison should depend on the void/voidable distinction (p. 104). Lords Reid, Tucker and Simonds agreed with Lord Somervell's reservations. Lord Denning's approach is difficult to follow. If the error here is correctly analysed as a non-jurisdictional error of law, the label "voidable" is appropriate (*cf.* above, p. 837). However, it is difficult to see that the error was anything other than a jurisdictional error. On the other hand, Lord Denning arguably goes too far in attributing *absolute* nullity to jurisdictional error.

In *R.* v. *Paddington Valuation Officer, ex p. Peachey Property Corporation Ltd.* [1966] 1 Q.B. 380, the applicants challenged, without success, the validity of a new valuation list. Lord Denning M.R. drew the same distinction as in *D.P.P.* v. *Head* between cases "where the invalidity is so grave that the list is a nullity altogether" and cases where "the valuation officer—acting within his jurisdiction—exercised that jurisdiction erroneously," where the list would be voidable not void. The allegation here fell into the latter category. The difficulty with this is that it was not argued that there was an error of law on the face of the record, the allegation being one of excess of jurisdiction. Lord Denning's approach might therefore be construed as an attempt to distinguish between different categories of *jurisdictional* error, grave errors making the decision void, less grave errors, voidable. This would be complex and unattractive, and inconsistent with his Lordship's statement that the valuation officer was "acting within his jurisdiction," although it may be compared with his Lordship's remarks in *ex p. Ostler* (below, p. 883). Perhaps it should simply be disregarded as incoherent.

Subsequently, Lord Denning seemed to recant, accepting in *Firman* v. *Ellis* [1978] Q.B. 886 and extra-judicially (*The Discipline of Law* (1979), p. 77) that a decision in breach of natural justice, on being set aside, is void *ab initio* and not voidable. Finally, he grew tired of the question. In *Lovelock* v. *Minister of Transport*

(1980) 40 P. & C.R. 336, it was alleged that compulsory purchase orders affecting green belt land made by the Minister for a motorway scheme were invalid, *inter alia*, on the ground that the necessary consent of the Secretary of State for the Environment to encroachment on the green belt had not validly been given. Lord Denning M.R. said (at p. 345):

"Assuming that [the Secretary of State] did fail to take into account a relevant consideration, the result is that, in point of legal theory, his consent was 'void.' It was made without jurisdiction. It was a nullity. Just as if he had failed to observe the rules of natural justice. But, in point of practice, it was 'voidable.' I have got tired of all the discussion about 'void' and 'voidable.' It seems to me to be a matter of words—of semantics—and that is all. The plain fact is that, even if such a decision as this is 'void' or a 'nullity,' it remains in being unless and until some steps are taken before the court to have it declared void. As Lord Radcliffe said long ago in *Smith* v. *East Elloe Rural District Council* [1956] A.C. 736, 769–770: 'It bears no brand of invalidity upon its forehead. Unless the necessary proceedings are taken at law to establish the cause of invalidity and to get it quashed or otherwise upset, it will remain as effective for its ostensible purpose as the most impeccable of orders.' That point of view was adopted by the House of Lords in *F. Hoffman-La Roche & Co. A.G.* v. *Secretary of State for Trade and Industry* [1975] A.C. 295 by Lord Reid (p. 341) and by Lord Morris of Borth-y-Gest (p. 350).

So, even if there was anything wrong in what the Secretary of State did—even if he did fail to take into account a relevant consideration—even if there was any failure of natural justice in that or any other regard—this consent remained valid and effective for all purposes, and for people to act on it, unless and until steps were taken to call it in question. No steps were taken until the appeal was opened in this court.

Meanwhile, what has happened? As a result of the consent having been given, the Minister of Transport has gone through all the machinery leading to the making of the compulsory purchase orders. He has given all the notices in the newspapers. He has held an inquiry lasting for many, many days. Eventually, he made the orders. We are told that tenders have been put out for the work to be done. All this has been done in the belief that the consent was valid—as, indeed, it was unless and until it was set aside.

That having been done, it seems to me impossible now to challenge the orders on the ground that the statutory procedures or requirements have not been satisfied."

(*Cf.* Waller L.J. to similar effect at p. 350; Dunn L.J. agreed with both Lord Denning and Waller L.J.: see p. 353). See Comment, [1980] J.P.L. 821.

3. Local authorities when seeking an injunction by virtue of the Local Government Act 1972, s.222, to enforce the criminal law are not necessarily to be required to give an undertaking in damages: *Kirklees Metropolitan Borough Council* v. *Wickes Building Supplies Ltd.*, *The Times*, June 29, 1992, H.L. They are entitled to the special exemption enjoyed by the Crown. The House accepted that if the grant of an injunction was subsequently held to be in breach of Community Law, the U.K. might be obliged to make good damage caused to individuals by the breach. However, that obligation would arise irrespective of any undertaking in damages.

(C) A Discretionary Approach

In *London and Clydeside Estates Ltd.* v. *Aberdeen District Council*, above, p. 461, Lord Hailsham deprecated the use of the terms "void" and "voidable" (just as he disapproved of the terms "mandatory" and "directory" in respect of procedural requirements). See *Craig*, pp. 334–337, for an argument that Lord Hailsham's view that matters should largely be left to the discretion of the court goes too far:

> "That the concept of retrospective nullity can give rise to awkward problems is no doubt true. But to infer that therefore it ought to be totally discarded is a *non sequitur*."

(D) Partial Invalidity

D.P.P. v. HUTCHINSON

[1990] 2 A.C. 783; [1990] 3 W.L.R. 196; [1990] 2 All E.R. 836; (1990) 89 L.G.R. 281 (House of Lords)

Section 14(1) of the Military Lands Act 1892 provides:

> "Where any land belonging to a Secretary of State . . . is for the time being appropriated by . . . a Secretary of State for any military purpose, a Secretary of State may make byelaws for regulating the use of the land for the purposes for which it is appropriated, and for securing the public against dangers arising from that use, with power to prohibit all intrusion on the land and all obstruction of the use thereof. Provided that no byelaws promulgated under the section shall authorise the Secretary of State to take away or prejudicially affect any right of common."

The Secretary of State for Defence, acting under section 14 of the Act of 1892, made the R.A.F. Greenham Common Byelaws 1985 in respect of common land appropriated for military purposes. Byelaw (2)(b) provided that no person should, *inter alia*, enter or remain in the protected area without the authority or permission of an authorised person. The defendants, who were not commoners, entered the land and were charged with and convicted by the justices of entering it contrary to byelaw 2(b). The Crown Court allowed their appeals, holding that the byelaws were *ultra vires* in that they prejudicially affected rights of common. The Divisional Court of the Queen's Bench Division allowed an appeal by case stated by the Director of Public Prosecutions. The defendants appealed to the House of Lords.

Lord Bridge: . . . The Divisional Court (Mann L.J. and Schiemann J.) [1989] Q.B. 583 allowed the Crown's appeal and restored the convictions. They held that the Greenham byelaws, although *ultra vires* on their face, could be severed, so that they might be upheld and enforced as against all except persons entitled to exercise rights of common over the protected area. It mattered not that the severance could only be achieved by reading into the byelaws, where necessary, appropriate exceptions and exemptions, provided that the court was satisfied, as Schiemann J. stated, at p. 599, that it was, that the Secretary of State, if he had appreciated the limitation on his powers would:

"nevertheless have gone on to make the byelaws in such a way that the proviso to section 14(1) was given effect but that all the world save commoners would still have been within their ambit. . . ."

When a legislative instrument made by a law-maker with limited powers is challenged, the only function of the court is to determine whether there has been a valid exercise of that limited legislative power in relation to the matter which is the subject of disputed enforcement. If a law-maker has validly exercised his power, the court may give effect to the law validly made. But if the court sees only an invalid law made in excess of the law-maker's power, it has no jurisdiction to modify or adapt the law to bring it within the scope of the law-maker's powers. These, I believe, are the basic principles which have always to be borne in mind in deciding whether legislative provisions which on their face exceed the law-maker's power may be severed so as to be upheld and enforced in part.

The application of these principles leads naturally and logically to what has traditionally been regarded as the test of severability. It is often referred to inelegantly as the "blue pencil" test. Taking the simplest case of a single legislative instrument containing a number of separate clauses of which one exceeds the law-maker's power, if the remaining clauses enact free-standing provisions which were intended to operate and are capable of operating independently of the offending clause, there is no reason why those clauses should not be upheld and enforced. The law-maker has validly exercised his power by making the valid clauses. The invalid clause may be disregarded as unrelated to, and having no effect upon, the operation of the valid clauses, which accordingly may be allowed to take effect without the necessity of any modification or adaptation by the court. What is involved is in truth a double test. I shall refer to the two aspects of the test as textual severability and substantial severability. A legislative instrument is textually severable if a clause, a sentence, a phrase or a single word may be disregarded, as exceeding the law-maker's power, and what remains of the text is still grammatical and coherent. A legislative instrument is substantially severable if the substance of what remains after severance is essentially unchanged in its legislative purpose, operation and effect.

The early English authorities take it for granted, I think, that if byelaws are to be upheld as good in part notwithstanding that they are bad in part, they must be both textually and substantially severable. Thus, Lord Kenyon C.J. said in *R.* v. *Company of Fishermen of Faversham* (1799) 8 Durn. & E. 352, 356:

"With regard to the form of the byelaw indeed, though a byelaw may be good in part and bad in part, yet it can be so only where the two parts are entire and distinct from each other."

[His Lordship also cited *R.* v. *Lundie* (1862) 8 Jur.N.S. 640 and *Strickland* v. *Hayes* [1896] 1 Q.B. 290. He then referred to United States and Australian authorities that emphasised the need for both textual and substantial severability.]

Our attention has been drawn to a number of more recent English authorities on the severability of provisions contained in various documents of a public law character. I doubt if these throw much light on the specific problem of severance in legislative instruments. The modern authority most directly in point and that on which the Divisional Court relied is *Dunkley* v. *Evans* [1981] 1 W.L.R. 1522. The West Coast Herring (Prohibition of Fishing) Order 1978 (S.I. 1978 No. 930) prohibited fishing for herring in an area defined in the Schedule to the Order as within a line drawn by reference to co-ordinates and coastlines. The Order was made by the Minister of Agriculture, Fisheries and Food under the Sea Fish (Conservation) Act 1967. The prohibited area included a stretch of sea adjacent to the coast of Northern Ireland, representing 0.8 per cent. of the total area covered by the Order, to which the enabling power in the Act of 1967 did not extend. The defendants admitted fishing in part of the prohibited area to which the enabling power did extend but submitted that, by including the area to which the enabling power did not extend, the Minister had acted *ultra vires* and, since textual severance was not possible, the whole Order was invalid. The justices accepted this submission and dismissed the informations. The Divisional Court allowed the prosecutor's appeal. Delivering the judgment of the court, Ormrod L.J. cited, at pp. 1524–1525, the following passage from the judgment of Cussen J. in the Supreme Court of Victoria in *Olsen* v. *City of Camberwell* [1926] V.L.R. 58, 68:

> " 'If the enactment, with the invalid portion omitted, is so radically or substantially different a law as to the subject-matter dealt with by what remains from what it would be with the omitted portions forming part of it as to warrant a belief that the legislative body intended it as a whole only, or, in other words, to warrant a belief that if all could not be carried into effect the legislative body would not have enacted the remainder independently, then the whole must fail.' "

It is to be noted that this quotation is from the judgment in a case where textual severance was possible. Following the quotation the judgment of Ormrod L.J. continued:

> "We respectfully agree with and adopt this statement of the law. It would be difficult to imagine a clearer example than the present case of a law which the legislative body would have enacted independently of the offending portion and which is so little affected by eliminating the invalid portion. This is clearly, therefore, an order which the court should not strive officiously to kill to any greater extent than it is compelled to do. . . . We can see no reason why the powers of the court

to sever the invalid portion of a piece of subordinate legislation from the valid should be restricted to cases where the text of the legislation lends itself to judicial surgery, or textual emendation by excision. It would have been competent for the court in an action for a declaration that the provisions of the Order in this case did not apply to the area of the sea off Northern Ireland reserved by section 23(1) of the Act of 1967, as amended, to make the declaration sought, without in any way affecting the validity of the Order in relation to the remaining 99·2 per cent. of the area referred to in the Schedule to the Order. Such an order was made, in effect, by the House of Lords in *Hotel and Catering Industry Training Board* v. *Automobile Proprietary Ltd.* [1969] 1 W.L.R. 697, and by Donaldson J. in *Agricultural, Horticultural and Forestry Industry Training Board* v. *Aylesbury Mushrooms Ltd.* [1972] 1 W.L.R. 190."

I do not think any light is thrown on the point at issue by the last two cases referred to by Ormrod L.J. In *Hotel and Catering Industry Training Board* v. *Automobile Proprietary Ltd.* the subordinate legislation in question was textually severable. In *Agricultural, Horticultural and Forestry Industry Training Board* v. *Aylesbury Mushrooms Ltd.* the text was not severable but the issue of severance was never canvassed in argument and I cannot help thinking that the outcome might have been different if it had been.

Another case on which the Divisional Court relied was *Thames Water Authority* v. *Elmbridge Borough Council* [1983] Q.B. 570. This concerned the validity of a resolution passed by a local authority under section 163 of the Local Government Act 1933 appropriating land for certain purposes. The land to which the resolution, on its face, applied included a small area which the local authority had no power to appropriate. The court held the resolution to be a valid exercise of the power in relation to land which the authority had power to appropriate. What the court was doing in this case was simply construing the local authority's resolution in relation to facts affecting land to which it applied. I do not think the case can be regarded as authoritative as to the severability of legislative instruments. It is one thing to determine the effect of an exercise of statutory power, as in this case an appropriation of land, which is exercised once and for all. It is quite another to decide whether an instrument purporting to make a law to which all will be subject so long as the law operates as a valid exercise of the law-maker's limited power.

The modern English authority to which I attach most significance is *Daymond* v. *Plymouth City Council* [1976] A.C. 609, where severability was not in issue, but where it appears to have been taken for granted without question that severance was possible. Section 30(1) of the Water Act 1973 gave power to water authorities:

"to fix, and to demand, take and recover such charges for the services performed, facilities provided or rights made available by them including separate charges for separate services, facilities or rights or combined charges for a number of services, facilities or rights) as they think fit."

The subsection was silent as to who was liable to pay the charges. The Water Authorities (Collection of Charges) Order 1974 (S.I. 1974 No. 448) embodied provisions which required a rating authority to collect on behalf of a water authority a "general services charge" (article 7(2)) referable to sewerage services "from every person who is liable to pay the general rate in respect of a hereditament . . ." (article 10(1)). A householder whose property was not connected to a sewer, the nearest sewer being 400 yards away from his house, refused to pay the charge and brought an action for a declaration that the Order could not properly apply to him. This House held, by a majority of three to two, that on the true construction of the enabling legislation there was no power to impose a charge for sewerage services upon occupiers of property not connected to a sewer. As I have said, the question of severability was not raised, but there is no hint in the speeches that the invalidation of the charging provision in relation to properties not connected to sewers would affect their validity in relation to properties which were so connected.

The test of textual severability has the great merit of simplicity and certainty. When it is satisfied the court can readily see whether the omission from the legislative text of so much as exceeds the law-maker's power leaves in place a valid text which is capable of operating and was evidently intended to operate independently of the invalid text. But I have reached the conclusion, though not without hesitation, that a rigid insistence that the test of textual severability must always be satisfied if a provision is to be upheld and enforced as partially valid will in some cases, of which *Dunkley* v. *Evans* and *Daymond* v. *Plymouth City Council* are good examples, have the unreasonable consequence of defeating subordinate legislation of which the substantial purpose and effect was clearly within the law-maker's power when, by some oversight or misapprehension of the scope of that power, the text, as written, has a range of application which exceeds that scope. It is important, however, that in all cases an appropriate test of substantial severability should be applied. When textual severance is possible, the test of substantial severability will be satisfied when the valid text is unaffected by, and independent of, the invalid. The law which the court may then uphold and enforce is the very law which the legislator has enacted, not a different law. But when the court must modify the text in order to achieve severance, this can only be done when the court is satisfied that it is effecting no change in the substantial purpose and effect of the impugned provision. Thus, in *Dunkley* v. *Evans*, the legislative purpose and effect of the prohibition of fishing in the large area of the sea in relation to which the Minister was authorised to legislate was unaffected by the obviously inadvertent inclusion of the small area of sea to which his power did not extend. In *Daymond* v. *Plymouth City Council* the draftsman of the Order had evidently construed the enabling provision as authorising the imposition of charges for sewerage services upon occupiers of property irrespective of whether or not they were connected to sewers. In this error he was in the good company of two members of your Lordships' House. But this extension of the scope of the charging power, which, as the majority held, exceeded its proper limit, in no way affected the legislative purpose and effect of the charging power as applied to occupiers of properties which were connected to sewers.

To appreciate the full extent of the problem presented by the Greenham byelaws it is necessary to set out the full text of the prohibitions imposed by byelaw (2) which provides:

> "No person shall: (a) enter or leave or attempt to enter or leave the protected area except by way of an authorised entrance or exit. (b) enter, pass through or over or remain in or over the protected area without authority or permission given by or on behalf of one of the persons mentioned in byelaw 5(1). (c) cause or permit any vehicle, animal, aircraft or thing to enter into or upon or to pass through or over or to be or remain in or upon or over the protected area without authority or permission given by or on behalf of one of the persons mentioned in byelaw 5(1). (d) remain in the protected area after having been directed to leave by any of the persons mentioned in byelaw 4. (e) make any false statement, either orally or in writing, or employ any other form of misrepresentation in order to obtain entry to any part of the protected area or to any building or premises within the protected area. (f) obstruct any constable (including a constable under the control of the Defence Council) or any other person acting in the proper exercise or execution of his duty within the protected area. (g) enter any part of the protected area which is shown by a notice as being prohibited or restricted. (h) board, attempt to board, or interfere with, or interfere with the movement or passage, of any vehicle, aircraft or other installation in the protected area. (i) distribute or display any handbill, leaflet, sign, advertisement, circular, poster, bill, notice or object within the protected area or affix the same to either side of the perimeter fences without authority of permission given by or on behalf of one of the persons mentioned in byelaw 5(1). (j) interfere or remove from the protected area any property under the control of the Crown or the service authorities of a visiting force or, in either case, their agents or contractors. (k) wilfully damage, destroy, deface or remove any notice board or sign within the protected area. (l) wilfully damage, soil, deface or mark any wall, fence, structure, floor, pavement, or other surface within the protected area."

It is at once apparent that paragraphs (a), (b), (c), (d), (g), (j) and (l) are *ultra vires* as they stand. Paragraphs (e), (f), (i) and (k) appear to be valid and paragraph (h) is probably good in part and bad in part, since the exercise by a commoner of his rights may well interfere with the movement or passage of vehicles. Textual severance can achieve nothing since it is apparent that the valid provisions are merely ancillary to the invalid provisions.

There is exhibited to the case stated by the Crown Court a letter written by an official of the Ministry of Defence to an objector at the time the byelaws were made which concludes with the sentence:

> "Finally I can confirm that in accordance with the enabling Act, the Military Lands Act 1892, the byelaws will not affect rights of common."

Mr. Laws has invited us to infer from this that the Secretary of State for Defence made the byelaws in the belief that the law would imply the necessary exceptions to prevent the byelaws from prejudicially affecting rights of common. I do not think we are entitled to take account of the letter in considering whether the byelaws may be upheld as valid in part. But in any event it is a matter of pure speculation as to what the writer of the letter had in mind. The draftsman of the byelaws cannot possibly have been in ignorance of the terms and effect of the proviso to section 14(1) of the Act of 1892 and the theory of an inadvertent omission appears the less plausible since five sets of byelaws in relation to common lands used for military purposes which were made by the Secretary of State for Defence under section 14 of the Act of 1892 in the years 1976 to 1980 all contain careful express provisions to safeguard rights of common.

I think the proper test to be applied when textual severance is impossible, following in this respect the Australian authorities, is to abjure speculation as to what the maker of the law might have done if he had applied his mind to the relevant limitation on his powers and to ask whether the legislative instrument

> "with the invalid portions omitted would be substantially a different law as to the subject-matter dealt with by what remains from what it would be with the omitted portions forming part of it": *R.* v. *Commonwealth Court of Conciliation and Arbitration, ex p. Whybrow & Co.*, 11 C.L.R. 1, 27.

In applying this test the purpose of the legislation can only be inferred from the text as applied to the factual situation to which its provisions relate. Considering the Greenham byelaws as a whole it is clear that the absolute prohibition which they impose upon all unauthorised access to the protected area is no less than is required to maintain the security of an establishment operated as a military airbase and wholly enclosed by a perimeter fence. Byelaws drawn in such a way as to permit free access to all parts of the base to persons exercising rights of common and their animals would be byelaws of a totally different character. They might serve some different legislative purpose in a different factual situation, as do some other byelaws to which our attention has been drawn relating to areas used as military exercise grounds or as military firing ranges. But they would be quite incapable of serving the legislative purpose which the Greenham byelaws, as drawn, are intended to serve.

For these reasons I conclude that the invalidity of byelaw 2(b) cannot be cured by severance. It follows that the appellants were wrongly convicted and I would allow their appeals, set aside the order of the Divisional Court and restore the order of the Crown Court at Reading.

LORDS GRIFFITH, OLIVER and GOFF agreed with LORD BRIDGE.

LORD LOWRY [agreed with Lord Bridge's conclusion that the byelaw could not survive the test of substantial severability, but also made a reservation in favour of the traditional test of textual severability].

A helpful modern review of severability is found in *R.* v. *Secretary of State for Transport, ex p. Greater London Council* [1986] Q.B. 556 in the judgment of McNeill J., at pp. 578–579:

> "At the end of this part of the argument, it is clear to me that in principle and in appropriate proceedings, the court may hold to be unlawful part of an administrative order or decision having effect in public law while holding valid the remainder of the order or decision. The qualifications which limit the application of this principle are as follows. (1) The words 'administrative order or decision' include at least delegated legislation and statutory orders: see *Dunkley* v. *Evans* [1981] 1 W.L.R. 1522 and *Olsen* v. *City of Camberwell* [1926] V.L.R. 58; orders under delegated statutory powers: see *Blackpool Corporation* v. *Locker* [1948] 1 K.B. 349; byelaws: see *Strickland* v. *Hayes* [1896] 1 Q.B. 290; resolutions of local authorities: see *Thames Water Authority* v. *Elmbridge Borough Council* [1983] Q.B. 570; planning consents: see *Hall & Co. Ltd.* v. *Shoreham-by-Sea Urban District Council* [1964] 1 W.L.R. 240 and *Kingsway Investments (Kent) Ltd.* v. *Kent County Council* [1971] A.C. 72; and statutory demands for information: see *Dyson* v. *Attorney-General* [1912] 1 Ch. 158 and *Potato Marketing Board* v. *Merricks* [1958] 2 Q.B. 316. I am satisfied that the direction presently under consideration would be such a decision.
>
> "(2) The striking down or striking out of a part only of such an order or decision cannot be done if the order or decision is 'one and indivisible' (*Dyson's* case [1912] 1 Ch. 158); if the 'excess is so intertwined with the valid as to be separable from it only with difficulty' (*Royal Bank of Canada* v. *Inland Revenue Commissioners* [1972] Ch. 665); if the 'good part is so inextricably mixed up with the bad that the whole must go'

(*Kingsway Investments* case [1971] A.C. 72); if the 'parts are so interwoven that the rest should fall with the inadmittedly invalid part' (*Olsen's* case [1926] V.L.R. 58); if 'the invalid part is inextricably interconnected with the valid' (*Halsbury's Laws of England*, 4th ed., Vol. 1 (1973), para. 26); or unless 'the good and bad parts are clearly identifiable and the bad part can be separated from the good and rejected without affecting the validity of the remaining part' (*per* Stephenson L.J. in *Thames Water Authority* v. *Elmbridge Borough Council* [1983] Q.B. 570, 585).

"(3) The court may not rewrite such an order or decision. This is not open to argument; but, for illustration only, Lord Reid, in *Kingsway Investments (Kent) Ltd.* v. *Kent County Council* [1971] A.C. 72, 90, said: 'It is a general rule that the court will not remake a contract and to strike out one term and leave the rest in operation is remaking the contract.' In *Dunkley* v. *Evans* [1981] 1 W.L.R. 1522, 1525, Ormrod L.J. said: 'the court will not and cannot rewrite contracts, and so confines itself to deleting part of the text when it is able to do so.'

"(4) Proceedings in which the principle has been applied in public law, so far as the cases cited to me are concerned, have included appeals from decisions of the High Court (*Dyson's* case [1912] 1 Ch. 158 and, after special case stated by an arbitrator, the *Thames Water Authority* case [1983] Q.B. 570), an appeal from the county court (*Blackpool Corporation* v. *Locker* [1948] 1 K.B. 349), cases stated on appeal from justices or quarter sessions (*Strickland* v. *Hayes* [1896] 1 Q.B. 290 and *Dunkley* v. *Evans* [1981] 1 W.L.R. 1522), on special case stated by a disciplinary board (*Potato Marketing Board* v. *Merricks* [1958] 2 Q.B. 316) and applications for declaratory relief (*Kingsway Investments* case [1971] A.C. 72 and *Hall & Co. Ltd.* v. *Shoreham-by-Sea Urban District Council* [1964] 1 W.L.R. 240, both relating to conditions imposed on planning consents)."

My noble and learned friend, Lord Bridge, has in the course of his speech noted some of the cases which might be taken to suggest that the traditional test of textual severability does not strictly apply and it is really unnecessary for me to add to what he has so percipiently said about them. If *Dunkley* v. *Evans* [1981] 1 W.L.R. 1522 is correct (and it certainly produces a very sensible result), it may, by reference to an imaginary map, based on the co-ordinates given in the impugned Order, be justified on "blue pencil" principles. *Thames Water Authority* v. *Elmbridge Borough Council* [1983] Q.B. 570 was concerned with the Planning Acts and with a local authority's exercise of its statutory powers. The judgment of Stephenson L.J. is worthy of careful study. I quote the opening paragraphs, at p. 585:

"For some centuries our courts have been applying to the benevolent interpretation of written instruments of all kinds, including statutes, the common-sense principle preserved in Latin as 'ut res magis valeat quam pereat': *Coke upon Littleton* 36a; *Broom's Legal Maxims*, 10th ed. (1939), p. 361.

By applying that principle they have been able, not only to make sense of near nonsense, but also to give effect to what is good and enforce what is valid, while refusing to enforce what is bad and giving no effect to what is invalid. This latter exercise can be carried out, and can, of course, be carried out only, where the good and bad parts are clearly identifiable and the bad part can be separated from the good and rejected without affecting the validity of the remaining part. But this ought to be done whenever the good and bad parts can be so identified and separated and what remains is clearly valid in the sense that there is nothing inherently unenforceable about it and all the surrounding circumstances indicate that common sense and the intention of the maker of any document which includes both good and bad parts would give effect to it."

The really important case, however, which my noble and learned friend has mentioned, and to which I shall presently return, is *Daymond* v. *Plymouth City Council* [1976] A.C. 609 where, as he puts it, "severability was not in issue, but where it appears to have been taken for granted without question that severance was possible."

Other cases are noted in *Wade, Administrative Law*, 6th ed. (1988), p. 875, but they do not cast a great deal of light on the problem which has concerned me. . . .

My Lords, the accepted view in the common law jurisdictions has been that, when construing legislation the validity of which is under challenge, the first duty of the court, in obedience to the principle that a law should, whenever possible, be interpreted *us res magis valeat quam pereat*, is to see whether the impugned provision can reasonably bear a construction which renders it valid. Failing that, the court's duty, subject always to any relevant statutory provision such as the Australian section 15A, is to decide whether the whole of the challenged legislation or only part of it must be held invalid and ineffective. That problem has traditionally been resolved by applying first the textual, and then the substantial, severability test. If the legislation failed the first test, it was condemned in its entirety. If it passed that test, it had to face the next hurdle. This approach, in my opinion, has a great deal in its favour.

The basic principle is that an *ultra vires* enactment, such as a byelaw, is void *ab initio* and of no effect. The so-called blue pencil test is a concession to practicality and ought not to be extended or weakened. In its traditional form it is acceptable because, once the offending words are ignored, no word or phrase needs to be given a meaning different from, or more restrictive than, its original meaning. Therefore the court has not legislated; it merely continues to apply that part of the existing legislation which is good.

It may be argued that a policy split has developed and that it is time to show common sense and bring our thinking up to date by a further application of the *ut res magis valeat quam pereat* principle. I am, however, chary of yielding to this temptation for a number of reasons. 1. The blue pencil test already represents a concession to the erring law-maker, the justification for which I have tried to explain. 2. When applying the blue pencil test (which actually means ignoring the offending words), the court cannot cause the text of the instrument to be altered. It will remain as the ostensible law of the land unless and until it is replaced by something else. It is too late now to think of abandoning the blue pencil method, which has much to commend it, but the disadvantage inherent in the method ought not to be enlarged. 3. It is up to the law-maker to keep within his powers and it is in the public interest that he should take care, in order that the public may be able to rely on the written word as representing the law. Further enlargement of the court's power to validate what is partially invalid will encourage the law-maker to enact what he pleases, or at least to enact what may or may not be valid, without having to fear any worse result than merely being brought back within bounds. 4. *Dunkley* v. *Evans* [1981] 1 W.L.R. 1522 and *Thames Water Authority* v. *Elmbridge Borough Council* [1983] Q.B. 570 are very special cases. I recall in that regard what McNeill J. said in *R.* v. *Secretary of State for Transport, ex p. Greater London Council* [1986] Q.B. 556, 582D. 5. To liberalise the test would, in my view, be anarchic, not progressive. It would tend in the wrong direction, unlike some developments in the law of negligence, which have promoted justice for physically or economically injured persons, or the sounder aspects of judicial review, which have promoted freedom and have afforded protection from power. 6. The current of decisions and relevant authority has flowed in favour of the traditional doctrine.

[His Lordship concluded by noting that the sole question considered in *Daymond* v. *Plymouth City Council* [1976] A.C. 609 was whether section 30 of the Water Act 1973 empowered the water authority to charge occupiers of property who did not receive the benefit of the authority's services directly.]

No case was cited, and no argument was advanced, on the question whether the invalidity of the authority's demand against such occupiers as the plaintiff would nullify the Order of 1974 in relation to occupiers who were receiving the services, and both the initial judgment and their Lordships' speeches were entirely devoted to the complicated and strenuously contested issue concerning the scope of section 30. . . .

It would therefore not be surprising if, having regard to the remedy sought and granted, the residual effect of the Order of 1974 on those who admittedly were liable for the charge was never mentioned.

I am therefore very reluctant to treat the case as an authority which by implication contradicts the established doctrine of textual severability for the purposes of the present appeal. Accordingly, I would allow this appeal on two grounds, (1) that there is no valid part of byelaw 2(b) which can be severed from the invalid part and stand by itself and (2) that the byelaw would not in any event survive the test of substantial severability.

Appeals allowed.

Notes

1. See comments by A. W. Bradley, [1989] P.L.1. (on the decision of the Divisional Court), and [1990] P.L. 293 (on the decision of the House of Lords). Bradley is critical of the fact that it appeared:

> "that the Ministry of Defence knew of the limitation upon the Secretary of State's powers and knowingly departed from the previous practice of taking care to comply with the intent of the legislation" (p. 295).

He also noted that Lord Lowry's view had "the edge in terms of the previous authorities" (p. 300). Lord Bridge's approach, while more generous to the law-maker, still gave "salutary substance to the spectre of the judge over Whitehall's shoulder" (p. 300).

> "What previously may have seemed in danger of being entirely at the discretion of the court is now subject to a more structured review" (p. 299).

2. In *R.* v. *Secretary of State for Transport, ex p. Greater London Council* [1986] Q.B. 556, McNeill J. quashed a direction by the Secretary of State requiring the GLC to pay a specified sum to London Regional Transport by way of grant. Through a miscalculation, this figure was too high by some £10·2m. McNeill J. held that the direction was "single and indivisible"; that the deduction of £10·2m. would involve rewriting and changing the character of the direction; and that this could not be justified by reference to the authorities on severance. The direction "stands or falls as one."

3. *D.P.P.* v. *Hutchinson* was applied by the House in *R.* v. *Inland Revenue Commissioners, ex p. Woolwich Equitable Building Society* [1990] 1 W.L.R. 1400. The Revenue conceded that part of a regulation was *ultra vires* in that it purported to prescribe a rate of income tax for which building societies were accountable different from that of the year of assessment; the House held (reversing the Court of Appeal on this point) that this could not be severed from the rest of the regulation and that this and a linked regulation were wholly *ultra vires*. The fact that the offending part could be deleted without altering the grammatical sense of what was left was insufficient for severance:

> "One has to ask also the question whether the deletion of that which is in excess of the power so alters the substance of what is left that the provision in question is in reality a substantially different provision from that which it was before deletion" (*per* Lord Oliver at p. 1413).

Here it was "beyond argument" that the regulation without the offending part:

> "is in substance quite different from the regulation which the draftsman actually produced and intended.... What form the regulation might have taken if the invalidity of paragraph (4) had been appreciated is a matter of pure speculation." (*per* Lord Oliver at pp. 1415–1416).

(*cf.* Lord Goff at pp. 1417–1419.)

CHAPTER 15

EXCLUSION OF JUDICIAL REVIEW

PARLIAMENT may attempt to make a particular act or decision "judge-proof." One general method is to entrust powers in subjective form (see above, pp. 408 *et seq.*). Another general method is to use explicit exclusion clauses, purporting for example, to exclude a particular remedy, or to prevent any recourse to the courts at all. Historically these clauses have been controversial both politically and legally. Section 11 of the Tribunals and Inquiries Act 1958 (see now s.12 of the 1992 Act, above p. 78) reduced the effects of such clauses in statutes passed before July 1958. One of the exclusion clauses expressly preserved by the 1958 Act was considered in the *Anisminic* case (above, p. 237). Another variety frequently found in legislation is the "finality" clause, which seems to have little effect beyond taking away a right of appeal which would otherwise exist. (See *R.* v. *Medical Appeal Tribunal, ex p. Gilmore,* below.) The other significant modern exclusionary formula is that built into the typical "statutory *ultra vires*" clause (see above, pp. 622–639). These protect compulsory purchase orders, etc., from any judicial review apart from on an application to the High Court within six weeks on the stated grounds. The effect of these clauses is discussed in *Smith* v. *East Elloe R.D.C.*, below, p. 871, and *ex p. Ostler*, below, p. 880. In the latter case, the Court of Appeal held that the authority of the House of Lords in *Smith* v. *East Elloe* has not been affected by the *Anisminic* case, and that an order cannot be challenged other than in accordance with the statutory procedure.

Another technique is that of empowering a public authority to "define" expressions used in the enabling Act which sets it up. See, for example, the Counter-Inflation Act 1973, s.23 and Sched. 3, para. 1, discussed by V. Korah at (1976) 92 L.Q.R. 42.

One variety of clause to which effect has been given is a "conclusive evidence" clause (see below, p. 870). Then the courts may hold that Parliament has entrusted a matter exclusively to another tribunal (above, p. 786). Finally, the courts may refuse a particular remedy in the exercise of their discretion where an alternative remedy is available (see above, pp. 772–773).

One limiting factor is that statutory ouster clauses of whatever kind cannot be relied on to defeat actions against the state relying on community law: P. Oliver, (1987) 50 M.L.R. 881, 897–898, citing Case 224/84, *Johnston* v. *Chief Constable of the Royal Ulster Constabulary* [1987] Q.B. 129, E.C.J., which concerned a "conclusive evidence" certificate under Art. 53(2) of the Sex Discrimination (Northern Ireland) Order 1976.

R. v. MEDICAL APPEAL TRIBUNAL, ex p. GILMORE

[1957] 1 Q.B. 574; [1957] 2 W.L.R. 498; 101 S.J. 248; *sub nom. Re Gilmore's Application* [1957] 1 All E.R. 796 (Court of Appeal)

In 1936 the applicant, a colliery pick sharpener, sustained an injury to both eyes while at work, his right eye being rendered almost blind. In March, 1955, he suffered a further injury at work, by which the condition of his left eye was so severely aggravated that in the result he was almost totally blind. On his claim for disablement benefit under the National Insurance (Industrial Injuries) Act 1946, two medical boards provisionally assessed the degree of disablement at 100 per cent.; but a third board made no award. The claimant appealed to a medical appeal tribunal which had before it and incorporated in its award an extract from a specialist's report setting out the facts as to the state of both eyes; but in making its award the tribunal assessed the aggravation at only 20 per cent., showing thereby that they had failed to assess in accordance with regulation 2(5) of the National Insurance (Industrial Injuries) (Benefit) Regulations 1948 (relating to industrial injuries to paired organs). If a one-eyed man should lose the sight of his remaining good eye in an industrial accident, this regulation required his disablement to be assessed as if the blindness in the bad eye were itself the result of losing the good eye, (*i.e.* as 100 per cent. disablement).

Section 36(3) of the National Insurance (Industrial Injuries) Act 1946, provided that: "... any decision of a claim or question ... shall be final." The applicant applied for an order of certiorari to quash the decision of the tribunal on the ground that there was a manifest error of law on the face of the record.

The Divisional Court refused leave to apply for certiorari, and so the applicant moved the Court of Appeal *ex parte*, which granted his request. The court was of opinion that they ought to extend the usual time limit of six months because he had not been guilty of any delay in seeking redress, and that there was some ground for thinking that there was an error on the face of the record.

On February 12, 1957, the application came on for hearing in the Court of Appeal. After the case had been opened, counsel for the Ministry of Pensions and National Insurance and for the tribunal informed the court that he had carefully considered the matter with the responsible officers of the Ministry and, as a result, he conceded that the decision of the medical appeal tribunal of June 13, 1956, was erroneous in point of law; he added that the Ministry were in some difficulty because the chairman of the tribunal had died.

Despite that concession, the court of its own motion considered that as the application raised points of considerable importance, judgment should be reserved.

DENNING L.J.: The first point is whether the error of the tribunal appears on the face of the record. It does not appear on the face of their written adjudication of June 13, 1956. There is not a word there about the right eye, or even the left eye for that matter. But the tribunal gave an extract from the specialist's report and thereby, I think, they made that report a part of the record. Just as a pleading is taken to incorporate every document referred to in it, so also does an adjudication. Once the specialist's report is read with the record, we have before us the full facts about the previous injury to the right eye and the subsequent injury to the left. These facts are sufficient to disclose the error in law: for it is then apparent that the award of 20 per cent. must be wrong. No reasonable person, who had proper regard to regulation 2(5), could have come to such a conclusion. It is now settled that when a tribunal come to a conclusion which could not reasonably be entertained by them if they properly understood the relevant enactment, then they fall into error in point of law: see *Edwards (Inspector of Taxes)* v. *Bairstow* [1956] A.C. 14. When the primary facts appear on the record, an error of this kind is sufficiently apparent for it to be regarded as an error on the face of the record such as to warrant the intervention of this court by certiorari.

I may add that, even if we had not been able to have recourse to the specialist's report, we would have been able to get the facts by ordering the tribunal to complete the record by finding the facts, as the regulations require them to. By regulation 13 of the National Insurance (Industrial Injuries) (Determination of Claims and Questions) Regulations 1948, it is enacted that "A tribunal shall in each case record their decision in writing . . . and shall include in such record, . . . a statement of the reasons for their decision, including their findings on all questions of fact material to the decision." It seems to me that the tribunal cannot, by failing to find the material facts, defeat an application for certiorari. The court has alway had power to order an inferior tribunal to complete the record. Abbott C.J. long ago gave very good reasons in this behalf. He said: "If an inferior court . . . send up an incomplete record, we may order them to complete it . . . If we are not to order, or allow the officers of the court below to make a perfect record, which unquestionably they are at liberty to do, it will be in their power, by making an imperfect record, to defeat a writ of error whenever it shall be brought. The power of doing that lies in their hands, unless we prevent it": see *Williams* v. *Lord Bagot* (1824) 4 Dow. & Ry. 315. Likewise a tribunal could defeat a writ of certiorari unless the courts could order them to complete or correct an imperfect record. So the courts have power to give such an order: see *R.* v. *Warnford* (1825) 5 Dow. & Ry. 489.

The second point is the effect of section 36(3) of the Act of 1946 which provides that "any decision of a claim or question . . . shall be final." Do those words preclude the Court of Queen's Bench from issuing a certiorari to bring up the decision?

This is a question which we did not discuss in *R.* v. *Northumberland Compensation Appeal Tribunal, ex p. Shaw* [1952] 1 K.B. 338, because it did not there arise. It does arise here, and on looking again into the old books I find it very well settled that the remedy by certiorari is never to be taken away by any statute except by the most clear and explicit words. The word "final" is not enough. That only means "without appeal." It does not mean "without recourse to certiorari." It makes the decision final on the facts, but not final on the law. Notwithstanding that the decision is by a statute made "final," certiorari can still issue for excess of jurisdiction or for error of law on the face of the record. . . .

[His Lordship reviewed the authorities.]

In my opinion, therefore, notwithstanding the fact that the statute says that the decision of the medical appeal tribunal is to be final, it is open to this court to issue a certiorari to quash it for error of law on the face of the record. It would seem to follow that a decision of the national insurance and industrial insurance commissioners is also subject to supervision by certiorari (a point left open by the Divisional Court in *R.* v. *National Insurance Commissioner, ex p. Timmis* [1955] 1 Q.B. 139); but they are so well versed in the law and deservedly held in such high regard that it will be rare that they fall into error such as to need correction.

In contrast to the word "final" I would like to say a word about the old statutes which used in express words to take away the remedy by certiorari by saying that the decision of the tribunal "shall not be removed by certiorari." Those statutes were passed chiefly between 1680 and 1848, in the days when the courts used certiorari too freely and quashed decisions for technical defects of form. In stopping this abuse the statutes proved very beneficial, but the court never allowed those statutes to be used as a cover for wrongdoing by tribunals. If tribunals were to be at liberty to exceed their jurisdiction without any check by the courts, the rule of law would be at an end. Despite express words taking away certiorari, therefore, it was held that certiorari would still lie if some of the members of the tribunal were disqualified from acting: see *R.* v. *Cheltenham Commissioners* (1841) 1 Q.B. 467, where Lord Denman C.J. said (*ibid.* at p. 474): "The statute cannot affect our right and duty to see justice executed." So, also, if the tribunal exceeded its jurisdiction: see *ex p. Bradlaugh* (1878) 3 Q.B.D. 509; or if its decision was obtained by fraud: see *R.* v. *Gillyard* (1848) 12 Q.B. 527, the courts would still grant certiorari. I do not pause to consider those cases further; for I am glad to notice that modern statutes never take away in express words the right to certiorari without substituting an analogous remedy. This is probably because the courts no longer use it to quash for technical defects but only in case of a substantial miscarriage of justice. Parliament nowadays more often uses the words "final" or "final and conclusive," or some such words which leave intact the control of the Queen's courts by certiorari.

The value of this ancient writ of certiorari is well shown by the present case in which it is only by reason of it that a workman blinded at work obtains the industrial insurance benefit to which he is by law entitled, as now acknowledged on all hands. The order must issue to quash the declaration of the medical appeal tribunal of June 13, 1956. There is no need for a mandamus because the tribunal will no doubt consider the claim afresh and come to a right decision on it.

ROMER and PARKER L.JJ. delivered concurring judgments.

Notes

1. *Ex p. Gilmore* considers both "finality" and "no certiorari" clauses. As to the former, it has been held that it would not even prevent an appeal by case stated on a question that might otherwise be resolved by certiorari or a declaration (*Tehrani* v. *Rostron* [1972] 1 Q.B. 182). In *Pearlman* v. *Keepers and Governors of Harrow School* [1979] Q.B. 56, Lord Denning M.R. at p. 71 stated *obiter* that a finality clause would only exclude an appeal on the facts and not on a point of law. Eveleigh L.J. was inclined to agree on this point (p. 79). Geoffrey Lane L.J. disagreed (p. 74) and his view was subsequently endorsed by Lord Diplock and Lord Keith in *Re Racal Communications Ltd.* [1981] A.C. 374, 382. The House of Lords held in that case that a provision that a decision of a High Court judge shall not be appealable meant exactly that: see pp. 254–260. On "no certiorari" clauses see further the *Pearlman* case, above p. 258. Lord Denning M.R. held at p. 69 that the "no certiorari" clause (County Courts Act 1959, s.107) only applied to proceedings under the 1959 Act, *Pearlman* arising under the Housing Act 1974. Both Geoffrey Lane L.J. and Eveleigh L.J. treated the clause as applicable.

2. A "finality" clause may help a court decide that no duty of care in negligence is owed: see *Jones* v. *Department of Employment* [1989] Q.B. 1, above, p. 810.

3. "Conclusive evidence" clauses were considered by the Court of Appeal in *R.* v. *Registrar of Companies, ex p. Central Bank of India* [1986] Q.B. 1114. The Registrar of Companies registered a charge under section 95(1) of the Companies Act 1948. The Court of Appeal held, on an application for judicial review, that the registrar, in deciding to register the charge in default of delivery of the original documents by which the charge was created or evidenced, had erred in law. However, section 98(2) of the 1948 Act provided that the registrar's certificate:

> "shall be conclusive evidence that the requirements of this Part of this Act as to registration have been complied with."

The court held that this precluded it from considering evidence adduced to show non-compliance with the requirements for registration and, accordingly, from quashing the registration. This form of clause, although in a pre-1958 statute, was not negatived by section 14 of the Tribunals and Inquiries Act 1971 (now section 12 of the 1992 Act, above, p. 78). Lawton L.J. was of the view that the Registrar had acted in excess of jurisdiction; Slade and Dillon L.JJ. that he had made an error of law within jurisdiction. Slade L.J. at pp. 1175–1176 followed Lord Diplock's approach in *Re Racal Communications Ltd.* (above p. 257), concluding that the presumption that administrative authorities, in accordance with *Anisminic*, cannot determine questions of law conclusively was here rebutted in view of s.98(2). His Lordship also noted that counsel for the Registrar accepted that s.98(2) did not bind the Crown, so there was nothing to prevent intervention by the Attorney-General. Moreover, the provisions might not apply where a purported certificate disclosed an error on its face, (*per* Slade L.J. at p. 1177), or was procured by fraud (*per* Lawton L.J. at p. 1169, Dillon L.J. at p. 1183).

Ex p. Central Bank of India was followed in *R.* v. *Secretary of State for Foreign Affairs, ex p. Trawnik, The Times*, February 21, 1986. Section 40(3) of the Crown Proceedings Act 1947 provides that:

> "A certificate of a Secretary of State: (*a*) to the effect that any alleged liability of the Crown arises otherwise than in respect of His Majesty's Government in the United Kingdom . . . shall, for the purposes of this Act, be conclusive as to the matter so certified."

The applicant sought a judicial review of two certificates under s.40(3)(*a*) relating to the possible liability of the Crown in nuisance in respect of the establishment of a machine-gun range in West Berlin. The Court of Appeal held on a preliminary issue that evidence in contradiction of the terms of the certificates was inadmissible. May L.J. said that:

> "As a matter of construction, the words 'shall . . . be conclusive as to the matter so certified' in section 40(3)(*a*) are equivalent to a provision that the certificate shall be conclusive evidence of the matters certified, whether these be questions of fact or law or of mixed fact and law.
>
> Such words do not preclude an application for judicial review of the certificate but such an application if based on the proposition that that which has been certified is so clearly wrong that the certificate must be a nullity, would be bound to fail because the evidence which counsel would wish to call to prove this very thing could not be adduced."

Emery and Smythe, p. 54, argue that this reasoning cannot be reconciled with *Anisminic*.

SMITH v. EAST ELLOE RURAL DISTRICT COUNCIL AND OTHERS

[1956] A.C. 736; [1956] 2 W.L.R. 888; 120 J.P. 263; 100 S.J. 282; [1956] 1 All E.R. 855; 54 L.G.R. 233; 6 P. & C.R. 102 (House of Lords)

[For earlier litigation concerning the dispute between S. and the authorities, see p. 793.]

By paragraph 15(1) of Part IV of Schedule 1 to the Acquisition of Land (Authorisation Procedure) Act 1946: "If any person aggrieved by a compulsory purchase order desires to question the validity thereof . . . on the ground that the authorisation of a compulsory purchase thereby granted is not empowered to be granted under this Act . . . he may, within six weeks from the date on which notice of the confirmation or making of the order . . . is first published . . . make an application to the High Court. . . ."

By paragraph 16: "Subject to the provisions of the last foregoing paragraph, a compulsory purchase order . . . shall not . . . be questioned in any legal proceedings whatsoever. . . ."

On November 29, 1948, the Minister of Health confirmed a compulsory purchase order in respect of 8½ acres of land owned by Kathleen Rose Smith, following a public local inquiry. A notice to treat and a notice of entry were duly served on the appellant, and in due course the compulsory purchase price for the said house and land was fixed by the Lands Tribunal at £3,000. The respondent council caused a firm of builders to demolish the house and to erect on its site and on the said land a number of houses.

On July 6, 1954, the appellant issued a writ, claiming:

1. Against the East Elloe Rural District Council: (a) Damages for trespass to the plaintiff's land; (b) An injunction restraining them by their officers, servants and agents and each and every one of them from trespassing upon the aforesaid land and premises; (c) A declaration that the compulsory purchase order was wrongfully made and in bad faith.
2. Against the Ministry of Health: A declaration that the compulsory purchase order was wrongfully confirmed and in bad faith.
3. Against the respondent J. C. Pywell: A declaration that he knowingly acted wrongfully and in bad faith in procuring the said order and confirmation of the same.
4. Against the Ministry of Housing and Local Government: As having taken over the functions of the [Ministry of Health] a declaration that the said compulsory purchase order and confirmation of the same are in bad faith.
5. Further and other relief.
6. Damages.
7. Costs.

The writ was set aside by Master Clayton on the ground that the court had no jurisdiction to grant the relief sought as the result of paragraph 16 of Part IV of Schedule 1 to the 1946 Act. S. appealed unsuccessfully to Havers J., the Court of Appeal, and the House of Lords.

VISCOUNT SIMONDS: . . . [stated the facts, read section 1(1) and paragraphs 15 and 16 of Part IV of Schedule 1 to the 1946 Act, and referred to a point of construction which was the main argument advanced by the appellant before the Court of Appeal, and which His Lordship shortly rejected.]

In this House a more serious argument was developed. It was that, as the compulsory purchase order was challenged on the ground that it had been made and confirmed "wrongfully" and "in bad faith," paragraph 16 had no application. It was said that that paragraph, however general its language, must be construed so as not to oust the jurisdiction of the court where the good faith of the local authority or the Ministry was impugned and put in issue. Counsel for the appellant made his submission very clear. It was that where the words "compulsory purchase order" occur in these paragraphs they are to be read as if the words "made in good faith" were added to them.

My Lords, I think that anyone bred in the tradition of the law is likely to regard with little sympathy legislative provisions for ousting the jurisdiction of the court, whether in order that the subject may be deprived altogether of remedy or in order that his grievance may be remitted to some other tribunal. But it is our plain duty to give the words of an Act their proper meaning and, for my part, I find it quite impossible to qualify the words of the paragraph in the manner suggested. It may be that the legislature had not in mind the possibility of an order being made by a local authority in bad faith or even the possibility of an order made in good faith being mistakenly, capriciously or wantonly challenged. This is a matter of speculation. What is abundantly clear is that words are used which are wide enough to cover any kind of challenge which any aggrieved person may think fit to make. I cannot think of any wider words. Any addition would be mere tautology. But, it is said, let those general words be given their full scope and effect, yet they are not applicable to an order made in bad faith. But, my Lords, no one can suppose that an order bears upon its face the evidence of bad faith. It cannot be predicated of any order that is has been made in bad faith until it has been tested in legal proceedings, and it is just that test which paragraph 16 bars. How, then, can it be said that any qualification can be introduced to limit the meaning of the words? What else can "compulsory purchase order" mean but an act apparently valid in the law, formally authorized, made, and confirmed?

It was urged by counsel for the appellant that there is a deep-rooted principle that the legislature cannot be assumed to oust the jurisdiction of the court, particularly where fraud is alleged, except by clear words, and a number of cases were cited in which the court has asserted its jurisdiction to examine into an alleged abuse of statutory power and, if necessary, correct it. Reference was made, too, to *Maxwell on the Interpretation of Statutes* to support the view, broadly stated, that a statute is, if possible, so to be construed as to avoid injustice. My Lords, I do not refer in detail to these authorities only because it appears to me that they do not override the first of all principles of construction, that plain words must be given their plain meaning. There is nothing ambiguous about paragraph 16; there is no alternative construction that can be given to it; there is in fact no justification for the introduction of limiting words such as "if made in good faith," and there is the less reason for doing so when those words would have the effect of depriving the express words "in any legal proceedings whatsoever" of their full meaning and content. . . .

[His Lordship thought that the construction of paragraph 16 was not affected by paragraph 15. He did not express a final opinion on paragraph 15, but inclined to the opinion that it covered challenges "on the ground of bad faith or any other ground which would justify the court in setting aside a purported exercise of statutory power."]

I come, then, to the conclusion that the court cannot entertain this action so far as it impugns the validity of the compulsory purchase order, and it is no part of my present duty to attack or defend such a provision of an Act of Parliament. But two things may, I think, fairly be said. First, if the validity of such an order is open to challenge at any time within the period allowed by the ordinary Statute of Limitations with the consequence that it and all that has been done under it over a period of many years may be set aside, it is not perhaps unreasonable that Parliament should have thought fit to impose an absolute bar to proceedings even at the risk of some injustice to individuals. Secondly, the injustice may not be so great as might appear. For the bad faith or fraud upon which an aggrieved person relies is that of individuals, and this very case shows that, even if the validity of the order cannot be questioned and he cannot recover the land that has been taken from him, yet he may have a remedy in damages against those individuals. . . .

Lord Morton of Henryton: My Lords, I think there can be no doubt that the respondents were never entitled to have the writ set aside so far as it claims relief against the respondent Pywell. The relief claimed by paragraph 3 of the writ and the further relief claimed by paragraphs 5, 6 and 7, in so far as that relief affects the respondent Pywell, in no way call in question the validity of the compulsory purchase order of August 26, 1948, or of its confirmation. It is simply alleged, as against Mr. Pywell personally, that he knowingly acted wrongfully and in bad faith in procuring the order and the confirmation thereof. It is equally clear that claims 1, 2 and 4 do put in issue the validity of the order. . . .

Mr. Roy Wilson, for the appellant, puts forward propositions which I summarize as follows: (1) Paragraph 15 gives no opportunity to a person aggrieved to question the validity of a compulsory purchase order on the ground that it was made or confirmed in bad faith. (2) Although, *prima facie*, paragraph 16 excludes the jurisdiction of the court in all cases, subject only to the provision of paragraph 15, it is inconceivable that the legislature can have intended wholly to exclude all courts from hearing and determining an allegation that such an order was made in bad faith. (3) Therefore, paragraph 16 should be read as applying only to an order or a certificate made in good faith. . . . The Attorney-General, on behalf of the respondents, contends that the opportunity of objection given by paragraph 15 extends to cases where bad faith is alleged, but, whether or not this is so, if the person aggrieved fails to apply to the court within the six weeks' period there mentioned, the jurisdiction of the court is completely ousted by paragraph 16, the terms whereof are unambiguous.

My Lords, I accept that Mr. Wilson's first proposition. I cannot construe paragraph 15 as covering a case in which all the requirements expressly laid down by statute have been observed, but the person aggrieved has discovered that in carrying out the steps laid down by statute the authority has been actuated by improper motives. It is to be observed that both in the earlier and in the later part of paragraph 15 there is only one ground upon which the validity of the order can be questioned.... These words seem to me to restrict the complainant to alleging non-compliance with some requirement to be found in the relevant statutes or regulations. If paragraph 15 had been intended to apply to cases of bad faith, surely the restrictive words "on the ground that," etc., would have been left out in both parts....

My Lords, having accepted Mr. Wilson's first proposition, ... I reject his second and third propositions, on the short and simple ground that the words of paragraph 16 are clear, and deprive all courts of any jurisdiction to try the issues raised by paragraphs 1, 2 and 4 of the writ, whereby the appellant undoubtedly seeks to question the validity of the order of August 26, 1948.

Turning first to counsel's second proposition, it does not seem to me inconceivable, though it does seem surprising, that the legislature should have intended to make it impossible for anyone to question in any court the validity of a compulsory purchase order on the ground that it was made in bad faith. It may have been thought that the procedure which has to be followed before such an order is made and confirmed affords sufficient opportunity for allegations of bad faith to be ventilated, and it may have been thought essential, if building schemes were to be carried out, that persons alleging bad faith in the making of an order after the order has been made, should be limited to claims sounding in damages against the persons who, in bad faith, caused or procured the order to be made. The present action started nearly six years after the order now in question was made and confirmed, and illustrates the difficulty which might arise if no such limit were imposed, since houses have already been erected on the land which was the subject of the order....

LORD REID: ... If the words of these paragraphs, [*i.e.* 15 and 16 of Sched. 1] are held to have their ordinary meanings, then an order can never be questioned or attacked in any court on the ground that it has been obtained by corrupt or fraudulent means, no matter how serious the corruption or how wide the conspiracy by which it has been obtained. Admittedly no other tribunal is given jurisdiction to deal with such a case, and the Minister has no power to act if, after he has confirmed an order, it were found that the making of the order had been due to corruption or malice. The only reason suggested for depriving the subject of redress in such a case is administrative convenience, and I find it necessary to examine these paragraphs narrowly to see whether I am forced to reach the conclusion that that must be held to have been the intention of Parliament. . . . [I]n order to determine how far the 1946 Act has limited the jurisdiction of the courts I must see what were the grounds on which the court could give relief under the ordinary law or the 1933 Act. . . . It seems to me that there were four grounds on which the courts could give relief. First, informality of procedure; where, for example, some essential step in procedure had been omitted. Secondly, *ultra vires* in the sense that what was authorized by the order went beyond what was authorized by the Act under which it was made. Thirdly, misuse of power in *bona fide*. And, fourthly, misuse of power in *mala fide*. In the last two classes the order is *intra vires* in the sense that what it authorizes to be done is within the scope of the Act under which it is made, and every essential step in procedure may have been taken: what is challenged is something which lies behind the making of the order. I separate these two classes for this reason. There have been few cases where actual bad faith has even been alleged, but in the numerous cases where misuse of power has been alleged judges have been careful to point out that no question of bad faith was involved and that bad faith stands in a class by itself.

Misuse of power covers a wide variety of cases, and I am relieved from considering at length what amounts to misuse of power is *bona fide* because I agree with the analysis made by Lord Greene M.R. in *Associated Provincial Picture Houses Ltd.* v. *Wednesbury Corporation*. [See above, pp. 395–398].

[His Lordship read the passages from Lord Greene's judgment "The exercise of such a discretion must be a real exercise . . . disregard these irrelevant collateral matters" . . . "a person entrusted . . . to be acting 'unreasonably.' " . . . "It is true to say . . . something overwhelming." . . . "The court is entitled to investigate . . . Parliament has confided in them." . . . and continued:]

None of those cases need involve *mala fides*. A local authority may have had regard to quite irrelevant considerations or may have acted quite unreasonably but yet be entirely innocent of dishonesty or malice.

I can draw no other conclusion from the form in which paragraph 15 is now enacted than that Parliament intended to exclude from the scope of this paragraph the whole class of cases referred to in the passages which I quoted. No doubt in one sense it might be said that in none of these cases is authority "empowered to be granted," but that would be a stained and unnatural reading of these words only to be accepted if there were in the Act some clear indication requiring it. But, to my mind, all the indications are the other way, and this part of the paragraph only refers to cases of *ultra vires* in the narrow sense in which I have used it.

If other cases of misuse of power in *bona fide* are excluded, can a distinction be made where mala fides is in question? As I shall explain when I come to paragraph 16, I am of opinion that cases involving *mala fides* are in a special position in that mere general words will not deprive the court of jurisdiction to deal with them, and, if that is so, then no question would arise under paragraph 15. But, if I am wrong about cases of *mala fides* being in this special position, I do not see how there can be a distinction under paragraph 15 between cases of *bona fide* and *mala fide* misuse of power. I can see nothing to indicate any intention to that effect, and if Parliament intended to treat bad faith as a special case it would be very strange to introduce the exception here. The time limit under paragraph 15 is six weeks, which is appropriate for grounds which appear from the terms of the order but not appropriate for grounds based on facts lying behind the order which may not be discoverable for some time after it is confirmed;...

In my view, the question whether authority is empowered to be granted is intended to be capable of immediate answer: if it can depend on facts lying behind the order, then neither the Minister nor the owner could know for certain at the time of confirmation whether any order is empowered to be granted or not, because facts showing misuse of power might subsequently emerge. Accordingly, in my opinion, the appellant could not have brought her case within paragraph 15, even if she had raised it immediately after the order was confirmed.

I turn to paragraph 16. Not only does it prevent recourse to the court after six weeks in cases to which paragraph 15 does apply, but, on the face of it, it prevents any recourse to the court at all in cases to which paragraph 15 does not apply. It uses words which are general and emphatic, and, to my mind, the question is whether this use of general words necessarily leads to the conclusion that the jurisdiction of the court is entirely excluded in all cases of misuse of powers in *mala fide* where those acting in *mala fide* have been careful to see that the procedure was in order and the authority granted by the order was within the scope of the Act under which it was made. A person deliberately acting in bad faith would naturally be careful to do this. In my judgment, paragraph 16 is clearly intended to exclude, and does exclude entirely, all cases of misuse of power in *bona fide*. But does it also exclude the small minority of cases where deliberate dishonesty, corruption or malice is involved? In every class of case that I can think of the courts have always held that general words are not to be read as enabling a deliberate wrongdoer to take advantage of his own dishonesty. Are the principles of statutory construction so rigid that these general words must be so read here? Of course, if there were any other indications in the statute of such an intention beyond the mere generality of the words that would be conclusive: but I can find none.

There are many cases where general words in a statute are given a limited meaning. That is done, not only when there is something in the statute itself which requires it, but also where to give general words their apparent meaning would lead to conflict with some fundamental principle. Where there is ample scope for the words to operate without any such conflict it may very well be that the draftsman did not have in mind and Parliament did not realize that the words were so wide that in some few cases they could operate to subvert a fundamental principle. . . . So, general words by themselves do not bind the Crown, they are limited so as not to conflict with international law, they are commonly read so as to avoid retrospective infringement of rights, and it appears to me that they can equally well be read so as not to deprive the court of jurisdiction where bad faith is involved. . . . I think that there is still room for reason to point out that the general words in this case must be limited so as to accord with the principle, of which Parliament cannot have been ignorant, that a wrongdoer cannot rely on general words to avoid the consequences of his own dishonesty. As I have said, we must take this case on the footing that the appellant might allege deliberate dishonesty of the grossest kind.

It is said that Parliament may have intended that even cases of gross dishonesty should be excluded from redress because otherwise it would be embarrassing to deal with allegations of this kind after a long interval, and, if the case were proved, a local authority and ultimately the ratepayers might be involved in grievous loss. I am not entirely satisfied that the law is powerless to deal justly with such a situation. But, even if that were a possible consequence, I would hesitate to attribute to Parliament the view that considerations of that kind justify hushing up a scandal.

In my judgment this appeal should be allowed.

LORD RADCLIFFE: . . . It is an abuse of power to exercise it for a purpose different from that for which it is entrusted to the holder, not the less because he may be acting ostensibly for the authorized purpose. Probably most of the recognized grounds of invalidity could be brought under this head: the introduction of illegitimate considerations, the rejection of legitimate ones, manifest unreasonableness, arbitrary or capricious conduct, the motive of personal advantage or the gratification of personal ill-will. However that may be, an exercise of power in bad faith does not seem to me to have any special pre-eminence of its own among the causes that make for invalidity. It is one of several instances of abuse of power, and it may or may not be involved in several of the recognized grounds that I have mentioned. Indeed, I think it plain that the courts have often been content to allow such circumstances, if established, to speak for themselves rather than to press the issue to a finding that the group of persons responsible for the exercise of the power have actually proceeded in bad faith.

It must be assumed that the legislature which enacted the Acquisition of Land (Authorization Procedure) Act 1946, was aware that the law protected persons disturbed by an exercise of statutory powers in that it allowed them to come to the courts to challenge the validity of the exercise on any of such grounds. But, if so, I do not see how it is possible to treat the provisions of paragraphs 15 and 16 of Part IV of Schedule 1 to the Act as enacting anything less than a complete statutory code for regulating the extent to which, and the conditions under which, courts of law might be resorted to for the purpose of questioning the validity of a compulsory purchase order within the protection of the Act. I should myself read the words of paragraph 15(1), "on the ground that the authorization of a compulsory purchase thereby granted is not empowered to be granted under this Act," as covering any case in which the complainant sought to say that the order in question did not carry the statutory authority which it purported to. In other words, I should regard a challenge to the order on the ground that it had not been made in good faith as within the purview of paragraph 15. After all, the point which concerns the aggrieved person is the same in all cases: an order has been made constituting an ostensible exercise of statutory power and his purpose in resorting to the courts is to show that there is no statutory authority behind the order. I do not see any need to pick and choose among the different reasons which may support the plea that the authorization ostensibly granted does not carry the powers of the Act. But, even if I did not think that an order could be questioned under paragraph 15 on the ground that it had been exercised in bad faith, and I thought, therefore, that the statutory code did not allow for an order being questioned on this ground at all, I should still think that paragraph 16 concluded the matter, and that it did not leave to the courts any surviving jurisdiction.

The appellant's argument for an exception rests on certain general reflections which do not seem to me to make up into any legal principle of construction as applied to an Act of Parliament. It is said that the six weeks which are all the grace that, on any view, paragraph 15 allows an aggrieved person for his taking action, are pitifully inadequate as an allowance of time when bad faith, which may involve concealment or deception, is thought to be present. And indeed they are. Further, it is said that it would be an outrageous thing if a person who by ordinary legal principles would have a right to upset an order affecting him were to be precluded from coming to the courts for his right, either absolutely or after six weeks, when the order is claimed by him to have been tainted by bad faith. And perhaps it is. But these reflections seem to me to be such as must or should have occurred to Parliament when it enacted paragraph 16. They are not reflections which are capable of determining the construction of the Act once it has been passed, unless there is something that one can lay hold of in the context of the Act which justifies the introduction of the exception sought for. Merely to say that Parliament cannot be presumed to have intended to bring about a consequence which many people might think to be unjust is not, in my opinion a principle of construction for this purpose. In point of fact, whatever innocence of view may have been allowable to the lawyers of the eighteenth and nineteenth centuries, the twentieth-century lawyer is entitled to few assumptions in this field. It is not open to him to ignore the fact that the legislature has often shown indifference to the assertion of rights which courts of law have been accustomed to recognize and enforce, and that it has often excluded the authority of courts of law in favour of other preferred tribunals.

At one time the argument as shaped into the form of saying that an order made in bad faith was in law a nullity and that, consequently, all references to compulsory purchase orders in paragraphs 15 and 16 must be treated as references to such orders only as had been made in good faith. But this argument is in reality a play on the meaning of the word nullity. An order, even if not made in good faith, is still an act capable of legal consequences. It bears no brand of invalidity upon its forehead. Unless the necessary proceedings are taken at law to establish the cause of invalidity and to get it quashed or otherwise upset, it will remain as effective for its ostensible purpose as the most impeccable of orders. And that brings us back to the question that determines this case: Has Parliament allowed the necessary proceedings to be taken?

I am afraid that I have searched in vain for a principle of construction as applied to Acts of Parliament which would enable the appellant to succeed. On the other hand, it is difficult not to recall in the respondents' favour the dictum of Bacon: "*Non est interpretatio, sed divinatio, quae recedit a litera.*"

LORD SOMERVELL OF HARROW: . . . The words of paragraph 15 are plainly appropriate to *ultra vires* in the ordinary sense. They do not in their ordinary meaning, in my opinion, cover orders which "on the face of it" are proper and within the powers of the Act, but which are challengeable on the ground of bad faith. . . .

This construction is strengthened by the context. The jurisdiction of the court under paragraph 15 is ousted after six weeks. If Parliament had intended that this should apply in the case of a person defrauded it would have made it plain, and not left it to be derived from a doubtful syllogism which would certainly not occur to a layman and would not, I think, occur ordinarily to a lawyer unless he happened to have recently to familiarize himself with passages such as that I have cited from Lord Warrington.

The limited right under paragraph 15, therefore, does not apply to applications based on bad faith. Pausing there, the victim of *mala fides* would have his ordinary right of resort to the courts. It is said, however, that paragraph 16 takes away this right. In other words, Parliament without ever using words which would suggest that fraud was being dealt with has deprived a victim of fraud of all right of resort to the courts, while leaving the victim of a *bona fide* breach of a regulation with such a right. If Parliament has done this it could only be by inadvertence. The two paragraphs fall to be construed together. *Mala fides* being, in my opinion, clearly excluded from paragraph 15, it should not, I think, be regarded as within the general words of paragraph 16. Construing general words as not covering fraud is accepted as right in many contexts. This seems to me an appropriate context for that principle. The Act, having provided machinery for access to the courts in cases of *ultra vires*, cannot have intended to exclude altogether a person defrauded. General words, therefore, should not be construed as affecting such an exclusion.

The respondents sought to rely on the word "whatsoever." It is a word which in certain contexts may bring comfort to those who seek to include fraud under general words. Here it is applied, not to the grounds of challenge, but to the legal proceedings. Orders of this kind may be challenged in various ways, by injunction, by prerogative writ or the procedure now substituted, or, as here, by an ordinary writ. The word "whatsoever" is apt to cover this multiplicity.

It is finally said there might be great inconvenience if after, say, houses had been built the validity could be challenged. There are two grounds which lead me to give little weight to this. First, there is a possibility of fraud in the subsequent proceedings following on a notice to treat. No one suggests there is any ouster or special limitation of jurisdiction in that case. Further, if there is a possibility of bad faith in matters of this kind, I would think it much more inconvenient to the administration, national and local, as a whole that a person defrauded should be deprived of any remedy in the courts. I, therefore, would allow the appeal.

Appeal allowed in part.

Note

1. See J. S. Hall, (1957) 21 Conv. (N.S.) 455; *Smith* v. *Pywell* (1959) *The Times*, April 28.

2. In *Webb* v. *Minister of Housing and Local Government* [1965] 1 W.L.R. 755, Lord Denning M.R. stated (at p. 770) that the differing voices in *Smith* v. *East Elloe R.D.C.* were such that the case offered no clear or binding guidance on the scope of review within six weeks on a statutory application to quash. The courts have subsequently adopted a broad approach: see pp. 622–639.

R. v. SECRETARY OF STATE FOR THE ENVIRONMENT, ex p. OSTLER

[1976] 3 W.L.R. 288; [1977] Q.B. 122; [1976] 3 All E.R. 90; (1976) 75 L.G.R. 45; 120 S.J. 332 (Court of Appeal)

The applicant, a corn merchant with business premises in the market square of Boston, Lincolnshire, applied in December 1975 to the Queen's Bench Divisional Court for leave to apply for an order of certiorari to quash a stopping-up order made under the Highways Act 1959 and a compulsory purchase order made under the Acquisition of Land (Authorisation Procedure) Act 1946. Those orders were made to carry out a road scheme to relieve traffic congestion in the town centre. Both orders had been confirmed by the Secretary of State for the Environment on May 8, 1974. In support of his application he claimed that he had not objected to the original proposals when they were published in 1972 because they appeared not to touch his premises and for that reason had not attended the first public inquiry in September 1973, but that after the orders had been confirmed a supplementary proposed order had been published which would, if carried out, affect his premises; and that he had objected to the supplementary proposals at a further public inquiry in December 1974 but had not been allowed to question the original orders confirmed in May on the ground that they had become final. He alleged that after the supplementary order had been confirmed, it had come to his knowledge that before the 1973 inquiry there had been a secret agreement between an officer of the Department and local wine merchants who were intending to object to the original proposals, guaranteeing that if they were confirmed, the supplementary proposal would be made; that the wine merchants' objections had thereupon been withdrawn; that if he had known of the secret agreement he would have objected before the first proposals were confirmed; and that by reason of his having been deprived of the opportunity to object, the confirmed orders were invalidated by want of natural justice and bad faith verging on fraud.

A preliminary objection was taken on behalf of the Secretary of State that, whatever the facts, any attack on the validity of the confirmed orders was barred in any legal proceedings whatever because the prescribed six-week period under paragraph 2 of Schedule 2 to the Act of 1959 and paragraph 15 of Schedule 1 to the Act of 1946 had expired; that there was binding House of Lords authority (*Smith* v. *East Elloe R.D.C.*, above, p. 871) to that effect on the provisions of the Act of 1946 (which were in terms identical with those of the Act of 1959) and that the application for certiorari should not be permitted to proceed. The Divisional Court, after considering whether speeches in the House of Lords in the *Anisminic* case (above, p. 237) had undermined the earlier authority, adjourned the application to go into the merits but later granted the Secretary of State leave to appeal on the preliminary point of law.

LORD DENNING M.R.: . . . Now it is quite clear that if Mr. Ostler had come within six weeks, his complaint could and would have been considered by the court. . . .

[His Lordship read paragraph 2 of Schedule 2 to the 1959 Act.]

That is a familiar clause which appears in many statutes or schedules to them. Although the words appear to restrict the clause to cases of *ultra vires* or non-compliance with regulations, nevertheless the courts have interpreted them so as to cover cases of bad faith. On this point the view of Lord Radcliffe has been accepted (which he expressed in *Smith* v. *East Elloe Rural District Council* [1956] A.C. 736, 769). In addition this court has held that under this clause a person aggrieved—who comes within six weeks—can upset a scheme or order if the Minister has taken into account considerations which he ought not to have done, or has failed to take into account considerations which he ought to have done, or has come to his decision without any evidence to support it, or has made a decision which no reasonable person could make. It was so held in *Ashbridge Investments Ltd.* v. *Minister of Housing and Local Government* [1965] 1 W.L.R. 1320, and the Minister did not dispute it. It has been repeatedly followed in this court ever since and never disputed by any Minister. So it is the accepted interpretation. But the person aggrieved must come within six weeks. That time limit has always been applied. . . .

[His Lordship then read paragraph 4.]

So those are the strong words, "shall not . . . be questioned in any legal proceedings whatever. . . ."

[His Lordship summarised *Smith* v. *East Elloe R.D.C.*, and the *Anisminic* case.]

Some of their Lordships seem to have thrown doubt on *Smith* v. *East*

Elloe Rural District Council [1956] A.C. 736: see what Lord Reid said at [1969] 2 A.C. 147, 170–171. But others thought it could be explained on the ground on which Browne J. explained it. Lord Pearce said, at p. 201: "I agree with Browne J. that it is not a compelling authority in the present case"; and Lord Wilberforce said, at p. 208: "After the admirable analysis of the authorities made by Browne J. . . . no elaborate discussion of authority is needed."

I turn therefore to the judgment of Browne J. His judgment is appended as a note to the case at p. 223 *et seq*. He put *Smith* v. *East Elloe Rural District Council*, at p. 224, as one of the "cases in which the inferior tribunal has been guilty of bias, or has acted in bad faith, or has disregarded the principles of natural justice." He said of those cases:

> "It is not necessary to decide it for the purposes of this case, but I am inclined to think that such decisions are not nullities but are good until quashed (*cf.* the decision of the majority of the House of Lords in *Smith* v. *East Elloe Rural District Council* [1956] A.C. 736, that a decision made in bad faith cannot be challenged on the ground that it was made beyond powers and Lord Radcliffe's dissenting speech . . .)."

In these circumstances, I think that *Smith* v. *East Elloe Rural District Council* must still be regarded as good and binding on this court. It is readily to be distinguished from the *Anisminic* case [1969] 2 A.C. 147. The points of difference are these:

First, in the *Anisminic* case the Act ousted the jurisdiction of the court altogether. It precluded the court from entertaining any complaint at any time about the determination. Whereas in the *East Elloe* case the statutory provision has given the court jurisdiction to inquire into complaints so long as the applicant comes within six weeks. The provision is more in the nature of a limitation period than of a complete ouster. That distinction is drawn by Professor Wade, *Administrative Law*, 2nd ed. (1967), pp. 152–153, and by the late Professor S. A. de Smith in the latest edition of *Halsbury's Laws of England*, 4th ed., vol. 1 (1973), para. 22, note 14.

Second, in the *Anisminic* case, the House was considering a determination by a truly judicial body, the Foreign Compensation Tribunal, whereas in the *East Elloe* case the House was considering an order which was very much in the nature of an administrative decision. That is a distinction which Lord Reid himself drew in *Ridge* v. *Baldwin* [1964] A.C. 40, 72. There is a great difference between the two. In making a judicial decision, the tribunal considers the rights of the parties without regard to the public interest. But in an administrative decision (such as a compulsory purchase order) the public interest plays an important part. The question is, to what extent are private interests to be subordinated to the public interest.

Third, in the *Anisminic* case, the House had to consider the actual determination of the tribunal, whereas in the *Smith* v. *East Elloe* case the

House had to consider the validity of the process by which the decision was reached.

So *Smith* v. *East Elloe Rural District Council* [1956] A.C. 736 must still be regarded as the law in regard to this provision we have to consider here. I would add this: if this order were to be upset for want of good faith or for lack of natural justice, it would not to my mind be a nullity or void from the beginning. It would only be voidable. And as such, if it should be challenged promptly before much has been done under it, as Lord Radcliffe put it forcibly in *Smith* v. *East Elloe Rural District Council* [1956] A.C. 736, 769–770.

[His Lordship read the passage: "But this argument is in reality a play on the meaning of the word nullity.... Has Parliament allowed the necessary proceedings to be taken?"]

The answer which he gave was "No." That answer binds us in this court today.

Since the *Anisminic* case the court has considered the position in *Routh* v. *Reading Corporation*, December 2, 1970, Bar Library Transcript No. 472 of 1970. Salmon L.J., supported by Karminski and Cairns L.JJ., held that *Smith* v. *East Elloe Rural District Council* was of good authority, even after the *Anisminic* case. In Scotland, too, it has been applied, in *Hamilton* v. *Secretary of State for Scotland*, 1972 S.L.T. 233.

Looking at it broadly, it seems to me that the policy underlying the statute is that when a compulsory purchase order has been made, then if it has been wrongly obtained or made, a person aggrieved should have a remedy. But he must come promptly. He must come within six weeks. If he does so, the court can and will entertain his complaint. But if the six weeks expire without any application being made, the court cannot entertain it afterwards. The reason is because, as soon as that time has elapsed, the authority will take steps to acquire property, demolish it and so forth. The public interest demands that they should be safe in doing so. Take this very case. The inquiry was held in 1973. The orders made early in 1974. Much work has already been done under them. It would be contrary to the public interest that the demolition should be held up or delayed by further evidence or inquiries. I think we are bound by *Smith* v. *East Elloe Rural District Council* [1956] A.C. 736 to hold that Mr. Ostler is barred by the statute from now questioning these orders. He ought to be stopped at this moment. I would allow the appeal accordingly.

GOFF L.J.: ... In my judgment, in *Smith* v. *East Elloe Rural District Council* the majority did definitely decide that those statutory provisions preclude the order from being challenged after the statutory period allowed, then by paragraph 15, and now by paragraph 2, and we are bound by that unless *Anisminic Ltd.* v. *Foreign Compensation Commission* [1969] 2 A.C. 147 has to cut across it that we are relieved from the duty of following *Smith* v. *East Elloe Rural District Council* and, indeed, bound not to follow it.

That raises a number of problems. With all respect to Lord Denning M.R. and Professor Wade, I do myself find difficulty in distinguishing *Anisminic* on the ground that in that case there was an absolute prohibition against recourse to the court, whereas in the present case there is a qualified power for a limited period, because the majority in the *Smith* case said either that fraud did not come within paragraph 15, so that, in effect, it was an absolute ouster, or that it made no difference to the construction if it did.

Nevertheless, it seems to me that the *Anisminic* case is distinguishable on two grounds. First, the suggestion made by Lord Pearce [1969] 2 A.C. 147, 201, that *Anisminic* dealt with a judicial decision, and an administrative or executive decision might be different. I think it is. It is true that the Minister has been said to be acting in a quasi judicial capacity, but he is nevertheless conducting an administrative or executive matter, where questions of policy enter into and must influence his decision.

I would refer in support of that to a passage from the speech of Lord Reid in the well-known case of *Ridge* v. *Baldwin* [1964] A.C. 40, 72. I need not read it. It sets out what I have been saying.

Where one is dealing with a matter of that character and where, as Lord Denning M.R. has pointed out, the order is one which must be acted upon promptly, it is, I think, easier for the courts to construe Parliament as meaning exactly what it said—that the matter cannot be questioned in any court, subject to the right given by paragraph 2, where applicable, and where application is made in due time—than where, as in *Anisminic*, one is dealing with a statute setting up a judicial tribunal and defining its powers and the question is whether it has acted within them. I think that is supported by the passage in the speech of Lord Reid in the *Anisminic* case [1969] 2 A.C. 147, 170, where he said:

> "But I do not think that it is necessary or even reasonable to construe the word 'determination' as including everything which purports to be a determination but which is in fact no determination at all."

The second ground of distinction is that the ratio in the *Anisminic* case was that the House was dealing simply with a question of jurisdiction, and not a case where the order is made within jurisdiction, but it is attacked on the ground of fraud or *mala fides*. There are, I am fully conscious, difficulties in the way of that distinction, because Lord Somervell of Harrow in *Smith* v. *East Elloe Rural District Council* [1956] A.C. 736, 771, in his dissenting speech, said that fraud does not make the order voidable but a nullity. Lord Reid said the same in the *Anisminic* case [1969] 2 A.C. 147, 170; and at p. 199 Lord Pearce equated want of natural justice with lack of jurisdiction.

Nevertheless, despite those difficulties, I think there is a real distinction between the case with which the House was dealing in *Anisminic* and the case of *Smith* v. *East Elloe Rural District Council* on that ground, that in the one case the determination was a purported determination only, because the tribunal, however eminent, having misconceived the effect of the statute, acted outside its jurisdiction, and indeed without any jurisdiction at all, whereas here one is dealing with an actual decision made within jurisdiction though sought to be challenged.

It cannot be gainsaid that some of the speeches in *Anisminic* do appear to cast doubts upon the correctness of the decision in *Smith* v. *East Elloe Rural District Council*, but it certainly was not expressly overruled, nor did any of their lordships, as I see it, say that it was wrong. There are substantial differences, such as Lord Denning M.R. and I have indicated, between the two cases, and it seems to me that *Smith* v. *East Elloe Rural District Council* stands, is binding on this court, and is a decision directly in point. . . .

SHAW L.J. agreed with the reasons given by Lord Denning M.R.

Appeal allowed.

Notes

1. The House of Lords refused leave to appeal: [1977] 1 W.L.R. 258.

2. For discussions of the relationship between *Smith* v. *East Elloe R.D.C.* and the *Anisminic* case written before *Ostler* was decided, see K. Davies, (1971) 35 Conv. (N.S.) 316; J. E. Trice, [1973] J.P.L. 227; E. Young, [1973] J.P.L. 221; J. Alder, (1975) 38 M.L.R. 274.

3. For case notes on *Ostler*, see H. W. R. W[ade], (1977) 93 L.Q.R. 8; C. A. Whomersley, [1977] C.L.J. 4; J. Alder, [1976] J.P.L. 270; C. Harlow, [1976] P.L. 304. For a more extended discussion see the debate between Alder and Gravells: J. E. Alder, (1975) 38 M.L.R. 274 and (1980) 43 M.L.R. 670; N. P. Gravells, (1978) 41 M.L.R. 383 and (1980) 43 M.L.R. 173. Alder argues that *Anisminic* and *Smith* v. *East Elloe R.D.C.* can be reconciled by a process of conceptual reasoning; Gravells that the *Anisminic* principle, "formulated in an entirely different factual context," could have no relevance to the treatment of time limit clauses. See also L. H. Leigh, "Time Limit Clauses and Jurisdictional Error" [1980] P.L. 34.

4. *Anisminic* is the leading example of a case where a "shall not be questioned clause" has been held not to prevent judicial review of an *ultra vires* decision. Others include *Att.-Gen.* v. *Ryan* [1980] A.C. 718, where the Privy Council held that a minister's refusal of an application for citizenship without a fair hearing could be challenged notwithstanding a provision that such a decision "shall not be subject to appeal or review in any court." *Cf. South East Asia Fire Bricks Sdn. Bhd.* v. *Non-Metallic Mineral Products Manufacturing Employees Union* [1981] A.C. 363, where the company sought certiorari to quash a decision of the Malaysian Industrial Court that favoured the union for an error of law on the face of the record. The Privy Council held that this remedy was barred by a provision that read:

> "Subject to this Act, an award of the Court shall be final and conclusive, and no award shall be challenged, appealed against, reviewed, quashed or called in question in any court of law."

Lord Fraser of Tullybelton stated that this result was achieved not by the finality clause (following *ex p. Gilmore*, above, p. 866), but by the provision that the award should not be "quashed" either alone or in conjunction with the words "shall not be questioned in any court of law." The error alleged here was an error of law within jurisdiction, the Privy Council rejecting the view that all errors of law went to jurisdiction (see above, p. 260). (If that view were to be accepted, little if any effect is left to a "shall not be questioned clause":

> "... [I]f every error is now to be jurisdictional, ouster clauses will have no sphere of operation at all, and the judicial attitude will be exposed as one of naked disobedience to Parliament." (H.W.R. W[ade], (1979) 95 L.Q.R. 163, 166.))

5. *Ex p. Ostler* was applied by Pill J. in *R.* v. *Secretary of State for the Environment, ex p. Kent* (1988) 57 P. & C.R. 431, where the applicant applied on February 11, 1988, for judicial review of the decision of a planning inspector dated November 12, 1987, allowing an appeal against a refusal of planning permission. His Lordship rejected an argument to the effect that the six-week time limit did not apply as the Secretary of State had not had jurisdiction to entertain the appeal under section 245 of the Town and Country Planning Act 1971 as the local authority's procedure of consultation had been flawed. An appeal to the Court of Appeal was dismissed: [1990] J.P.L. 124. Here, the applicant did not find out until after the six-week period that an application for planning permission had been made in respect of land near his home or had subsequently gone on appeal to the Secretary of State.

Ex p. Ostler was also applied in *Khan* v. *Newport Borough Council* [1991] C.O.D. 157, in respect of a tree preservation order. Staughton L.J. commented that it was not at first sight obvious why any short time limits should be necessary in the case of such an order, as opposed to a compulsory purchase order as in *ex p. Ostler*. Then, in *R.* v. *Cornwall County Council, ex p. Huntingdon, The Times*, March 5, 1992, the Divisional Court applied *ex p. Ostler* in rejecting an application for judicial review of an order under the Wildlife and Countryside Act 1981, s.53(2)(*b*). The court rejected an argument that the order here was "fundamentally invalid" whereas the orders in *Smith* v. *East Elloe R.D.C.* and *ex p. Ostler* were not; Mann L.J. expressed the view that there were no "degrees of invalidity."

6. Lord Denning writing extra-judicially recanted most of his arguments in *ex p. Ostler*, accepting that a breach of natural justice or bad faith renders a decision a nullity, and expressing the view that the decisions should rest simply on the last paragraph of his judgment (*The Discipline of Law* (1979), pp. 108–109).

7. The Interception of Communications Act 1985, s.7(8), provides that the decisions of the tribunal set up under that Act to investigate complaints concerning interception of mail or telephone-tapping, "(including any decisions as to their jurisdiction) shall not be subject to appeal or liable to be questioned in any court." A similar provision appears in the Security Service Act 1989, s.5(4), in respect of decisions of the Security Service Commissioner and Tribunal.

Questions

1. Has *Smith* v. *East Elloe R.D.C.* been overruled by *Anisminic* or can it be distinguished as suggested by *Ostler*?

2. Is the distinction made in *Ostler* between "administrative" decisions (*East Elloe*) and "judicial ones" (*Anisminic*) supportable in view, *inter alia*, such decisions as *R.* v. *Liverpool Corporation* (p. 502)?

3. Why should a decision made on the basis of irrelevant considerations of personal animosity be protected because it may also have been influenced by policy considerations and can be called an "administrative" decision?

4. Is it possible to draft an exclusion clause that effectively excludes the jurisdiction of the courts to review a decision of an administrative agency in *all* circumstances? Consider the provisions summarised in n. 7, *supra*.

CHAPTER 16

DELEGATED LEGISLATION

"Parliament and government would grind to a halt if there were not built into our constitution an adequate system of Executive legislation" (First Special Report from the Joint Committee on Statutory Instruments, 1977–78 (1977–78 H.C. 169), para. 37). In the early part of this century there was considerable debate about the constitutional propriety of the delegation by Parliament, particularly to the government, of powers to legislate. The Committee on Ministers' Powers (Cmd. 4060, 1932) concluded (p. 58) that the delegation of legislative powers:

> "is legitimate for certain purposes, within certain limits, and under certain safeguards. It is plain that it is in fact inevitable."

Various reasons were put forward for this conclusion (below, p. 888). The committee noted a number of criticisms of delegated legislation that had been voiced, but did not think that the evidence justified "an alarmist view of the constitutional situation" (p. 54). What was lacking was coherence and uniformity in operation. There were "real dangers incidental to delegated legislation" and "safeguards" were necessary. The Committee recommended that the existing Rules Publication Act 1893, which required certain categories of delegated legislation to be published, should be replaced by a more comprehensive measure. The many different forms in which an enabling statute might require delegated legislation to be laid before Parliament should be replaced by a standardised procedure. These two matters were addressed by the Statutory Instruments Act 1946 (below, p. 895). It was also recommended that each House of Parliament should set up a Standing Committee for the purpose of considering and reporting (a) on every Bill containing a proposal to confer law-making power on a Minister; and (b) on delegated legislation that was subject to a laying requirement. The House of Commons acted on recommendation (b) in 1944. The House of Lords continued to scrutinise delegated legislation that required the approval of the House under arrangements that had commenced in 1925. Following the recommendations of the Joint Committee on Delegated Legislation (The Brooke Committee Report, 1971–72 H.L. 184, H.C. 475), these separate arrangements were replaced by a Joint Committee on Statutory Instruments (below, pp. 908–911).

(A) THE NECESSITY FOR DELEGATION

REPORT OF THE COMMITTEE ON MINISTERS' POWERS

(Cmd. 4060) pp. 51–52

Necessity for Delegation

11. We have already expressed the view that the system of delegated legislation is both legitimate and constitutionally desirable for certain

purposes, within certain limits, and under certain safeguards. We proceed to set out briefly—mostly by way of recapitulation—the reasons which have led us to this conclusion:—

Pressure on Parliamentary time

(1) Pressure upon Parliamentary time is great. the more procedure and subordinate matters can be withdrawn from detailed Parliamentary discussion, the greater will be the time which Parliament can devote to the consideration of essential principles in legislation.

Technicality of subject matter

(2) The subject matter of modern legislation is very often of a technical nature. Apart from the broad principles involved, technical matters are difficult to include in a Bill, since they cannot be effectively discussed in Parliament. . . .

Unforeseen contingencies

(3) If large and complex schemes of reform are to be given technical shape, it is difficult to work out the administrative machinery in time to insert in the Bill all the provisions required; it is impossible to foresee all the contingencies and local conditions for which provision must eventually be made. . . .

Flexibility

(4) The practice, further, is valuable because it provides for a power of constant adaptation to unknown future conditions without the necessity of amending legislation. Flexibility is essential. The method of delegated legislation permits of the rapid utilisation of experience, and enables the results of consultation with interests affected by the operation of new Acts to be translated into practice. In matters, for example, like mechanical road transport, where technical development is rapid, and often unforeseen, delegation is essential to meet the new positions which arise.

Opportunity for experiment

(5) The practice, again, permits of experiment being made and thus affords an opportunity, otherwise difficult to ensure, of utilising the lessons of experience. The advantage of this in matters, for instance, like town planning, is too obvious to require detailed emphasis.

Emergency Powers

(6) In a modern State there are many occasions when there is a sudden need of legislative action. For many such needs delegated legislation is

the only convenient or even possible remedy. No doubt, where there is time, on legislative issues of great magnitude, it is right that Parliament itself should either decide what the broad outlines of the legislation shall be, or at least indicate the general scope of the delegated powers which it considers are called for by the occasion.

Note

One of the members of the Committee, Miss Ellen Wilkinson added a note (pp. 137–138) which commenced:

> "While agreeing generally with this report I would like to add a note regarding the tone of certain passages which rather give the impression that the delegating of legislation is a necessary evil, inevitable in the present state of pressure on parliamentary time, but nevertheless a tendency to be watched with misgiving and carefully safeguarded.
>
> I feel that in the conditions of the modern state, which not only has to undertake immense new social services, but which before long may be responsible for the greater part of the industrial and commercial activities of the country, the practice of Parliament delegating legislation and the power to make regulations, instead of being grudgingly conceded, ought to be widely extended, and new ways devised to facilitate the process."

She went on to argue that Parliament could only deal really effectively with the principle and general plan of proposed legislation. "The details should be left to the experts." In practice, the distinction between "principle" (for primary legislation) and "detail" (for delegated legislation) can be difficult to draw. (See, *e.g.* J. A. G. Griffith, "The Place of Parliament in the Legislative Process" (1951) 14 M.L.R. 279, 425). In recent years the Joint Committee on Statutory Instruments (see below, pp. 908–911) has expressed concern:

SPECIAL REPORT FROM THE JOINT COMMITTEE ON STATUTORY INSTRUMENTS 1985–86

Report on Proceedings 1981–86 (1985–86 H.L. 216, HC. 31–xxxvii) p. 2

General Aspects of Secondary Legislation

2. Since [1982], there have been several significant developments in the field of secondary legislation. While the number of statutory instruments in each session has not increased unduly, their volume and complexity have done so. The character of some secondary legislation has also continued to change. The Committee's concern at the nature of the change was expressed in a letter sent by the Chairman of the Committee to the Leaders of both Houses in February 1986 of which the following is an extract:

> "Since the establishment of this Committee in 1973, secondary legislation has increased not only in volume, but in scope. Instead of simply implementing the "nuts and bolts" of Government policy, statutory

instruments have increasingly been used to change policy, sometimes in ways that were not envisaged when the enabling primary legislation was passed. In view of the volume and complexity of much modern legislation and the difficulty of finding time for its preparation and consideration by Parliament, we accept that this trend is not one which it will necessarily be easy to reverse. We feel strongly, however, that the procedures for scrutinising secondary legislation should, like all other Parliamentary procedures, evolve to take account of historic change."

3. The Chairman subsequently wrote to the Chairman of the House of Commons Procedure Committee in similar terms, proposing that that Committee should undertake an enquiry into some of the issues involved. He also gave evidence to the Procedure Committee during their enquiry into the use of time on the floor of the House [HC (1985–86) 257–i]. What fruits will be borne by these various representations remains to be seen.

(B) The Forms of Delegated Legislation

REPORT FROM THE JOINT COMMITTEE ON DELEGATED LEGISLATION 1971–72

(1971–72 H.L. 184, H.C. 475). pp. x–xii

Delegated legislation:

6. In his memorandum of evidence to Your Committee, Counsel to Mr. Speaker (Sir Robert Speed) has defined delegated legislation thus:—

(1) Delegated legislation covers every exercise of a power to legislate conferred by or under an Act of Parliament or which is given the force of law by virtue of an Act of Parliament. It can be expressed in a variety of forms:—

(*a*) Measures passed by the General Synod of the Church of England.

(*b*) Provisional orders confirmed by a Provisional Order Confirmation Act, including those made under the Private Legislation Procedure (Scotland) Act, 1936.

(*c*) Orders in Council and regulations, orders, rules, schemes or other instruments made by a Minister or Government Department or Rule Committee or similar authority.

(*d*) Orders, bye-laws or other instruments, made by public or local authorities (in some cases confirmed by the Privy Council, a Minister or a Government Department).

(2) In some cases the power to legislate may be conferred by legislation which is itself a piece of delegated legislation, *e.g.* an Order in Council.

(3) The documents by which a power of delegated legislation is exercised are, in the main, statutory instruments.

(4) The definition of statutory instruments varies according to whether the Act under which the instrument is made was passed before or after January 1, 1948, the date on which the Statutory Instruments Act 1946 [below, pp. 895–899] was brought into operation.

(5) In regard to post-1947 Acts, under section 1(1) of the Statutory Instruments Act 1946 every Order in Council made in exercise of a statutory power is a statutory instrument, and every instrument made by a Minister of the Crown in exercise of a statutory power is a statutory instrument if the Act conferring the power expressly so provides.

(6) As regards pre-1948 Acts, broadly speaking, every instrument made under an Act of Parliament—

(i) by Her Majesty in Council, or
(ii) by a Minister of the Crown, or
(iii) relating to any court in the United Kingdom,

is a statutory instrument if it is of a legislative and not an executive character.

(7) Measures are not statutory instruments, although in some cases the Measure does apply the Statutory Instruments Act 1946 to the subordinate legislation made thereunder. Also, as a general rule, the instruments referred to in category 1(*d*) above are not statutory instruments.

(8) Statutory instruments are classified as local or general according to their subject matter. Unless there are special reasons to the contrary, a statutory instrument which is in the nature of a local and personal or private Act is classified as local, and a statutory instrument which is in the nature of a public general Act is classified as general.

(9) The classification is done in the first place by the Minister responsible for the preparation of the Order in Council or the Minister by whom the instrument is made. He, when sending the instrument to the Queen's Printer, certifies it as local or general.

(10) There is a procedure under which a Committee composed of Officers of both Houses, called the Statutory Instruments Reference Committee, may determine any question referred to them regarding the classification of instruments as general or local. About 2,000 statutory instruments nowadays are registered each year, approximately half being general and half local.

Notes

1. A number of significant categories of subordinate legislation are not "statutory instruments." These include (1) the bye-laws of local authorities, made under powers conferred by the Local Government Act 1972 and other statutes (see *Cross*, Ch. 6) and below, pp. 912–918; (2) special procedure orders (see S. H. Bailey and M. J. Gunn, *Smith and Bailey on the Modern English Legal System* (2nd ed., 1991), p. 248); Orders in Council made under the royal prerogative (*ibid.* p. 269).

2. Between 1954 and 1983 the total number of statutory instruments made each year varied between 1,641 (1966) and 2,877 (1962). In 23 of the years, the annual total was between 1,900 and 2,400. (61 H.C. Deb., June 6, 1984, cols. 166–167, written answer). It has been noted that while the numbers of instruments remain reasonably constant, they have increased in length, complexity and scope (see above, pp. 889–890).

(C) The Preparation of Delegated Legislation

REPORT OF THE JOINT COMMITTEE ON DELEGATED LEGISLATION 1971–72

(1971–72 H.L. 184, H.C. 475) pp. 194 ff

Memorandum by the Civil Service Department on Departmental Procedures in Producing Delegated Legislation

ANNEX D

MACHINERY FOR THE PRODUCTION OF DELEGATED LEGISLATION

Note by the Department of the Environment

1. The Secretary of State is the initiating or confirming authority for a wide range of orders, regulations, rules and bye-laws. The instruments made or confirmed in the Department vary from those which are delegated legislation in the fullest sense of the expression to orders which apply to small localities, are not subject to any form of Parliamentary procedure or scrutiny and are made in a well-precedented form. No single procedure would be suitable for the preparation of all these instruments. It is proposed therefore to describe the procedure normally followed in the case of a statutory instrument of general application which is laid before Parliament.

2. The decisions whether and how to exercise the enabling power are ones of policy. In some cases the terms of the enabling legislation require the instrument to be made, or to be made at regular intervals, so that no initial decision to exercise the power is necessary. These policy decisions are taken at a high level in the Department, after full consideration of the policy issues.

3. In some cases the enabling Act prescribes consultation with specified bodies before an instrument is made. In all cases there is full consultation

with interests affected. This is done either on the basis of a memorandum of proposals for inclusion in the instrument, or on the basis of a draft of the instrument, or sometimes both.

4. The instrument is drafted by a barrister or solicitor in the Department's Legal Branch. The Legal Branch is sub-divided into sections each under an Assistant Solicitor and these sections correspond broadly to the administrative directorates. All lawyers in the Branch (subject to experience) are expected to draft subordinate legislation as the need arises. Consequently instruments are normally drafted by a lawyer who advises on the functions concerned and is familiar with the legislative and case-law background to the subject matter of the instrument.

5. The administrator dealing with the exercise of the power will instruct his legal counter-part as to the content of the proposed instrument. The draftsman's first task is to verify that any conditions precedent to the exercise of the power have been fulfilled (or will be by the time the instrument is made), the procedure to which the order is subject and that the Department's proposals are *intra vires* the enabling legislation. Before preparing a first draft he may have to have meetings with the administrators and other persons involved (such as other professional and technical Departmental advisers) in order to deal with the questions arising out of the instructions. At all stages close liaison between administrators and draftsman is maintained.

6. To help him in the preparation of the instrument, the draftsman will have the Handbook on Statutory Instrument Procedure published by the Statutory Publications Office as this is issued to every lawyer on joining the Branch. The reports of the Select Committee on Statutory Instruments are circulated in the Legal Branch and copies are readily available for inspection. On occasion the special attention of all members of the Branch is drawn to particular points raised by the Committee. One of the Assistant Solicitors acts as liaison officer between the Department and the Committee and he is always available for consultation by the draftsman of an instrument. All lawyers in the Branch work as the need arises on the preparation of legislation, and in the case of an instrument of difficulty or importance the draftsman will generally have worked on Bills and so have had close connection with drafting by Parliamentary Counsel.

7. The Department's lawyers (with the exception of those engaged on litigation) all work in one building, in close proximity to one another. This enables a great deal of informal consultation to take place and a draftsman, if he encounters difficulties, has easy access to other lawyers who may be able to help him with the benefit of greater experience. Advice, particularly on questions of *vires*, may be taken from outside the Department. It is always open to the Department to consult the Law Officers or to obtain an Opinion from the appropriate standing Junior Counsel. Parliamentary Counsel are also most helpful if in special circumstances they are consulted.

8. When a satisfactory draft of an instrument has been prepared copies

(often with an explanatory document) will be circulated for comment to persons in the Department and any other Departments who might be expected to have an interest in the content of the instrument and sometimes to outside organisations too. It is normally the administrator dealing with the instrument who circulates copies and obtains comments. The draft instrument is reconsidered in the light of any comments received. When the draft is thought to be sufficiently firm it will be put to the appropriate Minister by a senior administrator with a comprehensive submission explaining its content and background and drawing attention to the main points which have arisen in the consultations. Previous to this, however, the Minister concerned may well have been consulted either generally or on individual points that have arisen in the course of the preparation of the instrument.

9. Once Ministerial clearance has been obtained the way is clear for the instrument to be made. Printed copies are obtained from the Stationery Office by one of the non-professional staff of the Legal Branch who deal particularly with statutory instrument procedures and arrangements for the laying of instruments before Parliament. The head of the non-professional section works direct to the Legal Adviser. The section maintains close liaison with the Stationery Office and the Editor of Statutory Instruments. This section submits the instrument to the appropriate Minister, usually the Secretary of State, for signature, together with a brief supplied by the administrator concerned; in the case of instruments requiring additional Ministerial signatures from outside the Department, the section sees that these are obtained.

10. The instrument having been made it is sent for printing, the date of laying have been agreed in advance with the Stationery Office. When the instrument is laid, the requisite forms are completed and copies of the instrument, with all relevant documents, are passed to the Parliamentary Clerk for presentation to Parliament and to the Select Committee on Statutory Instruments.

11. Time is often of the essence in the making of an instrument and the procedures set out above have, on occasions, to be telescoped in order to comply with a very tight timetable. Close personal contact between administrators, the draftsman and the section dealing with printing and laying make flexibility possible when occasion demands.

Notes

1. The other annexes to the memorandum concerned the Home Office, the Ministry of Defence, the Ministry of Agriculture, Fisheries and Food and the Scottish Office (pp. 196–203).

2. An example of a statutory advisory body is the Council on Tribunals, which must be consulted before procedural rules are made for a large number of statutory tribunals (Tribunals and Inquiries Act 1992, s.8 and Schedule 1). Another is the Social Security Advisory Committee set up by the Social Security Act 1980 to replace the National Insurance Advisory Committee and the Supplementary Benefits Commission (see A. I. Ogus and E. M. Barendt, *The Law of Social*

Security (3rd ed., 1988) pp. 535–537). One of its functions is to comment on regulations concerning social security benefits other than industrial injuries benefits, war pensions and occupational pensions (for which there are separate bodies). Draft regulations must be sent for it to comment on unless it appears to the Secretary of State "that by reason of the urgency of the matter it is inexpedient so to refer them" or the Committee agrees (Social Security Administration Act 1992, s.173(1)); other exceptions are set out in Schedule 7, Part I, and temporary exceptions are set out in section 173(5). If the Secretary of State subsequently lays the regulations before Parliament, he must lay, in addition, the Committee's report and a statement indicating the extent to which any recommendations have been implemented, and in so far as effect has not been given to them, his reasons why not (1992 Act, s.174). Where draft regulations have not been submitted to the Committee because of urgency, the final regulations must be submitted as soon as practicable, unless the Committee agrees. Moreover, the Secretary of State may, in urgent cases where he has referred drafts to the Committee make the regulations before receiving the Committee's advice (1992 Act, s.173(3)). In these cases, the Secretary of State must lay the Committee's report before Parliament, with a statement of the extent (if any) to which he proposes to give effect to any recommendations (1992 Act, s.173(4)).

3. Where a statute requires consultation with particular interests, that is likely to be regarded by the courts as a mandatory procedural requirement, failure to comply with which will render the regulations *ultra vires*, at least as regards the interests not consulted (see above, pp. 454–460). In many areas of government decision-making, the courts have been prepared to imply into a statute a requirement of prior consultation with affected interests. This is one aspect of the requirements of "natural justice" and apply to those with a "legitimate expectation" of being consulted (see Chap. 9). However, the courts have been unwilling to imply such requirements prior to the making of delegated legislation. See *Bates* v. *Lord Hailsham of St. Marylebone* [1972] 1 W.L.R. 1373 (above, p. 538).

(D) Printing, Publication and Laying before Parliament

These matters are regulated by the Statutory Instruments Act 1946 and the Statutory Instruments Regulations 1947.

STATUTORY INSTRUMENTS ACT 1946

Definition of "Statutory Instrument"

1.—(1) Where by this Act or any Act passed after the commencement of this Act to make, confirm or approve orders, rules, regulations or other subordinate legislation, is conferred on His Majesty in Council or on any Minister of the Crown then, if the power is expressed—

(*a*) in the case of a power conferred on His Majesty, to be exercisable by Order in Council;

(*b*) in the case of a power conferred on a Minister of the Crown, to be exercisable by statutory instrument,

any document by which that power is exercised shall be known as a "statutory instrument" and the provisions of this Act shall apply thereto accordingly.

(2) Where by any Act passed before the commencement of this Act

power to make statutory rules within the meaning of the Rules Publication Act 1893, was conferred on any rule-making authority within the meaning of that Act, any document by which that power is exercised after the commencement of this Act shall, save as is otherwise provided by regulations made under this Act, be known as a "statutory instrument" and the provisions of this Act shall apply thereto accordingly.

Numbering, printing, publication and citation

2.—(1) Immediately after the making of any statutory instrument, it shall be sent to the King's printer of Acts of Parliament and numbered in accordance with regulations made under this Act, and except in such cases as may be provided by any Act passed after the commencement of this Act or prescribed by regulations made under this Act, copies thereof shall as soon as possible be printed and sold by the King's printer of Acts of Parliament.

(2) Any statutory instrument may, without prejudice to any other mode of citation, be cited by the number given to it in accordance with the provisions of this section, and the calendar year.

Supplementary provisions as to publication

3.—(1) Regulations made for the purposes of this Act shall make provision for the publication by His Majesty's Stationery Office of lists showing the date upon which every statutory instrument printed and sold by the King's printer of Acts of Parliament was first issued by that office: and in any legal proceedings a copy of any list so published purporting to bear the imprint of the King's printer shall be received in evidence as a true copy, and an entry therein shall be conclusive evidence of the date on which any statutory instrument was first issued by His Majesty's Stationery Office.

(2) In any proceedings against any person for an offence consisting of a contravention of any such statutory instrument, it shall be a defence to prove that the instrument had not been issued by His Majesty's Stationery Office at the date of the alleged contravention unless it is proved that at that date reasonable steps had been taken for the purpose of bringing the purport of the instrument to the notice of the public, or of persons likely to be affected by it, or of the person charged.

(3) Save as therein otherwise expressly provided, nothing in this section shall affect any enactment or rules of law relating to the time at which any statutory instrument comes into operation.

Statutory Instruments which are required to be laid before Parliament

4.—(1) Where by this Act or any Act passed after the commencement of this Act any statutory instrument is required to be laid before Parliament after being made, a copy of the instrument shall be laid before each House of Parliament and, subject as hereinafter provided, shall be so laid before the instrument comes into operation:

Provided that if it is essential that any such instrument should come into operation before copies thereof can be so laid as aforesaid, the instrument may be made so as to come into operation before it has been so laid; and where any statutory instrument comes into operation before it is laid before Parliament, notification shall forthwith be sent to the Lord Chancellor and to the Speaker of the House of Commons drawing attention to the fact that copies of the instrument have yet to be laid before Parliament and explaining why such copies were not so laid before the instrument came into operation.

(2) Every copy of any such statutory instrument sold by the King's printer of Acts of Parliament shall bear on the face thereof:

(*a*) a statement showing the date on which the statutory instrument came or will come into operation; and

(*b*) either a statement showing the date on which copies thereof were laid before Parliament or a statement that such copies are to be laid before Parliament.

(3) Where any Act passed before the date of the commencement of this Act contains provisions requiring that any Order in Council or other document made in exercise of any power conferred by that or any other Act be laid before Parliament after being made, any statutory instrument made in exercise of that power shall by virtue of this Act be laid before Parliament and the foregoing provisions of this section shall apply thereto accordingly in substitution for any such provisions as aforesaid contained in the Act passed before the said date.

Statutory Instruments which are subject to annulment by resolution of either House of Parliament

5.—(1) Where by this Act or any Act passed after the commencement of this Act, it is provided that any statutory instrument shall be subject to annulment in pursuance of resolution of either House of Parliament, the instrument shall be laid before Parliament after being made and the provisions of the last foregoing section shall apply thereto accordingly, and if either House within the period of forty days beginning with the day on which a copy thereof is laid before it, resolves that an Address be presented to His Majesty praying that the instrument be annulled, no further proceedings shall be taken thereunder after the date of the resolution, and His Majesty may by Order in Council revoke the instrument, so, however, that any such resolution and revocation shall be without prejudice to the validity of anything previously done under the instrument or to the making of a new statutory instrument.

(2) Where any Act passed before the date of the commencement of this Act contains provisions requiring that any Order in Council or other document made in exercise of any power conferred by that or any other Act shall be laid before Parliament after being made and shall cease to be in force or may be annulled, as the case may be, if within a specified period either House presents an address to His Majesty or passes a resolution to that effect, then, subject to the provisions of any Order in Council made under this Act, any statutory instrument made in exercise of the said power shall by virtue of this Act be subject to annulment in pursuance of a resolution of either House of Parliament and the provisions of the last foregoing subsection shall apply thereto accordingly in substitution for any such provisions as aforesaid contained in the Act passed before the said date.

Statutory Instruments of which drafts are to be laid before Parliament

6.—(1) Where by this Act or any Act passed after the commencement of this Act it is provided that a draft of any statutory instrument shall be laid before Parliament, but the Act does not prohibit the making of the instrument without the approval of Parliament, then, in the case of an Order in Council the draft shall not be submitted to His Majesty in Council, and in any other case the statutory instrument shall not be made, until after the expiration of a period of forty days beginning with the day on which a copy of the draft is laid before each House of Parliament, or, if such copies are laid on different days, with the later of the two days, and if within that period either House resolves that the draft be not submitted to His Majesty or that the statutory instrument be not made, as the case may be, no further proceedings shall be taken thereon, but without prejudice to the laying before Parliament of a new draft.

(2) Where any Act passed before the date of the commencement of this Act contains provisions requiring that a draft of any Order in Council or other document to be made in exercise of any power conferred by that or any other Act shall be laid before Parliament before being submitted to His Majesty, or before being made, as the case may be, and that it shall not be so submitted or made if within a specified period either House presents an address to His Majesty or passes a resolution to that effect, then, subject to the provisions of any Order in Council made under this Act, a draft of any statutory instrument made in exercise of the said power shall by virtue of this Act be laid before Parliament and the provisions of the last foregoing subsection shall apply thereto accordingly in substitution for any such provisions as aforesaid contained in the Act passed before the said date.

Supplementary provisions as to ss.4, 5 and 6

7.—(1) In reckoning for the purposes of either of the last two foregoing sections any period of forty days, no account shall be taken of any time during which Parliament is dissolved or prorogued or during which both Houses are adjourned for more than four days.

(2) In relation to any instrument required by any Act, whether passed before or after the commencement of this Act, to be laid before the House of Commons only, the provisions of the last three foregoing sections shall have effect as if references to that House were therein substituted for references to Parliament and for references to either House and each House thereof.

(3) The provisions of sections four and five of this Act shall not apply to any statutory instrument being an order which is subject to special Parliamentary procedure, or to any other instrument which is required to be laid before Parliament, or before the House of Commons, for any period before it comes into operation. . . .

Interpretation

11.—(1) For the purposes of this Act, any power to make, confirm or approve orders, rules, regulations or other subordinate legislation conferred on the Treasury, . . ., the Board of Trade or any other government department shall be deemed to be conferred on the Minister of the Crown in charge of that department.

(2) If any question arises whether any board, commissioners or other body on whom any such power as aforesaid is conferred are a government department within the meaning of this section, or what Minister of the Crown is in charge of them, that question shall be referred to and determined by [the Minister for the Civil Service].

THE STATUTORY INSTRUMENTS REGULATIONS 1947

(S.I. 1948 No. 1)

1. , . .

(2) In these Regulations—

(*a*) "Principal Act" means the Statutory Instruments Act, 1946:

(*b*) "responsible authority" means—

(i) in relation to an Order in Council, the Minister responsible for the preparation of the draft of the Order submitted to His Majesty in Council, and

(ii) in relation to any other instrument, the Minister by whom the instrument is made;

and in this definition references to a Minister include references to the Treasury, the Admiralty, the Board of Trade, and any other Government department, and to any other authority making a document which by virtue of Regulation 2 of these Regulations is such a statutory rule as is referred to in subsection (2) of Section 1 of the Principal Act:

(*c*) "general instrument" and "local instrument" mean, respectively, an instrument classified as such under these Regulations: and

(*d*) "Reference Committee" means the Statutory Instruments Reference Committee provided for by these Regulations.

2. . . .

(3) Notwithstanding anything in this Regulation, subsection (2) of Section 1 of the Principal Act shall not apply to—

(*a*) any document which, although of a legislative character, applies only to a named person or premises and is not required to be laid before or subject to confirmation or approval by Parliament or the House of Commons; or

(*b*) any Order in Council which, being an Order for which the Lord President of the Council is the responsible authority, confirms or approves subordinate legislation in the nature of a local and personal or private Act; or

(*c*) any such document as is mentioned in the Schedule to these Regulations.

Numbering, Printing and Sale

3. Numbering.—All statutory instruments received by the King's printer of Acts of Parliament under subsection (1) of Section 2 of the Principal Act shall be allocated to the series of the calendar year in which they are made and shall be numbered in that series consecutively as nearly as may be in the order in which they are received:

Provided that where any such instrument—

(*a*) will not take effect unless it is confirmed or approved by Parliament or the House of Commons, or

(*b*) is subject to special parliamentary procedure, or will become subject thereto in certain events,

the instrument may be allocated and numbered as if it had been made and received on the date on which the responsible authority notifies the King's printer that the instrument has become operative or will become operative: and

Provided also that any statutory instrument made before the commencement of the Principal Act shall be allocated to the series of the calendar year in which that Act commences.

4. Classification.—(1) For the purpose of these Regulations, statutory instruments shall be classified as local or general according to their subject matter.

(2) Unless there are special reasons to the contrary in any particular case, a statutory instrument which is in the nature of a local and personal or private Act shall be classified as local, and a statutory instrument which is in the nature of a Public General Act shall be classified as general.

(3) The responsible authority shall, on sending a statutory instrument

to the King's printer of Acts of Parliament, certify it as local or general as the case may be; and, unless the Reference Committee otherwise direct under these Regulations, the instrument shall be classified accordingly.

5. Exemption for local instruments and instruments otherwise regularly published.—The following statutory instruments shall, unless the Reference Committee in any particular case otherwise direct under these Regulations, be exempt from the requirements of subsection (1) of Section 2 of the Principal Act with respect to the printing and sale of copies, that is to say:—

(*a*) any local instrument, and

(*b*) any general instrument certified by the responsible authority to be of a class of documents which is or will be otherwise regularly printed as a series and made available to persons affected thereby:

Provided that the responsible authority may, on sending to the King's printer of Acts of Parliament any statutory instrument certified by that authority as local, request him to comply with the requirements aforesaid.

6. Exemption for temporary instruments.—If the responsible authority considers that the printing and sale of copies of a statutory instrument in accordance with the requirements of subsection (1) of Section 2 of the Principal Act is unnecessary having regard to the brevity of the period during which that instrument will remain in force and to any other steps taken or to be taken for bringing its substance to the notice of the public, he may, on sending it to the King's printer of Acts of Parliament, certify accordingly; and any instrument so certified shall, unless the Reference Committee otherwise direct under these Regulations, be exempt from the requirements aforesaid.

7. Exemption for certain schedules, etc.—If the responsible authority considers that the printing and sale in accordance with the requirements of subsection (1) of Section 2 of the Principal Act of any schedule or other document which is identified by or referred to in a statutory instrument and would, but for the provisions of this Regulation, be required to be included in the instrument as so printed and sold, is unnecessary or undesirable having regard to the nature or bulk of the document and to any other steps taken or to be taken for bringing its substance to the notice of the public, he may, on sending it to the King's printer of Acts of Parliament, certify accordingly; and any instrument so certified shall, unless the Reference Committee otherwise direct under these Regulations, be exempt from the requirements aforesaid so far as concerns the document specified in the certificate.

8. Exemption for confidential instruments.—If the responsible authority considers that the printing and sale of copies of a statutory instrument in accordance with the requirements of subsection (1) of Section 2 of the Principle Act would, if effected before the coming into operation of that instrument, be contrary to the public interest, he may, on sending it to the King's printer of Acts of Parliament, certify accordingly; and any instrument so certified shall, so long as it has not come into operation, be exempt from the requirements aforesaid:

Provided that if at any time after the instrument has been so certified and before the instrument has come into operation it appears to the said authority that the printing and sale of copies of the instrument as aforesaid would no longer be contrary to the public interest, he shall notify the King's printer of Acts of Parliament to that effect, and thereupon the foregoing provisions of this Regulation shall cease to apply to that instrument.

Notes

1. The 1946 Act was of considerable importance in that it brought a measure of order into what had previously been a highly convoluted area, by providing one basic procedure (albeit with some variants) for the making of delegated legislation by central government. On the history of delegation, see C. K. Allen, *Law and Orders* (3rd ed., 1965), Chap. 2.

2. The 1947 Regulations were made under section 8 of the 1946 Act, which enables the Minister for the Civil Service, with the concurrence of the Lord Chancellor and the Speaker, to make regulations for the purposes of the Act. They were amended by S.I.s 1977 No. 641 and 1982 No. 1728. Regulation 9 requires H.M.S.O. to publish a "Statutory Instruments Issue List" showing the serial number, short title and date of issue of each instrument issued by the office. Regulation 10 requires the publication of an "Annual Edition" comprising copies of all instruments issued (except spent and local instruments), an Annual Numerical and Issue List of Statutory Instruments, a classified list of local instruments, a table showing the effects on existing statutes and statutory instruments, and an index. Regulation 11 establishes a Statutory Instruments Reference Committee, consisting of two or more persons nominated by the Lord Chancellor and the Speaker. Its functions include that of determining any question arising as to numbering, printing or publication of instruments, their classification as general in the nature of a Public General Act or of a local and personal or private Act, and whether a document constitutes a "statutory rule" within the meaning of s.1(2) of the 1946 Act. The schedule mentioned in reg. 2(3)(*c*) now comprises three documents only: see S.I. 1982 No. 1728.

3. Section 9(1) of the 1946 Act enables the Queen in Council to apply the provisions of the 1946 Act to powers in pre-1948 statutes to confirm or approve subordinate legislation conferred on a Minister of the Crown, where the exercise of such a power would not constitute the making of a statutory rule within the 1893 Act and so would fall outside section 1(2). See the Statutory Instruments (Confirmatory Powers) Order 1947 (S.I. 1948 No. 2), which applied the Act to certain classes of subordinate legislation authorised by pre-1948 statutes. Most of the classes are no longer important, the legislation in question having since been repealed. One general class that is still provided for is where (1) a minister has power under a pre-1948 statute to confirm or approve subordinate legislation made by an authority which is not a "rule-making authority" under the 1893 Act, (2) the legislation is "of a legislative and not an executive character" and (3) the legislation is required to be laid before Parliament or the House of Commons.

4. Section 1 of the Laying of Documents Before Parliament (Interpretation) Act 1948 provides:

Meaning of references to laying before Parliament

"**1.**—(1) For the removal of doubt it is hereby declared that a reference in any Act of Parliament or subordinate legislation, whether passed or made before or after the passing of this Act, to the laying of any instrument, report, account or other document before either House of Parliament is, unless the contrary intention appears, to be construed as a reference to the taking, during the existence of a Parliament, of such action as is directed by virtue of any Standing Order, Sessional Order or other direction of that House for the time being in force to constitute the laying of that document before that House, or as is accepted by virtue of the practice of that House for the time being as constituting such laying, notwithstanding that the action so directed or accepted consists in part or wholly in action capable of being taken otherwise than at or during the time of a sitting of that House; and that a reference in any such Act or subordinate legislation to the laying of any instrument, report, account or other document before Parliament is, unless the contrary intention appears, to be construed accordingly as a reference (construed in accordance with the preceding declaration) to the laying of the document before each House of Parliament.

(2) It is hereby further declared that nothing in section four of the Statutory Instruments Act 1946, is to be taken as indicating an intention that any reference in that section to the laying of copies of certain statutory instruments as therein mentioned is to be construed otherwise than in accordance with the preceding declaration."

By Standing Order No. 141, the House of Commons has directed that the delivery of a copy of a statutory instrument to the Votes and Proceedings Office on any day during the existence of a Parliament shall be deemed to be laying before the House. In practice, it is normally then placed in the House of Commons Library. S.O. No. 141 does not, however, apply to instruments required to be laid for any period before it comes into operation. These can only be laid on sitting days. (See *Erskine May's Parliamentary Practice* (21st ed., 1989) pp. 543–545).

5. It is unclear whether a requirement that an instrument be laid before Parliament is "mandatory" or "directory" (*i.e.* whether laying is or is not a pre-condition to the validity of the instrument: see pp. 448 *et seq.*). The position appears to be that the matter depends on the exact wording and context of the particular case. There are authorities that suggest that laying requirements are directory: see *Bailey* v. *Williamson* (1873) L.R. 8 Q.B. 118; *Starey* v. *Graham* [1899] 1 Q.B. 406, 412; *Springer* v. *Doorly* (1950) L.R.B.G. 10 (West Indian Court of Appeal); A. I. L. Campbell, [1983] P.L. 43; but see *de Smith*, p. 148, for the argument that they should be mandatory. In *R.* v. *Secretary of State for Social Services, ex p. Camden London Borough Council* (Unreported, February 26, 1986), Macpherson J. held that the requirement in section 33(3)(*c*) of the Supplementary Benefits Act 1976 that certain social security regulations "shall not be made unless a draft of the regulations has been laid before Parliament and approved by a resolution of each House . . ." was mandatory. Indeed, the words were "clear, strong and mandatory." On appeal, the Court of Appeal assumed this to be so without deciding the point: [1987] 1 W.L.R. 819. The other point that arose for consideration in this case was whether the laying requirement was applicable to a document referred to in the regulations. The regulations in question concerned allowances for board and lodgings and were designed to limit the maximum benefits payable according to areas, and to limit the time for which in any area those benefits would be payable to individual claimants. The regulations provided that in any particular case,

the relevant amount was the amount shown as applicable for that area in a booklet entitled *Supplementary Benefit Maximum Amounts, Initial Periods and Board and Lodging Areas,* published by H.M.S.O. The Booklet was not laid before Parliament. Macpherson J. held that the booklet did not fall within the laying requirement, as it was not "part of" the statutory instrument, and was not a "document by which the Secretary of State exercises his actual powers" for the purposes of the 1946 Act. See A. I. L. Campbell, [1987] P.L. 328.

R. v. SHEER METALCRAFT LTD.

[1954] 1 Q.B. 586; [1954] 2 W.L.R. 777; [1954] 1 All E.R. 542
Streatfeild J.

Trial on indictment at Kingston-upon-Thames Assizes. The company, and its managing director were prosecuted for infringement of the Iron and Steel Prices Order 1951 (S.I. 1951 No. 252). The defendants argued that it was not a valid statutory instrument as its schedules, which set out maximum prices for different commodities of steel, had not been printed with the instrument by the Queen's Printer, as required by section 2(1) of the Statutory Instruments Act 1946 (above, p. 896), and the minister had not certified under regulation 7 of the 1947 regulations (above, p. 901) that this was unnecessary. Streatfeild J. ruled on this submission.

STREATFEILD J.: ... [read sections 1, 2 and 3 of the 1946 Act (above pp. 895–896), and regulation 7 of the 1947 Regulations.]

There does not appear to be any definition of what is meant by "issue" [in section 3(1)] but presumably it does mean some act by the Queen's Printer of Acts of Parliament which follows the printing of the instrument. That section, therefore requires that the Queen's Printer shall keep lists showing the date upon which statutory instruments are printed and issued.

It seems to follow from the wording of this subsection that the making of an instrument is one thing and the issue of it is another. If it is made it can be contravened; if it has not been issued then that provides a defence to a person charged with its contravention. It is then upon the Crown to prove that, although it has not been issued, reasonable steps have been taken for the purpose of bringing the instrument to the notice of the public or persons likely to be affected by it.

I do not think that it can be said that to make a valid statutory instrument it is required that all of these stages should be gone through; namely, the making, the laying before Parliament, the printing and the certification of that part of it which it might be unnecessary to have printed. In my judgment the making of an instrument is complete when it is first of all made by the Minister concerned and after it has been laid before Parliament. When that has been done it then becomes a valid statutory instrument, totally made under the provisions of the Act.

The remaining provisions to which my attention has been drawn, in my view, are purely procedure for the issue of an instrument validly made—

namely, that in the first instance it must be printed by the Queen's Printer unless it is certified to be unnecessary to print it; it must then be included in a list published by Her Majesty's Stationery Office showing the dates when it is issued and it may be issued by the Queen's Printer of Acts of Parliament. Those matters, in my judgment, are matters of procedure. If they were not and if they were stages in the perfection of a valid statutory instrument, I cannot see that section 3(2) would be necessary, because if each one of those stages were necessary to make a statutory instrument valid, it would follow that there could be no infringement of an unissued instrument and therefore it would be quite unnecessary to provide a defence to a contravention of any such instrument. In my view the very fact that subsection (2) of section 3 refers to a defence that the instrument has not been issued postulates that the instrument must have been validly made in the first place otherwise it could never have been contravened.

In those circumstances I hold that this instrument was validly made and approved and that it was made by or signed on behalf of the Minister on its being laid before Parliament; that so appears on the face of the instrument itself. In my view, the fact that the Minister failed to certify under regulation 7 does not invalidate the instrument as an instrument but lays the burden upon the Crown to prove that at the date of the alleged contraventions reasonable steps had been taken for bringing the instrument to the notice of the public or persons likely to be affected by it. I, therefore, rule that this is admissible.

[When evidence of the steps taken to bring the instrument to the notice of the public and of the contravention of it by the accused had been given. His Lordship summed up and the jury, after a retirement of two minutes, found both the accused guilty on all counts.]

Verdict: Guilty on all counts.

Notes

1. The report at [1954] 1 All E.R. 542, 545–546, states that evidence was given that the Minister of Supply issued information regarding the deposited schedules to trade journals; that the maximum permitted prices during the relevant months appeared in the *Board of Trade Journal*, the *Metal Bulletin* and the *Ironmonger*; and that the British Iron and Steel Federation sent copies of the schedules to the defendant company when the order of 1951 came into existence.

2. Some support for *Sheer Metalcraft* is provided by *Jones* v. *Robson* [1901] 1 K.B. 673. By section 6 of the Coal Mines Regulation Act 1896:

> "a Secretary of State on being satisfied that any explosive is or is likely to become dangerous, may, by order, of which notice shall be given in such manner as he may direct, prohibit the use thereof in any mine . . . either absolutely or subject to conditions."

The Secretary of State made an Order imposing conditions as to the handling of detonators on and after October 1, 1899. The defendant, the manager of a mine, was prosecuted for breach of the Order. He was aware of the Order, but no notice of it had been published as required by section 6. The Divisional Court held that the defendant could properly be convicted. The Order came into force when it was made by the Secretary of State, and the provisions as to notice were "directory" only.

However, the ruling in *Sheer Metalcraft* that an instrument can come into effect before it is issued is inconsistent with the decision of Bailhache J. in *Johnson* v. *Sargant & Sons* [1918] 1 K.B. 101. The Food Controller made an Order under the Defence of the Realm regulations requisitioning, *inter alia*, imported beans. The Order was dated May 16, 1917, but only became known to the public on May 17. It stated that it did not apply to beans "which have been sold by the original consignees and paid for by the purchasers." On May 16, the plaintiff paid for and took delivery of a cargo of beans from the defendants. They subsequently claimed that the contract had been cancelled by the Order. They referred to the rule that a statute takes effect from the first moment of the day on which it is passed, unless another day is expressly named, in which case it comes into operation immediately on the expiration of the previous day. They argued that, by analogy with the position with statutes, the Order came into operation immediately after midnight on May 15. As the beans were only paid for on May 16, the transaction was caught by the Order. However, Bailhache J. did not regard the analogy as appropriate:

> "there is about statutes a publicity even before they come into operation which is absent in the case of many Orders such as that with which we are now dealing; indeed, if certain Orders are to be effective at all, it is essential that they should not be known until they are actually published. In the absence of authority upon the point I am unable to hold that this Order came into operation before it was known, and, as I have said, it was not known until the morning of May 17."

Accordingly, the transaction fell within the exemption in the Order.

Jones v. *Robson* was not cited in *Johnson* v. *Sargant*, and neither case was cited in *R.* v. *Sheer Metalcraft*.

3. In *Simmonds* v. *Newell* [1953] 1 W.L.R. 826, the Defiant Cycle Co. and two of its directors were prosecuted before justices for selling steel at a price in excess of the maximum permitted by the Iron and Steel Prices Order 1951, as amended. The Order had been made by the Minister of Supply. The maximum prices were set out in schedules. An Assistant Secretary in the Ministry of Supply decided, having regard to regulation 7 of the 1947 Regulations (above, p. 901), that the printing and sale of the schedules was not necessary. She so decided in view of the bulk of the schedules, because they would be available for inspection at Steel House in London, and because trade associations would be distributing copies of the schedules that were most in demand. The Assistant Secretary wrote to the editor of Statutory Instruments that the schedules had been certified under reg. 7 to be exempted from printing and sale, but there was not in fact a certificate to that effect. The Divisional Court held that the letter did not constitute a certificate. The Solicitor General had accepted that while this did not render the Order invalid, it threw upon the Crown the burden of proving that reasonable steps had been taken to bring the purport of the instrument to the notice of the public, or of persons likely to be affected by it or the person charged (section 3(2) of the 1946 Act). Lord Goddard C.J. commented (p. 830):

> "That is certainly a very reasonable attitude for the Solicitor-General to take up, because it is not desirable, in criminal matters, that people should be prosecuted for breaches of orders unless the orders can fairly be said to be known to the public."

As no evidence had been given that steps had been taken to publicise the Order, the defendants should have been acquitted.

The court left open arguments—

(1) that a contravention of section 2 of the 1946 Act in not causing to be printed an instrument required to be printed would have the effect that the instrument was invalid; and
(2) that the defence in section 3(2) was available even where the instrument was exempt from the printing requirements.

4. In *Lim Chin Aik* v. *The Queen* [1963] A.C. 160, the question before the Privy Council was whether a person could properly be convicted of the offence of remaining in Singapore while the subject of an order prohibiting his entry if he was unaware of the existence of the order. Most of the advice of their Lordships was directed to the issue whether the offence required the proof of *mens rea* (their Lordships held that it did). In addition, they rejected the Crown's argument that once made the Order became part of the law of Singapore and that ignorance of the law is no excuse. *Per* Lord Evershed (p. 171):

> "In their Lordships' opinion, even if the making of the order by the Minister be regarded as an exercise of the legislative as distinct from the executive or administrative function (as they do not concede), the maxim cannot apply to such a case as the present where it appears that there is in the State of Singapore no provision, corresponding, for example, to that contained in section 3(2) of the English Statutory Instruments Act of 1946, for the publication in any form of an order of the kind made in the present case or any other provision designed to enable a man by appropriate inquiry to find out what 'the law' is."

This appears to suggest that in the context "ignorance of the law" can be an excuse even though (and, indeed, because) there is no express statutory defence.

Lord Evershed noted that the case concerned an order directed at an individual, and that the relevant Ordinance drew a distinction between such orders and an order directed to a class of persons. It expressly provided in the latter case for "publication in the Gazette and presentation to the Legislative Assembly" (p. 172).

5. These cases raise two questions: (1) can delegated legislation come into effect before it is published?; (2) can a person be properly convicted of an offence created by delegated legislation unless either reasonable steps have been taken to make it public or the defendant is actually aware of it? Justice requires the answer to (2) to be no (*cf.* Lord Goddard's remark in *Simmonds* v. *Newell*). That could be achieved by a broad general rule that delegated legislation does not come into force until published. Alternatively, and more narrowly, it could be achieved by a special defence in the criminal law. Such a defence would operate as an exception to the maxim that ignorance of the law is no excuse: the justification is that the maxim would operate harshly if even the best of endeavours would not enable the "law" to be ascertained. Section 3(2) of the 1946 Act provides a defence of that kind. *Lim Chin Aik* v. *The Queen* suggests such a defence might be available even in the absence of a statutory provision. This would make it more acceptable for the answer to question (1) to be yes. Note that question (2) did not arise in *Jones* v. *Robson*, and that the section 3(2) defence was potentially available in *Simmonds* v. *Newell* and *R.* v. *Sheer Metalcraft*, although not made out on the facts in the second case. *Johnson* v. *Sargant* did not concern a criminal prosecution. Thus in none of these reported cases in this country has a person been convicted of an offence under delegated legislation the details of which had not been published at the time of contravention.

6. Some commentators reconcile *Johnson* v. *Sargant* with the other cases by treating it as authority for the proposition that a piece of delegated legislation *which does not itself state a commencement date* comes into effect on the date of publication and not that on which it was made (see 44 *Halsbury's Laws of England*, 4th ed., para. 1003). *Jones* v. *Robson*, *Simmonds* v. *Newell* and *R.* v. *Sheer Metalcraft* all concerned instruments with specified commencement dates. Nothing was, however, made of this point in the cases themselves. Since 1947, all statutory instruments required to be laid before Parliament will show the dates they came into operation (see the 1946 Act, s.4(2)(*a*), (3), above p. 896).

7. D. J. Lanham, ("Delegated Legislation and Publication" (1974) 37 M.L.R. 510) argues strongly that the principle of *Johnson* v. *Sargant* is to be preferred, as a matter of justice, and that the general common law rule is that delegated legislation does not come into force until it is published. The contrary view is expressed by A. I. L. Campbell, [1982] P.L. 569, reply by Professor Lanham, [1983] P.L. 395.

8. Consider section 3(2) of the 1946 Act (above, p. 896). To what kinds of statutory instrument does it apply? (see Lanham, *op. cit.*, pp. 521–523). This question turns on the meaning of the words "any such statutory instrument." The possibilities are that:

(i) These words refer back to the kinds of statutory instruments specified in section 3(1), *i.e.* "every statutory instrument printed and sold by the King's printer." This would have the result that the defence would only be available where an instrument *is issued at some time*, but the contravention precedes the date of issue. It would not be available if the instrument is never issued, even where that was in breach of publication requirements. *Simmonds* v. *Newell* and *R.* v. *Sheer Metalcraft* are against this narrow interpretation.

(ii) The words are to be read as referring to "any statutory instrument," no weight being attached to the word "such." The defence would then be available wherever the instrument has not been issued at the date of contravention. This interpretation gives the broadest scope to the s.3(2) defence. Would this be an appropriate occasion for the exercise of the limited power of judges to ignore statutory words to prevent statutory provisions having an absurd result?

(iii) The defence would only be available where the instrument has not been issued at the date of contravention, *and this is in breach of a duty to publish*. This was the situation that arose in *Simmonds* v. *Newell* and *Sheer Metalcraft*. Does the wording of section 3 justify this reading?

9. The defence in section 3(2) appears, with the language but not the substance modified, as clause 50 in the proposed Criminal Code Bill (see *Codification of the Criminal Law: A Report to the Law Commission* (1984–85 H.C. 270) pp. 129–130, 198).

(E) Parliamentary Scrutiny

FIRST REPORT FROM THE SELECT COMMITTEE ON PROCEDURE, 1977–78

(1977–78 H.C. 588–I)

Categories of parliamentary control

3.5 Delegated legislation may be divided into categories according to the kind of Parliamentary control which is applied to it. The category into which an instrument falls is determined by its parent Act. The Act may provide that:

(i) the instrument shall expire or shall not come into effect unless it, or a draft of it, is approved by a resolution of both Houses of Parliament (or in certain cases, usually if finance is involved, of the House of Commons only) (the affirmative procedure);
(ii) the instrument shall come into effect automatically but shall be subject to annulment in pursuance of a resolution of either House of Parliament (or the House of Commons only); or shall come into effect only if no annulling resolution is passed while it is laid in draft; a motion to annul such an instrument is referred to as a "prayer" (the negative procedure);
(iii) the instrument shall be laid before both Houses of Parliament (or the House of Commons only) with no provision for Parliament to take any action upon it;
(iv) the instrument shall be a statutory instrument, with no provision that it shall be laid before either House.

According to the provisions of the parent Act, instruments subject to the affirmative procedure may either have immediate effect but expire unless approved within a specified period (usually 28 or 40 days); or may be laid in draft but only be made after approval by one or both Houses; or they be made but not have effect until approved. Under the provisions of the Statutory Instruments Act 1946 a standard period of 40 days is stipulated as the "praying" time against an instrument subject to the negative procedure, although no account is taken of any time during which Parliament is dissolved or prorogued or during which both Houses are adjourned for more than four days.

The terms of reference of the Joint Committee on Statutory Instruments are indicated in the following extract:

HOUSE OF COMMONS STANDING ORDERS

124. Statutory Instruments (Joint Committee) (1) A select committee shall be appointed to join with a committee appointed by the Lords to consider:

(A) every instrument which is laid before each House of Parliament and upon which proceedings may be or might have been taken in either House of Parliament, in pursuance of an Act of Parliament, being—

(*a*) a statutory instrument, or a draft statutory instrument;
(*b*) a scheme, or an amendment of a scheme, or a draft thereof, requiring approval by statutory instrument;

(*c*) any other instrument (whether or not in draft), where the proceedings in pursuance of an Act of Parliament are proceedings by way of an affirmative resolution; or

(*d*) an order subject to a special parliamentary procedure;

but excluding any Order in Council or draft Order in Council made or proposed to be made under paragraph 1 of Schedule 1 to the Northern Ireland Act 1974;

(B) every general statutory instrument not within the foregoing classes, and not required to be laid before or to be subject to proceedings in this House only, but not including measures under the Church of England Assembly (Powers) Act 1919 and instruments made under such measures:

with a view to determining whether the special attention of the House should be drawn to it on any of the following grounds—

(i) that it imposes a charge on the public revenues or contains provisions requiring payments to be made to the Exchequer or any government department or to any local or public authority in consideration of any licence or consent or of any services to be rendered, or prescribes the amount of any such charge or payment;

(ii) that it is made in pursuance of any enactment containing specific provisions excluding it from challenge in the courts, either at all times or after the expiration of a specific period;

(iii) that it purports to have retrospective effect where the parent statute confers no express authority so to provide;

(iv) that there appears to have been unjustifiable delay in the publication or in the laying of it before Parliament;

(v) that there appears to have been unjustifiable delay in sending a notification under the proviso to subsection (1) of section four of the Statutory Instruments Act 1946, where an instrument has come into operation before it has been laid before Parliament;

(vi) that there appears to be a doubt whether it is *intra vires* or that it appears to make some unusual or unexpected use of the powers conferred by the statute under which it is made;

(vii) that for any special reason its form or purport call for elucidation;

(viii) that its drafting appears to be defective;

or on any other ground which does not impinge on its merits or on the policy behind it and to report its decision with the reasons thereof in any particular case.

Note

It is generally accepted that the Joint Committee does useful work in the technical scrutiny of statutory instruments. However, weaknesses identified by the 1977–78 Procedure Committee in securing that instruments are considered by the Joint Committee before they are debated in the House and indeed in obtaining time for such debates have not been tackled. The first of these points was partly met in 1971 when the government undertook to make every effort to ensure that instruments subject to the negative procedure are laid before Parliament and the Committee at least 21 days before they come into operation (Report from the Joint Committee on Delegated Legislation, 1971–72 (1971–72 H.L. 184, H.C. 475) p. xxv). In 1978 the Joint Committee on Statutory Instruments reported that this was now an established part of departmental practice, that observance of the rule was in general adequate, and that where there was a breach of the rule, the Committee were informed of the reasons at the time when the offending instrument was laid (First Special Report, 1977–78 (1977–78 H.L. 51, H.C. 169) p. 11). The government declined to accept the Committee's suggestion that the rule be extended to other kinds of instrument, but departments were reminded that Parliament should have as much notice as possible of the coming into operation of all kinds of delegated legislation (Second Special Report, 1977–78 (1977–78 H.L. 236, H.C. 579) p. 10) (letter from Michael Foot, Lord President of the Council). Unjustified delay may be the subject of adverse comment under ground (iv), above.

The most recent survey concluded that the technical process of scrutiny now appears to work as effectively as a parliamentary committee can be expected to function. Nevertheless, the increasing use of delegated legislation for major policy implementation, the lack of parliamentary time for debate, an increase in decisions taken before the Committee's report is published and the emphasis on political rather than legal points in debates on the merits have led to "the reality that parliamentary scrutiny of delegated legislation is not effective democratic control." (J. D. Hayhurst and P. Wallington, "The Parliamentary Scrutiny of Delegated Legislation" [1988] P.L. 547, 573–576: the conclusions are Wallington's.)

(F) *VIRES*

Apart from the procedural matters already considered in this chapter, the validity of a statutory instrument may be challenged on the ground that it is *ultra vires* as a matter of substance.

Notes

1. Examples of challenge on this ground include the following: In *Hotel and Catering Industry Training Board* v. *Automobile Proprietary Ltd.* [1969] 1 W.L.R. 697, the House of Lords held that a power to make an order establishing a Training Board for persons employed "in any activities of industry or commerce" did not enable an order to be made in respect of members' clubs. In *R.* v. *Customs and Excise Commissioners, ex p. Hedges and Butler* [1986] 2 All E.R. 164, a power to demand production of the whole of the records of a business, including records concerning non-dutiable goods, was held not to be "incidental" or "supplementary" to powers concerning the regulation of excise warehouses and dealings in dutiable goods.

2. On the question whether the invalid part of an instrument can be severed, see *R.* v. *Inland Revenue Commissioners, ex p. Woolwich Equitable Building Society*, above, p. 865.

3. It is not clear whether a statutory instrument, as distinct from a bye-law (see below, pp. 914–918) can be challenged for unreasonableness. In *Maynard* v. *Osmond* [1977] Q.B. 240, regulations which did not allow police officers (other than Chief Constables and Assistant and Deputy Chief Constables) to be legally represented in disciplinary proceedings were challenged on this ground; the Court of Appeal did not express any doubt as to its jurisdiction to entertain such a challenge, but dismissed the argument on its merits. A provision in the Immigration Rules (which are not published as statutory instruments) was held to be

unreasonable in *R.* v. *Immigration Appeal Tribunal, ex p. Manshoora Begum* [1986] Imm.A.R. 385.

The scope of review may be narrower where an instrument is approved by Parliament (*cf.* above, pp. 400–403).

4. See generally, K. Puttick, *Challenging Delegated Legislation* (1988).

(G) Byelaws

LOCAL GOVERNMENT ACT 1972

Byelaws

Power of councils to make byelaws for good rule and government and suppression of nuisances

235.—(1) The council of a district and the council of a London borough may make byelaws for the good rule and government of the whole or any part of the district or borough, as the case may be, and for the prevention and suppression of nuisances therein.

(2) The confirming authority in relation to byelaws made under this section shall be the Secretary of State.

(3) Byelaws shall not be made under this section for any purpose as respects any area if provision for that purpose as respects that area is made by, or is or may be made under, any other enactment.

Procedure etc., for byelaws

236.—(1) Subject to subsection (2) below, the following provisions of this section shall apply to byelaws to be made by a local authority under this Act [and to byelaws made by a local authority, [or a metropolitan county passenger transport authority] under any other enactment and conferring on the authority] a power to make byelaws and for which specific provision is not otherwise made.

(2) This section shall not apply to byelaws made [. . .] by the Civil Aviation Authority under [section 29 of the Civil Aviation Act 1982].

(3) The byelaws shall be made under the common seal of the authority, or, in the case of byelaws made by a parish or community council not having a seal, under the hands and seals of two members of the council, and shall not have effect until they are confirmed by the confirming authority.

(4) At least one month before application for confirmation of the byelaws is made, notice of the intention to apply for confirmation shall be given in one or more local newspapers circulating in the area to which the byelaws are to apply.

(5) For at least one month before application for confirmation is made, a copy of the byelaws shall be deposited at the offices of the authority by

whom the byelaws are made, and shall at all reasonable hours be open to public inspection without payment.

(6) The authority by whom the byelaws are made shall, on application, furnish to any person a copy of the byelaws, or of any part thereof, on payment of such sum, not exceeding 10p for every hundred words contained in the copy, as the authority may determine.

(7) The confirming authority may confirm, or refuse to confirm, any byelaw submitted under this section for confirmation, and may fix the date on which the byelaw is to come into operation and if no date is so fixed the byelaw shall come into operation at the expiration of one month from the date of its confirmation.

(8) A copy of the byelaws, when confirmed, shall be printed and deposited at the offices of the authority by whom the byelaws are made, and shall at all reasonable hours be open to public inspection without payment, and a copy thereof shall, on application, be furnished to any person on payment of such sum, not exceeding 20p for every copy, as the authority may determine.

(9) The proper officer of a district council shall send a copy of every byelaw made by the council, and confirmed, to the proper officer of the council, whether separate or common, of every parish or community to which they apply or, in the case of a parish not having a council, to the chairman of the parish meeting, and the proper officer of the parish or community council or chairman of the parish meeting, as the case may be, shall cause a copy to be deposited with the public documents of the parish or community.

A copy so deposited shall at all reasonable hours be open to public inspection without payment.

(10) The proper officer of a county council shall send a copy of every byelaw made by the council, and confirmed, to the council of every district in the county, and the proper officer of the council of a district shall send a copy of every byelaw made by the council, and confirmed, to the council of the county.

(11) In this section the expression "the confirming authority" means the authority or person, if any, specified in the enactment (including any enactment in this Act) under which the byelaws are made, or in any enactment incorporated therein or applied thereby, as the authority or person by whom the byelaws are to be confirmed, or if no authority or person is so specified means the Secretary of State.

Offences against byelaws

237. Byelaws to which section 236 above applies may provide that persons contravening the byelaws shall be liable on summary conviction to a fine not exceeding such sum as may be fixed by the enactment conferring the power to make the byelaws, or, if no sum is so fixed, the sum of [level 2 on the standard scale] and in the case of a continuing offence a further fine not exceeding such sum as may be fixed as aforesaid, or, if no sum is so fixed, the sum of £5 for each day during which the offence continues after conviction thereof.

Evidence of byelaws

238. The production of a printed copy of a byelaw purporting to be made by a local authority [or a metropolitan county passenger transport authority] upon which is endorsed a certificate purporting to be signed by the proper officer of the authority stating—

(*a*) that the byelaw was made by the authority;
(*b*) that the copy is a true copy of the byelaw;
(*c*) that on a specified date the byelaw was confirmed by the authority named in the certificate or, as the case may require, was sent to the Secretary of State and has not been disallowed;
(*d*) the date, if any, fixed by the confirming authority for the coming into operation of the byelaw,

shall be *prima facie* evidence of the facts stated in the certificate, and without proof of the handwriting or official position of any person purporting to sign the certificate.

Note

These sections, which replaced almost verbatim corresponding sections in the Local Government Act 1933, have been very widely used by local authorities throughout the country. They cover a wide range of matters, including controls over the sale of contraceptives, the riding of cycles on footpaths or horses on grass verges, the leading of bulls through streets, and prohibitions on spitting, allowing dogs to foul pavements, etc.

KRUSE v. JOHNSON

[1898] 2 Q.B. 91; 67 L.J.K.B. 782; 78 L.T. 647; 14 T.L.R. 416; 62 J.P. 469; 42 S.J. 509; [1895–1899] All E.R. Rep. 105; 46 W.R. 630; 19 Cox C.C. 103
(Divisional Court (Q.B.D.)

Kent County Council made a bye-law prohibiting any person from playing music or singing in a public place within 50 yards of any dwelling-house after being required by any constable, or by an inmate of such house to desist. The bye-law was made under section 16 of the Local Government Act 1888 and section 23(1) of the Municipal Corporations Act 1882, which gave power to "make such bye-laws as to them [the council], seem meet for the good rule and government of the . . . [county], and for the prevention and suppression of nuisances not already punishable in a summary manner by virtue of any Act. . . ." K. was convicted by justices of an offence against this bye-law, in that he had conducted an open-air religious service within 50 yards of a house, after being required to desist by a constable. K. appealed by way of case stated to the Divisional Court, contending that the bye-law was *ultra vires* for unreasonableness.

LORD RUSSELL OF KILLOWEN C.J.: ... [stated the facts, outlined the relevant legislation, and continued:] We thus find that Parliament has thought fit to delegate to representative public bodies in town and cities, and also in counties, the power of exercising their own judgment as to what are the bye-laws which to them seem proper to be made for good rule and government in their own localities. But that power is accompanied by certain safeguards. There must be antecedent publication of the bye-law with a view, I presume, of eliciting the public opinion of the locality upon it, and such bye-laws shall have no force until after they have been forwarded to the Secretary of State. Further, the Queen, with the advice of her Privy Council, may disallow the bye-law wholly or in part, and may enlarge the suspensory period before it comes into operation. I agree that the presence of these safeguards in no way relieves the Court of the responsibility of inquiring into the validity of bye-laws where they are brought in question, or in any way affects the authority of the Court in the determination of their validity or invalidity. It is to be observed, moreover, that the bye-laws having come into force, they are not like the laws, or what were said to be the laws, of the Medes and Persians—they are not unchangeable. The power is to make bye-laws from time to time as to the authority shall seem meet, and if experience shews that in any respect existing bye-laws work hardly or inconveniently, the local authority, acted upon by the public opinion, as it must necessarily be, of those concerned, has full power to repeal or alter them. It need hardly be added that, should experience warrant that course, the Legislature which has given may modify or take away the powers they have delegated. I have thought it well to deal with these points in some detail, and for this reason—that the great majority of the cases in which the question of bye-laws has been discussed are not cases of bye-laws of bodies of a public representative character entrusted by Parliament with delegated authority, but are for the most part cases of railway companies, dock companies, or other like companies, which carry on their business for their own profit, although incidentally for the advantage of the public. In this class of case it is right that the Courts should jealously watch the exercise of these powers, and guard against their unnecessary or unreasonable exercise to the public disadvantage. But, when the Court is called upon to consider the bye-laws of public representative bodies clothed with the ample authority which I have described, and exercising that authority accompanied by the checks and safeguards which have been mentioned, I think the consideration of such bye-laws ought to be approached from a different stand-point. They ought to be supported if possible. They ought to be, as has been said, "benevolently" interpreted, and credit ought to be given to those who have to administer them that they will be reasonably administered. This involves the introduction of no new canon of construction. But, further, looking to the character of the body legislating under the delegated authority of Parliament, to the subject-matter of such legislation, and to the nature and extent of the authority given to deal with matters which concern them, and in the manner which to them shall seem meet, I think courts of justice ought to be slow to condemn as invalid any bye-law, so made under such conditions, on the ground of supposed unreasonableness. Notwithstanding what Cockburn C.J. said in *Bailey* v. *Williamson* (1873) L.R. 8 Q.B. 118, 124, an analogous case, I do not mean to say that there may not be cases in which it would be the duty of the Court to condemn bye-laws, made under such authority as these were made, as invalid because unreasonable. But unreasonable in what sense? If, for instance, they were found to be partial and unequal in their operation as between different classes; if they were manifestly unjust; if they disclosed bad faith; if they involved such oppressive or gratuitous interference with the rights of those subject to them as could find no justification in the minds of reasonable men, the Court might well say, "Parliament never intended to give authority to make such rules; they are unreasonable and *ultra vires*." But it is in this sense, and in this sense only, as I conceive, that the question of unreasonableness can properly be regarded. A bye-law is not unreasonable merely because particular judges may think that it goes further than is prudent or necessary or convenient, or because it is not accompanied by a qualification or an exception which some judges may think ought to be there. Surely it is not too much to say that in matters which directly and mainly concern the people of the county, who have the right to choose those whom they think best fitted to represent them in their local government bodies, such representatives may be trusted to understand their own requirements better than judges. Indeed, if the question of the validity of bye-laws were to be determined by the opinion of judges as to what was reasonable in the narrow sense of that word, the cases in the books on this subject are no guide; for they reveal, as indeed one would expect, a wide diversity of judicial opinion, and they lay down no principle or definite standard by which reasonableness or unreasonableness may be tested.

So much for the general considerations which, it seems to me, ought to be borne in mind in considering bye-laws of this class. I now come to the bye-law in question.

It is admitted that the county council of Kent were within their authority in making a bye-law in relation to the subject-matter which is dealt with by the impeached bye-law. In other words, it is conceded, and properly so, that the local authority might make a bye-law imposing conditions under which musical instruments and singing might be permitted or prevented in public places; but it is objected that they had no authority to make a bye-law on that subject in the terms of this bye-law. Further, it is not contended that the bye-law should, in order to be valid, be confined to cases where the playing or singing amounted to a nuisance; but the objections are, as I understand them, that the bye-law is bad—first, because it is not confined to cases where the playing or singing is in fact causing annoyance, and next, because it enables a police constable to bring it into operation by a request on *his* part to the player or singer to desist. As to the first of these objections, if the general principles upon which these bye-laws ought to be dealt with are those which I have already stated, it is clear that the absence of this qualification cannot make the bye-law invalid. But, further, such a qualification in my judgment would render the bye-law ineffective. What is to be the standard of annoyance? What may be a cause of annoyance to one person may be no annoyance, and may even be pleasurable, to another person. Again, who is to be the judge in such case of whether there is or is not an annoyance? Is it to be the resident of the house within 50 yards of the playing or singing; or is it to be the magistrate who hears the charge? It is enough to say that, in my judgment, the absence of the suggested qualification cannot make the bye-law invalid, even if it be admitted that its presence would be an improvement.

As to the second objection—namely, that the policeman has the power of putting the bye-law into operation by requiring the player or singer to desist—I again say that, even if the absence of this power would be an improvement, and would make the bye-law in the apprehension of some more reasonable, it is not, on the principles I have already stated, any ground for declaring the bye-law to be invalid. In support of this objection pictures have in argument, been drawn—more or less highly coloured—of policemen who without rhyme or reason would or might gratuitously interfere with what might be a source of enjoyment to many. In answer, I say a policeman is not an irresponsible person without check or control. If he acts capriciously or vexatiously, he can be checked by his immediate superiors, or he can be taught a lesson by the magistrates should he prefer vexatious charges. If the policeman persisted in saying that the musician should desist when the people in the neighbourhood desired his music, his gratuitous interference would promptly come to an end. Nor is it correct to say, as has been erroneously stated in some of the cases cited, that the magistrate would be bound in every case to convict where the musician did not desist when called upon. It is clear that under s.16 of the Summary Jurisdiction Act 1879, the magistrate, if he thinks the case of so trifling a nature that it is inexpedient to inflict any punishment, may, without proceeding to conviction, dismiss the information. The facts of this case are certainly no illustration of the bye-law having been gratuitously or vexatiously put in force. The case states that, although it was not proved that the occupier of the house within 50 yards had, on the day in question, requested the constable to require the appellant to desist, yet it was proved that the singing was an annoyance to the occupier, and that he had on previous occasions complained to the police of such singing. Indeed, it was stated during the argument that the conviction here appealed from was the second conviction of the appellant for an offence against this bye-law. . . .

In my opinion, judged by the test of reasonableness, even in its narrower sense, this is a reasonable bye-law; but, whether I am right or wrong in this view, I am clearly of opinion that no Court of law can properly say that it is invalid.

SIR F. H. JEUNE P. delivered a concurring judgment. MATTHEW J. dissented.

CHITTY L.J., WRIGHT, DARLING AND CHANNELL JJ. concurred with LORD RUSSELL OF KILLOWEN C.J.

Conviction affirmed.

Notes

1. This case has been considered and applied on many occasions. See notes in [1895–1899] All E.R. Rep. 105–106; D. G. T. Williams, *Welsh Studies in Public Law* (ed. by J. A. Andrews), "The Control of Local Authorities," pp. 128 *et seq.*

2. On the validity of bye-laws in general, see Alan Wharam, (1973) 36 M.L.R. 611; *Cross*, Chap. 6.

3. There are many more cases raising the validity of bye-laws in commonwealth jurisdictions than in this country. See the reports on "Administrative Law" in the *Annual Survey of Commonwealth Law* (H. W. R. Wade; D. G. T. Williams; M. H. Matthews).

4. Bye-laws may be *ultra vires* for uncertainty. This ground of challenge has also been invoked against planning conditions (see the cases cited in Question 2, below) and against a nuisance order: *R.* v. *Fenny Stratford JJ., ex p. Watney Mann (Midlands) Ltd.* [1976] 2 All E.R. 888.

Questions

1. The doctrine of *Kruse* v. *Johnson* has been said to be one involving "unreasonableness," not "reasonableness." Why?

2. Is there any justification for these principles being applied to conditions imposed in a planning permission under the town and country planning legislation? This development is traced by Williams (*op. cit.* note 1, above). See Lord Denning in *Fawcett Properties Ltd.* v. *Buckingham C.C.* [1961] A.C. 636; Lord Upjohn in *Mixnam's Properties Ltd.* v. *Chertsey U.D.C.* [1965] A.C. 735; the Court of Appeal in *Mixnam's* case [1964] 1 Q.B. 214; *de Smith*, pp. 353–354; P. Robertshaw, [1975] P.L. 133.

INDEX